Microsoft® Office 2010

A Lesson Approach

Microsoft® Office 2010
A Lesson Approach

Deborah Hinkle

Kathleen Stewart

Pat R. Graves

Amie Mayhall

Jon Juarez

John Carter

McGraw Hill

Connect
Learn
Succeed™

The McGraw-Hill Companies

McGraw Hill

Connect
Learn
Succeed™

MICROSOFT® OFFICE 2010: A LESSON APPROACH

3 4 5 6 7 8 9 0 RMN/RMN 1 0 9 8 7 6 5 4 3 2 1

ISBN   978-0-07-745489-0
MHID   0-07745489-8

Vice president/Editor in chief: *Elizabeth Haefele*
Vice president/Director of marketing: *John E. Biernat*
Executive editor: *Scott Davidson*
Developmental editor: *Alan Palmer*
Marketing manager: *Tiffany Wendt*
Lead digital product manager: *Damian Moshak*
Digital development editor: *Kevin White*
Director, Editing/Design/Production: *Jess Ann Kosic*
Lead project manager: *Rick Hecker*
Buyer II: *Sherry L. Kane*
Senior designer: *Marianna Kinigakis*
Media project manager: *Cathy L. Tepper*
Interior design: *Kay Lieberherr*
Typeface: *10.5/13 New Aster*
Compositor: *Aptara®, Inc.*
Printer: *R. R. Donnelley*

Library of Congress Cataloging-in-Publication Data

Microsoft Office 2010 : a lesson approach / Deborah Hinkle ... [et al.].
      p. cm.
   Includes index.
   ISBN-13: 978-0-07-745489-0 (alk. paper)
   ISBN-10: 0-07-745489-8 (alk. paper)
     1. Microsoft Office. 2. Business—Computer programs. I. Hinkle, Deborah A.
   HF5548.4.M525M52499 2011
   005.5—dc22

                                                                                        2010026434

www.mhhe.com

CONTENTS

UNIT 2 *Paragraph Formatting, Tabs, and Advanced Editing*

UNIT 3 *Page Formatting*

EXCEL

Case Study   *EX-ii*

UNIT 1 *Introduction to Excel*

Contents

UNIT 2 *Working with Formulas and Functions*

UNIT 3 *Presenting and Analyzing Worksheet Data*

POWERPOINT

Unit 1 *Basic Skills*

Unit 2 *Presentation Illustration*

ACCESS

Unit 1 *Understanding Access Databases*

xvi

Contents

Unit 2 Designing and Managing Database Objects

We are proud to introduce the 1st edition of *Microsoft Office 2010: A Lesson Approach*, written to help you master Microsoft Office. The text guides you step by step through the Office features you are likely to use in both your personal and business life.

Case Study

Learning the features of Office is one component of the text, and applying what you learn is another component. A case study was created for each application to offer the opportunity to learn and apply features in a realistic business context. Take the time to read the case studies. All the documents for this course relate to the case study presented at the beginning of each application.

Organization of the Text

The text includes ten units, and each unit is divided into lessons. There are thirty-six lessons, each self-contained but building on previously learned procedures. This building-block approach, together with the case study and the following features, enables you to maximize the learning process.

Features of the Text

- Objectives are listed for each lesson.
- The estimated time required to complete each lesson up to the Summary section is stated.
- Within a lesson, each heading corresponds to an objective.
- Easy-to-follow exercises emphasize learning by doing.
- Key terms are italicized and defined as they are encountered.
- Extensive graphics display screen contents.
- Ribbon commands and keyboard keys are shown in the text when used.
- Lessons contain important notes, useful tips, and helpful reviews.
- The Lesson Summary reviews the important concepts taught in the lesson.
- The Command Summary lists the commands taught in the lesson.

Lesson Approach Web Site

Visit the Lesson Approach Web site at www.mhhe.com/lessonapproach2010 to access a wealth of additional materials.

- Concepts Review includes true-false, short answer, and critical thinking questions that focus on lesson content.
- Skills Review provides skill reinforcement for each lesson.
- Lesson Applications apply your skills in a more challenging way.
- On Your Own exercises apply your skills creatively.

- Unit Applications give you the opportunity to practice the skills you learn throughout a unit.

- Appendices contain Microsoft's Certification standards for each application, as well as additional information.

Conventions Used in the Text

This text uses a number of conventions to help you learn the program and save your work.

- Text to be keyed appears either in **red** or as a separate figure.

- File names appear in **boldface**.

- Options that you choose from tabs and dialog boxes, but that aren't buttons, appear in **green**; for example, "Choose **Print** from the File tab."

- You are asked to save each document with your initials followed by the exercise name. For example, an exercise might end with this instruction: "Save the document as *[your initials]*4-12." Documents are saved in folders for each lesson.

If You Are Unfamiliar with Windows

If you are not familiar with Windows, review the "Windows Tutorial" Lesson, available at www.mhhe.com/lessonapproach2010, before beginning Lesson 1. This tutorial provides a basic overview of Microsoft's operating system and shows you how to use the mouse. You might also want to review "File Management," also available on the Lesson Approach Web site, to get more comfortable with files and folders.

Screen Differences

As you practice each concept, illustrations of the screens help you follow the instructions. Don't worry if your screen is different from the illustration. These differences are due to variations in system and computer configurations.

Microsoft® Office Word 2010

A Lesson Approach, Complete

There is more to learning a word processing program like Microsoft Word than simply pressing keys. You need to know how to use Word in a real-world situation. That is why all the lessons in this book relate to everyday business tasks.

As you work through the lessons, imagine yourself working as an intern for Campbell's Confections, a fictional candy store and chocolate factory located in Grove City, Pennsylvania.

Campbell's Confections

It was 1950. Harry Truman was president. Shopping malls and supermarkets were appearing in suburban areas. And Campbell's Confections began doing business.

Based in Grove City, Pennsylvania, Campbell's Confections started as a small family-owned business. Originally, Campbell's Confections was a candy store, with a few display cases in the front of the building and a kitchen in the back to create chocolates and to try new recipes. The store was an immediate

success, with word traveling quickly about the rich, smooth, creamy chocolates made by Campbell's Confections. Today, the store includes several display cases for chocolates and hard candies and special displays for greeting cards and gifts. The factory is now located in a separate building on Monroe Street and offers tours for visitors.

Within a few years of opening the first store, the company expanded its business by opening Campbell's Confections candy stores in Mercer, New Castle, and Meadville. Today there are 24 stores in 3 states—Pennsylvania, Ohio, and West Virginia.

The goal of Campbell's Confections is to offer "quality chocolate," and the company has grown from its retail base to include wholesale and fund-raising divisions. E-commerce has been the latest venture with Internet sales increasing monthly.

Currently, Thomas Campbell is the president-owner, and Lynn Tanguay is the vice president.

To understand the organization of Campbell's Confections, take a look at Figure CS-1. Notice each of the specialty areas and management divisions.

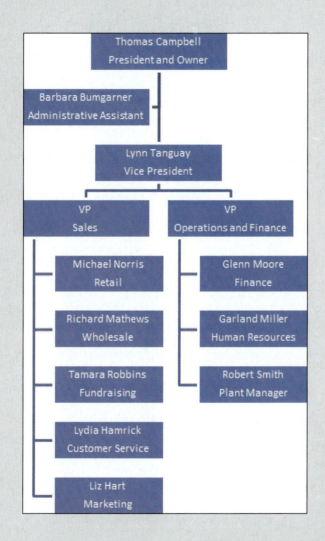

All the documents you will use in this text relate to Campbell's Confections. As you work through the documents in the text, take the time to notice the following:

- How the employees interact, and how they respond to customers' queries.
- The format and tone of the business correspondence (if you are unfamiliar with the standard formats for business documents, refer to Appendix B).

- References to the *Gregg Reference Manual*, a standard reference manual for business writing and correspondence.
- The content of the correspondence (and its relation to Campbell's Confections).

As you use this text and become experienced with Microsoft Word, you will also gain experience in creating, editing, and formatting the type of documents that are generated in a real-life business environment.

Unit 1

BASIC SKILLS

Creating and Editing a Document

OBJECTIVES *After completing this lesson, you will be able to:*

1. Start Word and identify parts of the Word screen.
2. Key and edit text.
3. Name and save a document.
4. Open an existing document.
5. Move within a document.
6. Select text.
7. Print a document.
8. Close a document and exit Word.

Estimated Time: 1½ hours

Microsoft Word is a versatile, easy-to-use word processing program that helps you create letters, memos, reports, and other types of documents. This lesson begins with an overview of the Word screen. Then you learn how to create, edit, name, save, print, and close a document. The documents you create for this unit will provide an overview of Campbell's Confections, its products, and the process of making chocolate.

Starting Word and Identifying Parts of the Word Screen

There are several ways to start Word, depending on your system setup and personal preferences. For example, you can use the Start button on the Windows taskbar or double-click a Word shortcut icon that might be on your desktop.

NOTE

Your screen may differ from the screen shown in Figure 1-1 depending on the programs installed on your computer.

Exercise 1-1   START WORD

1. Click the Start button on the Windows taskbar, and point to **All Programs**.

2. On the All Programs menu, click **Microsoft Office**, and then click **Microsoft Word 2010**. In a few seconds, the program loads, and the Word screen appears.

Figure 1-1
Start menu

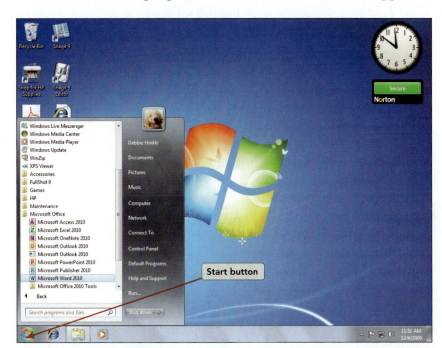

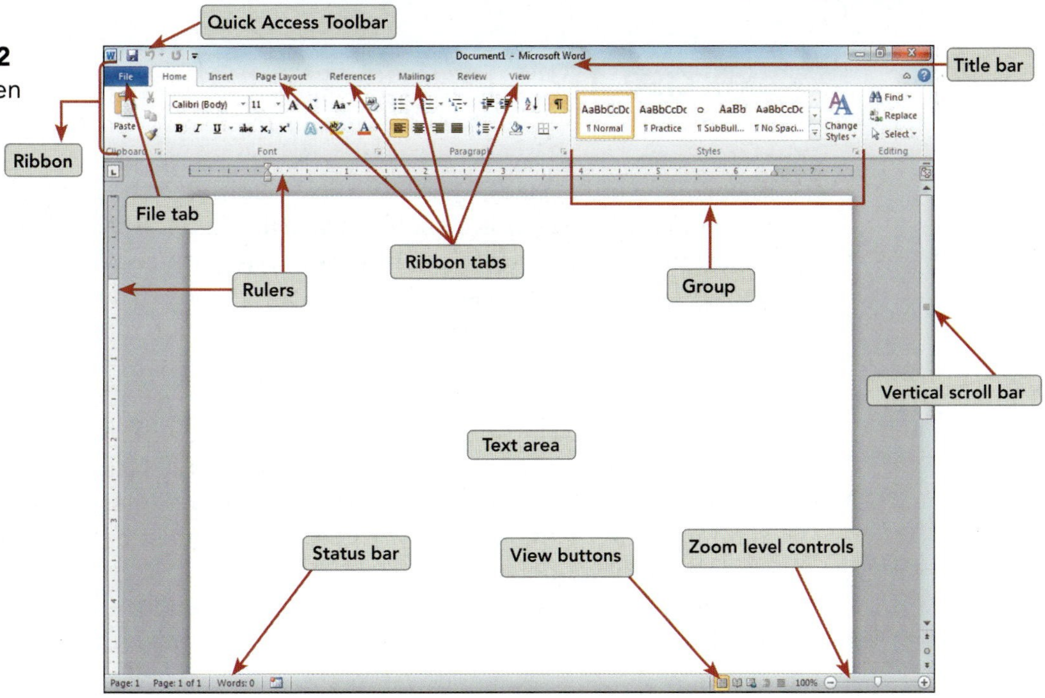

Figure 1-2
Word screen

TABLE 1-1 Parts of the Word Screen

Part of Screen	Purpose
Quick Access Toolbar	The Quick Access Toolbar is located at the top of the Word window, and its commands are available for all tabs on the Ribbon. By default, it displays icons for save, undo, and repeat. The Quick Access Toolbar can be customized to include commands that you use frequently.
Title bar	Displays the name of the current document. The opening Word screen is always named "Document1."
Ribbon	Displays contextual tabs. Each tab contains groups, and each group includes related commands. Commands can be buttons, menus, or drop-down list boxes.
File tab	Displays the Backstage view with options to create, save, open, and close documents. You can also display recently opened documents.
Ruler	The horizontal and vertical rulers display in Print Layout view. The horizontal ruler shows the placement of margins, indents, and tabs. Use the View Ruler button to show or hide the rulers.
Text area	Displays the text and graphics in the document.
Scroll bars	Used with the mouse to move right or left and up or down within a document.
Status bar	Displays the page number and page count of the document, the document view buttons, and the zoom control. It also displays the current mode of operation. The status bar can be customized.
View buttons	Used to switch from one document view to another. Available views include Print Layout, Full Screen Reading, Web Layout, Outline, and Draft View.

Exercise 1-2   IDENTIFY THE RIBBON AND THE QUICK ACCESS TOOLBAR

To become familiar with Word, start by identifying the parts of the screen you will work with extensively, such as the Ribbon and the Quick Access Toolbar. As you practice using Word commands, you will see *ScreenTips* to help you identify screen elements such as buttons. A ScreenTip appears when you point to a command on the Ribbon. It includes the name of the command and a brief description. ScreenTips also appear to help you identify parts of the Word screen.

When you start Word, the Ribbon appears with the Home tab selected. The Ribbon consists of eight tabs by default. Each tab contains a group of related commands, and the number of commands for each tab varies. A command can be one of several formats. The most popular formats include buttons and drop-down lists.

The *Quick Access Toolbar* contains frequently used commands and is positioned above the Ribbon by default. You can minimize the Ribbon so that only the names of the tabs display, or you can place the Quick Access Toolbar below the Ribbon. The commands on the Quick Access Toolbar are available for all tabs on the Ribbon, and you can customize the Quick Access Toolbar to include the commands you frequently use.

1. Move the mouse pointer to the **File** tab on the Ribbon. Click the left mouse button to open the Backstage view. The Backstage view replaces the Microsoft Office Button and the File menu from earlier versions of Microsoft Word. It lists commands to create, open, save, and print documents. The Navigation Pane appears on the left side of Backstage view and includes a list of the Quick commands. Click the **Info** command to view information about your document. When a document is open, the Info tab displays the document properties such as size, number of pages, and number of words. You can also see when your document was last modified.

Figure 1-3
Backstage view

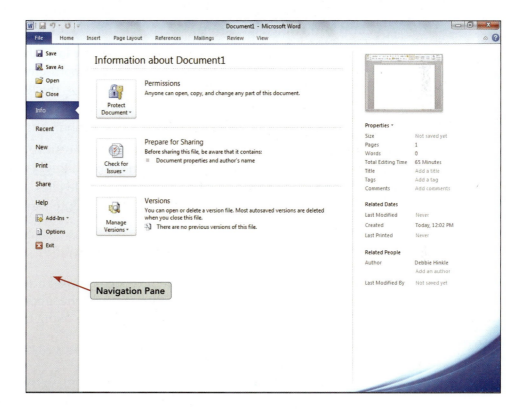

Navigation Pane

2. Click the **File** tab to close Backstage view. You can also close the Backstage view by pressing Esc or clicking another tab on the Ribbon.

3. Move the mouse pointer above the File tab to the Quick Access Toolbar, and point to the Save button 🖫. A ScreenTip and a keyboard shortcut to save a document display.

TIP

Commands may appear in more than one location. For example, you can save a document by choosing Save from the File tab, by clicking the Save command on the Quick Access Toolbar, or by pressing Ctrl + S.

NOTE

The width of the application window affects the size and shape of the Ribbon commands.

NOTE

Any Ribbon command with a light gray icon is currently not available. However, you can still identify the button by pointing to it with the mouse.

4. Point to the commands to the right of the Save command. Notice each command includes descriptive text and a keyboard shortcut. The Save, Undo, and Repeat commands are located on the Quick Access Toolbar by default.

5. Move the mouse pointer to the **Insert** tab on the Ribbon, and click **Insert**. Notice the change in the number and types of groups displayed. When you point to a Ribbon tab, the name of the tab is outlined but not active. Click the Ribbon tab to display the commands.

6. Click the **Page Layout** tab. There are five groups of commands on the Page Layout tab. Point to the **Margins** command. Read the ScreenTip.

7. Click the **Home** tab. Notice the groups and buttons available for formatting and editing.

8. Move the mouse pointer to the right of the last tab on the Ribbon, and locate the caret symbol (^). This symbol represents a button and is used to minimize the Ribbon. Click the Minimize the Ribbon button ⌃ , and notice that only the Ribbon tabs and ruler display. The Minimize the Ribbon button changes to Expand the Ribbon button.

9. Click the Expand the Ribbon button ⌄ to restore the Ribbon. The keyboard shortcut to minimize the Ribbon is Ctrl + F1 . To restore the Ribbon, press Ctrl + F1 . You can also double-click any tab on the Ribbon to minimize the Ribbon. Double-click a tab to restore the Ribbon.

Exercise 1-3   IDENTIFY COMMANDS

Use the Ribbon to locate and execute commands to format and edit your document. Commands also control the appearance of the Word screen. You can access Ribbon commands by using the mouse or keyboard Access Keys.

1. Activate the **Home** tab.

2. Locate the **Paragraph** group, and click the Show/Hide ¶ button ¶ . This button shows or hides formatting marks on the screen. Formatting marks display for spaces, paragraph marks, and tab characters. The command toggles between show and hide.

3. Press the ⌐Alt⌐ key. Small lettered or numbered squares, called *Key Tips*, appear on the File tab, Quick Access Toolbar, and Ribbon to access or execute a command.

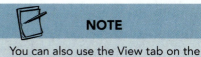

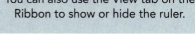

Figure 1-4
Key Tips

4. Press the letter ⌐P⌐ on the keyboard to select the **Page Layout** tab.

5. Press the letter ⌐M⌐ on the keyboard to display the **Margins** gallery. Press ⌐Esc⌐ to close the gallery. Press ⌐Esc⌐ twice to turn off the Key Tips.

NOTE

You can also use the View tab on the Ribbon to show or hide the ruler.

NOTE

Drag the Zoom slider to the right to zoom in, and drag the Zoom slider to the left to zoom out. You can also use ⌐Ctrl⌐+the wheel on your mouse to zoom in and zoom out. The View tab on the Ribbon contains Zoom commands.

6. Locate the vertical scroll bar, and click the View Ruler button. Notice the rulers disappear from the Word screen. Click the View Ruler button again to display the rulers.

7. Locate the Zoom button ⌐100%⌐ on the status bar.

8. Click the Zoom button to open the Zoom dialog box, and click **200%**. Click **OK**. The text area is magnified, and you see a portion of the page.

9. Point to and click the Zoom Out button ⊖. The document magnification changes to 190%. Click the Zoom In button ⊕ twice to change the magnification to 210%. Drag the Zoom slider to 100%. The document returns to normal display.

Keying and Editing Text

When keying text, you will notice various shapes and symbols in the text area. For example:

*   The *insertion point* │ is the vertical blinking line that marks the position of the next character to be entered.

*   The mouse pointer takes the shape of an *I-beam* I when it is in the text area. It changes into an arrow when you point to a command on the Quick Access Toolbar or the Ribbon.

*   The *paragraph mark* ¶ indicates the end of a paragraph. The paragraph mark displays when the Show/Hide ¶ button ¶ is selected.

Exercise 1-4 KEY TEXT AND MOVE THE INSERTION POINT

1. Before you begin, make sure the Show/Hide ¶ button ¶ on the **Home** tab, **Paragraph** group is selected. When this feature is "turned on," you can see paragraph marks and spacing between words and sentences more easily.

2. Key the words **Campbell's Confections** (don't worry about keying mistakes now—you can correct them later). Notice how the insertion point and the paragraph mark move as you key text. Notice also how a space between words is indicated by a dot.

Figure 1-5
The insertion point marks the place where you begin keying

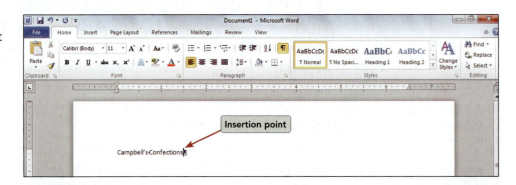

NOTE

The documents you create in this course relate to the case study about Campbell's Confections, a fictional candy store and chocolate factory (see the Case Study in the front matter).

3. Move the insertion point to the left of the word "Campbell's" by positioning the I-beam and clicking the left mouse button.

4. Move the insertion point back to the right of "Confections" to continue keying.

Exercise 1-5 WRAP TEXT AND CORRECT SPELLING

As you key additional text, you will notice Word performs several tasks automatically. For example, Word does the following by default:

*   Wraps text from the end of one line to the beginning of the next line.
*   Alerts you to spelling and grammatical errors.
*   Corrects common misspellings, such as "teh" for "the" and "adn" for "and."
*   Suggests the completed word when you key the current date, day, or month.

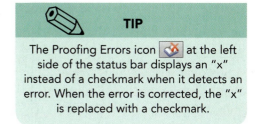

TIP

The Proofing Errors icon at the left side of the status bar displays an "x" instead of a checkmark when it detects an error. When the error is corrected, the "x" is replaced with a checkmark.

1. Continue the sentence you started in Exercise 1-4, this time keying a misspelled word. Press [Spacebar], and then key **is western Pennsylvania's leeding candy maker** (don't key a period). Word recognizes that "leeding" is misspelled and applies a red, wavy underline to the word. The status bar displays a Proofing Errors icon to indicate an error exists in the document.

2. To correct the misspelling, use the mouse to position the I-beam anywhere on top of the red, underlined word and click the *right* mouse button. A shortcut menu appears with suggested spellings. Click "leading" with the *left* mouse button. The misspelled word is corrected. Notice the change in the icon that displays in the status bar. The Proofing Errors icon changes to a No Proofing Errors icon on the status bar.

Figure 1-6
Choose the correct spelling from the shortcut menu

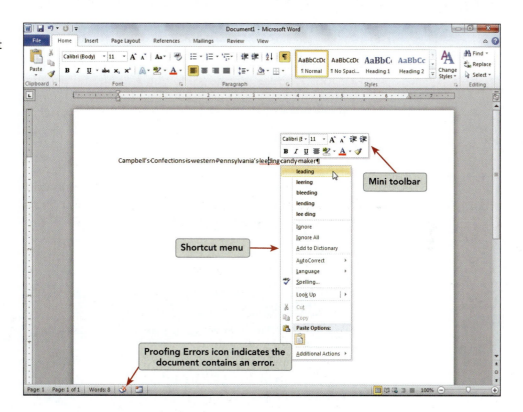

3. Move the insertion point to the right of "maker," and press [Spacebar]. Continue the sentence with another misspelled word by keying **adn**, and press [Spacebar]. Notice that "adn" is automatically corrected to "and" when you press [Spacebar].

4. Complete the sentence by keying **is located in Grove City on Main Street**.

5. Verify that the insertion point is to the immediate right of the period following Street, and then press the ⌈Spacebar⌉ once. Key the following text:

It is a family-owned business with several stores located in western Pennsylvania, eastern Ohio, and northern West Virginia.

Notice how the text automatically wraps from the end of the line to the beginning of the next line.

6. Press ⌈Enter⌉ once to start a new paragraph.

7. Key the second paragraph shown in Figure 1-7. When you key the first four letters of "Monday" in the first sentence, Word suggests the completed word in a small box. Press ⌈Enter⌉ to insert the suggested word, and then press ⌈Spacebar⌉ before you key the next word. Follow the same procedure for "Saturday."

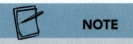

NOTE

Throughout this text, one space is used after a period to separate sentences. This is the standard format for word processing and desktop publishing.

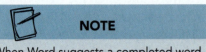

NOTE

When Word suggests a completed word as you key text, you can ignore the suggested word and continue keying or insert it by pressing ⌈Enter⌉.

Figure 1-7

```
For more information about Campbell's Confections, visit one
of our stores Monday through Saturday, or visit our Web site
anytime. Our sales associates will be happy to assist you.
```

Exercise 1-6 DELETE TEXT

The keyboard offers many options for basic text editing. For example, you can press ⌈Backspace⌉ to delete a single character to the left of the insertion point or press ⌈Ctrl⌉+⌈Delete⌉ to delete an entire word.

TABLE 1-2 Basic Text Editing

Key	Result
⌈Backspace⌉	Deletes the character to the left of the insertion point.
⌈Ctrl⌉+⌈Backspace⌉	Deletes the word to the left of the insertion point.
⌈Delete⌉	Deletes the character to the right of the insertion point.
⌈Ctrl⌉+⌈Delete⌉	Deletes the word to the right of the insertion point.

1. Move the insertion point to the right of the word "It" in the second sentence of the first paragraph. (Use the mouse to position the I-beam, and click the left mouse button.)

2. Press [Backspace] twice to delete both characters, and key **Campbell's Confections**.

3. Move the insertion point to the left of "one" in the second paragraph.

4. Press [Delete] three times and key **any**.

5. Move the insertion point to the left of the word "information" in the second paragraph.

6. Hold down [Ctrl] and press [Backspace]. The word "more" is deleted.

7. Move the insertion point to the right of "Grove City" in the first sentence of the first paragraph.

8. Hold down [Ctrl] and press [Delete] to delete the word "on." Press [Ctrl]+[Delete] two more times to delete the words "Main Street."

NOTE

When keyboard combinations (such as [Ctrl]+[Backspace]) are shown in this text, hold down the first key as you press the second key. Release the second key, and then release the first key. An example of the entire sequence is this: Hold down [Ctrl], press [Backspace], release [Backspace], and release [Ctrl]. With practice, this sequence becomes easy.

Exercise 1-7   INSERT TEXT

When editing a document, you can insert text or key over existing text. When you insert text, Word is in regular *Insert mode,* and you simply click to position the insertion point and key the text to be inserted. To key over existing text, you switch to *Overtype mode.* The Overtype feature is turned off by default.

1. In the first sentence of the first paragraph, move the insertion point to the left of the "G" in "Grove City." Key **downtown**, and press [Spacebar] once to leave a space between the two words.

2. Move the insertion point to the beginning of the document, to the left of "Campbell's."

3. Click the **File** tab, and click the **Options** command.

4. Click **Advanced** in the Navigation Pane of the Word Options dialog box. Locate **Editing options**, and click to select **Use overtype mode.** Click **OK**.

5. Press [Caps Lock]. When you key text in Caps Lock mode, the keyed text appears in all uppercase letters.

6. Key **campbell's confections** over the existing text.

7. Move the mouse pointer to the status bar, and press the right button on the mouse. Locate **Overtype** in the shortcut menu, and click the left mouse button to select the option. Click in the text area to hide the shortcut menu. Notice that the Overtype mode indicator appears in the status bar.

8. Position the insertion point to the left of "Campbell's Confections" in the second sentence of the first paragraph. Verify that Caps Lock is still active, and key **campbell's confections**.

9. Click the Overtype mode indicator Overtype to turn off Overtype.

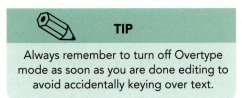

TIP

Always remember to turn off Overtype mode as soon as you are done editing to avoid accidentally keying over text.

10. Press Caps Lock to turn off Caps Lock mode. Click the **File** tab, and click the **Options** command. Click **Advanced**, locate **Editing options**, and verify that the **Use overtype mode** is deselected. Click **OK**.

11. Right-click the status bar, and deselect **Overtype**. Click in the text area to close the shortcut menu.

Exercise 1-8 COMBINE AND SPLIT PARAGRAPHS

1. At the end of the first paragraph, position the insertion point to the left of the paragraph mark (after the period following "West Virginia").

2. Press Delete once. The two paragraphs are now combined, or merged, into one.

3. Press Spacebar once to insert a space between the sentences.

4. With the insertion point to the left of "For" in the combined paragraph, press Enter once to split the paragraph.

Figure 1-8
Edited document

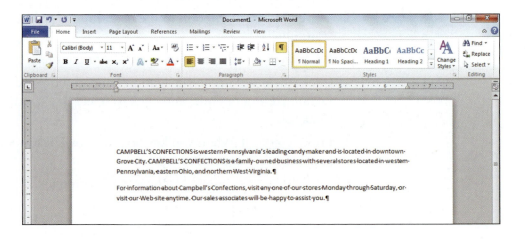

Naming and Saving a Document

Your document, called "Document1," is stored in your computer's temporary memory. Until you name and save the document, the data can be lost if you have a power failure or a computer hardware problem. It is always good practice to save your work frequently.

The first step in saving a document for future use is to assign a *file name*. Study the following rules about naming documents:

- File names can contain up to 260 characters, including the drive letter, the folder name, and extension. The following characters cannot be used in a file name:

  / \ > < * ? " : |

- File names can include uppercase letters, lowercase letters, or a combination of both. They can also include spaces. For example, a file can be named "Business Plan."

- Throughout this course, document file names will consist of [your initials] (which might be your initials or the identifier your instructor asks you to use, such as **rst**), followed by the number of the exercise, such as **1-12**. The file name would, therefore, be **rst1-12**.

You can use either the Save command or the Save As command to save a document. Here are some guidelines about saving documents:

- Use Save As when you name and save a document the first time.

- Use Save As when you save an existing document under a new name. Save As creates an entirely new file and leaves the original document unchanged.

- Use Save to update an existing document.

NOTE

Your instructor will advise you on the proper drive and folder to use for this course.

Before you save a new document, decide where you want to save it. Word saves documents in the current drive and folder unless you specify otherwise. For example, to save a document to a removable storage device, you need to change the drive to F:, or whichever is appropriate for your computer.

Document files are typically stored in folders that are part of a hierarchal structure similar to a family tree. At the top of the tree is a disk drive letter (such as C:) that represents your computer, network, removable storage device, or CD/DVD drive. Under the disk drive letter, you can create folders to organize your files. These folders can also contain additional folders.

For this course, you will create a new folder for each lesson and store your completed exercise documents in these folders.

Exercise 1-9   NAME AND SAVE A DOCUMENT

1. Click the **File** tab to open the Backstage view, and click **Save As**. The Save As dialog box appears. The appearance of the Save As dialog box is determined by the operating system. The Save As dialog box in Windows 7 is different from the Save As dialog box shown in Windows XP.

Figure 1-9
Save As dialog box using Windows 7

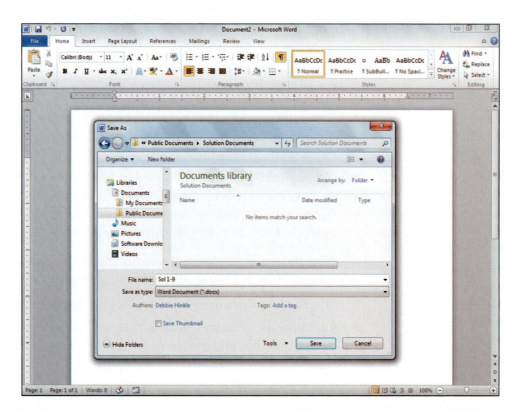

NOTE

To save a document as a PDF file, open the Save As dialog box, choose the appropriate drive and folder for saving the document, key the file name, open the Save as type drop-down list, and choose PDF (*.pdf). Click Save.

2. Locate the **File name** text box. A suggested file name is highlighted. Replace this file name by keying *[your initials]* **1-9**.

3. Drag the scroll box in the Navigation Pane, and choose the appropriate drive for your removable storage device—Removable Disk (F:), for example.

NOTE

When no document is open, the document window displays a shaded background. If you want to create a new document, click the File tab, click New, click Blank document, and click Create. The keyboard shortcut to start a new document is Ctrl+N.

4. Click the New Folder button New folder. A New Folder icon appears in the File list section. Key the folder name *[your initials]* **Lesson1**, and press Enter. The folder name appears in the Address bar and in the Navigation Pane. Word is ready to save the file in the new folder.

5. Click the Save button Save. Your document is named and saved for future use.

6. Open the **File** tab and click **Close**. The Close command in Backstage view closes the current document but does not exit the Word program. If you click the Close button located on the title bar and no other documents are open, you exit Word.

Opening an Existing Document

Instead of creating a new document for this exercise, you start this exercise by opening an existing document. There are several ways to open a document:

- Choose Open from the File tab.
- Press Ctrl+O.
- Use the document links in the Recent Documents file listing.

The Open command displays the Open dialog box. The commands and features listed in the Open dialog box resemble the commands and features you studied in the Save As dialog box. Remember the operating system determines the appearance of the Open dialog box.

TIP

The keyboard shortcut to open the File tab is Alt+F.

NOTE

The push pin icon that appears to the right of files listed under Recent Documents is used to pin a document to the list so that it does not disappear from view. Click the pinned icon to unpin the document from the list.

Exercise 1-10   OPEN AN EXISTING FILE

1. Click the **File** tab to open the Backstage view. Click the **Recent** command. The file names listed under Recent Documents are files opened from this computer. If the file you want is listed, click its name to open it. The Recent Documents section displays up to 22 documents by default.

2. Click **Open** to display the Open dialog box. You are going to open a student file named **Campbell-1**.

3. Locate the appropriate drive and folder according to your instructor's directions.

Figure 1-10
Files listed in the Open dialog box using Windows 7

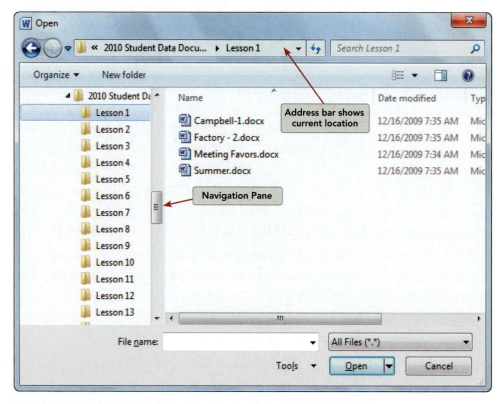

TABLE 1-3 Open Dialog Box Buttons

Button	Name	Purpose
« Public Docume... ▸ Student Data Files ▾ ↻	Address bar	Navigates to a different folder.
←	Back button	Works with the Address bar, and returns to previous location.
→	Forward button	Works with the Address bar, and returns to location already opened.
Search Documents 🔍	Search box	Looks for a file or subfolder.
Organize ▾	Organize	Opens a menu of file functions, such as cutting a file, copying a file, pasting a file, deleting a file, or renaming a file. Includes the Layout option to display the Navigation Pane, Details Pane, and the Preview Pane.
New folder	New Folder	Creates a new folder to organize files.
▤ ▾	View	Displays a menu of view options for displaying drives, folders, files, and their icons.

4. After you locate the student files, click the arrow next to the View button in the Open dialog box to display a list of view options.

5. Choose **List** to list the files by file name.

Figure 1-11
View menu in the
Open dialog box

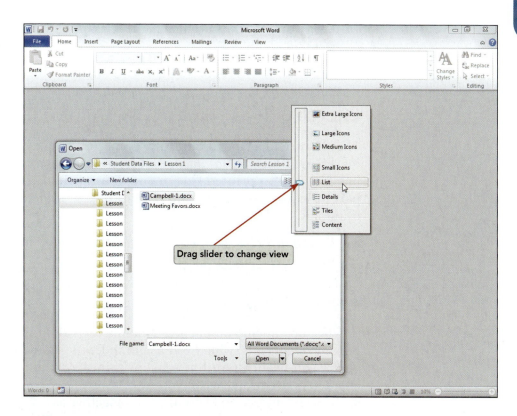

TIP

You can also double-click a file name to open a file.

6. From the list of file names, locate **Campbell-1** and click it once to select it.

7. Click **Open**.

NOTE

Documents created in earlier versions of Word display Compatibility Mode in the Title bar when opened. Compatibility Mode enables you to open, edit, and save documents that were created using earlier versions of Word. New features in Microsoft Word 2010 are not available in Compatibility Mode. To check for features not supported by earlier versions of the Word program, click the File tab, and click the Info command. Click the Check for Issues button. Click Check Compatibility. To convert a document created in an earlier version of Word to Microsoft Word 2010, click the Info command, and click Convert. Click OK.

8. Click the **File** tab, and choose **Save As**. You are going to save **Campbell-1** under a new file name.

9. Use the **Navigation Pane** to locate the appropriate drive and the folder you created for Lesson 1.

10. Verify that the file's original name (**Campbell-1**) is selected. If it is not selected, double-click it.

11. Key the file name *[your initials]***1-10**, and click **Save**.

Exercise 1-11   ENTER FORMATTING CHARACTERS

The Show/Hide ¶ button on the Home tab displays or hides paragraph marks and other *formatting marks*. These characters appear on the screen, but not in the printed document. Formatting marks are included as part of words, sentences, and paragraphs in a document. Here are some examples:

- A word includes the space character that follows it.

- A sentence includes the end-of-sentence punctuation and at least one space.

- A paragraph is any amount of text followed by a paragraph mark.

The document you opened contains two additional formatting characters: *tab characters,* which you use to indent text, and *line-break characters,* which you use to start a new line within the same paragraph. Line-break characters are useful when you want to create a paragraph of short lines, such as an address, and keep the lines together as a single paragraph.

Another formatting character is a *nonbreaking space,* which you use to prevent two words from being divided between two lines. For example, you can insert a nonbreaking space between "Mr." and "Smith" to keep the name "Mr. Smith" undivided on one line.

TABLE 1-4 Formatting Characters

Character	To Insert, Press
Tab (→)	`Tab`
Space (·)	`Spacebar`
Nonbreaking space (°)	`Ctrl`+`Shift`+`Spacebar`
Paragraph mark (¶)	`Enter`
Line-break character (↵)	`Shift`+`Enter`

1. Click the Show/Hide ¶ button ¶ if the formatting characters in the document are hidden.

2. Move the insertion point to the end of the document (after "family recipes.").

3. Press Enter to begin a new paragraph, and key **Campbell's Confections has been a member in good standing of the NCA for over 50** (do not press Spacebar).

4. Insert a nonbreaking space after "50" by pressing Ctrl+Shift+Spacebar. Then key **years.** (including the period). Word now treats "50 years" as a single unit.

Figure 1-12
Formatting characters

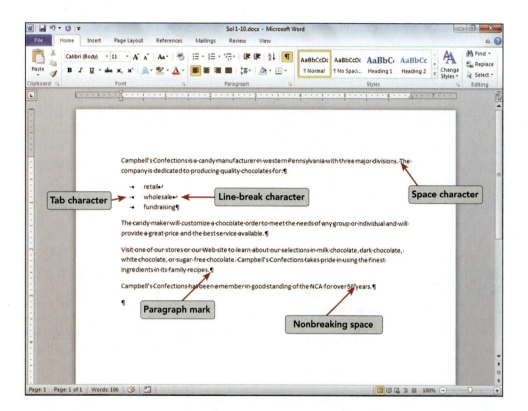

5. Press Enter and key the following text as one paragraph at the end of the document, pressing Shift+Enter at the end of the first and second lines instead of Enter.

Campbell's Confections
25 Main Street
Grove City, PA 16127

6. Click the Show/Hide ¶ button ¶ to hide the formatting characters, and click it again to redisplay them.

Moving within a Document

You already know how to move around a short document by positioning the I-beam pointer with the mouse and clicking. This is the easiest way to move around a document that displays in the document window. If a document is too long or too wide to view in the window, you need to use different methods to navigate within a document.

Word offers two additional methods for moving within a document:

- *Using the keyboard:* You can press certain keys on the keyboard to move the insertion point. The arrow keys, for example, move the insertion point up or down one line or to the left or right one character. Key combinations quickly move the insertion point to specified locations in the document.

- *Using the scroll bars:* Use the vertical scroll bar at the right edge of the document window to move through a document. The position of the scroll box indicates your approximate location in the document, which is particularly helpful in long documents. To view and move through a document that is wider than the document window, use the horizontal scroll bar at the bottom of the document window.

NOTE

Scrolling through a document does not move the insertion point. It moves only the portion of the document you are viewing in the document window. When you use the keyboard to move within a document, the insertion point always moves to the new location.

TIP

Word remembers the last three locations in the document where you edited or keyed text. You can press Shift + F5 to return the insertion point to these locations. For example, when you open a document you worked on earlier, press Shift + F5 to return to the place where you were last working before you saved and closed the document.

Exercise 1-12 USE THE KEYBOARD TO MOVE THE INSERTION POINT

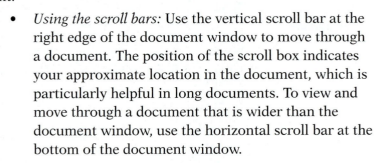

1. Press Ctrl + Home to move to the beginning of the document. Press End to move to the end of the first line.

2. Press Ctrl + ↓ several times to move the insertion point down one paragraph at a time. Notice how the text with the line-break characters is treated as a single paragraph.

3. When you reach the end of the document, press [PageUp] until you return to the beginning of the document.

TABLE 1-5 Keys to Move the Insertion Point

To Move	Press
One word to the left	[Ctrl]+[←]
One word to the right	[Ctrl]+[→]
Beginning of the line	[Home]
End of the line	[End]
One paragraph up	[Ctrl]+[↑]
One paragraph down	[Ctrl]+[↓]
Previous page	[Ctrl]+[PageUp]
Next page	[Ctrl]+[PageDown]
Up one window	[PageUp]
Down one window	[PageDown]
Top of the window	[Alt]+[Ctrl]+[PageUp]
Bottom of the window	[Alt]+[Ctrl]+[PageDown]
Beginning of the document	[Ctrl]+[Home]
End of the document	[Ctrl]+[End]

NOTE

The horizontal scroll bar does not display if the document window is wide enough to display the document text. To display the horizontal bar, resize the window.

Exercise 1-13 SCROLL THROUGH A DOCUMENT

Using the mouse and the scroll bars, you can scroll up, down, left, and right. You can also set the Previous and Next buttons on the vertical scroll bar to scroll through a document by a specific object, such as tables or headings. For example, use these buttons to jump from one heading to the next, going forward or backward.

1. Locate the vertical scroll bar, and click below the scroll box to move down one window.

Figure 1-13
Using the scroll bars

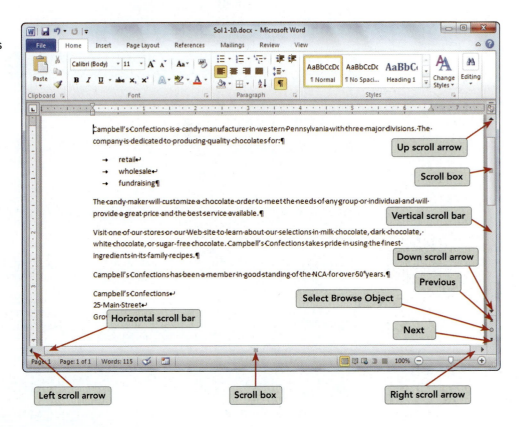

---

2. Drag the scroll box to the top of the scroll bar.

3. Click the down scroll arrow on the scroll bar three times. The document moves three lines.

4. Click the up scroll arrow on the vertical scroll bar three times to bring the document back into full view.

Notice that as you scroll through the document, the insertion point remains at the top of the document.

5. Click the Select Browse Object button ⊙, located toward the bottom of the vertical scroll bar. A palette of icons appears.

6. Move the pointer over each icon to identify it. These browse options become significant as your documents become more complex. Click the Browse by Page icon ▢.

TABLE 1-6 Scrolling through a Document

To Move	Do This
Up one line	Click the up scroll arrow ▲.
Down one line	Click the down scroll arrow ▼.
Up one window	Click the scroll bar above the scroll box.
Down one window	Click the scroll bar below the scroll box.
To any relative position	Drag the scroll box up or down.
To the right	Click the right scroll arrow ▶.
To the left	Click the left scroll arrow ◀.
Into the left margin	Hold down [Shift] and click the left scroll arrow ◀.
Up or down one page	Click Select Browse Object ◯, click Browse by Page ▯, and then click Next ▼ or Previous ▲.

Selecting Text

Selecting text is a basic technique that makes revising documents easy. When you select text, that area of the document is called the *selection,* and it appears as a highlighted block of text. A selection can be a character, group of characters, word, sentence, or paragraph or the whole document. In this lesson, you delete and replace selected text. Future lessons show you how to format, move, copy, delete, and print selected text.

You can select text several ways, depending on the size of the area you want to select.

TABLE 1-7 Mouse Selection

To	Use the Mouse to Select
A series of characters	Click and drag, or click one end of the text block, and then hold down [Shift] and click the other end.
A word	Double-click the word.
A sentence	Press [Ctrl] and click anywhere in the sentence.
A line of text	Move the pointer to the left of the line until it changes to a right-pointing arrow, and then click. To select multiple lines, drag up or down.
A paragraph	Move the pointer to the left of the paragraph and double-click. To select multiple paragraphs, drag up or down. You can also triple-click a paragraph to select it.
The entire document	Move the pointer to the left of any document text until it changes to a right-pointing arrow, and then triple-click (or hold down [Ctrl] and click).

Exercise 1-14 SELECT TEXT WITH THE MOUSE

1. Select the first word of the document by double-clicking it. Notice that the space following the word is also selected. When text is selected, a Mini toolbar appears with formatting options.

Figure 1-14
Selecting a word

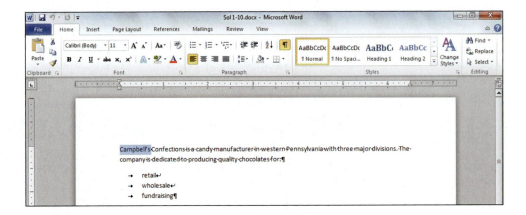

2. Cancel the selection by clicking anywhere in the document. Selected text remains highlighted until you cancel the selection.

3. Select the first sentence by holding down Ctrl and clicking anywhere within the sentence. Notice that the period and space following the sentence are part of the selection. Cancel the selection.

4. Locate the paragraph that begins "Visit one of our."

5. To select the text "milk chocolate," click to the left of "milk." Hold down the left mouse button and slowly drag through the text, including the comma and space after "chocolate." Release the mouse button. Cancel the selection.

6. To select the entire paragraph by dragging the mouse, click to position the insertion point to the left of "Visit." Hold down the mouse button, and then drag across and down until all the text and the paragraph mark are selected. Cancel the selection.

7. Select the same paragraph by moving the pointer into the blank area to the left of the text "Visit." (This is the margin area.) When the I-beam pointer changes to a right-pointing arrow , double-click. Notice that the first click selects the first line and the second click selects the paragraph, including the paragraph mark. Cancel the selection.

TIP

When selecting more than one word, you can click anywhere within the first word and then drag to select additional text. Word "smart-selects" the entire first word.

TIP

You can also triple-click within a paragraph to select it.

Figure 1-15
Selecting text

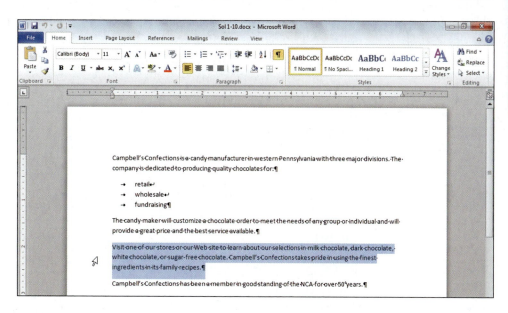

Exercise 1-15   SELECT NONCONTIGUOUS TEXT

In the previous exercise, you learned how to select *contiguous text,* where the selected characters, words, sentences, or paragraphs follow one another. But sometimes you would like to select *noncontiguous text,* such as the first and last items in a list or the third and fifth word in a paragraph. In Word, you can select noncontiguous text by using Ctrl and the mouse.

1. Select the first line of the list ("retail").

2. Press Ctrl and select the third line of the list ("fundraising"). With these two separate lines selected, you can delete, format, or move them without affecting the rest of the list.

3. Cancel the selection, and go to the paragraph that begins "Visit one of our."

4. In the paragraph that begins "Visit one of our," double-click the word "our" before "Web site." With the word now selected, hold down Ctrl as you double-click the word "selections" in the same sentence and "finest" in the next sentence. (See Figure 1-16.) All three words are highlighted.

UNIT 1 LESSON 1

Figure 1-16
Selecting
noncontiguous
words

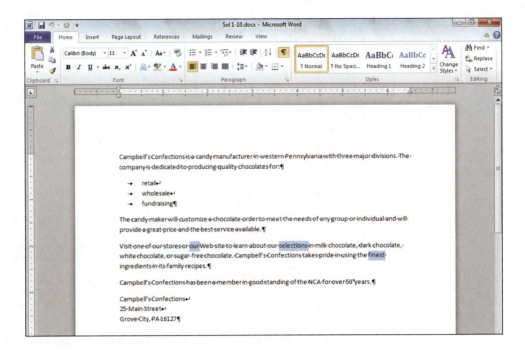

5. Cancel the selection.

Exercise 1-16 ADJUST A SELECTION USING THE MOUSE AND THE KEYBOARD

NOTE

Another way to extend a text selection is to turn on Selection mode by pressing [F8]. In Selection mode, you can press [F8] to select a word, press it again to select a sentence, press it again to select a paragraph, and press it again to select the entire document. Press [Shift]+[F8] to shorten the selection. Press [Esc] to turn off Selection mode. Right-click the status bar, and click Selection Mode to turn on or turn off the status bar indicator.

1. Select the paragraph beginning "Visit one of our."

2. Hold down [Shift] and press [←] until the last sentence is no longer highlighted. Release [Shift].

3. Increase the selection to include the last sentence by holding down [Shift] and pressing [End] and then pressing [↓]. Release [Shift].

4. Increase the selection to include all the text below it by holding down [Shift] and clicking at the end of the document (after the ZIP Code).

5. Select the entire document by pressing [Ctrl]+[A]. Cancel the selection.

TABLE 1-8 Keyboard Selection

To Select	Press
One character to the right	Shift + →
One character to the left	Shift + ←
One word to the right	Ctrl + Shift + →
One word to the left	Ctrl + Shift + ←
To the end of a line	Shift + End
To the beginning of a line	Shift + Home
One line up	Shift + ↑
One line down	Shift + ↓
One window down	Shift + PageDown
One window up	Shift + PageUp
To the end of a document	Ctrl + Shift + End
To the beginning of a document	Ctrl + Shift + Home
An entire document	Ctrl + A

Exercise 1-17 EDIT TEXT BY REPLACING A SELECTION

You can edit a document by selecting text and deleting or replacing the selection.

NOTE

Although keying over selected text is an excellent editing feature, it sometimes leads to accidental deletions. Remember, when text is selected in a document (or even in a dialog box) and you begin keying text, Word deletes all the selected text with your first keystroke. If you key text without realizing a portion of the document is selected, use the Undo command to restore the text.

1. Locate the paragraph that begins "Visit one of our," and select the word "our" in the first sentence that follows the word "about."

2. Key **the variety of** to replace the selected text.

3. Locate the paragraph that begins "Campbell's Confections has been," and select "NCA." Key **National Confectioners Association**. Notice that, unlike using Overtype mode, when you key over selected text, the new text can be longer or shorter than the selection.

Exercise 1-18 UNDO AND REDO ACTIONS

Word remembers the changes you make in a document and lets you undo or redo these changes. For example, if you accidentally delete text, you can use the Undo command to reverse the action and restore the text. If you change your mind and decide to keep the deletion, you can use the Redo command to reverse the canceled action.

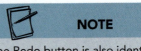

NOTE

The Redo button is also identified as the Repeat button. Use the Repeat command to repeat the last action performed.

There are two ways to undo or redo an action:

- Click the Undo button 🔄 or the Redo button 🔁 on the Quick Access Toolbar.
- Press Ctrl+Z to undo or Ctrl+Y to redo.

1. Delete the first word in the document, "Campbell's," by moving the insertion point to the right of the space after the word and pressing Ctrl+Backspace. (Remember that a word includes the space that follows it.)

2. Click the Undo button 🔄 to restore the word.

3. Move the insertion point to the left of the word "candy" in the first line of the first paragraph.

4. Key **midsize** and press Spacebar once. The text now reads "midsize candy manufacturer."

5. Press Ctrl+Z. The word "midsize" is deleted.

6. Click the Redo button 🔁 to restore the word "mid-size."

7. Click the down arrow to the right of the Undo button 🔄. Word displays a drop-down list of the last few actions, with the most recent action at the top. You can use this feature to choose several actions to undo rather than just the last action. Click Cancel to close the list.

8. Click the Undo button 🔄.

Figure 1-17
Undo drop-down list

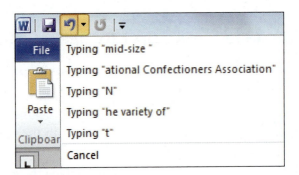

Exercise 1-19 REPEAT ACTIONS

Suppose you key text you want to add to other areas of a document. Instead of rekeying the same text, you can use the Repeat command to duplicate the text. To use the Repeat command, press either:

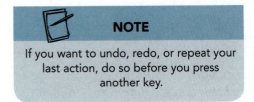

NOTE

If you want to undo, redo, or repeat your last action, do so before you press another key.

- Ctrl+Y
- F4

1. In the first paragraph position the insertion point to the left of the word "candy."

2. Key **popular** and press Spacebar once. The sentence now begins "Campbell's Confections is a popular candy."

3.   Move the insertion point to the left of the word "selections" in the paragraph that begins "Visit one of our."

4.   Press F4 and the word "popular" is repeated.

Printing a Document

After you create a document, printing it is easy. You can use any of the following methods:

- Choose Print from the File tab.

- Press Ctrl + P.

The Print command in Backstage view and the keyboard shortcut to print display the Print tab, where you can select printing options and preview the document. Clicking the Print button 🖶 sends the document directly to the printer, using Word's default settings.

Exercise 1-20 PRINT A DOCUMENT

1.   Click the **File** tab to open the Backstage view. Click the **Print** command. The Print tab displays Word's default print settings and a preview of the document.

Figure 1-18
Print tab

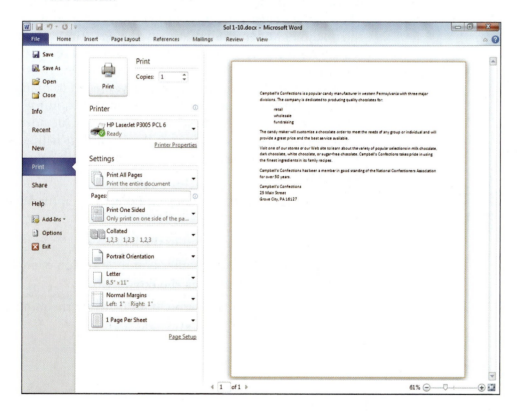

2.   Click the Print button 🖶 to accept the default print settings.

Closing a Document and Exiting Word

NOTE

If you wanted to save the current document with a different file name, you would use the Save As command.

Exercise 1-21 SAVE A REVISED DOCUMENT

You have already used the Save As command to rename the document you opened earlier in this lesson. Now that you have made additional revisions, you can save a final version of the document by using the Save command. The document is saved with all the changes, replacing the old file with the revised file.

1.   Click the Save button on the Quick Access Toolbar. This action saves the changes to the document. Since the document was saved earlier in the lesson, the Save As dialog box does not display.

Exercise 1-22 CHECK WORD'S AUTORECOVER SETTINGS

Word's *AutoRecover* feature can automatically save open documents at an interval you specify. However, this is not the same as saving a file yourself, as you did in the preceding exercise. AutoRecover's purpose is to save open documents "in the background," so a recently saved version is always on disk. Then if the power fails or your system crashes, the AutoRecover version of the document opens automatically the next time you launch Word. In other words, AutoRecover ensures you always have a recently saved version of your document.

Even with AutoRecover working, you need to manually save a document (by using the Save command) before closing it. AutoRecover documents are not always available. If you save and close your file normally, the AutoRecover version is deleted when you exit Word. Still, it is a good idea to make sure AutoRecover is working on your system and to set it to save recovery files frequently.

1.   Open the **File** tab, and click **Options** to open the Word Options dialog box.

2.   Click the **Save** command in the left pane.

3.   Make sure the **Save AutoRecover information every** box is checked. If it is not checked, click the box.

4.   Click the up or down arrow buttons to set the **minutes** to 5. Click **OK**.

Figure 1-19
Setting AutoRecover
options

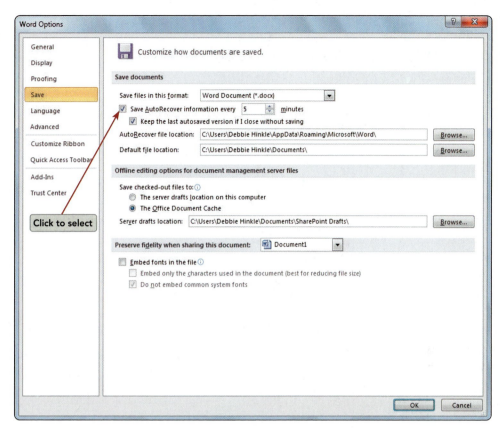

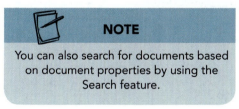
Click to select

Exercise 1-23 REVIEW AND EDIT DOCUMENT PROPERTIES

Information that describes your document is called a *property*. Word automatically saves your document with certain properties, such as the file name, the date created, and the file size. You can add other properties to a document, such as the title, subject, author's name, and keywords. This information can help you organize and identify documents.

> **NOTE**
>
> You can also search for documents based on document properties by using the Search feature.

1. With the file *[your initials]*1-10 still open, click the **File** tab and click the **Info** command. Locate the Properties button ⌷Properties ▾⌷ under the document preview. Click the down arrow, and click **Advanced Properties**. The Document Properties dialog box displays.

Figure 1-20
Entering Summary
information

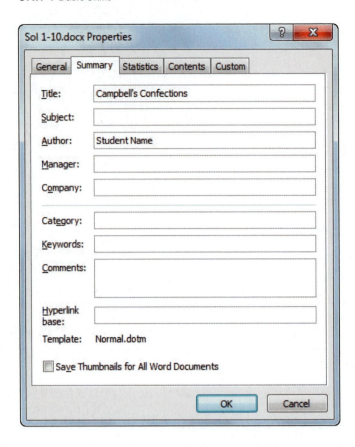

2. Click the **General** tab. This tab displays basic information about the file, such as file name, file type, location, size, and creation date.

3. Click the **Statistics** tab. This tab shows the exact breakdown of the document in number of paragraphs, lines, words, and characters.

4. Click the **Summary** tab. Here you can enter specific document property information or change existing information.

5. Key or edit the title to read **Campbell's Confections**, and key *[your name]* as the author. Click **OK**.

6. Save the document, and submit your work.

Exercise 1-24   CLOSE A DOCUMENT AND EXIT WORD

When you finish working on a document and save it, you can close it and open another document, or you can exit Word.

The easiest ways to close a document and exit Word include using the following:

- The Close button in the upper right corner of the Word window.
- The Close command from the File tab.
- Keyboard shortcuts:

    Ctrl + W closes a document.

    Alt + F4 exits Word.

>
> **NOTE**
>
> When no document is open, the document window is gray. If you want to create a new document, choose New from the File tab, click Blank Document, and click the Create button. The keyboard shortcut to create a new document is Ctrl + N.

1. Click the **File** tab, and choose **Close** from the Backstage view Navigation Pane.

2. Click the Close button ▉ X ▉ in the upper right corner of the screen to exit Word and to display the Windows desktop.

Using Online Help

Online Help is available to you as you work in Word. Click the Help button ❓ or press F1 to open the Word Help window. You can click a Word Help link or key a word or phrase in the Search box.

FIND OUT MORE ABOUT USING HELP

1. Start Word.

2. Locate the Help button ❓ in the upper right corner of the screen. Click the button to open the Word Help window.

3. Locate and click the link **Getting started with Word 2010**.

Figure 1-21
Using the Word
Help window

4. Review the list of topics.

5. Click the topic "What's new in Microsoft Word," and review the information.

6. Click the Back button ⊙ to return to the list of categories.

7. Close Help by clicking the Word Help window's Close button ⬛.

Lesson 1   Summary

- To start Microsoft Word, click the Start button on the Windows taskbar, point to All Programs, click Microsoft Office, and click Microsoft Word 2010.

- The File tab is located to the left of the Home tab on the Ribbon. Click the tab to open the Backstage view.

- The title bar is at the top of the Word screen and displays the current document name.

- The Quick Access Toolbar displays icons for Save, Undo, and Repeat.

- The Ribbon contains tabs which include groups of related commands. Commands can be buttons, menus, or drop-down list boxes.

- Click a tab name to display related groups of commands. The number of groups and commands varies for each tab.

- Identify a command by name by pointing to it with the mouse. Word displays a ScreenTip with the command name.

- The horizontal ruler appears below the Ribbon.

- Scroll bars appear as shaded bars to the right and bottom of the text area. They are used to view different portions of a document.

- The status bar is located at the bottom of the Word screen. It displays the page number and page count of the document, the document view buttons, and the zoom control. It also displays the current mode of operation. Right-click the status bar to customize it.

- Use the Zoom feature to change the magnification of the text area.

- The blinking vertical line in the text area is called the insertion point. It marks the position of the next character to be keyed.

- The mouse pointer displays as an I-beam when it is in the text area and as an arrow when you point to a command outside the text area.

- When the Show/Hide ¶ button is turned on, a paragraph mark symbol appears at the end of every paragraph. A dot between words represents a space.

- Word automatically wraps text to the next line as you key text. Press Enter to start a new paragraph or to insert a blank line.

- Word flags spelling errors as you key text by inserting a red, wavy line under the misspelled word. To correct the spelling, point to the underlined word, click the right mouse button, and choose the correct spelling.

- Word automatically corrects commonly misspelled words for you as you key text. Word can automatically complete a word for you, such as the name of a month or day. Word suggests the completed word, and you press Enter to insert it.

- Delete a single character by using Backspace or Delete. Ctrl + Backspace deletes the word to the left of the insertion point. Ctrl + Delete deletes the word to the right of the insertion point.

- To insert text, click to position the insertion point, and key the text.

- To key text over existing text, turn on Overtype mode.

- Insert one space between words and between sentences.

- Document names, or file names, can contain 260 characters, including the drive letter, folder name, and extensions. The file name can contain spaces. The following characters cannot be used in a file name: **/ \ > < * ? " : |**

- Save a new document by using the Save As command and giving the document a file name. Use the Save command to update an existing document.

- Create folders to organize your files. You can do this in the Save As dialog box, using the New Folder button. Rename folders by locating and selecting the folder. Right-click the folder name, and choose Rename from the shortcut menu

- To start a new blank document, press Ctrl+N, or click the File tab. Click New, click Blank document, and click Create.

- Use the Open dialog box to open an existing file. Use the Views button in the dialog box to change the way files are listed.

- Formatting characters—such as blank spaces or paragraph marks—appear on-screen, but not in the printed document. Insert a line-break character to start a new line within the same paragraph. Insert a nonbreaking space between two words to make sure they appear on the same line.

- When a document is larger than the document window, use the keyboard or the scroll bars to view different parts of the document. Keyboard methods for moving within a document also move the insertion point.

- Keyboard techniques for moving within a document include single keys (such as PageUp and Home) and keyboard combinations (such as Ctrl+↑). See Table 1-5.

- Scrolling techniques for moving within a document include clicking the up or down scroll arrows on the vertical scroll bar or dragging the scroll box. Scrolling does not move the insertion point. See Table 1-6.

- Selecting text is a basic technique for revising documents. A selection is a highlighted block of text you can format, move, copy, delete, or print.

- There are many different techniques for selecting text, using the mouse, the keyboard, or a combination of both. Mouse techniques involve dragging or clicking. See Table 1-7. Keyboard techniques are listed in Table 1-8.

- You can select any amount of contiguous text (characters, words, sentences, or paragraphs that follow one another) or noncontiguous text (such as words that appear in different parts of a document). Use Ctrl along with the mouse to select noncontiguous blocks of text.

- When text is selected, Word replaces it with any new text you key, or it deletes the selection if you press Delete.

- If you make a change in a document that you want to reverse, use the Undo command. Use the Redo command to reverse the results of an Undo command.

- If you perform an action, such as keying text in a document, and you want to repeat that action elsewhere in the document, use the Repeat command.

- Choose Print from the File tab, or press Ctrl+P to print a document.

- Use the Save command to save any revisions you make to a document.
- Word's AutoRecover feature periodically saves open documents in the background so you can recover a file in the event of a power failure or system crash.
- Document properties are details about a file that help identify it. Properties include the file name, file size, and date created, which Word updates automatically. Other properties you can add or change include title, subject, author's name, and keywords. View or add properties for an open document by clicking the File tab and clicking Info.
- To use Word Help, click the Help button or press F1.

NOTE

Word provides many ways to accomplish a particular task. As you become more familiar with Word, you will find the methods you prefer.

LESSON		Command Summary	
Feature	**Button**	**Command**	**Keyboard**
Close a document	X	File tab, Close	Ctrl+W or Ctrl+F4
Document Properties	Properties ▾	File tab, Info command	
Exit Word	X	File tab, Exit	Alt+F4
Help	?		F1
Open	📂	File tab, Open	Ctrl+O or Ctrl+F12
Print	🖨	File tab, Print	Ctrl+P
Redo	↻	Quick Access Toolbar	Ctrl+Y or Alt+Shift+Backspace
Repeat	↻	Quick Access Toolbar	Ctrl+Y or F4
Save	💾	Quick Access Toolbar	Ctrl+S or Shift+F12
Save As	📄	File tab, Save As	F12
Select entire document		Home tab, Editing group, Select All	Ctrl+A
Undo	↩	Quick Access Toolbar	Ctrl+Z or Alt+Backspace

- **Concepts Review**

    True/False Questions

    Short Answer Questions

    Critical Thinking Questions

- **Skills Review**

    Review Exercises that target single skills

    Lesson Applications

    Review Exercises that challenge students by testing multiple skills in each exercise

- **On Your Own**

    Open-ended exercises that require students to synthesize multiple skills and apply creativity and problem-solving as they would in a real world business situation

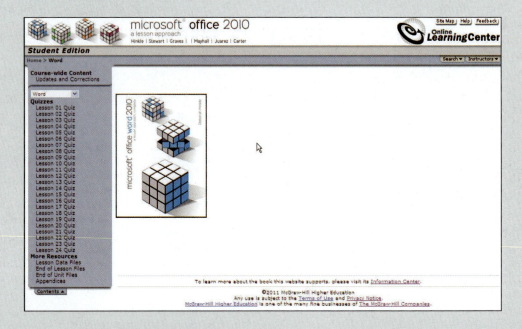

Lesson 2
Formatting Characters

After completing this lesson, you will be able to:

1. Work with fonts.
2. Apply basic character formatting.
3. Work with the Font dialog box.
4. Repeat and copy character formats.
5. Change case and highlight text.
6. Apply special effects

Estimated Time: 1 hour

Every document is based on a theme. A *theme* is a set of formatting instructions for the entire document and includes fonts, colors, and object effects. The default theme is Office, and you can easily change the theme by selecting an option from the Themes gallery.

Character formatting is used to emphasize text. You can change character formatting by applying bold or italic format, for example, or by changing the style of the type. Word also provides special features to copy formats, highlight text, and apply text effects for visual emphasis.

Working with Fonts

A *font* is a type design applied to an entire set of characters, including all letters of the alphabet, numerals, punctuation marks, and other keyboard symbols. Every theme defines two fonts—one for headings and one for body text.

Figure 2-1
Examples of fonts

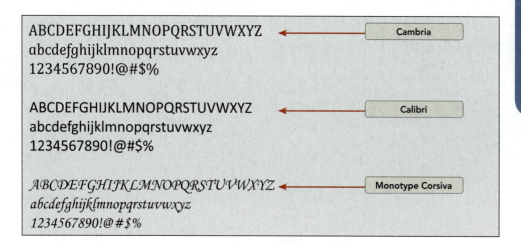

The Office theme includes a Heading font and a Body font. Calibri is the default Body font, and it is an example of a plain font. Cambria is more ornate, and it is the default Heading font. Monotype Corsiva is an example of a script font. Calibri is a *sans serif* font because it has no decorative lines, or serifs, projecting from its characters. Cambria is a *serif* font because it has decorative lines. Fonts are available in a variety of sizes and are measured in *points*. There are 72 points to an inch. Like other character formatting, you can use different fonts and font sizes in the same document.

> **NOTE**
>
> The default Office theme fonts are Calibri, a sans serif font, and Cambria, a serif font. The default font size is 11 points.

Figure 2-2
Examples of different point sizes

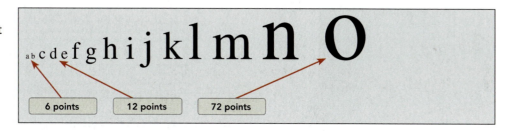

Exercise 2-1   CHANGE FONTS AND FONT SIZES USING THE RIBBON

The easiest way to choose fonts and font sizes is to use the Ribbon. The Home tab includes the Font group that contains frequently used character formatting commands.

> **TIP**
>
> Press Ctrl + Shift + * to display formatting characters. (Do not use the asterisk on the numeric keypad.)

1. Open the file **Festival**. This document is a text document that will be used to practice character formatting and to create a flyer for the Chocolate Festival.

NOTE

The fonts you used most recently appear below the Theme Fonts. Shaded divider lines separate the Theme Fonts, Recently Used Fonts, and the list of All Fonts.

2. Click the Show/Hide ¶ button ¶ to display paragraph marks and space characters if they are not already showing.

3. Move to the beginning of the document, and select the first two lines of text, which begins "Campbell's Confections." (Remember, you can press Ctrl + Home to move to the beginning of a document.)

4. Click the **Home** tab, and locate the **Font** group. Click the down arrow next to the **Font** box to open the Font drop-down list. Fonts are listed alphabetically by name and are displayed graphically.

Figure 2-3
Choosing a font

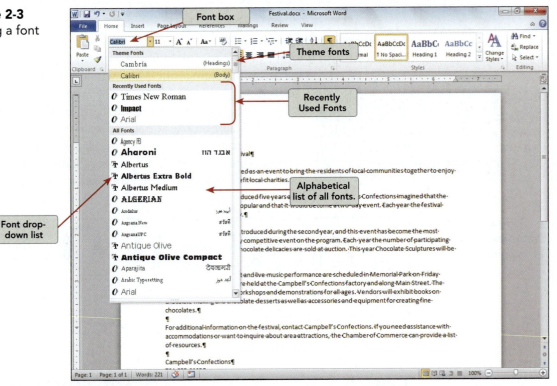

NOTE

As you scroll the list of fonts and font sizes, the Live Preview feature enables you to preview the change in the document before you select an option.

5. Use the ↓ on the keyboard or the scroll box on the font list's scroll bar and choose **Arial**.

6. Click the down arrow button to open the **Font Size** drop-down list, and choose 16 points. When you point to 16 in the drop-down list, the selected text previews the change in format. Now the first two lines stand out as a headline.

Figure 2-4
Choosing a font size

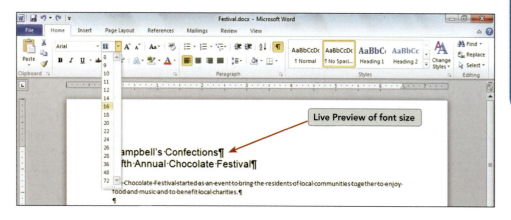

Exercise 2-2 CHANGE FONT SIZE USING KEYBOARD SHORTCUTS

If you prefer keyboard shortcuts, you can press Ctrl+Shift+> to increase the font size or Ctrl+Shift+< to decrease the font size. You can also press Ctrl+] to increase the font size by one point, or press Ctrl+[to decrease the font size by one point.

TIP

Sometimes text might appear bold on your screen when it is simply a larger font size.

1. Move the insertion point to the end of the document, and press Enter to start a new paragraph.

2. Press Ctrl+Shift+>, and key **Save the Date!**. The new text appears in 12-point type.

3. Press Enter to begin another paragraph. Press Ctrl+Shift+< to reduce the font size to 11 points, and key **September 26, 20--**.

Basic Character Formatting

NOTE

The underline feature is rarely used for emphasis because it affects the readability of text. Use bold or italic for emphasis.

The basic font styles or character formats are bold, italic, and underline. Text can have one or more character formats.

TABLE 2-1 Character Formatting

Attribute	Example
Normal	This is a sample.
Bold	**This is a sample.**
Italic	*This is a sample.*
Underline	<u>This is a sample</u>.
Bold and italic	***This is a sample.***

The simplest ways to apply basic character formatting are to use:

- Commands on the Ribbon, Home tab, Font group
- Keyboard shortcuts
- Commands on the Mini toolbar

You can apply character formatting to existing text, including text that is noncontiguous. You can also turn on a character format before you key new text and turn it off after you enter the text. For example, you can click the Bold button **B**, key a few words in bold, click the button again to turn off the format, and continue keying regular text.

Exercise 2-3   APPLY BASIC CHARACTER FORMATTING USING THE RIBBON

1. Select "Chocolate Festival" in the first paragraph below the heading.
2. Click the Bold button **B** on the Ribbon to format the text bold. (The Bold command is located in the Font group.)
3. With the text still selected, click the Italic button *I* on the Ribbon to format the text bold and italic.
4. Click the Bold button **B** again to turn off the bold format and to leave the text as italic only. Click the Bold button **B** again to restore the bold-italic formatting.

> **NOTE**
>
> The Home tab on the Ribbon displays by default. If the Home tab is not the active tab, click the Home tab to make it active and to display the Font group commands.

Figure 2-5
Using the Ribbon to apply character formatting

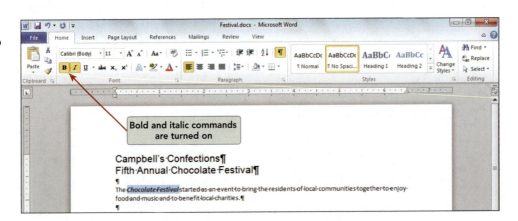

5. Move the insertion point to the end of the same paragraph, and press the [Spacebar] once.

6. Click the Bold button **B** and the Italic button *I*, and key **Visitors to the festival will be able to sample and purchase chocolate creations as well as listen to area musicians throughout the festival celebration.** in bold italic.

7. Click both buttons to turn off the formatting.

8. Select the bold-italic text "Chocolate Festival."

9. Press [Ctrl], and select the bold-italic sentence that begins "Visitors to the festival" as well.

10. Click the Underline button **U** on the Ribbon to underline the noncontiguous selections.

11. Click the Undo button ↰ to remove the underline.

12. Select the first line in the document.

13. Click the Change Case button **Aa**, and click **UPPERCASE.**

NOTE

When text is selected, a Mini toolbar appears with character and paragraph formatting commands.

Exercise 2-4 APPLY AND REMOVE BASIC CHARACTER FORMATTING USING KEYBOARD SHORTCUTS

If you prefer to keep your hands on the keyboard instead of using the mouse, you can use keyboard shortcuts to turn basic character formatting on and off. You can press [Ctrl]+[B] for bold, [Ctrl]+[I] for italic, and [Ctrl]+[U] for underline. To remove character formatting from selected text, press [Ctrl]+[Spacebar].

1. Select the text "Chamber of Commerce" near the end of the document.

2. Press [Ctrl]+[B] to apply bold format to the selected text, and press [Ctrl]+[I] to add italic format.

3. Move the insertion point to the end of the document, and press [Enter] to start a new paragraph.

4. Press [Ctrl]+[B] to turn on the bold option, and key **Visit our Web site for a list of events.**

5. Select the bold-italic text "Chocolate Festival" in the first paragraph, and press [Ctrl]+[Spacebar] to remove the formatting.

6. Click the Undo button ↰ to restore the bold-italic formatting.

Exercise 2-5   APPLY AND REMOVE BASIC CHARACTER FORMATTING USING THE MINI TOOLBAR

The Mini toolbar appears when you select text in a document. You can click any of the buttons on the toolbar to apply or remove character formatting from the selected text.

1. Select the first line of text. Notice the Mini toolbar displays.

Figure 2-6
Mini toolbar

2. Click the drop-down arrow beside the Font Color button **A**. Locate Standard Colors in the palette, and click **Blue**.

3. Click the Grow Font button **A** two times, and notice the change in the font size. Click the Shrink Font button **A** one time.

Using the Font Dialog Box

The Font dialog box offers a wider variety of options than those available on the Ribbon, and you can conveniently choose several options at one time.
There are several ways to open the Font dialog box:

*   Click the Font Dialog Box Launcher.

*   Right-click (use the right mouse button) selected text to display a *shortcut menu,* and then choose Font. A shortcut menu shows a list of commands relevant to a particular item you click.

*   Use keyboard shortcuts.

Figure 2-7
Shortcut menu

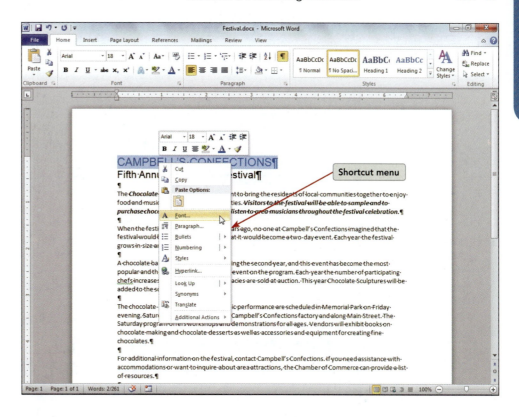

Exercise 2-6   CHOOSE FONTS AND FONT STYLES USING THE FONT DIALOG BOX

1. Select the first line of text, which is currently 18-point Arial and blue.

2. Click the Font Dialog Box Launcher ⬛ in the lower right corner of the Font group on the Ribbon. The Font dialog box displays.

Figure 2-8
Font Dialog Box
Launcher

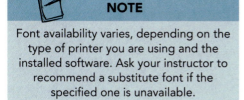

NOTE

Font availability varies, depending on the type of printer you are using and the installed software. Ask your instructor to recommend a substitute font if the specified one is unavailable.

3. Choose **ITC Bookman Demi** from the **Font** list, **Italic** from the **Font style** list, and **20** from the **Size** list. Look at your choices in the **Preview** box, and click **OK**.

Figure 2-9
Using the Font
dialog box

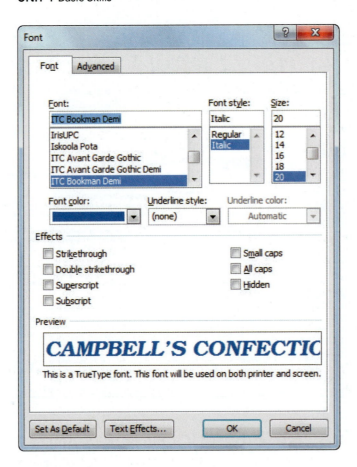

Exercise 2-7   APPLY UNDERLINE OPTIONS AND CHARACTER EFFECTS

In addition to choosing font, font size, and font style, you can choose font color, a variety of underlining options, and special character effects from the Font dialog box.

1. Select the text "Save the Date!" near the end of the document.

2. Press Ctrl + D to open the Font dialog box.

TIP

Press Ctrl+Shift+F to open the Font dialog box with the Font box active. Press Ctrl+Shift+P to open the Font dialog with the Size box active.

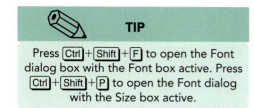

3. Click the down arrow ▾ to open the **Underline style** drop-down list. Drag the scroll box down to see all the available underline styles. Choose one of the dotted-line styles.

4. Click the down arrow ▾ next to the Font color box, and choose Green in the Standard Colors palette. (Each color is identified by name when you point to it.)

Figure 2-10
Font color options in the Font dialog box

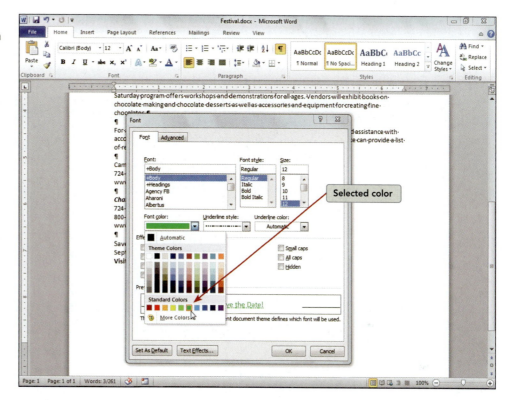

5. Click the down arrow next to the **Underline color** box, and choose Red.

6. Click **OK**. The text is green with a red dotted underline.

TIP

As a rule, punctuation such as colons and periods should not be underlined.

7. Select the sentence in the first paragraph below the heading that begins "Visitors to the festival."

8. Move the mouse pointer to the Ribbon, and click the Clear Formatting button 🗛.

9. Select the text "Chocolate Festival" in the first paragraph.

10. Click the selected text with the right mouse button, and from the shortcut menu, choose **Font** to open the Font dialog box. Locate **Effects**, click the **Small caps** check box, and click **OK**. The text that was formerly lowercase now appears in small capital letters.

11. Select the text "Save the Date."

12. Click the Strikethrough button 🔠 on the Ribbon. The text appears with a horizontal line running through it.

13. Click the Undo button 🔙 to undo the strikethrough effect.

TABLE 2-2 Font Effects in the Font Dialog Box

Effect	Description and Example
Strikethrough	Applies a ~~horizontal line~~.
Double strikethrough	Applies a ~~double horizontal line~~.
Superscript	Raises text ᵃᵇᵒᵛᵉ other characters on the same line.
Subscript	Places text ᵦₑₗₒw other characters on the same line.
Small Caps	Makes lowercase text SMALL CAPS.
All Caps	Makes all text UPPERCASE.
Hidden	Hidden text does not print and appears on-screen only if Word's Display options are set to display hidden text. See File tab, Options.

Exercise 2-8 USE KEYBOARD SHORTCUTS FOR UNDERLINE OPTIONS AND FONT EFFECTS

Word provides keyboard shortcuts for some underlining options and font effects as an alternative to using the Ribbon or opening the Font dialog box.

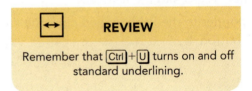

REVIEW

Remember that Ctrl+U turns on and off standard underlining.

1. Locate and select the text "Campbell's Confections" near the end of the document. Press Ctrl and select the text "Chamber of Commerce."

2. Press Ctrl+Shift+K to apply small caps to the selected text.

3. Select the text "chocolate bake-off" in the third paragraph that begins "A chocolate bake-off."

4. Press Ctrl+Shift+D to apply double underlining, and press Ctrl+Shift+K to apply small caps format.

TABLE 2-3 Keyboard Shortcuts for Underlining and Character Effects

Keyboard Shortcut	Action
Ctrl + Shift + W	Turn on or off words-only underlining.
Ctrl + Shift + D	Turn on or off double underlining.
Ctrl + Shift + =	Turn on or off superscript.
Ctrl + =	Turn on or off subscript.
Ctrl + Shift + K	Turn on or off small capitals.
Ctrl + Shift + A	Turn on or off all capitals.
Ctrl + Shift + H	Turn on or off hidden text.

Exercise 2-9   CHANGE CHARACTER SPACING

The Character Spacing tab in the Font dialog box offers options for changing the space between characters or the position of text in relation to the baseline. Character spacing can be expanded or condensed horizontally, as well as raised or lowered vertically.

1. Select the first line of text, which begins "Campbell's Confections."

2. Open the **Font** dialog box, and click the **Advanced** tab.

3. Click the down arrow to open the **Scale** drop-down list. Click **150%**, and notice the change in the **Preview** box. Change the scale back to **100%**.

Figure 2-11
Font dialog box—
Advanced tab

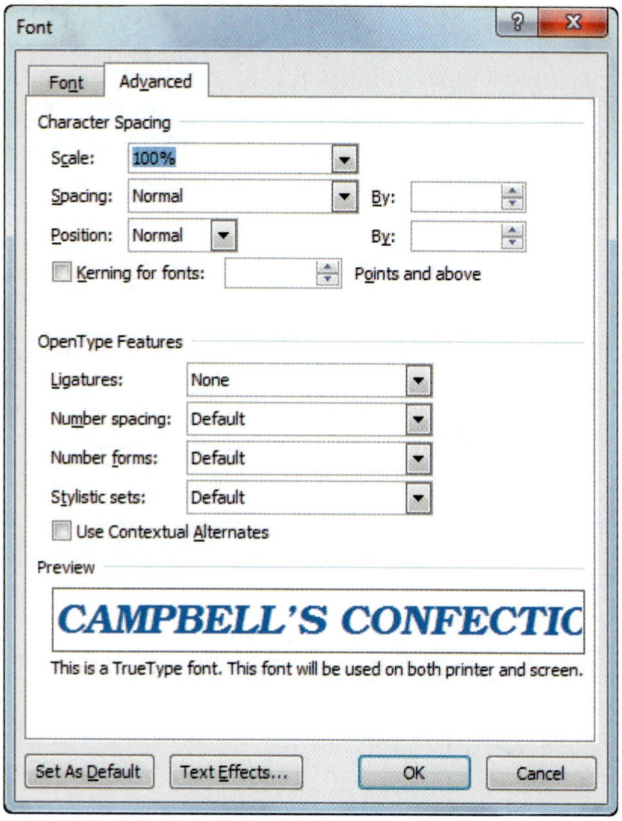

> **TIP**
>
> You can increase the space between characters even more by increasing the number in the By box (click the arrows or key a specific number). Experiment with the Spacing and Scale options on your own to see how they change the appearance of text.

4. Click the down arrow to display the **Spacing** options. Click **Expanded**, and then click **OK**. The text appears with more space between each character. When you expand or condense text spacing, you change the spacing between all the selected characters.

5. Select the first line if necessary, and use the Mini toolbar to change the font to **Arial**.

6. Open the **Save As** dialog box, create a new folder for your Lesson 2 files, and save the document as *[your initials]2-9*.

> **NOTE**
>
> Remember to use this folder for all the exercise documents you create in this lesson.

Repeating and Copying Formatting

You can use F4 or Ctrl+Y to repeat character formatting. You can also copy character formatting with a special tool on the Ribbon—the Format Painter button .

Exercise 2-10   REPEAT CHARACTER FORMATTING

Before trying to repeat character formatting, keep in mind that you must use the Repeat command immediately after applying the format. In addition, the Repeat command repeats only the last character format applied. (If you apply multiple character formats from the Font dialog box, the Repeat command applies all formatting.)

1. Select "chocolate tasting event" in the fourth paragraph, and click the Italic button *I* to italicize the text.

2. Select "chocolate delicacies" in the third paragraph, and press F4 to repeat your last action (turning on italic format).

3. Select the text "Save the Date!"

4. Open the **Font** dialog box. Click the **Font** tab, if it is not already displayed, and choose another font, such as Impact. Select the font size **14** points, and change the font color to Red. Click **OK**. The text appears with the new formatting.

5. Select the text "September 26, 20--" and press [F4]. Word repeats all the formatting you chose in the Font dialog box. If you apply each character format separately, using the Ribbon, the Repeat command applies only the last format you chose.

Figure 2-12
Repeating character formatting

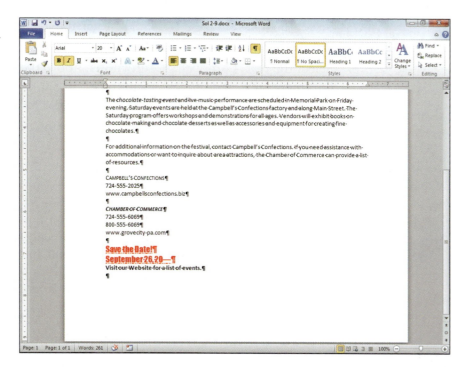

Exercise 2-11   COPY CHARACTER FORMATTING

The Format Painter button 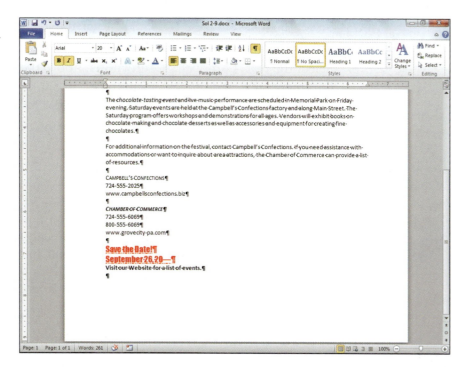 makes it easy to copy a character format. This is particularly helpful when you copy text with multiple formats, such as bold-italic small caps.

To use Format Painter to copy character formatting, first select the text with the formatting you want to copy, and then click the Format Painter button. The mouse pointer changes to a paintbrush with an I-beam pointer. Use this pointer to select the text to which you want to apply the copied formatting.

1. In the paragraph that begins "When the," select "festival" and click the Font color button. Change the font color to Dark Blue. Apply bold and italic format to the selected text.

2. With the text still selected, locate the **Clipboard** group on the **Home** tab, and click the Format Painter button. When you move the pointer back into the text area, notice the new shape of the pointer.

3. Use the paintbrush pointer to select "festival" in the next sentence. This copies the font color, bold, and italic format to the selected text, and the pointer returns to its normal shape.

4. Select the text "*CHAMBER OF COMMERCE*" near the end of the document.

5. Press Ctrl + D to open the **Font** dialog box. Change the **Font color** to Blue, and change the **Size** to 12. Click **OK**. Do not deselect the text.

6. Double-click the Format Painter button 🖌. You double-click the Format Painter button to copy formatting repeatedly.

7. Select the text "Save the Date!" The copied formatting is applied to the text, and the pointer remains the paintbrush pointer.

8. Select the text "Campbell's Confections" above the Chamber of Commerce text and the text "September 26, 20--." The paintbrush pointer copies the new formatting over the old formatting.

9. Press Esc or click the Format Painter 🖌 to stop copying and to restore the normal pointer.

Changing Case and Highlighting Text

You have used Caps Lock to change case, and you have seen the Small Caps and All Caps options in the Font dialog box. You can also change the case of characters by using keyboard shortcuts and the Change Case command on the Ribbon. The Change Case command includes options for Sentence case, lowercase, UPPERCASE, Capitalize Each Word, and tOGGLE cASE.

Exercise 2-12   CHANGE CASE

1. Locate the paragraph that begins "For additional," and select the text "Campbell's Confections." Press Shift + F3. This keyboard shortcut changes case. Now the text appears in all uppercase letters.

2. With the text still selected, press Shift + F3 again. Now the sentence appears in all lowercase letters.

3. Press Shift + F3 again, and the original capitalization is restored.

4. Select the first line of the document, and click the Change Case button **Aa** on the Ribbon.

5. Click **tOGGLE cASE**. This option changes the text to lowercase. Click the Change Case button **Aa**, and click **UPPERCASE**.

6. Click anywhere in the document to deselect the text.

Exercise 2-13   HIGHLIGHT TEXT

To emphasize parts of a document, you can mark text with a color highlighter by using the Highlight button on the Ribbon, Home tab, Font group. As with the Format Painter button, when you click the Highlight button, the pointer changes shape. You then use the highlight pointer to select the text you want to highlight. In addition, you can choose from several highlighting colors.

1. Make sure no text is selected. On the Ribbon, click the down arrow next to the Highlight button to display the color choices. Click **Yellow** to choose it as the highlight color. This turns on the Highlight button, and the color indicator box on the button is now yellow.

Figure 2-13
Choosing a highlight color

2. Move the highlight pointer 🖉 into the text area.

3. Drag the pointer over the telephone numbers below "Chamber of Commerce."

4. Press ⌨Esc to turn off the highlighter and restore the normal pointer.

5. Select the first line of text in the document.

6. Click the Highlight button to highlight the selection. This is another way to use the highlighter—by selecting the text and then clicking the Highlight button.

7. Select the first line of text again. Remove the highlight by clicking the down arrow to display the highlight color choices and choosing **No Color**.

8. Select the remaining highlighted text, and click the Highlight button . Because "No Color" was last chosen (as shown in the color indicator box on the button), this action removes the highlight from the selected text.

Applying Special Effects

One way to call attention to a paragraph is to use a dropped capital letter, or a *drop cap.* A drop cap is a large letter that appears below the text baseline. It is usually applied to the first letter in the first word of a paragraph.

A second way to add visual emphasis to your text is to use the Text Effects feature. Text Effects include the following features: Outline, Shadow, Reflection, Glow, and Bevel. Each of these features includes special options for a variety of effects.

UNIT 1 LESSON 2

Exercise 2-14 CREATE A DROP CAP

1. Place the insertion point at the beginning of the first paragraph that begins "The Chocolate Festival."

2. Click the **Insert** tab on the Ribbon, and click the Drop Cap button. Click **In margin**.

3. Undo the drop cap.

4. Click the Drop Cap button, and click **Drop Cap Options**. The Drop Cap dialog box opens.

Figure 2-14
Drop Cap dialog box

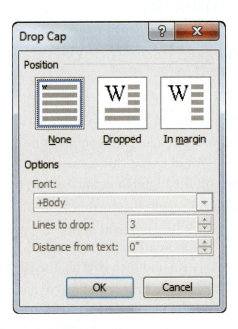

5. Under **Position**, click **Dropped**. This option is used to wrap the paragraph around the letter.

6. Change the **Distance from text** to **.1**, and click **OK**. Click within the document to deselect the "T." Notice the appearance of "The" and that it is dropped three lines.

Exercise 2-15 APPLY TEXT EFFECTS

1. Select the second line of text in the document that begins "Fifth Annual."

2. Click the Home tab, and click the Text Effects button to display a gallery of options. Click the fourth option in the third row **Gradient Fill–Blue, Accent 1**.

Figure 2-15
Text Effects gallery

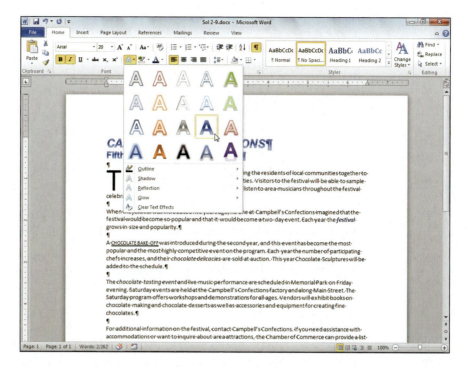

3. Select the first line of text in the document, and display the Text Effects gallery.

4. Click **Shadow**, and click an option in the **Outer** group.

5. Click the Text Effects button , point to **Shadow**, and click **Shadow Options**. The Format Text Effects dialog box displays with the Shadow option selected.

6. Click the Color button , and select a color. Drag the **Transparency** slider to **65** percent. Drag the **Blur** slider to **6** points, and drag the **Distance** slider to **5** points. Change the **Angle** option to **180** degrees. Click **Close** to return to the document.

7. Save the document as *[your initials]***2-15** in your Lesson 2 folder.

8. Submit your work, and close the document.

NOTE

An alternative to dragging the slider is to use the increment arrows to move the value up or down one percent, one point, or one degree, or to key a value in the text box.

NOTE

Each of the text effects listed in the Text Effects gallery has additional options for changing the appearance of the text.

Lesson 2   Summary

- A font is a type design applied to an entire set of characters, including all the letters of the alphabet, numerals, punctuation marks, and other keyboard symbols.

- A font can be serif (with decorative lines) or sans serif (with no decorative lines).

- Fonts are available in a variety of sizes, which are measured in points. There are 72 points to an inch.

- You can use the Ribbon to change fonts and font sizes.

- Keyboard shortcuts can also be used to change font sizes: Ctrl + Shift + > increases the text size and Ctrl + Shift + < decreases the text size.

- Use the Ribbon, Home tab, Font group to apply basic character formatting (for example, bold, italic, and/or underline) to selected contiguous (text that is together) or noncontiguous text (text that is not together).

- Use keyboard shortcuts to apply and remove basic character formatting.

- Use the Mini toolbar to apply character formatting to selected text.

- The Font dialog box can be used to change fonts, font sizes, and font styles. The Font dialog box also has settings for underline styles, font and underline colors, effects such as small caps (see Table 2-2), and character spacing.

- A hyperlink often appears as blue underlined text you click to open a software feature (such as a dialog box or a Help topic) or to go to an e-mail or a Web address.

- Keyboard shortcuts are available for some underline styles and font effects (see Table 2-3).

- A shortcut menu shows a list of commands relevant to a particular item. To display a shortcut menu, point to the item and right-click the mouse.

- Use F4 or Ctrl + Y to repeat character formatting.

- Use Format Painter to copy character formatting. Double-click the Format Painter button to apply formatting to more than one selection.

- To change the case of selected characters, use the keyboard shortcut Shift + F3 or the Change Case command on the Ribbon, Home tab.

- Use the Highlight button to apply a color highlight to selected text you want to emphasize on-screen.

- Use Drop Cap from the Insert tab to create a dropped cap. A drop cap is a large letter that appears below the text baseline. It is usually applied to the first letter in the first word of a paragraph.

- Text Effects add visual emphasis to your text. Choose an Outline, Shadow, Reflection, Glow, or Bevel effect.

LESSON 2 — Command Summary

Feature	Button	Command	Keyboard
Bold	**B**	Home tab, Font group	Ctrl + B
Change case	Aa	Home tab, Font group	Shift + F3
Decrease font size	A˅	Home tab, Font group	Ctrl + Shift + <
Drop Cap	A≡	Insert tab, Text group	
Font color	A	Home tab, Font group	
Format Painter	🖌	Home tab, Clipboard group	
Highlight text	ab̲ ▾	Home tab, Font group	
Increase font size	A˄	Home tab, Font group	Ctrl + Shift + >
Italic	*I*	Home tab, Font group	Ctrl + I
Remove character formatting	A̲	Home tab, Font group	Ctrl + Spacebar
Text effects	A	Home tab, Font group	
Underline	U̲	Home tab, Font group	Ctrl + U

Please visit our Online Learning Center, *www.lessonapproach2010.com*, **where you will find the following review materials:**

- **Concepts Review**

  True/False Questions

  Short Answer Questions

  Critical Thinking Questions

- **Skills Review**

  Review Exercises that target single skills

  Lesson Applications

  Review Exercises that challenge students by testing multiple skills in each exercise

- **On Your Own**

  Open-ended exercises that require students to synthesize multiple skills and apply creativity and problem-solving as they would in a real world business situation

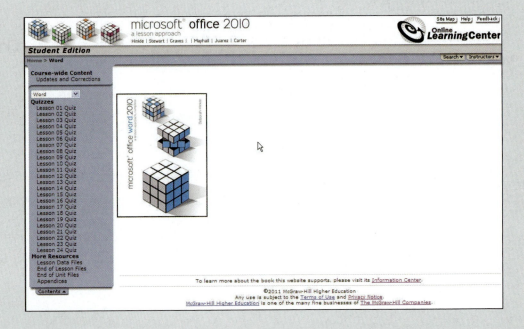

Writing Tools

OBJECTIVES *After completing this lesson, you will be able to:*

1. Use AutoComplete, AutoCorrect, and Actions.
2. Work with Building Blocks.
3. Insert the date and time as a field.
4. Check spelling and grammar.
5. Use the thesaurus and Research task pane.

Estimated Time: 1 hour

Word provides several automated features that save you time when keying frequently used text and correcting common keying errors. Word also provides important writing and research tools: a spelling and grammar checker, a thesaurus, and access to research services. These tools help you create professional-looking documents.

Using AutoComplete and AutoCorrect

By now, you might be familiar with three of Word's automatic features, though you might not know their formal names:

- *AutoComplete* suggests the completed word when you key the first four or more letters of a day, month, or date. If you key "Janu," for example, Word displays a ScreenTip suggesting the word "January," which you can insert by pressing Enter. Continue keying if you do not want the word inserted.

- *AutoCorrect* corrects commonly misspelled words as you key text. If you key "teh" instead of "the," for example, Word automatically changes the spelling to "the." You can create AutoCorrect entries for text you frequently use, and you can control AutoCorrect options.

- *Actions* help you save time by pressing the right mouse button for certain words or phrases and displaying a shortcut menu of actions. Word recognizes names, dates, addresses, and telephone numbers, as well as user-defined data types.

Exercise 3-1   PRACTICE AUTOCOMPLETE AND AUTOCORRECT

1. Open a new document. Click the **File** tab, and click **Options**. Click **Proofing**, and click **AutoCorrect Options** to open the AutoCorrect dialog box. Notice the available AutoCorrect options.

2. Scroll down the list of entries, and notice the words that Word corrects automatically (assuming the **Replace text as you type** option is checked).

Figure 3-1
AutoCorrect dialog
box

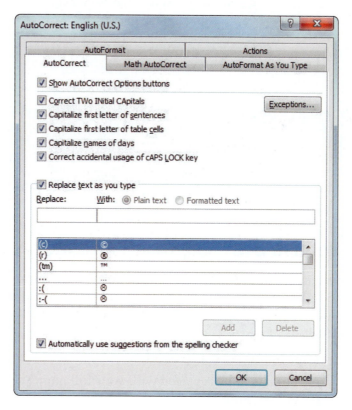

3. Click Cancel to close the dialog box. Click Cancel to close the Word
    Options dialog box.

4. Key **i am testing teh AutoCorrect feature.** Press [Enter]. Word corrects the
    "i" and "teh" automatically.

5. Try keying another incorrect sentence. Using the exact
    spelling and case as shown, key **TOdya is**. AutoCorrect
    corrects the spelling and capitalization of "Today."

6. Key today's date, beginning with the month, and then
    press [Spacebar]. When you see the AutoComplete
    ScreenTip that suggests the current date, press [Enter].

7. Key a period at the end of the sentence.

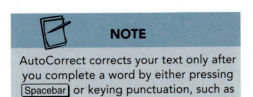

NOTE

AutoCorrect corrects your text only after
you complete a word by either pressing
[Spacebar] or keying punctuation, such as
a period or comma.

TABLE 3-1 AutoCorrect Options

Options	Description
Correct TWo INitial Capitals	Corrects words keyed accidentally with two initial capital letters, such as "WOrd" or "THis."
Capitalize first letter of sentences	Corrects any word at the beginning of a sentence that is not keyed with a capital letter.
Capitalize first letter of table cells	Corrects any word at the beginning of a table cell that is not keyed with a capital letter.
Capitalize names of days	Corrects a day spelled without an initial capital letter.
Correct accidental usage of cAPS LOCK key	If you press [Caps Lock] accidentally and then key "tODAY," AutoCorrect changes the word to "Today" and turns off [Caps Lock].
Replace text as you type	Makes all corrections automatically.

Exercise 3-2 CREATE AN AUTOCORRECT ENTRY

You can create AutoCorrect entries for words you often misspell. You can
also use AutoCorrect to create shortcuts for text you use repeatedly, such as
names or phrases. Here are some examples of these types of AutoCorrect
entries:

*   "asap" for "as soon as possible"
*   Your initials to be replaced with your full name, such as "**jh**" for
    "**Janet Holcomb**"
*   "cc" for "Campbell's Confections"

1. Click the **File** tab, and click **Options**. Click **Proofing**.

2. Click **AutoCorrect Options** to open the AutoCorrect dialog box. Click the **AutoCorrect** tab if necessary. In the **Replace** box, key **fyi.**

3. Press ⌨Tab, and key **For your information** in the **With** box.

4. Click the **Add** button to move the entry into the alphabetized list. Click **OK** to close the AutoCorrect dialog box. Click **OK** to close the Word Options dialog box.

5. Start a new paragraph in the current document, and key **fyi, this really works.** Word spells out the entry, just as you specified in the AutoCorrect dialog box. It is not necessary to capitalize text keyed in the Replace text box.

Exercise 3-3   CONTROL AUTOCORRECT OPTIONS

Sometimes you might not want text to be corrected. You can undo a correction or turn AutoCorrect options on or off by clicking the AutoCorrect Options button and making a selection.

1. Move the I-beam over the word "For" until a small blue box appears beneath it.

Figure 3-2
Controlling
AutoCorrect options

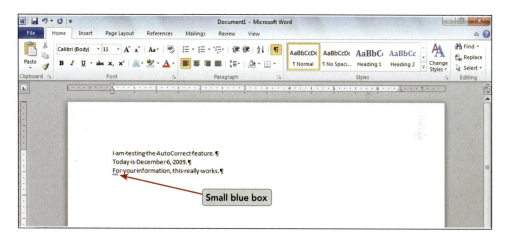

2. Drag the I-beam down over the small blue box until your mouse becomes a pointer and the box turns into the AutoCorrect Options button.

3. Click the button, and choose **Change back to "fyi"** from the menu list.

Figure 3-3
Undoing Automatic
corrections

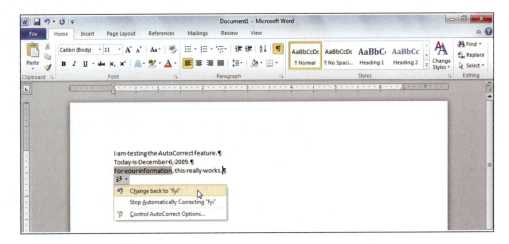

4. Click the AutoCorrect Options button 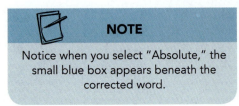 again, and choose **Redo AutoCorrect** from the list. The words "For your information" are restored.

5. Click the button again, and choose **Control AutoCorrect Options**. The AutoCorrect dialog box opens.

6. Position the insertion point in the Replace text box, and key **fyi**. The AutoCorrect entry displays and is highlighted. Click **Delete**, and then click **OK**.

Exercise 3-4 CREATE AN AUTOCORRECT EXCEPTION

Another way to keep Word from correcting text you do not want corrected is to create an AutoCorrect exception. For example, you might have a company name that uses nonstandard capitalization such as "tuesday's bookstore." In such a case, you can use the AutoCorrect Exceptions dialog box to prevent Word from making automatic changes.

1. In a new paragraph, key the following on two separate lines:
    The ABCs of chocolate:
    ABsolute

    Press the ⟨Spacebar⟩. Notice that AutoCorrect automatically changes the "B" in "ABsolute" to lowercase.

NOTE

Notice when you select "Absolute," the small blue box appears beneath the corrected word.

2. Open the AutoCorrect dialog box by moving the mouse over the word "Absolute" and clicking the AutoCorrect Options button 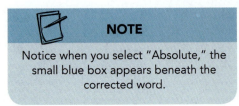. Click **Control AutoCorrect Options**. Click **Exceptions**. The AutoCorrect Exceptions dialog box displays.

3. Click the **INitial CAps** tab.

4. Key the exception **ABsolute** in the **Don't Correct** text box. Click **Add**. The entry is now in the list of exceptions.

Figure 3-4
AutoCorrect Exceptions dialog box

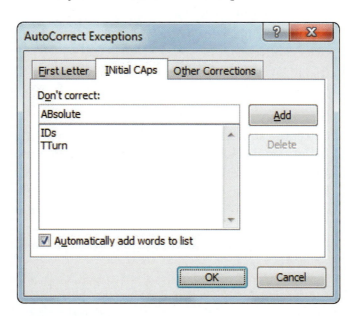

5. Click **OK,** to close the AutoCorrect Exceptions dialog box, and then click **OK** again to close the AutoCorrect dialog box.

6. Select "Absolute" and then key **ABsolute storage temperature is a must.**

7. Right-click "Absolute," and choose **AutoCorrect** from the shortcut menu. Click **AutoCorrect Options** from the submenu, and click **Exceptions**. Select "ABsolute" from the list, and click **Delete**. Click **OK** to close the AutoCorrect Exceptions dialog box, and click **OK** to close the AutoCorrect dialog box.

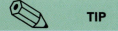
TIP

Another good example of an AutoCorrect exception is the use of lowercase initials, which are sometimes entered at the bottom of a business letter as reference initials (see Appendix B, "Standard Forms for Business Documents"). In this case, you would not want Word to capitalize the first letter. To add your initials to AutoCorrect Exceptions, click the First Letter tab, and key your initials (lowercase) in the Don't capitalize after text box. Click OK twice.

Exercise 3-5   DEFINE ACTIONS

Just as Word recognizes an e-mail or Web address and automatically creates a hyperlink, it also recognizes names, dates, addresses, telephone numbers, and user-defined data types. You can right-click a word or phrase, and perform actions in Word for which you would normally open other programs, such as Microsoft Outlook. For instance, you can add a contact, schedule a meeting, or display your calendar.

1. Open the **File** tab, and click **Options**. Click **Proofing**, and click **AutoCorrect Options**.

2. Click the **Actions** tab, and click the **Enable additional actions in the right-click menu** check box if it is not selected.

3. Locate the heading **Available Actions**, and select **Address (English)** and **Date (XML)**. Deselect all other options.

4. Click **OK** to close the AutoCorrect dialog box. Click **OK** to close the Word Options dialog box.

5. Position the insertion point at the end of the document, press [Enter] twice, and key:

    Campbell's Confections
    25 Main Street
    Grove City, PA 16127

6. Select the address, and click the right-mouse button. Choose **Additional Actions,** and click **Add to Contact**. Microsoft Outlook launches, and an Untitled-Contact dialog box opens. You can add contact information including name, business, e-mail address, and telephone numbers. You can also search for directions using the Map It link.

Figure 3-5
List of actions

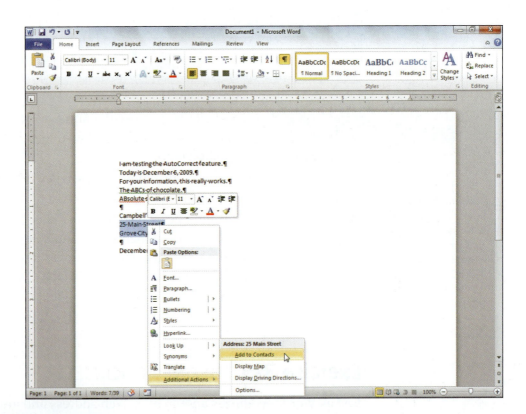

NOTE

Microsoft Outlook is a program included in the Microsoft Office suite. If it is not set up on your machine, just close the dialog box when it asks you to configure it, or ask your instructor for help. If Outlook does launch, the Add to Contacts option lets you record information about individuals and businesses.

7. Close the Contact window without saving.

8. Select the date near the top of the document. Right-click to display the shortcut menu, and click **Additional Actions.** Choose **Show my Calendar**. Microsoft Outlook Calendar launches. Study the calendar features, and then close the Calendar window.

9. Close the document without saving.

Working with AutoText and Building Blocks

AutoText is another feature you can use to insert text automatically. This feature is extremely versatile. You can use it to create AutoText entries for text you use repeatedly (the AutoText entry can even include the text formatting). The text for which you create an AutoText entry can be a phrase, a sentence, paragraphs, logos, and so on.

After you create an entry, you can insert it with just a few keystrokes.

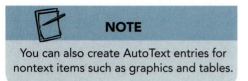

NOTE

You can also create AutoText entries for nontext items such as graphics and tables.

Exercise 3-6 CREATE AN AUTOTEXT ENTRY

To create an AutoText entry, you key the text that you want to save and select it, or you select text that already exists in a document. When you select the text to be used for an AutoText entry, be sure to include the appropriate spaces, blank lines, and paragraph marks.

1. Open the file **Letter - 1**.
2. Press Ctrl+A to select the document.
3. Click the **Insert** tab on the Ribbon.
4. Locate the Text group, and click **Quick Parts**. Click **AutoText**, and an AutoText gallery displays. Click **Save selection to AutoText gallery**. The Create New Building Block dialog box displays.

Figure 3-6
Quick Parts menu

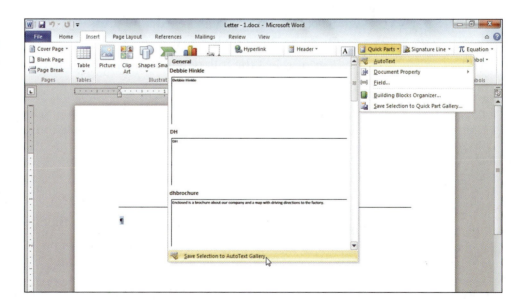

5. Key *[your initials]*Letterhead in the **Name** box. Each AutoText entry must have a unique name.

6. Select **AutoText** from the **Gallery** drop-down list box if necessary.

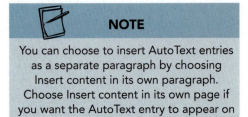

NOTE

You can choose to insert AutoText entries as a separate paragraph by choosing Insert content in its own paragraph. Choose Insert content in its own page if you want the AutoText entry to appear on a new page.

7. Verify that **General** is selected in the **Category** drop-down list box.

8. Key **Grove City Letterhead** in the **Description** text box.

9. Select **Normal.dotm** from the **Save in** drop-down list.

10. Select **Insert content only** from the **Options** drop-down list. Click **OK**.

11. Press Ctrl+End to move to the end of the document. Key the text in Figure 3-7.

Figure 3-7

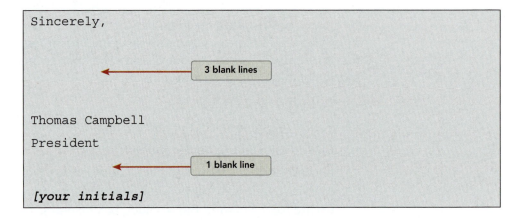

12. Select the text you just keyed, and press Alt+F3 to open the Create New Building Block dialog box.

13. Key or select the following information in the Create New Building Block dialog box.

Name:	*[your initials]*Closing
Gallery:	**AutoText**
Category:	**General**
Description:	**Closing**
Save in:	**Normal.dotm**
Options:	**Insert content only**

14. Click **OK** to close the Create New Building Block dialog box.

15. Close the document, and do not save the changes.

Exercise 3-7 INSERT AUTOTEXT ENTRIES

There are several ways to insert an AutoText entry. If the AutoText entry is stored in the Normal.dotm, key the first four letters of the entry, and an AutoComplete box displays. Press Enter or Tab to insert the text. If you have an AutoText entry that is unique or short, you can key the first few letters of the entry name and press F3 to insert the entry. A third method is to click the Insert tab, click Quick Parts, click AutoText, and click the AutoText entry from the AutoText gallery. To insert an AutoText entry using the Building Blocks Organizer, position the insertion point and open the Building Blocks Organizer. When the Building Blocks Organizer dialog box opens, click one of the column headings to sort the entries. Click the Name heading to sort the text alphabetically by name. Click the Gallery heading to display the entries by gallery type. AutoText entries appear at the top of the Gallery listing. Select the entry, and click the Insert button.

1. Create a new document.
2. Click the **Insert** tab, and locate the Text group. Click **Quick Parts**, and click **Building Blocks Organizer**. The Building Blocks Organizer dialog box displays.

Figure 3-8
Building Blocks
Organizer dialog box

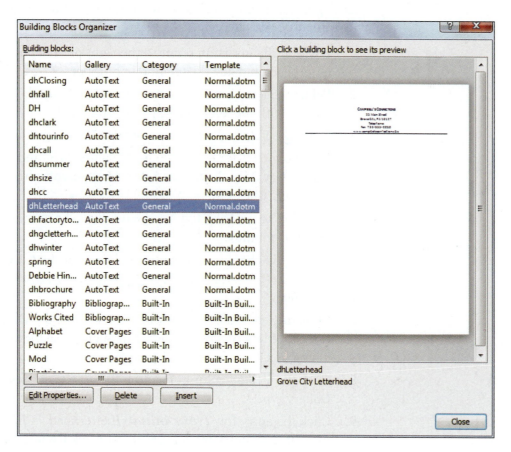

3. Click the **Gallery** heading, and the list sorts by gallery type.
4. Click the **Name** heading, and the list is sorted alphabetically by name.

5. Click the Gallery heading, and locate the "*[your initials]*Letterhead" AutoText entry.

6. Click the *[your initials]*Letterhead entry, and click Insert. The letterhead information is automatically inserted.

7. Click the Undo button to remove the AutoText entry.

8. Key *[your initials]*Letterhead, and press Enter to insert the Autotext entry when the AutoComplete box displays.

9. Begin keying *[your initials]*Closing, and press the Enter key when the AutoComplete box displays.

> **TIP**
>
> Check Appendix B, "Standard Forms for Business Documents," to double-check that your letter has the correct number of blank lines between items.

Exercise 3-8   EDIT AND DELETE AUTOTEXT ENTRIES

After you create an AutoText entry, it may need to be edited. If you no longer use an entry, you can delete it.

1. Position the insertion point to the right of "Telephone:" in the letterhead, and key the telephone number 724-555-2025.

2. Select the letterhead text beginning with "Campbell's Confections" and ending with the left-aligned paragraph mark.

3. Press Alt+F3 to open the Create New Building Block dialog box.

4. Key *[your initials]*Letterhead in the Name box, and select AutoText from the Gallery drop-down list. Select Normal.dotm from the Save in drop-down list. Click OK.

5. Click Yes to redefine the AutoText entry. The entry now includes the telephone number.

6. To test the change, delete all the document text. Key *[your initials]*Letterhead, and press Enter to insert the letterhead AutoText.

7. Click the Insert tab on the Ribbon, and click the Quick Parts command. Click Building Blocks Organizer to open the Building Blocks Organizer dialog box.

8. Click the Gallery column heading to sort the entries in the list by Gallery type.

9. Click the entry for "*[your initials]*Letterhead." Click Delete to remove the AutoText entry from the Gallery. Click No to prevent the deletion of the AutoText entry. Click Close to return to your document.

Inserting the Date and Time

You have seen that when you begin keying a month, AutoComplete displays the suggested date, and you press Enter to insert the date as regular text. You can also insert the date or time in a document as a field. A *field* is a hidden code that tells Word to insert specific text that might need to be updated automatically, such as a date or page number. If you insert the date or time in a document as a field, Word automatically updates it each time you print the document.

There are two ways to insert the date or time as a field:

- Click the Insert tab on the Ribbon, and click the Date and Time command. Select the desired format from the Date and Time dialog box.

- Press Alt + Shift + D to insert the date and Alt + Shift + T to insert the time.

Exercise 3-9   INSERT THE DATE AND TIME

You can enter date and time fields that can be updated automatically. You can also choose not to update these fields automatically.

1. Move the insertion point to the end of the current document.

2. Press Alt + Shift + D to enter the default date field.

3. Press Ctrl + Z to undo the date insertion.

4. Click the **Insert** tab on the Ribbon, and click the **Date and Time** command to open the Date and Time dialog box.

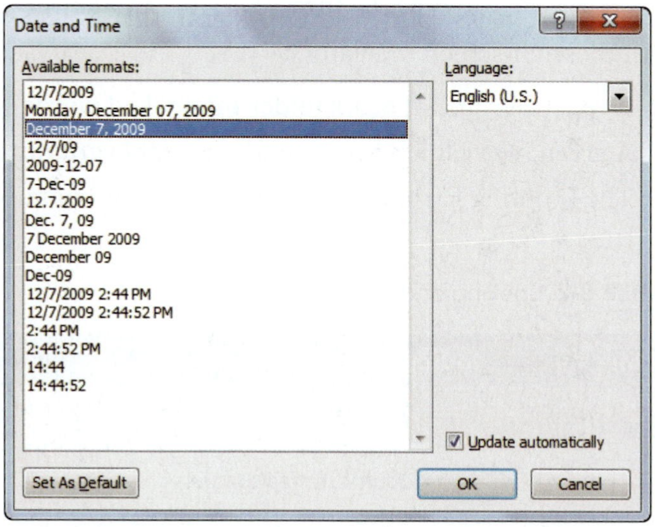

Figure 3-9
Date and Time
dialog box

Date and Time dialog box:

Available formats:
12/7/2009
Monday, December 07, 2009
December 7, 2009
12/7/09
2009-12-07
7-Dec-09
12.7.2009
Dec. 7, 09
7 December 2009
December 09
Dec-09
12/7/2009 2:44 PM
12/7/2009 2:44:52 PM
2:44 PM
2:44:52 PM
14:44
14:44:52

Language:
English (U.S.)

☑ Update automatically

Set As Default   OK   Cancel

NOTE

You can also use the Date and Time dialog box to insert the date and time in a particular text format without inserting it as an updatable field.

TIP

Although printing updates a field, you can also update a field on-screen by clicking the field and pressing F9. To change the date or time format, right-click the field, and choose Edit Field.

5. Scroll the list of available time and date formats, and choose the third format in the list (the standard date format for business documents).

6. Check the **Update automatically** check box so the date is automatically updated each time you print the document. Click **OK**.

7. Move the insertion point after the date field, and press Spacebar twice.

8. Press Alt + Shift + T to insert the time as a field.

9. Save the document as *[your initials]*3-9 in your Lesson 3 folder.

10. Submit your work, and close the document.

TIP

Remember that the Update Automatically option will change the date in your document. If you are sending correspondence, do not choose this option because the date in the letter will then always reflect the current date, not the date on which you wrote the letter.

Checking Spelling and Grammar

Correct spelling and grammar are essential to good writing. As you have seen, Word checks your spelling and grammar as you key text and flags errors with these on-screen indicators:

- A red, wavy line appears under misspelled words.
- A green, wavy line appears under possible grammatical errors.
- The Proofing Errors icon on the status bar contains an "X."

TABLE 3-2 Spelling and Grammar Status

Icon	Indicates
	Word is checking for errors as you key text.
	The document has errors.
	The document has no errors.

Exercise 3-10 SPELL- AND GRAMMAR-CHECK ERRORS INDIVIDUALLY

NOTE

If no green, wavy lines appear in your document, open the File tab, and click Options. Click Proofing in the left pane. Click the Check grammar with spelling check box, and click OK.

TIP

Word's spelling and grammar tools are not foolproof. For example, it cannot correct a word that is correctly spelled but incorrectly keyed, such as "sue" instead of "use." It might also apply a green, wavy line to a type of grammatical usage, such as the passive voice, which might not be preferred, but is not incorrect.

You can right-click text marked as either a spelling or a grammar error and choose a suggested correction from a shortcut menu.

1. Open the file **Milk Chocolate - 2**. This document has several errors, indicated by the red and green wavy lines.

2. At the top of the document, press [Enter] and move the insertion point to the blank paragraph mark. Notice that the Proofing Errors indicator on the status bar contains an "X."

3. Using 14-point bold type, key a misspelled word by keying the title **Mlk Chocolate**. When you finish, "Mlk" is marked as misspelled.

4. Right-click the misspelled word, and choose "Milk" from the spelling shortcut menu.

5. Right-click the grammatical error "It contain" in the second sentence. Choose "contains" from the shortcut menu.

Exercise 3-11 SPELL- AND GRAMMAR-CHECK AN ENTIRE DOCUMENT

Instead of checking words or sentences individually, you can check an entire document. This is the best way to correct spelling and grammar errors in a long document. Use one of these methods:

*   Click the Spelling and Grammar button on the Review tab of the Ribbon.

*   Press [F7].

1. Position the insertion point at the beginning of the document, and click the **Review** tab. Click the Spelling & Grammar button. Word locates the first misspelling, "choclate."

UNIT 1 LESSON 3

Figure 3-10
Checking spelling
and grammar

TIP

To check spelling without also checking grammar, click the Check grammar check box to clear it.

2. Click **Change** to correct the spelling to the first suggested spelling, "chocolate." Next, Word finds a word choice error, "hole."

3. Click **Change** to correct the word choice. Next, Word finds two words that should be separated by a space.

4. Click **Change** to correct the spacing. Next Word finds a repeated word, "of."

5. Click **Delete** to delete the repeated word. Next Word finds a grammatical error—"it" is not capitalized.

6. Click **Change** to correct the capitalization in the document.

7. Click **OK** when the check is complete. Notice there are no more wavy lines in the document, and the Proofing Errors indicator shows a checkmark.

8. Read the paragraph, and check for errors that were not found by the Spelling and Grammar checker.

9. Locate "10 per cent" in the second sentence. Delete the space between "per" and "cent."

10. Locate the sentence that begins "It is mild," and change "type" to "**types.**"

11. Locate the sentence that begins "It used," and change it to read "**It is used.**"

NOTE

You can create or add a custom dictionary for technical and specialized vocabulary. Open the File tab, click Options, and click Proofing. Click Custom Dictionaries, click New, and key a name for the custom dictionary. To add a custom dictionary that you purchased, follow the steps listed above, except choose Add instead of New. Locate the folder, and double-click the dictionary file.

TABLE 3-3 Dialog Box Options When Checking Spelling and Grammar

Option	Description
Ignore Once	Skips the word.
Ignore All	Skips all occurrences of the word in the document.
Add to Dictionary	Adds the word to the default dictionary file in Word. You can also create your own dictionary and add words to it.
Change	Changes the word to the entry in the Change To box or to the word you chose from the Suggestions list.
Change All	Same as Change, but changes the word throughout the document.
AutoCorrect	Adds the word to the list of corrections Word makes automatically.
Options	Lets you change the Spelling and Grammar options in Word.
Undo	Changes back the most recent correction made.
Cancel	Discontinues the checking operation.

Using the Thesaurus and Research Task Pane

The *thesaurus* is a tool that can improve your writing. Use the thesaurus to look up a *synonym* (a word with a similar meaning) for a selected word to add variety or interest to a document. You can look up synonyms for any of the synonym recommendations to get additional word choices. The thesaurus sometimes displays *antonyms* (words with the opposite meaning) and related words.

After selecting a word to change, you can start the thesaurus in one of three ways:

- Click the Review tab, and click Thesaurus.
- Press Shift + F7.
- Right-click the word, and choose Synonyms from the shortcut menu.

Exercise 3-12   USE THE THESAURUS

1. Select the word "best" in the first sentence, or place the insertion point in the word.
2. Press Shift + F7. The Research task pane appears with a list of synonyms for "best."

Figure 3-11
Using the thesaurus

3. Point to the word "finest," and click the drop-down arrow. Click **Look Up**. A list of additional synonyms appears for "finest" in the task pane.

4. Go back to the word "finest" by clicking the Previous search button [Back ▾].

5. Point to "finest," click the down arrow, and choose **Insert**. Word replaces "best" with "finest" and returns to the document.

6. Save the document as *[your initials]*3-12 in your Lesson 3 folder.

7. Submit the document, but do not close it.

Exercise 3-13   USE REFERENCES

If you are connected to the Internet, you can access several research sources, such as a dictionary, an encyclopedia, and research sites such as Factiva iWorks, HighBeam Research, and Live Search. From the Review tab on the Ribbon, you can click the Research button; right-click a word and click Look Up in the shortcut menu; or press [Alt] and click a word to open the Research task pane.

1. Press [Alt] and click the word "chocolate" in the first sentence.

Figure 3-12
Using references

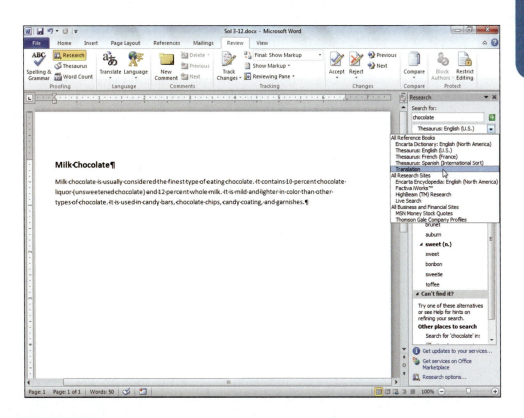

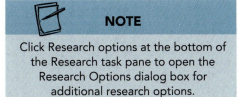

NOTE

Click Research options at the bottom of the Research task pane to open the Research Options dialog box for additional research options.

2. Click the drop-down arrow beside the **All Reference Books** box, and choose **Encarta Dictionary**. The task pane indicates the part of speech, syllabication, and several definitions for "chocolate."

3. Click the drop-down arrow beside the All Reference Books box, and choose **Translation**.

4. Choose **English** in the **From** box and **French (France)** in the **To** box. The bilingual dictionary displays the French word for chocolate—*chocolat*.

5. Close the document.

Lesson 3   Summary

- The AutoComplete feature suggests the completed word when you key the first four or more letters of a day, month, or date.
- The AutoCorrect feature corrects some misspelled words and capitalization errors for you automatically as you key text.

- Use the AutoCorrect dialog box to create entries for words you often misspell and the AutoCorrect Options button to control AutoCorrect options.

- Use the AutoCorrect Exceptions dialog box to create an AutoCorrect exception so Word will not correct it.

- Use Actions to perform Microsoft Outlook functions, such as creating entries in Outlook's contact list.

- AutoText is another versatile feature you can use to insert text automatically. You create AutoText entries for text you use repeatedly, including text formatting.

- Use the Building Blocks Organizer to edit and delete AutoText entries.

- Insert the date and time in a document as an automatically updated field, which is a hidden code that tells Word to insert specific information—in this case, the date and/or time. Use the Date and Time dialog box to choose different date and time formats.

- Use the spelling and grammar checker to correct misspelled words in your document as well as poor grammar usage. Check errors individually or throughout your entire document.

- Use the thesaurus to look up synonyms (words with similar meaning) or sometimes antonyms (words with the opposite meaning) for a selected word to add variety and interest to your document.

- Use the Research task pane to look up words or phrases in a dictionary, to research topics in an encyclopedia, or to access bilingual dictionaries for translations. You can also access research sites such as Live Search.

LESSON 3		Command Summary	
Feature	**Button**	**Command**	**Keyboard**
Check spelling and grammar		Review tab, Proofing group, Spelling & Grammar	F7
Create AutoText entry		Insert tab, Text group, Quick Parts, AutoText	Alt + F3
Insert Date		Insert tab, Text group, Date & Time	Alt + Shift + D
Insert Time		Insert tab, Text group, Date & Time	Alt + Shift + T
Research		Review tab, Proofing group, Research	Alt + Click
Thesaurus		Review tab, Proofing group, Thesaurus	Shift + F7
Translate		Review tab, Language group, Translate	

Please visit our Online Learning Center, *www.lessonapproach2010.com*, **where you will find the following review materials:**

- **Concepts Review**

  True/False Questions

  Short Answer Questions

  Critical Thinking Questions

- **Skills Review**

  Review Exercises that target single skills

  Lesson Applications

  Review Exercises that challenge students by testing multiple skills in each exercise

- **On Your Own**

  Open-ended exercises that require students to synthesize multiple skills and apply creativity and problem-solving as they would in a real world business situation

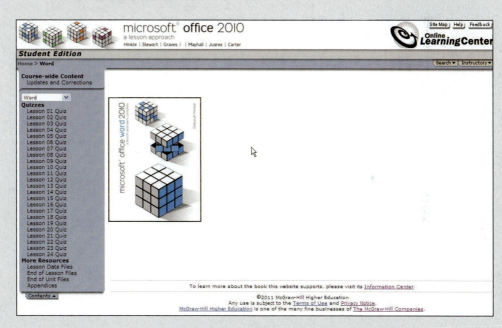

Please visit our Online Learning Center, *www.lessonapproach2010.com*, **where you will find Unit Applications review materials.**

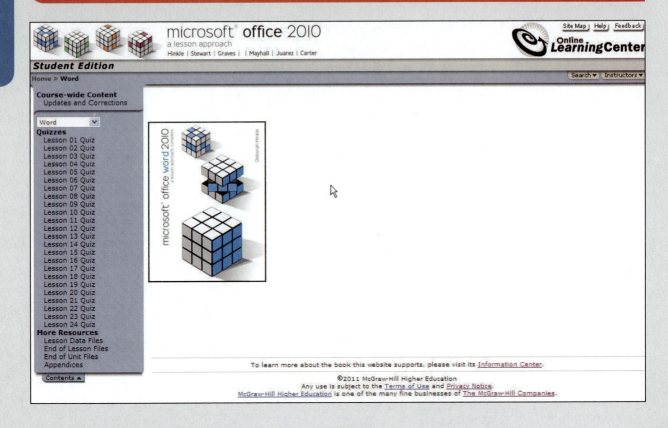

Unit 2

PARAGRAPH FORMATTING, TABS, AND ADVANCED EDITING

Lesson 4
Formatting Paragraphs

After completing this lesson, you will be able to:

1. Align paragraphs.
2. Change line spacing.
3. Change paragraph spacing.
4. Set paragraph indents.
5. Apply borders and shading.
6. Repeat and copy paragraph formats.
7. Create bulleted and numbered lists.
8. Insert symbols and special characters.

Estimated Time: 1½ hours

In Microsoft Word, a *paragraph* is a unique block of information. Paragraph formatting controls the appearance of individual paragraphs within a document. For example, you can change the space between paragraphs or change the space between lines. For emphasis, you can indent paragraphs, number them, or add borders and shading.

A paragraph is always followed by a *paragraph mark*. All the formatting for a paragraph is stored in the paragraph mark. Each time you press Enter, you copy the formatting instructions in the current paragraph to a new paragraph. You can copy paragraph formats from one paragraph to another and view paragraph formats in the Reveal Formatting task pane.

Paragraph Alignment

Paragraph alignment determines how the edges of a paragraph appear horizontally. There are four ways to align text in a paragraph, as shown in Figure 4-1.

Figure 4-1
Paragraph alignment
options

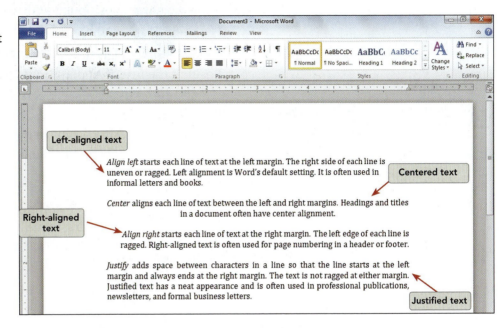

Exercise 4-1   CHANGE PARAGRAPH ALIGNMENT

The easiest way to change paragraph alignment is to use the alignment buttons on the Ribbon, Home tab, Paragraph group. You can also use keyboard shortcuts: left align, Ctrl+L; center, Ctrl+E; right align, Ctrl+R; and justify, Ctrl+J. To change the alignment of one paragraph, position the insertion point in the paragraph. To change the alignment of multiple paragraphs, select the paragraphs and then apply the alignment format.

Figure 4-2
Alignment buttons
on the Ribbon

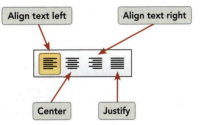

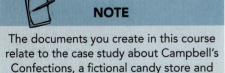
NOTE

The documents you create in this course relate to the case study about Campbell's Confections, a fictional candy store and chocolate factory (see the Case Study in the front matter).

1. Open the file **Corporate Gifts**. Click the Show/Hide ¶ button ¶ to display paragraph marks if they are turned off.

2. Position the insertion point anywhere in the first paragraph.

3. Click the Center button on the Ribbon (Home tab, Paragraph group) to center the paragraph.

4. Continue to change the paragraph's formatting by clicking the Align Right button ▤, the Justify button ▤, and the Align Left button ▤. Notice how the lines of text are repositioned with each change.

5. Position the insertion point in the second paragraph, and press [Ctrl]+[E] to center the paragraph.

6. Position the insertion point in the third paragraph. Use the keyboard shortcut [Ctrl]+[R] to right-align the third paragraph.

7. Position the insertion point in the fourth paragraph, and press [Ctrl]+[J] to justify the fourth paragraph.

NOTE

When applying paragraph formatting, you do not have to select the paragraph—you just need to have the insertion point within the paragraph or just before the paragraph mark.

REVIEW

If you do not see one of the alignment buttons, check the Ribbon to verify that the Home tab is active.

Exercise 4-2   USE CLICK AND TYPE TO INSERT TEXT

You can use *Click and Type* to insert text or graphics in any blank area of a document. This feature enables you to position the insertion point anywhere in the document without pressing [Enter] repeatedly. Word automatically inserts the paragraph marks before that point and also inserts a tab.

1. Open the file **Factory**, and leave the Corporate Gifts document open.

2. Click the **File** tab, and click **Options**. Click **Advanced** in the left pane, and locate the **Editing options** group. Click **Enable click and type** if it is not already selected. Click **OK**.

3. Press [Ctrl]+[End] to move to the end of the document.

4. Position the I-beam about five lines below the last line of text, in the center of the page. The I-beam is now the Click and Type pointer [I], which includes tiny lines that show left, right, or center alignment.

Figure 4-3
Using Click and Type

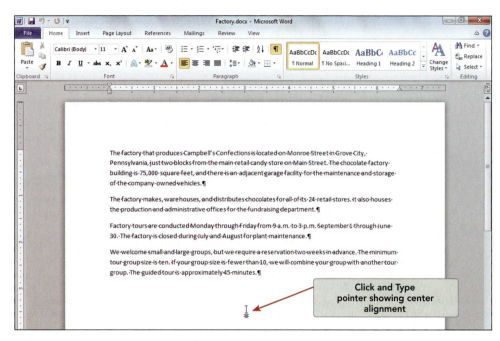

Click and Type
pointer showing center
alignment

5. Move the I-beam back and forth until it shows center alignment. Double-click, and key **Visit us at www.campbellsconfections.biz.** The text is centered, and paragraph marks are inserted before the new line.

6. Save the document as *[your initials]*4-2 in your Lesson 4 folder.

7. Submit your work, and close the document.

Line Spacing

Line space is the amount of vertical space between lines of text in a paragraph. Line spacing is typically based on the height of the characters, but you can change it to a specific value. For example, some paragraphs might be single-spaced and some double-spaced. The default line spacing is Multiple 1.15.

Exercise 4-3　CHANGE LINE SPACING

You can apply the most common types of line spacing by using keyboard shortcuts: single space, Ctrl+1; 1.5-line space, Ctrl+5; and double space, Ctrl+2. Additional spacing options, as well as other paragraph formatting options, are available in the Paragraph dialog box or from the Line and Paragraph Spacing button.

1. Position the insertion point in the first paragraph.

2. Press Ctrl+2 to double-space the paragraph.

3. With the insertion point in the same paragraph, press [Ctrl]+[5] to change the spacing to 1.5 lines. Press [Ctrl]+[1] to change the paragraph format to single spacing.

4. With the insertion point in the same paragraph, click the down arrow to the right of the Line and Paragraph Spacing button ⬚ on the Ribbon, Home tab, Paragraph group, and choose **2.0** to change the line spacing to double. Click the down arrow again, and choose **1.0** to restore the paragraph to single spacing.

5. Right-click the first paragraph, and choose **Paragraph** from the shortcut menu. (You can also open the Paragraph dialog box by clicking the Dialog Box Launcher ⬚ in the right corner of the Paragraph group.)

6. Click the down arrow to open the **Line spacing** drop-down list, and choose **Double**. The change is reflected in the **Preview** box.

Figure 4-4
Line-spacing options
in the Paragraph
dialog box

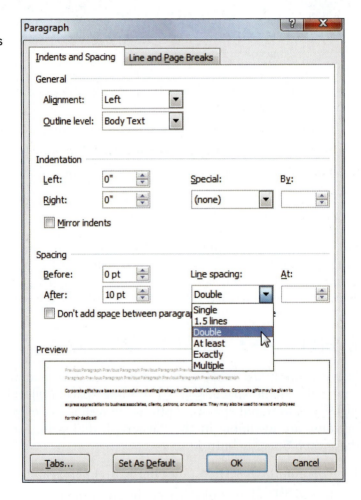

NOTE

The At Least option applies minimum line spacing that Word adjusts to accommodate larger font sizes. The Exactly option applies fixed line spacing that Word does not adjust. This option makes all lines evenly spaced. The Multiple option increases or decreases line spacing by the percentage you specify. For example, setting line spacing to a multiple of 1.25 increases the space by 25 percent, and setting line spacing to a multiple of 0.8 decreases the space by 20 percent.

7. With the dialog box still open, choose **Single** from the Line spacing drop-down list. The **Preview** box shows the change.

8. Choose **Multiple** from the Line spacing drop-down list. In the **At** box, key **1.25**. (Select the text that appears in the box and key over it.) Press Tab to see the change displayed in the **Preview** box.

9. Click **OK**. Word adds an extra quarter-line space between lines in the paragraph.

Figure 4-5
Examples of line spacing

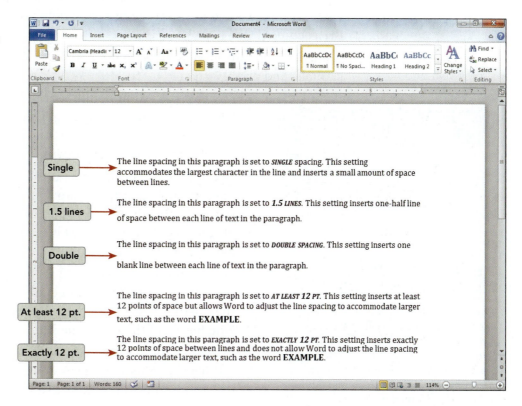

Paragraph Spacing

In addition to changing spacing between lines of text, you can change *paragraph space*. Paragraph space is the amount of space above or below a paragraph. Instead of pressing Enter multiple times to increase space between paragraphs, you can use the Ribbon or the Paragraph dialog box to set a specific amount of space before or after paragraphs.

Paragraph spacing is set in points. If a document has 12-point text, one line space equals 12 points. Likewise, one-half line space equals 6 points, and two line spaces equal 24 points. By default, paragraph spacing is 0 points before and 10 points after.

Exercise 4-4   CHANGE THE SPACE BETWEEN PARAGRAPHS

1. Press Ctrl + Home to move the insertion point to the beginning of the document. Select the whole document by pressing Ctrl + A. Press Ctrl + L to left-align all paragraphs.

2. Use the keyboard shortcut Ctrl + 1 to change the entire document to single spacing.

3. Deselect the text, and position the insertion point at the beginning of the document.

4. Click the Bold button **B** to turn on bold, key **CORPORATE GIFTS** in all capitals, and press Enter.

5. Move the insertion point into the heading you just keyed. Although this heading includes only two words, it is considered a paragraph. Any text followed by a paragraph mark is a paragraph.

6. Open the Paragraph dialog box by clicking the Paragraph Dialog Box Launcher. You use the text boxes labeled **Before** and **After** to choose an amount of space for Word to insert before or after a paragraph.

7. Set the **Before** text box to 72 points (select the "0" and key **72**). Because 72 points equal 1 inch, this adds to the existing 1-inch top margin and places the title 2 inches from the top of the page.

8. Press Tab, set the **After** text box to **24** points, and click **OK**. The heading now starts 2 inches from the top of the page and is followed by two line spaces.

9. Right-click the **status bar** and click **Vertical Page Position**. Deselect the shortcut menu. The status bar displays **At 2"** on the left side.

10. Click the Center button ☰ to center the heading.

NOTE

Many business documents start 2 inches from the top of the page. You can set this standard by using paragraph formatting, as done here, or by changing margin settings.

TIP

The keyboard shortcut to add or remove 12 points of spacing before a paragraph is Ctrl + 0. Ctrl + Shift + N removes all paragraph and character formatting, restoring the text to default formatting. The Line Spacing button on the Ribbon includes an option to add or remove space before paragraph and an option to add or remove space after paragraph. The default is to add 12 points before or after the paragraph.

Paragraph Indents

An *indent* increases the distance between the sides of a paragraph and the two side margins. Indented paragraphs appear to have different margin settings. Word provides a variety of indents to emphasize paragraphs in a document, as shown in Figure 4-6.

Figure 4-6
Types of paragraph indents

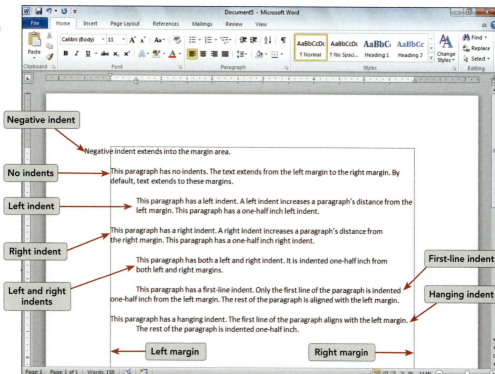

To set paragraph indents, you can use one of these methods:

- Indent buttons on the Ribbon, Home tab, Paragraph group
- Paragraph dialog box
- Keyboard shortcuts
- Ruler

Exercise 4-5 SET INDENTS BY USING INDENT BUTTONS AND THE PARAGRAPH DIALOG BOX

1. Select the paragraph that begins "Our line" through the end of the document.
2. Click the Increase Indent button ▤ on the Ribbon. The selected text is indented 0.5 inch from the left side.
3. Click the Increase Indent button ▤ again. Now the text is indented 1 inch.

4. Click the Decrease Indent button twice to return the text to the left margin.

NOTE

To set a *negative indent,* which extends a paragraph into the left or right margin areas, enter a negative number in the Left or Right text boxes. Any indent that occurs between the left and right margins is known as a *positive indent.*

5. With the text still selected, open the Paragraph dialog box by clicking the Paragraph Dialog Box Launcher

6. Under **Indentation**, change the **Left** setting to **0.75** inch and the **Right** setting to **0.75** inch.

7. Click to open the **Special** drop-down list in the Paragraph dialog box, and choose **First line**. Word sets the **By** box to 0.5 inch by default. Notice the change in the Preview box.

Figure 4-7
Setting indents

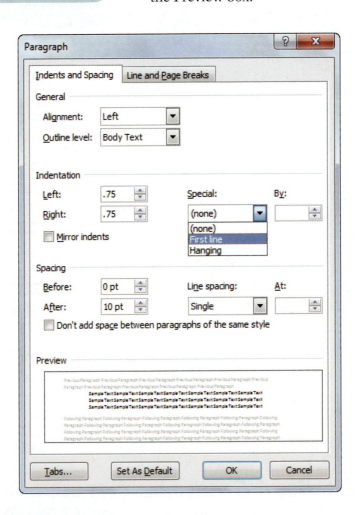

8. Click **OK**. Now each paragraph is indented from the left and right margins by 0.75 inch, and the first line of each paragraph is indented another 0.5 inch.

TIP

Word provides these keyboard shortcuts to set indents: Ctrl+M increases an indent; Ctrl+Shift+M decreases an indent; Ctrl+T creates a hanging indent; and Ctrl+Shift+T removes a hanging indent.

Exercise 4-6   SET INDENTS BY USING THE RULER

You can set indents by dragging the *indent markers* that appear at the left and right of the horizontal ruler. There are four indent markers:

- The *first-line indent marker* is the top triangle on the left side of the ruler. Drag it to the right to indent the first line of a paragraph.

- The *hanging indent marker* is the bottom triangle. Drag it to the right to indent the remaining lines in a paragraph.

- The *left indent marker* is the small rectangle. Drag it to move the first-line indent marker and the hanging indent marker at the same time.

- The *right indent marker* is the triangle at the right side of the ruler, at the right margin. Drag it to the left to create a right indent.

Figure 4-8
Indent markers on
the ruler

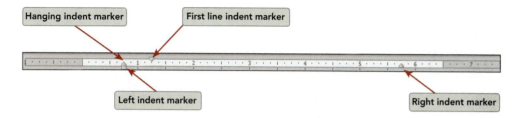

1. Make sure the horizontal ruler is displayed. If it is not, click the View Ruler button , or click the **View** tab, and click **Ruler** in the Show group.

2. Position the insertion point in the first paragraph below the title.

3. Point to the first-line indent marker on the ruler. A ScreenTip appears when you are pointing to the correct marker.

4. Drag the first-line indent marker 0.5 inch to the right. The first line of the paragraph is indented by 0.5 inch.

5. Press Shift+F1 to display the **Reveal Formatting** task pane. Locate the **Paragraph** section, and notice the settings under **Indentation**.

> **NOTE**
>
> To make sure you are pointing to the correct indent marker, check the ScreenTip identifier before you drag the marker.

6. Drag the first-line indent marker back to the zero position. Point to the hanging indent marker, and drag it 0.5 inch to the right. The lines below the first line are indented 0.5 inch, creating a hanging indent.

7. Drag the hanging indent marker back to the zero position. Drag the left indent marker (the small rectangle) 1 inch to the right. The entire paragraph is indented by 1 inch.

8. Select the first two paragraphs below the title, and press [Ctrl]+[Shift]+[N] to remove all formatting from the paragraphs. Notice that the line spacing and spacing after format return to the default settings.

9. Position the insertion point in the second paragraph, which begins "Our line," and re-create the indents by using the ruler:

   • Drag the left indent marker 0.75 inch to the right to indent the entire paragraph.

   • Drag the first-line indent marker to the 1.25-inch mark on the ruler.

   • Drag the right indent marker 0.75 inch to the left (to the 5.75-inch mark on the ruler). Now the paragraph is indented like the paragraphs below it.

10. Select all the indented paragraphs, and drag the first-line indent marker to the 1-inch mark on the ruler. Now the opening line of each paragraph is indented only 0.25 inch.

Figure 4-9
Document with indented text

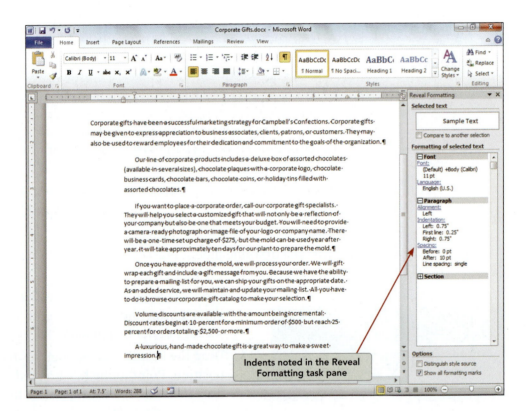

11. Close the Reveal Formatting task pane.

12. Save the document as *[your initials]*4-6 in a new folder for Lesson 4.

13. Submit the document, but do not close it.

Borders and Shading

To add visual interest to paragraphs or to an entire page, you can add a *border*—a line, box, or pattern—around text, a graphic, or a page. In addition, you can use *shading* to fill in the background behind the text of a paragraph. Shading can appear as a shade of gray, as a pattern, or as a color. Borders can appear in a variety of line styles and colors.

This lesson explains how to use the Borders and Shading dialog box to set border and shading options, and how to use the Borders button on the Ribbon (which applies the most recently selected border style). The Borders button ScreenTip will change to display the most recently selected border style.

Exercise 4-7   ADD BORDERS TO PARAGRAPHS

1. With the file *[your initials]*4-6 open, go to the end of the document. Press Enter to start a new paragraph, and press Ctrl+Q to remove the paragraph formatting carried over from the previous paragraph.

2. Key the text shown in Figure 4-10.

Figure 4-10

> Let Campbell's Confections help you with your marketing strategy and your employees' recognition plan! We can provide you with a unique and personalized gift that will create a lasting impression. Call us today at 724-555-2025 for more information.

3. Make sure the insertion point is to the left of the current paragraph mark or within the paragraph.

NOTE

The appearance of the Borders button and the ScreenTip change according to the most recently selected border style.

4. Click the down arrow beside the Borders button ⊞▾ and click **Borders and Shading** at the bottom of the drop-down list. The Borders and Shading dialog box appears. Click the **Borders** tab if it is not displayed.

5. Under **Setting**, click the **Box** option. The **Preview** box shows the Box setting. Each button around the Preview box indicates a selected border.

6. Scroll to view the options in the **Style** box. Choose the first border style (the solid line).

7. Open the **Color** drop-down list, and choose Green in the Standard Colors section. (ScreenTips identify colors by name.)

8. Open the **Width** drop-down list and choose **2¼ pt**.

9. Click the top line of the box border in the **Preview** box. The top line is deleted, and the corresponding button is no longer selected. Click the Top Border button 🔲 or the top border area in the diagram to restore the top line border.

Figure 4-11
Borders and Shading dialog box

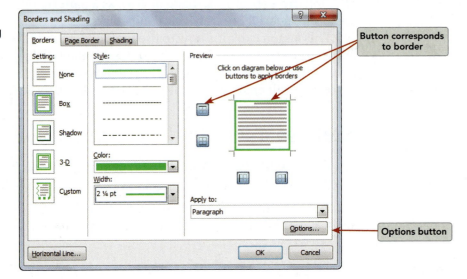

10. Click the **Options** button. In the Border and Shading Options dialog box, change the **Top** setting to 5 pt, press [Tab], and change the **Bottom** setting to 5 pt. Press [Tab], and change the **Left** and **Right** settings to 5 pt to increase the space between the text and the border. Click **OK**.

11. Change the **Setting** from Box to **Shadow**. This setting applies a black shadow to the green border. Notice that the **Apply to** box is set to **Paragraph**. Click **OK**. The shadow border is applied to the paragraph.

12. Click anywhere within the title "CORPORATE GIFTS."

13. Click the down arrow next to the Borders button 🔲▾ on the Ribbon. A drop-down menu of border options appears.

Figure 4-12
Border options on the Ribbon

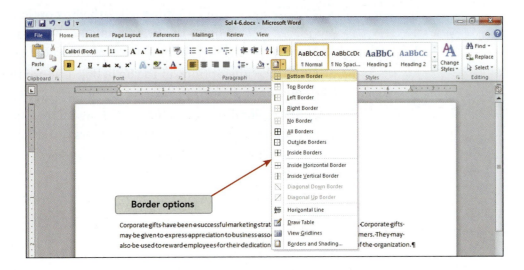

14. Click **Bottom Border**. A bottom border with the options previously set in the Borders and Shading dialog box is applied to the title.

15. Click the down arrow next to the Borders button ⊞▾. Click the No Border button ⬚ to delete the border.

16. Reapply the bottom border, and click the Top Border button ⬚ to add a top border as well.

17. Open the **Paragraph** dialog box, and change the left and right indents to **.5 inch**. Click **OK**, to close the Paragraph dialog box. Notice the border is indented from the left and right margins.

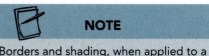

NOTE

Borders and shading, when applied to a paragraph, extend from the left margin to the right margin or, if indents are set, from the left indent to the right indent.

Exercise 4-8 APPLY BORDERS TO SELECTED TEXT AND A PAGE

In addition to paragraphs, you can apply borders to selected text or to an entire page. When you apply a border to a page, you can choose whether to place the border on every page, the current page, the first page, or all but the first page in a document.

1. In the third paragraph below the title (which begins "If you"), select the text "$275." Open the **Borders and Shading** dialog box.

2. From the **Style** box, scroll to the fifth line style from the bottom. Word automatically applies this style as the **Box** setting.

3. Change the **Color** to Blue. Notice that the **Apply to** box indicates **Text**.

Figure 4-13
Applying borders to selected text

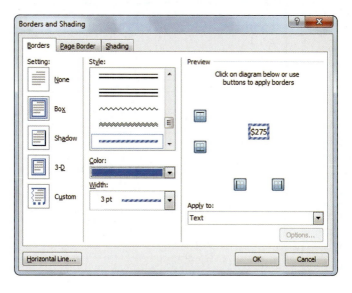

4. Click the **Page Border** tab. Choose the third-to-last line style (a band of three shades of gray), and click the **3-D** setting. The width should be **3 pt**.

5. Click **OK**. Notice the text border added to "$275" and the page border. Deselect the text so you can see the border color.

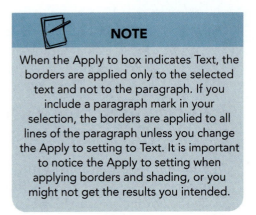

NOTE

When the Apply to box indicates Text, the borders are applied only to the selected text and not to the paragraph. If you include a paragraph mark in your selection, the borders are applied to all lines of the paragraph unless you change the Apply to setting to Text. It is important to notice the Apply to setting when applying borders and shading, or you might not get the results you intended.

Figure 4-14
Document with border formatting

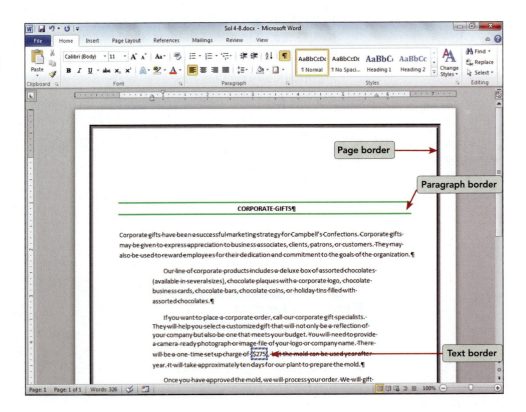

6. Save the document as *[your initials]*4-8 in your Lesson 4 folder. Submit the document. Leave it open.

Exercise 4-9   ADD A HORIZONTAL LINE

Word includes special horizontal lines to divide or decorate a page. These lines are actually picture files (or "clips") in the shape of horizontal lines that are normally used when creating Web pages.

NOTE

The Borders button drop-down list includes an option to insert a horizontal line. If you choose this option, the horizontal line inserted is based on the last horizontal line or border definition. Choose Horizontal Line from the Borders and Shading dialog box to select a style from the gallery.

1. Position the insertion point anywhere in the last paragraph, and click the down arrow beside the Borders button ⊞▾. Click the **No Border** option.

2. Position the insertion point at the beginning of the last paragraph.

3. Open the **Borders and Shading** dialog box. Click **Horizontal Line** at the bottom of the dialog box.

Figure 4-15
Inserting a horizontal line

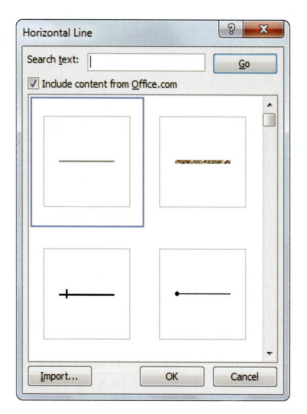

NOTE

Available horizontal line clips might vary, depending on which files are installed on your computer. Check with your instructor if the specified line is not available.

4. In the Horizontal Line dialog box, click the first box in the third row. Click **OK**. The line is inserted in the document.

Exercise 4-10   APPLY SHADING TO A PARAGRAPH

The Shading feature adds color and contrast to your document. You can apply shading to a single paragraph or to a group of paragraphs by using the Borders and Shading dialog box or the Shading button ⬛▾ on the Ribbon. Shading can affect the readability of text, especially when you use dark colors or patterns. It is a good idea to choose a larger type size and bold text when you use the shading feature.

1. Click anywhere in the last paragraph, and open the **Borders and Shading** dialog box.

2. Click the **Shading** tab.

3. Click the down arrow in the **Fill** box. Notice that you can apply theme colors or standard colors or select another color. Click a gray color in the first column.

Figure 4-16
Shading options in the Borders and Shading dialog box

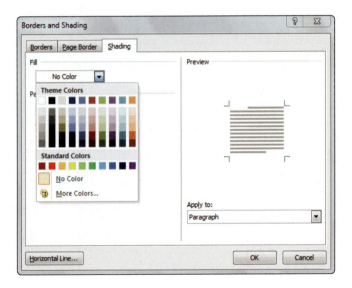

4. Open the **Style** drop-down list to view other shading options. Close the **Style** drop-down list without choosing a style.

5. Click **OK** to apply the gray shading to the paragraph.

6. With the insertion point still in the last paragraph, remove the gray shading by clicking the Shading button ⬛▾ on the Ribbon. Click **No Color**.

7. Click the Undo button 🔄 to restore the shading.

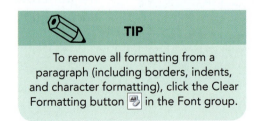

TIP

To remove all formatting from a paragraph (including borders, indents, and character formatting), click the Clear Formatting button 🔲 in the Font group.

Exercise 4-11   APPLY BORDERS AUTOMATICALLY

Word provides an AutoFormat feature to apply bottom borders. Instead of using the Borders button or the Borders and Shading dialog box, you can key a series of characters and Word automatically applies a border.

1. Press Ctrl+N to create a new document and leave the current document open.

2. Key --- (three consecutive hyphens) and press Enter. Word applies a bottom border. Press Enter two times.

3. Key === (three consecutive equal signs) and press Enter. Word applies a double-line bottom border. Press Enter two times.

4. Key ___ (three consecutive underscores) and press Enter. Word applies a thick bottom border.

5. Close the document without saving.

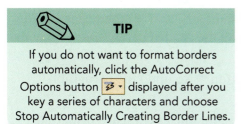

TIP

If you do not want to format borders automatically, click the AutoCorrect Options button ✎ ▾ displayed after you key a series of characters and choose Stop Automatically Creating Border Lines.

TABLE 4-1 Auto Formatting Borders

You Key	Word Applies
Three or more underscores (_) and press Enter	A thick bottom border
Three or more hyphens (-) and press Enter	A thin bottom border
Three or more equal signs (=) and press Enter	A double-line bottom border

Repeating and Copying Formats

You can quickly repeat, copy, or remove paragraph formatting. For example, press F4 or Ctrl+Y to repeat paragraph formatting and click the Format Painter button ✔ to copy paragraph formatting.

Exercise 4-12   REPEAT, COPY, AND REMOVE PARAGRAPH FORMATS

1. Click anywhere in the first paragraph under the title (which begins "Corporate Gifts"), and change the paragraph alignment to justified.

2. Select the rest of the indented paragraphs, starting with the paragraph that begins "Our line" through the paragraph that begins "A luxurious." Press F4 to repeat the formatting.

> **NOTE**
>
> You can click in a paragraph when repeating, copying, or removing formatting. You do not have to select the entire paragraph.

3. Click anywhere in the last paragraph (with the shading).

4. Click the Format Painter button ; then click within the paragraph above the shaded paragraph to copy the formatting.

5. Click the Undo button to undo the paragraph formatting.

6. Click anywhere in the shaded paragraph. Click the Clear Formatting button on the Ribbon to remove the formatting.

7. Click the Undo button to restore the formatting.

8. Click just before the paragraph mark for the horizontal line you inserted above the last paragraph. Open the **Paragraph** dialog box, add 24 points of spacing before the paragraph, and click **OK**.

9. Save the document as *[your initials]***4-12** in your Lesson 4 folder.

10. Submit and close the document.

Bulleted and Numbered Lists

Bulleted lists and *numbered lists* are types of hanging indents you can use to organize important details in a document. In a bulleted list, a bullet (•) precedes each paragraph. In a numbered list, a sequential number or letter precedes each paragraph. When you add or delete an item in a numbered list, Word automatically renumbers the list.

To create bulleted lists or numbered lists, use the Bullets button or the Numbering button on the Ribbon (which apply the most recently selected bullet or numbering style).

Exercise 4-13   CREATE A BULLETED LIST

1. Open the file **Memo - 1**. This document is a one-page memo. Key the current date in the memo date line.

2. Locate and select the four lines of text beginning with "Monday" and ending with "Thursday."

3. Click the Bullets button on the Ribbon, Home tab, Paragraph group. Word applies the bullet style that was most recently chosen in the Bullets list.

Figure 4-17
Bulleted list

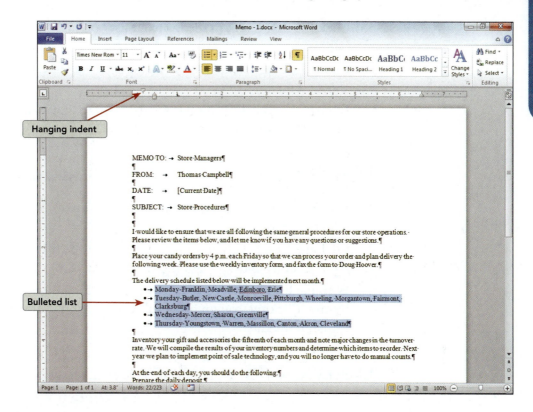

NOTE

When you create bulleted or numbered lists, Word automatically sets a 0.25-inch hanging indent.

4. With the list still selected, click the down arrow beside the Bullets button ▤▾, and click one of the bullet shapes listed in the **Bullet Library**. The list is formatted with a different bullet shape. Deselect the list.

Figure 4-18
Bullet options

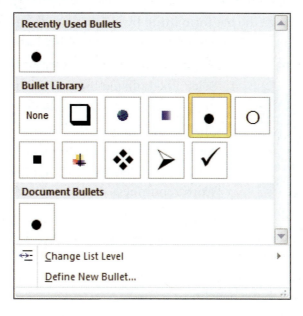

5. Click the first bullet in the bulleted list you just created to select all bullets.

6. Right-click the selected bullets, and click **Adjust List Indents** from the shortcut menu.

7. Change the **Bullet position** text box value to **.4**. Change the **Text indent** to **.65**. Click **OK**.

Exercise 4-14   CREATE A NUMBERED LIST

1. Select the last four paragraphs in the document, from "First Quarter" to "Fourth Quarter."

2. Click the Numbering button to format the list with the style that was most recently chosen from the Numbering list.

3. With the list still selected, click the down arrow beside the Numbering button. Click the roman numeral format. Word reformats the list with roman numerals.

Exercise 4-15   CHANGE A BULLETED OR NUMBERED LIST

Word's bulleting and numbering feature is very flexible. When a list is bulleted or numbered, you can change it in several ways. You can:

- Convert bullets to numbers or numbers to bullets in a list.
- Add or remove items in a bulleted or numbered list, and Word renumbers the list automatically.
- Interrupt a bulleted or numbered list to create several shorter lists.
- Customize the list formatting by changing the symbol used for bullets or changing the alignment and spacing of the bullets and numbers.
- Turn off bullets or numbering for part of a list or the entire list.

> **NOTE**
>
> When you select a bulleted or numbered list by dragging over the text, the list is highlighted but the bullets or numbers are not. You can select a list by clicking a bullet or number.

1. Select the bulleted list that starts with "Monday."

2. Click the down arrow beside the Numbering button.

3. Choose a numbered format that starts with "1" to convert the bullets to numbers.

4. Select and delete the line that begins "Wednesday." Word renumbers the list automatically.

5. Press Ctrl+Z to undo.

6. Place the insertion point at the end of the last item in the numbered list, after "Cleveland."

7. Press Enter and key **Friday-Emergency deliveries**. The formatting is carried to the new line.

8. Place the insertion point at the end of the fourth item (after "Cleveland.") and press Enter.

9. Key in italic ***When absolutely necessary:***

TIP

To change the shape, size, and color of a bullet, click the down arrow on the Bullets button and click Define New Bullet. Click the Symbol button to choose a new shape. Click the Font button to change size and color. Click the drop-down arrow of the Alignment box to change the bullet alignment. If you click the Picture button, you can insert a picture bullet—a decorative bullet often used in Web pages. You can format numbers or bullets of a list in a format different from the text of the list.

NOTE

After you format a list with bullets or numbering, each time you press Enter the format carries forward to the next paragraph. Pressing Enter twice turns off the format.

10. Click within the italic text, and click the Numbering button ⊞ ▾ on the Ribbon to turn off numbering for this item. The list continues with the following paragraph.

11. Select and right-click the numbered text below the italic text (the numbered item that begins "Friday").

12. Choose **Restart at 1**. The new list starts with "1."

13. Insert a blank line above the italic text (click to the left of *"When"* and press Enter).

14. Select the list beginning with "At the" through "Check and organize."

15. Click the down arrow beside the Bullets button ⊞ ▾, and click **Define New Bullet**.

16. Click **Symbol**, and change the **Font** to **Wingdings**. Scroll to locate and select the small, solid black square (■). Click **OK** to close the Symbol dialog box, and click **OK** to close the Define New Bullet dialog box.

Exercise 4-16   CREATE LISTS AUTOMATICALLY

Word provides an AutoFormat feature to create bulleted and numbered lists as you key text. When this feature is selected, you can enter a few keystrokes, key your list, and Word inserts the numbers and bullets automatically.

1. Press Ctrl+End to move to the end of the document.

2. Key the following: **Create a list of all equipment and fixtures in the store. Provide the following:**

3. Press Enter. Key * and press Spacebar.

4. Key **Description/Model number** and press Enter. Word automatically formats your text as a bulleted list.

5. Key the following text to complete the list, pressing Enter at the end of each line except the last line:

   Serial number
   Date acquired
   Purchase price
   Location
   Inventory number

TABLE 4-2 AutoFormatting Numbered and Bulleted Lists

You Key	Word Creates
A number; a period, closing parenthesis, or hyphen; a space or tab; and text. Press Enter. Example, **1.**, **1)**, or **1-**	A numbered list
An asterisk (*) or hyphen (-); a space or tab; and text. Press Enter.	A bulleted list

Exercise 4-17   CREATE A MULTILEVEL LIST

A *multilevel list* has indented subparagraphs. For example, your list can start with item number "1)," followed by another level of indented items numbered "a)," "b)," and "c)." An outline numbered list can have up to nine levels and is often used for technical or legal documents. The Multilevel List button ⯐ is located on the Ribbon, Home tab, Paragraph group.

1. Go to the end of the document and press Enter four times.
2. Click the arrow beside the Multilevel List button ⯐. Notice the outline numbering styles available in the List Library.

Figure 4-19
Multilevel List Library

3. Click the outline numbering style that begins with "I." Notice the uppercase roman numeral in the text. Click the **View** tab, and click to select the **Navigation Pane** check box. The Navigation Pane displays on the left and is used to move quickly from one heading to another.

4. Key **January** and press Enter. Word automatically formats the text with bold, 14 point text. The text may also appear in another font color.

5. Click the Increase Indent button 📇 (or press Tab), and key **A.** Spacebar **Prepare memo to employees regarding changes to W-4 forms.**

6. Press Enter and key **B.** Spacebar **Prepare and mail W-2 forms to employees.** The numbered list now has two indented subparagraphs. Press Enter. Key **C.** Spacebar **Prepare and mail 1099 forms.** Press Enter.

7. Position the insertion point at the left margin. (If necessary, click the Decrease Indent button 📇. You can now add a second first-level paragraph to your list.

8. Key **II. February**.

9. Review the Navigation Pane. Notice that the headings in the multilevel list appear in the Navigation Pane. Click the January heading in the Navigation Pane to move the heading to the top of the screen. Click the February heading to move it to the top of the screen.

10. Close the Navigation Pane by clicking the Navigation Pane Close button ✖.

NOTE

You can create and define a multilevel list style and add it to the List Library. Click the arrow beside the Multilevel List button, and click Define New Multilevel List. Enter the text and format for each level. Click OK.

Symbols and Special Characters

The fonts you use with Word include *special characters* that do not appear on your keyboard, such as those used in foreign languages (for example, ç, Ö, and Ω). There are additional fonts, such as *Wingdings* and *Symbol* that consist entirely of special characters.

To insert symbols and special characters in your documents, click the Insert tab on the Ribbon, locate the Symbols group, and click the Symbol command.

Exercise 4-18   INSERT SYMBOLS

1. Scroll toward the beginning of the document. Position the insertion point to the immediate left of the paragraph that begins "*When absolutely*."

2. Click the **Insert** tab. Locate the **Symbols** group, and click the Symbol button Ω Symbol ▾. Click **More Symbols**. The Symbol dialog box appears.

3. Make sure the **Symbols** tab is displayed, and choose **(normal text)** from the **Font** drop-down list box.

4. Scroll through the grid of available symbol characters for normal text, and notice that the grid contains diacritical marks that you can use for foreign languages. You will also see the symbol for cents (¢) and degrees (°).

5. Click the arrow to open the **Font** drop-down list box and choose **Symbol**. Review the available symbol characters.

6. Change the font to **Wingdings**. The characters included in the Wingdings font appear in the grid.

TIP

Notice the recently used symbols shown at the bottom of the Symbol dialog box. Word displays the 16 most recently used symbols.

Figure 4-20
Symbol dialog box

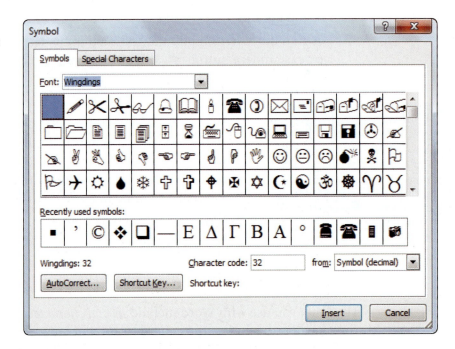

TIP

You can assign shortcut keys or AutoText to a symbol by clicking Shortcut Key or AutoCorrect in the Symbol dialog box. You can also press Alt and key the numeric code (using the numeric keypad, if you have one) for a character. For example, if you change the font of the document to Wingdings and press Alt+0040, you will insert the character for a Wingdings telephone. Remember to change the Wingdings font back to your normal font after inserting a special character.

7. Scroll down several rows until you see symbols similar to an asterisk (*). Click one of the symbols.

8. Click **Insert,** and then click **Close**. The symbol appears in the document.

9. Select the list with roman numerals beginning with "I. First Quarter" through "IV. Fourth Quarter."

10. Click the **Home** tab, and click the arrow beside the Bullets button ⊞▾.

11. Click **Define New Bullet** and click **Picture**. Click one of the picture bullets, and click **OK**, and then click **OK** again. The roman numerals are replaced with your chosen picture bullet.

Exercise 4-19 INSERT SPECIAL CHARACTERS

You can use the Symbol dialog box and shortcut keys to insert characters such as an en dash, an em dash, or smart quotes. An *en dash* (–) is a dash slightly wider than a hyphen. An *em dash* (—), which is twice as wide as an en dash, is used in sentences where you would normally insert two hyphens. *Smart quotes* are quotation marks that open a quote curled in one direction (") and close a quote curled in the opposite direction (").

NOTE

By default, Word inserts smart quotes automatically.

1. Make sure nonprinting characters are displayed in the document. If they are not, click the Show/Hide ¶ button ¶.

2. On page 1, locate the paragraph that begins "1. Monday." Position the insertion point to the immediate right of "Monday." Press Delete to remove the hyphen.

3. Click the **Insert** tab, and click the Symbol button Ω Symbol ▾. Click **More Symbols**, and click the **Special Characters** tab.

4. Choose **Em Dash** from the list of characters. (Notice the keyboard shortcut listed for the character.) Click **Insert**, and then click **Close**. The em dash replaces the hyphen.

5. Select the hyphen immediately following "Tuesday." Press Alt + Ctrl + – (the minus sign on the numeric keypad). An em dash is inserted. (If you don't have a numeric keypad, press F4 to repeat the character.)

6. Insert em dashes after "Wednesday," "Thursday," and "Friday."

Exercise 4-20 CREATE SYMBOLS AUTOMATICALLY

You can use Word's AutoCorrect feature to create symbols as you type. Just enter a few keystrokes, and Word converts them into a symbol.

1. Scroll to the "SUBJECT" line, and click to the left of "Store."

2. Key **< = =** and notice that Word automatically creates an arrow (←).

NOTE

To review the symbols AutoCorrect can enter automatically, open the Word Options dialog box, and click Proofing. Click AutoCorrect Options, and click the AutoCorrect tab.

3. Position the insertion point to the right of "Procedures." Key **= = >**. Word creates another arrow pointing to the right.

4. Format the first line of the memo with 72 points of paragraph spacing before it. This starts the first line two inches from the top of the page. (See Appendix B, "Standard Forms for Business Documents.")

5. Save the document as *[your initials]*4-20 in your Lesson 4 folder.

6. Submit and close the document.

Lesson 4   Summary

- A paragraph is any amount of text followed by a paragraph mark.

- Paragraph alignment determines how the edges of a paragraph appear horizontally. Paragraphs can be left-aligned, centered, right-aligned, or justified.

- The Click and Type feature enables you to insert text in any blank area of a document by simply positioning the insertion point and double-clicking.

- Line space is the amount of vertical space between lines of text in a paragraph. Lines can be single-spaced, 1.5-line-spaced, double-spaced, or set to a specific value.

- Paragraph space is the amount of space above or below a paragraph. Paragraph space is set in points—12 points of space equals one line space for 12-point text. Change the space between paragraphs by using the Before and After options in the Paragraph dialog box or by using the Ctrl+0 keyboard shortcut to add or remove 12 points before a paragraph.

- A left indent or right indent increases a paragraph's distance from the left or right margin. A first-line indent indents only the first line of a paragraph. A hanging indent indents the second and subsequent lines of a paragraph.

- To set indents by using the horizontal ruler, drag the left indent marker (small rectangle), the first-line indent marker (top triangle), or the hanging indent marker (bottom triangle), which are all on the left end of the ruler, or drag the right indent marker (triangle) on the right end of the ruler.

- A border is a line or box added to selected text, a paragraph, or a page. Shading fills in the background of selected text or paragraphs. Borders and shading can appear in a variety of styles and colors.

- In addition to regular borders, Word provides special decorative horizontal lines that are available from the Borders and Shading dialog box.

- The AutoFormat feature enables you to create a border automatically. Key three or more hyphens ⊡, underscores ⊡, or equal signs ⊡, and press Enter. See Table 4-1.

- Repeat paragraph formats by pressing F4 or Ctrl+Y. Copy paragraph formats by using the Format Painter button. Remove paragraph formats by pressing Ctrl+Q or choosing Clear Formatting from the Font group.

- Format a list of items as a bulleted or numbered list. In a bulleted list, each item is indented and preceded by a bullet character or other symbol. In a numbered list, each item is indented and preceded by a sequential number or letter.

- Remove a bullet or number from an item in a list by clicking the Bullets button or the Numbering button on the Ribbon. Press Enter in the middle of the list to add another bulleted or numbered item automatically. Press Enter twice in a list to turn off bullets or numbering. Change the bullet symbol or the numbering type by clicking the arrow beside the Bullets button to display the Bullet Library or the arrow beside the Numbering button to open the Numbering Library.

- The AutoFormat feature enables you to create a bulleted or numbered list automatically. See Table 4-2.

- Create a multilevel list by clicking the Multilevel List button. A multilevel list has indented subparagraphs, such as paragraph "1)" followed by indented paragraph "a)" followed by indented paragraph "i)." To increase the level of numbering for each line item, click the Increase Indent button or press Tab. To decrease the level of numbering, click the Decrease Indent button or press Shift+Tab.

- Insert symbols, such as foreign characters, by clicking the Insert tab and clicking the Symbol command. Wingdings is an example of a font that contains only symbols.

- Insert special characters, such as an em dash (—), by using the Special Characters tab in the Symbol dialog box.

- Create symbols automatically as you type by keying AutoCorrect shortcuts, such as keying :) to produce the ☺ symbol.

LESSON 4 — Command Summary

Feature	Button	Command	Keyboard
1.5-line space		Home tab, Paragraph group	Ctrl+F5
Borders		Home tab, Paragraph group	
Bulleted list		Home tab, Paragraph group	
Center text		Home tab, Paragraph group	Ctrl+E
Decrease indent		Home tab, Paragraph group	Ctrl+Shift+M
Double space		Home tab, Paragraph group	Ctrl+2
Hanging indent		Home tab, Paragraph group	Ctrl+T
Increase indent		Home tab, Paragraph group	Ctrl+M
Justify text		Home tab, Paragraph group	Ctrl+J
Left-align text		Home tab, Paragraph group	Ctrl+L
Multilevel List		Home tab, Paragraph group	
Numbered list		Home tab, Paragraph group	
Remove paragraph formatting		Home tab, Paragraph group	Ctrl+Q
Restore text to Normal formatting		Home tab, Font group	Ctrl+Shift+N
Right-align text		Home tab, Paragraph group	Ctrl+R
Shading		Home tab, Paragraph group	
Single space		Home tab, Paragraph group	Ctrl+1
Symbols and special characters	Ω Symbol	Insert tab, Symbols group	

Please visit our Online Learning Center, *www.lessonapproach2010.com*, **where you will find the following review materials:**

- **Concepts Review**

    True/False Questions

    Short Answer Questions

    Critical Thinking Questions

- **Skills Review**

    Review Exercises that target single skills

    Lesson Applications

    Review Exercises that challenge students by testing multiple skills in each exercise

- **On Your Own**

    Open-ended exercises that require students to synthesize multiple skills and apply creativity and problem-solving as they would in a real world business situation

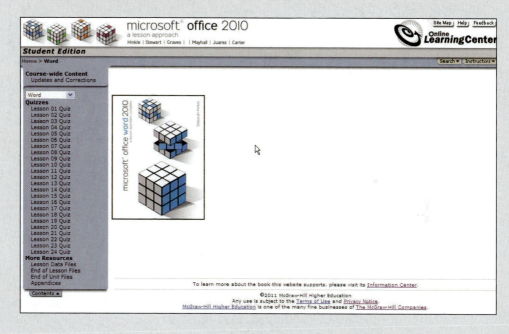

Tabs and Tabbed Columns

OBJECTIVES   *After completing this lesson, you will be able to:*

1. Set tabs.
2. Set leader tabs.
3. Clear tabs.
4. Adjust tab settings.
5. Create tabbed columns.
6. Sort paragraphs and tabbed columns.

Estimated Time: 1 hour

A *tab* is a paragraph-formatting feature used to align text. When you press Tab, Word inserts a tab character and moves the insertion point to the position of the tab setting, called the *tab stop*. You can set custom tabs or use Word's default tab settings.

As with other paragraph-formatting features, tab settings are stored in the paragraph mark at the end of a paragraph. Each time you press Enter, the tab settings are copied to the next paragraph. You can set tabs before you key text or set tabs for existing text.

In this lesson you will create documents with tabbed columns by setting tabs. Use the tab feature to create documents requiring an open table format and less complex layout. Use the table feature to create documents with tabbed columns requiring advanced formatting and design layout.

Lesson 5 introduces the memo format that is used for internal business communication. The printed memo format is not as popular today as it was a few years ago due to the increased use of e-mail. Use the memo format for documents that require a permanent record of the document content. When the document content does not require a permanent record, such as scheduling a meeting, create an e-mail message. The heading information for both a memo and an e-mail message include the name(s) of the recipient(s), the current date, and the subject of the message.

Setting Tabs

Word's default tabs are left-aligned and set every half-inch from the left margin. These tabs are indicated at the bottom of the horizontal ruler by tiny tick marks.

Figure 5-1
Default tabs

If you don't want to use the half-inch default tab settings, you have two choices:

- Change the distance between the default tab stops.
- Create custom tabs.

The four most common types of custom tabs are left-aligned, centered, right-aligned, and decimal-aligned. Custom tab settings are indicated by *tab markers* on the horizontal ruler. Additional custom tab options, such as leader tabs and bar tabs, are discussed later in the lesson.

Figure 5-2
Types of tabs

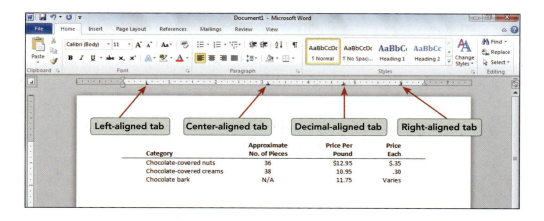

UNIT 2 LESSON 5

TABLE 5-1 Types of Tabs

Ruler Symbol	Type of Tab	Description
L	Left-aligned	The left edge of the text aligns with the tab stop.
⊥	Centered	The text is centered at the tab stop.
⅃	Right-aligned	The right edge of the text aligns with the tab stop.
⅃.	Decimal-aligned	The decimal point aligns with the tab stop. Use this option for columns of numbers.
I	Bar	Inserts a vertical line at the tab stop. Use this option to create a divider line between columns.

There are two ways to set tabs:

- Use the Tabs dialog box.
- Use the ruler.

Exercise 5-1 SET TABS BY USING THE TABS DIALOG BOX

1. Open the file **Memo - 2**.
2. Click the View Ruler button 🖳 to display the horizontal ruler, if necessary.
3. Select the text near the end of the document that begins "Item New Price" through the end of the document.
4. Click the **Home** tab, and locate the **Paragraph** group. Click the Paragraph Dialog Box Launcher 🖳. Click the **Tabs** button ⎡ Tabs... ⎤ at the bottom of the dialog box. The Tabs dialog box appears. Notice that the **Default tab stops** text box is set to 0.5 inch.

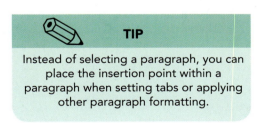

TIP

Instead of selecting a paragraph, you can place the insertion point within a paragraph when setting tabs or applying other paragraph formatting.

Figure 5-3
Tabs dialog box

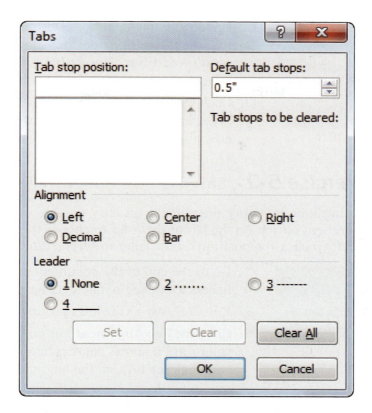

5. Key **.25** in the **Tab stop position** text box. The alignment is already set to left, by default.

6. Click **OK**. The ruler displays a left tab marker 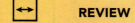, the symbol used to indicate the type and location of a tab stop on the ruler.

7. Move the insertion point to the left of the first word on the first line of the selected text, "Item."

REVIEW

Tabs are nonprinting characters that can be displayed or hidden. Remember, to display or hide nonprinting characters, click the Show/Hide ¶ button on the Home tab, Paragraph group.

NOTE

When you set a custom tab, Word clears all default tabs to the left of the new tab marker.

8. Press ⟦Tab⟧. The first line of the group is now indented 0.25 inch. This produces the same effect as creating a first-line indent.

9. Press ⟦Tab⟧ at the beginning of each of the lines that you formatted with the 0.25-inch left tab ("1.25 oz.," "1 lb.," "1 lb.," "4 oz.," and "4 oz.").

10. Select the same six lines of text ("Item" through "2.25") at the end of the document. Notice that there are tab characters between some of the words and that the text is crowded and difficult to read. The text is aligned at the default tab settings (every 0.5 inch).

11. Open the **Tabs** dialog box by double clicking the tab marker at 0.25 on the ruler. Key **3.0** in the **Tab stop position** text box.

UNIT 2 LESSON 5

NOTE

The column heading "New Price" does not contain a decimal, but is aligned at the decimal point. You will adjust the tab for this heading later in this lesson.

12. Under **Alignment**, choose **Decimal**. Click **Set**. Notice that the tab setting appears below the Tab stop position text box. The setting is automatically selected so that another tab setting can be keyed.

13. Click **OK**. The column headings "Item" and "New Price," along with the text below the headings, are now aligned at the tab stops.

Exercise 5-2 SET TABS BY USING THE RULER

Setting tabs by using the ruler is an easy two-step process: Click the Tab Alignment button on the left of the ruler to choose the type of tab alignment, and then click the position on the ruler to set the tab.

TIP

When choosing tab settings for information in a document, keep in mind that left-aligned text and right- or decimal-aligned numbers are easier to read.

1. Go to the end of the document, and press Enter if necessary to begin a new paragraph.

2. Key **Category** at the left margin.

3. Click the Tab Alignment button on the horizontal ruler until it shows center alignment. Each time you click the button, the alignment changes.

Figure 5-4
Tab Alignment button on the ruler

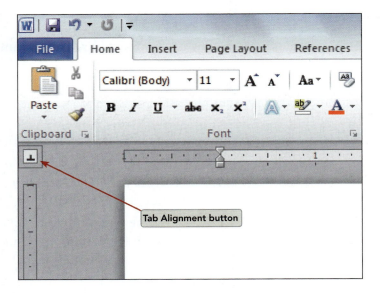

Tab Alignment button

TIP

As you toggle through the Tab Alignment button symbols, notice the appearance of the first-line indent symbol and the hanging indent symbol. You can display one of these symbols, and then just click the ruler to the desired indent position instead of using the point-and-drag method.

4. Click the ruler at 3.25, and a center tab marker displays.

5. Press Tab, and key **No. of Pieces**.

6. Click the **Tab Alignment** button on the horizontal ruler until it shows right alignment, and then click the ruler at 5.5.

7. Press Tab, and key **Price/Pound**.

TIP

You can copy tab settings from one paragraph to another. Click in the paragraph whose tab settings you want to copy. Click the Format Painter button. Click in the paragraph to which you are copying the tab settings.

8. Press [Enter] to start a new line. The tab settings will carry forward to the new line.

9. Key **Chocolate-covered nuts**, press [Tab], key **36**, press [Tab], and key **$12.95**.

10. Press [Enter] and key **Chocolate-covered creams**, press [Tab], key **38**, press [Tab], and key **10.95**. Press [Enter].

Figure 5-5
Document with tabbed text

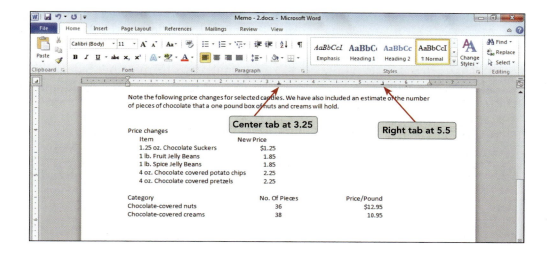

Setting Leader Tabs

You can set tabs with *leader characters,* patterns of dots or dashes that lead the reader's eye from one tabbed column to the next. Leaders may be found in a table of contents, in which dotted lines fill the space between the headings on the left and the page numbers on the right.

Word offers three leader patterns: dotted line, dashed line, and solid line.

Figure 5-6
Leader patterns

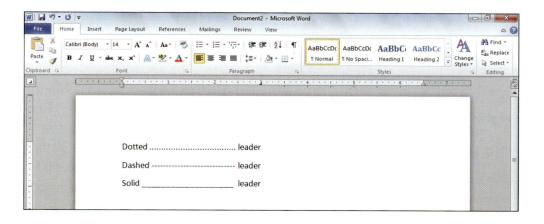

Exercise 5-3   SET LEADER TABS

1. Select the two columns of text under the headings "Item" and "New Price." The prices are aligned at a 3-inch decimal tab.

2. Open the **Tabs** dialog box. The tab settings for the selected text are displayed in the **Tab stop position** text box with the 0.25-inch tab highlighted.

3. Click to select **3"**, and under **Leader**, click the second leader pattern (the dotted line).

4. Click **Set** and click **OK**. A dotted-line leader fills the space to the left of the 3-inch tab setting.

5. Select the heading "Price Changes" and apply bold, small caps formatting. Select the headings "Item" and "New Price" and apply bold and italic.

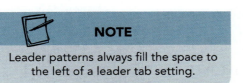

NOTE

Leader patterns always fill the space to the left of a leader tab setting.

Clearing Tabs

You can clear custom tabs all at once or individually. When you clear custom tabs, Word restores the default tab stops to the left of the custom tab stop. There are three ways to clear a tab:

- Use the Tabs dialog box.
- Use the ruler.
- Press [Ctrl]+[Q].

Exercise 5-4   CLEAR A TAB BY USING THE TABS DIALOG BOX AND THE KEYBOARD

1. Select the six lines of text under the heading "Price Changes."

2. Open the **Tabs** dialog box. The 0.25-inch tab is highlighted in the **Tab stop position** text box.

3. Click **Clear** and click **OK**. Word clears the 0.25-inch custom tab, and the text moves to the right to align at the tab stop at 3.0. (The text moves because each line is preceded by a tab character (→).

4. Delete the tab character (→) at the beginning of each line. The text in the first column moves to the left margin, and the text in the second column is aligned at the tab setting.

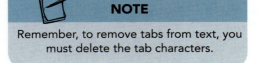

NOTE

Remember, to remove tabs from text, you must delete the tab characters.

5. Select the six lines of text under the heading "Price Changes" once again. Press [Ctrl]+[Q]. The remaining tab setting is deleted, and the text is no longer aligned.

6. Click the Undo button 🔙 to restore the 3-inch custom tab.

7. Save the document as *[your initials]*5-4 in your Lesson 5 folder.

Exercise 5-5   CLEAR A TAB BY USING THE RULER

1. Position the insertion point at the beginning of the line of text with the heading "Category."
2. Position the pointer on the 5.5-inch right-aligned tab marker on the ruler.

NOTE

When clearing or adjusting tabs by using the ruler, watch for the ScreenTip to correctly identify the item to which you are pointing. If no ScreenTip appears, you might inadvertently add another tab marker.

3. When the ScreenTip "Right Tab" appears, drag the tab marker down and off the ruler. The custom tab is cleared, and the heading "Price/Pound" moves to a default tab stop.
4. Undo the last action to restore the tab setting.
5. Select the headings "Category," "No. of Pieces," and "Price/Pound," and apply bold, small caps formatting.

Adjusting Tab Settings

You can adjust tabs inserted in a document by using either the Tabs dialog box or the ruler. Tabs can be adjusted only after you select the text to which they have been applied.

Exercise 5-6   ADJUST TAB SETTINGS

1. Select the line with the headings "Item" and "New Price." The second heading is not aligned with the text below.
2. Point to the tab marker at 3 inches on the ruler.
3. Drag the tab marker to the right until the heading aligns with the text below.
4. Select the last three lines of text in the document ("Category" through "10.95").

NOTE

When you change tab settings with the ruler, be careful to drag the tab marker only to the right or to the left. If you drag the tab marker up or down, you might clear it from the ruler. If you inadvertently clear a tab marker, undo your action to restore the tab.

5. Open the **Tabs** dialog box.
6. Click to select the tab setting **5.5** in the **Tab stop position** text box.
7. Change the tab alignment setting by clicking **Left**. Click **OK**. Notice the change in the alignment of the heading and the text below.
8. Click the Undo button.

Figure 5-7
Using the ruler to
adjust a tab setting

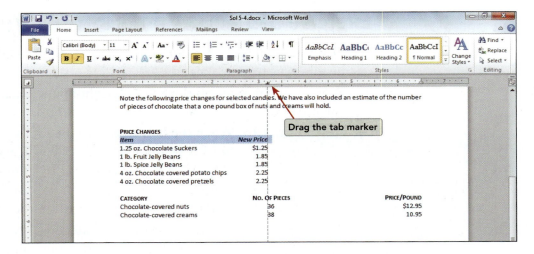

9. With the text still selected, drag the 5.5-inch tab marker to 6.5 inches on the ruler. The text is now aligned at the right margin.

Creating Tabbed Columns

As you have seen in these practice documents, you can use tabs to present information in columns.

When you format a table using tabbed columns, follow these rules for existing text or text to be keyed.

- The table should be centered horizontally within the margins.
- Columns within the table should be between 6 and 10 spaces apart.
- The width of the table should not exceed the width of the document's body text.
- At least one blank line should separate the top and bottom of the table from the body text of the document.

Exercise 5-7   SET TABBED COLUMNS

1. Position the insertion point at the end of the document, and press Enter twice.
2. Press Ctrl + Q to remove the tab settings from the paragraph mark; then key the text shown in Figure 5-8. Use single spacing.

Figure 5-8

> The following stores offer a complete line of gifts and accessories in addition to our fine chocolates. Other stores offer a limited selection of gifts and accessories due to space limitations.

3. Press Enter twice.

4. Study Figure 5-9 to determine the longest item in each column. (Pennsylvania is the longest item in the first column. Youngstown is the longest item in the second column, and West Virginia is the longest item in the third column.)

Figure 5-9

Pennsylvania	Ohio	West Virginia
Grove City	Akron	Clarksburg
Pittsburgh	Canton	Fairmont
Erie	Cleveland	Morgantown
Monroeville	Youngstown	Wheeling

5. Create a guide line that contains the longest item in each column by keying the following with 10 spaces between each group of words:

   Pennsylvania   Youngstown   West Virginia

6. Click the Center button ▤ on the Ribbon to center the line.

7. Change the Tab Alignment button to left alignment ⌐. Using the I-beam as a guide, click the ruler to set a left-aligned tab at the beginning of each group of words.

Figure 5-10
Guide line for
centering tabbed
columns

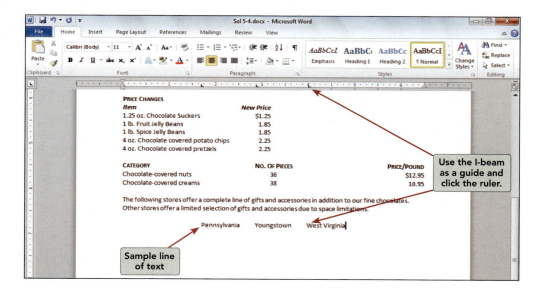

8. Delete the text in the guide line up to the paragraph mark. Do not delete the paragraph mark, which is now storing your left-aligned tab settings.

9. Click the Align Left button ▤ to left-align the insertion point.

10. Key the table text as shown in Figure 5-9, pressing Tab before each item and single-spacing each line. Underline each column heading.

11. Select the text near the top of the document beginning with "Item No." and ending with the line that begins "BC32."

12. Change the Tab Alignment button to left alignment ⌐, and click the ruler at 2.5.

13. Change the Tab Alignment button to right alignment 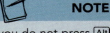, and click the ruler at 5.5.

14. Select the text if necessary, and click the Increase Indent button ⯈ two times to move the text away from the left margin.

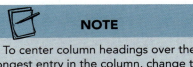

15. Drag the left tab marker (right or left) to position the middle column an equal distance from the first and third columns.

16. Bold and center the heading "Standard-Size Boxes." Format the title with all caps and 12 points spacing after. Apply bold and italic formatting to the column headings.

Exercise 5-8 SELECT A TABBED COLUMN

After text is formatted in tabbed columns, you can select columns individually by selecting a vertical block of text. Selecting tabbed text can be helpful for formatting or deleting text. You use Alt to select a vertical block of text.

1. Scroll to the end of the document. Hold down Alt and position the I-beam to the immediate left of "Ohio."

2. Drag across the heading, and then down until the heading and all four cities are selected.

Figure 5-11
Selecting text vertically

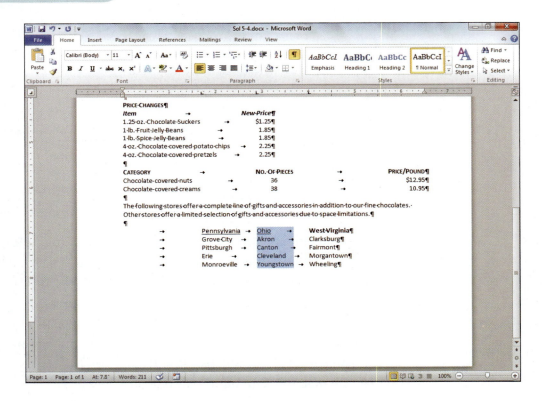

3. Press ⌈Delete⌋ to delete the column.

4. Undo the deletion.

5. Select the column again, this time selecting only the names under the column heading "Ohio."

6. Click the Italic button ⌈*I*⌋ to format the text.

Exercise 5-9   INSERT BAR TABS

Bar tabs are used to make tabbed columns look more like a table with gridlines. A bar tab inserts a vertical line at a fixed position, creating a border between columns. You can set bar tabs by using the ruler or the Tabs dialog box.

1. At the bottom of the document, select the four lines of tabbed text below the headings "Pennsylvania," "Ohio," and "West Virginia."

2. Open the **Tabs** dialog box. Key **2.5** in the text box, click **Bar**, and click **OK**. The vertical bar is placed between the first and second columns. Do not deselect the tabbed text.

3. To set bar tabs by using the ruler, click the Tab Alignment button until it changes to a bar tab ⌈▣⌋. Click the ruler at 3.75 inches. The bar tab markers appear as short vertical lines on the ruler.

4. Adjust the bar tab markers on the ruler to make them more evenly spaced, as needed.

5. Deselect the tabbed text. Click the Show/Hide ¶ button ⌈¶⌋ to view the document without nonprinting characters. The bar tabs act as dividing borders between the columns.

Figure 5-12
Tabbed text with bar tabs

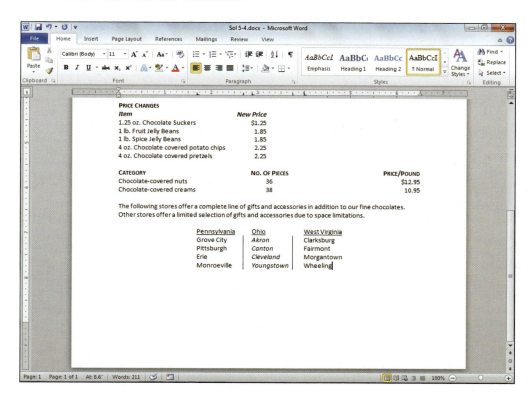

6. Position the insertion point in the line that contains "Grove City."

7. Point to the 3.75-inch bar tab on the ruler, and drag it off the ruler. The vertical line in the table disappears.

8. Undo the deletion to restore the bar tab.

9. Save the document as *[your initials]*5-9 in your Lesson 5 folder.

10. Submit the document.

Sorting Paragraphs and Tabbed Columns

Sorting is the process of reordering text alphabetically or numerically. You can sort to rearrange text in ascending order (from lowest to highest, such as 0–9 or A–Z) or descending order (from highest to lowest, such as 9–0 or Z–A).

You can sort any group of paragraphs, from a single-column list to a multiple-column table, such as one created by tabbed columns. When sorting a tabbed table, you can sort by any of the columns.

Figure 5-13
Sorting paragraphs and tables

PENNSYLVANIA STORES	NO. OF EMPLOYEES
Butler	14
Edinboro	15
Erie	18
Franklin	12
Greenville	10
Grove City	20
Meadville	12
Mercer	10
Monroeville	18
New Castle	14
Pittsburgh	20
Sharon	14

Alphabetical sort in ascending order

PENNSYLVANIA STORES	NO. OF EMPLOYEES
Grove City	20
Pittsburgh	20
Erie	18
Monroeville	18
Edinboro	15
Butler	14
New Castle	14
Sharon	14
Franklin	12
Meadville	12
Greenville	10
Mercer	10

Numerical sort in descending order

Exercise 5-10   SORT TABBED TABLES

1. Select the headings "Pennsylvania," "Ohio," and "West Virginia" and the four lines of text below the headings.

2. Click the Sort button 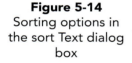 on the Ribbon, Paragraph group.

3. Open the **Sort by** drop-down list to view the other sort options. Field numbers represent each of the columns. Open the **Type** drop-down list. Notice that the type options include **Text**, **Number**, and **Date**.

4. Click **Descending** to change the sort order, and click the **Header row** option to select it. Click **OK**. The text in the first column is sorted alphabetically in descending order.

5. Press Ctrl+Z to undo the sort. Do not deselect the text.

6. Click the Sort button 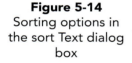 to open the Sort Text dialog box.

7. Click **Header row** at the bottom of the dialog box. This option indicates that the selection includes column headings, which should not be sorted with the text.

8. Open the **Sort by** drop-down list. Now you can sort by the table's column headings instead of by field numbers.

9. Choose **Ohio** from the drop-down list. Click **Descending** and click **OK**.

Figure 5-14
Sorting options in the sort Text dialog box

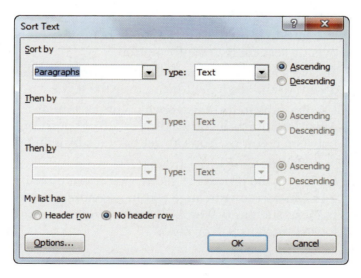

10. Save the document as *[your initials]*5-10 in your Lesson 5 folder.

11. Submit and close the document.

Lesson 5   Summary

- Tabs are a paragraph-formatting feature used to align text. When you press Tab, Word inserts a tab character and moves the insertion position to the tab setting, called the tab stop.

- Word's default tabs are left-aligned and set every half-inch from the left margin, as indicated at the bottom of the horizontal ruler.

- The four most common types of custom tabs are left-aligned, centered, right-aligned, and decimal-aligned. Custom tab settings are indicated on the horizontal ruler by tab markers.

- Set tabs by using the Tabs dialog box or the ruler. To use the ruler, click the Tab Alignment button on the left of the ruler to select the type of tab alignment, and then click the position on the ruler to set the tab. See Table 5-1.

- A leader tab uses a series of dots, dashes, or solid underlines to fill the empty space to the left of a tab stop. Use the Tabs dialog box to set a leader tab.

- Clear custom tabs all at once or individually. To clear a tab, use the Tabs dialog box, the ruler, or press Ctrl+Q.

- To adjust tab settings, position the insertion point in the tabbed text (or select the text), and then either open the Tabs dialog box or drag the tab markers on the ruler.

- Use tabs to present information in columns. Tabbed columns are a side-by-side vertical list of information.

- To select a tabbed column (for formatting or deleting the text), hold down Alt and drag the I-beam over the text.

- Use bar tabs to format tabbed columns similar to a table with gridlines. A bar tab inserts a vertical line at a fixed position, creating a border between columns. You can set bar tabs by using the ruler or the Tabs dialog box.

- Sorting is the process of reordering text alphabetically or numerically. You can sort to rearrange text in ascending order (from lowest to highest, such as 0–9 or A–Z) or descending order (from highest to lowest, such as 9–0 or Z–A).

LESSON 5		Command Summary	
Feature	Button	Command	Keyboard
Bar tab	▯	Home tab, Paragraph group	
Center tab	⊥	Home tab, Paragraph group	
Clear tabs		Home tab, Paragraph group	Ctrl + Q
Decimal tab	⊥	Home tab, Paragraph group	
Leader tabs		Home tab, Paragraph group	
Left tab	L	Home tab, Paragraph group	
Right tab	⅃	Home tab, Paragraph group	
Sort text	A↓Z	Home tab, Paragraph group	

Please visit our Online Learning Center, *www.lessonapproach2010.com*, **where you will find the following review materials:**

- **Concepts Review**

    True/False Questions

    Short Answer Questions

    Critical Thinking Questions

- **Skills Review**

    Review Exercises that target single skills

    Lesson Applications

    Review Exercises that challenge students by testing multiple skills in each exercise

- **On Your Own**

    Open-ended exercises that require students to synthesize multiple skills and apply creativity and problem-solving as they would in a real world business situation

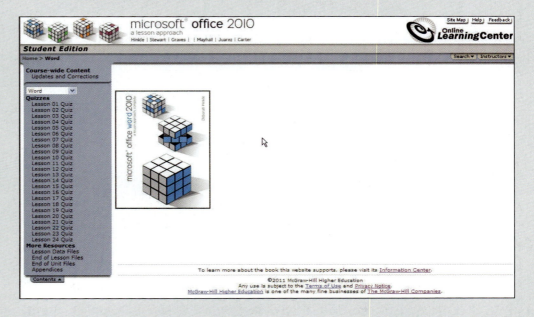

Lesson 6
Moving and Copying Text

OBJECTIVES

After completing this lesson, you will be able to:

1. Use the Office Clipboard.
2. Move text by using cut and paste.
3. Move text by dragging.
4. Copy text by using copy and paste.
5. Copy text by dragging.
6. Work with multiple document windows.
7. Move and copy text among windows.

Estimated Time: 1 hour

One of the most useful features of word processing is the capability to move or copy a block of text from one part of a document to another or from one document window to another, without rekeying the text. In Word, you can move and copy text quickly by using the Cut, Copy, and Paste commands or the drag-and-drop editing feature.

Using the Office Clipboard

Perhaps the most important tool for moving and copying text is the *Clipboard*, which is a temporary storage area. Here is how it works: Cut or copy text from your document, and store it on the Clipboard. Then move to a different location in your document, and insert the Clipboard's contents using the Paste command.

There are two types of clipboards:

- The system Clipboard stores one item at a time. Each time you store a new item on this Clipboard, it replaces the previous item. This Clipboard is available to many software applications on your system.

- The Office Clipboard can store 24 items, which are displayed on the Clipboard task pane. The Office Clipboard collects multiple items without erasing previous items. You can store items from all Office applications.

Exercise 6-1 DISPLAY THE CLIPBOARD TASK PANE

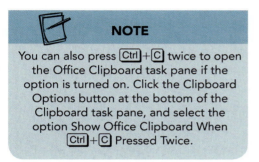

NOTE

You can also press Ctrl + C twice to open the Office Clipboard task pane if the option is turned on. Click the Clipboard Options button at the bottom of the Clipboard task pane, and select the option Show Office Clipboard When Ctrl + C Pressed Twice.

1. Click the **Home** tab. The first group is the **Clipboard** group, and it contains a Dialog Box Launcher 🔲 to open the Clipboard task pane.

2. Click the **Clipboard Dialog Box Launcher**. The Clipboard task pane opens. At the top of the task pane, notice the Paste All 🔲 Paste All and Clear All 🔲 Clear All buttons. At the bottom of the screen, at the right end of the taskbar in the Notification Area, notice the Clipboard icon 📋, indicating that the Office Clipboard is in use.

Figure 6-1
Clipboard task pane

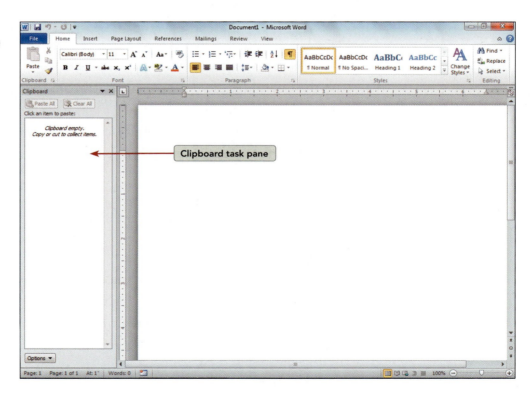

3. If the Office Clipboard contains items from previous use, click the Clear All button to empty the Clipboard.

4. Click the **Options** button at the bottom of the task pane. Notice the options available for using the Office Clipboard.

5. Click outside the task pane, making sure not to choose any of the options in the list.

> **NOTE**
>
> If the option Show Office Clipboard Automatically is selected, the Clipboard task pane will open automatically when you copy twice in a row without pasting.

Moving Text by Using Cut and Paste

To move text by using the *cut-and-paste* method, start by highlighting the text you want to move and using the Cut command. Then move to the location where you want to place the text, and use the Paste command. When you use cut and paste to move paragraphs, you can preserve the correct spacing between paragraphs by following these rules:

• Include the blank line below the paragraph you are moving as part of the selection.

• When you paste the selection, click to the left of the first line of text following the place where your paragraph will go—not on the blank line above it.

There are multiple ways to cut and paste text. The most commonly used methods are:

• Use the Cut and Paste buttons on the Ribbon, Home tab.

• Use the shortcut menu.

• Use the keyboard shortcuts Ctrl+X to cut and Ctrl+V to paste.

• Use the Clipboard task pane.

Exercise 6-2   USE THE RIBBON TO CUT AND PASTE

1. Open the file **Festival Memo**.

2. Key the current year in the date line of the memo heading.

3. Select the text "Strawberry Days" in the subject line of the memo.

4. Click the **Home** tab, and click the Cut button to remove the text from the document and place it on the Clipboard. Notice the Clipboard item in the task pane.

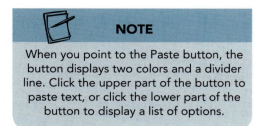

5. Position the insertion point to the left of "Art" in the subject line to indicate where you want to insert the text.

6. Click the Paste button 📋 to insert "Strawberry Days" in its new location. The Paste Options button 📋 (Ctrl) ▾ appears below the pasted text, and the Clipboard item remains in the task pane. The Paste Options button is available to make sure the text you paste has the type of formatting you want.

7. Move the I-beam over the Paste Options button 📋 (Ctrl) ▾. (The I-beam will change to an arrow when it passes over the Paste Options button.) Click the button's drop-down arrow to view the Paste Options gallery. A ScreenTip displays when you point to the gallery icons. Click in the document window to close the gallery.

Figure 6-2
Paste options

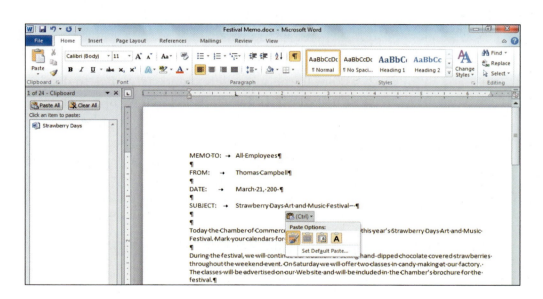

8. Delete the em dash and extra spaces at the end of the subject line.

Exercise 6-3 USE THE SHORTCUT MENU TO CUT AND PASTE

1. Select the paragraph near the bottom of the document that begins "All hotels are." Include the paragraph mark on the blank line following the paragraph.

Figure 6-3
Using the shortcut menu to cut

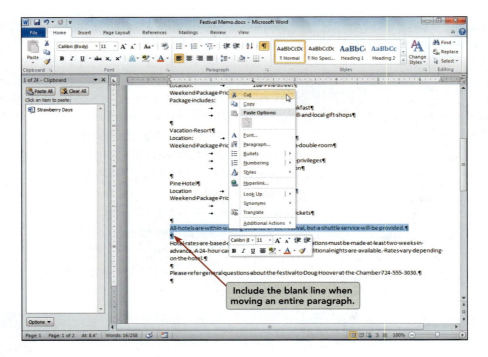

2. Point to the selected text and right-click to display the shortcut menu.

3. Click **Cut**. The item is added to the Clipboard task pane.

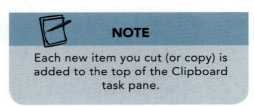

NOTE

Each new item you cut (or copy) is added to the top of the Clipboard task pane.

4. Position the I-beam to the left of the paragraph that begins "Several special." Right-click and click the first Paste Option—(Keep Source Formatting)—from the shortcut menu. The paragraph moves to its new location, and the Paste Options button (Ctrl) appears below the pasted text.

Figure 6-4
Using the shortcut menu to paste

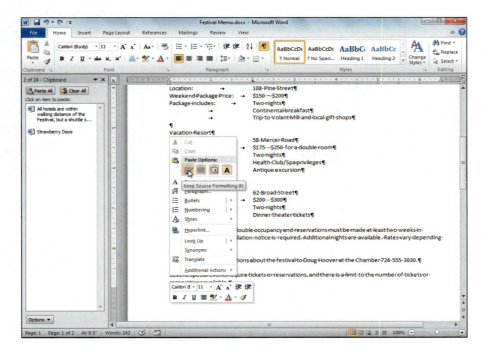

Exercise 6-4 USE KEYBOARD SHORTCUTS TO CUT AND PASTE

If you prefer using the keyboard, you can press Ctrl+X to cut text and Ctrl+V to paste text. You can also use Ctrl+Z to undo an action. The location of these shortcut keys is designed to make it easy for you to move your mouse with your right hand while you press command keys with your left hand.

1.   Select the paragraph that begins "Several special" and the blank line that follows the paragraph. Press Ctrl+X to cut the text. A new item appears in the task pane.

2.   Position the insertion point just before the paragraph that begins "Please refer." Press Ctrl+V to paste the text.

3.   Press Ctrl+Z to undo the paste. Press Ctrl+Y to redo the paste. (Remember, you can also click the Undo button ↰ to undo actions.) Notice that the Clipboard item remains in the task pane.

Exercise 6-5 USE THE OFFICE CLIPBOARD TO PASTE

Each time you cut text in the previous exercises, a new item was added to the Office Clipboard. You can paste that item directly from the task pane.

1.   Select all the information that goes with the "Pine Hotel," including the title "Pine Hotel" and the blank line that follows the hotel information.

2.   Cut this text, using the Cut button ✂ on the Ribbon. The text is stored as a new item at the top of the Clipboard task pane.

3.   Position the insertion point to the left of the paragraph that begins "Wolf Creek Hotel."

> **NOTE**
>
> Choosing the Paste option from the drop-down list pastes that item, just like clicking directly on the item. The Paste All button 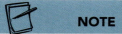 on the Clipboard task pane is used to copy all Office Clipboard items to the location of the insertion point.

4.   Click the task pane item for the Pine Hotel text that you just cut. (Do not click the drop-down arrow.) The text is pasted at the location of the insertion point.

5.   Press Ctrl+Z to undo the paste. Press Ctrl+Z again to undo the cut. The Clipboard item remains in the task pane.

6.   Point to this Clipboard item in the task pane, and click the drop-down arrow that appears to its right.

7.   Choose **Delete** from the list to delete the item from the Clipboard.

Moving Text by Dragging

You can also move selected text to a new location by using the *drag-and-drop* method. Text is not transferred to the Clipboard when you use drag and drop.

Exercise 6-6   USE DRAG AND DROP TO MOVE TEXT

1. Select all the information related to "Vacation Resort," including the title "Vacation Resort" and the blank line below the information.

2. Point to the selected text. Notice that the I-beam changes to a left-pointing arrow.

3. Click and hold down the left mouse button. The pointer changes to the drag-and-drop pointer . Notice the dotted insertion point near the tip of the arrow and the dotted box at the base of the arrow.

4. Drag the pointer until the dotted insertion point is positioned to the left of the line beginning "Wolf Creek Hotel." Release the mouse button. The paragraph moves to its new location, and the Paste Options button 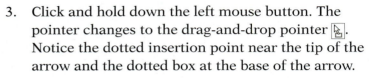 appears.

> **TIP**
>
> Use cut and paste to move text over long distances—for example, onto another page. Use drag and drop to move text short distances where you can see both the selected text and the destination on the screen at the same time.

Figure 6-5
Drag-and-drop pointer

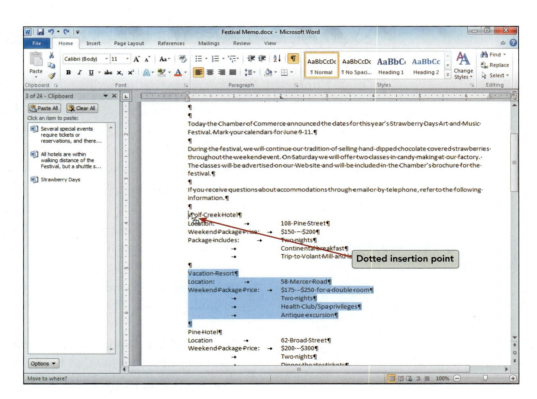

Copying Text by Using Copy and Paste

Copying and pasting text is similar to cutting and pasting text. Instead of removing the text from the document and storing it on the Clipboard, you place a copy of the text on the Clipboard.

There are several ways to copy and paste text. The most common methods are:

- Use the Copy and Paste buttons on the Ribbon, Home tab.
- Use the shortcut menu.
- Use keyboard shortcuts Ctrl+C to copy and Ctrl+V to paste.
- Use the Clipboard task pane.

Exercise 6-7   USE COPY AND PASTE

1. Under "Wolf Creek Hotel," select the entire line that contains the text "Continental breakfast." Include the tab character to the left of the text and the paragraph mark to the right of the text. If necessary, click the Show/Hide ¶ button ¶ to display formatting characters. (The selected text should begin at the left margin and end with the paragraph mark.)

2. Click the Copy button on the Ribbon to transfer a copy of the text to the Clipboard. Notice that the selected text remains in its original position in the document.

3. Position the insertion point to the left of the paragraph that begins with a tab character and includes "Health Club/Spa privileges" in the text under "Vacation Resort."

4. Click the Paste button. A copy of the paragraph is added to the "Vacation Resort" package description, and the Paste Options button (Ctrl) appears.

5. Point to the Paste Options button (Ctrl). When you see the down arrow, click the button. Notice that the same options are available when you copy and paste text. Click in the document window to close the list of options and keep the source formatting.

6. Position the insertion point to the left of the paragraph that begins "Dinner theater tickets." Press Ctrl+V to paste the text into the "Pine Hotel" package description.

Exercise 6-8   USE THE OFFICE CLIPBOARD TO PASTE COPIED TEXT

A new item is added to the Office Clipboard each time you copy text. You can click this item to paste the text into the document.

NOTE

You can store up to 24 cut or copied items on the Office Clipboard. When the Clipboard is full and you cut or copy text, the bottom Clipboard item is deleted and the new item is added to the top of the task pane.

1. Under "Vacation Resort," select the text "for a double room." Include the space character to the left of the text.

2. Press Ctrl+C to copy this text.

3. Position the insertion point to the right of the text that begins "$150–$200" in the Wolf Creek Hotel information.

4. Click the Clipboard that contains the text "for a double room." The Clipboard content is pasted into the document at the location of the insertion point.

Copying Text by Dragging

To copy text by using the drag-and-drop method, press Ctrl while dragging the text. Remember, drag and drop does not store text on the Clipboard.

Exercise 6-9   USE DRAG AND DROP TO COPY TEXT

NOTE

You may already have noticed that when you delete, cut, move, or paste text, Word automatically adjusts the spacing between words. For example, if you cut a word at the end of a sentence, Word automatically deletes the leftover space. If you paste a word between two other words, Word automatically adds the needed space as part of its Smart Cut-and-Paste feature. The Smart Cut-and Paste feature is turned on by default.

1. Scroll until you can see the text under "Wolf Creek Hotel" and "Pine Hotel."

2. Select the text under the Wolf Creek Hotel beginning with "for a double room."

3. While pressing Ctrl, drag the selected text to the immediate right of the text "$200–$300" in the "Pine Hotel" section. The plus (+) sign attached to the drag-and-drop pointer indicates the text is being copied rather than moved.

4. The text is copied, and a space is automatically inserted between "$300" and "for."

Figure 6-6
Copying with the drag-and-drop pointer

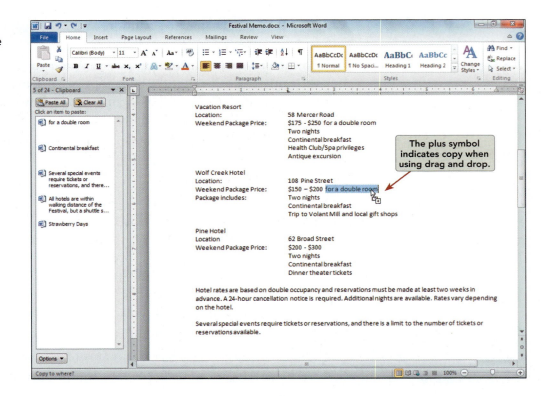

5. Move to the top of the document, and change the spacing before to 72 points, and insert your reference initials at the end of the document.

TIP

Dragging is not effective over long distances within a document. Try these alternative methods: To cut, select the text, hold down [Ctrl], scroll as needed, and right-click where you want to paste the text. To copy, select the text, hold down [Ctrl] and [Shift], scroll as needed, and right-click where you want to paste the text.

6. Open the **File** tab, and click **Print**. The Print tab displays. Drag the Zoom slider in the lower right corner to approximately 25% to see both pages of the document.

7. Save the document as *[your initials]*6-9 in a new folder for Lesson 6.

8. Click the Clear All button 🔊 Clear All on the Office Clipboard to clear all items. Click the Close button ✖ on the task pane to close the Office Clipboard.

9. Submit and close the document.

Working with Multiple Document Windows

In Word, you can work with several open document windows. Working with multiple windows makes it easy to compare different parts of the same document or to move or copy text from one document to another.

Exercise 6-10   SPLIT A DOCUMENT INTO PANES

Splitting a document divides it into two areas separated by a horizontal line called the *split bar*. Each of the resulting two areas, called *panes*, has its own scroll bar.

To split a screen, click the View tab and click the Split button or use the split box at the top of the vertical scroll bar.

1. Open the file **Fund2**.

2. Click the **View** tab and click the Split button 🔲. A gray bar appears along with the split pointer ⬍.

3. Move your mouse up or down (without clicking) until the gray bar is just below the second paragraph of the letter.

Figure 6-7
Splitting a document
into two panes

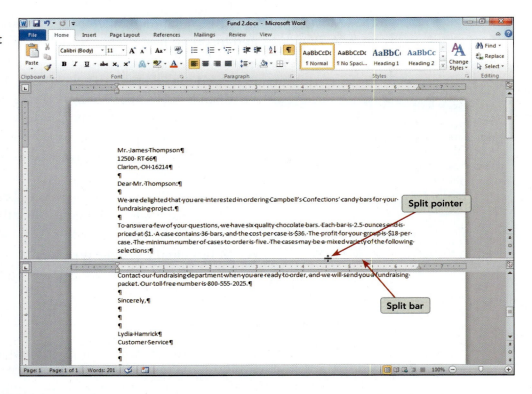

4. Click the left mouse button to set the split. The document divides into two panes, each with its own ruler and scroll bar.

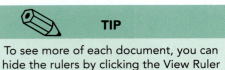
TIP

To see more of each document, you can hide the rulers by clicking the View Ruler button 🖼 on the vertical scroll bar.

5. To change the split position, move the mouse pointer over the split bar (between the top and bottom panes) until you see the split pointer ⬍ and a ScreenTip that says "Resize." Then drag the bar above the list.

6. To remove the split bar, move the mouse pointer over it. When you see the split pointer, double-click. The split bar is removed.

7. Position the pointer over the *split box*—the thin gray rectangle at the top of the vertical scroll bar.

8. When you see the split pointer ⬍, double-click. Once again the document is split into two panes. (You can also remove the split bar by choosing Remove Split 🖳 from the View tab.)

Figure 6-8
Double-clicking the
split box to create
two window panes

Exercise 6-11 MOVE BETWEEN PANES TO EDIT TEXT

After you split a document, you can scroll each pane separately and easily move from pane to pane to edit separate areas of the document. To switch panes, click the insertion point in the pane you want to edit.

1. Click in the top pane.

2. With the insertion point in the top pane, click the insertion point in the bottom pane.

3. Use the scroll bar in the bottom pane to scroll to the top of the document. Both panes should now show the inside address.

NOTE

Editing in a pane is the same as editing in a single window. It is important to understand that the changes you make to one pane affect the entire document.

4. In the bottom pane, change the street address to **12575 Route 66** and the state to **PA**. Notice that the changes also appear in the top pane.

5. In the bottom pane, scroll until the paragraph beginning "Specialty fundraising" is displayed. Click within the top pane, and scroll until the paragraphs beginning "Specialty fundraising" and "There are no" are both displayed.

6. Go back to the bottom pane. Select the paragraph beginning "Specialty fundraising," and click the Cut button ✂ on the Home tab. (Remember to include the blank line after the paragraph when selecting it.)

7. Move to the top pane, position the insertion point to the left of "There are no," and click the Paste button 📋. The paragraph is moved from one part of the document to another.

8. Drag the split bar to the top of the screen. This is another way to remove the split bar. The document is again displayed in one pane.

TIP

See Appendix B, "Standard Forms for Business Documents," for standard business letter formatting.

9. Apply the correct letter formatting to the document by adding the date and your reference initials. Use the correct spacing between all letter elements, and place 72 points spacing before the date.

10. Save the document as *[your initials]***6-11** in your Lesson 6 folder.

11. Submit and close the document.

Exercise 6-12 OPEN MULTIPLE DOCUMENTS

In addition to working with window panes, you can work with more than one document file at the same time. This is useful if you keyed text in one document that you want to use in a second document.

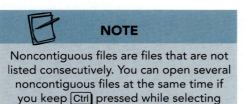

NOTE

Noncontiguous files are files that are not listed consecutively. You can open several noncontiguous files at the same time if you keep [Ctrl] pressed while selecting additional files.

1. Display the **Open** dialog box. Simultaneously open the noncontiguous files **Bittersweet** and **Milk Chocolate**. To do this, click **Bittersweet** once, press [Ctrl], and click **Milk Chocolate** once. With both files selected, click **Open**.

2. Click the **View** tab. Click the Switch Windows button 🔲, and notice that the two open files are listed at the bottom of the list. The active file has a check next to it. Switch documents by clicking the file that is not active.

3. Press [Ctrl]+[F6] to switch back.

4. Point to the Word button 🔲 in the Windows taskbar. The button expands to display thumbnails for each open document. Move the mouse from one thumbnail to another to preview the documents and to change the active document. Click the **Bittersweet** button to activate that document.

Figure 6-9
Switching document windows using the taskbar

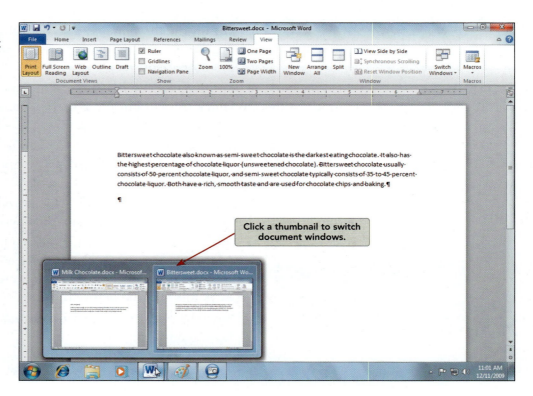

5. Click the **View** tab, if necessary. Click the Arrange All button 🔲 to view both documents at the same time. The two documents appear one below the other.

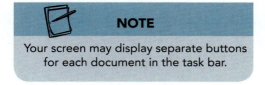

NOTE

Your screen may display separate buttons for each document in the task bar.

Figure 6-10
Two documents
displayed on one
screen

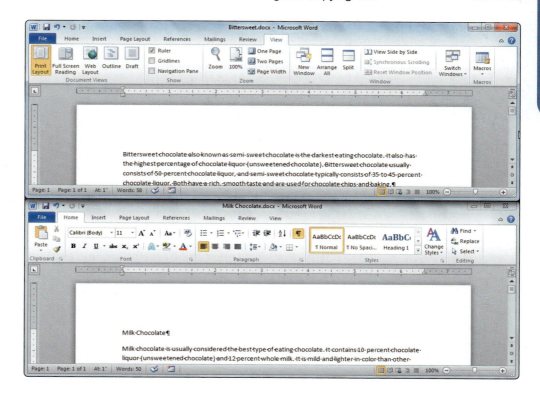

6. Press Ctrl+F6 to switch between documents. Press Ctrl+F6 again. Notice that the active window—the one containing the insertion point—has a highlighted title bar.

7. Close the **Bittersweet** and **Milk Chocolate** documents.

8. Start Word if necessary, or click the Maximize button 🔲 to maximize the Word window.

9. Simultaneously open three files, **Bittersweet**, **Chocolate - 2**, and **Milk Chocolate**, by accessing the Open dialog box. Select the first file, **Bittersweet**, and then press Ctrl and select the other two files. Click Open.

10. Choose Arrange All from the View tab to display all three documents simultaneously.

Exercise 6-13 REARRANGE AND RESIZE DOCUMENT WINDOWS

You can rearrange the open documents in Word by using basic Windows techniques for minimizing, maximizing, restoring, and sizing windows.

1. Click the **Bittersweet** title bar, and drag this document's window toward the top of the screen. Click the Close button ❌ for **Chocolate - 2**. Click the Maximize button 🔲 for **Milk Chocolate**.

2. Minimize the **Milk Chocolate** window by clicking its Minimize button ▭. The document disappears from view. The **Milk Chocolate** button is on the taskbar, indicating that Word is still running.

3. Restore the **Milk Chocolate** document for viewing by clicking its taskbar button.

4. Click the Close button ✕ for **Milk Chocolate**. Close the **Bittersweet** document.

Moving and Copying Text among Windows

When you want to copy or move text from one document to another, you can work with either multiple (smaller) document windows or full-size document windows. Either way, you can use cut and paste or copy and paste. If you work with multiple windows, you can also use drag and drop. To use this technique, you must display both documents at the same time.

Exercise 6-14   COPY TEXT FROM ONE DOCUMENT TO ANOTHER BY USING COPY AND PASTE

When moving or copying text from one document into another, the paste default is to paste text in the format of the document from which it was cut or copied. To control the formatting of pasted text, you can use the Paste Options gallery or the Paste Special function. In this exercise, you will use the Paste Options gallery to paste text without formatting.

1. Open the files **Bittersweet**, **Chocolate - 2**, and **Milk Chocolate**. Click the **Bittersweet** button on the taskbar to make it the active document. Maximize the window if necessary.

2. In the **Bittersweet** document, select the entire document and change the font to 12-point Arial. Click the Copy button 🗐.

3. Switch to the **Chocolate - 2** document. Maximize the window if necessary.

4. Click the insertion point at the beginning of the paragraph that begins "Sweet or." Press Ctrl+V to insert the text copied from **Bittersweet**. Notice the format of the new text does not match the format of the current document.

5. Click the Paste Options button 🖹 (Ctrl)▾, or press Ctrl to display the Paste Options gallery.

6. Point to the first option in the gallery. The Keep Source Formatting button 🖹 previews the pasted text, and the text retains the 12-point Arial format.

TIP

You can insert an entire file into the current document by using the Insert tab. Move the insertion point to the place in the document where you want to insert the file. Then from the Insert tab, click the Object button. Click Text from File and double-click the file name. The text from the entire file is inserted at the insertion point.

7. Point to the second option in the Paste Options gallery. The Merge Formatting button previews the pasted text, and the text matches the destination document format.

8. Point to the fourth option in the Paste Options gallery. The Keep Text Only button 🅰 previews the text with no format. The format from the destination document (12-point Arial) is removed from the text.

9. Choose the second option, Merge Formatting.

TABLE 6-1 Paste Options

Paste Gallery Icon	Option	Description
	Keep Source Formatting (K)	Text retains format from the source (original) document.
	Merge Formatting (M)	Format for copied text matches the destination document format.
	Use Destination Theme (H)	Format for copied text matches the destination styles format.
🅰	Keep Text Only (T)	The formatting from the source (original) document is removed, and the pasted text displays as plain, unformatted text.
Set Default Paste...	Set Default Paste	Use this feature to control the default settings. When pasting within the same document, pasting between documents, or pasting from other programs, the default setting is to keep source formatting.

10. Click the **View** tab, and click the Switch Windows button to activate **Bittersweet** again. Close this document without saving it.

Exercise 6-15 MOVE TEXT FROM ONE DOCUMENT TO ANOTHER BY USING DRAG AND DROP

1. Arrange the two open documents (**Milk Chocolate** and **Chocolate - 2**), so they are both displayed.

2. Switch to the **Milk Chocolate** document, and select the paragraph below the title.

3. Drag the selected paragraph to the **Chocolate - 2** document, and position the insertion point in front of the paragraph that begins "Sweet or."

Figure 6-11
Dragging a
paragraph between
document windows

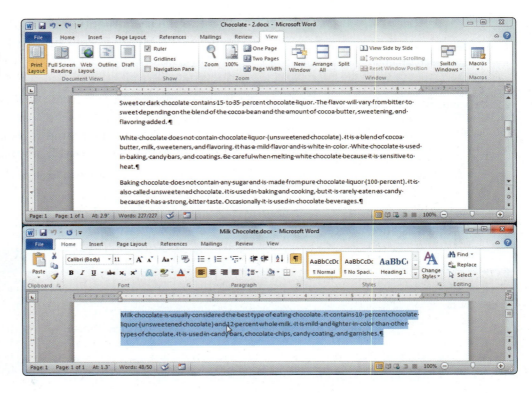

4. Close the **Milk Chocolate** document without saving.

5. Maximize the **Chocolate - 2** document. Correct the spacing between paragraphs (if you have extra paragraph marks, for example).

6. At the top of the document, add the title **TYPES OF CHOCOLATE**, formatted as 14-point bold and centered. Add 72 points spacing before and 24 points spacing after the title.

7. Save the document as *[your initials]6-15* in your Lesson 6 folder; then submit and close it.

Lesson 6 Summary

- The most important tool for moving and copying text is the Clipboard, which is a temporary storage space.

- When you display the Clipboard task pane, you are activating the Office Clipboard, which can store up to 24 cut or copied items. With the Clipboard task pane open, cut or copied text appears as a new item in the task pane.

- You move text by cutting and pasting—cut the text from one location and paste it to another.

- Copy and paste is similar to cut and paste, but instead of removing the text from the document, you place a copy of it on the Clipboard.

- There are many methods for cutting, copying, and pasting text. Use buttons on the Ribbon, keyboard shortcuts, or the shortcut menu. Use the Clipboard task pane to paste stored text items.
- Use the Paste Options button to control the formatting of pasted text.
- You can use the drag-and-drop method to copy or move text from one location to another in a document or between documents.
- Split a document into panes to compare different parts of the document or to cut or copy text from one part of the document to another. Use the View tab or the split box above the vertical scroll bar to split a document.
- Open multiple documents and arrange them to fit on one screen to move or copy text from one document to another.

LESSON 6		Command Summary	
Feature	**Button**	**Command**	**Keyboard**
Arrange multiple windows		View tab, Window group	
Copy		Home tab, Clipboard group	Ctrl + C
Cut		Home tab, Clipboard group	Ctrl + X
Insert file	Object ▾	Insert tab, Text group	
Next window		View tab, Window group, Switch Windows, *<file name>*	Ctrl + F6
Open Office Clipboard		Home tab, Clipboard group	Ctrl + C twice
Paste		Home tab, Clipboard group	Ctrl + V
Previous window		View tab, Window group, Switch Windows, *<file name>*	Ctrl + Shift + F6
Split a document		View tab, Window group	

Please visit our Online Learning Center, *www.lessonapproach2010.com,* **where you will find the following review materials:**

- **Concepts Review**
  - True/False Questions
  - Short Answer Questions
  - Critical Thinking Questions

- **Skills Review**
  - Review Exercises that target single skills
  - Lesson Applications
  - Review Exercises that challenge students by testing multiple skills in each exercise

- **On Your Own**
  - Open-ended exercises that require students to synthesize multiple skills and apply creativity and problem-solving as they would in a real world business situation

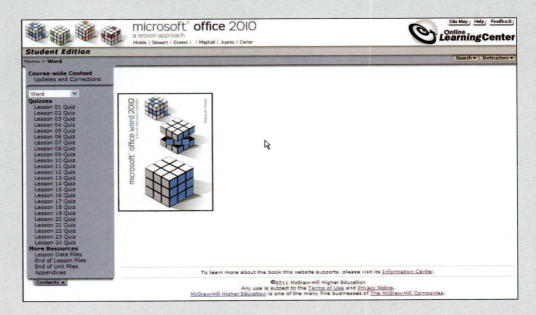

Lesson 7
Find and Replace

OBJECTIVES   *After completing this lesson, you will be able to:*

1. Find text.
2. Find and replace text.
3. Find and replace special characters.
4. Find and replace formatting.

Estimated Time: 1¼ hours

When you create documents, especially long documents, you often need to review or change text. In Word, you can do this quickly by using the Find and Replace commands.

The *Find* command locates specified text and formatting in a document. The *Replace* command finds the text and formatting and replaces it automatically with a specified alternative.

Finding Text

Instead of scrolling through a document, you can use the Find command to locate text or to move quickly to a specific document location.

Two ways to use find are:

- Ribbon, Home tab, Editing group, Find command.
- Press Ctrl + F.

You can use the Find command to locate whole words, words that sound alike, font and paragraph formatting, and special characters. You can search an entire document or only selected text and specify the direction of the search. In the following exercise, you use find to locate all occurrences of the word "Campbell."

Exercise 7-1   FIND TEXT

1. Open the file **Stevenson - 1**.
2. Click the **Home** tab, and locate the **Editing** group. Click the Find button 🔍 to open the Navigation Pane.

Figure 7-1
Navigation Pane

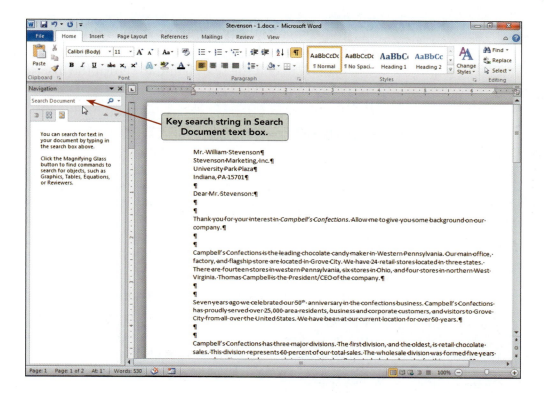

3. Delete any text in the **Search Document** text box, and key **Campbell**.
4. Notice that each occurrence of Campbell appears highlighted in the document and that 10 matches were located. The Campbell text string was located as a whole word and within a word such as "Campbell's."
5. Click the Next Search Result button ▼ to move to the first occurrence of Campbell. A box displays around the first entry in the Navigation Pane, and the first occurrence in the document appears highlighted. Notice that the search text "Campbell" is embedded within "Campbell's" and includes italic formatting.
6. Click the Next Search Result button ▼ two more times. Each time you click the Next Search Result button ▼ the next block of text appears highlighted in the Navigation Pane.
7. Click the Previous Search Result button ▲ two times to return to the first occurrence of "Campbell."
8. Click the Browse the pages button ▦ to display document pages in the Navigation Pane. Click the thumbnail for page 2 of the document. The second page of the document displays in the document window. Click the thumbnail for page 1.

9. Click the Browse the results button 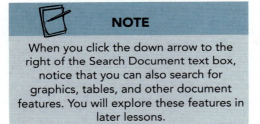 to display the search results in the Navigation Pane.

10. Click the Navigation Pane Close button ✖ to close the Navigation Pane.

11. Place the insertion point at the beginning of the paragraph that begins "Thank you." Press [Ctrl]+[F] to open the Navigation Pane.

12. Key **Campbell's Confections** in the **Search Document** text box. Every occurrence of the text appears highlighted.

13. Click the End Search button ⊠ to the right of the Search Document text box to end the search and to return the insertion point to the first paragraph of the document.

Exercise 7-2   FIND TEXT BY USING THE MATCH CASE OPTION

The Find command includes options for locating words or phrases that meet certain criteria. One of these options is Match case, which locates text that matches the case of text keyed in the Search text box. The next exercise demonstrates how the Match case option narrows the search when using the Find command.

1. Move to the end of the document by pressing [Ctrl]+[End]. Position the insertion point to the right of "Hamrick" in the closing.

> **NOTE**
>
> When you click the down arrow to the right of the Search Document text box, notice that you can also search for graphics, tables, and other document features. You will explore these features in later lessons.

2. Delete any text in the **Search Document** text box, and key **confections**. Eight matches appear highlighted in the document.

3. Click the End Search button ⊠ to end the search.

4. Click the down arrow ▾ to the right of the **Search Document** text box, and click **Options** to open the **Find Options** dialog box.

Figure 7-2
Find Options dialog box

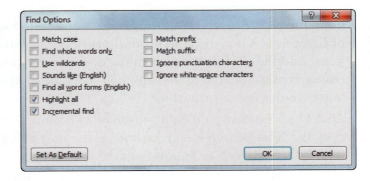

5. Click the **Match case** check box to select this option. Click **OK** to close the Find Options dialog box.

6. Key **confections** in the **Search Document** text box, and notice that only one occurrence appears highlighted.

7. Close the Navigation Pane.

Exercise 7-3   FIND TEXT BY USING THE FIND WHOLE WORDS ONLY OPTION

The Find whole words only option is another way to narrow the search criteria. Word locates separate words but not characters embedded in other words.

1. Move the insertion point to the beginning of the document. Press Ctrl+F to open the Navigation Pane.

2. Key **or** in the Search Document text box. Forty-nine matches appear highlighted. Notice that almost every occurrence appears as embedded text within a word.

3. Click ⊠ to clear the Search text box.

4. Click the down arrow to the right of the **Search Document** text box, and click **Options** to open the Find Options dialog box.

5. Click the **Find whole words only** check box to select the option, click to deselect the **Match case** option, and click **OK** to close the Find Options dialog box.

6. Key **or** in the Search Document text box. Only two matches appear highlighted as a result of narrowing the search to whole words.

7. Open the **Find Options** dialog box, and clear the **Find whole words only** option. Close the Navigation Pane.

> **NOTE**
>
> When you select Match case, Find whole words only, or other options in the Find Options dialog box, the options are selected until you deselect them. When you finish a search, the selected options are not deselected automatically. You must open the Find Options dialog box to deselect the options.

Exercise 7-4   FIND TEXT BY USING THE WILDCARD OPTION

You can use the wildcard option to search for text strings using special search operators. A *wildcard* is a symbol that stands for missing or unknown text. For example, the Any Character wildcard "?" finds any character. Using the "?" wildcard, a search for "b?te" would find both "bite" and "byte." The question mark is replaced by a character that follows "b" and precedes "te."

Search options are available in the Find Options dialog box and the Find and Replace dialog box. The Find and Replace dialog box includes options to find formatting and special characters.

TABLE 7-1 Search Options in the Find and Replace Dialog Box

Option	Description
Sounds like	Word locates words that have a similar pronunciation to the keyed text. Example: In the practice document, key "ur" in the Find what text box, and study the results.
Find all word forms (English)	Use this feature to find noun or adjective forms or verb tenses. Example: In the practice document, key "are" in the Find what text box.
Match prefix	Select this feature to locate text that appears at the beginning of a word.
Match suffix	Select this feature to locate text that appears at the end of a word.
Ignore punctuation characters	Select this feature to ignore punctuation in the search.
Ignore white-space characters	Select this feature to ignore space between words.

1. Position the insertion point at the beginning of the document, and click the down arrow 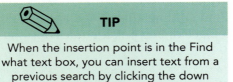 to the right of the Find command in the Editing group on the Home tab. Click **Advanced Find** to open the **Find and Replace** dialog box with the **Find** tab displayed.

Figure 7-3
Find and Replace
dialog box

2. Click the More button (More >>) to display the expanded dialog box and click **Use wildcards** to select this option.

3. Select and delete text in the **Find what** text box, and key **ca**.

4. Click the Special button (Special ▾), and choose **Any Character** from the list. The "^?" is inserted.

Figure 7-4
Choosing a special search operator

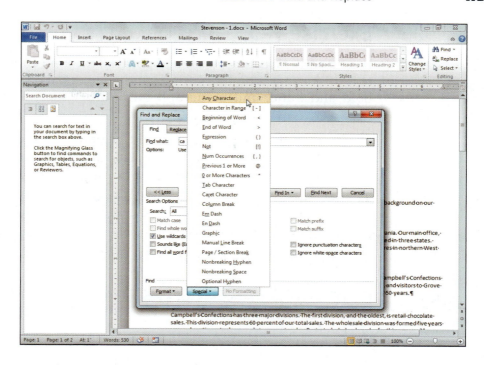

TIP

Press Esc to cancel a search. You can also interrupt a search by clicking outside the Find and Replace dialog box, editing the document text, and then clicking the dialog box to reactivate it.

TIP

After you initiate a find by using the Find and Replace dialog box, you can close the dialog box and use the Next Find/Go To button and Previous Find/Go To button located at the bottom of the vertical scroll bar to continue the search without having the dialog box in your way. (See Figure 7-5.)

5. Choose **All** from the **Search** direction drop-down list, if it is not already selected. Then click **Less** to collapse the dialog box.

6. Click **Find Next**. The first occurrence appears highlighted.

7. Continue clicking **Find Next** and notice all the occurrences of "ca^?" in the document. Both lowercase and uppercase words are highlighted in the search for "ca^?"

8. Click **OK** in the dialog box that says Word finished searching the document.

9. Click **Cancel** to close the Find and Replace dialog box.

Figure 7-5
Finding text without the Find and Replace dialog box

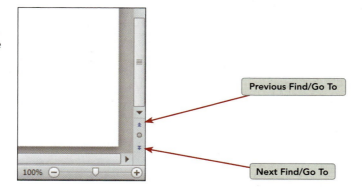

Exercise 7-5   FIND FORMATTED TEXT

In addition to locating words and phrases, the Find command can search for text formatting. The formatting can include character formatting, such as bold and italic, and paragraph formatting, such as alignment and line spacing.

1. Position the insertion point at the beginning of the document. Open the **Find and Replace** dialog box by clicking the down arrow to the right of the Find command on the Home tab and choosing **Advanced Find**.

2. Key **Campbell's Confections** in the **Find what** text box. Click **More** to expand the dialog box, and choose **All** from the **Search** direction drop-down list. Click any checked search options to clear them.

3. Click the Format button [Format ▾], and choose **Font**.

Figure 7-6
Format options

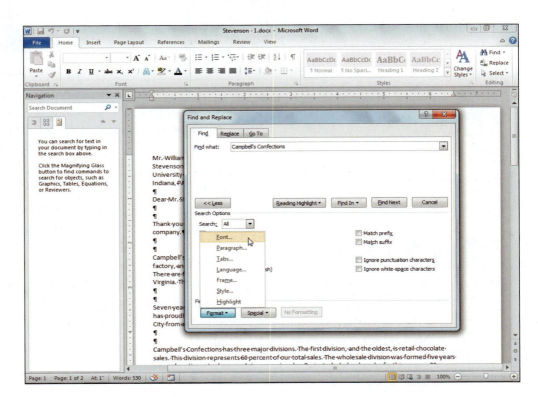

4. In the Find Font dialog box, choose **Italic** from the **Font style** list and click **OK**. The italic format now appears below the **Find what** text box.

5. Click **Less**, and then click **Find Next**. Word locates *"Campbell's Confections."*

6. Click **Cancel** to close the Find and Replace dialog box.

Finding and Replacing Text

The Replace command searches for specific text or formatting and replaces it with your specified alternative. You can replace all instances of text or formatting at once, or you can find and confirm each replacement.

   Two ways to replace text are:

- Ribbon, Home tab, Editing group, Replace command.
- Press [Ctrl]+[H].

Exercise 7-6   REPLACE TEXT BY USING FIND NEXT

1. Position the insertion point at the beginning of the document, locate the **Editing** group, and click the Replace button ⬛. The Find and Replace dialog box displays with the **Replace** tab selected.

2. Key **traveler** in the Find what text box. Expand the dialog box, and click the No Formatting button No Formatting to remove formatting from previous searches. Make sure no options under **Search Options** are selected.

3. Press [Tab] to move to the **Replace with** text box, and key **visitor**. Click the No Formatting button No Formatting if it is active.

Figure 7-7
Replacing text

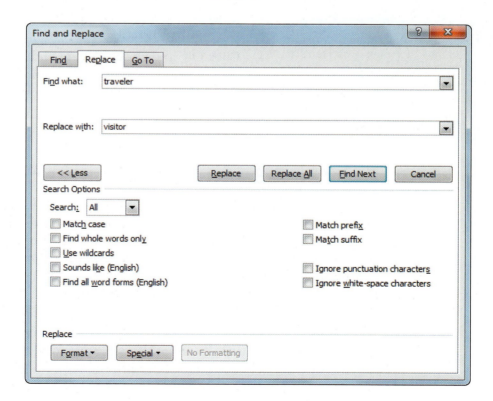

NOTE

Remember, pressing Tab in a dialog box moves the insertion point from one text box to another and highlights existing text, or pressing Tab moves from one option or command to the next option or command in the dialog box. Pressing Enter executes the dialog box command.

4. Adjust the position and size (click **Less** to reduce the size, and drag the title bar to move the dialog box) of the dialog box so you can see the document text. Click **Find Next**. Click **Replace** to replace the first occurrence of "traveler" with "visitor."

5. Continue to click **Replace** until Word reaches the end of the document.

6. Click **OK** when Word finishes searching the document.

7. Close the Find and Replace dialog box.

Exercise 7-7   REPLACE TEXT BY USING REPLACE ALL

The Replace All option replaces all occurrences of text or formatting in a document without confirmation.

1. Move the insertion point to the beginning of the document, and press Ctrl+H to open the Find and Replace dialog box with the **Replace** tab selected.

2. Key **Campbell's Confections** in the **Find what** text box. Press Tab and key **CAMPBELL'S CONFECTIONS** in the **Replace with** text box.

NOTE

After replacing text or formatting, you can always undo the action. If you used replace all, all changes are reversed at once. If you used replace, only the last change is reversed, but you can undo the last several changes individually by selecting them from the Undo drop-down list.

3. Expand the dialog box, clear the **Match case** check box if necessary, and click **Replace All**. Word will indicate the number of replacements made.

4. Click **OK**, and close the Find and Replace dialog box. "Campbell's Confections" now appears as "CAMPBELL'S CONFECTIONS" throughout the document.

5. Click the Undo button ↩ to undo the Replace All command.

Exercise 7-8   DELETE TEXT WITH REPLACE

You can also use the Replace command to delete text automatically. Key the text to be deleted in the Find what text box and leave the Replace with text box blank. You can find and delete text with confirmation by using the Find Next option or without confirmation by using the Replace All option. When keying text in the Find what text box, be sure to key the text exactly as it appears in the document including blank spaces and punctuation. You may need to include a blank space after the text to ensure correct spacing between words.

1. Position the insertion point at the beginning of the document, and open the **Find and Replace** dialog box with the Replace tab selected.

2. Key **Campbell's** in the **Find what** text box, and press Spacebar once. The space character is not visible in the text box.

3. Press [Tab] to move to the **Replace with** text box, and press [Delete] to remove the previous entry.

4. Click the Replace All button [Replace All].

5. Click **OK** and close the dialog box. The word "Campbell's" followed by a space is deleted from the company name throughout the document. If the word "Campbell's" was followed by a punctuation mark, the word would not be deleted.

6. Click the Undo button .

7. Save the document as *[your initials]*7-8 in a new folder for Lesson 7. Leave the document open for the next exercise.

TIP

Another option in the Find and Replace dialog box is Find all word forms. Use this option to find different forms of words and replace the various word forms with comparable forms.

Finding and Replacing Special Characters

The Find and Replace features can search for characters other than ordinary text. Special characters include paragraph marks and tab characters. Special characters are represented by codes that you can key or choose from the Special drop-down list.

Exercise 7-9 FIND AND REPLACE SPECIAL CHARACTERS

NOTE

The dialog box that appears when you end the search process is determined by the search direction and the position of the insertion point when you begin the search. When Word searches through the entire document, the dialog box tells you Word is finished searching, and the insertion point returns to its original position. When you search from a point other than the top or bottom of the document and choose up or down as your search direction, Word asks if you want to continue the search. If you choose not to continue, the insertion point remains at the last occurrence found.

1. Click the Show/Hide ¶ button [¶] to display special characters in the document if they are not showing.

2. Position the insertion point at the top of the document. Open the **Find and Replace** dialog box with the **Replace** tab selected. Expand the dialog box, if necessary. Delete the text that appears in the **Find what** text box.

3. Click the **Special** button and choose **Paragraph Mark**. A code (^p) is inserted in the **Find what** text box. Add two additional paragraph mark codes in the **Find what** text box to search for three consecutive paragraph marks in the document. (Use the **Special** drop-down list or key **^p^p**.)

4. Move to the **Replace with** text box, and insert two paragraph mark codes.

5. Clear any **Search Options** check boxes and click **Less**.

6. Click **Find Next**. Word locates the extra paragraph mark after the salutation of the letter.

Figure 7-8
Replacing special characters

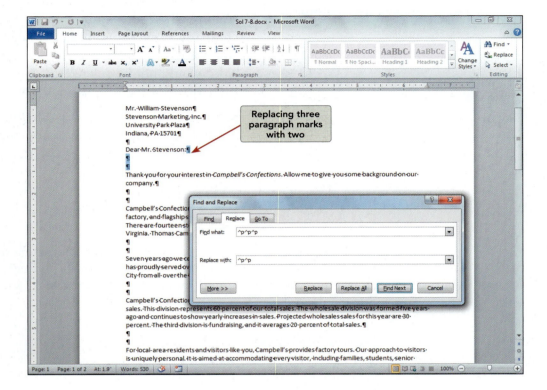

7. Click **Replace**. Notice the elimination of the extra paragraph mark. Continue to click **Replace** for each paragraph mark until you reach the paragraph marks after "Sincerely."

8. Close the Find and Replace dialog box. The document paragraphs are now correctly spaced.

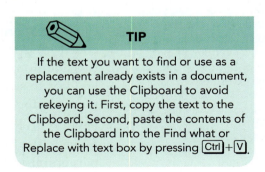

TIP

If the text you want to find or use as a replacement already exists in a document, you can use the Clipboard to avoid rekeying it. First, copy the text to the Clipboard. Second, paste the contents of the Clipboard into the Find what or Replace with text box by pressing Ctrl + V.

TABLE 7-2 Find and Replace Special Characters

Find or Replace	Special Character Code to Key
Paragraph mark (¶)	^p (must be lowercase)
Tab character (→)	^t (must be lowercase)
Any character (find only)	^?
Any digit (find only)	^#
Any letter (find only)	^$
Column break	^n
Clipboard contents (replace only)	^c
Em dash	^+
En dash	^=
Field (find only)	^d
Footnote mark (find only)	^f
Graphic (find only)	^g
Manual line break	^l
Manual page break	^m
Nonbreaking hyphen	^~
Nonbreaking space	^s
Section break (find only)	^b
White space (find only)	^w

Finding and Replacing Formatting

Word can search for and replace both character and paragraph formatting. You can specify character or paragraph formatting by clicking the Format button in the Find and Replace dialog box or using keyboard shortcuts.

Exercise 7-10   FIND AND REPLACE CHARACTER FORMATTING

1. Position the insertion point at the top of the document, and open the **Find and Replace** dialog box with the **Replace** tab selected. Expand the dialog box.

2. Key **Campbell's Confections** in the **Find what** text box. Press Tab and delete the text in the **Replace with** text box.

3. Click the **Format** button and choose **Font**. Choose **Bold** and **Small caps**. Click **OK**.

4. Click **Replace All**.

5. Click **OK** when Word finishes searching the document, and close the dialog box. "Campbell's Confections" appears bold and in small caps throughout the document.

6. Reopen the **Find and Replace** dialog box with the **Replace** tab selected. Expand the dialog box.

7. Highlight the text in the **Find what** text box, if it is not already. Click the **Format** button and choose **Font**. Choose **Bold** and **Small caps** and click **OK**.

8. Press Tab to move the insertion point to the **Replace with** text box. Click the No Formatting button [No Formatting] to clear existing formatting.

9. Click the Format button [Format ▾] and choose **Font**. Choose the **Not Bold** style, deselect **Small caps**, and click **OK**.

10. Press Ctrl+I (the keyboard shortcut for italic text). Now the format for the **Replace with** text box is "Not Bold, Not Small caps, Not All caps, Italic."

11. Click **Replace All**.

12. Click **OK** and close the Find and Replace dialog box. "Campbell's Confections" is now italic, and not bold, small caps, throughout the document.

TIP

You can use keyboard shortcut keys to apply or remove formatting in the Find what or Repace with text boxes. To apply bold, press Ctrl+B, and Font: Bold displays below the Find what text box. To remove bold, press Ctrl+B twice, and you will see Font: Not Bold below the Find what or Replace with text box.

Exercise 7-11   FIND AND REPLACE PARAGRAPH FORMATTING

1. Position the insertion point at the beginning of the second paragraph that begins "Campbell's Confections." Open the Find and Replace dialog box with the Replace tab selected.

2. In the **Find what** text box, insert two paragraph mark special characters (use the **Special** list or key **^p^p**). Clear existing formatting.

3. Move to the **Replace with** text box, enter two paragraph mark special characters, and clear existing formatting.

4. Click the **Format** button and choose **Paragraph**. Click the **Indents and Spacing** tab if it is not active. Deselect **Mirror indents** if necessary.

5. Choose **First Line** from the **Special** drop-down list. If "0.5" is not the measurement displayed in the **By** text box, select the text in the **By** box and key **0.5**. Click **OK**.

Figure 7-9
Defining paragraph formatting

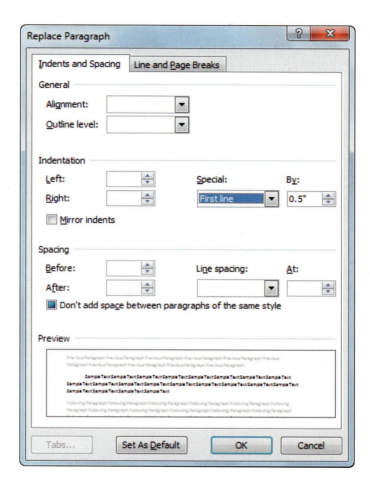

6. Click **Find Next** and Word highlights the paragraph marks after "company." Click **Replace** to format that paragraph.

7. Click **Replace** seven more times (through the paragraph ending "enclosed brochure").

8. Close the Find and Replace dialog box. Scroll through the document to view the paragraph formatting changes. The paragraphs should now have a 0.5-inch first-line indent.

9. Position the insertion point at the top of the document. Open the Find and Replace dialog box with the Replace tab selected.

10. Delete the text in the **Find what** text box, and set the text box to look for a 0.5-inch first-line indent. Deselect **Mirror indents** if necessary. Close the Paragraph dialog box.

11. Delete the text in the **Replace with** text box, and clear the formatting. Click the **Format** button, and click **Paragraph**. Deselect **Mirror indents**, key **0.25** in the **Left** and **Right** indent text boxes. Choose **(none)** from the **Special** drop-down list. Click **OK**.

Figure 7-10
Replacing paragraph formatting

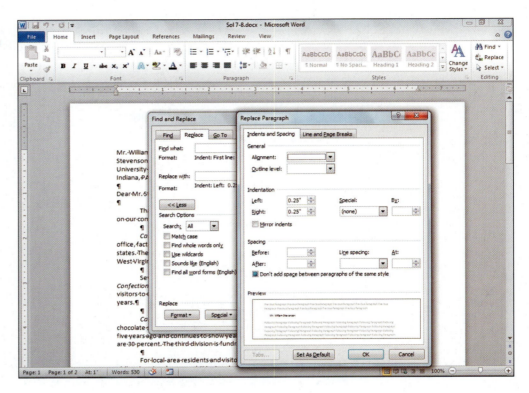

12. Click **Replace All** and click **OK**. Close the Find and Replace dialog box.

13. Scroll through the document to observe the replacement of first-line indented paragraphs with 0.25-inch left- and right-indented paragraphs.

14. Enter the date at the top of the document, with 72 points spacing before and three blank lines after it. Replace "xx" with your reference initials. Add an enclosure notation.

15. Save the document as *[your initials]*7-11 in your Lesson 7 folder.

16. Submit and close the document.

TABLE 7-3 Find and Replace Formatting Guidelines

Guideline	Procedure
Find specific text with specific formatting.	Key the text in the Find what text box and specify its formatting (choose Font or Paragraph from the Format drop-down list or use a keyboard shortcut).
Find specific formatting.	Delete text in the Find what text box, and specify formatting.
Replace specific text but not its formatting.	Key the text in the Find what text box. Click the No Formatting button to clear existing formatting. Key the replacement text in the Replace with text box, and clear existing formatting.
Replace specific text and its formatting.	Key the text in the Find what text box, and specify its formatting. Delete any text in the Replace with text box, key the replacement text, and specify the replacement formatting.
Replace only formatting for specific text.	Key the text in the Find what text box, and specify its formatting. Delete any text in the Replace with text box, and specify the replacement formatting.
Replace only formatting.	Delete any text in the Find what text box, and specify formatting. Delete any text in the Replace with text box, and specify the replacement formatting.

Lesson 7 Summary

- The Find command locates specified text and formatting in a document. The Replace command finds text and formatting and replaces it automatically with specified alternatives.

- Use the Find command to locate whole words, words that sound alike, font and paragraph formatting, and special characters. Using the Find command, you can search an entire document or selected text. You can also specify the direction of the search.

- Use the Match case option to locate text that matches the case of document text. Example: When searching for "Confections," Word would not find "confections."

- When you want to locate whole words and not parts of a word, use the Find whole words only option. Example: When searching for the whole word "can," Word would find only "can," but not "candy" or "candidate."

- Use the Use wildcards option to search for text strings by using special search operators. A wildcard is a symbol that stands for missing or unknown text. Example: A search for "b^?yte" would find "bite" and "byte." See Table 7-2.

- Use the Sounds like option to find a word that sounds similar to the search text but spelled differently or to find a word you do not know how to spell. When you find the word, you can stop the search process and edit your document.

- Use the Find command to search for formatted text. The formatting can include character formatting, such as bold and italic, and paragraph formatting, such as alignment and line spacing. Use the Replace command to replace the formatting. See Table 7-3.
- Use the Replace command to search for all instances of text or formatting at once or to find and confirm each replacement.
- Use the Replace command to delete text automatically. Key the text to be deleted in the Find what text box, and leave the Replace with text box blank.

LESSON 7		Command Summary	
Feature	**Button**	**Command**	**Keyboard**
Find		Home tab, Editing group	Ctrl + F
Replace		Home tab, Editing group	Ctrl + H

Please visit our Online Learning Center, *www.lessonapproach2010.com*, **where you will find the following review materials:**

- **Concepts Review**

  True/False Questions

  Short Answer Questions

  Critical Thinking Questions

- **Skills Review**

  Review Exercises that target single skills

  Lesson Applications

  Review Exercises that challenge students by testing multiple skills in each exercise

- **On Your Own**

  Open-ended exercises that require students to synthesize multiple skills and apply creativity and problem-solving as they would in a real world business situation

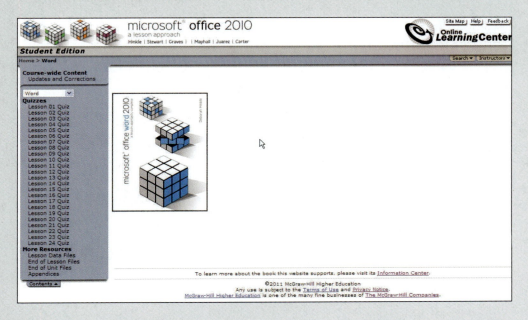

Please visit our Online Learning Center, *www.lessonapproach2010.com,* **where you will find Unit Applications review materials.**

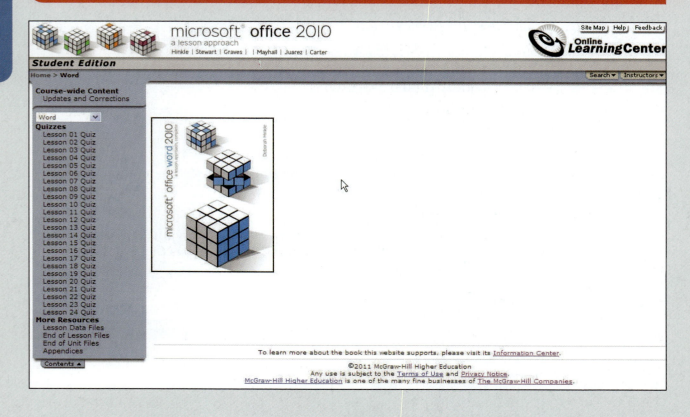

Unit 3

PAGE FORMATTING

Lesson 8

Margins and Printing Options

OBJECTIVES   *After completing this lesson, you will be able to:*

1. Change margins.

2. Preview a document.

3. Change paper size and orientation.

4. Print envelopes and labels.

5. Choose print options.

Estimated Time: 1½ hours

In a Word document, text is keyed and printed within the boundaries of the document's margins. *Margins* are the spaces between the edges of the text and the edges of the paper. Adjusting the margins can significantly change the appearance of a document.

Word offers many useful printing features: changing the orientation (the direction, either horizontal or vertical, in which a document is printed), selecting paper size, and printing envelopes and labels.

Changing Margins

By default, a document's margin settings are:

- Top margin: 1 inch
- Bottom margin: 1 inch
- Left margin: 1 inch
- Right margin: 1 inch

Figure 8-1
Default margin
settings

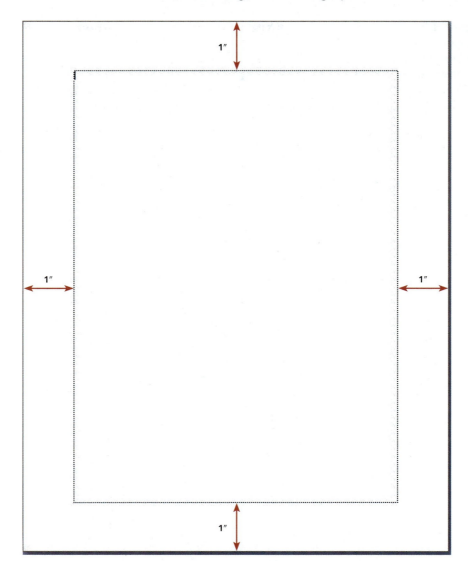

Using standard-size paper (8.5 by 11 inches) and Word's default margin settings, you have 6.5 by 9 inches on the page for your text. To increase or decrease this workspace, you can change margins by using the Page Setup dialog box or the rulers or the Print tab.

To set margins, you can use one of these methods:

- Choose a preset margin setting from the Margin command list.
- Change settings in the Page Setup dialog box.
- Drag margins using the horizontal and vertical rulers.
- Change settings when previewing the document using the Print tab.

UNIT 3 LESSON 8

Figure 8-2
Actual workspace using default margin settings and standard-size paper

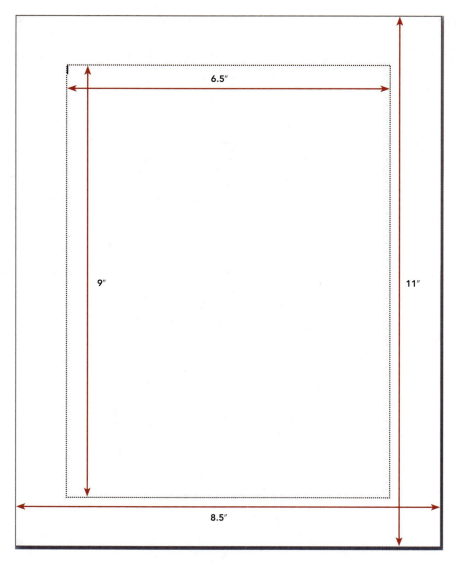

Exercise 8-1 CHANGE MARGINS FOR A DOCUMENT USING THE PAGE SETUP DIALOG BOX

One way to change margins for a document is to use the Page Setup dialog box. You can change margins for an entire document or selected text. You can open the Page Setup dialog by clicking the Margins button on the Page Layout tab, clicking the Page Setup Dialog Box Launcher, or double clicking the vertical or horizontal ruler.

NOTE

The documents you create in this course relate to the case study about Campbell's Confections, a fictional candy store and chocolate factory (see the Case Study in the front matter).

TIP

You can view page margins by opening the Word Options dialog box. Click Advanced, scroll to Show document content, and click Show text boundaries.

1. Open the file **Corporate Gifts**. (Make sure no text is selected.)

2. Click the **Page Layout** tab and click the Margins button ▯. Locate the **Normal** option, and notice that it displays the default margin settings.

3. Click **Custom Margins** at the bottom of the Margins gallery, and click the **Margins** tab, if it is not active. The dialog box shows the default margin settings.

TIP

Press Tab to move from one margin text box to the next and to see the new settings in the Preview box. Press Shift + Tab to move to the previous margin text box.

4. Edit the margin text settings so they have the following values (or click the arrow to change the settings). As you do so, notice the changes in the **Preview** box.

Top	**1.5**
Bottom	**1.5**
Left	**2**
Right	**2**

Figure 8-3
Changing margins in the Page Setup dialog box

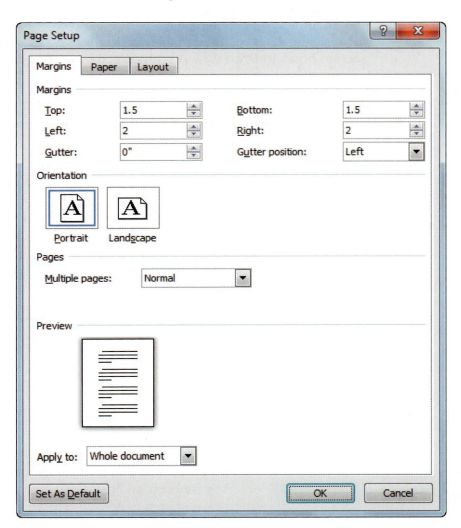

5. Click the down arrow to open the **Apply to** drop-down list. Notice that you can choose either **Whole document** or **This point forward** (from the insertion point forward). Choose **Whole document** and click **OK** to change the margins of the entire document.

NOTE

You can also open the Page Setup dialog box by pressing Shift + F1 to display the Reveal Formatting task pane. Click the + to the left of Section to display the section formatting, and click the Margins link. Use the Reveal Formatting task pane to verify margin settings.

Exercise 8-2   CHANGE MARGINS FOR SELECTED TEXT BY USING THE PAGE SETUP DIALOG BOX

When you change margins for selected text, you create a new section. A *section* is a portion of a document that has its own formatting. When a document contains more than one section, *section breaks* indicate the beginning and end of a section. When you insert a next page section break, the document view determines the appearance of the section break. Print layout view displays a next page section break as a new page. A next page section break in Draft view is represented by double-dotted lines.

1. Select the text from the second paragraph to the end of the document.

2. Click the **Page Layout** tab. Click the **Page Setup Dialog Box Launcher** (see Figure 8-4) to display the Page Setup dialog box.

Figure 8-4
Page Setup Dialog
Box Launcher

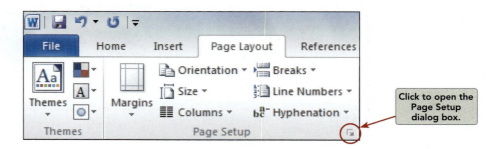

Click to open the Page Setup dialog box.

3. Change the margins to the following settings:

Top	2
Bottom	2
Left	1.5
Right	1.5

4. Choose **Selected text** from the **Apply to** box. Click **OK**.

5. Deselect the text, and scroll to the beginning of the selection. Word applied the margin changes to the selected text and created a new section. The section appears on a new page. The status bar displays section numbers and page numbers to help you identify the position of the insertion point in the document. To display section numbers and page numbers in the status bar, right-click the status bar, and click to select Section and Page Number. Click in the document to close the shortcut menu.

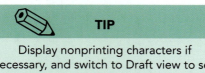

TIP

Display nonprinting characters if necessary, and switch to Draft view to see the section break double-dotted line in the document. Remember that Draft view does not display documents as they will appear when printed.

Figure 8-5
Creating a new section by changing margins for selected text

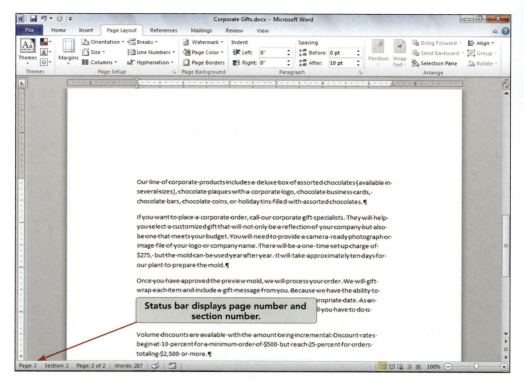

Exercise 8-3 CHANGE MARGINS FOR A SECTION BY USING THE PAGE SETUP DIALOG BOX

After a section is created, you can change the margins for just the section (not the entire document) by using the Page Setup dialog box. To help you know which section you are formatting, customize the status bar to display section numbers.

1. Move the insertion point anywhere in the new section (section 2), and right-click the status bar. Click **Section** to select the display option, and click in the document to close the shortcut menu. Open the **Page Setup dialog box**.

2. Change the left and right margin settings to **1.25** inches.

3. Open the **Apply to** drop-down list to view the options. Notice that you can apply the new margin settings to the current section, to the whole document, or from the insertion point forward.

4. Choose **This section** and click **OK** to apply the settings to the new section.

Exercise 8-4   CHANGE MARGINS USING THE RULERS

To change margins using the rulers, use Print Layout view. The status bar includes five buttons for changing document views. This lesson discusses two of the document views. The default view for Word documents is Print Layout, which displays text as it will appear on the printed page. Use Print Layout view to display headers, footers, and other page elements. Draft view displays the main text of the document. It does not display headers, footers, multicolumn layout, or graphics.

There are two ways to switch document views:

- Click a view button on the right side of the status bar.

- Click the View tab, and click a view button.

Figure 8-6
View buttons on the status bar and the View tab

Status Bar View Buttons

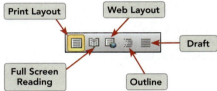

View Tab Buttons

1. Place the insertion point at the beginning of the document (Ctrl + Home). In bold uppercase letters, key **CORPORATE GIFTS**, and then press Enter. Center the title and add 24 points spacing after. The Page Layout tab includes a Paragraph group and an option to change paragraph spacing.

2. Click the View Ruler button at the top of the vertical scroll bar if necessary to display the rulers.

3. Click in the new section (page 2). The status bar shows that the document contains two pages and two sections. Notice the extra space at the top of the page. The new section has a large top margin (2 inches).

4. To see more of the page, including the margin areas, click the Zoom button on the status bar 100% , and then choose **Whole page**. Click **OK**. Review the document then drag the Zoom slider to 100%.

5. Move the insertion point to the top of the document (the first section). The shaded area at the top of the vertical ruler represents the 1.5-inch top margin. The shaded area on the left and right side of the horizontal ruler represents the 2-inch left and right margins. The white area between the shaded areas on the horizontal ruler shows the text area, which is a line length of 4.5 inches. (See Figure 8-7.)

NOTE

You can also use the View tab to change the Zoom level. Click the One Page option to view the entire page. Click the Zoom button to display the Zoom dialog box, and click the 100% button to return the zoom level to 100% of the normal size. The Page Width button changes the zoom level so that the width of the page matches the width of the document window.

Figure 8-7
Rulers in Print Layout
view

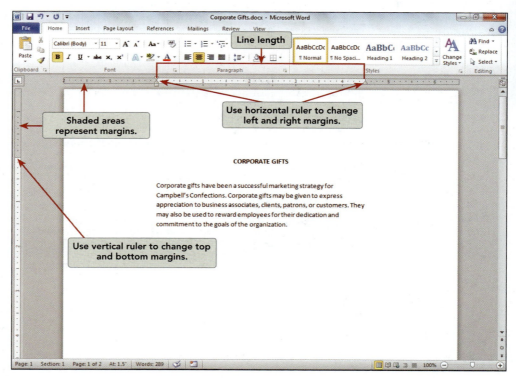

Figure 8-7
Rulers in Print Layout
view

6. To change the top margin, position the pointer over the top margin boundary on the vertical ruler. The top margin boundary is the line between the shaded area and the white area on the ruler. The pointer changes to a two-headed vertical arrow and a ScreenTip displays the words "Top Margin."

7. Press and hold down the left mouse button. The margin boundary appears as a dotted horizontal line.

8. Drag the margin boundary slightly up, and release the mouse button. The text at the top of the document moves up to align with the new top margin.

9. Click the Undo button to restore the 1.5-inch top margin.

10. Hold down the Alt key, and drag the top margin boundary down until it is at 2 inches on the ruler. Release Alt and the mouse button. Holding down the Alt key as you drag shows the exact margin and text area measurements.

11. To change the left margin, position the pointer over the left margin boundary on the horizontal ruler. The left margin boundary is between the shaded area and the white area on the ruler. Move the mouse to the point where the first-line indent marker meets the hanging indent marker. The pointer changes to a two-headed horizontal arrow, and a ScreenTip displays the words "Left Margin."

UNIT 3   LESSON 8

Figure 8-8
Adjusting the left
margin

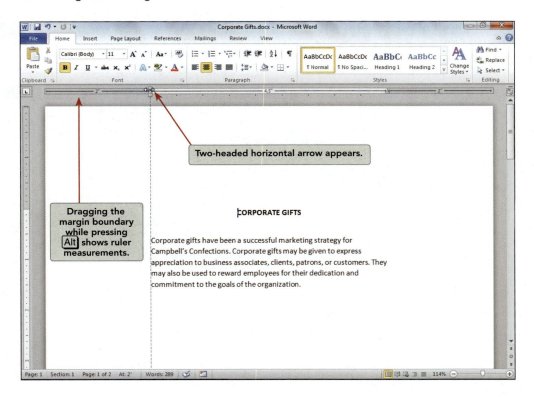

12. Hold down the [Alt] key, and drag the margin boundary to the left to create a 1.75-inch left margin.

13. Using the same procedure, drag the right margin boundary until it is located 1.75 inches from the right. Be sure to watch for the two-headed arrow before dragging. The first section now has 1.75-inch left and right margins and a 2-inch top margin.

14. Scroll to the next page (section 2). Click within the text to activate this section's ruler. Change the top margin to 1.75 inches.

15. Click the **File** tab, and click the **Options** command. Click **Advanced** in the left pane and scroll to **Show document content**. Click **Show text boundaries**, and click **OK**. Dotted lines mark the page margins.

16. Remove the page margins from view by clicking the **File** tab, clicking the **Options** command, clicking **Advanced**, scrolling to **Show document content**, and deselecting **Show text boundaries**. Click **OK**.

17. Save the document as *[your initials]*8-4 in a new Lesson 8 folder, and close the document.

NOTE

You might have to fine-tune the pointer position to place it directly on the left margin boundary. Move the pointer slowly until you see the two-headed arrow and the "Left Margin" ScreenTip.

NOTE

If you move the pointer to the top edge of the page in Print Layout view, you will see the Hide White Space button. Double-click the button to hide the white space (the margin area) at the top and bottom of each page and the shaded space between pages so you can see more document text. Point to the top of the page, and double-click the Show White Space button to restore the space.

Exercise 8-5   SET FACING PAGES WITH GUTTER MARGINS

If your document is going to be bound—put together like a book, with printing on both sides of the paper—you will want to use mirror margins and gutter margins. *Mirror margins* are inside and outside margins on facing pages that mirror one another. *Gutter margins* add extra space to the inside or top margins to allow for binding.

Figure 8-9
Mirror margins

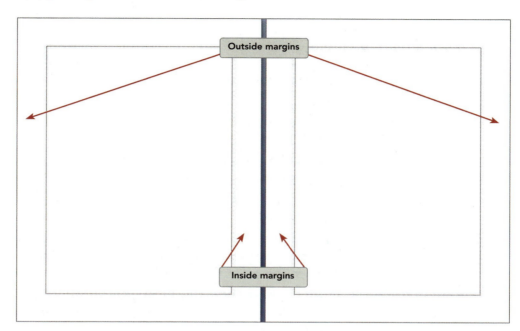

1. Open the file **Festival Planning**. Position the insertion point at the top of the document. Open the **Page Setup** dialog box, and click the down arrow to display the **Multiple pages** drop-down list. Choose **Mirror margins**. Notice that the **Preview** box now displays two pages. The left and right margin text boxes are now labeled inside and outside margins.

2. Change the **Inside** margin setting to **1.25** inches and the **Outside** margin setting to **1** inch.

3. Set the **Gutter** margin to **1** inch, and press Tab to reflect the change in the **Preview** box. Click **OK**. A 1-inch gutter margin is added to the document. (Make sure you use at least 1-inch gutter margins to allow room for binding and to prevent the inside margin text from disappearing into the document binding.)

4. Click the Zoom button 100% on the status bar, and click the **Many pages** button . Move the mouse over the grid of pages that displays, and select three pages in the first row. Click **OK**. Notice that the first page and the third page have wide margins on the left side of the page (outside margins). The second page has a wide right (inside) margin.

TIP

Visualize the document as double-sided, facing pages in a book by placing the back of page 2 against the back of page 1 and placing page 3 beside page 2. The gutter margin of page 1 is on the left. The gutter margin on the right of page 2 and on the left of page 3 allows space for the binding and represents facing pages. *Facing pages* appear as a two-page spread with odd-numbered right pages and even-numbered left pages.

Figure 8-10
Facing pages and
gutter margins

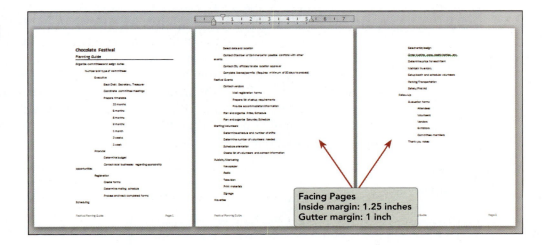

5. Drag the Zoom slider to 100%, and position the insertion point at the top of the document.

6. Open the **Page Setup** dialog box, and open the **Multiple pages** drop-down list. Choose **Normal**. Change the **Gutter** setting to **0.75**, and change the **Gutter position** to **Top**. Click **OK**. The document is ready for top binding.

7. Drag the **Zoom slider** to 35% to see the changes in the document. Notice the additional space at the top of the document to allow for binding. Change the zoom level to 100%.

8. Open the **Page Setup** dialog box. Change the **Left** and **Right** margins to **1** inch, change the **Gutter** setting to **0** inch, and change the **Gutter position** to **Left**. Click **OK**.

9. Save the document as *[your initials]*8-5 in your Lesson 8 folder.

10. Submit the document, and leave it open for the next exercise.

Previewing a Document

Use the Print tab to preview a document and to check how the document will look when you print it. You can view multiple pages at a time, adjust margins, and change page orientation using the Print tab.

To preview a document, click the File tab, and click the Print command to display the Print tab. The keyboard shortcut to preview a document is Alt + Ctrl + I or Ctrl + F2.

Exercise 8-6   VIEW A DOCUMENT IN PRINT PREVIEW

The Print tab displays a document in reduced size. You can view one page of a document or multiple pages. The Print tab includes buttons to navigate from one page to another and to change the zoom level of a document.

1. Move the insertion point to the beginning of the document.

2. Click the **File** tab, and click the **Print** command. The Navigation Pane displays on the left. The Print tab displays print settings and a preview of the document.

Figure 8-11
Print tab

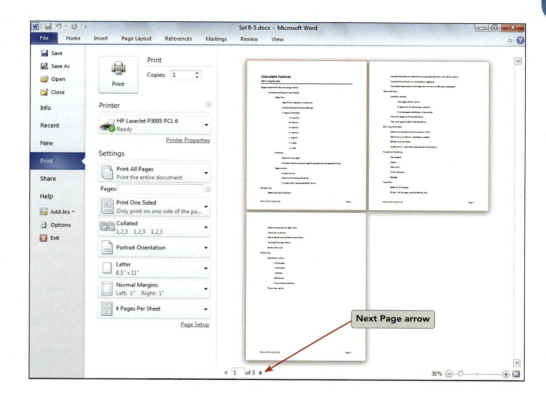

3. Change the zoom level to 60%. To move to page 2, click the Next Page arrow ▶.

4. Drag the **Zoom slider** to 25% to view all the pages of the document.

5. Drag the **Zoom slider** to 100%, and click the **Home** tab to return to Print Layout view.

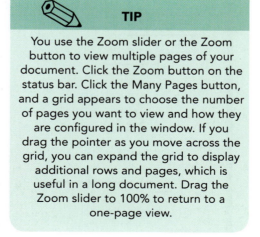

TIP

You use the Zoom slider or the Zoom button to view multiple pages of your document. Click the Zoom button on the status bar. Click the Many Pages button, and a grid appears to choose the number of pages you want to view and how they are configured in the window. If you drag the pointer as you move across the grid, you can expand the grid to display additional rows and pages, which is useful in a long document. Drag the Zoom slider to 100% to return to a one-page view.

Exercise 8-7   CHANGE MARGINS USING THE PRINT TAB

The Print tab displays a preview of the active document and includes print and page formatting settings. Once you have had a chance to study the preview of your document, it is easy to make changes to the margin settings.

1. Move the insertion point to the beginning of the document (page 1, section 1).
2. Click the **File** tab, and click the **Print** command.
3. Locate the **Settings** gallery, and click the down-arrow for **Margins**. Click **Custom Margins** to open the Page Setup dialog box.
4. Change the top margin to **2** inches and click **OK**.
5. Save the document as *[your initials]*8-7.

Paper Size and Orientation

When you open a new document, the default paper size is 8.5 by 11 inches. You can change the paper size to print a document on legal paper (8.5 by 14) or define a custom-size paper.

The Page Layout tab, the Page Setup dialog box, and the Print tab display options to choose orientation settings: portrait or landscape. A *portrait* page is taller than it is wide. This orientation is the default in new Word documents. A *landscape* page is wider than it is tall. You can apply page-orientation changes to sections of a document or to the entire document.

Exercise 8-8   CHANGE PAPER SIZE AND PAGE ORIENTATION

Figure 8-12
Changing page orientation

1. Display the **Page Layout** tab.
2. Locate the **Page Setup** group, and click the **Orientation** command.
3. Click **Landscape**, and drag the Zoom slider to 65% to view the change. Change the zoom level to 100%.

4. Click the **Size** command in the Page Setup group. Notice the default paper size for letter paper.
5. Click the **More Paper Sizes** option, and choose **Legal** from the Paper size drop-down list. Click the **Margins** tab, and choose **Portrait**. Click **OK**. Notice how the orientation and paper size changed.
6. Press Ctrl+Z twice to undo the changes to paper size and orientation.
7. Display the **Print** tab, and locate the **Settings** gallery.
8. Click the **Orientation** command, and click **Landscape Orientation**.
9. Save the document as *[your initials]*8-8.
10. Submit and close the document.

Printing Envelopes and Labels

Word provides a tool to print different-size envelopes and labels. Using the Envelopes and Labels command, you can:

- Print a single envelope without saving it, or attach the envelope to a document for future printing. The envelope displays at the beginning of the document as a separate section.
- Print labels without saving them, or create a new document that contains the label text. You can print a single label or a full page of the same label.

Exercise 8-9   PRINT AN ENVELOPE

Printing envelopes often requires that you manually feed the envelope to your printer. If you print labels on paper that is a different size than 8.5- by 11-inch sheets, you might need to feed the labels manually. Your printer will display a code and not print until you feed an envelope or label sheet manually.

1. Open the file **Matthews**. This document is a one-page business letter.
2. Click the **Mailings** tab, and locate the **Create** group. Click the Envelopes button.
3. Click the **Envelopes** tab if it is not active. Notice that Word detected the inside address in the document and placed this text in the **Delivery address** text box. You can edit this text as needed.

UNIT 3   LESSON 8

Figure 8-13
Envelopes and
Labels dialog box

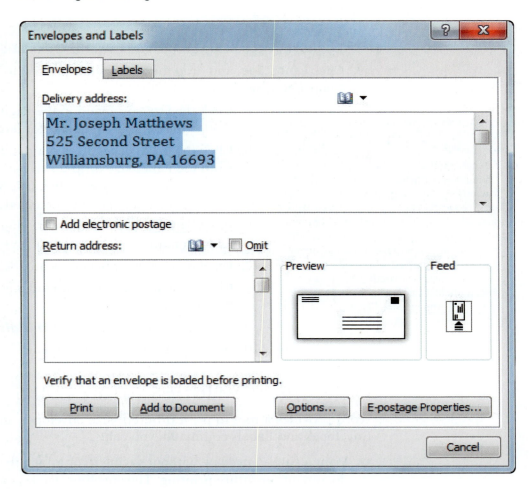

4. In the **Delivery address** text box, enter the full ZIP+4 Code by keying **-1129** after "16693."

5. Make sure the **Omit** box is not checked. Select and delete any text in the **Return address** text box, and then key the following return address, starting with your name:

   [your name]
   Campbell's Confections
   25 Main Street
   Grove City, PA 16127-0025

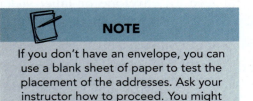

NOTE

If you don't have an envelope, you can use a blank sheet of paper to test the placement of the addresses. Ask your instructor how to proceed. You might have to feed the envelope or blank sheet manually.

6. Place a standard business-size envelope in your printer. The **Feed** box illustrates the feeding method accepted by your printer. Before proceeding with the next step, check with your instructor for guidelines for printing envelopes.

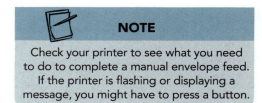

NOTE

Check your printer to see what you need to do to complete a manual envelope feed. If the printer is flashing or displaying a message, you might have to press a button.

7. Click **Print**. When Word asks if you want to save the return address as the default return address, click **No**. Word prints the envelope with the default font and text placement settings. If the envelope does not print, check with your instructor. Do not create a second envelope.

Exercise 8-10   CHOOSE ENVELOPE OPTIONS

Before printing an envelope, you can choose additional envelope options. For example, you can add the envelope content to the document for future use. You can also click the Options button in the Envelopes and Labels dialog box to:

- Change the envelope size. The default size is Size 10, which is a standard business envelope.
- Change the font and other character formatting of the delivery address or return address.
- Verify printing options.

1. Open the **Envelopes and Labels** dialog box again.
2. Key your name and address in the **Return address** box.
3. Click the **Options** button in the Envelopes and Labels dialog box to open the Envelope Options dialog box. Click the **Envelope Options** tab if it is not active.
4. Under **Envelope size**, click the down arrow to look at the different-size options. Click the arrow again to close the list.

Figure 8-14
Envelope Options
dialog box

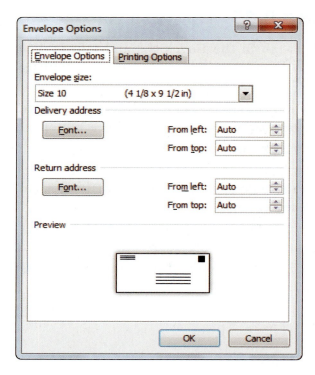

5. Click the Font button for the **Delivery address**. The Envelope Address dialog box for the delivery address opens.

6. Format the text as bold and all caps, and change the font size to 10. Click **OK** to close the Envelope Address dialog box. Click **OK** to close the Envelope Options dialog box.

7. Delete the punctuation from the delivery address, and add **-1129** to the ZIP Code.

8. Click **Add to Document** to add the envelope information to the top of the document as a separate section. Do not save the return address as the default address. Once the envelope is added to the document, you can also format or edit the envelope text just as you would any document text. The default font for envelope addresses is Cambria.

NOTE

The delivery address format preferred by the U.S. Postal Service is all caps with no punctuation.

NOTE

If you are asked to feed the envelope manually, you might be asked to feed the letter manually as well.

9. Replace "[Today's date]" with the current date. Correct any spacing between the elements of the letter. Add your reference initials followed by **Enclosures (2)**. To make sure the letter follows the correct format, see Appendix B, "Standard Forms for Business Documents."

10. Preview the letter and envelope using the Print tab.

11. Save the document as *[your initials]***8-10** in your Lesson 8 folder.

12. Submit the document.

13. Leave the document open for use in the next exercise.

Exercise 8-11   PRINT LABELS

The Labels tab in the Envelopes and Labels dialog box makes it easy to print different-size labels for either a return address or a delivery address.

1. Position the insertion point in the envelope section of the document. Click the **Mailings** tab. Click the Labels button ⊞.

2. Click the **Use return address** check box to create labels for the letter sender.

3. Select the address text, and press Ctrl+Shift+A to turn on all caps. Delete the comma after the city.

4. Click the option **Full page of the same label**, if it is not active, to create an entire page of return address labels.

5. Click the Options button [Options...] to choose a label size.

Figure 8-15
Label Options dialog
box

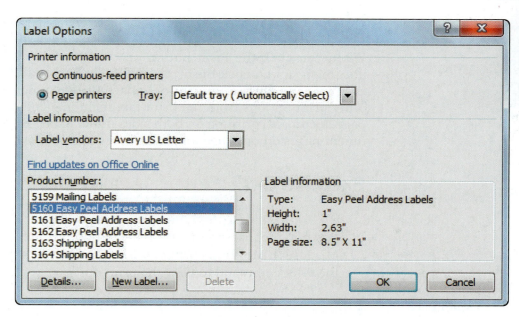

NOTE

Be sure to verify the options selected in the Printer information and Label information sections.

NOTE

When you select a product number in the Label Options dialog box, the Label information section displays the type of label, the height and width of the label, and the page size. There are several types of labels available including address labels, identification labels, media labels, file folder labels, and shipping labels. Labels are available for laser and ink jet printers. Read the label description, size information, and printer type before purchasing labels.

6. Verify that **Page printers** is selected under **Printer information** and that **Avery US Letter** is listed in the **Label vendors** list box.

7. Scroll the **Product number** list to see the various label options, and choose **5160**, the product number for a standard Avery address label.

8. Click **OK**, and then click **New Document** to save the labels as a separate document. (If you click Print, you can print the labels without saving them.) Do not save the return address.

9. Select all text in the new document, and reduce the font size to 11 points.

10. Save the document as *[your initials]*8-11 in your Lesson 8 folder.

11. Change the zoom level to view the labels on the page.

12. Submit the document, or prepare the printer for a sheet of 5160-size labels, or feed a blank sheet of paper into the printer, and then print the labels.

13. Close the document containing the full sheet of labels.

Setting Print Options

When you click the Print button on the Print tab, Word prints the entire document. If you click the arrow beside the Print All Pages command, however, you can choose to print only part of a document. You can also select other print options from the Print tab, including collating copies of a multipage document, printing on both sides of the paper, or printing multiple document pages on one sheet of paper.

Exercise 8-12   CHOOSE PRINT OPTIONS FROM THE PRINT TAB

1. Position the insertion point to the left of the date in the letter to Mr. Joseph Matthews (*[your initials]*8-10). Click the **File** tab, and click the **Print** command to view the print options.

Figure 8-16
Print tab

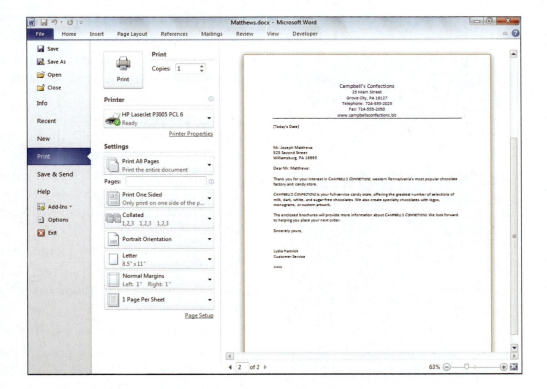

2. Click the down arrow of the **Print All Pages** option, and choose **Print Current Page**. Click **Print**. Word prints the business letter.

3. Open the **Print** tab again. Key **1-2** in the **Pages** text box. You can enter specific page numbers or page ranges.

4. In the **Copies** text box, use the up arrow to change the number of copies to **2**.

5. Click the down arrow beside the **Collated** option, and verify that **Collated** is selected. Click the **Uncollated** option. Word will print two copies of page 1 and then two copies of page 2.

NOTE

Each time you select an option in the Print tab, the name of the setting changes. For example, when you open the Print tab, the first print setting is identified as Print All Pages. If you choose the Print Current Page option, the print setting name changes to Print Current Page. The settings remain in effect until you make the next change.

6. Change the number of copies back to 1.

7. Click the down arrow to open the **Print Current Page** drop-down list. It shows the various elements you can print in addition to the entire document. Click again to close the list.

8. Click the down arrow to open the **1 Page Per Sheet** drop-down list, which gives you the option to print your selection over a specified number of sheets. Choose the **2 Pages Per Sheet** setting. This option prints two pages on one sheet of 8.5- by 11-inch paper, with each page reduced to fit on the sheet.

9. Click the down arrow to open the **2 Pages Per Sheet** list, and locate the **Scale to Paper Size** option. Point to the Scale to Paper Size command to view the option to print on a different paper or envelope size (Word adjusts the scaling of the fonts, tables, and other elements to fit the new size). Click **No Scaling** to close the list.

TABLE 8-1 Print Tab Settings

Button	Description	Function
Print	Print	Print the document in the Print Preview window.
Copies: 1	Number of copies	Prints one or multiple copies of document.
HP LaserJet P3005 PCL 6 Ready	Printer	Select printer to use.
Print All Pages / Print the entire document	Print All Pages	Options include the entire document, selected text, current page, specific pages, document properties, odd and even pages.
Pages:	Pages	Specify print range. Example: Key 1-4, 6 to print pages 1 through 4 and page 6.
Print One Sided / Only print on one side of the p...	Print One Sided	Use the option to print on both sides of the paper.
Collated / 1,2,3 1,2,3 1,2,3	Collated	Choose to collate or not to collate a document. In a three-page document, uncollated prints all first-page copies before printing copies of the second page or the third page. The collated option prints one set of pages 1 through 3 and then prints the second set.
Portrait Orientation	Portrait Orientation	Switch between portrait and landscape orientation.
Letter / 8.5" x 11"	Paper Size	Choose a paper size for the document or the current active section.
Normal Margins / Left: 1" Right: 1"	Margins	Change margin settings.
1 Page Per Sheet	Pages Per Sheet	Choose the number of pages to print per sheet of paper, or choose an option to scale the document to a different paper size.

10. Click the Print button 🖨. Word prints reduced versions of pages 1 and 2 on one sheet of paper.

11. Close the document without saving.

Lesson 8   Summary

- In a Word document, text is keyed and printed within the boundaries of the document's margins. Margins are the spaces between the edges of the text and the edges of the paper.

- Change the actual space for text on a page by changing margins (left, right, top, and bottom). You can key new margin settings in the Page Setup dialog box.

- Changing margins for selected text results in a new section for the selected text. A section is a portion of a document that has its own formatting. When a document contains more than one section, you see double-dotted lines, or section breaks, between sections to indicate the beginning and end of a section.

- Print Layout view shows the position of text on the printed page. Use the View buttons on the right of the status bar to switch between Print Layout view and Draft view.

- The Print tab shows how an entire document looks before printing. Use the navigation buttons, Zoom slider, and the scroll bar to view all or part of the document. Change the zoom level as needed.

- Change margins in Print Layout view by positioning the pointer over a margin boundary on the ruler and dragging. Press Alt to see the exact ruler measurement as you drag.

- For bound documents, use mirror margins and gutter margins. Mirror margins are inside and outside margins on facing pages that mirror one another. Gutter margins add extra space to allow for top or inside binding.

- A document can print in either portrait (8.5- by 11-inch) or landscape (11- by 8.5-inch) orientation. Choose an orientation using the Orientation command on the Page Layout tab, in the Page Setup dialog box, Margins tab, or using the Print tab.

- Scale a document to fit a particular paper size. Choose paper size options by clicking the Pages Per Sheet down arrow, and choosing Scale to Paper Size.

- Use Word to print different-size envelopes. You can change address formatting and make the envelope part of the document for future printing. Use Word to print different-size address labels—either a single label or a sheet of the same label.

- Choose print options such as printing only the current page, specified pages, selected text, collated copies of pages, and reduced pages by opening the Print tab.

LESSON 8		Command Summary	
Feature	Button	Command	Keyboard
Choose print options		File tab, Print	Ctrl + P
Margins		Page Layout tab, Page Setup group	
Print envelopes or labels		Mailings tab, Envelopes or Mailings tab, Labels command	
Print Layout view		View tab, Print Layout command	Alt + Ctrl + P
Print Preview		File tab, Print	Ctrl + F2 or Alt + Ctrl + I

Please visit our Online Learning Center, *www.lessonapproach2010.com*, where you will find the following review materials:

- **Concepts Review**
    True/False Questions
    Short Answer Questions
    Critical Thinking Questions

- **Skills Review**
    Review Exercises that target single skills
    Lesson Applications
    Review Exercises that challenge students by testing multiple skills in each exercise

- **On Your Own**
    Open-ended exercises that require students to synthesize multiple skills and apply creativity and problem-solving as they would in a real world business situation

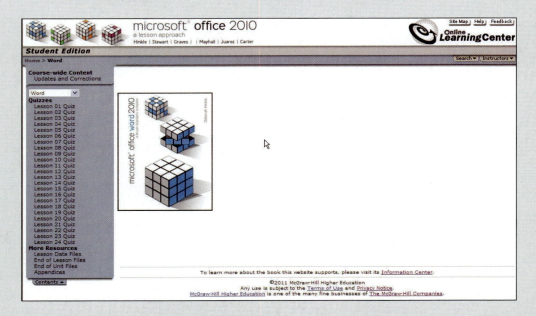

Lesson 9
Page and Section Breaks

After completing this lesson, you will be able to:

1. Use soft and hard page breaks.
2. Control line and page breaks.
3. Control section breaks.
4. Format sections.
5. Use the Go To feature.

Estimated Time: 1 hour

In Word, text flows automatically from the bottom of one page to the top of the next page. This is similar to how text wraps automatically from the end of one line to the beginning of the next line. You can control and customize how and when text flows from the bottom of one page to the top of the next. This process is called *pagination*.

Sections are a common feature of long documents and have a significant impact on pagination. This lesson describes how to insert and manage sections.

Using Soft and Hard Page Breaks

As you work on a document, Word is constantly calculating the amount of space available on the page. Page length is determined by the size of the paper and the top and bottom margin settings. For example, using standard-size paper and default margins, page length is 9 inches. When a document exceeds this length, Word creates a *soft page break*. Word adjusts this automatic page break as you add or delete text. A soft page break appears as a horizontal dotted line on the screen in Draft view. In Print Layout view, you see the actual page break—the bottom of one page and the top of the next. Draft view is frequently used to edit and format text. It does not show the page layout as it appears on a printed page, nor does it show special elements of a page such as columns, headers, or footers.

Exercise 9-1   ADJUST A SOFT PAGE BREAK AUTOMATICALLY

NOTE

When you format and edit long documents, check the status bar settings to make sure section and page numbers display. To verify the settings, right-click the status bar, and click to select the options.

NOTE

The page breaks described in this lesson might appear in slightly different locations on your screen.

1. Open the file **History**. Switch to Draft view by clicking the Draft view button on the status bar. Change the zoom level to **100%** if necessary. Click the Show/Hide button if necessary to turn on the display of formatting characters.

2. Scroll to the bottom of page 3. Notice the soft page break separating the heading "Gourmet Chocolate" from the paragraph below it.

3. Locate the paragraph just above the heading "Gourmet Chocolate" (it begins "In 2001"). Move the insertion point to the left of "The Web site has proven" in the middle of the paragraph, and press Enter to split the paragraph. Notice the adjustment of the soft page break. Press Ctrl+Z to undo the paragraph split.

Figure 9-1
Adjusting the position of a soft page break

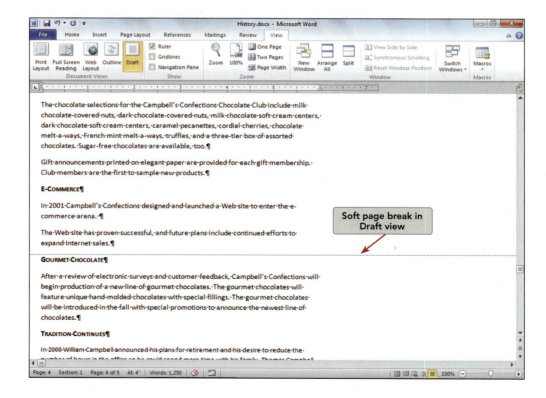

Soft page break in Draft view

TIP

Remember the various methods for moving within a long document. For example, you can drag the scroll box on the vertical scroll bar and use the scroll arrows to adjust the view. You can also use keyboard shortcuts: Ctrl+↑ or Ctrl+↓ to move up or down one paragraph, PageUp or PageDown to move up or down one window, and Ctrl+Home or Ctrl+End to move to the beginning or end of a document.

TIP

You can also insert a page break by clicking the Page Layout tab, clicking the Breaks button, and clicking Page.

Figure 9-2
Insert tab, pages group

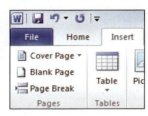

Exercise 9-2   INSERT A HARD PAGE BREAK

When you want a page break to occur at a specific point, you can insert a *hard page break*. In Draft view, a hard page break appears on the screen as a dotted line with the words "Page Break." In Print Layout view you see the actual page break.

There are three ways to insert a hard page break:

- Use the keyboard shortcut Ctrl+Enter.
- Click the Insert tab, and click the Page Break button.
- Click the Page Layout tab, and click the Breaks button.

1. Move the insertion point to the bottom of page 2, to the beginning of the paragraph that starts "The most popular."

2. Press Ctrl+Enter. Word inserts a hard page break so the paragraph and bulleted text are not divided between two pages.

3. Move to the middle of page 4, and place the insertion point to the left of the heading text that begins "Chronology."

4. Click the **Insert** tab, and click the Page Break button 🖹 to insert a page break. Word inserts a hard page break and adjusts pagination in the document from this point forward.

Figure 9-3
Inserting a hard page break

[Screenshot of Microsoft Word — History.docx]

TRADITION·CONTINUES¶

In·2000·William·Campbell·announced·his·plans·for·retirement·and·his·desire·to·reduce·the·number·of·hours·in·the·office·so·he·could·spend·more·time·with·his·family.·Thomas·Campbell·became·the·president·of·Campbell's·Confections·on·August·1,·2000.·William·continues·to·visit·the·office·on·a·regular·basis·and·provides·guidance·and·support·to·Thomas.¶

——————Page·Break——————¶   *Hard page break in Draft view*

CHRONOLOGY·OF·CAMPBELL'S·CONFECTIONS·STORES¶

Year	City	State¶
1950	Grove·City	Pennsylvania¶
1953	Mercer	Pennsylvania¶
1954	New·Castle	Pennsylvania¶
1955	Meadville	Pennsylvania¶
1960	Franklin	Pennsylvania¶
1962	Butler	Pennsylvania¶
1964	Pittsburgh	Pennsylvania¶
1966	New·Wilmington	Pennsylvania¶
1968	Clarion	Pennsylvania¶
1970	Greenville	Pennsylvania¶

Page: 4   Section: 1   Page: 6 of 6   At: 1"   Words: 1,250   100%

Exercise 9-3   DELETE A HARD PAGE BREAK

You cannot delete a soft page break, but you can delete a hard page break by clicking the page break and pressing Backspace or Delete.

1. Select the page break you just inserted by dragging the I-beam over the page break. Be sure to select the paragraph mark.

2. Press Delete to delete the page break.

3. Scroll back to the hard page break you inserted at the top of page 3. Position the insertion point to the left of "The most popular" and press Backspace two times (one time to delete the paragraph mark and one time to delete the page break). The page break is deleted, and Word adjusts the pagination.

Controlling Line and Page Breaks

To control the way Word breaks paragraphs, choose one of four line and page break options from the Paragraph dialog box:

*   *Widow/orphan control:* A *widow* is the last line of a paragraph and appears by itself at the top of a page. An *orphan* is the first line of a paragraph and appears at the bottom of a page. By default, this option is turned on to prevent widows and orphans. Word moves an orphan forward to the next page and moves a widow back to the previous page.

*   *Keep lines together:* This option keeps all lines of a paragraph together on the same page rather than splitting the paragraphs between two pages.

*   *Keep with next:* If two or more paragraphs need to appear on the same page no matter where page breaks occur, use this option. This option is most commonly applied to titles that should not be separated from the first paragraph following the title.

*   *Page break before:* Use this option to place a paragraph at the top of a new page.

Exercise 9-4   APPLY LINE AND PAGE BREAK OPTIONS TO PARAGRAPHS

TIP

To reopen the file quickly, click the File tab and click Recent. Click the file name **History** under Recent Documents.

1. Close **History** without saving; then reopen the document. Switch to Draft view.

2. At the bottom of page 3, click within the heading "Gourmet Chocolate." You are going to format this heading so it will not be separated from its related paragraph.

3. Click the **Home** tab, and click the **Paragraph Dialog Box Launcher** 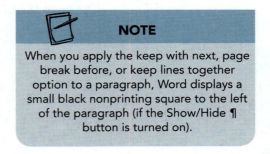 to open the Paragraph dialog box. Click the **Line and Page Breaks** tab.

Figure 9-4
Line and Page Breaks
tab in the Paragraph
dialog box

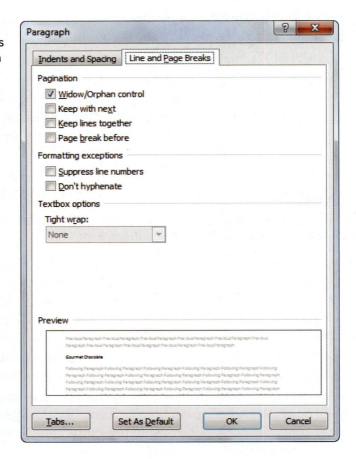

4. Click **Keep with next** to select it, and click **OK**. Word moves the soft page break, keeping the two paragraphs together.

NOTE

When you apply the keep with next, page break before, or keep lines together option to a paragraph, Word displays a small black nonprinting square to the left of the paragraph (if the Show/Hide ¶ button is turned on).

Figure 9-5
Applying the Keep
with next option

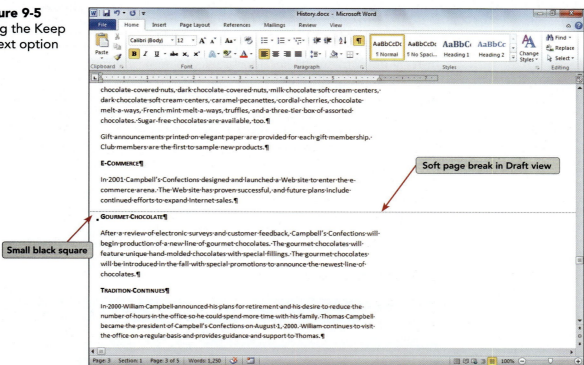

Soft page break in Draft view

Small black square

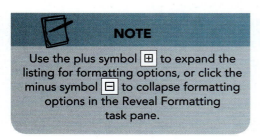

5. Press Ctrl + Home to go to the top of the document. Select the title, and apply 48 points spacing before.

6. Locate the text at the bottom of page 1 that begins "By 1980." The paragraph is divided by a soft page break.

7. Right-click the paragraph to open the shortcut menu. Click **Paragraph**. Click the **Line and Page Breaks** tab if necessary.

8. Choose **Keep lines together** and click **OK**. The soft page break moves above the paragraphs to keep the lines of text together.

9. Move to page 4, and place the insertion point in the paragraph that begins "Chronology." You will format this paragraph so it begins at the top of the page.

10. Open the **Paragraph** dialog box, click **Page break before**, and click **OK**. Word starts the paragraph at the top of page 5 with a soft page break.

11. Press Shift + F1 to open the **Reveal Formatting** task pane. Click the plus symbol ⊞ to the left of **Paragraph** to display the paragraph formatting. Notice the link for Line and Page Breaks. When you click the link, the Paragraph dialog box opens. Close the Paragraph dialog box and the Reveal Formatting task pane.

12. Save the document as *[your initials]***9-4** in a new folder for Lesson 9. Leave it open for the next exercise.

NOTE

Use the plus symbol ⊞ to expand the listing for formatting options, or click the minus symbol ⊟ to collapse formatting options in the Reveal Formatting task pane.

Controlling Section Breaks

When you create a new document, the document is formatted with one section by default. Insert section breaks to separate parts of a document that have formatting different from the rest of the document. For example, you may want to insert a section at the beginning of a document to include a title page with special formatting and centered vertically. When you change the left and right margins of selected text, a separate section is created.

For better control in creating section breaks, you can insert a section break directly into a document at a specific location by using the Break dialog box. You can also specify the type of section break you want to insert. Insert a *next page* section break to start a section on a new page. Insert a *continuous* section break to start a new section on the same page. Switch to Draft view to see the double-dotted section break lines.

TABLE 9-1 Types of Section Breaks

Type	Description
Next page	Section starts on a new page.
Continuous	Section follows the text before it without a page break.
Even page or odd page	Section starts on the next even- or odd-numbered page. Useful for reports in which chapters must begin on either odd- or even-numbered pages.

Exercise 9-5   INSERT SECTION BREAKS BY USING THE BREAK COMMAND

1. Place the insertion point to the left of the paragraph at the top of page 5 that begins "Chronology."

2. Press Ctrl+Q. This clears the formatting for the paragraph, removing the soft page break you applied earlier.

3. Click the **Page Layout** tab, and click the Breaks button. Under **Section Breaks**, click **Continuous**. Word begins a new section on the same page, at the position of the insertion point.

4. Click above and below the section mark. Notice that the section number changes on the status bar but the page number stays the same.

Figure 9-6
Inserting a
continuous section
break

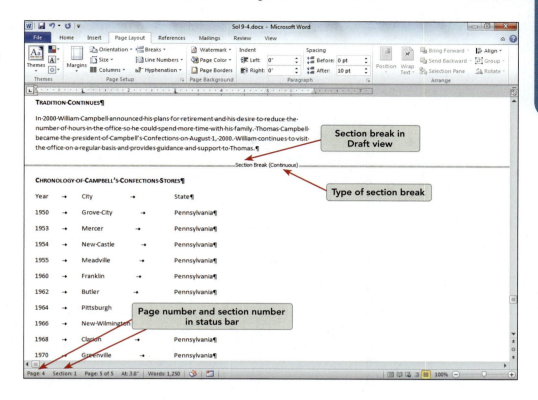

TRADITION·CONTINUES¶

In·2000·William·Campbell·announced·his·plans·for·retirement·and·his·desire·to·reduce·the·
number·of·hours·in·the·office·so·he·could·spend·more·time·with·his·family.·Thomas·Campbell·
became·the·president·of·Campbell's·Confections·on·August·1,·2000.·William·continues·to·visit·
the·office·on·a·regular·basis·and·provides·guidance·and·support·to·Thomas.¶

Section break in Draft view

Section·Break·(Continuous)

CHRONOLOGY·OF·CAMPBELL'S·CONFECTIONS·STORES¶

Type of section break

Year	→	City	→	State¶
1950	→	Grove·City	→	Pennsylvania¶
1953	→	Mercer	→	Pennsylvania¶
1954	→	New·Castle	→	Pennsylvania¶
1955	→	Meadville	→	Pennsylvania¶
1960	→	Franklin	→	Pennsylvania¶
1962	→	Butler	→	Pennsylvania¶
1964	→	Pittsburgh		
1966	→	New·Wilmington		
1968	→	Clarion	→	Pennsylvania¶
1970	→	Greenville	→	Pennsylvania¶

Page number and section number in status bar

Page: 4   Section: 1   Page: 5 of 5   At: 3.8"   Words: 1,250   100%

Formatting Sections

After you create a new section, you can change its formatting, or you can specify the section break to be a different type of section break. This is often useful for long documents, which sometimes contain many sections that require different page formatting, such as different margin settings or page orientation. For example, you can change a next page section break to a continuous section break, or you can change the page orientation of a section, without affecting the rest of the document.

NOTE

The formatting you apply to the section is stored in the section break. If you delete a section break, you also delete the formatting for the text above the section break. For example, if you have a two-section document and you delete the section break at the end of section 1, the document becomes one section with the formatting of section 2.

Exercise 9-6   APPLY FORMATTING TO SECTIONS

1. Position the insertion point before the text "Wholesale" on page 2. Use the **Page Layout** tab, Breaks button to insert a **Next page** section break.

2. With the insertion point in the new section (section 2), open the **Page Setup** dialog box by clicking the **Page Setup Dialog Box Launcher**.

3. Click the **Layout** tab, and click to open the **Section start** drop-down list. From this list you can change the section break from New page to another type.

4. Choose **Continuous** so the section does not start on a new page.

Figure 9-7
Using the Page
Setup dialog box to
modify the section

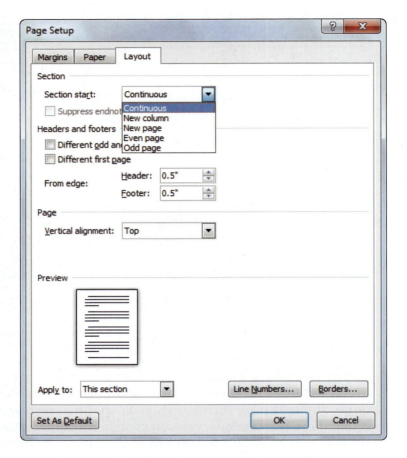

5. Click the **Margins** tab.

6. Set 1.5-inch left and right margins. Make sure **This section** appears in the **Apply to** box, and click **OK**. Section 2 of the document now has new margin settings. Click the Print Layout button on the status bar to view the change.

Exercise 9-7   CHANGE THE VERTICAL ALIGNMENT OF A SECTION

Another way to format a section is to specify the vertical alignment of the section on the page. For example, you can align a title page so the text is centered between the top and bottom margins. Vertical alignment is a layout option available in the Page Setup dialog box.

1. Move the insertion point to the last section of the document (which begins "Chronology"). Notice that the section type is continuous. Because this section does not start on a new page, a page break interrupts the list of stores.

2. Open the **Page Setup** dialog box, and click the **Layout** tab.

3. Use the **Section start** drop-down list to change the section from **Continuous** to **New page**.

4. Open the **Vertical alignment** drop-down list and choose **Center**. Click **OK**.

TABLE 9-2 Vertical Alignment Options

Options	Description
Top	Aligns the top line of the page with the top margin (default setting).
Center	Centers the page between the top and bottom margins with equal space above and below the text.
Justified	Aligns the top line of the page with the top margin and the bottom line with the bottom margin, with equal spacing between the lines of text (similar in principle to the way Word justifies text between the left and right margins).
Bottom	Aligns the bottom line of a partial page along the bottom margin.

Figure 9-8
Vertical alignment options

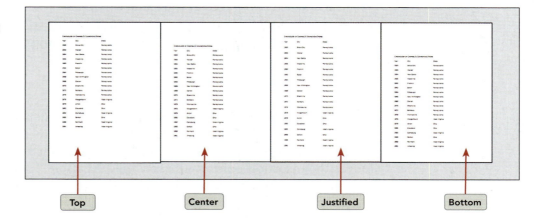

Top   Center   Justified   Bottom

Exercise 9-8 CHECK PAGINATION USING THE PRINT TAB OR PAGE LAYOUT VIEW

After you apply page breaks, section breaks, or section formatting, use Print Preview on the Print tab or Print Layout view to check the document. Viewing the pages in relation to one another provides ideas for improvement before printing.

Remember, you can change the page formatting of a document using Print Layout view or the Print tab.

1. Click the **File** tab, and click **Print**. Notice that the text is centered between the top and bottom margins. Notice also that viewing a document using the Print tab does not show the dotted lines of the section breaks, but it does show how the page will look when you print it.

NOTE

The appearance of the buttons in the Settings section will vary depending on the last formatting option selected.

2. While still displaying the document using the Print tab, click the **Margins Setting** option, and choose **Custom Margins** at the bottom of the list. Click the **Layout** tab, and change the vertical alignment to **Justified**. Click **OK**. Word justifies the last page of the document so the text extends from the top margin to the bottom margin.

3. Click the Previous Page button ◀ to scroll back, page by page, to page 2, section 1, of the document.

4. Drag the Zoom slider to 50%. You cannot see the continuous section break before "Wholesale," but you can check the formatting and see how the document will look when printed.

5. Click the **Home** tab, and switch to Print Layout view.

6. Scroll to page 2, section 1. Notice that in Print Layout view, page breaks are indicated by the actual layout of each page as it will look when printed.

7. Click the Zoom button 100% on the status bar to open the Zoom dialog box. Click the **Many Pages** button, and click on the grid to display **1 × 2** (one row, two pages). Click **OK**. This reduces the document display so you can see two pages at the same time.

8. Scroll to the end of the document. Click the Draft View button ▤ to switch to Draft view. Drag the **Zoom slider** to **100%** if necessary.

Using the Go To Feature

You use the Go To feature to move through a document quickly. For example, you can go to a specific section, page number, comment, or bookmark. *Go To* is a convenient feature for long documents—it is faster than scrolling, and it moves the insertion point to the specified location.

There are three ways to initiate the Go To command:

- Click the Home tab, and click the drop-down arrow beside the Find 🔍 command, and choose Go To or click the Replace button ᵇⁱⁱ to open the Find and Replace dialog box. Click the Go To tab.

- Double-click on the status bar (anywhere to the left of "Words").

- Press Ctrl+G or press F5.

Exercise 9-9 GO TO A SPECIFIC PAGE OR SECTION

1. With the document in Draft view, press F5. Word displays the **Go To** tab, located in the Find and Replace dialog box.

Figure 9-9
Using the Go To feature

2. Scroll through the **Go to what** list to review the options. Choose **Section** from the list, and click **Previous** until you reach the beginning of the document.

3. Click **Next** until the insertion point is located at the beginning of the last section, which is section 3.

4. Choose **Page** from the **Go to what** list and click **Previous**. The insertion point moves to the top of the previous page.

5. Key **2** in the **Enter page number** text box, and click **Go To**. The insertion point moves to the top of page 2.

6. Close the dialog box.

Exercise 9-10 GO TO A RELATIVE DESTINATION

You can use the Go To command to move to a location relative to the insertion point. For example, with Page selected in the Go to what list, you can enter "+2" in the text box to move forward two pages from the insertion point. You can move in increments of pages, lines, sections, and so on. Another option is to move by a certain percentage within the document, such as 50%—the document's midpoint.

1. Double-click the word "Page" on the status bar to open the Find and Replace dialog box with the Go To tab active.

2. Choose **Line** from the **Go to what** list, and key **4** in the text box. Click **Go To**. The insertion point moves to the fourth line in the document.

3. Key **+35** in the text box, and click **Go To**. The insertion point moves forward 35 lines from the previous location.

NOTE

You must select Page in the Go to what list to use a percentage.

TIP

You can use the Go To feature to delete a single page of content. Position the insertion point, and open the Find and Replace dialog box. Click the Go To tab, and key \page in the text box. Click Go To. Click Close (the text will be highlighted), and press Delete.

4. Key **-35** in the text box, and click **Go To**. The insertion point moves back to the previous location.

5. Click **Page** in the **Go to what** list, key **50%** in the text box, and click **Go To**. The insertion point moves to the midpoint of the document.

6. Close the dialog box.

7. Save the document as *[your initials]*9-10 in the Lesson 9 folder.

8. Open the **Print** tab, and choose **4 Pages Per Sheet** in the **1 Page Per Sheet** list box. Click **Print**.

9. Close the document.

Lesson 9   Summary

- Pagination is the Word process of flowing text from line to line and from page to page. Word creates a soft page break at the end of each page. When you edit text, you adjust line and page breaks. You can adjust the way a page breaks by manually inserting a hard page break (Ctrl + Enter).

- Delete a hard page break by selecting it and pressing Delete or Backspace.

- The Paragraph dialog box contains line and page break options to control pagination. To prevent lines of a paragraph from displaying on two pages, click in the paragraph and apply the Keep lines together option. To keep two paragraphs together on the same page, click in the first paragraph and apply the Keep with next option. To insert a page break before a paragraph, click in the paragraph and choose the Page break before option.

- Use section breaks to separate parts of a document that have different formatting. Apply a next page section break to start a section on a new page or a continuous section break to continue the new section on the same page. Apply an even page or odd page section break to start a section on the next even- or odd-numbered page.

- Change the vertical alignment of a section by clicking within the section and opening the Page Setup dialog box. On the Layout tab, under Vertical alignment, choose an alignment option (top, center, justified, or bottom).

- Check pagination using the Print tab or Print Layout view. Scroll through the document or change the zoom to display a different view.
- Use the Go To command to go to a specific page or section in a document. You can also go to a relative destination, such as the midpoint of the document or the 50th line.

LESSON 9		Command Summary	
Feature	Button	Command	Keyboard
Formatting sections		Page Layout tab, Page Setup group, Page Setup dialog box	
Go To	🔍 or ᵃᵇ⁄ₐc	Home tab, Editing group, Find or Replace command, Go To tab	Ctrl+G or F5
Hard page break	▤	Insert tab, Pages group, Page Break	Ctrl+Enter
Line and page break options		Home tab, Paragraph group, Paragraph dialog box, Line and Page Breaks tab	
Section breaks	▤	Page Layout tab, Page Setup group, Breaks command	

Please visit our Online Learning Center, *www.lessonapproach2010.com,* **where you will find the following review materials:**

- **Concepts Review**

  True/False Questions

  Short Answer Questions

  Critical Thinking Questions

- **Skills Review**

  Review Exercises that target single skills

  Lesson Applications

  Review Exercises that challenge students by testing multiple skills in each exercise

- **On Your Own**

  Open-ended exercises that require students to synthesize multiple skills and apply creativity and problem-solving as they would in a real world business situation

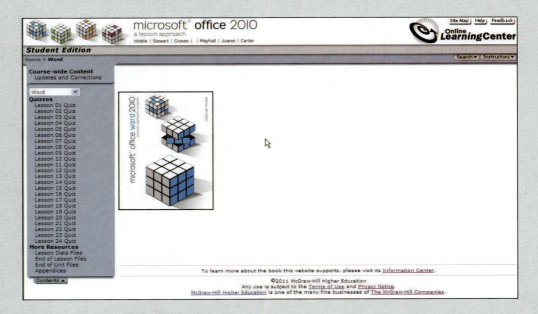

Lesson 10
Page Numbers, Headers, and Footers

OBJECTIVES *After completing this lesson, you will be able to:*

1. Add page numbers.
2. Change the starting page number.
3. Add headers and footers.
4. Add headers and footers within sections.
5. Link section headers and footers.
6. Create continuation page headers.
7. Create alternate headers and footers.

Estimated Time: 1½ hours

Page numbers, headers, and footers are useful additions to multiple-page documents. Page numbers can appear in either the top or bottom margin of a page. The text in the top margin of a page is a *header;* text in the bottom margin of a page is a *footer.* Headers and footers can also contain descriptive information about a document, such as the date, title, and author's name.

Adding Page Numbers

Word automatically keeps track of page numbers and indicates on the left side of the status bar the current page and the total number of pages in a document. Each time you add, delete, or format text or sections, Word adjusts page breaks and page numbers. This process, called *background repagination,* occurs automatically when you pause while working on a document. Right-click the status bar to select formatted page number, section, and page number options when working with long documents.

Figure 10-1
Status bar indicators
for a multiple-page
document

Exercise 10-1 ADD AND PREVIEW PAGE NUMBERS

Page numbers do not appear on a printed document unless you specify that
they do. The simplest way to add page numbers is to click the Insert tab and
click Page Number.

1. Open the file **History**.

2. With the insertion point at the top of the document, click the **Insert** tab
   and click the Page Number button. Word displays a list of options
   for placing your page number in the document. Notice that you can
   choose top of page, bottom of page, or page margins. Once you
   choose a position for the page number, you select a design from the
   gallery. A *gallery* is a list of design options for modifying elements of
   a page.

Figure 10-2
Page number
options

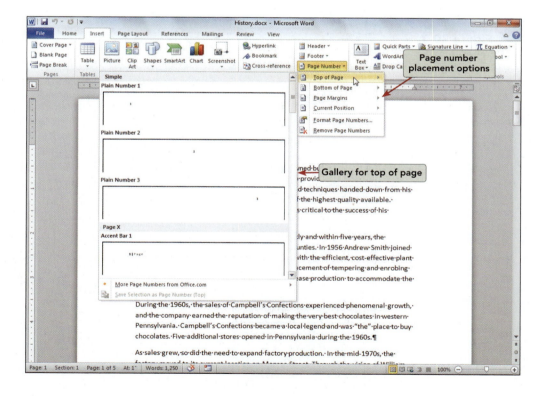

NOTE

If you key the number 2 in the header or footer pane, the document will print the number 2 on every page of the document instead of the page number. Remember to use the Insert Page Number button to add page numbers to a document.

3. Click **Top of Page** to display the gallery for placing numbers at the top of the page. Click **Plain Number 3** to place a page number in the upper right corner of the document.

4. Scroll through the document to view the page numbers. By default Word places page numbers on every page. Notice the divider line that separates the header pane from the document text.

5. Notice that the **Ribbon** adds a new tab when page numbers have been added to a document. The **Header & Footer Tools Design** tab includes additional options for formatting the document.

6. Click the Close Header and Footer button ![x].

NOTE

You can see page numbers when Print Layout view is the selected view, when the Print tab is displayed, or on the printed page.

7. Click the **Insert** tab, and click the Page Number button ![icon]. Click **Bottom of Page**, and scroll to the bottom of the gallery. Click **Triangle 2**. A page number appears at the bottom right corner of each page.

8. Click the Zoom button 100%, and choose **Whole page**. Click **OK**. Notice that page numbers appear in the header and footer of the page.

Figure 10-3
Viewing page numbers

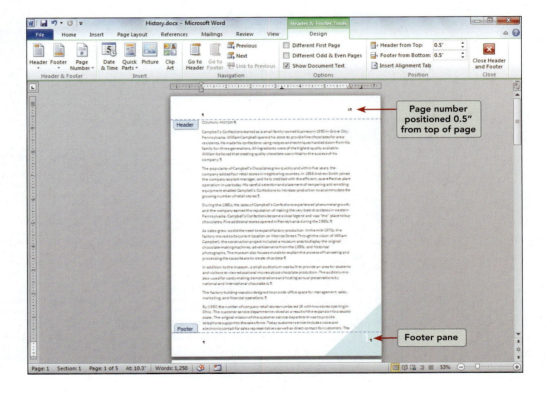

9. Change the zoom level to 100%, and scroll to view the first page of the document. The page number appears within the 1-inch top margin and is positioned 0.5 inch from the top edge of the page at the right margin.

10. Click the Undo button 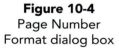 to remove the page number in the footer.

Exercise 10-2 CHANGE THE POSITION AND FORMAT OF PAGE NUMBERS

Not only can you change the placement of page numbers and decide if you want to number the first page or not, but you can also change the format of page numbers. For example, instead of using traditional numerals such as 1, 2, and 3, you can use roman numerals (i, ii, iii) or letters (a, b, c). You can also start page numbering of a section with a different value. For instance, you could number the first page ii, B, or 2.

1. Double-click the header on page 1. This activates the header pane (the area at the top of the page that contains the page number), displays the Header & Footer Tools Design tab, and dims the document text.

2. Select the page number, and change the format of the number to italic using the Mini toolbar. Press Ctrl+E to center the number. Press Ctrl+Z to undo the center alignment.

NOTE

You can apply character formatting to page numbers by selecting the page number and applying the desired format.

3. Locate the **Header and Footer** group on the Header & Footer Tools Design tab. Click the Page Number button and click **Format Page Numbers**.

4. Open the **Number format** drop-down list, and choose uppercase roman numerals (I, II, III). Click **OK**.

Figure 10-4
Page Number
Format dialog box

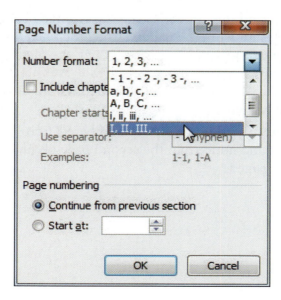

5. Locate the **Options** group on the Header & Footer Tools Design tab, and click **Different First Page**. Selecting the Different First Page option creates a separate header for the first page of the document and removes the page number from page 1 of the document.

6. Locate the **Navigation** group on the Header & Footer Tools Design tab, and click the Previous button 🖳. Scroll to the top of page 1, and notice that the page number does not display on the first page of the document. Click the Next button 🖳 to return to page 2 of the document. Click the Close Header and Footer button ❌.

7. View the document using the Print tab, and note that page 1 does not display a page number. Click the Next Page button ▶ to display page 2. The header page numbering format is now italic, starting with roman numeral II on page 2.

8. Click the **Home** tab to return to the document.

Changing the Starting Page Number

In addition to formatting page numbers and changing the page number placement, you can change the starting page numbering. You can format a document to include a cover page and change the page number options to display no page number on page 1 and to display page number 1 on the actual page 2 of the document.

To add a cover page, click the Insert tab and click the Cover Page button. Select a design from the gallery, and the cover page automatically appears at the beginning of the document. You can also insert a blank page by clicking the Blank Page button on the Insert tab.

Exercise 10-3   ADD A COVER PAGE

1. Position the insertion point at the beginning of the document. Click the **Insert** tab, and click the Cover Page button 📄. Click the **Sideline** design from the gallery. Click the placeholder "[Type the document title]," and key **History**. Click the placeholder for "[Type the company name]," and key **Campbell's Confections**. Key your name in the Author section. Click the Pick the Date control, and select today's date.

2. Notice that the cover page is not numbered. Scroll to page 2 of the document, and notice that the second page of the document is numbered page I.

3. Position the insertion point at the top of the second page of the document. Click the **Insert** tab, and click the Page Number button. Click **Format Page Numbers**. Click the option **Continue from previous section**. Click **OK** to close the dialog box. The second page of the document is now numbered page II.

Figure 10-5
Preview page numbers

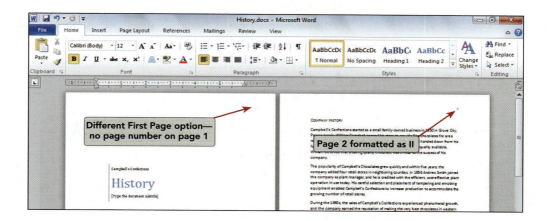

4. Click the Zoom button 100%, and click the Many Pages button. Drag to select three pages on the first row. Click **OK**. Notice that the cover page is not numbered and that page numbering starts with page 2. Return the zoom level to 100%.

5. Double-click the page number of page 2 of the document. Position the insertion point to the immediate left of the page number. Key **Page** and press Spacebar once.

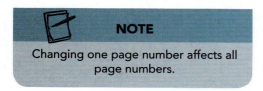

NOTE

Changing one page number affects all page numbers.

6. Scroll to the header pane on page 3 to view the revised header text.

7. Close the Header and Footer pane.

8. Save the document as *[your initials]*10-3 in your Lesson 10 folder.

Figure 10-6
Formatted page number with "Page" added

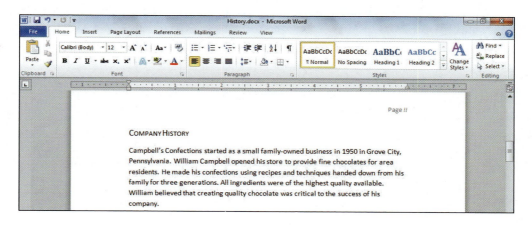

Exercise 10-4   REMOVE PAGE NUMBERS

To remove page numbers, delete the text in the header or footer area or click the Remove Page Numbers button.

1. Click the **Insert** tab, and click the Page Number button 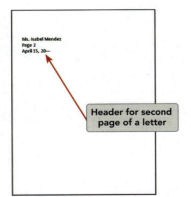. Click **Remove Page Numbers**.

2. Scroll through the document, and notice that the page number has been deleted from all pages.

3. Click the Cover Page button, and click **Remove Current Cover Page**.

4. Close the document without saving it.

Adding Headers and Footers

Headers and footers are typically used in multiple-page documents to display descriptive information. In addition to page numbers, a header or footer can contain:

- The document name
- The date and/or the time you created or revised the document
- An author's name
- A graphic, such as a company logo
- A draft or revision number

This descriptive information can appear in many different combinations. For example, the second page of a business letter typically contains a header with the name of the addressee, the page number, and the date. A report footer could include the report name and a header with the page number and chapter name. A newsletter might contain a header with a title and logo on the first page and a footer with the title and page number on the pages that follow.

Figure 10-7
Examples of headers and footers

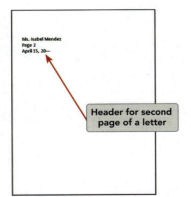

Ms. Isabel Mendez
Page 2
April 15, 20—

Header for second page of a letter

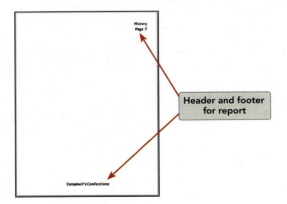

History
Page 7

Header and footer for report

Campbell's Confections

Exercise 10-5   ADD A HEADER TO A DOCUMENT

1. Open the file **History - 2**. This file is a six-page document with a title page. You will add a header and footer to pages 2 through 6.

2. Click the **Insert** tab, and click the Header button 📄. Click the **Blank** design at the top of the Header gallery. Word displays the Header & Footer Tools Design tab and the blank header pane.

3. Locate the **Options** group on the Header & Footer Tools Design tab, and click the **Different First Page** check box. This enables you to give the document two different headers—a header for the title page (the first page), which you will leave blank, and a header for the rest of the document, which will contain identifying text. Notice that this header pane is labeled "First Page Header."

4. Click the Next button 📑. Notice that this header pane is labeled "Header." The Previous button 📑 and the Next button 📑 are useful when you move between different headers and footers within sections of a document.

5. Key **Campbell's Confections History** in the page 2 header pane. This text now appears on every page of the document except the first page.

NOTE

These preset tab settings in the header and footer pane are default settings for a document with the default 1-inch left and right margins. In such a document, the 3.25-inch tab centers text and the 6.5-inch tab right-aligns text. This document, however, has 1.25-inch left and right margins, so it is best to adjust the tabs.

6. Press Tab once. Notice that the ruler has two preset tab settings: 3.25-inch centered and 6.5-inch right-aligned. Drag the center tab marker to 3 inches on the ruler, and drag the right-aligned tab marker to the right margin (6 inches). Press Tab again to move to the right-aligned tab setting.

7. Click the Page Number button 📄, and click **Current Position**. Click the **Plain Number** option. Word inserts the page number at the right margin. Click to the immediate left of the page number, and key **Page**, and press Spacebar.

8. Click the Previous button 📑, and notice that the first-page header pane is still blank. Click the Next button 📑 to return to the header you created on page 2.

TABLE 10-1 Header and Footer Tools Design Tab

Button	Name	Purpose
	Header	Edit the document header.
	Footer	Edit the document footer.
	Insert Page Number	Insert page numbers.
	Date and Time	Insert the current date or time.
	Quick Parts	Insert common header or footer items, such as running total page numbers (for example, page 1 of 10) or document properties.
	Picture	Insert a picture from a file.
	Clip Art	Insert clip art.
	Go to Header	Activates header for editing.
	Go to Footer	Activates footer for editing.
	Previous	Show the header or footer of the previous section.
	Next	Show the header or footer of the next section.
Link to Previous	Link to Previous	Link or unlink the header or footer in one section to or from the header or footer in the previous section.
Different First Page	Different First Page	Create a header and footer for the first page of the document.
Different Odd & Even Pages	Different Odd and Even Pages	Specify a header or footer for odd-numbered pages and a different header or footer for even-numbered pages.
Show Document Text	Show Document Text	Display or hide the document text.
	Header from Top	Specify height of header area.
	Footer from Bottom	Specify height of footer area.
	Insert Alignment Tab	Insert a tab stop.

Exercise 10-6   ADD A FOOTER TO A DOCUMENT

1. With the header on page 2 displayed, click the Go to Footer button ⬛ to display the footer pane.

2. Key your name and press [Tab].

3. Save the document as *[your initials]*10-6 in your Lesson 10 folder.

4. With the insertion point at the center of the footer, click the Date & Time button ⬛ on the Header & Footer Tools Design tab.

5. Click the third option in the **Available formats** list. Remove the check from the **Update automatically** check box. Click **OK**. The current date is inserted in the footer.

6. Press [Tab] to move to the right margin, and click the Quick Parts button ⬛. Click **Field** and scroll the list of **Field names** to locate **FileName**. Click **FileName**, and notice that a list of **Field properties** appears in the middle of the dialog box. Click **First capital**. Click **OK**.

Figure 10-8
Inserting fields

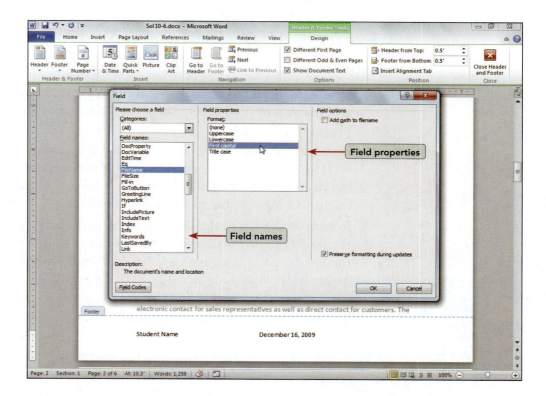

7. View the footer text. The document's file name is inserted at the right margin. This footer information prints at the bottom of each page except the first.

8. Improve the footer tab positions by dragging the center tab marker to 3 inches and the right tab marker to 6 inches. (Remember, this document has 1.25-inch left and right margins, not the default 1-inch margins.)

9. Click the Close Header and Footer button ⊠ to return to the document.

10. Switch to the Print tab. Check that no header or footer appears on the title page. Click the Next Page button ▶ to move through each page of the document and to view the header and footer.

11. Return to Page Layout view and save the document. Leave it open for the next exercise.

Adding Headers and Footers within Sections

Section breaks have an impact on page numbers, headers, and footers. For example, you can number each section differently or add different headers and footers for each section.

When you add page numbers to a document, it is best to add the page numbers first and then add the section breaks. Otherwise, you have to apply page numbering to each individual section.

Exercise 10-7   ADD SECTIONS TO A DOCUMENT WITH HEADERS AND FOOTERS

1. Delete the hard page break that follows the title page of the document, and insert a next page section break. Delete blank paragraph marks if necessary.

2. Insert a next page section break before the heading "Fundraising" in section 2 (page 3 of the document) and a next page section break before the heading "Chronology" in section 3 (page 5 of the document). The document layout now includes four sections.

3. Return to the top of the document (by pressing Ctrl + Home), and click the **Insert** tab. Click the Header button 📄. Click **Edit Header**. Notice that the header pane label indicates the section number.

NOTE

If a document has two sections, there are multiple variations for headers and footers. For example, section 1 can display a header and section 2 can display a different header. If the Different First Page option is selected, the document could have four different headers or footers. Section 1 would include a header for the first page and a header for the remaining pages in the section. Section 2 would include a header for the first page and a header for the remaining pages in section 2. To avoid confusion, read carefully the label for each header and footer pane.

4. Click the Next button 📄 to move to the header, in section 2. Notice that this header is also blank, and it is labeled "First Page Header – Section 2." Earlier in the lesson you selected the Page Setup option **Different First Page**, and the option was applied to the entire document. This means the first page of each section can be formatted separately from the other pages in the section. It can include the same text and format as the other pages in the section, or it can contain different text and formatting.

5. Click the Next button 📄 again to move to Header – Section 2. The header and footer text begin on page 3.

6. Click the Next button 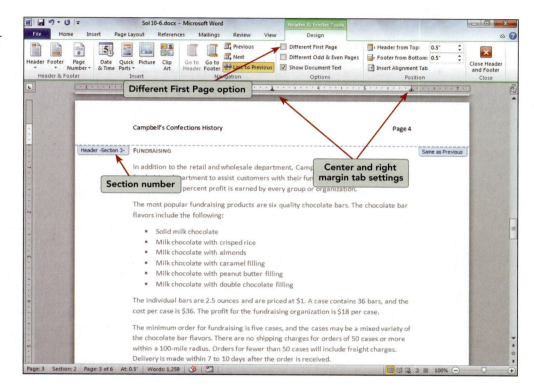 to move to section 3. Because the **Different First Page** option applies to the entire document, the first page of this section contains no header or footer.

7. Turn off the Different First Page option for section 3 by clicking the **Different First Page** option on the Header & Tools Design tab to clear the check box. Page 1 of section 3 displays the document header and footer text. Turning off this option applies only to this section, as you will see in the next step.

Figure 10-9
The header text for section 3

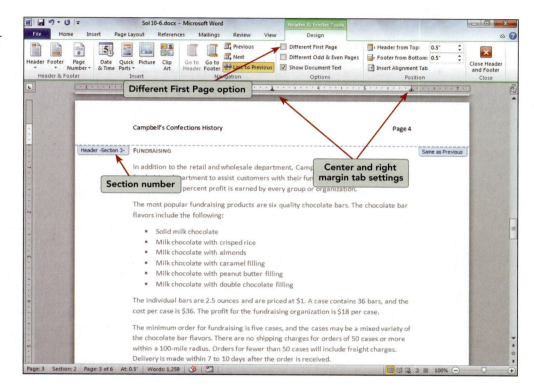

8. Click the Previous button 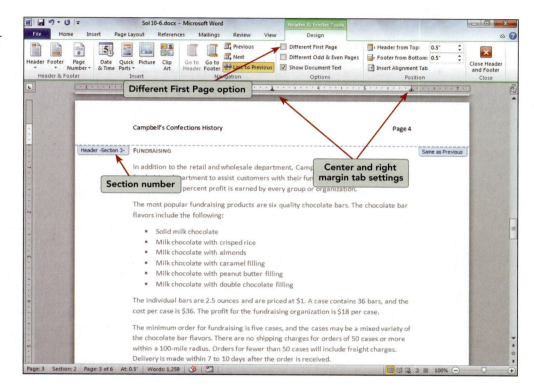 twice to move to the header on page 1 of section 2. The header pane should read **First Page Header–Section 2**. Notice that the header pane is still blank because the **Different First Page** option is still checked for this section.

9. Click to deselect the **Different First Page** option for this section. Now the header and footer display for page 1 of section 2.

10. Click the Next button 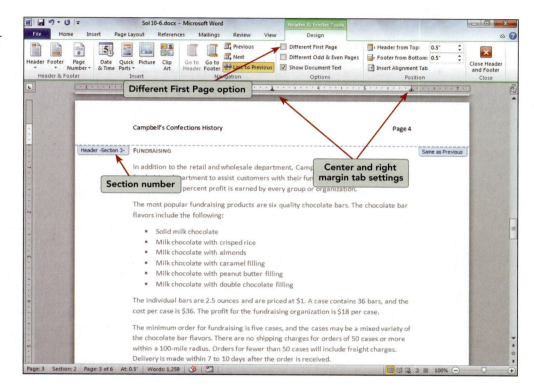 two times to move to the first-page header of section 4. Click to deselect the **Different First Page** option. The header appears on page 1 of section 4.

11. View each header in the document by dragging the scroll box (on the vertical scroll bar) up one page at a time. As you display each page's header, notice the page numbering. Also notice that the text "Same as Previous" appears on the header panes. Same as previous means the header or footer is linked to the header or footer in the previous section.

Linking Section Headers and Footers

By default, the Link to Previous button is "on" when you work in a header or footer pane. As a result, the text you key in the header (or the footer) is the same from section to section. Any change you make in one section header or footer is reflected in all other sections. You can use the Link to Previous button to break the link between header or footer text from one section to another section. Breaking the link enables you to key different header or footer text for each section.

> **NOTE**
>
> Breaking the link for the header does not break the link for the footer. You must unlink them separately.

Exercise 10-8   LINK AND UNLINK SECTION HEADERS AND FOOTERS

1. Scroll to the header for section 3, and select the text "Campbell's Confections History" and apply italic formatting.

2. Click the Previous button to move to the header in section 2. The header text is italic, demonstrating the link that exists between the headers.

3. Click the Next button 🔽 to return to section 3. Click the Link to Previous button 🔳 Link to Previous to turn off this option. Now sections 2 and 3 are unlinked, and you can create a different header for section 3.

> **TIP**
>
> To select text in a header or footer, you can point and click from the area to the immediate left of the header or footer pane.

4. Delete all the text in the header for section 3, including the page number.

5. Press ⌷Tab⌷ to move to the center tab setting and key **Supplement**. Press ⌷Tab⌷ again and click the Date & Time button 🔳. Select the first number format, and click **OK**. Drag the center tab marker to 3 inches and the right tab marker to 6 inches.

6. Click the Go to Footer button 🔳 to switch to the footer for section 3. The footer text between sections 2 and 3 is still linked, so click the Link to Previous button 🔳 Link to Previous to break the link.

> **NOTE**
>
> By default, page numbering continues from the previous section.

7. Delete all the footer text in section 3 except your name. Click the Previous button 🔳 to view the footer text in section 2. The footer text has not been affected. Click the Next button 🔽 to return to the footer in section 3.

8. Click the Link to Previous button 🔳 Link to Previous to restore the link between section footers. When Word asks if you want to delete the current text and connect to the text from the previous section, click **Yes**.

Figure 10-10
Restoring the link
between section
footers

9. Move to the header pane by clicking the Go to Header button 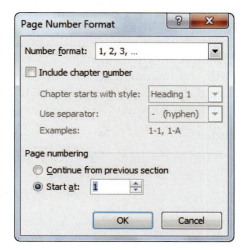. Click the Next button to move to section 4.

10. Click the Link to Previous button [Link to Previous] to disconnect the section 4 header from the section 3 header.

11. Move to the header for section 3, and click the Link to Previous button [Link to Previous], and click **Yes** to connect the section 3 header to the header in section 2.

12. Click the Close Header and Footer button.

13. Format the title page attractively. Adjust page breaks throughout the document as needed.

14. Save the document as *[your initials]*10-8. Submit the document.

Exercise 10-9   CHANGE THE STARTING PAGE NUMBER

So far, you have seen page numbering start either with 1 on page 1 or 2 on page 2. When documents have multiple sections, you might need to change the starting page number. For example, in the current document, section 1 is the title page and the header on section 2 begins numbering with page 2. You can change this format so that section 2 starts with page 1.

1. Double-click the page number in section 2, page 1, to display the header pane.

2. Click the Page Number button, and click **Format Page Numbers** to open the Page Number Format dialog box.

3. Click to select the **Start at** option, and key **1** in the text box.

Figure 10-11
Changing the
starting page
number for section 2

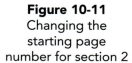

> **NOTE**
>
> You can change the starting page number for any document, with or without multiple sections. For example, you might want to number the first page of a multiple-page document "Page 2" if you plan to print a cover page as a separate file.

4. Click **OK.** Section 2 now starts with page 1. Close the Header and Footer pane.

5. Save the document as *[your initials]*10-9 in your Lesson 10 folder.

6. Submit and close the document.

Creating Continuation Page Headers

It is customary to use a header on the second page of a business letter or memo. A continuation page header for a letter or memo is typically a three-line block of text that includes the addressee's name, the page number, and the date.

There are three rules for letters and memos with continuation page headers:

- Page 1 must have a 2-inch top margin.
- Continuation pages must have a 1-inch top margin.
- Two blank lines must appear between the header and the continuation page text.

Exercise 10-10   ADD A CONTINUATION PAGE HEADER TO A LETTER

The easiest way to create a continuation page header using the proper business format is to apply these settings to your document:

- Top margin: 2 inches.
- Header position: 1 inch from edge of page.
- Page Setup layout for headers and footers: Different first page.
- Additional spacing: Add two blank lines to the end of the header.

By default, headers and footers are positioned 0.5 inch from the top or bottom edge of the page. When you change the position of a continuation page header to 1 inch, the continuation page appears to have a 1-inch top margin, beginning with the header text. The document text begins at the page's 2-inch margin, and the two additional blank lines in the continuation header ensure correct spacing between the header text and the document text.

1. Open the file **Mendez**.

2. Add the date to the top of the letter, followed by three blank lines.

3. Open the **Page Setup** dialog box, and display the **Layout** tab. Check **Different First Page** under **Headers and Footers**. Locate the section **From edge**, and set the **Header** to 1 inch from the edge.

4. Click the **Margins** tab, and set a 2-inch top margin and 1.25-inch left and right margins. Click **OK**.

5. Click the **Insert** tab, and click the Header button . Click **Edit Header** to display a blank header pane.

6. Click the Next button to move to the header pane on page 2.

7. Create the header in Figure 10-12, inserting the information as shown. Press Enter twice after the last line. Use appropriate format for the page number and date.

TIP

Letters and memos should use the spelled-out date format (for example, December 12, 2012), and the date should not be a field that updates each time you open the document. To insert the date as text, with the correct format, click the Date and Time button and clear the Update automatically check box.

Figure 10-12

```
Ms. Isabel Mendez

Page [Click Page Number, Current Position, Plain Number
for the page number.]

Date [Click Date & Time, and choose the third format to
insert the current date.]
```

Figure 10-13
Continuation page header for a letter

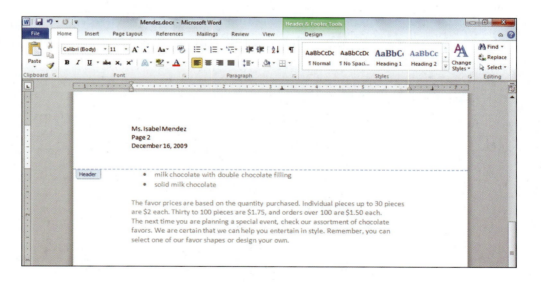

8. Close the header pane, and change the zoom level to view both pages. Return the zoom level to 100%.

9. Add a complimentary closing, and key **Lydia Hamrick** and the title **Customer Service** at the end of the letter, followed by your reference initials.

10. Save the document as *[your initials]*10-10 in your Lesson 10 folder.

11. Submit, and close the document.

Creating Alternate Headers and Footers

In addition to customizing headers and footers for different sections of a document, you can also change them for odd and even pages throughout a section or document. For example, this textbook displays the unit name for even pages and displays the lesson name for odd pages.

Exercise 10-11   CREATE ALTERNATE FOOTERS IN A DOCUMENT

To create alternate headers or footers in a document, you use the Different odd and even check box and then create a header or footer for both even and odd pages.

1. Open the file **History - 2**. Delete the page break on page 1, and insert a next page section break. Delete blank paragraph marks if necessary.

2. Position the insertion point in section 1, click the **Insert** tab, and click the Footer button 📄.

3. Click **Edit Footer**, and click the **Different Odd and Even Pages** option. Click the **Different First Page** option so the first page does not display a footer.

4. Click the Next button 📄, and verify that the insertion point is in the Even Page Footer pane for section 2.

5. Click the Footer button 📄, and scroll through the gallery. Select **Contrast (Even Page)**. Click the Pick the Date control, and choose today's date. The footer displays on page 2.

Figure 10-14
Even page footer

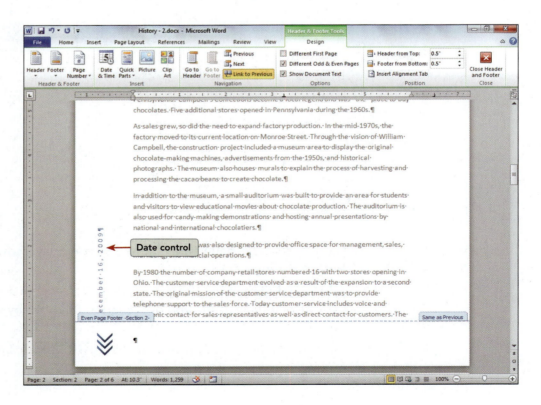

6. Click the Next button 🖳 to move to the footer on page 3. The footer pane is labeled "Odd Page Footer–Section 2" and is blank.

7. Click the Footer button 🖻, and scroll through the gallery. Select **Contrast (Odd Page)**. The footer displays on page 3.

8. Click the Close Header and Footer button ❌.

9. Click the Zoom button ⎡ 100% ⎤, and click the Many Pages button 🖳. Drag over the grid to select six pages. Click **OK**. View each page of the document. Notice the position of the page number on the odd and even pages.

10. Change the zoom level to 100%. Add 72 points of paragraph space before the title on page 1, and center the text on page 1 horizontally. Apply a page border to section 1. Adjust page breaks throughout the document as needed.

11. Save the document as *[your initials]*10-11 in your Lesson 10 folder.

12. Print the document four pages per sheet, or submit the document, and then close it.

NOTE

To create different odd and even headers or footers within a section, you must first break the link between that section's header or footer and the previous section's header or footer.

Lesson 10   Summary

- A header is text that appears in the top margin of the printed page; a footer is text that appears in the bottom margin. These text areas are used for page numbers, document titles, the date, and other information.

- Always add page numbers to long documents. You can choose the position of page numbers (for example, bottom centered or top right) and the format (for example, 1, 2, 3 or A, B, C). You can also choose to number the first page or begin numbering on the second page.

- Check page numbers using the Print tab or Print Layout view (page numbers are not visible in Draft view). In Print Layout view, you can activate the header or footer pane that contains the page number by double-clicking the text and then modifying the page number text (for example, apply bold format or add the word "Page" before the number).

- To remove page numbers, activate the header or footer pane that contains the numbering, select the text, and then delete it. You can also click the Page Number button and choose Remove Page Numbers.

- To add header or footer text to a document, click the Insert tab, and click Header or Footer. Select a design from the gallery. Use the Header & Footer Tools Design tab buttons to insert the date and time or to insert Quick Parts for the file name, author, print date, or other information. See Table 10-1.

- Adjust the tab marker positions in the header or footer pane as needed to match the width of the text area.
- A document can have a header or footer on the first page different from the rest of the pages. Apply the Different First Page option in the Page Setup dialog box (Layout tab), or use the Different First Page button on the Header & Footer Tools Design tab.
- Header and footer text is repeated from section to section because headers and footers are linked by default. To unlink section headers and footers, click the Link to Previous button. To relink the header or footer, click the button again.
- Sections can have different starting page numbers. Click the Page Number button to open the Page Number Format dialog box, and then set the starting page number.
- Memos or letters that are two pages or longer should have a continuation page header—a three-line block containing the addressee's name, page number, and date. Set the header to 1 inch from the edge, add two blank lines below the header, and use a 2-inch top margin. Apply the Different First Page option, and leave the first-page header blank.
- Use the Header & Footer Tools Design Tab or the Page Setup dialog box to change the position of the header or footer text from the edge of the page. The default position is 0.5 inch.
- A document can have different headers and footers on odd and even pages. Apply the Different odd and even option.

LESSON 10		Command Summary	
Feature	**Button**	**Command**	**Keyboard**
Add or edit footer		Insert tab, Footer	
Add or edit header		Insert tab, Header	
Add page numbers		Insert tab, Page Number	
Change layout settings		Page Layout tab, Page Setup dialog box, or Header & Footer Tools Design tab	
Change page number format		Insert tab, Page Number, Format Page Numbers	

Please visit our Online Learning Center, *www.lessonapproach2010.com,* **where you will find the following review materials:**

Concepts Review

True/False Questions

Short Answer Questions

Critical Thinking Questions

Skills Review

Review Exercises that target single skills

Lesson Applications

Review Exercises that challenge students by testing multiple skills in each exercise

On Your Own

Open-ended exercises that require students to synthesize multiple skills and apply creativity and problem-solving as they would in a real world business situation

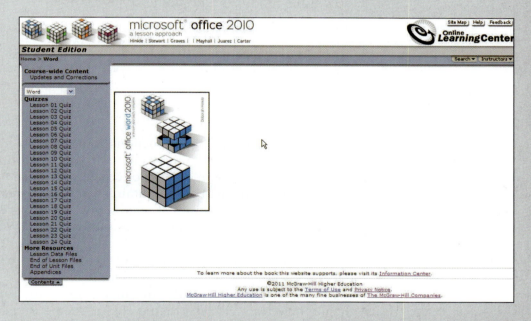

Lesson 11
Styles and Themes

OBJECTIVES *After completing this lesson, you will be able to:*

1. Apply styles.
2. Create new styles.
3. Redefine, modify, and rename styles.
4. Use style options.
5. Apply and customize a theme.

Estimated Time: 1¼ hours

A *style* is a set of formatting instructions you can apply to text. Styles make it easier to apply formatting and ensure consistency throughout a document. You can apply styles, modify them, or create your own.

In every document, Word maintains *style sets*—a list of style names and their formatting specifications. A style set, which is stored with a document, includes standard styles for body text and headings. Word includes several built-in styles, and a few of the built-in styles appear in the Quick Style Gallery on the Home tab. When you point to a style in the Quick Style Gallery, you can see a preview of the style formatting.

A *theme* is a set of formatting instructions for the entire document. A theme includes style sets, theme colors, theme fonts, and theme effects. Themes can be customized and are shared across Office programs.

Applying Styles

The default style for text is called the *Normal* style. Unless you change your system's default style, the Normal style is a paragraph style with the following formatting specifications: 11-point Calibri, English language, left-aligned, 1.15-line spacing, 10 points spacing after, and widow/orphan control.

To change the appearance of text in a document, you can apply five types of styles:

- A *character style* is formatting applied to selected text, such as font, font size, and font style.
- A *paragraph style* is formatting applied to an entire paragraph, such as alignment, line and paragraph spacing, indents, tab settings, borders and shading, and character formatting.
- A *linked style* formats a single paragraph with two styles. It is typically used to assign a heading style to the first few words of a paragraph.
- A *table style* is formatting applied to a table, such as borders, shading, alignment, and fonts.
- A *list style* is formatting applied to a list, such as numbers or bullet characters, alignment, and fonts.

Exercise 11-1   APPLY STYLES

There are two ways to apply styles:

NOTE

Define a style set before you apply formatting to ensure you are using the appropriate styles.

- Open the Styles task pane and select a style to apply. To open the Styles task pane, click the Styles Dialog Box Launcher or press [Alt]+[Ctrl]+[Shift]+[S]. The Styles task pane includes the built-in styles featured in the Quick Style Gallery plus all available styles.
- Click the Home tab, and click a Quick Style.

1. Open the file **Volume 1**.
2. Click the **Home** tab, and click the **Styles Dialog Box Launcher** to open the Styles task pane. The task pane lists formatting currently used in the document and includes some of Word's built-in heading styles. Each style has a drop-down list of options to help you manage the styles.

NOTE

To apply a style to a paragraph, you can simply click anywhere in the paragraph without selecting the text. Remember, this is also true for applying a paragraph format (such as line spacing or alignment) to a paragraph.

3. Activate the **Home** tab, and click the Change Styles button. Click **Style Set**, and click **Word 2010**. The style set defines the built-in styles for the document.
4. Click in the line "Choc Talk," and place the mouse pointer (without clicking) over the Heading 1 style in the task pane. A ScreenTip displays the style's attributes.
5. Click the **Heading 1** style in the Styles task pane. The text is formatted with 14-point bold Cambria, blue, 24 points spacing before, and 1.15-line spacing.

Figure 11-1
Using the Styles task pane to apply a style

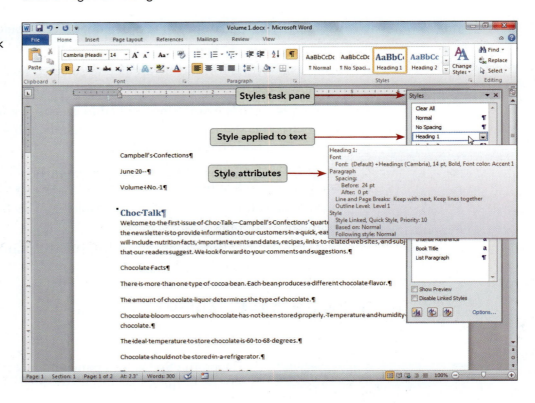

6. Close the Styles task pane by clicking the Styles task pane Close button .

7. Position the insertion point in the text "Chocolate Facts."

8. Click the **Home** tab, and locate the **Styles** group. The Styles group includes a gallery of styles that provides a quick and convenient way to apply styles. One row of the styles gallery displays by default. Click the More arrow ⊡ to display all the styles in the Quick Style Gallery. Move the mouse pointer over each of the quick styles to preview the format.

9. Choose **Heading 2**. Notice the applied formatting.

TIP

Style sets may only show those styles already used in the document. To see all styles available, click **Options** in the Styles task pane, and click the arrow beside Select styles to Show. Select All styles.

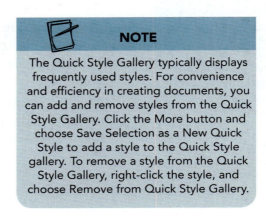

NOTE

The Quick Style Gallery typically displays frequently used styles. For convenience and efficiency in creating documents, you can add and remove styles from the Quick Style Gallery. Click the More button and choose Save Selection as a New Quick Style to add a style to the Quick Style gallery. To remove a style from the Quick Style Gallery, right-click the style, and choose Remove from Quick Style Gallery.

Figure 11-2
Using the Quick
Style Gallery

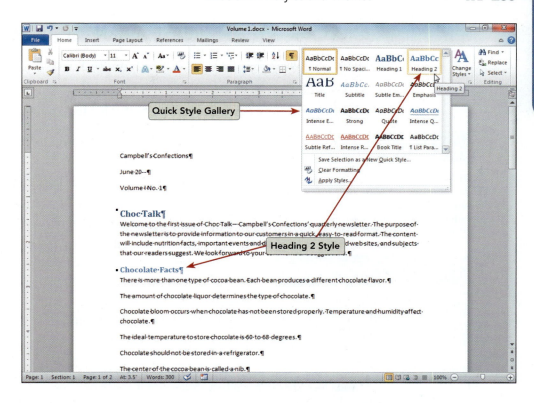

TIP

You can use keyboard shortcuts to apply three popular heading styles. Press Ctrl+Alt+1 to apply the Heading 1 style. Press Ctrl+Alt+2 to apply the Heading 2 style, and press Ctrl+Alt+3 to apply the Heading 3 style.

TIP

To remove a style from text and restore the Normal style, choose Clear All from the Styles task pane or Clear Formatting from the Quick Style Gallery. The keyboard shortcut for the Normal style is Ctrl+Shift+N.

10. Position the insertion point in the heading "Nutrition." Press F4 to repeat the Heading 2 style.

Creating New Styles

Creating styles is as easy as formatting text and then giving the set of formatting instructions a style name. Each new style name must be different from the other style names already in the document.

Word saves the styles you create for a document when you save the document.

Exercise 11-2 CREATE A PARAGRAPH STYLE

There are two ways to create a new paragraph style:

- Use the Quick Style Gallery.

- Click the New Style button in the Styles task pane.

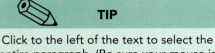

TIP

Click to the left of the text to select the entire paragraph. (Be sure your mouse is in the margin area and the mouse pointer changes to a white arrow.)

NOTE

Click to select the Show Preview check box in the Styles task pane to display style names with formatting.

1. Reopen the Styles task pane by clicking the **Styles Dialog Box Launcher**.

2. Select the heading "Chocolate Facts."

3. Increase the font size to 14 points, and press ⌈Ctrl⌉+⌈Shift⌉+⌈K⌉ to apply small caps.

4. Click the New Style button 🔠 at the bottom of the Styles task pane. The Create New Style from Formatting dialog box opens.

5. Key **Side Heading** in the **Name** box. Verify that **Paragraph** is the **Style type**.

Figure 11-3
Create New Style from Formatting dialog box

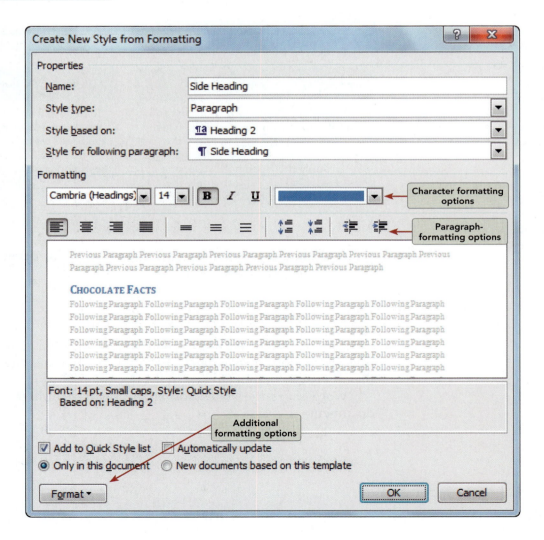

NOTE

If you key a style name that already exists in the Style box, you apply the existing style; you do not create a new one.

TIP

Use the formatting buttons in the Create New Style from Formatting dialog box to apply basic font and paragraph formatting. For more formatting options, click the Format button, and choose Font, Paragraph, Tabs, Border, or Numbering to open the corresponding dialog boxes.

6. Notice the two rows of buttons under **Formatting**. The first row applies character formatting, and the second row applies paragraph formatting.

7. Click **OK**. The style appears in the Quick Style Gallery and in the Styles task pane.

8. Locate the heading "Nutrition." Click in the paragraph, and click the **Side Heading** style in the task pane. The new style is applied.

9. Repeat the formatting to the side headings "Pets and Chocolate" and "Important Chocolate Dates."

10. Select the text "June 20—" at the top of the document, and change the font size to 12.

11. Right-click the selected text, and click **Styles** in the shortcut menu. The Styles Gallery displays as well as options to update the Normal style to match the selected text or to save the selection as a new style. Click **Save Selection as a New Quick Style**.

Figure 11-4
Creating a new style

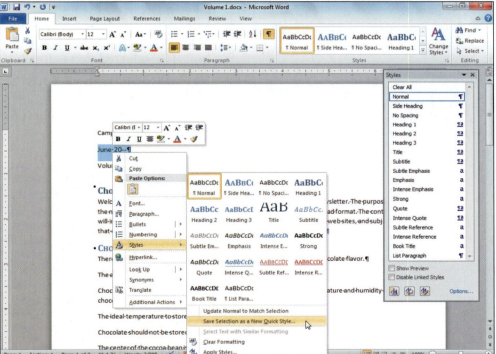

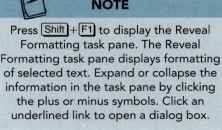

NOTE

Press ⌈Shift⌋+⌈F1⌋ to display the Reveal Formatting task pane. The Reveal Formatting task pane displays formatting of selected text. Expand or collapse the information in the task pane by clicking the plus or minus symbols. Click an underlined link to open a dialog box.

12. Key **Issue Date** in the **Name** text box, and click **OK**.

13. Notice that the Side Heading style and the Issue Date style appear in the Styles task pane and the Quick Style Gallery.

Exercise 11-3 CREATE A CHARACTER STYLE

A character style is applied to selected text and only contains character formatting.

NOTE

When you change the style type to character, the paragraph format buttons in the Create New Style from Formatting dialog box dim. Paragraph, Tabs, and Numbering options in the Format button menu are also unavailable for character styles.

NOTE

In a list of styles, paragraph styles display a paragraph symbol (¶) and character styles display a text symbol (<u>a</u>) to the right of the style name. Linked styles display both a paragraph symbol (¶) and a text symbol (<u>a</u>).

1. Select the text "Choc Talk" in the first paragraph under the heading "Choc Talk." Open the Create New Style from Formatting dialog box by clicking the New Style button , and key **Accent** in the **Name** text box.

2. Choose **Character** from the **Style type** drop-down list box. Once the style type is defined as a character style, paragraph-formatting options are not available.

3. Click the **Format** button, choose **Font**, and set the formatting to 11-point Calibri and italic.

4. Click **OK** to close the Font dialog box. Click **OK** to close the Create New Style from Formatting dialog box. The selected text is formatted, and the Accent style appears in the Styles task pane and the Quick Style Gallery.

5. Note that a character style is applied to selected text, not the entire paragraph.

TIP

At the bottom of the Styles task pane, you can click the Options link to choose which types of styles are displayed. The default setting, "Recommended," lists styles and unnamed formats available to the current document. "In use" lists styles and unnamed formats applied in the current document. "In current document" lists styles and unnamed formats available in the current document. "All styles" lists styles in the current document and all of Word's built-in styles. You can also specify how the styles are sorted: alphabetical, as recommended, font, based on, and by type.

Figure 11-5
Applying the
character style

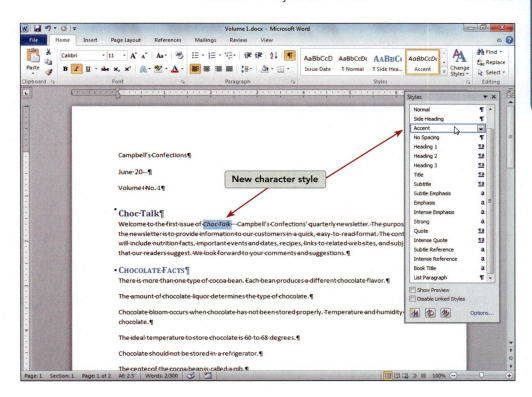

6. Save the document as ***[your initials]*11-3** in a new folder for Lesson 11. Do not print the document; leave it open for the next exercise.

Modifying and Renaming Styles

After creating a style, you can modify it by changing the formatting specifications or renaming the style. When you modify a style, the changes you make affect each instance of that style. You can quickly replace one style with another by using the Replace dialog box, the Styles task pane, or the shortcut menu.

Exercise 11-4   MODIFY AND RENAME STYLES

To modify a style, right-click the style in the Styles task pane and then choose Modify. Or select the styled text, modify the formatting, right-click the style name in the Styles task pane, and choose Update to Match Selection. You can also select and modify text formatting. Right-click the selected text, choose Styles, and click Update to Match Selection.

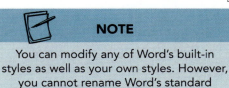

NOTE

You can modify any of Word's built-in styles as well as your own styles. However, you cannot rename Word's standard heading styles.

1. In the Styles task pane, right-click the style name **Heading 1**. Choose **Modify** from the shortcut menu.

TIP

Instead of using the right mouse button to open this drop-down list of style options, you can use the left mouse button to click the down arrow next to a style name. Remember, if you click a style name (not its down arrow) with the left mouse button, you will apply the style to the text containing the insertion point.

2. In the Modify Style dialog box, change the point size to 18, and click **OK** to update the style.

3. Select the text "June 20—" and open the **Paragraph** dialog box. Change the **Spacing After** to 0 points and click **OK**. Right-click the selected text "June 20—." Choose **Styles**, then choose **Update Issue Date to Match Selection**. The style is updated to match the selected text formatting.

TIP

You can also click the Select All Instances option in the Styles task pane to select all instances of a style.

Figure 11-6
Modifying a style by updating

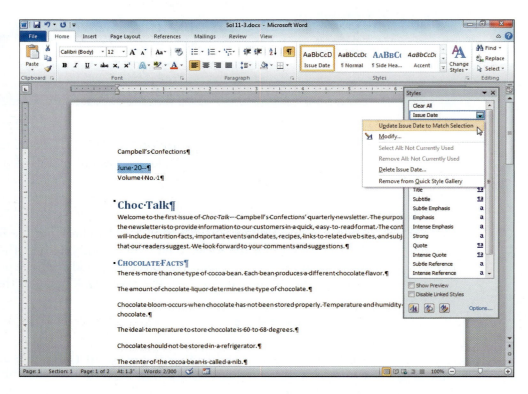

NOTE

After modifying or renaming a style, you can undo your action (for example, click Undo from the Quick Access Toolbar).

4. Position the insertion point in the text "June 20—." Right-click the **Issue Date** style in the task pane, and choose **Modify**.

5. Rename the Issue Date style by keying **Pub Date** in the **Name** text box. Click **OK**. The style Pub Date appears in the task pane, replacing the style name Issue Date.

Exercise 11-5   REPLACE A STYLE

1. Click the **Home** tab, and locate the **Editing** group. Click the Replace button. Click the **More** button, if needed, to expand the dialog box. Clear any text or formatting from a previous search.

2. Click the **Format** button and choose **Style**. The Find Style dialog box displays.

3. Click **Side Heading** from the **Find what style** list, and click **OK**.

Figure 11-7
Find Style dialog box

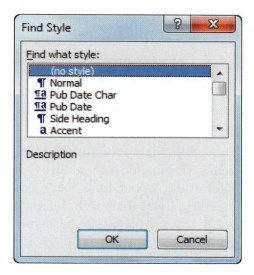

4. Tab to the **Replace with** text box, click **Format**, and choose **Style**.

5. Choose **Heading 3** from the **Replace With Style** list, and click **OK**.

6. Click **Replace All**. Click **OK**. Word replaces all occurrences of the Side Heading style with the Heading 3 style. Close the Find and Replace dialog box. Notice the change in the format. Click the Undo button.

TIP

You can also use the Styles task pane to replace one style with another style: Right-click a style name in the task pane, choose Select All Instances, and then click another style name in the Styles task pane. An alternative method is to right click the styled text, choose Styles from the shortcut menu, choose Select text with Similar Formatting, and then click another style name in the Styles task pane.

Exercise 11-6   DELETE A STYLE

1. Click the Manage Styles button at the bottom of the Styles task pane. Click the **Edit** tab. Select the **Pub Date** style in the **Select a style to edit** list box. Click **Delete**.

2. Click **Yes** when prompted to verify the deletion. Click **OK**. The Pub Date style is deleted, and the paragraph returns to Normal, the default style.

3. Click the Undo button to reverse the style deletion.

UNIT 3   LESSON 11

4. Right-click the Pub Date style in the Styles task pane. Choose **Delete Pub Date** from the drop-down list. Click **Yes** to verify the deletion. The Pub Date style is deleted, and the paragraph returns to the Normal style.

NOTE

When you delete a style from the style sheet, any paragraph that contained the formatting for the style returns to the Normal style. You cannot delete the standard styles (Word's built-in styles) from the style sheet.

NOTE

When you right-click a style in the Quick Style Gallery, and choose Remove from Quick Style Gallery, the style is removed from the Style Gallery but not deleted from the Styles task pane.

Using Style Options

Word offers two options in the Create New Style from Formatting dialog box to make formatting with styles easier:

*   *Style based on:* This option helps you format a document consistently by creating different styles in a document based on the same underlying style. For example, in a long document, you can create several different heading styles that are based on one heading style and several different body text styles that are based on one body text style. Then if you decide to change the formatting, you can do so quickly and easily by changing just the base styles.

*   *Style for following paragraph:* This option helps you automate the formatting of your document by applying a style to a paragraph and then specifying the style that should follow immediately after the paragraph. For example, you can create a style for a heading and specify a body text style for the next paragraph. After you key the heading and apply the heading style, press Enter, and the style changes to the body text style.

NOTE

The standard styles available with each new Word document are all based on the Normal style.

Exercise 11-7   USE THE STYLE FOR FOLLOWING PARAGRAPH OPTION

1. Go to the end of the document, and position the insertion point in the blank paragraph above "Copyright."
2. Click the **New Style** button 🔠 in the Styles task pane.
3. Key **StaffName** in the **Name** text box.
4. Click **Format** and choose **Font**. Set the font to 11-point Cambria, and click **OK** to close the Font dialog box. Click **OK** to close the Create New Style from Formatting dialog box.

5. Click the New Style button 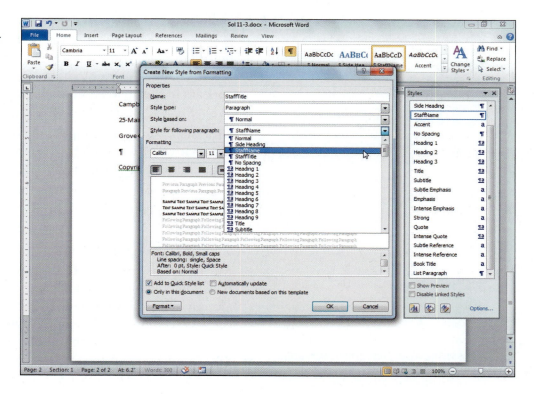 in the Styles task pane. Key **StaffTitle** in the **Name** text box. The **Style type** is **Paragraph**. Change the **Style based on** to **Normal**. Click **Format** and choose **Font**. Set the font to 11-point Calibri, with bold and small caps, and click **OK**.

6. Check that the Align Left button is selected. Click **Format**, and choose **Paragraph**. Change the **Spacing After** to 0 points, and change the **Line spacing** to single. Click **OK**. Click the down arrow for **Style for following paragraph**, and select **StaffName**. Click **OK**.

Figure 11-8
Choosing a style for the following paragraph

7. Key **President** on the blank line above "Copyright," and apply the **StaffTitle** style. Notice the format of the text. Press [Enter]. Key **Thomas Campbell**.

8. Note that the style automatically changes from StaffTitle to StaffName, which was the style indicated as the style for the following paragraph.

9. Key the text shown in Figure 11-9. Apply the appropriate styles.

Figure 11-9

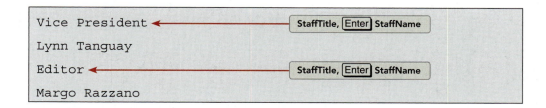

Exercise 11-8   USE THE BASED ON OPTION

1. Select the text near the bottom of page 2, from "Choc Talk" to "16127." Click the New Style button on the Styles task pane. Key **BaseBody** in the **Name** box. Verify that **Paragraph** is selected for the **Style type**, and **Normal** is selected for **Style based on**.

2. Change the font to Times New Roman, 12 points. Change the paragraph formatting to 0 points spacing after and single spacing. Click **OK** to close the Create New Style from Formatting dialog box.

3. Click the New Style button in the task pane.

> **TIP**
>
> When you want to use an existing style as the based on style, select the text with that style before opening the New Style dialog box. The style will automatically appear in the Style based on box.

4. Key **Body2** as the name of the new style. Click the Italic button in the Create New Style from Formatting dialog box to change the font to italic. Check that **Basebody** appears in the **Style based on** list box. Click **OK**.

5. Notice that the selected paragraph(s) are formatted with the Body2 style. Apply the BaseBody text to the text that was formatted by the new style. Deselect the text, and press Enter after the ZIP Code.

6. Place the mouse pointer over (without clicking) the Body2 style in the task pane. The ScreenTip indicates that the Body2 style is based on the Basebody style.

7. Click the New Style button in the task pane to create another style.

> **TIP**
>
> An alternative to using the Quick Style Gallery or the Styles task pane to apply styles is to use the Apply Styles window. To display the Apply Styles window, choose Apply Styles from the Quick Style Gallery drop-down list or press Ctrl + Shift + S. You can choose a style from the list or key the first few letters of the style name.

8. Key **Body3** as the name of the new style. Choose **Basebody** from the **Style based on** list, if it is not already selected. Change the font size to 10 points. Click **OK**. Apply the BaseBody style to any text or paragraph that was formatted by the new style.

9. Move to the top of the document. Select the text from "June 20—" to "Volume 1 No. 1." Apply the Body2 style. Deselect the text.

10. Right-click the style **Basebody** in the task pane, and choose **Modify**.

11. Change the font to Calibri. Click **OK**. All the text using or based on the Basebody style changes to the Calibri font.

Exercise 11-9   DISPLAY AND PRINT STYLES

To make working with styles easier, you can display a document's styles on the screen and print the style sheet. To see the styles, switch to Draft view.

1. Switch to Draft view. Open the Word Options dialog box, and click **Advanced** in the left pane. Scroll to the **Display** group of options.

2. Set the **Style area pane width** box to **0.5** inch and click **OK**. The style area appears in the left margin.

Figure 11-10
Styles shown in Style area

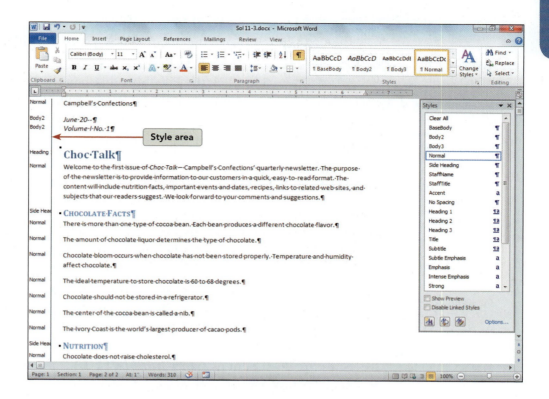

Figure 11-10
Styles shown in Style area

3. Right-click the **Normal** style in the Styles task pane. Click **Select All Instance(s)**. Click the **Basebody** style in the Styles task pane. Text previously formatted with the Normal style is now formatted with the Basebody style.

4. Select the text under "Chocolate Facts" beginning with "There is" through "cacao pods." Format the list as a bulleted list using a small square bullet.

5. Select the bulleted list you just formatted if necessary. Right-click the selected bulleted list, and select **Styles** from the shortcut menu. Select **Save Selection as a New Quick Style**. Name the style **BaseBullet**, and click **Modify**. Set the **Style based on** setting to Basebody. Click **OK** to close the dialog box.

6. Apply the BaseBullet style to the text under the headings "Nutrition," "Pets and Chocolate," and "Important Chocolate Dates."

7. Modify the Heading 2 style so it is based on Basebody. Apply the Heading 2 style to the first line of the document "Campbell's Confections." Move to the last page of the document, and repeat the Heading 2 format for the "Choc Talk" line.

NOTE

The style area is intended for on-screen purposes in Draft view only (it is not available in Print Layout view). If you open the Print tab and preview the document, this area does not display or appear on the printed document. Additionally, when you display the Style area, it will be displayed for any document you open unless you reduce the view to 0 inches. The default Style area pane width is 0 inches.

NOTE

You can assign a shortcut key to a style you use frequently. In the Styles task pane, right-click the style to which you want to assign a shortcut key. Choose Modify. Click Format and then click Shortcut key. In the Customize Keyboard dialog box, press an unassigned keyboard combination, such as Alt + B, for a body text style. The shortcut key is saved with the document.

8. Open the Word Options dialog box, and click **Advanced**. Scroll to the **Display** section, set the **Style area pane width** box to **0** inch, and click **OK**. Switch to Print Layout view.

9. Save the document as *[your initials]*11-9 in your Lesson 11 folder.

10. Click the File tab, and open the **Print** tab. Choose **Styles** from the **Print All Pages** drop-down list, and click **Print**. Word prints the styles for your active document.

11. Submit the document.

Exercise 11-10   CHANGE STYLE SET

Word provides several style sets to format your document. The number and types of styles available varies for each style set. You can choose Word 2010 as the style set or try Elegant, Fancy, Formal, or other style sets. Each style set affects the format of your document.

1. Position the insertion point at the top of the document. Click the Change Styles button ![AA], and click **Style Set**. The default style set is currently selected. Click **Fancy**, and scroll through the document to notice the changes in format.

2. Save the document as *[your initials]*11-10.

3. Submit and close the document.

Apply and Customize a Document Theme

You can use document themes to format an entire document quickly. A gallery of theme designs is available to format your document, or you can go to Microsoft Online for additional theme selections. Themes can also be customized and saved. Themes define the fonts used for body text and the fonts used for headings. For example, the default theme is Office, and Calibri is the default font for body text, and Cambri is the default font for headings. Themes affect the styles of a document.

Exercise 11-11   APPLY A THEME

1. Reopen the file **Volume 1**. Make sure the Styles task pane displays.

2. Click the **Page Layout** tab, and click the Themes button ![Aa]. The design gallery for themes displays.

Figure 11-11
Themes Gallery

3. Move your mouse over each of the theme designs, and preview the changes in your document. Click the **Technic** theme.

4. Scroll through the document, and notice the changes made. The default body text font is 11-point Arial, and the default heading font is Franklin Gothic Book.

5. View the style names in the Styles task pane. When you change a document theme, styles are updated to match the new theme.

6. Using the new styles, change the text "Campbell's Confections" at the beginning of the document to the Heading 2 style, and change "Choc Talk" to the Heading 1 style.

Exercise 11-12   CUSTOMIZE A THEME

Theme colors include text and background colors, accent colors, and hyperlink colors. The Theme Colors button displays the text and background colors for the selected theme.

1. Click the **Page Layout** tab, and locate the **Themes** group. Click the Theme Colors button ▮. The design gallery for theme colors displays with the current theme colors selected.

Figure 11-12
Theme colors

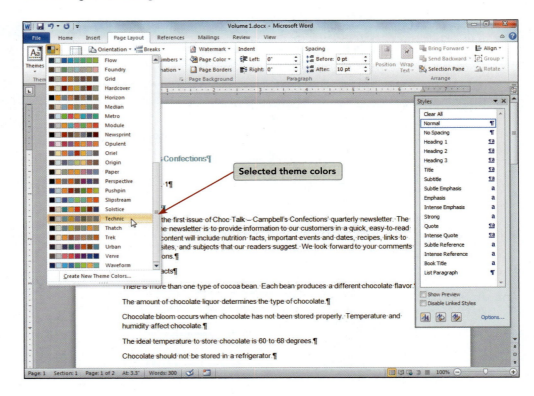

2. Click **Create New Theme Colors**. Notice that there is a button for each element of the theme. Click the down arrow beside the Accent 1 button ▣ ▾, and notice that the first color in the fifth row of Theme Colors is selected. Click the last color in the fifth row, **Aqua, Accent 1, Darker 50%**. Key **Custom Accent 1** in the **Name** box. Click **Save**. The accent color for the heading text in the document changes.

Figure 11-13
Create New Theme Colors dialog box

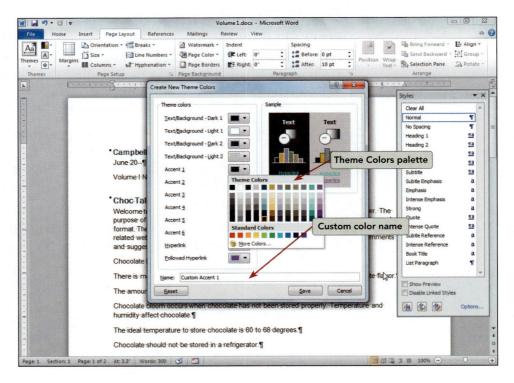

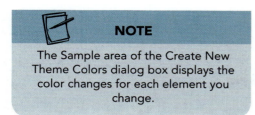

NOTE

The Sample area of the Create New Theme Colors dialog box displays the color changes for each element you change.

3. Click the Theme Colors button ▮ on the Page Layout tab, and notice that the Custom Accent 1 theme color appears at the top of the list. Right-click the Custom Accent 1 color, and click **Delete**. Click **No**.

4. Click the **Page Layout** tab, and click the Theme Fonts button ▮A▮. The heading and body text font for each theme displays.

5. Click the option to **Create New Theme Fonts**. The current heading font and body font are selected in the Create New Theme Fonts dialog box.

Figure 11-14
Create New Theme Fonts dialog box

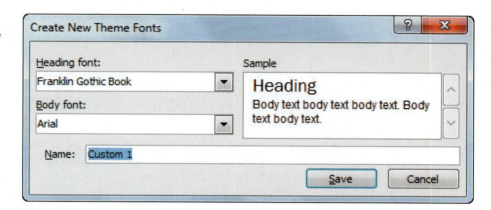

6. Change the **Heading font** to **Footlight MT Light**, and change the **Body font** to **Arial Narrow**. Key **Custom Font** in the **Name** box. Click **Save**.

7. Click the Theme Fonts button ▮A▮, and notice that "Custom Font" appears at the top of the list. Right-click **Custom Font**, and click **Edit**. Change the **Heading font** to **Eras Medium ITC**, and change the **Body font** to **Footlight MT Light**. Click **Save**.

8. Select the headings "Chocolate Facts," "Nutrition," "Pets and Chocolate," and "Important Chocolate Dates," and apply the Heading 3 style.

9. Apply the Heading 4 style to the line that begins "Volume." Apply the Heading 5 style to the second line "June 20—."

10. Select the lines of text under each of the headings formatted with the Heading 3 style, and format the lines as a bulleted list.

11. At the end of the document, delete the text that begins "Choc Talk" through the end of the document.

12. Click the **Page Layout** tab, and click the Themes button ▮Aa▮. Click **Save Current Theme**. Key **Custom Theme** in the File name box. Click **Save**.

13. Click the Themes button ▮Aa▮, and notice that the design gallery displays built in designs and custom designs. Right-click the **Custom Theme** at the top of the gallery, and click **Delete**. Click **Yes** to delete the theme.

14. Save the document as *[your initials]*11-12 in your Lesson 11 folder.

15. Submit and close the document.

Lesson 11   Summary

- A style is a set of formatting instructions you can apply to text to give your document a unified look. The five types of styles are character, paragraph, linked, table, and list.

- Word's default style for text is called the Normal style. The default settings for body text are 11-point Calibri, left-aligned, 1.15-line spacing, 10 points spacing after, with widow/orphan control. Word provides nine built-in heading styles (for example, Heading 1, Heading 2). The default font for heading text is Cambria.

- To apply a style, select the text you want to style (or click in a paragraph to apply a paragraph style). Then choose the style from the Styles task pane or the Quick Style Gallery.

- View the attributes of a style by placing the mouse pointer over the style name in the Styles task pane and reading the text in the ScreenTip. Preview the style by placing the mouse pointer over the style name in the Quick Style Gallery.

- Select all instances of a style by clicking the arrow for the style name in the Styles task pane or by right-clicking a style name in the task pane and choosing Select All Instance(s). You can use the Quick Style Gallery to select all instances too.

- To create a new paragraph style: Select text, modify the text, right-click the text, select Styles from the shortcut menu, select Save Selection as a New Quick Style, key a new style name, and click OK. Or click the New Style button in the Styles task pane, and set the style's attributes in the Create New Style from Formatting dialog box.

- To create a character style, select the text and apply the font formatting. Click the New Style button in the Styles task pane, and key the style name. Change the Style type to Character, and click OK. An alternative is to select text, modify the text, right-click the text, select Styles from the shortcut menu, choose Save Selection as a New Quick Style, key a new style name, and click Modify. Change the Style type to character, and click OK.

- To modify or rename a style, right-click the style name in the Styles task pane (or point to the style name and click the down arrow), choose Modify, and then change the attributes. Or select text that uses the style, change the format, right-click the style name in the task pane, and choose Update to Match Selection.

- After applying a style throughout a document, you can replace it with another style. Click the Replace command on the Home tab (in the dialog box, click Format, choose Style, and select the style name in both the Find what and Replace with boxes).

- You can also replace styles by using the Styles task pane (select all instances of a style and then choose another style).

- To delete a style, right-click the style name in the Styles task pane, and choose Delete. Click Yes to delete the style. You can also click the Manage Styles button in the Styles task pane, select the style, and click Delete. Click Yes to delete the style, and click OK.

- When creating new styles, you can specify that they be based on an existing style. You can also specify that one style follows another style automatically. Both these options are offered in the Create New Style from Formatting dialog box.

- Display styles along the left margin of a document in Draft view by opening the Word Options dialog box, clicking Advanced, and scrolling to the Display group. Change the Style area width box to 0.5 inch. Do the reverse to stop displaying styles.

- Print a style sheet by choosing Print from the File tab and choosing Styles from the Print All Pages drop-down list.

- The theme feature formats an entire document using design elements. Themes include theme colors, theme fonts, and theme effects.

LESSON 11		Command Summary	
Feature	**Button**	**Command**	**Keyboard**
Apply styles		Home tab, Styles group	
Create styles		Home tab, Styles group, Styles task pane	
Styles task pane		Home tab, Styles group, Styles Dialog Box Launcher	Shift + Ctrl + Alt + S
Theme colors		Page Layout tab, Themes group	
Theme fonts		Page Layout tab, Themes group	
Themes		Page Layout tab, Themes group	
View style area		Word Options, Advanced, Display	

Please visit our Online Learning Center, *www.lessonapproach2010.com,* **where you will find the following review materials:**

Concepts Review

True/False Questions

Short Answer Questions

Critical Thinking Questions

Skills Review

Review Exercises that target single skills

Lesson Applications

Review Exercises that challenge students by testing multiple skills in each exercise

On Your Own

Open-ended exercises that require students to synthesize multiple skills and apply creativity and problem-solving as they would in a real world business situation

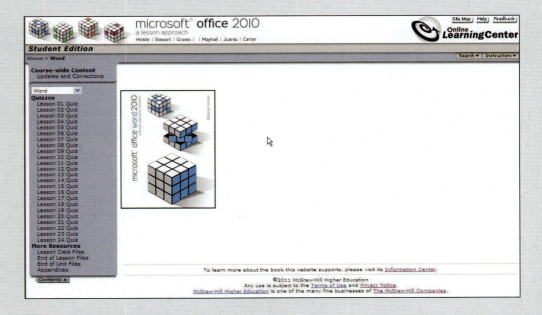

Lesson 12
Templates

OBJECTIVES   *After completing this lesson, you will be able to:*

1. Use Word templates.
2. Create new templates.
3. Attach templates to documents.
4. Modify templates.
5. Use the Organizer.

Estimated Time: 1½ hours

If you often create the same types of documents, such as reports or letters, you can save time by using templates. Word provides a variety of sample templates and templates online that contain built-in styles to help you produce professional-looking documents. You can also create your own templates and reuse them as often as you like.

Using Word's Templates

A *template* is a file that contains formatting information, styles, and sometimes text for a particular type of document. For instance, a company letterhead could be created and stored as a template. The template would include the company name and address, corporate logo, and telephone and fax numbers. The template would also include the margins, font, and font size for the letter. The letterhead template provides a reusable model for all documents requiring the company letterhead.

The following features can be included in templates:

• Formatting features, such as margins, columns, and page orientation.

• Standard text that is repeated in all documents of the same type, such as a company name and address in a letter template.

- Character and paragraph formatting that is saved within styles.
- Macros (automated procedures).

Templates also include *placeholder text* that is formatted and replaced with your own information when you create a new document.

Every Word document is based on a template. The default template file in Word is called *Normal.* New documents that you create in Word are based on the Normal template and contain all the formatting features assigned to this template, such as the default font, type size, paragraph alignment, margins, and page orientation. The Normal template differs from other templates because it stores settings that are available globally. In other words, you can use these settings in every new document even if it is based on a different template. The file extension for template files is .dotx or .dotm. (A .dotm file is used to enable macros in the file.)

Exercise 12-1   USE A WORD TEMPLATE TO CREATE A NEW DOCUMENT

Starting Word opens a new blank document that is based on the Normal template.

1. Click the **File** tab, and click **New**.

Figure 12-1
Available templates

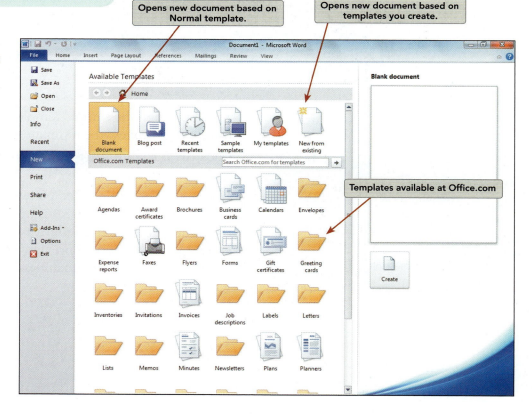

Opens new document based on Normal template.

Opens new document based on templates you create.

Templates available at Office.com

NOTE

Some templates might not be installed on your computer. Check with your instructor for instructions on locating the template.

2. Under **Available Templates**, click **Sample Templates**.

3. Click the **Equity Fax** sample template. Notice the design of the template in the **Preview** pane.

Figure 12-2
Sample templates

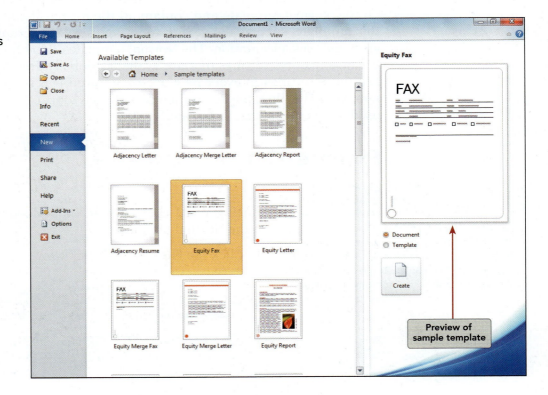

4. Scroll through the sample templates, and click the thumbnails to view the templates in the Preview pane.

5. Click the Back button to return to the Available Templates Home page.

6. Locate the **Office.Com Templates** section, and click the **Letters** icon. Click the **Business** folder, and click the folder named **Sales letters**. Click **Follow-up to exhibit booth visitors** to preview the letter. Click the Download button. The document displays in a new window.

NOTE

The formatting stored in templates is often complex and highly stylized and does not necessarily conform to the traditional formatting for business documents as described in *The Gregg Reference Manual*.

Figure 12-3
Creating a document from the downloaded template

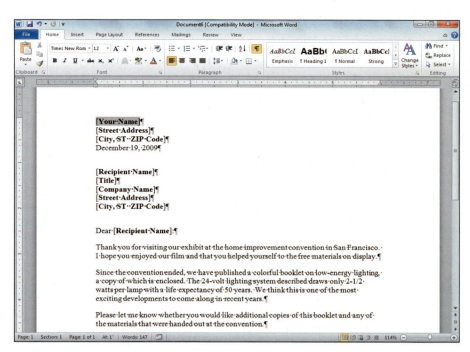

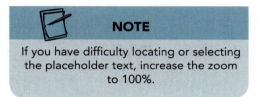
NOTE

If you have difficulty locating or selecting the placeholder text, increase the zoom to 100%.

7. Select the first line of the return address, "[Your Name]," and key **Campbell's Confections**. Click to select the placeholder text that reads "[Street Address]." Key **25 Main Street**. Click to select the placeholder that reads "[City, ST ZIP Code]," and key **Grove City, PA 16127**.

8. Click each of the placeholders for the inside address, and key the following replacement text.

   Mr. Paul Sakkal
   President
   Wholesale Nut Company
   1000 Millington Court
   Cincinnati, OH 45242

9. Click the placeholder in the salutation, and key **Mr. Sakkal**.

10. Edit the first paragraph that begins "Thank you for" as shown in Figure 12-4.

Figure 12-4

Thank you for visiting our exhibit at the **National Confections Association Conference** in **Chicago**. I hope you enjoyed our **video** and that you helped yourself to the free materials on display.

11. Change the second paragraph to read as follows:

    Since the convention ended, we have published a colorful booklet on **our complete line of candy**, a copy of which is enclosed. **Our most popular selections include cordial cherries, caramel pecanettes, and chocolate melt-a-ways.**

12. Key **Lynn Tanguay** in the placeholder for [Your Name] and **Vice President** in the [Title] placeholder. Key your initials at the end of the document before the enclosure notation.

13. Format the first line of the return address (Campbell's Confections) using 14-point bold and small caps.

14. Save the document as **[your initials]12-1** in a new Lesson 12 folder. Click **OK**, if a message box appears.

15. Submit and close the document.

Creating New Templates

You can create your own templates for different types of documents by using one of three methods:

- Create a blank template file by using the default template, and define the formatting information, styles, and text according to your specifications.

- Open an existing template, modify it, and save it with a new name.

- Open an existing document, modify it, and save it as a new template.

Exercise 12-2 CREATE A NEW TEMPLATE

1. Click the **File** tab, click **New**, and click **My Templates**. Click the **Blank Document** icon.

Figure 12-5
New dialog box showing personal templates

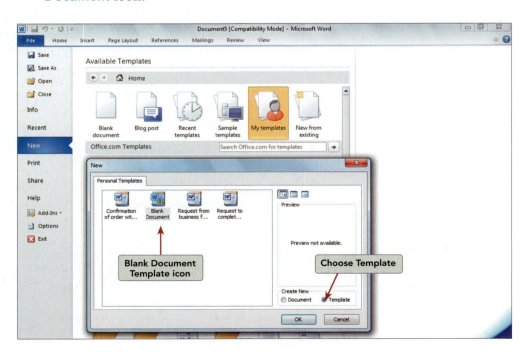

NOTE

If you select Blank Document or Recent Templates, you open a document window which can be saved as a template. If you select My Templates, you can choose to open a document or template window.

2. In the lower right corner of the dialog box, under **Create New**, click **Template** and then click **OK**. A new template file opens with the default name Template1.

3. Change the top margin to 0.5 inch.

4. Key the text shown in Figure 12-6.

Figure 12-6

```
Campbell's Confections

25 Main Street

Grove City, PA 16127

Telephone: 724-555-2025

Fax: 724-555-2050

www.campbellsconfections.biz
```

5. Select the letterhead information, and center the text horizontally. Select the first line, and apply 14-point bold and small caps formatting.

6. Modify the Normal style to 0 points spacing after and single spacing. Press Enter three times to insert blank lines after the Web address, and change the paragraph alignment to left.

NOTE

By default, Word saves new templates in a User template folder on your hard disk. The specific location is C:\Users\ [Username]\AppData\Roaming\Microsoft\ Templates (or a similar location in your computer). Before proceeding, ask your instructor where you should save your templates. If you use the default location, you can create new documents from your templates by using the New tab. If you use your Lesson 12 folder, you create new documents from your templates by using Windows Explorer or Computer.

7. Insert the date as a field at the third blank paragraph mark after the letterhead by clicking the **Insert** tab, and clicking **Date and Time**. Use the third date format in the **Available formats** list in the Date and Time dialog box. Check **Update automatically** so the date field is updated each time the document is printed. Click **OK**.

8. Press Enter four times.

9. Click the last line of the letterhead text, and apply a bottom border. If necessary, right-click the Web address, and remove the hyperlink format.

10. Click the **File** tab, and click **Save As**. A folder named "Templates" appears in the address bar of the Save As dialog box, and "Word Template" should appear in the Save as type list box.

UNIT 3 LESSON 12

Figure 12-7
Save As dialog box

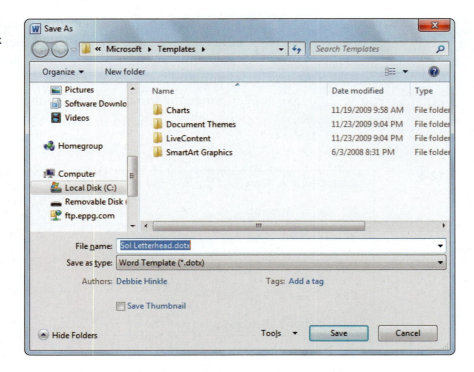

11. Save the template with the file name *[your initials]***Letterhead** in your Lesson 12 folder (unless your instructor advises you to save in the default Templates folder).

12. Close the template.

Exercise 12-3   CREATE A NEW TEMPLATE BY USING AN EXISTING DOCUMENT

1. Reopen the New tab by choosing **New** from the **File** tab. Click **New from Existing**.

2. Locate and click to select the student data file **Memo - 1**. Click the Create New button ⬚ Create New ▼ . Word opens a copy of the document.

3. Change the top margin to 2 inches. Select the document, and change the font size to 12 points.

4. Delete all text to the right of each tab character in the memo heading.

5. Insert the date as a field; use the third date format. Check **Update automatically** so the date field is updated each time the document is printed.

6. Delete all the document paragraphs, but include the blank paragraph marks after the subject line.

7. Open the **File** tab, click **Save As**. Change the **Save as type** drop-down list box to display Word Template (*.dotx).

8. Save the file as *[your initials]*Memo in your Lesson 12 folder (unless your instructor advises you to save in the default Templates folder).

9. Close the template.

Attaching Templates to Documents

All existing documents have an assigned template—either Normal or another template that was assigned when the document was created. You can change the template assigned to an existing document by *attaching* a different template to the document. When you attach a template, that template's formatting and elements are applied to the document, and all the template styles become available in the document.

Exercise 12-4   ATTACH A TEMPLATE TO A DOCUMENT

1. Open the New tab. Click the Memos icon in the Office.com Templates section.

2. Click Credit memo (Blue Gradient design), and click the Download button. You may see a dialog box that indicates that downloading a template is only available for machines with genuine Microsoft Office software.

> **NOTE**
>
> If you do not see a list of Word documents, check that All Word Documents displays in the Files of type box.

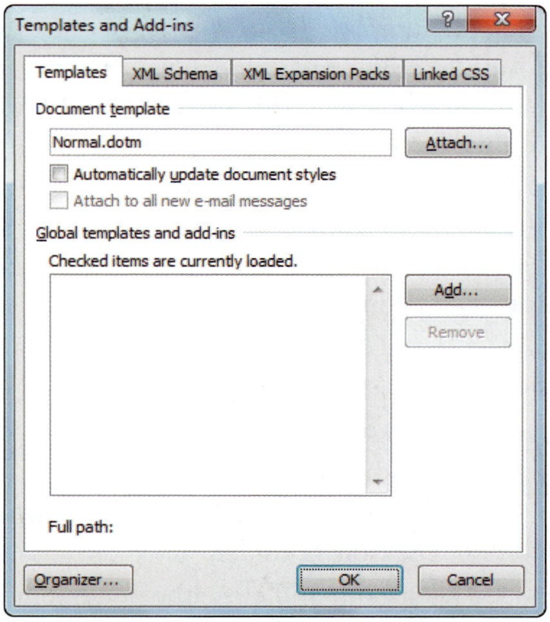

3. Save the credit memo as a template file named *[your initials]*CreditMemo in your Lesson 12 folder (unless your instructor advises you to save in the default Templates folder). Click OK if necessary, and close the template.

4. Open the student data file **Memo - 4**.

Figure 12-8
Templates and
Add-ins dialog box

5. Open the Word Options dialog box, and click Customize Ribbon in the left pane. Locate the section entitled Customize the Ribbon on the right side of the dialog box. Click to select Developer under Main Tabs. Click OK.

6. Click to select the Developer tab on the Ribbon. Click the Document Template button 📄. The Templates and Add-ins dialog box shows that the document is currently based on the Normal template.

7. Click **Attach**. The Attach Template dialog box opens, displaying available templates and folders in the current folder.

8. Locate your Lesson 12 folder, and display **All Word Templates** in the **Files of type** box.

Figure 12-9
Attach template
dialog box

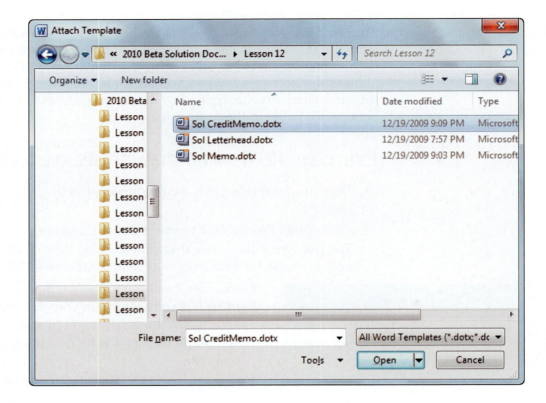

9. Double-click the template *[your initials]*CreditMemo.

10. Click the **Automatically update document styles** check box, and click **OK**. Formatting from the *[your initials]*Credit Memo template is applied to this document, and you can now apply any of the Credit Memo styles.

11. Display the Styles task pane.

12. Right-click the **Normal style**, and click **Modify**. Change the spacing after to 12 points, and change the line spacing to single.

13. Delete the text in the date line, and key today's date. Select the subject line, and change the spacing after to 24 points.

14. Set a 2-inch top margin.

15. Add your reference initials.

16. Save the document as *[your initials]*12-4 in your Lesson 12 folder.

17. Submit and close the document.

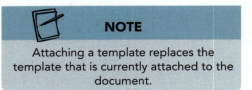

NOTE

Attaching a template replaces the template that is currently attached to the document.

Modifying Templates

After you create a template, you can change its formatting and redefine its styles. You can also create new templates by modifying existing templates and saving them with a new name.

NOTE

Any changes you make to the formatting or text in a template affect future documents based on that template. The changes do not affect documents that were created from the template before you modified it.

TIP

You can point to a file name to check its file type.

Exercise 12-5　MODIFY TEMPLATE FORMATTING

1. Click the **File** tab, and click **Open**. From the **Files of type** drop-down list, choose **All Word Templates**.

2. Locate the folder you used to save your templates (for example, the Templates folder on your hard disk under either C:\Users\[*Username*]\AppData\Roaming\ Microsoft or your Lesson 12 folder).

3. Locate the file *[your initials]*Letterhead.

4. Double-click the file *[your initials]*Letterhead to open it. Display the Styles task pane.

5. Click the **Page Layout** tab, and click the Themes button . Change the document theme to **Flow**.

6. Modify the Normal style font size to 12 points.

7. Click the Save button to save the changes. The earlier version of the template is overwritten by the new version.

8. Close the template.

TIP

Opening a template through the Open dialog box opens the actual template. Double-clicking a template in Windows Explorer, Computer, or the Templates dialog box opens a new document based on the template. Changes that you make to the new document do not affect the template.

NOTE

To create a new template based on an existing template, modify the existing template as desired and then save the template with a new name.

Using the Organizer

Instead of modifying template styles, you can copy individual styles from another document or template into the current document or template by using the Organizer. The copied styles are added to the style sheet of the current document or template. When you copy styles, remember these rules:

- Copied styles replace styles with the same style names.
- Style names are case sensitive—if you copy a style named "HEAD" into a template or document that contains a style named "head," the copied style is added to the style sheet and does not replace the existing style.

You can also copy styles by using the Organizer. To open the Organizer, display and activate the Developer tab if necessary. Click the Document Template button. Click the Organizer button; then select the Styles tab.

Exercise 12-6   COPY STYLES TO ANOTHER TEMPLATE

1. Open the **New** tab, and click **Sample Templates**. Click to select the **Equity Lettter** template, click **Template**, and click **Create**.

2. Save the document as a template named *[your initials]***EquityLetter** in your Lesson 12 folder. Display the Styles task panel, and notice the list of styles. Close the document.

3. Open the template *[your initials]***Letterhead** revised in Exercise 12-5.

4. Click the **Developer** tab, and click the Document Template button 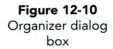. Click the **Organizer** button [Organizer...].

5. Click the **Styles** tab in the Organizer dialog box. On the left side of the dialog box, the Organizer lists the template and styles currently in use. You use the right side of the dialog box to copy styles to or from another template.

6. Click the **Close File** button [Close File] on the right side of the dialog box. The Normal template closes, and the **Close File** button changes to **Open File**.

7. Click the Open File button [Open File...]. In the Open dialog box, make sure **All Word Templates** appears in the **Files of type** box.

8. Locate the folder that contains the *[your initials]***EquityLetter** template.

9. Double-click the *[your initials]***EquityLetter** template. You can now choose styles from this template to copy into your letterhead template.

Figure 12-10
Organizer dialog box

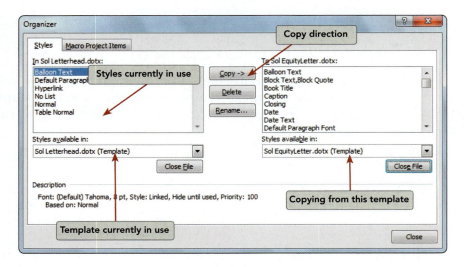

10. Scroll down the list of styles in the Equity Letter template. Click **Date Text** and click **Copy**.

11. Choose the **Normal** style from the Equity Letter style list. Notice the style description.

12. Click **Copy** and then click **Yes** to overwrite the existing style Normal.

13. Close the Organizer dialog box. The styles you chose from the Equity Letter template are copied to the current template. Notice that the Normal style from the Equity Letter template replaced the previous Normal style, so the text is formatted in Constantia 11 point with 8 points spacing after.

14. Click the Options link at the bottom of the Styles task pane. Click the down arrow for **Select styles to show** and select **All styles**. Click **OK**.

15. Apply the newly copied style Date Text to the date line. Modify the Normal style by changing the spacing after to 0 and changing the line spacing to single.

16. Close the template without saving changes.

Lesson 12   Summary

- A template is a reusable model for a particular type of document. Templates can contain formatting, text, and other elements. By default, all new documents are based on the Normal template.

- Word provides a variety of templates upon which you can base a new document or a new template. You can modify an existing template and save it with a new name. You can also modify an existing document and save it as a new template.

- Every document is based on a template. You can change the template assigned to an existing document by attaching a different template to the document, thereby making the new template's styles available in the document.

- To modify a template you created, open the Open dialog box and choose All Word Templates from the Files of type drop-down list. Locate and open the file.

- Instead of modifying template styles, use the Organizer to copy individual styles from one document or template to another.

LESSON 12		Command Summary	
Feature	Button	Command	Keyboard
Attach template	⊞	Developer tab, Templates group, Document Template	
Copy styles	⊞	Developer tab, Templates group, Document Template, Organizer	
Use a template		File tab, New	

Please visit our Online Learning Center, *www.lessonapproach2010.com*, where you will find the following review materials:

Concepts Review

True/False Questions

Short Answer Questions

Critical Thinking Questions

Skills Review

Review Exercises that target single skills

Lesson Applications

Review Exercises that challenge students by testing multiple skills in each exercise

On Your Own

Open-ended exercises that require students to synthesize multiple skills and apply creativity and problem-solving as they would in a real world business situation

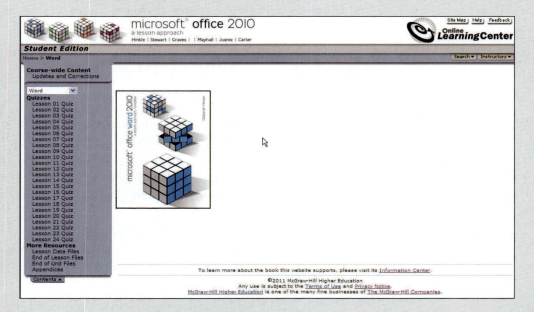

Please visit our Online Learning Center, *www.lessonapproach2010.com*, where you will find Unit Applications review materials.

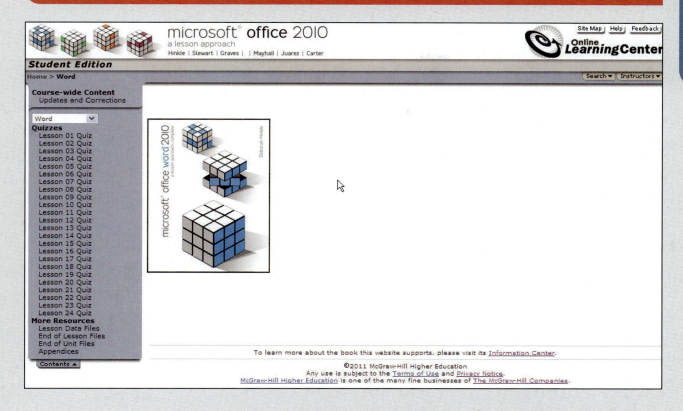

Site Map | Help | Feedback

microsoft® office 2010
a lesson approach
Hinkle | Stewart | Graves | | Mayhall | Juarez | Carter

Online
LearningCenter

Student Edition

Home > Word

Search ▼ | Instructors ▼

Course-wide Content
Updates and Corrections

Word ▼
Quizzes
Lesson 01 Quiz
Lesson 02 Quiz
Lesson 03 Quiz
Lesson 04 Quiz
Lesson 05 Quiz
Lesson 06 Quiz
Lesson 07 Quiz
Lesson 08 Quiz
Lesson 09 Quiz
Lesson 10 Quiz
Lesson 11 Quiz
Lesson 12 Quiz
Lesson 13 Quiz
Lesson 14 Quiz
Lesson 15 Quiz
Lesson 16 Quiz
Lesson 17 Quiz
Lesson 18 Quiz
Lesson 19 Quiz
Lesson 20 Quiz
Lesson 21 Quiz
Lesson 22 Quiz
Lesson 23 Quiz
Lesson 24 Quiz
More Resources
Lesson Data Files
End of Lesson Files
End of Unit Files
Appendices

Contents ▲

To learn more about the book this website supports, please visit its Information Center.

©2011 McGraw-Hill Higher Education
Any use is subject to the Terms of Use and Privacy Notice.
McGraw-Hill Higher Education is one of the many fine businesses of The McGraw-Hill Companies.

Microsoft® Office Excel 2010

A Lesson Approach, Complete

CASE STUDY

There's more to learning a spreadsheet program like Microsoft Office Excel than simply keying data and formulas. You need to know how to use Excel in a real-world situation. That's why all the lessons in this book relate to common business tasks.

As you work through the lessons, imagine yourself working at AllAround Vision Care, a fictional eye care group that offers eye exams, eyeglasses and contact lenses, corrective vision surgery, and more. In addition to its eye care centers, AllAround Vision Care cooperates with a nonprofit entity named the WorldWide Campaign. It works to identify adults and children who need medical and financial assistance with corrective eyewear, sunglasses, vision exercises, and surgery.

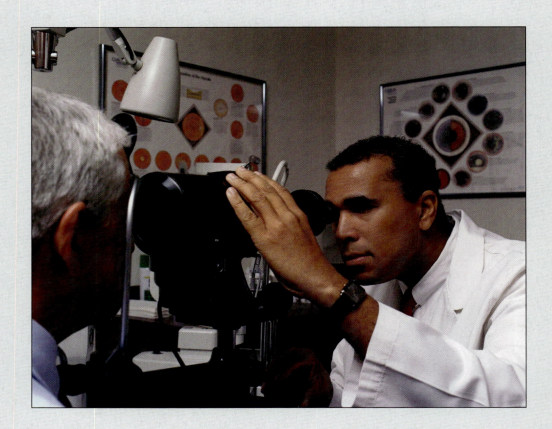

AllAround Vision Care

AllAround Vision Care was started in 2006 by Henry Conrad. Henry, an ophthalmologist with 10 years of experience, opened two offices in the Chicago area and entered into agreements with other ophthalmologists and optometrists for staffing these locations. Henry's sister, Rita, helped set up the offices and was instrumental in starting work with the WorldWide Campaign. AllAround Vision Care now has eye care centers in Chicago, Boston, Seattle, and Dallas. Its work with the WorldWide campaign is global.

The worksheets, data, and graphics you will use in this course relate to AllAround Vision Care eye centers and its not-for-profit work with the WorldWide Campaign. As you work with the worksheets in the text, take notice of the following:

- The *data*, *formulas*, and *worksheets* required to carry on day-to-day activities.
- The *layout* and *design* of worksheets. Worksheets prepared for customers and patients, contributors, or regulatory agencies require a professional look. Formatting is less important for internal worksheets.
- The types of business *activities* required by an organization such as AllAround Vision Care. It must deal with receipts and expenditures, customer and patient data, insurance information, employee records, government records, supplies, and more.

As you use this text and become more experienced with Microsoft Office Excel, you will gain expertise in creating, editing, and formatting worksheets generated in a real-life professional environment.

Unit 1

INTRODUCTION TO EXCEL

Getting Acquainted with Excel

OBJECTIVES *After completing this lesson, you will be able to:*

1. Navigate in a workbook.

2. Edit data in a worksheet.

3. Work with columns and rows.

4. Save workbook files.

5. Print Excel files.

6. Get acquainted with Excel functions.

7. Use alignment, borders, and fill.

8. Get acquainted with an Excel chart.

Estimated Time: 1½ hours

Microsoft Excel is an *electronic spreadsheet*. The term "spread" comes from ledger sheets that spread across facing pages in a journal used many years ago by bookkeepers and accountants. These paper pages had rows and columns used for entering names and numbers that allowed the accountant to track, calculate, and analyze business activities. The accountant used a separate calculator and manually entered arithmetic results when needed into a paper worksheet. If a letter, report, or presentation were needed, data might need to be copied or reentered somewhere else to prepare it.

Figure 1-1 is a sample of a ledger page that tracks sales of eyeglass frames for AllAround Vision Care for a 4-year period. It shows the name of the frame and the total number sold per year. There is also a column that shows the average for the 4-year period and another column for the total.

Figure 1-1
Illustration of ledger page

AllAround Vision Care						
Web Sales of Frames (Worldwide)						
Frame Name	Year 1	Year 2	Year 3	Year 4	Average	Total
1 Antilles	100	110	90	100	100	400
2 Chaos	120	130	80	120	113	450
3 Flashy	140	120	110	130	125	500
4 Independence	170	140	100	120	133	530
5 Moonlight	120	80	120	110	108	430
6 Never Blue	180	160	140	90	143	570
7 Newton	100	120	130	70	105	420
8 Now or Never	180	190	170	60	150	600
9 Poppy	200	180	160	100	160	640
10 Techno	210	170	150	120	163	650
11 Ubie	190	150	120	140	150	600
12 Vermont	170	140	140	130	145	580
13 Winifred	150	130	180	120	145	580
14 Zonked	120	110	120	110	115	460
15 Frame Totals	2,150	1,930	1,810	1,520	1,853	7,410

An Excel workbook moves this type of work to the computer. Data are entered in a similar way, in rows and columns. Arithmetic results, when needed, are calculated by Excel. Changes to the data are accomplished by keying new values, and arithmetic results are automatically updated. The data are easily formatted into an attractive report that can be printed or electronically distributed. You will be working with the data shown in Figure 1-1 throughout this lesson and will be able to compare your Excel worksheet to this illustration.

Companies and individuals use Excel to monitor and track information, to compute various results, and to prepare easy-to-read formatted reports. AllAround Vision Care, an eye care center, uses Excel to keep and track patient accounts, to monitor sales of products, to compare and analyze office procedures and surgeries, to manage payroll and insurance information, and much more. In this course, you will be working with workbooks from AllAround Vision Care to learn about Excel's features and commands.

Navigating in a Workbook

A *workbook* is the file Excel creates to store your data. Generally, a workbook should deal with related data. A company such as AllAround Vision Care might keep one workbook for current patient accounts. In that workbook, there might be a sheet for each doctor that lists his or her patients. Or the company might list all patients on one worksheet with doctors and insurance companies shown on separate sheets. The company might then have another workbook that maintains employee payroll information, separate from the patient data.

A *worksheet* is an individual page or sheet in a workbook. A workbook must have at least one worksheet and can have as many as your computer's memory allows.

Each worksheet is divided into *rows* and *columns*. The rows are numbered and reach row 1,048,576. There are 16,384 columns, lettered from A to Z, then AA to AZ, BA to BZ, AAA to AAZ, ABA to ABZ, and so on, up to column XFD.

The intersection of a row and a column forms a rectangle known as a *cell*. You enter data (text, a number, or a formula) into a cell. Cells have *cell addresses* or *cell references*, which identify where a cell is located on the worksheet. Cell B2, for example, is the cell in column B, row 2.

The *active cell* is the cell that appears outlined with a thick border. It is ready to accept data or a formula, or if it already contains data or a formula, it is ready to be modified. When you open a new workbook, the active cell is cell A1, the top-left cell in the worksheet. Cell A1 is referred to as "Home."

The mouse pointer displays as a thick white cross when you move it across cells in a worksheet. When you point at a Ribbon or worksheet tab, a command button, or a menu item, the pointer turns into a white arrow.

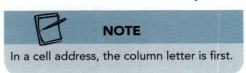

NOTE

In a cell address, the column letter is first.

NOTE

Pointing and resting the mouse pointer on a button or command name is known as "hovering."

Figure 1-2
Excel worksheet screen

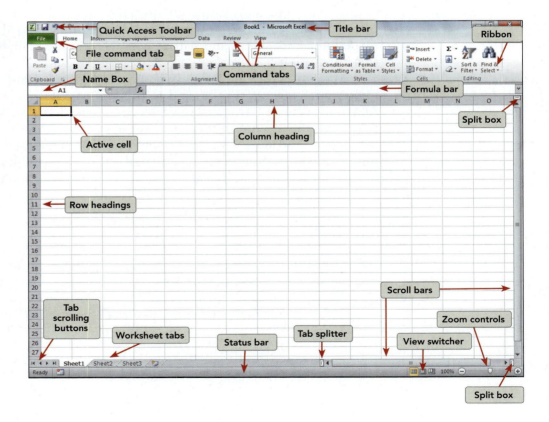

TABLE 1-1 Parts of the Excel Screen

Part of Screen	Purpose
Active cell	The cell outlined in a heavy black border. It is ready to accept new data, a formula, or your edits.
Column headings	Alphabetic characters across the top of the worksheet that identify columns.
Command tabs	Ribbon tab controls with command buttons, galleries, and other controls for creating, managing, editing, and formatting data.
Formula bar	Displays the contents of the active cell. You can enter text, numbers, or formulas in the formula bar. It can be expanded and collapsed.
File command tab	Opens Backstage view with information about the current state of the workbook and access to commands for saving, printing, and distributing workbooks.
Name Box	A drop-down combo box that shows the address of the active cell. You can use it to move the pointer to a specific location.
Quick Access Toolbar	Toolbar with shortcut command buttons for common tasks.
Ribbon	Organizes and displays command tabs.
Row headings	Numbers down the left side of the worksheet that identify rows.
Scroll bars	Used to move different parts of the screen into view.
Split box	Divides the window into two panes showing the same worksheet. There is a vertical and a horizontal split box.
Status bar	Displays information about the current task and mode of operation as well as view choices and the Zoom control.
Tab scrolling buttons	Navigation buttons to scroll through worksheet tabs.
Tab splitter	Adjusts the width of the horizontal scroll bar to show more or fewer worksheet tabs.
Title bar	Contains the program name and the name of the workbook.
View switcher	Buttons to change the current view to Normal, Page Layout, or Page Break Preview.
Worksheet tabs	Indicators at the bottom of the worksheet to identify sheets in the workbook.
Zoom controls	Buttons and slider to change the view magnification.

Exercise 1-1 EXPLORE THE EXCEL WINDOW

Excel opens with a new, blank workbook. You can see the the Quick Access Toolbar and the Ribbon (see Figure 1-2). New workbooks are named **Book1**, **Book2**, and so on during a work session; those names are replaced by the file names you provide when you save your work.

The *File* command tab is the green tab at the left of the window. It opens Backstage view, an interactive window that consolidates information about the workbook and provides access to Save, Print, and Share commands. Backstage view has a Navigation pane to choose a category of tasks. Then each pane has Quick commands for saving, printing, or distributing your workbook. The *Ribbon* is a set of command tabs across the top of the Excel window. Each command tab (except the File tab) has buttons, galleries, or other controls related to a specific task group or object. Some command tabs are context-sensitive and appear only when needed to accommodate what you are doing. The *Quick Access Toolbar* is above the Ribbon and provides one-click access to frequently used commands. You can add command buttons to this toolbar, and you can reposition it below the Ribbon. In Excel 2010, you can also customize the Ribbon to add your own group (or tab) with command buttons.

NOTE

The command tabs in the Ribbon are similar to panes or tabs in a dialog box.

Your screen size and resolution affect how the command buttons look and how much data you see at once. Your buttons may include explanatory text, and you may see more or fewer rows and columns than what appears in illustrations in this text.

Use the left mouse button to carry out commands unless the instructions explicitly say to right-click.

1. Start Excel. A blank workbook named **Book1** opens.

2. Click the **File** command tab. When a workbook is open, Backstage view opens to the Information pane. The Quick command groups are Permissions, Prepare for Sharing, and Versions. The right panel displays some of the file properties and provides access to others. A *property* is a piece of information about the workbook. It might include a descriptive title, file size, revision dates, and more.

Figure 1-3
Backstage view information

3. Click the **Home** command. Commands on this tab are organized into seven groups: Clipboard, Font, Alignment, Number, Styles, Cells, and Editing.

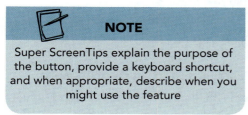

NOTE

Super ScreenTips explain the purpose of the button, provide a keyboard shortcut, and when appropriate, describe when you might use the feature

4. In the **Font** group, rest the mouse pointer on the Bold button ⃞ᴮ . A *super ScreenTip* includes the button name, a brief description of the button's function, and its keyboard shortcut.

5. In the **Font** group, rest the mouse pointer on the Dialog Box Launcher. A super ScreenTip describes and previews the dialog box that will be opened when you click this button. Many command groups have a dialog box launcher, and it opens the dialog box that includes commands for that group.

Figure 1-4
Dialog Box Launcher for the Font group

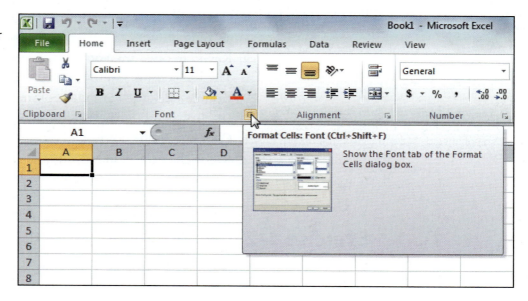

6. Click the Dialog Box Launcher for the **Font** group. The Format Cells dialog box opens with the **Font** tab visible.

7. Click **Cancel** to close the dialog box.

8. Click the **View** command tab. Commands on this tab are organized into five groups: Workbook Views, Show, Zoom, Window, and Macros.

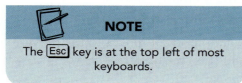

NOTE

The ⃞Esc key is at the top left of most keyboards.

9. In the **Workbook Views** group, move the mouse pointer to the Full Screen button ⃞ and click. A Full Screen view shows only worksheet cells with row and column headings.

10. Press ⃞Esc on the keyboard to return to normal view.

11. Click the Page Layout view button ⃞. This view is an interactive preview of how the page will print and shows margins, the ruler, header, and footer areas.

NOTE

When Key Tips are visible, press Tab or an arrow key to move through tasks in the current group.

TIP

The keyboard shortcut to collapse or expand the Ribbon is Ctrl + F1. You can also collapse or expand it from the up or down arrow next to the Microsoft Office Excel Help button 🔵.

12. Click the Normal button 🔲 .

13. Press and release the Alt key. *Key Tips* appear over a command name when you press the Alt key. They show keyboard shortcuts.

14. Key **h** to activate the **Home** command tab.

15. Press Tab. The focus moves to the Paste button 📋 in the Clipboard group, and the Key Tips are no longer visible.

16. Press Tab again. The focus moves to the Cut button ✂ in the Clipboard group.

17. Press Esc.

18. Press F10. This is another keyboard shortcut to display Key Tips. Note that the keyboard shortcuts for commands in the Quick Access Toolbar use numbers rather than letters.

19. Key **m** to open the **Formulas** command tab. Press Tab. The focus moves to the Insert Function button ƒx .

20. Double-click the **Formulas** command tab. The Ribbon collapses and more working space is available.

21. Click the **Home** command tab.

22. Right-click the **Home** command tab. Remove the checkmark for **Minimize the Ribbon**. You can right-click any tab to expand or collapse the Ribbon.

Exercise 1-2   MOVE BETWEEN WORKSHEETS

As you work with a new or an existing workbook, you must know how to move around within it. A new workbook has three worksheets named **Sheet1**, **Sheet2**, and **Sheet3**. **Sheet1** is displayed when a new workbook is opened. The worksheet names appear on the tabs, located along the bottom of the sheet above the status bar. Colors on your computer may be different from illustrations in this text if your workstation is set to use a different color scheme.

NOTE

Cell A1 is the active cell on all three worksheets in a new workbook.

NOTE

When keyboard combinations (such as Ctrl + PageUp) are shown in this text, hold down the first key without releasing it and press the second key. Release the second key and then release the first key.

1. Click the **Sheet2** worksheet tab. The tab for the active sheet is white, and the tab name is bold.

2. Click the **Sheet3** tab. All three sheets are empty.

3. Press Ctrl + PageUp. This shortcut moves to the previous worksheet, **Sheet2**, in this case.

4. Press Ctrl + PageDown. This command moves to the next worksheet, **Sheet3**.

5. Click the **Sheet1** tab to return to **Sheet1**.

Exercise 1-3 GO TO A SPECIFIC CELL

When you move the mouse pointer to a cell and click, the cell you click becomes the active cell. The active cell is the one that will be affected when you give a command. It is outlined with a black border, and you see its address in the *Name Box*. The Name Box is a drop-down combo box at the left edge of the formula bar. You can also determine the active cell address by the orange-shaded column and row headings. Rows and columns are separated by *gridlines* on screen which, as a default, do not print.

1. Move the mouse pointer to cell D4 and click. Cell D4 is the active cell, and its address appears in the Name Box. The column D and row 4 headings are shaded.

Figure 1-5
Active cell showing a thick border

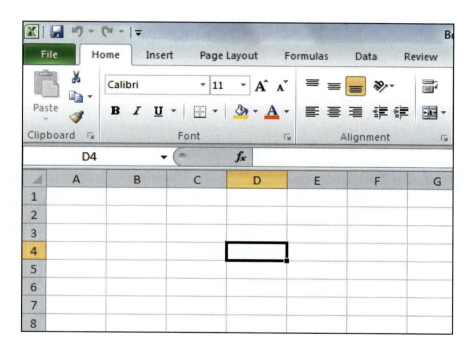

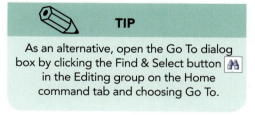
TIP

As an alternative, open the Go To dialog box by clicking the Find & Select button in the Editing group on the Home command tab and choosing Go To.

2. Press [Ctrl]+[Home]. This shortcut makes cell A1 the active cell.

3. Press [Ctrl]+[G] to open the Go To dialog box.

4. Key **b19** in the **Reference** box and press [Enter]. Cell B19 becomes the active cell, and its address is shown in the Name Box.

5. Press [Ctrl]+[G]. Recently used cell addresses are listed in the **Go to** list in the Go To dialog box.

6. Key **c2** and click **OK**.

7. Click in the **Name Box**. The current cell address is highlighted.

8. Key **a8** in the Name Box and press [Enter].

9. Click in the **Name Box**. Key **b2:d4** in the Name Box and press [Enter]. This identifies and highlights a *range* or group of cells (see Figure 1-6 on the next page).

Figure 1-6
Keying a range
address in the Name
Box

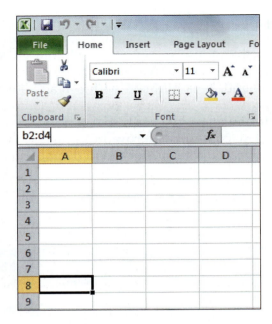

10. Press Ctrl+Home to return to cell A1.

TABLE 1-2 Navigation Commands in a Workbook

Press	To Do This
Ctrl+Home	Move to the beginning of the worksheet.
Ctrl+End	Move to the last used cell on the worksheet.
Home	Move to the beginning of the current row.
Click	Move to the cell that is clicked.
Ctrl+G or F5	Open the Go To dialog box.
Enter	Move one cell down in the current column.
Shift+Enter	Move one cell up in the current column.
Tab	Move to the next cell in a left-to-right sequence.
Shift+Tab	Move to the previous cell in a right-to-left sequence.
PageUp	Move up one screen.
PageDown	Move down one screen.
Alt+PageUp	Move one screen to the left.
Alt+PageDown	Move one screen to the right.
↑, ↓, ←, →	Move one cell up, down, left, or right.
Ctrl+arrow key	Move to the edge of a group of cells with data.
Ctrl+Backspace	Move to the active cell when it has scrolled out of view.
Ctrl+PageUp	Move to the previous worksheet.
Ctrl+PageDown	Move to the next worksheet.

Exercise 1-4   SCROLL THROUGH A WORKSHEET

Because a worksheet has millions of cells, it can hold a lot of data, much of which are out of view at any given time. If you need to verify a name or number in row 235, you need to scroll through the sheet. Scrolling through a worksheet does not change the active cell. Instead, the worksheet moves on the screen so that you see different columns or rows. The number of rows and columns you see at once depends on screen resolution and the Zoom size in Excel.

TABLE 1-3 Scrolling Through a Worksheet

To Move the View	Do This
One row up	Click the up scroll arrow.
One row down	Click the down scroll arrow.
Up one screen	Click the scroll bar above the scroll box.
Down one screen	Click the scroll bar below the scroll box.
To any relative position	Drag the scroll bar up or down.
One column to the right	Click the right scroll arrow.
One column to the left	Click the left scroll arrow.

1. On the vertical scroll bar, click below the scroll box. The worksheet has been repositioned so that you see the next group of about 20 to 30 rows.

2. Click above the vertical scroll box. The worksheet has scrolled up to show the top rows.

3. Click the right scroll arrow on the horizontal scroll bar once. The worksheet scrolls one column to the right.

4. Click the left scroll arrow once to bring the column back into view.

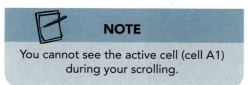

NOTE

You cannot see the active cell (cell A1) during your scrolling.

5. Click the down scroll arrow on the vertical scroll bar twice.

6. Drag the vertical scroll box to the top of the vertical scroll bar. As you drag, a ScreenTip displays the row number at the top of the window. During all this scrolling, the active cell is still cell A1.

Exercise 1-5   CHANGE THE ZOOM SIZE

The *Zoom size* controls how much of the worksheet you see on the screen, how large the data appear, and your need to scroll. The 100% size shows the data close to print size. A Zoom slider and two buttons are at the right edge of the status bar.

1. Click the Zoom In button ⊕ on the status bar. The worksheet is resized to 110%, and you see fewer columns and rows (see Figure 1-7 on the next page).

Figure 1-7
Changing the zoom
size

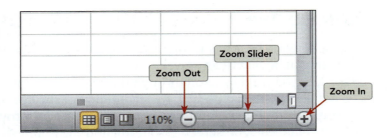

2. Click the Zoom Out button ⊖. The worksheet is reduced to 100% magnification.

3. Click the Zoom Out button ⊖ again. Each click changes the magnification by 10%.

4. Point at the Zoom slider ⬜, hold down the mouse button, and drag the slider slowly in either direction. You can set any magnification size.

5. Click the **View** command tab. There is a Zoom button 🔍 on this tab.

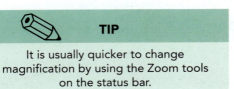

TIP

It is usually quicker to change magnification by using the Zoom tools on the status bar.

6. Click the Zoom button 🔍. The Zoom dialog box opens.

7. Choose **200%**. Click **OK**.

8. Click **200%** in the status bar. The same dialog box opens.

9. Choose **100%** and click **OK**.

Exercise 1-6 CLOSE A WORKBOOK WITHOUT SAVING

Generally, you should save your work when closing a workbook. To ensure that you do, Excel will display a message box asking you to save the workbook if there have been changes made. However, you can close a workbook without saving. You might do this when you are experimenting with a new calculation or a new format for your work.

To close a workbook, you can:

*   Click the Close Window button ⊠ at the right end of the Ribbon.

*   Click the **File** command tab and choose **Close**.

*   Use keyboard shortcuts, Ctrl + W or Ctrl + F4.

1. Click the Close Window button ⊠ at the right top edge of the Ribbon.

2. If you have made a change to the workbook, a dialog box asks if you want to save the changes. Click **Don't Save** if this message box opens.

3. The workbook closes, and a blank blue-gray screen appears. No workbook is open.

4. Click the **File** command tab. When no workbook is open, Backstage view opens with the Recent Workbooks pane. This view lists the most recently used workbooks at your computer. You can choose one from the list when it is what you want to open.

5. Choose **New** from the navigation list. Available templates are categorized in Backstage view. A template is a model workbook with margin settings, font choices, and more. To create a new blank workbook, you choose **Blank workbook**. You can either double-click that icon or click **Create** in the preview area.

Figure 1-8
Creating a new
workbook from
Backstage view

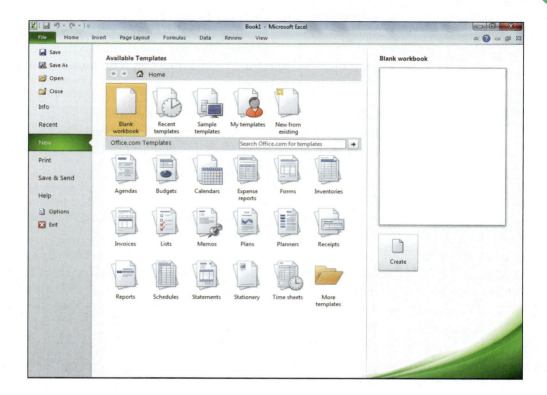

6. Create a new workbook.

7. Click the **File** command tab and choose **Close**. You are back to the blank blue-gray screen with no workbook open.

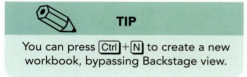

TIP

You can press Ctrl + N to create a new workbook, bypassing Backstage view.

Editing Data in a Worksheet

For AllAround Vision Care, common tasks include editing a patient's account, updating payment information, or adding a new eyeglass frame to the inventory. If calculations are involved, they are automatically updated as soon as changes are made. You can edit data by keying new data or by changing existing information.

Worksheet cells contain text, numbers, or formulas. Any of these data types can be keyed, edited, or deleted. A *formula* calculates an arithmetic result and is placed in the cell where the results are to be displayed. The formula bar above the column headings displays the contents of the active cell, whether it is text, a number, or a formula.

Exercise 1-7   OPEN A WORKBOOK

NOTE

All workbooks in this course relate to the case study about AllAround Vision Care, a fictional eye care establishment (see frontmatter).

You will use the **Excel_Lesson1** workbook for your work in this lesson. This workbook has two worksheets. The sheets have been named **EyeglassSales** and **Chart** to indicate what is on each sheet. The **EyeglassSales** worksheet shows an eyeglass frame name in the first column (A). The next four columns (B through E) show values, the number of each frame sold per year. The sixth column (F) calculates the total number sold for each frame style. The numbers in this column were not keyed; they are calculated.

The worksheet named **Chart** is a chart sheet. It does not have worksheet cells; instead it has a bar chart that depicts the values shown in column F and names in column A on the **EyeglassSales** worksheet.

There are several ways to open an existing workbook.

- Click the File command tab and choose Open.
- Use the keyboard shortcut Ctrl+O or Ctrl+F12.
- Navigate through folders in Windows Explorer or Computer to find and double-click the workbook name.

When you open a workbook from the Internet, from an e-mail attachment, or from a potentially unsafe location, it will open in Protected View. In Protected View, a workbook cannot be edited. A default setting in Excel's Trust Center Settings opens workbooks from such locations with restricted editing because they might contain malware which can harm your computer. You can view the workbook to evaluate its source and its contents. When you are confident that the file is safe, you can exit Protected View and edit the workbook as usual. Protected View displays a security message panel across the top of the worksheet, below the command tabs. The file name in title bar shows [Protected View].

Figure 1-9
Protective View

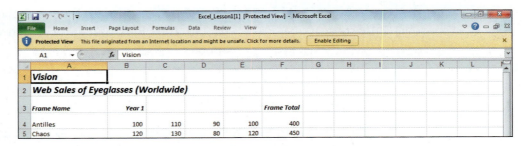

1. Click the **File** command tab and choose **Open**. The navigation line shows the most recently used folder.

2. Navigate to the drive and folder where the data files for this lesson are located.

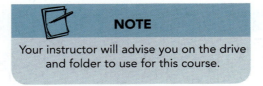

NOTE

Your instructor will advise you on the drive and folder to use for this course.

3. Find and double-click **Excel_Lesson1**. The workbook opens with the **EyeglassSales** worksheet visible. If you have opened this workbook from an Internet location, you'll see the security message panel below the command tabs.

4. If the security message panel for Protected View is open, click **Enable Editing** to continue.

5. Click the **Chart** worksheet tab. This bar chart illustrates total sales for each eyeglass frame listed.

6. Press Ctrl+PageUp. This moves to the **EyeglassSales** worksheet.

7. Press Ctrl+PageDown. The active tab is the **Chart** sheet.

8. Click the **EyeglassSales** tab.

Exercise 1-8 REVIEW AND EDIT CELL CONTENTS

When the workbook is in Ready mode, you can key, edit, or replace the contents of a cell. To replace a cell's contents, make it the active cell, key the new data, and press Enter. You can also click the Enter button ✓ in the formula bar or press any arrow key on the keyboard to complete any editing. The Enter button ✓ appears to the left of the formula bar only when you are keying or editing a cell's contents.

If you replace a number used in a formula, the formula automatically recalculates when you complete your change.

REVIEW

If you cannot see column F or row 21, adjust the zoom size.

Figure 1-10
Editing cell contents
**Excel_Lesson1.xlsx
EyeglassSales
Sheet**

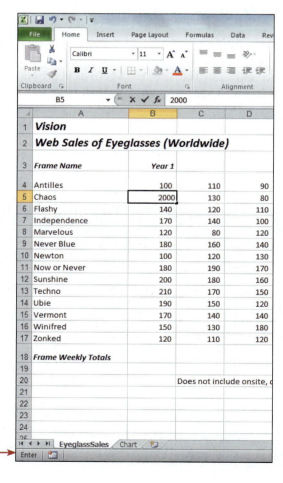

1. Press F5 to open the Go To dialog box.

2. Key **a5** and press Enter. The active cell is changed to cell A5. This cell contains the name of one of the frames (Chaos), which you can see in the formula bar and on the worksheet.

3. Press F5, key **c10**, and press Enter. Cell C10 contains a number, a value.

4. Click cell F17. Cell F17 contains a formula, which you can see in the formula bar. Formulas calculate a result.

5. Click cell B5 to make it the active cell.

6. Key **2000** without a comma. As you key the number, it appears in the cell and in the formula bar. The status bar shows "Enter" to indicate that you are in Enter mode (at the far left).

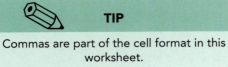

TIP

Commas are part of the cell format in this worksheet.

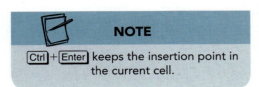

NOTE

Ctrl + Enter keeps the insertion point in the current cell.

7. Press Enter. Excel inserts a comma, and the next cell in column B is active. The "Frame Total" (cell F5, 2,330) is recalculated. The worksheet returns to Ready mode.

8. Press ↑ to move to cell B5. Key **1000** without a comma. Click the Enter button ✔ at the left in the formula bar. Notice that when you use the Enter button ✔, the pointer stays in cell B5.

9. Click the **Chart** sheet tab. Notice the length of the Chaos bar; Excel also adjusted the number scale to better show the value differences.

10. Click the **EyeglassSales** worksheet tab.

11. In cell B5, key **0**, and press Ctrl + Enter. Notice that cell B5 is active, and that a zero is represented as a short dash in this worksheet.

12. Click the **Chart** sheet tab. The chart is based on the data in the **EyeglassSales** sheet. Everything has been recalculated.

13. Click the **EyeglassSales** worksheet tab, and key **100** in cell B5. Press →.

Exercise 1-9   USE EDIT MODE

If a cell contains a long or complicated text entry or a formula with a minor error, you can edit it rather than rekeying an entire entry. This, of course, saves time and can contribute to accuracy since fewer keystrokes are required. There are several ways to start Edit mode:

- Double-click the cell.
- Click the cell and press F2.
- Click the cell, and then click anywhere in the formula bar.

TABLE 1-4   Keyboard Shortcuts in Edit Mode

Key	To Do This
Enter	Complete the edit, return to Ready mode, and move the insertion point to the next cell.
Alt + Enter	Move the insertion point to a new line within the cell, a line break.
Esc	Cancel the edit and restore the existing data.
Home	Move the insertion point to the beginning of the data.
End	Move the insertion point to the end of the data.
Delete	Delete one character to the right of the insertion point.
Ctrl + Delete	Delete everything from the insertion point to the end of the line.
Backspace	Delete one character to the left of the insertion point.
← or →	Move the insertion point one character left or right.
Ctrl + ←	Move the insertion point one word left.
Ctrl + →	Move the insertion point one word right.

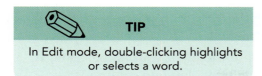

TIP

In Edit mode, double-clicking highlights or selects a word.

1. Click cell A2. The text in cell A2 is longer than the width of column A, and its display overlaps into columns B and C.

2. Press F2. Edit mode is shown in the status bar. An insertion point appears in the cell at the end of the text.

3. Double-click **Eyeglasses** in the cell. A *Mini toolbar* appears with buttons for font editing. This toolbar appears when text within a cell or a chart object is highlighted.

4. Point at the Mini toolbar. Its appearance brightens for easy viewing. The Mini toolbar duplicates buttons in the Font group on the Home command tab.

Figure 1-11
Using Edit mode
Excel_Lesson1.xlsx
EyeglassSales Sheet

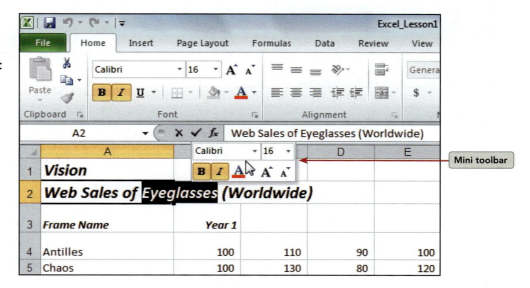

5. Key **Frames**. It replaces the word "Eyeglasses." The Mini toolbar has disappeared.

6. Press Enter to complete the edit. Pressing Enter does not start a new line in the cell when the worksheet is in Edit mode.

7. Double-click cell A1. This starts Edit mode, and an insertion point appears in the cell.

8. Press the Home key on the keyboard. The insertion point moves to the first position in the cell.

9. Key **AllAround** and press Spacebar.

10. Press the End key on the keyboard. The insertion point moves to the end of the text.

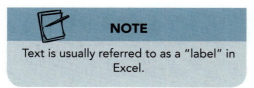

NOTE

Text is usually referred to as a "label" in Excel.

11. Press Spacebar and key **Care**. Press Enter.

12. Double-click cell A18. Edit mode starts.

13. Double-click **Weekly** and press Delete on the keyboard two times. The first press of the key deletes the word; the second press deletes the space.

14. Press Enter. The new label is "Frame Totals."

15. Click cell A22. There is nothing in this cell.

16. Key *[Your First and Last Name]* and press Enter. If your name is longer than column A, part of its display might overlap into column B.

Exercise 1-10 CLEAR CELL CONTENTS

When you clear the contents of a cell, you delete the text, number, or formula in that cell. You can clear cell contents by simply pressing the Delete key on the keyboard while the cell is active. You can also click the Clear button on the Home command tab in the Editing group.

> **NOTE**
>
> A green triangle in the top left corner of a cell indicates that a formula error has occurred if this error type is active at your computer. Ignore the triangles for now.

1. Click cell B5. Press Delete on the keyboard. The number is deleted, and Excel recalculates the formula results in cell F5. This cell is now empty, and there may be a small green triangle in the top left corner.

2. Press → to move the pointer to cell C5.

3. On the **Home** command tab in the **Editing** group, click the Clear button .

4. Choose **Clear Contents**. The value is deleted, and formula is recalculated.

Exercise 1-11 USE UNDO AND REDO

The Undo command reverses the last action you performed in the worksheet. For example, if you delete the contents of a cell, the Undo command restores what you deleted. The Redo command reverses the action of the Undo command. It "undoes" your Undo. These commands enable you to try a value or a format and then change your mind.

To use the Undo command, you can:

• Click the Undo button 🔄 on the Quick Access Toolbar.

• Press Ctrl+Z or Alt+Backspace.

To use the Redo command, you can:

• Click the Redo button 🔄 on the Quick Access Toolbar.

• Press Ctrl+Y or F4.

> **NOTE**
>
> The ScreenTip for the Undo button includes the most recent task, such as Undo Clear.

Excel keeps a history or list of your editing commands, and you can undo several at once.

1. Click the Undo button . The number in cell C5 is restored.

2. Click the Redo button 🔄. The number is cleared again.

3. Click cell A8 and key **Moonlight**. Press Enter.

4. In cell A12 key **Poppy** and press Enter.

5. Click the arrow next to the Undo button ↺ to display the history list.

6. Move the mouse to highlight the top two actions and click. The last two changes are undone, and the original frame names are restored.

Figure 1-12
Undoing multiple edits
Excel_Lesson1.xlsx
EyeglassSales Sheet

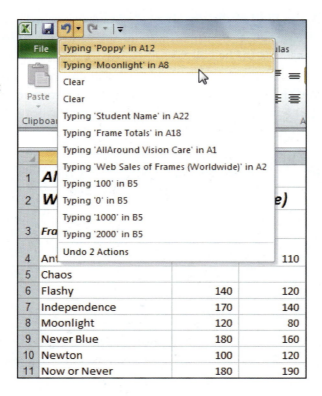

7. Click the Redo button ↻. The first action is restored.

8. Click the Redo button ↻ again. The revised names are back.

NOTE

Depending on the actions that have been undone and redone on your computer, your list might be different from the one shown in Figure 1-11.

Exercise 1-12 FILL A LABEL SERIES

A *series* is a list of labels (text), values (numbers), dates, or times that follows a pattern. An example of a label series for this worksheet is "Year 1, Year 2, Year 3, and Year 4" in row 3. Excel can complete many series automatically which speeds data entry. Some series are recognized by your keying one of the items; others require that you key at least two of the items.

The *Fill handle* is the easiest way to fill a series. The Fill handle is a tiny square at the lower right corner of a selected cell. Depending on the cell contents, the Fill handle can fill or copy data.

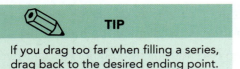

TIP

If you drag too far when filling a series, drag back to the desired ending point.

1. Click cell B3. This label is correct and is the first in a series that should end with "Year 4" in cell E3.

2. Rest the mouse pointer on the Fill handle for cell B3. The Fill handle is active when the pointer changes to a black cross.

3. Click the Fill handle, and drag right across cells C3 and D3 to reach cell E3. The labels are completed, and the AutoFill Options button appears next to the cell E3.

4. Rest the mouse pointer on the AutoFill Options button. Click its arrow. The options depend on the type of data and whether you gave the Fill command using the handle or the Ribbon. In this case, you just want to fill a series.

Figure 1-13
Filling a label series
Excel_Lesson1.xlsx
Eyeglass Sheet

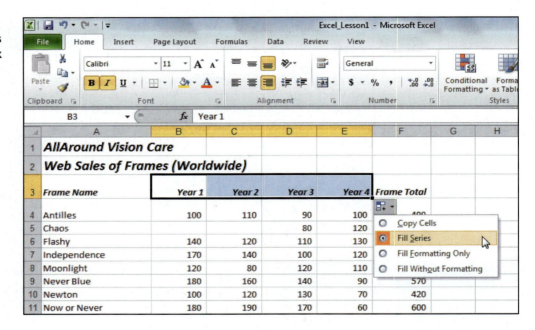

5. Press Esc on the keyboard. The option menu is closed, and no changes are made.

6. Press Ctrl+Home.

Working with Columns and Rows

In a new workbook, columns are 8.43 spaces (64 pixels) wide, usually not wide enough to accommodate a long name or large number. If the column on the right of a cell is empty, a label (text) wider than 8.43 spaces spills into it so that you can see the entire label or name on screen. If the column on the right is not empty, the label is truncated or cut off so that you only see part of it. If a number is too long or wide for a cell, the cell displays a series of number symbols (####). In either situation, you can widen the column so that the data are visible.

Rows in a new workbook are 15 points (20 pixels) high to fit the default 11-point Calibri font. Font size is measured in points; a *point* is 1/72 inch. If you format labels or values with larger font sizes, the row may not be tall enough. Generally, Excel resizes the row height if you use a larger font, but you can size it manually too.

Resizing column widths and row heights is a formatting method to increase readability. Here are the ways you can resize column widths and row heights:

- Drag a column or row border to a different size.

- Double-click a column's right border to autofit the column. *Autofit* means the column is widened to fit the longest entry in the column.

- Double-click a row's bottom border to autofit the row height. A row is autofitted to fit the largest font size currently used in the row.

- On the Home tab in the Cells group, click the Format button 🗒 and then choose **Row Height** or **Column Width**.

When you use the mouse to change the row height or column width, you will see the size in a ScreenTip. For rows, the height is shown in points (as it is for fonts) as well as in pixels. For columns, the width is shown in character spaces and in pixels. A *pixel* is a screen dot, a single point of color on the screen. A *character space* is the average width of a numeric character in the standard font used in the worksheet.

If you use Ribbon commands to change the column width or row height, you must key the entry by using points for row height or character spaces for column width.

Exercise 1-13 MODIFY ROW HEIGHT

As you adjust the row height and column width in these exercises, use settings as close as possible to the values shown in the step.

1. Place the pointer on the horizontal border between the headings for rows 4 and 5. The pointer turns into a two-headed, solid black arrow.

2. Drag up until the ScreenTip shows **15.00 (20 pixels)** and release the mouse button.

Figure 1-14
Resizing rows

	A	B	C	D
1	**AllAround Vision Care**			
2	**Web Sales of Frames (Worldwide)**			
3	*Frame Name*	*Year 1*	*Year 2*	*Year 3*
4	Height: 15.00 (20 pixels)			
5	Antilles	100	110	90
6	Chaos			80
7	Flashy	140	120	110
8	Independence	170	140	100
9	Moonlight	120	80	120
10	Never Blue	180	160	140

3.   Click anywhere in row 18.

4.   In the **Cells** group, click the Format button and choose **Row Height**. The Row Height dialog box opens.

5.   Key **15** and press Enter. The row is 15 points (20 pixels) high.

Exercise 1-14   MODIFY COLUMN WIDTH

1.   Place the pointer on the vertical border between the column headings for columns A and B. The pointer changes to a two-headed arrow with a wide vertical bar.

> **TIP**
>
> Be careful about autofitting columns that include titles in rows 1 or 2. Excel will autofit a column to accommodate long labels.

2.   Drag the sizing pointer to the left until the ScreenTip shows **17.86 (130 pixels)**, and release the mouse button.

3.   Place the pointer between the column headings for columns A and B. Double-click. Excel autofits column A to fit the longest label in the column in cell A2.

4.   Place the pointer on the vertical border between the column headings for columns A and B. Drag the sizing pointer to set **17.86 (130 pixels)**.

5.   Double-click the border between the column headings for columns B and C. Excel autofits column B.

6.   Click anywhere in column C.

> **NOTE**
>
> If you change data in a column that you've autofitted, the column does not automatically autofit for the new entry.

7.   In the **Cells** group, click the Format button and then choose **Column Width**. The Column Width dialog box opens.

8.   Key **10** and press Enter. The column width is changed to 10 spaces (75 pixels).

Exercise 1-15   INSERT ROWS

In the worksheet you are editing, the eyeglass frame names are in alphabetical order. If the company acquires a new frame named "Beacon," it should be positioned at row 5 between "Antilles" and "Chaos." To make this update, you simply insert a row at that location.

Inserted or deleted rows and columns extend across or down the entire worksheet. If you have used different parts of the worksheet (columns A to F and columns AA to FF), you could interrupt data elsewhere on the sheet (which you may not see) when adding or deleting rows or columns.

1.   Right-click cell A13 and choose **Insert**. The Insert dialog box opens.

2.   Choose **Entire row** and click **OK**. A new row is inserted, and the existing rows shift down. The new row spans the worksheet, and the Insert Options button appears.

3.   Rest the mouse pointer on the Insert Options button. Click its arrow. The options depend on what has been inserted.

4. Press [Esc] on the keyboard. The option menu is closed, and the new row uses the same format as the row above it.

5. Click the row heading for row 15. The entire row is selected.

6. With the black right arrow pointer, drag to select the row headings for rows 15 through 17. Three rows are selected or highlighted.

7. Right-click any of the selected row headings. The Mini toolbar and a shortcut menu opens.

8. Choose **Insert**. Three rows are inserted, because you selected three rows before giving the Insert command.

Figure 1-15
Inserting three rows at once
Eyeglass_Sheet.xlsx
EyeglassSales Sheet

	A	B	C	D	E	F
1	**AllAround Vision Care**					
2	**Web Sales of Frames (Worldwide)**					
3		Year 1	Year 2	Year 3	Year 4	Frame Total
4		100	110	90	100	400
5				80	120	200
6		140	120	110	130	500
7		170	140	100	120	530
8		120	80	120	110	430
9		180	160	140	90	570
10		100	120	130	70	420
11		180	190	170	60	600
12		200	180	160	100	640
13						
14		210	170	150	120	650
15		190	150	120	140	600
16	Vermont	170	140	140	130	580
17				180	120	580
18				120	110	460
19						
20						

Shortcut menu items shown over the table:
- Cut
- Copy
- Paste Options:
- Paste Special...
- Insert
- Delete
- Clear Contents
- Format Cells...
- Row Height...
- Hide
- Unhide

Mini toolbar: Calibri | 11 | A^ A^ | $ ▾ % , | B I ≡ ▾ A ▾ ▾ ▾ .00 .00

Exercise 1-16   DELETE ROWS

Data below deleted rows shift up in the worksheet.

1. Click cell A13 and press [Ctrl]+[-]. The Delete dialog box opens.

2. Choose **Entire row** and click **OK**. The row is deleted.

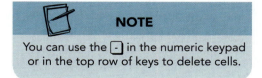

NOTE

You can use the [-] in the numeric keypad or in the top row of keys to delete cells.

3. Click the row heading for row 14. Drag to select the row headings for rows 14, 15, and 16.

4. Right-click one of the selected row headings. Choose **Delete**. Three rows are deleted.

UNIT 1 LESSON 1

Exercise 1-17 INSERT A COLUMN

When you insert a column, it extends from row 1 to row 1,048,576. If you insert a column in a location that affects an existing formula, Excel may update the formula depending on how it was created.

1. Click cell F4. The cells in column F include a formula that sums or adds the contents of cells B4 through E4. The formula does not specifically refer to each cell but identifies a group of cells (B4:E4), meaning those two cells and everything between them.

2. Right-click the column F heading. The column is selected and the shortcut menu opens. The Mini toolbar appears, too.

NOTE

When you choose **Insert** or **Delete** from the shortcut menu, the dialog box does not open.

3. Choose **Insert**. One column is inserted, and what was column F is now column G.

4. Click cell G4. The formula still sums the contents of cells B4 to E4. However, if you key a value in column F, the formula will update to include it.

5. Click cell F4. Key **100** and press →. The formula in cell G4 now sums cells B4 to F4.

6. Delete the contents of cell F4. The formula recalculates.

7. Click cell F3. Key **4-Year** and press Alt + Enter. This inserts a *line break* within the cell which places the next word on a new line.

8. Key **Average** and press Enter. Excel copies the format from the columns that precede the new column.

9. Click cell F3. In the formula bar, you initially see only the first line of the entry.

TIP

If you place the pointer in cell A1 when you save a workbook, cell A1 is the active cell the next time you open the workbook.

10. Click the Expand Formula Bar button ⌄. The formula bar is taller so that you can see more than one line of the entry.

11. Double-click the border between the column headings for columns F and G to autofit the column.

12. Press Ctrl + Home to place the pointer in cell A1.

Saving Workbook Files

When you create a new workbook or make changes to an existing one, you must save the workbook to keep your changes. Until you save your changes, your work can be lost if there is a power failure or a computer problem.

To save a new workbook, give it a file name. A *file name* is what you see in the Information pane in Backstage view, in the Recent Workbooks list, in the Open dialog box, in Computer, or in Windows Explorer. You can use up to 255 characters in a file name. Included in those 255 characters are the drive and folder names, so the actual file name is limited to fewer than 255 characters. Generally, it is a good idea to keep file names as short and descriptive as possible. However, some companies develop a naming convention for all documents. This might include a department name, a client name, and/or the date. AllAround Vision Care, for example, might name all workbooks like this: **AA_Boston_SalesOrders**, indicating company initials, the city, and the topic.

You can use upper- or lowercase letters, or a combination of both, for file names. Windows is case-aware, which means it does recognize upper- and lowercase that you key. However, it is not case-sensitive, so it does not distinguish between "BOOK1" and "book1." You can use spaces in a file name, but you cannot use the following characters: \ ? : * " < > |

File names are followed by a period and a three- or four-letter extension, supplied automatically by the software. Excel 2010 workbooks have the extension ".xlsx." Extensions identify the type of file.

For a new workbook, you can use either the Save or the Save As command. If you make changes to a workbook and want to save it with the same file name, use Save. If you want to save a workbook with a different file name and preserve the original, use Save As.

Excel saves workbooks in the current drive or folder unless you specify a different location. A *folder* is a named location on a disk, network, or other media. You can navigate to any folder in the Save dialog box.

The exercises in this book use a naming convention. The main workbook for the lesson is named **Excel_Lesson***N*. The Skills Review exercises are named **Excel_SR***N-n* in which *N* is the lesson number and *n* is the exercise number. Lesson Applications follow the form **Excel_LA***N-n*.

The exercise instructions will suggest a similar naming convention for saving your work. These names consist of two parts:

- ***[your initials]***, which might be your initials, such as **kms**, or an identifier that your instructor provides
- The number of the exercise, such as **1-18** or **Lesson1-18**

Exercise 1-18   USE THE SAVE AS COMMAND

1. Click the **File** command tab. Backstage view displays more information about this workbook than a blank one. You can see the location from which you opened the file, the author, size, and dates.

Figure 1-16
Backstage view for
existing workbook
**Excel_Lesson1.xlsx
Eyeglass Sheet**

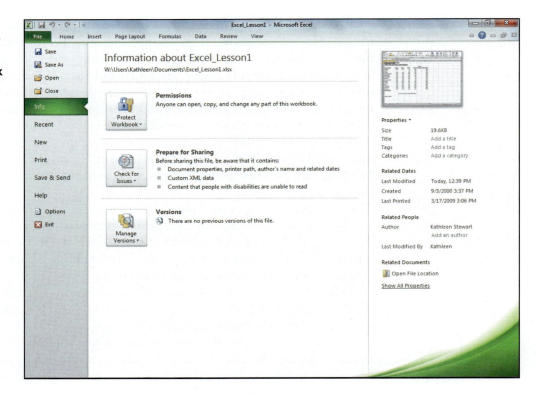

2. Choose **Save As** in the Navigation pane. The Save As dialog box opens. This will allow you to save **Excel_Lesson1** with a new file name in a lesson folder.

3. Navigate to and create or choose the drive and folder location for your work.

4. In the **File name** box, make sure the file name **Excel_Lesson1** is highlighted or selected. If it is not highlighted, click to select it.

5. Key *[your initials]*1-18 and click **Save**. The dialog box closes, and your new file name appears in the title bar.

6. Click the **File** command tab. The new file name and location are now shown.

7. Click the **Home** command tab.

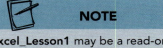

NOTE

Excel_Lesson1 may be a read-only file if you opened it from a protected or restricted location. You cannot save such a file with its existing file name.

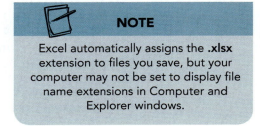

NOTE

Excel automatically assigns the **.xlsx** extension to files you save, but your computer may not be set to display file name extensions in Computer and Explorer windows.

Printing Excel Files

Printed output remains a commonly used method of distributing work, so it is necessary to know what options are available for printing worksheets. Backstage view for printing has Quick commands for choosing the printer, setting margins, and specifying what should be printed.

You can use any of these methods to print a worksheet or a chart sheet:

- Click the **File** command tab and choose **Print**.
- Press Ctrl + P.
- Click the Quick Print button 🖨 on the Quick Access Toolbar.

The Quick Print button 🖨, if it is on the Quick Access Toolbar, sends the active sheet to the printer with your default print settings. The other methods open Backstage view for printing where you can set printing options.

Exercise 1-19 USE BACKSTAGE VIEW FOR PRINTING

Most Excel users work in Normal view, a view that is optimized for working on the screen. Because there are often differences in how you perceive things on the screen versus how it looks printed, Backstage view provides a preview of the printed page. For example, it may look like the data fit on a single page on the screen, but when printed, it requires two pages.

Page Layout view displays your worksheet with margin and header-footer areas visible. This can give you a better idea of the overall layout of the data on a printed page. You can edit your work in Page Layout view just as in Normal view. Backstage view also shows your worksheet as it will print in a normal or reduced view, but you cannot make data changes in this view.

1. In the status bar, click the Page Layout view button ▦. The page shows margin areas and the horizontal and vertical rulers.

2. Click the Zoom Out button ➕ in the status bar. The worksheet is reduced to 90% magnification.

3. Click the Zoom Out button ➕ to reach 50% magnification. Unused pages appear grayed out.

4. Click **50%** in the status bar. Choose **100%** and click **OK**.

5. Click the Normal button ▦ in the status bar.

6. Click the **File** command tab and choose **Print**. Backstage view includes a preview of the current sheet as well as basic printing commands and choices. The worksheet is shown in a reduced size so that you can see the entire page. Note that there are no gridlines or borders; the grid that appears in Normal and Page Layout view does not print by default. Column and row headings do not print either.

Figure 1-17
Worksheet in
Backstage view for
printing
1-18.xlsx
EyeglassSales Sheet

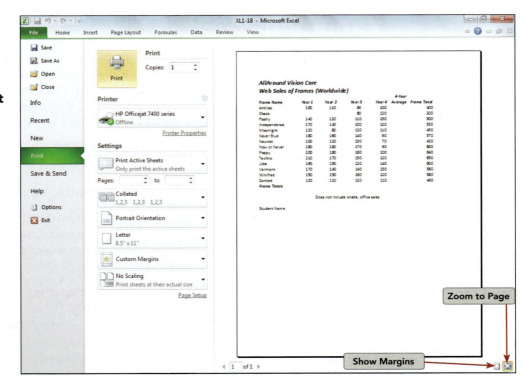

7. Click the Zoom to Page button. The worksheet is shown close to actual print size. Scroll bars appear too, so that you can view different areas of the worksheet.

8. Click the Zoom to Page button to return to a reduced view.

9. Click the **Home** command tab.

10. Click the **Chart** sheet tab. Click the **File** command tab and choose **Print**. Charts usually are set to print in landscape orientation.

11. Click the **Home** command tab.

Exercise 1-20 PRINT A WORKBOOK

By default, Excel prints the active sheet. You can print all sheets in a workbook with one command from the Print dialog box. Make sure that you have access to a printer that is ready.

1. Click the **Eyeglass Sales** worksheet tab.

2. Press Ctrl + P. This is the keyboard shortcut to open Backstage view. Your default print settings and the active sheet are shown.

3. In the **Settings** group, click **Print Active Sheets**. Choose **Print Entire Workbook**. The reduced size shows the first page, the **EyeglassSales** sheet. Below the thumbnail image, you can see that this is page "1 of 2."

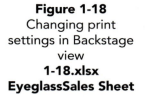

Figure 1-18
Changing print
settings in Backstage
view
**1-18.xlsx
EyeglassSales Sheet**

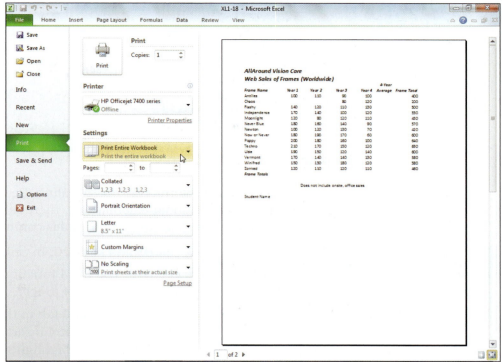

4. Click the Next Page button ▶. This is the second sheet, the **Chart** sheet. It is set to print in landscape orientation.

5. Click the Previous Page button ◀ to return to the worksheet.

6. Click the Print button 🖨. Both sheets are sent to the printer and Backstage view closes.

Getting Acquainted with Excel Functions

Formulas and functions are a primary reason for using Excel, and it is essential that you start learning how easy they are to master. Although there are some subtle differences between a formula and a function, many people use the words interchangeably.

The AllAround Vision Care worksheet you are using has a formula in column G that adds the values in each of the cells indicated in the formula. A *formula* is an equation that performs a calculation. You enter a formula in a cell at a location when some arithmetic is required. When you press ⌷Enter⌷, the results are displayed in the cell. A *function* is a built-in Excel formula. These built-in formulas cover many categories of commonly used mathematical, statistical, financial, and scientific operations.

An Excel function has *syntax*, which defines the necessary parts of the formula and the order of those parts. The syntax consists of an equal sign and the name of the function, followed by parentheses. Inside the parentheses, you place arguments. An *argument* is the information the function needs to complete its calculation, usually one or more values or cell addresses. Many functions use a cell range as an argument, a group of cells with a single address. A cell-range address includes the first cell, a colon, and the last cell.

Figure 1-19
Syntax for the SUM
function

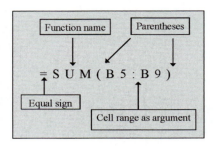

Exercise 1-21   USE SUM

The SUM function adds columns or rows of values. Because it is so commonly used in business and personal calculations, there is a SUM button on the Home command tab as well as on the Formulas command tab.

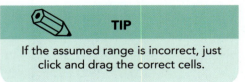

TIP

If the assumed range is incorrect, just click and drag the correct cells.

1. Click cell B5 and key **120**. In cell C5, key **130**.

2. Click cell B18. The SUM function in this cell will add the values from cells B4 to B17.

3. On the **Home** command tab in the **Editing** group, click the SUM button Σ. Excel inserts the function in the cell and automatically highlights the assumed range.

Figure 1-20
Using SUM
1-18.xlsx
EyeglassSales Sheet

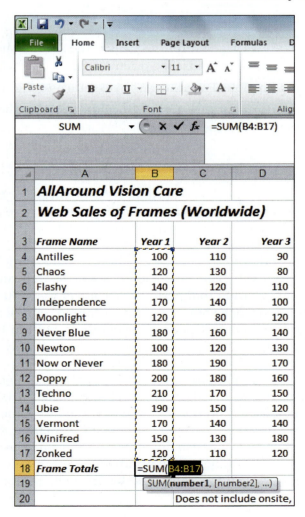

4. Press Enter. The results are calculated as 2,150.
5. Click cell B18. The formula bar shows the formula, and the cell displays the results.

Exercise 1-22 COPY A FUNCTION

When a cell contains a function or a formula, the Fill handle acts as a copy tool. It copies the formula across the dragged range, adjusting the cell references as needed. The SUM function in cell B18, when copied to column C, should be =SUM(C4:C17). This concept is known as *relative reference*. It means that, when copying a formula, Excel knows to change it to reflect the row and/or column in which the copy is located.

1. Click cell B18, and rest the mouse point on the Fill handle.
2. Click and drag the Fill handle right to cell E18. The formulas are copied, and the AutoFill Options button appears next to the cell E18.
3. Rest the mouse pointer on the AutoFill Options button. Click its arrow. The options are slightly different from those for a Fill command.
4. Press Esc.
5. Click cell D18. Look at the formula bar to see that the cell references are relative to where this copy is located.

Exercise 1-23 USE AVERAGE AND EDIT A FUNCTION

AVERAGE adds values and divides by the number of values. It is a widely used calculation and is an option next to the SUM button. In your worksheet, you can calculate an average yearly sales number for each eyeglass frame.

1. Click cell F4. The AVERAGE function will add the values from cells B4 to E4 and then divide the result by 4.
2. Click the arrow next to the SUM button Σ and choose **Average**. Excel inserts the function and highlights the assumed range.

Figure 1-21
Using AVERAGE
1-18.xlsx
EyeglassSales Sheet

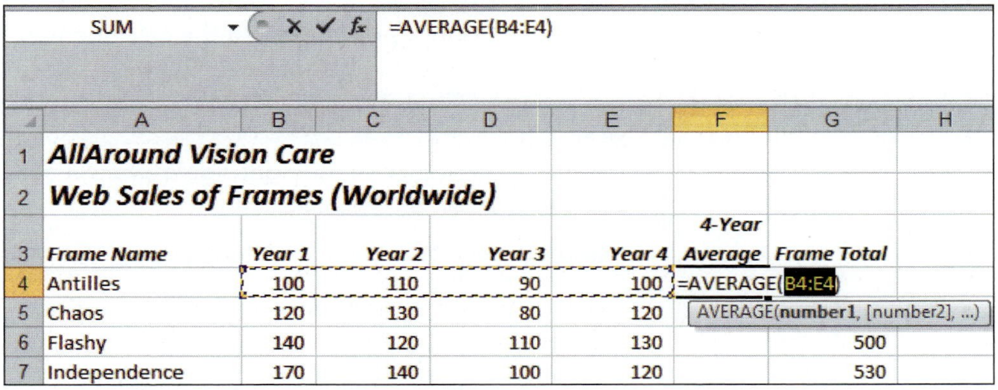

3. Press Ctrl+Enter. The result is 100, and the insertion point stays in cell F4.
4. Rest the mouse point on the Fill handle for cell F4.
5. Click and drag the Fill handle down to cell F18. The formulas are copied.

6. Click cell F10. The formula was adjusted during copying to show the correct row.

7. Click cell G4. Excel has updated this formula to include the inserted column (from Exercise 1-17). The average, however, should not be included in this sum.

8. Press F2. The function appears in the cell and in the formula bar. The cells are highlighted, too.

9. In the cell, edit the formula to show **e4** in place of "F4." Press Enter. The other formulas in this column are unchanged, because you never keyed values in column F for rows 5 through 17.

10. Click cell G18. Click the SUM button Σ and press Enter. The results are calculated as 7,410.

11. Click the Collapse Formula Bar button ⌃. More screen space is available for the rows.

> **NOTE**
>
> There is a green error triangle in cell F18, because Excel notes that this formula is different from others in the row. The function is correct, so ignore the triangle for now.

Using Alignment, Borders, and Fill

There are many elements of formatting a worksheet including cell alignment, borders, and fill (shading). As you key data in a cell, it is formatted as *General*. This style or format displays a label so that it is aligned at the left of the cell. It formats a value so that it is right-aligned in the cell and displays any decimal numbers that you key. The General format does not usually contribute to the best readability of your work, so you will likely choose more appealing formats.

Cell alignment establishes how the contents of a cell are positioned in the cell. Cell contents can be aligned horizontally and vertically.

TABLE 1-5 Horizontal Alignment Options

Setting	Result
General	Aligns numbers and dates on the right, text on the left, and centers error and logical values.
Left (Indent)	Aligns cell contents on the left of the cell indented by the number of spaces entered in the Indent box.
Center	Aligns contents in the middle of the cell.
Right (Indent)	Aligns cell contents on the right side of the cell indented by the number of spaces entered in the Indent box.
Fill	Repeats the cell contents until the cell's width is filled.
Justify	Spreads text to the left and right edges of the cell. This works only for wrapped text that is more than one line.
Center across selection	Places text in the middle of a selected range of columns.
Distributed (Indent)	Positions text an equal distance from the left and right edges including the number of spaces entered in the Indent box.

If a label (or text) is too wide for a cell, it generally spills into the cell to the right if that cell is empty and if the label is left-aligned. If the adjacent cell is not empty, the label is partially visible in the cell but completely visible in the formula bar.

Exercise 1-24   CHANGE HORIZONTAL ALIGNMENT

The Alignment group on the Home command tab contains three horizontal alignment buttons: the Align Text Left button, the Center button, and the Align Text Right button.

1. Click cell A3. This label is left-aligned, the default for text.
2. Click the Center button 🔳 in the **Alignment** group on the **Home** command tab. The label is centered within the cell.
3. Click cell A18. Click the Align Text Right button 🔳. This label is emphasized by right alignment and stands out from the other left-aligned data in the column.
4. Click cell B3 and then cell C3. These labels are right-aligned to balance with the right-aligned values below them.
5. Click cell G3. This label is centered. You can determine that by noting which button is active in the Alignment group.
6. Click the Align Text Right button 🔳.
7. Click cell A1. This label is left-aligned as is the label in cell A2.
8. With the white cross pointer, click cell A1 and drag right and then down to reach cell G2. Cells A1:G2 represent the selection. This range or group of cells includes the labels to be centered and identifies the width over which they should be centered.
9. Click the Dialog Box Launcher in the **Alignment** group. The Format Cells dialog box opens to the Alignment tab.
10. Click the arrow for the **Horizontal** box to display the options.
11. Choose **Center Across Selection** and then click **OK** (see Figure 1-22).

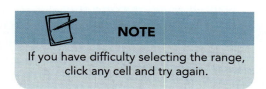

NOTE

If you have difficulty selecting the range, click any cell and try again.

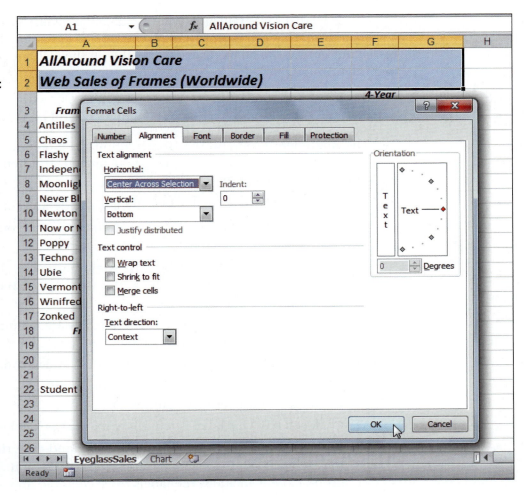

Figure 1-22
Centering across a
selection
1-18.xlsx
EyeglassSales Sheet

Exercise 1-25   APPLY BORDERS

A *border* is a line around a cell or a range of cells. You can use borders to draw attention to a part of a worksheet, to show totals, or to group information in your worksheet. Borders are also used to display a grid on the printed page, making it easier for a reader to follow the data from left to right. Although your worksheet has gridlines on the screen, these do not automatically print. They can be printed, but you can build more eye-appealing borders.

Cells share borders, so adding a border to the bottom of cell A1 has the same effect as adding a border to the top of cell A2.

You should first select the cell(s) to which the border is to be applied. Excel provides two methods to apply a border to a cell or a range of cells:

- Use the Borders button ⊞ in the Font group.

- Use the Format Cells dialog box.

1. Click cell A4 and press [F8]. This starts Extend Selection mode, indicated in the status bar.

2. Press [→] 6 times to highlight up to column G.

3. Press ↓ 13 times to reach row 17. Cells A4:G17 will be formatted with the border you design.

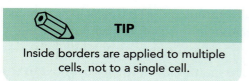

TIP

Inside borders are applied to multiple cells, not to a single cell.

4. Click the Dialog Box Launcher for the **Font** group. Click the **Border** tab. When setting a border, set the **Style**, then the **Color**, and finally the location.

5. In the **Style** box, choose a dotted line (first column, first choice below **None**).

6. Click the arrow for the **Color** box. Note that Automatic, which is black, is the current color.

7. Press Esc to remove the color palette.

8. Click **Outline**. The Border buttons around the preview show the top, bottom, and left and right side borders active in an outline border.

9. Click **None** in the **Presets** group to remove the border in the preview.

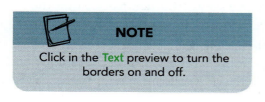

NOTE

Click in the **Text** preview to turn the borders on and off.

10. In the **Text** preview area, click where a bottom horizontal border will be located.

11. In the **Text** preview area, click where a middle horizontal border will be located.

Figure 1-23
Border tab in the Format Cells dialog box
1-18.xlsx
EyeglassSales Sheet

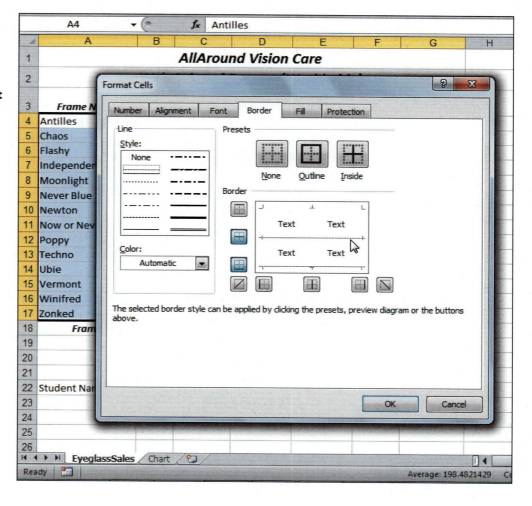

12. Click **OK**.

13. Click a cell in column H to better see the borders.

14. Click cell **A3**. Hold down the Shift key and press → 6 times. This selects up to and including cell G3. Holding down the Shift key while pressing any arrow key works in all the Office applications for selecting data.

15. In the **Font** group on the **Home** command tab, click the arrow next to the Borders button ▦. A gallery of border styles opens.

16. Choose **Bottom Border**. A thin solid bottom border is applied to the cell range.

17. Select cells A18:G18.

18. Click the arrow next to the Borders button ▦. Click **Top and Double Bottom Border**.

19. Click an empty cell to see the border. Notice that the Borders button ▦ shows the last-used style.

20. Click cell **A3**. Hold down the Shift key and press → 6 times. Continue holding down the Shift key, and press ↓ 15 times to reach row 18.

TIP

Totals in accounting and financial reports are often shown with a single border above and a double border below.

21. Press Ctrl+1. Click the **Border** tab.

22. In the **Style** box, choose a single line (first column, last line).

23. Click the Middle Vertical button ▥ below the preview box. Click **OK**.

Exercise 1-26 ADD SOLID FILL

Shading or *fill* is a background color or pattern for a cell or a range of cells. You can use fill in much the same way as a border—to group data or to add emphasis. Fill can be used to differentiate one row from the next, too. Excel provides two methods for applying fill to a cell or a range of cells:

• Use the Fill Color button ▧ in the Font group.

• Use the Format Cells dialog box.

1. Select cells A1:G2. In the **Font** group, click the Fill Color button ▧. Excel applies the color shown beneath the paint bucket icon.

2. Click in row 5 to see the fill.

3. Click the Undo button ↺. The fill is removed, and the cells are still selected.

4. Click the arrow next to the Fill Color button ▧. The color palette opens.

5. Choose **White, Background 1, Darker 25%** in the first column.

6. Select cells A18:G18. Press Ctrl+1 and click the **Fill** tab.

7. For the **Background Color**, choose the first color in the third row below the horizontal line that separates theme colors from the variations. Click **OK**.

8. Press Ctrl+Home.

Getting Acquainted with an Excel Chart

A *chart* uses cells in a worksheet to create a graph of the data. Your workbook for this lesson includes a 3-D bar chart that illustrates the total number of frames sold over a 4-year period. The higher the sales, the longer the bar. The chart is on a separate sheet and uses data from columns A and G in the worksheet. From a quick glance at the chart, you can identify the best and worst sellers and compare the sales of all frames to one another.

Many organizations can use an Excel chart to better illustrate and highlight data. Your school, for example, could use a chart to track enrollment patterns, illustrating how numbers go up and down from semester to semester. Your phone service provider might include a chart in your monthly statement to compare minutes used each month.

A chart is an *object*, a clickable element that you can select and edit. A chart has smaller objects within it that can also be edited.

Exercise 1-27   CHANGE THE CHART STYLE

A *chart style* is a preset selection of colors and special effects for the overall appearance of the chart. There are many chart styles available from the Chart Tools Design command tab. A style is assigned when you create the chart, but it is a simple step to apply a different design.

1. Click the **Chart** sheet tab.
2. Click in the white chart background near the top middle of the chart. The chart is selected, and the Chart Tools command tabs are available. These command tabs are *context-sensitive* because they are available only when a chart is selected.
3. Click the **Chart Tools Design** command tab. The tab includes groups with commands for building charts.

Figure 1-24
Chart Tools Design tab
1-18.xlsx Chart Sheet

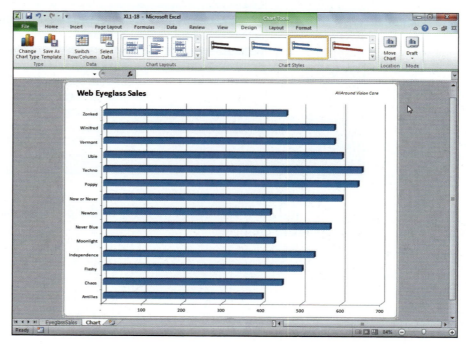

4. Click the Select Data button ⊞ in the **Data** group. The worksheet is displayed, and the data used to build the chart is highlighted by a moving marquee. The data include the labels in column A and the values in column G.

5. Click **Cancel**. The chart sheet is active.

6. Click the **Chart Tools Layout** command tab. This tab has commands for working with parts of a chart. The **Chart Area** is active and listed in the **Chart Elements** box in the **Current Selection** group.

7. Click the **Chart Tools Format** command tab. The commands available on this tab affect the style of various elements in the chart, the size, and the layering. This command tab also has a **Chart Elements** box.

8. Click the **Chart Tools Design** tab. The Chart Layouts and Chart Styles commands are located on this tab.

9. Click the More button ⊟ in the **Chart Styles** group. The Chart Styles gallery opens. A style consists of colors, shadows, bevels, and backgrounds.

Figure 1-25
Chart Styles gallery
1-18.xlsx Chart Sheet

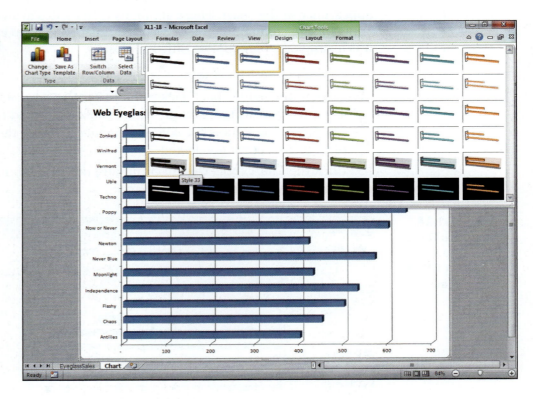

10. Find and click **Style 33**. The color of the bars, the background, and labels are changed.

Exercise 1-28   EDIT THE CHART TITLE AND ADD DATA LABELS

The chart has a title, "Web Eyeglass Sales" in the top left corner. This is an individual chart element or object that you can edit. The bars in the chart are plotted against the horizontal axis, which are the numbers along the bottom of the chart. In the chart, you can estimate the number of units sold but cannot determine the specific number. A *data label* is the actual value from the worksheet displayed on the chart near the bar. It is another chart element or object that can be added and edited.

1. Click the chart title. There is a solid border around the words along with its selection handles. A *selection handle* is a tiny circle or square at the corner and/or edges of a selected object to indicate it is active and ready for editing.
2. Click inside the title's bounding box. A text insertion point and a dashed line border mean you can edit the text.
3. Click to the left of the **S** in "Sales." Key **Frame** and press [Spacebar]. Click in the white chart background to deselect the title.
4. Select the title again and click the **Home** command tab. You can use basic format commands from this tab for chart objects.
5. In the **Font** group, click the **Font Size** arrow. Choose **24**.
6. Right-click any one of the bars. All the bars are selected, because they represent values from one column. This is a single data series. A shortcut menu has opened with available commands for the data series.
7. Choose **Add Data Labels**. The actual value from column G in the worksheet is displayed next to each bar.
8. Point and click one of the data labels. All of them are selected.
9. Click the **Home** command tab and change the font size to **14**.
10. Click in the blue-gray window background. The chart is deselected, and the Chart Tools command tabs are no longer visible.
11. Click the **EyeglassSales** worksheet tab. Compare your completed Excel worksheet to the handwritten version in Figure 1-1.

Exercise 1-29   SAVE A WORKBOOK AND EXIT EXCEL

You can exit Excel and close the workbook at the same time. If you give the command to exit Excel, you will see a reminder to save the workbook if you have not yet done so.

There are several ways to close a workbook and exit Excel:

- Click the File command tab and choose Exit.
- Use the Close button ⊠ to first close the workbook and then to close Excel.
- Use the keyboard shortcut [Alt]+[F4] to exit Excel.

1. Click the **File** command tab. The Info tab displays for an open workbook.

2. Choose **Save As**. You will save **[*your initials*]1-18** with a new file name in the lesson folder.

3. Navigate to and choose your lesson folder.

4. In the **File name** box, key *[your initials]*1-29 and click **Save**. Your new file name appears in the title bar.

5. Click the **File** command tab. Choose **Exit**. Do not save changes if asked.

Using Online Help

Online Help is available at your computer and on the Microsoft Office Web site. An easy way to use Help is to key a short request in the search text box at the top of the opening Help window.

GET ACQUAINTED WITH USING HELP

1. Start Excel and click the Microsoft Office Excel Help button 🔵.

2. In the search box, key **backstage view** and press Enter. Click the topic and read the information.

3. In the search box, key **protected view** and press Enter. Choose a topic and read the Help information. Close the Help window.

Lesson 1 Summary

- An Excel workbook provides functionality similar to handwritten ledger pages used to track financial information.

- Data in an Excel worksheet can be quickly edited and formatted to build a professional report.

- Excel opens with a blank workbook and the Ribbon. The File command tab provides information about the open workbook and access to Open, Print, and Save & Send commands.

- A new workbook opens with three worksheets. A worksheet is an individual page or tab in the workbook.

- Press Ctrl+PageUp and Ctrl+PageDown to move between worksheets in a workbook.

- Worksheets are divided into cells, which are the intersections of rows and columns. The location of the cell is its address (also called its cell reference).

- Move the pointer to a specific cell with the Go To command or by clicking the cell.

- The active cell is outlined with a black border. It is ready to accept new data or a formula or to be edited.

- The Name Box shows the address of the active cell. You can also use it to change the active cell.
- If you use the scroll box or arrows to reposition the worksheet on the screen, the active cell does not change.
- The Zoom size controls how much of the worksheet you can see at once.
- Replace any entry in a cell by clicking the cell and keying new data. Edit long or complicated cell data rather than rekeying them.
- The Undo and Redo buttons have history arrows so that you can undo or redo multiple commands at once.
- Use the Fill handle to fill a series of labels or to copy a formula.
- Column widths and row heights can be changed, and columns and/or rows can be inserted or deleted.
- A workbook file has an **xlsx** file name extension.
- Preview your worksheet or the entire workbook before printing it. To preview and print all the sheets in a workbook, open Backstage view for printing and choose Entire workbook from the Print What group.
- A function is a built-in formula. Commonly used functions such as SUM and AVERAGE can be inserted from a button on the Home tab.
- Cell alignment affects how the contents are horizontally or vertically positioned within the cell.
- Fill and borders can be used to differentiate and emphasize parts of the worksheet for greater readability.
- A chart is a graphic representation of data in a worksheet.
- Charts have various elements that can be edited to change the look of the chart.

LESSON 1		Command Summary	
Feature	**Button**	**Ribbon Location**	**Keyboard**
Align text right		Home, Alignment	
AutoFill options			
Average	Σ	Home, Editing	
Backstage view for printing		File, Print	Ctrl + F2
Borders		Home, Font	
Center		Home, Alignment	
Chart style		Chart Tools, Design, Chart Styles	
Clear cell contents		Home, Editing	Delete

continues

LESSON 1		Command Summary *continued*	
Feature	Button	Ribbon Location	Keyboard
Close window		File, Close	Ctrl+W or Ctrl+F4
Collapse formula bar			Ctrl+Shift+U
Collapse Ribbon			Ctrl+F1
Column width		Home, Cells	
Delete column or row		Home, Cells	Ctrl+-
Exit Excel		File, Exit	Alt+F4
Expand formula bar			Ctrl+Shift+U
Fill		Home, Font	
Full screen		View, Workbook Views	
Go To		Home, Editing, Find & Select	Ctrl+G or F5
Insert column or row		Home, Cells	Ctrl++
Key Tips			Alt or F10
Line break			Alt+Enter
Normal view		View, Workbook Views	
Open workbook		File, Open	Ctrl+O
Page Layout view		View, Workbook Views	
Print		File, Print	Ctrl+P
Redo			Ctrl+Y or F4
Row height		Home, Cells	
Save as		File, Save As	F12 or Alt+F2
Sum		Home, Editing	Alt+=
Undo			Ctrl+Z or Alt+Backspace
Zoom in			
Zoom out			
Zoom size		View, Zoom	

Please visit our Online Learning Center, *www.lessonapproach2010.com*, where you will find the following review materials:

- **Concepts Review**

  True/False Questions

  Short Answer Questions

  Critical Thinking Questions

- **Skills Review**

  Review Exercises that target single skills

  Lesson Applications

  Review Exercises that challenge students by testing multiple skills in each exercise

- **On Your Own**

  Open-ended exercises that require students to synthesize multiple skills and apply creativity and problem-solving as they would in a real world business situation

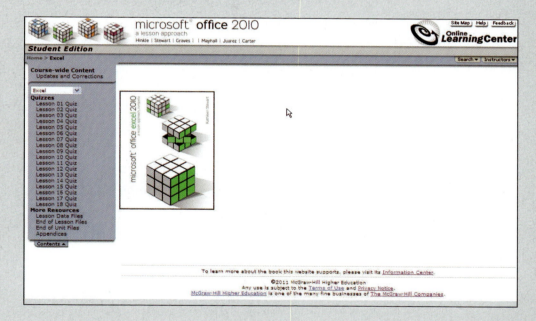

Developing Workbooks

OBJECTIVES *After completing this lesson, you will be able to:*

1. Enter labels, values, and dates.
2. Create formulas.
3. Apply cell styles and font commands.
4. Apply number and date formats.
5. Create a pie chart.
6. Change the document theme.
7. Use Page Layout view.

Estimated Time: 1½ hours

The first step in developing a workbook is determining your purpose or goal. AllAround Vision Care, for example, monitors the time and costs associated with its marketing campaigns. From this information, it can analyze the effectiveness of its advertising and calculate one of its operating expenses. This results in a relatively simple single-worksheet workbook with most of the data keyed. In another workbook, it tracks insurance payables and receivables per month. In this case, it may keep a separate sheet for each month, resulting in a workbook with 12 worksheets. For the workbook, it downloads some of the data from a billing program.

Whether you are developing a new workbook at your place of employment or for your personal needs, you will have a general idea of what needs to be shown and calculated. Consider these questions to help you refine what you need for a new workbook.

- What information are you analyzing? What type of answer or solution are you looking for?
- What data will be used? Will you be required to key it? Will it be downloaded or copied from another source?
- Will arithmetic be required in the worksheet? If so, what type of calculations will they be?

- Are there Excel functions that perform the required arithmetic? Or will you build your own formulas?
- Will it be a workbook that is used on a routine basis? Will data be added to the workbook regularly? Or is it a one-time report?
- Will other workers use your workbook?
- Is there a particular style or format that is expected?
- Will it be distributed outside your place of employment? How will it be distributed?

Depending on your preference, you can sketch a worksheet plan using paper and pencil. As you learn more about Excel's editing capabilities, however, you may find that it is fairly easy to lay out, test, and rearrange your data and ideas on the screen. You may also develop a preference for formatting the worksheet as you go along or for keying all the data and then applying all formatting.

Entering Labels, Values, and Dates

There are essentially two types of data that can be entered or copied into a worksheet: either a label or a value. When data begin with or include a letter, Excel recognizes it as a *label*. Labels are aligned at the left edge of the cell and are not used in calculations.

TIP

You can format a value as a label by keying an apostrophe before the number. The number is then not used in calculations.

When an entry starts with a number or an arithmetic symbol, Excel assumes it is a *value*. Dates are treated as values, as are formulas. A value is right-aligned in the cell and can be included in calculations. Arithmetic symbols used to introduce a value entry other than a date include =, −, and +.

As you key data, the keystrokes appear in the active cell and in the formula bar. If you make an error, press Esc to start over. You can also press Backspace to edit the entry.

There are several ways you can complete a cell entry.

TABLE 2-1 Ways to Complete a Cell Entry

Key or Button	Result
Press Enter	Completes entry and moves the pointer to the cell below
Press Ctrl + Enter	Completes entry and leaves the pointer in the current cell
Press Tab	Completes entry and moves the pointer to the cell to the right
Press Shift + Tab	Completes entry and moves the pointer to the cell to the left
Press an arrow key	Completes entry and moves the pointer one cell in the direction of the arrow
Click another cell	Completes entry and moves the pointer to the clicked cell
Click the Enter button ✓	Completes entry and leaves the pointer in the current cell

Exercise 2-1   ENTER LABELS IN A WORKSHEET

This new workbook will analyze marketing costs for a specific time period in each of AllAround Vision Care's cities. Excel, when started, opens with **Book1**, a blank workbook. New workbooks started after that are numbered consecutively. In a new workbook, cell A1 is active on **Sheet1**. Start Excel with a blank new workbook.

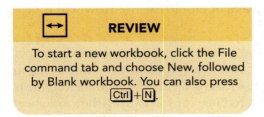
REVIEW

To start a new workbook, click the File command tab and choose New, followed by Blank workbook. You can also press Ctrl + N.

1. In cell A1, key **AllAround Eye** to start a label but do not press Enter. The worksheet is in Enter mode, shown in the status bar. The label appears in the formula bar and in the cell.

2. Press Backspace to delete **Eye**.

3. Key **Vision Care**. Notice that an Enter button ✔ and a Cancel button ✖ appear in the formula bar in Enter mode.

Figure 2-1
Label appearing in the formula bar and the cell

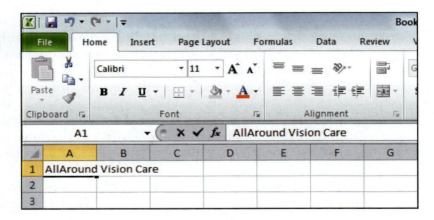

4. Press Enter. The label is completed in cell A1, and the pointer moves to cell A2. The label is longer than column A's width, so it appears to spill into columns B and C.

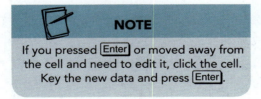
NOTE

If you pressed Enter or moved away from the cell and need to edit it, click the cell. Key the new data and press Enter.

5. In cell A2, key **Worldwi** to start a label. Press Esc on the keyboard. You can use Esc to delete an entry if you haven't yet pressed Enter or moved away from the cell.

6. Key **Nationwide Marketing Effort** and click the Enter button ✔ in the formula bar. The label appears to spill into cells B2:C2.

7. Click cell B3. Key **Starting Date** and press →. The label is too long for column B and spills into column C. The pointer is now in cell C3.

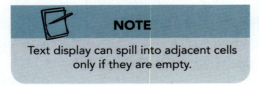
NOTE

Text display can spill into adjacent cells only if they are empty.

8. In cell C3, key **Ending Date** and press Tab. This label cuts off the label from cell B3 and spills into cell D3.

9. In cell D3, key **Last Year Cost** and press Tab. This label is not cut off, because there is nothing in the cell to the right.

10. Click cell B3. Although the label appears cut off in the cell, the complete text is visible in the formula bar.

Exercise 2-2   USE AUTOCORRECT WHILE KEYING LABELS

AutoCorrect makes spelling corrections while you key labels. It recognizes a common error such as "teh," and changes it to "the." It capitalizes the days of the week and the months and corrects capitalization errors, such as THis. You can also set AutoCorrect options to help you key routine data automatically.

AutoCorrect makes its change when you press the spacebar, the Enter key, or a punctuation mark.

1. Click cell A4.

Figure 2-2
Keying a deliberate error

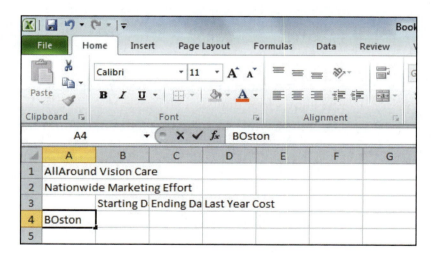

2. In cell A4, make an error by keying **BOston** and press Enter. The two incorrect uppercase letters are corrected.

3. In cell A5, make another error by keying **ChicaGO**. Press Enter. This error is not automatically corrected, because only two initial uppercase characters are recognized as an error.

4. Click cell A5 and press F2 to start Edit mode. Change **GO** to **go** and press Enter.

5. In cell A6, press Caps Lock. This is the error, turning on caps lock.

6. In cell A6, key **Dallas**. It appears as **dALLAS**. Press Enter. Accidental use of caps lock is recognized as an error.

7. In cell A7, key **Seattle** and press Enter.

8. Double-click the border between the column headings for columns B and C to autofit the column.

9. Autofit columns C and D.

10. In cell E3, key **Planned** and press Alt+Enter. Key **Increase** and press Enter. The height of row 3 is increased to accommodate the label.

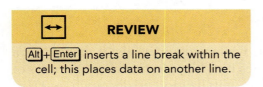

REVIEW

Alt+Enter inserts a line break within the cell; this places data on another line.

11. Click cell F3 and key **New Cost**. Key **Difference** in cell G3.

12. Autofit column G.

Exercise 2-3   ENTER DATES AND VALUES

Excel recognizes dates if you key them in a typical date style. For example, if you key "1/1/11," Excel formats that value as a date. Dates have their own formatting choices and can be used in date arithmetic.

For other values, Excel does recognize some format symbols if you key them. For example, if you key a value such as $67.34, it is automatically formatted in a currency format.

1. Click cell B4.

2. Key **12/1/11** and press Enter. Excel recognizes the numbers as a date and shows four digits for the year.

3. Continue keying the following dates in column B. Press Enter after each one:

   3/15/11
   8/1/11
   10/15/11

4. Key these dates in cells C4:C7:

   12/31/11
   4/15/11
   8/31/11
   11/15/11

5. Click cell D4. Hold down the Shift key and press → one time. Continue holding down Shift and press ↓ three times. With the cells selected, you can press Enter to move from cell to cell, going top to bottom and then left to right.

6. Key the values and percents in the "Last Year Cost" and "Planned Increase" columns shown here. Values and dates are right-aligned within the cell. When you key a percent sign, Excel assigns the percent style format.

Last Year Cost	Planned Increase
750	106%
825	106%
725	105%
650	107%

7. Press Ctrl + Home .

Exercise 2-4 NAME AND SAVE A WORKBOOK

When you have not yet named and saved a workbook, the Save button 🖫 in the Quick Access Toolbar opens the Save As dialog box. After you have named and saved a workbook, however, clicking this button automatically resaves the workbook with the same name; no dialog box opens.

1. In the Quick Access Toolbar, click the Save button 🖫 .

2. Navigate to and choose the drive and folder location for your work. Create a new lesson folder if that is your usual procedure.

3. In the **File name** box, make sure the file name **Book1** is highlighted or selected. If it is not highlighted, click to select it.

4. Key *[your initials]*2-4 and click **Save**. The dialog box closes, and the file name appears in the title bar.

Creating Formulas

A *formula* is an equation that performs a calculation on values in the worksheet and displays an answer. It is a calculation that you build using arithmetic operators and cell references. You enter a formula in a cell. After you press a completion key, the formula results appear in the cell. The formula itself is visible in the formula bar.

Formulas are fundamental to using Excel. If you enter the correct symbols and references, Excel does the math for you quickly and accurately. When you update any of the values used in a formula, Excel recalculates the results. In the worksheet that you are building for this lesson, you can build a multiplication formula to determine new costs in column F. Then in column G you can create a simple subtraction formula to calculate the difference between

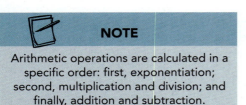

NOTE

Arithmetic operations are calculated in a specific order: first, exponentiation; second, multiplication and division; and finally, addition and subtraction.

the new cost and last year's cost. These formulas are not handled by any of Excel's built-in functions.

Like functions, formulas begin with an = sign as an identifier. After the = sign, you usually enter a cell address whose contents are to be added, subtracted, multiplied, or divided. The cell address is followed by an *arithmetic operator*. You probably recognize the arithmetic operators shown in Table 2-2. The *exponentiation* operator raises a number to a power. For example, 2^3 represents 2 to the third power, or 2^3, which means $2 \times 2 \times 2$ or 8.

TABLE 2-2 Arithmetic Operators

Key or Symbol	Operation
^	Exponentiation
*	Multiplication
/	Division
+	Addition
−	Subtraction

Exercise 2-5   KEY A FORMULA

In your workbook, the new increased cost is calculated by a multiplication formula. For Boston, you multiply last year's cost by 106% to determine the increased cost. To key a multiplication symbol, use the asterisk (*) in the 10-key pad or the asterisk in the row of numbers at the top of the keyboard.

1. Click cell F4.

2. Key **=d** to start the formula. *Formula AutoComplete* shows a list of built-in functions that begin with the letter "d." You can ignore this list when you are keying your own formula.

Figure 2-3
Formula
AutoComplete list
2-4.xlsx
Sheet1 sheet

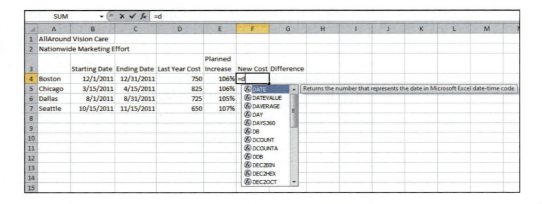

3. Key **4*e4** in cell F4. You'll see another Formula AutoComplete list when you key **e**. Your formula should be "=d4*e4," and it appears in the cell and in the formula bar. The cells are outlined in colors that match the colors of the formula in the cell.

Figure 2-4
Keying a formula
2-4.xlsx
Sheet1 sheet

			SUM	▾	✕ ✓ *fx*	=d4*e4			
◢	A	B	C	D	E	F	G	H
1	AllAround Vision Care							
2	Nationwide Marketing Effort							
3		Starting Date	Ending Date	Last Year Cost	Planned Increase	New Cost	Difference	
4	Boston	12/1/2011	12/31/2011	750	106%	=d4*e4		
5	Chicago	3/15/2011	4/15/2011	825	106%			
6	Dallas	8/1/2011	8/31/2011	725	105%			
7	Seattle	10/15/2011	11/15/2011	650	107%			
8								

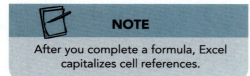

NOTE

After you complete a formula, Excel capitalizes cell references.

4. Press ⌜Enter⌟. The result is 795, which is 6% more than 750 (106% of 750).

5. Press ⌜↑⌟ to return to cell F4. Notice that the formula bar shows the formula, but the cell displays the results of the formula.

Exercise 2-6 ENTER A FORMULA BY POINTING

It is often easier to use the mouse to point to cells when building a formula. This increases accuracy, because you don't have to worry about keying the wrong cell address. To key a minus symbol, you can use the hyphen (-) in the 10-key pad or the hyphen in the top row of the keyboard.

1. Click cell F5. Key **=** to start the formula.

2. Click cell D5. The address appears in cell F5 and in the formula bar. Cell D5 has a moving marquee.

3. Key ***** to multiply by the next cell.

4. Click cell E5. It is placed in the formula after the asterisk and now has the moving marquee.

Figure 2-5
Entering a formula
by pointing
2-4.xlsx
Sheet1 sheet

			SUM	▾	✕ ✓ *fx*	=D5*E5			
◢	A	B		D	E	F	G	H
1	AllAround Vision Care		Enter					
2	Nationwide Marketing Effort							
3		Starting Date	Ending Date	Last Year Cost	Planned Increase	New Cost	Difference	
4	Boston	12/1/2011	12/31/2011	750	106%	795		
5	Chicago	3/15/2011	4/15/2011	825	106%	=D5*E5		
6	Dallas	8/1/2011	8/31/2011	725	105%			
7	Seattle	10/15/2011	11/15/2011	650	107%			
8								

5. Click the Enter button ✔ in the formula bar. The new cost of 874.5 is calculated. Values are assigned a general format which shows as many decimal places as will fit in the cell.

6. Rest the mouse pointer on the Fill handle for cell F5. Click the Fill handle and drag down to cell F7 to copy the formula.

7. Click cell G4. Key **=** to start the formula. Click cell F4.

8. Key **-** to subtract the value in the next cell.

9. Click cell D4 and press Ctrl + Enter . The difference is 45.

Exercise 2-7   COPY A FORMULA BY USING THE COPY AND PASTE BUTTONS

The formula in cell G5 will be the same as the one in cell G4 except for the row references. When you use the Fill handle to copy a formula, Excel makes this adjustment automatically. The same concept applies when you use the Copy and Paste buttons. The formula is relative to its location on the worksheet.

1. Click cell G4. In the **Clipboard** group, click the Copy button. The cell now has a moving marquee. The status bar tells you to select the destination for the copy.

2. Click cell G5. Hold down Shift and press ↓ two times to select the range G5:G7.

3. In the **Clipboard** group, click the Paste button. The formula is copied to all cells in the selected range. The Paste Options button appears just below the pasted data.

4. Hover over the Paste Options button and click its arrow. Options for copying the data are listed in the gallery. You need not change the option.

5. Press Esc twice to cancel the moving marquee and finish the Paste command.

6. Click cell G5 and review the formula. Click cell G6. Excel has adjusted the formulas relative to the row.

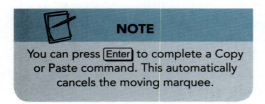

NOTE

You can press Enter to complete a Copy or Paste command. This automatically cancels the moving marquee.

Applying Cell Styles and Font Commands

Styles and fonts can be applied to labels and values in an Excel worksheet. The steps are similar to other programs, such as your e-mail client or Microsoft Word. You can use preset styles or apply your own font choices, colors, and special effects. There are formats that are appropriate for labels and others that are suited to values. In any case, you use styles and fonts to make your worksheet look good and be readable.

Often when changing fonts or using styles, you work with a range of cells. A *range* is a group of cells that forms a rectangle on the screen. For example, you can format all the cells in rows 3 through 7 at once by first selecting that range.

Like an individual cell, a range has an address. A *range address* consists of the upper-left cell address and the lower-right cell address, separated by a colon.

TABLE 2-3　Examples of Range Addresses

Range Address	Cells in the Range
A1:B3	6 cells on 3 rows and in 2 columns
B1:B100	100 cells, all in column B
C3:C13	11 cells, starting at cell C3, all in column C
D4:F12	27 cells on 9 rows and in 3 columns
A1:XFD1	16,384 cells or the entire row 1

Exercise 2-8　SELECT CELL RANGES WITH THE MOUSE

When a cell range is selected, it is highlighted or shaded on the screen. The *selection pointer* within the worksheet grid is a thick white cross shape. When you point at a row or column heading, the selection pointer appears as a solid black arrow. There are several ways to select a range of cells by using the mouse:

- Drag across adjacent cells to select the range.

- Click the first cell in the range. Hold down $\boxed{\text{Shift}}$ and click the last cell in the range.

- Click a column heading letter to select a column or click a row heading number to select a row.

- Drag across adjacent column heading letters or row heading numbers to select multiple columns or rows.

- Click the Select All button ⬜ (see Figure 2-6 on the next page) to select every cell on the worksheet.

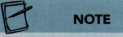

NOTE

If the correct cells are not selected, click any other cell and try selecting the cells again.

1. With the thick white cross-shaped pointer, click cell B3 and drag to the right to cell G3.

2. Release the mouse button. Cells B3 through G3 are selected. The Name Box shows the first cell in the range, and the formula bar shows the first label. Cell B3 appears white, and the remaining cells are light blue-gray (see Figure 2-6).

Figure 2-6
Selecting a range
of cells
**2-4.xlsx
Sheet1 sheet**

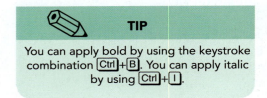

Select All

	A	B	C	D	E	F	G	H
	B3		fx	Starting Date				
1	AllAround Vision Care							
2	Nationwide Marketing Effort							
3		Starting Date	Ending Date	Last Year Cost	Planned Increase	New Cost	Difference	
4	Boston	12/1/2011	12/31/2011	750	106%	795	45	
5	Chicago	3/15/2011	4/15/2011	825	106%	874.5	49.5	
6	Dallas	8/1/2011	8/31/2011	725	105%	761.25	36.25	
7	Seattle	10/15/2011	11/15/2011	650	107%	695.5	45.5	
8								

TIP

You can apply bold by using the keystroke combination Ctrl+B. You can apply italic by using Ctrl+I.

3. Click the Bold button [B] in the **Font** group. The labels in the selected range are bold. Bold data are often slightly larger than data in the regular style of the same font.

4. While the cells are selected, click the Align Text Right button [≡] in the **Alignment** group.

5. Click cell A1. This makes cell A1 active and deselects the range.

6. Click cell A1 and drag to cell G1. Do not release the mouse button. Drag down to cell G2 and then release the mouse button. The selected range is A1:G2.

7. Click cell A1 to deselect the range.

8. Point to the row 1 heading. The pointer changes shape and is a solid black arrow.

9. Click the row 1 heading to select the row.

10. Click cell B2. You can click any cell to deselect a range.

11. Point to the row 1 heading. Click and drag down through the row headings from row 1 to row 5.

12. Release the mouse button. Five rows are selected.

13. Click any cell to deselect the rows.

14. Click the column A heading. This selects the column.

15. Click any cell to deselect the column.

16. Click the column B heading and drag to the column G heading. This selects a range that includes all the cells in columns B through G.

17. Click cell B3. Hold down [Shift] and click cell G7. This is another way to select a range. This range is B3:G7.

Exercise 2-9 USE KEYBOARD SHORTCUTS AND APPLY FONT COMMANDS

You can select a range of cells by using keyboard shortcuts. These shortcuts work for selecting data in many Windows programs.

TABLE 2-4 Keyboard Shortcuts to Select Cell Ranges

Keystroke	To Do This
Shift + arrow key	Select from the active cell, moving in the direction of the arrow.
Shift + Spacebar	Select the current row.
Shift + PageDown	Extend selection from active cell down one screen in the same column.
Shift + PageUp	Extend selection from active cell up one screen in the same column.
Ctrl + A	Select the entire range with data or the entire worksheet.
Ctrl + Spacebar	Select the current column.
Ctrl + Shift + Home	Extend selection from active cell to beginning of data.
Ctrl + Shift + End	Extend selection from active cell to end of data.
F8	Start Extend Selection mode.
F8 + arrow key	Extend selection from active cell in the direction of the arrow.
Esc	End Extend Selection mode.

1. Click cell A1. Hold down Shift and press ↓ one time. The range is A1:A2.

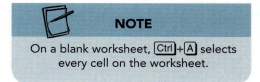

NOTE

On a blank worksheet, Ctrl + A selects every cell on the worksheet.

2. Click the arrow next to the **Font** box. Choose **Cambria**.

3. Click the arrow next to the **Font Size** box. Scroll to **16**. As you scroll down the list of font sizes, *Live Preview* displays the selected range with the size applied. Click **16** to complete the formatting.

4. Click cell B3 and press F8. This starts Extend Selection mode. "**Extend Selection**" appears in the status bar.

5. Press → five times. Click the Bold button **B** to remove bold. This cancels Extend Selection mode too.

6. Click cell A3. Hold down the Shift key and press ↓ to reach row 15. While holding down Shift, press → to reach column G. The range is A3:G15.

7. Click the arrow next to the **Font Size** box. Choose **12**. Existing data are changed, and the empty cells will use a 12-point font when data are entered.

8. Click cell A3. The range is deselected.

9. Hold down Shift and click cell G15. This is another way to select the range.

10. Hold down Ctrl. Click cell A17 and drag across to cell G18. Release the Ctrl key. Two different-sized ranges that are not next to each other are selected at the same time.

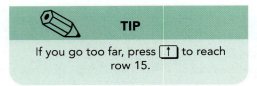

TIP

If you go too far, press ↑ to reach row 15.

Figure 2-7
Selecting two ranges
2-4.xlsx
Sheet1 sheet

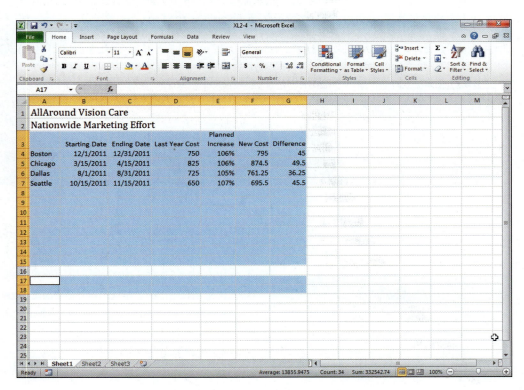

11. Press Ctrl+Home.

Exercise 2-10 APPLY CELL STYLES

A *cell style* is a set of format attributes that can include font style, font color, font size, borders, alignment, and fill. Excel has many predefined cell styles used to differentiate and emphasize data. The preset styles are organized into categories to illustrate how they might be used. In your workbook, you might use a heading or title style for the labels in cells A1:A2. You might also use a currency style to better illustrate the money values in the worksheet. The Cell Styles button 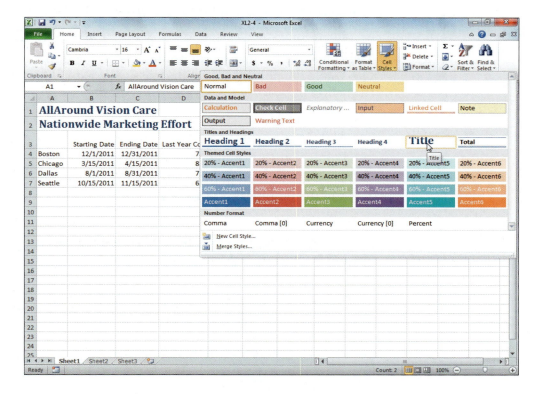 is in the Styles group on the Home command tab.

1. Select cells A1:A2. You have already changed the font style and size for this range.

2. In the **Styles** group on the **Home** command tab, click the Cell Styles button. The Cell Styles gallery opens. The five categories are guidelines.

Figure 2-8
Cell Styles gallery
2-4.xlsx
Sheet1 sheet

3. Hover the mouse pointer over several cell style names. Live Preview shows how the labels will appear with the style applied.

4. Find and click the **Title** style (under **Titles and Headings**). The labels are reformatted as Cambria 18 point in a different color.

5. Select cells B3:G3. Click the Cell Styles button.

6. Find and click the **Accent1** style (under **Themed Cell Styles**). The labels are set in white with blue fill, and the font size is set to 11.

7. Click the arrow next to the **Font Size** box. Choose **12**. You can use a combination of cell styles and your own format choices. The most recent choice applies.

8. Click the Bold button ⓑ.

9. Click the column heading for column B. Click and drag to select up to and including column G. Double-click the border between columns G and H.

10. Adjust the width of column E so that the label occupies two lines if needed.

11. Adjust the height of row 3 to **30.00 (40 pixels)**.

Exercise 2-11   USE THE FORMAT PAINTER

With the Format Painter, you can copy cell formats from one cell to another. This can be faster than applying formats individually, especially when you have designed your own settings.

To use the Format Painter, make the cell with formatting the active cell. Then click the Format Painter button 🖌 in the Clipboard group on the Home tab. While the pointer is a white cross with a small paintbrush, click and drag the cell(s) to be formatted.

1. Click cell A1.

2. In the **Clipboard** group, hover the mouse pointer over the Format Painter button 🖌 and read its ScreenTip.

3. Click the Format Painter button 🖌. Cell A1 shows a moving marquee, and the pointer is a thick white cross with a paintbrush.

Figure 2-9
Using the Format Painter
2-4.xlsx
Sheet1 sheet

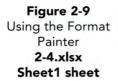

Formula painted here

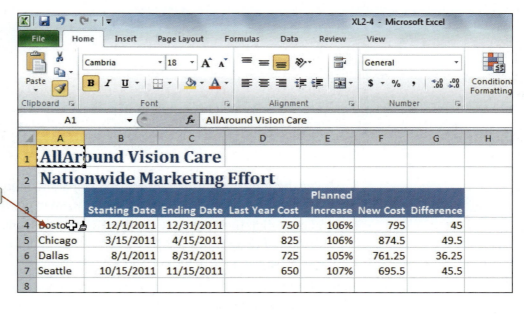

4. Click cell A4. The settings from the Title cell style are copied, and row 4 becomes taller. The column was not made wider. The Format Painter command is canceled.

5. Click the Undo button 🔄 and press [Esc] to cancel the marquee.

6. Click cell B3.

7. Double-click the Format Painter button 🖌. This locks the painter on so that you can format more than one cell.

8. Click cell A4 to copy the format. Then click cells A5, A6, and A7. Notice that right alignment has been copied.

9. Click the Format Painter button 🖌 to cancel the command.

10. Click the arrow next to the Undo button 🔄. Excel shows Format Painter as **Paste Special** in the Undo history list.

11. Undo four **Paste Special** commands. The labels in column A return to the initial format.

12. Click cell B3. Click the Format Painter button 🖌.

13. Drag across cells A4:A7. When you release the mouse button, the Format Painter command is canceled.

Applying Number and Date Formats

Professionally formatted worksheets are reports that can be distributed to patients, customers, employees, and others. Effective use of formatting enables you to create a report that is easy to understand. Your worksheet for AllAround Vision Care has some color and alignment features applied by the cell styles, but it is not particularly well designed at this point. You can start developing this workbook into a more expertly constructed report by styling the dates and values.

Exercise 2-12   APPLY NUMBER AND DATE FORMATS FROM THE RIBBON

By default, a value is formatted as General when you key it. This format shows only digits, no commas, and as many decimal places as you key or as will fit in the cell. If the value is 1.23456, five decimal places are displayed. A value such as 1.00 has insignificant zeros that are not shown. There are many predesigned number and date formats available. Dates use the Short Date format by default, which shows a date according to this layout: *m/d/yyyy*. Those symbols mean one or two digits for the month, a forward slash, one or two digits for the date, another forward slash, and four digits for the year. You can see that format in your worksheet.

1. Select cells D4:D7. These are money values.

2. In the **Number** group, click the Accounting Number Format button $. The cells are formatted to show a dollar sign and two decimal places. Dollar signs are aligned at the left edge of the cell.

3. In the **Number** group, click the arrow with the **Number Format** box. Commonly used number formats are listed in this gallery.

4. Choose **Currency**. This format includes the dollar sign and two decimal places, but the dollar signs are immediately left of the first digit. This is referred to as a *floating symbol*.

5. Select cells F4:G7 and apply the **Currency** format.

6. Select cells B4:C7.

7. In the **Number** group, click the arrow with the **Number Format** box. There are two preset date formats available in the gallery.

8. Choose **Long Date**. This is too much for the worksheet.

9. Click the Undo button ↩ .

Exercise 2-13   APPLY DATE FORMATS FROM THE FORMAT CELLS DIALOG BOX

Excel includes several date formats (besides long and short) in the Format Cells dialog box. If you want to show the month abbreviated or two digits for the year, you can choose or build a date format for that look using the Format Cells dialog box. You can open the Format Cells dialog box for the active cell or range by:

- Clicking the Dialog Box Launcher for the Number group on the Home tab.

- Right-clicking the cell or range and choosing **Format Cells** from the shortcut menu.

- On the Home tab in the Cells group, clicking the Format button 📄 and then choosing **Format Cells**.

- Pressing Ctrl + 1 .

1. Select cells B4:C7 if necessary.

2. Click the Dialog Box Launcher for the **Number** group. The Format Cells dialog box opens to the Number tab with the format for the selected range highlighted. Preset date formats are displayed in the **Type** list on the right. The dates shown are placeholders or samples.

3. Click the type in the list that shows the date first, a hyphen, an abbreviation for the month, another hyphen, and a two-digit year ("14-Mar-01") and click **OK**. All the dates in your worksheet are reformatted.

Figure 2-10
Choosing a date
format
2-4.xlsx
Sheet1 sheet

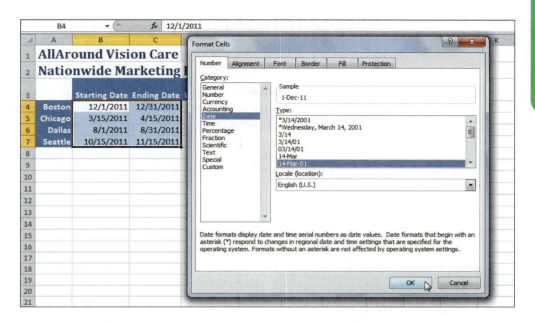

4. Select cell A3. Click the Cell Styles button . Choose **Accent1** from the **Themed Cell Styles**.

5. Select cells A1:G2. Click the Dialog Box Launcher for the **Alignment** group, and center the cells across the selection.

6. Select cells A3:G7. Click the Dialog Box Launcher for the **Font** group. Click the **Border** tab.

7. In the **Style** box, choose a dotted line. Set middle and bottom horizontal borders. Do not click **OK** yet.

8. In the **Style** box, choose a solid line. Set a middle vertical border. Click **OK**.

9. Press Ctrl + Home.

10. Click the Save button 🖫 in the Quick Access Toolbar. Your workbook is saved with the same name.

Creating a Pie Chart

Handwritten ledger pages have no quick way of transforming data into a visual presentation. In addition to its calculation features, a major capability of Excel is its generation of charts. By choosing the appropriate data in a worksheet, a graph can be built with a few clicks of the mouse.

A *pie chart* is a commonly used and easily recognized graph. It illustrates one set of values, and each slice represents one value from the set. By the size of the slice in relation to the whole pie, you can compare the values. A pie chart is best when you have fewer than eight values to be compared. The values must be positive numbers (greater than zero).

In your workbook for this lesson, you will build a pie chart that compares increased costs for the four cities. The pie represents the total cost for AllAround Vision Care. From the slices, it will be easy to determine the distribution of costs across the four locations.

Exercise 2-14   CREATE A PIE CHART

The first step to creating any chart is to select the labels and the values to be plotted. As you become more experienced building charts, it becomes easier to identify what data should be used. After the data are selected, choose the type of chart from the Chart group on the Insert command tab. Excel creates a chart object on the same worksheet as the data. An *object* is any clickable element or part of a worksheet or a chart.

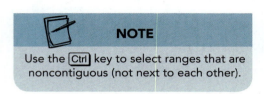

NOTE

Use the [Ctrl] key to select ranges that are noncontiguous (not next to each other).

1. Select cells A4:A7. These are the labels for the pie slices.

2. Hold down the [Ctrl] key and select cells F4:F7. These are the values that will be represented by the slices.

3. Click the **Insert** command tab. Click the Pie button in the **Chart** group. A gallery of pie-chart types opens.

4. In the **3-D Pie** group, click **Pie in 3-D**. A pie chart is inserted in the worksheet and may cover some of the data.

Figure 2-11
Creating a pie chart
2-4.xlsx
Sheet1 sheet

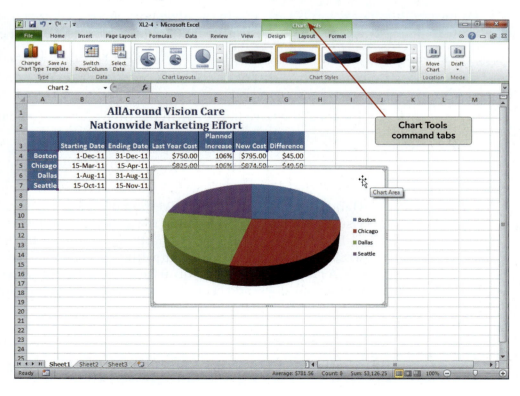

5. Click in the top-right white background of the chart object. Click the **Chart Tools Layout** command tab. In the **Current Selection** group, check that the **Chart Area** is active.

6. Point at the top-right corner of the chart object to display the four-headed move pointer.

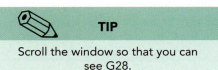

TIP

Scroll the window so that you can see G28.

7. Drag the chart object so that its top-left corner aligns in cell A9.

8. Point at the bottom-right selection handle (three dots arranged in a triangle shape). The sizing pointer is two-headed.

9. Drag the bottom-right selection handle down to cell G28.

Exercise 2-15 ADD A CHART TITLE AND MOVE THE LEGEND

Most charts have titles to explain what they illustrate. Your chart does not have a title, but you can easily add one. Your chart does have a legend, the list of city names at the right. A *legend* is a chart element that explains the colors used to differentiate the values.

1. Click in the top-right white background of the chart object.

2. Click the **Chart Tools Layout** command tab. In the **Labels** group, click the Chart Title button ▣.

3. Choose **Above Chart**. A chart-title placeholder is inserted on the chart.

4. Point at the **Chart Title** placeholder and click. The object is selected and shows a bounding box and four selection handles.

5. Triple-click **Chart Title** and point at the Mini toolbar.

6. Set the font size to **24**.

7. Triple-click **Chart Title** again, and key **Cost Distribution for This Year**. Click in the white chart background.

8. Point at the legend and click to select it. In the **Current Selection** group, you can determine which chart object is active.

9. On the **Chart Tools Layout** command tab in the **Labels** group, click the Legend button ▣.

10. Choose **Show Legend at Bottom**. This allows for the actual pie to be wider.

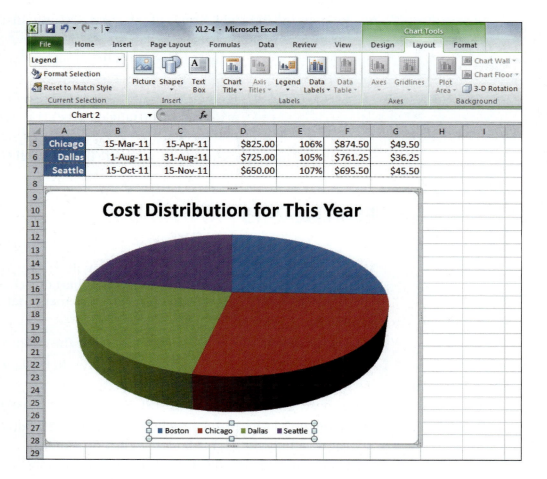

11. Click an empty worksheet cell. The chart is deselected, and the **Chart Tools** command tabs are no longer visible.

12. Press Ctrl + Home.

13. Click the **File** command tab and choose **Save As**. Navigate to your folder.

14. In the **File name** box, change the file name to *[your initials]*2-15. Click **Save**.

Changing the Document Theme

A *document theme* is a combination of 2 fonts, 12 colors, and special effects. The default for a new workbook is the Office theme. The Office document theme uses 11-point Calibri as a body text font; that is the default font. There is also a font for headings, Cambria. In any workbook, however, you can use any font that is listed in your font list. Although a theme lists specific colors, you can use any color available in a color palette, or you can build your own color. Cell styles are based on the document theme, too, using the fonts and colors from the theme.

Document themes have been developed by designers to use fonts, colors, and effects that are coordinated and balanced. Microsoft Excel installs with more than 40 predesigned themes. There are additional professionally designed themes available online from Microsoft and from third-party sources. You or your company can also design, save, and use a custom theme. AllAround Vision Care, for example, may decide to design its own theme using colors and fonts that work well at each of its four locations. Many offices contemplate designing a custom theme so that their work has a distinctive look. When you use only Microsoft themes, you are using the same color palette as all Office users worldwide.

Exercise 2-16　CHANGE THE DOCUMENT THEME

If you use theme fonts and colors in a workbook, those fonts and colors are modified when you apply a different document theme. Nontheme fonts are all the other fonts available on your computer. These are not updated when you change the document theme.

Theme fonts are identified at the top of your font list. Theme colors are displayed when you open a color palette. The Live Preview feature allows you to see any changes before they are applied so you can better judge if the results are what you want.

1. Click the **Home** command tab. Click the arrow next to the **Font** box. The theme fonts are at the top of the list, Cambria for headings and Calibri for body data. Other fonts on your computer are listed below these two.

NOTE

Although a theme includes 12 colors, 2 are for hyperlinks and do not appear in color palettes.

2. Press [Esc]. Click the arrow next to the Font Color button [A]. There are ten theme colors with light-to-dark variations of each. There are also standard colors and **More Colors**.

3. Click **More Colors**. You can choose any color from the spectrum or build your own color on the **Custom** tab.

4. Click **Cancel**.

5. Click the arrow next to the Fill Color button [🎨]. The same theme colors are shown.

6. Click the **Page Layout** command tab. The first group is **Themes**.

7. Hover over the Themes button [Aa]. The ScreenTip includes the current Office theme name.

8. Click the Themes button [Aa] to open its gallery (see Figure 2-13 on the next page).

Figure 2-13
The Document
Themes gallery
2-15.xlsx
Sheet1 sheet

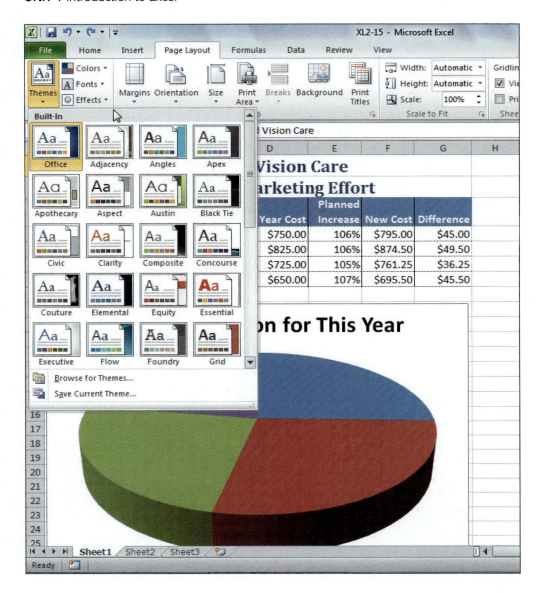

9. Hover over each theme icon and note how the worksheet and chart are formatted.

10. Find and click the **Urban** theme.

11. Click the **Home** command tab.

12. Click the arrow next to the **Font** box. The Urban theme fonts are Trebuchet MS for headings and Georgia for body text.

13. Click cell A1 and check the font name in the **Font** box. This cell uses the Title cell style, which applies the headings font for the current theme.

14. Click cell A4 and check the font name in the **Font** box. This cell uses the Accent1 cell style and the body text font.

15. Click cell B4. The body text font for this theme is Georgia.

Exercise 2-17   RENAME A WORKSHEET AND CHANGE THE TAB COLOR

You can rename a worksheet tab with a more descriptive name to help you and others remember the worksheet's purpose. Use names that contribute to your understanding of what is included in the workbook. Worksheet names can be up to 31 characters, and you can use spaces in the name. You can also change the color shown on the worksheet tab. This can serve as a visual cue for quickly locating a specific sheet. In some of its workbooks, AllAround Vision Care assigns a specific color to each city so that a worker can quickly identify which sheet to use.

1.   Double-click the worksheet tab for **Sheet1**. The tab name is selected.

2.   Key **MarketingCosts** and press Enter.

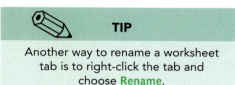

TIP

Another way to rename a worksheet tab is to right-click the tab and choose **Rename**.

3.   Double-click **Sheet2** and name it **Plans**. The **Plans** sheet is empty.

4.   Right-click the **MarketingCosts** tab and choose **Tab Color**. The Theme Colors palette are colors for the Urban theme.

5.   Choose **Purple, Accent 3, Darker 25%** in the seventh column.

Figure 2-14
Changing the tab color
2-15.xlsx
MarketingCosts sheet

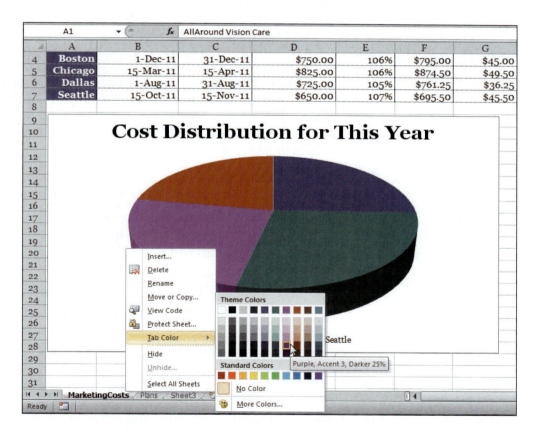

6. Click the **Plans** tab. Now you can better see the color of the **MarketingCosts** tab.

7. Click the **MarketingCosts** tab.

Using Page Layout View

Workbooks open in Normal view which provides the most screen space for rows and columns. Page Layout view is interactive and simulates a printed page. It includes horizontal and vertical rulers so that you can change the margins by dragging a marker. You can adjust column widths and row heights as well as edit data from this view. Many users like Page Layout view for building headers and footers too. With all these additional choices, there is less space for your actual data in Page Layout view.

Headers and footers are used to display the page number, a company name, a department, the date, a company logo, or many other types of documentation. Corporations or government bodies might use a header/footer for a disclaimer that appears on every page. A *disclaimer* is a statement that specifies or limits an obligation or legal right associated with the document.

You can switch to Page Layout view by clicking the Page Layout button 🔲 in the status bar or the Page Layout button 📄 on the View command tab.

Exercise 2-18   EDIT DATA AND CHANGE PAGE MARGINS

Excel sets 0.70 inch for left and right margins in a new workbook. The top and bottom margins are both set at 0.75 inch. You can change margins and column widths in Page Layout view by dragging a margin marker or a column heading border. As you drag, the margin setting or column width is shown in inches or character spaces in a ScreenTip. Column headings are just below the horizontal ruler. Margin markers are located at the left, right, top, and bottom ends of the rulers.

1. Click the Page Layout button 🔲 in the status bar. You can see that the worksheet is too wide to fit on a portrait page. A *portrait* page is taller than it is wide.

2. Click the Zoom Out button ⊖ in the status bar two times. In 80% magnification, you can better see how this data do not fit on the page.

3. Double-click cell B3 to start Edit mode. Click in front of the "D" in "Date." Press Alt+Enter and then press Enter.

4. Insert a line break in cell C3 using the same steps. Insert a line break in cell D3 after "Year."

5. Center the contents in cells B3:C3. Then autofit columns B:D.

6. In Page Layout view, hover over the left margin marker. The pointer changes to a two-headed arrow, and a ScreenTip shows the setting.

7. Click and drag left to set a left margin of about **0.65 inch**. Your margin setting does not need to be exact.

Figure 2-15
Changing page
margins in Page
Layout view
**2-15.xlsx
MarketingCosts
sheet**

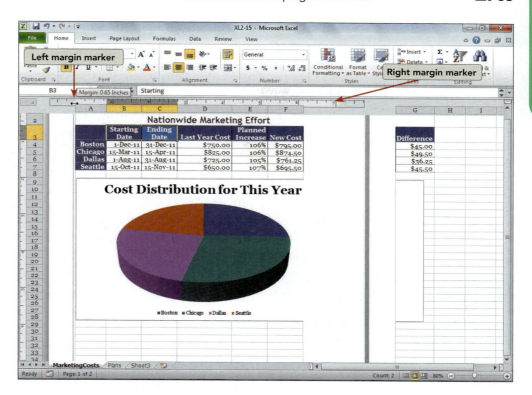

---

8. Hover the pointer over the right margin marker. Click and drag right to reach **0.65 inch**.

9. Hover the pointer over the top margin marker. Click and drag down to reach **1.00 inch**.

Exercise 2-19   SET A HEADER AND A FOOTER

A *header* prints at the top of each page in a worksheet. A *footer* prints at the bottom of each page. Excel has preset headers and footers, or you can create your own. In Normal view, you cannot see headers or footers.

A header or footer can have up to three sections. The left section prints at the left margin. The center section prints at the horizontal center of the page. The right section aligns at the right margin. Header and footer margins are preset to print 0.3 inch from the top and bottom of the page, within the top and bottom margin areas.

You can create headers and footers by:

- Clicking the Page Layout view button 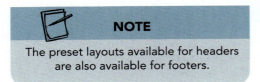 on the status bar.
- Clicking the Page Layout button in the Workbook View group on the View tab.
- Clicking the Header & Footer button in the Text group on the Insert tab.
- Clicking the Dialog Box Launcher in the Page Setup group on the Page Layout tab.
- Clicking **Page Setup** in Backstage view for printing.

1. Click **Click to add header** above the main labels. The insertion point is in the middle section of the header area. The Header & Footer Tools Design tab is a context-sensitive tab that opens when the insertion point is within a header or footer section.

> **NOTE**
>
> The preset layouts available for headers are also available for footers.

2. In the **Header & Footer** group at the left, click the Header button. A gallery of preset header arrangements opens. Sections are separated by commas. A single item prints in the center section. Two items print with the first in the center and the second in the right section. Three items print with one each at the left, in the center, and at the right.

Figure 2-16
Choosing a Preset
Header
2-15.xlsx
MarketingCosts
sheet

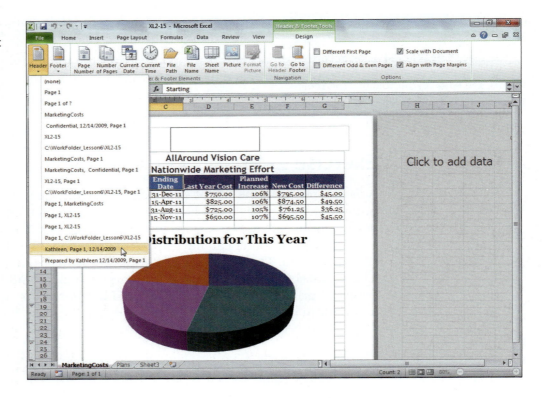

3. Find and choose the three-item layout that shows the user name, the page number, and the date. You will see the header on the sheet.

4. Point at the date in the header and click. The code for displaying the current date is **&[Date]**.

5. Point at the page number and click. The code includes the word "Page" and then the code **&[Page]**.

6. Point at the user name and click. This name is taken from the user name settings in the Excel Options dialog box. Edit it now to be *[Your First and Last Name]*.

7. Click the **Header and Footer Tools Design** tab. In the **Navigation** group, click the Go to Footer button. The window has scrolled, and you likely do not see the top of the worksheet.

8. Point inside the right footer section and click.

9. In the **Header and Footer Elements** group, click the File Name button. The code is **&[File]**.

10. Click a cell above the footer area. This completes the footer and returns the focus to your worksheet.

11. Press Ctrl+Home. If you see **Click to add data** on the right, the data fits horizontally on the current page. If your workbook shows the header for page 2 on the right, it means that the page is still too wide. You can reduce the chart width to fit the sheet to a single page if necessary.

TIP

You may see **Click to add data** below the page, too, if your screen resolution settings allow for more information to be visible.

NOTE

Follow your class procedures for submitting work.

12. Click the white chart background near the chart title. Rest the mouse pointer on the bottom-right selection handle to display the two-headed sizing handle.

13. Drag the handle left as little as possible until you do see **Click to add data** on the right. This marks an empty page.

14. Click the Normal button in the status bar. You do not see headers and footers in Normal view.

15. Press Ctrl+Home. Click the **File** command tab and choose **Save As**. Navigate to your folder.

16. Change the file name to *[your initials]*2-19. Click **Save**.

17. Close the workbook.

Using Online Help

Understanding formulas is a vital skill to develop in order to become a proficient Excel user.

LOOK UP FORMULAS

1. Click the Microsoft Office Excel Help button.

2. In the Search box, key **create formula**, and press Enter.

3. In the list of topics, choose a topic related to creating formulas.

4. When you finish investigating formulas, close the Help window.

Lesson 2   Summary

- Before beginning a workbook, analyze what you want to show and what data you will use.
- Take some time to plan your worksheet layout and experiment until you develop a logical, easy-to-read report.
- In a blank workbook, you can key values, labels, dates, and formulas. Excel recognizes data by the first character you key in a cell.
- To complete a cell entry, press Enter, Tab, or any arrow key or click another cell. You can also click the Enter button ✔ in the formula bar.
- Labels are aligned at the left edge of a cell. If they are longer than the column width, they spill into the next column if it is empty. Otherwise, they appear cut off on the screen.
- AutoCorrect automatically corrects some typographical errors for labels as you key them.
- Values and dates are right-aligned in the cell. There are several preset formats for both values and dates.
- Common formats, such as accounting number, can be applied to cells from the Number group on the Home tab. Many other formats are available in the Format Cells dialog box.
- Formulas are keyed in a cell using arithmetic symbols and cell references. You can also point to a cell to add its address to a formula.
- Many formulas, when copied, use a relative reference so that they are updated to reflect the row and column in which they are located.
- Many commands can be applied to a cell range, or group of cells. Ranges can be selected using the mouse or keyboard commands.
- A cell style is a preset collection of format settings.
- A pie chart is a popular chart type used to represent one set of numbers from the worksheet.
- A document theme is a preset arrangement of colors, fonts, and effects for a workbook. New workbooks use the Office document theme.
- The worksheet tab name can be changed to a more descriptive name. You can also change the worksheet tab color for visual cues.
- Page Layout view provides quick access to changing margins, adjusting column widths, and setting headers and footers.
- A header prints at the top of every page. It usually includes some type of documentation for the worksheet. A footer prints at the bottom of every page.

LESSON 2		Command Summary	
Feature	Button	Ribbon Location	Keyboard
Accounting Number Format	$	Home, Number	
Align Text Left		Home, Alignment	
Cell style		Home, Styles	
Chart title		Chart Tools Layout, Labels	
Copy		Home, Clipboard	Ctrl + C
Currency format		Home, Number	
Document Theme		Page Layout, Themes	
Font Color		Home, Font	Ctrl + 1
Format Painter		Home, Clipboard	
Header/footer		Insert, Text	
Legend		Chart Tools Layout, Labels	
Page Layout view		View, Workbook Views	
Paste		Home, Clipboard	Ctrl + V
Pie chart		Insert, Chart	
Rename sheet		Home, Cells	
Save		File, Save	
Tab color		Home, Cells	

Please visit our Online Learning Center, *www.lessonapproach2010.com,* **where you will find the following review materials:**

- **Concepts Review**

  True/False Questions

  Short Answer Questions

  Critical Thinking Questions

- **Skills Review**

  Review Exercises that target single skills

  Lesson Applications

  Review Exercises that challenge students by testing multiple skills in each exercise

- **On Your Own**

  Open-ended exercises that require students to synthesize multiple skills and apply creativity and problem-solving as they would in a real world business situation

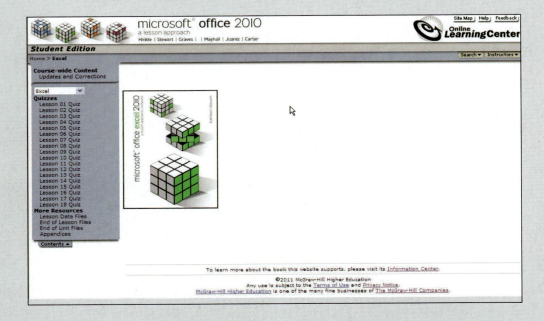

Developing Editing and Formatting Skills

OBJECTIVES *After completing this lesson, you will be able to:*

1. Insert and delete sheets and cells.
2. Copy, cut, and paste cell contents.
3. Use AutoComplete and Pick From Drop-down List.
4. Use Find and Replace commands.
5. Work with the Alignment group.
6. Use the Format Cells dialog box.
7. Format with data bars.

Estimated Time: 1¼ hours

Your ability to edit, update, rearrange, and format worksheets enables you to develop a well-designed report for any audience. Excel's editing tools are similar to features available in Word and PowerPoint, especially those related to text and objects. For example, you can cut, copy, and paste labels or values from one worksheet to another to save time keying data. If a function name has been keyed incorrectly throughout a large worksheet, you can use Find and Replace commands to quickly correct such an error. Formatting tools in Excel include preset styles as well as individual commands for setting alignment, fill, borders, and more.

Inserting and Deleting Sheets and Cells

When you plan a new workbook, you may know how many sheets will be required to accomplish your work. In other cases, you may start with the default three worksheets and develop a workbook that has one sheet for each month of a year. If your instructor uses Excel to manage course grades, he or she may maintain separate sheets for each course and/or semester. Or he or she may keep a separate workbook for each course.

A new Excel workbook starts with three blank worksheets, but you can insert as many sheets as your computer's memory allows. The number of sheets allowable also depends on how much data are stored on each sheet. And if you discover that you have more sheets than you need, you can delete sheets to create a more compact file.

You insert a new worksheet when you:

- Click the Insert Worksheet tab.
- Press [Shift] + [F11].
- In the Cells group on the Home tab, click the arrow with the Insert Cells button and choose Insert Sheet.
- Right-click a worksheet tab and choose Insert. Then choose Worksheet in the dialog box.

You delete a worksheet when you:

- Right-click the worksheet tab and choose Delete.
- In the Cells group on the Home tab, click the arrow with the Delete Cells button and choose Delete Sheet.

Exercise 3-1 INSERT, MOVE, AND DELETE WORKSHEETS

Excel names inserted sheets starting with the next number in sequence. For example, if the workbook already has **Sheet1**, **Sheet2**, and **Sheet3**, a new, inserted sheet would be named **Sheet4**. The workbook for Lesson 3 has a single sheet that tracks number of service hours donated by AllAround Vision Care ophthalmologists. The data list a date, the doctor's name, hours, a reference number, and a service code. There is a section on the worksheet for the main data and two supporting areas with related labels.

> **TIP**
>
> You can change the default number of sheets in a new workbook in the General pane in the Excel Options dialog box (File command tab).

1. Open **Excel_Lesson3**. This workbook has one worksheet named **DonatedService**. Notice that there is no **Sheet1**.

2. Click the **Insert Worksheet** tab. A blank sheet is inserted after the **DonatedService** sheet, named **Sheet1**.

3. Double-click the **Sheet1** tab. Key **Doctors** and press [Enter]. The worksheet tab is renamed.

> **NOTE**
>
> Your sheet numbers might be different if you or someone else was working in Excel before you started this lesson.

4. Right-click the **Doctors** tab. Choose a color different from the color of the **DonatedService** sheet.

5. Press [Shift] + [F11]. A new worksheet named **Sheet2** is placed in front of the **Doctors** sheet with this keyboard shortcut.

6. Right-click the **DonatedService** tab and choose **Insert**. The Insert dialog box opens.

7. Click the **General** tab if necessary. This tab shows the types of objects you can insert in your workbook. You may have objects different from the text figure. The **Spreadsheet Solutions** tab lists sample Excel templates (model workbooks) that are available on your computer.

Figure 3-1
Insert Worksheet
dialog box

8. On the **General** tab, make sure **Worksheet** is selected and click **OK**. A new **Sheet3** is placed before the **DonatedService** worksheet.

9. Click the **DonatedService** tab, and point at the tab to display a white arrow pointer.

10. Click and drag the tab to the left of **Sheet3**. As you drag, you see a small sheet icon and a triangle that marks the new position of the sheet.

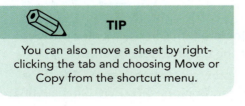

TIP

You can also move a sheet by right-clicking the tab and choosing Move or Copy from the shortcut menu.

11. Release the mouse button. The **DonatedService** sheet is now the leftmost tab.

12. Right-click the **Sheet3** tab. Choose **Delete**. The sheet is deleted, and **Sheet2** is active.

13. On the **Home** command tab in the **Cells** group, click the arrow with the Delete Cells button. Choose **Delete Sheet**. The sheet is deleted, and the **Doctors** worksheet is active.

14. Right-click any one of the tab scrolling buttons to the left of the **Donated Service** tab. A list of the worksheet names appears so that you can choose which one to make active.

15. Choose **DonatedService**.

Exercise 3-2 INSERT AND DELETE CELLS

It is not unusual to have to insert rows or columns in a worksheet. In your workbook, the company may decide to insert data from the month of March between rows 9 and 10. It may realize it needs to insert a column for displaying the doctors' cities. Although it is common to insert and/or delete rows and columns, you can also insert and delete cells. When you do this, you can accidentally rearrange data if you don't watch the entire sheet.

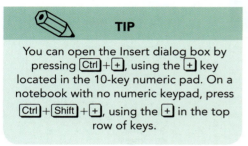

TIP

You can open the Insert dialog box by pressing Ctrl + +, using the + key located in the 10-key numeric pad. On a notebook with no numeric keypad, press Ctrl + Shift + +, using the + in the top row of keys.

1. Set the zoom size so that you can see columns A through I.

2. Click cell D15. This label belongs in column E. One way to solve this problem is to insert a cell at this location, moving the label to the right.

3. Right-click cell D15 and choose **Insert**. An Insert dialog box opens with choices about what happens after the cell is inserted.

Figure 3-2
Insert dialog box
Excel_Lesson3.xlsx
DonatedSheet
sheet

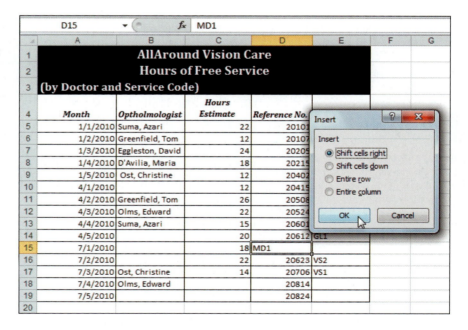

4. Choose **Shift cells right** and click **OK**. A blank cell is inserted, making room for the missing reference number. The service code is now in the correct column. But everything in row 15 to the right of cell D15 has been moved one cell to the right.

5. Point at the Insert Options button 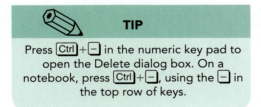 and click its arrow. None of the choices would eliminate the problem.

6. Click the Undo button in the Quick Access Toolbar. It would be better to move the label rather than insert a cell in this case.

NOTE

You will see the Mini toolbar when you right-click a cell.

7. Select cells I7:I9. Right-click any cell in the range and choose **Insert**.

8. Choose **Shift cells down** and click **OK**. Everything in column I has shifted down three cells, and the data are out of alignment now.

Figure 3-3
Three cells inserted, with other cells shifted down
Excel_Lesson3.xlsx DonatedService sheet

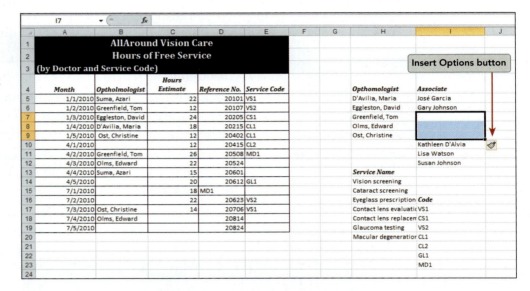

9. Click the Undo button.

10. Right-click cell H7 and choose **Delete**. The Delete dialog box opens.

TIP

Press Ctrl + − in the numeric key pad to open the Delete dialog box. On a notebook, press Ctrl + −, using the − in the top row of keys.

11. Choose **Shift cells up** and click **OK**. The error is not apparent in the doctors' names, but it is in the service code list.

12. Click the Undo button.

Copying, Cutting, and Pasting Cell Contents

The capability to move and/or copy data enables you to rearrange or duplicate your work when necessary. The Clipboard group of commands on the Home command tab is the same in the major Office applications. These commands include cut, copy, and paste with all the variations and options for these tasks.

You can copy or cut (move) cell contents in a worksheet. When you copy or cut a cell or range of cells, a duplicate of the data is placed on the *Windows Clipboard*. This is a temporary memory area used to keep data you have copied or cut.

Data that is cut can be pasted once. Data that is copied can be pasted many times and in many locations. Copied data stays on the Windows Clipboard until you copy or cut another cell or range. Then that data replaces the data on the Windows Clipboard.

The Cut and Paste commands are used to move labels and values from one cell to another. To use cut and paste, first select the cells you want to cut, and then:

- Click the Cut button ✂ in the Clipboard group. Position the pointer at the new location and click the Paste button 📋 or press Enter.

- Right-click the selected cells. Choose Cut. Right-click the new cell location and choose Paste.

- Select the cell or range. Drag it to a new location.

- Press Ctrl+X. Position the pointer at the new location and press Ctrl+V or press Enter.

The Copy and Paste commands make a duplicate of the data in another location. To use copy and paste, select the cells you want to copy, and then:

- Click the Copy button 📋 in the Clipboard group. Position the pointer at the new location, and click the Paste button 📋 or press Enter.

- Right-click the selected cells. Choose Copy. Right-click the new cell location and choose Paste.

- Select the cell or range. While holding down the Ctrl key, drag it to a new location.

- Press Ctrl+C. Position the pointer at the new location and press Ctrl+V or press Enter.

Exercise 3-3 CUT AND PASTE CELL CONTENTS

When you paste cells that have been cut, the cut data replace existing data unless you tell Excel to insert the cut data. Formatting is also cut, often with unexpected results. Inserting cut cells is one way to rearrange data too.

1. Click cell B11. Click the Cut button ✂. A moving marquee surrounds the cell.

2. Click cell B15 and then click the Paste button 📋. The name is removed from cell B11 and pasted in cell B15. The marquee is canceled.

3. Select cells B12:B13 and right-click either cell. Choose **Cut**. The range displays the moving marquee.

4. Click cell B16 and press [Enter] to paste. This time, the names originally in cells B12:B13 are moved, the borders are cut, and the original name in cell B17 has been replaced.

Figure 3-4
Cutting cell contents
Excel_Lesson3.xlsx
DonatedService
sheet

	A	B	C	D	E	F
	B16		fx	Olms, Edward		
1		**AllAround Vision Care**				
2		**Hours of Free Service**				
3	**(by Doctor and Service Code)**					
4	*Month*	*Optholmologist*	*Hours Estimate*	*Reference No.*	*Service Code*	
5	1/1/2010	Suma, Azari	22	20101	VS1	
6	1/2/2010	Greenfield, Tom	12	20107	VS2	
7	1/3/2010	Eggleston, David	24	20205	CS1	
8	1/4/2010	D'Avilia, Maria	18	20215	CL1	
9	1/5/2010	Ost, Christine	12	20402	CL1	
10	4/1/2010		12	20415	CL2	
11	4/2/2010		26	20508	MD1	
12	4/3/2010		22	20524		
13	4/4/2010		15	20601		
14	4/5/2010		20	20612	GL1	
15	7/1/2010	Greenfield, Tom	18	MD1		
16	7/2/2010	Olms, Edward	22	20623	VS2	
17	7/3/2010	Suma, Azari	14	20706	VS1	
18	7/4/2010	Olms, Edward		20814		
19	7/5/2010			20824		
20						

REVIEW

Cells share borders, so the top border from cell B12 affected the bottom border of cell B11.

5. Select cells H17:I17. Click the Cut button .

6. Click cell H16 and then click the Paste button. A regular Paste command replaces existing data. One of the service code lines is missing now.

7. Click the Undo button and press [Esc] to cancel the marquee.

8. Select cells H17:I17 again. Click the Cut button.

9. Right-click cell H16 and choose **Insert Cut Cells**. The data from cells H17:I17 are inserted, and the other codes have shifted down.

Exercise 3-4   COPY AND PASTE CELL CONTENTS

1. Click cell B15 and click the Copy button. The cell is surrounded by the moving marquee.

NOTE

Close the Clipboard task pane if it opens.

2. Click cell B11 and click the Paste button. The label is pasted, and the Paste Options button appears.

3. Right-click cell B16 and choose **Copy**. The data replace the previous data in the Windows Clipboard.

4. Right-click cell B12 and hover on the Paste button  in the shortcut menu. The menu fades, and Paste Preview shows the name that will be pasted (Olms Edward). Do not click anything yet.

5. Point in the menu area and hover at **Paste Special** to see the choices.

Figure 3-5
Paste Special Options
Excel_Lesson3.xlsx DonatedService sheet

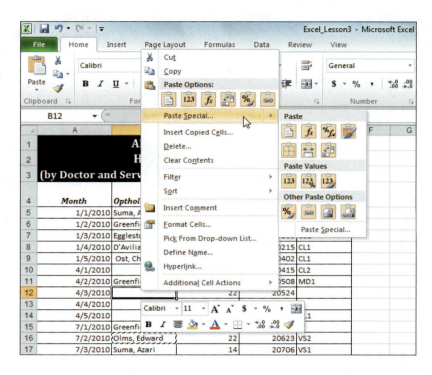

TIP

The marquee is not canceled after you click the Paste button  to remind you that you can paste data again in a different location.

6. In the Other Paste Options group, hover at and then click the Formatting button. This command copies only the formatting; the name is not copied.

7. Select cells C13:C14. Press Ctrl+C. Excel displays a marquee around the range.

8. Click cell C18. You only need to click in the first cell for the copy as long as the destination range is empty.

9. Press Ctrl+V. The values are duplicated. The marquee remains as well as the Paste Options button.

10. Click cell C20. Press Ctrl+V to paste again.

11. Press Esc to cancel the marquee.

NOTE

Copied cells replace existing data unless you choose the option to insert them.

12. Select the range A18:E19 and right-click any cell in the range. Choose **Copy**.

13. Right-click cell A20 and paste the data.

14. Select the range A5:E7 and press Ctrl+C.

15. Right-click cell A10. Choose **Insert Copied Cells**. The Insert Paste dialog box opens.

16. Choose **Shift cells down**. Click **OK**. The copied cells are inserted, and the existing cells are shifted down in the column. Notice that the data in columns H and I are not affected.

17. Press [Esc] to cancel the marquee.

18. Select the range H4:I20 and click the Copy button 📋.

19. Click the **Doctors** worksheet tab and right-click cell A1.

20. Hover at the Paste button 📋 in the shortcut menu to see the Paste Preview.

21. Point to redisplay the menu and hover at **Paste Special**. Click the Keep Source Column Widths button 📋. The data are copied, and column widths are maintained.

22. Click the **DonatedService** worksheet tab and press [Esc] to cancel the marquee.

TIP

The Paste Options keyboard shortcuts are [Ctrl] plus the letter shown with the command.

Exercise 3-5   USE DRAG AND DROP

The easiest way to copy or cut data when you can see both the original and the destination cells on-screen is to drag and drop. This is a Windows feature that works in almost all software programs. In Excel, the *drag-and-drop pointer* is a four-headed arrow. You see it when you point at any edge of a cell. When you just drag the data from one cell to another, it is a cut and paste. If you hold down the [Ctrl] key while dragging, the command is copy and paste.

1. Select cell D18. Place the pointer at the top or bottom edge or border of the cell. The drag-and-drop pointer ✥ appears.

2. Hold down the mouse button and drag to cell E18. A ScreenTip identifies the destination cell. You can also see a ghost highlight that shows where the data will be placed.

Figure 3-6
Using drag and drop to cut
Excel_Lesson3.xlsx
DonatedService sheet

15	4/3/2010		22	20524	
16	4/4/2010		15	20601	
17	4/5/2010		20	20612	GL1
18	7/1/2010	Greenfield, Tom	18	MD1	
19	7/2/2010	Olms, Edward	22	20623	VS2
20	7/3/2010	Suma, Azari	14	20706	VS1

3. Release the mouse button. This was a cut and paste.

4. Place the pointer at the top or bottom edge or border of cell B20 to display the drag-and-drop pointer. Notice the missing borders in row 18 though.

5. Hold down [Ctrl]. You will see a tiny plus sign (+) with a solid white arrow to signify this will be a copy and paste. Do not release [Ctrl].

6. Click and drag cell B20 to cell B23. Release the mouse button first and then release [Ctrl]. This is a drag and drop to perform a copy and paste. The original name in cell B23 has been replaced.

7. Select cells H4:I9. Place the pointer at the top or bottom edge of the range to display the drag-and-drop pointer.

8. Hold down the [Ctrl] key to display the plus sign (+) and the white arrow pointer. Do not release the [Ctrl] key.

9. Click and drag down to cells H23:I28. Release the mouse button first and then [Ctrl]. The entire range is copied.

Exercise 3-6   USE THE OFFICE CLIPBOARD

The *Office Clipboard* is a temporary memory area that can hold up to 24 copied items. It is separate from and in addition to the Windows Clipboard. The Office Clipboard is available when any Office application (Excel, Access, Word, or PowerPoint) is running. It is shared among these programs, so something you copy in Excel can be pasted in Word. The options for the Office Clipboard allow you to set it to open automatically when you first copy an object and to show a screen message after copying.

1. Click the Dialog Box Launcher in the Clipboard group. The Clipboard task pane opens at the left of the window. You may see values and labels from your last copy task.

2. Click the Clear All button 🗋 in the Clipboard task pane. If the Clear All button 🗋 is grayed or dimmed, you have nothing on the Clipboard and can continue.

3. Select the range A6:E6 and click the Copy button 🗋. An Excel icon and the data appear in the task pane. There is an icon 🗋 in the lower right corner of the Windows taskbar too. You'll see a ScreenTip if you rest the mouse pointer on it.

4. Select the range H23:I24 and click the Copy button 🗋. Another icon and data appear in the pane, above the first set.

5. Press [Esc]. The marquee is removed.

6. Click cell A25. Click the second object in the Clipboard task pane to paste an entry.

Figure 3-7
Using the clipboard task pane
Excel_Lesson3.xlsx DonatedService sheet

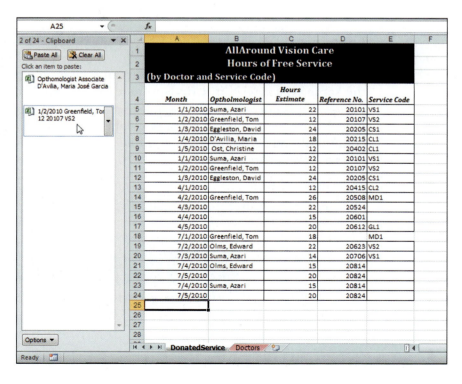

7. Click cell C28. Click the first object in the task pane.

8. Click the Clear All button 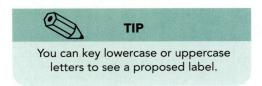 in the task pane, and then close the task pane.

9. Delete the contents of cells C28:D29. Then delete the contents of cells H23:I28. Press [Ctrl]+[Home].

Using AutoComplete and Pick From Drop-Down List

In many workbooks, there is repetition of labels in a column. Your workbook includes the same doctors' names, the same reference numbers, and the same service codes in columns B, D, and E. These labels are routine in this worksheet. A business that tracks sales data might repeat a product name or a sales location many times in a column. If you keep your check and debit transactions in a worksheet, you would probably use the same label for routine expenses or payees. There are several ways of streamlining repetitive or routine data entry like this. Two such features depend on labels already in the column.

*   *AutoComplete* displays a suggested label after you key the first character(s) in a cell. AutoComplete works for labels that are all text or a combination of text and numbers.

*   *Pick From Drop-down List* displays a list of labels already in the column for your selection. This method is helpful when it is important that you use exactly the same data as already entered. It's a simple way to validate data as they are entered.

Exercise 3-7   USE AUTOCOMPLETE

When you key the first few characters of a label, Excel scans the column for the same characters. If it finds a match, it displays a proposed entry. If the suggestion is correct, press [Enter]. If the suggested label is not what you want, ignore it and continue to key a new label. Depending how many rows in the column already contain data, you may need to key more than one character before Excel proposes a label.

1. Click cell B13.

2. Key **d** to see an AutoComplete suggestion. In this case, Excel's suggestion is correct.

> **TIP**
>
> You can key lowercase or uppercase letters to see a proposed label.

Figure 3-8
An AutoComplete
suggestion
**Excel_Lesson3.xlsx
DonatedService
sheet**

	A	B	C	D	E
			B13	▾ ◉ ✗ ✓ *fx*	d'Avilia, Maria
1		AllAround Vision Care			
2		Hours of Free Service			
3	(by Doctor and Service Code)				
4	Month	Optholmologist	Hours Estimate	Reference No.	Service Code
5	1/1/2010	Suma, Azari	22	20101	VS1
6	1/2/2010	Greenfield, Tom	12	20107	VS2
7	1/3/2010	Eggleston, David	24	20205	CS1
8	1/4/2010	D'Avilia, Maria	18	20215	CL1
9	1/5/2010	Ost, Christine	12	20402	CL1
10	1/1/2010	Suma, Azari	22	20101	VS1
11	1/2/2010	Greenfield, Tom	12	20107	VS2
12	1/3/2010	Eggleston, David	24	20205	CS1
13	4/1/2010	d'Avilia, Maria	12	20415	CL2
14	4/2/2010	Greenfield, Tom	26	20508	MD1

3. Press [Enter]. The label is entered with the same capitalization as the existing label in the column.

4. In cell B15, key **e** and press [Enter].

5. Click cell H21. Key **c**. No suggestion is made, because two labels in the column start with "c." Excel needs more information.

6. Key **a** to see a suggestion for "cataract screening."

7. Press [Enter]. The first character is uppercase.

8. Click cell H10 and key an uppercase **G**. Excel has found a match, but you can ignore it.

9. Key **olden, Dan** and press [Enter].

10. Click cell D18 and key **20**. Excel does not make AutoComplete suggestions for values.

11. Key **712** to complete the reference number and press [Enter].

Exercise 3-8   USE PICK FROM DROP-DOWN LIST

The Pick From Drop-down List option appears on the shortcut menu when you right-click a cell. Do this before you key any character.

1. Right-click cell B16.

2. Choose **Pick From Drop-down List**. Excel displays a list of labels already in column B.

3. Click **Olms, Edward** (see Figure 3-9 on the next page). The name is inserted in the cell.

Figure 3-9
Using Pick From
Drop-down List
**Excel_Lesson3.xlsx
DonatedService
sheet**

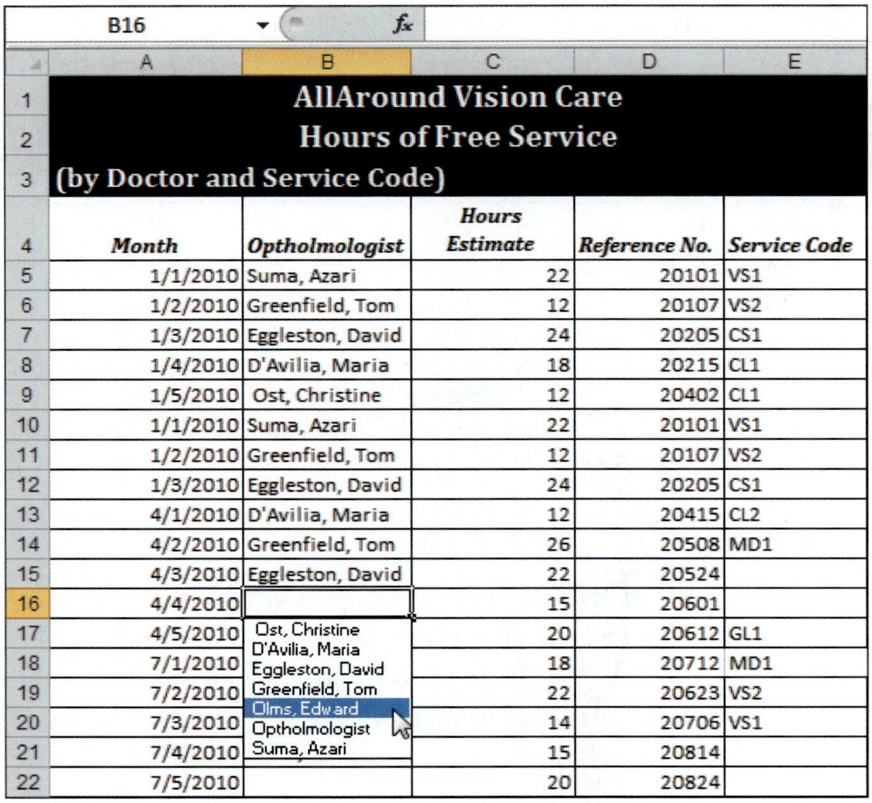

4. Right-click cell E15. Choose **Pick From Drop-down List**. All labels in the column are listed.

5. Click **MD1**.

6. Right-click cell A20. Choose **Pick From Drop-down List**. Only labels from rows 1:3 are listed. Dates are values and not available for AutoComplete or Pick From Drop-down List.

7. Press ⌈Esc⌋. Select cells D18:E18.

8. Click the Dialog Box Launcher in the **Font** group. Click the **Border** tab. Add the missing vertical borders and click **OK**.

Exercise 3-9   SPELL-CHECK A LABEL

The data in this workbook are labels and values. Labels are usually titles, names, addresses, or list-type information, not necessarily dictionary words. Excel does have a spelling command, and it is a worthwhile task to spell-check your work before distributing it. The Excel speller checks labels in a worksheet against its dictionary and highlights all that have no match. You can check the entire worksheet, or you can simply select a range of cells to check a label or two.

1. Click cell B4.

2. Click the **Review** command tab.

3. Click the Spelling button ⌨ in the **Proofing** group. The Spelling dialog box indicates that the word is misspelled and offers the correction.

Figure 3-10
Checking the spelling
Excel_Lesson3.xlsx DonatedService sheet

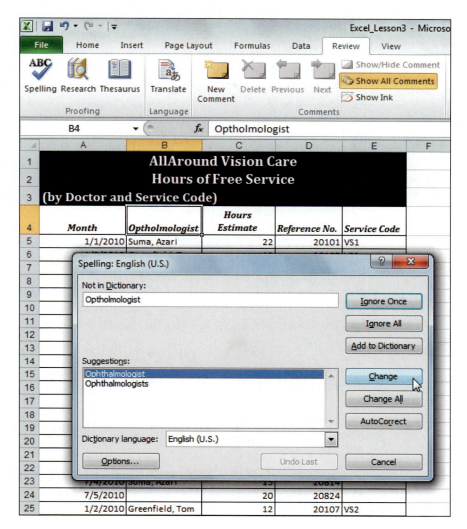

4. Click **Ophthalmologist** in the **Suggestions** list, and then click **Change**. The correction is made and the next error is located.

5. Click **Change**. The second error is corrected, and one of the doctor's names is highlighted as an error.

6. Click **Ignore All**. This option ignores all occurrences of the exact same spelling of the name.

7. Click **Ignore All** for several more names. Excel will highlight many names as misspelled, but it will not flag common first and last names.

8. Choose **Yes** in the message box that shows **Do you want to continue checking at the beginning of the sheet?** The company name is noted.

9. Click **Close** and then click **OK**.

10. Press ⌈Ctrl⌉+⌈Home⌉. Save the workbook as *[your initials]*3-9.

Using Find and Replace Commands

Find and Replace commands are time-saver steps for updating and/or correcting data. In your workbook, one of the doctor's names has been misspelled each time it appears. To fix it, you can find the incorrect label and replace it with the correct one. Find and Replace commands are especially helpful for large worksheets with hundreds or thousands of rows and/or columns, because you don't need to look through all that data to find what you are looking for.

The Find command locates a *character string,* a sequence of letters, numbers, or symbols. You can also use the Find command to locate formats, such as everything in a worksheet that is bold.

There are two ways to start the Find command:

- Click the Find & Select button ![binoculars icon] in the **Editing** group on the **Home** command tab and choose **Find**.

- Press [Ctrl]+[F] or [Shift]+[F5].

The Replace command locates occurrences of a character string and substitutes a replacement string. A *replacement string* is a sequence of characters that are exchanged for existing data. The Replace command can also search for a format, replacing it with another format.

There are two ways to start the Replace command:

- Click the Find & Select button ![binoculars icon] in the **Editing** group on the **Home** command tab and choose **Replace**.

- Press [Ctrl]+[H].

Find and Replace commands share a dialog box, so you can actually use any of these four methods to start either command.

Exercise 3-10   FIND AND REPLACE A LABEL

The Find command searches cells in the worksheet or the workbook, depending on your choice. You can search by column or row. If you know that the name you are looking for is in column A or B, it is faster to search by column. You can be quite specific, too, and choose an option to search formulas and values. Other options let you match the capitalization or the entire cell contents.

In find and replace character strings, do not key format symbols such as the dollar sign or a comma. Format symbols are not treated as part of the data in Excel.

NOTE

The Find command does not search separate clickable objects in a workbook such as a chart.

1. Click the Find & Select button ![binoculars icon] in the **Editing** group on the **Home** command tab. Choose **Find**. The Find and Replace dialog box opens. Notice that each command has a separate tab.

2. Key **suma** in the **Find what** box. A search string is not case-sensitive.

NOTE

Cell addresses in the Find and Replace dialog box are shown with dollar signs ($) to indicate an absolute reference. "Absolute" means only that particular cell address holds a match.

TIP

You can size the Find dialog box by dragging one of its corners. Move it by dragging it by the title bar.

NOTE

If the dialog box shows Options <<, it is expanded.

3. Click **Find All**. The dialog box expands to list information about each cell that includes this string of characters. The first occurrence is outlined in the worksheet (cell B5) and highlighted in the list.

4. Click the **Replace** tab in the dialog box.

5. Click in the **Replace with** box and key **Sumah**. The replacement string is case-sensitive, and you should use capitalization exactly as you want it to be replaced.

6. Click **Options >>** to expand the dialog box. You can set search formats, how the search is made, and upper- and lowercase letters.

7. Make sure there is no checkmark for **Match case**. If checked, Excel would only locate "suma" in lowercase letters, of which there is none.

8. Make sure there is no checkmark for **Match entire cell contents**. If checked, your Find string would have to include the entire last and first names with the comma.

9. Verify that your search will be within the **Sheet**, **By Rows**, and in **Formulas**. In this relatively small worksheet, these options do not affect the speed of the command.

10. Click **Find Next**. An occurrence of the misspelled name (cell B10) is outlined.

Figure 3-11
Find and Replace dialog box, Replace tab
3-9.xlsx DonatedService sheet

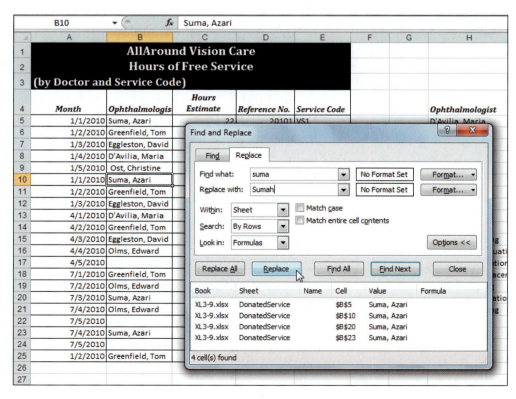

11. Click **Replace**. The change is made, and Excel locates the next occurrence (cell B20). It is a good idea to do the first replace and check it before replacing all occurrences.

12. Click **Replace All**. The message box notes how many replacements were made (four).

13. Click **OK**. The dialog box shows what has been replaced.

14. Click **Close**.

Exercise 3-11   USE WILDCARDS

A *wildcard* is a character that represents one or more numbers or letters. Wildcards help you locate groups of data such as all reference numbers that start with "207" in your workbook. Wildcards are also used when you are not sure about the spelling of a label or the exact value. For example, you might remember that the code for eyeglass prescriptions begins with a "V" but cannot recall the actual code. A wildcard search string will help you locate that data.

Excel recognizes two common wildcard characters:

- * Represents any number of characters.
- ? Represents any single character.

TIP

If you want to find a word or value that includes an asterisk or a question mark, precede the wildcard with a tilde (~). For example, "**25~***" would find **25***.

The character string "12*" would find all data in a worksheet that include "12" followed by any number of letters or values. This might include "123," "12345," and "12AB." The character string "1?3" would locate data that have a "1" followed by any single character or value and then a "3." Examples are "123," "1B3," and "193."

1. Select cells D5:D25. You can limit a find and replace activity to selected cells.

2. Click the Find & Select button 🔍 in the **Editing** group and choose **Find**.

3. Double-click **suma** in the **Find what** box if it is still there, and key **204***. This character string will find cells with an entry that begins with "204."

4. Click **Find All**. Two values in the worksheet match this character string.

5. Select cells E5:E25.

6. Double-click **204*** in the **Find what** box, and key ***1**. This will locate cells with an entry that ends in the number "1."

7. Click **Find All**. There are 11 cells that match.

8. Click the **Doctors** worksheet tab.

9. Click **Options >>** to expand the dialog box if it is collapsed.

10. Double-click the **Find what** entry and key **screen???**. This string will find a word that begins with "screen" and ends with any three characters.

Figure 3-12
Changing the Find options
3-9.xlsx
Doctors sheet

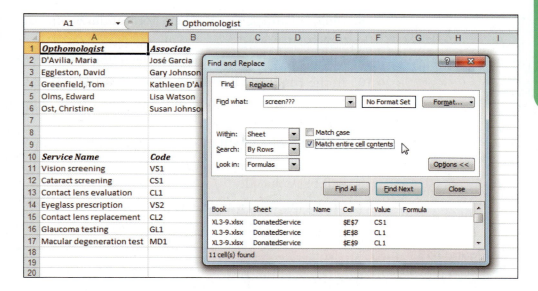

11. Select **Match entire cell contents**. Click **Find All**. There are no cells that contain only this word. The message box says that Excel cannot find data to match.

12. Click **OK** to close the message box.

13. Click to remove the checkmark for **Match entire cell contents**. Click **Find All**. Two cells are found.

14. Click **Close** to close the Find and Replace dialog box.

Exercise 3-12 FIND AND REPLACE FORMATS

In addition to finding or replacing character or value strings, you can find and replace formats. You can replace labels or values formatted as bold italic to be shown without bold and in a different color. When you replace formats, you should not show any characters in the Find what or Replace with boxes.

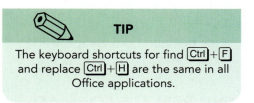

TIP

The keyboard shortcuts for find Ctrl+F and replace Ctrl+H are the same in all Office applications.

1. Press Ctrl+Home. Press Ctrl+H to open the Find and Replace dialog box.

2. Double-click in the **Find what** box and press Delete. The box is empty.

3. Double-click in the **Replace with** box and press Delete.

4. Click the arrow next to **Format** to the right of the **Find what** box.

5. Click **Choose Format From Cell**. The dialog box collapses, and the pointer shows the selection pointer with an eyedropper. This pointer will copy the format of the clicked cell to the dialog box.

6. Click cell A1. The dialog box expands. The format from cell A1 (11-point bold-italic Cambria) is shown in the **Preview** area for **Find what**. These cells are also left-aligned.

7. Click the arrow next to **Format** to the right of the **Replace with** box.

8. Choose **Format**. The Replace Format dialog box opens. You can set a new format here.

9. Click the **Font** tab. In the **Font** list, choose **Calibri (Body)**.

10. In the **Font style** list, choose **Bold Italic**. In the **Size** list, choose **12**.

11. Click the arrow for the **Color** box, and choose **Purple, Accent 4** in the eighth column.

12. Click the **Alignment** tab. In the **Horizontal** list, choose **Center**.

13. Click **OK**. The previews show the format that will be found and how it will be replaced.

14. Click **Find All**. Four cells are listed.

Figure 3-13
Replacing formats
3-9.xlsx
Doctors sheet

15. Click **Replace All**. The formats for the labels in rows 1 and 10 have been replaced.

16. Click **OK** in the message box and then click **Close**.

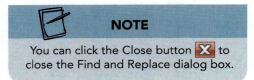

> **NOTE**
>
> You can click the Close button ▨ to close the Find and Replace dialog box.

Exercise 3-13   RESET FIND AND REPLACE FORMATS

After replacing formats, it is important to reset the Find and Replace dialog box. If you don't, the formats will be in effect the next time you use Find and Replace and could affect your results.

1. Click the Find & Select button ▨ and choose **Replace**.

2. Click the arrow next to **Format** for the **Find what** box.

3. Choose **Clear Find Format**. The area shows **No Format Set**.

4. Click the arrow next to **Format** for the **Replace with** box.

5. Choose **Clear Replace Format**. Click **Close**.

6. Click the **DonatedService** worksheet tab.

7. Save the workbook as *[your initials]*3-13.

Working with the Alignment Group

Cell alignment establishes how the contents of a cell are positioned in the cell. These settings affect the overall balance and readability of your workbook. Labels are left-aligned by default, and values are right-aligned, which can result in titles positioned at the far left of a column and numerical data positioned at the far right. Vertical alignment settings have similar effects but relate to how data are positioned within the row.

Cell alignment includes horizontal and vertical positioning, indents, wrapping text, and merge and center. The Alignment group on the Home command tab has buttons for many of the options.

Exercise 3-14   USE MERGE AND CENTER

The Merge and Center command combines a selected range of cells into one cell that occupies the same amount of space and centers the contents. You can merge any number of columns and rows to create special effects and alignment settings. The range of cells to merge should be empty except for the top-left cell. When only one row is merged, the Merge and Center command formats the data like the Center Across Selection command.

1. Select the range A3:E3.

2. In the **Alignment** group on the **Home** command tab, click the Merge and Center button . Cells A3:E3 are now one cell (A3), and the label is horizontally centered within it.

3. Click the **Doctors** worksheet tab.

4. Select the range A1:B1.

5. Click the Merge and Center button . A message box tells you that only the top-left data will be preserved.

6. Click **OK**. The cells are merged and centered, but the label that was in cell B1 is removed.

> **NOTE**
>
> You can unmerge cells by clicking the Merge and Center button to turn off the command.

7. Click cell A10, and point at its top or bottom border to display the four-headed drag-and-drop pointer.

8. Drag the label to cell C10.

9. Select cells C10:C17.

10. Click the Merge and Center button . Cells C10:C17 become one cell (C10) that occupies the same amount of space. The label is bottom-aligned in the cell and only partially visible (see Figure 3-14 on the next page).

Figure 3-14
Cells merged
vertically
3-13.xlsx
Doctors sheet

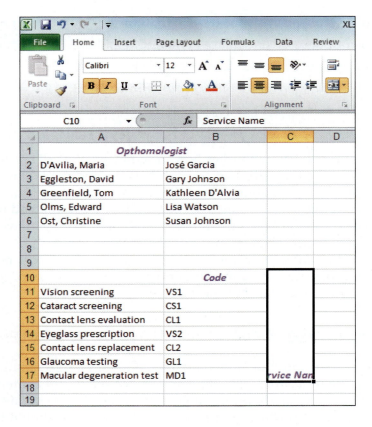

Exercise 3-15   CHANGE THE VERTICAL ALIGNMENT

As a default, data in a cell are aligned at the bottom of the cell. The Alignment group contains three vertical alignment buttons: Top Align ⬜, Middle Align ⬜, and Bottom Align ⬜. You can also set an alignment choice from the Format Cells dialog box.

TABLE 3-1 Vertical Alignment Options

Setting	Result
Top	Aligns cell contents at the top of the cell.
Center	Aligns cell contents in the vertical middle of the cell.
Bottom	Aligns cell contents at the bottom of the cell.
Justify	Spreads text to fill to the top and bottom edges of the cell. This works only for wrapped text that is more than one line.
Distributed	Positions text an equal distance from the top and bottom edges.

1. With cell C10 selected, click the Middle Align button ≣ in the **Alignment** group. Notice that the contents are horizontally centered. Check the Center ≣ in the **Alignment** group. Do not widen the column yet.

2. Click the **DonatedService** worksheet tab.

3. Select the range A4:E4.

4. Press Ctrl+1 to open the Format Cells dialog box.

5. On the **Alignment** tab, click the arrow for the **Vertical** box.

6. Choose **Center** and then click **OK**. The labels are vertically centered in the row.

Exercise 3-16 WRAP TEXT AND CHANGE INDENTS

Multiple-word labels can be split into multiple lines in a cell using the Wrap Text setting. This format choice is similar to pressing Alt+Enter as you key a label. When you key your own line break, it is stationary. When you use Wrap Text, the line break depends on the width of the column.

You can improve the readability of adjacent labels and values by adding an indent to one or the other. This moves the data away from the edge of the cell but maintains the alignment.

1. Click the column heading for column D and drag to the column E heading. Point at the border between columns E and F and set the width to **9.29 (70 pixels)**. This is wide enough for the data, but not wide enough for the labels in row 4.

2. Click cell D4 and click the Wrap Text button in the **Alignment** group. The label splits into two lines.

NOTE

Your screen size and resolution setting affect how buttons look in the Ribbon. They may or may not include text. The arrow may be next to or below the icon.

TIP

If the Wrap Text command splits a label in a poor location, adjust the column width.

3. Click the Center button ≣ in the **Alignment** group. The wrapped label looks better centered.

4. Click cell E4 and click the Wrap Text button. Click the Center button ≣.

5. Make column B **19.29 (140 pixels)** wide.

6. Click cell B5. Press F8 to start Extend Selection mode. Press Ctrl+↓. This shortcut selects contiguous cells with data in the column. Press ↓ as many times as necessary to select the remaining names.

7. Click the Increase Indent button in the **Alignment** group. The labels are moved one character space to the right and are still left-aligned.

8. Select cells A5:A25. These dates are right-aligned.

Figure 3-15
Wrapped text and indents increased
3-13.xlsx
DonatedService sheet

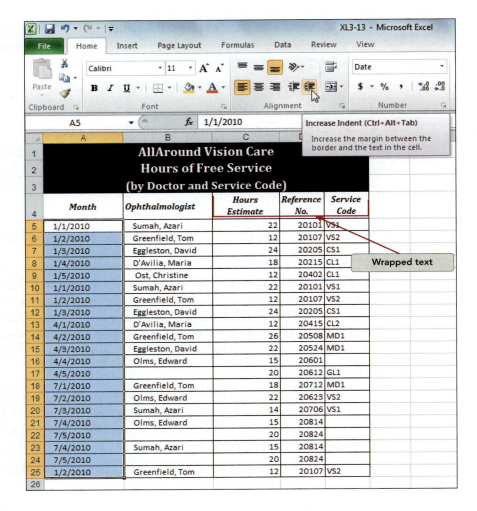

9. Click the Increase Indent button ⊞. The dates are moved so that they begin one character space from the left cell edge and are still right-aligned.

10. Click the Increase Indent button ⊞ two times. Each click moves them one character to the right.

11. Make column C **10.71 (80 pixels)** wide. Select cells C5:C25. These values are right-aligned.

12. Click the Increase Indent button ⊞ three times.

13. Increase the indent two times for cells E5:E25.

14. Verify that all the labels in row 4 are center-aligned.

Exercise 3-17   CHANGE CELL ORIENTATION

Cell orientation affects the rotation of data within the cell. By default, all cells use horizontal orientation. The label in the merged cell C10 on the Doctors worksheet has a horizontal orientation like the rest of the data. Because the cells were merged vertically, however, the label will look better if rotated.

1. Click the **Doctors** worksheet tab and click cell C10.

2. Click the Orientation button in the **Alignment** group. Choose Vertical Text. That's not the best choice.

3. Click the Orientation button and choose **Rotate Text Down**.

4. Click in the formula bar and edit the label to add **and Codes** at the end of the entry. Press Enter. Now the merged cell is not tall enough.

5. Select cells C10:C19 and click the Merge & Center button. This toggles off the merge and center command.

6. Click the Merge & Center button again. This toggles the command on.

7. Widen column A to show the longest service name. Autofit columns B and C.

Using the Format Cells Dialog Box

Most format commands can be applied using buttons on the Home and other tabs in the Ribbon. There are some, though, that must be built in the Format Cells dialog box. These formats include custom number and date styles and fills other than solid colors. In addition to customized formats, all the basic format choices are available from the Format Cells dialog box, too. This dialog box opens from the Dialog Box Launchers in the Font, Alignment, and Number groups on the Home command tab. The keyboard shortcut to open the Format Cells dialog box is Ctrl+1.

Exercise 3-18   APPLY A GRADIENT FILL

A *gradient* is a blend of colors. Depending on what is selected in the worksheet, you can build gradients that use one, two, or more colors. For worksheet cells, you can apply a two-color gradient. You can select any two colors from the theme colors as well as standard colors. A gradient fill also has a shading style and a variant. These options set the direction or way in which the colors blend.

> **TIP**
>
> Patterns usuallly make worksheet data difficult to read and are not a good choice for a fill.

1. Click cell C10 and click the Dialog Box Launcher in the **Font** group. The Format Cells dialog box opens to the Font tab.

2. Click the **Fill** tab.

3. Click the arrow for the **Pattern Style** box. Patterns include dots, stripes, and crosshatches.

4. Click **Fill Effects** on the left side of the dialog box. This closes the pattern palette. For your current selection, a gradient fill with two colors is the only option.

5. Click the arrow for **Color 1** and choose **Purple, Accent 4, Lighter 60%** in the eighth column.

6. Click the arrow for **Color 2** and choose **White, Background 1** in the first column.

Figure 3-16
Building a gradient fill
3-13.xlsx
Doctors sheet

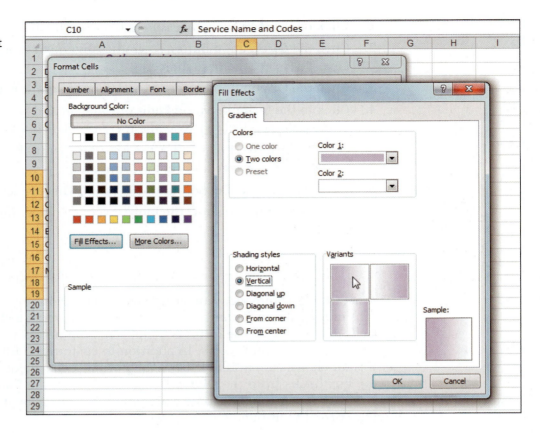

7. In the **Shading styles** group, choose **Vertical**. Choose the top-left variant. Click **OK** two times.

8. Click an empty cell to see the gradient better.

Exercise 3-19 CREATE A CUSTOM NUMBER FORMAT

A *custom* number *format* is one that is not shown in any of the type lists but that you design using Excel formatting codes. Custom formats can be built for values, dates, and times. A common custom format is one that shows a *leading zero,* which is a zero (0) as the first digit in a number, as in a decimal number (example "0.59"). Postal and international telephone codes sometimes have leading zeros. Item inventory numbers or numbers assigned by a digital camera can also use leading zeros. Excel does not show a leading zero because it has no value. If you key "059," in the cell, Excel displays "59" unless you create your own format to display that leading zero.

Custom formats are built in the Format Cells dialog box. For a leading zero format, use a zero (0) as the *placeholder*. A placeholder in a custom format is one of Excel's formatting codes. The number of placeholders signifies how many digits must be shown in the value. If the value has fewer digits than there are placeholders, zeros are added at the beginning of the value so that the value has the specified number of digits. Zeros at the beginning of a value are considered insignificant. An *insignificant zero* does not affect the value. For example, 0050 has the same value as 50.

1. Click the **DonatedService** worksheet tab and select cells D5:D25. You will display these numbers with a leading zero.

2. Click the Dialog Box Launcher in the **Number** group.

3. Choose **Custom** in the **Category** list. Click **0** in the **Type** list. A single zero appears in the entry box under **Type**.

4. Click after the **0** in the box and key **00000** to show six zeros. This custom format requires that the value show six digits. If the value has five digits, Excel inserts a zero in the first position.

Figure 3-17
Custom format for reference numbers **3-13.xlsx DonatedService sheet**

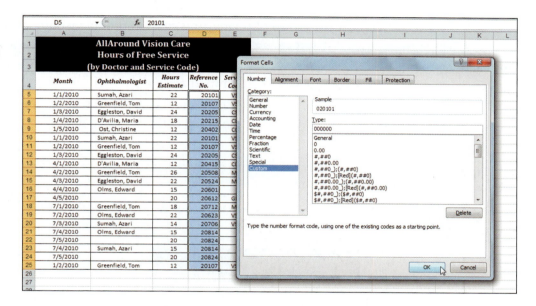

5. Click **OK**. All the reference numbers include a leading zero.

6. Press ⌃Ctrl+Home. Save the workbook as *[your initials]*3-19.

Formatting with Data Bars

Conditional formatting commands enable you to set formatting based on what's in the cell. A *data visualization* displays bars, colors, or icons in cells with or without the actual values. Data visualization is a variation of conditional formatting. Data visualizations allow the reader to quickly identify trends and exceptions in the data or to compare values. They might be compared to minicharts within the column or row.

Excel has three types of data visualizations.

*   *Data bars* fill each cell with varying lengths and shades of a color based on the highest and lowest values.

*   A *color scale* shades each cell with varying colors based on the values. There are two- and three-color scales.

*   An *icon set* displays an icon at the left of each cell based on the values. There are sets of three, four, and five icons.

Exercise 3-20 FORMAT CELLS WITH DATA BARS

With data bars, you can determine the value of a cell relative to other cells in the range by a quick glance. The highest value displays the longest bar, and the lowest value displays the shortest bar. Data bar options include gradient fill and solid fill. In the workbook for this lesson, you can apply data bars to the number of donated service hours. This will illustrate the dates and doctors with the most and fewest hours spent.

1. Select cells C5:C25.

2. In the **Styles** group, click the Conditional Formatting button 📊. A subgroup of formatting rules and data visualizations opens.

TIP

If a value in the range is negative, the bar is shown in red and clearly demonstrates that the value is negative.

3. Hover over **Data Bars**. Hover over each of the data bar options. Live Preview displays the visualization immediately on screen.

4. Click **Blue Data Bar** in the **Gradient Fill** group. The selected cells show the data bars.

Figure 3-18
Choosing a data bar format
3-19.xlsx
DonatedService
sheet

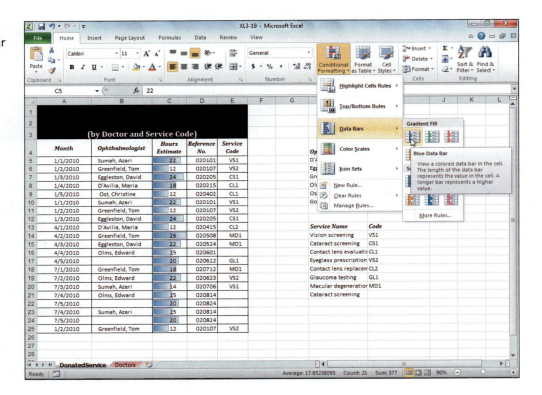

5. Click in column F. The length of the bars compares the values in the range. The greatest number of hours has a bar that fills the column width (cell C14, 26). The smallest value (cell C6, 12) displays a bar that is slightly less than half the width of the longest bar.

Exercise 3-21 EDIT A DATA BAR RULE

Data bars are applied based on comparison or relational rules. You can view and edit these rules to change the colors or to reset whether values, percentages, or percentiles are used to compare the data. To determine the proportional length of each bar, Excel looks for a minimum and a maximum value. Zero or the lowest negative number is assumed as the minimum. If a cell range includes zero (0), no bar is displayed; a red bar is displayed for a negative value. The maximum value displays a bar that occupies 100% of the column width.

1. Select cells C5:C25 again.
2. Click the Conditional Formatting button 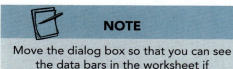.
3. Choose **Manage Rules**. The Conditional Formatting Rules Manager dialog box opens. You can see that a data bar is applied to the current selection.
4. Choose **Edit Rule**. The Edit Formatting Rule dialog box shows that the cells are formatted with a blue gradient-fill bar based on automatic settings. In this case, automatic uses the actual values in the cells.

NOTE

Move the dialog box so that you can see the data bars in the worksheet if necessary

5. In the **Bar Appearance** group, click the arrow for **Color**. Choose **Black, Text 1** in the second column.
6. Click to select **Show Bar Only**. Click **OK**. Click **OK** again.

Figure 3-19
Edit Formatting Rule dialog box
**3-19.xlsx
DonatedService
sheet**

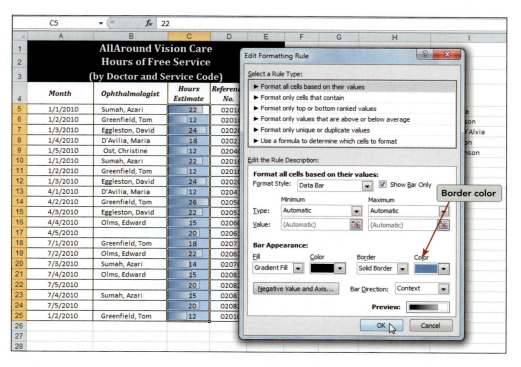

7. Click a cell in column F. This option hides the values.
8. Select cells C5:C25. Click the Conditional Formatting button 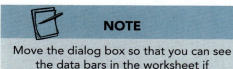. Choose **Manage Rules** and then click **Edit Rule**.

9. Click to deselect **Show Bar Only**.

10. In the **Bar Appearance** group, click the arrow for **Border**. Choose **Solid Border** (it may already be selected). This setting can make it easier to discern the ends of the bars in the cell.

11. Click **OK**. Click **OK** again. The values become more difficult to see with the black gradient fill.

12. Edit the formatting rule once more to use a light gray bar color instead of black. Then set the border color to a slightly darker gray.

13. Key your first and last name in cell A27. Key your first and last name in cell A20 on the **Doctors** worksheet.

14. Press Ctrl + Home. Save the workbook as *[your initials]*3-21.

15. Close the workbook.

Using Online Help

In addition to data bars, color scales and icon sets are quick ways to visualize your data. Use Help to learn about these aspects of conditional formatting.

EXPLORE CONDITIONAL FORMATTING

1. In a new workbook, press F1.

2. In the Search box, key **conditional formatting** and press Enter.

3. Find and review topics to learn more about data bars, color scales, icon sets, and other rules. Read the help information.

4. Close the Help window.

Lesson 3 Summary

- Excel's editing and formatting commands contribute to your quick updating and revising of worksheet data and their appearance.
- You can insert, delete, move, and rename worksheets in a workbook.
- Insert or delete cells if data have been improperly positioned in a worksheet and space is needed for missing data.
- When you cut or copy an item, it is placed on the Windows Clipboard and the Office Clipboard. Copied data can be pasted more than once.
- The Office Clipboard stores up to 24 copied elements. It is shared among Word, Excel, Access, and PowerPoint.
- Use drag and drop to quickly cut or copy cells.
- The AutoComplete feature makes suggestions when you key a label that begins with the same characters as labels already in the column.
- The Pick From Drop-down List displays a list of all labels already in the current column.

- Excel can spell-check individual labels or the entire worksheet.
- The Find command locates and lists all occurrences of data that match the Find what character string. You can use wildcards in the character string.
- The Replace command locates and substitutes new data for existing data. You can complete the changes one at a time or all at once.
- The Merge and Center command combines a selected cell range into one cell and center-aligns the data within the new single cell.
- Vertical alignment settings are available on buttons in the Alignment group and in the Format Cells dialog box.
- Wrapped text splits into multiple lines when the column is not wide enough.
- Indents move the data away from the left or right edge of the cell for better readability.
- The orientation of data within the cell can be rotated.
- A gradient fill for a cell uses a blend of two colors. It is available from the Format Cells dialog box on the Fill tab.
- To display a leading zero with values, create a custom format with a zero (0) as a placeholder.
- Data bars are conditional formatting that displays bars of different widths in a range of cells based on each cell's value.

LESSON 3		Command Summary	
Feature	Button	Ribbon Location	Keyboard
Bottom align		Home, Alignment	Ctrl + 1
Middle align		Home, Alignment	Ctrl + 1
Top align		Home, Alignment	Ctrl + 1
Copy		Home, Clipboard	Ctrl + C
Cut		Home, Clipboard	Ctrl + X
Data bars		Home, Styles	
Data bars, edit		Home, Styles	
Delete cell, row, column		Home, Cells	Ctrl + −
Increase indent		Home, Alignment	Ctrl + Alt + Tab

continues

UNIT 1 LESSON 3

LESSON 3	Command Summary *continued*		
Feature	**Button**	**Ribbon Location**	**Keyboard**
Insert cell, row, column		Home, Cells	Ctrl + +
Merge and center		Home, Alignment	
Paste		Home, Clipboard	Ctrl + V
Text orientation		Home, Alignment	Ctrl + 1
Wrap text		Home, Alignment	Ctrl + 1
Find		Home, Editing	Ctrl + F or Shift + F5
Replace		Home, Editing	Ctrl + H or Shift + F5

Please visit our Online Learning Center, *www.lessonapproach2010.com,* **where you will find the following review materials:**

- **Concepts Review**

    True/False Questions

    Short Answer Questions

    Critical Thinking Questions

- **Skills Review**

    Review Exercises that target single skills

    Lesson Applications

    Review Exercises that challenge students by testing multiple skills in each exercise

- **On Your Own**

    Open-ended exercises that require students to synthesize multiple skills and apply creativity and problem-solving as they would in a real world business situation

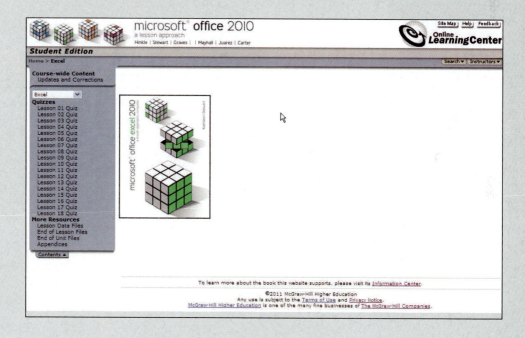

Please visit our Online Learning Center, *www.lessonapproach2010.com*, where you will find Unit Applications review materials.

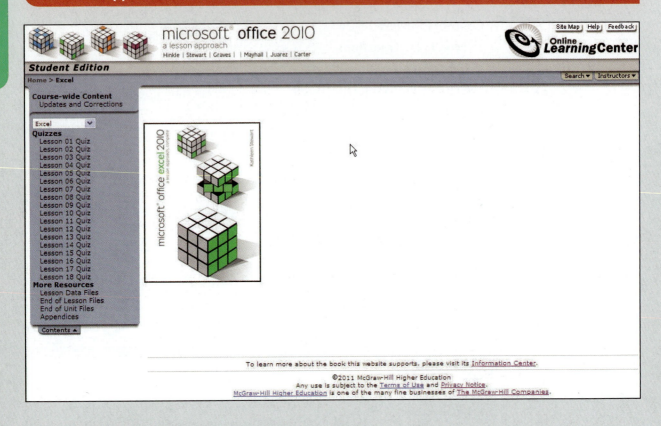

Unit 2

WORKING WITH FORMULAS AND FUNCTIONS

Lesson 4
Exploring Formula Basics

OBJECTIVES *After completing this lesson, you will be able to:*

1. Build addition and subtraction formulas.

2. Build multiplication and division formulas.

3. Set highlight cells rules.

4. Use order of precedence in a formula.

5. Use relative, absolute, and mixed references.

6. Work with the Page Layout tab.

7. Copy and group worksheets.

Estimated Time: 1½ hours

Excel's capabilities in performing arithmetic and scientific calculations are invaluable to business, government, education, and individuals. Excel computes results automatically and constantly, highlights many types of common errors, offers suggestions in correcting errors, and aids in the proper entering of many calculations. It does this through its formulas.

A formula executes a computation, similar to any problem that might be solved on a calculator. For people who are averse to mathematics, Excel helps them to get work accomplished with speed and accuracy. For those who enjoy math, Excel provides challenging opportunities to build and refine all types of calculations.

NOTE

The workbooks you create and use in this course relate to the case study about AllAround Vision Care, a fictional eye care practice (see frontmatter).

Excel formulas use common arithmetic operations (addition, subtraction, multiplication, and division). For any problem, you enter an = sign in the cell to start, followed by cell addresses to indicate which values are to be used, and then arithmetic operator(s). When you press [Enter] or click the Enter button ✔ in the formula bar, Excel calculates and displays the results of the formula.

Building Addition and Subtraction Formulas

Addition and subtraction problems can be relatively straightforward. When you plan your monthly budget, you know how much money you'll have and subtract what you spend to determine what is available for savings or special activities. Business organizations have many similar types of calculations. AllAround Vision Care, in the workbook for this lesson, monitors kilowatt-hours used and gallons of water consumed to help it achieve its conservation goals. One of its first formulas determines the difference between what was estimated and what was actually used.

Addition formulas total or sum cell values using the plus sign (+). Subtraction formulas compute the difference between cell values using the minus sign (−).

TIP

When cells are next to each other in a row or a column, it is quicker to use AutoSum than to key a formula for addition.

Exercise 4-1 CREATE ADDITION FORMULAS

REVIEW

If you open a workbook from an Internet location, it opens in Protected View. Enable editing so that you can continue working.

When there is no workbook open, Backstage view will show the Recent files list when you click the File command tab. You can choose a workbook name in the list or choose Open to locate a different workbook name. In the workbook for this lesson, you build the formulas first, without all the related data being present. This is not unusual, because many companies have model workbooks or "shell" workbooks in which the daily, weekly, or monthly figures are added when available. The **ElectricUse** worksheet includes only the estimated values, and the actual hours are entered later.

1. Open **Excel_Lesson4**. Click the Zoom Out button ⊖ in the status bar one or two times to see row 28. This worksheet has the gridline display off.

2. Click cell B26. In this cell you will add each of the four weeks to determine a monthly estimate

3. Key **=** to start a formula.

4. Click cell B7, estimated hours for Week 1 for Boston. A marquee appears around the cell.

5. Key **+** to add the next cell. Cell B7 is outlined in a color.

TIP

You can use ⊞ on the numeric keypad or at the top of the keyboard to key the plus symbol in a formula.

6. Click cell B12, the second week estimate.

7. Key **+** and click cell B17, the third estimate.

8. Key **+** and click cell B22, the fourth week. This addition formula determines the total monthly estimate for Boston.

Figure 4-1
Entering an addition
formula
Excel_Lesson4.xlsx
ElectricUse sheet

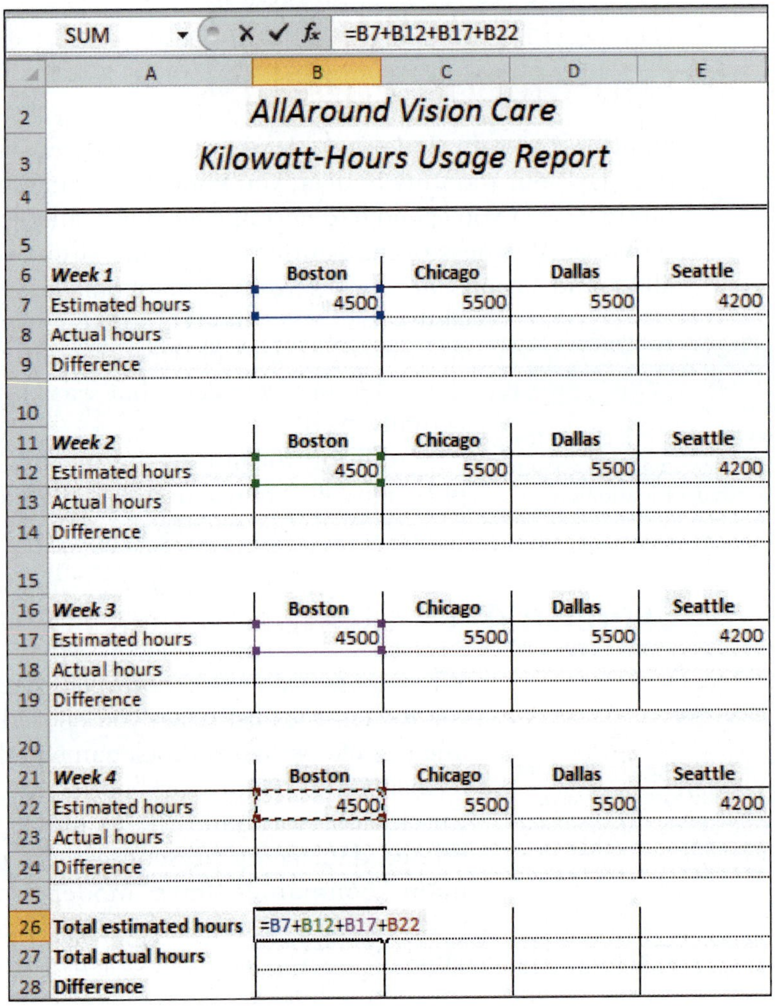

SUM	▼	✕ ✓ *fx*	=B7+B12+B17+B22	

	A	B	C	D	E
2		**AllAround Vision Care**			
3		**Kilowatt-Hours Usage Report**			
4					
5					
6	*Week 1*	**Boston**	**Chicago**	**Dallas**	**Seattle**
7	Estimated hours	4500	5500	5500	4200
8	Actual hours				
9	Difference				
10					
11	*Week 2*	**Boston**	**Chicago**	**Dallas**	**Seattle**
12	Estimated hours	4500	5500	5500	4200
13	Actual hours				
14	Difference				
15					
16	*Week 3*	**Boston**	**Chicago**	**Dallas**	**Seattle**
17	Estimated hours	4500	5500	5500	4200
18	Actual hours				
19	Difference				
20					
21	*Week 4*	**Boston**	**Chicago**	**Dallas**	**Seattle**
22	Estimated hours	4500	5500	5500	4200
23	Actual hours				
24	Difference				
25					
26	Total estimated hours	=B7+B12+B17+B22			
27	Total actual hours				
28	Difference				

9. Press [Enter]. The result is 18,000.

10. Click cell C26. Although you can copy the formula, you'll create the same formula with a deliberate error to see how Excel helps you.

11. Key = to start.

12. Click cell C7, key +, and click cell C12. Key + and click cell C17.

13. Key + and click cell C22. This should end the formula.

14. Key +. This operator is unnecessary.

15. Click the Enter button ✔ in the formula bar. A message box opens. That final plus sign is not necessary, and Excel proposes a correction, eliminating it.

Figure 4-2
Error message box
about incorrect
formula

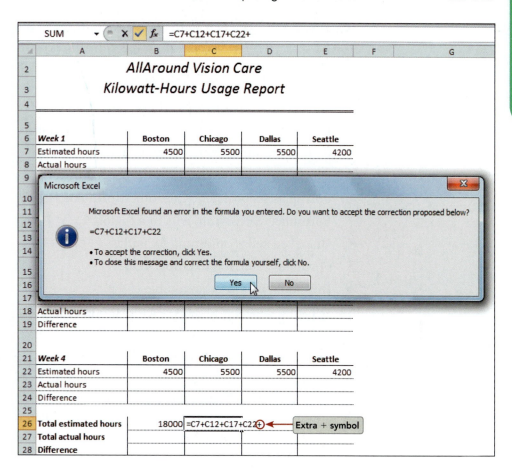

16. Choose **Yes**. The result is 22,000.

17. Rest the mouse pointer on the Fill handle for cell C26.

18. Drag the handle to the right to cell E26 to copy the formula. The AutoFill Options button appears ▦, and there may be one Error Checking Options button ◈ for the range. The Fill command copies the solid vertical border; you may not see it since the cells are selected.

19. Click the AutoFill Options button ▦, and choose **Fill Without Formatting**. The formatting that was already set is maintained with no additional formats.

20. Click cell D26, and view the formula in the formula bar. It is relative to its location.

Exercise 4-2 SET ERROR CHECKING RULES

Excel automatically alerts you to problems with formulas by showing an error indicator and an Error Checking Options button. The error indicator is a small green triangle in the top left corner of the cell. The Error Checking Options button is a small exclamation point within a diamond. It appears when you click the cell with the error indicator. When an error indicator warns of a potential error, you can review the type of error, fix it, or ignore the error.

Excel checks for the following types of errors.

- Cells containing formulas that result in an error.
- Inconsistent calculated column formula in tables.
- Cells containing years represented as two digits.
- Numbers formatted as text or preceded by an apostrophe.
- Formulas inconsistent with other formulas in the region.
- Formulas which omit cells in a region.
- Unlocked cells containing formulas.
- Formulas referring to empty cells.
- Invalid data entered in a table.

1. Click the **File** command tab and choose **Options**. Open the **Formulas** pane.

2. In the **Error checking rules**, verify that all rules show a checkmark.

3. Rest the mouse pointer on **Formulas referring to empty cells**, and read the ScreenTip. This rule is not toggled on by default.

4. Click to place checkmarks if necessary, and click **OK**. You'll see an error indicator after the next exercise.

Exercise 4-3   USE SUM WITH MULTIPLE ARGUMENTS

The SUM function is an addition formula. It sums or adds the arguments shown within the parentheses. When you click the Sum button Σ, the SUM function assumes a contiguous range of cells for its argument (C5:C10) and separates the two addresses with a colon. You can use SUM with cells that are not next to each other by listing each cell address and separating them with commas. To add the actual hours used per week, you'll use the SUM function in row 27. This function will refer to empty cells.

1. Click cell B27. Click the Sum button Σ on the **Home** command tab. The function initially identifies the single cell above it.

2. Click cell B8, actual hours for Week 1 for Boston. This is the first argument.

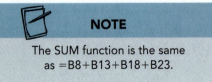

NOTE

The SUM function is the same as =B8+B13+B18+B23.

3. Key **,**. A comma separates the arguments.

4. Click cell B13 and key **,**, a second comma.

5. Click cell B18, key **,**, and click cell B23.

Figure 4-3
Separating
arguments with
commas
Excel_Lesson4.xlsx
ElectricUse sheet

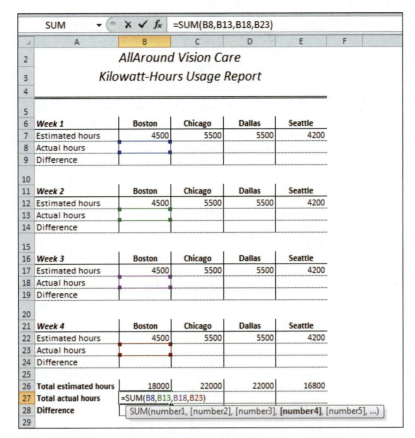

6. Press **Enter**. The result is 0, and the cell displays an error indicator (a green triangle) in the top left corner.

Exercise 4-4   REVIEW ERROR CHECKING

1. Click cell B27. The Error Checking Options button ⬦ appears to the left of the cell.

2. Position the mouse pointer on the Error Checking Options button ⬦ to see a ScreenTip that describes the type of error (see Figure 4-4 on the next page). The cells in the function have no values yet.

Figure 4-4
Error Checking
Options
Excel_Lesson4.xlsx
ElectricUse sheet

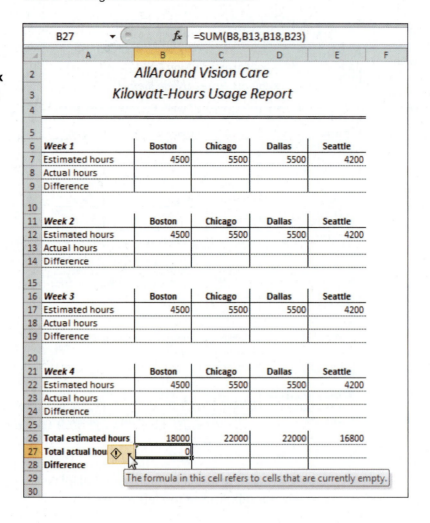

3. Click the arrow next to the button. Although Excel tags empty cells as an error, it is acceptable to build a formula before the data are entered.

4. Choose **Ignore Error**. The small triangle is removed.

5. Rest the mouse pointer on the Fill handle for cell B27. Drag right to cell E27 to copy the formula. The error indicators appear for all three copied formulas. The AutoFill Options button appears .

6. Click the AutoFill Options button , and choose **Fill Without Formatting**.

7. Select cells C27:E27. There is one Error Checking Options button for the range.

8. Click the arrow and choose **Ignore Error**. All three error triangles are cleared.

Exercise 4-5 CREATE SUBTRACTION FORMULAS

The difference between estimated and actual kilowatt-hour usage is computed by subtracting actual hours from estimated hours. You can use ⊟ on the numeric keypad or the hyphen at the top of the keyboard.

When you plan a subtraction problem, it is necessary to identify which cell address/value is first. In this worksheet, for example, the subtraction problem has the formula, estimated hours – actual hours.

1. Click cell B9, and key **=** to start a formula.

2. Click cell B7, the estimated hours.

3. Key **-**, and click cell B8, the cell that will display actual hours. Press [Enter].

4. Click cell B9. Rest the mouse pointer on the Error Checking Options button ⬦. This is the same type of error, a reference to empty cells. You need not do anything.

5. Drag the Fill handle for cell B9 to cell E9 to copy the formula.

6. Click the AutoFill Options button, and choose, **Fill Without Formatting**.

7. Click the Error Checking Options button ⬦, and choose **Ignore Error**. All error triangles are cleared.

8. While cells B9:E9 are selected, click the Copy button in the **Clipboard** group.

9. Click cell B14 and click the Paste button. The copy is made, and new error indicators appear.

10. Click the Paste Options button, and choose **Keep Source Formatting**. You must do this first, because the Paste Options button is removed when you ignore the error(s).

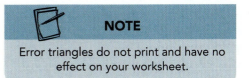

NOTE

Error triangles do not print and have no effect on your worksheet.

11. Click the arrow with the Error Checking Options button ⬦, and choose **Ignore Error**.

12. Click cell B19 and click the Paste button. Choose the option to keep the source formatting. Click the arrow with the Error Checking Options button ⬦, and choose **Ignore Error**.

13. Paste again in row 24, set the paste options, and ignore the error indicators. Then paste in row 28; there are no errors noted here.

14. Press [Esc] to clear the marquee.

15. Click cell B14. When this formula was copied, it was adjusted to subtract the cell directly above from the cell two rows above.

Exercise 4-6   ENTER DATA IN A RANGE

If you select a range of cells before keying data, you can press [Enter] to move from cell to cell in top-to-bottom, left-to-right order as you key new data. If you are accustomed to pressing [Enter] to complete a command, this can enable you to enter data more quickly.

1. Select cells B8:E8. When you press [Enter] after keying each value, the pointer will move to the next cell to the right.

2. Key **4200** and press [Enter]. As you key values, the difference is calculated in row 9.

3. Key **4850** and press Enter.

4. Key **5200** and press Enter. Key **3900** and press Enter.

5. Select cells B13:E13 and key these values. Press Enter after each value.

     4150   5300   4800   4100

6. Select cells B18:E18 and key the values shown here; some of these result in negative values in rows 19 and 24. Select cells B23:E23 and complete the row. The formulas in rows 27 and 28 are calculated as you go along.

Row 18	4600	5700	5400	4100
Row 23	4250	5500	5600	4300

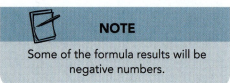

NOTE

Some of the formula results will be negative numbers.

7. Press F12 and save the workbook as *[your initials]*4-6.

Building Multiplication and Division Formulas

Division and multiplication, like addition and subtraction, are common business and personal calculations. If you hire a painter to work in your home, he calculates how many hours the job requires and multiplies by his hourly rate to price the job. On the other hand, if he gives you a job price and an estimate of the hours, you can divide the cost by the number of hours to determine his hourly rate.

In the worksheet for this lesson, AllAround Vision Care wants to determine what percentage the actual kilowatt-hours are in relation to the estimated hours, a sort of usage rate. This is a division problem that results in a decimal that is formatted as a percentage. It also wants to calculate what the target hours should be for next year. This is a multiplication problem, multiplying the current usage by an increase or decrease percentage.

Multiplication formulas use an asterisk (*) to multiply, and they begin with an = sign like all formulas. A division formula uses a forward slash (/) to mark its operation.

Results of multiplication or division formulas can be values that are not whole numbers. A *whole number* is a value without a fraction or decimal.

TIP

You can use * and / on the numeric keypad or * at the top of the keyboard and / at the bottom.

Exercise 4-7   CREATE DIVISION FORMULAS AND APPLY THE PERCENT STYLE

When a formula result or a keyed value is not a whole number, Excel displays it as a value with decimal positions. It will show as many decimal positions as will fit in the cell and as are necessary. Excel converts a decimal value to a percentage when you apply the Percent style and rounds the value to two digits. It multiplies the decimal value by 100 to do this conversion. For example, 0.94625 is 0.94625*100 which displays as 95%.

Excel copies formats and formulas to match other rows if the format and/or formula appears at least three times in the five rows preceding the new data. This is the *Extend data range formats and formulas* choice in the Excel Options dialog box (Advanced tab).

1. On the **ElectricUse** worksheet in *[your initials]4-6*, reduce the zoom size to 80%.

2. In cell A30, key **Actual/Estimate**. The label uses the bold format like the three rows that precede it.

3. In cell A31, key **Next year estimate**. The bold format is applied.

4. Click cell B30, and key **=** to start a formula.

5. Click cell B27, and key **/** for division. Dividing the actual hours (cell B27) by the estimated hours (cell B26) determines a ratio or a percentage. It represents how small or large the actual hours are in relation to the estimated hours.

Figure 4-5
Building a division formula
4-6.xlsx
ElectricUse sheet

SUM	▾	X ✓ *fx*	=B27/B26	

	A	B	C	D	E
2		*AllAround Vision Care*			
3		*Kilowatt-Hours Usage Report*			
4					
5					
6	*Week 1*	Boston	Chicago	Dallas	Seattle
7	Estimated hours	4500	5500	5500	4200
8	Actual hours	4200	4850	5200	3900
9	Difference	300	650	300	300
10					
11	*Week 2*	Boston	Chicago	Dallas	Seattle
12	Estimated hours	4500	5500	5500	4200
13	Actual hours	4150	5300	4800	4100
14	Difference	350	200	700	100
15					
16	*Week 3*	Boston	Chicago	Dallas	Seattle
17	Estimated hours	4500	5500	5500	4200
18	Actual hours	4600	5700	5400	4100
19	Difference	-100	-200	100	100
20					
21	*Week 4*	Boston	Chicago	Dallas	Seattle
22	Estimated hours	4500	5500	5500	4200
23	Actual hours	4250	5500	5600	4300
24	Difference	250	0	-100	-100
25					
26	Total estimated hours	18000	22000	22000	16800
27	Total actual hours	17200	21350	21000	16400
28	Difference	800	650	1000	400
29					
30	Actual/Estimate	=B27/B26			
31	Next year estimate				
32					

6. Click cell B26 and press [Enter]. The result is 0.955555556, formatted as a decimal. You may see more or fewer decimal positions depending on your screen size and resolution.

7. Click cell B30. Click the Percent Style button [%]. The percent symbol is added, and the value is converted and rounded to 96%.

8. In the **Number** group on the Ribbon, click the Increase Decimal button. One decimal position is added and the percent is now 95.6%.

9. Click the Increase Decimal button three times. The percent is now 95.5556%, the decimal equivalent of 0.95556. This level of precision is not required for this worksheet.

10. In the **Number** group, click the Decrease Decimal button. One decimal position is removed.

11. Click the Decrease Decimal button so that only one decimal position is shown.

12. Copy the formula in cell B30 to cells C30:E30. All the copies are formatted as a percentage with one decimal position.

Exercise 4-8   CREATE MULTIPLICATION FORMULAS AND APPLY THE COMMA STYLE

As a conservation goal, AllAround Vision Care would like each office to reduce its kilowatt-hour usage by 3%. In a multiplication formula, you can calculate the actual number of hours to be saved or the new total. Multiplying by 97% (100% – 3%) will result in the city's proposed usage; multiplying by 3% will calculate how many hours it needs to save. When you multiply by a percentage, you can key the value with the percent sign (%) in the formula. If you do not key the percent sign, you must key the decimal equivalent of the value.

TIP

Convert a percentage to its decimal equivalent by dividing the percentage amount by 100. For example, 89% is 89/100 or 0.89 (89 divided by 100).

1. Click cell B31 and key **=**.

2. Click cell B27, key *****, and then key **3%**. Press [Ctrl]+[Enter]. Multiplying by 3% does not calculate a new estimate. This amount is 3% of the actual total and represents the number of hours that must be saved or not used.

3. With cell B31 active, click in the formula bar. A text insertion point appears, and the cell in the worksheet is outlined in the same color as the cell address in the formula bar.

4. Click in front of **3** and delete it in the formula bar.

5. Key **97** to change the percentage to **97%**. To calculate a new estimate, multiply the actual total by 97%.

Figure 4-6
Editing a formula in
the formula bar
4-6.xlsx
ElectricUse sheet

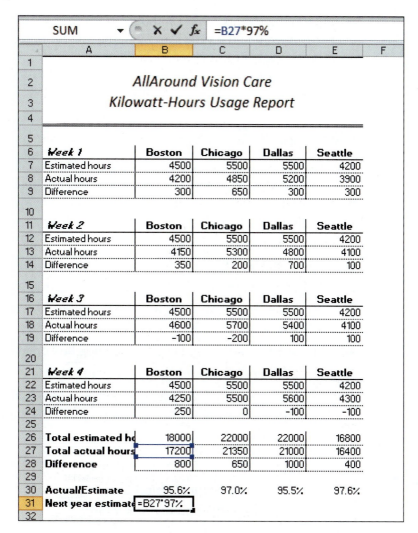

6. Press Ctrl+Enter. The new estimate is 16,684.

7. Copy cell B31 to cells C31:E31.

8. Select cells B31:E31. Click the Comma Style button. Commas are added as well as two decimal positions.

9. In the **Number** group, click the Decrease Decimal button two times. The decimals are removed.

10. Select cells B7:E9 and apply Comma style. Remove the decimal positions.

11. Repeat this command for all the values, except those in rows 30:31. You can select all the cells at once and give the command only once too.

12. Click cell B19. This is a *negative value*, one that is less than zero. Comma style shows negative values in parentheses, a common business practice.

Setting Highlight Cells Rules

Conditional formatting, like data bars, is cell formatting that is applied under specific conditions. Its purpose might be to emphasize, to draw attention, and/or to visualize the data. Conditional formatting is interactive, because it changes as your data change. You might, for example, set a conditional format that highlights a value in bold red text if it greater than 100. Then if the data are edited and the values are updated, the formatting adjusts as needed.

You can set several types of *highlight cells rules*. These rules or settings use comparison or relational operators to determine if the value or label should be formatted. You set the format or style to be applied.

Exercise 4-9   CREATE A HIGHLIGHT CELLS RULES

A few of the relational operators are listed in the Highlight Cells Rules menu. They are listed in English, so you need not worry about keying a symbol. For those operators that are not listed, you can access them in the New Formatting Rule dialog box. In your worksheet, you will set a rule to show negative numbers with a light red fill so that such values are quickly identified.

1. Select cells B9:E9.

2. Click the Conditional Formatting button 🔳 in the **Styles** group.

3. Hover over **Highlight Cells Rules**. The gallery lists several commonly used operators.

4. Choose **Less Than**. The Less Than dialog box opens.

5. Key **0**. A negative value is less than zero.

6. Click the arrow with the format choices. Choose **Light Red Fill**. Click **OK**. There are no cells in the selected range less than zero.

Figure 4-7
Building a Less Than rule
4-6.xlsx
ElectricUse sheet

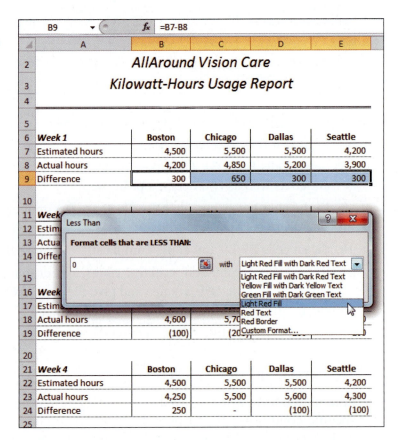

7. In cell B8, key **4700** and press Enter. Click a cell in column F to see the format better.

16. Choose **Formulas**. There are four categories of formulas. Click **OK**. All cells with a formula are selected.

17. Press Ctrl + Home . Save your work as *[your initials]*4-10.

Using Order of Precedence in Formulas

Excel follows mathematical rules as it calculates formulas and functions. These rules include an *order of precedence,* sometimes called *order of operation* or *math hierarchy.* The order of precedence determines which part of a formula is calculated first. Generally, a formula is calculated from left to right, but some arithmetic operators take priority over others. For example, if you key a formula with both a multiplication symbol (*) and an addition symbol (+), Excel calculates the multiplication first even if it is the second symbol as you move from left to right. You can override the order of precedence by enclosing parts of the formula within parentheses.

When two operators have the same order of precedence—for example, multiplication and division—the operations are performed from left to right (see Table 4-1).

Figure 4-10 shows three formulas with the same values and the same operators. The results differ depending on the placement of the parentheses.

TIP

You can memorize the order of precedence for parentheses and the first five operators: "Please excuse *my dear Aunt Sally*" (parentheses, exponentiation, multiplication, division, addition, subtraction).

Figure 4-10
Parentheses change the order of operations

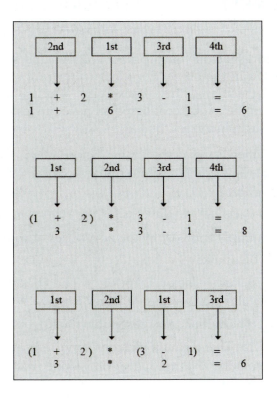

TABLE 4-1 Operator Precedence in Excel

Operator	Precedence	Description
( )	1st	Parentheses
^	1st	Exponentiation
*	2nd	Multiplication
/	2nd	Division
+	3rd	Addition
–	3rd	Subtraction
&	4th	Concatenation (symbol used to join text strings)
=	5th	Equal to
<	5th	Less than
>	5th	Greater than

Exercise 4-11 BUILD A FORMULA WITH MULTIPLE OPERATORS

On another worksheet in your workbook, AllAround Vision Care keeps track of pages printed in the office. For a particular range of pages, an ink toner cost has been calculated. In this exercise, you use a formula that seems logical to determine a total cost based on page ranges. You will see, however, that it results in an incorrect total.

1. Click the **TonerUse** worksheet tab. Click cell E15. You need to sum or add the values for each city and multiply by the relevant cost for the specified range.

2. Key **=**, and click cell C6, the cost for the 1000-pages-or-fewer range.

3. Key ***** to multiply this cost by the next series of values.

4. Select cell D6 and key **+**.

5. Click cell E6, key **+**, click cell F6, key **+**, and click cell G6. This part of the formula adds the number of pages per city.

6. Press Enter. The value looks reasonable (3080), but it is wrong.

7. Click cell E15. This formula includes a multiplication symbol and three addition symbols. The multiplication is done first (C6*D6). That result is added to E6+F6+G6.

Exercise 4-12 CHECK RESULTS WITH AUTOCALCULATE

The *AutoCalculate* feature displays formula results for a selected range in the status bar. AutoCalculate can display sums, averages, counts, maximums, or minimums.

1. Right-click the status bar. Find the AutoCalcuate group in the menu (Average, Count, and others).

2. Verify that there are checkmarks for **Average**, **Count**, and **Sum**. Press [Esc].

3. Select the range D6:G6. AutoCalculate shows the average, the count, and the sum for these cells. The sum is 4000.

Figure 4-11
Using AutoCalculate
4-6.xlsx
TonerUse sheet

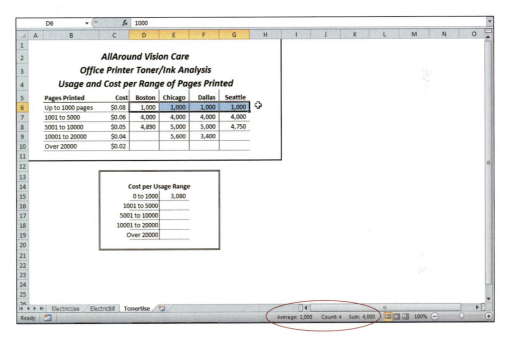

4. Click cell J14 and key **=**. Click cell C6, key ***4000**, and press [Enter]. This is the correct amount—the total pages (4000) multiplied by the cost for that usage range.

5. Delete the contents of cell J14.

6. Select cells B6:B10. These are labels, so AutoCalculate only shows a count.

Exercise 4-13 SET ORDER OF PRECEDENCE

1. Double-click cell E15 to start Edit mode.

2. In the worksheet cell, click in front or to the left of **D6**.

3. Key a left parenthesis **(** in front of **D6**.

4. Press End. The insertion point moves to the end of the formula.

5. Key a right parenthesis **)**.

Figure 4-12
Changing the order
of precedence
4-10.xlsx
TonerUse sheet

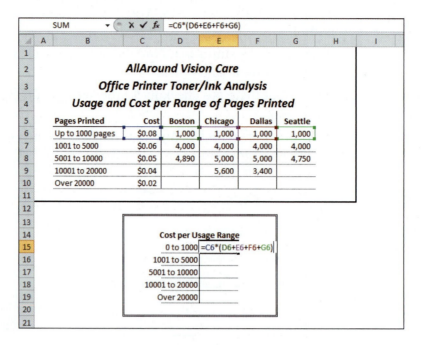

6. Press Enter. These parentheses force the additions to be calculated first. That result (4000) is multiplied by the cost in cell C6; the cost is 320.

7. Apply Currency format to cell E15.

8. Copy the formula in cell E15 to cells E16:E19. You'll see error indicators in cells E18 and E19.

9. Click cell E18 and click the Error Checking Options button ◈. The empty cells are in row 9.

10. Choose **Ignore Error**. Ignore the error for cell E19.

11. Press Ctrl+Home.

12. Save the workbook as *[your initials]4-13*.

REVIEW

The Currency format is available from the list of number formats in the Ribbon. The Accounting Number format on the button aligns the dollar symbol at the left edge of the cell.

Using Relative, Absolute, and Mixed References

When you copy a formula, Excel adjusts cell addresses relative to the row or column where the copy is located. Your formula in cell E15 in the **TonerUse** worksheet referred to cells in row 6. When you copied that formula down to row 16, the cell references in the formula were adjusted down to show row 7, 8, 9, or 10. This was correct. Your references in cell E15 were relative. An example of a cell address with a *relative reference* is C6.

There are worksheets, however, when this would result in an error. Suppose that there was only one cost in cell C6 and that cells C7:C10 were empty. If you copied the formula in cell E15 to cell E16, you would want it to continue to refer to cell C6 (not cell C7). This reference to cell C6 is an *absolute reference*. In this case, the address does not change when the formula is copied to another cell. An absolute reference displays two dollar signs ($) in its address, one in front of the column letter and one in front of the row number. $C$6 is an absolute reference to cell C6.

In a *mixed reference*, part of the cell address is adjusted when a formula is copied; the other is not. A *mixed reference* displays one dollar sign, either with the column letter or the row number. $C6 is a mixed reference with an absolute reference to column C but a relative reference to row 6.

Dollar signs used within a cell address do not signify currency. They are reserved symbols used to mark the type of cell reference. Because absolute references are common to many calculations, Excel has a quick way of adding dollar signs to a cell reference with the F4 key.

Cell references can also be described as 3-D. A *3-D reference* is a cell address on a different sheet in the same workbook. It includes the name of the worksheet followed by an exclamation point. A 3-D reference can be absolute, relative, or mixed.

TABLE 4-2 Cell References

Address	Type of Reference	Description
B1	Relative	
$B$1	Absolute	
$B1	Mixed	Column letter is absolute; row number is relative.
B$1	Mixed	Row number is absolute; column letter is relative.
Sheet2!B1	3-D, relative	Cell is on a different worksheet.
Sheet2!$B$1	3-D, absolute	Cell is on a different worksheet.
Sheet2!B$1	3-D, mixed	Row number is absolute; column letter is relative. Cell is on a different worksheet.

Exercise 4-14   CREATE A 3-D RELATIVE REFERENCE

In large worksheets, working with related columns or rows on-screen at the same time can be tedious if you have to scroll the window back and forth often. You can split the workbook window into multiple panes and then adjust what shows in each pane. The result is that you can position data that are otherwise many columns or rows apart so that they appear side by side. When a worksheet has split windows, you can work in any pane because it is all still the same worksheet. The **ElectricBill** worksheet has a split window that allows for columns J:K to be positioned immediately to the right of column E.

1. In *[your initials]*4-13, click the **ElectricBill** worksheet tab. There is a vertical split bar between columns E and J. Columns F:I are blank and scrolled out of view.

2. Click cell B7. To calculate an amount for Boston, you need the number of kilowatt-hours here. Those data are on the **ElectricUse** worksheet.

3. Key **=** in cell B7, and click the **ElectricUse** worksheet tab.

4. Click cell B27 (total actual hours for Boston), and press ⌈Enter⌋. The focus returns to the **ElectricBill** worksheet. The number of hours is 17,700.

5. Click cell B7. The formula bar shows the sheet name, an exclamation point, and the cell address (=ElectricUse!B27). This is a 3-D relative cell address.

6. Drag the Fill handle for cell B7 to cell E7. Click the AutoFill Options button 🔡 and choose **Fill without Formatting**.

7. Click cell C7. The cell address shows the sheet name and cell 27 for the Chicago value. Because it is a relative reference, it adjusts to the worksheet position.

Exercise 4-15   CREATE AN ABSOLUTE REFERENCE

1. Click cell B8 and key **=**. The customer charge is displayed in cell K4 and is the same for all cities.

2. Click cell K4 and press ⌈Enter⌋. This is a relative address. Watch what happens when you copy this cell address.

3. Drag the Fill handle for cell B8 to cell E8. Cells C8:E8 show zero (0) and have error indicators.

4. Click cell C8. When copied, the original cell address of K4 was reset one column to the right, cell L4. Cell L4 is empty.

5. Click the Undo button ⟲.

6. Click cell B8 and press ⌈F2⌋. Edit mode starts.

7. Press ⌈F4⌋. Two dollar signs are inserted, one before "K" and one before "4."

Figure 4-13
Making a cell
reference absolute
4-13.xlsx
ElectricBill sheet

	A	B	C	D	E	J	K	L
1								
2		*AllAround Vision Care*						
3		*Kilowatt-Hours Analysis Report*				Commercial Service Rates		
4						Customer Charge	$25.32	
5						Distribution charge per kWh	$0.03450	
6	Week 1	Boston	Chicago	Dallas	Seattle	Supply charge per kWh	$0.04350	
7	Actual hours	17700	21350	21000	16400	Transmission charge per kWh	$0.08450	
8	Customer charge	=$K$4						
9	Distribution charge							
10	Supply charge							
11	Transmission charge							
12	Total bill							
13								
14								
15								
16								
17								
18								

NOTE

If you do not specify that the AutoFill should be without formatting, the vertical right border from the cell in column B is copied and creates a formatting error in column E.

8. Press F4 again. The dollar sign appears only in front of the row reference "4." Each press of F4 cycles through a choice.

9. Press F4 again. The dollar sign appears only with the column reference "K."

10. Press F4 again. The dollar signs are removed, and the reference is relative.

11. Press F4 once more. This is an absolute reference.

12. Press Ctrl+Enter. Look in the formula bar.

13. Drag the Fill handle for cell B8 to cell E8. Click the AutoFill Options button 🔡 and choose **Fill without Formatting**.

14. Click each copied cell and look in the formula bar. The cell address did not change as the reference was copied.

Exercise 4-16　USE MIXED REFERENCES

The next three cost items depend on the kilowatt-hours used (row 7) and the associated costs in columns J:K.

1. Click cell B9. You need to multiply the hours for Boston by the appropriate cost in column K.

2. Key **=** and click cell B7. When this address is copied to column C, it should be adjusted to show C7. So the row 7 is absolute.

3. Press F4 two times to show "B$7." When copied, this part of the formula will always refer to row 7, but the column will increment once for each column.

4. Press ***** and click cell K5. The costs are in column K, but the other two costs are on different rows.

5. Press F4 three times to show "**$K5**." This part of the formula will refer to column K, but the row will implement once for each copy.

Figure 4-14
Mixed reference formula
4-13.xlsx
ElectricBill sheet

SUM	▾ ⌃ ✕ ✓ *fx*	=B$7*$K5						
	A	B	C	D	E	J	K	L
1								
2		*AllAround Vision Care*						
3		*Kilowatt-Hours Analysis Report*				Commercial Service Rates		
4						Customer Charge	$25.32	
5						Distribution charge per kWh	$0.03450	
6	*Week 1*	Boston	Chicago	Dallas	Seattle	Supply charge per kWh	$0.04350	
7	Actual hours	17700	21350	21000	16400	Transmission charge per kWh	$0.08450	
8	Customer charge	$25.32	$25.32	$25.32	$25.32			
9	Distribution charge	=B$7*$K5						
10	Supply charge							
11	Transmission charge							
12	Total bill							
13								

6. Press Ctrl+Enter.

7. Drag the Fill handle for cell B9 to cell E9 and choose **Fill without Formatting**.

8. Click the copied formulas and check the formula bar.

9. Select cells B9:E9. Drag the Fill handle down to row 11. Ignore the AutoFill Options button .

10. Click a few cells in the copied range, and review the formulas.

11. Select cells B12:E12. Click the Sum button Σ .

12. Click cell B12. The SUM function assumed all the cells above the row should be included. Row 7 should not be included in this sum.

13. Press F2 and change **B7** to **B8**. Press Enter.

14. Copy the formula in cell B12 to cells C12:E12.

15. Check that the values in row 7 show Comma style with no decimals.

16. Click the **View** command tab in the Ribbon.

17. In the **Window** group, click the Split button. The split bar is removed, and the empty columns are visible.

18. Fix the border for cell E12.

19. Save the workbook as *[your initials]*4-16.

Working with the Page Layout Tab

For worksheets that are printed, there are several properties or settings that can be adjusted so that the document is optimized for easy reading. A worksheet on-screen often looks somewhat different when printed. Many times you can see more on the screen than will fit on a printed page, or you cannot assess the margins as easily on-screen. Sometimes on-screen, you cannot determine if the page is portrait or landscape. Backstage View for printing does provide a way to check these attributes before actually sending the worksheet to the printer.

NOTE

Not all worksheets are printed; some are incorporated into Web pages or PowerPoint presentations.

The Page Layout command tab in the Ribbon includes many commands for adjusting work before printing. From the Page Layout command tab, you can:

- Change page margins.
- Set the page orientation.
- Choose a paper and page size.
- Set a print area and/or print titles.
- Scale the worksheet to fit the page or print larger than the page.
- Print worksheet gridlines and column-row headings.
- Define page breaks.
- Add a background color or image.

Exercise 4-17   CHANGE ORIENTATION AND SCALING

Page orientation determines if the worksheet prints landscape or portrait. The default is portrait orientation, a page that is taller than it is wide. A *landscape* orientation is horizontal—the page is wider than it is tall. Whether you choose portrait or landscape depends on the amount of data and how the worksheet will be used.

Scaling refers to the printed size of the worksheet. By default, worksheets print at a full size, 100%. If you reduce that percentage, the entire worksheet is proportionally shrunk by that ratio, but only for printing or other output. You might shrink a worksheet if you want to print it on an index card or some other specialty paper. If you need the worksheet for a large display board, you can scale it larger and piece the pages together. Excel automatically breaks the worksheet into sections and prints one section per page.

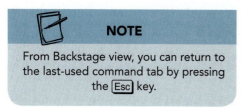

NOTE

From Backstage view, you can return to the last-used command tab by pressing the [Esc] key.

1. In *[your initials]*4-16, click the **ElectricBill** worksheet tab. This worksheet has two sections of data and is rather wide.

2. Click the **File** command tab and choose **Print**. In Backstage view, you can see that the worksheet, as it is laid out, occupies two portrait pages.

3. Click the Next Page arrow ▶. Press [Esc] to close Backstage view.

4. Click the Zoom Out button ⊖ to reach **80%**. You'll be better able to see the page breaks at this size.

5. Click the **Page Layout** command tab.

6. In the **Page Setup** group, click the Page Orientation button 📄. Choose **Landscape**. The worksheet still does not fit on a single page. The dotted lines on the screen represent where new pages start; these are automatic page breaks. Automatic page breaks depend on your printer and its settings.

Figure 4-15
Scaling the worksheet
**4-16.xlsx
ElectricBill sheet**

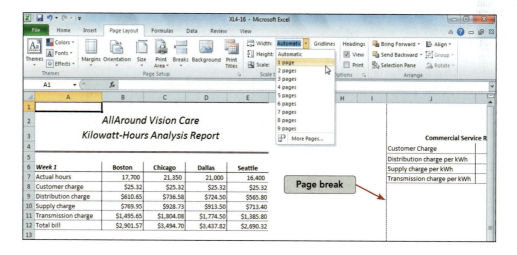

7. In the **Scale to Fit** group, click the arrow for the **Width** box. Choose **1 page**. The worksheet is automatically scaled to about 75–77%, visible in the **Scale** box. The actual percentage depends on your default printer. Since the **Height** of the page is not a problem in this case, you can leave it at **Automatic**.

8. Press [Ctrl]+[F2] to open Backstage view for printing. The Scaling group displays **Fit All Columns on One Page**, the result of scaling the width of the worksheet. You can set scaling from this group, too.

9. Return to a normal view. Adjust column widths to display all the data if necessary.

Exercise 4-18   HIDE COLUMNS AND CENTER A PAGE

This worksheet leaves several empty columns between the data sections. For better printing, you can temporarily hide those columns. You can hide any column or row that need not be viewed or printed. Even though a row or column may be hidden, any values used in a formula are still referenced.

You can determine if columns or rows are hidden, because their headings are hidden. There is also a slightly thicker border between the headings.

1. Click the column heading for column F and drag to select columns F:H.
2. Right-click any of the selected column headings, and choose **Hide**. Three columns are hidden.
3. Click an empty cell. Notice the border between the headings for column E and I. It is slightly wider or thicker than the others.
4. Press [Ctrl]+[Home]. The worksheet has been automatically rescaled to about 90–95%. Scaling is dynamic.
5. Open Backstage view for printing and view the worksheet.
6. Close Backstage view and click the **ElectricUse** worksheet tab.
7. Open Backstage view for printing and view this worksheet. The sheet is positioned toward the left side of the page.
8. Click **Page Setup** below the **Settings** command group. Click the **Margins** tab. The Page Setup dialog box opens with default top, bottom, left, and right margins (0.75 inch and 0.7 inch).

Figure 4-16
Page Setup dialog box
4-16.xlsx
ElectricBill sheet

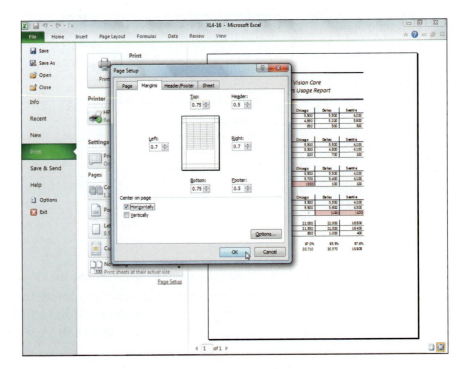

9. In the **Center on page** group, click to place a checkmark for **Horizontally**.
10. Click **OK**. The page appears centered on the page now.
11. Close Backstage view. You cannot see horizontally page centering in Normal view.

Exercise 4-19   ADD A BACKGROUND IMAGE

A *background* is an image that appears with a worksheet on screen and on the Web. If a worksheet is to be posted to the company's Web site for viewing by clients or patients, a background can draw attention to the frame on the Web page. It can also contribute to the worksheet being more easily viewed.

A background fills or spans the entire worksheet, and it does not print. As a background, you can use common image formats such as TIF, JPG, or PNG. You need to be careful about what you select as a background, however, because it can also mask or hide some data if its colors or design is wrong. Before beginning this exercise, place a copy of the student data file named **Background** in an accessible folder.

1. Click the **TonerUse** worksheet tab. This sheet will be posted on the Web site for AllAround Vision Care employees.

2. On the **Page Layout** command tab in the **Page Setup** group, click the Background button . The Sheet Background dialog box opens.

3. Navigate to the folder with the **Background** file. This is a TIF file that is a color gradient.

4. Click once to select the file. If the dialog box is set to display a preview, you will see a thumbnail of the image. You can turn on a preview from the Organize menu (Layout).

5. Click **Insert**. The background is a blend of gold and yellow colors and fills the worksheet.

6. Select cells A1:H11. Click the **Home** command tab. Click the arrow with the Fill Color button and choose **White, Background 1**.

7. Apply the same fill to the other data.

Figure 4-17
Using a sheet background
4-16.xlsx
WaterUse sheet

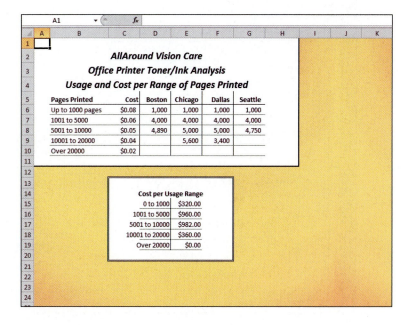

8. Press Ctrl+Home. Press Ctrl+F2. Backgrounds do not print, so they are not visible in Backstage view for printing.

9. Close Backstage view.

Exercise 4-20   SAVE A WORKBOOK AS A WEB PAGE

There are many ways to make data visible to others in the company as well as to the public. If you have the use of a Web site, you can easily post a workbook for viewing by those who have access to the site. It is a simple step of saving the workbook as a Web page from the Save As dialog box.

Although Excel is not a Web design tool, you can save a workbook as a simple HTML file ready for posting on the Web. An *HTML* file uses *hypertext markup language,* a widely used and recognized format for Web pages. Excel Web pages are saved with an .htm extension. You can save the entire workbook or an individual worksheet as a Web page. When you save the entire workbook, the Web page shows the worksheet tabs.

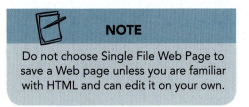

NOTE

Do not choose Single File Web Page to save a Web page unless you are familiar with HTML and can edit it on your own.

1. Click the **File** command tab and choose **Save As**. The Save As dialog box opens.

2. Click the arrow for **Save as type** and choose **Web Page**.

3. Set the **Save in** to your usual folder.

4. In the **Save** area, choose **Entire workbook**.

5. Click **Change Title**. This title appears in the title bar of the Web browser.

Figure 4-18
Saving a Web page
4-16.xlsx
WaterUse sheet

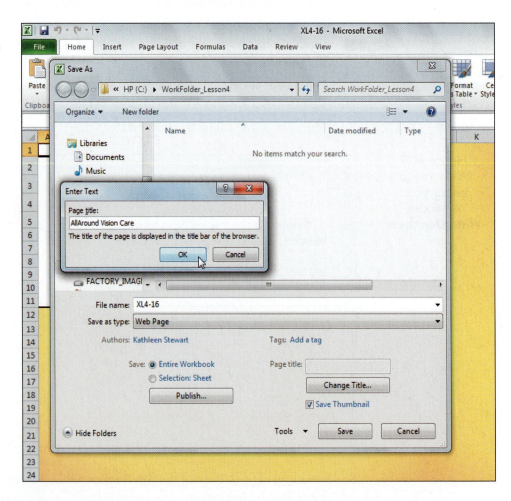

6. Key **AllAround Vision Care** and click **OK**.

7. Name the file *[your initials]*4-20. Click **Publish**. The Publish as Web Page dialog box verifies what will be published. Click the arrow and choose **Entire workbook** in the **Choose** group.

8. Click **Open published web page in browser**. Click **Publish**. The Web page should open in your browser.

9. Look for the title and the background.

10. Click the Close button to close the browser.

11. On the **Page Layout** command tab, click the Delete Background button in the **Page Setup** group. The background is removed. The white fill for the cells does not matter when the worksheet is printed on white paper, but you should remove it.

12. Select cells A1:H11. Click the **Home** command tab. Click the arrow with the Fill Color button, and choose **No Fill**.

13. Remove the fill for the remaining data.

14. Press Ctrl+Home. Save the workbook as *[your initials]*4-20.

Copying and Grouping Worksheets

You know that you can copy data from one worksheet to another. With the Move or Copy dialog box, however, you can copy all the data and the formatting, creating a duplicate of the entire worksheet. AllAround Vision Care employees make a copy of a worksheet in order to prepare a documentation sheet that shows the formulas and other explanatory notes. For other tasks, they copy the sheet for one month to start the next month's worksheet and delete the previous month's data. This saves time and effort and increases accuracy since labels and formatting are maintained. If you keep a monthly expenditure worksheet to track your personal budget, you can copy the initial sheet each month, delete the old expenses, and start anew.

When you have many worksheets in a workbook, you can group the sheets to edit or format them with a single command too. For many tasks, this does assume that the worksheets are identical. If you key a formula in cell C10, for example, it is entered in that cell on every sheet in the group. You could, however, group sheets that are not identical and change the font size.

Exercise 4-21   COPY A SINGLE WORKSHEET

1. Right-click the **ElectricUse** worksheet tab. Choose **Move or Copy Sheet**.

2. In the Move or Copy dialog box, the **To book** box shows the name of the current workbook. The **Before sheet** list allows you to move or copy the sheet to a specific location in the active workbook.

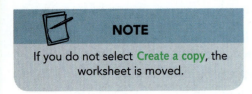

NOTE

If you do not select **Create a copy**, the worksheet is moved.

3. Choose **(move to end)** in the **Before sheet** list.
4. Click to place a checkmark for **Create a copy**.
5. Click **OK**. The new worksheet named **ElectricUse (2)** is an exact duplicate of the **ElectricUse** sheet.
6. Rename the **ElectricUse (2)** tab as **ElectricUse (Formulas)**.

Exercise 4-22 GROUP AND COPY WORKSHEETS

When you have many worksheets in a workbook, you may not be able to see all the tab names at once. The tab scrolling buttons enable you to scroll through the tab names; these buttons are to the left of the first tab name. The first button scrolls the tab names so that the first name is visible; the second button scrolls one tab name to the left, a "previous sheet" button. The last button scrolls so that the last tab name is visible; the third button is a "next sheet" button. The tab scrolling buttons do not change the active worksheet; you still need to click the tab name to do that.

1. Click the **ElectricBill** worksheet tab.
2. Hold down Ctrl and click the **TonerUse** tab. Both worksheets are selected, and the word "[Group]" appears in the title bar after the file name.

REVIEW

You can use the Ctrl or the Shift key to select adjacent worksheets tabs.

3. Click the Format button 📄 in the **Cells** group, and choose **Move or Copy Sheet**.
4. Choose **(move to end)** in the **Before sheet** list.
5. Click to place a checkmark for **Create a copy**.

Figure 4-19
Copying grouped sheets
4-20.xlsx
Grouped sheets

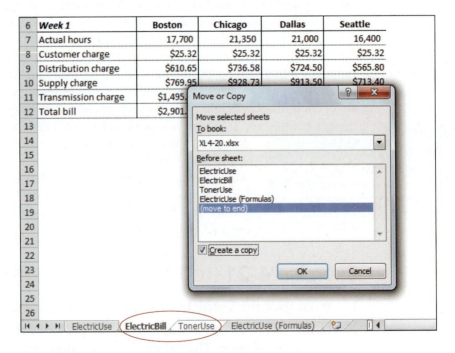

6. Click **OK**. Both copies are made.
7. Rename the **ElectricBill (2)** tab as **ElectricBill (Formulas)**. Rename the **TonerUse (2)** tab as **TonerUse (Formulas)**.

8. Right-click one of the tab scrolling buttons at the left of the worksheet tabs. A list of the worksheets opens.

9. Choose **ElectricBill** to make it the active worksheet.

10. Click the rightmost worksheet scrolling tab. This acts as a "last tab" button and moves the rightmost tab into view.

11. Click the leftmost worksheet scrolling tab. This acts as a "first tab" button.

12. Click each of the middle buttons, which serve as "next tab" and "previous tab." The tab scrolling buttons do not change the active worksheet; they only move a sheet into view.

Exercise 4-23   DISPLAY FORMULAS

A formula is visible in the formula bar, but only the results are shown in the cell. When you are reviewing work or trying to decipher what someone else has done in a worksheet, you can display the formulas on screen in the cells. In fact, this is a good way to troubleshoot errors. It is easy to switch between a formula view and a regular view of the worksheet, but many workers keep a duplicate copy of the sheet for formula display.

1. Click the **ElectricUse (Formulas)** worksheet tab.

2. Click the **Formulas** command tab in the Ribbon.

3. In the **Formula Auditing** group, click the Show Formulas button. The actual formulas are displayed, and the worksheet is made wider. The dotted vertical line, if you see one, represents an automatic page break.

Figure 4-20
Displaying formulas
4-20.xlsx
ElectricUse
(Formulas) sheet

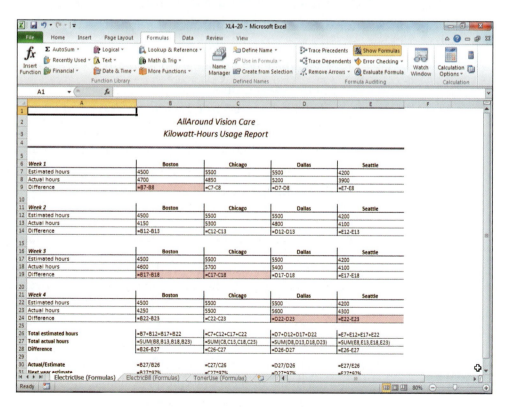

NOTE

The tilde (~) key is located at the top left of the keyboard. It also shows the accent grave (`).

4. Click the **ElectricBill (Formulas)** tab. Hold down Ctrl and click the **TonerUse (Formulas)** tab.

5. Press Ctrl+~. The formulas on both sheets are displayed.

6. Right-click the **ElectricBill (Formulas)** tab and choose **Ungroup Sheets**.

7. Open Backstage View for printing. This sheet was scaled to fit one landscape page, and scaling is dynamic.

8. Close Backstage view.

9. Click the **TonerUse (Formulas)** tab. Press Ctrl+F2. This sheet was not scaled and is too wide to print on a single page with the formulas visible.

10. Close Backstage view.

Exercise 4-24   PRINT GRIDLINES AND HEADINGS

When a formula sheet is prepared as documentation, it is used for checking the location and accuracy of formulas. That is easier to do when row and column headings and gridlines are printed too. These are the elements that you see on the screen while working. They include the column heading letters (A, B, C, and so on) and row numbers. The gridlines are the lines that form the cells. Both these elements can be set to display or be hidden on screen as well as printed.

1. Click the **ElectricUse (Formulas)** worksheet tab.

2. Hold down Shift and click the **TonerUse (Formulas)** tab. All three worksheets are grouped.

3. Click the **Page Layout** command tab.

4. In the **Sheet Options** group, click to place checkmarks for **Gridlines: View**, **Gridlines: Print**, **Headings: View**, and **Headings: Print**.

5. Press Ctrl+F2. Press the Next Page arrow ▶ to see all the pages. Each worksheet would require more than one page when printed.

6. Close Backstage view, and right-click any worksheet tab in the group. Ungroup the sheets.

Exercise 4-25   ADD A FOOTER TO GROUPED SHEETS

When multiple sheets each need the same header or footer, you can group the sheets and create the header-footer layout once. To do this, you use the Page Setup dialog box, opened from the Page Layout command tab or from Backstage view for printing. You should be aware that any changes you make in the dialog box will pertain to each sheet in the group, too.

1. Click the leftmost (first) tab scrolling button. This button scrolls so that the first worksheet tab name is visible.

2. Click the **ElectricUse** worksheet tab, the first worksheet at the left.

3. Click the rightmost (last) tab scrolling button. This button scrolls so that the tab name on the far right is visible.

4. Hold down (Shift) and click the **TonerUse (Formulas)** tab. All six worksheets are grouped.

5. Click the **Page Layout** command tab. Click the Dialog Box Launcher in the **Page Setup** group. Click the **Header/Footer** tab.

6. Click the arrow for the **Footer** box. Scroll to find the three-item choice that displays the user name, the page number, and the date.

Figure 4-21
Header/Footer
tab in Page Setup
dialog box
**4-20.xlsx
ElectricUse
(Formulas) sheet**

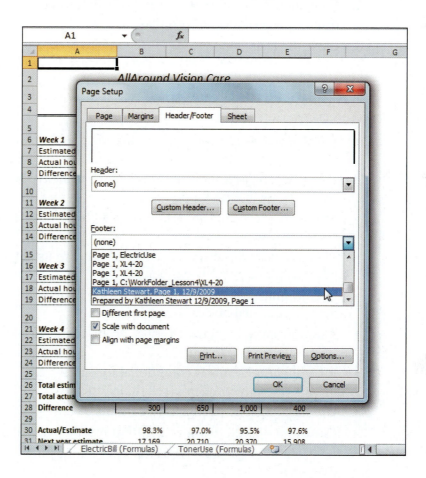

7. Click the **Page** tab. Notice that the **Orientation** group shows **Portrait**, the default setting. Choose **Landscape**.

8. In the **Scaling** group, note that the sheets would be reset to the default 100%. Choose **Fit to**. In the option boxes, choose **1 page** wide by **1 page** tall.

9. Click **Print Preview**. This opens Backstage view for printing.

10. Click the Next Page arrow ▶ to review each sheet.

11. Close Backstage view. Right-click any worksheet and ungroup the sheets.

12. Save the workbook as *[your initials]*4-25 and close it.

Using Online Help

Use Help to view additional information about operators and order of precedence:

1. In a new workbook, press F1. In the Search box, key **operators** and press Enter.
2. Find and review topics to learn more about mathematical operators and order of precedence in formulas.
3. Close the Help window.

Lesson 4   Summary

- Excel formulas use common arithmetic operators to perform different types of calculations.
- Formulas are automatically checked for some types of errors, such as a reference to an empty cell.
- Although Excel can tag certain types of formula errors, it does not correct them.
- The Percent style converts a decimal value to its percentage equivalent and includes a percent symbol.
- The Comma style displays values with a thousands' separator (a comma) and two decimal places.
- There are buttons in the Number group to increase or decrease decimals in a value.
- A highlight cells rule is conditional formatting that applies formatting based on a rule set using a relational operator.
- Use Paste Special to copy only formats.
- Use Go to Special to select cells that meet a particular criteria.
- In calculating formulas, Excel follows mathematical order of precedence.
- You can establish the order of precedence in a formula by keying parentheses around the calculations to be performed first.
- AutoCalculate is a feature located in the status bar that displays sums, averages, and counts for selected cells.
- Cell addresses in a formula can be specified as relative, absolute, or mixed. These references determine what happens when the formula is copied.
- A 3-D reference is a cell address that refers to a cell on a different worksheet in the same workbook.

- Portrait orientation prints a vertical page. Landscape orientation prints a horizontal page.
- The Scale to Fit group on the Page Layout command tab enables you to print the worksheet in a reduced or enlarged size.
- Worksheet columns and/or rows can be hidden from view and unhidden when necessary.
- You can add an image as a sheet background for display on a Web page. These backgrounds do not print.
- Workbooks or individual sheets can be saved as Web pages for viewing in most browsers.
- The entire worksheet with data and formatting can be copied using the Move and Copy dialog box.
- Many commands can be applied to several worksheets at once by grouping the sheets.
- Formulas can be displayed in full for documentation or help in locating problems.
- The gridlines and row and column headings can be set to display and/or to print.

LESSON 4		Command Summary	
Feature	**Button**	**Ribbon Location**	**Keyboard**
Absolute reference			F4
Background		Page Layout, Page Setup	
Center page		Page Layout, Page Setup	
Comma Style	,	Home, Number	Ctrl+1
Copy sheet		Home, Cells	
Decrease decimal	.00→.0	Home, Number	Ctrl+1
Fit to page		Page Layout, Scale to Fit	
Go To Special		Home, Editing	Ctrl+G or F5
Gridlines		Page Layout, Sheet Options	
Headings, row/column		Page Layout, Sheet Options	

continues

LESSON 4		Command Summary *continued*	
Feature	**Button**	**Ribbon Location**	**Keyboard**
Highlight cells rule		Home, Styles	
Increase decimal		Home, Number	Ctrl + 1
Page Orientation		Page Layout, Page Setup	
Paste Special		Home, Clipboard	
Percent Style	%/o	Home, Number	Ctrl + Shift + %
Scaling		Page Layout, Scale to Fit	
Show/hide column		Home, Cells	
Show/hide formulas		Formulas, Formula Auditing	Ctrl + ~
Split window		View, Window	
Web page		File, Save As	F12

Please visit our Online Learning Center, *www.lessonapproach2010.com,* **where you will find the following review materials:**

- **Concepts Review**

    True/False Questions

    Short Answer Questions

    Critical Thinking Questions

- **Skills Review**

    Review Exercises that target single skills

    Lesson Applications

    Review Exercises that challenge students by testing multiple skills in each exercise

- **On Your Own**

    Open-ended exercises that require students to synthesize multiple skills and apply creativity and problem-solving as they would in a real world business situation

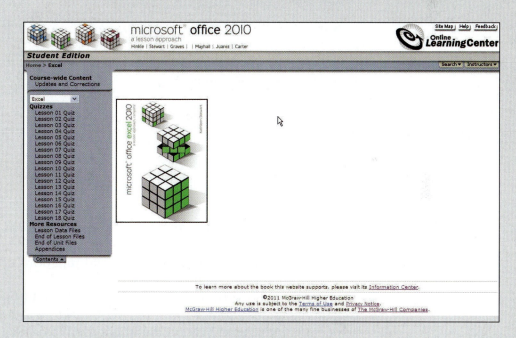

Exploring Function and Argument Basics

OBJECTIVES   *After completing this lesson, you will be able to:*

1 Use Insert Function.

2 Key and point to enter functions.

3 Navigate with and create named ranges.

4 Use range names in functions.

5 Explore function categories.

6 Use a constant.

7 Format data using icon sets.

Estimated Time: 1½ hours

When you key operators and cell addresses to perform a calculation, it is generally called a "formula." A *function* is a built-in formula like SUM or AVERAGE. These two words (formula and function) are often used interchangeably and share many features.

Functions do things automatically that would be difficult or time-consuming to do manually. Take the SUM function as an example. In some worksheets, AllAround Vision Care might need to calculate a sum of cells in 25 or more rows. Imagine having to key or point to create this formula (=B5+B6+B7+ . . . up to B29). The function to accomplish the same result is =SUM(B5:B29), much shorter and easier to verify. The built-in functions also have dialog boxes, ScreenTips, and Help screens to guide you in building your formulas.

Excel has over 300 built-in functions that cover a wide variety of business, statistical, mathematical, and other categories. The Formulas command tab in the Ribbon has a Function Library group with buttons for the most commonly used categories. You can start with easy-to-understand functions, learn how they are built, and progress to becoming more proficient.

Using Insert Function

Excel functions have or follow *syntax*, the rules for how the calculation is built. Syntax consists of the equal sign and the name of the function, followed by parentheses. Inside the parentheses, there may be one or multiple arguments, although there are a couple of functions that do not have any arguments.

An *argument* is data required for the function to complete its calculation. If a function has more than one argument, the arguments are separated by commas. Arguments can be:

- Cell references (individual cells or ranges)
- Constants (a number keyed in the formula)
- Another function (known as a nested function)
- Range names

Figure 5-1
Syntax for the SUMIF function

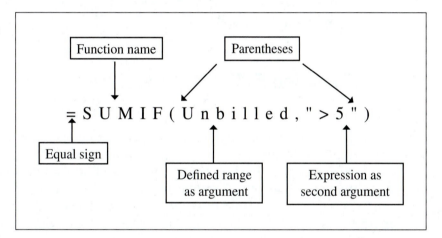

If cell references in an argument include a cell with any of the following types of data, many functions ignore that argument:

- Text
- Blank or empty cells (not zeros)
- Error values such as #NAME?
- Logical values such as TRUE or FALSE

TABLE 5-1 Function Examples

Function(arguments)	Cell Data	Result
=AVERAGE(A1:A3)	A1=10, A2=20, A3=30	20
=COUNT(A1, B2)	A1=25, B2="Ice Cream"	2
=COUNTA(A1:A3)	A1=20, A2=0, A3=TRUE	2; cell A3 is ignored
=COUNTBLANK(A1, B2)	A1=25, B2=#NAME?	0
=SUM(50,60)	None	110
=SUM(A1:A3)	A1=20, A2=Empty, A3=40	60; cell A2 is ignored
=SUMIF(Boston,">100")	Boston=named range of cells	Sum of only those cells that have a value greater than 100
=AVERAGEIF(Chicago, ">50")	Chicago=named range of cells	Average of only those cells that have a value greater than 50

Exercise 5-1   USE INSERT FUNCTION WITH A CELL RANGE

The Insert Function command opens a dialog box that lists Excel functions alphabetically or by category. After you choose the function, the Function Arguments dialog box opens with entry boxes and explanatory text to guide you in building the formula. There is an Insert Function button _fx_ at the left end of the formula bar. The same button _fx_ is available on the Formulas tab in the Function Library.

In the workbook for this lesson, AllAround Vision Care will total the number of selected procedures performed in each of its offices. In addition, it wants to get numbers for certain categories of patients and/or procedures.

REVIEW

If you open data files from an Internet location, you must enable editing to work with the workbook.

1. Open **Excel_Lesson5**. Click cell B18. The SUM function in this cell can calculate a total of all the values in cells B6:E14.

2. Click the Insert Function button _fx_ in the formula bar. The Insert Function dialog box opens. The prompt in the **Search for a function** box is highlighted and ready to be replaced.

3. Key **sum** and press ⏎. Functions that match your search string are listed in the **Select a function** list. **SUM** is highlighted. The syntax and a brief explanation of the function are below the list.

Figure 5-2
Insert Function
dialog box
Excel_Lesson5.xlsx
Procedures sheet

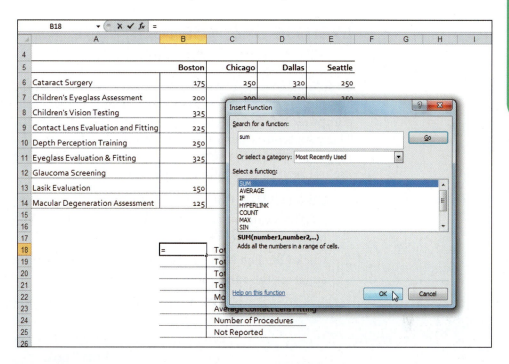

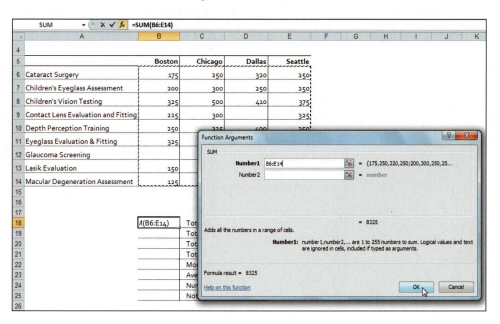

NOTE

Move a dialog box when it covers your data. Move it by pointing at its title bar and dragging.

---

4. Click **OK**. The Function Arguments dialog box provides an entry box for keying or pointing to cell addresses.

5. With the insertion point in the **Number1** box, click cell B6 and drag to select cells B6:E14. The dialog box collapses as you drag and expands when you release the mouse button. The range address appears in the **Number1** box, and the actual sum (8325) appears in the dialog box too.

Figure 5-3
Function Arguments
dialog box
Excel_Lesson5.xlsx
Procedures sheet

6. Click **OK**. The results are shown, and the dialog box closes. The Error Checking Options button ◈ notes that there are empty cells within the range. Leave the error triangles for now.

Exercise 5-2 USE INSERT FUNCTION WITH MULTIPLE RANGES

To calculate some of the totals in this worksheet, you cannot drag to select a contiguous range of cells. Instead you can click each cell to be included in the computation separately, placing each cell address in its own Number box. The procedures performed on patients who are identified as seniors are cataracts, glaucoma screening, and macular degeneration. Those cell ranges are not next to each other in the worksheet.

1. Click cell B19. Click the Insert Function button 𝑓𝑥 . The **Select a function** list shows the most recently used functions, so **SUM** is listed and highlighted.

2. Click **OK**. The **Number1** box in the Function Arguments dialog box suggests the range above the current address.

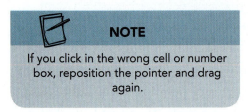

NOTE

If you click in the wrong cell or number box, reposition the pointer and drag again.

3. With the suggested range highlighted in the **Number1** box, click cell B6 and drag to select cells B6:E6. When you release the mouse button, the range address is entered in the **Number1** box.

4. Click in the **Number2** box and click cell B12. Drag to select cells B12:E12. Notice that the formula appears in the formula bar and in the cell. When arguments are entered separately, they are separated by commas in the function.

5. Click in the **Number3** box. Drag to select cells B14:E14. Excel provides the commas to separate the arguments when you use the Function Arguments dialog box.

Figure 5-4
Function Arguments dialog box with ranges entered separately
Excel_Lesson5.xlsx Procedures sheet

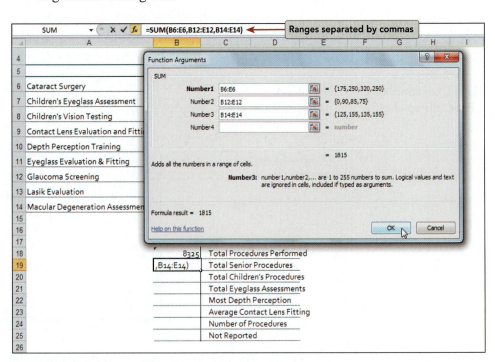

6. Press [Enter]. The dialog box closes; the result (1815) is displayed in the cell.

Keying and Pointing to Enter Functions

When you become more accomplished using some functions, you may find it faster to key the function, especially if you have keyboard speed. The syntax is the same. And as a help to you, Excel displays screen messages. The *Formula AutoComplete* list is a pop-up list that opens after you key the first character in the function name. From this list, you can select the function and need not key the entire name. Then while you are entering the arguments, an *Argument ScreenTip* appears and highlights what is next.

Exercise 5-3 KEY A SUM FUNCTION

To choose a function from the Formula AutoComplete list, you first highlight it. Then you can either double-click it or press Tab. If you press Enter at this point, an incomplete function is entered, and you'll see an error message such as #NAME? in the cell. If this happens, delete the cell contents and try again.

1. Click cell B20.

2. Key **=sum**. Each character that you key opens a list that matches your keystroke(s). You should now see a list of functions that begin with "sum." SUM is at the top of the list with its explanatory ScreenTip to its right.

3. Double-click **SUM** in the list. The opening parenthesis is inserted with the function name. An Argument ScreenTip illustrates the syntax with the first argument **number1** shown in bold.

4. Click cell B7 and drag to select cells B7:E7. As you drag, the ScreenTip shows the number of rows and columns. **1R × 4C** means 1 row, 4 columns.

5. Key **,** to separate the arguments. The second argument, **number2**, is shown in bold in the ScreenTip.

Figure 5-5
SUM function with its
argument ScreenTip
Excel_Lesson5.xlsx
Procedures sheet

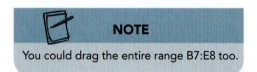

	A	B	C	D	E	F
4						
5		Boston	Chicago	Dallas	Seattle	
6	Cataract Surgery	175	250	320	250	
7	Children's Eyeglass Assessment	200	300	250	250	
8	Children's Vision Testing	325	500	410	375	
9	Contact Lens Evaluation and Fitting	225	300		325	
10	Depth Perception Training	250	325	400	350	
11	Eyeglass Evaluation & Fitting	325	400	375		
12	Glaucoma Screening		90	85	75	
13	Lasik Evaluation	150	150	125	200	
14	Macular Degeneration Assessment	125	155	135	155	
15						
16						
17						
18		8325	Total Procedures Performed			
19		1815	Total Senior Procedures			
20		=SUM(B7:E7,	en's Procedures			
21		SUM(number1, [number2], [number3], ...)	ments			
22			Most Depth Perception			
23			Average Contact Lens Fitting			
24			Number of Procedures			
25			Not Reported			
26						

Formula bar: SUM ▼ ✕ ✓ *fx* =SUM(B7:E7,

NOTE

You could drag the entire range B7:E8 too.

6. Click cell B8 and drag to select cells B8:E8.

7. Press [Ctrl]+[Enter]. The result is 2610. You do not need to key the closing parenthesis; it is assumed and inserted for you.

8. Look in the formula bar.

9. Click cell B21. Key **=sum**.

10. Press the [Tab] key on the keyboard. The opening parenthesis is inserted with the function name. The ScreenTip shows **number1** in bold.

11. Click cell B7 and drag to select cells B7:E7.

12. Key **,** to separate the arguments.

13. Click cell B11 and drag to select cells B11:E11.

14. Press [Enter]. The result is 2100.

15. Save the workbook as *[your initials]***5-3**.

Navigating with and Creating Named Ranges

A *defined name* is a name that you create and assign to a single cell or a group of cells. It is a *range name* or *named range*. There are several reasons for using range names:

- You can use range names for navigation.

- Range names can be used instead of cell addresses in formulas.

- Range names are easier to remember and recognize than cell addresses.

- You are less likely to make an error selecting a range name than by keying a cell address in a formula or function.

- Range names make formulas easier to understand.

- Named ranges appear in Formula AutoComplete lists.

Range names make it easier for you and others to find data in a workbook. In the workbook for this lesson, for example, there is a range name for "Contacts." When you select that range name, the relevant cells are highlighted. You don't need to spend time reading through all the labels to find the data.

Here are some rules for named cell ranges:

- Begin cell range names with a letter.

- Do not use single-letter range names, such as "n."

- Do not use range names that resemble cell addresses, such as "A5."

- Keep range names relatively short.

- Use uppercase letters, an underscore, or a period to separate words (FirstQuarter, First_Quarter, or First.Quarter). Do not use spaces.

- Do not use special characters such as hyphens (-) or symbols ($, %, &, #).

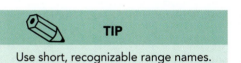

TIP

Use short, recognizable range names.

Excel has a few reserved, built-in range names that you should not use. These special names include Print_Area, Print_Titles, Consolidate_Area, and Sheet_Title. If you name a range on your worksheet with one of these names, you override Excel's use of the names and could have unexpected results.

TABLE 5-2 Examples of Acceptable and Unacceptable Range Names

Acceptable Names	Unacceptable Names
Week1	Week 1
Week_1	Week-1
Week.1	Week:1
WeekNo1	Week#1
Wk1	W1 or W

Exercise 5-4 NAVIGATE USING RANGE NAMES

The Name Box is a text box with a drop-down arrow to the left of the formula bar. You can use this Name Box to quickly move the insertion point to a named range in a workbook. The Name Box and the formula bar share space in the Excel window, and there is a small round indented button between them that can be used to size either element. Rest the mouse pointer on this button, and you'll see a two-pointed arrow that you can drag left or right. You can size the Name Box to see lengthy range names in full.

The Go To dialog box lists all range names in the workbook so that you can use it for navigation too.

1. Click the down arrow in the Name Box. The range names in the workbook are listed.

Figure 5-6
Range names in the workbook
5-3.xlsx
Procedures sheet

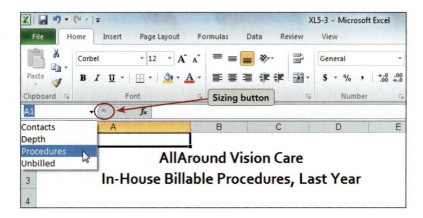

2. Choose **Procedures**. The range A6:A14 is highlighted on the worksheet.
3. Press ⌃Ctrl+G. The Go To dialog box shows defined range names and recently used cell addresses.
4. Double-click **Contacts**. Cells B9:E9 are defined as the "Contacts" range.
5. Click the down arrow in the Name Box. Choose **Unbilled**. This range is located on the **Boston** worksheet.
6. Click the down arrow in the Name Box. Choose **Procedures**. The focus resets to the **Procedures** worksheet.

Exercise 5-5 NAME A DEFINED RANGE

There are several ways to create a named range. After selecting the cells on the worksheet, you can:

• Click the Name Box, key the range name, and press Enter.

• Click the Define Name button 🔲 on the Formulas tab. Key the range name and click **OK**.

• Click the Name Manager button 📖 on the Formulas tab. Click **New**, key the range name, and click **OK**.

If you use one of the button commands, Excel suggests a range name based on the worksheet layout. You can accept it, or key a name of your own choice.

1. Select the range B6:B14. Click the Name Box (not its arrow).
2. Key **Boston** and press Enter.

3. Select the range C6:C14. Click the Name Box, key **Chicago**, and press ⏎Enter⏎.

4. Click the **Formulas** command tab.

5. Select cells D6:D14. In the **Defined Names** group, click the Define Name button. The New Name dialog box opens with the highlighted range indicated and a suggested name from row 5.

Figure 5-7
New Name
dialog box
5-3.xlsx
Procedures sheet

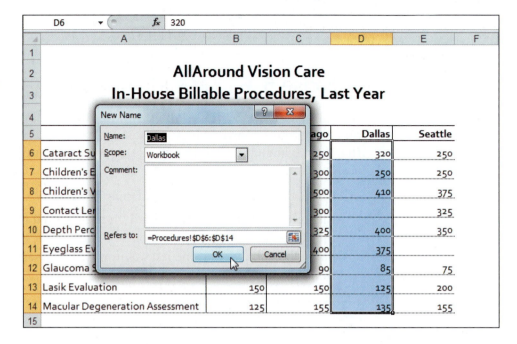

6. Click **OK**.

7. Select cells E6:E14. In the **Defined Names** group, click the Name Manager button. The Name Manager dialog box lists the existing defined names in the workbook.

Figure 5-8
Name Manager
dialog box
5-3.xlsx
Procedures sheet

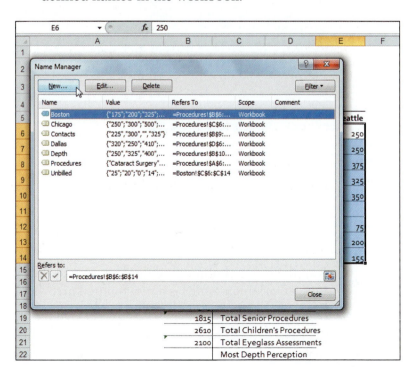

8. Click **New**. The New Name dialog box opens with the suggested name.

9. Click **OK**. Close the Name Manager dialog box.

10. Click the arrow in the Name Box, and choose one of your new ranges.

11. Press F5 and choose a range from the Go To dialog box. Click **OK**.

12. Press Ctrl + Home.

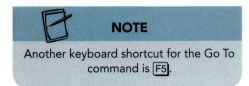

NOTE

Another keyboard shortcut for the Go To command is F5.

Exercise 5-6 CREATE RANGE NAMES AUTOMATICALLY

If columns and rows have labels and data that follow a pattern, you can quickly name several ranges with one command. You begin by selecting the entire range, and Excel will use the top row and/or the left column to assign names.

1. On the **Boston** worksheet, select cells A6:B14.

2. Click the **Formulas** command tab. In the **Defined Names** group, click the Create from Selection button ⊞. The Create Names from Selection dialog box shows that the left column will be used as the basis for range names.

Figure 5-9
Creating range names automatically
5-3.xlsx
Boston sheet

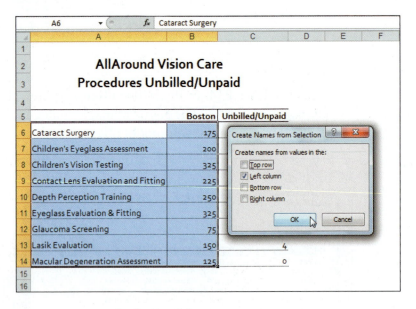

3. Click **OK**. Range names have been created for each of the procedures.

4. Press Ctrl + Home.

5. Click the arrow in the Name Box. You can see now that some of the names are lengthy. Press Esc.

6. Rest the mouse button on the size button at the right edge of the Name Box. The sizing pointer is a two-pointed arrow.

7. Drag to the right to make the Name Box slightly wider.

8. Click the arrow in the Name Box. Choose **Cataract_Surgery**. The range is the value in column B; the label in column A was used to name the range.

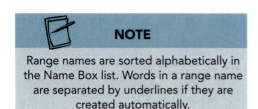

NOTE

Range names are sorted alphabetically in the Name Box list. Words in a range name are separated by underlines if they are created automatically.

9. Click the down arrow in the Name Box and choose another procedure name.

Exercise 5-7 DELETE RANGE NAMES

Defined names can be deleted from the Name Manager dialog box. Since range names can be used in formulas, you should assess what might happen when you delete range names. If you delete a range name that is used in a formula, Excel displays the error message #NAME? in the cell, because it no longer has the name as a reference. You have not used range names in any of your formulas yet.

1. Click the **Procedures** worksheet tab. Click the **Formulas** command tab.

2. In the **Defined Names** group, click the Name Manager button 📇. The named ranges in the workbook are listed in the dialog box.

3. Drag the bottom right corner of the dialog box to expand it.

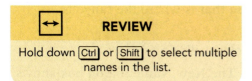

REVIEW

Hold down Ctrl or Shift to select multiple names in the list.

4. Widen the **Name**, **Value**, and **Refers to** columns to see more of the information. The **Refers to** column identifies the worksheet and cell range. The **Scope** column indicates if the name is limited to a particular sheet.

5. Click **Unbilled** and click **Delete**. Click **OK**. This name was on the **Boston** worksheet.

6. Click **Cataract_Surgery**. Hold down Ctrl and click **Children's_Eyeglass_ Assessment**. Hold down Ctrl and click **Children's_Vision_Testing**. Click **Delete** and click **OK**. Close the dialog box.

Figure 5-10
Deleting named ranges
5-3.xlsx
Procedures sheet

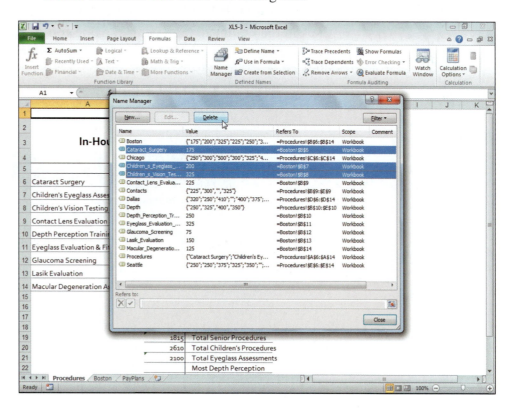

7. Click the Name Box arrow. There are fewer range names now.

8. Press [Esc] to remove the menu.

Exercise 5-8 SETTING THE SCOPE FOR A NAMED RANGE

The *scope* for a range name is its location applicability. By default, range names are assigned to the workbook. If you use a range name on **Sheet1**, you should not use the same name on a different sheet in the same workbook. You can, however, set a scope for a new range name as you create it so that it is assigned to a particular sheet. Then you can use the same range name several times, scoping each use to the appropriate worksheet. A name that is scoped to a worksheet only appears in the Name Box list for that sheet.

1. Click the Name Box arrow. Choose **Lasik_Evaluation**. The pointer returns to the **Boston** sheet, because that is where the range is located.

2. Click the **Formulas** command tab. Select cells C6:C14.

3. Click the Define Name button . The New Name dialog box shows the selected range with a suggested name that uses the label in the row above the range.

4. Click the **Scope** arrow. The sheets in the workbook are listed as well as the workbook itself.

5. Choose **Boston**. This name will apply only on this sheet.

6. Click in the **Comment** box. Defined name comments appear with the range name in Formula AutoComplete lists and in the Name Manager dialog box.

7. Key **As of current date**. Click **OK**.

> **NOTE**
>
> If you create names from a selection, you are not able to change the scope.

Figure 5-11
Changing the scope
for a name
5-3.xlsx
Boston sheet

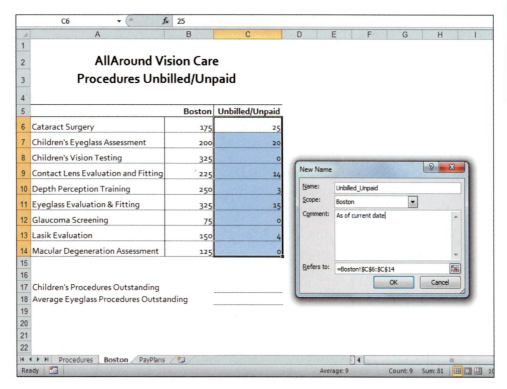

8. Click the Name Box arrow. These are the named ranges on both sheets.

9. Choose **Boston**. The pointer returns to the **Procedures** sheet.

10. Click the Name Box arrow. The **Unbilled_Unpaid** name does not appear in the list because it is scoped to the **Boston** sheet.

11. Click the **Boston** sheet tab. Click the Name Box arrow. Look for the **Unbilled_Unpaid** name in the list.

12. Press [Esc]. Save the workbook as *[your initials]*5-8.

Using Range Names in Functions

Companies use range names for work that is routine. If you always have to check the monthly totals in a worksheet with 5,000 rows, it's much easier if you can simply choose the "Totals" range and quickly see the results. If this "Totals" range is used in a forecast formula for next month, you know that the formula is =TOTALS*10%.

Named ranges can be used as arguments in a formula or a function. When you use a range name in a function/formula, the formula is easy to understand at first glance. For example, a formula such as =SUM(FirstQtrSales) conveys its purpose more quickly than =SUM(B12:F12).

When you use the Insert Function dialog box, you can access the Paste Names dialog box to add named ranges to a formula. You can also simply key the range name if you remember it. When you key a function, Formula AutoComplete provides some help, too. If you key a display trigger, you'll see defined range names in a list. A *display trigger* is one or more keyboard characters that open a dialog box or show a prompt or ScreenTip. The display trigger for range names is any alphabetic character; it lists the range names that begin with that character.

Exercise 5-9 USE NAMED RANGES WITH MAX AND AVERAGE

The Function Library on the Formulas command tab includes a button that is labeled AutoSum. It is the same as the Sum button Σ on the Home command tab.

1. Click the **Procedures** sheet tab.

2. Click the Name Box arrow and choose **Depth**. This range identifies the values for each city for this procedure. You can use the name **Depth** in a formula instead of B9:E9.

3. Click cell B22. Click the arrow with the AutoSum button Σ in the **Function Library** group on the **Formulas** tab.

4. Choose **Max**. The function is inserted and the range immediately above cell B22 is assumed.

5. Press F3. This keyboard shortcut opens the Paste Names dialog box.

6. Click **Depth** in the list and click **OK**. The range name replaces the assumed cell range in the formula.

7. Press Enter. The result is 400 for the highest value in the Depth range.

8. Click cell B23. Key **=aver** and press Tab. The ScreenTip indicates that the first argument is **number1**, but there is no assumed range. You need the "Contact Lens" range here.

9. Key **c** to display defined names and functions that begin with *C*. The range name does not appear in the list at this point.

10. Key **on** to refine the list. Function names include a function icon, and range names have a worksheet icon.

Figure 5-12
Using range names in Formula AutoComplete
5-8.xlsx
Procedures sheet

8325	Total Procedures Performed
1815	Total Senior Procedures
2610	Total Children's Procedures
2100	Total Eyeglass Assessments
400	Most Depth Perception
=AVERAGE(con	tact Lens Fitting

AVERAGE(**number1**, [number2], ...) edures

- *fx* CONCATENATE
- *fx* CONFIDENCE.NORM
- *fx* CONFIDENCE.T
- Contact_Lens_Evaluation_and_Fitting
- Contacts
- *fx* CONVERT
- CONFIDENCE

11. Double-click **Contact_Lens_Evaluation_and_Fitting** and press ⌷Enter⌷. This is the wrong range name, and you can use AutoCalculate to check.

12. Right-click the AutoCalculate area in the status bar. Make sure there is a checkmark for **Average**.

13. Select cells B9:E9, and note the average indicated in AutoCalculate (283.333).

14. Click cell B23 and press ⌷Delete⌷.

15. Key **=aver** and press ⌷Tab⌷. Key **con**. Double-click **Contacts** and press ⌷Enter⌷. The general number format shows as many decimal places as will fit in the cell at its current width.

Exercise 5-10 USE COUNT, COUNTA, AND COUNTBLANK

Five functions in the statistical category include COUNT in their names. The COUNT function tallies or counts the number of values in a range; it does not include labels. The COUNTA function tallies values and labels. You might think of it as "count all." The COUNTBLANK function counts empty cells in a range. These functions can be used in numerous ways to help any business determine how many of whatever it is they need to know.

1. Click cell B24 and click the **Formulas** command tab. Click the More Functions button ▥.

2. Choose **Statistical** to display its list of functions.

3. Choose **COUNT**. The Function Arguments dialog box opens. You will count the number of procedures listed.

4. Press ⌷F3⌷ to open the Paste Names dialog box.

5. Scroll the list of range names and double-click **Procedures**. The range appears in the **Value1** box. You can see that the result is zero (0).

6. Click **OK**. The COUNT function does not count labels.

7. Click in the formula bar, and position the insertion point to key **a** after **COUNT**. Press ⌷Enter⌷.

8. Click cell B24. The function COUNTA includes labels; there are nine procedures listed.

9. Click cell B25. The function here should count how many cells are empty in the value range. There is no range name for all the values on this worksheet.

10. Click the Insert Function button *fx*. The Insert Function dialog box opens.

NOTE

The Count option in AutoCalculate shows the same results as the COUNTA function. AutoCalculate's Numerical Count option shows the same results as the COUNT function.

11. Click the arrow for the **Or select a category** list, and choose **Statistical**. Scroll the list and click **COUNTBLANK**. Click **OK**. The argument for this function is **Range**.

12. Click cell B6 and drag to select cells B6:E14. Click **OK**. There are three cells that are empty.

Figure 5-13
Using COUNTBLANK
5-8.xlsx
Procedures sheet

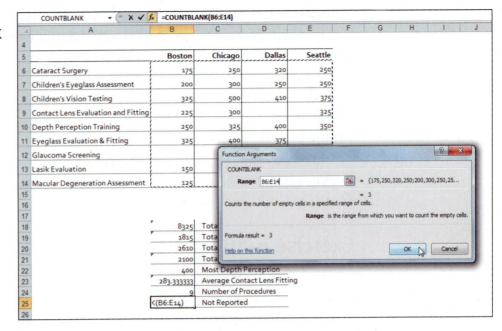

Exercise 5-11   INSERT DATA WITHIN A NAMED RANGE

If you insert a row or column within a defined name range, it is included in any formulas that reference the range.

1.   On the **Procedures** sheet, insert a row at row 9.

2.   In cell A9, key **Color Vision Testing**.

3.   Select cells B9:E9. Key the following values for the cities and press [Enter] to move from column to column.

   250   325   175   100

4.   Click the arrow in the Name Box and choose **Procedures**. The new label in cell A9 is included in the named range.

5.   Click the arrow in the Name Box and choose **Chicago**. The new value is included in the range.

6.   Click cell B25. The results have been updated to include the new row. There are now ten procedures.

Exercise 5-12   MODIFY DEFINED NAMES

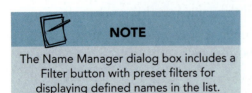

NOTE

The Name Manager dialog box includes a Filter button with preset filters for displaying defined names in the list.

You can change a range name or redefine the range to which it refers. Formulas are automatically updated to show the new name or include the new data.

1.   Click the **Formulas** command tab. Click the Name Manager button 📇.

2. Select **Contacts** in the list. Click **Edit**. The Edit Name dialog box is the same as the New Name dialog box, but scope choices are not available.

3. In the **Name** box, edit the name to **Contacts Procedures**. Click **OK**.

4. A message box opens stating that the name is not valid. You cannot use spaces in a range name. Click **OK**.

5. In the **Name** box, edit the name to **Contacts_Procedures**. Click **OK**. The new name is listed.

6. Close the Name Manager dialog box.

7. Click cell B24 and view the formula bar. The formula has been updated to show the new range name.

8. Click the Name Manager button .

9. Choose **Boston** in the list. This range currently refers to the values in column B on the **Procedures** sheet.

> **NOTE**
>
> Many dialog boxes include a RefEdit button when choosing a range is an option. The button is a toggle and looks slightly different depending on whether it collapses or expands the dialog box.

10. Click **Edit**. The **Refers to** entry shows the cell range. The button at the right end of the **Refers to** box is the RefEdit button ; it toggles reference editing for a command. It may also be referred to as the Range Finder button, because you use it to select a range of cells.

11. Click the RefEdit button . The dialog box collapses so that you can find and select a new cell range.

12. Click the **Boston** worksheet tab. Select cells B6:B14 and click the Range Finder button . Click **OK**. Click **Close**.

Figure 5-14
Changing the range for a defined name
5-8.xlsx
Procedures sheet

	B6		fx =AVERAGE(Contacts_Procedures)				
	A	B	C	D	E	F	G
1							
2	**AllAround Vision Care**						
3	**Procedures Unbilled/Unpaid**						
4							
5		Boston	Unbilled/Unpaid				
6	Cataract Surgery	175	25				
7	Children's Eyeglass Assessment	200	20			RefEdit or Range Finder button	
8	Children's Vision Testing	325	0				
9	Contact Lens Evaluation and Fitting	225	14				
10	Depth Perception Training	250	3				
11	Eyeglass Evaluation & Fitting	325		Edit Name - Refers to:			
12	Glaucoma Screening	75		=Boston!$B$6:$B$14			
13	Lasik Evaluation	150					
14	Macular Degeneration Assessment	125	0				
15							
16							

13. Click the Name Box arrow and choose **Boston**. The values on the **Boston** sheet are selected.

Exercise 5-13 DELETE A RANGE NAME USED IN A FORMULA

Now that you have formulas with range names as arguments, you can experiment with deleting a range name. Excel displays the error message #NAME? in the cell if you delete a range name that was used in the formula or function.

1. Click the **Procedures** worksheet tab. Click cell B23. You used the named range **Depth** in the MAX function.

2. Click the Name Manager button 🖳. Choose **Depth** and click **Delete**. The message box asks you to confirm the deletion.

3. Click **OK**. Click **Close**. #NAME? appears in cell B23.

4. Click the Error Checking Options button ◈ for cell B23. This error is described as an **Invalid Name Error**. It refers to a name, "Depth," that no longer exists in this workbook.

5. Press [Esc] to remove the options menu.

6. Press [Ctrl]+[Z], the keyboard shortcut for the Undo command. The range name "Depth" has been restored, and the formula is acceptable.

7. Save the workbook as *[your initials]*5-13.

Exploring Function Categories

Excel functions are organized into categories based on their uses and purposes. There is a date and time category, for example, that includes a variety of formulas for formatting, converting, and calculating dates and times. There are database functions that are meant to be used with large lists of data. There are also engineering and cube categories for more technical and scientific work. Most of the function categories are available from a button on the Formulas command tab, but you have access to all functions, regardless of category, in the Insert Function dialog box.

TABLE 5-3 Function Categories

Category		Purpose
Compatibility	📄	Provides downward compatibility with earlier versions of Excel. An improved 2010 version of each of the functions in this group is in its designated category
Cube	📦	Locates data from tables in SQL Analysis Services, a separate Microsoft product
Database	f_x	Statistical and mathematical calculations performed with criteria on large tables of data
Date & Time	📅	Converts dates and times to values and sets how dates and times are displayed

continues

TABLE 5-3 Function Categories   *continued*

Category		Purpose
Engineering		Determines complex numbers, coefficients, conversions, and measurements
Financial		Calculates accounting and financial concepts, such as depreciation, interest paid, payment amounts, and rates of return
Information		Finds and displays cell contents, errors, and other cell properties or settings
Logical		Determines if an expression or condition is true or false
Lookup & Reference		Finds and displays cell addresses or values from tables or lists of data
Math & Trig		Includes common mathematical and trigonometry calculations such as rounding, showing integers, summing, and showing sines and cosines
Statistical		Determines standard deviations, distributions, square roots, averages, medians, and other statistical computations
Text		Formats or converts text strings

Some companies, no doubt, use functions from every category. Most, however, use the more common business functions such as SUM, AVERAGE, and COUNT. As you learn about functions, you'll see that some categories have highly specialized uses. They require that you have previous experience and knowledge about what they are calculating. You'll find, too, that you can become an expert Excel user, knowing how to use less sophisticated functions from several categories.

Exercise 5-14   USE A MATH & TRIG FUNCTION

The SUMIF function belongs to the Math & Trig category, like SUM. SUMIF adds cell values only if they meet a condition. In your workbook, AllAround Vision Care can determine how many unpaid bills cover children's procedures. It will set a condition that the procedure include the word "children" for the cell to be included in the total.

The SUMIF function has two required arguments, Range and Criteria. *Range* is the group of cells that are checked for the criteria. *Criteria* is the condition that must be met for a cell to be included in the addition. There is a third argument, *Sum_range,* which can be omitted if the cells to be added are the same as the ones that are matched against the criteria.

1. Click the **Boston** worksheet tab. Click cell C17. Outstanding accounts for children's procedures are to be summed.

2. Click the **Formulas** command tab. Click the Math & Trig button.

3. Scroll to find **SUMIF** and click. The Function Arguments dialog box opens with the insertion point in the **Range** entry box. Argument names that are bold in the dialog box are required; others are optional.

4. Click cell A6 and drag to select the range A6:A14. As you drag, the dialog box collapses. When you release the mouse button, the dialog box expands.

5. Click in the **Criteria** box. This argument is explained in the dialog box.

6. Key **child***to set a rule that the cells in the range must start with the string "child." You can use the wildcard (*) to shorten what you have to key as long as it still distinguishes the data.

7. Click in the **Sum_range** box. The range of cells to be summed is C6:C14.

8. Select cells C6:C14. The range name **Unbilled_Unpaid** is automatically substituted.

Figure 5-15
SUMIF function in the Function Arguments dialog box
5-13.xlsx
Boston sheet

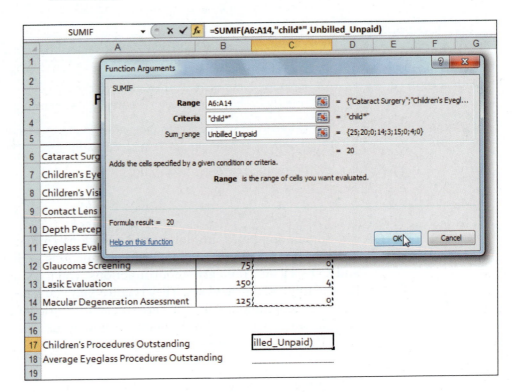

9. Click **OK**. The result is 20.

10. View the formula bar. The criteria have been inserted with quotation marks.

Exercise 5-15 USE A STATISTICAL FUNCTION

AVERAGEIF, like AVERAGE, belongs to the statistical category. An average is the *arithmetic mean*. The arithmetic mean adds the values and divides the results by the number of values. The AVERAGEIF function averages cell values only if they meet a condition. Like SUMIF, AVERAGEIF has two required arguments, *Range* and *Criteria*. The *Average_range* argument is used when the cells that are matched against the criteria are different from those to be averaged. In cell B18, you can calculate an average for eyeglass procedures outstanding.

1. Click cell B18. Click the Insert Function button f_x.

2. In the **Or select a category** list, choose **Statistical**. In the **Select a function** list, find **AVERAGEIF**.

3. Click **AVERAGEIF** and click **OK**. The Function Arguments dialog box opens.

4. Click cell A6 and drag to select the range A6:A14.

5. Click in the **Criteria** box.

6. Key ***eye***to include those cells that have "eye" somewhere in the label.

7. Click in the **Average_range** box.

8. Press F3 to open the Paste Names dialog box. Scroll the list to find **Unbilled_Unpaid** and click it. Click **OK**.

9. Click **OK**. The result is 17.5.

10. Click the **Home** command tab. Click the Decrease Decimal button one time. The value is rounded up and shows 18.

Exercise 5-16   USE A FINANCIAL FUNCTION

The PMT function belongs to the financial group of functions. The PMT (payment) function calculates a monthly payment for money owed. If you have ever borrowed money and paid it back over a period of time, this calculation was likely used to determine your payments. The PMT function has three required arguments: Rate, Nper, and Pv. *Rate* is the interest rate, a percentage added to the original amount. *Nper* is the number of payments to be made. *Pv* represents the loan amount. PMT has two optional arguments, *Fv* and *Type*.

In your workbook, another worksheet calculates monthly payments for AllAround Vision Care patients who have a balance due. It shows the payment based on the amount owed and whether the patient chooses a 1- or 2-year payback period.

1. Click the **PayPlans** worksheet tab.

2. Click cell B5. Click the **Formulas** command tab.

3. Click the Financial button. Scroll and click **PMT**. The PMT Function Arguments dialog box opens with the insertion point in the **Rate** box, the first argument.

4. Key **2.75%/12** in the **Rate**. The annual interest rate is indicated in the label in cell A3 and must be divided by 12 to calculate a monthly payment for a year.

5. Click in the **Nper** box. This argument is the total number of payments. For one year, it's 12 payments.

6. Key **12** in the **Nper**.

NOTE

The formula uses a relative reference for the Pv argument so that it can be copied to the other rows.

7. Click in the **Pv** box and click cell A5. This argument represents the present value which is the amount owed now.

8. Click in the **Fv** box. This is an optional argument for how much money might not have to be paid back. Usually this argument is left blank.

9. Click in the **Type** box, and key **1** for a payment at the beginning of the month.

Figure 5-16
PMT function in the Function Arguments dialog box
5-13.xlsx
PayPlans sheet

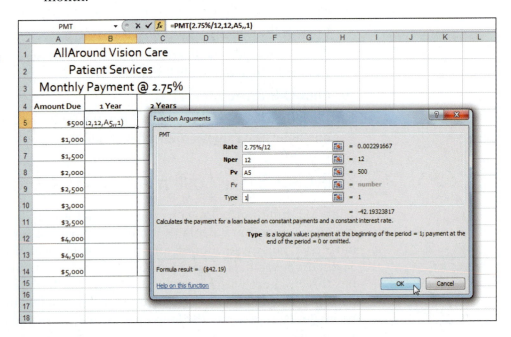

10. Click **OK**. The result ($42.19) is a negative number, because it is money that the patient is expected to pay. Negative values are formatted in red with parentheses in this worksheet, based on the currency format (already applied).

TIP

You can show the formula results as positive values by keying a hyphen (-) as a minus sign in front of the reference to cell A5 in the PMT formula.

11. Rest the mouse pointer on the Fill handle for cell B5. Drag the handle to cell B14 to copy it.

12. Click cell C5. Click the Recently Used button 📖 and choose **PMT**.

13. Key **2.75%/12** in the **Rate**.

14. Key **24** in the **Nper** for a 2-year loan.

15. Click in the **Pv** box and click cell A5.

16. Key **1** in the **Type** box. Click **OK**.

17. Copy the formula to row 14.

18. Select cells B5:C14, and click the Dialog Box Launcher in the **Number** group on the **Home** command tab. For the currency format, there are four options for displaying negative values.

19. Click **($1,234.10)** in the black font color, and click **OK**.

20. Save the workbook as *[your initials]*5-16.

Using a Constant

A *constant* is a value that does not change. It can be a value that is keyed in a formula or in the Function Arguments dialog box. In the PMT function used by AllAround Vision Care to determine monthly payments, the interest rate of 2.75% is a constant. In the city where you live, there may be a tax rate that is used for most purchases. This is a constant that is always applied at the cash register to your purchases.

Constants can be named, just like cell ranges. The same features and guidelines apply to named constants as to named cell ranges. Named constants do appear in Formula AutoComplete lists unless they have been scoped to a particular worksheet.

Exercise 5-17　NAME A CONSTANT

You must use the New Name dialog box to name a constant. You cannot use the Name Box next to the formula bar to create a named constant, because it is not a cell that is selected on the worksheet. It is a value that you key, and it does not and need not appear anywhere on the sheet. It does not matter which worksheet is active when you create a constant.

1. In *[your initials]*5-16, press Ctrl+F3. This is the keyboard shortcut to open the Name Manager dialog box.

2. Click **New**. In the **Name** box, key Increase.

3. In the **Comment** box, key **This is a projected percentage increase in number of procedures**.

4. In the **Refers to** text box, delete existing data and key **=8%**.

Figure 5-17
Naming a constant
5-16.xlsx
PayPlans sheet

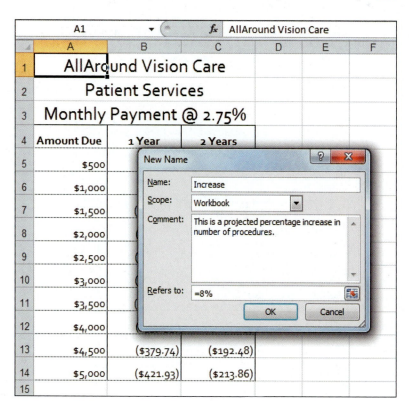

UNIT 2 LESSON 5

5. Click **OK**. The constant name appears in the list with the defined names. The **Value** column does not show cell references like the other defined names.

6. Click **Close**.

7. Click the arrow in the Name Box. Named constants do not appear in this list.

8. Press [Esc] to close the list.

Exercise 5-18 USE FILL ACROSS WORKSHEETS

Before you can make a forecast about the number of procedures for next year, you need to create a copy of the existing data on another sheet. Fill Across Worksheets is a copy command that copies selected data to one or more worksheets. To use this command, you first select the worksheet with the data and the sheet(s) where the data should be copied.

1. In *[your initials]*5-16, insert a new worksheet. You'll copy selected cells to this new sheet.

2. Click the **Procedures** worksheet tab.

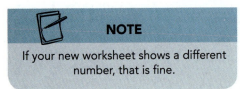

NOTE

If your new worksheet shows a different number, that is fine.

3. Select cells A1:E15. These are the data that will be copied.

4. Hold down the [Ctrl] key and click the **Sheet1** worksheet tab. This is where the data will be copied. The title bar shows "[Group]."

5. On the **Home** command tab in the **Editing** group, click the Fill button.

Figure 5-18
Using Fill Across Worksheets
5-16.xlsx
Procedures sheet

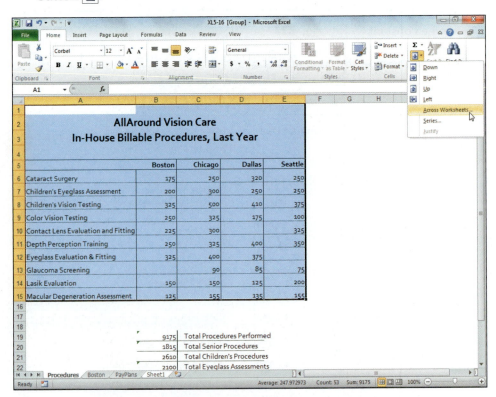

6. Choose **Across Worksheets**. The Fill Across Worksheets dialog box has options to copy everything, only the data, or only the formatting.

7. Choose **All** and click **OK**.

8. Right-click the **Sheet1** worksheet tab. Choose **Ungroup Sheets**. Column widths are not copied.

9. Click the column heading for column B, and drag to select columns B:E. Make these columns **10.00 (75 pixels)** wide. Make column A **35.00 (250 pixels)** wide.

10. Select and delete all the values.

11. Rename **Sheet1** as **NextYear**.

Exercise 5-19   USE A CONSTANT IN A FORMULA

To determine projected procedure numbers for next year, you will multiply the current numbers by the Increase constant.

1. Click cell B6. Key **=** and click the **Procedures** worksheet tab.

2. Click cell B6. Key ***** to multiply.

3. Key **in** to open the Formula AutoComplete list. This list includes named ranges or constants and functions that begin with "in." Your constant **Increase** should be first in the list and highlighted.

4. Press [Enter]. The error message #NAME? appears in the cell.

5. Click cell B6 and look at the formula bar. You cannot press [Enter] to choose from the Formula AutoComplete list, because your constant name is incomplete.

6. Key **=** and click the **Procedures** worksheet tab.

7. Click cell B6 and key *****.

8. Key **in** and press [Tab]. This inserts the complete constant name in the formula bar, but the formula is not finished.

9. Press [Enter]. The focus returns to the **NextYear** sheet.

10. Click cell B6. The constant value (8%) is multiplied by the value in cell B6 on the **Procedures** sheet, resulting in how many additional procedures are the goal. To calculate the actual new value, the constant should be 108%, not 8%.

11. Press [Ctrl]+[F3]. Find **Increase** in the list and click it. Then click **Edit**.

12. Click in the **Refers to** box, and edit the value to **108%**.

13. Click **OK** and then click **Close**. The formula on the **NextYear** sheet is recalculated with the new constant.

14. Copy the formula in cell B6 to column E and then to row 15. Fix any borders after copying. If all Excel error checking rules are active, you will see error triangles for formulas that refer to empty cells. You need not do anything about these errors now.

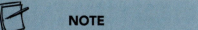

NOTE

A constant is an absolute reference.

Exercise 5-20   CREATE A RANGE NAME LIST

In large workbooks there can be many range names. It can become difficult to recall them and to remember what sheet they are located on. The Paste List command in the Paste Name dialog box creates a table of the workbook's range names. You can use this command to create a list of range names on a separate worksheet. This form of workbook documentation is for your and for others who might use your work.

1. Insert a new worksheet and name it **Documentation**.

2. In cell A1, key **Procedures Report Range Names**.

3. In cell A2, press Ctrl + ; and press Enter. This keyboard shortcut inserts the current date using mm/dd/yyyy format.

4. In cell A3, key **Name**. In cell B3, key **Range**.

5. Click cell A4. On the **Formulas** command tab in the **Defined Names** group, click the Use in Formula button. The range names are listed.

6. Choose **Paste Names** at the bottom of the list. The Paste Name dialog box opens.

7. Click **Paste List**. The range names and cell references are pasted in two columns starting in cell A4.

Figure 5-19
A pasted range name list
5-16.xlsx
Documentation sheet

	A	B	C	D	E
1	Procedures	Report Range Name			
2	12/11/2009				
3	Name	Range			
4	Boston	=Boston!$B$6:$B$14			
5	Chicago	=Procedures!$C$6:$C$15			
6	Contact_Le	=Boston!$B$9			
7	Contacts_P	=Procedures!$B$10:$E$10			
8	Dallas	=Procedures!$D$6:$D$15			
9	Depth	=Procedures!$B$11:$E$11			
10	Depth_Perc	=Boston!$B$10			
11	Eyeglass_E	=Boston!$B$11			
12	Glaucoma_	=Boston!$B$12			
13	Increase	=108%			
14	Lasik_Evalu	=Boston!$B$13			
15	Macular_De	=Boston!$B$14			
16	Procedures	=Procedures!$A$6:$A$15			
17	Seattle	=Procedures!$E$6:$E$15			
18					
19					

8. Adjust column widths and row heights to make the data easy to follow. Apply **All Borders** starting at row 3.

Formatting Data with Icon Sets

In addition to its format options and cell styles, Excel provides more graphic ways to illustrate data. These features enable you to create a professional report that, with a quick look, highlights some aspect of the data. The Conditional Formatting command includes, in its gallery, three types of data visualizations: data bars, color scales, and icon sets.

An icon set consists of three to five icons that appear with or without the value in a range of cells. The icon shown in a particular cell depends on the value. For example, there is an icon set that shows three circle symbols—red, yellow, and green. The green icon is assigned to the highest values in the range, the yellow to the middle range, and the red to those cells with the lowest values in the range.

Exercise 5-21   APPLY ICON SETS

On the Boston worksheet, the company wants to draw attention to the procedures that have resulted in unpaid or unbilled accounts. It wants to learn, by a quick glance, which procedures may need to be handled differently. Excel's Live Preview feature displays the icon sets in the selected range before you apply them, so you can experiment to see which set best matches the company's goal.

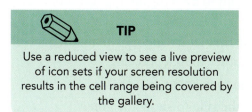

TIP

Use a reduced view to see a live preview of icon sets if your screen resolution results in the cell range being covered by the gallery.

1. Click the **Boston** worksheet tab. Select cells C6:C14.

2. Click the **Home** command tab. In the **Styles** group, click the Conditional Formatting button.

3. Hover at **Icon Sets**. A gallery opens with four categories of icon sets.

4. Hover at several sets to see the results in the worksheet.

Figure 5-20
Choosing an icon set
5-16.xlsx
Boston sheet

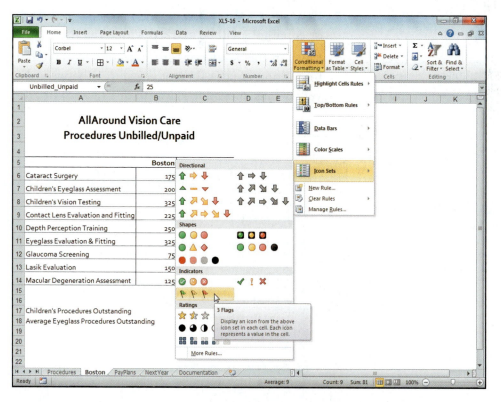

5. Choose **3 Flags** in the **Indicators** category. The icons appear at the left edge of the cell.

6. Click an empty worksheet cell. The highest values display green flags. Values in the middle display the yellow icon. Those below a particular value show the red icon.

Exercise 5-22   EDIT THE ICON FORMATTING RULE

The 3 Flags icon set divides the values into three groups, each representing one-third of the total number. It assigns green to the highest value, but in this worksheet, it should be opposite. The procedures with the most unbilled or unpaid accounts are problematic and should display the red icon as a warning. You can edit a conditional formatting rule but may need to spend some time determining what you want to display.

1. Select cells C6:C14 and click the Conditional Formatting button 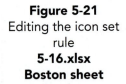.
2. Choose **Manage Rules**. The icon set is listed in the Conditional Formatting Rules Manager dialog box.
3. Click **Edit Rule**. In the **Edit the Rule Description** group, note that the icons are set based on percentages rather than the actual value. A value that computes to greater than or equal to 67% (of the highest number) gets a green flag.
4. Click the arrow with **Percent** for the first icon. Choose **Number**. This will set the rule to use a specific value rather than a percent.
5. Change the **Type** for the second icon to **Number**.
6. Click **Reverse Icon Order**. This sets the rule to show the green checkmark for the lowest value, already visible in the dialog box.
7. Key **5** in the **Value** box for the first icon (red flag). Values greater than or equal to 5 will be marked with a red flag.
8. Key **1** in the **Value** box for the second icon (yellow flag). If a value is less than 5 and greater than or equal to 1 (between 1 and 5), it will display a yellow flag. If a value is less than 1 or zero (0), it gets a green flag.

Figure 5-21
Editing the icon set rule
5-16.xlsx
Boston sheet

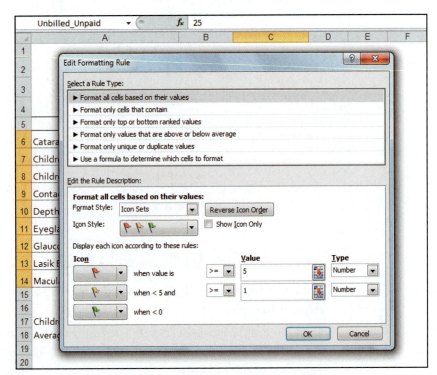

9. Click **OK**. Click **OK** again. The most troublesome procedures now include a red flag, and those with no unbilled accounts have the green flag.

10. Press Ctrl + Home. Save the workbook as *[your initials]*5-22. Close the workbook.

Using Online Help

Use Help to view additional information about range names:

1. In a new workbook, press F1.

2. In the Search box, key **range names** and press Enter.

3. Review several topics to learn more about defined names. Close the Help window.

Lesson 5   Summary

- Formulas and functions are calculations, and the names can be used interchangeably.

- Formulas are user-created; functions are built-in and follow specific syntax or rules.

- Arguments for a function or formula can be cell addresses, named ranges, constants, or another function.

- You can use the Insert Function command to place built-in functions in the worksheet. The Function Arguments dialog box provides help in choosing the arguments.

- If you key a function name, Formula AutoComplete and ScreenTips appear to provide guidance in building the formula.

- Multiple arguments in a function are separated by commas.

- Many functions ignore text, blank cells, error values (#NAME?), and logical values (TRUE or FALSE).

- A range of cells can be defined with a name.

- Range names can be used in place of cell addresses in formulas and to navigate in a workbook.

- Range names can be edited and deleted. When a range name is deleted, the worksheet may show an error message if that name was used in a formula.

- The COUNT function counts the number of values in a range. COUNTA does the same and includes labels. COUNTBLANK counts empty cells in a range.

- The function categories classify Excel's built-in functions based on their purposes. Some categories include sophisticated scientific, engineering, and business formulas.

- The SUMIF and the AVERAGEIF functions add and average values only if they meet the criteria specified in the argument.
- The financial function category includes PMT, which is used to calculate regular payments for money owed.
- A constant is a named value. It is a value that does not change.
- A constant name appears like a defined name in the Name Manager dialog box and in Formula AutoComplete.
- A list of range names in the workbook can serve as documentation. It is created from the Paste Names dialog box.
- An icon set is a data visualization that displays an icon at the left edge of the cell based on the value.
- Icon sets can use three, four, or five icons to represent the values.
- Copy selected data from one worksheet to another using the Fill Across Worksheets command.

LESSON 5		Command Summary	
Feature	**Button**	**Ribbon Location**	**Keyboard**
Constant, create		Formulas, Defined Names	Ctrl + F3
Defined name, create		Formulas, Defined Names	Ctrl + F3
Defined name, from selection		Formulas, Defined Names	Ctrl + Shift + F3
Delete range name		Formulas, Defined Names	Ctrl + F3
Fill across worksheets		Home, Editing, Fill	
Icon set		Home, Styles, Conditional Formatting	
Insert function	f_x	Formulas, Function Library	Shift + F3
Modify name or range		Formulas, Defined Names	Ctrl + F3
Paste names	f_x	Formulas, Defined Names	F3
Scope, set		Formulas, Defined Names	Ctrl + F3

Please visit our Online Learning Center, *www.lessonapproach2010.com,* **where you will find the following review materials:**

- **Concepts Review**

    True/False Questions

    Short Answer Questions

    Critical Thinking Questions

- **Skills Review**

    Review Exercises that target single skills

    Lesson Applications

    Review Exercises that challenge students by testing multiple skills in each exercise

- **On Your Own**

    Open-ended exercises that require students to synthesize multiple skills and apply creativity and problem-solving as they would in a real world business situation

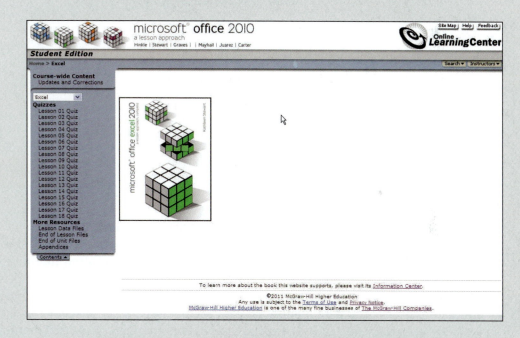

Lesson 6
Using Dates, Times, and Logical Functions

OBJECTIVES *After completing this lesson, you will be able to:*

1. Key and format dates and times.
2. Use Date & Time functions.
3. Use date and time arithmetic.
4. Use the IF function.
5. Create and edit cell styles.
6. Use the AND, OR, and NOT functions.
7. Prepare worksheets for output.

Estimated Time: 1½ hours

Dates and times are an important data element in many worksheets. Birth dates, hire dates, order dates, ship dates, time elapsed, starting time, and ending time are all examples of data that are often maintained in a workbook. Airlines monitor times and dates as they schedule and watch their flights. Shipping companies maintain time-date records to supervise the movement of merchandise. In the workbook that you'll use for this lesson, AllAround Vision Care keeps the date of each patient's last visit, manufacture and expiration dates for eyedrops, and start and end times for certain office procedures. With these values, it can determine when to send an appointment reminder, when to discard perishable products, and how to schedule equipment use.

In addition to its date and time function category, Excel has a logical category. A *logical function* is a formula that calculates if a statement or an expression is true. Unlike most functions, these functions do not display the results of a calculation. They display either the word "true" or "false" as a result in the cell. These functions are used to get yes-no answers to questions. Airlines, for example, might match expected arrival times to actual arrival times to show if the flight was on time. AllAround Vision Care uses logical functions to test if patients have multiple diagnoses.

Keying and Formatting Dates and Times

Dates and times can be shown in many ways in business documents. In the United States, it is common to show the month, the date, and the year, in that order. In many other countries, the date is shown in date-month-year order. And it is not uncommon to see dates like this: 2011/01/30. Times, too, have many different formats. Most time representations in the United States are shown using a 12-hour clock and specifying a.m. or p.m. But you may have seen airline and/or ship schedules utilize a 24-hour clock, widely used across the world.

You'll probably find it easiest to enter a date in *mm/dd/yy* format. After it is recognized as a date, Excel assigns a default date format. In the English version of Excel, if you key the year with four digits, Excel will recognize the date even if you key the year first. Times are more likely to appear as you key them if you know what to include. In any case, you may sometimes notice that what you see in the cell does not match what you key with times and dates. You can, however, apply one of many built-in date-time formats or create your own format after the data are entered.

Exercise 6-1 KEY AND FORMAT DATES

It may be natural for you to key dates in this format: *mm/dd/yy*. You'll see, though, that there are other styles that are recognized as dates. For years between 1900 and 1929, you must key "19" with the year to distinguish the twentieth century from the twenty-first century. In the workbook for this lesson, AllAround Vision Care monitors manufacture dates for eyedrops so that it knows whether any product needs to be disposed. You'll key dates in various formats to compare how they appear on screen.

1. Open **Excel_Lesson6**. Click the **ExpireDate** worksheet tab.

2. In cell A4, key **01/01/10** and press Enter. The date is formatted without leading zeros and shows the year with four digits.

3. In cell A5, key **15-jan-10** and press Enter. The default format is applied, although you keyed the date in date-month-year order.

4. In cell A6, key **january 29, 2010** and press Enter. The dates are all formatted the same.

5. In cell A7, key **2010/02/12** and press Enter. As long as you key enough information for Excel to recognize the date, it is usually accurate.

TIP

While keying a date, you generally do not need to capitalize months; Excel will do so automatically.

6. In cell A8, key **10/02/26** and press Enter. The same format is applied, but the date is recognized as being in 2026. It is supposed to be February 26, 2010.

7. Delete the contents of cell A8.

8. Select cells A4:A7, and click the Dialog Box Launcher in the **Number** group. The Format Cells dialog box should open to the **Number** tab.

9. If necessary, choose **Date** in the **Category** list.

10. Choose **March 14, 2001** in the **Type** list. Click **OK**.

11. Use the Fill handle for the selected range to extend the dates to July 30 in cell A19.

Exercise 6-2 CREATE A CUSTOM DATE FORMAT

A *custom format* is one that you create using Excel's formatting codes. A custom number format has up to four sections; the sections have codes for how to display positive values, negative values, zero, and text. A custom date format has one section, so it's a bit easier to build. Usually, you can choose one of the preset formats and edit it to be your own. Table 6-1 shows a list of the codes used for building date formats. You can also add spaces and commas within the code.

TABLE 6-1 Date Format Codes

Code	Results	Example
m	Month without a leading zero	1
mm	Month with a leading zero when needed	01
mmm	Month as a three-letter abbreviation	Jan
mmmm	Month spelled in full	January
mmmmm	Month as a single character	J
d	Date as a number without a leading zero	1
dd	Date as a number with a leading zero when needed	01
ddd	Day as an abbreviation	Tue
dddd	Day spelled in full	Tuesday
y	Year as a two-digit number	11
yyy or yyyy	Year as a four-digit number	2011

1. Select cells A4:A19 and right-click anywhere in the selection. Choose **Format Cells**.

2. Click the **Number** tab if necessary and choose **Date** in the **Category** list.

3. Scroll through the **Type** list. There is no preset format to show the date, the month spelled out, and a two-digit year (14 March 10).

4. Click **Custom** in the **Category** list. The **Type** list displays codes for number, date, and time formats. The date formats use *d*, *m*, and *y* in their codes (*d*ate, *m*onth, *y*ear).

5. Scroll the **Type** list to find **d-mmm**. You can choose a sample code as a starting point for building your own format.

6. Click the code to select it. The **Sample** box above the **Type** list shows the first date in the selected range with that format.

7. Click in the **Type** box above the **Type** list.

8. Delete the hyphen and press ⌷Spacebar⌷.

9. Edit the code to show **dd mmmm y**. Two *dd*'s show the date with a leading zero. Four *mmmm*'s spell out the month. A single *y* shows a two-digit year.

10. Look at the **Sample** box.

Figure 6-1
Creating a custom
date format
**Excel_Lesson6.xlsx
ExpireDate sheet**

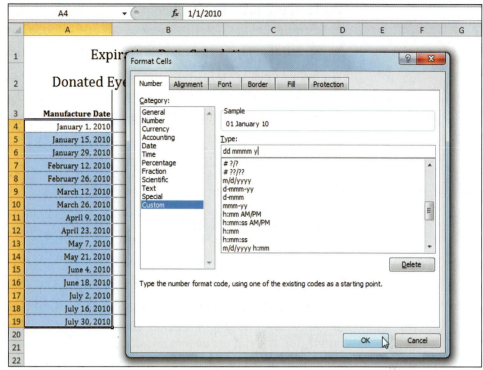

11. Click **OK**. The dates are reformatted without a comma.

Exercise 6-3 KEY AND FORMAT TIMES

When you key a time for a 12-hour clock, you should key "am" to specify morning and "pm" to specify after 12 noon. If you don't key either of those identifiers, Excel may not recognize the value as a time and format it as a general number. If you key a colon with values, however, Excel assumes it is a time. You don't need to key a colon, though, for on-the-hour times as long as you key "am" or "pm." On another sheet in your workbook, AllAround Vision Care calculates the time elapsed for Lasik procedures as a guide for scheduling appointments.

1. Click the **Surgeries** worksheet tab.

2. Click cell C6 and key **9 am**.

3. Press [Ctrl]+[Enter]. The time is shown with a colon and zeros (for minutes and seconds), and "AM" is capitalized.

4. Look in the formula bar to see seconds.

5. Click cell D6, key **10:30**, and press [Ctrl]+[Enter]. If you do not key *am* or *pm*, Excel assumes it is morning.

6. In cell C7, key **13:30** and press [→]. Excel shows the time using the 24-hour clock. With this format, you do not specify a.m. or p.m. because the value itself signifies that.

7. In cell D7, key **3:30 pm** and press [Enter].

8. In cell C8, key **2:45 pm**, and in cell D8 key **16:30**.

UNIT 2 LESSON 6

9. Select cells C6:D11 and right-click anywhere in the selection. Choose **Format Cells**. Click the **Number** tab and choose **Time** in the **Category** list.

10. Scroll the **Type** list. Then choose **1:30 PM** and click **OK**.

11. Select cells C9:D11. When cells are selected, you can move from cell to cell down one column at a time by pressing ⏎.

12. Key the following times, and press ⏎ after each time.

	C	D
9	10 am	11:30 am
10	12:30 pm	2 pm
11	9 am	10:45 am

Using Date and Time Functions

The Date & Time function category includes built-in formulas that convert dates to serial numbers, display the current date and time, count workdays, and more. A *serial number* is a unique value that is assigned to every date. Serial numbers allow Excel to do date and time arithmetic.

Excel's serial number system starts with January 1, 1900, being assigned number 1. Number 2 is January 2, 1900. Excel assigns the next consecutive number to every date up to December 31, 9999 (which is number 2,958,465).

Probably the two most widely used functions in the Date & Time category are TODAY() and NOW(). Both functions are used to display the current date and/or time.

TIP

Macintosh systems start counting at January 1, 1904. You can use this numbering system by choosing it from the Advanced pane in the Excel Options dialog box.

Exercise 6-4   USE THE TODAY() FUNCTION

The TODAY() function displays the current date, using the computer's clock. This function has no arguments, but it is still necessary to include the parentheses. Excel formats the results in its default date format. The TODAY() function is *volatile*, which means that the formula results depend on the computer on which the workbook is opened and that computer's internal clock.

1. Click the **Diagnoses** worksheet tab. Hold down ⇧Shift and click the **ExpireDate** tab. Four worksheets are grouped.

2. Click cell A25. The date will be entered in this cell on all four sheets.

3. Click the **Formulas** command tab. In the **Function Library** group, click the Date & Time button 🕐. Choose **TODAY**. The Function Arguments dialog box notes that no arguments are necessary.

4. Click **OK**. The current date is entered in the default date format.

5. Click the **Home** command tab. Click the **Number Format** box and choose **General**. The General format displays a date as its serial number.

6. Click the Undo button ↩. The format change is reversed.

Exercise 6-5 USE NOW() AND WEEKDAY

The NOW() function is similar to the TODAY() function. In fact, these two functions can generally be used interchangeably. NOW() has no arguments and is volatile. The current date and time are displayed based on the moment that the function is entered or when the workbook is opened. The time and date also update if you change the cell format.

WEEKDAY uses Excel date system to calculate which day of the week is indicated by a particular date. To do this, it displays a value from 1 to 7 as results.

The Shrink to Fit setting is a text control command. It resizes the label or value on screen so that it will fit in the cell but does not change the actual font size.

1. Click cell A26. The worksheets are still grouped.

2. Key **=now(** and press Enter. Excel supplies the closing parenthesis. A series of ##### symbols indicate that the column is not wide enough to show the time in the current font size. Do not widen the column.

3. Click cell A26. Click the Dialog Box Launcher in the **Alignment** group on the **Home** command tab.

4. Click to place a checkmark for **Shrink to fit** in the **Text control** group. Click **OK**. The NOW() function shows the date and the time.

5. Click cell A26. Check the current font size in the **Font** group. It is unchanged.

6. Press Ctrl+1 while cell A26 in selected to open the Format Cells dialog box.

7. Click the **Number** tab and choose **Time** in the **Category** list.

8. Scroll through the **Type** list. Then choose **1:30 PM** and click **OK**. The NOW() function shows only the time, and the data are resized or unshrunk.

9. Click cell B25. You'll determine the weekday for cell A25.

10. Click the **Formulas** command tab. In the **Function Library** group, click the Date & Time button . Choose **WEEKDAY**. The Function Arguments dialog box requires the **Serial_number** argument. You can click a cell reference for this argument.

11. Click cell A25.

12. Click in the **Return_type** box. This argument sets which day of the week is counted as "1." Read the explanation and then key **1**. This means "1" is Sunday, "2" is Monday, etc.

13. Click **OK**. The result is volatile and is a number between 1 and 7.

Exercise 6-6 CREATE A CUSTOM TIME FORMAT

A custom time format has one section, and it is often quickest to choose a preset format and edit it. Table 6-2 shows codes used for showing times. As you work more with formatting dates and times, the codes become easy to remember. Since you see the results in the dialog box, you can verify that they are correct, too.

TABLE 6-2 Time Format Codes

Code	Results	Example
h	Hour without a leading zero	3
hh	Hour with a leading zero when needed	03
m	Minutes without a leading zero	7
mm	Minutes with a leading zero when needed	07
s	Seconds without a leading zero	4
ss	Seconds without a leading zero	04
AM/PM	Displays time as 12-hour clock	3:07:12 AM

1. Click cell A26 and press Ctrl + 1.
2. Click **Custom** in the **Category** list.
3. Scroll the **Type** list to find **h:mm AM/PM**.
4. Click the code to select it. The **Sample** box shows the date and time with that format.
5. Click in the **Type** box before the **h**.
6. Edit the code to show **mmmm d, h:mm AM/PM**. Be sure to insert the spaces and the comma. Check the **Sample** box to verify your format as you build it.

Figure 6-2
Creating a custom
time format
**Excel_Lesson6.xlsx
Grouped sheets**

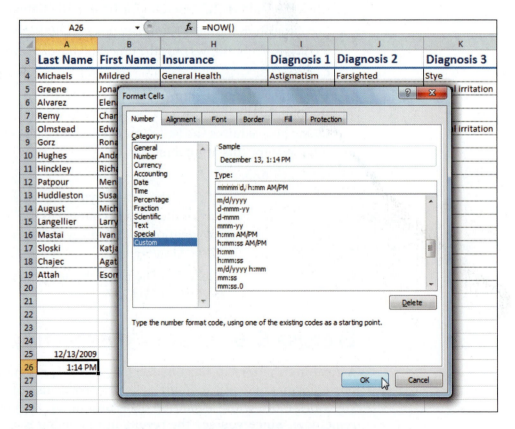

7. Click **OK**. The time is reformatted and shrunk to fit again.

8. Save the workbook as *[your initials]*6-6. If you save a workbook while the sheets are grouped, that's how it will reopen.

Using Date and Time Arithmetic

Date and time arithmetic is used in many business and personal activities. AllAround Vision Care calculates days until the next appointment, time spent using equipment, number of days for overdue accounts, and more. In your personal records, you could determine how many days until your next birthday, how long it takes to complete a remodeling project, or how many hours you sleep each night. Because Excel's serial number system assigns a unique value to each date and time, Excel can calculate ages, days passed, or days until.

Date and time arithmetic is usually simple and mimics what you would do manually. The results may initially be formatted incorrectly, so you'll also need to check everything carefully to make sure your data are understandable. Other times, you'll see that you need to add some of the same elements that you would use if you did the calculation manually.

Exercise 6-7   DETERMINE DATES AND AGES

For date arithmetic that concerns years, you may need to clarify how many days are in a year. Common business practice uses 365.25 days, which averages for a leap year occurring every 4 years. Some built-in functions actually use 360 days as a year, which may be acceptable for some transactions.

In your workbook, you are to calculate the expiration date for perishable eyedrops. You have the manufacture date and can add the number of days in 2 years to determine the expiry date. Then you can also calculate how old the product is as of today.

1. In *[your initials]*6-6, right-click the **ExpireDate** worksheet tab and choose **Ungroup Sheets**.

2. Select cells A4:A19 and replace all occurrences of the year with last year. This is more likely to give you real expiration dates as your formula results.

3. Click cell B4 and key **=** to start a formula.

4. Click cell A4 and key **+** to add days to the manufacture date. You can multiply 365.25 by 2 to determine the number of days in 24 months (2 years).

5. Key a left parenthesis **(** after the plus sign. Order of precedence is a factor here, because you have addition and multiplication in the same formula.

 REVIEW

Multiplication is calculated before addition so using parentheses to order the formula is optional.

6. Key **365.25*2)**. The parentheses force the multiplication to be calculated first.

Figure 6-3
Calculating a future date
6-6.xlsx
ExpireDate sheet

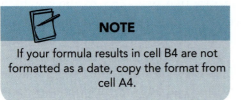

WEEKDAY	▾	X ✔ *fx*	=A4+(365.25*2)	
	A	B	C	D
1		**Expiration Date Calculation**		
2		**Donated Eye Drops for Seniors Program**		
3	**Manufacture Date**	**24 Months after Manufacture**	**Product Age Today**	
4	01 January 09	=A4+(365.25*2)		
5	15 January 09			
6	29 January 09			
7	12 February 09			
8	26 February 09			

7. Press **Enter**. The results may be formatted as a serial number that represents the date. If necessary, apply the same date format used in cells A4:A19.

8. Copy this formula down to cell B19.

9. In cell C4, key **=today()** to start the formula.

10. Key **–** to subtract and click cell A4. This formula subtracts the manufacture date from today.

11. Press **Enter**. The result is probably formatted as a date, so it doesn't make sense. You might also see a series of ### symbols if you have a "negative" date. If this happens, replace the years in column A with an earlier year.

12. Click cell C4. Click the arrow with the **Number Format** box in the **Number** group on the **Home** command tab. Choose **General**. The results are shown as number of days. Your results are volatile—they depend on last year (cell A4) and today.

13. Press **F2**. Press **Home**. The insertion point is at the first position in the formula. You are now going to convert the results so that they are shown as years or partial years.

14. Position the insertion point between **=** and **T**.

15. Key **(**, the left parenthesis. Press **End**. The insertion point moves to the end of the current formula.

16. Key **)**, the right parenthesis. This entire formula should be divided by 365.25 to convert the days to years.

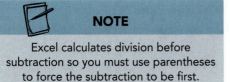

NOTE

If your formula results in cell B4 are not formatted as a date, copy the format from cell A4.

NOTE

Excel calculates division before subtraction so you must use parentheses to force the subtraction to be first.

Figure 6-4
Converting the age
formula to years
6-6.xlsx
ExpireDate sheet

WEEKDAY		f_x =(TODAY()-A4)/365.25	
	A	B	C	D

Expiration Date Calculation

Donated Eye Drops for Seniors Program

	Manufacture Date	24 Months after Manufacture	Product Age Today
4	01 January 09	01 January 11	=(TODAY()-A4)/365.25
5	15 January 09	15 January 11	
6	29 January 09	29 January 11	
7	12 February 09	12 February 11	
8	26 February 09	26 February 11	

17. Key **/365.25** and press Enter. The result shows as many decimals as will fit in the cell, or the results are formatted as a date.

18. Click cell C4. Click the arrow with the **Number Format** box and choose **Number**. This format shows two decimal places. This is the age in years. Remember TODAY() is volatile, so your results are specific to the current date.

19. Copy this formula down to cell C19. You may have negative amounts depending on the year in column A.

Exercise 6-8 DETERMINE TIME PASSED AND SHOW FRACTIONS

Calculating time passed is similar to determining an age. You subtract the beginning time from the ending time. Excel usually shows time results as a fraction of a 24-hour day. To convert such results to hours, you multiply the results by 24. On another sheet in your workbook, you'll determine time used for Lasik procedures.

1. Click the **Surgeries** worksheet tab. Notice how small the date and time in cells A25:A26 were shrunk on this sheet. That is because column A is very narrow.

2. Select cells A25:A26 and drag them to B26:B27.

3. In cell E6, key **=** and click cell D6, the ending time.

4. Key a minus sign (that is, a hyphen, **-**), and click cell C6, the starting time. Press Enter. The results are shown as a decimal part of a 24-hour day (0.06).

5. Click cell E6. Click the Increase Decimal button two times. Unrounded, the value is 0.0625.

6. Click the arrow with **Number Format** and choose **Fraction**. The fraction format, when selected from the gallery, uses one digit, and this value is so small that it appears as zero (0).

7. Click the Dialog Box Launcher in the **Number** group. In the **Type** list, choose **As sixteenths (8/16)**. Click **OK**. Now the company can see that this procedure takes 1/16 of a day.

8. Copy the formula to row 11 without formatting to preserve the borders. Without the formatting, the fraction style is not copied.

9. Select the cells and apply the **As sixteenths (8/16)** fraction format. All the results show 1/16.

10. Right-click the column E heading and choose **Copy**. Right-click the column F heading ,and choose **Insert Copied Cells**. Press Esc. The formula is copied with a relative reference initially, and the fractions are negative.

11. Delete the contents of cells F6:F11.

12. In cell F6, key **=** and click cell E6, the fractional value. You can convert a fraction of a day to hours.

Figure 6-5
Converting time to hours
6-6.xlsx
Surgeries sheet

	WEEKDAY		X ✓ ƒx	=E6*24			
	A	B	C	D	E	F	G	H
2		Time Spent on Lasik Surgeries					
3		Wednesday, September 15					
4							
5		Doctor and Location	Start Time	End Time	Total Time	Total Time	
6		Christine Ost, Chicago	9:00 AM	10:30 AM	1/16	=E6*24	
7		Michael Everst, Dallas	1:30 PM	3:30 PM	1/16		
8		Sahallie Dia, Seattle	2:45 PM	4:30 PM	1/16		
9		Rich Van Lente, Chicago	10:00 AM	11:30 AM	1/16		
10		Erin McCarthy, Boston	12:30 PM	2:00 PM	1/16		
11		George Panton, Dallas	9:00 AM	10:45 AM	1/16		
12							
13							
14							

13. Key ***24** to multiply by the number of hours in a day. Press Enter.

14. Copy this formula to row 19 without formatting.

15. Select cells F6:F11. Click the Dialog Box Launcher in the **Number** group. Choose a fraction shown, **As quarters (2/4)**. Click **OK**.

Using the IF Function

The IF function is probably the most commonly used function from the logical category. It's used to determine whether some situation or circumstance exists. Then it specifies what should be done when the situation exists and what should be done when it doesn't. AllAround Vision Care, for example, can use an IF formula to determine which patients have a balance due so that notices can be sent. If your instructor assigns extra points for some activity, he or she might use an IF statement to determine if the points are added to your final score. IF statements are used in many programming languages. They can become quite sophisticated and are able to automate tasks that might otherwise be very tedious.

The IF function is one of the functions from the Logical category that shows a result other than TRUE or FALSE. It has three arguments and follows this form: "If X, then Y; otherwise Z." Think of X, Y, and Z as the arguments.

The syntax for an IF function is

=IF(*logical_test, value_if_true, value_if_false*)
Example: =IF(C5>50,C5*2,"None")

- *Logical_test* is the first argument, the condition. It's a statement or expression that is either true or false, yes or no. In the example, the expression C5>50 is either true or false, depending on the value in cell C5.

- *Value_if_true,* the second argument, is what the formula shows if the logical_test is true. In the example, if C5 is greater than 50 (C5>50), the value in cell C5 is multiplied by 2 (C5*2). The value_if_true can be a formula, a value, text, or a cell address.

- *Value_if_false,* the third argument, is what the formula shows if the logical_test is not true. The value_if_false can be a formula, a value, text, or a cell address. In the example, if the value in cell C5 is 50 or less (C5=49), the result is the word "None."

IF functions can use relational or comparison operators as well as the arithmetic operators (see Table 2-2, page EX-58).

Exercise 6-9   USE IF TO SHOW TEXT

In your workbook for this lesson, you can determine if AllAround Vision Care should send an invoice to a patient. This is necessary if the patient owes money.

When you use the Function Arguments dialog box, Excel inserts quotation marks around text that you key in an argument text box. If you key the IF function, you must key quotation marks around text that should appear on screen as a result.

1. In *[your initials]*6-6, click the **AR** worksheet tab. Notice that this worksheet has hidden columns. There is a slightly thicker border between columns B and H to indicate that several columns are hidden from view. You'll show them later in this lesson.

2. Click cell M4. If the patient owes any amount greater than $0, an invoice should be sent. So the cell should display the word "Invoice" if the value in column L is greater than zero (>0).

3. Click the **Formulas** command tab.

4. Click the Logical button . Choose **IF** from the list. The insertion point is in the **Logical_test** box, the first argument.

5. Press F3 to open the Paste Names dialog box. Choose **Due** and click **OK**. The range name appears in the **Logical_test** box.

> **NOTE**
>
> Move the Function Arguments dialog box so that you can see the cells you want to click.

6. Key **>0** in the **Logical_test** box after **Due**. This logical test will determine if the value in the Due column (cell L4) is greater than 0.

7. Click in the **Value_if_true** box.

8. Key **Invoice**. If the value in cell L4 is greater than 0, cell M4 will display the word "Invoice."

9. Click in the **Value_if_false** box. Note the quotation marks for "Invoice."

10. Leave this box empty. If the value in cell L4 is zero or less, you would like cell M4 to be blank.

Figure 6-6
Function Arguments
dialog box for IF
6-6.xlsx
AR sheet

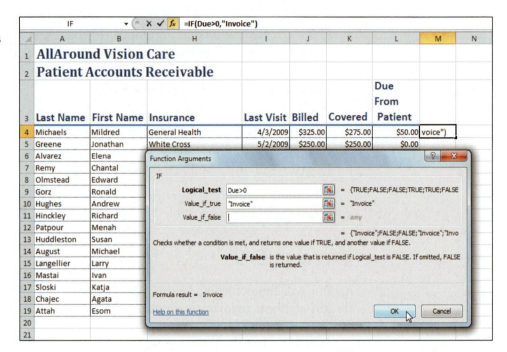

11. Click **OK**. The result of this IF formula for cell L4 is **Invoice**.

12. Look at the formula in the formula bar. You can see the quotation marks for **Invoice** now.

13. Copy the formula to row 19. The cells that should be blank show the word FALSE. It would be better if the cell showed nothing.

14. Click the Undo button.

15. Click cell M4 and click the Insert Function button f_x. The Function Arguments dialog box opens with the current data.

16. Click in the **Value_if_false** box and read the explanatory text. If you omit an entry for this box, the result is false.

17. Key **" "** (2 double quotation marks with nothing between them). This is text that will show nothing.

18. Click **OK**. Copy the formula to row 19. The cell in column M is empty for patients who do not owe money.

Exercise 6-10 KEY AN IF FUNCTION TO CALCULATE A VALUE

If the patient currently owes money, the account is overdue. In the next column, you can calculate a late fee.

1. Click cell N4. Key **=if** to see the Formula AutoComplete list.

2. Press Tab. The ScreenTip displays the syntax for the function, and the argument to be keyed is in bold.

3. Click cell M4. A marquee appears around the cell, and the address appears after the left parenthesis. This starts the **Logical_test**.

4. Key **="invoice"** after **M4**. This logical test will determine if cell M4 shows the word "Invoice."

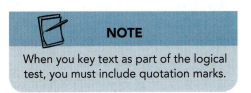
NOTE

When you key text as part of the logical test, you must include quotation marks.

5. Key **,** after **"invoice"** to separate the logical test from the value_if_true. Value_if_true in the ScreenTip is in bold.

6. Press F3 and choose **Due**. Click **OK**.

7. Key ***5%** after **Due**. The formula multiplies the value in the Due column by 5% if cell M4 shows "Invoice."

8. Key **,** after **5%** to separate the value_if_true from the value_if_false. Value_if_false in the ScreenTip is in bold.

9. Key **" "** (two quotation marks with nothing between them). This represents no text, or nothing. If cell M4 does not show "Invoice," cell N4 will show nothing. It will be blank.

Figure 6-7
Keying an IF statement
6-6.xlsx
AR sheet

	A	B	H	I	J	K	L	M	N	O	P	Q
	IF			=IF(M4="invoice",Due*5%,"")								
1	AllAround Vision Care											
2	Patient Accounts Receivable											
3	Last Name	First Name	Insurance	Last Visit	Billed	Covered	Due From Patient					
4	Michaels	Mildred	General Health	4/3/2009	$325.00	$275.00	$50.00	Invoice	=IF(M4="invoice",Due*5%,""			
5	Greene	Jonathan	White Cross	5/2/2009	$250.00	$250.00	$0.00		IF(logical_test, [value_if_true], [value_if_false])			
6	Alvarez	Elena	UAB	4/3/2009	$125.00	$125.00	$0.00					
7	Remy	Chantal	General Health	6/1/2009	$225.00	$185.00	$40.00	Invoice				

10. Press Enter. Excel added the closing right parenthesis for you. Cell N4 shows 2.5 or 5% of the value in cell L4. This is the late fee.

11. Format the results in cell N4 as currency. Copy the formula to row 19.

12. Set borders for your results in columns M:N to match the rest of the data.

13. Click cell M3 and key **Send**. Press Alt+Enter and key **Invoice**.

14. In cell N3, key **Late**. Press Alt+Enter and key **Fee**.

15. Click cell L3, and click the Format Painter button 🖌 in the **Clipboard** group on the **Home** command tab.

16. Drag across cells M3:N3 to copy the format. Adjust column widths if necessary.

17. Save the workbook *[your initials]*6-10.

Creating and Editing Cell Styles

A cell style includes format attributes from the tabs in the Format Cells dialog box. Formatting with a style is generally faster than applying each command separately. A Title cell style, for example, includes font style, size, and color and applies all three attributes with one click. You can apply each setting on its own but that would require three clicks. Many companies create their own styles with preferred or required settings and make them available to all employees. This helps the company accomplish a unified look to all its documents.

Cell styles are connected to the document theme. If you change the theme, each style is updated to show the new fonts, colors, and other attributes. Excel provides a selection of built-in cell style names for a document theme, categorized according to purpose. You can modify those styles as well as create new ones. Cell styles are saved with the workbook in its document theme.

Exercise 6-11   CLEAR FORMATS

In order to better see your own cell styles in your workbook, you can reset some values to the default general format. You do that by clearing formats already applied.

NOTE

If you are opening the workbook to resume work, choose its file name from the Recent list in Backstage view if it is there.

1. In *[your initials]*6-10, click the **AR** worksheet tab.

2. Click cell A1. Click the Cell Styles button 📝 in the **Styles** group. This cell has the **Title** style applied, marked by the outline with the style name in the gallery.

3. Click cell A3. Click the Cell Styles button 📝. These cells have the Heading 1 style applied.

4. Select cells A1:N3, click the Clear button 🖉 in the **Editing** group. Choose **Clear Formats**. The cells are returned to the Normal style.

5. Click cell A1. Click the Cell Styles button 📝. Look for the **Normal** style. This style applies the general format and 11-point Calibri as the font.

6. Select cells in row 3 that still show a border. Click the Borders button ⊞ and choose **No Border**.

7. Click an empty worksheet cell.

Exercise 6-12   CREATE A CELL STYLE

When you create a new style, settings from the default Normal style are listed as a starting point. You name the new cell style with a name of your choice, and then from the Format Cells dialog box, you make your design choices. Cell styles that you create are listed in the Custom category at the top of the Cell Styles gallery.

1. Click the Cell Styles button 📝. Click **New Cell Style**. These are the settings for the Normal style for the six properties shown.

2. In the **Style name** box, key **MyTitle** and click **Format**. The Format Cells dialog box opens.

Figure 6-8
Creating a new style
6-10.xlsx
AR sheet

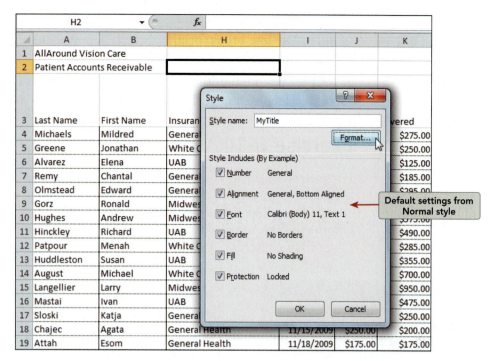

3. Click the **Font** tab. Choose 18-point italic Cambria. Click **OK** in the Format Cells dialog box. Click **OK** in the Style dialog box.

4. Select cells A1:A2. Click the Cell Styles button. Click **MyTitle** in the **Custom** group.

5. Click an empty cell. Click the Cell Styles button. Click **New Cell Style**.

6. In the **Style name** box, key **MyHeading** and click **Format**.

7. On the **Font** tab, choose 16-point italic Cambria. Do not click **OK** yet.

8. Click the **Border** tab. Set a single bottom black border using the fifth icon in the second column for the **Style**. Do not click **OK** yet.

9. Click the **Alignment** tab. Choose **Center** in the **Horizontal** list.

10. Click **OK** in the Format Cells dialog box. Click **OK** in the Style dialog box.

11. Select cells A3:N3. Click the Cell Styles button. Choose **MyHeading**.

Exercise 6-13   MODIFY A CELL STYLE

Notice that the labels in cells L3:N3 no longer show the text wrapping to a second line. When you key a line break (Alt+Enter), the Wrap Text property is automatically activated. The cell style that you created, however, does not have wrapped text on. You can modify the style to include that property as well as adjust the font size.

1. Click the Cell Styles button. Right-click **MyHeading** and choose **Modify**.

2. Click **Format**. The Format Cells dialog box opens.

3. Click the **Alignment** tab. Click to place a checkmark for **Wrap Text** in the **Text control** group.

4. Change the font size to 14.

5. Click **OK** in the Format Cells dialog box. Click **OK** in the Style dialog box. The line break, originally keyed, now splits the labels to two or three lines.

6. Adjust column widths so that columns L:N show the labels on two lines. Other labels should display on a single line.

Exercise 6-14   REPEAT A COMMAND

For your worksheet, you'll create another cell style to add fill, apply it to one row, and then repeat the command for the remaining rows. The Repeat command redoes the most recent action, such as applying a cell style. This command does not appear on the Ribbon by default in Excel. You can add it to your Quick Access Toolbar or use the keyboard shortcut [Ctrl]+[Y].

1. Click an empty worksheet cell.

2. Click the Cell Styles button . Click **New Cell Style**.

3. In the **Style name** box, key **AddFill** and click **Format**.

4. Click the **Fill** tab. Choose a light gray fill, one of the color tiles in the first column. Click **OK** in the Format Cells dialog box. Click **OK** in the Style dialog box.

> **NOTE**
>
> The Repeat button appears on the Quick Access Toolbar in Word and PowerPoint.

5. Select cells A5:N5. Click the Cell Styles button. Choose **AddFill** at the top of the gallery. The style has added fill but also reformatted the values.

6. Click the Undo button.

7. Click the Cell Styles button. Right-click **AddFill** and choose **Modify**.

8. In the **Style** dialog box, the **Style includes** group notes what attributes are part of the style. These are the names of the tabs from the Format Cells dialog box. Any that you did not edit maintain default settings from the Normal style.

9. Click to remove the checkmarks for **Number**, **Alignment**, **Font**, **Border**, and **Protection**. Only the settings you made on the **Fill** tab will be included in this cell style.

10. Click **OK** in the Style dialog box.

11. Select cells A5:N5. Click the Cell Styles button. Choose **AddFill**. Only fill is applied.

12. Select cells A7:N7. Press [Ctrl]+[Y]. This is the keyboard shortcut to repeat the most recent command.

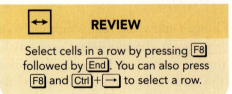

> **REVIEW**
>
> Select cells in a row by pressing [F8] followed by [End]. You can also press [F8] and [Ctrl]+[→] to select a row.

13. Repeat these steps to apply the style to every other row in the sheet, up to and including row 19.

14. Save the workbook *[your initials]*6-14.

Using the AND, OR, and NOT Functions

The Logical functions provide a method of determining when multiple situations exist or one or the other of a circumstance is true. In the workbook for this lesson, there is a sheet that lists patient diagnoses in separate columns. Some patients have multiple diagnoses; they are farsighted and color blind, for example.

AllAround Vision Care can use logical functions to flag when a patient has a particular combination of diagnoses. If your instructor keeps project, quiz, and test grades in a worksheet, he or she could use a logical function to identify which students have certain score ranges on two or three particular items.

AND, OR, and NOT are logical functions. They are often used as arguments in other functions, but you'll learn in this lesson how to use them in simple formulas. The results of these three functions insert either "TRUE" or "FALSE" in the cell. They do not calculate a numerical result or show a value or label result like the IF function.

Exercise 6-15   USE THE AND FUNCTION

The AND function has one argument named *LogicalN* in which "N" is a number. There can be, however, up to 255 variations or possibilities for that argument. In an AND function, you create multiple logical tests or statements. All of them must be true for the formula to show true. Otherwise, the formula result is false.

TABLE 6-3 Examples of the AND Function

Expression	Result
AND(C4>10, D4>10)	True if both C4 and D4 are greater than 10; false if either C4 or D4 is 10 or less.
AND(C4>10, C4<100)	True if C4 is greater than 10 but less than 100; false if C4 is 10 or less than 10 or 100 or greater than 100.
AND(C4="john", D4="doe")	True only if C4 shows John and D4 shows Doe.
AND(C4="yes", D4<100)	True if C4 shows yes and D4 is less than 100; false if C4 shows no but D4 is greater than 100; false if C4 shows no.

In your workbook, you will determine which patients have multiple diagnoses of astigmatism and farsightedness. When you key a label as part of an argument in a logical function, you usually need to include the quotation marks to identify or mark it clearly. You also must spell the label in the argument exactly as it is spelled in the worksheet.

1. In *[your initials]*6-14, click the **Diagnoses** worksheet tab.

2. In cell L3, key **Astigmatism** and press ⎇Alt+↵Enter. Key **and Farsighted** and press ↵Enter.

3. Apply the **Heading 1** cell style to cell L3, and adjust the column width so that the label splits to two lines. Make row 3 **56.25 (75 pixels)** tall.

4. Click cell L4. Click the **Formulas** command tab.

5. Click the Logical button . Choose **AND** in the list. The insertion point is in the **Logical1** box.

6. Click cell I4. The address appears in the **Logical1** box.

> **NOTE**
>
> Your new cell styles are available on each worksheet in your workbook, but you have not applied them to all the sheets.

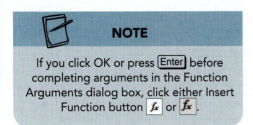

NOTE

If you click OK or press [Enter] before completing arguments in the Function Arguments dialog box, click either Insert Function button f_x or f_x.

7. Key **="astigmatism"** in the **Logical1** box after **I4**. Because there is a cell reference in the entry box in addition to a label, you must key the quotation marks with the label to distinguish it.

8. Click in the **Logical2** box. Click cell J4 and key **="farsighted"**. This AND function will show true if the patient has both diagnoses.

Figure 6-9
Function Arguments
dialog box for AND
6-14.xlsx
Diagnoses sheet

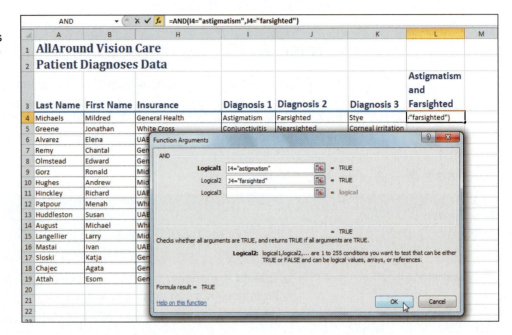

9. Click **OK**. The first patient does have both diagnoses.

10. Copy the formula to cells L5:L19.

Exercise 6-16   USE THE OR FUNCTION

In an OR function, any one of your logical tests can be true for the result cell to show true. All tests must be false for the formula result to be false. In this worksheet, you will determine if a patient suffered from either conjunctivitis or a stye.

TABLE 6-4 Examples of the OR Function

Expression	Result
OR(C4>10, D4>10)	True if either C4 or D4 is greater than 10; false only if both C4 and D4 are less than or equal to 10.
OR(C4>10, D4<100)	True if C4 is greater than 10 or if D4 is less than 100; false only if C4 is equal to or less than 10 and if D4 is equal to or greater than 100.
OR(C4="mary", D4="sue")	True if C4 is Mary and D4 is any name. True if D4 is Sue and C4 is any name. False if C4 is not Mary and D4 is not Sue.

1. In cell M3, key **Conjunctivitis** and press ⌐Alt⌐+⌐Enter⌐. Key **or Stye** and press ⌐Enter⌐.

2. Apply the **Heading 1** cell style and adjust the column width.

3. Click cell M4. Key **=or** and press ⌐Tab⌐. The first argument **logical1** is in bold in the ScreenTip.

4. Click cell I4. Key **="conjunctivitis"**.

5. Key a comma after **"conjunctivitis"**. The second argument is **logical2**.

6. Click cell J4 and key **="stye"**. This OR function will show true if the patient has conjunctivitis as a first diagnosis or stye as a second.

NOTE

You must key each condition accurately.

Figure 6-10
Keying an OR function
6-14.xlsx
Diagnoses sheet

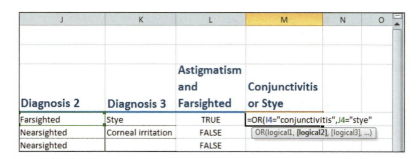

7. Press ⌐Enter⌐. The first patient does not have either of these diagnoses in column I or J; you did not check the third diagnosis.

8. Copy the formula to row 19. If all error checking rules are active at your computer, error triangles indicate formulas that refer to empty cells.

Exercise 6-17   USE THE NOT FUNCTION

In a NOT function, the reverse or opposite of the logical test must be true for the result cell to show true. This may not be the easiest way to think about many circumstances, but the function is helpful in certain situations. If a worksheet has data that were received from an outside source, it may show data that do not illustrate what is needed. If AllAround Vision Care got data from another group that listed 150 patients with a diagnosis of astigmatism and just a few with other diagnoses, it could find those other diagnoses with a NOT function. If you download a mailing list and want to find all names that are in a city other than your own, you could also use a NOT function.

The NOT function has only one argument, and it is what you are not looking for.

TABLE 6-5 Examples of the NOT Function

Expression	Result
NOT(C4>10)	True if C4 is 10 or less than 10; false if C4 is 11 or greater.
NOT(C4="tom")	True if C4 contains any name other than Tom. False if C4 does show Tom.

1. Click cell N3. Key **Not** and press Alt+Enter. Key **Astigmatism** and press Enter.

2. Click cell M3, and click the Format Painter button in the **Clipboard** group. Click cell N3 to copy the format.

3. Adjust the column width. Center the labels in cells L3:N3.

4. Click cell N4. Click the Logical button. Choose **NOT** in the list. The argument is **Logical**.

5. Click cell I4. Key **=astigmatism**. The formula tests if the value in cell I4 is *not* astigmatism. If it is something other than astigmatism, cell N4 will show true.

Figure 6-11
Editing a NOT function
6-14.xlsx
Diagnoses sheet

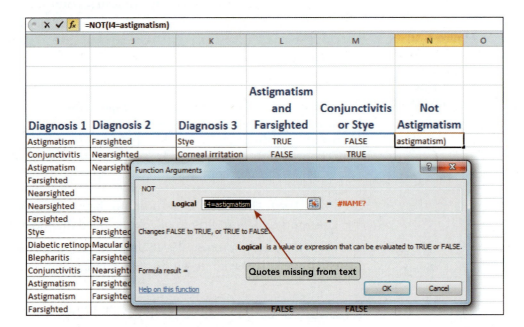

6. Click **OK**. "#NAME?" appears in the cell. This error message is a result of your not keying the quotation marks.

7. Click cell N4 and click the Insert Function button.

8. Edit the argument to include the quotation marks and press Enter.

9. Copy the formula to row 19. The trues are the patients who have a diagnosis other than astigmatism.

Exercise 6-18 FORMAT LOGICAL RESULTS WITH HIGHLIGHT CELLS RULES

Logical function results are automatically generated by Excel and use uppercase letters. This makes it somewhat difficult to distinguish true from false. You can, however, apply a highlight cells rule to better differentiate the results.

1. Select cells L4:N19. Click the Conditional Formatting button. Choose **Highlight Cells Rules** and **Equal To**.

2. Key **true**. Click the arrow for the format choices and choose **Red Text**.

3. Click **OK**. If you see error triangles, they mark formulas that refer to empty cells if that rule is active on your computer. You can ignore error triangles; they do not print.

4. Complete the borders for the results columns.

5. Press Ctrl + Home

Preparing Worksheets for Output

After data are entered, formulas are inserted, and formatting is completed, a workbook is ready for its intended audience. That may be as a printed page, an e-mail attachment, or another file format. Depending on how you plan to distribute a workbook, you will use various commands to get it ready. Most of these are routine tasks such as checking margins, adding headers and/or footers, and adjusting page breaks. Backstage view helps you see what things still need to be done to finalize your workbook.

Exercise 6-19   UNHIDE COLUMNS AND VIEW PAGES

Both the Diagnoses and the AR worksheets have hidden columns. Since both sheets have columns C:G hidden, you can group the sheets to unhide these columns.

1. Click the **Diagnoses** worksheet tab.

2. Hold down Shift and click the **AR** worksheet tab. Look for "[Group]" in the title bar.

3. Click the column heading for column B, and drag right to the heading for column H. The hidden columns are between these two columns.

4. Right-click either column heading and choose **Unhide**.

5. Right-click either worksheet in the group and choose **Ungroup Sheets**.

6. Click the **Diagnoses** tab. Click the **AR** tab. Columns C:G are visible on both sheets.

NOTE

In Backstage view, the Info pane includes a Prepare for Sharing group which provides access to the Document Inspector. This command is covered in Lesson 10.

7. With the **AR** worksheet visible, click the **File** command tab. In Info view, you can see the thumbnail image of the worksheet on the right as well as some general properties.

8. Choose **Print** in the navigation commands at the left. In Backstage view for printing, you can see that this worksheet would print on two or three pages in portrait orientation. Variation in the number of pages depends on your printer and your current default settings in Excel.

9. Click **Portrait Orientation** and choose **Landscape Orientation**. In landscape orientation, the worksheet requires two pages.

10. Close Backstage view. You may see a page break as a dotted line in Normal view.

Exercise 6-20   PREVIEW PAGE BREAKS

A *page break* is a code that tells the printer to start a new page. Excel inserts automatic page breaks as you work depending on the data, the font size, the column widths, and the page margins. An automatic page break appears as a dashed vertical and/or horizontal line on the screen. You can accept Excel's location for page breaks, you can move the break to a new location, or you can insert your own page breaks.

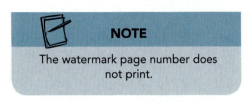

NOTE

The watermark page number does not print.

1. Click the Page Break Preview button ▦ in the status bar. A message box explains how you can adjust page breaks.

2. Click **OK**. Page Break preview is a reduced view size. Pages are arranged in top-to-bottom, left-to-right order with a watermark page number. Automatic page breaks are blue dashed lines.

Figure 6-12
Page Break preview
6-14.xlsx
AR sheet

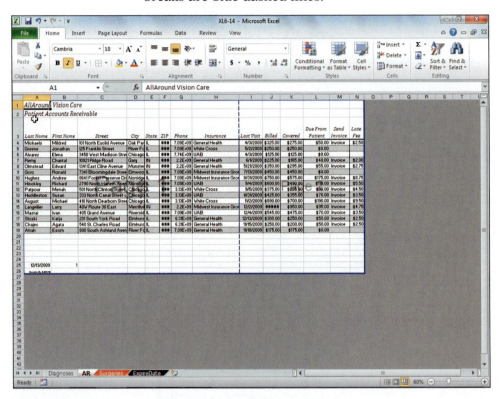

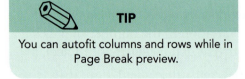

TIP

You can autofit columns and rows while in Page Break preview.

3. Widen any column in which the data are not completely visible. The phone number may appear as an exponent if the column is too narrow.

4. Click and drag the vertical blue dashed line so that it is between columns G and H. If it is already there, drag it and reposition it to the same location for practice.

5. Click the Normal button ▦ in the status bar. Look for the dashed line in Normal view to mark the page break.

Exercise 6-21 SET PRINT TITLES

When data are too wide to fit on a single page, you can repeat columns or rows that identify the data on each printed page. In the AR worksheet, for example, AllAround Vision Care would probably print the patient's name on all sheets to identify the data.

A *print title* is a print-only command that does not change the worksheet margins. Print titles are visible in Page Layout view and in Print Preview. They are not visible in Normal view nor in Page Break preview.

1. Click the Print Titles button 🖼 on the **Page Layout** command tab. The Page Setup dialog box opens with the **Sheet** tab active.

2. Click in the **Rows to repeat at top** text box.

3. Click anywhere in row 1 and drag to row 2. The dialog box shows **$1:$2**. These labels will print at the top on each page of the worksheet.

4. Click in the **Columns to repeat at left** text box.

5. Click anywhere in column A and drag to column B. The dialog box shows **$A:$B**. These labels will print at the left of each page.

Figure 6-13
Setting Print titles
6-14.xlsx
AR sheet

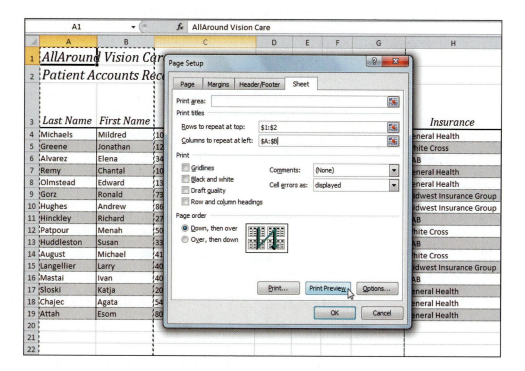

6. Click **Print Preview** in the dialog box. Backstage view shows the print titles on each page.

7. Click the Next Page arrow ▶ to view the pages. The label in cell A1 may be cut off on the second page.

8. Close Backstage view.

Exercise 6-22 CHANGE PAGE BREAKS

Because of the repeated data from columns A and B, each printed page includes the identifying information and is as wide as necessary. Print titles that refer to labels that spill into the adjacent cells usually need to be set to a width that accommodates the label without spillover. Otherwise, a label may be truncated on second and succeeding pages.

When Excel inserts an automatic page break, it does so only between columns. It will never split the data from a column across printed pages.

1. Click the Page Layout button ▥ in the status bar. Click the Zoom Out button ⊝ to reach **60%** or smaller so that you can see page 1 and the left half of page 2.

2. Widen column A a few pixels at a time until the labels in rows 1 and 2 are completely visible on page 2.

3. Click the Page Break Preview button ▤ in the status bar. Click **OK**. The page break between columns G and H may be solid or dashed right now. Look for a second page break, an automatic one that became necessary as you widened the column. If you do not see this second page break, widen column A until you do see it.

4. Drag the first page break line to position it between columns F and G. The automatic page break readjusts.

5. Drag the second page break line so that it is between columns I and J. Now the worksheet requires three printed pages. The solid blue lines indicate page breaks that you positioned.

6. Click the Normal button ▤ in the status bar. Press [Ctrl]+[F2] to open Backstage view for printing.

7. Click the Next Page arrow ▶. You can see all three pages now with the print titles.

8. Click the **Page Layout** command tab. Click the Dialog Box Launcher in the **Page Setup** group. On the **Margins** tab, choose **Horizontally** in the **Center on page** group. Click **OK**.

Exercise 6-23 INSERT AND REMOVE PAGE BREAKS

The ability to control page breaks enables you to define what appears on each page. You may want to do this to separate related data so that they are easier to digest. In the Diagnoses worksheet for this lesson, AllAround Vision Care wants to show patient address information on its own page and the insurance and diagnoses data on a separate page.

In addition to or in place of automatic page breaks, you can insert your own breaks where you want each separate page to start. Page breaks are inserted from the Page Layout command tab. When you insert a page break, it is placed to the left of and/or above the active cell or column or row.

1. Click the **Diagnoses** worksheet tab.

2. Click cell H1. If you insert a page break here, it will be between columns G and H.

3. Click the **Page Layout** command tab. In the **Page Setup** group, click the Breaks button ▤.

Figure 6-14
Inserting a page
break
6-14.xlsx
Diagnoses sheet

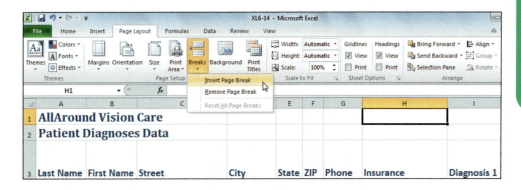

4. Choose **Insert Page Break**. In Normal view, you should see a dashed line, slightly different from the automatic page break.

5. Press Ctrl + F2. Click the Next Page arrow ▶ to view the pages. Your manual page break and automatic page breaks may result in pages with very little data.

6. Click the **Page Layout** command tab.

7. Click cell H1 if necessary. The page break is to the left of this column.

8. Click the Breaks button 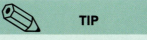 and choose **Remove Page Break**. You may now see an automatic page break again.

9. Click cell I1. Click the Breaks button and choose **Insert Page Break**.

10. Click the Orientation button and choose **Landscape**. Automatic page breaks are fluid and adjust according to other page settings. Manual page breaks stay where you placed them.

11. View both pages in Backstage view. Do not close Backstage view yet.

Exercise 6-24   SET MARGINS AND COLUMN WIDTH IN BACKSTAGE VIEW

From Backstage view for printing, you can display margin markers and adjust margins by dragging those markers. This helps you to see how the data adjust and can aid in your quickly choosing settings that accomplish your goals.

1. In Backstage view for printing, click the Show Margins button in the lower-right corner. The page shows markers for all margins, including the header and footer. The top margin is the lower of the two horizontal lines; the marker is the tiny rectangle at either edge.

2. Click the top margin marker and drag it down a bit (see Figure 6-15 on the next page). You can check your new margin setting by clicking **Last Custom Margins Settings**.

Figure 6-15
Changing margins in
Backstage view
6-14.xlsx

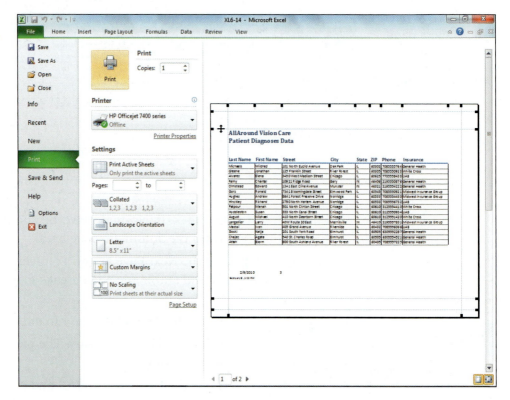

3. Display the second page, and make the **Diagnosis 1** column slightly wider.

4. Return to the **Page Layout** command tab.

Exercise 6-25 CREATE A CUSTOM FOOTER

You have seen that a footer (or a header) prints on all pages of a worksheet. Excel has preset header and footer layouts, but you can also design your own by keying your labels or using Excel's codes in the Header/Footer dialog box or directly in the sections in Page Layout view. You can also specify different footers for even and odd pages or set a unique footer for the first page.

1. Click the Dialog Box Launcher in the **Page Setup** group. Click the **Header/Footer** tab.

2. Click to place a checkmark for **Different first page**. Then click **Custom Footer**. The Footer dialog box includes two tabs, one for the first page and one for all other pages.

3. On the **Footer** tab, click the Format Text button [A]. Choose **10** as the size and click **OK**.

4. Key **AllAround Vision Care** in the left section. The font size is applied as you type.

5. Click in the center section. Click the Format Text button [A]. Choose **10** and click **OK**.

6. Click the Insert Page Number button ⊞. The code is **&[Page]**.

7. Press [Spacebar] to insert a space after **&[Page]**.

8. Key **of** and press [Spacebar].

9. Click the Insert Number of Pages button ⊞. The code is **&[Pages]**.

Figure 6-16
Printing page
numbers
6-14.xlsx
Diagnoses sheet

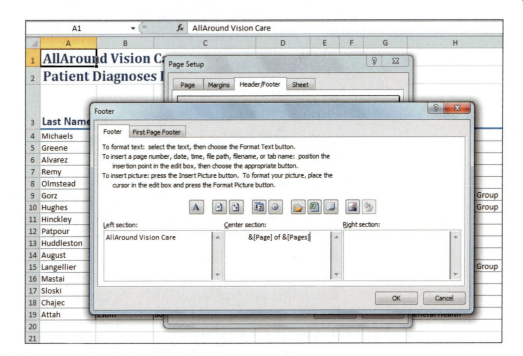

10. Insert your name in the right section with the same size font.

11. Click the **First Page Footer** tab. Click in the center section.

12. Set the font size to **10**.

13. Click the Insert Page Number button ⊞. Press [Spacebar], key **of**, and press [Spacebar].

14. Click the Insert Number of Pages button ⊞.

15. Insert your name in the right section with the same size font.

16. Click **OK** to close the Footer dialog box. Click **OK** to close the Page Setup dialog box.

17. View your worksheet in Backstage view. Return to a Normal view.

18. Save the workbook *[your initials]***6-25**.

Exercise 6-26   SAVE A WORKBOOK IN AN EARLIER EXCEL VERSION

Not all Excel users update to the latest version of the software immediately. Even though you are using Excel 2010, you will find that there are many companies and individuals who may still be using Excel 2007, Excel 2003, or earlier versions. As a result, you may find that you need to somehow enable those who don't have the latest version to access your work.

Excel 2010 can open workbooks saved in earlier versions of Excel. The reverse is not true; that is, a person using Excel 2003 cannot open a workbook saved in Excel 2010 format. You, however, can save an Excel 2010 workbook as an Excel 97-2003 workbook so that others can open and edit your work. When you save a workbook in the earlier version format, the Compatibility Checker automatically runs. This is a command that alerts you to elements of your workbook that might not be available in the earlier version. Most of these issues are insignificant and are related to formatting.

1. Click the **File** command tab. Click **Save & Send**. The Save & Send commands enable you to save workbooks in different formats and to distribute your work.

2. Click **Change File Type**. The different formats in which you can save a workbook are listed.

3. Choose **Excel 97-2003 Workbook**. Click **Save As** near the bottom of the screen. The Save As dialog box opens, and the same name and folder are assumed. You can use the same file name, because the Excel 97-2003 version uses a different extension, **xls**.

4. Navigate to your folder if necessary. Click **Save**. The Microsoft Office Excel Compatibility Checker runs. The dialog box notes commands or formatting that may not work in the earlier version.

Figure 6-17
The Compatibility Checker dialog box
6-25.xlsx
Diagnoses sheet

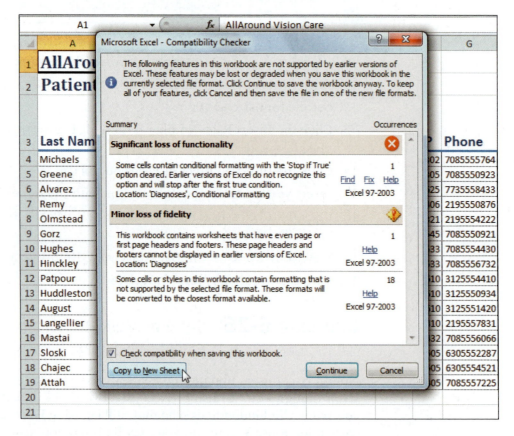

5. Click **Copy to New Sheet**. This creates a documentation sheet in the workbook to explain the potential issues. The sheet is named **Compatibility Report**. Your workbook has not been saved in the 97-2003 format.

6. Click the **Diagnoses** worksheet tab. Click the **File** command tab. Click **Send & Save**.

7. Click **Change File Type**. Choose **Excel 97-2003 Workbook**. The same file name and folder are shown.

8. Click **Save As** at the bottom of the screen. The Compatibility Checker runs each time you save a workbook in this format.

9. Click **Continue**. Save the workbook in Excel 2010 format now with a different file name.

10. Click the **File** command tab. Click **Send & Save**. Click **Change File Type**.

11. Choose **Workbook**. This is the default Excel 2010 format. Click **Save As** near the bottom of the screen.

12. Key or edit the file name to *[your initials]*6-26.

13. Click **Save**. The workbook is resaved. You now have two versions of the workbook, one in Excel 2010 format and one in Excel 97-2003.

Exercise 6-27   SAVE A PDF FILE

A *PDF* file is an Adobe portable document file format. It might be described as a snapshot of your document. A company might use PDF format for distributing information to customers or employees, because these documents are easily viewed. To read a PDF file, the receiver only needs to install Adobe Reader, free software from Adobe Corporation. In addition, PDF files can be smaller than some application files, which makes them more easily distributed electronically.

A PDF file cannot be edited in Excel nor in Adobe Reader. It can only be viewed.

1. Click the **File** command tab and choose **Save & Send**.

2. Click **Create PDF/XPS Document**. Backstage view lists some information about these formats; a "fixed" format is one that cannot be edited.

3. Click the Create a PDF/XPS button 🖻 The dialog box titled "Publish as PDF or XPS" is opened. Note that the **Save As type** is **PDF**. The file name and folder are the same. This is acceptable, because a PDF file uses the file name extension **pdf**.

4. As the **Optimize for** setting, choose **Standard (publishing online and printing)**.

5. Click **Options**. From this dialog box, you set whether to include all pages or only certain pages. Notice that the default shows that only the **Active sheet** will be included.

6. Choose **Entire workbook** in the **Publish what** group (see Figure 6-18 on the next page). Click **OK**.

7. Click **Open file after publishing**. This assumes that your computer has Adobe Reader installed. If you are not sure, deselect that option for now.

Figure 6-18
Saving a PDF file
6-26.xlsx
Diagnoses sheet

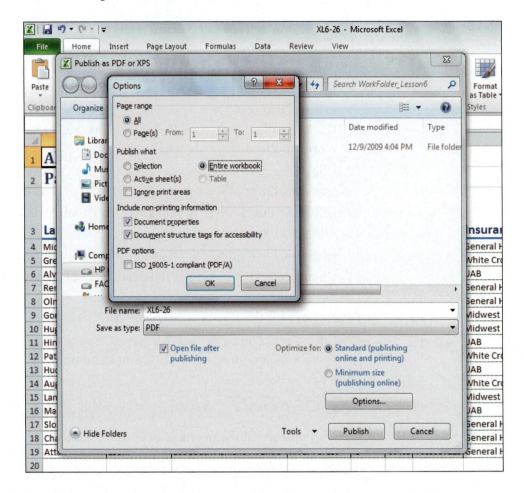

8. Click **Publish**. The PDF file is saved separately and is opened in Adobe Reader. The workbook is still open.

9. Scroll through the pages in Adobe Reader. Then close the program and return to your workbook.

10. Save and close the workbook.

Using Online Help

Excel has many date and time functions that calculate or convert common calculations related to dates and schedules.

USE HELP TO VIEW ADDITIONAL INFORMATION ABOUT DATE AND TIME FUNCTIONS

1. In a new workbook, click the Microsoft Office Excel Help button 🔵. In the Search box, key **date and time functions** and press Enter.

2. Find and review topics about several of the functions.

3. Close the Help window.

Lesson 6   Summary

- Dates and times are an important and widely used type of data.

- Dates and times, if keyed in an order that is recognized by Excel, are automatically formatted in a default setting.

- Custom date and time formats use codes to specify how the data appear.

- Excel uses a serial number system to assign a value to each date and time. With this, date and time arithmetic is possible.

- The Date & Time function category displays or converts dates and times into various formats, allowing the data to be used in different ways.

- The TODAY() and NOW() functions display the current date and/or time based on the computer's clock.

- Shrink to Fit is a setting in the Format Cells dialog box that sizes data on screen so that they are completely visible in the cell.

- Date and time arithmetic may require converting days to years or fractional days to hours or vice versa.

- The fractions format for values converts a decimal to its fractional equivalent. You can specify how many digits to use in the fraction for your degree of precision.

- The logical function category is a small group that determines if a particular circumstance is true or false. Most of them show true or false as results.

- The IF function enables you to create formulas that test whether a condition is true and then specify what should be shown or done. You also set what appears or is done if the condition is false.

- The IF function can show text in its result, it can calculate a value, or it can show a cell reference.

- You can remove all formatting from a cell and return to the default general style.

- A cell style includes the format attributes from the Format Cells dialog box. You can create your own cell styles which are saved with the worksheet.

- AND, OR, and NOT are logical functions. AND and OR are used to check for multiple conditions. NOT checks for the opposite of what you specify.

- Page breaks determine where a new printed page starts. Excel inserts automatic page breaks based on the paper size, margins, font size, and data.

- You can insert and delete manual page breaks, and you can adjust any page break.

- If a worksheet requires more than one page, you can repeat column or row headings on the printed page by setting the print titles.

- You can print each page number as well as the total number of pages in a worksheet as a header or a footer.

- Excel has options to show different footers on even and odd pages or the first page of a worksheet.
- A workbook can be saved in an earlier Excel format. When you do so, the Compatibility Checker runs and notes formats and/or features that may not work or may work differently in the older version.
- An Excel workbook can be saved as a PDF file, an Adobe Acrobat format. This type of document is readable by anyone who has the free Reader software.

LESSON 6		Command Summary	
Feature	**Button**	**Ribbon Location**	**Keyboard**
Clear format		Home, Editing	
Compatibility checker		File, Info	
Create cell style		Home, Styles	
Delete page break		Page Layout, Page Setup	
Edit cell style		Home, Styles	
Fractions		Home, Number	Ctrl + 1
Insert page break		Page Layout, Page Setup	
Page break preview		View, Workbook Views	
PDF file		File, Send & Save	F12
Print titles		Page Layout, Page Setup	
Repeat command			Ctrl + Y

Please visit our Online Learning Center, *www.lessonapproach2010.com,* **where you will find the following review materials:**

- **Concepts Review**

    True/False Questions

    Short Answer Questions

    Critical Thinking Questions

- **Skills Review**

    Review Exercises that target single skills

    Lesson Applications

    Review Exercises that challenge students by testing multiple skills in each exercise

- **On Your Own**

    Open-ended exercises that require students to synthesize multiple skills and apply creativity and problem-solving as they would in a real world business situation

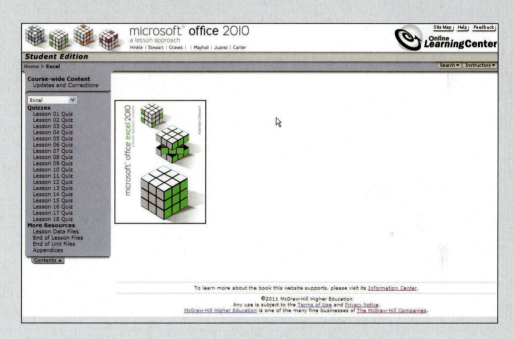

Please visit our Online Learning Center, *www.lessonapproach2010.com*, where you will find Unit Applications review materials.

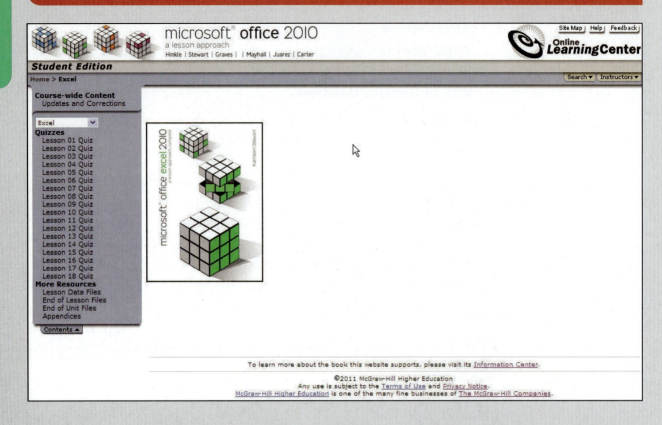

Unit 3

PRESENTING AND ANALYZING WORKSHEET DATA

Lesson 7
Building Worksheet Charts

OBJECTIVES   *After completing this lesson, you will be able to:*

1. Use the Chart Tools Design tab.
2. Use the Chart Tools Layout and Format tabs.
3. Create chart sheets and chart objects.
4. Edit the data source.
5. Format data series with images, gradients, and textures.
6. Create combination charts.
7. Insert sparklines.

Estimated Time: 2 hours

Excel is unmatched in its ability to portray worksheet data in a chart. Charts can help you illustrate comparisons, identify patterns, and recognize trends in data. AllAround Vision Care uses many types of charts. It uses charts to compare sales of products, to identify growth in revenues, and to monitor changes in utility expenses. In this lesson, you'll work with a bar chart that compares dollar contributions from the four cities for a particular year. It is easier to determine which city did the best from the chart than it is from looking at the actual values. Your instructor might use a similar type of chart to compare average exam or quiz scores throughout the semester. He or she would be able to quickly determine which exams resulted in the best scores. Utility companies sometimes include a bar or column chart with their bills to show how home energy consumption changes from month to month.

NOTE

The workbooks you create and use in this course relate to the Case Study about AllAround Vision Care, a fictional eye care company (see frontmatter).

A *chart* is a visual representation of numerical data. A chart can plot one or more sets of numbers from a worksheet. The number of data sets to be displayed usually determines the type of chart to use. Experience helps you identify which data to use as well as which type of chart to choose.

Using the Chart Tools Design Tab

Charts are clickable elements within a workbook. When a chart is selected or active, the three Chart Tools command tabs in the Ribbon are visible: Design, Layout, and Format. The Chart Tools Design tab includes five command groups: Type, Data, Chart Layout, Chart Styles, and Location.

Charts can be located on the same sheet as the data or on separate sheets in the workbook. In either case, a chart is dynamically linked to the data used to create it and is updated when you edit the data. A chart that appears on the same sheet as the data is a graphic object. An *object* is a separate, clickable part of a worksheet.

Exercise 7-1   OPEN THE SELECTION AND VISIBILITY PANE

When a workbook has objects such as charts or images, you can use the Selection and Visibility pane to select, view, and rearrange the objects. Remember that, if you access a student data file from a Web site or an e-mail attachment, the workbook opens in Protected View. Click **Enable Editing** to exit Protected View.

1. Open **Excel_Lesson7**. The zoom size is set to 80% so that you can see the worksheet and the chart without scrolling.

2. Click in the white chart background area between the two titles above the columns. The Chart Tools command tabs are visible. The chart is surrounded by a light rounded-corner frame, and the data used in the chart are outlined (cells B6:B11 and cells G6:G11).

3. Press [Alt] to see the Key Tips. Key **jo** to select the Chart Tools Format tab. The Current Selection group shows that the chart area is the active chart element. If it doesn't show that item name, click the arrow with the entry box and choose **Chart Area**.

4. In the **Arrange** group, click the Selection Pane button. The Selection and Visibility pane opens at the right of the window. This worksheet has a chart and a text box, two objects. The Eye button toggles the object's visibility on and off.

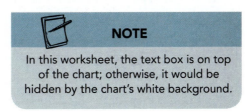

NOTE

In this worksheet, the text box is on top of the chart; otherwise, it would be hidden by the chart's white background.

Figure 7-1
Selection and
Visibility pane
Excel_Lesson7.xlsx
$Contributions
sheet

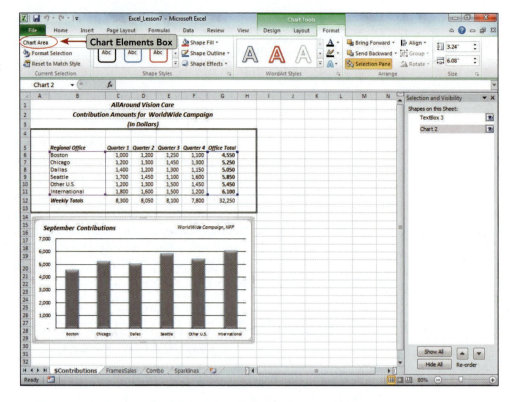

5. Click the Eye button 🔲 for **TextBox 3**. The text box is the campaign name in the top right corner of the chart (WorldWide Campaign, NFP). It's hidden now.

6. Click the Eye button 🔲 for **TextBox 3** again to display it.

7. Toggle the visibility of **Chart 2** on and off. Finish with the chart visible.

Exercise 7-2   CHANGE THE CHART TYPE AND LAYOUT

The chart type in this worksheet is clustered column. It plots one series or one column of values, column G. The labels in column A represent the category and are the city names in this case. In column charts, the category is along the bottom, and the values are along the side.

Chart layout sets what elements are included on the chart and where they are located. Some layouts include a chart title and a legend; others may include data labels and axes titles. These preset layouts can be changed to suit your plans for the chart.

1. Click the chart background. Click the **Chart Tools Design** tab.

2. In the **Type** group, click the Change Chart Type button 📊. The Change Chart Type gallery shows various charts and subtypes.

3. Click **Stacked Column** in the first row, and click **OK**. There is no change, because that chart type does not fit the data.

4. Click the Change Chart Type button 📊. Scroll the gallery list and choose **Pie**. Click **OK**. This is not a good fit for the data, because you cannot see any distinction.

5. Click the Change Chart Type button 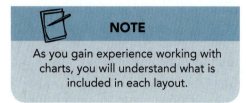. Choose **Bar** in the pane on the left, and then choose **Clustered Bar** as the chart subtype. Click **OK**. This chart type does fit the data and does provide a visual comparison of the data. It is similar to a column chart but shows the categories along the side and the values along the bottom.

6. Click the Change Chart Type button . Choose **Clustered Column** and click **OK**. Bar and column charts are good for comparing one or a few sets of values.

7. Click the More button ⇊ in the **Chart Layouts** group. The Chart Layout gallery shows 11 preset layouts for this chart type. The thumbnails give an indication of what is included in the layout.

NOTE

As you gain experience working with charts, you will understand what is included in each layout.

Figure 7-2
The Chart Layout gallery
Excel_Lesson7.xlsx
$Contributions
sheet

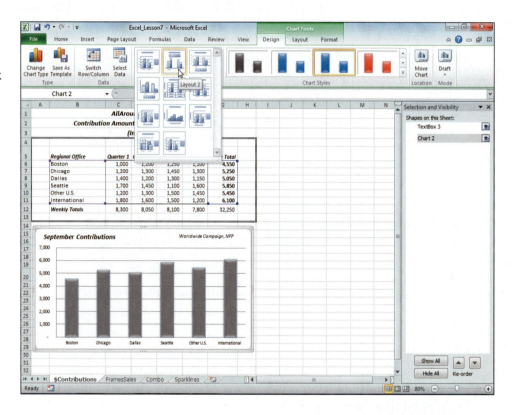

8. Click **Layout 2**. The chart is redesigned to show values above the columns with no values along the vertical axis. The chart title is centered, and there is a legend ("Series 1" above the columns). A legend clarifies what is shown in the columns.

9. In the **Chart Layouts** group, click the More button ⇊. Choose **Layout 3**. This is similar to Layout 1 but with a legend at the bottom.

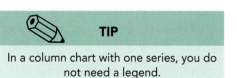

TIP

In a column chart with one series, you do not need a legend.

10. Choose **Layout 4**. This layout does not include a chart title, so the title is removed. There is still a legend.

11. Choose **Layout 3**. A chart title placeholder is inserted and will need to be rekeyed (later in the lesson).

Exercise 7-3 APPLY A CHART STYLE

A *chart style* is a preset selection of colors and effects for the chart, its background, and its components. The Chart Styles gallery provides variations based on the current document theme and the chart type. Changing the chart style does not alter the layout of the chart. But it can have unexpected results.

1. In the **Chart Styles** group, click the More button ⏷. The Chart Styles gallery opens. The chart currently uses Style 19, but the column colors were modified separately.

2. Find and click **Style 34**. The columns show a flat effect in a new color.

3. In the **Chart Styles** group, find and choose **Style 41**. This style changes the background color and resets a beveled effect. Notice that the text box (with the campaign name) is no longer visible, because it uses black text.

Exercise 7-4 PREVIEW A CHART OBJECT

By default, a chart object prints with the worksheet. When you open Backstage view for printing, you'll see a preview of the data and the chart. If you select the chart, however, Backstage view for printing shows only the chart and that is what will print.

1. Click the Close button ⊠ in the **Selection and Visibility** pane.

2. Click cell A1 to deselect the chart. The background frame is removed from the chart.

NOTE

When a chart is selected, the keyboard shortcut to open Backstage view for printing does not work.

3. Press Ctrl+F2. Backstage view for printing shows the data and chart on a single page.

4. Close Backstage view.

5. Click the black background chart area to select the chart. Be sure not to select the invisible text box.

6. Click the **File** command tab and choose **Print**. In the **Settings** group, **Print Selected Chart** is chosen. The chart by itself is previewed in landscape orientation resized to a full page.

7. Close Backstage view. Click cell A1.

Using the Chart Tools Layout and Format Tabs

A chart is composed of many clickable elements or objects. These elements are initially formatted by the chart layout and style, but you can change each object individually. Most changes to a chart element are made from the Chart Tools Layout or Format command tabs.

• The *chart area* is the background for the chart. It can be filled with a color, gradient, or pattern.

• An *axis* is the horizontal or vertical boundary that identifies what is plotted.

- The *horizontal (category) axis* is created from row or column headings in the data. A category describes what is shown in the chart. In a bar chart, the category axis is the vertical axis; it's the horizontal axis in a column chart.

- The *vertical (value) axis* shows the numbers on the chart. Excel creates a range of values (the *scale*) based on the data. In a bar chart, the value axis is along the bottom. In a column chart, it is along the side.

- An *axis title* is an optional title for the categories or values.

- The *plot area* is the rectangular area bounded by the horizontal and vertical axes.

- The *chart title* is an optional title or name for the chart.

- A *data series* is a collection of related values from the worksheet. These values are in the same column or row and translate into the columns, lines, pie slices, and so on.

- A *data point* is a single value or piece of data from the data series.

- A *data marker* is the object that represents individual values. The marker can be a bar, a column, a slice, a point on a line, or an image.

- A *data label* is an optional object that displays the values with the marker.

- A *legend* is an element that explains the symbols, textures, or colors used to differentiate series in the chart.

- A *gridline* is a horizontal or vertical line that extends across the plot area to make it easier to read and follow the values.

- A *tick mark* is a small line or marker on the horizontal (category) and vertical (value) axes to help in reading the values.

- A *chart wall* is the vertical background or wall for a 3-D chart.

- A *chart floor* is the base or bottom for a 3-D chart.

Figure 7-3
Excel chart elements

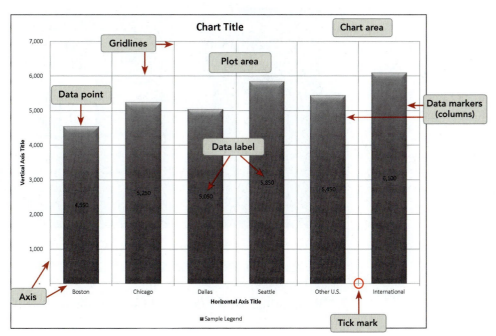

Exercise 7-5   EDIT THE CHART TITLE PLACEHOLDER

A chart element shows a ScreenTip when you hover over it. To edit an object, select it. When an object is selected, it shows a bounding frame and selection handles, and its name appears in the Chart Elements box on the Chart Tools Format tab. *Selection handles* are small circles, rectangles, or dots at the corners and along each border of the bounding frame. They can be used to size the element.

1. Point at the placeholder text **Chart Title** on the chart and click. The object is selected and shows a bounding border with four selection handles. Its name appears in the Chart Elements box in the Current Selection group.

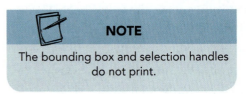

NOTE

The bounding box and selection handles do not print.

2. Click the **Chart Tools Layout** tab. Point at an edge of the chart title object to display a four-pointed arrow. This is the move pointer.

3. Drag the placeholder left to align near the values on the vertical axis.

4. Triple-click **Chart Title**. This is temporary text.

5. Key **Contribution Dollars**. The placeholder text is replaced.

6. Triple-click **Contribution Dollars** to select it. The Mini toolbar appears when data within an element are selected.

Figure 7-4
Editing the chart title
Excel_Lesson7.xlsx
$Contributions
sheet

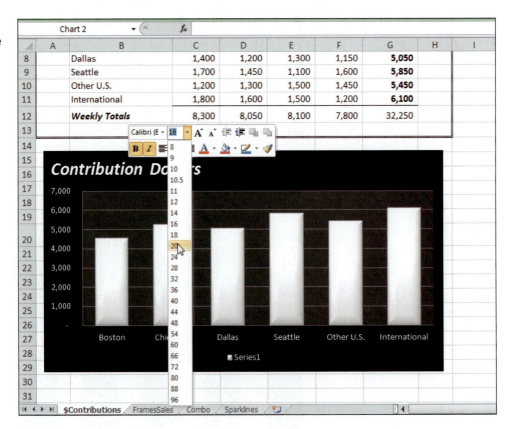

7. Point at the Mini toolbar. Click the Italic button I. Change the font size to 20.

NOTE

If you accidentally select the text box, the Drawing Tools Format command tab is activated. Click away from that area in the chart background.

8. Click the legend below the city names, **Series 1**. It is selected and shows a bounding border with selection handles. Its name is in the Chart Elements box.

9. Press ⌨Delete on the keyboard. The columns are resized to fill the space.

Exercise 7-6   SET THE SHAPE STYLE

On the Chart Tools Format tab, there is a group named Shapes Styles. A shape in a chart refers to the bars, the columns, the pie slices, the lines, or whatever element is used in a particular chart type. In the chart you are using, the shape is a column.

There is one data series in this chart, the values from column G. Each value is represented by the height of its column shape. The values are plotted against the value (vertical) axis, the numbers at the left in the chart area. The category for this chart is the city name, shown along the horizontal axis.

TIP

In a column or line chart, the value axis may be referred to as the *y* axis and the category (horizontal) axis as the *x* axis.

1. Make sure the chart is selected. Click the **Chart Tools Format** tab.

2. Rest the mouse pointer on the Dallas column to see its ScreenTip. It is one data point from the series.

3. Click the Dallas column. The entire data series is selected, and the Chart Elements box shows **Series 1**. This is the first (and only) series in this chart.

4. In the **Shape Styles** group on the **Chart Tools Format** tab, click the More button ⏷ for the **Shape Styles**. The style icons show "abc" in a rounded-corner rectangle. Some shape styles include an outline but no fill, others have both outline and fill, and others have beveled or shadow effects.

Figure 7-5
Changing the shape's style
Excel_Lesson7.xlsx
$Contributions
sheet

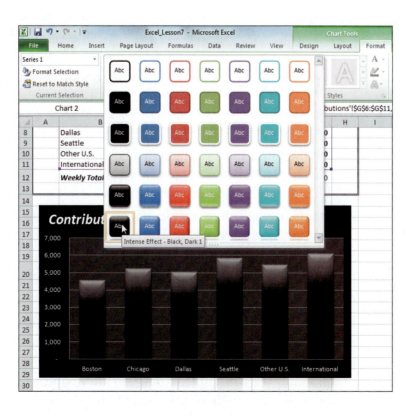

5. Choose **Intense Effect, Black, Dark 1** in the bottom row of the gallery. Make sure the data series is selected.

6. In the **Shape Styles** group, click the Shape Fill button .

7. Choose **White, Background 1, Darker 35%** in the first column.

8. Click the chart background.

Exercise 7-7   FORMAT THE PLOT AND CHART AREAS

The chart area is the solid black chart background. The plot area is the slightly lighter rectangle that appears behind the columns with horizontal gridlines. These are both elements that can be formatted within a chart.

1. Click the **Chart Tools Format** tab. Click the **Chart Elements** arrow and choose **Plot Area**. You can select any chart element from this box.

2. In the **Current Selection** group, click the Format Selection button. The Format Plot Area dialog box opens. It has six panes with format options.

3. On the **Fill** pane, choose **No fill**. Click **Close**. The color (light gray) is removed and the area is transparent.

4. Click the **Chart Elements** arrow and choose **Chart Area**. The chart's background is selected; it is black.

5. Click the Format Selection button.

6. On the **Fill** pane, choose **No fill**. Click **Close**. The fill color is removed, but now you cannot see the white axes text.

7. In the **Shape Styles** group, click the Shape Fill button. Choose **Black, Text 1**. You can make format choices from the galleries in the command tab or from the dialog box.

> **TIP**
>
> Choosing no fill color means your chart will print faster than with a white fill color and look the same on white paper.

Exercise 7-8   FORMAT THE AXES

The horizontal (category) axis is the x axis in this chart, the city names. The vertical axis is the value axis in a column chart.

1. On the **Chart Tools Format** tab, click the **Chart Elements** arrow and choose **Horizontal (Category) Axis**. The labels are selected and show a bounding box and selection handles.

2. On the **Home** command tab, change the font size to 9 points. Many format choices can be made from the Home tab.

3. Click one of the values along the vertical (value) axis, the y axis, the sales in dollars. Look for the bounding box to make sure the axis is selected.

4. On the **Chart Tools Format** tab, click the Format Selection button.

5. On the **Number** pane, choose **Currency**. Set **Decimal places** to **0** and **Symbol** to **$**.

6. Click **Axis Options**. You can specify how the values are scaled. **Auto** is probably the best choice when you are first learning about charts, because you can distort the data if you choose inappropriate numbers.

Figure 7-6
Setting axis options
**Excel_Lesson7.xlsx
$Contributions
sheet**

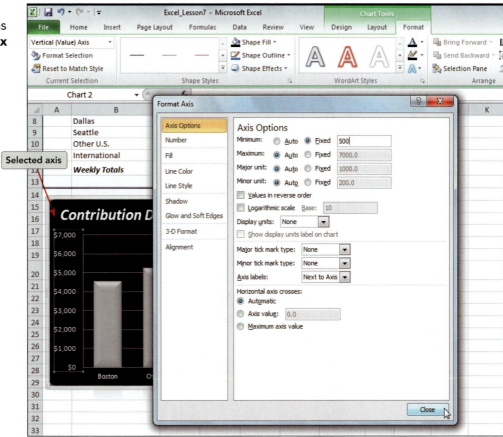

7. For **Minimum**, choose **Fixed**. Then key **500** in the entry box. Click **Close**. The columns now assume that $500 is the bottom or floor for the values.

Exercise 7-9   SET A GRADIENT FILL

Gradient fills are available for most of the elements in a chart. A gradient is a blend of two or more colors. Each color used in a gradient is a *stop;* it refers to a position on the color bar. You can define each color stop, add stops, or remove them.

1. Click the **Chart Elements** arrow and choose **Plot Area**.

2. Right-click inside the plot area and choose **Format Plot Area**.

3. On the **Fill** pane, choose **Gradient fill**. The default gradient has three stops, represented by the down-pointing block arrows on the color bar below **Gradient stops**.

4. Rest the mouse pointer on the rightmost (third) arrow. The ScreenTip identifies this color as **Stop 3 of 3**. You will build a two-color gradient and can delete this stop.

5. Click **Stop 3 of 3**. Click the Remove gradient stop button 🔲. The stop is removed, but the other two stops have not changed.

6. Click **Stop 2 of 2**, and drag it to the right end of the color bar. This is identified as the 100% position.

7. In the **Gradient stops** group, click **Stop 1 of 2**.

8. Click the arrow for **Color** and choose **White, Background 1, Darker 5%**.

9. Click **Stop 2 of 2**.

10. Click the arrow for **Color** and choose **White, Background 1, Darker 15%**.

Figure 7-7
Building a gradient fill
Excel_Lesson7.xlsx
$Contributions
sheet

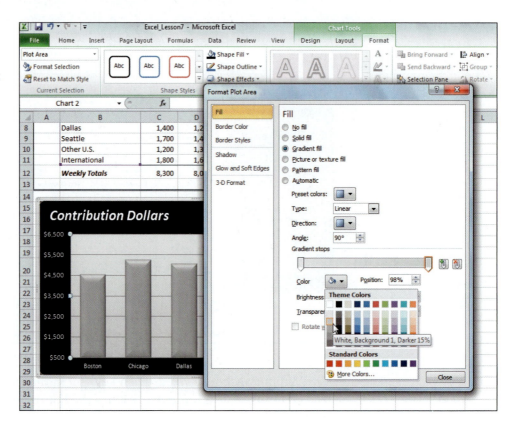

11. Click **Close**.

12. Click a worksheet cell to deselect the chart.

Exercise 7-10   ADD DATA LABELS

A *data label* is an optional title shown for each value. It is the actual value from column G in this case. Data labels add specificity to the chart, because a reader can only estimate the exact value from most charts.

1. Click the chart to select it. Click the **Chart Tools Layout** tab.

2. Hover over the Data Labels button and read its ScreenTip.

3. Click the Data Labels button and choose **Outside End**. The value of each data point appears above its column. The white color does not show well with your current design choices.

4. Rest the mouse pointer on one of the data labels to see the ScreenTip. Click a label to select the object. The data labels are selected and show bounding boxes and selection handles.

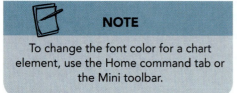

NOTE

To change the font color for a chart element, use the Home command tab or the Mini toolbar.

5. Click the **Home** command tab. Click the arrow for the Font Color button ![A] and choose **Black, Text 1**.

6. Right-click one of the data labels and choose **Format Data Labels**. Click **Number** and set currency with no decimals. Click **Close**. The labels might be better positioned in the middle of the column.

7. Click the **Chart Tools Layout** tab. Click the Data Labels button ![icon] and choose **Center**.

Exercise 7-11   CHANGE FONT COLOR IN A TEXT BOX

There is a text box on the chart that has black as its font color. It is invisible now on the black background. A text box is a drawing object on the Insert command tab.

1. Click the **Chart Tools Format** tab. In the **Arrange** group, click the Selection Pane button ![icon]. The Eye button ![icon] is on for both the chart and the text box, meaning both are shown (not hidden).

2. Click **TextBox 3** in the Selection and Visibility pane. The text box is selected in the top right corner of the chart, but you still cannot read the text.

3. Point inside the text box to display an I-beam pointer.

4. Triple-click to select all the text in the text box. You still cannot see it.

Figure 7-8
Choosing the invisible text box
Excel_Lesson7.xlsx
$Contributions
sheet

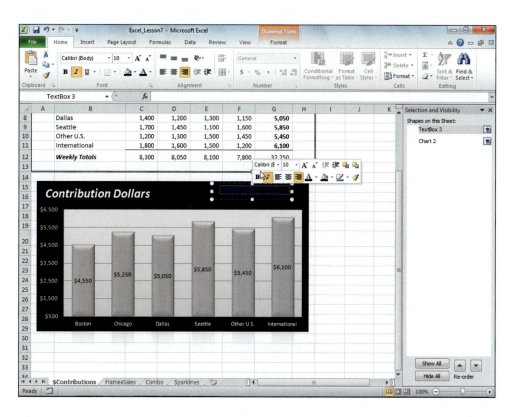

5. Click the **Home** command tab. Click the arrow for the Font Color button ![A] and choose **White, Background 1**. Then click the Bold button ![B].

6.   Click the Close button ⊠ in the **Selection and Visibility** pane. Click cell A1.

7.   Save the workbook as *[your initials]***7-11**.

Creating Chart Sheets and Chart Objects

With practice and experience, you can develop skill in identifying data and choosing chart types. Keep a few questions in mind as you decide to build a chart.

- Can a chart help analysis of the data?
- What data will be used to build a chart?
- What type of chart is best for that data?

> **NOTE**
>
> The appearance of a button in the Ribbon is affected by the screen resolution setting, so you may or may not see text with command buttons. All buttons have ScreenTips for clarification.

The most popular chart types for business and personal use are column charts, bar charts, pie charts, and line charts. There are also specialized charts such as doughnut, scatter, and radar charts. Table 7-1 describes the chart types available in Excel.

TABLE 7-1 Chart Types in Excel

Type		Definition
	Column	A column chart is the most popular chart type. Column charts make comparisons among items, or they might show how values change over a period of time. They can be prepared with 3-D effects or stacked columns. Categories are on the horizontal axis (*x*), and values are on the vertical axis (*y*). The shape can also be a cone, a cylinder, or a pyramid.
	Line	Line charts show trends in data over a period of time. They emphasize the rate of change. 3-D effects are available. Lines can be stacked and can show markers, a character, or symbol on the line that indicates the value at that point.
	Pie	Pie charts show one data series (one set of values) and compare the size of each value to the whole. Pie charts should have fewer than seven data points (slices) to be easy to interpret. A pie chart can use 3-D effects and can show exploded slices.
	Bar	Bar charts illustrate comparisons among items or show individual figures at a specific time. Bar charts can use 3-D effects and stacked bars. Categories are on the vertical axis (*y*). Values are on the horizontal axis (*x*). The shape can also be a cone, a cylinder, or a pyramid.
	Area	Area charts look like colored-in line charts. They show the rate of change and emphasize the magnitude of the change. 3-D effects are available.
	Scatter	Scatter charts are used to show relationships between two values, such as additional advertising dollars and increased sales amounts. Scatter charts do not have a category; both axes show numbers or values.
	Stock	Stock charts are often called "high-low-close charts." They use three series of data (three sets of values) in high, low, close order. They can also use volume as a fourth series.

continues

TABLE 7-1 Chart Types in Excel *continued*

Type	Definition
Surface	Surface charts illustrate optimum combinations of two sets of data. They show two or more series on a surface. Surface charts can use 3-D effects.
Doughnut	Doughnut charts compare the sizes of parts. A doughnut chart has a hole in the middle. A doughnut chart shows the relative proportion of the whole. A doughnut chart can show more than one data series, with each concentric ring representing a series.
Bubble	Bubble charts compare sets of three values. They are like scatter charts with the third value displayed as the size of the bubble. Bubble charts can be 3-D.
Radar	Radar charts show the frequency of data relative to a center point and to other data points. There is a separate axis for each category, and each axis extends from the center. Lines connect the values in a series.

Exercise 7-12 CREATE A CHART SHEET

A *chart sheet* is a chart that is located on its own sheet in the workbook, separate from its underlying data. A chart sheet does not display any columns or rows, like a regular worksheet. To build a chart sheet, select the values and labels to be plotted and press F11 to create a default chart, a clustered column chart on its own sheet. You can now build a column chart that graphs and compares unit sales of a particular eyeglass frame from each city and from the company's Web site.

1. In *[your initials]*7-11, click the FrameSales worksheet tab.
2. Select cells B6:C10. This range includes the city name (the category) and the values (the series).
3. Press F11. A default clustered column chart is inserted on its own sheet named Chart1.
4. On the Chart Tools Design tab in the Chart Layouts group, click the More button ▼.
5. Choose Layout 3. This layout includes a chart title and a legend ("Series 1" at the bottom).
6. Click the chart title placeholder. Its bounding box and selection handles are visible.
7. Triple-click the placeholder text. Key Number of JetSetter Frames Sold.
8. Click any column in the chart, and notice that the entire series (all the columns) is selected.
9. While all columns are selected, click the "Chicago" column. It alone is selected. The Chicago column (and value) is a data point (see Figure 7-9 on the next page).
10. Click the Chart Tools Format tab. In the Shape Styles group, click the Shape Fill button.
11. Choose Red, Accent 2 in the sixth column (see Figure 7-9 on the next page). Only the selected column is redesigned.

Figure 7-9
Changing an
individual column
7-11.xlsx
Chart1 sheet

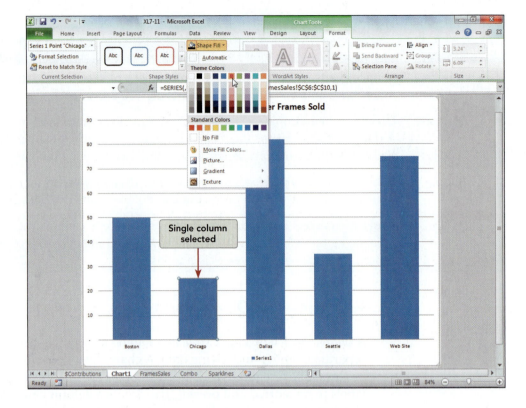

12. Click the legend below the columns and press Delete. It is not necessary in this chart, because the horizontal axis includes the city names.

Exercise 7-13 CREATE A CHART OBJECT

A *chart object* appears on the same sheet as the data; it may be called an *embedded chart*. There are no design, layout, or format differences between a chart object and a chart sheet. In fact, you can convert one to the other when necessary. You create a chart object by selecting the data and choosing a chart type from the Insert command tab. The data about the JetSetter frame sales can also be illustrated in a pie chart.

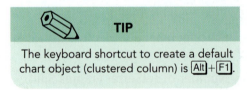

TIP

The keyboard shortcut to create a default chart object (clustered column) is Alt + F1.

1. Click the **FrameSales** worksheet tab. Cells B6:C10 are still selected.

2. Click the **Insert** command tab.

3. Click the Pie button 🥧. A ScreenTip describes each chart subtype when you hover over its icon.

4. In the **2-D Pie** group, choose **Pie**. The simple pie chart is inserted on the worksheet.

Exercise 7-14 MOVE AND SIZE A CHART OBJECT

The selection handles on the corners for a chart object are three dots arranged in a triangle shape. The handles are four dots arranged in a row in the middle of each edge. The move pointer is a four-pointed arrow; the sizing pointer is two-pointed. If you hold down Alt while dragging a chart object, its position snaps to the nearest cell.

1. Point at the top edge of the chart object to display a four-pointed arrow. Drag the chart so that its top left corner aligns at cell A14.

NOTE

Change the zoom size or scroll the worksheet so that you can see cell A14 and row 32.

2. Point at the bottom-right selection handle. A two-pointed sizing pointer appears.

3. Click and drag the bottom-right selection handle to cover cell E32. As you drag, the chart is made larger.

4. Click the **Chart Tools Design** tab. In the **Chart Layouts** group, click the More button ⊡.

5. Choose **Layout 5**. This layout includes a chart title, no legend, and data labels inside the pie slices.

6. In the **Chart Styles** group, click the More button ⊡. Choose **Style 17**. The slices are shown in shades of gray with a raised effect.

Exercise 7-15   DISTINGUISH AMONG CHART ELEMENTS

As you prepare a chart, you'll need to select various parts of the chart. Whatever element or part is selected at the time you give a command is what is changed. Some parts or objects in a chart consist of more than one other part or object. For example, the actual pie (the series object) has several slices (data point objects). The Chart Elements box is available on both the Chart Tools Layout or Format tabs. From the list, you can select a specific object in the chart. You can also select an individual object by simply clicking it. Then you can verify its selection in the Chart Elements box.

1. Click the **Chart Tools Format** tab. Make sure that the chart area is the current selection.

2. In the **Shape Styles** group, click the More button ⊡ for the **Shape Styles**.

3. Hover over a few different styles. Since the chart area is selected, the entire chart is restyled.

4. Press Esc to close the gallery without making a change.

5. Point at any pie slice, away from the label, and click. The pie is selected, and **Series 1** is the current selection.

6. For **Shape Styles**, click the More button ⊡.

7. Hover over several styles. Now the slices would be affected, not the background.

8. Press Esc.

9. While the slices are selected, click only the Chicago slice. You should see selection handles for just this slice (see Figure 7-10 on the next page). Be careful not to select the data label.

Figure 7-10
Pie chart with a
single slice selected
**7-11.xlsx
FrameSales sheet**

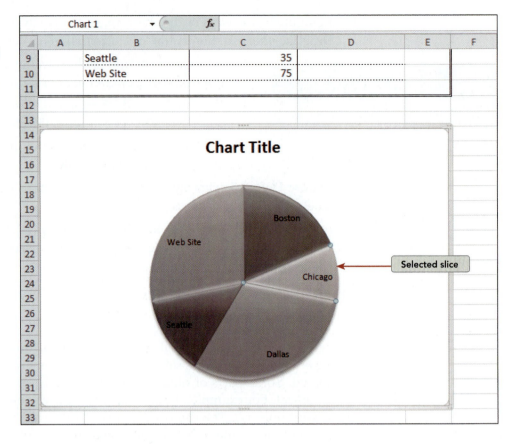

10. Click the More button ⏷ for **Shape Styles**.

11. Hover over several styles. Now just one slice would be affected.

12. Press Esc.

13. Click the chart title object. Press ↑. Another chart object is selected, probably the data labels.

14. Press ↑ several times to cycle through selecting the chart objects.

15. Click the **Chart Elements** arrow and choose **Series 1**. The pie object is selected; it is the single data series. It does include other objects, the slices.

16. Press →. One of the slices is selected.

17. Press → several times to cycle through selection of the slices.

18. Select the chart title object. Triple-click the placeholder text and key **JetSetter Sales**.

19. Right-click the pie and choose **Format Data Labels**. The data labels are the city names within the slices.

20. On the **Label Options** pane, click to place a checkmark for **Percentage**. Click **Close**. The slices now show category names and percentages, which represent which part of the whole pie is illustrated by the slice.

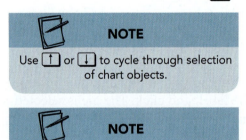

NOTE

Use ↑ or ↓ to cycle through selection of chart objects.

NOTE

If, when you triple-click to select text, you accidentally open a Format dialog box, just close it.

Exercise 7-16   MOVE A CHART OBJECT TO ITS OWN SHEET

A chart object can be relocated to its own sheet. When you do this, the chart is sized to fill the page. You can create a second chart object for the data about the JetSetter frame, a bar chart.

1. Select cells B6:C10 and click the **Insert** command tab.
2. In the **Charts** group, click the Bar button ![bar icon].
3. In the **3-D Bar** group, choose **Clustered Bar in 3-D**, the first icon. The chart object appears on the worksheet.
4. In the **Location** group, click the Move Chart button ![move chart icon]. The Move Chart dialog box allows you to move the chart to its own new sheet, creating a chart sheet. You could also move the object to another worksheet in this workbook.

Figure 7-11
Move Chart dialog box
7-11.xlsx
FrameSales sheet

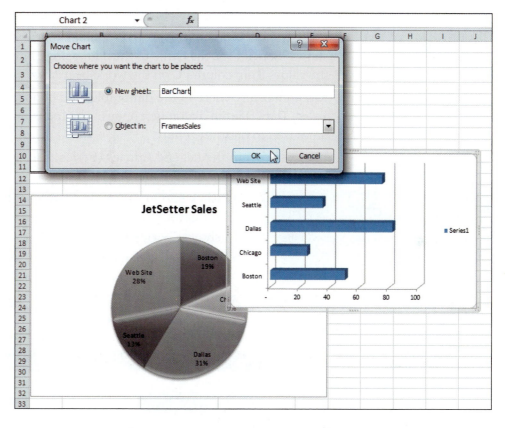

5. Choose **New sheet** and key **BarChart** in the entry box. Click **OK**. The chart is placed on a new sheet.
6. Click **Series 1**, the legend at the right, and press [Delete].
7. Click the **Chart Tools Layout** tab. In the **Labels** group, click the Chart Title button ![title icon].
8. Choose **Above Chart**. A placeholder object is inserted.
9. Triple-click **Chart Title**, and key **Comparison of JetSetter Frame Sales**.

TIP

Most charts that have only one data series do not need a legend.

10. Click anywhere in the light blue-gray side panel to deselect the chart.

Exercise 7-17   SHOW GRIDLINES AND A DATA TABLE

Gridlines in a chart are horizontal and vertical lines on the plot area that aid in relating numbers to the bars or columns. Major vertical gridlines are shown in the bar chart you just created. They connect to the values along the horizontal axis so that you can make a reasonable assumption of the number represented by the bar. Gridlines can be major and minor, vertical and horizontal.

A *data table* is a matrix that lists the values and categories illustrated in the chart. It is separate from the chart and appears below the horizontal axis. It is one way to include the actual data used to build the chart and serves as clarification to the reader.

1. Click the white chart background to select the chart area.
2. On the **Chart Tools Layout** tab, click the Gridlines button 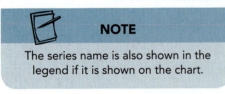.
3. Choose **Primary Vertical Gridlines**, and then choose **Major and Minor Gridlines**. More lines help identify the data point.
4. In the **Labels** group, click the Data Table button .
5. Choose **Show Data Table**. A matrix (a table) appears below the chart and shows "Series 1" as the name of the data being plotted. The data series are the values from column C on the worksheet; there is only one set of values.
6. Right-click anywhere in the data table, and choose **Select Data**. The Select Data Source dialog box opens. The focus moves to the worksheet data used to build the chart.
7. Click **Series 1** in the Legend Entries (Series) list. On the right, you can see the category names for this data series.

> **NOTE**
>
> The series name is also shown in the legend if it is shown on the chart.

8. Click **Edit** in the **Legend Entries (Series)** box. There is no series name at this point; that's why the data table shows "Series 1."
9. In the **Series name** box, key **Unit Sales** and click **OK**. Click **OK** again. The data table shows the new series name.

Figure 7-12
Editing the series name
7-11.xlsx
BarChart sheet

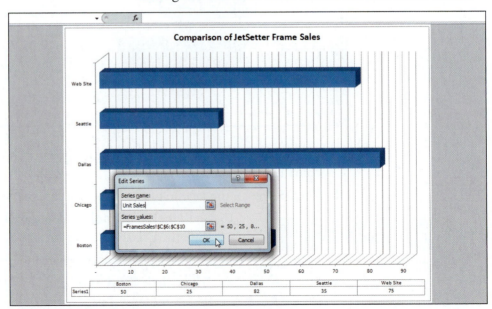

10. Save the workbook as *[your initials]***7-17**.

Editing a Chart's Data Source

The *data source* for a chart are the worksheet rows and columns used to build the chart. This information can be changed. If you build a chart, do all the formatting, and then realize that you used the wrong set of values, you can simply edit the data source. Many companies use the same chart each month or quarter, with different data for each period. The chart need not be built from scratch each month; it can be copied and the copy's data source updated.

In addition to using different or new data, you can add categories or values to an existing chart. In the charts for this lesson, you might need to add a row for catalog sales for the JetSetter frame. You might also add a second eyeglass frame to the data being plotted. Some changes to the underlying data for a chart are automatically reflected in the chart. Others require that you update the data source with the appropriate command.

Exercise 7-18   EDIT CHART DATA

Changes made to the underlying data for a chart are automatically shown in the chart. These include entering new values or changing city names.

1. Click the **FrameSales** worksheet tab in *[your initials]*7-17. Notice the pie slice size for Dallas and its corresponding value in the worksheet.
2. Click the **BarChart** tab. Note the length of the bar for Dallas.
3. Click the **Chart1** tab. Note the height of the Dallas column.
4. Click the **FrameSales** worksheet tab.
5. Click cell C8, key **150**, and press ⏎Enter. Notice the larger pie slice for Dallas.
6. Click the **Chart1** tab. The height of the Dallas column is increased proportionally as the chart is redesigned.
7. Click the **BarChart** tab. Note the length of the Dallas bar.

Exercise 7-19   ADD A DATA POINT

If you add another city location and its total, you add a data point to the data series. If you insert these additional data within the chart's current data range, they appear automatically in all charts linked to the data. If you add new data below or above the chart's original source data range, you need to reset the data range for each chart.

1. On the **FrameSales** sheet, insert a row at row 10. This row is within the current data range for the chart.
2. Key **Catalog Sales** in cell B10. Key **125** in cell C10 and press ⏎Enter. The pie chart object is redrawn.
3. Click the **Chart1** tab. Click the **BarChart** tab. The charts are automatically redrawn to include the new data.
4. Click the **FrameSales** worksheet tab. Insert a row at row 12. This row is outside the current data range for the charts.

5. Key **Exhibition Sales** in cell B12. Key **45** in cell C12 and press Enter. The pie chart object is not changed.

6. Click the **Chart1** tab. Click the **BarChart** tab. None of the charts has been changed.

7. Click the **FrameSales** worksheet tab. Click the white background area for the pie chart. The data range in the worksheet shows sizing handles at each corner.

8. Position the pointer on the bottom-right handle for cell C11. A two-pointed sizing arrow appears.

9. Drag the sizing arrow to include the Exhibition Sales information. The pie chart is updated when you release the mouse button. You have edited its data source.

Figure 7-13
Adding a data point
7-17.xlsx
FrameSales sheet

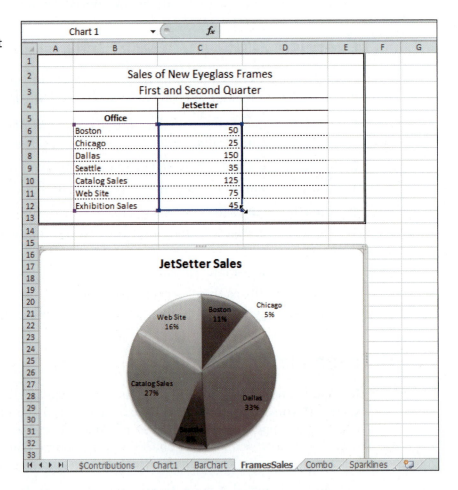

10. Click the **Chart1** tab. You must update the data source for each chart separately.

11. Right-click the white chart background. Choose **Select Data**. The Select Data Source dialog box opens on top of the **FrameSales** worksheet with the current data range selected (see Figure 7-14 on the next page).

12. In the **Chart data range** entry box, edit the address to show **$C$12** instead of $C$11. Click **OK**. The column chart is updated to include Exhibition Sales.

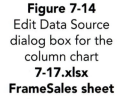

Figure 7-14
Edit Data Source
dialog box for the
column chart
7-17.xlsx
FrameSales sheet

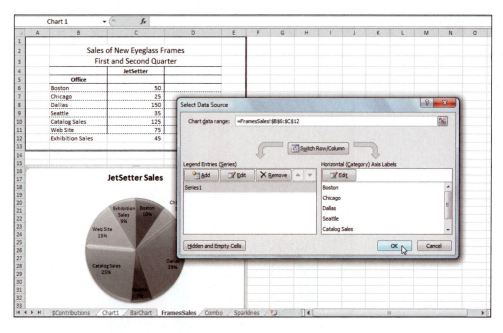

13. Click the **BarChart** tab. Right-click the white chart background.

14. Choose **Select Data**. Click cell B6 and drag to select cells B6:C12. Click **OK**. There is now an Exhibition Sales bar.

Exercise 7-20 ADD AND RENAME DATA SERIES

Your charts currently graph one set of values, one data series. If you add a second eyeglass frame to the worksheet data, another column, you can create a second series for the column and bar charts. A pie chart can have only one data series.

1. On the **FrameSales** worksheet, key **Kallie** in cell D4. Copy the format from cell C4.

2. Key the following values in cells D6:D12:

D6	60
D7	120
D8	45
D9	15
D10	30
D11	25
D12	10

3. Format the values and borders to match the rest of the worksheet.

4. Click the **Chart1** tab. Right-click the white chart background and choose **Select Data**.

5. In the **Chart data range** entry box, edit the address to show **$B$6:d12**. Click **OK**. The column chart now shows two columns for each city location, one for each frame. The Chicago data have a different color scheme due to your earlier change (see Figure 7-15 on the next page). Your colors may be different from the text figures.

Figure 7-15
Adding a data series
7-17.xlsx
FrameSales sheet

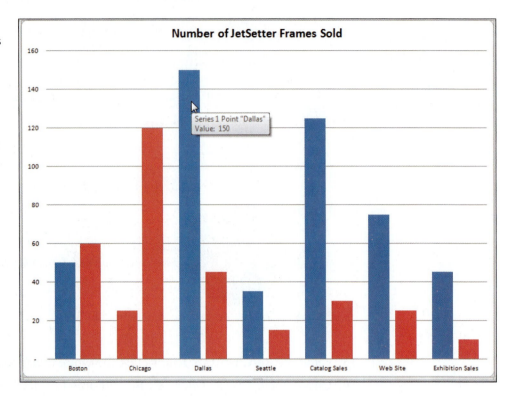

NOTE

A legend is important when you have more than one data series. Hover over a column to determine which one represents "Series 1."

6. Right-click any column for **Series 1** (JetSetter). Choose **Select Data**.

7. Click **Series 1** in the Legend Entries (Series) list and click **Edit**.

8. Key **JetSetter** and click **OK**.

9. Click **Series 2** in the list and click **Edit**. Key **Kallie** and click **OK**.

10. Click **OK** again. Hover over several columns to view the series' names.

11. Right-click the **JetSetter** column for Chicago. Choose **Reset to Match Style**. The column color resets to its original color.

12. Click the white background. Click the **Chart Tools Layout** tab. Click the Legend button in the **Labels** group and choose **Show Legend at Bottom**.

13. On the **Chart Tools Design** tab, choose **Style 30**.

Formatting Data Series with Images, Gradients, and Textures

Data series are represented by the columns, the slices, and the bars. By default, these elements use a solid fill color, although the preset styles do add effects such as bevels or shadows. There are other possibilities for the fill. They include gradients, textures, or even images. These fill types can better distinguish bars, columns, or slices when the worksheet is output in black and white. They might also be used to clearly stamp a chart with a company's identity. Well-known logos such as the Pepsi-Cola circle or the Nike icon can be used inside bars or columns instead of a plain color.

You can insert an image, a gradient, or texture as fill by selecting the data series and doing the following:

- Clicking the Shape Fill button on the Chart Tools Format tab.
- Clicking the Format Selection button 🖉 on the Chart Tools Format tab or the Chart Tools Layout tab.
- Right-clicking the object and choosing Format Data Series or Format Data Point.

Exercise 7-21   USE AN IMAGE FOR A DATA SERIES

Be careful when using images as fill in any chart. It can detract from the purpose if it creates a cluttered look. If you want to use an image as fill in a bar or column chart, it looks best if you use a 2-D chart rather than 3-D. You can convert your 3-D bar chart into a 2-D chart.

The data files for this lesson include a JPEG file named **Eyeglasses**; make sure you know where to find it.

> **NOTE**
>
> JPEG stands for joint photographic experts group. It is a commonly used format for storing digital images on the Web and one of the formats used by digital cameras.

1. Click the **BarChart** tab. Select the chart, and then click the **Chart Tools Design** tab.
2. Click the Change Chart Type button 📊. In the **Bar** group, choose **Clustered Bar** (first icon, first row) to change the chart to a two-dimensional chart. Click **OK**.
3. Click any bar in the chart. All the bars show selection handles.
4. Click the **Chart Tools Format** tab. Click the Format Selection button 🖉. The Format Data Series dialog box opens.
5. On the **Fill** pane, choose **Picture or texture fill**. Additional options appear in the dialog box, and the bars fill with the last-used choice.
6. In the **Insert from** group, click **File** to locate an image on disk.
7. Navigate to the folder with **Eyeglasses** to find the image.
8. Choose **Eyeglasses** and click **Insert**. Do not click **Close**. The picture is inserted and stretched to fit the length of the bar. Move the dialog box if necessary to see the chart.
9. In the dialog box, click to select **Stack**. The image is scaled to fit and repeats across the bars (see Figure 7-16 on the next page).

Figure 7-16
Inserting a picture
7-17.xlsx
BarChart sheet

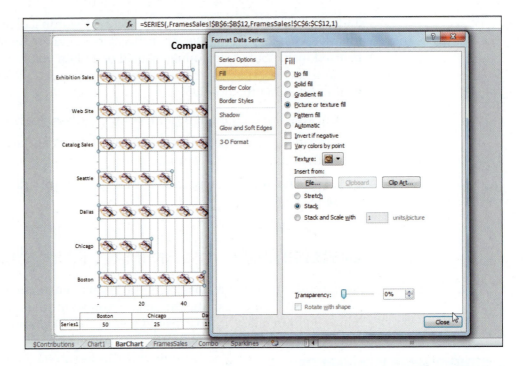

10. Click **Close**.

Exercise 7-22   ADD A BORDER AND A SHADOW

The bars now display an image with no visible border. This can be effective, or you can choose to add a border to the shapes. You can also add a shadow to give it more of a 3-D look.

1. Click the blue-gray window background to deselect the chart. The bounding box border for a selected object is not the same as a border that prints.

2. Click any bar in the chart.

3. Click the **Chart Tools Format** tab. Click the Format Selection button 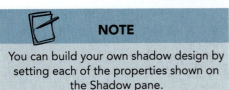.

4. On the **Border Color** pane, choose **Solid line**.

5. For the **Color**, click the arrow and choose **Black, Text 1**.

6. On the **Border Styles** pane, click the down spinner arrow to set the **Width** at **0.5 pt**.

7. On the **Shadow** pane, click the arrow for **Presets**. In the **Outer** group, choose **Offset Diagonal Bottom Right** (first icon).

8. Click **Close**.

9. Click the white chart background. On the **Chart Tools Layout** tab, click the Gridlines button.

10. Choose **Primary Vertical Gridlines** and then choose **None**. The chart looks less busy without the lines.

11. Click the blue-gray window background to deselect the chart.

> **NOTE**
>
> You can build your own shadow design by setting each of the properties shown on the Shadow pane.

Exercise 7-23   USE GRADIENTS FOR DATA SERIES FILL

From the Fill pane in the Format Data Series dialog box, you can build color blends (gradients) that use two or more colors. There are also several preset gradients.

1. Click the **Chart1** tab.

2. Right-click any column that represents the "Kallie" frame and choose **Format Data Series**.

3. On the **Fill** pane, choose **Gradient fill**. The dialog box updates to show the related options.

4. Click the arrow for **Preset colors**. A gallery of preset color blends opens.

5. Find and click **Calm Water** (third tile, second row). The gradient fill is immediately visible. This gradient uses six colors, identified in the **Gradient stops** group. Do not close the dialog box yet.

6. Click any JetSetter column in the chart. Choose **Fill** and **Gradient fill**. The most recently used gradient is applied. You can build your own gradient by removing stops and setting new colors.

7. In the **Gradient stops** group, click **Stop 2 of 6**. Click the Remove gradient stop button 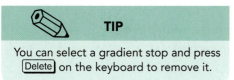. The stop is removed.

> ✎ **TIP**
>
> You can select a gradient stop and press ⌈Delete⌋ on the keyboard to remove it.

8. Remove stops 2, 3, and 4 so that you have a two-color bar.

9. Click **Stop 1 of 2**. Click the arrow for **Color** and choose **White, Background 1**.

10. Click **Stop 2 of 2**. Set its color to **Olive Green, Accent 3, Darker 25%**.

11. Click the arrow for **Direction**. Several variations of the way in which the colors blend are shown in a gallery.

12. Find and choose **Linear Up**. The white shades will be at the bottom of the column.

Figure 7-17
Setting a gradient direction
7-17.xlsx
Chart1 sheet

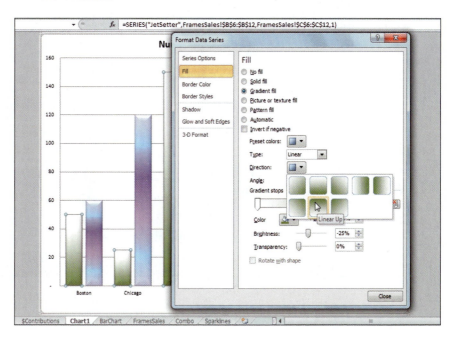

13. Click **Close**.

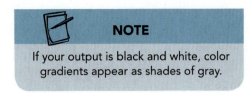

NOTE

If your output is black and white, color gradients appear as shades of gray.

Exercise 7-24 USE TEXTURE AS FILL

A *texture* is fill that appears as a grainy, nonsmooth surface or background. Use textures carefully, because they can detract from the purpose of a chart if they are too intricate.

1. Click the **FrameSales** worksheet tab.

2. Click the pie (away from a data label) to select it. Click the Web Site slice to select that slice only.

REVIEW

Point at the slice, not the data label within the slice.

3. Right-click the slice and choose **Format Data Point**.

4. On the **Fill** pane, choose **Picture or texture fill**. The slice may fill with the last-used image or texture.

5. Click the arrow for **Texture**. A gallery of available textures opens. Textures simulate marble, wood, canvas, and similar surfaces.

Figure 7-18
Using a texture as fill
7-17.xlsx
FrameSales sheet

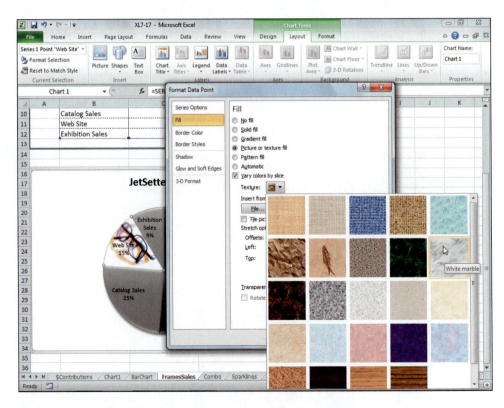

6. Hover over several texture tiles to see each ScreenTip.

7. Choose **White marble**. Click **Close**.

8. Select only the Catalog Sales slice. Click the **Chart Tools Format** tab, and then click the Shape Fill button 🖌. Hover at **Texture** to see the gallery.

9. Choose **Granite**.

10. Click a cell in the worksheet. Save your workbook as *[your initials]7-24*.

Creating Combination Charts

A *combination chart* uses more than one chart type or different number scales for two sets of values. For example, a column chart with a line chart can be used to compare daily phone minutes used (columns) and daily cost (lines). By using different chart types, it is generally easier to distinguish that there are two different sets of values illustrated. Another type of combination chart uses the same chart type for each set of values but includes a second number scale at the right. If a chart were comparing driving speed and miles per gallon for a car fleet, it might be best to show the speed values on one side of the chart and the MPG values on the other side.

Exercise 7-25   CREATE A CHART WITH TWO CHART TYPES

Most chart types cannot be combined. You can combine a column chart with a line or an area chart. Or you might combine a line with an area chart. In fact, if you try to create a combination chart that is not workable, Excel displays a message telling you that.

You'll create a new column chart in this exercise that initially shows the number of units sold and the selling price in two columns. By changing one of the columns to a line, you can better see what happens as the price increases.

1. In *[your initials]7-24*, click the arrow with the Name Box and choose **Frames**. This is a named range on the **Combo** worksheet tab.

2. Select cells J6:L15 and press [F11]. A clustered column chart sheet is inserted. It plots the units sold and the cost per unit.

3. On the **Chart Tools Design** tab, apply Style 25.

4. On the **Chart Tools Design** tab, click the Select Data button 🖽.

5. Choose **Series 1** in the Legend Entries (Series) list and click **Edit**. Key **Units Sold** and click **OK**.

6. Edit **Series 2** to display **Unit Cost** and click **OK**.

7. Click **OK** again. The legend is updated to show the series names.

8. Right-click any Units Sold column and choose **Change Series Chart Type**.

9. In the **Line** category, choose **Line with Markers**. Click **OK**. The Unit Sold series is now a line chart. The marker is a diamond shape that identifies the data point. Notice that the higher the selling price, the fewer units sold (see Figure 7-19 on the next page). This was not apparent when two columns were used.

Figure 7-19
Changing the chart
type for a data series
7-24.xlsx
Chart3 sheet

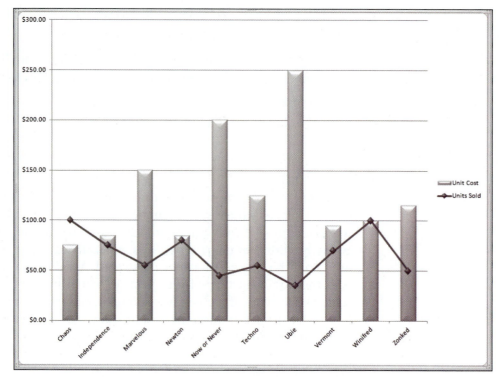

10. Right-click the line and choose **Format Data Series**.

11. On the **Line Color** pane, choose **Solid line**. Then choose **Black, Text 1** as the **Color**.

12. On the **Marker Options** pane, choose **Built-in**. Set the **Size** to **10**. Click **Close**.

13. Click the white chart background. The markers should be the same color as the line.

14. Right-click the line and choose **Format Data Series**. On the **Marker Fill** pane, choose **Solid fill**. Then set the color to match the line color.

15. On the **Marker Line Color** pane, choose **Solid line** and the same color.

16. On the **Shadow** pane, click the arrow for **Presets**. Choose **Offset Diagonal Bottom Right** in the **Outer** group.

17. Click **Close**. Click the white chart background.

Exercise 7-26   BUILD A COMBINATION CHART WITH A SECONDARY AXIS

The column-line combination chart is one way to demonstrate the difference in values. Another way to accomplish the same thing is to use a second set of values. A *secondary axis* is a set of axis values that are different from the first (primary) set. It appears at the right side of the chart.

The data for the chart in this exercise list the number of promotional pieces purchased and the cost. The chart compares dollars to units, and you'll use a column chart combined with an area chart.

1. Click the **Combo** worksheet tab. Click the arrow with the Name Box and choose **Promo**.

NOTE

The formulas in columns E and F multiply the number of pieces by a constant.

NOTE

Ranges for a chart need not be contiguous. Use Ctrl to select noncontiguous ranges.

2. Select cells B6:C11 and cells E6:E11. They represent the number of promotional pieces printed and the costs for the English version.

3. Click the **Insert** command tab. Choose a **Clustered Column** 2-D chart.

4. Click the Move Chart button 📊, and place the chart on its own sheet named **PromoPieces**. There are two series, one for the units and one for the dollars. Both series use the same value axis, and the number printed columns are disproportionately taller.

5. Right-click the legend and choose **Select Data**.

6. Change the name for **Series 1** to display **Units Printed**. Change the name for **Series 2** to **Cost**, and click **OK**. Click **OK** again.

7. On the **Chart Tools Layout** tab, click the Chart Title button 📊. Choose **Above Chart**.

8. Edit the placeholder to show **Costs and Units Printed**.

9. Right-click any Cost column and choose **Change Series Chart Type**.

10. Click **Area** in the left pane, and then choose **Area** as the chart subtype. Click **OK**.

11. Right-click somewhere in the Cost data area and choose **Format Data Series**.

12. On the **Fill** pane, choose **Gradient fill**. Click the arrow with **Preset colors** and choose **Moss**. Click **Close**.

13. Right-click a Units Printed column, and choose **Format Data Series**.

14. On the **Series Options** pane in the **Plot Series On** group, choose **Secondary Axis**. The selected series (Units Printed) will be plotted on a separate value axis. Click **Close**. The values on the right are units and relate to the Units Printed columns. The currency values on the left axis are the costs associated with the area chart.

Figure 7-20
Using a secondary axis in a chart
7-24.xlsx
PromoPieces sheet

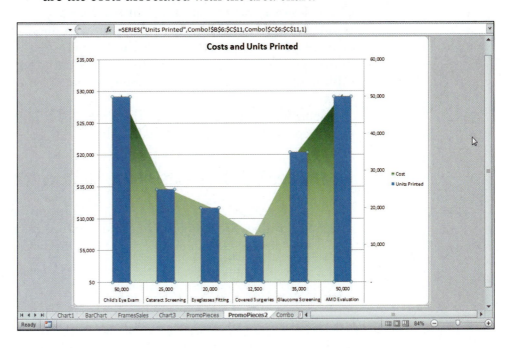

15. Right-click the legend and choose **Format Legend**. On the **Legend Options** pane, choose **Bottom** and click **Close**.

Exercise 7-27   ADD AXES TITLES

Since you are using two axes in this chart, you should add axes titles to clarify which set of values pertain to the shapes in the chart. An axis title appears at the left or right, in this case.

1. On the **Chart Tools Layout** tab, click the Axis Titles button 📊. Choose **Primary Vertical Axis Title**. Choose **Rotated Title**. The primary axis is at the left and a title placeholder is inserted.

2. Triple-click the placeholder text and key **Cost**. Click the white chart background.

3. Click the Axis Titles button 📊. Choose **Secondary Vertical Axis Title**. Choose **Rotated Title**. The secondary axis is at the right.

4. Triple-click the placeholder text and key **Units**. Click the white chart background.

5. Point at the secondary axis title and right-click. Choose **Format Axis Title**. Click **Alignment**. This pane includes options for rotating the title.

6. Click the arrow for **Text direction**. Choose **Rotate all text 90°**. Click **Close**.

7. Click the blue window background. Save the workbook as *[your initials]*7-27.

Inserting Sparklines

A *sparkline* is a miniature chart placed in its own cell alongside the data. Sparklines can be used to show trends for data without the need for building a separate chart. If you were to list your monthly expenditures for several categories of items in separate columns for each month (12 columns), you could insert sparklines in the 13th column to illustrate how your expenses progressed from month to month. In your workbook for this lesson, AllAround Vision Care has listed the cash donations per month in each city. Within this worksheet data, it can use sparklines to monitor the general trend in gift giving in each city.

Sparklines are a new feature in Excel 2010, and they are placed on a worksheet from the Insert command tab.

Exercise 7-28   INSERT LINE SPARKLINES

There are three styles of sparklines: line, column, and win/loss. Line and column sparklines are similar to line and column charts. A win/loss sparkline plots values in a stacked column chart. Sparklines can be inserted all at once by selecting the range and giving the command. You can also select the first sparkline in a column and copy it, like a formula. Sparklines are usually placed next to the data to which they refer. In this case, you will insert a column at the left of the data.

1. In *[your initials]*7-27, click the **Sparklines** worksheet tab. These are more detailed data about contributions for one year.

2. Insert a column at column C. The sparklines will be inserted in the new column C.

3. Click cell C6 and click the **Insert** command tab.

4. In the **Sparklines** group, click the Insert Line Sparkline. The Create Sparklines dialog box has two entry boxes, one for the data to be plotted and the other for the location of the sparkline.

5. In the **Data Range** box, select cells D6:O6, the values for each month.

6. In the **Location Range** box, verify that cell C6 has been assumed. If not, click that cell.

Figure 7-21
Create Sparklines dialog box
7-27.xlsx
Sparklines sheet

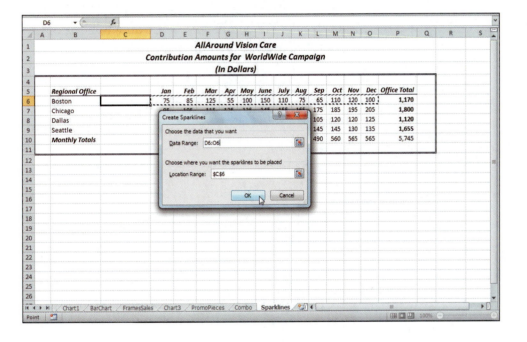

7. Click **OK**. One sparkline for Boston is displayed. You can see that AllAround Vision Care had some peaks and valleys in its cash collection.

8. Select rows 6:10 and make them **22.50 (30 pixels)** tall. The greater height will give the sparkline more visibility and clarity.

Exercise 7-29 FORMAT SPARKLINES

The Sparkline Tools Design command tab becomes available when you choose a cell that includes a sparkline. There are groups on this command tab with options for changing the data range, showing data points, and setting the color.

1. Click cell C6 and click the **Sparkline Tools Design** tab.

2. In the **Style** group, click the More button ⏷. The colors are from the current document theme.

3. Find and click **Sparkline Style Dark #3**.

4. In the **Show** group, click to place a checkmark for **Markers**. The marker is the symbol that designates the value on the line. It is a tiny diamond on your sparkline.

5. In the **Style** group, click the Marker Color button 🔲. You can change the color for all the markers or only for certain ones.

6. Choose **High Point**, and choose **Tan, Background 2, Darker 90%** in the third column. The marker that represents the highest value is recolored.

7. Click the Fill handle for cell C6 and drag to copy the sparkline to cell C10. Each sparkline illustrates the data in its row.

Figure 7-22
Restyled and copied sparklines
7-27.xlsx
Sparklines sheet

	A	B	C	D	E	F	G	H	I	J	K	L	M	N	O	P	Q	R
1							*AllAround Vision Care*											
2							*Contribution Amounts for WorldWide Campaign*											
3							*(In Dollars)*											
4																		
5		*Regional Office*			*Jan*	*Feb*	*Mar*	*Apr*	*May*	*June*	*July*	*Aug*	*Sep*	*Oct*	*Nov*	*Dec*	*Office Total*	
6		Boston			75	85	125	55	100	150	110	75	65	110	120	100	1,170	
7		Chicago			95	105	115	125	135	145	155	165	175	185	195	205	1,800	
8		Dallas			125	105	85	65	45	60	75	90	105	120	120	125	1,120	
9		Seattle			100	120	110	130	150	170	165	155	145	145	130	135	1,655	
10		*Monthly Totals*			395	415	435	375	430	525	505	485	490	560	565	565	5,745	
11																		
12																		

8. Save the workbook as *[your initials]*7-29. Close the workbook.

Using Online Help

In addition to the popular column, bar, line, and pie charts, there are several charts that are more specialized for certain types of data. Use Help to explore some of these chart types.

Use Help to learn about charts:

1. In a new workbook, press [F1].

2. Find and review topics about bubble charts and high-low charts.

3. Close the Help window when finished.

Lesson 7   Summary

- Charts can be objects in a worksheet, or they can be separate chart sheets.
- A chart is linked to the data that it is plotting. If the data are edited, the chart automatically reflects the changes.
- There are three Charts Tools command tabs: Design, Layout, and Format. They are available when the chart or one of its objects is selected.
- The Selection and Visibility pane aids in selecting and layering objects, such as charts, in a worksheet.
- The chart layout specifies where various elements are positioned. The layout can be changed at any time.
- All chart elements have formatting attributes that include fill, outline, and effects. There are preset styles, or you can design your own formats.
- If you select data and press F11, Excel creates an automatic clustered column chart sheet.
- Move a chart object by selecting it and dragging it. Size a chart object by dragging one of its selection handles.
- After a chart is created, you can add or delete data points and/or an entire data series.
- There are various labels that can be placed on a chart including a main title, data labels, axes labels, a legend, or a data table.
- Although charts typically use solid color for columns, slices, and bars, you can use images, textures, or gradients to add visual appeal to your charts.
- There are preset gradients with multiple color stops. You can edit them or create your own gradients by adding and removing color stops.
- Combination charts have at least two series and use different chart types for each series.
- Some combination charts use a secondary axis, because the values for what is being plotted are disproportionate.
- Sparklines are charts within cells. They can use lines or columns to graph a data range on the worksheet.

LESSON 7		Command Summary	
Feature	**Button**	**Ribbon Location**	**Keyboard**
Axis titles, add		Chart Tools Layout, Labels	
Axis, add		Chart Tools Layout, Axes	
Axis, format		Chart Tools Format, Current Selection	Ctrl + 1
Chart layout		Chart Tools Design, Chart Layouts	
Chart object, create		Insert, Charts	Alt + F1
Chart sheet, create		Insert, Charts	F11
Chart title, add		Chart Tools Layout, Labels	
Chart type		Chart Tools Design, Type	
Data labels		Chart Tools Layout, Labels	
Data labels, format		Chart Tools Format, Current Selection	Ctrl + 1
Data series, format		Chart Tools Format, Current Selection	Ctrl + 1
Data source		Chart Tools Design, Data	
Data table, add		Chart Tools Layout, Labels	
Gridlines		Chart Tools Layout, Axes	
Marker color		Sparkline Tools Design, Style	
Move chart		Chart Tools Design, Location	
Selection and visibility pane		Chart Tools Format, Arrange	
Shape fill		Chart Tools Format, Shape Styles	
Shape style		Chart Tools Format, Shape Styles	
Sparkline		Insert, Sparklines	

Please visit our Online Learning Center, *www.lessonapproach2010.com,* **where you will find the following review materials:**

- **Concepts Review**

  True/False Questions

  Short Answer Questions

  Critical Thinking Questions

- **Skills Review**

  Review Exercises that target single skills

  Lesson Applications

  Review Exercises that challenge students by testing multiple skills in each exercise

- **On Your Own**

  Open-ended exercises that require students to synthesize multiple skills and apply creativity and problem-solving as they would in a real world business situation

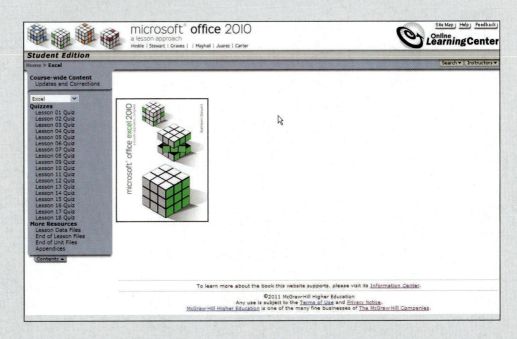

Lesson 8
Working with Excel Tables

OBJECTIVES *After completing this lesson, you will be able to:*

1. Create an Excel table.
2. Work with the Table Tools Design tab.
3. Sort and filter records in a table.
4. Identify structured references.
5. Use COUNTIFS and SUMIFS.
6. Create a calculated column in a table.
7. Set print areas and custom views.

Estimated Time: 1½ hours

With its table features, Excel provides a way to manage data similar to database software such as Access. Excel is not a relational database manager like Access, but it does provide commands to arrange, display, group, and perform calculations on list-style data. An Excel *table* is a list of related information with a row of headers (titles) followed by rows of data. Each row represents a single entity, such as a product, an employee, or an account.

Companies like AllAround Vision Care can use Excel tables in worksheets that list employee data. It can keep patient information in a table arrangement too. Any data that is list-like can be formatted as an Excel table and take advantage of special Table commands.

Creating an Excel Table

Data that can be formatted as a table are keyed in a regular worksheet using columns and rows. It includes a *header row* with descriptive labels or titles, followed immediately by rows of data. A worksheet can have multiple tables, and each can be managed independently.

There is terminology that is common to tables or lists whether you use Excel, Access, or Word. A row of data is referred to as a *record*. A record includes all the categories of information for that row. A *field* is a single category of information; each column in a table is a field. In an employee table, for example, there is a field for "Last Name," and a field for "First Name." A unique *field name* is the label in the header row for each column. An individual piece of data in a column is a *field value*.

When you prepare data that will be formatted as an Excel table, follow these guidelines:

- Key field names or descriptive labels in the first row. This is the header row.

- Do not repeat field names in the header row.

- Start field names with a letter.

- Do not mix data types in the columns. For example, do not enter values and text in the same column.

- Do not leave blank rows within the data.

Figure 8-1
Excel data that can be formatted as a table

	A	B	C	D	E	F	G
1	AllAround Vision Care						
2	Exempt and Nonexempt Personnel						
3	ID #	Last Name	First Name	Hire Date	Birth Date	Position/Department	Location
4	1	Conrad	Rita	2/3/2006	12/20/1953	Vice-President	Chicago
5	7	Conrad	Henry	2/3/2006	12/25/1957	President	Chicago
6	9	Steinbeck	Sarah	2/5/2010	1/28/1982	Treasurer	Chicago
7	17	Lopez	Harriet	7/10/2009	7/16/1979	Executive Assistant	Chicago
8	5	Sante	Juan	3/18/2007	5/8/1970	Fund-Raising	Dallas
9	8	Eassa	Nassar	3/1/2010	3/2/1972	Fund-Raising	Boston
10	11	Calcivechia	Maria	10/5/2009	9/14/1961	Fund-Raising	Seattle
11	14	Johnson	Alfred	2/3/2006	6/9/1975	Fund-Raising	Boston
12	16	Pawlowski	Jane	5/29/2009	4/3/1980	Fund-Raising	Chicago
13	3	Ladewig	Glenn	2/23/2007	6/3/1959	Human Resources	Boston
14	4	McDonald	Robin	7/6/2005	7/23/1975	Human Resources	Chicago
15	12	Alverez	Toni	7/31/2009	3/30/1979	Human Resources	Dallas
16	19	Engledahl	Bobbi	6/16/2008	10/14/1980	Human Resources	Chicago
17	20	Hughes	Brittany	11/21/2009	5/19/1984	Human Resources	Seattle
18	2	Stewart	Kathleen	5/2/2006	9/7/1975	Marketing	Dallas
19	6	Sumara	Keiko	2/3/2008	2/20/1982	Marketing	Seattle
20	10	Artagnan	Ted	12/4/2009	8/3/1961	Marketing	Seattle
21	15	Chavez	José	5/5/2010	8/15/1980	Marketing	Chicago
22	18	Gaylord	David	8/1/2009	3/17/1981	Marketing	Boston

Exercise 8-1   ARRANGE WINDOWS AND COPY DATA TO A NEW WORKBOOK

AllAround Vision Care currently lists employee data on separate sheets according to department. Each sheet includes the same header row with the same field names. To take advantage of table features, you can copy all the data into a worksheet in a new workbook. Copying or moving data from one workbook to another is the same as copying or moving data within a worksheet or from one sheet to another. For the paste destination, however, you switch to the other workbook and its appropriate sheet. When you work with multiple workbooks at a time, you can arrange them so that they are side by side on the screen, or you can leave each workbook in a maximized view.

1. Open **Excel_Lesson8**. (If the workbook opens in Protected View, click **Enable Editing**.) This workbook has a separate sheet for each of four departments.

2. Click each worksheet tab to review the data. Then return to the **Administration** worksheet.

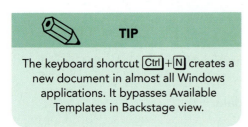

TIP

The keyboard shortcut Ctrl+N creates a new document in almost all Windows applications. It bypasses Available Templates in Backstage view.

3. Press Ctrl+N. A new workbook opens. It is maximized and active or on top of the **Excel_Lesson8** workbook. You have two workbooks open and can see that in the Windows taskbar. The new workbook is named **Book***N* where *N* is the next consecutive number in your work session.

4. Click the **View** command tab. The **Window** group includes commands to arrange open workbooks.

5. Click the Arrange All button . The Arrange Windows dialog box opens. The workbook that is active when you arrange windows horizontally appears in the top half of the screen.

6. Choose **Horizontal** and click **OK**. Both workbooks are displayed in equally sized windows. The active workbook has scroll bars and shaded row and column headings for the active cell.

Figure 8-2
Tiled windows

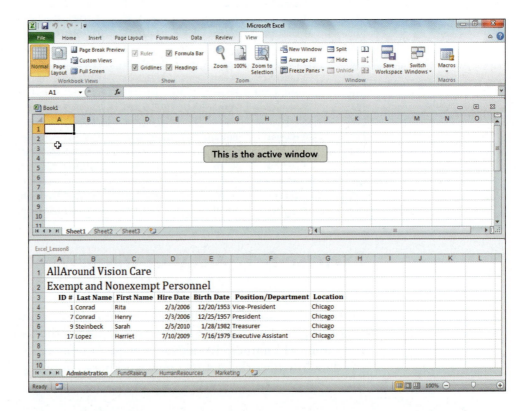

7. On the **Administration** worksheet tab, click cell A1. Press F8, and then press → to extend the selection to column G.

8. Press Ctrl+↓ to extend the selection to row 7.

9. On the **Home** command tab, click the Copy button 📋.

10. Click cell A1 in the blank workbook, and click the Paste button 📋. The data are copied, and the Paste Options button 📋 appears.

11. Click the Paste Options button 📋 and choose 📋 **Keep Source Column Widths**. The columns widths from the original data are applied.

12. Click cell A8 in the new workbook. Click the **FundRaising** worksheet tab.

13. Select cells A4:G8 and press Ctrl+C.

14. Press Ctrl+F6 to switch to the new workbook, and press Ctrl+V. The keyboard shortcut to switch to another open file is the same in all Windows applications.

15. Click cell A13 in the new workbook and maximize its window. The windows are no longer tiled.

16. Press Ctrl+F6. The command to switch windows is the same.

TIP

You can click the workbook name on the Windows taskbar to move between open workbooks.

17. Click the **HumanResources** worksheet tab. Select cells A4:G8, and copy them to cell A13 in your new workbook.

18. Copy the appropriate cells from the **Marketing** worksheet tab in **Excel_Lesson8** to your workbook.

19. Close the **Excel_Lesson8** workbook.

20. Press Ctrl+Home. Save the workbook as *[your initials]*8-1.

Exercise 8-2   CREATE AN EXCEL TABLE

To create an Excel table, you select the data and choose a table style. So it is basically a format command. The Table Styles gallery offers light, medium, and dark color schemes, some with borders, some without. After the table is identified and formatted, the Table Tools Design tab provides commands and options for refining the table.

1. Click any name in the **First Name** column.

2. On the **Home** command tab in the **Styles** group, click the Format as Table button 📊. The gallery of table styles opens.

3. Find and click **Table Style Medium 1**. The Format as Table dialog box shows assumed table cells, A1:G22, all the contiguous data to the active cell. You should not include the labels in rows 1:2.

4. Click cell A3. Drag to select cells A3:G22.

5. Click to place a checkmark for **My table has headers**. The header row is row 3.

6. Click **OK**. The row data are formatted as a table, and the Table Tools Design tab is visible.

7. Click cell F1. The table is deselected. Filter arrows with drop-down lists have been added to the header row, and fill is applied to every other row by the table style. The labels in row 3 are invisible, because they are the same color as the fill used in this particular table style.

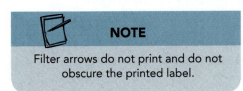

NOTE

Filter arrows do not print and do not obscure the printed label.

Figure 8-3
Excel table
**8-1.xlsx
Sheet1 sheet**

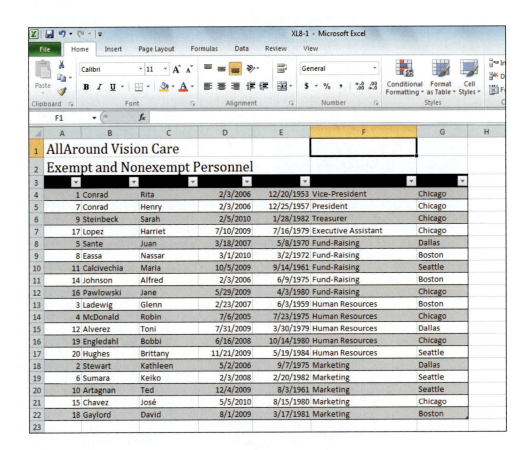

Working with the Table Tools Design Tab

The Table Tools Design tab appears when the active cell is any cell within the table. The command tab has four groups for managing the contents and the look of a table. The Properties group allows you to name a table and resize it. The Tools group has a command button to convert the table to a simple data range and another button to remove duplicate records. A third button pertains to PivotTables, a more sophisticated table layout for data.

NOTE

A PivotTable is a special type of table in which you can arrange data interactively by dragging elements into the design.

The External Table Data group on the Table Tools Design tab has commands for managing data when they are linked or downloaded from an outside source. This is a common business task, because many offices are linked nonstop to corporate headquarters, supplier Web sites, or governmental agencies. The Table Style Options group relates to the design of the table as do the Table Styles.

Exercise 8-3   SET TABLE STYLE OPTIONS

From the Table Style Options and the Table Styles groups, you can change the color scheme, set whether alternate rows have shading, and show or hide header and total rows.

1. Click any cell within the table. Click the **Table Tools Design** command tab.
2. In the **Table Style Options** group, click to deselect **Header Row**. The first row of labels and the filter arrows are toggled off.
3. Click to deselect **Banded Rows**. This removes the fill in alternate rows.
4. Click to select **Banded Columns**. The fill is applied to every other column.
5. Click to select **First Column**. This style shows the data in the first column in bold to emphasize it.
6. Click to deselect both **Banded Columns** and **First Column**.
7. Click to select **Header Row** and **Banded Rows**.
8. Click to select **Total Row**. This row appears at the bottom of the table. Each cell in row 23, when clicked, will display a drop-down list from which you can choose a function.

Figure 8-4
Choosing a function for the total row
8-1.xlsx
Sheet1 sheet

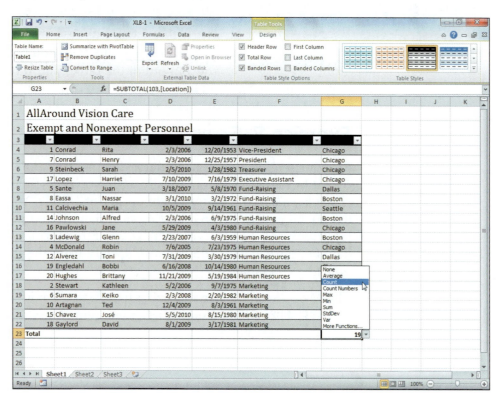

9. Click cell G23 and click its arrow. A **Count** has been calculated since the data are labels.

10. Click cell B23 and click its arrow. Choose **Sum**. The result is zero (0) because the SUM function ignores labels.

11. Click cell B23 and its arrow. Choose **None**.

12. Click to remove the checkmark for **Total Row** in the **Table Style Options** group.

13. Click the More button ⊽ for **Table Styles**. Hover over several different styles to see a preview of your table with a different style.

14. Choose **Table Style Light 15**. Now the header row labels are visible.

Exercise 8-4   ADD A RECORD TO A TABLE

When AllAround Vision Care hires a new worker, that person's data are added to the end of the table. A table grows to accommodate a new row if you press Tab when the insertion point is in the last column of the last row. AutoComplete and Pick From Drop-down List both work in tables too.

1. Click cell G22, currently the last row in your table.

2. Press Tab. A new row with appropriate fill is added.

3. Key **21** in the **ID** column for row 23 and press Tab.

4. Key your first and last name in the appropriate columns.

5. In cell D23, press Ctrl+; to insert today's date in cell D23 and press Tab. Key your birth date in mm/dd/yy format in cell E23.

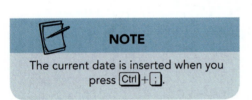

NOTE

The current date is inserted when you press Ctrl+;.

6. Key **f** in the **Position/Department** column, and press Tab. AutoComplete works in a table.

7. Key a character to choose any city from column G, and press Enter. The insertion point moves to the next row but out of the table. The Table Tools Design tab is no longer visible.

Exercise 8-5   RESIZE A TABLE

Resizing a table involves adding or deleting rows and/or columns. Although the table does grow automatically when you press Tab to add a row, there is a *sizing handle* at the bottom right corner of a table. You can drag this handle to expand a table before entering new data, if you prefer. If you contract a table with this handle, you remove the table formatting from the data; the data are not deleted. You can also specify from the Resize Table dialog box how to size a table.

1. Place the pointer on the sizing handle at the bottom right corner of cell G23. The pointer changes to a two-pointed arrow.

2. Drag down to expand the table to row 28. The blank rows include the appropriate fill.

3. Place the pointer on the sizing handle, and drag to shrink the table to row 22. Data are not deleted; it is just not part of the table.

4. Size the table to include your data.

5. Click any cell in the table and click the **Table Tools Design** tab.

6. In the **Properties** group, click the Resize Table button .

7. In the Resize Table dialog box, edit the range address to show **$A$3:h23**.

Figure 8-5
Resizing a table
8-1.xlsx
Sheet1 sheet

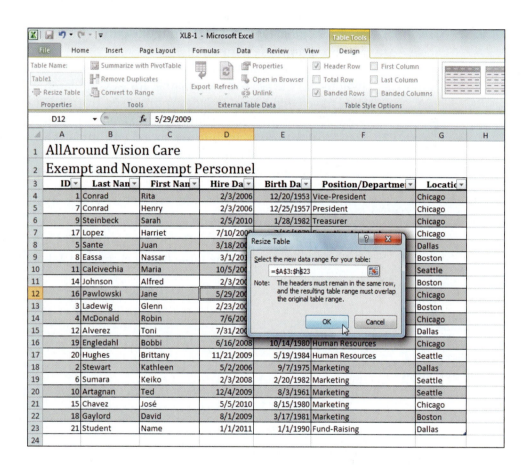

8. Click **OK**. A new column is inserted at the right with matching formats and a default label in the header row.

9. Click cell H3 and key **Group** and press Alt+Enter. Key **Assignment** and press Enter. Widen the column to show the label on two lines.

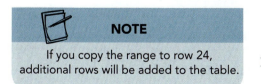

NOTE

If you copy the range to row 24, additional rows will be added to the table.

10. In cell H4, key **1**. Key **2** in cell H5. Key **3** in cell H6. Continue with **4** and **5** in cells H7:H8.

11. Select cells H4:H8 and press Ctrl+C.

12. Click cell H9 and press Ctrl + V. Click cell H14 and press Ctrl + V. Continue until you reach row 23.

13. Press Esc to remove the marquee.

Exercise 8-6 NAME A TABLE AND REMOVE DUPLICATES

Each table that you create in a workbook is given a default defined name. It is Table*N*, *N* being a consecutive number during your work session. You can rename a table to provide a more descriptive name. The table name, like any range name, can be used in formulas rather than referring to cells A3:H23. In addition, table names appear in the Formula AutoComplete list for functions and programming commands.

It is not unusual to find duplicates in large tables. Entering data can be tedious, so the person responsible for keying data can make an error. If the data have been downloaded or purchased from a list provider, they may not have been monitored carefully. A *duplicate row* is a row that has exactly the same information in one or more columns. The table tools include a command to remove duplicate rows from a table. It does not preview which rows will be removed, so be careful when using this command.

NOTE

Tables are named and numbered during a work session. Your table number may be different.

1. Click any cell in the table. Click the **Table Tools Design** tab.

2. In the **Properties** group, click the **Table Name** box. The table has been named **Table1** by default.

Figure 8-6
Renaming a table
8-1.xlsx
Sheet1 sheet

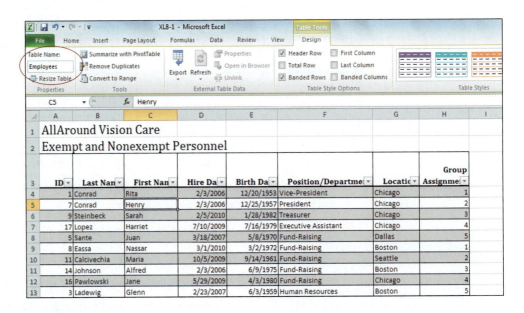

3. Key **Employees** and press Enter. The table is renamed.

4. Click cell H23 and press Tab.

NOTE

As you copy a date, you'll first see the serial number for that date.

5. Press Ctrl + ' (apostrophe) in cell A24. This keyboard shortcut copies the data from the cell directly above.

6. Press [Tab]. Press [Ctrl]+['] in each cell in row 24 to create an exact copy of your record.

7. If you have accidentally added a blank row to your table, delete that row.

8. Click any cell in the table. In the **Tools** group, click the Remove Duplicates button . The Remove Duplicates dialog box opens. You can specify which columns might contain duplicate data.

9. Click **Unselect All**. If the table has thousands of records, it is faster to select only those fields that would clearly identify duplicates.

10. Click to select **Last Name** and **First Name**.

Figure 8-7
Removing Duplicates
dialog box
8-1.xlsx
Sheet1 sheet

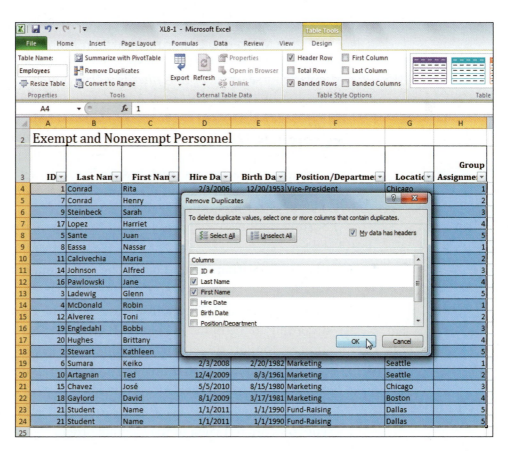

11. Click **OK**. One duplicate row has been removed, and the remaining 20 records are unique. You did not have an opportunity to confirm what was deleted.

12. Click **OK** in the message box.

TIP

You can undo a Remove Duplicates task.

Sorting and Filtering Records

The capability to manage rows of data is a major purpose for formatting your work as a table. Two such management tasks are sorting and filtering. These two commands can be carried out separately or together.

Records in a table are often entered in no particular order or in chronological order as the data are available. The Sort commands enable you to reorder and display the records in the way that best meets your work needs. For example, an office manager who needs to contact all employees in a particular city can arrange the rows by city. In its patient table, AllAround Vision Care could sort the rows by insurance company to identify which carriers are most often billed.

Filters enable you to keep a large list but display only required information. In its employee table, AllAround could filter the list to show only personnel in the Marketing Department. If your school uses an Excel table to list students' enrollments, it can filter the table to show all students enrolled in a particular course or section. A *filter* is a criterion, a requirement or a condition. A filter hides rows that do not meet your criteria.

Exercise 8-7   SORT RECORDS IN A TABLE

An *ascending sort* arranges rows in A-to-Z order or lowest value to highest value using the data in one of the columns. A *descending sort* organizes rows in Z-to-A order or highest value to lowest.

Sorting options are available from the filter arrows next to the header row labels.

1. Click the **Last Name** filter arrow. The sort choices are listed first in the gallery.

2. Choose **Sort A to Z**. The gallery closes, and the rows are alphabetized according to the name in column B. The filter arrow includes an icon to indicate the sort direction (ascending).

3. Click the **Last Name** filter arrow. Choose **Sort Z to A**. The rows are alphabetized in reverse, from Z to A.

4. Click the arrow next to the Undo button ⟲. Undo the two **Sort** actions. The rows are returned to the original order.

Exercise 8-8   SORT BY MULTIPLE COLUMNS

Sorting by more than one column sorts within a sort. If people have the same last name, records can be further sorted using the first name. So "Smith, Alice" would come before "Smith, Carol" in an ascending sort. In your table, you can sort first by position and department and then by city. Multiple-level sorting requires that you use the Sort dialog box.

1. Click the **Position/Department** filter arrow.

2. Choose **Sort A to Z**. The rows are alphabetized by department name. But notice the city names for the Fund-Raising Department; they are in random order.

3. Click the **Position/Department** filter arrow.

4. Choose **Sort by Color** and then choose **Custom Sort**. This opens the Sort dialog box, which shows your existing sort. Because this table has fill color, you can arrange the rows by color too. Color choices are listed in the **Sort On** list.

5. Click **Add Level**. A **Then by** group opens for the second sort order.

6. Click the arrow for the **Then by** box and choose **Location**.

7. Verify that **Sort On** shows **Values** and that **A to Z** is the **Order**.

Figure 8-8
Sorting by more than one column
8-1.xlsx
Sheet1 sheet

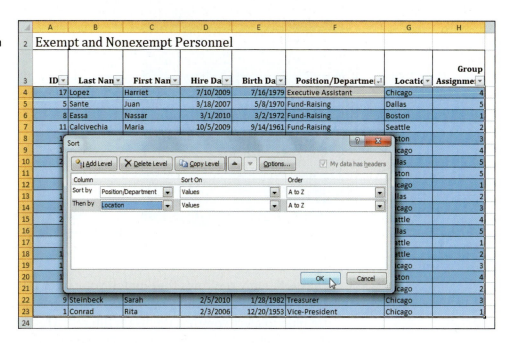

8. Click **OK**. The records are still sorted by the position and department name. Now, however, the records from a given department are organized in alphabetical order by the city name.

9. Click the **ID** filter arrow. The sort choices refer to a column that has values rather than labels.

10. Choose **Sort Smallest to Largest**. This sort arranges the rows by ID number and removes the previous sort.

Exercise 8-9 USE TEXT FILTERS

Filter commands are available from the filter arrow lists and depend on the type of data in the column.

1. Click the **Position/Department** filter arrow. Since this column has labels, text filters are available. Below the Search box, all labels are selected, so all are shown.

2. Click to remove the checkmark for **(Select All)**. Then click to place a checkmark for **Human Resources**. This is the filter, the criterion.

Figure 8-9
Filtering by department
8-1.xlsx
Sheet1 sheet

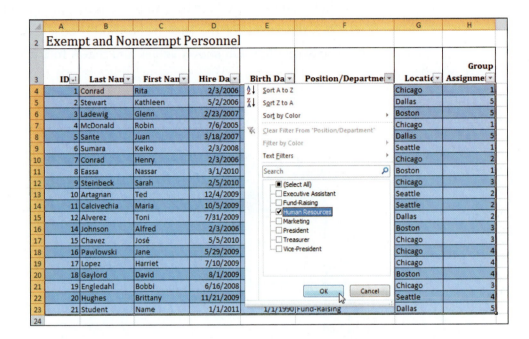

3. Click **OK**. Only the rows that match your filter (Human Resources) are displayed. The other rows are hidden. The row headings for visible rows are blue to alert you that the list is filtered. The filter arrow for **Position/Department** includes a filter icon. The status bar indicates "5 of 20 records found."

TIP

This type of filter is described as an "Or condition" in database terminology, because either Boston or Chicago meets the criteria.

4. Click the **Position/Department** filter arrow, and click to place a checkmark for **(Select All)**. Click **OK**.

5. Click the **Location** filter arrow, and remove the checkmark for **(Select All)**.

6. Select **Boston** and **Chicago**. Click **OK**. Employees in both cities are listed.

7. Click the **Position/Department** filter arrow. Deselect all the choices and choose **Marketing**. Click **OK**. This adds a second filter, which now displays only employees (two) in the Marketing Department in Boston or Chicago.

8. Click the **Position/Department** filter arrow and choose **(Select All)**. Click **OK**. Repeat for the **Location** column.

Exercise 8-10   USE DATE FILTERS

Date filters provide choices that include only the year, only a month, or any combination.

1. Click the **Hire Date** filter arrow. Each year is listed with a plus symbol to indicate that the year can be expanded. Don't do that yet.

2. Click to deselect **(Select All)**.

3. Click to select **2010** and click **OK**. Persons hired during 2010 are listed.

4. Click the **Hire Date** filter arrow. Choose **Clear Filter from "Hire Date"** from the list. The filter is removed, the same as if you had selected **(Select All)**.

5. Click the **Hire Date** filter arrow. Click to deselect **(Select All)**. Click the plus symbol with **2010**. The year data expand and list only those months during which an employee was hired.

6. Click the plus symbol with **2009**. Employees were added in more months during this year.

7. Click to place checkmarks for **May** for **2010** and **2009**. Click **OK**. (Two matches, unless your data fit the criteria).

Figure 8-10
Building a date filter
8-1.xlsx
Sheet1 sheet

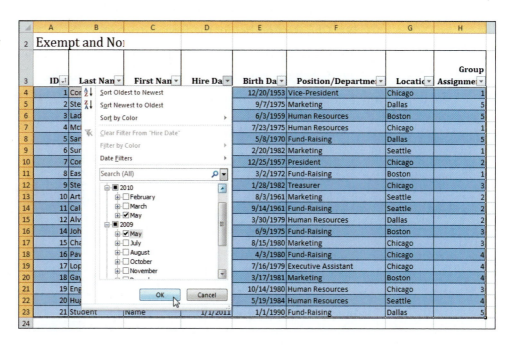

8. Click the **Hire Date** filter arrow. Choose **Clear Filter from "Hire Date"** from the list.

9. Click the **Hire Date** filter arrow. Hover at **Date Filters**. Many date filters are listed.

10. Choose **All Dates in the Period** and then choose **September**. No employees were hired in September of any year (unless you added yourself in September).

11. Click the **Hire Date** filter arrow. Choose **Date Filters**.

12. Choose **All Dates in the Period** and then choose **May**. Three employees were hired in May of any year (four, if you added yourself in May).

13. Click the **Hire Date** filter arrow. Choose **Clear Filter from "Hire Date"**.

14. Click the **Birth Date** filter arrow.

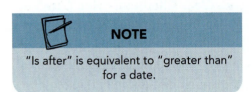

NOTE

"Is after" is equivalent to "greater than" for a date.

15. Choose **Date Filters** and then choose **Custom Filter**. The Custom AutoFilter dialog box opens. In a custom filter, you can key a date rather than choose one from the list.

16. In the first entry box, click the arrow and choose **is after or equal to**.

17. Click in the entry box to the right and key **6/1/80**. This filter specifies that the birth date be on or after June 1, 1980.

18. Click **OK**. Six employees meet the criteria (and maybe yourself).

19. Click the **Birth Date** filter arrow. Choose **Date Filters** and then **Custom Filter**. Your current filter is indicated.

20. Choose **And** below the first entry box.

21. Click the down arrow for the box below the And and Or buttons.

22. Scroll the list and choose **is before or equal to**.

23. Click in the entry box to the right and key **12/31/80**. You can enter a year with two or four digits.

Figure 8-11
Building a custom filter
8-1.xlsx
Sheet1 sheet

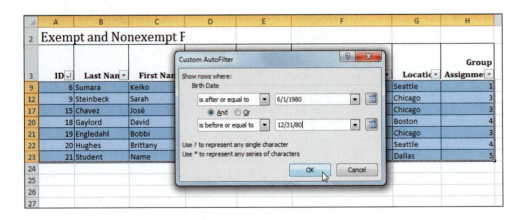

24. Click **OK**. These employees (two, plus yourself) were born between June 1 and December 31, 1980.

25. Clear the **Birth Date** filter.

Identifying Structured References

When you create an Excel table, the columns are automatically assigned a defined name based on the label in the header row. It is similar to a range name but is known as a structured reference. A *structured reference* is a defined name that refers to an identifiable range within an Excel table. Structured references include all the header row labels. Other structured references for a table are #All, #Data, #Headers, #This Row, and #Total Row; these are built-in, reserved names and include the # symbol. Structured reference names appear in Formula AutoComplete after their trigger character is keyed, but they do not appear in the Paste Names list.

Exercise 8-11   IDENTIFY STRUCTURED REFERENCES

The total row in a table appears as the last row when you toggle it on. It includes calculation choices for each column and automatically shows a sum for numeric columns. The total row uses the SUBTOTAL function from the Math & Trig category and structured references from the table. The first argument in this function is a number which specifies the calculation that is performed.

TABLE 8-1 SUBTOTAL Function_Num Argument Options

Function_Num	Function_Num	Function
1	101	AVERAGE
2	102	COUNT
3	103	COUNTA
4	104	MAX
5	105	MIN
6	106	PRODUCT
7	107	STDEV
8	108	STDEVP
9	109	SUM
10	110	VAR
11	111	VARP

1. Click the **Formulas** command tab and the Name Manager button 🗐. The table name **Employees** appears as a range name, but there are no structured reference names listed.
2. Click **Close**.
3. Click any table cell. Click the **Table Tools Design** tab. In the **Table Style Options** group, click to select **Total Row**.

4. Click cell B24 and click its arrow. Choose **Count**. There are 20 names in the list.

5. Look at the formula bar. The Total Row uses SUBTOTAL. Its arguments include a number (103) that specifies which subtotal function is being used. The second argument is the column or field [Last Name].

6. Click the Insert Function button f_x in the formula bar. The Function Arguments dialog box shows the two arguments. "[Last Name]" is a structured reference to the column. The first argument **Function_num 103** uses COUNTA and ignores hidden values.

Figure 8-12
Structured reference
to a table column
8-1.xlsx
Sheet1 sheet

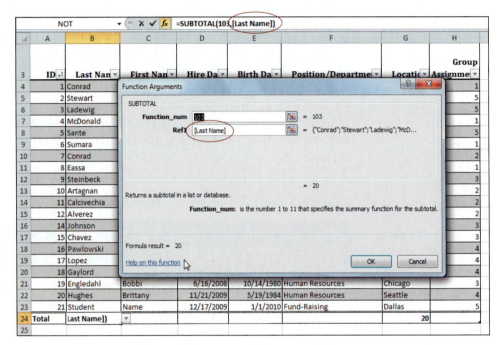

7. Click **Cancel** in the Function Arguments dialog box.

8. Click cell H24, and choose **Max** as the total row function.

9. Click the Expand Formula Bar button. Look in the formula bar to see the structured reference to "[Group Assignment]." Note also that SUBTOTAL 104 is the MAX function.

10. Collapse the formula bar.

11. Click cell H24. Click the arrow and choose **None** as the total row function.

Exercise 8-12   USE COUNTIF WITH A STRUCTURED REFERENCE

When you key a formula, you can trigger the display of function and range names in Formula AutoComplete by keying the first character in the function name. A *trigger* is a key that starts some action. This initial Formula AutoComplete list includes table names. After the function, range, or table is selected, you can trigger the display of structured reference names. The key to trigger the display of structured reference names is [(left square bracket).

COUNTIF, from the statistical category, works like AVERAGEIF and SUMIF. It counts nonblank cells that meet the criteria that you set as an argument.

1. Click cell F25. In this cell, you'll count how many persons are in the Fund-Raising Department.

2. Key **=coun** and double-click **COUNTIF**. The first argument is the range, which is the Position/Department column in the Employees table.

3. Key **e** to display the Formula AutoComplete list for functions and defined names beginning with the letter "E." Table names are included and show the defined name icon to distinguish them from function names.

4. Double-click **Employees**, the table name. Next you need the column name.

5. Key **[** to trigger the display of the structured references.

Figure 8-13
Structured references in Formula AutoComplete
8-1.xlsx
Sheet1 sheet

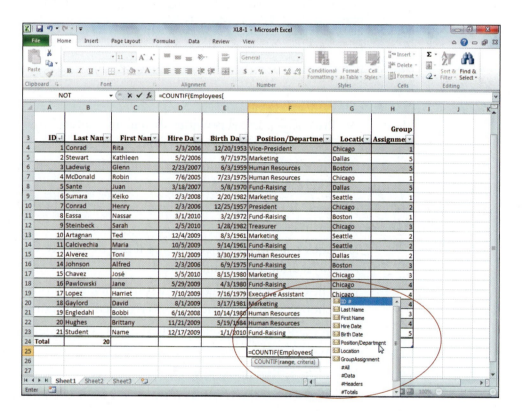

6. Double-click **Position/Department** and key **]** to complete the reference.

7. Key a comma to move to the **criteria** argument.

8. Key **"fund*"** to count records that show "Fund-Raising." The quotation marks are necessary when you key a formula; they identify text. You need not capitalize the criteria, and you can use a wildcard to save having to key the entire label (see Figure 8-14 on the next page).

REVIEW

The COUNTIF function has two arguments, the range and the criteria. It is similar to SUMIF and AVERAGEIF.

Figure 8-14
Keying a COUNTIF
function
8-1.xlsx
Sheet1 sheet

`=COUNTIF(Employees[Position/Department],"fund*"`

First Name	Hire Date	Birth Date	Position/Department	Location	Group Assignment
...ita	2/3/2006	12/20/1953	Vice-President	Chicago	1
...athleen	5/2/2006	9/7/1975	Marketing	Dallas	5
...lenn	2/23/2007	6/3/1959	Human Resources	Boston	5
...obin	7/6/2005	7/23/1975	Human Resources	Chicago	1
...uan	3/18/2007	5/8/1970	Fund-Raising	Dallas	5
...eiko	2/3/2008	2/20/1982	Marketing	Seattle	1
...enry	2/3/2006	12/25/1957	President	Chicago	2
...assar	3/1/2010	3/2/1972	Fund-Raising	Boston	1
...arah	2/5/2010	1/28/1982	Treasurer	Chicago	3
...ed	12/4/2009	8/3/1961	Marketing	Seattle	2
...Maria	10/5/2009	9/14/1961	Fund-Raising	Seattle	2
...oni	7/31/2009	3/30/1979	Human Resources	Dallas	2
...lfred	2/3/2006	6/9/1975	Fund-Raising	Boston	3
...osé	5/5/2010	8/15/1980	Marketing	Chicago	3
...ane	5/29/2009	4/3/1980	Fund-Raising	Chicago	4
...arriet	7/10/2009	7/16/1979	Executive Assistant	Chicago	4
...avid	8/1/2009	3/17/1981	Marketing	Boston	4
...obbi	6/16/2008	10/14/1980	Human Resources	Chicago	3
...rittany	11/21/2009	5/19/1984	Human Resources	Seattle	4
...ame	12/17/2009	1/1/2010	Fund-Raising	Dallas	5
				20	

`=COUNTIF(Employees[Position/Department],"fund*"`
COUNTIF(range, **criteria**)

9. Press Enter. Excel provides the closing parenthesis for the formula. There are six employees in fund-raising.

10. Click cell F8. Hold down Ctrl, and click each cell in column F that shows **Fund-Raising**.

11. Look at the AutoCalculate area in the status bar to confirm your formula results "Count: 6."

12. Click cell D25. In this cell, you'll use COUNTIF to count employees hired after a particular date.

13. Click the **Formulas** command tab. Click the More Functions button. Choose **Statistical** and COUNTIF. The first argument is the range.

14. In the **Range** box, select cells D4:D23. The structured reference name is supplied.

15. In the **Criteria** box, key **>1/1/10**.

16. Click **OK**. If the result is formatted as date, change it to general. Verify that there are three persons hired after January 1, 2010 (four, counting yourself).

17. Save the workbook as *[your initials]***8-12**. Close the workbook.

Using COUNTIFS and SUMIFS

Filtering and sorting data are common tasks in Excel tables. In large lists of data, however, there are also functions that can quickly analyze the data in various ways. Two functions that are well suited to large lists of data, whether they are formatted as tables or not, are COUNTIFS and SUMIFS. COUNTIFS belongs to the statistical function category, and SUMIFS is part of the Math & Trig group.

Exercise 8-13 UNHIDE A SHEET AND CREATE A TABLE

A worksheet might be hidden to protect sensitive information or to unclutter the worksheet tab area. The workbook for this lesson has two hidden worksheets with list-type data that can be formatted as an Excel table.

1. Open **Excel_Lesson8**. Right-click any worksheet tab. Choose **Unhide Sheet**. The Unhide dialog box lists the names of hidden sheets.

2. Choose **VolunteerFunds** and click **OK**. This worksheet lists volunteer names, address information, and additional data about money they have raised for the WorldWide Campaign.

3. Select cells A3:K21. The table includes the header row but not the main labels. You can select the appropriate range before giving the Format as Table command.

4. On the **Home** command tab, click the Format as Table button 🖼. Find and choose **Table Style Light 1**. Place a checkmark for **My table has headers**. Click **OK**.

5. Key the following labels in cells O3:O6. You'll use this section of the sheet to find which volunteers meet this criteria.

   Connecticut, Over $100 Raised
   Massachusetts, Over $100 Raised
   Connecticut, Goal > $650
   Massachusetts, Goal > $650

6. Make column O **29.29 (210 pixels)** wide.

7. Click the column heading for column A. Hold down [Shift] and click the column heading for column F. Right-click any selected heading and hide the columns. Now you can see the data that you'll use in your analysis.

Exercise 8-14 USE COUNTIFS

The COUNTIFS function counts cells based on more than one criterion. In your worksheet, for example, you will count how many volunteers from Connecticut have already raised over $100. The two criteria are "Connecticut" and ">100." For this function, you can use multiple columns or more than one condition in a single column as criteria. There are two argument groups: the criteria_range and the criteria.

Criteria_range is the range of cells in which you want to count cells. In a table, this is usually a column. *Criteria* is a number, a date, or an expression that determines whether to include a cell in the count. For COUNTIFS, you can use *criteria_range1* which is subject to *criteria1*. Then you might set *criteria_range2* to meet the condition in *criteria2*. All criteria ranges must have the same number of rows and columns as *criteria_range1*.

1. Click cell P3 and click the Insert Function button *fx*. Choose **COUNTIFS** in the **Statistical** category, and click **OK**.

2. In the **Criteria_range1** box, click and select cells G4:G21. This identifies that the cells in the State/Province column will be counted. Excel automatically supplies the structured reference.

3. Click in the **Criteria1** box.

4. Key **ct**. The rows will be counted if the state is CT; criteria are not case-sensitive.

5. Click in the **Criteria_range2** box. Select cells J4:J21. This specifies that the rows in the Funds Raised column will be counted.

6. Click in the **Criteria2** box.

7. Key **>100**. The rows will be counted if the state is CT and if the funds raised amount is greater than 100. This function uses two columns (criteria ranges) each with its own criteria.

Figure 8-15
Using COUNTIFS
Excel_Lesson8.xlsx
VolunteerFunds
sheet

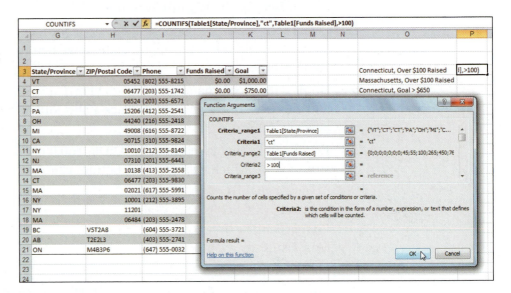

8. Click **OK**. There is one record that meets the requirements.

9. Click cell P4 and key **=countifs** and press ⌐Tab⌐. The Argument ScreenTip shows that **Criteria_range1** is the first argument.

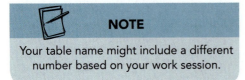

NOTE

Your table name might include a different number based on your work session.

10. Key **t** to trigger the display of Formula AutoComplete options. Although you have not named the table, it has a default name, **Table1**.

11. Double-click **Table1**.

12. Key **[** to trigger the list of structured references.

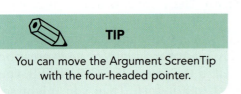

TIP

You can move the Argument ScreenTip with the four-headed pointer.

13. Double-click **State/Province** and key **]** to close the reference.

14. Key a comma to separate the arguments. **Criteria1** is the next argument.

15. Key **"ma"** and key a comma **,**. You must key the quotation marks when you key arguments.

16. For the **Criteria_range2** argument, key **t** and double-click **Table1**.

17. Key **[**, double-click **Funds Raised**, and key **]** to close the reference.

18. Key a comma, and key **">100"** for **Criteria2**.

Figure 8-16
Keying a COUNTIFS
formula
Excel_Lesson8.xlsx
VolunteerFunds
sheet

✕ ✓ *fx*	=COUNTIFS(Table1[State/Province],"ma",Table1[Funds Raised],">100"							
N	O	**P**	Q	R	S	T	U	V
	Connecticut, Over $100 Raised	1						
	Massachusetts, Over $100 Raised	=COUNTIFS(Table1[State/Province],"ma",Table1[Funds Raised],">100"						
	Connecticut, Goal > $650	COUNTIFS(criteria_range1, criteria1, [criteria_range2, **criteria2**], [criteria_range3, ...])						
	Massachusetts, Goal > $650							

19. Press Enter. There are two volunteers in Massachusetts who raised more than $100.

20. Key **250** in cell J13. The formula results for cell P4 are updated.

21. In cells P5:P6, use COUNTIFS for the circumstances indicated in cells O5:O6. Both cells will show a result of 2.

22. Click the Select All button ⬜ to the left of the column G heading. This selects all the rows, columns, and cells on the worksheet.

23. Right-click the column G heading and unhide all columns.

24. Click cell A1. Save the workbook as *[your initials]*8-14.

Exercise 8-15   USE SUMIFS

The SUMIFS function adds cell values using multiple criteria. There are three argument groups: the sum_range, the criteria_range, and the criteria. *Sum_range* is the range of cells to be added. The *criteria_range* and *criteria* arguments are numbered like those in COUNTIFS. Each criteria_range argument must have the same number of rows and columns as the sum_range argument.

1. Right-click any worksheet tab. Choose **Unhide Sheet**. Choose **InsuranceInfo** and click **OK**.

2. Select cells A3:I23. On the **Home** command tab, click the Format as Table button 📊. Choose **Table Style Dark 4**. Place a checkmark for **My table has headers**. Click **OK**.

3. Click the **ID** filter arrow and choose **Sort Smallest to Largest**.

4. Make column L **37.86 (270 pixels)** wide.

5. Click cell M4. In this cell, you will sum the number of dependents for employees in fund-raising in Boston.

6. Click the Insert Function button *fx*. Choose **SUMIFS** in the **Math & Trig** category.

7. In the **Sum_range** box, select cells H4:H23. This identifies that rows in the # of Dependents column will be summed. Note the table number and that you may not see the complete structured reference name in the entry box.

8. Click in the **Criteria_range1** box and select cells G4:G23. This identifies that the first criteria will be the location.

9. Click in the **Criteria1** box. Key **boston**. The cells in the Dependents column will be summed if the city is Boston.

10. In the **Criteria_range2** box, select cells F4:F23 for the Position/ Department column.

11. Click in the **Criteria2** box. Key **fund***. The cells in the Dependents column will be summed if the city is Boston and if the department is Fund-Raising.

Figure 8-17
Using SUMIFS
8-14.xlsx
InsuranceInfo sheet

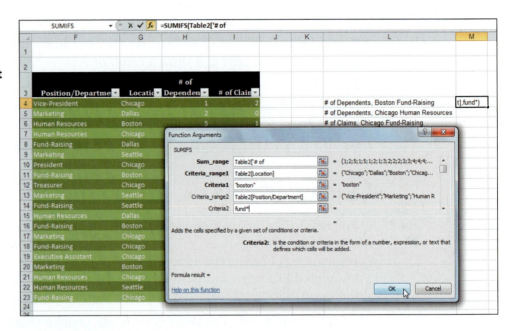

12. Click **OK**. There are four total dependents in the Fund-Raising Department in Boston.

13. Click cell M5 and key **=sumifs**. Press Tab.

14. Key **t** to trigger Formula AutoComplete. Double-click **Table2** to start the **Sum_range** argument.

15. Key **[** to trigger the list of structured references. Double-click **# of Dependents** and key **]** to close the reference. The **Sum_range** argument is complete.

16. Key a comma to move to the **Criteria_range1** argument. Key **t** and double-click **Table2**. Key **[**, double-click **Location**, and key **]**. The **Criteria_range1** argument is complete.

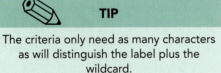

TIP

The criteria only need as many characters as will distinguish the label plus the wildcard.

REVIEW

Table1 is on the Volunteers worksheet.

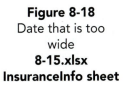

TIP

You can copy the formula and edit it.

17. Key a comma and key **"chicago",** for the **Criteria1** argument. The second comma introduces the **Criteria_range2** argument.

18. Select cells F4:F23 and key a comma.

19. Key **"hum*"** as the **Criteria2** argument and press Enter. The result is 4.

20. Use SUMIFS in cells M6:M7 with the conditions specified in L6:L7. Sort the table as needed to verify your results.

21. Sort the table by ID and save it as *[your initials]*8-15.

Exercise 8-16   SET DATE ALIGNMENT WITH THE TEXT FUNCTION

Dates are values and are right-aligned within a cell. Right-aligned values do not spill over into the adjacent column on the left when they are too wide to be seen. Instead you see the series of #####. To see a value that is too wide, you can widen the column or reduce the font size if those steps are acceptable in your document.

When those options are not appropriate, you can use a text function that formats how a date is shown in the cell. The TEXT function displays a value as text in the format that you specify. The value is then treated as text, follows label alignment rules, and is not used in calculations.

1. In *[your initials]*8-15 key **=today()** in cell I1. Press Enter.

2. Set the date to use 16-point Cambria to match the labels in cells A1:A2. You should see a series of #### symbols, because the column is not wide enough.

3. Format the cell to show the date with the month spelled out, the date, a comma, and four digits for the year. You'll still see the series of ###.

Figure 8-18
Date that is too wide
8-15.xlsx
InsuranceInfo sheet

4. Delete the contents of cell I1. Rather than widen the column or change the font size, you'll display the date using the TEXT function.

5. In cell I1, click the Insert Function button ƒx. Choose **TEXT** in the Text category.

6. In the **Value** box, key **today()** to use the current date.

7. Click in the **Format_text** box. In this box, you key format codes to display the date as you want it to appear.

8. Key **mmmm** to show the month spelled out.

9. Press [Spacebar] for a space after the month.

10. Key **d** to show the date without a leading zero. Key a comma to appear after the date.

11. Press [Spacebar] for a space after the comma. Key **yyyy** to show four digits for the year.

Figure 8-19
Using the TEXT function
8-15.xlsx
InsuranceInfo sheet

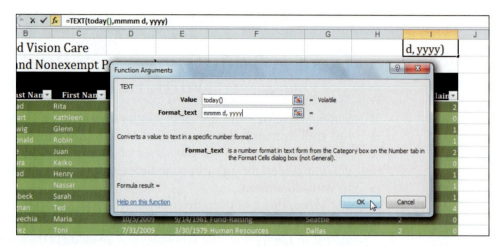

12. Click **OK**. The date as text is left-aligned and spills into column J.

13. Right-align the date. It spills, like any label, into the empty adjacent cell on the left.

14. Change the page orientation to landscape.

15. Save the workbook as *[your initials]*8-16.

Creating a Calculated Column in a Table

A *calculated column* in a table is one that has a formula. If you key the formula in the first data row, it is automatically extended to the remaining rows in the table. This means that you don't need to worry about copying the formula. This feature contributes to the many reasons why Excel tables are so widely used to manage large lists of data. After a formula is extended down a table, you can edit an individual cell if necessary to delete the formula or revise it for just that cell.

This Table AutoExpansion feature is toggled on and off in the AutoCorrect Options dialog box. You can access this dialog box from the Proofing pane in the Excel Options dialog box.

Exercise 8-17   CREATE A CALCULATED COLUMN

In your workbook for this lesson, you can calculate how much money is still pending from each volunteer. This can be calculated by subtracting what they have already collected from the goal. A calculated column will use the structured reference names preceded by an @ symbol.

1. Click the **VolunteerFunds** worksheet tab in *[your initials]***8-16**.

2. Click cell L4. If you enter a formula here, it will be extended to row 21.

3. Key **=** and click cell K4. Excel supplies the structured reference.

4. Key **-** to subtract and click cell J4. Press Enter. A new column is added to the table.

5. Click cell L3 and key **Pending**.

6. Format the formula cells as currency.

Exercise 8-18   CREATE A CALCULATED COLUMN EXCEPTION

A *calculated column exception* is a different formula or different data in a cell in a table column with a formula. Most exceptions are marked with error triangles. If you delete a formula, however, it is not marked.

1. Click cell L7. Note the @ symbol with the structured references in the formula bar.

2. Press Delete. The formula is removed and no error is noted.

3. Click cell L12 and click in the formula bar.

4. Key **+100** at the end of the formula and press Enter. An error triangle appears at the left of the cell, and the Formula AutoCorrect Options button 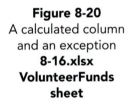 is shown.

5. Click the arrow with the Formula AutoCorrect Options button 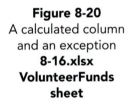. In a table, your option is to update the formula in all the other rows to this new one. Do not make any changes.

Figure 8-20
A calculated column and an exception
8-16.xlsx
VolunteerFunds sheet

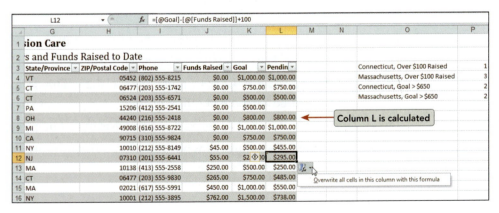

6. Click cell L12 and click the Error Checking Options button ◈. The options note the calculated column with an option to restore the original formula. Do not make any changes.

7. Click cell L16 and key **N/A**. Press ⌷Enter⌷. The label is noted as an inconsistency, but there is no Formula AutoCorrect Options button for this type of exception.

Setting Print Areas and Custom Views

For many companies, the main reason for using an Excel table is that it manages many rows of data like a database. But with large sets of data, it is challenging to decide how to print the information. You can, of course, fit all data to a single page, but this may result in information that is difficult to read because it is so small. You can let Excel split the pages as it prints, but this too results in awkward review as you try to match the correct pages side by side or top to bottom.

Print areas are one way to print only portions of a worksheet. A *print area* is the range of cells to be printed. The default print area is the entire worksheet, but you can define a part of a large worksheet for printing. You can define and save one print area with a workbook, and this print area can be removed and reset as many times as needed.

Sometimes it's difficult to view relevant data in a large table. If you convert the table to a simple range, you can then develop custom views. A *custom view* is a set of display and print settings. They are helpful for large data lists, because you can create various layouts for the data with elements shown or hidden. Custom views are named and saved with the workbook.

Exercise 8-19   SET AND CLEAR A PRINT AREA

1. On **VolunteerFunds** worksheet in *[your initials]*8-16, open Backstage view for printing. The default print area is everything that is on the sheet. It would require two pages.

2. Click the **Insert** command tab.

3. Add a preset header to the worksheet that includes your name, the page number, and the date.

4. Select cells A1:L21. This is the table and its related labels.

5. On the **Page Layout** command tab, click the Print Area button 🖹.

6. Choose **Set Print Area** and click cell E23. The defined print area is outlined by a dashed line border.

7. In the **Scale to Fit** group, set the **Width** to one page.

8. Open Backstage view for printing. The print area includes only the table, fit to one page.

9.　On the **Page Layout** command tab, click the Print Area button 🖻. Choose **Clear Print Area**. The print area is removed.

10.　In the **Scale to Fit** group, reset the **Width** to **Automatic** and the **Scale** to 100%.

Exercise 8-20　PRINT SELECTIONS

In addition to defining a print area, you can select any range of cells to be printed using the Selection choice in the Print what area of Backstage view for printing. This type of print selection cannot be saved with the workbook.

1.　Select cells O3:P6. This is the selection to be printed.

2.　Open Backstage view for printing.

3.　Click the arrow with Print **Active Sheets** in the **Settings** group. Choose **Print Selection**. Only the selected cells would be printed with the header. Notice that they are positioned as if they are the first items on the page.

Figure 8-21
Printing Selections
8-16.xlsx
VolunteerFunds
sheet

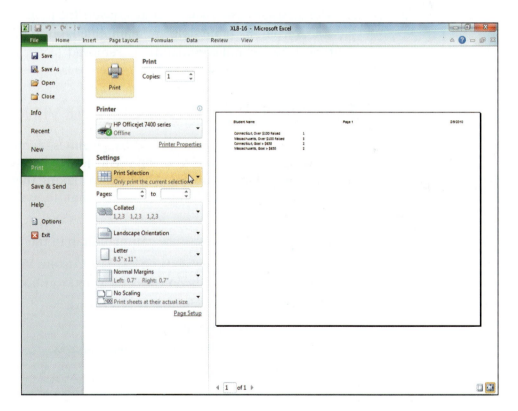

4.　Close Backstage view.

Exercise 8-21   CONVERT A TABLE TO A RANGE

Just as you can format a range as a table, you can convert an Excel table into simple data columns and rows. Before you can create a custom view, you must convert a table into a range. Custom views are not available if a workbook has a table.

1. In *[your initials]*8-16, click the **InsuranceInfo** worksheet tab.
2. Click the **View** command tab in the Ribbon. Notice that the Custom Views button ⬚ is unavailable.
3. Select and group all the worksheet tabs except **InsuranceInfo**.
4. When the five worksheets are grouped, right-click any tab in the group. Choose **Delete** and delete the grouped sheets. Your workbook now has only one sheet.
5. Click any cell in the range.
6. Click the **Table Tools Design** tab. In the **Tools** group, click the Convert to Range button ⬚.
7. The message asks if you want to convert the table. Choose **Yes**. The colors from the table style are maintained, but the filter arrow and all table features and commands are removed.

Exercise 8-22   CREATE CUSTOM VIEWS

A *custom view* includes column widths, gridlines, window size and position, the active sheet, and more. You can use a view to keep certain arrangements of your data so that you do not need to keep making the same layout changes. The first view you should create is one that shows the worksheet in its existing layout.

1. Click cell A1. Click the **View** command tab in the Ribbon.
2. Click the Custom Views button ⬚. The Custom Views dialog box shows that there are currently no views for your workbook.
3. Click **Add**. The Add View dialog box opens.
4. Key **Original** as the name for this view.
5. Make sure that **Print settings** and **Hidden rows, columns and filter settings** are selected.

Figure 8-22
Creating a custom
view
8-21.xlsx
InsuranceInfo sheet

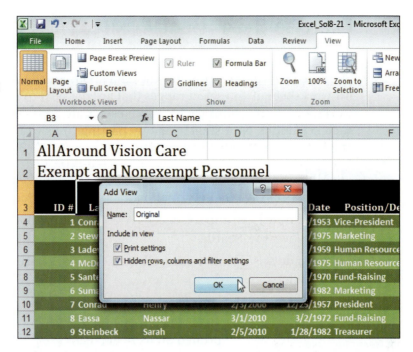

6. Click **OK**.

7. Click the **View** command tab. Remove the checkmark for **Gridlines**.

8. Select cells A4:I23 and set the font color to black and bold.

9. Drag across the column headings for columns D:E and hide them. Then hide columns H:I and L:M.

10. Press [Ctrl]+[Home]. On the **View** command tab, click the Custom Views button [⊞]. The dialog box shows your first view name.

11. Click **Add**. Key **Compact** as the name for this view.

12. Make sure **Print settings** and **Hidden rows, columns and filter settings** are selected. Click **OK**.

13. Save the workbook as *[your initials]***8-22**. Close the workbook.

Exercise 8-23   DISPLAY VIEWS

TIP

You cannot create a custom view while worksheets are grouped.

1. Open *[your initials]***8-22**. It opens in the **Compact** view.

2. On the **View** command tab, click the Custom Views button [⊞].

3. Choose **Original** and click **Show**. Font color and style are attributes, not display settings. Those changes became a permanent part of the data.

Exercise 8-24   PASTE A LINK TO PRINT NONCONTIGUOUS SELECTIONS

Suppose you want to print only the data about Seattle employees. In a regular list worksheet, if you select ranges that are not next to each other on the same worksheet, Excel prints each one on a separate page. You can, however, print such selections on a single page by pasting links to each range somewhere else in the worksheet. A *link*, in this case, is a simple 3-D reference to a cell.

1. Hide columns H:I.
2. Select cells A9:G9, information about an employee in Seattle.
3. Hold down Ctrl and select cells A13:G14, data about two more employees in Seattle.
4. Hold down Ctrl and select cells A22:G22. You have three noncontiguous selections.

REVIEW

When these data were formatted as an Excel table, you could filter the data to show only Seattle personnel and print.

NOTE

Formatting is not copied for a link, but you can reformat the data if necessary or choose the Paste Options choice to keep the formatting.

5. Open Backstage view for printing. Choose **Print Selection** in the **Settings** group. Each selection will be printed on its own page.
6. Scroll through the pages in Backstage view, and then return to the worksheet in Normal view.
7. Select cells A9:G9 and click the Copy button 📋.
8. Right-click cell A25. Choose Paste Link 📋. The range is copied to cell A25 with a 3-D reference to each of the cells in row 9.
9. Press Esc to remove the marquee and click cell A25. Look at the 3-D reference in the formula bar.
10. Click a few of the other copied cells to view the reference.
11. Paste a link for cells A13:G14 starting in cell A26. Then paste a link to cells A22:G22 in cell A28.
12. Select cells A25:G28. Press Ctrl+P to open Backstage view. Choose **Print Selection** in the **Settings** group. The data could now be printed on a single sheet.
13. Close Backstage view. Save the workbook as *[your initials]*8-24.
14. Close the workbook.

Using Online Help

Structured references are found only in Excel tables but work somewhat like range names.

USE HELP TO LEARN ABOUT STRUCTURED REFERENCES

1. In a new workbook, press F1 and search for information about structured references in a table.
2. Read and then close the Help windows.

Lesson 8   Summary

- An Excel table is a list of data with a row of labels as titles (header row), followed by any number of rows of data.
- A table column is a field; a row is a record.
- You can copy data from one workbook to another in tiled windows. Windows can be arranged horizontally or vertically.
- An Excel table is created from the Styles group on the Home tab. The styles include light, medium, and dark color schemes with or without borders.
- When a table is selected or active, the Table Tools Design command tab is available with commands for managing the table.
- Table style options include a header row, banded rows or columns, a total row, and emphasized first and last columns.
- Table AutoExpansion makes it easy to add rows or columns to a table. Just position the insertion point in the last table cell and press Tab to insert a row. To add a column, just key a label in the header row.
- A table is automatically named, but you can assign a more descriptive name from the Properties group.
- The Remove Duplicates command automatically searches for and deletes data rows that are duplicates based on the fields that you specify.
- You can sort a table by single or multiple columns. Sorts are described as ascending or descending.
- A filter displays only certain rows from a table. The filter arrow lists are quick ways to choose which records should be shown.
- Excel creates structured references for the parts of a table. These are similar to defined range names, but the names do not appear in the Name Manager dialog box.
- COUNTIFS and SUMIFS are functions that count and sum ranges based on multiple criteria. They are especially useful in large sets of data.
- A calculated column in a table is automatically completed when you enter a formula in the first data row.
- Data that are formatted as a table can be converted to a simple data range.
- The TEXT function displays a value (or date) as text using the format keyed in its second argument. The value is then not used in calculations and can be formatted with text attributes.
- You can set a print area that is different from the entire worksheet. One print area can be saved with the workbook.

- A print selection is not saved. If you choose more than one selection, each one prints on a separate page.
- A custom view is a set of display and print choices for a workbook. You can save several views with a workbook.

LESSON 8		Command Summary	
Feature	Button	Ribbon Location	Keyboard
Arrange windows		View, Window	
Convert table to range		Table Tools Design, Tools	
Custom view		View, Workbook Views	
Duplicate data			Ctrl+'
Paste link		Home, Clipboard	
Print area, clear		Page Layout, Page Setup	
Print area, set		Page Layout, Page Setup	
Remove duplicates		Table Tools Design, Tools	
Table, create		Home, Styles	Ctrl+L
Table, name		Table Tools Design, Properties	
Table, redesign		Table Tools Design, Table Style Options	
Table, resize		Table Tools Design, Properties	
Table, style		Table Tools Design, Table Styles	
Unhide worksheet		Home, Cells	

Please visit our Online Learning Center, *www.lessonapproach2010.com*, where you will find the following review materials:

Concepts Review

True/False Questions

Short Answer Questions

Critical Thinking Questions

Skills Review

Review Exercises that target single skills

Lesson Applications

Review Exercises that challenge students by testing multiple skills in each exercise

On Your Own

Open-ended exercises that require students to synthesize multiple skills and apply creativity and problem-solving as they would in a real world business situation

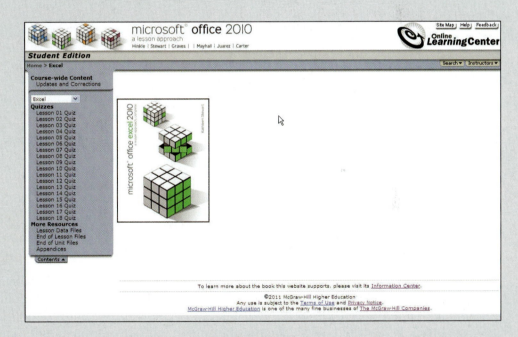

Lesson 9

Using What-If Analysis Tools

OBJECTIVES   *After completing this lesson, you will be able to:*

1. Monitor workbook security.
2. Create a scenario.
3. Set conditional formatting.
4. Manage scenarios.
5. Forecast with a trendline.
6. Use Goal Seek.
7. Use Solver.
8. Use the Research tool.
9. Work with the Info pane.

Estimated Time: 1½ hours

What-if analysis is a procedure in which you vary values to predict or test future results or values. Although many people feel that all Excel commands provide some type of analysis, there are specialized tools that are options for the What-If Analysis button on the Data command tab. These analytical tools enable you to enter, save, and review sets of possible values; to work out mathematical problems in reverse; or to add forecast lines to charts.

The Review command tab in the Ribbon includes a Research tool that provides a different type of analysis or investigation in a worksheet. With the Research command group, you can find a label with the same or opposite meaning, look for general information about a label or topic, or translate a label into another language. These commands are similar to commands found in Microsoft Word and PowerPoint.

Monitoring Workbook Security

With widespread use of networks and the Internet, document security has become an important concern for all companies and individuals. You have already learned how a workbook accessed from an e-mail attachment or a Web site opens in Protected View. You will learn about two other security settings in this lesson.

Marked as Final is a document property or setting, listed in the Permissions group (Info pane) in Backstage view. When a document has been marked as final by its creator, it is uneditable until that property is reset. This property is a simple reminder and warning to anyone using the workbook, because the setting can be easily bypassed. When you open a workbook that has been marked as final, you'll see a message panel above the formula bar. There is also an icon in the status bar. You do need to acknowledge or accept the warning before you can make any edits in the workbook.

The Lesson 9 workbook has a macro. A *macro* is a Visual Basic routine or program included in a workbook that performs some task. Because macros can be hiding places for computer viruses, you can adjust settings in the Trust Center for your computer to protect against your opening an infected macro file.

Exercise 9-1   OPEN A MARKED AS FINAL WORKBOOK AND RUN A MACRO

The macro in your workbook will automatically insert the company name in cell A1. A workbook with a macro is a *macro-enabled workbook* with an **xlsm** file name extension, different from a regular workbook with an **xlsx** extension. Before opening the workbook, you'll check the macro settings for your computer.

1. With a blank or no workbook open, click the **File** command tab and choose **Options**.

2. Click **Trust Center** to open the pane. The first two groups enable you to view privacy settings and to search online for additional security information.

3. Click **Trust Center Settings**. There are several locations, documents, and other elements that can be allowed or restricted to protect your work.

4. Click **Macro Settings**.

5. Click to select **Disable all macros with notification** if it is not selected (see Figure 9-1 on the next page). This is the default setting. With this choice, you will see an opening Security Warning panel if a workbook contains a macro, and the macro is disabled.

Figure 9-1
Macro Settings pane

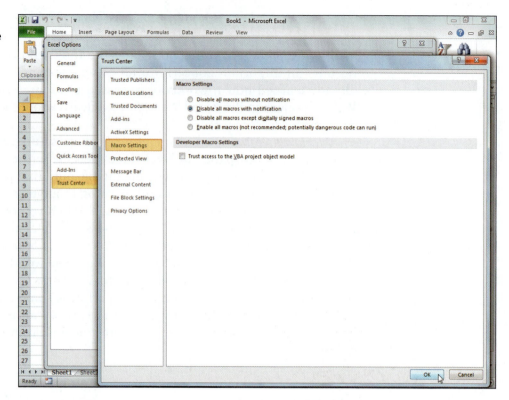

6. Click **OK** to close the Trust Center. Click **OK** to close the Excel Options dialog box.

7. Open **Excel_Lesson9**. If the workbook is in Protected View, click **Enable Editing**. The message panels above the formula bar alerts you that the workbook is marked as final and that macros have been disabled. The Ribbon is collapsed.

8. In the Security Warning panel, click **Enable Content**. You will now be able to run the macro.

9. Note the Marked as Final icon 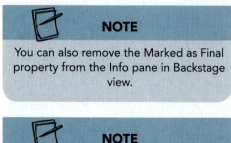 next to **Ready** in the status bar. This is a second reminder.

10. Click the **Home** command tab. Notice that most of the buttons are grayed out or dimmed, meaning they are unavailable. The title bar shows "[Read Only]" after the file name.

> **NOTE**
>
> You can also remove the Marked as Final property from the Info pane in Backstage view.

> **NOTE**
>
> This workbook is set at 80% view size.

11. Key any characters in cell A1. You cannot do so.

12. In the security message bar, click **Edit Anyway**. The Marked as Final property is removed.

13. Make sure the insertion point is in cell A1.

14. Click the **View** command tab. Click the Macros button . The Macro dialog box shows that there is one macro in this workbook named **CompanyName**.

15. Click **Run**. This macro inserts the company name in cell A1.

Creating a Scenario

A *scenario* is a set of values, built from the What-If Analysis button  on the Data command tab. Scenarios allow you to display new values for selected cells with recalculated formulas. In the workbook for this lesson, AllAround Vision Care has data about unit and dollar sales for the five most popular eyeglass frames. As it forecasts sales possibilities and probabilities for next year, it can experiment with higher and lower unit prices. This will allow it to make a calculated estimate of the effect on sales of changing prices.

A scenario is named and saved with the workbook. You can create and keep multiple scenarios for a worksheet and then, with a few clicks, view different solutions for your data.

Exercise 9-2   NAME RANGES AND CREATE A SCENARIO

In a scenario, you normally refer to ranges of cells. These include cells that can change and cells that show results. If you name these ranges, managing scenarios becomes easier.

1. Select cells E22:E26. Click the **Name Box** and key **Prices**. Press [Enter].
2. Name cells G14:G18 as **DollarSales**.
3. Name cell G19 as **TotalSales**.
4. Select cells D22:E26. Click the Create from Selection button ⊞ on the **Formulas** command tab. Use the **Left column** to create range names automatically.
5. Click the **Data** command tab. In the **Data Tools** group, click the What-If Analysis button 📊.
6. Choose **Scenario Manager**. The Scenario Manager dialog box opens. There are now no scenarios defined in your workbook.
7. Click **Add**. The Add Scenario dialog box opens.
8. In the **Scenario name** box, key **Current Prices**. Press [Tab].

REVIEW

When you press [Tab] to move to the next text box, the existing entry is highlighted and ready to be replaced.

9. In the **Changing cells** box, press [F3]. The Paste Name dialog box opens with the named ranges.
10. Choose **Prices** and click **OK**. The Add Scenario dialog box is still open.
11. Press [Tab]. In the **Comment** box, key **This scenario shows sales at current prices.** This text replaces the default comment inserted by the Scenario Manager.
12. Notice the Protection options. *Protection* is another worksheet property that allows or prevents editing. The two options here are relevant only if the Protection setting is enabled.

Figure 9-2
Adding a scenario
**Excel_Lesson9.xlsm
Sheet1 sheet**

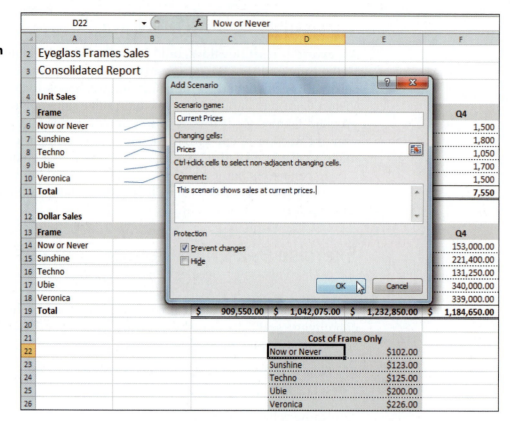

13. Click **OK**. The Scenario Values dialog box shows each of the cells from the Prices range with its current value, formatted as a general number. Do not change any values.

14. Click **OK**. The Scenario Manager dialog box lists the name of the scenario you just created.

Exercise 9-3   ADD SCENARIOS TO THE WORKBOOK

1. With the Scenario Manager dialog box open, click **Add**.

2. In the **Scenario name** box, key **Reduced Prices**.

3. Press ⌨Tab. Excel shows the last range you used for **Changing cells**, the Prices range, cells E22:E26. A marquee appears around the range in the worksheet. Your new scenario will be for this same range of cells.

4. Press ⌨Tab. In the **Comment** box, key **This scenario shows sales at reduced prices.**

5. Click **OK**. The Scenario Values dialog box opens. Now you will change each price.

6. Key the values shown, pressing ⌨Tab to move from one text box to the next. If you press ⌨Enter before you have completed the changes, click **Edit** and then click **OK** to return to the Scenario Values dialog box.

Now or Never	99
Sunshine	99
Techno	105
Ubie	165
Veronica	175

Figure 9-3
Changing scenario values
Excel_Lesson9.xlsm Sheet1 sheet

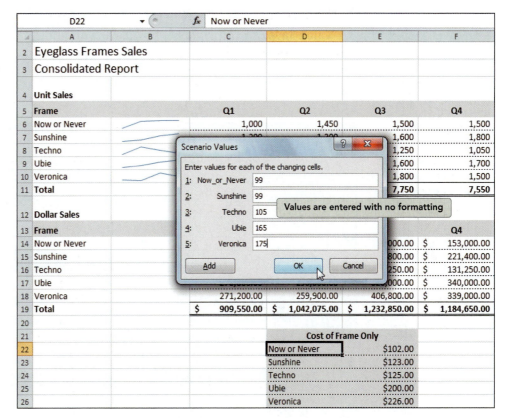

7. Click **OK**. The Scenario Manager shows the names of both scenarios.

8. Click **Add**. In the **Scenario name** box, key **Increased Prices**.

9. Press [Tab] two times. In the **Comment** box, key **This scenario shows sales at higher prices.**

10. Click **OK**. The original prices are shown. Key each new price as shown.

Now or Never	120
Sunshine	135
Techno	150
Ubie	225
Veronica	250

11. Click **OK**. The Scenario Manager shows all three scenario names.

12. Click **Close**. The "Current Prices" scenario is displayed in the worksheet, so you still see the original prices.

13. Click a blank cell in the worksheet.

Exercise 9-4   SAVE A MACRO-FREE WORKBOOK

When you resave this workbook, you can keep it as a macro-enabled workbook, or you can save it as a macro-free workbook. This does mean that you would no longer be able to run the macro.

1. Press F12 and name the workbook *[your initials]9-4*.

2. Click the **Save as type** arrow and choose **Excel Workbook**.

3. Click **Save**. An information box alerts you about the macro. Macros are stored in Visual Basic (VB) modules. Visual Basic is a programming language that works within Excel.

Figure 9-4
Message box when saving a macro-free workbook
Excel_Lesson9.xlsm

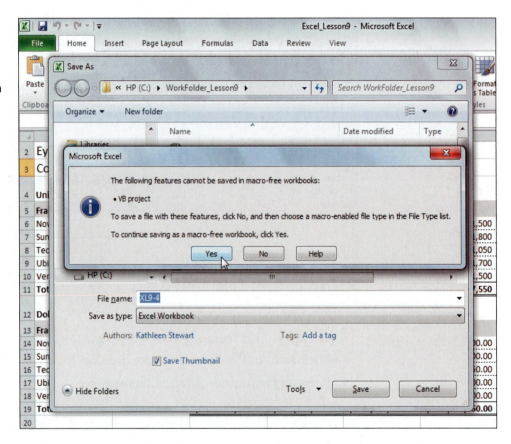

4. Click **Yes**.

5. Close the workbook. Then reopen *[your initials]9-4*. Notice that there is no security warning about the macro.

6. Click the **View** command tab. Click the Macros button 🔲. Macros have been removed.

7. Click **Cancel**.

Setting Conditional Formatting

Color scales are data visualizations that help you see a variation in values across a range of cells. They are part of the Conditional Formatting group. There are two-color and three-color scales. Each uses gradation of color to show the high, middle, and low values.

Highlight cells rules apply the formatting when the cell meets the conditions set by the operators. Several common comparison and relational operators are listed in the gallery, but you can choose from others when you create your own rule.

Exercise 9-5   SET A COLOR SCALE

In your workbook, you can use a color scale for the unit sales values. With a two-color scale, the range will display more than two colors, because each color has several variations. The preset color scales include options that show the largest or the smallest value in either the lightest or the darkest color.

1. Select cells C6:F10. In the **Styles** group on the **Home** command tab, click the Conditional Formatting button 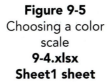.

2. Choose **Color Scales** and the **Green-Yellow Color Scale** in the third row, third icon. This two-color scale shows the highest values in the darkest color.

Figure 9-5
Choosing a color scale
9-4.xlsx
Sheet1 sheet

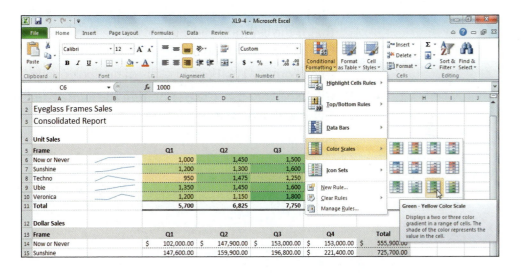

3. Click in column H to better see the color scale.

4. Select cells C6:F10 and click the Conditional Formatting button 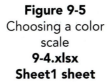.

5. Choose **Manage Rules**. The Conditional Formatting Rules Manager dialog box shows that a color scale is applied to the current selection.

6. Click **Edit Rule**. The Edit Formatting Rule dialog box is the same as the one for data bars.

7. Click the **Color** arrow for the **Minimum** group. Choose **White, Background 1** in the first row.

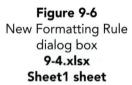

8. Click the **Color** arrow for the **Maximum** group. Choose **White, Background 1, Darker 50%**. The color ramp may look like it has some red in the middle, but that shade does not appear in the worksheet.

9. Click **OK** to close both dialog boxes. Click a cell in column H.

Exercise 9-6 CREATE A NEW FORMATTING RULE

The "greater than or equal to" operator is not listed in the Highlight Cells Rules gallery. With the More Rules option, you can choose this operator as well as any format from the Format Cells dialog box.

1. Click the **Name Box** arrow and choose **DollarSales**. Cells G14:G18 are selected.

2. Click the Conditional Formatting button 📊.

3. Hover over **Highlight Cells Rules** and choose **More Rules**. The New Formatting Rule dialog box opens. The rule type is **Format only cells that contain**.

4. In the **Edit the Rule Description** group, click the arrow with **Cell Value**. In addition to formatting values, you can use other conditions for applying the format.

5. Choose **Cell Value**.

6. Click the arrow with **greater than** and choose **greater than or equal to**.

7. Click in the rightmost text box and key **750000**. Your condition states that if the cell value is equal to or greater than 750,000, formatting will be applied. Next, you'll define the formatting.

8. Click **Format**. The Format Cells dialog box opens.

9. Click the **Font** tab. Choose **Bold** in the **Font style** list. Click the arrow for **Color** and choose **Blue, Accent 1**.

Figure 9-6
New Formatting Rule
dialog box
9-4.xlsx
Sheet1 sheet

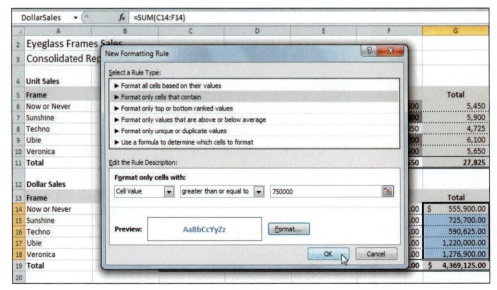

10. Click **OK**. The preview area shows your conditional formatting.

11. Click **OK**. Click any cell to deselect the range. Two cells in the range are formatted.

Exercise 9-7 SET MULTIPLE CONDITIONAL FORMATTING RULES

A range of cells can have more than one conditional formatting rule applied. The unit sales values already have a color scale, and you can now add another rule to show values equal to 1500 in a different color.

1. Select cells C6:F10, the range with a color scale.

2. Click the Conditional Formatting button ▦. Hover over **Highlight Cells Rules** and choose **Equal To**.

3. Key **1500** and press Tab. Click the arrow for the format choices.

4. Choose **Custom Format**. On the Font tab, choose the same blue and bold. Click **OK**. Some cells meet this condition and are formatted with this rule in addition to the color scale.

5. Click a blank cell to see your formatting.

Exercise 9-8 CLEAR AND INSERT SPARKLINES

Your workbook currently includes line sparklines in column B that graph the values in columns C:F. You are going to clear these sparklines and insert column sparklines instead.

1. Click cell B6. Sparklines are treated as a group, so you'll see that the entire range is selected.

2. Press Delete. Nothing happens. Because sparklines are grouped and linked to the entire range of data, a simple delete command does not work.

3. Click the **Sparkline Tools Design** tab. In the **Group** group, click the Clear button ✐. One sparkline (cell B6) is cleared.

4. Click cell B7. The remaining sparklines are still a group.

5. Click the arrow with the Clear button ✐, and choose **Clear Selected Sparkline Groups**. All the sparklines are removed.

6. Select cells B6:B10, the range for the new sparklines.

7. Click the **Insert** command tab. In the **Sparklines** group, click the Insert Column Sparkline button ▮▮.

8. For the **Data Range**, select cells C6:F10. Verify that the **Location Range** is identified as cells B6:B10. Click **OK**.

9. From the **Sparkline Tools Design** tab, choose **Sparkline Style Dark #1**.

10. Make rows 5:26 **27.00 (36 pixels)** tall.

11. Click cell B6. The sparkline group is selected. When sparklines are initially drawn, Excel uses an automatic setting to size the smallest column sparkline for the lowest value. This results in almost invisible columns for the low values.

12. Click the **Sparkline Tools Design** tab. Click the Sparkline Axis button . In the **Vertical Axis Minimum Value Options** group, choose **Custom Value**. With a minimum value of 0, the column sparklines will better graph the actual values.

13. Verify that the minimum value is **0.0** and click **OK**.

Managing Scenarios

While the workbook is open, you can display each scenario one at a time to assess results and make a decision about your data. In your workbook, for example, AllAround Vision Care can see what its dollar sales might be if it raises or lowers prices. Its current scenarios assume that the unit sales numbers do not change, only the prices. In addition to displaying scenarios individually, you can create a summary report that shows the changing and results sales for each scenario.

Exercise 9-9   SHOW SCENARIOS

You can watch the changes in the relevant cells as you switch from one scenario to another. Conditional formatting in the DollarSales range will adjust, because those cells are affected by the prices. The color scales and the sparklines will not update, because the unit sales numbers are not changing.

1. Set a zoom size that enables you to see all the data.

2. Click the **Data** command tab. In the **Data Tools** group, click the What-If Analysis button. Choose **Scenario Manager**.

3. Position the Scenario Manager dialog box so that you can see individual frame costs and total dollar sales.

4. Select **Reduced Prices** in the **Scenarios** list.

5. Click **Show**. The worksheet shows reduced frame prices and the resulting total dollar sales.

> **NOTE**
> You can delete a scenario by clicking its name and clicking Delete.

6. Double-click **Increased Prices** in the **Scenarios** list. The worksheet now shows higher prices with new dollar results, three displayed now in the red color.

7. Double-click **Current Prices**. The worksheet shows current prices and dollar results.

Exercise 9-10   EDIT A SCENARIO

1. With the Scenario Manager dialog box open, choose **Increased Prices** in the **Scenarios** list.

2. Click **Edit**. The Edit Scenario dialog box is the same as the Add Scenario dialog box.

3. Press [Tab] to reach the **Comment** box. Each time you edit a scenario, Excel adds a line to the comment with the user's name and the current date.

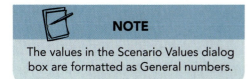

NOTE

The values in the Scenario Values dialog box are formatted as General numbers.

4. Click **OK**. The Scenario Values dialog box opens.
5. Change the **Sunshine** price to **250**. Click **OK**. The **Current Prices** scenario is still displayed.
6. Double-click **Increased Prices** in the **Scenarios** list.

Exercise 9-11   CREATE A SCENARIO SUMMARY REPORT

A *scenario summary report* is a formatted description for each scenario in the worksheet. It shows data from the cells that change and the result cells in outline format on a separate worksheet. An *outline* groups and summarizes rows and/or columns with the ability to hide or show parts of the data. An outline has levels that are indicated by numbers and buttons above the column headings and to the left of the row headings.

1. With the Scenario Manager dialog box open, click **Summary**. The Scenario Summary dialog box opens.
2. Make sure the **Report type** is **Scenario summary**.
3. In the **Result cells** box, press F3. Choose **DollarSales**. Click **OK**.

Figure 9-7
Scenario Summary
dialog box
**9-4.xlsx
Sheet1 sheet**

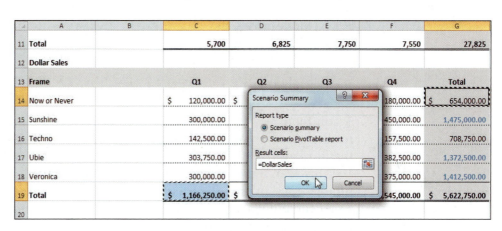

4. Click **OK**. A new worksheet **Scenario Summary** appears. Above the column letter headings and to the left of the row number headings, you can see the outline level indicators. This outline has two levels.

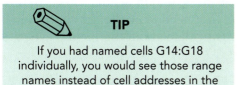

TIP

If you had named cells G14:G18 individually, you would see those range names instead of cell addresses in the report.

5. Click the Level 1 symbol (1) to the left of the column A heading. The outline collapses and shows no details.
6. Click the Level 2 symbol (2) to the left of the column A heading. The outline expands and shows all details. Each section in the report now has a collapse button (–).
7. Click the collapse symbol (–) to the left of row 5. The **Changing Cells** section (rows 6:10) is hidden.
8. Click the expand symbol (+) to the left of row 5 to display the **Changing Cells** section again (see Figure 9-8 on the next page).

Figure 9-8
Scenario summary
report
9-4.xlsx
**Scenario Summary
sheet**

	Current Values:	Current Prices	Reduced Prices	Increased Prices
Scenario Summary				
		This scenario shows sales at current prices.	This scenario shows sales at reduced prices.	This scenario shows sales at higher prices. Modified by Kathleen on 12/19/2009
Changing Cells:				
Now_or_Never	$120.00	$102.00	$99.00	$120.00
Sunshine	$250.00	$123.00	$99.00	$250.00
Techno	$150.00	$125.00	$105.00	$150.00
Ubie	$225.00	$200.00	$165.00	$225.00
Veronica	$250.00	$226.00	$175.00	$250.00
Result Cells:				
$G$14	$ 654,000.00	$ 555,900.00	$ 539,550.00	$ 654,000.00
$G$15	1,475,000.00	725,700.00	584,100.00	1,475,000.00
$G$16	708,750.00	590,625.00	496,125.00	708,750.00
$G$17	1,372,500.00	1,220,000.00	1,006,500.00	1,372,500.00
$G$18	1,412,500.00	1,276,900.00	988,750.00	1,412,500.00

Notes: Current Values column represents values of changing cells at
time Scenario Summary Report was created. Changing cells for each
scenario are highlighted in gray.

Column and row outline levels

9. Rename **Sheet1** as **Scenarios**.

10. Save the workbook as *[your initials]*9-11.

Forecasting with a Trendline

A common way to analyze and predict business data is to forecast future
results based on past performance. If AllAround Vision Care can determine
that it recruited 100 new patients last year, it might predict that it can recruit
105 this year. If it can accomplish this several years in a row, there is an identifiable trend in growth of its services. With this type of data in a worksheet,
Excel can build a chart and a related trendline. A *trendline* is a line in a chart
that illustrates and predicts general tendencies or directions in the values.

Exercise 9-12   CREATE A CHART WITH A TRENDLINE

A trendline makes sense in a column, line, area, and/or scatter chart. Before
you can add a trendline to your data, you first need to create the chart. You'll
create a column chart sheet for this task using data about the Techno eyeglass
frame.

NOTE

You would not use a trendline in a pie
chart, because a pie chart does not graph
changes in the values; it graphs
proportions.

1. In *[your intials]*9-11, click the **Scenarios** worksheet
   tab. Click the **Data** command tab.

2. Click the What-If Analysis button 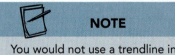. Choose **Scenario
   Manager**. Show the **Current Prices** scenario. Click **Close**.

3. Select the range C8:F8, quarterly unit totals for the
   Techno frame.

4. Press F11. A column chart on its own sheet is created.

5. Click the **Chart Tools Design** tab and choose **Style 25**.

6. Click the **Chart Tools Layout** tab. Click the Chart Title button 🖼 and choose **Above Chart**. Edit the chart title object to **Projected Sales of Techno Frame**.

7. Select and delete the legend.

8. Click the **Chart Tools Layout** tab. Click the Trendline button 📈. There are four types of trendlines listed in the gallery.

9. Choose **Linear Trendline**. A linear trendline is a straight line and is well suited to data that increase or decrease at a steady rate. The default line does not forecast past the existing data yet.

10. Click the **Chart Elements** arrow in the **Current Selection** group. Choose **Series 1 Trendline 1**. Then click the Format Selection button 🖋. The Format Trendline dialog box has four panes.

11. Click **Trendline Options**. There are actually six types of trendlines that can be used, but only four are listed in the gallery.

12. In the **Forecast** group, in the **Forward** box, key **4** to project sales for the next four quarters.

Figure 9-9
Forecasting four future periods
9-11.xlsx
Chart1 sheet

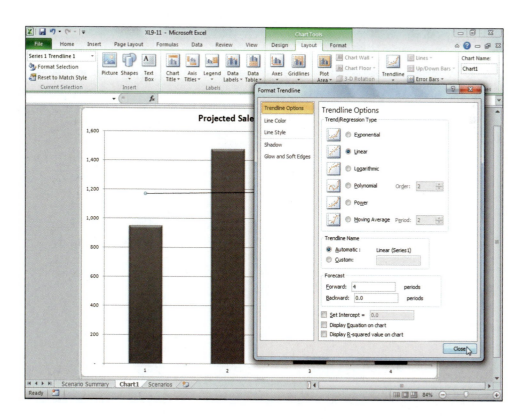

13. Click **Close**. Given current sales, the trendline shows that sales will increase slightly in each of the next four quarters.

Exercise 9-13   FORMAT A TRENDLINE

1. Click the **Chart Elements** arrow and choose **Series 1 Trendline 1**. Then click the Format Selection button 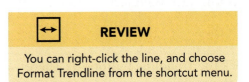.

REVIEW
You can right-click the line, and choose Format Trendline from the shortcut menu.

2. Click **Line Style**, and choose **3 pt** in the **Width** box. Click the **Dash type** arrow, and choose **Dash** (fourth option).

3. In the **Arrow Settings** group, click the **End type** arrow and choose **Arrow**.

4. Click **Line Color**, and choose **Blue, Accent 1** as the **Color**.

5. Click **Trendline Options**.

6. In the **Trendline Name** group, choose **Custom**.

7. Key **Next Four Quarters** in the **Custom** box. Click **Close**.

8. Click the **Chart Tools Layout** tab and click the Legend button.

9. Choose **Overlay Legend at Right**.

10. Click the **Chart Tools Design** tab. Click the Select Data button.

11. Choose **Series1** and click **Edit**. Change the series name to **This Year**. Click **OK** twice.

Figure 9-10
Formatted trendline
9-11.xlsx
Chart1 sheet

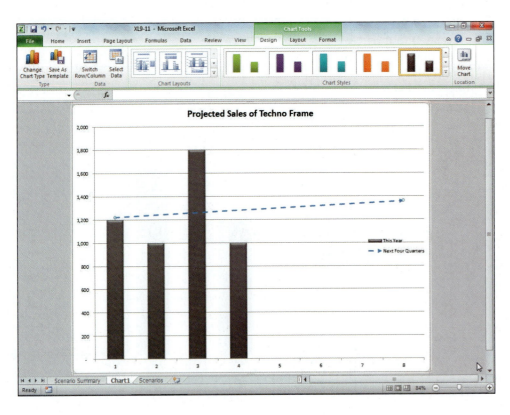

12. Click the blue-gray window background. Click the **Scenarios** sheet tab.

13. In the range C8:F8, key these values.

    1200   1000   1800   1000

14. Click the **Chart1** tab. Even with lower sales in two quarters, the trend is for higher sales.

15. Save the workbook as *[your initials]9-13.*

Using Goal Seek

In your use of analysis tools so far, you've worked with the current data to see what the future results might be. Another type of analysis is one in which a goal is identified, and then you determine how to reach that goal. In your workbook for the lesson, AllAround Vision Care can seek a dollar sales value that it would like to attain. From that, it can then test ways of reaching that number and determine which method might be the easiest to accomplish.

Goal Seek allows you to "backsolve" a cell value to reach a desired outcome. *Backsolving* might be described as what-if analysis in reverse. That is, you know what you would like as results for a formula. With that information, adjust values or arguments used in the formula to reach your desired results.

Goal Seek is an option on the What-If Analysis button. It can be used to vary one value or cell from the formula.

Exercise 9-14   USE GOAL SEEK TO DETERMINE A PRICE

Suppose that AllAround Vision Care has decided to promote the new Sunshine eyeglass frame with the hopes of reaching $1,000,000 in sales next year. You can use Goal Seek to determine a price for the frame that would enable the company to reach that level of sales without changing anything else.

1. In *[your initials]9-13*, click the **Scenarios** sheet tab. Click cell G15.

2. Click the **Data** command tab. Show the **Current Prices** scenario.

3. Click the What-If Analysis button. Choose **Goal Seek**. The Goal Seek dialog box opens. The **Set cell** box shows the active cell, G15. This cell has the formula that you would like to result in $1,000,000.

4. In the **To value** box, key **1000000**.

5. In the **By changing cell** box, click cell E23 in the worksheet, the price of the Sunshine frame. Goal Seek can adjust one cell at a time. The results assume unit sales do not change.

Figure 9-11
Using Goal Seek
to set a price
9-13.xlsx
Scenarios sheet

	Frame		Q1		Q2		Q3		Q4		Total
13	Frame		Q1		Q2		Q3		Q4		Total
14	Now or Never	$	102,000.00	$	147,900.00	$	153,000.00	$	153,000.00	$	555,900.00
15	Sunshine		147,600.00		159,900.00		196,800.00	$	221,400.00		725,700.00
16	Techno		150,000.00		125,000.00		225,000.00	$	125,000.00		625,000.00
17	Ubie		270,000.00						340,000.00		1,220,000.00
18	Veronica		271,200.00						339,000.00		1,276,900.00
19	Total	$	940,800.00	$					178,400.00	$	4,403,500.00
20											
21											
22						Now or Never		$102.00			
23						Sunshine		$123.00			
24						Techno		$125.00			
25						Ubie		$200.00			
26						Veronica		$226.00			
27											

Goal Seek
Set cell: G15
To value: 1000000
By changing cell: $E$23
OK   Cancel

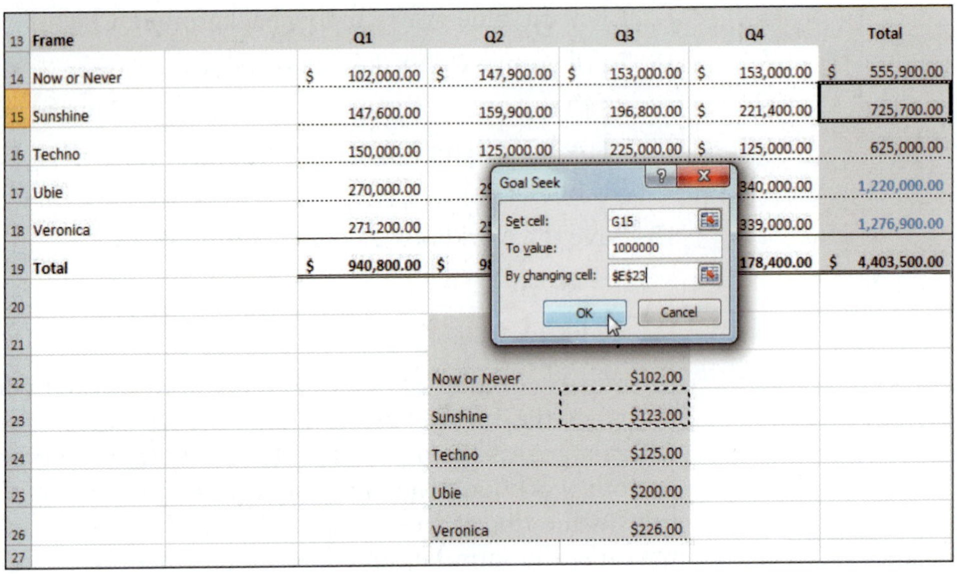

6. Click **OK**. The Goal Seek Status dialog box shows that a solution was found. A new price is shown in cell E23. You would have to increase the price to $169.49 to reach dollar sales of $1,000,000 assuming the same number of frames are sold.

Figure 9-12
Goal Seek Status
after a solution is
found
9-13.xlsx
Scenarios sheet

	Frame		Q1		Q2		Q3		Q4		Total
13	Frame		Q1		Q2		Q3		Q4		Total
14	Now or Never	$	102,000.00	$	147,900.00	$	153,000.00	$	153,000.00	$	555,900.00
15	Sunshine		203,389.83		220,338.98		271,186.44	$	305,084.75		1,000,000.00
16	Techno		150,000.00		125,000.00		225,000.00	$	125,000.00		625,000.00
17	Ubie		270,000.00						340,000.00		1,220,000.00
18	Veronica		271,200.00						339,000.00		1,276,900.00
19	Total	$	996,589.83						1,262,084.75	$	4,677,800.00
20											
21											
22						Now or Never		$102.00			
23						Sunshine		$169.49			
24						Techno		$125.00			
25						Ubie		$200.00			
26						Veronica		$226.00			
27											

Goal Seek Status
Goal Seeking with Cell G15 found a solution.   Step
Target value: 1000000   Pause
Current value: 1,000,000.00
OK   Cancel

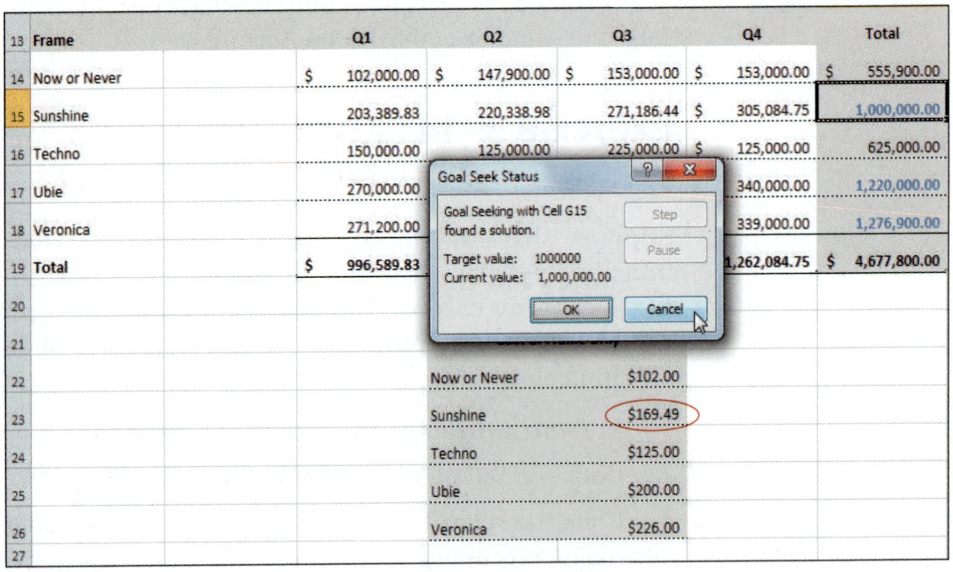

7. Click **Cancel**. Nothing is changed in the worksheet, and the original data are displayed.

Exercise 9-15   USE GOAL SEEK TO DETERMINE UNITS SOLD

Instead of changing the price, AllAround Vision Care wonders how many frames would have to be sold to reach $1,000,000 in sales for the frame. The total number of frames for the Sunshine frame is calculated in cell G7 by a SUM formula.

1. Click the What-If Analysis button . Choose **Goal Seek**. The **Set cell** entry shows the active cell (G15).

2. In the **To value** box, key **1000000**.

3. Click in the **By changing cell** box.

4. Click cell G7 in the worksheet, the current total number of Sunshine frames sold. This cell has a SUM formula.

5. Click **OK**. Excel displays an error message, because Goal Seek cannot change the value in a cell that has a formula. It can change only a cell that has a value.

6. Click **OK** in the error message box.

7. While the Goal Seek dialog box is open, select cells C7:F7 for the **By changing cell** box and click **OK**. Another message box informs you that the reference must be to a single cell.

8. Click **OK** in the error message box.

NOTE

Goal Seek can change one adjustable cell with a value. It cannot be used for more than one cell at a time.

9. Select cell E7 for the **By changing cell** box and click **OK**. A solution is found and requires a lot of frames to be sold during the third quarter, realistically probably too many.

10. Click **Cancel**. Nothing is changed in the worksheet.

Using Solver

Solver backsolves the value for a cell with a formula. It is an analysis tool that can address problems more complex than those handled by Goal Seek. As you learned in the previous exercise, you were not able to use the sales unit numbers from each quarter as adjustable values in Goal Seek, because it can solve for only one value at a time.

Solver is a sophisticated tool, often used in *optimization modeling*, which is a method of finding the most desirable results for a formula. Solver has the following components:

- An *objective* formula that you want to result in a particular value.

- *Variable cells* that relate directly or indirectly to the objective (formula) cell. Solver changes the values in these cells to produce the desired result.

- Limitations, or *constraints,* placed on the objective cell, the variable cells, or other cells directly or indirectly related to the target cell.

Solver is an Excel add-in. An *add-in* is a feature or command that supplies some type of enhanced capability. Excel has several add-ins, some of which are installed separately from the main program. When the Solver add-in is installed, its button appears on the Data command tab in the Analysis group.

Exercise 9-16   USE SOLVER TO DETERMINE UNITS SOLD

A *parameter* is the information that Solver needs to determine a solution. In your worksheet, you will again try to reach sales of $1,000,000 for the Sunshine frame. This time, however, you'll have Solver adjust the quarterly sales units, shown in row 7.

1. Select cell G15. This cell has a SUM formula.

2. Click the **Data** command tab. In the **Analysis** group, click the Solver button . The Solver Parameters dialog box opens.

3. In the **Set Objective** box, verify that "$G$15" is shown.

4. In the **To** group, choose **Value of**.

5. Key **1000000** in the **Value of** box. This tells Solver that you want the formula in cell G15 to compute to 1,000,000 (more or less).

6. Click in the **By Changing Variable Cells** box. Move the dialog box if necessary so that you can see cell C7.

7. Select cells C7:F7 in the worksheet, quarterly unit sales for the Sunshine frame. These values affect the formula results in cell G15.

NOTE

If Solver does not appear on the Data command tab, click the File command tab and choose Options. On the Add-Ins pane, choose Solver Add-in in the list and click Go. Continue to follow on-screen directions to install Solver.

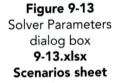

NOTE

Set Objective shows the active cell address, but you can change the reference if necessary.

Figure 9-13
Solver Parameters
dialog box
9-13.xlsx
Scenarios sheet

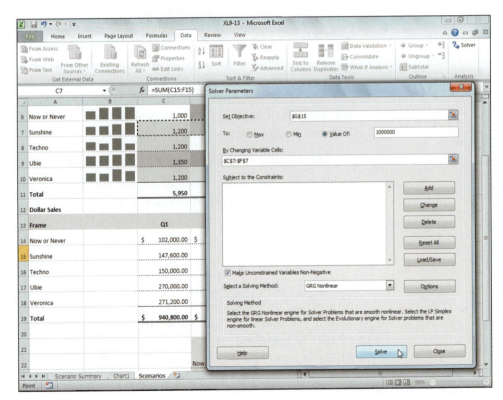

8. Click **Solve**. Each of the values in cells C7:F7 has been adjusted. The Solver Results dialog box allows you to keep the solution or return to the original values. You can also save the values from the solution as a scenario.

9. Click **Save Scenario**. In the **Scenario Name** box, key **Solver 1**.

10. Click **OK**. The Solver Results dialog box is still open.

11. Choose **Restore Original Values** and click **OK**. The worksheet is not changed, but you have saved one set of possible values.

Exercise 9-17   ADD SOLVER CONSTRAINTS

Without any constraints or limitations, Solver can find solutions that may not be realistic. In the previous exercise, for example, AllAround Vision Care may realize that it tends to get higher sales during the third and fourth quarters, not during the first and second quarters. It can incorporate these issues as constraints in a Solver problem.

1. With cell G15 selected, click the Solver button 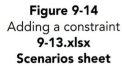. Your most recent parameters are shown.

2. In the **To** group, verify that the **Value of** box shows "1000000."

3. Verify that the **By Changing Variable Cells** box shows "$C$7:$F$7."

4. In the **Subject to the Constraints** area, click **Add**. The Add Constraint dialog box opens.

5. With the insertion point in the **Cell Reference** text box, select cell C7 in the worksheet.

6. Click the arrow for the middle (operator) box and choose **>=**.

7. In the **Constraint** box, key **1300**. This sets a requirement that the value in cell C7 (unit sales for the first quarter) be greater than or equal to 1300 units.

Figure 9-14
Adding a constraint
9-13.xlsx
Scenarios sheet

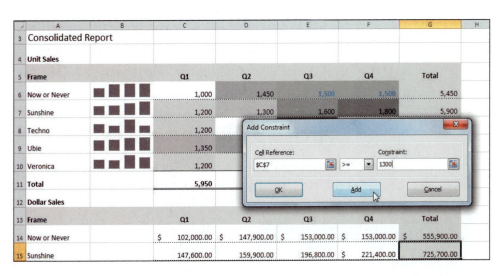

8. Click **Add**. The Add Constraint dialog box opens for a second constraint.

9. With the insertion point in the **Cell Reference** box, select cell D7.

10. Click the arrow for the operator box and choose **>=**.

11. In the **Constraint** box, key **1400**. This requirement is that the value in cell D7 (second quarter sales) be slightly more than its current value.

12. Click **Add**. With the insertion point in the **Cell Reference** box, select cell E7. Click the arrow for the operator box and choose **>=**. In the **Constraint** box, key **1700**.

13. Click **Add**. Add one more constraint for cell F7. It should be greater than or equal to 1850. When this constraint is complete, click **OK**. The Solver Parameters dialog box lists four constraints.

Figure 9-15
Using multiple constraints
9-13.xlsx
Scenarios sheet

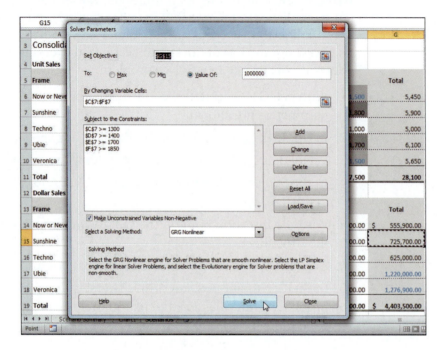

14. Click **Solve**. The sales for each quarter are adjusted as needed.

15. Click **Save Scenario**. Key **Solver 2** and click **OK**.

16. Choose **Restore Original Values** and click **OK**. The worksheet returns to its original values.

Exercise 9-18   EDIT A SCENARIO REPORT

Because you saved your Solver solutions as scenarios, you could show either possibility at any time. You now can create another scenario summary report to show those two possibilities.

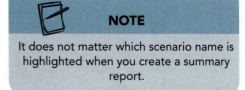

NOTE

It does not matter which scenario name is highlighted when you create a summary report.

1. Click the What-If Analysis button. Choose **Scenario Manager**. Your solver solutions are included in the Scenario Manager dialog box.

2. Choose **Summary**. Make sure **Scenario summary** is selected. Move the dialog box if row 15 is obscured.

3. Specify the **Result cells** by selecting cells C15:G15 in the worksheet. Click **OK**.

4. Hide columns D:G (Current Values through Increased Prices). Hide rows 6:10.

5. Click cell C11 and key **Quarter 1**. AutoFill to **Quarter 4** in cell C14. Copy these cells to cells C16:C19. Key **Year Total** in cell C20.

6. Insert a row at row 1 and key **Sunshine Sales Analysis** in cell B1. Set the font size to 16.

7. Save the workbook as ***[your initials]*9-18**.

Using the Research Tool

The Research task pane helps you find and insert data from an outside source into a worksheet. These outside sources can be built-in or online tools. Excel includes a Research Library with a multilanguage thesaurus and dictionary, a translation utility, and an encyclopedia. Although these tools are probably most often used in text documents, they can be used to better manage your use and choice of labels in a worksheet.

You can open the Research task pane by:

- Clicking the Research button 🔖 on the Review command tab.
- Clicking a word while holding down the Alt key.
- Clicking the Thesaurus button 📖 on the Review command tab.
- Clicking the Translate button 📑 on the Review command tab.

Exercise 9-19   FIND SYNONYMS

A *thesaurus* is a reference that lists words that mean the same thing as the word you select. A *synonym* is a word that means the same thing as another word. Many thesauruses include words with opposite meanings (antonyms) too. The thesaurus component of Excel's Research tool can look up labels in cells and suggest alternative words with the same or a similar meaning. In the workbook for this lesson, there is a hidden sheet with information for the Canadian market. The eyeglass frame names will be changed to an English alternative that means the same thing.

NOTE

If you have different reference books and resources on your computer, expand and collapse each one and check its findings.

1. Right-click any worksheet tab and choose **Unhide Sheet**. Unhide the **CanadianInfo** sheet.

2. Hold down Alt and click cell A4. The Research task pane opens with results for the word "now" based on the reference component that is in effect. The All Reference Books box shows the Research component that was most recently used at your computer.

3. Click the arrow for the All Reference Books list (below the Search for box). Choose **All Reference Books**. All reference books on your computer are searched. Each resource has an expand or collapse arrow to indicate whether its information is hidden or shown (see Figure 9-16 on the next page).

Figure 9-16
Using the Research task pane
9-18.xlsx
CanadianInfo sheet

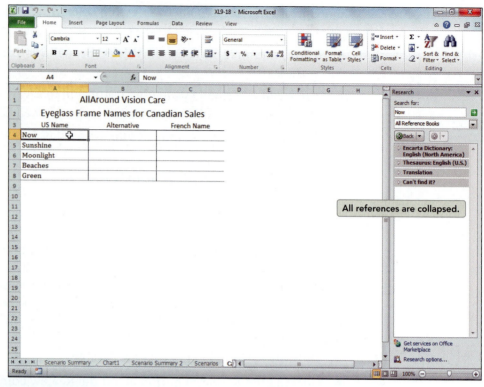

NOTE

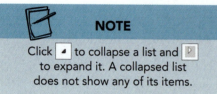

Click ◢ to collapse a list and ▷ to expand it. A collapsed list does not show any of its items.

4. Collapse each of the resource components to start.

5. Click the Expand button ▷ for **Thesaurus: English (U.S.)**. There are many words or word combinations that mean the same as "now."

6. Click cell B4. Your alternative word goes here.

7. Place the mouse pointer on **pronto** in the **immediately (adv.)** group.

Figure 9-17
Choosing a word from the thesaurus
9-18.xlsx
CanadianInfo sheet

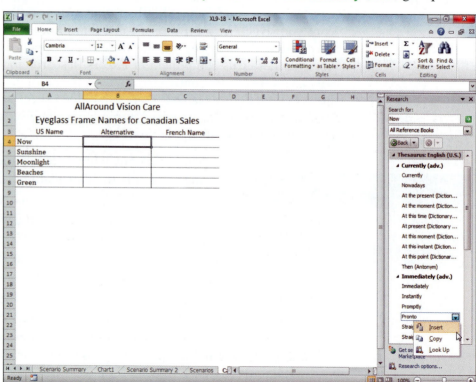

8. Click the arrow and choose **Insert**. The word is inserted in cell B4.

9. Hold down [Alt] and click cell A5. The task pane updates to show similar words for "sunshine."

10. Click cell B5. Your new word goes here.

11. Find **sunbeams**, click its arrow, and choose **Insert**.

12. Click cell A6. Click the **Review** command tab. Click the Thesaurus button [🔲]. There are several results for this word.

13. Click cell B6 and insert an alternative name of your choice.

14. Click cell A7 and click the Thesaurus button [🔲].

15. Click cell B7 and insert a new name of your choice.

16. Click cell A8 and click the Thesaurus button [🔲].

17. Click cell B8 and insert **jade**.

18. Close the Research task pane.

Exercise 9-20   TRANSLATE WORDS

As part of the Research tool, Excel can translate words into another language. Although this is a handy feature, you will find that you must be familiar with the language so that you can use correct grammar, including noun gender and verb tenses. In the Translation tool, possible word translations are shown but are not selectable. You must key the new word.

In your worksheet, AllAround Vision Care would like to provide a French translation for the English frame names. Excel includes Spanish and French language dictionaries, and there are many other language dictionaries available from Microsoft.

1. Click cell A4. Click the **Review** command tab. Click the Translate button [🔲]. Results are shown in one of your online language dictionaries.

2. Click the Expand button [▷] for **Translation** in the Research task pane if necessary.

3. In the **To** box, choose **French (France)**. Click the Expand button [▷] for **Bilingual Dictionary** if the list is not expanded. There are many translation possibilities for the word "now." If you do not know something about French, you could easily make a poor choice here.

4. Click cell C4 and key **Tout de Suite** (see Figure 9-18 on the next page).

Figure 9-18
Using Translation in
the Research task
pane
9-18.xlsx
CanadianInfo sheet

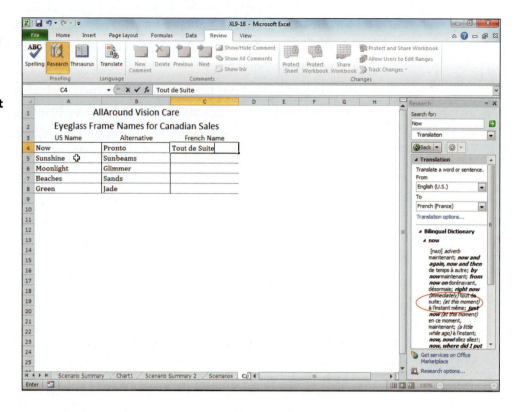

5. Click cell A5. Click the Translate button [icon]. These results are more streamlined than "now."

6. Click cell C5 and key **Soleil**.

7. Hold down [Alt] and click cell A6. You can probably see already why it is important that you know something about the language you are translating to.

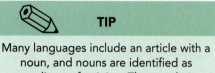

TIP

Many languages include an article with a noun, and nouns are identified as masculine or feminine. The translation tool does not include the article, although it does specify whether the noun is masculine or feminine.

8. Click cell C6 and key **Clair de Lune**.

9. Hold down [Alt] and click cell A7. The tool provides a singular, masculine noun.

10. Click cell C7 and key **Les Plages**.

11. Look up the word in cell A8. Key **Vert** as the French name.

12. Close the Research task pane.

Exercise 9-21   INSERT A SPECIAL SYMBOL

Many words in international languages include accents on individual characters. An *accent* is a mark or symbol above or below a character that indicates a change in pronunciation or meaning. Accented characters are special symbols and can be easily inserted in a label.

1. Insert a row at row 3.

2. In cell A3 key **Bon March**. The next character is an accented lowercase e (é).

3. While in **Edit** mode for cell A3, click the **Insert** command tab.

4. In the **Symbols** group, click the Symbol button Ω. The Symbol dialog box opens.

5. Click the **Font** arrow and key **c**. Set the font to **Cambria**.

6. Click the **Subset** arrow and choose **Basic Latin**.

7. Scroll to find **é**, the accented lowercase "e." This is an *acute* accent.

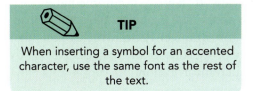

TIP

When inserting a symbol for an accented character, use the same font as the rest of the text.

Figure 9-19
Inserting a symbol
9-18.xlsx
CanadianInfo sheet

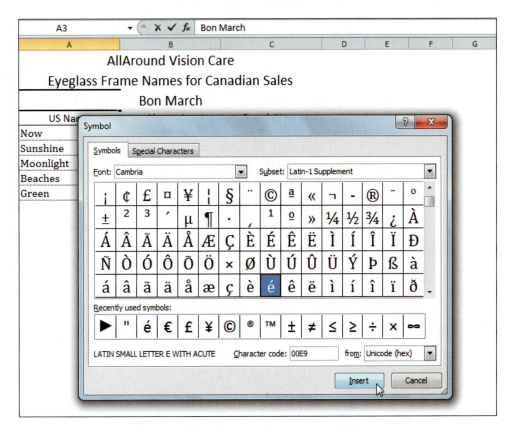

8. Click the character to select it and click **Insert**. Click **Close**. The accented é is inserted.

9. Complete the label in cell A3 to show "Bon Marché Department Store."

10. Press Ctrl + Home .

Working with the Info Pane

The Info pane in Backstage view, in its own way, provides an overview or analysis of your workbook's status. What you see in this view depends on settings and properties in the workbook. Generally, you'll see a Protect Workbook group, a Check for Issues group, and a Manage Versions group.

A workbook *property* is a setting or metadata that are stored with the workbook when it is saved. *Metadata* include the computer name, the user name, the storage folder, hidden data, and more. Some Excel workbook properties are visible in the Info pane in Backstage view. If they are not immediately visible, you can open a related dialog box to access the property. Workbook properties are also shown in the Document Information Panel which opens just below the Ribbon. You can also see many properties in an Open dialog box by setting and organizing its view to show such information.

Exercise 9-22   SET DOCUMENT PROPERTIES

Standard properties for Microsoft Office documents include author name, document title, and subject. These are optional settings, and you key your own data for these properties. There are other properties that are automatically set and maintained. They include data such as the file size or the dates when a workbook was created or edited. You cannot edit automatically updated properties.

1. Click the **File** command tab. When a workbook is open, Backstage view opens to the Info pane. You should see **Permissions**, **Prepare for Sharing**, and **Versions** quick command groups. On the right, you can see a small image of the active sheet and some of the document properties.

2. Click the arrow with **Properties**. Choose **Show Document Panel**. Backstage view closes, and the Document Information Panel opens below the Ribbon at the top of the worksheet.

3. Triple-click in the **Author** box and key *[your first and last name]*.

4. Press [Tab]. Key **Frame Info** in the **Title** box.

5. Click in the **Comments** box and key the following:

   This workbook will be saved in Excel 97-2003 format for review by all locations and suppliers.

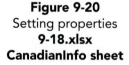

Figure 9-20
Setting properties
9-18.xlsx
CanadianInfo sheet

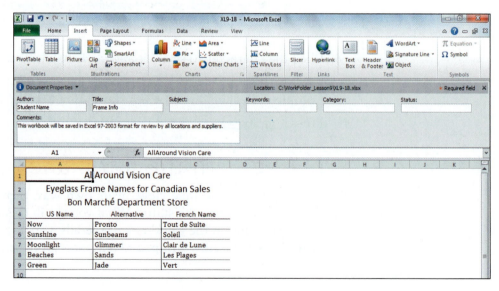

6. Close the Document Information Panel.

7. Press F12. The Save As dialog box shows the current file name.

8. Click the **Save as type** arrow and choose **Excel 97-2003 Workbook**.

NOTE

If the message box says that the Compatibility Checker could not finish and formatting may be lost, click Yes to continue.

9. Edit the file name to *[your initials]*9-22 and click **Save**. The Compatibility Checker runs and alerts you that some of the formatting is not supported in earlier versions of Excel.

10. Click **Continue**. Close the workbook.

Exercise 9-23 SET ADVANCED PROPERTIES

From the File command tab, you can choose the Open command or the Recent command to open a workbook. The Recent command is usually faster if your workbook appears in the list of file names, because you do not need to navigate to the folder. The list includes the workbook name and its location. You can set how many workbooks are shown in the list in the Excel Options dialog box (Advanced tab). And, of course, the list constantly changes as you work.

As you have seen, Info in Backstage view displays several document properties. You'll see, too, that the quick commands listed on the left are context-sensitive, because they reflect what is included in the workbook. For example, when you open the workbook you just saved, you'll see a Compatibility Mode group because the file is in Excel 97-2003 format.

For any workbook, you can include a thumbnail preview of the worksheet that is visible in other dialog boxes or windows. This preview displays part of the data on the active sheet as an aid to identification of the file from Explorer, Computer, or the Open dialog box.

1. Click the **File** command tab. When no workbook is open, Backstage view opens to the **Recent** choice.

2. Find and click *[your initials]*9-22 to open the workbook. Because this workbook was saved in Excel 97-2003 format, the title bar shows "[Compatibility Mode]." In this mode you have access to all Excel 2010 features and commands. However, if you use a feature that is not available in an earlier version (sparklines, for example), it would not be editable if you resave the file in this format.

3. Click the **File** command tab. The **Compatibility Mode** group includes a command that can convert the file to Excel 2010 format.

4. View the information on the right. You can now see your name and the title, but the comment is not visible.

5. Click the arrow with **Properties** and choose **Advanced Properties**. The Properties dialog box includes five panes of metadata about your workbook.

6. Click the **General** tab. This tab shows properties that are automatically maintained.

7. Click the **Summary** tab. This tab shows the information you keyed earlier with a few additional choices.

8. Key your school or business as the company.

9. Click to select **Save Thumbnails for All Excel Documents**. This will create a tiny image of the worksheet for previewing the contents of the file in Open and Explorer dialog boxes.

Figure 9-21
Saving a thumbnail
as a property
9-22.xls
CanadianInfo sheet

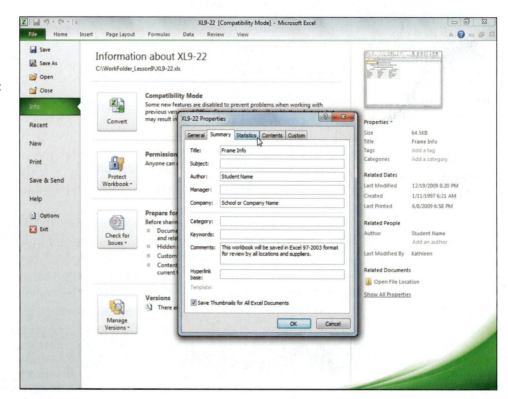

10. Click the **Statistics** tab. These settings are automatically updated.

11. Click the **Contents** tab. This contains the metadata that are saved with this workbook. It summarizes what is in the workbook and includes the sheet names, range names, and chart sheet names.

12. Click the **Custom** tab. This tab provides settings that can be created specific to a company or individual. AllAround Vision Care, for example, might set a property that indicates the office location where a workbook was originated.

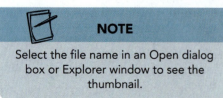

NOTE

Select the file name in an Open dialog box or Explorer window to see the thumbnail.

13. Click **OK** to close the Properties dialog box.

14. Click **Save As**. The Save As dialog box shows the current file type.

15. Click the **Save as type** arrow and choose **Excel Workbook**. This is 2010 format.

16. Edit the file name to *[your initials]*9-23 and click **Save**. Close the workbook.

17. Press Ctrl+O. Find *[your initials]*9-23 and click once to select it.

18. Set the Open dialog box to show the preview if necessary. Close the dialog box without opening the file.

Using Online Help

Solver, Goal Seek, and scenarios can be used to find solutions to fairly sophisticated business problems. Learn more about what-if analysis in general.
   Ask a question about what-if analysis:

1. Look for Help topics about what-if analysis, projecting values, data tables, and Solver.

2. Read the information and close the windows.

Lesson 9   Summary

- The Mark as Final command is a simple way to protect a workbook from being edited. This property is easily reset and provides minimum security.

- Macros are recorded programming routines that might contain malicious code, so you can set a computer to disable them and notify you when you open a workbook with a macro.

- What-if analysis tests and displays values in a worksheet as a way to predict future results.

- A scenario is a set of values for specific cells, saved with a name in the workbook.

- You can add multiple scenarios to a workbook.

- Scenarios can be edited, displayed, or deleted when necessary.

- A scenario summary report is an outline about each scenario in the worksheet.

- Color scales are conditional formatting for cells that fills each cell with a color variation based on its value.

- Highlight cells rules can use operators in addition to those shown in the gallery if you use the New Formatting Rule dialog box.

- Multiple conditional formatting rules and/or data visualizations can be set for a range of cells.

- A trendline illustrates and predicts general tendencies of values in a chart.

- In backsolving, you specify the desired results of a formula and adjust values to reach those results.

- Goal Seek is an analysis command that adjusts a single cell value to reach a desired outcome in a formula.

- Solver is a what-if analysis tool. Its parameters are a target cell, adjustable cells, and constraints or limitations on the target or adjustable cells.

- Research tools in Excel include a thesaurus and translation dictionaries.
- The Thesaurus command proposes alternative labels with the same and/or opposite meanings.
- Translation tools look up a word and list possible words with the same meaning in the chosen language.
- Basic information about an open workbook is assembled and show in Backstage view from the Info command.
- Document properties are metadata that are saved with the workbook. Some settings are automatic, and others are set by the user.
- Document properties include an optional thumbnail preview that is visible in the Open and Explorer dialog boxes.

LESSON 9		Command Summary	
Feature	Button	Ribbon Location	Keyboard
Color scale		Home, Styles	
Goal Seek		Data, Data Tools	
Properties		File, Info	
Research		Review, Proofing	Alt+Click
Scenario, create		Data, Data Tools	
Scenario, edit		Data, Data Tools	
Solver		Data, Analysis	
Symbol	Ω	Insert, Symbols	
Thesaurus		Review, Proofing	Alt+Click
Thumbnail preview		File, Info	
Translate		Review, Language	Alt+Click
Trendline, add		Chart Tools Layout, Analysis	
Sparkline, axis		Sparkline Tools Design, Group	

Please visit our Online Learning Center, *www.lessonapproach2010.com,* **where you will find the following review materials:**

Concepts Review

True/False Questions

Short Answer Questions

Critical Thinking Questions

Skills Review

Review Exercises that target single skills

Lesson Applications

Review Exercises that challenge students by testing multiple skills in each exercise

On Your Own

Open-ended exercises that require students to synthesize multiple skills and apply creativity and problem-solving as they would in a real world business situation

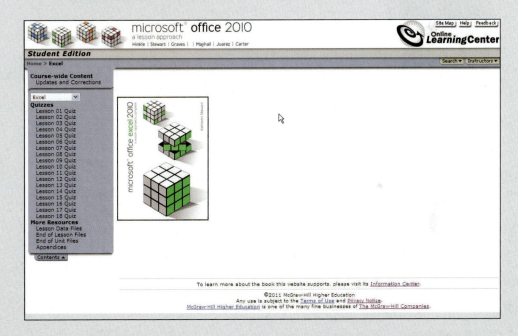

Please visit our Online Learning Center, *www.lessonapproach2010.com,* **where you will find Unit Applications review materials.**

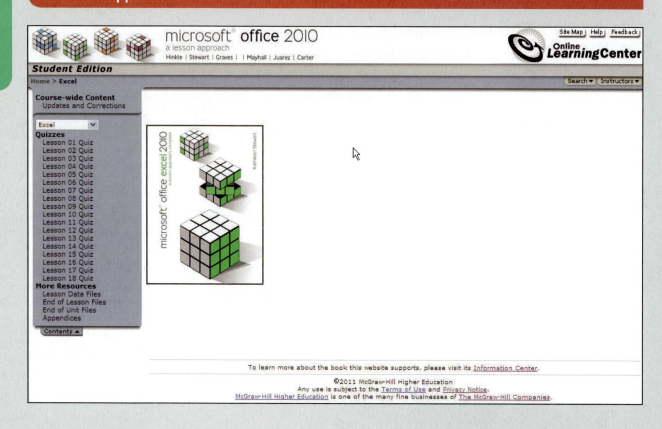

Microsoft® Office PowerPoint 2010

A Lesson Approach, Complete

CASE STUDY

Microsoft PowerPoint 2010 is a powerful and persuasive tool that can be used in many creative ways. It is the industry standard for business presentations. The possibilities for how you combine color, text, and graphics to illustrate your presentation are almost endless. However, making good choices requires more than just understanding how the program works. You need knowledge of your presentation situation and your audience to design your slides in an effective way. Also, speaking with the computer support of a slide show can be more demanding than speaking impromptu. You can appear very professional when you deliver your presentation with confidence and handle your software and equipment well.

To better understand the context of how PowerPoint is used in business, all the lessons in this text relate to everyday business tasks. Imagine yourself working as an intern for Good 4 U, a fictional New York restaurant. Through your work in this position you will develop design skills to prepare slides that are attractive and contribute to audience understanding.

Good 4 U Restaurant

The Good 4 U restaurant has been in business for only a little over three years, but it's been a success from the time it served its first veggie burger. The restaurant—which features healthy food and has a theme based on "everyday active life"—seems to have found an award-winning recipe for success. (Figure CS-1 shows the interior of the largest dining room in the restaurant. It features plants and a wide expanse of windows looking out over Central Park South, a tree-lined avenue on the south side of New York's Central Park.)

All the food at Good 4 U is low-fat and contains low sodium. The menu features a variety of vegetables (all organic, of course!), as well as fish and chicken. The restaurant doesn't serve alcohol, offering instead fruit juices and sparkling water. Good 4 U's theme of "everyday active life" is reflected on the restaurant's walls with running, tennis, and bicycling memorabilia. This theme really reflects the interests of the two co-owners: Julie Wolfe, who led the New York Flash to two Women's Professional Basketball Association championships in her 10 years with the team, and Gus Irvinelli, who is an avid tennis player and was selected for the U.S. Amateur team. Even the chef, Michele Jenkins, leads an active everyday life—she rides her bicycle 10 miles a day in and around Central Park.

Two years ago, Roy Olafsen was a marketing manager for a large hotel chain. He was overweight and out of shape. In the same week that his doctor told him to eat better and exercise regularly, Roy received a job offer from Good 4 U. "It was too good to pass up," he said. "It was my chance to combine

Figure CS-1 Interior of Good 4 U restaurant and a sampling of the fresh food prepared daily.

work and a healthy lifestyle." As you work through the text, you'll discover that Good 4 U is often involved in health-oriented products, as well as events that focus on athletics. Since Roy has been hired, he has worked to expand opportunities outside the restaurant walls and educate others about the healthy food available at Good 4 U. He has encouraged the restaurant to sponsor workshops, classes, marathons, and other health- and activity-based events. Roy has also encouraged Julie and Gus to expand their business by adding a catering component and by opening restaurants in two other cities.

As an intern at Good 4 U, you will work with the four key people shown in Figure CS-2 to help them develop presentations for potential customers, new hires, and community members. Each lesson will describe who will be presenting the material, the purpose of the presentation, and the intended audience. As you work with these presentations, notice the following things:

• The types of presentations needed in a small business to carry on day-to-day operations.

Figure CS-2 Key employees

Julie Wolfe
Co-Owner

Gus Irvinelli
Co-Owner

Michele Jenkins
Head Chef

Roy Olafsen
Marketing Manager

- The design of presentations. Real businesses must often focus on designing eye-catching, informative presentations for customers. The business's success is often influenced by the compelling presentations that sell its services to customers.
- The "Tips for Designing Presentations" at the end of this Case Study. Good presentations generally follow these basic guidelines.

As you use this text and become more experienced with Microsoft PowerPoint 2010, you will gain experience in creating, editing, and designing presentations for business that you can apply to your classes and work situations.

In your first meeting with Roy Olafsen, he gave you the following tips for designing presentations. These tips can be applied to any presentation.

Tips for Designing Presentations

- Prepare a distinctive title slide. Make sure the title identifies the presentation content.
- Maintain a consistent color scheme throughout the presentation for a sense of unity.
- Keep the background simple, and modify it to help create a unique theme for your presentation.
- Choose colors carefully so that all text can be seen clearly. You must have a high contrast between background colors and text colors for easy reading.
- Write lists with parallel wording, and be concise. Limit bulleted text to no more than seven words on a line and no more than seven lines on a slide.
- Avoid small text. Body text on slides, such as that for first-level bulleted lists, should be no smaller than 24 points. Text for second-level bulleted text or annotations may be slightly smaller, but not less than 20 points. Establish a hierarchy for text sizes based on text importance, and then use those sizes consistently.
- Think and design visually to express your message. Use graphics such as boxes, lines, circles, and other shapes to highlight text or to create SmartArt diagrams that show processes and relationships. Illustrate with pictures and other images as appropriate.
- Select all images carefully to make your presentation content more understandable. They should not detract from the message. Avoid the temptation to "jazz up" a slide show with too much clip art.
- Keep charts simple. The most effective charts are pie charts with three or four slices and column charts with three or four columns. Label charts carefully for easy interpretation.
- Provide some form of handout so that your audience can keep track of the presentation or make notes while you are talking.
- Include multimedia elements of animation, transitions, audio, and video if these elements strengthen your message, engage your audience, aid understanding, or make your presentation more compelling.
- Your final slide should provide a recommendation or summary to help you conclude your presentation effectively.

Unit 1

BASIC SKILLS

Lesson 1
Getting Started in PowerPoint

OBJECTIVES *After completing this lesson, you will be able to:*

1. Explore Microsoft PowerPoint.
2. View a presentation.
3. Add text using placeholders.
4. Prepare presentation supplements.
5. Name, save, and close a presentation.

Estimated Time: 2 hours

Microsoft PowerPoint is a presentation program widely used in business and in education. It enables you to show your presentation content in a visual way through on-screen slides that are displayed in a slide show. For example, a hotel manager may develop a presentation to help market the hotel at conferences and meetings, or an instructor may display notes for a lecture to help students keep focused. A financial analyst may present investment information to prospective clients, or a builder may present construction plans to an urban development commission for approval. Also, PowerPoint is an effective tool for creating flyers and other printed products because of its versatile drawing and layout tools.

In this lesson, you will be working as an intern with Roy Olafsen, Good 4 U marketing manager, to make revisions to a presentation he has developed. This lesson provides an overview of PowerPoint features so that you will become accustomed to the application screen and to the way slides move within a slide show. You will also see examples of graphics you will learn to create later in this text.

Exploring PowerPoint

NOTE

The presentations in this text relate to the case study about Good 4 U, a fictional restaurant.

To become familiar with PowerPoint, identify parts of the window such as the Ribbon, tabs, and command buttons shown in Figure 1-1. Several tabs are unique to PowerPoint, while others are very similar to tabs used in Word and Excel. The Quick Access Toolbar is located above the Ribbon.

TABLE 1-1 The PowerPoint Window

Part of Window	Purpose
Command buttons	Buttons designed to perform a function or display a gallery of options.
Groups	Logical sets of related commands and options.
Notes pane	The area where you can add speaker notes for the presenter.
Quick Access Toolbar	Located by default at the top of the PowerPoint window and provides quick access to commands that you use frequently.
Ribbon	Consists of task-oriented tabs with commands organized in groups.
Scroll bars	Used with the pointer to move a slide or outline text right or left and up or down. You can also use the vertical scroll bar to move from slide to slide.
Slide pane	The area where you create, edit, and display presentation slides.
Slides and Outline pane	The area that can display either an outline of the presentation's text or thumbnails—miniature pictures—of the presentation's slides. You choose either Outline or Slides by clicking the appropriate tab. (If this pane is not displayed, click the Normal view button.)
Status bar	Displays information about the current presentation.
Tabs	Task-oriented collections of commands. In addition to the standard tabs, contextual tabs appear relevant to the selected object.
Title bar	Contains the name of the presentation.
View buttons	Buttons used to switch between Normal view, Slide Sorter view, and Slide Show view.

Figure 1-1
PowerPoint window
in Normal view

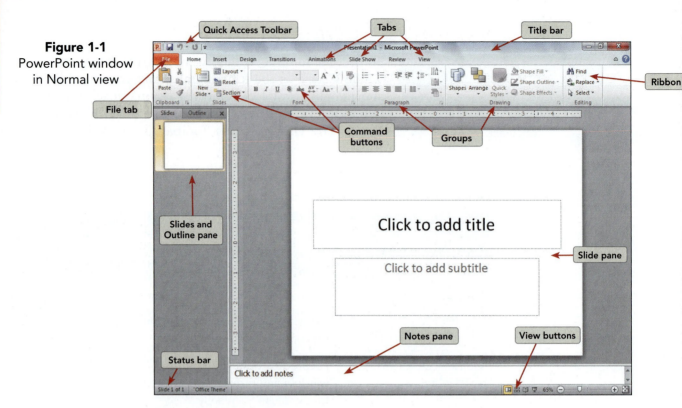

Exercise 1-1 IDENTIFY PARTS OF THE POWERPOINT WINDOW AND QUICK ACCESS TOOLBAR

The PowerPoint *Ribbon* contains nine task-oriented tabs: File, Home, Insert, Design, Transitions, Animations, Slide Show, Review, and View. Commands on each tab are organized in logical groups. A *ScreenTip* is the box displaying a command or object name that pops up when you point to it; sometimes a brief description will also appear. Within the Ribbon groups you will find drop-down galleries that easily present formatting options, graphics choices, layouts, and more.

The *Quick Access Toolbar* is a customizable toolbar located above the Ribbon. It contains common commands that function independently of the tab currently displayed. It can be moved under the Ribbon, but that location requires more space.

1. Open PowerPoint. Using Figure 1-1 as a guide, move your pointer over items in the PowerPoint window to identify them by name using ScreenTips similar to Figure 1-2.

Figure 1-2
ScreenTip over the
New Slide command
button

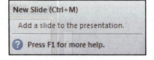

2. Click the drop-down arrow at the end of the Quick Access Toolbar.

3. Choose **Show Below the Ribbon**.

4. Click the drop-down arrow again, and choose **Show Above the Ribbon** to return to the default position.

Exercise 1-2 OPEN AN EXISTING PRESENTATION

When you first open PowerPoint, you will often start a new blank presentation. However, in this exercise you open an existing PowerPoint presentation that Roy Olafsen developed for a local business organization to explain the background of the Good 4 U restaurant. You will make several revisions to this presentation.

1. Click the **File** tab to open Backstage view which displays quick commands.

2. Click **Open**.

3. In the Open dialog box, navigate to the appropriate drive and folder for your student files according to your instructor's directions.

4. When you locate the student files, click the arrow next to the Views button ▤ (see Figure 1-3) in the Open dialog box to display a menu of view options.

Figure 1-3
Folders listed in the Open dialog box

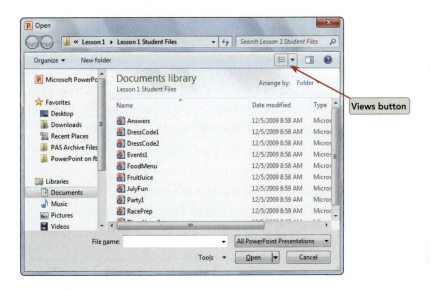

Views button

NOTE

Your instructor will tell you where to locate the files for this text. For more information about working with files, folders, and directories in Windows, refer to "File Management" at the Professional Approach Online Learning Center at www.mhhe.com/lessonapproach2010.

5. Choose **Small Icons** to list all files by name.

6. Click the Views button ▤ again, and choose **Details** to see the type of file and the date on which it was last modified.

7. Locate the file **ThreeYears2** (use the scroll bar if necessary), and click once to select the file.

8. Click **Open**. (You can also double-click the file's name to open it.) PowerPoint opens the file in Normal view.

Exercise 1-3 WORK WITH RIBBONS, TABS, GROUPS, AND COMMAND BUTTONS

On the Ribbon, tabs reflect tasks you commonly perform, and they provide easy access to the commands organized in related groups of buttons and other controls. *Live Preview* is a feature that shows what your changes will look like before clicking or selecting an effect. Sometimes the group of available effects is presented in a *gallery* that displays thumbnails of different options you can choose.

1. Click the **Insert** tab.
2. Identify each of the groups located on the Insert tab: Tables, Images, Illustrations, Links, Text, Symbols, and Media. These groups contain command buttons that provide options through dialog boxes or galleries of options.

Exercise 1-4 USE MICROSOFT POWERPOINT HELP

Microsoft Office provides a *Help* feature that is an excellent reference tool for finding more information on any PowerPoint feature.

1. Click the Microsoft PowerPoint Help button 🔵 located on the upper right of the Ribbon, or you can press F1. The Help window will appear on top of your open PowerPoint presentation.
2. Key **Ribbon** in the search box located on the Help window, and press Enter (or click the Search button 🔍 Search ▾).
3. Scroll through the list of options that display, and click **Familiarize yourself with the fluent Office user interface**.
4. Read and scroll through the entire Help window.
5. When you have finished reading, click the Close button 🔲 X 🔲 in the upper right corner of the Help window to close it and return to PowerPoint.

Viewing a Presentation

PowerPoint provides multiple views for working with your presentations based on what you need to do.

- *Normal view.* Enter information directly on a slide or in outline format.
- *Slide Sorter view.* Display multiple slides as thumbnails, or miniature slides, for a presentation overview, to rearrange slides, and to add special transition effects for the movements between slides.

- *Notes Page view.* Add speaker notes to accompany a slide.
- *Reading view.* Browse through your slides in sequence.
- *Slide Show view.* Display your presentation to an audience.

Views can be changed by using the View tab or by using the status bar at the bottom of the PowerPoint window.

Exercise 1-5   USE NORMAL AND SLIDE SORTER VIEWS

Normal view is the default view when PowerPoint opens and is the best view for writing text directly on a slide and designing your presentation. In this exercise, you will change to *Slide Sorter view* and rearrange slides by dragging.

1. Your PowerPoint window should be in Normal view. From the View tab, in the Presentation Views group, choose the Slide Sorter button ▦. You may also use the Slide Sorter button ▦ on the status bar.

2. Click slide 7 and hold down your left mouse button and drag until you see a vertical line before slide 6, then release the mouse button. This change creates a better sequence.

3. From the View tab, in the Presentation Views group, click the Normal view button ▤ to return to Normal view. You may also click the Normal view button ▣ on the status bar.

Exercise 1-6   USE THE SLIDES AND OUTLINE PANE

In Normal view, the *Slides and Outline pane* is at the left of the Slide pane. The Outline tab allows you to quickly enter text in an outline format because it shows only slide titles and listed text with *bullets,* small circular shapes, in front of each listing. The Slides tab provides thumbnails so that you can see or rearrange slides; it is similar to the Slide Sorter view.

1. Click the **Outline** tab at the top of the Slides and Outline pane to see only the presentation's text.

2. Point to the right border of the Slides and Outline pane. When the splitter ⬌ appears, drag the border about an inch to the right to increase the size of the Slides and Outline pane.

3. Scroll in the outline text until you see the text for slide 4.

Figure 1-4
Working with the
Slides and Outline
pane

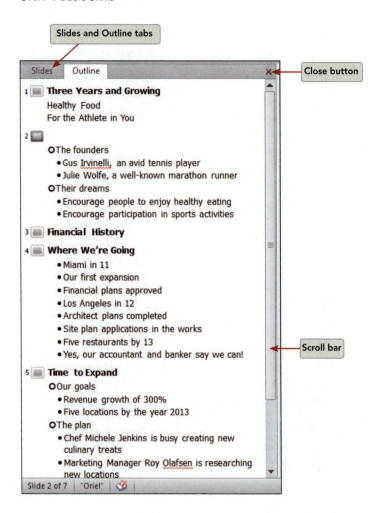

4. Working in the Outline tab, change each of the years (11, 12, and 13) to **2011, 2012**, and **2013**. The first line, for example, should read "Miami in 2011." Notice that, as you work, your changes are reflected in the Slide pane.

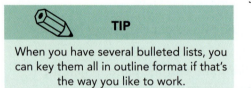

TIP

When you have several bulleted lists, you can key them all in outline format if that's the way you like to work.

5. Click in front of "Miami"; then from the Home tab, in the Paragraph group, click the Decrease List Level button ⊞ to promote the item by moving it to the left. Apply this same treatment to "Los Angeles in 2012" and "Five Restaurants by 2013." This distinguishes the main items in the list from the more detailed items under them.

6. Click the Close button ⊠ on the Slides and Outline pane to hide it. The Slide pane expands to fill the space.

7. From the View tab, in the Presentation Views group, click the Normal view button ⊞. The Slides and Outline pane is displayed again.

8. Click the **Slides** tab at the top of the Slides and Outline pane. The Slides and Outline pane becomes smaller and the size of the Slide pane increases.

Exercise 1-7 MOVE FROM SLIDE TO SLIDE

PowerPoint provides several ways to move from slide to slide when using Normal view:

- Drag the vertical scroll box, or click on the vertical bar above and below the box.
- Click the Previous Slide ⬆ or Next Slide ⬇ button located below the vertical scroll bar.
- Press PageUp and PageDown.

Figure 1-5
Moving from slide to slide

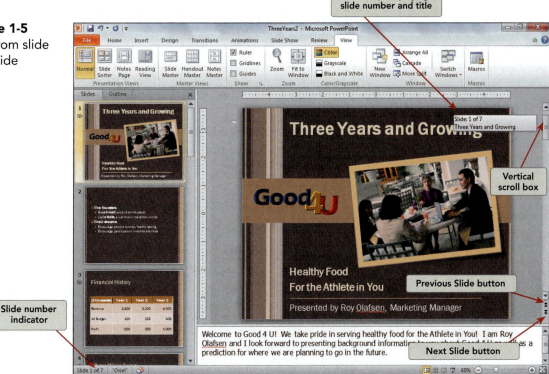

1. At the right of the Slide pane, drag the box on the vertical scroll bar. Notice the pop-up box that displays slide numbers and slide titles as you drag. When you drag the box to the bottom of the scroll bar and release the mouse button, slide 7 appears in your window. Notice that slide 7 has a highlighted border around it in the Slides and Outline pane. This identifies it as the current slide.

2. Drag the scroll box up to display slide 6. Notice that "Slide 6 of 7" appears on the left side of the status bar to also identify the current slide.

3. Click the Previous Slide button ⬆ at the bottom of the vertical scroll bar several times to move back in the presentation. Use the Next Slide button ⬇ to move forward.

4. Press PageDown and PageUp on your keyboard several times to move to different slides. Use this method to move to slide 2. Check the status bar for the slide number.

Exercise 1-8   USE ZOOM AND FIT TO WINDOW

PowerPoint provides two different ways to change the size of the current slide in both Normal view and Slide Sorter view. The *Zoom* command can magnify your slide so that you can see small details for precise alignment and corrections. The *Fit to Window* command will change from the current zoom settings to fit your slide in the window that is open.

- From the View tab, in the Zoom group, click the Zoom or Fit to Window command button.

- Use the Zoom slider or Fit slide to current window button on the right end of the status bar.

1. From the View tab, in the Zoom group, click the Zoom button 🔍.

2. On the Zoom dialog box, click the radial button beside "200%" and click OK.

3. From the View tab, in the Zoom group, click the Fit to Window button 🔲 to reduce slide size so that the slide is viewable in the window.

4. On the right end of the status bar, click the Zoom In button (a plus) ⊕ until you reach "170%."

5. On the right end of the status bar, click the Fit slide to current window button 🔲 so that the entire slide is viewable again.

Exercise 1-9   USE READING AND SLIDE SHOW VIEWS

Both *Reading view* and *Slide Show view* display your slides at full-screen size beginning on the current slide. The Reading view command is on the View tab. From the Slide Show tab, you can start a slide show from the beginning or from the current slide. The Reading View and Slide Show commands are also available on the status bar.

Reading view is used to browse through your presentation with the title bar showing. The status bar is displayed with navigation tools to move from slide to slide. Slide Show view is used to show your presentation to an audience because only the slide is displayed. Navigation tools are available if you point to them.

In both views, slides can be changed by pressing the ⌷Spacebar⌷, ⌷PageUp⌷, ⌷PageDown⌷, ⌷N⌷, or ⌷P⌷ key or the arrow keys or by clicking the left mouse button.

1. Move to slide 1. From the View tab, in Presentation Views, click the Reading view button 🔲. The first slide in the presentation fills the screen, with the title bar at the top and status bar at the bottom.

2. On the status bar, click the right arrow to move to slide 2.

3. Press ⌷N⌷ on the keyboard to move to the next slide, slide 3.

4. Press ⌷P⌷ twice to return to slide 1. Press ⌷Esc⌷ to exit Reading view.

5. On slide 1, click the Slide Show button ⊞ located on the status bar to the left of the Zoom slider. The first slide in the presentation fills the screen.

6. Click the left mouse button to move to slide 2, and repeat to move to slide 3.

Exercise 1-10   OBSERVE ANIMATION AND TRANSITION EFFECTS

Animation effects are the special visual or sound effects that appear as objects are displayed on the screen or removed from view. *Transition effects* are the visual and sound effects that appear when changing slides. When developing this slide show, Roy Olafsen placed several different effects in the show to feature items on the slides and to control the way text appears on a slide while he is talking.

1. In Slide Show view and with slide 3 "Financial History" displayed, Press N to move to slide 4, which is titled "Where We're Going."

2. Using the left mouse button, click anywhere to see a sample of a PowerPoint text animation.

3. Press N again to move to slide 5 "Time to Expand." Notice the Box transition effect between slides 4 and 5.

4. Click the left mouse button two times to bring in the text on slide 5.

5. Press N to move to slide 6 "We've Come a Long Way." Press N three more times to bring in the text for slide 6. Notice the Entrance and Emphasis effects placed on this text. If your sound is on, you should also hear sound effects with each text item.

6. Press N to move to slide 7 and N again to finish the presentation.

7. Press Esc or − (minus) to end the slide show.

Adding Text Using Placeholders

Adding and editing text in PowerPoint is very similar to editing text in Word. When you point to an object on your screen that contains text, an *I-beam*, a vertical blinking bar in the shape of an uppercase "I," will appear and you can click in the position where you want to insert text. You can also drag the I-beam to select existing text. The Enter key moves the insertion point to the next line or bullet. The Delete key removes the character to the right of the insertion point. The Backspace key removes the character to the left of the insertion point.

Exercise 1-11   KEY PLACEHOLDER TEXT

Text *placeholders* are used for *title text* (the text that usually appears at the top of a slide), *body text* (text in the body of a slide such as a list), and other objects, such as picture captions. When you click inside a text placeholder, you *activate* it so that it is ready for editing or for inserting new text.

Placeholders help keep slide layout and formatting consistent within a presentation.

Body text often contains *bullets* (small dots, squares, or other symbols) to indicate the beginning of each item in a list; therefore, this text is called bulleted text. Bullets can also be decorative for an attention-getting effect.

NOTE

Notice that the pointer changes from an I-beam inside the border to an arrow pointer outside the border. When the pointer rests on top of the border, it becomes a four-pointed arrow, which can be used to move the text placeholder. When the pointer rests on top of a sizing handle, a two-pointed arrow appears for changing the placeholder size.

1. Move to slide 2, and click in the title text placeholder to activate the placeholder. Notice the border, a dashed line, that surrounds the placeholder, indicating that the placeholder is activated and you can edit or insert text. Sizing handles appear on the corners and edges.

2. Key the text **Where We Came From**.

3. In the body text placeholder, click anywhere on the line of text that begins "Gus Irvinelli."

4. Without clicking, move the pointer outside the placeholder border to the right and then back inside.

5. Drag the I-beam across the text "an avid" to select it, as shown in Figure 1-6. (Click to the left of "an avid," hold down the left mouse button, drag the I-beam across the two words, and then release the mouse button.)

Figure 1-6
Selecting text to edit

6. Key **a professional** to replace the selected text. (New text will automatically replace the selected text.)

7. Click the I-beam after the words "healthy eating," and press ⟨Enter⟩ to insert a new bulleted line. The new bullet is dimmed until you key text.

NOTE

Bulleted text lists the points being made in a slide presentation. This presentation uses open-circle and solid-dot bullets. Bullets can be changed to fit your presentation needs.

8. Key **Make their financial investments grow** after the new bullet.

9. Deactivate the placeholder by clicking a blank area of the slide. Be sure your pointer is a simple arrow, not an I-beam or a four-pointed arrow.

Exercise 1-12   CHANGE AND RESET PLACEHOLDER LAYOUT

Placeholders can be moved, resized, and rearranged on your slide. The *Layout* command of PowerPoint provides different slide layouts or can reset the placeholder to the original layout.

1. Still working on slide 2, click in the title placeholder to activate it.

2. Move your pointer to the outer border of the title placeholder.

3. When your pointer turns to a four-pointed arrow ⊕ (see Figure 1-7), click and drag the title placeholder to the bottom of the slide.

Figure 1-7
Selecting a placeholder

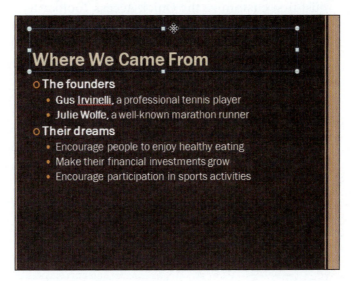

4. From the Home tab, in the Slides group, click the Reset button 📄 to reposition the title placeholder in its original position.

Preparing Presentation Supplements

Although the primary way of viewing a presentation is as a slide show, you can also print PowerPoint slides in several different ways to create materials you will use as a speaker or to create documents for your audience. You should carefully review the way your document will look before printing and select settings appropriate for each presentation situation.

NOTE

Throughout this text you will be instructed to submit your work. Your instructor may require that you submit your files to an electronic drop box or that you print slides. To conserve paper and speed up printing, you may print a *handout* instead of full-size slides.

- *Slides.* Individual slides are printed in full size on separate pages.

- *Notes pages.* Individual slides are printed at the top of a page with speaker notes printed below.

- *Outline.* Only the slide titles and bulleted text are printed.

- *Handouts.* Multiple scaled-down slide images are printed on each page (one, two, three, four, six, or nine to a page) and are often given to an audience during a presentation. Printing several slides on a single page is also a good way to review your work away from your computer and a convenient way to print class assignments.

Exercise 1-13   PRINT FULL-PAGE SLIDES

You can start the printing process in one of the following ways:

- From the File tab, choose **Print**. The area that appears is called *Print Backstage* view. It displays PowerPoint's default print settings and indicates the designated printer. A preview of the current slide is shown with navigation and zoom controls on the bottom. A scroll bar is on the right.
- Press Ctrl+P to open the File tab with Print Backstage view displayed.
- From the Quick Access Toolbar, click the Quick Print button . You must first customize the Quick Access Toolbar to make this button available. Use it with caution. This feature does not allow you to control print options. It prints with the most recently used print options and could result in printing your entire presentation with one slide on each page.

1. To print the first slide in your presentation, display slide 1 and then, from the File tab, choose **Print**. The Print Backstage view appears, as shown in Figure 1-8. Some of the settings may appear differently on your computer depending on how PowerPoint was installed.

Figure 1-8
Print Backstage view

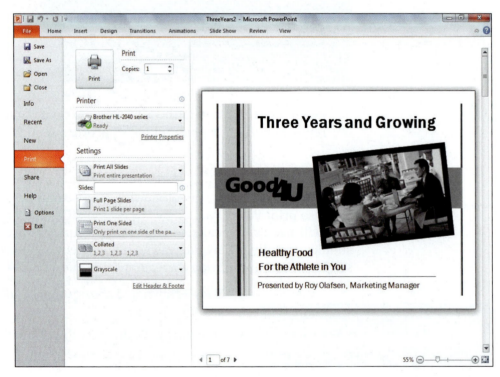

2. Notice that Print has the number of copies set for "1".

3. For Printer, the current printer is displayed. Click the down arrow to see the list of available printers. Follow your instructor's directions to choose an appropriate printer from the list.

4. Under Settings, look at the categories that are arranged as buttons with down arrows that display all your options. The option displayed on each button will change on the basis of the previous setting used. Make these changes:

    -   Click the down arrow for Print All Slides and choose **Print Current** Slide. This controls which slides will print.

        -   If **Full Page Slides** is displayed, it requires no change. This controls what you print, such as slides, notes pages, outlines, or handouts in a variety of layouts in both horizontal and vertical orientations.

        -   If **Collated** is displayed, it requires no change. This controls the printing order by choosing collated or uncollated.

        -   **Color** or **Grayscale** may be displayed depending on whether you are sending to a color printer or not; no change is required.

> **TIP**
>
> You can create a presentation that uses overhead transparencies by printing your slides on transparency film. Before printing, insert transparency sheets directly into your printer (choosing the correct type of transparency for a laser or ink-jet printer).

5. Click the Print button 🖨 to print the current slide.

Exercise 1-14 PRINT NOTES PAGES AND OUTLINES

Roy Olafsen has written some notes on two slides of this presentation to remind himself about what he needs to say when those slides are displayed for his audience. In this exercise you will print those pages, review outline printing, and print a handout page.

In addition to the print settings covered previously, you will learn about printing in black and white. The *Grayscale* option converts the presentation colors to shades of gray. The *Pure Black and White* option converts all colors to either black or white, eliminating shades of gray.

1. On slide 1, press Ctrl+P.

2. Under Settings, make these changes to prepare an outline:

    -   Click the down arrow for Print Current Slide, and choose **Print All Slides**.

    -   Click the down arrow for Full Page Slides, and choose **Outline**. Notice the text-only page that appears in the preview area. If you wanted to study the text of your presentation away from your computer, then printing this page would be convenient. To save paper, we will not print this view.

3. Notes pages provide a slide image at the top of a page with speaker notes below. Since Roy Olafsen made notes on slides 1 and 2, you need to print only those notes pages.

TIP

To print consecutive slides, you can use a hyphen. For example, key **2-4** to print slides 2 through 4. To print a combination of slides, you can key the range **1, 3, 5-9, 12** to print slides 1, 3, 5 through 9, and 12.

4. Under Settings, make these changes to prepare notes pages:
   - Click the down arrow for Outline, and choose **Notes Pages**.
   - Click the down arrow for Print All Slides, and choose **Custom Range**.
   - In the Slides text box, key **1,2** to print only slides 1 and 2.
   - Click the down arrow for Notes Pages, and choose the option **Scale to fit paper** to expand items to the full width of the page (or check the box beside Scale to fit paper).

5. If **Color** is displayed, click the list box down arrow and then **Grayscale**. If you have a color printer, you can choose Color from the list box but the grayscale setting will conserve your color ink or toner.

6. Click the Print button 🖨.

Exercise 1-15 PRINT HANDOUTS

For handouts, the number of slide images on a page can range from one to nine. You can use either landscape or portrait orientation, and the slides will be slightly larger if you choose **Fit to Paper**. Placing a line around the slides will make them more distinct on the page, especially if the slides have a light-colored background. You can choose to arrange the slides vertically or horizontally.

Roy Olafsen has seven slides in this presentation, and he has requested that you prepare a handout with all the slides on one page.

1. On slide 1, press Ctrl+P.

2. Under Settings, make these changes to prepare handouts:
   - Click the down arrow for Custom Range, and choose **Print All Slides**.
   - Click the down arrow for Notes Pages, and choose **9 Slides Horizontal** to print the entire presentation on one page.
   - Click the down arrow for 9 Slides Horizontal, and select **Scale to fit paper** and **Frame Slides** (or check the box beside **Scale to fit paper** and **Frame Slides**).
   - Click the down arrow for Portrait Orientation. Click the list box down arrow and then **Landscape Orientation** so that the slides will be larger on the page. (If **Landscape Orientation** appears, it requires no change.)

3. For Print, change the **Number of copies** to **2**. The **Collated** list box by default is set to print the slide show from beginning to end two times.

4. For Color, click the list box down arrow and examine the options: Color, Black and White, or Grayscale. Click **Grayscale**. (If Grayscale appears, it requires no change.)

5. Click the Print button 🖨.

Naming, Saving, and Closing a Presentation

When you create a new presentation or make changes to an existing one, you must save the presentation to make your changes permanent. Until your changes are saved, they can be lost if you have a power failure or a computer problem; therefore, it is a good idea to save frequently.

The first step in saving a document is to give it a *file name*. File names can be up to 255 characters long, but short file names are generally preferred. You can use uppercase letters, lowercase letters, hyphens, underlines, and spaces. For example, you can use "Good 4 U Sales Report" as a file name. File names cannot include these characters: / \ < > * ? " : |

Throughout this text, your document file names will consist of **your initials** or an identifier your instructor asks you to use, such as **rst**, followed by the number of the exercise, such as **1-15**. PowerPoint assigns the file extension pptx, but you may not see this extension when you look at file names on your computer, depending on how the software is installed.

To save your presentation, you can use either the Save command or the Save As command.

- Use Save to update an existing document. The current file replaces the previously saved file. To save, click the Save button 💾 on the Quick Access Toolbar; from the File tab, choose **Save**; or press Ctrl + S.

- Use Save As to name your presentation for the first time or to save your presentation using a different file name. In the latter case, the original presentation remains unchanged, and a second presentation with a new name is saved as well. To use Save As, from the File tab, choose **Save As**.

Exercise 1-16 CREATE A FOLDER AND SAVE YOUR PRESENTATION

NOTE

Your instructor will advise you on the proper drive or folder to use when creating your lesson folders.

Before saving a presentation file, decide where you want to save it: in a folder on your computer's hard drive, on a network drive, or on a removable drive. It's a good idea to create separate folders for specific categories to help keep your work organized. For example, you might want to create folders for different projects or different customers. In this text, you will follow these steps to create a new folder for each lesson's work before you begin the lesson.

1. From the File tab, choose **Save As**. The Save As dialog box appears.

2. Using the list box at the top or folders on the left, follow your instructor's directions to navigate to the location where you should create your folder.

3. Click the New Folder button on the Save As dialog box toolbar, as shown in Figure 1-9.

Figure 1-9
Save As dialog box

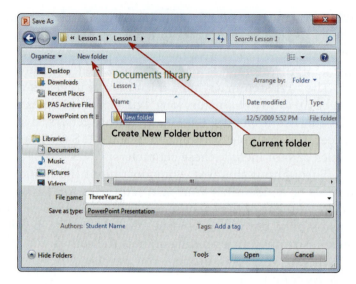

4. With the words "New folder" selected, key **Lesson 1** and click off the folder. A yellow folder icon appears with the name "Lesson 1."

5. Double-click the **Lesson 1** folder to open it.

6. In the File name text box, key *[your initials]*1-16.

7. Click **Save**. Your document is saved for future use. Notice that the title bar displays the new file name.

NOTE

When saving presentations in the future, remember to navigate to the appropriate folder before saving your file.

Exercise 1-17 REVIEW PRESENTATION PROPERTIES AND PERMISSIONS

When a presentation is saved, PowerPoint automatically saves information about it such as the date created, file size, author name, and other information.

1. With your presentation still open, from the File tab, the Info group of quick commands will be automatically highlighted.

2. Notice the information on the right of the Backstage view.

3. Click the Properties button `Properties ▾`, and then click **Advanced Properties**. The General tab displays basic information about the file.

4. Click the **Statistics** tab. This tab shows precise information about the dates the file was created, modified, and accessed as well as the number of slides and other statistics.

5. Click the **Summary** tab. Here you can change existing information or add new information. Key *[your name]* as the author.

6. Click **OK**.

7. In the middle of the Backstage view, notice the Permissions category. The current setting indicates that the presentation is not restricted and anyone can open, copy, and change it.

8. Click the **File** tab again to close Backstage view.

9. Press Ctrl+S to save your changes to the properties of the document.

Exercise 1-18 CLOSE A PRESENTATION AND EXIT POWERPOINT

After you finish a presentation and save it, you can close it and open another presentation or you can close it and exit the program. Use one of these methods:

- From the File tab, choose **Close** or **Exit PowerPoint**.
- Use keyboard shortcuts. Ctrl+W closes a presentation, and Alt+F4 exits PowerPoint.
- Use the Close button [X] in the upper right corner of the window.

1. From the File tab, choose **Close** to exit the presentation.

2. Click the Close button [X] in the upper right corner of the window to exit PowerPoint.

Lesson 1 Summary

- Microsoft PowerPoint is a powerful graphics program used to create professional-quality presentations for a variety of settings.
- Identify items in the PowerPoint window by pointing to them and waiting for their ScreenTips to appear.
- PowerPoint command buttons are arranged in groups that can be accessed by clicking on the Ribbon tabs.
- The Quick Access Toolbar contains a set of commands independent of the tab that is currently displayed. The toolbar includes commonly used commands such as save, undo, redo, and print.
- The PowerPoint Help window is a great place to look for additional information on a topic or for steps in completing a task.
- Key and edit text on a slide in the same way as you would in Word.
- Use the Slide Show button to run a slide show. A slide show always starts with the slide that is currently selected.

- The Print Navigation pane provides a variety of ways to print your presentation: as slides, handouts, notes pages, and outlines.
- To print handouts that contain more than one slide on a page, use the Print Navigation pane to select from the Print Settings options.

LESSON 1		Command Summary	
Feature	**Button**	**Ribbon**	**Keyboard**
Close a presentation		File tab, Close	Ctrl+W or Ctrl+F4
Display Slides and Outline pane		View tab, Presentation Views group, Normal	
Document Properties		File tab, Document Properties	
End a slide show		Right-click, End Show	Esc or −
Exit PowerPoint		File tab, Exit PowerPoint	Alt+F4
Help		Help Button	F1
Next Slide			Page Down
Next Slide (Slide Show view)		Right-click, Next	N, Page Down
Normal view		View tab, Presentation Views group, Normal	
Open a presentation		File tab, Open	Ctrl+O
Permissions		File tab	
Previous Slide			Page Up
Previous Slide (Slide Show view)		Right-click, Previous	P, Page Up, Backspace
Print		File tab, Print; Quick Access Toolbar, Print button	Ctrl+P
Reading view		View tab, Presentation Views group, Reading view	
Reset		Home tab, Slides group, Reset	
Save		File tab, Save; Quick Access Toolbar, Save button	Ctrl+S
Save with a different name		File tab, Save As	
Slide Show		Slide Show tab, Start Slide Show group, From Beginning or From Current Slide buttons or View buttons, Slide Show	F5
Slide Sorter view		View tab, Presentation Views group, Slide Sorter	
Zoom		View tab, Zoom group, Zoom	

Please visit our Online Learning Center, *www.lessonapproach2010.com*, **where you will find the following review materials:**

- **Concepts Review**

  True/False Questions

  Short Answer Questions

  Critical Thinking Questions

- **Skills Review**

  Review Exercises that target single skills

  Lesson Applications

  Review Exercises that challenge students by testing multiple skills in each exercise

- **On Your Own**

  Open-ended exercises that require students to synthesize multiple skills and apply creativity and problem-solving as they would in a real world business situation

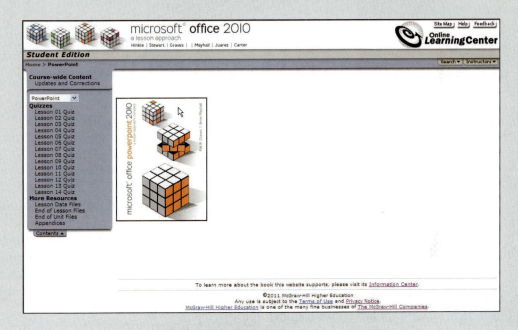

Lesson 2

Developing Presentation Text

OBJECTIVES *After completing this lesson, you will be able to:*

1. Create a new blank presentation.
2. Use the font group commands.
3. Adjust text placeholders.
4. Work with bullets and numbering.
5. Work with text boxes.

Estimated Time: 1¾ hours

You can add interest to a PowerPoint presentation by varying the appearance of text—this includes changing the font, text style, bullet shape, or position of text. You can change text appearance before or after you key it. Always strive for readability and continuity within your presentation.

In this lesson, you will learn how to change text attributes such as color, font, font style, and font size. You will also work with bullets and numbering for easy-to-read lists and modify paragraph indents. Several keystrokes you will use to quickly move around on slides or within your presentation are shown in Table 2-1.

As an intern at Good 4 U, you are developing content for a promotional presentation. Co-owner Julie Wolfe will be using this presentation when speaking to large corporations in the area to persuade them to get healthy and choose Good 4 U for their upcoming events.

NOTE

The documents you create in this course relate to the case study about Good 4 U, a fictional restaurant business (see frontmatter).

Creating a New Blank Presentation

PowerPoint provides several ways to begin a presentation. With any method, as you add new slides for your content, you choose an appropriate slide layout and key slide text.

TABLE 2-1 Using the Keyboard to Navigate on a Slide and in a Presentation

Keystrokes	Result
Ctrl + Enter	Selects and activates the next text placeholder on a slide. If the last placeholder (subtitle or body text) is selected or activated, pressing Ctrl + Enter inserts a new slide after the current slide. Pressing Ctrl + Enter never selects any objects on a slide (including text boxes) that are not placeholders.
Ctrl + M	Inserts a new slide after the current slide.
Enter	If a text box or text placeholder is activated so that the text can be edited, inserts a new paragraph, including a bullet if in a body text placeholder. If a text box or text placeholder is selected but not activated, selects all the text in the object.
Esc	Deactivates the currently activated text placeholder or text box and selects the entire text box instead. If a text box is selected but not activated, pressing Esc deselects the text box.
Esc, Tab	Moves to the next object on a slide, regardless of whether a text box is activated. It never inserts a new slide.
Shift + Enter	If a text box or text placeholder is activated, inserts a new line (but not a new paragraph) at the insertion point.
Shift + Tab	If a text box or text placeholder is not activated, selects the previous object on a slide. If the insertion point is between a bullet and the first text character on the line, promotes the bulleted text.
Tab	If a text placeholder or text box is activated, inserts a tab character at the insertion point; if not activated, selects the next object on the slide. If the insertion point is between a bullet and the first text character on a line, pressing Tab demotes the bulleted text. Pressing Tab repeatedly when no objects are activated cycles through all the objects on a slide but never moves to another slide.

- *Blank presentation.* Provides a plain background with simple text treatments and minimal color use. The very basic theme called Office is applied.
- *Theme.* Adds coordinated colors, font styles, background designs, and placeholder positioning to fit the background for an entire presentation. Themes give a unified and professional appearance.
- *Templates.* Provide a theme plus sample content as a guide in developing a presentation.

Since you will be learning how to create slides and key text in different ways, you will start this lesson with a blank presentation. Templates and Themes will be used in a different lesson.

Exercise 2-1 START A NEW BLANK PRESENTATION

Julie Wolfe would like to see the content for this presentation put together before deciding on colors and a design theme. Therefore, you will begin this exercise with a blank presentation.

1. Start PowerPoint. A blank title slide appears, ready for your text input, as shown in Figure 2-1.

Figure 2-1
Title slide

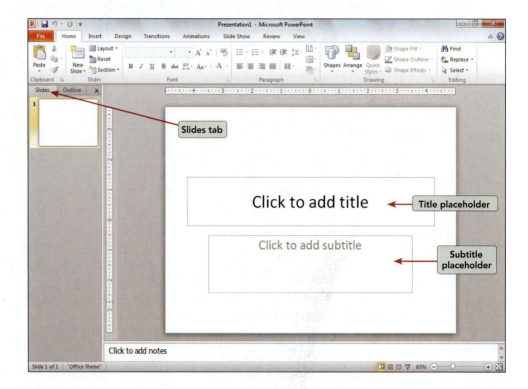

2. Click the title placeholder to activate it, and key **For the Pleasure of Your Company**.

3. Click the subtitle placeholder, and key **Plan Your Next Event with Good 4 U**.

4. Position the insertion point after the word "Event" in the subtitle; then press Shift+Enter to insert a new line in the same paragraph. The subtitle is now split into two lines. Delete the space before "with" on the second line of the subtitle.

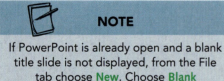

NOTE

If PowerPoint is already open and a blank title slide is not displayed, from the File tab choose **New**. Choose **Blank Presentation**, and click **Create**.

5. Using the same procedure, split the title text into two lines so that "Your Company" appears on the second line.

Exercise 2-2   ADD NEW SLIDES AND USE SLIDE LAYOUTS

To add a new slide after the current slide in a presentation, you can do one of the following:

- From the Home tab, in the Slides group, click the New Slide button.
- Press Ctrl+M.
- When a placeholder is selected, press Ctrl+Enter one or more times until a new slide appears.

When a new slide first appears on your PowerPoint window, you don't need to activate a placeholder to start keying text. When no placeholder is selected, as long as your slide pane is active, the text you key automatically goes into the title text placeholder. Knowing this can speed up the process of inserting new slides.

1. From the Home tab, in the Slides group, click the top of the New Slide button 🖼. A new slide appears, containing a title text placeholder and a body text placeholder.

2. Key **Excellent Service**. The text appears automatically in the title placeholder.

Figure 2-2
Keying text on a slide

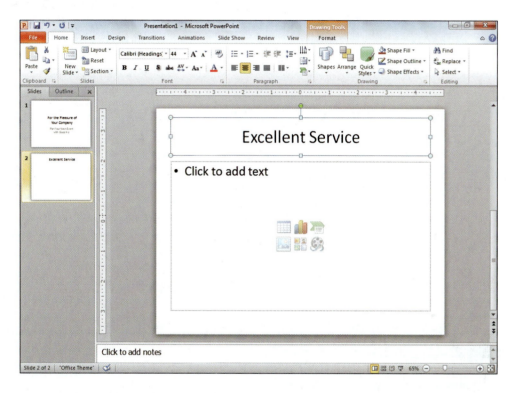

3. Press ⌈Ctrl⌉+⌈Enter⌉ or click the body text placeholder to activate it, and key the following text, pressing ⌈Enter⌉ at the end of each bulleted line:

- **We put your employees and guests at ease**
- **We make your company look good**
- **We adhere to promised schedules**
- **We provide a professional and courteous staff**
- **We guarantee customer satisfaction**

4. Press ⌈Ctrl⌉+⌈M⌉ to create a new text slide.

5. Key **A Delightful Menu** as the title, and then key the following text in the body text placeholder:

- **High-quality, healthy food**
- **Variety to appeal to a broad range of tastes**

TIP

When you insert a new slide, it uses the same layout as the previous slide (unless the previous slide was the title slide).

6. From the Home tab, in the Slides group, click the down arrow on the New Slide button to see thumbnail *slide layouts* with their names, as shown in Figure 2-3. Layouts contain placeholders for slide content such as titles, bulleted lists, charts, and shapes.

Figure 2-3
Inserting a new slide by using the slide layouts

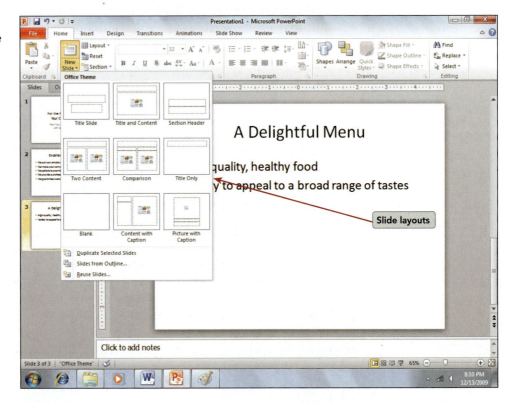

7. Click the **Title and Content** slide layout.

8. Key **High-Energy Fun** as the title, and then key the following body text. Notice that PowerPoint's AutoCorrect feature automatically adds an accent mark to the word "décor."

    • **Athletic decor**

    • **Sports promotions**

9. Press Ctrl+M to insert another slide; then key **A Healthy Atmosphere** as the title, and key the following body text:

    • **Smoke-free**

    • **Alcohol optional**

    • **We sell none**

    • **We'll gladly serve your own**

10. Notice how each slide is numbered in the Slides and Outline pane.

11. Move to slide 4 "High-Energy Fun" by clicking on the slide 4 thumbnail, and from the Home tab, in the Slides group, click the down arrow on the New Slide button . Click the **Two Content** slide layout.

12. Key **Events That Are Good 4 U** as the title, and then key the following bulleted text in the left body text placeholder:

    - **High-energy meetings**
    - **Productive lunches**
    - **Company celebrations**
    - **Celebrity promotions**

13. Key the following bulleted text in the right body text placeholder:

    - **Entertaining customers**
    - **Demonstrating products**

14. Create a new folder for Lesson 2, and save the presentation *[your initials]*2-2 in your new Lesson 2 folder.

15. Close the presentation.

Using the Font Group Commands

One way to change the appearance of text in your presentation is by changing the font. A font is a set of characters with a specific design. You can change the *font face* (such as Times New Roman or Arial) and the *font size*. Fonts are measured in *points* (with 72 points in an inch), indicating how tall a font is.

Different fonts can take up different amounts of horizontal space, even though they are the same size. For example, a word formatted as 20-point Arial will be wider than a word formatted as 20-point Garamond, as shown in Figure 2-4.

Figure 2-4
Comparing fonts

20 point Arial:	**Formatting**
20 point Garamond:	Formatting

Another way to change the appearance of text is by applying text attributes. For example, you can apply a text style (such as bold or italic) and effect (such as underline or shadow). You use the Font group commands, shown in Figure 2-5 and described in Table 2-2, to change selected text.

Figure 2-5
The Font group on the Home tab

Font command buttons

TABLE 2-2 The Font Group Formatting Command Buttons

Button	Purpose
B Bold	Applies the bold attribute to text.
Aa Change Case	Applies different capitalizations such as uppercase, lowercase, or sentence case.
AV Character Spacing	Increases or decreases the space between characters.
Aa Clear All Formatting	Removes all formatting from the selected text.
A▼ Decrease Font Size	Decreases the size of selected text by one font size.
Verdana ▼ Font	Enables you to choose a font face for selected text or for text to be keyed at the insertion point.
A Font Color	Changes text color.
28 ▼ Font Size	Enables you to choose a font size for selected text or for text to be keyed at the insertion point.
A▲ Increase Font Size	Increases the size of selected text by one font size.
I Italic	Applies the italic attribute to text.
S Shadow	Applies a text shadow.
abc Strikethrough	Draws a line through selected text.
U Underline	Applies the underline attribute to text.

Exercise 2-3   CHANGE THE FONT FACE AND FONT SIZE

One convenient way to apply text formatting is to first key the text, focusing on content, and then select the text and apply formatting, such as by changing the size or font. Keep in mind that no more than two or three fonts should be used in a presentation. The font you use influences the tone of your presentation.

The Font drop-down list displays all the fonts available for your computer. On the left side of each font name is a symbol indicating the font type; most of them are *TrueType* fonts **T**, while others are *OpenType* fonts **O**. These fonts work well in most situations and remain very readable when scaled to different sizes. OpenType fonts provide more detailed letter shapes and more variations of character sets. If you plan to show your presentation on a different computer or print it with a different printer, it is best to choose a TrueType font.

The font size should be large enough for easy reading when the presentation is displayed on a large projection screen. The Increase Font Size **A▲** and Decrease

Font Size $\boxed{\text{A}}$ buttons change the size of all the text in a selected placeholder by one font-size increment. If several sizes of text are used in the placeholder, each size is changed proportionately. For example, if a text placeholder contains both 24-point text and 20-point text, clicking the Increase Font Size button $\boxed{\text{A}}$ will change the respective text sizes to 28 and 24 points at the same time.

Figure 2-6
Font drop-down list

Many of the buttons used to format text are toggle buttons. A *toggle button* switches between on and off when you click it. The Shadow button $\boxed{\text{S}}$ is an example of a toggle button: Click it once to apply a shadow and once again to remove it. Other examples of toggle buttons are Bold $\boxed{\text{B}}$, Italic $\boxed{\text{I}}$, and Underline $\boxed{\text{U}}$.

The presentation that you will be working on throughout the rest of this lesson promotes heart smart living through a diet and exercise plan. You will be representing the Good 4 U restaurant by appearing at an annual community event. The goal of your presentation is to encourage customers to get healthy and think about joining the Good 4 U team.

Figure 2-7
Font size drop-down list

1. Open the file **Health**. Examine the Font group, and locate the command buttons listed in Table 2-2.

2. On slide 1, click the title placeholder to activate it, and key **Heart**.

3. Double-click on the word "Heart" to select this text.

4. In the Font group, click the down arrow next to the Font box. A drop-down list of available fonts appears, as shown in Figure 2-6.

5. From the drop-down list, choose **Arial**.

6. With "Heart" still selected, click the down arrow next to the Font Size box, as shown in Figure 2-7. Choose **66**. The text size increases to 66 points.

7. Click the Decrease Font Size button $\boxed{\text{A}}$. The font size decreases by one size increment. Notice the number "60" displayed in the Font Size box.

8. Click the Increase Font Size button $\boxed{\text{A}}$ twice. The font size increases by two size increments, to 72 points (the equivalent of 1 inch tall).

Exercise 2-4   APPLY BOLD, ITALIC, COLOR, AND SHADOW

It can be convenient to apply basic text formatting as you key. This is particularly true with bold, italic, underline, and shadow if you use the following keyboard shortcuts:

- $\boxed{\text{Ctrl}}$ + $\boxed{\text{B}}$ for bold

- $\boxed{\text{Ctrl}}$ + $\boxed{\text{I}}$ for italic

- $\boxed{\text{Ctrl}}$ + $\boxed{\text{U}}$ for underline

- $\boxed{\text{Ctrl}}$ + $\boxed{\text{S}}$ for shadow

The color drop-down gallery is composed of theme and standard colors. Theme colors span the top of the gallery, with variations of those colors, which represent shades (percentages) of the theme colors, below. Standard colors are arranged much like a rainbow at the bottom of the gallery. When you move the mouse over a color or a variation of a theme color, a ScreenTip is provided that identifies which theme or standard color it is and the percentage of variation.

TIP

Theme colors are preselected groups of colors that provide variations suitable for many presentation needs. However, font colors or other graphic colors may need more emphasis than the theme colors provide.

1. Position the insertion point to the right of "Heart," and press [Spacebar]. Click the Bold button **B** (or press [Ctrl]+[B]), and then the Italic button *I* (or press [Ctrl]+[I]) to turn on these attributes.

Figure 2-8
Font Color gallery

2. Key **Smart!** The word is formatted in bold italic as you key. Notice that this word is also 72-point Arial, like the previous word.

3. Double-click the word "Heart" to select it; then press [Ctrl]+[B] to make it bold.

4. With "Heart" still selected, from the Home tab, in the Font group, click the Font Color button **A** down arrow to open the Font Color gallery showing Theme Colors and Standard Colors, as shown in Figure 2-8.

TIP

A shadow can help make the shapes of characters more distinctive. Be sure you always have a high contrast in color between your text colors and your background colors (light on dark or dark on light) for easy reading. Apply a shadow when it helps to make your text stand out from the background color, and apply the same type of shadow in a similar way for unity of design in your presentation.

5. Drag your pointer over the row of standard colors, and you will see a live preview of that color before it is applied. Click the red box to apply a red font color.

6. Click in the word "Smart" to deselect "Heart." "Heart" is now red.

7. Select both words in your title placeholder. From the Home tab, in the Font group, click the Shadow button **S**. Now the text appears to "float" above the slide background with a soft shadow behind it.

Exercise 2-5   CHANGE THE CASE OF SELECTED TEXT

Figure 2-9
Change Case drop-down list

If you find that you keyed text in uppercase and want to change it, you don't have to rekey the text. By using the Change Case button **Aa**, as shown in Figure 2-9, you can change any text to **Sentence case, lowercase, UPPERCASE, Capitalize Each Word,** or **tOGGLE cASE.** You can also cycle through uppercase, lowercase, and either title case or sentence case (depending on what is selected) by selecting text and pressing [Shift]+[F3] one or more times.

1. Move to slide 3.

2. Select "walk to good health" which has no letters capitalized.

3. From the Home tab, in the Font group, click the Change Case button **Aa** down arrow, and choose **Capitalize Each Word** so that each word begins with a capital letter (uppercase).

4. Select the word "To" in the title. Press ⌈Shift⌉+⌈F3⌉ two times to change it to lowercase.

5. Select the first bulleted item by clicking its bullet. This text was keyed with ⌈Caps Lock⌉ accidentally turned on.

6. From the Home tab, in the Font group, click the Change Case button **Aa**, and choose **tOGGLE cASE**. This option reverses the current case, changing uppercase letters to lowercase and lowercase letters to uppercase.

7. Select the two bulleted items under "Walking" (beginning with "reduces" and "lowers").

8. From Home tab, in the Font group, click the Change Case button **Aa**, and choose **Sentence case**. Now only the first word in each item is capitalized.

Exercise 2-6 CHANGE LINE SPACING WITHIN PARAGRAPHS

Line spacing can add space between the lines in a paragraph or space between paragraphs. Increased line spacing can make your text layout easier to read and enhance the overall design of a slide.

Figure 2-10
Line spacing sizes

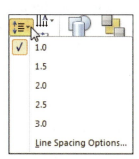

To change spacing between lines within a paragraph, you can use the Line Spacing button ⧉. Line spacing is changed in increments of .5 lines.

1. Move to slide 2. Click within the first bulleted item, which is considered a paragraph in the placeholder.

2. From the Home tab, in the Paragraph group, click the Line Spacing button ⧉, and a drop-down list of sizes appears, as shown in Figure 2-10.

3. Click **2.0**, and the line spacing of the first paragraph increases.

4. Usually you will want to change the line spacing for an entire text placeholder. Click the placeholder border to select it.

5. From the Home tab, in the Paragraph group, click the Line Spacing button ⧉, and change the line spacing to **1.5** lines.

Exercise 2-7 CHANGE LINE SPACING BETWEEN PARAGRAPHS

The default paragraph line-spacing measurement is single. Using the Paragraph dialog box, you can add space by inserting points before or after paragraphs to expand the space between them. In PowerPoint, each bulleted item in a list is treated as a paragraph.

1. Still working on slide 2, click within the second bulleted item (a paragraph); then in the Paragraph group, click the Dialog Box Launcher 🔲 to open the Paragraph dialog box, as shown in Figure 2-11.

Figure 2-11
Paragraph dialog box

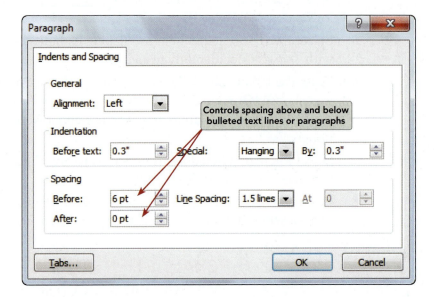

2. In the Spacing section, change the **Before** setting by clicking the spin-box up arrow twice to 18 points. Click **OK**.

3. To make all paragraph spacing uniform, select the entire text placeholder by clicking the placeholder border and open the Paragraph dialog box. Change the **Before** spacing to 12 points and the **After** spacing to 12. Change the Line spacing setting to **Single**. Click **OK**. The text is now evenly spaced in the placeholder.

Exercise 2-8   USE THE FONT DIALOG BOX TO MAKE MULTIPLE CHANGES

The Font dialog box is a convenient place to apply several font attributes all at one time. In addition to choosing a font, font style, and font size, this dialog box enables you to choose various effects, such as underline or shadow, and a font color.

1. Go to slide 1 and select the words "Diet and Exercise" in the subtitle. Notice that handles appear around the entire subtitle placeholder, but the colored area showing selection appears only around the text. This has happened because the placeholder is much bigger than the three words that are keyed in it.

2. Right-click the selected text to display the shortcut menu. Choose **Font** to open the Font dialog box, as shown in Figure 2-12.

TIP

Underlining is not the best way to emphasize text. Underlining can cut through the bottom of letters (the descenders) causing the text to be more difficult to read. And because underlining is used so much for hyperlinks on the Internet, underlining seems to have the connotation of a hyperlink. So emphasize your text in different ways, such as by using a larger font size, more dramatic color, or bold.

3.   Choose the following options in the Font dialog box:

- From the **Latin text font** list box, choose **Arial**.
- From the **Font style** list box, choose **Bold Italic**.
- From the **Size list** box, key **48**.
- For **Underline** style, choose **Wavy heavy line**.
- For **Underline** color, choose **Dark red** from the standard colors.
- Notice the additional options available in this dialog box.

Figure 2-12
Font dialog box

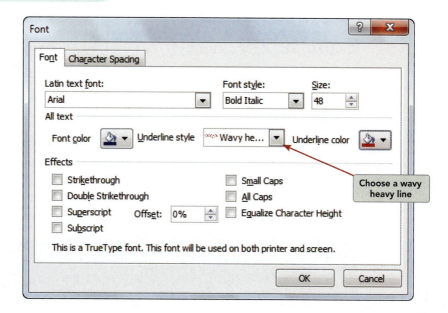

4.   Click **OK** to close this dialog box.

5.   Double-click the word "Heart" to select it, and then from the Home tab, in the Font group, click the Underline button ⟨U⟩ to turn on underlining. After looking at this underline feature, you decide that you would prefer it not be applied. Click the Underline button again to turn off this attribute.

TIP

You can change text attributes in the Outline tab in the same way as in the Slide pane.

6.   With the word "Heart" still selected, change the size to **80** points.

7.   Save the presentation as *[your initials]*2-8 in your Lesson 2 folder.

Adjusting Text Placeholders

The formatting for an entire placeholder, such as text size, color, or font, can be changed by first selecting the placeholder and then choosing the formatting. The placeholder border looks different depending on whether the placeholder is selected or text within the placeholder is selected.

You can select placeholders in several ways:

- Click the border of an active placeholder with the four-pointed arrow ⊕.

- Press [Esc] while a placeholder is active (when the insertion point is in the text).

- Press [Tab] to select the next placeholder on a slide (only when a text box or text placeholder is not active).

You can deselect placeholders in several ways:

- Press [Esc] to deselect a placeholder or other object. (Press [Esc] twice if a text placeholder or text box is active.)

- Click an area on the slide where there is no object.

Exercise 2-9   SELECT A TEXT PLACEHOLDER

Selecting and applying formatting to an entire placeholder can save time in editing.

1. On slide 3, click anywhere in the title text to make the placeholder active. Notice that the placeholder is outlined with small dashes to create a border showing the size of the rectangle. Circles are positioned on the corners and squares are positioned at the midpoint of all four sides, as shown in Figure 2-13. When the placeholder looks like this, the insertion point is active and you are ready to edit the text within the placeholder.

Figure 2-13
Selecting a text placeholder

Dashed line indicates text can be edited

Solid line indicates the entire placeholder can be edited

2. Point to any place on the dashed-line border but not on a circle or square. When you see the four-pointed arrow ⊕, click the border. Notice that the insertion point is no longer active and the border's appearance has changed to a solid line. This indicates that the placeholder is selected. You can make changes to all the text within it, the fill color of the placeholder, the size of the placeholder, or the position of the placeholder.

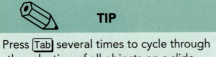

TIP

Press [Tab] several times to cycle through the selection of all objects on a slide—text placeholders or other objects.

3. Press [Tab]. Now the body text placeholder is selected.

4. Press [Esc] to deselect the body text placeholder. Now nothing on the slide is selected.

5. Still working on slide 3, click inside the title placeholder text and then press [Esc]. This is another way to select an active placeholder.

6. Click the Increase Font Size button $\boxed{A^{\cdot}}$ five times. The font size increases to 60 points.

7. Click the Decrease Font Size button $\boxed{A^{\cdot}}$ two times until the font size is 48 points.

8. Press $\boxed{\text{Tab}}$ to select the body text placeholder. Notice the 23+ in the Font Size box. This indicates that there is more than one font size in the placeholder, and the smallest size is 23 points.

9. Click any text in the first bullet. Notice that its font size is 26 points. Notice also that when you click text inside a placeholder, its border is no longer selected. (The dashed line returns to the border, showing that you are editing the text.)

10. Click the first sub-bullet text below it, which is 23 points.

11. Press $\boxed{\text{Esc}}$ to reselect the entire placeholder.

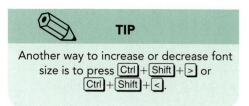

TIP

Another way to increase or decrease font size is to press $\boxed{\text{Ctrl}}$+$\boxed{\text{Shift}}$+$\boxed{>}$ or $\boxed{\text{Ctrl}}$+$\boxed{\text{Shift}}$+$\boxed{<}$.

12. Click the Increase Font Size button $\boxed{A^{\cdot}}$ twice so that 28+ appears in the Font Size box.

13. From the Home tab, in the Font group, click the down arrow on the Font Color button $\boxed{A}$, and choose Standard color **Dark Blue** (the color sample second from the right), making all the body text on this slide dark blue.

14. Still working in the Font group, click the Shadow button $\boxed{S}$ to test that effect. Now all the text has a shadow, but with the colors being used, the text looks blurred. Remove the Shadow by clicking the Shadow button $\boxed{S}$ again.

Exercise 2-10   CHANGE TEXT HORIZONTAL ALIGNMENT

Bulleted items, titles, and subtitles are all considered paragraphs in PowerPoint. Just as in a word-processing program, when you press $\boxed{\text{Enter}}$, a new paragraph begins. You can align paragraphs with either the left or right placeholder borders, center them within the placeholder, or justify long paragraphs so that both margins are even. However, the last alignment option should be reserved for longer documents such as reports, for which you want a formal appearance. Fully justified text is not appropriate for presentation slides.

You can change text alignment for all the text in a placeholder or for just one line, depending on what is selected.

1. Move to slide 5.

2. Position the insertion point in the first bulleted line, "Earn Good 4 U discounts."

3. From the Home tab, in the Paragraph group, click the Align Text Right button $\boxed{\equiv}$. The text in the first line aligns on the right.

4. Click the Align Text Left button $\boxed{\equiv}$, and the paragraph aligns on the left.

UNIT 1 LESSON 2

5. Select the placeholder border, and click the Center button ☰. Both lines are centered horizontally within the placeholder.

6. Click the Bold button **B**.

Exercise 2-11 RESIZE A PLACEHOLDER

You may need to make a text placeholder narrower or wider to control how text wraps to a new line, or you might want to move all the text up or down on a slide. You can change the size and position of a selected text placeholder in several ways:

*   Drag a *sizing handle* to change the size and shape of a text placeholder. Sizing handles are the four small circles on the corners and the squares on the border of a selected text placeholder or another object.

> **TIP**
>
> You can also change the size precisely using the Drawing Tools Format tab.

*   Drag the placeholder border to move the text to a new position.
*   Change placeholder size and position settings by using the Format Shape dialog box that is available from the shortcut menu when you right-click the placeholder.

By dragging a corner sizing handle, you can change both the height and the width of a placeholder at the same time.

1. Still working on slide 5, select the body text placeholder. Notice the small white circles and squares on the border. These are the sizing handles, as shown in Figure 2-14.

2. Position the pointer over the bottom center sizing handle.

3. When the pointer changes to a two-pointed vertical arrow ⭥, hold down your left mouse button and drag the bottom border up until it is just below the second line of text.

4. As you drag, the border moves and the pointer turns into a crosshair ✛. When you release the mouse, the border adjusts to the new position.

Figure 2-14
Resizing a placeholder

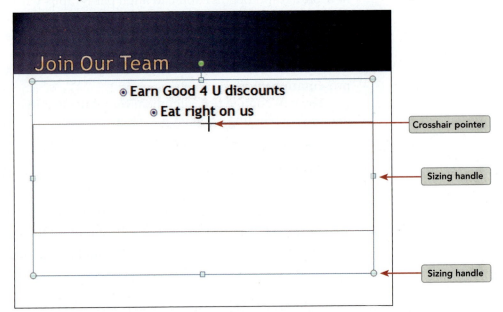

5. Position your pointer over the lower-left-corner sizing handle; then drag it toward the center of the text. Both the height and the width of the placeholder change.

6. Click the Undo button 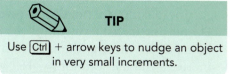 once to restore the placeholder to its previous size.

Exercise 2-12   MOVE A PLACEHOLDER

To change a placeholder's position, select it and point to any part of the placeholder border except the sizing handles. With your pointer showing the four-pointed arrow, drag to move the placeholder.

1. On slide 5, select the body text placeholder if it is not still selected.

2. Position the pointer over the placeholder border anywhere except on a sizing handle. The pointer changes to the four-pointed arrow ⊕.

3. Drag the four-pointed arrow ⊕ down until the placeholder appears approximately vertically centered on the white area of the slide, as shown in Figure 2-15.

Figure 2-15
Moving a placeholder

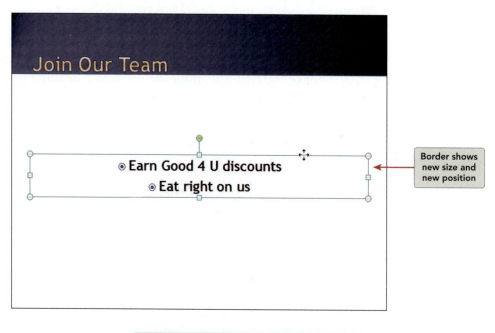

Border shows new size and new position

✎   **TIP**

Use Ctrl + arrow keys to nudge an object in very small increments.

---

4. Deselect the placeholder. The text is now attractively placed on the slide.

5. Move to slide 1, and save the presentation as *[your initials]*2-12. Leave the presentation open for the next exercise.

Working with Bullets and Numbering

When you work with body text placeholders, each line automatically starts with a bullet. However, you can turn bullets off when the slide would look better without them. You can remove bullets, add new ones, change the shape and color of bullets, and create your own bullets from pictures. The Bullets and Numbering buttons are both found in the Paragraph group.

Exercise 2-13 REMOVE BULLETS

The Bullets button ▤ is used to turn bullets off and on. Depending on how your text is selected, you can affect a single bullet or all the bulleted lines in a body placeholder when you use the Bullets button. The Bullets button is another example of a toggle button.

1. Display slide 2. Click within the body text to activate the placeholder. Press Esc to select the entire placeholder.

2. From the Home tab, in the Paragraph group, click the Bullets button ▤. This turns bullets off for the entire placeholder and moves the text to the left.

3. Click the Bullets button ▤ again to reapply the bullets.

4. Click within the first bulleted item, "Exercise regularly," and click the Bullets button ▤ to turn off the bullet. This technique could be used to make the first line in the list serve as a heading for the list.

5. Click the Bullets button ▤ again to reapply the bullet.

6. On slide 5, activate the body text placeholder and click the Bullets button ▤. When text is centered, bullets are unnecessary.

Exercise 2-14 INCREASE AND DECREASE LIST LEVEL OF BULLETED TEXT

As you create bulleted items, a new bullet is inserted when you press Enter to start a new line. When you want to expand on a slide's main points, you can insert indented bulleted text below a main point. This supplemental text is sometimes referred to as a sub-bullet or a level 2 bullet. PowerPoint body text placeholders can have up to five levels of indented text, but you will usually want to limit your slides to two levels.

Increasing an item's list level moves the bulleted item to the right. Decreasing its list level moves the bulleted item to the left. These changes can be made by moving the insertion point before the text and pressing Tab to increase the list level or Shift+Tab to decrease the list level or by using the Increase List Level ▤ or Decrease List Level ▤ buttons found on the Home tab, in the Paragraph group.

1. With slide 2 displayed, move your insertion point after "regularly"; then press Enter to create a new bulleted line.

2. Press [Tab] to increase the list level to the second-level bullet, and key **Walk 30 minutes daily**; then press [Enter].

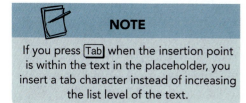

NOTE

If you press [Tab] when the insertion point is within the text in the placeholder, you insert a tab character instead of increasing the list level of the text.

3. Notice that the text is now indented automatically to the second-level bullet.

4. Key **Alternate aerobic and weight training**; then press [Enter].

5. To return to the first-level bullet, press [Shift]+[Tab].

6. Key **Get sufficient rest**.

Exercise 2-15   CHANGE THE COLOR AND SHAPE OF A BULLET

The Bullets gallery provides a few choices to change the shape of a bullet. The Bullets dialog box provides many more choices to change the bullet shape by choosing a character from another font. Fonts that contain potential bullet characters include Symbol, Wingdings, and Webdings. Another source of bullet characters is the Geometric Shapes subset available for most other fonts.

1. On slide 2, select the body text placeholder.

2. From the Home tab, in the Paragraph group, click the down arrow on the Bullets button ⊞ to see the gallery options, as shown in Figure 2-16.

3. Click the checkmark bullet option.

Figure 2-16
Bullets and Numbering gallery

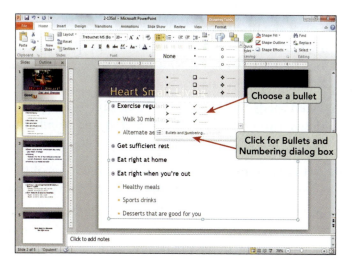

4. With the body text placeholder still selected, click the Bullets button ⊞ again, and then choose **Bullets and Numbering** at the bottom.

Figure 2-17
Bullets and
Numbering dialog
box

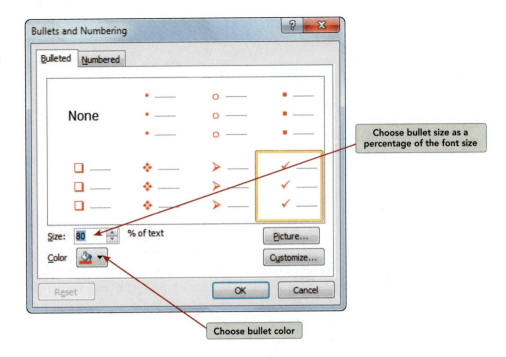

5. In the Bullets and Numbering dialog box, click the **Color** drop-down arrow, and choose a Standard **Red**, as shown in Figure 2-17.

6. In the Size box, click the down arrow several times until **80** is displayed. Click **OK**. All bullets on slide 2 are now red checkmarks, sized at 80 percent of the font size.

7. Select the first line of bulleted text; then press Ctrl while you use your I-beam pointer to select the text of the three remaining level-one bulleted text lines. Pressing Ctrl enables you to make multiple selections of non-adjacent text.

8. From the Home tab, in the Paragraph group, click the Bullets button down arrow ⊞; then choose **Bullets and Numbering**.

9. Click **Customize** to open the Symbol dialog box, shown in Figure 2-18.

10. In the Font drop-down list (upper left corner of the dialog box), scroll to the top and choose **Monotype Corsiva** if it is not displayed.

11. In the Subset drop-down list (upper right corner), choose **Geometric Shapes** (near the bottom of the list). Several characters suitable for bullets appear in the dialog box grid.

Figure 2-18
Symbol dialog box

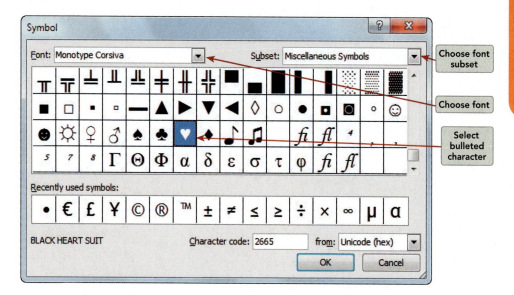

12. Click the heart bullet to select it; then click **OK**. The Symbol dialog box closes, and the Bullets and Numbering dialog box reappears.

13. Change the Size to **110**%, and leave the Color on a Standard **Red**. Click **OK**. The selected four bullets on the slide change to red hearts. While the percentage you use is related to the size of the font for that bulleted item, symbols vary in size. You may need to try more than one adjustment before you accept a size that is pleasing to you.

Exercise 2-16   CREATE A BULLET FROM A PICTURE

A picture bullet can add a unique or creative accent to your presentation. A picture bullet is made from a graphics file and can be a company logo, a special picture, or any image you create with a graphics program or capture with a scanner or digital camera.

1. Display slide 3, and select the first two bullets (but not the sub-bullets).

2. From the Home tab, in the Paragraph group, click the Bullets button down arrow ⊞; then choose **Bullets and Numbering**.

3. Click **Picture** to open the Picture Bullet dialog box. The Picture Bullet dialog box displays a variety of colorful bullets. You can choose from one of these bullets, or you can import a picture file of your own.

4. Click **Import**, and navigate to your student files and select **Walker.gif.** Choose **Add**.

5. Click the picture of a person walking to select it, and then click **OK**. The bullets are replaced with picture bullets, but they are too small.

Figure 2-19
Inserting a picture
bullet

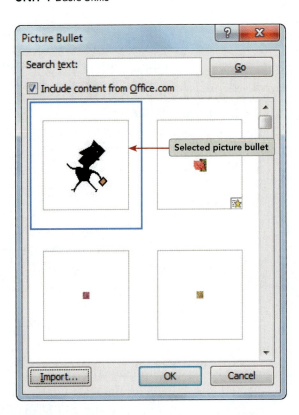

NOTE

If the AutoFit Options button 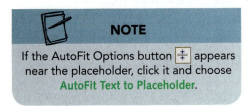 appears near the placeholder, click it and choose **AutoFit Text to Placeholder**.

6. With the two bullet items still selected, reopen the Bullets and Numbering dialog box. In the Size box, change the size to **175%**. Click **OK**.

7. Using the steps outlined above, change the bullet for the last bulleted item "Walking is a mood elevator" to the picture of the walker and size it to match the other bullets.

Exercise 2-17 CREATE NUMBERED PARAGRAPHS

Instead of using bullet characters, you can number listed items. A numbered list is useful to indicate the order in which steps should be taken or to indicate the importance of the items in a list.

Using the **Numbered** tab in the Bullets and Numbering dialog box, you can apply a variety of numbering styles, including numbers, letters, and Roman numerals. You can also create a numbered list automatically while you key body text.

1. Display slide 5, and select the body text placeholder.

2. From the Home tab, in the Paragraph group, click the Align Text Left button ☰.

3. Select all the text in the placeholder, and delete it.

4. With the placeholder activated, key **1.** and press Spacebar. Key **Walk with us**.

5. Press Enter. The second line is automatically numbered "2."

6. Key **Eat with us**, and press Enter.

7. Key **Do what's Good 4 U**. The slide now has three items, automatically numbered 1 through 3. Since AutoFit is on, your items can all be viewed even though you previously sized this text box for only two lines.

8. Press Esc to select the active placeholder.

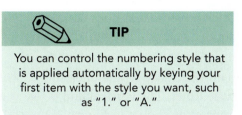

TIP

You can control the numbering style that is applied automatically by keying your first item with the style you want, such as "1." or "A."

9. From the Home tab, in the Paragraph group, click the down arrow on the Numbering button 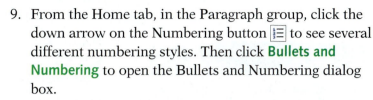 to see several different numbering styles. Then click **Bullets and Numbering** to open the Bullets and Numbering dialog box.

10. Click the first numbered option with the ScreenTip text **1.2.3.** In the Color box, choose the Standard **Red**, and change the size to **100**% of text. Click **OK**.

Exercise 2-18   USE THE RULER TO ADJUST PARAGRAPH INDENTS

A text placeholder will have one of three types of paragraph indents that affect all text in a placeholder. These paragraph indents are:

- *Normal indent.* All the lines of the paragraph are indented the same amount from the left margin.

- *Hanging indent.* The first line of the paragraph extends farther to the left than the rest of the paragraph.

- *First-line indent.* Only the first line of the paragraph is indented.

Paragraph indents are controlled by the Paragraph dialog box, shown in Figure 2-20, that is accessed through the Paragraph Dialog Box Launcher.

Figure 2-20
Paragraph dialog box

You can also set indents by using the ruler. If the ruler is displayed, you can see and manipulate *indent markers* when you activate a text object for editing. Indent markers are the two small triangles and the small rectangle that appear on the left side of the ruler.

At times you might want to change the distance between the bullets and text in a text placeholder. For example, when you use a large bullet (as you did in Exercise 2-16), the space that it requires may cause the text that follows it to word-wrap unevenly. You can easily adjust this spacing by dragging the indent markers. The following steps will guide you through this process.

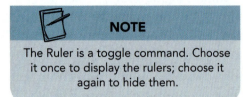

NOTE

The Ruler is a toggle command. Choose it once to display the rulers; choose it again to hide them.

1. Display slide 3. Notice how the text does not align correctly and the square second-level bullets are not indented enough.

2. From the View tab, in the Show group, click the checkbox to select the **Ruler**. The vertical and horizontal rulers appear, as shown in Figure 2-21.

Figure 2-21
Horizontal and vertical rulers

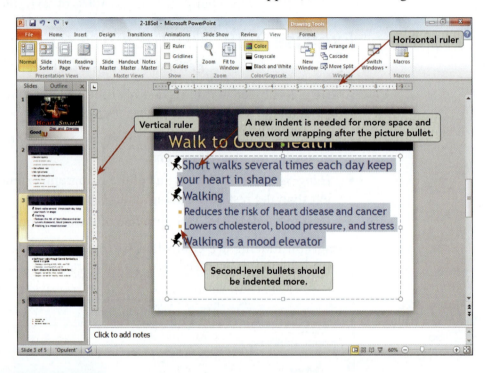

NOTE

You must have an insertion point somewhere inside a text box to change settings on the ruler. The appearance of the ruler reflects whether the entire placeholder is selected or the insertion point is active within the placeholder. If text is already in the placeholder, it must be selected for any ruler changes to apply to the text.

3. Click anywhere within the placeholder as if you were planning to edit some text. Notice the indent markers that appear on the horizontal ruler. Also notice that the white portion of the ruler indicates the width of the text placeholder.

4. Select all of the text in the placeholder.

5. Point to the first-line indent marker on the ruler (triangle at the top of the horizontal ruler, shown in Figure 2-22), and drag it to the right, to the 1-inch mark. The first line of each bulleted item is now indented the same way.

Figure 2-22
Indent markers

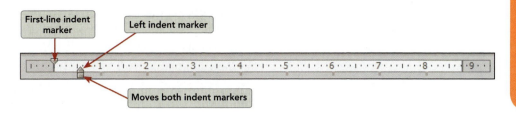

6. Drag the small rectangle (below the triangle on the bottom of the ruler) to the .5-inch mark on the ruler. Notice that both triangles move when you drag the rectangle.

7. Drag the left indent marker (triangle at the bottom of the ruler) to the right to the 1-inch mark on the ruler, and the text will word-wrap with even alignment after the picture bullet.

8. Select the text in the lines beginning with square bullets. Drag the first-line indent marker to the 1.5-inch mark on the ruler. Drag the left indent marker to the 2-inch mark on the ruler. Now the text has much better alignment.

9. Save the presentation as *[your initials]*2-18 in your Lesson 2 folder. Leave the presentation open for the next exercise.

Working with Text Boxes

Until now, you have worked with text placeholders that automatically appear when you insert a new slide. Sometimes you'll want to use *text boxes* so that you can put text outside the text placeholders or create free-form text boxes on a blank slide.

You create text boxes by clicking the Text Box button ⌨ found on the Insert tab, in the Text group, and then dragging the pointer to define the width of the text box. You can also just click the pointer, and the text box adjusts its width to the size of your text. You can change the size and position of text boxes the same way you change text placeholders.

Exercise 2-19 CREATE A TEXT BOX

TIP

You can also click and drag the text tool pointer to create a text box in a specific width. The text you key will wrap within the box if it does not fit on one text line. You can use the resizing handles to increase or decrease the text box width. You can practice making other text boxes on this slide and then click Undo as needed to return to just the first text box.

When you use the Text Box button ⌨ to create a single line of text, you are free to place that text anywhere on a slide, change its color and font, and rotate it. This type of text is sometimes called floating text.

Since the goal of this presentation is to encourage others to join the Good 4 U team, you decide to emphasize this idea by adding a text box and visually enhancing the text.

1. Display slide 5.

2. From the Insert tab, shown in Figure 2-23, in the Text group, click the Text Box button ⌨.

Figure 2-23
Insert tab

Text Box button

Figure 2-24
Creating floating text

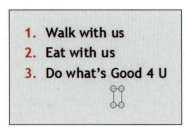

3. Place the pointer below the "G" in "Good 4 U," and click. A small text box containing an insertion point appears, as shown in Figure 2-24.

4. Key **Join Our Team Today!** Notice how the text box widens as you key text.

Exercise 2-20 CHANGE THE FONT AND FONT COLOR

You can select the text box and change the font and font color using the same methods as you did with text placeholders.

1. Click the text box border to select it. Change the text to 44 points, bold, shadowed.

2. With the text box selected, choose an attractive script font such as Monotype Corsiva or Script MT Bold.

3. Click the Font color button [A], and change the text color to **Red**.

4. Using the four-pointed arrow ⊕, move the floating text box to the bottom right corner of the slide. See Figure 2-25 for placement.

5. Increase the size of the placeholder surrounding the numbered list as needed to match Figure 2-25. Notice that AutoFit increases the size of the font as you increase the size of the placeholder up to 26-point font size.

Figure 2-25
Placement for floating text

Exercise 2-21 ROTATE AND CHANGE TEXT DIRECTION

You can *rotate* almost any PowerPoint object—including text boxes, placeholders, and clip art—by dragging the green rotation handle that appears at the top of a selected object. You can also control rotation of text boxes and placeholders by using the Format Shape dialog box.

To *constrain* the rotation of an object to 15-degree increments, hold down Shift while rotating.

1. On slide 5, click "Join Our Team Today!" and drag the text box up slightly so that you will have enough space to angle it on the slide.

2. Point to the green rotation handle at the top of the text box, and drag it to the left. Notice the circling arrow pointer that appears while you drag.

Figure 2-26
Rotating a text box

3. Position the text box as shown in Figure 2-26.

4. With the "Join Our Team Today!" text box selected, press Ctrl+C to copy.

5. Move to slide 4, and press Ctrl+V to paste.

6. Rotate the copied text box to make it straight again; then change the text to read **Offered Daily!**. The text box should resize itself to fit this text.

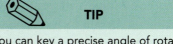

TIP

You can key a precise angle of rotation measurement on the 3-D Rotation tab of the Format Shape dialog box in the Z area.

7. With the text box selected, from the Home tab, in the Paragraph group, click Text Direction ; then choose **Rotate All Text 270°** to make the text read from the bottom up.

8. Reposition this rotated text on the right of the slide.

Exercise 2-22 WRAP TEXT AND CHANGE ALIGNMENT

When you drag the pointer to define the width of a text box, *word wrapping* is automatically turned on. As you key, your insertion point automatically jumps to a new line when it gets to the right side of the box. The height of the box automatically adjusts to accommodate additional text lines.

1. Move to slide 2, "Heart Smart Living."

2. From the Insert tab, in the Text group, click the Text Box button .

3. Position your pointer to the right of "Exercise regularly"; then drag to the right to create a rectangle that is about 4 inches wide (use the ruler as a guide).

4. In the text box, key **Be consistent wherever you are!**

Figure 2-27
Text wrapped in a
text box

5. Click the text box border to select it; then increase the font size to 28 points, and make the text bold and red; and then right-align the text. Resize the text box if necessary to match Figure 2-27, and position the text box as shown.

6. Save the presentation as *[your initials]* 2-22 in your Lesson 2 folder.

7. Close the presentation and submit your work.

Lesson 2   Summary

- Creating a presentation by starting with a blank presentation lets you concentrate on textual content. Anytime during the process, you can choose a design theme and theme colors.

- Keyboard shortcuts are a big time-saver when creating a presentation. For example, Ctrl+Enter moves to the next text placeholder; Ctrl+M inserts a new slide.

- When you add a new slide, you can choose a slide layout. Slide layouts can be either text layouts or content layouts containing different arrangements of placeholders.

- After a slide is added, you can change the layout of the current slide or of a group of selected slide thumbnails.

- Before keying text in a placeholder, activate the placeholder by clicking inside it.

- A font is a set of characters with a specific design, for example, Arial or Times New Roman.

- Font size (the height of a font) is measured in points, with 72 points to an inch. Fonts of the same size can vary in width, some taking up more horizontal space than others.

- Many formatting buttons are toggle buttons, meaning that the same button is clicked to turn an effect on and clicked again to turn it off.

- Change text attributes and effects such as bold, italic, and text color by first selecting the text and then clicking the appropriate buttons on the Home tab in the Font group. Or apply formatting before you key text.

- The Font dialog box, accessible through the Font Dialog Box Launcher, enables you to apply multiple formatting styles and effects all at one time.

- When a text placeholder is selected, formatting that you apply affects all the text in the placeholder.

- Text in placeholders can be aligned with the left or right side of the placeholder, centered, or justified.

- Body text placeholders are preformatted to have bulleted paragraphs. Bullets for selected paragraphs or placeholders are turned on or off by clicking the Bullets button.
- Use the Bullets and Numbering dialog box to change the shape, size, and color of bullets or numbers.
- Graphic files can be used as picture bullets.
- Paragraph indents can be adjusted in text placeholders and text boxes by dragging indent markers on the ruler when a text object is selected.
- To display the ruler for a text object, from the View tab, in the Show group, choose Ruler, and then activate the text object as if to edit the text.
- Bulleted text always uses a hanging indent. Changing the distance between the first-line indent marker (top triangle) and the left indent marker (bottom triangle) on the ruler controls the amount of space between a bullet and its text.
- Indent settings apply only to the selected text object and all the text in the text box.
- Line spacing and the amount of space between paragraphs are controlled using the Line Spacing button and dialog box. Line and paragraph spacing can be applied to one or more paragraphs in a text object or to the entire object.
- Text boxes enable you to place text anywhere on a slide. From the Insert tab, in the Text group, click the Text Box button; then click anywhere on a slide or draw a box and then start keying text.
- Text in a text box can be formatted by using options in the Font group. Change the width of a text box to control how the text will word-wrap.
- When you select a text box on a slide, a green rotation handle appears slightly above the top-center sizing handle. Drag the rotation handle left or right to rotate the object.

LESSON 2		Command Summary	
Feature	Button	Menu	Keyboard
Activate placeholder			Ctrl + Enter
Align Text Left	≡	Home tab, Paragraph group, Align Text Left	Ctrl + L
Align Text Right	≡	Home tab, Paragraph group, Align Text Right	Ctrl + R
Apply a font	Verdana	Home tab, Font group, Font	Ctrl + Shift + F
Bold	**B**	Home tab, Font group, Bold	Ctrl + B
Center	≡	Home tab, Paragraph group, Center	Ctrl + E

continues

LESSON 2   Command Summary *continued*

Feature	Button	Menu	Keyboard
Change case	Aa	Home tab, Font group, Change Case	Shift + F3
Change font size	28	Home tab, Font group, Font Size	Ctrl + Shift + P
Change paragraph spacing		Home tab, Paragraph group, Line Spacing	
Change text box options		Drawing Tools Format tab	
Create new presentation		File tab, New	Ctrl + N
Deactivate placeholder			Esc
Decrease Font Size	A	Home tab, Font group, Decrease Font Size	Ctrl + Shift + <
Decrease List Level			Shift + Tab or Alt + Shift + ←
Font Color	A	Home tab, Font group, Font Color	
Increase Font Size	A	Home tab, Font group, Increase Font Size	Ctrl + Shift + >
Increase List Level			Tab
Insert line break			Shift + Enter
Insert new slide		Home tab, Slides group, New Slide	Ctrl + M
Italic	I	Home tab, Font group, Italic	Ctrl + I
Justify		Home tab, Paragraph group, Justify	Ctrl + J
Move to next placeholder			Ctrl + Enter
Shadow	S	Home tab, Font group, Shadow	Ctrl + S
Text Box	A	Insert Tab, Text group, Text Box	
Turn bullets on or off		Home tab, Paragraph group, Bullets	
Turn numbering on or off		Home tab, Paragraph group, Numbering	
Underline	U	Home tab, Font group, Underline	Ctrl + U

Please visit our Online Learning Center, *www.lessonapproach2010.com*, where you will find the following review materials:

- **Concepts Review**
    - True/False Questions
    - Short Answer Questions
    - Critical Thinking Questions

- **Skills Review**
    - Review Exercises that target single skills
    - Lesson Applications
    - Review Exercises that challenge students by testing multiple skills in each exercise

- **On Your Own**
    - Open-ended exercises that require students to synthesize multiple skills and apply creativity and problem-solving as they would in a real world business situation

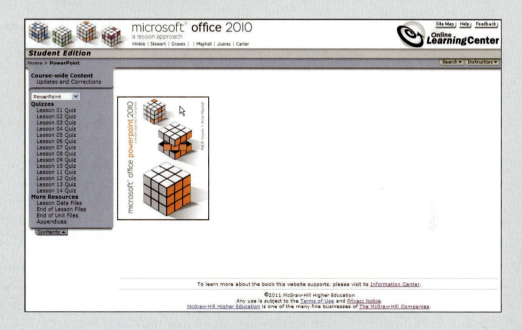

Revising Presentation Text

OBJECTIVES *After completing this lesson, you will be able to:*

1. Select slides, rearrange slides, add sections, and delete slides.
2. Use the Clipboard.
3. Check spelling and word usage.
4. Insert headers and footers.
5. Apply a consistent background and theme colors.
6. Add movement effects.

Estimated Time: 1½ hours

Loyal customers who enjoy dining at Good 4 U have asked Michele Jenkins, head chef, if she would consider catering meals for their businesses and meeting facilities. She is eager to try out this concept because of the success she had with catering in her previous job. Michele has set up a meeting with Julie Wolfe and Gus Irvinelli, co-owners of Good 4 U, to discuss some options she has in mind. She has developed a simple, text-based presentation to help her share these ideas in an organized way. She has asked you to help her rearrange some of the content and then apply a background with an attractive color scheme and interesting transitions. Because she put the presentation together quickly, she knows it has errors that must be fixed.

When using PowerPoint, it is important to review your presentation to ensure that it flows logically, is free of errors in spelling and grammar, and is consistent in its visual representation. Many PowerPoint tools will help with this important task.

Selecting Slides, Rearranging Slides, Adding Sections, and Deleting Slides

Just as you frequently rearrange paragraphs or sentences in a word-processing document, you will often need to rearrange or delete slides in a PowerPoint presentation. To change the arrangement of slides, you can drag them to a new position in the Slides tab, in the Outline tab, or in Slide Sorter view. You can also use sections to organize and rearrange content in the presentation.

You can delete selected slide thumbnails by pressing Delete on your keyboard.

Figure 3-1
Selecting contiguous slides

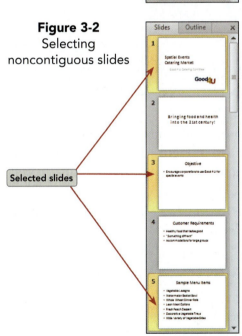

Selected slides

Figure 3-2
Selecting noncontiguous slides

Selected slides

TIP

You can change the number and size of slides displayed in the Slides tab by dragging its border to the right or to the left.

Exercise 3-1 SELECT MULTIPLE SLIDES

If you select multiple slides, you can move them to a new position or delete them all at one time. You can also apply transitions, animation schemes, and other effects to a group of selected slides.

Select multiple slides in one of these ways:

- To select *contiguous slides* (slides that follow one after another), click the first slide in the selection and then hold down Shift while you click the last slide in the selection.

- To select *noncontiguous slides* (slides that do not follow one after another), click the first slide and then hold down Ctrl while you click each slide you want to add to the selection, one at a time.

1. Open the file **Catering**.

2. Working in the Slides tab of the Slides and Outline pane, without clicking, point to each thumbnail one at a time and notice that a ScreenTip appears displaying the title of the slide.

3. Click the thumbnail for slide 2 "Bringing food and health . . ." to select it.

4. Hold down Shift, and click the slide 4 thumbnail "Customer Requirements". Release Shift.

   The heavy border around the slide 2, 3, and 4 thumbnails, as shown in Figure 3-1, indicates that they are selected. This is a contiguous selection.

5. With Shift released, click slide 3. Now it is the only slide selected.

6. Hold down Ctrl, and click slide 1. Slide 1 and slide 3 are both selected. This is a noncontiguous selection.

7. While holding down Ctrl, click slide 5. Now three noncontiguous slides are selected, as shown in Figure 3-2. You can add as many slides as you want to the selection if you hold down Ctrl while clicking each slide thumbnail.

Exercise 3-2 REARRANGE SLIDE ORDER

The Slides tab is a convenient place to rearrange slides. You simply drag selected slide thumbnails to a new position. *Slide Sorter view* enables you to see more thumbnails at one time and is convenient if your presentation contains a large number of slides. You select slides in Slide Sorter view in the same way as you do in the Slides tab.

1. Click the Slide Sorter view button ⊞.
2. Click the slide 2 thumbnail to select it.

Figure 3-3
Moving a slide in the Slide Sorter view

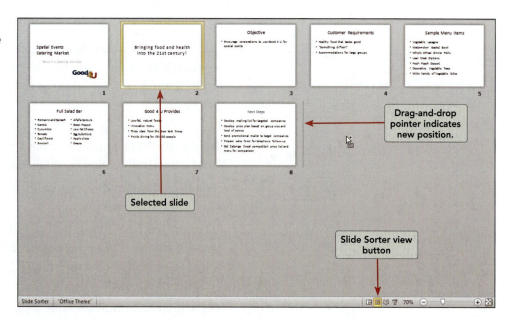

3. Click the slide 2 thumbnail, and drag the slide after the eighth slide, as shown in Figure 3-3. Notice the vertical line and the drag-and-drop pointer that shows where the slide will go.

4. Release the mouse button. Slide 2 "Bringing food and health . . ." becomes slide 8.

5. Using [Ctrl], make a noncontiguous selection of slides 3 "Customer Requirements" and 6 "Good 4 U Provides".

6. Point to either slide in the selection, and drag the selection after the first slide. Both slides move to the new position.

7. Check to make sure your slides are in the following order. If they are not, rearrange your slides to match this order.

   Slide 1: Special Events Catering Market (This slide has a spelling error that you will correct later.)

   Slide 2: Customer Requirements

   Slide 3: Good 4 U Provides

NOTE

While you are dragging, be sure not to release the left mouse button until the drag-and-drop pointer is in the position where you want the selection to go. Otherwise, you might either cancel the selection or drop the slide in the wrong place.

Slide 4: Objective

Slide 5: Sample Menu Items

Slide 6: Full Salad Bar

Slide 7: Next Steps

Slide 8: Bringing food and health into the 21st century!

8. Double-click slide 1 to display it in Normal view.

Exercise 3-3   INSERT SECTIONS

By creating sections, you can easily organize the content of a presentation into groups by topic. On the Home tab, in the Slides group, click the Section button 🔲 to open the drop-down list of available options. You can also right-click a slide thumbnail in the Slides tab to access this feature.

1. Working in Normal view on the Slides tab in the Slides and Outline pane, click the slide 1 thumbnail to select it.

2. From the Home tab, in the Slides group, click the Section button 🔲, and choose **Add Section**. Notice in the Slides tab that a line is added that says "Untitled Section" and all slides in the presentation are selected, as shown in Figure 3-4.

Figure 3-4
Adding a section

3. From the Home tab, in the Slides group, click the Section button 🔲, and choose **Rename Section**.

4. Key **Presentation Opening** in the Rename Section dialog box, and click **Rename**. Notice the section title changes in the Slides tab.

5. Still working in the Slides tab, select the slide 5 thumbnail, "Sample Menu Items."

6. Right-click the slide 5 thumbnail, and choose **Add Section**.

7. Right-click the line "Untitled Section," and choose **Rename Section**. Key **Menu Details**, and click **Rename**.

8. Add a section to slide 7 "Next Steps", and rename the section **Closing**.

TIP

Working with sections makes it easy to rearrange slide content by topic for reuse at different functions and makes a large amount of content in a presentation more manageable. The options of moving and removing sections can speed up the editing process.

9. Working in the Slides and Outline pane, click the "Presentation Opening" section title to select it and the slides below it.

10. From the Home tab, in the Slides group, click the Section button, and choose **Collapse All**. Notice that only the section titles are now showing in the Slides tab.

11. Right-click a section title, and notice the options for editing sections. Choose **Expand All** to expand the sections so that you can view the individual slides.

Exercise 3-4 DELETE SLIDES

When you want to delete slides, you first select them (in the Slides tab or in Slide Sorter view) the same way you select slides you want to move. Delete them by pressing Delete on your keyboard.

REVIEW

To advance through a slide show, click the left mouse button or press the Spacebar, PageDown, →, or N.

1. Working in Normal view on the Slides tab, click the slide 4 "Objective" thumbnail to select it.

2. Press Delete on your keyboard. Slide 4 is deleted, and the new slide 4 becomes selected.

3. Move to slide 1, and click the Slide Show button to view the presentation as a slide show.

4. Advance through the slides (using any method), reading the text and observing the built-in animation effects.

5. Create a new folder for Lesson 3. Save the presentation as *[your initials]*3-4 in the Lesson 3 folder. Leave the presentation open for the next exercise.

Using the Clipboard

The *Cut, Copy, Paste,* and *Duplicate* commands are almost universally available in computer programs. These commands work in the background using a temporary storage space called the *Clipboard* that can hold up to 24 items at a time.

- *Cut.* The selected text or object is removed and stored on the Clipboard.

- *Copy.* The selected text or object remains in its original place, and a copy is placed on the Clipboard.

- *Paste.* A copy of the item is placed at the location of the insertion point, and the item remains on the Clipboard.

- *Duplicate.* A copy of the item is made on the same slide, and a copy is placed on the Clipboard.

Items affected by these actions can be viewed and managed by using the Clipboard task pane. Duplicate works well when you need to create a second copy of something on the same slide; if you need to copy something and paste it on a different slide, then copy and paste is the best method to use. Unlike the Cut command, Delete does not save items to the Clipboard.

The following keyboard shortcuts are big time-savers when you do extensive editing:

- Ctrl+C　Copy
- Ctrl+X　Cut
- Ctrl+V　Paste
- Ctrl+D　Duplicate

Exercise 3-5　USE CUT, COPY, PASTE, AND DUPLICATE TO REARRANGE SLIDES

In the previous objective, you learned how to rearrange slides by dragging their thumbnails. This exercise presents another way to arrange slides: by using the clipboard. On the Home tab, in the Clipboard group, you can open the Clipboard task pane by clicking the Dialog Box Launcher.

Figure 3-5
Using the Clipboard task pane

Number of items in the Clipboard

Slide that has been cut

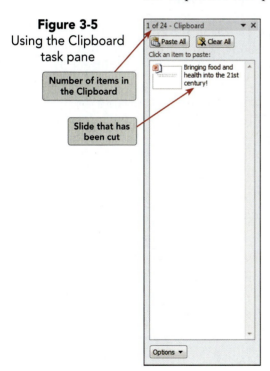

1. With the *[your initials]*3-4 presentation open, from the Home tab, in the Clipboard group, click the Dialog Box Launcher ⌐ to display the Clipboard task pane, as shown in Figure 3-5.

2. On the Slides tab, click the thumbnail of slide 7 "Bringing food and health into the 21st century!".

3. From the Home tab, in the Clipboard group, click the Cut button ✂. This removes the slide and stores it on the Clipboard.

4. Select the thumbnail for slide 1 "Spatial Events Catering Market". Later you will change the spelling of the first word and the subtitle text.

5. From the Home tab, in the Clipboard group, click the Paste button 📋. The cut slide (on the Clipboard) is inserted (or pasted) after slide 1. This accomplishes the same thing as does moving the slide by dragging its thumbnail.

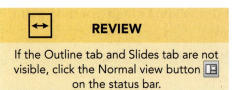

REVIEW

If the Outline tab and Slides tab are not visible, click the Normal view button 🔲 on the status bar.

6. Select the thumbnail for slide 2 "Bringing food and health . . .". From the Home tab, in the Clipboard group, click the down arrow on the Copy button 🖻; then click **Duplicate**. The duplicated slide appears immediately after the original slide but does not appear on the Clipboard.

7. Press ⌨Delete to remove the duplicate slide.

8. Select the slide 1 thumbnail "Spatial Events Catering Market". From the Home tab, in the Clipboard group, click the Copy button 🖻. Notice that two slides are stored on the Clipboard task pane.

9. Move to slide 7 "Next Steps". From the Home tab, in the Clipboard group, click the Paste button 📋 to paste the slide "Spatial Events Catering Market". A copy of the slide is inserted at the end of the presentation to use for making a concluding comment.

10. Move to slide 8, the copied slide.

11. Delete the subtitle text, and key the following text in its place on four lines:

    Catering Market Slogan:
    Make Your Event Special
    Call Good 4 U at
    800-555-1234

Exercise 3-6 USE CUT, COPY, AND PASTE TO REARRANGE TEXT

Figure 3-6
Text and slides stored on the Office Clipboard

The Cut, Copy, Paste, and Duplicate commands can be used for text, but some things are different when changing text compared to changing objects. The Paste Options button 📋 appears near a pasted item if the item's *source* formatting is different from the formatting of similar elements in its *destination* presentation. A Clipboard item's source is the presentation or other document from which text was cut or copied. Its destination is the presentation or other document in which it is pasted.

1. Display slide 7 "Next Steps".

2. Activate the body text placeholder; then click the second bullet to select all its text.

3. Press ⌨Ctrl+⌨X to cut the text from the slide. It appears on the Clipboard task pane. Notice the difference between text and slides on the Clipboard, as shown in Figure 3-6.

4. Click in front of the text in the first bulleted item.

5. Click the first item on the Clipboard task pane (Develop price plan . . .) to insert that text as the first bulleted item.

6. Move to slide 6 "Full Salad Bar".

7. Select the title text "Full Salad Bar," and press Ctrl+C to copy the text from the slide.

8. Move to slide 5, and click after the text "Wide Variety of Vegetable Sides"; press Enter to create a new bullet, and press Ctrl+V. Notice that a Paste Options button appears each time you paste.

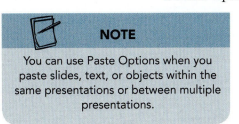

NOTE

You can use Paste Options when you paste slides, text, or objects within the same presentations or between multiple presentations.

9. Click the Paste Options button that appears underneath the new bulleted item, as shown in Figure 3-7, and choose the Keep Source Formatting button from the four choices. Notice that the new bulleted item font size does not match the size of the other bullets.

Figure 3-7
Viewing the Paste Options button

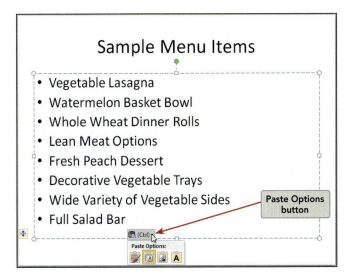

10. Click the Paste Options button again. This time, choose the Keep Text Only button. The bullet changes to match the size of the other bulleted items.

Exercise 3-7   CLEAR THE CLIPBOARD TASK PANE

The Clipboard task pane conveniently shows a series of items that have been cut or copied. The advantage of using the Clipboard to paste items is that you can have several items available and choose which ones you want to paste instead of having to paste immediately after copying or cutting. If you have copied a lot of items, you may find it beneficial to clear the Clipboard task pane.

The Clipboard Options button [Options ▾] allows you to control the settings of the Clipboard task pane.

Figure 3-8
Viewing the Clipboard task pane options

Show Office Clipboard Automatically
Show Office Clipboard When Ctrl+C Pressed Twice
Collect Without Showing Office Clipboard
✔ Show Office Clipboard Icon on Taskbar
✔ Show Status Near Taskbar When Copying
Options ▾

Clipboard Options button

1. If the Clipboard task pane is not open, click the Clipboard Dialog Box Launcher [⌄].

2. Click the Clipboard Options button [Options ▾] at the bottom of the task pane, as shown in Figure 3-8.

3. If it is not already selected, choose **Show Office Clipboard Automatically** to enable the Clipboard to automatically open when you use the Cut or Copy commands.

4. At the top of the Clipboard task pane, click the Clear All button [✕ Clear All] to clear all of the contents held on the Clipboard.

5. Click Close [✕] on the Clipboard task pane.

Exercise 3-8   USE UNDO, REPEAT, AND REDO

When a presentation opens, the Undo button [↩] and the Repeat button [↻] appear on the Quick Access Toolbar. The Repeat button duplicates any action taken. The Undo button [↩] reverses the last action taken. You can undo a series of editing actions, including keying or deleting text, promoting or demoting items, or deleting slides. By using Undo more than once, you can undo multiple actions.

Once Undo is used, the Redo button [↪] appears. It reapplies editing commands in the order you undid them.

TIP

By default, PowerPoint can undo the last 20 actions. You can increase or decrease this number by choosing File, Options, Advanced and changing the maximum number of undos. Increasing the number uses up more RAM memory on your computer.

1. Move to slide 7 "Next Steps". Click at the end of the second bulleted line, and press [Enter].

2. Click the Undo button [↩]. Notice that the new bullet is removed and your insertion point is back at the end of the second bulleted line.

3. Click the Redo button [↪]. The bullet is back and ready to accept text beside it.

4. On the new bulleted line, key the text below:

    Fully develop a menu choices plan

TIP

It's fairly common to make unintentional deletions and unintentional text moves. The [Ctrl]+[Z] key combination is very handy to use when the unexpected happens.

5. Press [Ctrl]+[Z], the keyboard shortcut for Undo. Part of your text will go away.

6. Press [Ctrl]+[Y], the keyboard shortcut for Redo. The text that was taken away in step 5 is now back on your screen.

7. In the Slides and Outline pane, click slide 6, and press [Delete] on your keyboard. Notice that the slide is deleted.

8. Press [Ctrl]+[Z] to undo this deletion and put the slide back into place.

Exercise 3-9   USE FORMAT PAINTER

Format Painter makes it easy to copy formatting such as the font size, color, and font face from one object to another object on the same slide or within a presentation. When you copy the format of an object, many default settings associated with that object are copied as well.

1. On slide 6, select the title "Full Salad Bar."

2. From the Home tab, in the Clipboard group, click the Format Painter button 🖌. The Format Painter picks up the font formatting of this title.

3. Click within the word "cucumber" on the same slide. The text appears with the same formatting as the title. Click the Undo button ↩.

4. Select the title "Full Salad Bar" once again, and double-click the Format Painter button 🖌. Double-clicking keeps the Format Painter active, so you can copy the formatting to more than one object.

5. Move to slide 7, and click "Next" in the title. Notice that when you click just a word, it changes only that single word.

6. Click the word "Steps" to format it the same way.

7. Click the Format Painter button 🖌 again or press Esc to restore the standard pointer.

8. Save the presentation as *[your initials]*3-9 in the Lesson 3 folder. Leave the presentation open for the next exercise.

Checking Spelling and Word Usage

PowerPoint provides many tools to edit and revise text and improve the overall appearance of a presentation:

- *Spelling Checker,* which corrects spelling by comparing words to an internal dictionary file.

- *Research,* which allows you to search through reference materials such as dictionaries, encyclopedias, and translation services to find the information you need.

- *Thesaurus,* which offers new words with similar meanings to the word you are looking up.

- *Find* and *Replace,* which allows you to find a certain word or phrase and replace it with a different word or phrase.

Exercise 3-10   CHECK SPELLING

The *Spelling Checker* flags misspelled words with a red wavy underline as you key text. It can also check an entire presentation at once. The Spelling Checker is an excellent proofreading tool, but it should be used in combination with your own careful proofreading and editing.

In your internship position at Good 4 U, you have been asked to spell-check every presentation and document you create. This should be completed to ensure that no spelling errors appear because they will reflect badly on the image of Good 4 U.

1. In slide 1, a word in the subtitle has a red wavy underline indicating a spelling error. Right-click the word. Choose the correct spelling (Committee) from the shortcut menu, and click to accept it.

2. Notice the spelling of "Spatial" in the title. This is an example of a word that is correctly spelled but incorrectly used. The Spelling Checker can't help you with this kind of mistake. Change the spelling to **Special**. Do this on slide 8 also.

3. Move to slide 1, and run the Spelling Checker for the entire presentation. From the Review tab, in the Proofing Group, click the Spelling button, or press F7.

4. PowerPoint highlights "diffrent," the first word it doesn't find in its dictionary. It displays the word in the Spelling dialog box and suggests a corrected spelling, as shown in Figure 3-9.

Figure 3-9
Using the Spelling Checker

5. Click **Change** to apply the correct spelling, "different."

6. When the Spelling Checker locates "Privite," click **Change** on the correct spelling, "Private."

7. At the next spelling error "Caterngo," click **Ignore** because this is the correct spelling of the company name.

8. Click **OK** when the spelling check is complete.

NOTE

If the Spelling dialog box is hiding a misspelled word, move the dialog box to a different position by dragging its title bar.

Figure 3-10
Research task pane
with definitions

Exercise 3-11 USE RESEARCH

Research is a handy reference tool for looking up many facets of a word. For example, when you research the word "catering," you find information about the definition of the word from the dictionary, synonyms in the thesaurus, and an area where you can translate this word into another language.

1. From the Review tab, in the Proofing group, click the Research button.

2. On the Research task pane in the **Search for** box, type **catering**.

3. Click the down arrow in the Live Search list box, and choose **Encarta Dictionary**.

4. Definition 2, as shown in Figure 3-10, is the correct one for how the word "catering" is used.

5. On the Research pane, click the Close button.

Exercise 3-12 USE THE THESAURUS

The *Thesaurus* is used to find words with similar meanings. This tool is extremely helpful when the same word becomes repetitious and you would like to use a similar word or when you are looking for a more appropriate word with a similar meaning.

1. On slide 6, put your insertion point in the word "Full." From the Review tab, in the Proofing group, click the Thesaurus button. In the Research task pane, the word "Full" is automatically placed in the **Search for** box, a search has already been performed, and the results displayed, as shown in Figure 3-11.

Figure 3-11
Highlighted search
word in Thesaurus
task pane

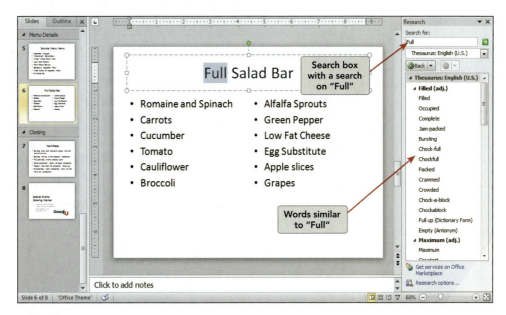

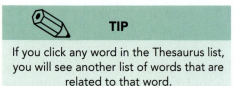

TIP

If you click any word in the Thesaurus list, you will see another list of words that are related to that word.

2. Scroll down until you find the word "Extensive" toward the bottom of the list. Click the down arrow beside "Extensive," and choose **Insert**. Notice that the word "Full" is replaced by the word "Extensive," and the slide now reads "Extensive Salad Bar."

3. On the Thesaurus task pane, click the Close button ⊠.

Exercise 3-13   USE FIND AND REPLACE

When you create presentations—especially long presentations—you often need to review or change text. In PowerPoint, you can do this quickly by using the Find and Replace commands. The *Find* command locates specified text in a presentation. The *Replace* command finds the text and replaces it with a specified alternative.

1. Move to slide 1. From the Home tab, in the Editing group, click the Find button 🔍 (or press Ctrl+F) to open the Find dialog box.

2. In the **Find what** text box, key **Full**, as shown in Figure 3-12.

3. Click the **Find Next** button. PowerPoint locates and selects the text.

Figure 3-12
Find dialog box with text selected

4. Click the Close button ⊠ to close the Find dialog box.

5. Move to slide 1. From the Home tab, in the Editing group, click the Replace button (or press Ctrl+H) to open the Replace dialog box.

6. In the **Find what** text box, key **Full** if it is not displayed already. In the **Replace with** text box, key **Extensive**, as shown in Figure 3-13.

7. Check **Match case** and **Find whole words only** to ensure that you find only the text "Full" and not words that contain these letters (such as "fuller" or "fullest").

Figure 3-13
Replace dialog box

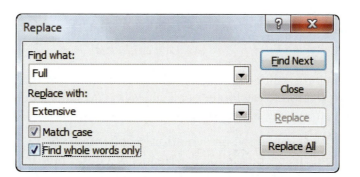

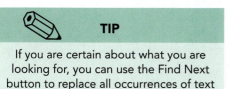

TIP

If you are certain about what you are looking for, you can use the Find Next button to replace all occurrences of text in one step.

8. Click the Find Next button [Find Next], and PowerPoint finds the first occurrence of "Full." Click the Replace button and "Extensive" replaces "Full." A dialog box appears to tell you the search is completed. Click **OK**.

9. In the Replace dialog box, click **Close**.

10. Return to slide 1, and save the presentation as *[your initials]*3-13 in your Lesson 3 folder. Leave the presentation open for the next exercise.

Inserting Headers and Footers

You can add identifying information to your presentation using the Header and Footer dialog box. In PowerPoint, the information appears in placeholders on slides, notes pages, and handout pages for the following:

- *Date and time.* Current date and time updated automatically or keyed as a fixed date.

- *Header.* Descriptive text printed at the top of the page on note and handout pages only.

- *Page number.* Number placed in the lower right corner of note and handout pages by default.

- *Slide number.* Number placed on slides, usually in the lower right corner.

- *Footer.* Descriptive text printed at the bottom of slides, notes pages, and handout pages.

The Header & Footer button is on the Insert tab in the Text group. This command opens the Header and Footer dialog box, which has two tabs: the Slide tab and the Notes and Handouts tab.

Exercise 3-14 ADD SLIDE DATE, PAGE NUMBER, AND FOOTER

Using the Slide tab in the Header and Footer dialog box, you can add information to the footer of all slides in a presentation by clicking **Apply to All**, or you can add footer information to only the current slide by clicking **Apply**.

1. Working on the presentation *[your initials]*3-13, from the Insert tab, in the Text group, click the Header & Footer button 📄. Notice the two tabs in the Header and Footer dialog box, one for adding information to slides and one for adding information to notes and handouts, as shown in Figure 3-14. Click the Slide tab.

Figure 3-14
Header and Footer
dialog box, Slide tab

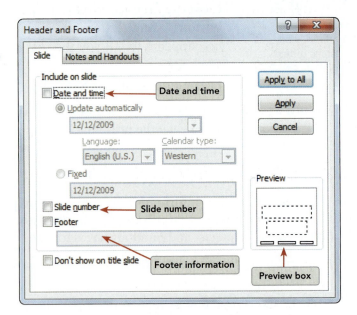

2. In the Preview box, notice the positions for the elements you can place on a slide. As you enable each element by selecting its check box, PowerPoint indicates where the element will print with a bold outline.

3. Click the **Slide number** check box to select it.

4. Click the check box labeled **Don't show on title slide**. When this box is checked, footer and page number information does not appear on the slides using the title slide layout.

5. Leave the **Date and time** check box unchecked.

6. Click the **Footer** check box, and key **Special Events Catering Market**.

7. Click **Apply to All**.

8. Move to slide 1, and click the Slide Show button 🖵 on the status bar to view the presentation as a slide show. Notice the footer information and slide number that appear at the bottom of the slide when you get to slide 3. Slides 1 and 2 do not contain this information since the slides are in the Title Slide layout.

9. Press [Esc] to exit the slide show.

Exercise 3-15   ADD HANDOUT DATE, PAGE NUMBER, AND HEADER

Using the Notes and Handouts tab, you can insert both header and footer information on notes pages and handouts.

1. From the Insert tab, in the Text group, click the Header and Footer button 📄. In the Header and Footer dialog box, click the Notes and Handouts tab, as shown in Figure 3-15.

2. Click the **Date and time** check box, and choose **Update automatically** to add today's date if it is not selected already. Each time you print the presentation handout, it will include the current date. You can choose different date and time formats from the drop-down list.

Figure 3-15
Header and Footer
dialog box, Notes
and Handouts tab

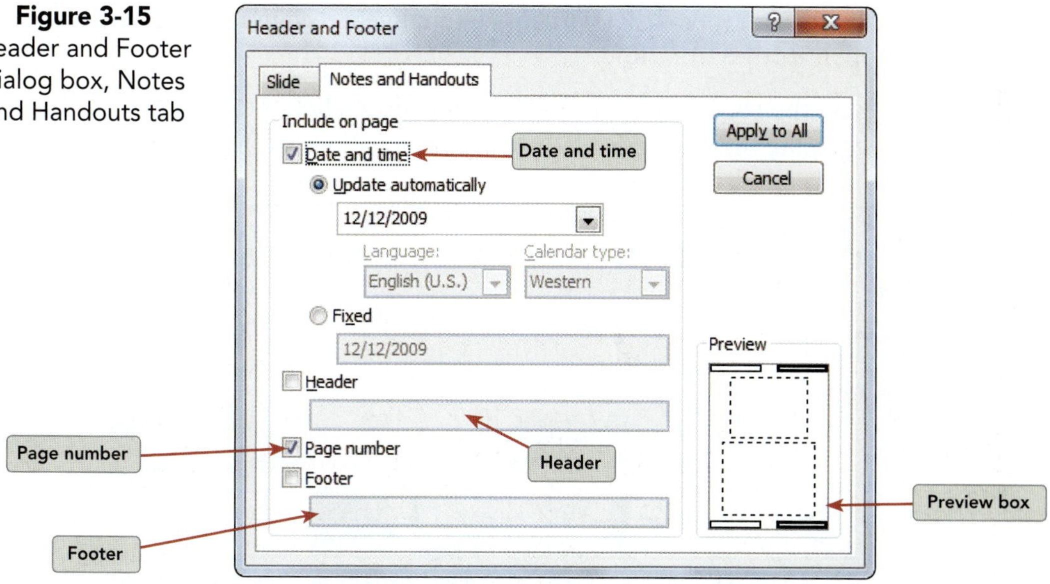

3. Click the **Header** check box to activate that feature, and key *[your name]* in the Header text box. The header is printed in the upper left corner of a note or handout page.

4. Leave the **Page number** check box checked. Page numbers are printed at the bottom right of the page.

5. Click the **Footer** check box to activate that feature, and key the file name *[your initials]*3-15 in the Footer text box.

6. Click **Apply to All** to add this information to all handout pages you print (but not to individual slides).

7. Save the presentation as *[your initials]*3-15 in your Lesson 3 folder. Leave the presentation open for the next exercise.

Applying a Consistent Background and Theme Colors

When you create a new blank presentation, the presentation contains no special formatting, colors, or graphics. Sometimes it's convenient to work without design elements so that you can focus all your attention on the presentation's text. Before the presentation is completed, however, you will usually want to apply a *design theme* to add visual interest. You can apply a design theme or change to a different one at any time while you are developing your presentation.

Exercise 3-16   SELECT A DESIGN THEME

The presentation that you have been working on in this lesson contains no theme. To select a design theme, from the Design tab, in the Themes group, click a design theme. The process to change a design theme is the same as to apply it for the first time.

1.   On the Design tab, in the Themes group, click the More button ⤓ to display the theme choices shown in a gallery as thumbnails.

Figure 3-16
Applying a design theme

2.   Use the vertical scroll bar in the All Themes window to view the design thumbnails. The window is divided by "This Presentation," "Built-In" (listed in alphabetical order by name), and "From Office.com." Links are available for "Browse for Themes" and "Save Current Theme," as shown in Figure 3-16.

3.   Point to one of the design theme thumbnails, and notice the live preview that automatically shows what that design theme will look like when applied to your presentation. A ScreenTip also appears to indicate the name of the theme you are previewing or choosing.

4. Point to several design themes to sample what your presentation will look like with them applied.

5. Right-click any design theme thumbnail. Notice that you can apply the slide design to matching slides, all slides, or selected slides.

6. Click **Apply to All Slides**. The design theme that you selected is applied to all the slides in your presentation.

7. Locate the **Austin** design theme thumbnail, and click it. All the slides are automatically changed.

8. Notice that each thumbnail on the Slides tab shows the new theme design. The theme name appears on the status bar.

9. Move to slide 1, and view the presentation as a slide show; then return to slide 1 in Normal view.

Exercise 3-17   CHANGE THEME COLORS

You can apply different built-in colors to the current design theme by changing the *theme colors*. Live preview displays the theme colors on your slide as you point to each different theme.

Figure 3-17
Theme Colors drop-down list

1. From the Design tab, in the Themes group, click the Colors button. Theme colors are listed alphabetically by name, as shown in Figure 3-17. Scroll through the whole list.

2. Point to any theme color set to see a preview of what it will look like when applied to your presentation.

3. Click any theme color to apply it to your presentation.

4. Click the **Equity** theme color to apply it to your presentation.

5. Sometimes, theme colors or other changes do not update automatically, and you must reset layouts to ensure that all of the slide content has been changed. Click the slide 1 thumbnail on the Slides tab.

6. Press Ctrl+A to select all the slides.

7. From the Home tab, in the Slides group, click the Reset button. The colors will all be updated to match the Equity theme colors.

8. View the presentation as a slide show; then return to Normal view. Notice that on slide 8 the logo overlaps the subtitle text. Press Esc to exit the slide show.

9. Move to slide 8. Move the title and subtitle placeholders up so that you can read the text.

10. Still working on slide 8, from the Design tab, in the Themes group, click the Colors button ▣.

11. Right-click the **Civic** theme color, and choose **Apply to Selected Slides**. Notice that the color of only slide 8 changes to make this closing slide contrast with the other slides.

Exercise 3-18   CHANGE THEME FONTS

You can apply different built-in fonts to the current design theme by changing the *theme font*. The built-in theme fonts include a heading and body font.

Figure 3-18
Theme Fonts drop-down list

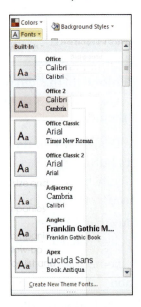

1. From the Design tab, in the Themes group, click the Fonts button ▣. Several choices for theme fonts are available, as shown in Figure 3-18.

2. Point to any theme font to see a preview of what it will look like applied to your presentation. A ScreenTip will pop up showing the name of the theme font.

3. Click any theme font to apply it to your presentation.

4. Point to the Fonts button ▣ again and click the **Grid** theme font (Franklin Gothic Medium) to apply it to your presentation.

5. Move to slide 1, view the presentation as a slide show, and then return to Normal view.

Exercise 3-19   CHANGE THEME EFFECTS

You can apply different built-in effects to the current design theme by changing the *theme effects*.

Figure 3-19
Theme Effects drop-down list

1. From the Design tab, in the Themes group, click the Effects button ▣. Several choices for theme effects are available, as shown in Figure 3-19.

2. Click any theme effect to apply it to your presentation. Right now you may not see any changes because these effects are most noticeable when applied to graphics you will use in later lessons.

3. Click the **Module** theme effect to apply it to your presentation.

4. View the presentation as a slide show; then return to Normal view.

Exercise 3-20 CREATE NEW THEME FONTS

Although there is a wide variety of built-in theme fonts, it is sometimes better to choose your own. You can accomplish this by creating new theme fonts.

1. From the Design tab, in the Themes group, click the Fonts button ⒜.
2. Click **Create New Theme Fonts** at the bottom of the Font Theme drop-down list.
3. Click the drop-down arrow beside **Heading font**, and choose **Gloucester MT Extra Condensed**, as shown in Figure 3-20.
4. Click the drop-down arrow beside **Body font**, and choose **Goudy Old Style**.
5. In the Name box, key **Special Event Fonts**.

Figure 3-20
Create New Theme
Fonts dialog box

6. Click **Save**. Notice the change in the fonts of your presentation.
7. Save the presentation as *[your initials]*3-20 in your Lesson 3 folder. Leave the presentation open for the next exercise.

Adding Movement Effects

A *slide transition* is a movement effect that appears as slides change during a slide show. You can choose to make one slide blend into the next in a checker-board pattern or fade pattern, or you can choose from many other effects as slides enter and exit display on the screen. Transitions can have an effect like turning pages of a book. Movement can be applied to all slides in a presentation or only to selected slides.

Exercise 3-21 APPLY SLIDE TRANSITIONS

Transitions can be applied to individual slides, to a group of slides, or to an entire slide show. To apply transitions, from the Transitions tab, in the Transition to This Slide group, click the More button ⯆ to display the gallery of transition options organized in groups: Subtle, Exciting, and Dynamic

Content. Click the transition to apply it. The Effect Options feature allows you to modify the chosen transition to fit your presentation needs.

1.   Move to slide 1.

2.   From the Transitions tab, in the Transition to This Slide group, click the More button ⬇ to view all the transition options as thumbnails.

3.   Point to several transitions, and notice the preview of how each transition effect will look applied to your slide.

4.   Choose Glitter from the gallery of transitions, as shown in Figure 3-21. This applies the transition to slide 1 only.

Figure 3-21
Choosing the Glitter transition

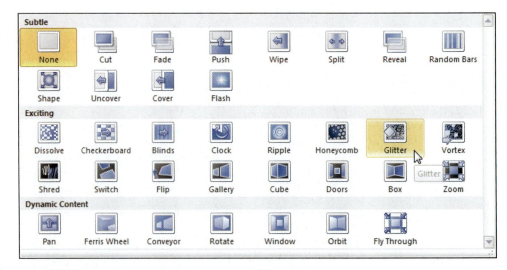

5.   From the Transitions tab, in the Transitions to This Slide group, click the Effect Options button 🖳, and choose Diamonds from Top so that the slide redraws from the top down using diamond shapes.

6.   From the Transitions tab, in the Timing group, click the Apply to All button 🗗. This applies the transition to all slides in the presentation.

7.   View the presentation as a slide show, and notice the transition you have applied.

Exercise 3-22   ADJUST SOUNDS AND DURATION

Transitions also have the option of including sounds during the transition, and you can adjust the speed at which the transition occurs.

1.   Move to slide 1. From the Transitions tab, in the Timing group, click the down arrow in the Duration box until you get to "02:00," which indicates a two-second duration time for the transition. This speeds up the transition time slightly.

2.   From the Transitions tab, in the Timing group, click Apply to All 🗗. This applies the duration changes to all slides in the presentation.

3. Click the drop-down arrow in the Sounds list box, and point to several sounds to listen to the possibilities for transition sounds.

4. Move to slide 1, and click **Applause** to apply the applause sound.

5. Still working in the Timing group, for **Advance slide** notice that **On mouse click** is selected. This option ensures that the transition from slide to slide occurs on a mouse click.

6. View the presentation as a slide show to hear this sound as slide 1 appears.

7. Save the presentation as *[your initials]*3-22 in your Lesson 3 folder.

8. Close the presentation and submit your work.

TIP

Try not to apply transition effects randomly. You might choose one transition for most of your presentation and then select one or two other effects to better emphasize the slide content as it appears. Be careful when using sounds, too, because they may detract from your presentation unless specifically suited to your content.

Lesson 3   Summary

- To change the order of slides in a presentation, use either the Slides tab on the Slides and Outline pane or the Slide Sorter view. Select the slides you want to move; then drag them to a new location. You can also delete selected slides.

- Sections can be used to organize and rearrange presentation content.

- The Clipboard can store up to 24 items that you cut or copy from a presentation. The items can be text, entire slides, or other objects. Insert a Clipboard item at the current location in your presentation by clicking the item.

- Text can be moved or copied by using the Cut, Copy, Paste, and Duplicate commands. Slides can also be rearranged by using these commands.

- The Paste Options button enables you to choose between a pasted item's source formatting and its destination formatting. The source is the slide or placeholder from which the item was cut or copied, and the destination is the location where it will be pasted.

- PowerPoint enables you to undo and—if you change your mind—redo multiple editing actions. The default number of available undos is 20.

- The Format Painter button enables you to copy formatting from one object to another.

- Double-clicking the Format Painter button keeps it active so that multiple objects can receive the copied format. Click the Format Painter button again to turn it off.

- Right-clicking a word flagged with a red wavy line provides a shortcut list of suggested spelling corrections. You can spell-check an entire presentation at one time by using the Spelling dialog box.

- Use the Research task pane to research items in the dictionary, thesaurus, and translator all at once.
- Use the Thesaurus task pane to find words with similar meanings.
- The Find command and the Replace command search your entire presentation for specified text. The Replace feature enables you to automatically make changes to matching text that is found.
- Headers and Footers can appear at the top and bottom of notes and handouts pages. Footers can appear at the bottom of slides. They are commonly used to provide page numbers, dates, and other identifying information common to an entire presentation.
- Design themes apply consistent color, design, fonts, and effects all at once.
- Built-in theme colors, theme fonts, and theme effects can be accessed from the Design tab, in the Themes group.
- Design themes, theme colors, theme fonts, and theme effects can be applied to individual slides, to a group of selected slides, or to an entire presentation.
- Slide transitions add visual interest to slide shows. They can be applied to individual slides, a group of slides, or an entire slide presentation.
- Effect options change the way a transition appears. They can be used to modify the direction of movement and sometimes the shape of the transition.
- Transition sounds and duration can be adjusted to add interest in a presentation.

LESSON 3		Command Summary	
Feature	**Button**	**Ribbon**	**Keyboard**
Add sections		Home, Slides, Section, Add Section	
Apply design theme		Design, Themes group, More	
Change list levels	or	Home, Font group, Decrease List Level or Increase List Level	
Choose theme colors		Design, Themes group, Colors	
Choose theme effects		Design, Themes group, Effects	
Choose theme fonts	A	Design, Themes group, Fonts	
Clear the Clipboard task pane	Clear All	Clipboard task pane, Clear All	
Copy formatting of an object		Home, Clipboard group, Format Painter	

continues

LESSON 3		Command Summary *continued*	
Feature	**Button**	**Ribbon**	**Keyboard**
Copy selected object or text		Home, Clipboard group, Copy	Ctrl + C
Cut selected object or text		Home, Clipboard group, Cut	Ctrl + X
Display Clipboard task pane		Home, Clipboard group, Dialog Box Launcher	
Duplicate		Home, Clipboard group, Copy, Duplicate	Ctrl + D
Find		Home, Editing group, Find	Ctrl + F
Header and footer		Insert, Text group, Header and Footer	
Modify section view (expand/collapse)		Home, Slides, Section, Expand All/Collapse All	
Paste (insert) cut or copied object or text		Home, Clipboard group, Paste	Ctrl + V
Paste options			
Redo		Quick Access Toolbar, Redo	Ctrl + Y
Rename Section		Home, Slides, Section, Rename	
Repeat		Quick Access Toolbar, Repeat	
Replace		Home, Editing group, Replace	Ctrl + H
Research definitions		Review, Proofing group, Research	
Select contiguous slides			Shift + click left mouse button
Select noncontiguous slides			Ctrl + click left mouse button
Slide transition		Transitions, Transition to This Slide group, More	
Spelling Checker		Review, Proofing group, Spelling	F7
Thesaurus		Review, Proofing group, Thesaurus	Shift + F7
Undo		Quick Access Toolbar, Undo	Ctrl + Z

Please visit our Online Learning Center, *www.lessonapproach2010.com*, where you will find the following review materials:

- **Concepts Review**

  True/False Questions

  Short Answer Questions

  Critical Thinking Questions

- **Skills Review**

  Review Exercises that target single skills

  Lesson Applications

  Review Exercises that challenge students by testing multiple skills in each exercise

- **On Your Own**

  Open-ended exercises that require students to synthesize multiple skills and apply creativity and problem-solving as they would in a real world business situation

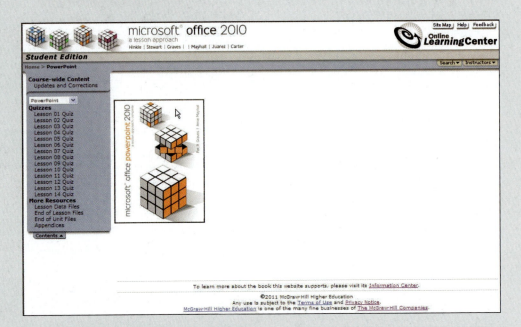

Please visit our Online Learning Center, *www.lessonapproach2010.com*, where you will find Unit Applications review materials.

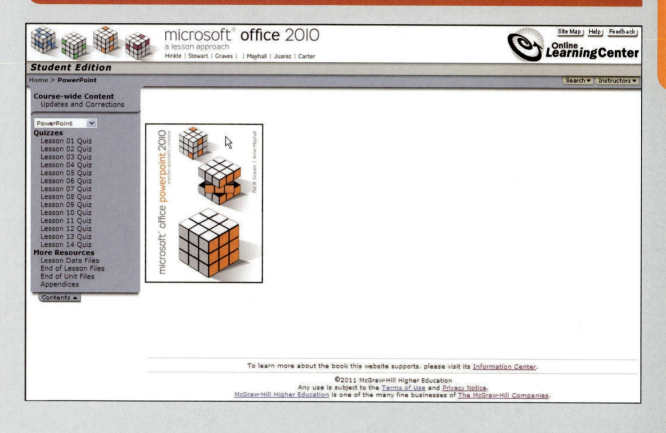

Unit 2

PRESENTATION ILLUSTRATION

Lesson 4
Working with Images

OBJECTIVES *After completing this lesson, you will be able to:*

1. Work with shapes.
2. Insert and adjust clip art images.
3. Insert and enhance a picture.
4. Create WordArt.
5. Create a photo album.

Estimated Time: 2 hours

An effective presentation slide show consists of more than text alone. Although text may carry most of the information, you can use several types of objects to help communicate your message or draw attention to key points. For example, you can add shapes, free-floating text objects, clip art images, and photographs to help illustrate your presentation.

After you add an object to a slide, you can change its size, position, and appearance. In this lesson, you will concentrate on some basic drawing skills and begin to explore some of the many special effects made possible in PowerPoint 2010. You will utilize these skills to add interest to a presentation, **Opening1**, that Gus Irvinelli has started and will use to unveil the plans for the new Good 4 U location in Miami Beach, Florida. Gus is counting on you to improve the appearance of this presentation to help make a great first impression about the new location. On some slides, you will show him comparison images that he may choose from for the final presentation.

Working with Shapes

PowerPoint provides a variety of tools for drawing on the Home, Insert, and Drawing Tools Format tabs. In this lesson, you will learn basic drawing techniques. In later lessons, you will learn to create more complex drawings.

When you are drawing shapes, the ruler helps you to judge size and positioning. When the ruler is displayed, it appears in two parts: The horizontal measurement is across the top of the slide, and the vertical measurement is on the left. By default, the ruler measures in inches; the center of the slide (vertically and horizontally) appears as zero. A dotted line on each ruler indicates the horizontal and vertical position of your pointer.

Gus Irvinelli has requested that you become familiar with fundamental drawing concepts because he wants to use a lot of images with a variety of effects in his presentation. Therefore, the first seven exercises in this chapter will help you become familiar with PowerPoint's drawing tools.

> **NOTE**
>
> The presentations you create in this course relate to the case study about Good 4 U, a fictional restaurant (see frontmatter).

TABLE 4-1 Tools for Basic Drawing

Button	Name	Purpose
	Arrow	Draws an arrow.
	Clip Art	Inserts a clip art object, which could be a drawing, sound, movie, or stock photograph.
	Line	Draws a straight line.
	Oval	Draws an oval or circle.
	Photo Album	Creates a presentation made of pictures with one, two, or four pictures on a separate slide.
	Picture	Inserts a bitmap or photo image from a file.
	Rectangle	Draws a rectangle or square.
	Select	Selects an object. This tool is automatically in effect when no other tool is in use.
	Shape Effects	Adds a visual effect such as shadow, glow, or bevel.
	Shape Fill	Fills a shape with colors, patterns, or textures.
	Shape Outline	Changes the color of a shape's outline or the color of a line.
	Shapes	Opens the Shapes gallery, which contains tools for drawing a variety of predefined shapes.
	Text Box	Inserts text anywhere on a slide.
	WordArt	Creates Microsoft WordArt text on a slide.

Exercise 4-1 DRAW SHAPES—RECTANGLES, OVALS, AND LINES

In this exercise, you practice drawing several *shapes* on a blank slide. To draw a shape, click the appropriate drawing tool button (such as the Line ⬂, Rectangle ▭, or Oval ⬭); then drag the *crosshair pointer* ➕ on your slide until the shape is the size you want.

You can draw multiple shapes with the same drawing tool by using the *Lock Drawing Mode* option. This keeps the button activated, so you can draw as many of the same shapes as you want without the need to reclick the button. This feature is deactivated when you click another button. If you decide not to keep a shape, you can easily remove it by selecting it and pressing ⌜Delete⌟.

As you draw with different tools, the ones you have used appear at the top of the Shapes gallery in the Recently Used Shapes category; however, each tool is also shown in a related group when you access the entire Shapes gallery.

Gridlines and guides are useful for positioning objects on a slide while you are developing a presentation. *Gridlines* are evenly spaced vertical and horizontal lines. The space between the lines can be modified by using the Grid and Guides dialog box available on the View tab, in the Show group, by clicking the Dialog Box Launcher. *Guides* are lines that are shown at the vertical and horizontal center of the slide, and their positioning can be adjusted by dragging the lines. Gridlines and guides do not show when slides are printed or during a slide show.

NOTE

Three of the slides in this presentation were created by using the Blank slide layout. The Blank slide layout contains no text placeholders. Any text that appears on the slides is placed in text boxes.

NOTE

If you are using a computer screen resolution higher than 1024 × 768 or a wide-screen monitor, the Shapes gallery will be displayed in the Drawing group without clicking the Shapes button.

1. Open the presentation started by Gus Irvinelli, **Opening1**.

2. Insert a new slide after slide 2, and use the **Blank** layout. You will use this slide to practice drawing.

3. If the rulers are not showing, right-click the blank slide and choose **Ruler** from the shortcut menu. Notice that zero is placed at the midpoint of the slide on both the vertical ruler and the horizontal ruler.

4. From the View tab, in the Show group, click the check box beside **Gridlines** and the check box beside **Guides** to select them.

5. While watching the horizontal ruler at the top of the slide, move your pointer back and forth, observing the dotted line on the ruler indicating the pointer's position. While moving your pointer up and down, observe the dotted line on the vertical ruler.

6. From the Home tab, in the Drawing group, click the Shapes button 🔲; then click the Rectangle button ▭. The pointer changes to a crosshair pointer ➕.

7. Move the crosshair pointer ➕ to the 3-inch mark to the left of the zero on the horizontal ruler and to the 2-inch mark above the zero on the vertical ruler.

NOTE

Your square might look more like a rectangle if your monitor's horizontal size and vertical size are not perfectly synchronized. Your square will print correctly, even if it is distorted on your screen.

3. Position the crosshair pointer $+$ on the left of your slide.

4. Press and hold Shift; then drag diagonally down and to the right, ending near the horizontal center of the slide. Release the mouse button first, and then release Shift. See Figure 4-6 for the approximate size and placement of the completed square.

Figure 4-6
Square and circle

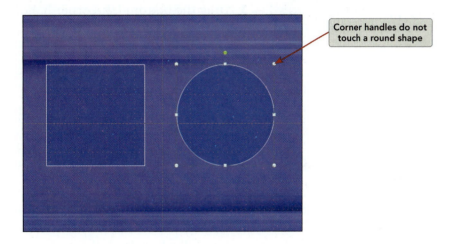

Corner handles do not touch a round shape

5. From the Home tab, in the Drawing group, click the Shapes button, and choose the Oval button.

6. Position your pointer to the right of the square.

TIP

To quickly verify the exact size of your object, click the Drawing Tools Format tab and check the Height and Width dimensions in the Size group.

7. While pressing Shift, drag diagonally down and to the right to create a circle the same size as the square. Your screen should resemble Figure 4-6. Both the square and the circle in this example have a **Height** and **Width** measurement of **3.5"**.

8. Notice that with a circular shape, the corner handles do not touch the shape.

Exercise 4-5   RESIZE AND MOVE SHAPES

A shape that you draw is resized in the same way as resizing a text placeholder: Select it, and then drag one of its sizing handles. Holding down Shift and/or Ctrl while dragging a sizing handle has the following effects on an object:

- Shift preserves a shape's *proportions,* meaning that its height grows or shrinks at the same rate as its width, preventing shapes from becoming too tall and skinny or too short and wide.

- Ctrl causes a shape to grow or shrink from the center of the shape, rather than from the edge that's being dragged.

- Ctrl+Shift together cause a shape to grow or shrink proportionately from its center.

To move a shape, point anywhere in the shape, and when you see the four-pointed arrow ⊕, drag the shape to another place on your slide.

1. Still working on slide 5, select the circle by clicking anywhere inside it, and then point to its bottom center sizing handle. Your pointer changes to a two-pointed vertical arrow ↕.

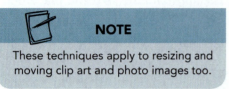

NOTE

These techniques apply to resizing and moving clip art and photo images too.

2. Drag the handle down. As you drag, the pointer changes to a crosshair +. The circle has changed into an oval and is now larger.

3. Drag the bottom-left-corner handle diagonally up and to the left. The oval is now wider and flattened, taking on an entirely new shape.

4. Click the Undo button ↺ twice to restore the circle to its original size and shape.

5. Point to the circle's lower-left-corner sizing handle. While holding down Shift, drag diagonally out from the circle's center, making it larger. (Don't worry if the circle overlaps the rectangle.) The circle retains its original shape. Press Ctrl+Z to undo this action and revert the circle to its original size.

6. While holding down both Ctrl and Shift, drag the lower-left-corner sizing handle toward the center of the circle. The circle becomes smaller, shrinking evenly from all edges. With this technique, all expanding and contracting of the size occurs from the shape's center, as shown in Figure 4-7.

Figure 4-7
Resizing a shape from its center

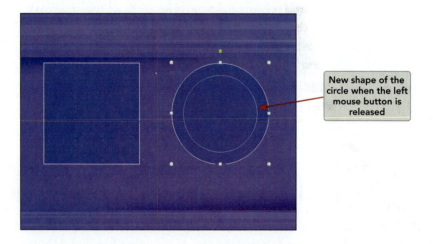

New shape of the circle when the left mouse button is released

7. Select the circle, and press Delete to remove it.

8. Select the square shape, and then from the Drawing Tools Format tab, in the Size group, key **4.5"** in both the **Height** and **Width** boxes.

9. Point in the square so that you see the four-pointed arrow ⊕; then drag the square to the middle of the slide.

10. To control precise sizing and positioning, from the Drawing Tools Format tab, in the Size group, click the **Dialog Box Launcher**.

TIP

If you like working with ruler measurements, you can precisely size and position objects without the need to open the Format Shape dialog box, but keep in mind that the rulers measure distances from the center of the slide. So, if you point to the 2-inch mark at the right of the zero mark on the horizontal ruler, you need to do some math to figure out how far you are from either edge of the slide. The Position option on the Format Shape dialog box, however, lets you choose to measure either from the center of the slide or from its top left corner.

11. In the **Format Shape** dialog box, click the **Size** option. Select the **Lock aspect ratio** option to keep the vertical and horizontal sizing in the same ratio as a shape (or some other object) is resized. This can be very important when working with photographs.

12. Click the **Position** option; then change the **Horizontal** position of the square to 2.75" from the top left corner and the **Vertical** position to 1.75" down from the top left corner.

13. Click the Close button [Close].

14. Create a new folder for Lesson 4. Save the presentation as *[your initials]***4-5** in your Lesson 4 folder. Keep the file open for the next exercise.

Exercise 4-6 USE ADJUSTMENT HANDLES TO MODIFY SHAPES

The rectangles, ovals, and lines that you have created are very simple shapes. Many additional shapes are available, as shown in Figure 4-8.

Figure 4-8
Additional shapes in the Shapes gallery

Shape tools are arranged in 10 different categories, including the Recently Used Shapes category, as shown in Figure 4-8. All of these shapes can be resized in the same way. Some shapes include one or more adjustment handles that enable you to change the shape dimensions, such as the tip of an arrow, after the shape is drawn.

1. You no longer need slides 3 and 4, on which you practiced making shapes. Click each of these slide thumbnails on the Slides tab, and press [Delete] to remove them.

2. Now working on slide 3, from the Home tab, in the Drawing group, click the Shapes button [ ] to display the Shapes gallery.

3. In the **Stars and Banners** category, point to the various shape buttons and read their ScreenTips to see what each one is called.

4. Right-click the 5-Point Star button [ ], and choose **Lock Drawing Mode**. Draw several stars in different sizes, positioned randomly on the slide with some stars overlapping. Place stars on the rectangle and on the blank area of the slide.

5. Press [Esc] to exit the locked drawing mode.

TIP

Use [Shift] to create symmetrical dimensions when drawing any shape.

6. Select one of the stars, and drag its yellow diamond-shaped adjustment handle 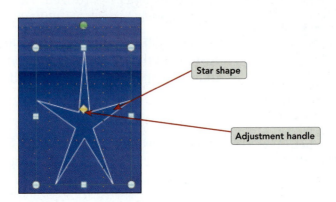 toward the center to make the points more narrow, as shown in Figure 4-9. Adjust each of the stars to look different from the others.

Figure 4-9
Dragging an adjustment handle

Star shape

Adjustment handle

7. Press Ctrl+Z several times to remove the stars so that only a square is left on the slide.

8. From the **Basic Shapes** category, click the Sun button 🔅. Draw a sun, about 2 inches in diameter, in the upper right corner of the slide.

9. Drag the adjustment handle ◆ toward the center of the Sun shape to make the center circle smaller and the points longer.

Exercise 4-7 PLACE TEXT IN A SHAPE AND ROTATE

You can easily transform a shape into an attention-getting background for text. Simply select the shape and key text (or paste it from the Clipboard). You can format and edit the text in the same way as you do in a text placeholder.

1. Select the Sun shape on slide 3, and press Delete.

2. From the Home tab, in the Drawing group, click the Shapes button 🔲 to display the Shapes gallery.

3. In the **Stars and Banners** category, choose the 16-Point Star button ⚙; then click and drag to draw this shape in the upper right of the slide. It should slightly overlap the large square.

4. Key **Grand Opening!** The text automatically appears in the center of the star in the same color as the star's outline.

5. Click the star's border anywhere between two sizing handles to select it.

6. From the Home tab, in the Font group, change the size from 18 points to 28 points, center the text, and apply bold. The text becomes too large for the star.

7. Drag the left-center sizing handle to make the star wide enough to contain the text without word wrapping. Part of the star shape will be over the square shape.

8. Drag the top-center sizing handle down to flatten the star, as shown in Figure 4-10.

Figure 4-10
Inserting text in a shape

9. Click the green rotation handle (the green circle at the top of the shape), and drag it slightly to the left to rotate the star.

10. Drag the star up and to the left until it just slightly overlaps the upper left corner of the square, as shown in Figure 4-11.

Figure 4-11
Rotating a shape with text

11. Compare slide 3 with Figure 4-11, and make any necessary adjustments.

12. Create a handout header and footer: Include the date, your name as the header, the page number, and *[your initials]*4-7 as the footer.

13. Move to slide 1, and save the presentation as *[your initials]*4-7 in your Lesson 4 folder. Keep the file open for the next exercise.

Inserting and Adjusting Clip Art Images

Included with Microsoft Office is a collection of ready-to-use images known as clip art, also called *clips,* that you can insert on PowerPoint slides. The *clip art* collection includes *vector drawings*—images made up of lines, curves, and shapes that are usually filled with solid colors. It also includes *bitmap pictures*—photographs made up of tiny colored dots that are made from scanned photographs or a digital camera. The Clip Art pane enables you to search for these clips by keyword. You can access this pane in two ways:

- From the Insert tab, in the Images group, click the Clip Art button 🖼.
- On a new slide content placeholder, click the Clip Art button 🖼.

Exercise 4-8   FIND CLIP ART AND MODIFY A SEARCH

Each clip art image that Microsoft provides has *keywords* associated with it that describe the subject matter of the picture. You use keywords to find the art you need for your presentation.

Clip art images (and other media such as photographs, sound, and movie files) are organized into collections and media types. You can choose to search all collections and types or to select a particular type. If you know that you want a photograph only, be sure to select only that type of media to make the search more efficient.

Figure 4-12
Clip Art pane

If you search for a keyword and don't find any images, or you don't find one you like, you can modify your search and try again.

1. If you have Internet access but are not connected, make a connection now (unless your instructor tells you otherwise).

2. Move to slide 2, and then from the Insert tab, in the Images group, click the Clip Art button 🖼. The Clip Art pane, as shown in Figure 4-12, is displayed on the right.

3. In the Clip Art pane, in the **Search for** box, key **food**.

4. Click the **Results should be** list box arrow. In this list box, you can choose to search all media types or limit your search to specific types. These options are helpful if you have a large number of media files stored on your computer or you are searching on the Internet. Check only the **Illustrations** category, and remove all other checks.

5. Notice that **Include Office.com content** is checked, meaning that all categories in the Microsoft Clip Organizer will be searched and, if you are connected to the Internet, the Microsoft Office Online collection will be searched too.

6. Click **Go**. Thumbnails of clips that match the search word will appear in the Clip Art pane, as shown in Figure 4-13.

Figure 4-13
Search results

NOTE

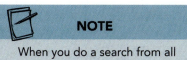

When you do a search from all categories, some clips will have a musical note, indicating that they are sound files. Some clips will have an animation icon 🌟 displayed in the lower right corner, indicating that they are videos.

7. Use the scroll bar to review some of the thumbnails.

8. In the **Search for** box, key **fruit**, and then click **Go**. Thumbnails of pictures with various types of fruit should appear in the pane. If you do not find a picture you like, modify the search using a different keyword.

Exercise 4-9   PREVIEW AND INSERT IMAGES

You can preview images in a larger format so that you can see more detail before choosing one of them.

1. Without clicking, point to a thumbnail in the Clip Art pane. As your pointer is over an image, a ScreenTip showing keywords, image dimensions, size, and file format appears. A gray bar with a downward-pointing triangle appears on the right side of the thumbnail. This bar changes to blue when you point to it.

2. Choose an image you would like to insert.

3. Click the gray bar beside the image you have chosen to display a list box of options. You can also display this list by right-clicking a thumbnail.

4. Choose **Preview/Properties**. In addition to displaying an enlarged picture, this dialog box also shows you the file name and more detailed information about the image, as shown in Figure 4-14.

Figure 4-14
Preview/Properties
dialog box

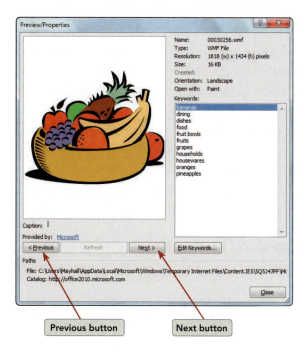

Previous button   Next button

5. Click the Next button  below the picture. The next picture in the pane is displayed.

6. Click the Next button several times more; then click the Previous button. Gus has requested that you choose a professional-looking image to insert. When you find an appropriate picture of healthful food, such as the one in Figure 4-14 or Figure 4-15, click **Close** on the Preview/Properties dialog box. Notice that the last image you previewed has a blue selection box around it.

> **TIP**
>
> You can also drag the image from the Clip Art pane onto your slide or select **Insert** from the list box that appears when you click the thumbnail bar.

7. Click the image thumbnail to insert the image on the current slide.

Figure 4-15
Positioning of an illustrated image

8. Drag the image above the text box, and resize or rotate it as necessary for a pleasing appearance. The image in Figure 4-15 was increased in size, rotated, and centered horizontally, and it overlaps the top edge of the text box. If you used a different image, then decide how to position it attractively on the slide.

9. Move to slide 1, and find another image that would be appropriate for Miami Beach. In the **Search for** box, key **palm tree**, and in the **Results should be** box, choose **Photographs**. Click **Go**.

10. When you find a photograph of a palm tree similar to the one in Figure 4-16, insert it on slide 1 and close the Clip Art pane.

Exercise 4-10   REARRANGE, DELETE, COPY, PASTE, AND DUPLICATE IMAGES

When developing a presentation, you might insert an image on one slide and later decide to move it to a different slide. You can rearrange, delete, copy, paste, and duplicate clip art images.

1. Still working on slide 1, click the photograph to select it. When you see the four-pointed arrow, drag the photograph down to center it vertically on the right edge of the text box.

2. Move to slide 4. This slide has four illustrations that were previously inserted. On the left, select the sunset beach scene, and notice the green rotation handle at the top. Practice dragging this handle to rotate the illustration.

3. Press ⌈Delete⌉ to remove the sunset beach scene from this slide.

4. On the right, select the palm tree image on the top, and press ⌈Ctrl⌉+⌈C⌉ to copy it and then ⌈Delete⌉ to remove it from this slide. The image is still on your Clipboard.

5. Insert a new slide after slide 4 using the **Blank** layout. Press ⌈Ctrl⌉+⌈V⌉ to insert the palm tree on the new slide 5.

NOTE

When moving objects on the screen that need precise positioning, you can use the directional arrow keys on the keyboard to *nudge* the image gradually. If you press ⌈Ctrl⌉+the arrow keys, the image will be nudged in very small increments.

6. When this image first appears, the size is 1.84 inches for both the height and the width. From the Picture Tools Format tab, in the Size group, change both **Height** and **Width** to **1.5"**.

7. Drag the palm tree to the upper left of the slide, aligning the bottom of the image with the darkest blue color on the background and the left edge of the image even with the left of the slide, as shown in Figure 4-16.

Figure 4-16
Duplicated images

8. Press ⌈Ctrl⌉+⌈D⌉ to *duplicate* this image. Move the second image over to align with the bottom of the first image and position it so that the branches almost touch.

NOTE

Using the Duplicate command is faster than using Copy and Paste when you want a second image on the same slide. Copy and Paste works best when you want to copy an image from one slide and paste it on another slide.

9. With the second image selected, press ⌈Ctrl⌉+⌈D⌉. Because the positioning information from your first duplication is remembered by PowerPoint, this image should go into the same alignment.

10. Press ⌈Ctrl⌉+⌈D⌉ five more times to create a row of palm trees across the top of the slide as shown in Figure 4-16. Your final palm tree may extend past the end of the slide. This row of trees will create a nice top border for a night scene added later in the lesson.

Exercise 4-11 GROUP AND UNGROUP IMAGES AND TEXT

When you *group* objects, you combine two or more shapes or images so that they behave as one. If you then move one object of the group, all the other objects move with it. Grouping ensures that objects meant to stay together don't accidentally get moved individually or deleted. When you apply formatting to a group, all the objects in the group receive the same formatting. If you need to work on the objects separately, then you can *ungroup* them. *Regrouping* can combine the objects again.

1. Move to slide 4. Press Shift while you click both the beach scene image and the text below it. Now selection handles appear on both images.

2. From the Picture Tools Format tab, in the Arrange group, click Group ; then select **Group**. Now the clip art image and the text are combined as one object.

3. Resize the group by stretching the corner sizing handle on the top right to make the image about as large as the palm tree on the right.

4. In resizing the group, the text has moved and is not in the best position. From the Picture Tools Format tab, in the Arrange group, click the Group button; then choose **Ungroup**. Now you can move the image and text separately.

5. Arrange the beach scene image on the left so that the bottom aligns evenly with the palm tree on the right. Move the beach scene text so that it is centered under the image and aligned with the palm tree text. You may need to resize the beach scene text box.

6. Now select the beach image. From the Picture Tools Format tab, in the Arrange group, click the Group button, and choose **Regroup**.

7. Select the palm tree image and the palm tree text, and group them.

8. Move to slide 6. Select the picture of Miami buildings, and press Ctrl+C.

9. Move to slide 3, and press Ctrl+V. Position the picture so that it is in the center of the square shape.

10. Resize the square shape to change it to a rectangle that evenly frames the picture.

11. If necessary, select the **16-Point Star** shape and move it up slightly so that the picture is not overlapping it.

Figure 4-17
Grouped shapes and picture

12. With the star selected, press ⌈Shift⌋ while you click the picture and the rectangle to select all three objects.

13. From the Drawing Tools Format tab, in the Arrange group, click the Group button ⿴▾, and choose **Group**.

14. From the View tab, in the Show group, uncheck the boxes for **Gridlines** and **Guides** since we are finished aligning objects.

15. Move to slide 1, and save the presentation as *[your initials]***4-11** in your Lesson 4 folder. Keep the file open for the next exercise.

Inserting and Enhancing a Picture

More than any other graphic element, pictures can add a sense of realism to a presentation. Microsoft's online collection offers an abundance of photograph images that you can search for using the Clip Art pane. Pictures that you take with a digital camera also can be inserted. Or pictures that are already printed can be turned into an appropriate digital format by scanning.

Once the picture is inserted into PowerPoint, you have many options for improving its appearance using the commands on the Picture Tools Format tab shown in Figure 4-18 and defined in Table 4-2. In the next exercises, you will learn to crop to remove unwanted details, adjust brightness and contrast, and apply many different styles and special effects.

Figure 4-18
Picture Tools Format ribbon

TABLE 4-2 Picture Tools Format Tab Commands

Button	Name	Purpose
	Align	Evenly spaces multiple objects.
	Artistic Effects	Adds interesting effects to pictures, including effects such as blur, pastels, light screen, cement, and painting.
	Bring Forward	Adjusts stacking order of pictures and other objects.
	Change Picture	Changes the selected picture to a different picture in the same size and format as a selected picture.
	Color	Enables you to change the color saturation and tone of a picture and select different monotone variations based on theme colors.
	Compress Pictures	Reduces resolution and removes unwanted information from a picture to make the presentation file size smaller.

continues

TABLE 4-2 Picture Tools Format Tab Commands   *continued*

Button	Name	Purpose
☼	Corrections	Increases or decreases a picture's brightness, contrast, or sharpness.
🖼	Crop	Enables you to trim away the edges of a picture, crop to shape, and adjust the aspect ratio of images.
⧉	Group	Fastens multiple objects together to act as one object.
⬍	Height	Adjusts the vertical size dimension.
✎	Picture Border	Places an outline around a picture in different colors, weights, or line styles.
◲	Picture Effects	Provides the effects of shadow, reflection, glow, soft edges, bevel, or 3-D rotation.
▤	Picture Layout	Converts the picture to a SmartArt graphic.
🖼	Picture Quick Styles	Provides a gallery of preset effects to add interest. Displays when the Ribbon is not expanded to its full size.
🖼	Remove Background	Removes unwanted portions of the picture background.
🖼	Reset Picture	Restores a picture's original attributes if changes were made by using the Picture Adjustment tools.
◭	Rotate	Angles pictures and other objects.
⬚	Selection Pane	Enables you to select individual pictures and other objects and change the visibility or order.
⬚	Send Backward	Adjusts the stacking order of pictures and other objects.
⬚	Width	Adjusts the horizontal size dimension.

Exercise 4-12   INSERT PHOTOGRAPH IMAGES

To search for a photograph image, use the same steps as you did for searching for illustrated images except choose Photographs instead of Illustrations under the **Results should be** list box.

1. Delete slide 6, since the photo is now used on slide 3.

2. Move to slide 5, and from the Insert tab, in the Images group, click the Clip Art button 🖼.

3. In the Clip Art pane, in the **Results should be** list box, check only **Photographs** and remove other checks. Be sure **Include Office.com content** is checked.

4. In the **Search for** box, key **Miami**, and then click **Go**. The pane shows thumbnails (miniature images) of clips that match the search word.

Figure 4-19
Photograph inserted
from search

5. Double-click the Miami night image. Drag the corner sizing handle to increase the picture height to about 4 inches. Notice that the width automatically adjusts to keep the image in proportion.

6. Position the image as shown in Figure 4-19. Close the Clip Art pane.

Exercise 4-13   CROP A PICTURE

When a picture (photograph) is selected and you click the Picture Tools Format tab, many options become available to you for adjusting the picture or applying picture styles and effects. You can also *crop* (trim) parts of a picture, just as you might do with a page from a magazine by using a pair of scissors to reduce its size or remove unwanted details around the edge.

When you click the cropping tool, a picture's sizing handles change to *cropping handles*—short black markers that you drag to trim a picture.

1. On slide 5, select the night scene picture. The colors of the lighted buildings and water reflections can be featured more if the picture is trimmed across the top and bottom.

2. From the Picture Tools Format tab, in the Size group, click the Crop button. The cropping handles appear around the edges of the picture, and your pointer changes to a cropping tool.

TIP

If you crop too far, either use the cropping tool to drag the handle in the opposite direction to restore that part of the picture or click the Undo button.

3. Position the cropping pointer on the top-center handle, and drag the handle down until the cropping line is positioned a little closer to the top of the tallest building, as shown in Figure 4-20. Notice the dark area showing what portion of the image will be removed.

4. Repeat this process to crop from the bottom so that the picture ends just below the reflection.

Figure 4-20
Cropping a picture

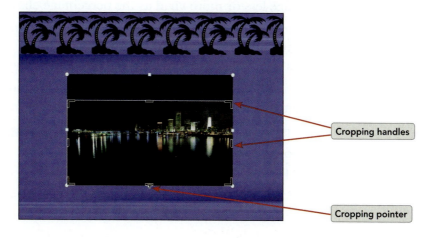

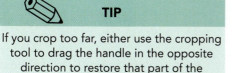

Cropping handles

Cropping pointer

5. Click a blank area of the slide to turn off the crop function and to remove the dark areas indicating the cropped part of the image.

Exercise 4-14   MODIFY COLORS

The appearance of a photograph can be changed in many ways using color settings. These effects might be used, for example, to improve the clarity of an image, make an image look aged, or create a subtle image to be placed behind other slide objects.

1. Move to slide 1, select the palm tree picture, and copy it. Insert a new slide **Blank** layout, and paste the picture.

2. Select the picture on slide 2; then from the Picture Tools Format tab, in the Adjust group, click the Color button 🖼. A gallery of color options will appear, as shown in Figure 4-21.

Figure 4-21
Color gallery

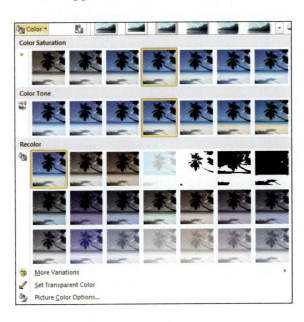

3. In the gallery, slowly drag your pointer over each of the options to see a preview on the picture.

    - *Color Saturation.* Controls the intensity of the colors, making the image less or more vivid as the percentage changes from 100%.

    - *Color Tone.* Creates cool or warm tones by changing the temperature of the image on a scale of 4,700 to 11,200. The low end of this scale has cool tones, and the high end has warm tones.

    - *Recolor.* Provides options for grayscale, black and white, or different light and dark monotone variations of the presentation's theme colors.

4. In the Recolor category in the last row, click **Dark Blue, Accent color 1 Light** to select this color change.

5. Move the picture to the upper left of the slide. Use the lower right sizing handle, and drag down to reach the bottom of the slide.

6. Drag the right sizing handle to the right of the slide so that the picture completely fills the slide (dimensions: 7.5 inches by 10 inches).

7. Move to slide 1, press Ctrl+A to select all objects on the slide, and then press Ctrl+C to copy them.

8. On slide 2, press Ctrl+V to paste all objects over the recolored palm tree picture.

9. Move back to slide 1, and press Delete to remove the original slide 1.

Exercise 4-15   APPLY A PICTURE STYLE

Many different *picture styles* are available to display your pictures in beautiful and interesting ways. As with any of the creative techniques you are using, be careful that the styles and other treatments you apply to your pictures add to the appearance of the picture and do not distort it or diminish its effectiveness.

1. On the new slide 1, select the smaller color picture of the palm tree. From the Picture Tools Format tab, in the Picture Styles group, slowly drag your pointer over each of the Picture Styles options, and the results of that option will be displayed on the picture.

2. Click the More button ▾ to see additional styles that are available, as shown in Figure 4-22.

Figure 4-22
Picture styles

3. Now click the Picture Style **Rounded Diagonal Corner, White**, as shown in Figure 4-23.

Figure 4-23
Picture with Rounded Diagonal Corner, White effect

4. On slide 5, select the picture, and apply the same Picture Style, **Rounded Diagonal Corner, White**.

5. From the Insert tab, in the Text group, click the Text Box button [A], and draw a text box at the bottom of the picture. In the text box, key **Beautiful Miami Skyline**. Change the font to **Bauhaus 93** in font size **36**, apply italics, and right-align the text. The title should fit nicely in the black water area of the image.

Exercise 4-16   INSERT A PICTURE FROM A FILE

When you begin to acquire a collection of digital images, you need to keep them organized in some logical way in folders on your computer that are appropriately named to identify the folder's contents. These folders might be saved in the Pictures folder that is automatically created on your computer when Microsoft Office is installed.

However, for this exercise you have a picture file stored in the same folder as all the other files for this lesson.

1. Display slide 5; then, from the Home tab, in the Slides group, click the New Slide button [icon] to add a new slide with a **Title Only** layout. Key **Outdoor Dining** as the slide title.

2. From the Insert tab, in the Images group, click the Picture button [icon].

3. In the Insert Picture dialog box, locate where your student data files for this lesson are stored, and select the file **Restaurant.jpg**. Click **Insert**.

4. With the picture selected, click the Picture Tools Format tab. In the Size group, change the height to **5"**, and the width will automatically change to **3.7"**.

5. Move the picture to the left of the slide, under the title.

Exercise 4-17   USE CORRECTIONS TO SHARPEN OR SOFTEN AND ADJUST CONTRAST AND BRIGHTNESS

Sometimes a picture may be too dark to show needed details, or colors are washed out from too much sunshine when the picture was taken. PowerPoint's *Corrections* feature can fix these problems. Adjusting the brightness changes the picture's overall lightness, while adjusting contrast affects the difference between the picture's lightest and darkest areas. Modifying the sharpness makes objects look more or less precise.

1. On slide 6, select the picture, and press [Ctrl]+[D] to duplicate it. Position the second image on the right of the slide. Use it to make the color adjustments in this exercise so that you can compare your changes to the original.

2. With the second picture selected, from the Picture Tools Format tab, in the Adjust group, click the Corrections button [icon]. A gallery of thumbnails appears showing the current picture selected and the effect of adjustments in 20 percent increments, as shown in Figure 4-24, that increase or decrease the brightness and contrast of the picture.

Figure 4-24
Corrections gallery

3. Drag your pointer over the thumbnails, and notice the effect on the picture and the ScreenTips that show brightness and contrast amounts. Click **Brightness: +20% and Contrast: +20%** (column 4, row 4) to increase the brightness and contrast by 20%.

4. Click the Corrections button ☀. The same gallery appears showing adjustments in the Sharpen and Soften category in 25 percent increments that increase or decrease the sharpness of the picture. Drag your pointer over the thumbnails, and study the effect on the picture. Click **Sharpen: 25%** (column 4) to increase the sharpness.

5. Now click the Reset Picture button 🖼 to restore the picture's original colors.

6. Sometimes these 20 and 25 percent increments change a picture's colors too much, so you might need to adjust them more gradually to get good results. On the Picture Tools Format tab, in the Adjust group, click the Corrections button ☀; then choose **Picture Corrections Options** to open the Format Picture dialog box. Move this dialog box away from the picture so that you can see the results of your changes as you make them.

7. Both the brightness and the contrast can be adjusted by dragging the slider to the left or right. You can also enter numbers in the spin boxes or click up or down to change in 1 percent increments.

8. Adjust the brightness to a positive **14%** and the Contrast to a positive **24%**. Modify the Sharpen setting to a positive **15%**. Click **Close**.

9. The picture appears a little clearer now when you compare the one changed on the right with the original version on the left, as shown in Figure 4-25. You will leave both images in the presentation, so Gus can decide which image he prefers to use.

Figure 4-25
Picture with corrections

10. Save the presentation as *[your initials]*4-17 in your Lesson 4 folder. Leave the presentation open for the next exercise.

Exercise 4-18   CROP TO A SHAPE

Any picture that is inserted on a slide can be cropped to fill a shape for an unusual and creative treatment.

1. On slide 6, from the Home tab, in the Slides group, click the New Slide button 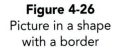 to add a new slide with a **Blank** layout.

2. On slide 7, insert another picture from your Clip Art pane. If the search from earlier in the lesson is not displayed, then search again for Miami photograph images.

3. Insert the image that is angled showing a beach and buildings.

4. With this image selected, from the Picture Tools Format tab, in the Size group, click the down arrow on the Crop button 🖼, and choose **Crop to Shape**. Try several of these shapes by clicking on the buttons in any of the categories. The image becomes the fill for that particular shape.

5. In the **Basic Shapes** category, select the **Heart** shape.

Exercise 4-19   ADD A BORDER TO A PICTURE

The line that surrounds shapes and pictures is referred to as a Picture Border. This line can be shown in different colors and *line weights* (thicknesses) or in different styles (solid lines or dashes) to create a border around a picture just as you have used an outline on other shapes.

1. With the heart-shaped picture selected, from the Picture Tools Format tab, in the Picture Styles group, click the Picture Border button 🖉. As you drag your pointer over the colors, you can see how the color will look if selected.

2. From the colors that appear, in the **Theme Colors** group, click the **White, Text 1** color.

3. Click the Picture Border button 🖉 again, and click **Weight**. Choose **4 ½ pt** for a thicker white line, as shown in Figure 4-26.

4. Continue to the next exercise.

Figure 4-26
Picture in a shape
with a border

Exercise 4-20   APPLY PICTURE EFFECTS

Special effects can be applied to pictures as well as other shapes you create using the Picture Effects button on the Picture Tools Format tab. Many different customized settings are possible. Picture effects are available in seven categories:

- *Preset.* Consists of a collection of images with several different settings already applied.
- *Shadow.* Displays a shadow behind the picture that can be adjusted in different ways to change direction, thickness, and blurring effect.
- *Reflection.* Causes a portion of the image to be displayed below the image as though it were reflecting in a mirror or on water.
- *Glow.* Adds a soft color around the picture edges that makes the picture stand out from the background.
- *Soft Edges.* Changes a picture's normal hard edges to a soft, feathered appearance that gradually fades into the background color.
- *Bevel.* Makes the picture look dimensional through several different options that can create a buttonlike effect.
- *3-D Rotation.* Enables the picture to be angled in different ways through perspective settings that change the illusion of depth.

Figure 4-27
Picture Effects

1. On slide 7, select the heart-shaped picture. From the Picture Tools Format tab, in the Picture Styles group, click the Picture Effects button.
2. The drop-down list of effects appears, as shown in Figure 4-27. Each of these effects has several variations that you can see on your image as you drag your pointer over the effect thumbnail.
3. Click **Shadow**, and then **Outer**. Choose the shadow named **Offset Diagonal Bottom Right** to apply a soft shadow.
4. Adjustments can be made to the way the shadow appears. Click the Picture Effects button, click **Shadow**, and then choose the **Shadow Options** at the bottom of this gallery.
5. From the dialog box that appears as shown in Figure 4-28, key these numbers for each of the following settings:

  - Transparency   **20%**
  - Size   **100%**
  - Blur   **10 pt**
  - Angle   **40°**
  - Distance   **15 pt**

6. Click **Close** to accept these settings.

TIP

You may also click the Picture Styles Dialog Box Launcher to access the Format Picture dialog box.

Figure 4-28
Format Picture,
Shadow settings

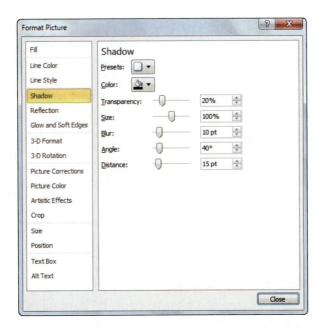

Exercise 4-21 APPLY ARTISTIC EFFECTS

Artistic Effects is a new feature in PowerPoint 2010 that applies photo filters to pictures. Previously, creating these interesting and unusual effects required photo editing software. The best way to become familiar with the Artistic Effects feature is to insert a picture image and apply different effects to observe how the image is modified. Artistic Effects include 23 different filters that can be adjusted in transparency or intensity. These include effects such as *Painting, Blur, Cement, Light Screen, Plastic Wrap, and Pastels.*

1. On slide 8, key **Innovative Dishes** as the slide title.

2. Use the Clip Art pane to search for and insert a photograph of a healthy salad or entrée similar to the one shown in Figure 4-29. Resize the picture to a height of **5"**, and position it on the right beside the waiter image.

3. With this image selected, from the Picture Tools Format tab, in the Adjust group, click the Artistic Effects button . Point to the options to preview the effect that each has on the image.

4. Since the image displays food, choose the **Plastic Wrap** effect. This effect might be appropriate to illustrate how take-home food could be packaged.

Figure 4-29
Artistic Effects

Exercise 4-22   REMOVE A PICTURE BACKGROUND

The *Background Removal* feature is new in PowerPoint 2010. It allows you to remove the background of an image to help the audience focus on the important part of that picture.

You will work with two images in this exercise. The first one has a solid-color background, so you will see how the Background Removal feature works really well with pictures like this to remove areas that may be distracting or that do not blend with your slide background. The second image has a little more color and details, so you will see how the Mark to Remove and Mark to Include options are used to control which parts of the picture are retained.

1. On slide 8, increase the waiter image size to **6"**, and position it attractively to the left of the salad image.

2. Because this image shows a person with a single-color background, the original background in the photo has probably been removed and replaced with white.

3. With the image selected, from the Picture Tools Format tab, in the Adjust group, click **Remove Background**. The background becomes pink as shown in Figure 4-30, indicating the area that is marked for removal, and handles appear on the area of the image to keep.

4. Resize the handles so that all of the waiter is within the rectangular shape.

5. On the Background Removal tab, in the Close group, click the Keep Changes button ✓, and the area marked in pink is removed. Now the waiter image looks more pleasing on the slide background.

Figure 4-30
Background
Removal, solid color

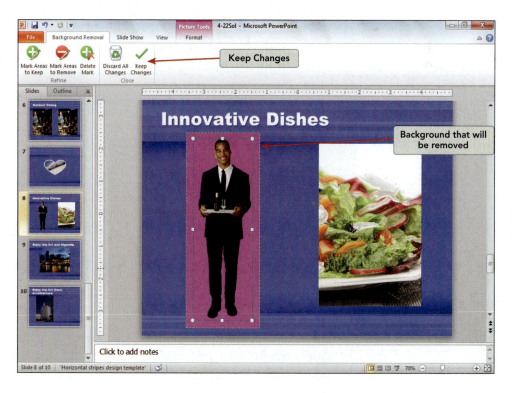

6. On slide 9, key **Enjoy the Art Deco Architecture** as the slide title.

7. Resize the image to a height of **6"**, and position it on the left with the bottom of the picture aligned with the bottom of the slide. Press Ctrl+D, and position the duplicated image on the right. Make your changes on this second image, and use the first one for comparison.

8. Use the Zoom slider on the status bar to increase the slide size to **90%** so that you can better see the details of the image.

9. With this image selected, from the Picture Tools Format tab, in the Adjust group, click the Remove Background button. The background becomes pink, indicating the area that is marked for removal, and handles appear on the area of the image to keep.

10. Resize the center handle on the bottom to extend the selected area to the bottom of the image.

11. On the Background Removal tab, in the Refine group, click the Mark Areas to Keep button, and your pointer becomes a pencil tool.

12. Very carefully click the edges of the building that should not be removed, and small plus marks will appear, indicating that this area is being added to the selected area. Include the palm tree on the right too.

13. If you mark the wrong area, click the Delete Mark button to again remove an area marked for removal from the selection. If areas that are not marked should be removed, click the Mark Areas to Remove button.

14. When finished, click the Keep Changes button. As shown in Figure 4-31, the final image now focuses on the one building, and surrounding buildings no longer appear.

15. Use the Fit to Window button on the status bar so that the slide fits in the available space of your monitor and you can compare this altered image to the original on the left.

Figure 4-31
Background Removal,
Mark Areas to Keep
and to Remove

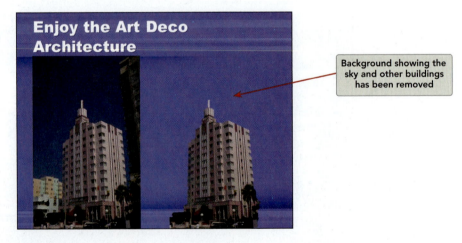

16. Move to slide 10 to make modifications to the final presentation slide. Apply the **Rotated, White** picture style, and resize the image so that the edges of the picture style touch the top and the bottom of the slide.

17. Apply the Artistic Effect **Paint Brush**.

18. Select the title text placeholder, and change the font to **Bauhaus 93**, bold, centered, with a font color of **Light Blue, Background 1**.

19. Resize the title text placeholder to fit the image, and rotate and reposition so that the title appears level with the bottom of the image.

20. Save the presentation as *[your initials]***4-22** in your Lesson 4 folder. Leave the presentation open for the next exercise.

Creating WordArt

WordArt provides special effects for text that are not possible with standard text-formatting tools. You can stretch or curve text and add special shading, 3-D effects, and much more to make text more readable or more decorative.

Exercise 4-23   CREATE AND MODIFY WORDART TEXT

In this exercise, you create WordArt text and then modify it by changing its shape and size.

Figure 4-32
WordArt Styles gallery

1. Display slide 3 with the building photograph.

2. From the Insert tab, in the Text group, click the WordArt button ⁴. The WordArt Styles gallery appears, as shown in Figure 4-32.

3. Point to the blue WordArt style **Fill – Blue, Accent 2, Warm Matte Bevel** (fifth row, third effect) and click to select it. WordArt appears in the middle of your slide with sample text as shown in Figure 4-33.

Figure 4-33
WordArt as it first appears

4. With the WordArt text selected, replace the text by keying **Good For You**.

TIP

Many different styles are displayed in the WordArt gallery using the colors of your current theme. When applied, some of the styles may need color adjustments so that the text is easily readable on the background color.

5. Click anywhere on the blank part of the slide to accept these changes, and the bevel effect of this style becomes more evident.

6. To edit WordArt text, simply select the text and change it. In this case, change the wording to **Good 4 U**.

7. Move the WordArt text to the lower left as shown in Figure 4-34.

Figure 4-34
WordArt positioning

8. Save the presentation as *[your initials]*4-23 in your Lesson 4 folder. Leave the presentation open for the next exercise.

Exercise 4-24   APPLY WORDART EFFECTS

Many of the same effects you applied to pictures can be applied to WordArt. From the Drawing Tools Format tab, in the WordArt Styles group, click the Text Effects Ⓐ. A drop-down list displays the effects, as shown in Figure 4-35. In Exercise 4-20 you were introduced to most of these effects when applying them to a picture: Shadow, Reflection, Glow, Bevel, and 3-D Rotation. But the last category, *Transform,* is unique to WordArt because it enables you to change your text into different shapes.

Figure 4-35
Transform effects

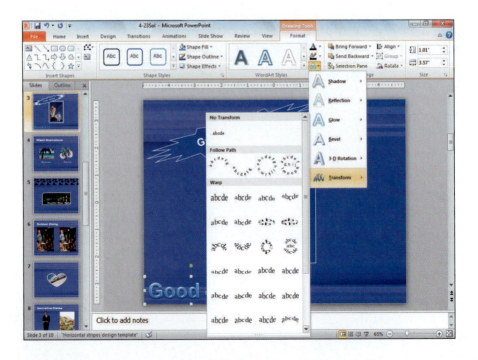

1. Still working on slide 3, with the Good 4 U WordArt selected, click the Drawing Tools Format tab; in the WordArt Styles group, click the Text Effects button ⒜, and choose **Transform**.

2. The default for WordArt text is No Transform because text will appear straight. When you drag your pointer over the various effects shown in this gallery, you will see a live preview showing that effect applied to your text. The text sample on each of the buttons gives you an indication of the particular effect.

3. From the Warp category, choose the effect **Deflate Top** (column 2, row 7), which causes the text in the middle of the WordArt to become smaller.

4. Move the WordArt to the bottom of the picture so that the letters "G" and "U" just slightly overlap with the blue rectangle, as shown in Figure 4-36.

Figure 4-36
Using Transform to apply the Deflate Top Warp effect

Exercise 4-25   EDIT WORDART FILL AND OUTLINE COLORS

The *Text Fill* color of WordArt text can be changed as well as the *Text Outline* color and the weight of the outline. The outline goes around the edge of each letter. Making it thick emphasizes the outline; making it thin provides less emphasis but still makes the text look quite different from the way it looks without an outline.

1. Move to slide 7.

2. From the Insert tab, in the Text group, click the WordArt button ⒜. For the style, click the white WordArt style that is called **Fill – White, Warm Matte Bevel**, and click to select it.

3. Key **We Love Miami Beach!** Select the text, and from the Home tab, in the Font group, change the font size to **44** points.

4. Move the WordArt text above the heart, centered horizontally on the slide.

5. With the WordArt selected, from the Drawing Tools Format tab, in the WordArt Styles group, click the Text Fill button ⒜. From the theme colors, choose **Gray-25%, Accent 4**.

6. With the WordArt selected, from the Drawing Tools Format tab, in the WordArt Styles group, click the Text Outline button  and choose **White, Text 1**.

7. Click the Text Outline button , click **Weight**, and choose **4½ pt**.

8. Now change the shadow effect so that it better matches the heart shape. From the Drawing Tools Format tab, in the WordArt Styles group, click the Dialog Box Launcher button .

9. From the Format Text Effects dialog box, choose **Shadow**. Change to these settings: Transparency **20%**, Size **100%**, Blur **4 pt**, Angle **45°**, Distance **2 pt**. Click **Close**.

10. From the Drawing Tools Format tab, in the WordArt Styles group, click the Text Effects button , click **Transform**, and from the Warp category, select **Wave 2**.

11. Resize and adjust any necessary spacing so that your slide resembles Figure 4-37.

Figure 4-37
Completed WordArt text

12. Update the handout footer to show *[your initials]***4-25**. View the presentation as a slide show.

13. Save the presentation as *[your initials]***4-25** in your Lesson 4 folder. The presentation is now ready for Gus's review. Close the presentation and submit your work.

Creating a Photo Album

A presentation consisting of mostly pictures can be created quickly using PowerPoint's *Photo Album* feature. Picture files can be inserted from different locations on your computer and will be displayed with one, two, or four pictures on a slide. The pictures can be displayed at full screen size or framed in different shapes. Also, text can accompany each picture at the time you create the photo album, or text can be added to the individual slides. When complete, your saved photo album can be displayed just as any other presentation.

While this feature can be important for business situations, it could also be very helpful for creating a display for open-house functions or even wedding or birthday celebrations.

As an intern at Good 4 U, you are to create a photo album showcasing the most popular salad choices. The images have been taken by Chef Michele and are included in your student files. She will later add more content to this slide show for the purpose of explaining menu options to people she talks to about catered events.

Exercise 4-26 CREATE ALBUM CONTENT BY INSERTING NEW PICTURES

In your Lesson 4 student data files you have a folder named **Salads** containing five pictures for this exercise. Copy the **Salads** folder to your storage location.

1. Open PowerPoint if necessary, and start a new blank presentation.

2. From the Insert tab, in the Images group, click the top of the Photo Album button 🖼. The Photo Album dialog box appears, as shown in Figure 4-38.

Figure 4-38
Photo Album dialog box

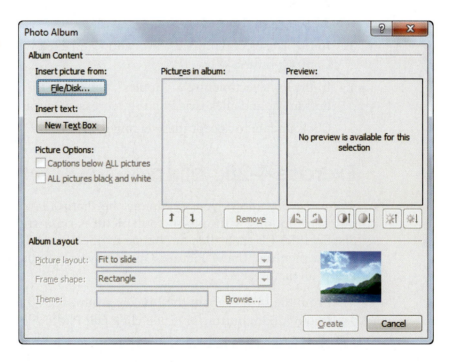

3. Click the File/Disk button [File/Disk...]; then choose the storage location where you have the Salads folder. Select the folder name, and then click **Insert**.

4. Select all the picture files (using contiguous selection methods), and click **Insert**.

5. At the bottom of the dialog box, notice the **Album Layout** options. By default, the **Picture layout** is **Fit to slide**. This option will expand each picture to fill your computer's screen. Click **Create**.

6. Each picture appears on a separate slide, and a title slide has been created.

Exercise 4-27 ADJUST PICTURE ORDER, BRIGHTNESS, AND CONTRAST

Using the Format Photo Album dialog box, you can easily reorder pictures by selecting the picture name and clicking the up or down arrow. Pictures can be rotated if their orientation needs to change, and even the brightness and contrast can be adjusted. These changes can be made at the time you create the Photo Album or later by editing the pictures individually.

1. From the Insert tab, in the Images group, click the lower half of the Photo Album button 🖼; then click **Edit Photo Album**.

2. Reorder the images using the up and down arrows below the image list to match the following order:

   1. apples
   2. avocado
   3. tuna
   4. chicken
   5. soup_salad

3. In the list select picture 2, "avocado," and click twice on the Increase Contrast button 🔲.

4. In the list select picture 1, "apples"; click once on the Increase Brightness button 🔲, and click twice on the Increase Contrast button 🔲.

5. Click **Update** to accept these changes.

Exercise 4-28 CONTROL ALBUM LAYOUT

Album Layout allows you to change the Picture layout from **Fit to slide** to different options with one to four pictures on a slide. You can choose to display titles for each slide or change to one of seven different Frame shapes for the pictures. Using Picture Options, you can choose to place captions below all pictures.

1. From the Insert tab, in the Images group, click the lower half of the Photo Album button 🖼; then click **Edit Photo Album**.

2. For **Picture Layout**, change to **1 picture**.

3. Now **Picture Options** are available. Click to place a check beside **Captions below ALL Pictures**.

4. For **Frame shape**, select several of the available options, and notice how the effect is displayed in the thumbnail area on the right. Select **Simple Frame, White**.

5. Now apply a background theme that will provide soft coloring on the background behind the pictures. For the theme, click Browse Browse... , and choose **Apex**; then click **Select**. (You may have to navigate to your themes for Office 2010.)

6. Be sure the options on your Edit Photo Album dialog box match those in Figure 4-39. Click **Update**.

Figure 4-39
Edit Photo Album
options

7. Now the pictures appear a little smaller on the slide and have a white
    frame with a subtle shadow effect, as shown in Figure 4-40. The **Apex**
    theme provides a soft background that is subtle and does not detract
    from the pictures.

Figure 4-40
Slide with framed
picture

8. Notice that the file name for each picture now appears in a text box
    below the picture. Chef Michele will later change this text to a more
    descriptive title for each salad.

9. On slide 1, key **New Salads** for the presentation title, and key **Good 4 U**
    for the subtitle. Change the subtitle text size to 36 points, and apply bold.

10. Add a header on the handout page with *[your initials]*4-28 in the
    header, remove the date, and put nothing in the footer.

11. Save the presentation as *[your initials]*4-28 in your Lesson 4 folder.

12. Close the presentation and submit your work.

Lesson 4 Summary

- In addition to providing text placeholders, PowerPoint offers a variety of objects to enhance the visual appearance of your slides. These include shapes, text boxes, clip art, pictures, and WordArt.

- PowerPoint has drawing tools for creating a variety of shapes including squares, circles, rectangles, ovals, and straight lines.

- To draw a shape, from the Insert tab, in the Illustrations group, click the Shapes button, choose a shape, and then drag diagonally on your slide to create the shape in the size you need.

- If you don't like a shape you drew, select it and press ⌈Delete⌋ to remove it from your slide, or press ⌈Ctrl⌋+⌈Z⌋ to undo the action.

- Use gridlines and guides to help with alignment and placement of objects on the slide.

- Press ⌈Shift⌋ while drawing a line or some other shape to constrain it. Constraining a shape makes it perfectly symmetrical, for example, a circle or a square, or it can make a line perfectly straight.

- Press ⌈Ctrl⌋ while drawing a shape to make it grow in size from the center instead of from one edge.

- Change the size of a drawn object by dragging one of its sizing handles (small white circles on its border) with a two-pointed arrow.

- To preserve an object's proportions when resizing it, hold down ⌈Shift⌋ while dragging a corner sizing handle.

- Move a drawn object by pointing to it and, when the four-pointed arrow appears, dragging the object to a new position.

- The Shapes gallery has many predefined shapes that are organized into several categories.

- When a shape is selected, text that you key appears inside the shape.

- Use the Clip Art pane to search for illustrations and photograph images. If you are connected to the Internet, Microsoft's Office.com content will automatically be searched.

- To see the file properties of an illustration or photograph in the Clip Art pane, point to a thumbnail and then click the vertical bar that appears on the right side of it (or right-click the thumbnail).

- Using the Cut, Copy, and Paste commands, you can easily move or copy objects from one slide to another or from one presentation to another.

- Using the Duplicate command is the quickest way to create a copy of an object on the same slide.

- Resize an image by dragging one of its sizing handles. If you want to preserve proportions, drag a corner handle. If you want to distort the proportions, drag one of the side handles.

- From the Picture Tools Format tab, in the Adjust group, use tools to change a picture's brightness, contrast, and colors.

- Illustrations and photograph images (vectors, bitmaps, or scanned images) can be cropped. Cropping is trimming away edges of a picture, much like using scissors to cut out a picture from a newspaper or magazine. Images can even be cropped to a shape.
- Artistic Effects enable you to alter a picture in some way, such as by making it look like a watercolor or oil painting.
- Picture Effects allow you to add shadows, reflection, glow, soft edges, bevel, and 3-D rotation effects. All of these can be customized.
- Remove Background enables you to take away unwanted portions of picture images.
- WordArt enables you to create special effects with text that are not possible with standard text-formatting tools.
- WordArt text is modified by using WordArt Styles and Text Effects to change its appearance in many different ways. These options are available on the Drawing Tools Format tab when WordArt text is selected.
- PowerPoint's Photo Album feature can be used to quickly create a presentation consisting mostly of pictures. One or more pictures can be placed on each slide, with a choice of different framing techniques.
- Once a photo album is created, it can be modified by choosing the Edit Photo Album option to rearrange pictures, request captions, and add a theme. A photo album is saved in the same way as any other presentation.

LESSON 4	Command Summary	
Feature	**Button**	**Ribbon**
Adjust Picture Brightness, Contrast, and Sharpness		Picture Tools Format tab, Adjust group, Corrections
Adjust Picture Color		Picture Tools Format tab, Adjust group, Color
Apply Artistic Effects		Picture Tools Format tab, Adjust group, Artistic Effects
Apply Picture Border		Picture Tools Format tab, Picture Styles group, Picture Border
Apply Picture Effects		Picture Tools Format tab, Picture Styles group, Picture Effects
Apply WordArt Styles		Drawing Tools Format tab, WordArt Styles group, More

continues

UNIT 2   LESSON 4

LESSON 4		Command Summary *continued*
Feature	**Button**	**Ribbon**
Apply WordArt Text Effects		Drawing Tools Format tab, WordArt Styles group, Text Effects
Change WordArt Color		Drawing Tools Format tab, WordArt Styles group, Text Fill
Change WordArt Outline		Drawing Tools Format tab, WordArt Styles group, Text Outline
Crop a Picture		Picture Tools Format tab, Size group, Crop
Crop a Picture to a Shape		Picture Tools Format tab, Size group, Crop down arrow, Crop to Shape
Insert Pictures		Insert tab, Images group, Picture
Insert Shapes		Home tab, Drawing group, Shapes or Insert tab, Illustrations group, Shapes
Insert WordArt		Insert tab, Text group, WordArt
Remove Background		Picture Tools Format tab, Adjust group, Remove Background
Search for Clip Art and Photographs		Insert, Images group, Clip Art, Clip Art pane, Search

Please visit our Online Learning Center, *www.lessonapproach2010.com*, **where you will find the following review materials:**

- **Concepts Review**

  True/False Questions

  Short Answer Questions

  Critical Thinking Questions

- **Skills Review**

  Review Exercises that target single skills

  Lesson Applications

  Review Exercises that challenge students by testing multiple skills in each exercise

- **On Your Own**

  Open-ended exercises that require students to synthesize multiple skills and apply creativity and problem-solving as they would in a real world business situation

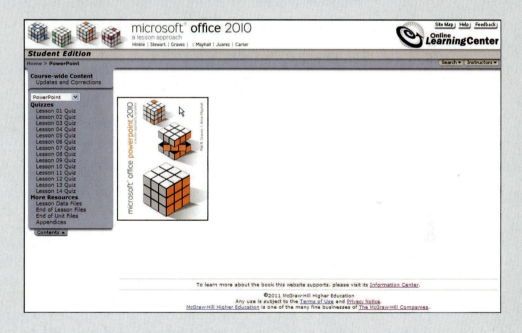

Creating Tables

After completing this lesson, you will be able to:

1. Create a table.

2. Draw a table.

3. Modify a table structure.

4. Align text and numbers.

5. Enhance the table.

6. Create a tabbed table.

Estimated Time: 2 hours

Julie Wolfe will soon be speaking to an economic development group about employee opportunities that Good 4 U provides to the community. So that this audience can easily compare the data she is presenting, she has asked you to prepare tables showing the number of employees in various positions and how the number of employees has changed in the last year.

Tables display information organized in rows and columns. Once a table is created, you can modify its structure by adding columns or rows, plus you can merge and split cells to modify your table's design. Table content can be aligned in different ways, and color can be applied to highlight selected table cells or to add table borders. In this lesson you will learn many different ways to make these changes that, ultimately, make a table easy to read.

Creating a Table

A *table* consists of rows, columns, and cells. *Rows* consist of individual cells across the table horizontally. *Columns* consist of individual cells aligned vertically down the table. The *cell* is the intersection between the column and a row.

PowerPoint provides several convenient ways to create a table. With each method listed below, you specify the number of columns and rows that you need.

- Insert a new slide, choose the **Title and Content** layout, and click the Insert Table button 🔲.

- From the Insert tab, in the Tables group, click the Table button 🔲, and choose **Insert Table**.

- From the Insert tab, in the Tables group, click the Table button 🔲, and drag the mouse to select the correct number of columns and rows.

- From the Insert tab, in the Tables group, click the Table button 🔲, and then click **Draw Table**. Using the pencil pointer, click and drag to create the size of the table, and then divide it into columns and rows.

- Create a table using tab settings.

When you insert a table into your presentation, your Ribbon will change to show the Table Tools Design and Layout tabs. These tabs contain many options for formatting and modifying tables.

Exercise 5-1 INSERT A TABLE

When you use the Table button 🔲 on the Insert tab, you may define a table's dimensions by dragging down and across a grid to determine the number of columns and rows.

1. Open the file **Briefing**. Insert a new slide after slide 1 that uses the **Title Only** slide layout. Julie Wolfe will show the number of employees for the previous year; therefore, key the title **Employment Levels 2009**.

2. From the Insert tab, in the Tables group, click the Table button 🔲. A grid appears for defining the size of the table.

3. Drag your pointer down three squares and across four squares to define a 4 by 3 table (four columns by three rows), as shown in Figure 5-1. A table is automatically placed on your slide.

Figure 5-1
Defining a table

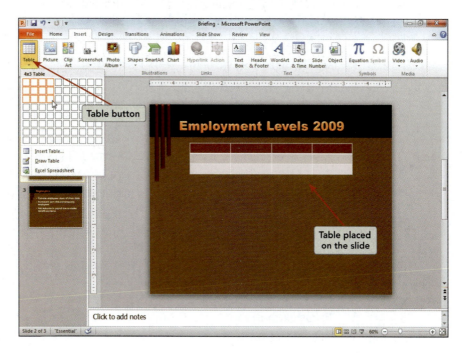

4. Point to the table's border so that the four-pointed arrow ✥ appears; then drag the table down about a half inch.

5. Key the text shown in Figure 5-2. Use your pointer to click in the first cell of the table, and then press Tab to move from cell to cell. Numbers will be right aligned later in the lesson.

Figure 5-2
Table with text

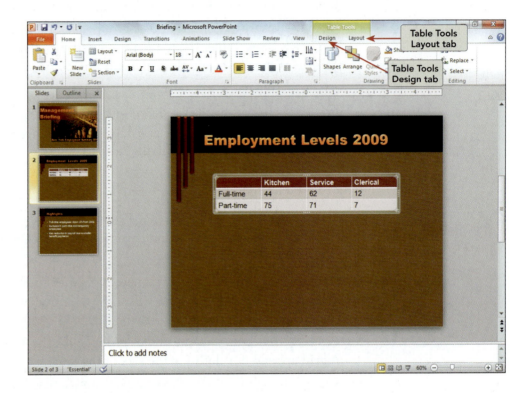

Exercise 5-2   NAVIGATE IN A TABLE

Use these methods to navigate in a table:

*   Click the cell with the I-beam.
*   Use the arrow keys: ←, →, ↑, and ↓.
*   Press Tab to move forward or Shift+Tab to move backward.

NOTE

When a cell is blank, pressing the left arrow key ← or the right arrow key → moves the insertion point left or right one cell. If text is in a cell, the left and right arrow keys move the insertion point one character to the left or right.

1. Click in the first table cell to put your insertion point there.

2. Press Tab several times. The insertion point moves through cells from left to right. When you reach the last cell in the last row, pressing Tab adds a new row with the insertion point in the first cell.

3. Since you do not need another row, click the Undo button to reverse this action.

4. Press Shift+Tab several times. The insertion point moves through cells from right to left.

5. Press each arrow key several times, and observe the movement of the insertion point.

Exercise 5-3   SELECT TABLE STYLES

A *table style* is a combination of formatting options based on your theme colors. A table style is applied automatically to any table that you add through the Insert Table command. These styles are applied using the Table Tools Design tab shown in Figure 5-3. When your pointer is over any thumbnail in the Table Styles gallery, you will see a preview of what your table will look like if you apply that style.

1. Right-click in any of the table cells, and choose **Select Table** from the shortcut menu.

2. From the Table Tools Design tab, in the Table Styles group, choose the More button ⊽ to open the Table Styles Gallery.

Figure 5-3
Table Tools
Design tab

3. Point to several thumbnails to see the ScreenTip with the name of the style and preview the effect on your table.

4. From the **Best Match for Document** category, choose **Themed Style 1, Accent 1** by clicking on the thumbnail. Notice how this table style blends well with the background.

Exercise 5-4   APPLY TABLE STYLE OPTIONS

The *Table Style Options* feature is used to modify specific parts of your table. The options include:

- *Header Row.* Emphasizes the first row of the table.
- *Total Row.* Emphasizes the last row of the table.
- *Banded Rows.* Provides rows in alternating colors.
- *First Column.* Emphasizes the first column of the table.
- *Last Column.* Emphasizes the last column of the table.
- *Banded Columns.* Provides columns in alternating colors.

1. With the table selected, from the Table Tools Design tab, in the Table Style Options group, click the **First Column** check box. Notice that the text in the first column now appears bold.

2. Click the **Header Row** check box to uncheck the box. Notice that the dark red disappears and the banded rows alternate starting with the first row.

3. Click the Undo button to reapply the Header Row formatting.

4. Click the **Banded Rows** check box to uncheck the box. Notice that the row alternating colors are removed.

5. Click the **Banded Columns** check box to apply alternating colors to the columns.

✎ **TIP**

If you were comparing the number of kitchen staff versus the number of clerical staff, the Banded Columns format would make the table easier to interpret because it emphasizes the staff categories. However, if you were comparing the number of full-time versus the number of part-time employees, the Banded Rows format would be a better choice.

Drawing a Table

The *Draw Table* command in PowerPoint allows you to control the exact size of the table and how it is divided by specifying where horizontal and vertical lines are placed. Once the table is created, all other table features can be applied.

Exercise 5-5   USE THE PENCIL POINTER TO DRAW A TABLE

To draw a table, you first drag the *pencil pointer* ✏ diagonally down and across to create a rectangle for the table's outside border. Then you draw horizontal and vertical lines within the table to divide it into rows and columns.

1. Insert a new slide after slide 3 that uses the **Title Only** slide layout. Julie Wolfe will show how employment numbers have increased from the previous year; therefore, key the title **Employment Levels 2010**.

2. From the Insert tab, in the Tables group, click the Table button 🔲, and then choose **Draw Table**.

3. Using the pencil pointer, drag from under the left edge of the title (down and to the right) to create a rectangle that fills the available space. See Figure 5-4 for size and placement. At this point, you have a one-cell table.

Figure 5-4
Using the pencil pointer

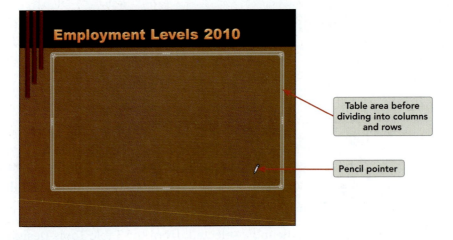

4. The pencil pointer creates rows and columns when you draw lines within the table area to create inside borders. Be sure the pointer is inside the table before you start drawing so that the lines you draw divide the table space. If the pointer touches the outside table border, a new table will be created. (If this happens, press Ctrl+Z to undo the action and try again.)

NOTE

For now, don't worry if your table cell sizes do not perfectly match those in Figure 5-5 or if your text wraps within the cell. You will learn how to adjust cell sizes later in this lesson.

5. With the table selected, from the Table Tools Design tab, in the Draw Borders group, click the Draw Table button 🖉, and draw a horizontal line through the middle of the table area. Each time you draw a line, one cell is

split into two cells. Because you are drawing horizontal lines now, the cells you are splitting create table rows. Draw two more horizontal lines to create four rows in the table, as shown in Figure 5-5.

6. Now split the table with four vertical lines to create five columns.

7. From the Table Tools Design tab, in the Draw Borders group, click **Draw Table** to turn off the pencil pointer.

8. Key the table text shown in Figure 5-5.

9. Right-click the table, and choose **Select Table**. From the Home tab, in the Font group, change Font Size to **24**.

Figure 5-5
Table text

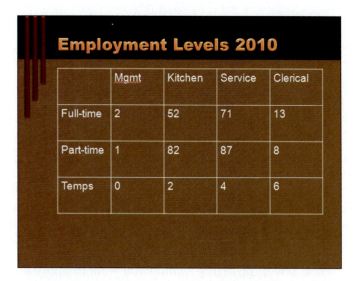

Employment Levels 2010				
	Mgmt	Kitchen	Service	Clerical
Full-time	2	52	71	13
Part-time	1	82	87	8
Temps	0	2	4	6

Exercise 5-6 CHANGE TABLE TEXT DIRECTION

Text direction changes can affect the appearance of a table and how it fits within a given space. If a column title is the only long text in the column, changing the column title text direction allows you to fit more columns in a given area. However, use this feature with caution because the text will not be as easy to read as horizontal text.

Text direction in a table can be changed using the Text Direction button available from the Home tab or the Table Tools Layout tab (see Figure 5-6).

Figure 5-6
Table Tools Layout tab

1. Click in the cell that reads **Mgmt**.

2. From the Table Tools Layout tab, in the Alignment group, click the Text Direction button.

Figure 5-7
Text Direction drop-down list

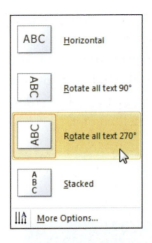

3. From the drop-down list, choose **Rotate all text 270°**, as shown in Figure 5-7.

4. Notice how the text reads going up in the cell. Change the text direction in the same manner for **Kitchen**, **Service**, and **Clerical**.

5. Select the entire first row of text by pointing to the left of the first table row and clicking when your pointer changes to a dark black arrow. From the Table Tools Layout tab, in the Cell Size group, change the **Table Row Height** to **1.3"**.

Exercise 5-7 APPLY SHADING AND BORDERS

When you first draw a table, the table cells contain no shading, allowing the slide's background to show. You can apply a shading color or other shading effects (such as a gradient or a picture effect) to one or more selected cells in your table. All the shading options are available from the Table Tools Design tab, in the Table Styles group, in the Shading button 🖌 gallery. This button works the same as the Shape Fill button 🖌.

Table borders are the lines forming the edges of cells, columns, and rows and the outline of the table. You can apply borders to all the cells in a selection, to just an outside border, or to just the inside borders separating one cell from another. Applying table borders is a three-step process:

- First, select the cells to which you want to apply the border effect.

- Second, select the border style, border width, and pen color you want.

- Third, click the Borders button ⊞, and choose an option from the drop-down list to control where the border appears.

1. On slide 4, with the table active, select all the cells in the top row by moving your pointer to the left of row 1 until you get a solid black arrow pointing at the row. Click to select the whole row.

2. From the Table Tools Design tab, in the Table Styles group, click the Shading button 🖌, and choose **Dark Red, Accent 5, Darker 25%** (column 9, row 5).

3. Change the font color for the selected row to **Light Yellow, Text 2**.

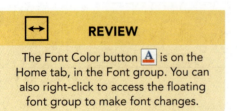

REVIEW

The Font Color button 🅰 is on the Home tab, in the Font group. You can also right-click to access the floating font group to make font changes.

4. Select the first column in the table by pointing to the top of the first column and clicking when you get a solid black arrow pointing down at the column. Apply the same **Dark Red, Accent 5, Darker 25%**, and change the font color to **Light Yellow, Text 2**.

5. Select all the cells that contain numbers by clicking in the first number cell and dragging your pointer down and to the right to the last number cell.

6. From the Table Tools Design tab, in the Table Styles group, click the Shading button ⬛, and apply **Brown, Background 2, Lighter 40%**. With these cells still selected, change the font color to **Black, Background 1**.

7. Click outside the table to observe the effect. Now the table has an appearance that distinguishes it from the slide background. Compare your table to Figure 5-8.

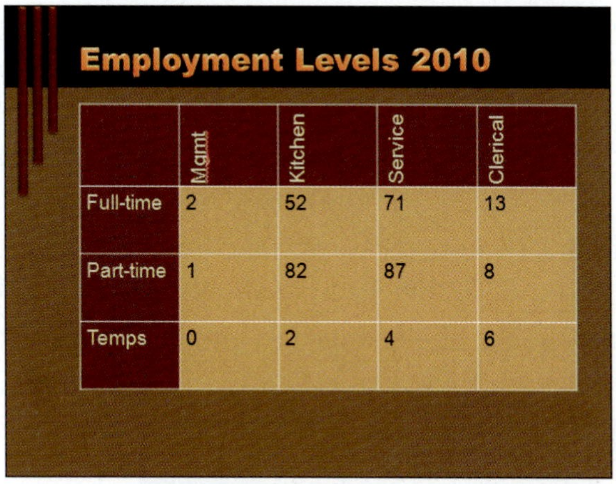

Figure 5-8
Shading applied to a table

Employment Levels 2010

	Mgmt	Kitchen	Service	Clerical
Full-time	2	52	71	13
Part-time	1	82	87	8
Temps	0	2	4	6

8. Select the whole table by right-clicking any cell within the table and choosing **Select Table** from the shortcut menu.

9. From the Table Tools Design tab, in the Draw Borders group, click the Pen Weight button [1 pt———▾], and change to **2¼ pt**.

10. Still working in the Draw Borders group, click the Pen Color button ✎, and choose **Brown, Background 2, Darker 50%**.

11. Click the Borders button ⊞ in the Table Styles group, and choose **Top Border**. Repeat this step for **Bottom Border**, **Left Border**, and **Right Border**. Click outside the table to deselect it, and notice the difference in the table with the borders in a different color.

Exercise 5-8   CHANGE BORDER AND SHADING COLORS

Table Border and Shading styles can be changed at any point while creating your presentation.

TIP

You can use the pencil tool to change the color and style of a border. Set the border options in the Draw Borders group. Then, instead of clicking the Borders button, use the pencil to click the borders you want to change.

1. Select any cell in your table. From the Table Tools Design tab, in the Draw Borders group, click Pen Style [———▾], and from the list box choose the dashed line (second style).

2. Click the Pen Weight button [1 pt———▾], and choose **1½ pt**.

Figure 5-9
Borders button
drop-down list

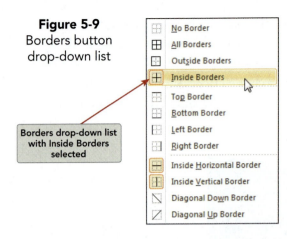

Borders drop-down list
with Inside Borders
selected

	No Border
	All Borders
	Outside Borders
	Inside Borders
	Top Border
	Bottom Border
	Left Border
	Right Border
	Inside Horizontal Border
	Inside Vertical Border
	Diagonal Down Border
	Diagonal Up Border

3. Click the Pen Color button, and choose **Brown, Background 2, Lighter 80%**.

4. Right-click in the table, and choose **Select Table**.

5. Click the Borders button list box arrow; then click **Inside Borders**, as shown in Figure 5-9. The inside borders of the table are now dashed lines.

6. Still working on slide 4, select row 3 of the table. From the Table Tools Design tab, in the Table Styles group, click the Shading button, and choose **Orange, Accent 2, Darker 25%**.

7. Repeat this process for row 1 of the table, using the same **Orange, Accent 2, Darker 25%**.

8. Repeat this process for rows 2 and 4 but apply the shading color **Brown, Background 2, Lighter 40%**, as shown in Figure 5-10.

9. Select the table, and change the font color to **Black, Background 1**.

Figure 5-10
Table with shaded
rows

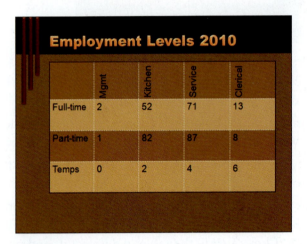

Exercise 5-9   ERASE CELL BORDERS

The *Eraser* can be used to delete borders between cells.

1. Click in the last cell of the table on slide 4. Click Tab one time. Notice that PowerPoint automatically inserts another row below the last row in the table. If this row causes your table to extend below the slide, resize the table from the bottom so it fits on the slide.

2. From the Table Tools Design tab, in the Draw Borders group, choose the Eraser button.

3. Click each of the four borders that divide the last row of the table into five cells. Notice that as you click each border, it disappears. When all four are removed, the last row has only one cell.

NOTE

You can press and hold Shift while the pointer is a pencil and perform the same alterations as those achieved with the Eraser.

4. Press Esc to turn off the Eraser. Click in the last row, and key **Estimated Projection**.

5. Create a new folder for Lesson 5, and save the presentation as *[your initials]***5-9** in your new Lesson 5 folder. Leave the presentation open for the next exercise.

Modifying a Table Structure

When creating a table, you decide how many rows and columns the table should have. After entering some data, you might discover that you have too many columns or perhaps too few rows. Or you might want one row or column to have more or fewer cells than the others. You can modify your table structure by inserting or deleting columns, merging a group of cells, or splitting an individual cell into two or more cells.

Exercise 5-10 INSERT AND DELETE ROWS AND COLUMNS

When you are inserting columns and rows, it is important to recognize which cell is active. Columns can be inserted either to the right or to the left of the column that contains the active cell. The column formatting of the active column is copied to the new column, or the table style is applied. Rows can be inserted above or below the row that contains the active cell. The row formatting of the active row is copied, or the table style is applied to the new row.

Insert columns and rows using one of these methods:

• From the Table Tools Layout tab, in the Rows & Columns group, choose which option you would like to insert.

• Right-click a cell in the table, and use commands on the shortcut menu.

• Insert a row at the bottom of the table by pressing Tab if you're in the last cell of the last table row. This is convenient if you run out of rows while you're entering data.

1. Move to slide 2, and click in the "Kitchen" cell.

2. Right-click, and from the shortcut menu, as shown in Figure 5-11, choose **Insert** and then **Insert Columns to the Left**. A new column appears to the left of "Kitchen." It is the same size as the "Kitchen" column and has the formatting of the table style applied. The table is wider to accommodate the extra column.

Figure 5-11
Inserting a column
through the shortcut
menu

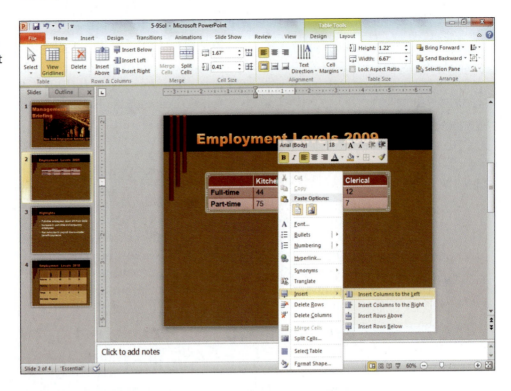

3. Click the blank cell in the upper-left corner of the table.

4. From the Table Tools Layout tab, in the Rows & Columns group, click the Insert Right button ▦. A new column appears to the right of the selected cell, and it is the same size and is formatted with the selected table style.

5. Click any cell in this new column.

6. From the Table Tools Layout tab, in the Rows & Columns group, click the Delete button ✖; then choose **Delete Columns**. The new column is deleted, and the table is resized. Your table should now have one blank column located to the left of the "Kitchen" column, and some of your titles may be wrapped to two lines. This will be fixed later.

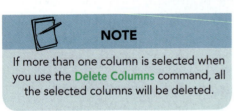

NOTE

If more than one column is selected when you use the **Delete Columns** command, all the selected columns will be deleted.

7. Click a cell in the second table row; then, from the Table Tools Layout tab, in the Rows & Columns group, click the Insert Below button ▦.

8. Click the last cell in the last row, containing the number "7." Press Tab. A new row is inserted at the bottom of the table.

9. Click in the blank row below the text "Full-time," right-click, and choose **Delete Rows** from the shortcut menu.

10. Complete the table by keying the information shown in Figure 5-12 into the blank row and blank column.

Figure 5-12
Modified table
structure

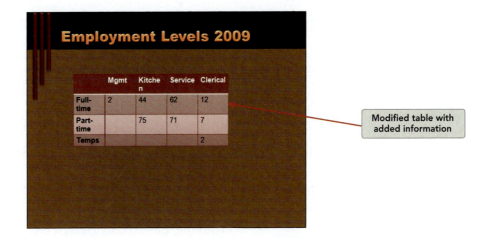

Modified table with
added information

Exercise 5-11 MERGE AND SPLIT CELLS

Cells can be merged and split in several ways. To split cells:

- Draw a line through them with the pencil pointer 🖉.
- Use the Split Cells button ▦ on the Table Tools Layout tab in the Merge group.
- Right-click the cell, and choose **Split Cells** from the shortcut menu.

To merge cells:

- Use the Eraser button 🖉 to remove borders between two adjacent cells to create one cell.
- Select two or more cells, and then, from the Table Tools Layout tab, in the Merge group, click the Merge Cells button ▦.
- Right-click the selected cells, and choose **Merge Cells** from the shortcut menu.

1. Move to slide 4. At the bottom of the table, click the cell containing the text "Estimated Projection."
2. From the Table Tools Layout tab, in the Merge group, click the Split Cells button ▦. Change the number of columns to **1** and the number of rows to **2**. The selected cell becomes two cells.
3. Click **OK**.
4. In the new cell, key **Revised Figures**.
5. Select the first three cells in the second row, which begins "Full-time."
6. Fom the Table Tools Layout tab, in the Merge group, click the Merge Cells button ▦. The three cells combine into one wide cell. The text and numbers from the merged cells all appear in one cell.
7. Click the Undo button ↩ to return the merged cells to their previous state.

Exercise 5-12 APPLY A DIAGONAL BORDER

Borders can be placed diagonally within a cell. For example, if you are using a PowerPoint table to create a calendar, you might want to put two dates in the same cell, separated by a diagonal line. Applying a diagonal border in this way does not create two separate cells; the border is merely a line drawn within one cell. You can make it look like two cells by carefully aligning text inside the cell.

1. Still working on slide 4, select the two rows at the bottom of the table. Then right-click, and choose **Merge Cells** from the shortcut menu to combine the two cells into one. The text "Revised Figures" now appears on a separate line below "Estimated Projection" in one cell.

NOTE

Be careful where you start drawing. If you touch one of the cell borders with the pencil, the formatting of that border will change if your pencil settings are different. If that happens, use Undo to restore it.

2. From the Table Tools Design tab, in the Draw Borders group, change the pen style to a dashed line and the color to **Brown, Background 2, Darker 50%**. Your pointer has been changed to a pencil.

3. Position the pencil pointer near, but not touching, the lower left corner of the cell in the last row. Draw a diagonal line across the cell to the upper right corner, as shown in Figure 5-13.

Figure 5-13
Using the pencil pointer to add a diagonal border

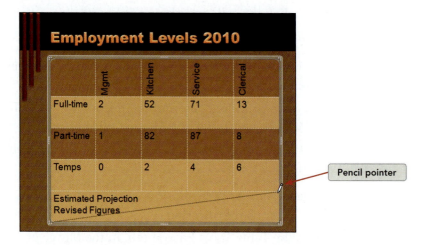

4. Press Esc to turn off the pencil pointer. Deselect the table to see the result. In a later exercise, you will align the text so that it appears to be in separate cells.

Exercise 5-13 DISTRIBUTE COLUMN WIDTH AND ROW HEIGHT

If you decide to add rows or columns, or if you decide to make a column wider, the table may no longer fit on a slide. You can make a table smaller or larger by dragging its sizing handles, and you can change the height of rows and the width of columns individually by dragging cell borders. You can also choose the exact height and width of the cells by using the Cell Size group on the Table Tools Layout tab.

From the Table Tools Layout tab, in the Cell Size group, use the *Distribute Columns* button 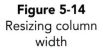 to easily adjust several columns to be the same width. The *Distribute Rows* button works in a similar way.

1. Move to slide 2, and move your pointer over the right border of the first column until the pointer changes to a resizing arrow.

2. Using this pointer, click and drag the column border to the right, making the column wide enough for the text "Part-time" to appear on one line, as shown in Figure 5-14. The column width increases, and the adjacent column becomes smaller. Now the second column might be too narrow for the word "Mgmt."

3. Use the resizing arrow to double-click the right border of the "Mgmt" column. Double-clicking a right border makes the column wide enough to accommodate the widest text line in the column.

4. Double-click the right border of each of the remaining columns to allow the widest text to be all on one line.

Figure 5-14
Resizing column width

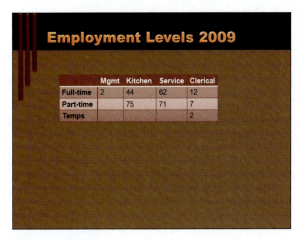

Employment Levels 2009

	Mgmt	Kitchen	Service	Clerical
Full-time	2	44	62	12
Part-time		75	71	7
Temps				2

NOTE

The same concepts work for resizing the row height except you must position your pointer on the row border instead of the column border.

5. Move to slide 4. Select the "Mgmt," "Kitchen," "Service," and "Clerical" columns by dragging across the second, third, fourth, and fifth cells in any row (or drag the small, black, down-facing arrow ⬇ just above the top border of the four columns).

6. From the Table Tools Layout tab, in the Cell Size group, click the Distribute Columns button. The four selected columns are now all the same width.

7. Select the second through fourth cells in the first column.

8. Click the Distribute Rows button. Now the second through fourth rows are exactly the same height.

9. Create a handout header and footer: Include the date and your name as the header, and the page number and *[your initials]*5-13 as the footer.

10. Save the presentation as *[your initials]*5-13 in your Lesson 5 folder. Leave the presentation open for the next exercise.

Aligning Text and Numbers

Table cell content can be aligned vertically at the top, middle, or bottom. The cell content can be aligned horizontally at the left, center, or right. You can use *Cell Margins* to refine even further the position of text and numbers in a cell. A cell margin is the space between cell borders and the contents of the cell.

Exercise 5-14   ALIGN TEXT AND NUMBERS HORIZONTALLY

Text is aligned horizontally within cells by using the alignment buttons on the Table Tools Layout tab, in the Alignment group, or on the Home tab, in the Paragraph group. You can also right-click to access the floating font group.

1. On slide 2, select the cells in the first row that contain the text "Mgmt," "Kitchen," "Service," and "Clerical."

2. From the Table Tools Layout tab, in the Alignment group, click the Center button ▤. The text is horizontally centered in each cell.

3. Select all the cells that contain numbers, and from the Table Tools Layout tab, in the Alignment group, click the Align Text Right button ▤.

4. Move to slide 4. In the last row of the table, select the text "Revised Figures." From the Home tab, in the Paragraph group, click the Align Text Right button ▤. This text arrangement helps to make the cell look split instead of just having a border in it.

Exercise 5-15   CHANGE THE VERTICAL POSITION OF TEXT IN A CELL

The appearance of a table can be affected by changing the vertical alignment of text or objects within cells. This change can improve the appearance when the cell is much larger than the text.

1. On slide 4, select the cells in the first row that contain the text "Mgmt," "Kitchen," "Service," and "Clerical."

2. From the Table Tools Layout tab, in the Alignment group, choose the Center Vertically button ▤. The text in the selected cells is now in the center of the cells.

3. Select all the cells in the second, third, and fourth rows.

4. Click the Align Bottom button ▤. The text moves to the bottom edge of the cells.

Exercise 5-16   USE MARGIN SETTINGS TO ADJUST THE POSITION OF TEXT IN A CELL

Sometimes, the horizontal and vertical alignment settings do not place text precisely where you want it in a cell. You might be tempted to use ⌈Spacebar⌉ to indent the text, but that usually doesn't work well.

You can precisely control where text is placed in a cell by using the cell margin settings, combined with horizontal and vertical alignment, as shown in Figure 5-15. For example, you can right-align a column of numbers and also have them appear centered in the column.

1. Move to slide 2. Select all the cells that contain numbers (include the blank cells too).

2. From the Table Tools Layout tab, in the Alignment group, click Cell Margins . From the drop-down list, click **Custom Margins**.

Figure 5-15
Using the Cell Text Layout dialog box to control cell margins

3. Click the **Vertical alignment** list box arrow to see the other settings. Choose **Middle**.

4. Under Internal margin, change the **Right** setting to **0.5″**, and then click **OK**. The numbers are still right-aligned, but some space is between the cell border and the numbers, as shown in Figure 5-16.

5. Select all the cells in the first column that contain text, and change the left margin to **0.2″**. Resize the column as needed to position each label on one line.

Figure 5-16
Table with improved alignment

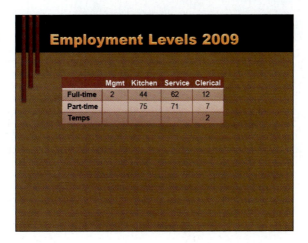

UNIT 2 LESSON 5

Exercise 5-17 RESIZE A TABLE

To resize an entire table, drag one of the sizing handles. When you drag, make sure the pointer is one of these object resizing arrows: ⇕, ⇔, ⤢; it should not be the resizing arrow used for changing column width ↔ or row height ⇳.

If you hold down Shift while dragging a corner sizing handle, the table will resize proportionately. Whenever possible, depending on how large or small you make the table, the relative proportions of row heights and column widths are preserved.

1. Move to slide 4, and click anywhere inside the table. Notice the eight sizing handles (shown as three or four dots) on the outside border (one in each corner and one in the middle of each side). They work just like sizing handles on other PowerPoint objects.

2. Using the diagonal two-pointed arrow ⤢, drag the lower right corner up and to the left about a half inch. The table becomes smaller, and the relative size of the rows and columns is preserved.

TIP

Click in the table, and then move your pointer to an outside border. When you get a four-pointed arrow, you may click and drag the table to position it.

3. Resize the rows and columns as necessary so that text does not word-wrap.

4. Position the table attractively on the slide by using the method that you use to move text boxes or other objects (see Figure 5-17).

Figure 5-17
Resized table

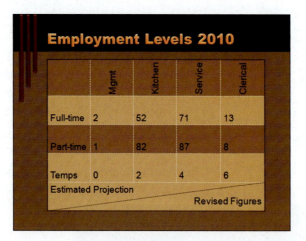

Enhancing the Table

You can enhance a table by adding one of the many three-dimensional effects available in PowerPoint 2010 or by inserting images. Images or special effects can be added to single cells or applied to an entire table.

Exercise 5-18   APPLY AND MODIFY A CELL BEVEL EFFECT

The *Cell Bevel* effect is a dimensional effect that makes cells look raised and rounded or pressed in, as shown in Figure 5-18. The Cell Bevel effect is found on the Table Tools Design tab, in the Table Styles group, under the Effects button.

1. On Slide 4, select the whole table. From the Table Tools Design tab, in the Table Styles group, click the Effects button.

2. Choose **Cell Bevel**; then choose **Riblet**. Notice the effect that is applied to the table.

3. With the table still selected, click the Effects button, choose **Cell Bevel** and then **No Bevel** to remove the bevel effect.

4. Click the Effects button again, choose **Cell Bevel**, and then choose **Relaxed Inset**.

Figure 5-18
Bevel effect applied to a table

Exercise 5-19   APPLY AND MODIFY A SHADOW EFFECT

Another dimensional effect is the *Shadow* effect. Just as you do when working with other objects, you can modify the shadow direction, its color, and many other settings. The Shadow effect can be applied from the Table Tools Design tab, in the Table Styles group, under the Effects button.

1. Still working on slide 4, select the table. From the Table Tools Design tab, in the Table Styles group, click the Effects button.

2. Choose **Shadow**, and move your pointer over several of the options. Notice the effect that the shadow has on the table.

3. Without selecting a shadow, choose **Shadow Options** at the bottom of the gallery. The Format Shape dialog box appears and allows you to control every aspect of the shadow.

4. For **Presets**, in the **Outer** group, choose **Offset Diagonal Bottom Right**.

5. For **Color**, choose **Dark Red, Accent 1, Darker 50%**.

6.   Change the other settings as follows:

- Transparency   **35%**
- Size   **100%**
- Blur   **5 pt**
- Angle   **50°**
- Distance   **15 pt**

7.   Click **Close** on the dialog box to return to your presentation. Deselect your table, and notice the shadow applied to the table, as shown in Figure 5-19.

Figure 5-19
Shadow effect
applied to a table

Exercise 5-20   APPLY AND MODIFY A REFLECTION EFFECT

The *Reflection* effect makes the table appear to be reflecting on a body of water or a mirror. Several preset reflection effects are available. The Reflection effect is found on the Table Tools Design tab, in the Table Styles group, under the Effects button ⬜.

1.   Move to slide 2, and select the table.

2.   From the Table Tools Design tab, in the Table Styles group, click the Effects button ⬜.

Figure 5-20
Reflection effect
applied to a table

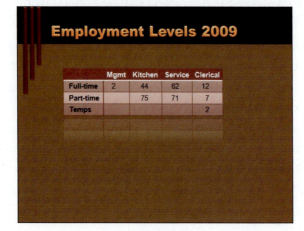

3.   Choose **Reflection**, and move your pointer over several of the options, noticing the effect that each reflection has on the table.

4.   Choose **Half Reflection, 8 pt offset**. The lower half of the table is reflected slightly below the table, as shown in Figure 5-20.

Exercise 5-21 INSERT A PICTURE AND APPLY GRADIENT SHADING

Pictures within a table can help viewers understand the context of the data in the table. A picture can be inserted in one cell, a selection of cells, or an entire table. Gradient shading on rows or columns can add interest or perhaps make text easier to read.

1. On slide 4, click in the first cell of the table.

2. From the Table Tools Design tab, in the Table Styles group, click the Shading button, and choose **Picture**.

3. Locate your student files for Lesson 5, and double-click **Employees** to insert the picture into the table.

4. Select the last four cells in the first row in the table, and change their color and effects following these steps:

    a. From the Table Tools Design tab, in the Table Styles group, click the Shading button, and choose **Gradient**.

    b. In the **Dark Variations** category, choose **From Bottom Right Corner**, which shows the blending of colors in a particular direction.

5. Repeat this process for all the cells on row 3.

6. Select row 5. From the Table Tools Design tab, in the Table Styles group, click the Shading button, and choose **Orange, Accent 2, Darker 25%**. Next, apply the same gradient fill as the one you applied to rows 1 and 3.

7. Click outside the table to observe the effects. Compare your table to Figure 5-21.

Figure 5-21
Gradient shading effects applied to a table

8. Update the handout footer to include the text *[your initials]*5-21.

9. Save the presentation as *[your initials]*5-21 in your Lesson 5 folder. Leave the presentation open for the next exercise.

Creating a Tabbed Table

In this lesson, you have learned several ways to create tables using Power-Point's table tools. You can also create tables through tab settings using the *Ruler* feature. Sometimes information can be effectively displayed with just a very simple table.

Exercise 5-22   SET AND EDIT TABS

In PowerPoint you set tabs on the ruler the same way you set tabs in Word, and they are left-aligned by default. However, PowerPoint's default tabs are set at 1-inch intervals. To set your own tabs, click the Tab Alignment button 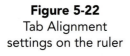 (above the vertical ruler) to choose the alignment type and then click the position on the horizontal ruler to set a tab.

1. Insert a new slide after slide 4 that uses the **Title Only** slide layout.

2. From the View tab, in the Show group, check the Ruler if it is not already checked.

3. Key the title **Full-time Employment Change**.

4. Draw a text box starting an inch below the slide title and extend it to the right (approximately 8 inches wide), as shown in Figure 5-22.

5. Key the following, pressing Tab where indicated: Tab **Department**, Tab **2009**, Tab **2010**, Tab **% Change**.

6. Select the text box, apply bold, and change the font color to **Brown, Background 2, Darker 50%**.

7. Click anywhere within the text box to activate the text box ruler.

Figure 5-22
Tab Alignment
settings on the ruler

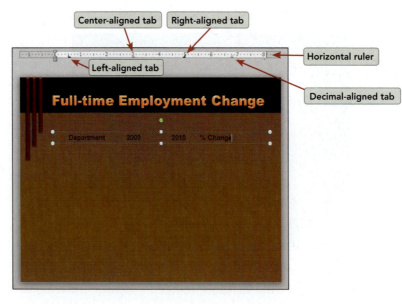

NOTE

Tabs are set when the Tab Alignment symbol appears on the ruler. The tabs you set override the default tabs, and the default tabs are removed. It might take some practice before you are comfortable with tab selection and placement.

8. Click the Tab Alignment button ⌊ above the vertical ruler. Each time you click the button, the alignment changes, enabling you to cycle through the four Tab Alignment choices, as shown in Table 5-1 and Figure 5-22.

TABLE 5-1 Tab Alignment Types

Tab	Purpose
⌊	Left-aligns text at the tab setting
⊥	Centers text at the tab setting
⌟	Right-aligns text at the tab setting
⊥	Aligns decimal points at the tab setting

9. Click the Tab Alignment button ⌊ one or more times until the left-aligned tab symbol ⌊ appears. Click the ruler at the 0.5-inch position to set a left tab.

10. Repeat this process for each of these tab settings:

    a. Center-aligned tab ⊥. Click the ruler at the 3-inch position. The text "2009" moves so that it is centered under the tab.

    b. Left-aligned tab ⌊. Click the ruler at the 3.5-inch mark to set a left tab.

    c. Right-aligned tab ⌟. Click the ruler at the 5-inch mark to set a right-aligned tab.

    d. Decimal-aligned tab ⊥. Click the ruler at the 6.75-inch mark to set a decimal-aligned tab.

11. Click the tab setting at the 3.5-inch mark, a left-aligned tab symbol, and click and drag it down and off the ruler. This removes the tab from the slide. The final tab settings are show in Figure 5-22.

TIP

When setting tabs, you might want to increase the zoom setting for an enlarged view of the ruler. After tabs are set, tabbed text that you key will automatically align under the tab symbols you placed on the ruler.

Exercise 5-23 CREATE A TABBED TABLE

Once the tabs are set for a tabbed table, the text can be entered by pressing Tab between each item. Tab spacing can be adjusted after the text is entered if necessary.

1. Working in the text box you created on slide 5, position the insertion point at the end of the text and press Enter to start a new text line.

2. Key the table text, shown in Figure 5-23, pressing [Tab] at the beginning of each line and between columns and pressing [Enter] at the end of each text line. The text box will increase in size as the text is keyed.

3. Select the entire text box by clicking its border. Increase the font size to 20 points.

4. With the text box still selected, from the Drawing Tools Format tab, in the Shape Styles group, click the Shape Fill button ⬛, and add the shape fill **Brown, Background 2, Lighter 80%**. Now the text is easier to read.

5. From the Drawing Tools Format tab, in the Shape Styles group, click the Shape Outline button ⬛, and add the shape outline **Brown, Background 2, Darker 50%**.

6. Select the text in the table, and from the Home tab, in the Paragraph group, change the line spacing to **1.5**.

7. Highlight the text in the text box. Drag the decimal-aligned tab symbol from the 6.75-inch position on the ruler to 7.5 inches. The entire column moves to the left.

Figure 5-23
Creating a tabbed table

8. Drag the center-aligned marker (at 3 inches) down and off the ruler to remove it. The table realigns in an unattractive way that does not make sense.

9. Click the Undo button ↩ once to restore the table's appearance.

10. Update the handout footer to include *[your initials]***5-23**.

11. View the presentation as a slide show to be sure all tables are appropriately positioned, and make any necessary adjustments.

12. Save the presentation as *[your initials]***5-23** in your Lesson 5 folder.

13. Close the presentation and submit your work.

Lesson 5   Summary

- Tables offer a convenient way to quickly organize material on a slide. From the Insert tab, in the Table group, you can use the Table button to insert a table. You can insert a table by choosing a content slide layout. You can "draw" a table directly on a slide by using the Draw Table button, or you can create a tabbed table through setting tabs.

- Before you can apply special formatting to table cells, you must first select the cells. You can select individual cells, groups of cells, rows, columns, or the entire table.

- Use the buttons on the Table Tools Design tab, in the Table Styles group, to apply fill effects and border effects to individual cells, a group of cells, or the entire table.

- Change the overall size of a table by dragging one of its sizing handles with a two-pointed arrow.

- Change the width of a column by dragging or double-clicking its border. Change the height of a row by dragging its border.

- Rows and columns can be easily inserted or deleted as you develop a table. Select at least one cell in the row or column where you want to insert or delete; then use buttons on the Table Tools Layout tab.

- While you are keying text in a table, a quick way to insert a new row at the bottom is to press Tab when you reach the last table cell.

- Occasionally, you might want one row or column to have more or fewer cells than the others. You can make this happen by merging a group of cells or splitting an individual cell into two or more cells.

- A diagonal line can be added to a cell to make it appear to be split into two cells. Careful placement of text within the cell completes this illusion.

- Applying and removing shading effects is similar to applying shading effects to other PowerPoint objects. Table and cell fills can be gradients, textures, or pictures.

- Before applying a border to cells or the entire table, choose the border style, border width, and border color from the Table Tools Design tab, in the Draw Borders group. Then select cells, and choose an option from the Borders button drop-down list or use the pencil pointer to apply it to the borders you want to change.

- Use the text alignment buttons on the Home tab, in the Paragraph group, to control the horizontal position of text in a cell.

- Use the Align Top, Center Vertically, and Align Bottom buttons on the Table Tools Layout tab in the Alignment group to control the vertical position of text in a cell.

- To fine-tune the horizontal or vertical position of text, change a cell's margin settings by using the Cell Margins button on the Table Tools Layout tab, in the Alignment group.

- Add and modify 3-D effects by selecting the table and clicking the Effects button on the Table Tools Design tab.

- Click the Tab Type button on the left edge of the ruler to change the type of tab. The button cycles through four tab types: left-aligned, centered, right-aligned, and decimal.
- Create a tabbed table by using a text box and setting tabs to control how the information is indented. Remove tabs or move tabs as needed by clicking and dragging.
- If table text has been entered in a tabbed table, then text must be highlighted before changes in tab settings will affect the text.

LESSON 5		Command Summary	
Feature	**Button**	**Ribbon**	**Keyboard**
Add Header Row		Table Tools Design tab, Table Style Options group, check Header Row	
Align Table Text vertically	, or	Table Tools Layout tab, Alignment group	
Apply Bevel, Shadow, or Reflection effects		Table Tools Design tab, Table Styles group, Effects	
Apply Borders		Table Tools Design tab, Table Styles group, Borders	
Apply Shading effect to cells		Table Tools Design tab, Table Styles group, Shading	
Change table style		Table Tools Design tab, Table Styles group, More	
Change Text Direction		Table Tools Layout tab, Alignment group, Text Direction	
Delete table columns		Table Tools Layout tab, Rows & Columns group, Delete	
Distribute Columns evenly		Table Tools Layout tab, Cell Size group, Distribute Columns	
Distribute Rows evenly		Table Tools Layout tab, Cell Size group, Distribute Rows	
Draw Table		Tables Tools Design tab, Draw Borders group, Draw Table	
Erase cell borders		Table Tools Design tab, Draw Table group, Eraser	
Insert Table		Insert tab, Tables group, Table	

continues

LESSON 5		Command Summary *continued*	
Feature	Button	Ribbon	Keyboard
Insert table columns		Table Tools Layout tab, Rows & Columns group, Insert Left or Insert Right	
Insert table rows		Table Tools Layout tab, Rows & Columns group, Insert Above or Insert Below	
Merge table cells		Table Tools Layout tab, Merge group, Merge Cells	
Navigate in a table			Tab; Shift + Tab; ↓; ↑; ←; →
Select column, row, or table		Table Tools Layout tab, Table group, Select	
Select table style		Table Tools Design tab, Table Styles group, More	
Set table cell margins		Table Tools Layout tab, Alignment group, Cell Margins	
Split a table cell		Table Tools Layout tab, Merge group, Split Cells	

Please visit our Online Learning Center, *www.lessonapproach2010.com,* **where you will find the following review materials:**

- **Concepts Review**

    True/False Questions

    Short Answer Questions

    Critical Thinking Questions

- **Skills Review**

    Review Exercises that target single skills

    Lesson Applications

    Review Exercises that challenge students by testing multiple skills in each exercise

- **On Your Own**

    Open-ended exercises that require students to synthesize multiple skills and apply creativity and problem-solving as they would in a real world business situation

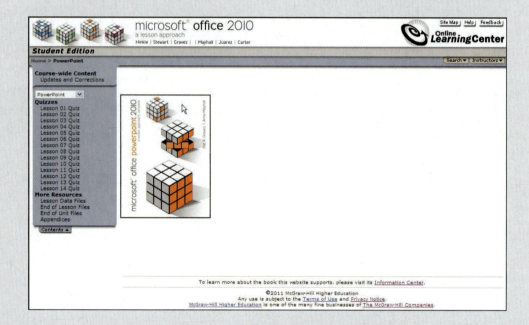

Lesson 6
Creating Charts

OBJECTIVES *After completing this lesson, you will be able to:*

1. Create a chart.
2. Format a column chart.
3. Use different chart types.
4. Work with pie charts.
5. Enhance chart elements.

Estimated Time: 1½ hours

Charts, sometimes called *graphs,* are diagrams that display numbers for visual comparison. Charts illustrate quantitative relationships and can help people understand the significance of numeric information more easily than viewing the same information as a table or a list of numbers. Charts are well suited for making comparisons or examining the changes in data over time.

Creating a Chart

PowerPoint provides several ways to start a new chart. You can add a chart to an existing slide, or you can select a slide layout with a chart placeholder at the time you create a new slide. Microsoft Excel is opened using either of these methods. Excel then holds the chart data in a *worksheet,* and these data are linked to PowerPoint where the chart is displayed. If changes are made to the data in Excel, the chart is automatically updated in PowerPoint.

If Excel is not installed on your computer when you start a new chart, Microsoft Graph will open with a sample *datasheet*. A datasheet provides rows and columns in which you key the numbers and labels used to create a chart. Advanced features of charting with Excel are not available with Graph.

Gus Irvinelli has requested that you create a presentation. The audience will be the general managers at each Good 4 U location. The presentation will include a progress report and a forecast for the future of Good 4 U. Gus prefers that the data be displayed in charts for an easy-to-understand visual representation.

Exercise 6-1 CHOOSE A SLIDE LAYOUT FOR A CHART

Several slide layouts are suitable for charts. Title and Content features one chart on a slide, while Two Content layouts make it easy to combine a chart and body text on the same slide.

1. Open the file **Finance1**.

2. Insert a new slide after slide 1 that uses the Title and Content slide layout, as shown in Figure 6-1. Key the slide title Sales Forecast. This layout contains a placeholder suitable for one chart.

Figure 6-1
Choosing a slide
layout for a chart

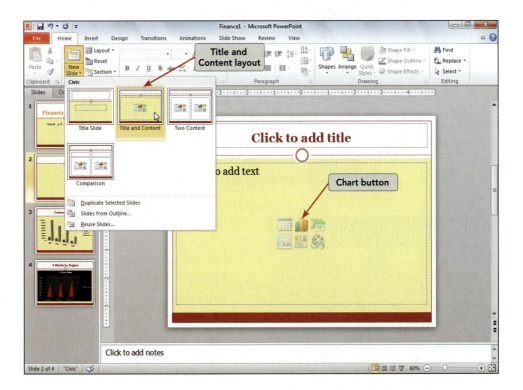

3. Click the Chart button in the center of the content placeholder.

4. On the Insert Chart dialog box, click the different chart categories on the left and notice the chart types that are displayed. From the Column category, click the 3-D Clustered Column Chart, and click OK. Excel opens, displaying a worksheet with sample data, and a chart is inserted into PowerPoint. Chart-related tabs appear on the Ribbon.

UNIT 2 LESSON 6

Exercise 6-2   EDIT THE DATA SOURCE

The worksheet contains rows and columns. Each number or label is in a separate *cell*—the rectangle formed by the intersection of a row and a column.

As you enter data, you can monitor the results on the sample chart. You key new information by overwriting the sample data or by deleting the sample data and keying your own data.

Figure 6-2
Creating a chart

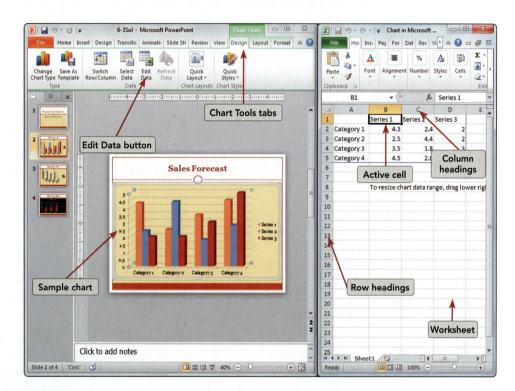

NOTE

If Excel is not installed on your computer, Microsoft Graph will open a datasheet that contains gray column headings and row headings with a buttonlike appearance that indicate column letters and row numbers. If you like, you can move the datasheet by dragging its title bar, and you can resize it by dragging its borders.

1. On the worksheet, click **Series 1**. A heavy black border, which indicates that this is the active cell, surrounds the cell that contains "Series 1," as shown in Figure 6-2. Notice that, when you are working on the worksheet, your pointer is a white cross ✛, called a *cell pointer*.

2. Move around the worksheet by clicking on individual cells. Then try pressing [Enter], [Tab], [Shift]+[Enter], [Shift]+[Tab], and the arrow keys to explore other ways to navigate in a worksheet.

3. Click cell **B2** (the cell in column B, row 2, that contains the value 4.3); then key **10**, and press [Enter]. The chart data will automatically update in PowerPoint.

4. Click cell **B2** with the value "10," which represents Category 1 of Series 1.

5. Press [Delete] to remove the contents of cell B2, and press [Enter]. Notice that the first column in the chart is no longer displayed.

6. Click and drag the pointer from cell B3 to cell B5 to select the rest of the numbers in the Series 1 column.

7. Press [Delete], and then for Series 1 no columns are displayed in the chart. Because the Series 1 column is still included on the worksheet, however, space still remains on the chart where the columns were removed and Series 1 shows in the legend.

8. Click the box in the upper left corner of the worksheet where the row headings meet the column headings, as shown in Figure 6-3. The entire worksheet is selected.

NOTE

If you leave gaps between columns or rows as you enter data, your chart will not display correctly.

Figure 6-3
Editing the worksheet

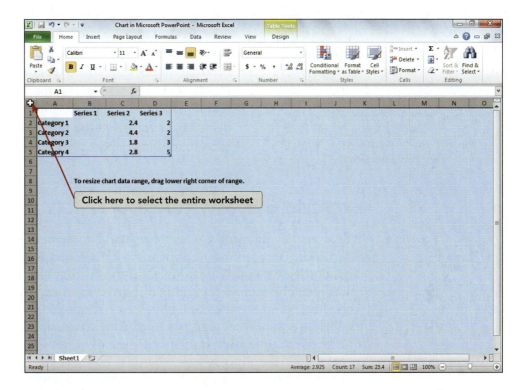

To resize chart data range, drag lower right corner of range.

Click here to select the entire worksheet

NOTE

If PowerPoint does not recognize your data from Excel, from the Chart Tools Design tab, in the Data group, click the Select Data button and then click the red arrow at the end of the Chart data range box. In Excel select the range of data you wish to use on the chart, click the red arrow again, and click OK.

9. Press [Delete]. The worksheet is now blank and ready for you to key new data. Notice that the columns in the chart have been removed.

10. Click the first cell in the upper left corner. All the cells in the worksheet are deselected.

11. Close Excel. The worksheet is not visible. The worksheet can be closed at any point and accessed when you wish.

12. From the Chart Tools Design tab, in the Data group, choose the Edit Data button . This reopens the worksheet, and you can now enter new data.

13. Key the numbers and labels shown in Figure 6-4. Be sure to put the labels in the top row and left-most column. Notice how the chart gets larger as you key data.

Figure 6-4
Worksheet with new data

	A	B	C	D	E
1		2011	2012	2013	
2	New York	920	1130	1450	
3	Miami	500	850	1210	
4	Los Angeles	350	760	990	
5	← Row heading				

TIP

You do not need to be concerned about number formatting in the worksheet. If any of the labels or numbers do not fit in a cell, move to the right of the column heading for the cell until you get the two-pointed arrow and double-click. This will adjust the column to fit the longest line of text.

14. Notice on the chart in PowerPoint that there is a blank area. In the sample chart, there were four categories. To fix this, row 5 must be deleted. Click the row heading number for row 5. Right-click, and choose **Delete**. This will update the chart by removing the blank space where the fourth-category columns were displayed before, and the remaining columns will expand to fill the chart area.

Exercise 6-3 SWITCH ROW OR COLUMN DATA

When you key data for a new chart, Excel interprets each row of data as a *data series*. On a column chart, each data series is usually displayed in a distinct theme color. For example, on the current chart, the 2011 worksheet column is one data series and is displayed in orange on the chart; the 2012 worksheet column is a second data series, displayed in blue on the chart; and the 2013 worksheet column is a third data series, displayed in a dark red.

When creating your worksheet, you might not know whether it is best to arrange your data in rows or columns. Fortunately, you can enter the data and easily change the way it is displayed on the chart.

1. In PowerPoint, click the slide 2 chart area to continue modifying this chart.

2. From the Chart Tools Design tab, click the Switch Row/Column button. The chart columns are now grouped by year instead of by city. The years are displayed below each group of columns.

3. Click the Switch Row/Column button again to group the chart columns by city. Your chart should look like the one shown in Figure 6-5.

4. Close Excel, but continue working in PowerPoint on the chart.

5. Create a slide footer for the current slide (slide 2 only) containing today's date, your name, and *[your initials]*6-3.

6. Create a new folder for Lesson 6. Save the presentation as *[your initials]*6-3 in your Lesson 6 folder.

Figure 6-5
Chart with new data

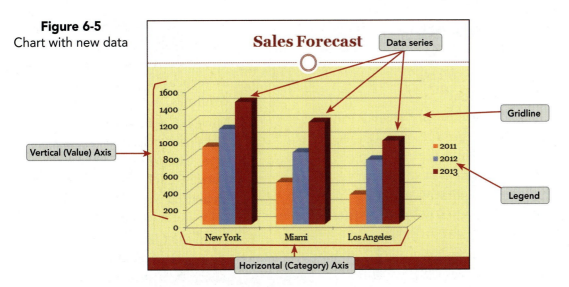

Formatting a Column Chart

You can apply a wide variety of format options to charts by changing the colors, gradients, fonts, and number formats of a chart. Some of these options are appropriate on the basis of the particular chart type being used. In this lesson you have been working with a 3-D Clustered Column chart.

You can alter the appearance of your chart's axes by changing text color, size, font, and number formatting. You can also change scale and tick mark settings. The *scale* indicates the values that are displayed on the value axis and the intervals between those values. *Tick marks* are small measurement marks, similar to those found on a ruler, that show increments on the *Vertical (Value) Axis* (on the left for column charts) and the *Horizontal (Category) Axis* (on the bottom for column charts).

To make these changes, use the Format Axis dialog box, which you display in one of the following ways:

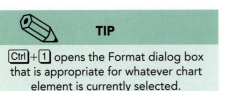

TIP

Ctrl + 1 opens the Format dialog box that is appropriate for whatever chart element is currently selected.

- From the Chart Tools Format tab, in the Current Selection group, choose the area you want to format, and click the Format Selection button.
- Right-click an axis, and choose **Format Axis** from the shortcut menu.

Exercise 6-4   EXPLORE PARTS OF A CHART

PowerPoint provides several tools that help you navigate around the chart and ScreenTips that help you select the part of the chart on which you want to work.

1. Click the chart to select it.
2. Move the pointer over the words "New York." The ScreenTip identifies this part of the chart as the Horizontal (Category) Axis.

Figure 6-6
Chart Elements list

3. Point to one of the horizontal gray lines (gridlines) within the chart. The ScreenTip identifies these lines as Vertical (Value) Axis Major Gridlines.

4. Move the pointer around other parts of the chart to find the Plot Area, Chart Area, and Legend Entries. Each of these areas can be formatted with fill colors, border colors, and font attributes.

5. From the Chart Tools Format tab, in the Current Selection group, the chart element that is currently selected is displayed. Click the **Chart Elements** down arrow to see a list of the various chart elements as shown in Figure 6-6.

6. Choose **Floor** from the list to select the chart floor. Sometimes it's easier to select the chart's smaller elements this way.

Exercise 6-5 CHANGE CHART STYLES

PowerPoint provides preset *Chart Styles* that can be applied to a chart to enhance its appearance. Chart Styles are sets of formatting combinations that can be applied to a chart as a group in one click.

1. On slide 2, click anywhere inside the chart to select it.

2. From the Chart Tools Design tab, in the Chart Styles group, click the More button ⏷.

3. Move your pointer over several of the style samples. Click the **Style 4** chart style, as shown in Figure 6-7.

Figure 6-7
Chart Styles gallery

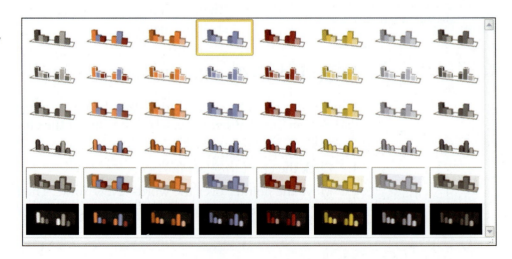

4. Notice the effect that applying a style has on the selected chart. The chart still coordinates with theme colors, but it has three blue colors applied.

Exercise 6-6 FORMAT THE VERTICAL (VALUE) AND HORIZONTAL (CATEGORY) AXES

The Vertical (Value) Axis and the Horizontal (Category) Axis are formatted through the Format Axis dialog box to change fonts, scales, units, and more options.

1. On slide 2, point to one of the numbers on the left side of the chart. When you see the Vertical (Value) Axis ScreenTip, right-click to open the shortcut menu.

2. Using the floating font group, change the font to **Arial**, **Bold**.

3. Right-click the Value Axis again to reopen the shortcut menu, and choose **Format Axis**. Click the **Number** option at the left of the dialog box; then, in the **Category** box, choose **Currency**. Change the decimal places to **0** because all numbers in the worksheet are even numbers. Change the symbol to **$ English (U.S.)**.

4. At the left of the dialog box, click **Axis Options**. In the **Maximum** box, choose **Fixed**, and key **1500** to set the largest number on the Value Axis.

5. In the **Major unit** box, choose **Fixed**, and key **500** to set wider intervals between the numbers on the Value Axis.

6. Click **Close**. The chart now shows fewer horizontal gridlines, and each value is formatted as currency with a dollar sign, as shown in Figure 6-8.

Figure 6-8
Formatting the Value Axis

7. Right-click the text **New York** on the Horizontal (Category) Axis.

8. Using the floating font group, change the font to **Arial**, **Bold**.

Exercise 6-7   APPLY DIFFERENT CHART LAYOUTS

The *Chart Layouts* feature controls the position where different chart elements appear. PowerPoint provides many different preset layouts.

1. Move to slide 3, and click anywhere within the chart area.

2. From the Chart Tools Design tab, in the Chart Styles group, click the More button ⏷, and choose **Style 2**.

3. From the Chart Tools Design tab, in the Chart Layouts group, click the More button ⏷. (Click the Quick Layout button 🔳 if your Layout Styles are not displayed.)

4. Select **Layout 2**. Notice the new position of several chart elements. Also, the Vertical (Value) Axis is gone, and it has been replaced with data labels showing the values on the columns, as shown in Figure 6-9.

Figure 6-9
Choosing a Chart Layout

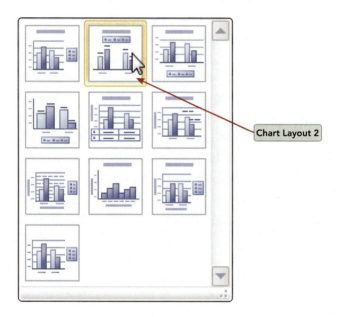

Chart Layout 2

5. Select the "Chart Title" text box, and press ⌨Delete to remove it.

Exercise 6-8   CHANGE OR REMOVE THE LEGEND

A *legend* is a box showing the colors assigned to the data series. You can customize a chart's legend by changing the border, background colors, and font attributes.

1. Move to slide 2, and right-click the legend box.

2. Using the floating font group, change the font to **Arial**, **Bold**.

3. Right-click the legend box again, and choose **Format Legend** so that you can make several changes at once. Click the **Fill** option at the left of the dialog box, choose **Solid Fill**, and select the **Gold, Accent 4** color to change the legend fill color.

TIP

Choosing a fill color, even if it is the same as the background, can make it difficult to choose good grayscale settings for printing.

4. At the left of the dialog box, click **Legend Options**, and choose **Top**. Click **Close**. The legend appears above the chart, and the fill color is changed. Note that sizing handles surround the legend.

5. Using a right or left sizing handle, resize the legend to make it wider (approximately 5 inches) so that there is more space between the legend items and all three items are still visible.

6. Select the legend, and drag it down so that it fits below the top gridline and above the columns, as shown in Figure 6-10. Adjust the width of the legend if it overlaps any columns.

Figure 6-10
Legend repositioned

Exercise 6-9   APPLY OR REMOVE GRIDLINES

Gridlines are the thin lines that can be displayed for major and minor units on vertical or horizontal axes. They align with major and minor tick marks on the axes when those are displayed. Gridlines make quantities easier to understand. In situations where numbers are displayed within the chart, gridlines may not be needed. The chart style you used on slide 3 did not display gridlines.

1. Still working on slide 2, click anywhere within the chart area.

2. From the Chart Tools Layout tab, in the Axes group, click the Gridlines button.

3. Choose **Primary Horizontal Gridlines** and **Minor Gridlines**. Notice that there are many horizontal gridlines now, as shown in Figure 6-11, instead of only gridlines on the major units.

Figure 6-11
Gridlines options

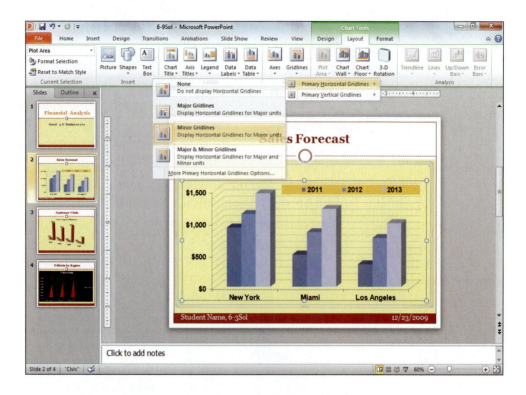

4. Update your slide footer for the current slide (slide 2 only) with today's date, your name, and *[your initials]*6-9.

5. Save the presentation as *[your initials]*6-9 in your Lesson 6 folder.

Using Different Chart Types

In addition to providing the 3-D Clustered Column chart, PowerPoint offers a wide variety of chart types, such as bar, area, line, pie, and surface, in both two- and three-dimensional layouts. In addition, you can include more than one chart type on a single chart, such as a combination of lines and columns.

If you are working on a two-dimensional (2-D) chart, you can add a secondary axis so that you can plot data against two different scales. For example, air temperature could be compared to wind speed, or number of customers could be compared to dollar sales. A secondary axis is also a good choice if you need to display numbers that vary greatly in magnitude; for example, sales generated by a small local brand could be compared with national sales trends.

Exercise 6-10 SWITCH TO OTHER CHART TYPES

Sometimes a different chart type can make data easier to understand. You can change chart types in the following ways:

*   From the Chart Tools Design tab, in the Type group, click the Change Chart Type button to open the Change Chart Type dialog box.

*   Right-click the chart area; then choose **Change Chart Type** from the shortcut menu.

1. Move to slide 3, and click the chart area to activate the chart. This chart compares dollar sales to number of customer visits. Because of the different types of data, the sales figures are not easy to understand.

2. Right-click the chart, and choose **Change Chart Type** from the shortcut menu. In the Change Chart Type dialog box, chart types are organized by category, as shown in Figure 6-12.

3. At the left of the dialog box, click **Bar**. Point to different thumbnails, and notice the description that appears in the ScreenTip. Choose **Clustered Bar in 3-D**, and click **OK**. The chart's vertical columns change to horizontal bars.

Figure 6-12
Changing to a different chart type

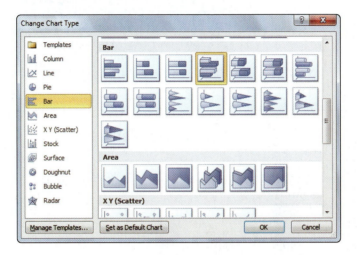

4. From the Chart Tools Design tab, in the Type group, click the Change Chart Type button. The Change Chart Type dialog box opens again.

5. At the left of the dialog box, click **Column**. Point to different thumbnails, and notice the description that appears in the ScreenTip. Click the **Clustered Column** type in the upper left of this category. Click **OK**. The chart changes to a two-dimensional column chart.

Exercise 6-11   ADD A SECONDARY CHART AXIS

The chart on slide 3 (Customer Visits) contains dollar values for apparel and food sales and also unit values for number of customer visits. Plotting customer visits on a secondary axis will improve the chart by making it easier to interpret.

If you are working with a 3-D chart, you must change it to a 2-D chart (as you did in the previous exercise), before you can add a secondary axis.

1. Select the chart on slide 3.

2. From the Chart Tools Design tab, in the Chart Layouts group, choose **Layout 1**, and delete the chart title text box.

3. Right-click one of the "Customers" columns, and choose **Format Data Series** from the shortcut menu. Click **Series Options** at the left of the dialog box.

4. In the **Plot Series On** area of the dialog box, select **Secondary axis**. Click **Close**. Now the orange and blue columns have become taller, and a new scale has been added on the right, as shown in Figure 6-13. In the following exercises you will improve the appearance of this chart.

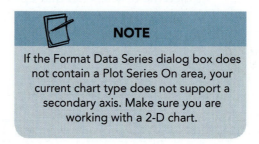

NOTE

If the Format Data Series dialog box does not contain a Plot Series On area, your current chart type does not support a secondary axis. Make sure you are working with a 2-D chart.

Figure 6-13
Adding a secondary axis

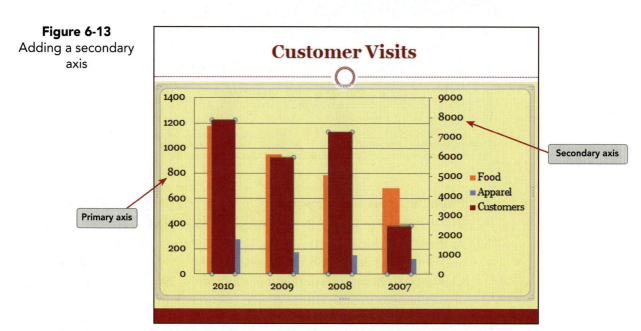

Exercise 6-12 COMBINE CHART TYPES

A good way to distinguish between different data types on a single chart is to assign different chart types. For example, with the current chart, the "Customers" data series can be shown as a line or an area, while the sales data can remain as columns, as shown in Figure 6-14.

1. On slide 3 select the "Customers" data series if not already selected.

2. Right-click the data series, and choose **Change Series Chart Type** from the shortcut menu. Click the **Area** category at the left of the dialog box, and choose the **Area** chart type. Click **OK**.

Figure 6-14
Area and Column
combination chart

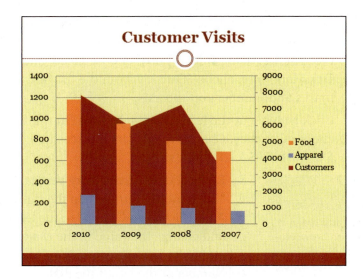

3. Click the "Customers" area to select it; then right-click, and choose **Change Series Chart Type** from the shortcut menu. Choose the **Line** category at the left of the dialog box, and click the **Line** chart type. Click **OK**.

4. Right-click the red line representing "Customers," and choose **Format Data Series** from the shortcut menu.

5. At the left of the dialog box, click **Line Style**, and change the **Width** to **3 points**.

6. At the left of the dialog box, click **Line Color**, and change the **Color** to **Red, Accent 3, Darker 50%**. Click **Close**.

Exercise 6-13   FORMAT PRIMARY AND SECONDARY AXES

Proper formatting and labeling on a chart is always important to ensure that viewers understand the information you want to convey. This is even more important when you have both primary and secondary axis scales on the chart.

1. On slide 3, click the chart area to select it.

2. From the Chart Tools Layout tab, in the Labels group, click the Axis Titles button [icon], and choose **Primary Vertical Axis Title** and **Rotated Title**.

3. In the Vertical (Value) Axis Title text box located on the primary vertical axis, delete the text and key **Sales (thousands)**. The size of the text box will adjust automatically. Figure 6-15 indicates the position of the text on the chart.

4. From the Chart Tools Layout tab, in the Labels group, click the Axis Titles button [icon], and choose **Secondary Vertical Axis Title** and **Rotated Title**. An Vertical (Value) Axis Title text box appears beside the secondary axis scale on the left.

5. In the Vertical (Value) Axis Title text box, delete the text and key **Customer Visits (hundreds)**. Descriptive titles now appear next to both the primary and the secondary axes.

6. Right-click the **Vertical (Value) Axis** (the "Sales" numbers on the left), and choose **Format Axis**. Click **Axis Options** at the left of the dialog box; then, in the **Major unit** text box, choose **Fixed**, and key **500**. Under **Major Tick Mark Type**, choose **Outside** from the list box. This will insert tick marks and numbers on the axis.

7. Click **Number** at the left of the dialog box. In the **Category** list box, choose **Currency**. Change the **Decimal places** to **0**. Under symbol, choose **$ English (U.S.)**. Click **Close**.

TIP

It is best to avoid using red and green in the same chart to distinguish between data sets. Some individuals have difficulty distinguishing between those two colors, so they would have difficulty comparing columns, bars, or pie slices.

8. Right-click the **Secondary Vertical (Value) Axis** (the "Customers" numbers on the right), and choose **Format Axis**. Click **Axis Options** at the left of the dialog box, and change the value in the **Major unit** text box to **Fixed** and **1500** to reduce some of the number labels. Click **Number** at the left of the dialog box. In the **Category** list box, choose **Number**. Change the **Decimal places** to **0**. The **Use 1000 Separator** should be checked. Click **Close**.

9. Click outside the chart area to view your changes.

10. Click the legend; then right-click, and choose **Format Legend**. For the Legend Position choose **Top**. Click **Close**. Now the chart appears more balanced, with the scales evenly spaced on each side.

Figure 6-15
Completed combination chart

11. Create a slide footer for only slide 3 that includes the date, your name, and *[your initials]***6-13**. Save the presentation as *[your initials]***6-13** in your Lesson 6 folder.

Working with Pie Charts

A *pie chart* is a simple, yet highly effective, presentation tool that shows individual values in relation to the sum of all the values—a pie chart makes it easy to judge "parts of a whole." Each value is displayed as a slice of the pie.

A pie chart can show only one data series. To show more than one data series, use more than one pie chart.

Exercise 6-14 CREATE A PIE CHART

In this exercise, you create a pie chart to display the breakdown of the restaurant's sales by category.

If your worksheet contains more than one data series, a pie chart uses the first column of numbers. You can change to a different row or column if you like.

1. Insert a new slide after slide 3 that uses the **Title Only** layout. This layout provides a white background.

2. Key the title **2010 Sales Categories**.

3. From the Insert tab, in the Illustrations group, click the Chart button 📊.

4. Click the **Pie** category, and choose the first chart type that appears in the pie chart category: **Pie**. Click **OK**. Excel opens and displays a sample worksheet, and in PowerPoint you will see a sample pie chart reflecting that data.

Figure 6-16
Worksheet for pie chart

	A	B
1		2010 Sales
2	Food	3339
3	Beverage	2933
4	Apparel	1529
5	Other	906

5. Replace the sample data with the data shown in Figure 6-16.

6. Close the Excel worksheet, and leave the presentation open for the next exercise.

Exercise 6-15 ADD PIE SLICE LABELS

You can add labels to the chart's data series and edit those labels individually. Labels help identify the categories being charted more easily than legends or datasheets.

1. Click one of the pie slices to select the Chart Series data.

2. From the Chart Tools Layout tab, in the Labels group, click the Data Labels button 📊, and click **More Data Label Options**.

3. Click **Label Options** at the left of the dialog box, and make several changes under the **Label Contains** heading:

    a. Select both **Category Name** and **Percentage**.

    b. Deselect **Value** and **Show Leader Lines**.

    c. Click **Close**.

NOTE

Depending on the pie chart, sometimes parts of the data labels might be hidden by the edges of the chart placeholder. In this case, you need to resize the pie by using the plot area sizing handles.

4. Data labels now appear on the pie slices. With the addition of the data labels, the pie is now smaller; however, the legend is no longer needed since the slices are each labeled, as shown in Figure 6-17.

5. Because the slide title identifies what the pie contains, the pie chart title for 2010 sales can be removed. Select this text box, and press ⌐Delete¬. The pie will expand to fill the available space.

6. Right-click the legend box, and choose **Delete** from the shortcut menu. The pie chart becomes a little larger.

Figure 6-17
Pie chart with data labels

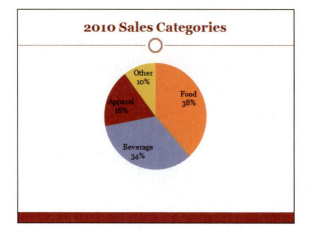

7. Click any data label. All the data labels are selected. Right-click one of the labels, and use the floating font group to change the font to **Arial**, **16 points**, **bold**, and **italic**. Click outside the pie to turn off this selection.

8. Click the data label "Other 10%" twice to select just that label. As with columns, click once to select all labels, and click again to select just one. You can now edit the selected label's text.

9. Click within the text to display an insertion point. Delete the word "Other" (but not "10%"), and key in its place **Take-out**.

10. Click the "Take-out 10%" label two times to select just that label. Right-click, and choose **Format Data Label**. Under the Label Position heading, choose **Inside End**. Click **Close**. Now the label is positioned on the slice. This will ensure that the new label stays on the pie.

Exercise 6-16   APPLY 3-D ROTATION

You can enhance the appearance of your pie chart with additional effects, such as changing to a 3-D appearance and rotating the angle of the pie or *exploding* a slice (dragging it out from the center of the pie) for emphasis.

1. Click to select the chart. From the Chart Tools Design tab, in the Type group, click the Change Chart Type button 📊, and select **Pie in 3-D**. The pie now has a perspective treatment. Click **OK**.

2. From the Chart Tools Layout tab, in the Background group, click the 3-D Rotation button 🔲. At the bottom of the Format Chart Area dialog box, click **Default Rotation**, and the pie becomes more dimensional but almost flat.

3. In the **Perspective** box, key **0.1°**.

4. Under the Rotation heading, change the **X degree** to **35°** to move the "Take-out 10%" slice to the right. Click **Close**.

5. Click the center of the pie once to select all the slices. Notice that each slice has selection handles where the slices join.

6. Click the "Food 38%" slice so that you have handles on that slice only (be careful not to select the label), and drag it slightly away from the center of the pie. This is called *exploding a slice,* as shown in Figure 6-18.

Figure 6-18
Pie chart with 3-D rotation and exploded slice

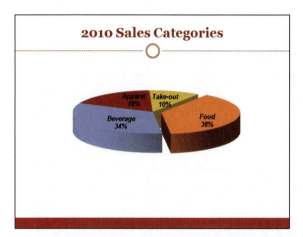

7. In Normal view, select the chart area, and use the corner sizing handles to make the pie chart larger to fill the slide.

8. Create a slide footer for slide 4 that includes the date, your name, and *[your initials]*6-16.

9. Save the presentation as *[your initials]*6-16 in your Lesson 6 folder. Keep the presentation open for the next exercise.

Enhancing Chart Elements

You can add many interesting effects to charts. In addition to changing colors, you can add shapes or pictures that help you make a particular point or highlight one aspect of the data. You can also annotate your charts with text to clarify or call attention to important concepts.

Exercise 6-17   ADD SHAPES FOR EMPHASIS

Shapes can be combined with text or layered to emphasize the point you need to make. For this exercise, you will combine an arrow and text.

1. Move to slide 5, titled "T-Shirts by Region."

2. Because this chart reflects only one data series, the legend at the side is not needed. Select the legend, and press ⌈Delete⌋.

3. Because the slide title identifies the content of this chart, the chart title is redundant; therefore, select the chart title, and press ⌈Delete⌋.

4. From the Insert tab, in the Text group, click the Text Box button 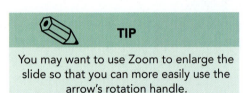, and click and drag above the Miami column to create a space to enter text. Change the font color to **White, Background 1**, and key **L.A. may top Miami in 2011**.

5. Select the text inside the text box, right-click, and use the floating font group to change the text to **Arial**, **bold**, **italic**.

> **TIP**
>
> You may want to use Zoom to enlarge the slide so that you can more easily use the arrow's rotation handle.

6. From the Insert tab, in the Illustrations group, click the Shapes button ; then, from the Block Arrow category, click the **Left Arrow** shape. Draw an arrow above the Los Angeles chart shape. Change the shape fill color to **Gold, Accent 4**, and remove the shape outline. Reposition and resize the arrow and text box as shown in Figure 6-19.

Figure 6-19
Chart with arrow and text box

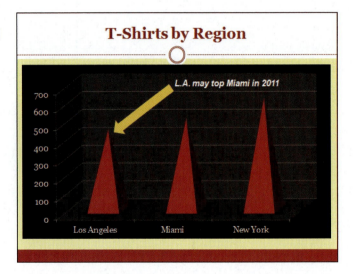

7. Create a slide footer for slide 5 that includes the date, your name, and *[your initials]*6-17.

8. Save the presentation as *[your initials]*6-17 in your Lesson 6 folder.

Exercise 6-18 CHANGE COLORS IN CHART AREAS

You can change the colors of individual chart areas, columns, or an entire data series. Shape fill effects, including textures and gradient fills, can be used the same way you use them for other PowerPoint shapes. You can also change the outline style of columns, bars, and other chart elements.

1. Move to slide 2, and point to one of the darkest blue columns, the 2011 series. Notice the ScreenTip that appears, identifying the data series.

2. Click any light-blue column, the 2013 series. All the light-blue columns are selected, as indicated by the box that is displayed around each selected column.

3. Click the light-blue column for Los Angeles. Now the Los Angeles column is the only one selected. Clicking once selects all the columns in a series; clicking a second time (not double-clicking) changes the selection to just one column.

4. Click one of the darkest blue columns to select all of the 2011 series.

5. From the Chart Tools Format tab, in the Shape Styles group, click the Shape Fill button . Choose **Blue, Accent 2, Darker 50%**.

> **TIP**
>
> You can change colors and fills on each part of the chart. Be sure to select the element that you would like to change before beginning to change colors or gradients or add a picture.

6. Click the darker blue column for Los Angeles, and then change the fill color to **Orange, Accent 1**. The Los Angeles column is now a different color from that of the other columns in its series. Click the Undo button to return the column to the darker blue to match the other columns in the series.

7. Select the columns that contain the light-blue fill color, the 2013 series. Click the Shape Fill button, and choose the blue color **Ice Blue, Accent 5**. Click the Shape Fill button again, and choose **Gradient**. Under the Light Variations category, select **Linear Up** so that the lightest color is at the top of the column.

Exercise 6-19   ADD A PICTURE FILL BEHIND A CHART

A picture can help communicate the meaning of the chart by illustrating the data in some way. For instance, if you are discussing T-shirts as in this exercise, it is appropriate to have a shirt picture in the chart background.

1. Move to slide 5. Change the font color of the text on both axes and in the text box font to **Black, Text 1** to make it easier to read once a picture has been added.

2. From the Chart Tools Layout tab, in the Current Selection group, choose **Chart Area** from the Chart Elements drop-down list. Click the Format Selection button.

3. At the left of the dialog box, click **Fill** then choose **Picture or texture fill**. For Insert from:, click **File**.

4. Navigate to your student files, and click the file **t-shirt**. Click **Insert**. Click **Close**. The picture fills the background of your chart. You need to recolor other parts of the chart so that the T-shirt is visible in the background, as shown in Figure 6-20.

5. Click the dark area behind the chart shapes, the back and side walls. Right-click, and choose **Format Walls**. Choose **No Fill**, and click **Close**.

6. Right-click the Vertical (Value) Axis numbers, and change the font to **Arial**, **Bold**.

7. Right-click the Horizontal (Category) Axis numbers, and change the font to **Arial**, **Bold**.

8. Adjust the position of the text box or arrow if necessary.

9. Update the slide footer for slide 5 to include the text *[your initials]*6-19.

Figure 6-20
Chart with picture
background

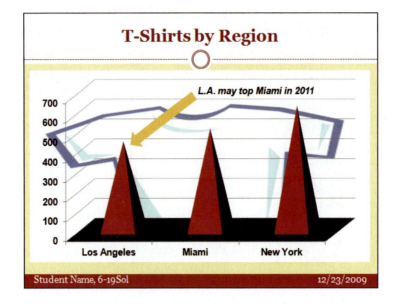

10. View the presentation as a slide show, starting with slide 1.

11. Create a handout header and footer: Include the date, your name as the header, the page number, and *[your initials]*6-19 as the footer.

12. Move to slide 1, and save the presentation as *[your initials]*6-19 in your Lesson 6 folder.

13. Close the presentation and submit your work.

Lesson 6   Summary

- Charts are diagrams that visually represent numeric information. Charts illustrate quantitative relationships and can help people understand the significance of numeric information more easily than viewing the same information as a list of numbers.

- When you start a new chart, a sample worksheet appears in Excel. On the worksheet, you key the numbers and labels that will be used to create a chart.

- The worksheet contains rows and columns. You key each number or label in a separate *cell*—the rectangle formed by the intersection of a row and a column.

- On the worksheet, key labels in the first row and column.

- A data series is a group of data that relate to a common object or category. Often, more than one data series is displayed on a single chart.

- Use the Switch Row/Column button to change how a data series is displayed on a chart.

- A wide variety of chart types are available, including column, bar, area, line, pie, and surface, with many different chart format options.

- Several content layouts are suitable for charts. Two Content layouts make it easy to combine a chart and body text on the same slide.

- Use the Chart Elements drop-down list to select specific parts of a chart, or use ScreenTips to identify parts as you point to them.

- Special fill and border effects, including textures and gradient fills, can be used in charts the same way you use them for other PowerPoint objects.

- Use the Format Axis dialog box to modify the units, font, and number format of the value axis or secondary value axis. Modify the unit settings to specify the range of numbers displayed and increments between numbers.

- Axis titles are an important part of charts. Careful labeling ensures that your charts will be interpreted correctly.

- A legend is a box showing the colors assigned to each data series. Customize a chart's legend by changing the border, background colors, and font attributes.

- Use a secondary axis when you need to plot two dissimilar types of data on the same chart. A secondary axis is available only for a 2-D chart type.

- Proper formatting and labeling on a chart is important when your chart has both a primary and a secondary axis.

- A good way to distinguish between different data types on a single chart is to assign different chart types. For example, use columns for one type of data and lines for the other type.

- A pie chart shows individual values in relation to the sum of all the values. Each value is displayed as a slice of the pie.

- A pie chart can show only one data series. To show more than one data series, use more than one pie chart.

- The plot area of a chart is the area containing the actual columns, bars, or pie slices. It can be formatted with or without a border and a fill effect.

- Exploding a pie slice (dragging it out from the center of the pie) emphasizes the slice.

- Use the Insert tab to add shapes and text boxes. Use text boxes wherever needed to annotate your chart to clarify its meaning.

- Charts can be enhanced by adding pictures, colors, and 3-D effects.

LESSON 6		Command Summary	
Feature	Button	Ribbon	Keyboard
Add a secondary axis		Chart Tools Format, Current Selection group, Format Selection (with data series selected)	
Add data labels		Chart Tools Layout, Labels group, Data Labels	
Add/remove gridlines		Chart Tools Layout, Axes group, Gridlines	
Apply different chart layouts		Chart Tools Design, Chart Layouts group, More	
Change chart style		Chart Tools Design, Chart Styles group, More	
Change chart type		Chart Tools Design, Type group, Change Chart Type	
Display worksheet		Chart Tools Design, Data group, Edit Data	
Format a chart object		Chart Tools Format, Current Selection group, Format Selection	Ctrl + 1
Insert a chart		Insert, Illustrations group, Chart	
Insert axis titles		Chart Tools Layout, Labels group, Axis Titles	
Insert or remove a legend		Chart Tools Layout, Labels group, Legend	
Switch data series between columns and rows		Chart Tools Design, Data group, Switch Row/Column	

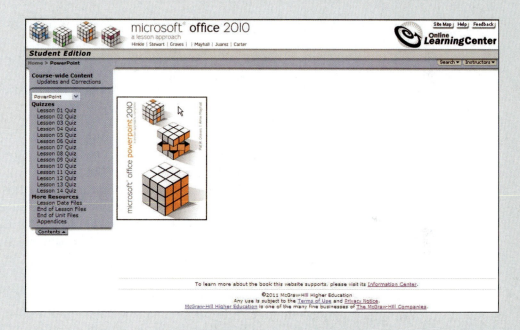

Please visit our Online Learning Center, *www.lessonapproach2010.com*, **where you will find the following review materials:**

- **Concepts Review**
    - True/False Questions
    - Short Answer Questions
    - Critical Thinking Questions

- **Skills Review**
    - Review Exercises that target single skills
    - Lesson Applications
    - Review Exercises that challenge students by testing multiple skills in each exercise

- **On Your Own**
    - Open-ended exercises that require students to synthesize multiple skills and apply creativity and problem-solving as they would in a real world business situation

Creating SmartArt Graphics

OBJECTIVES

After completing this lesson, you will be able to:

1. Create SmartArt graphics.
2. Enhance SmartArt layouts.
3. Prepare an organization chart.
4. Create other diagrams with SmartArt.
5. Change SmartArt graphics.

Estimated Time: 1½ hours

Diagrams provide a very effective way to illustrate data and have been important in business communication for a long time. Diagrams show a visual representation of information that can help an audience understand a presenter's message. For example, diagrams can be used to show the steps of a process or the relationship between managers and subordinates. An audience can see the process or relationship because it is portrayed with shapes and connecting lines or layered in some way.

PowerPoint's SmartArt graphics make it easy to create diagrams and other graphical layouts with a very professional appearance. A wide range of predesigned layouts can be customized in many different ways.

The slide show in this lesson is being developed for Julie Wolfe and Gus Irvinelli, Good 4 U co-owners, for a presentation to all employees at the New York location. They are announcing a new organizational structure and their philosophy behind the changes, which emphasizes a customer focus and the need for ongoing improvements. As you help them work on this presentation, you will create a variety of SmartArt graphics.

Creating SmartArt Graphics

A *SmartArt graphic* can be inserted on your slide, and the shapes of the graphical layout it creates can be filled in with identifying text. Or if you have text in a bulleted list or in text shapes, the text items can be converted to a graphical layout. You will use both of these techniques in this lesson.

From the Insert tab, in the Illustrations group, click the SmartArt button to display the Choose a SmartArt Graphic dialog box shown in Figure 7-1. You can display thumbnails of all possible layouts, or you can view them organized by the type of layout. On the right side of this dialog box, each layout is displayed in a larger size with a definition below to help you decide which layout best illustrates your communication needs. The white lines that you see on the sample diagram indicate where your text will appear when you label each part of the diagram.

Figure 7-1
Choose a SmartArt
Graphic dialog box

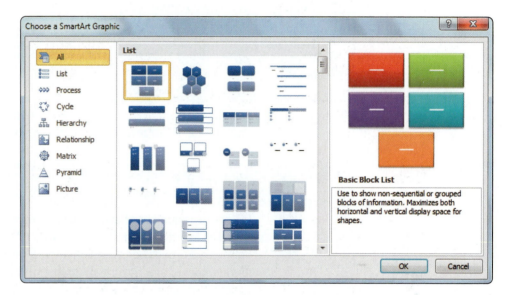

Preparing a few bulleted lists is a simple way to create a series of slides for a presentation. However, a presentation including only bulleted lists is not very appealing to an audience from a visual standpoint and may not be the best way to communicate the meaning of your message that an audience needs to understand.

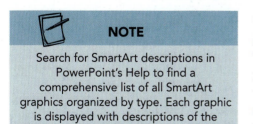
NOTE

Search for SmartArt descriptions in PowerPoint's Help to find a comprehensive list of all SmartArt graphics organized by type. Each graphic is displayed with descriptions of the layout and tips for situations in which each would be appropriate.

As you develop your presentation content, you should be considering your message from the viewpoint of the audience and not just thinking about what you need to say. To help your audience visualize the message concepts and remember them better, plan alternative ways to illustrate the concepts, such as by including pictures, charts, and shapes, to draw attention to key points. You can choose from an extensive array of SmartArt graphics. These graphics are diagrams that are arranged within eight types, as listed in Table 7-1.

TABLE 7-1 SmartArt Graphics Diagram Types

Diagram Type	Purpose
Cycle	Represents a continuous series of events such as an ongoing manufacturing or employee-review process. A cycle can be arranged in a circular pattern or with slices or gears to reflect interconnected parts. A radial cycle begins with a central part and then other parts extend from the center.
Hierarchy	Illustrates reporting relationships or lines of authority between employees in a company such as in an organization chart. These connections are sometimes called parent-child relationships. Hierarchy diagrams can be arranged vertically or horizontally such as in a decision tree used to show the outgrowth of options after choices are made.
List	Provides an alternative to listing text in bulleted lists. List diagrams can show groupings, labeled parts, and even directional concepts through the way the shapes are stacked. Several diagrams show main categories and then subtopics within those categories.
Matrix	Allows placement of concepts along two axes or in related quadrants. Emphasis can be on the whole or on individual parts.
Picture	Displays one or more pictures with a variety of other shapes to contain explanatory text or short captions.
Process	Shows a sequence of events or the progression of workflow such as in a flowchart. Process diagrams show connected parts of a process or even converging processes using a funnel technique. Several diagrams with arrows can portray conflict or opposing viewpoints.
Pyramid	Shows interconnected or proportional relationships building from one direction such as a foundational concept on which other concepts are built.
Relationship	Shows interconnected, hierarchical, proportional, or overlapping relationships. Some of these diagrams also appear in different categories too.

Exercise 7-1   USE GRAPHICAL LISTS TO SHOW GROUPS OF INFORMATION

In this exercise you will create a SmartArt graphic *list* in two different ways:

- Start with a Title and Content slide layout, click the SmartArt button ,
  and key content using a Text pane.

- Start with an existing bulleted list, and convert it to a SmartArt graphic.

  1. Open the file **Organize**. Julie and Gus started this presentation with a
     title slide and bulleted list on slide 2, but they have requested that you

Figure 7-2
Using the Text pane

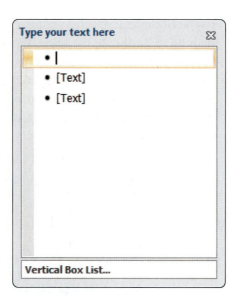

update the presentation to show the bulleted information in a more visual way that better emphasizes the content.

2. Move to slide 1, and from the Home tab, in the Slides group, click the New Slide button 🗐 and add a Title and Content slide. On the content placeholder, click the SmartArt button 🖼.

3. Click the **List** type. Click the **Vertical Box List** thumbnail; then click **OK**.

4. A Text pane appears on the left, as shown in Figure 7-2. When you key text here, it appears on shapes in the SmartArt layout.

5. For the three items in the list, key **New Procedure**, **New Philosophy**, and **New Department**. Use the arrow keys to move from bullet to bullet unless you want to add additional bullets.

6. Close the Text pane.

7. For the slide title, key **Organizational Changes**, as shown in Figure 7-3.

8. The Vertical Box List diagram works best when you have very concise information for first-level bulleted items. If you entered second-level items, they would appear in the white rectangle below each item. As you can see from the diagram, if you have three first-level items, very little space remains for second-level items.

NOTE

If you added a fourth bulleted item, the shapes on the slide would become a little smaller so that four could be displayed.

Figure 7-3
Vertical Box List
diagram

NOTE

If you already have bulleted text on a slide, then that text can be converted to a SmartArt diagram. In the following steps, you will show both the first-level and second-level text shown on slide 3.

9. In the Slides and Outline pane, click slide 3, and press Ctrl+D to duplicate the slide. Once your diagram is prepared on slide 4 and you have confirmed that all the text is appropriately displayed, you can delete slide 3 with the bulleted list. But for now, it is a good idea to leave one slide as originally prepared so that it is available for comparison.

10. Now highlight all the bulleted text on slide 4.

11. From the Home tab, in the Paragraph group, click the Convert to SmartArt button.

12. Click **More SmartArt Graphics** to access all the types, and choose the **List** type.

13. Double-click the **Horizontal Bullet List** thumbnail to insert it onto the slide.

14. The first-level bulleted items appear in the top rectangles, and the second-level bulleted items appear in the bottom rectangles with bullets. The color treatment is more dominant for first-level words than for second-level subpoints, as shown in Figure 7-4.

Figure 7-4
Horizontal Bullet List diagram

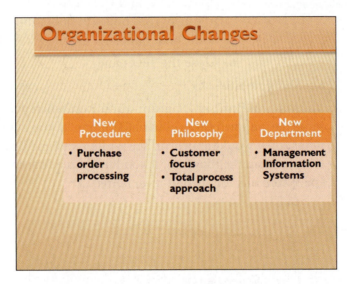

15. Confirm that the diagram on slide 4 includes all the text that is in the original slide 3 bulleted list. When you are sure that everything matches, delete slide 3.

Exercise 7-2   USE PROCESS DIAGRAMS TO SHOW SEQUENTIAL WORKFLOW STEPS

A *process diagram* reflects concepts or events that occur sequentially. Generally speaking, one part must be finished before the next part begins. Many variations for portraying these processes are available in SmartArt.

1. Move to slide 3. From the Home tab, in the Slides group, click the New Slide button.

2. On the slide 4 content area, click the SmartArt button 🖳 ; then choose the **Process** SmartArt type.

3. Examine the different options in this type. Double-click the **Basic Process** thumbnail. A three-part diagram appears, as shown in Figure 7-5. You can enter text by using the Text pane or keying directly in the diagram shapes. If the Text pane does not open automatically, click the Text pane border button ⁝ on the left border to open it.

4. For this exercise, key directly in each of the shapes. As you key, the text will automatically word-wrap in the shape and become smaller to fit within that shape. Therefore, when using this method, be careful to keep wording very concise.

5. Click in the first rectangle shape, and key **Survey customer needs**.

6. Click in the second rectangle shape, and key **Analyze survey results**.

7. Click in the third rectangle shape, and key **Develop product plans**.

Figure 7-5
Basic Process
diagram

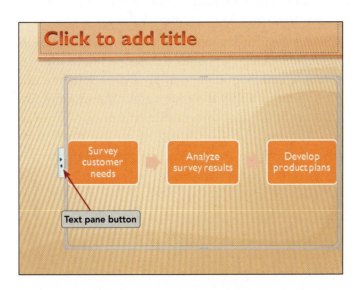

8. Because you need to include a fourth step in this process, you need to increase the size of the SmartArt area. Point to the top left corner of the SmartArt border, and drag it close to the left edge of the slide.

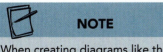
NOTE

When creating diagrams like this, be careful that your text does not become too small for easy reading. Later in this lesson you will make the text larger on this slide.

9. Select the third shape in the diagram; then click the Text pane button ⁝ to open the Text pane. The third shape is the third bulleted item that is highlighted.

10. Click at the end of the word "plans" in the text pane, and press [Enter]. Key **Introduce new products**. A fourth shape is added, and the text size is automatically adjusted again.

11. Close the Text pane.

12. For the slide title, key the text **New Development Process**.

Exercise 7-3 USE CYCLE DIAGRAMS TO SHOW A CONTINUING SEQUENCE

A *cycle diagram* is used to communicate a continuing process. In this exercise you will use the same information as you did for slide 4 but will display it in a cycle. Instead of creating the diagram first, however, you will enter text using a bulleted list and then convert the list into a SmartArt graphic.

1. Insert a new slide with the **Title and Content** layout after slide 4. Key the title **New Development Cycle**.

2. In the content placeholder key four bulleted items:

   Survey customer needs
   Analyze survey results
   Develop product plan
   Introduce new products

3. Select the listed text, and right-click. From the shortcut menu, choose **Convert to SmartArt**; then click **Basic Cycle**.

4. Select the four shapes. From the SmartArt Tools Format tab, in the Shape Styles group, click the Shape Fill button 🖌, and choose **Orange, Accent 1, Darker 25%** to apply a darker theme fill color. Select the four arrows, and apply the even darker theme color **Orange, Accent 1, Darker 50%**, as shown in Figure 7-6.

Figure 7-6
Completed cycle diagram

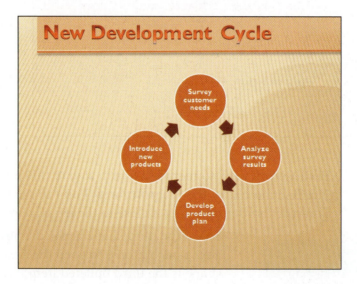

5. Create a handout header and footer: Include the date, your name as the header, the page number, and *[your initials]*7-3 as the footer.

6. Create a new folder for Lesson 7. Save the presentation as *[your initials]*7-3 in your new Lesson 7 folder.

Enhancing SmartArt Layouts

Once a SmartArt graphic is inserted on your slide, its appearance can be altered using the effects that you have learned to apply to shapes. However, additional options exist for customizing SmartArt layouts.

Exercise 7-4   APPLY SHAPE QUICK STYLES

One of the quickest ways to change the appearance of shapes within a diagram is to apply *Quick Styles*. These styles include more than one preset adjustment.

1. On slide 2, select the three rectangle shapes that contain text content.
2. From the Home tab, in the Drawing group, click the Quick Styles button 🟢 to see a gallery of styles in theme colors, as shown in Figure 7-7.

Figure 7-7
Shape Quick Styles

3. As you move your pointer horizontally, you will see different colors applied to the selected shapes. As you move your pointer vertically, you will see different effects such as outlines, beveling, and shadows.
4. To use a darker color and apply a shadow effect to the shapes, click **Light 1 Outline, Colored Fill – Brown, Accent 2** (third row, third column).

Exercise 7-5   ADJUST 3-D FORMAT AND ROTATION

In the previous exercises, the shapes have a *2-D* orientation—you see the shapes in dimensions of height (up/down measurement) and width (left/right measurement). Three-dimensional (*3-D*) settings add a perspective dimension to create the illusion of depth. For example, a square can look like a cube. Rotation settings enable you to tilt shapes on the screen.

1. Move to slide 4, and select the four rectangles.

2. From the Home tab, in the Drawing group, click the Shape Effects button ⌐; then choose **3-D Rotation**.

Figure 7-8
3-D Rotation effects

3. From the gallery of effects, choose **Perspective Heroic Extreme Left**, as shown in Figure 7-8.

4. Now add two more shape effects to customize this diagram. Select the rectangle shapes, and follow these steps on the Home tab, in the Drawing group:

   a. Click the Shape Effects button ⌐, choose **Bevel**, and then click **Circle**.

   b. Click the Shape Effects button ⌐, choose **Shadow**, and then from the Outer type, click **Offset Diagonal Top Right**.

   c. Click anywhere on the slide to turn off the selection.

5. Select the three arrows, and apply the same **Bevel** and **Shadow** effects.

Exercise 7-6   ADJUST THE OVERALL SIZE AND LAYOUT OF THE DIAGRAM

Diagrams can be resized like any other PowerPoint object. However, you must always be sure the text is still readable if the size of shapes is reduced. You may need to use only a single word on very small shapes. In this exercise, you will experiment with a couple of sizing techniques.

1. Duplicate slide 4; then make the following changes on the slide 5 diagram.

2. Notice that the four rectangles and connecting arrows extend across the complete slide, so you don't have any extra horizontal space unless the shapes become smaller. Resize the SmartArt area by dragging the right side about a half inch to the left. The text on the shapes becomes slightly smaller.

3. Resize the top and bottom of the SmartArt area so that it is just large enough to contain the shapes.

4. Drag this diagram up to fit directly under the slide title.

5. With the diagram selected, press Ctrl+D to duplicate the diagram. Position the second diagram evenly below the first one. Duplicating is a quick way to make a second diagram because you can simply edit the text on each shape for new wording without having to reset the Shape Effects.

6. On the second diagram, resize the bottom border of the SmartArt area to increase the available space for repositioning the shapes, as shown in Figure 7-9. Follow these steps:

    a. Select the first rectangle, and drag it to the upper left of the SmartArt area. Notice that the arrow between this rectangle and the second one automatically repositions itself.

    b. Select the second rectangle, and move it to the left.

    c. Select the third rectangle, and move it to the left and down slightly. Be careful that you allow enough space for the arrow.

    d. Select the fourth rectangle, and move it to the left and down slightly.

    e. Adjust rectangle positioning by nudging (using the arrow keys) so that the arrows remain approximately the same size.

7. Now you are still portraying the four-step process because of the connecting arrows that show the direction. However, with this curving arrangement, you will have enough room on the slide for a picture or some other graphic element to accompany the diagram.

Figure 7-9
A process diagram
arranged two ways

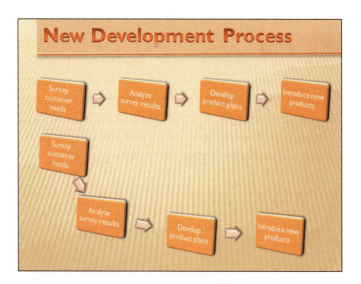

Exercise 7-7   ADD SHAPES

In Exercise 7-2 you added a shape, so you already have some experience in modifying the structure of a SmartArt graphic. While layouts add shapes in different places, the new shape is normally connected to the selected one in some way. Therefore, the shape that is selected when you add another shape is important.

1. Move to slide 6, and create a new slide with the **Title and Content** layout. Key **Adding SmartArt Shapes** as the slide title. Click the SmartArt button in the content placeholder.

2. From the **List** type, double-click the **Stacked List** thumbnail.

3. Now edit the text on each shape as follows:

    a. In the circle on the left, key **One**; then for the related text key **First item** and **Second item**.

    b. In the circle on the right, key **Two**; then for the related text key **First item** and **Second item**.

    c. Notice that the text automatically resizes and word-wraps for each shape.

4. Now under the left circle labeled "One," click the "First item" text to select that shape. From the SmartArt Tools Design tab, in the Create Graphic group, click the Add Shape button 🔲 down arrow; then choose **Add Shape After**. A new shape appears below the first item, and the diagram has been resized. Key **New item** in this shape.

5. Now select the left circle labeled "One." Click the Add Shape button 🔲 down arrow; then choose **Add Shape After**. This time a second circle with a related rectangle shape is added, as shown in Figure 7-10. Notice that you have the options of before and after as well as above and below when you are adding shapes, so it is very important that you choose where you want the shape to go.

6. In the added circle, key **New**; in the related shape, key **New item**.

7. Rearrange the order of the shapes in the diagram. Select the circle labeled "New." From the SmartArt Tools Design tab, in the Create Graphic group, click the Right to Left button 🔁, and the diagram is displayed from right to left. Click the button again to return the diagram to the previous arrangement.

Figure 7-10
Adding SmartArt shapes

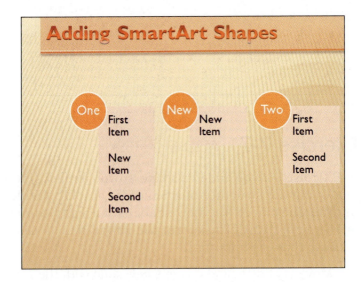

Exercise 7-8 CHANGE COLORS, APPLY SMARTART STYLES, AND RESET THE GRAPHIC

Using the Quick Styles feature is not the only way to change the appearance of a SmartArt layout. Many more options are available from the SmartArt Tools Design tab, in the SmartArt Styles group, as shown in Figure 7-11.

Figure 7-11
SmartArt Styles

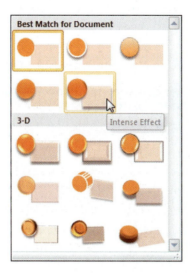

1. On slide 7 select the SmartArt layout. From the SmartArt Tools Design tab, in the SmartArt Styles group, click the More button ⧨ to see the gallery of SmartArt Styles arranged in two categories, Best Match for Document and 3-D. As you point to each thumbnail, you will see that effect applied to your diagram.

2. Choose **Intense Effect**.

3. With your SmartArt layout selected, from the SmartArt Tools Design tab, in the SmartArt Styles group, click the Change Colors button 🎨. Colors are arranged in eight categories: Primary Theme Colors, Colorful, and six Accent colors. The current color is selected, as shown in Figure 7-12.

Figure 7-12
Change Colors for a SmartArt layout

4. Point to different thumbnails in this gallery of colors, and consider the changes on your slide. Notice that, as you go down the list, colors change between the various accent colors in the presentation's design theme. Then as you go across, different line and shading treatments are used.

NOTE

As you work with diagrams, you will find the keyboard shortcuts listed in Table 7-2 helpful because they provide a quick way to move between shapes, select shapes, or select the text within the shapes.

5. Select the **Gradient Loop – Accent 5** color.

6. If you are not pleased with your change, it is easy to remove it. On the SmartArt Tools Design tab, in the Reset group, click the Reset Graphic button, and the original style of your layout is restored.

7. Update the handout footer text to *[your initials]*7-8.

8. Move to slide 1, and save the presentation as *[your initials]*7-8 in your Lesson 7 folder.

TABLE 7-2 Using the Keyboard to Navigate in SmartArt Graphics

Key	Result
Enter	Activated shape: Inserts a new text line.
Esc	Deactivates a selected shape.
F2	Toggles the current shape between being selected and activated.
← or →	Selected shape: Nudges the position of the shape left or right.
Shift+Tab	Selected shape: Moves to the previous shape. Activated shape: Inserts a tab at the insertion point.
Tab	Selected shape: Moves to the next shape. Activated shape: Inserts a tab at the insertion point.
↑ or ↓	Selected shape: Nudges the position of the shape up or down.

Preparing an Organization Chart

Organization charts are most commonly used to show a hierarchy such as the lines of authority or reporting relationships in a business. You start an organization chart in the same way as you start other SmartArt graphics, but it is important to consider superior and subordinate relationships.

Exercise 7-9   CREATE AN ORGANIZATION CHART

When you start a new organization chart, you begin with a default arrangement of five rectangular shapes. Each shape is positioned on a *level* in the chart, which indicates its position in the hierarchy. The top shape indicates the highest level (such as the president of a company) and shows a direct line down to the second level (such as the managers who report to the president). The shape that branches from the central line reflects a supporting position (such as an assistant to the president).

1. Insert a new slide after slide 7 that uses the **Title and Content** layout. Key the title **New Management Structure**.

2. In the content placeholder click the SmartArt button ⊞.

3. Choose the **Hierarchy** type; then double-click **Organization Chart**. A chart with five shapes appears, with text placeholders that show text in a large size. The text size will become smaller as you key text into the shapes.

4. Click the top shape in the chart. Notice the dashed outline that indicates the shape is activated, so you can key text.

5. Key **Julie Wolfe &**, press Enter, and key **Gus Irvinelli** to position the names on two lines. You will later format this text to fit on one line.

6. Press Enter to start a new line, and key **Co-owners**.

7. Press Esc to deactivate text editing. The shape now has a solid outline.

8. Press Tab to move to the first lower-level shape.

9. Key the following three items on three lines:

   Administration
   Michael Peters
   Administration Mgr

10. The text becomes smaller to fit in the shape. Press F2 to deactivate text editing.

11. Press Tab to move to the second shape on the lower level. Key the following items on three lines:

    Sales & Marketing
    Roy Olafsen
    Marketing Mgr

12. Press F2; then press Tab to move to the third shape, and key the following items on three lines:

    Operations
    Michele Jenkins
    Head Chef

13. Press F2; then press Tab to move to the shape that branches from the central line, and press Delete.

14. Click outside the SmartArt area to deactivate the organization chart, as shown in Figure 7-13.

UNIT 2   LESSON 7

Figure 7-13
Organization chart

Exercise 7-10   INSERT SUBORDINATE SHAPES

The organization of many companies changes frequently. You might need to promote, demote, or move organization chart shapes as the reporting structure changes or becomes more complex.

To expand an organization chart (see Figure 7-14), you can insert additional shapes of the following types:

- *Subordinate shapes.* Shapes that are connected to a superior shape (a shape on a higher level).

- *Coworker shapes.* Shapes that are connected to the same superior shape as another shape.

- *Assistant shapes.* Shapes that are usually placed below a superior shape and above subordinate shapes.

Figure 7-14
Structure of an
organization chart

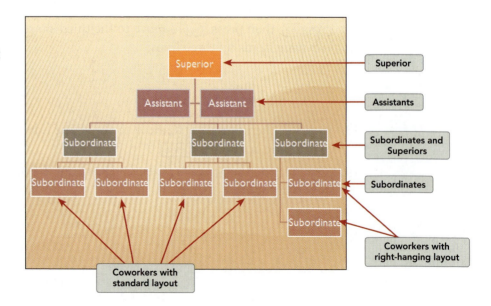

To add *subordinate shapes,* first select the shape that will be their superior and then, from the SmartArt Tools Design tab, in the Create Graphic group, click the Add Shape button 🔲.

1. Still working on slide 8, select the first shape on the second level, with the name "Michael Peters."

Figure 7-15
Adding organization chart shapes

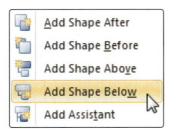

2. From the SmartArt Tools Design tab, in the Create Graphic group, click the Shape button 🔲 down arrow; then click **Add Shape Below**, as shown in Figure 7-15. A shape appears below the selected shape with a connecting line, and now the new shape is selected.

3. Click the Add Shape button 🔲 down arrow; then click **Add Shape Before**. Now two shapes show a reporting relationship to Michael Peters. They are currently shown with the **Right-Hanging Layout**. All the shapes automatically become smaller so that the chart will fit on the slide.

4. Repeat this process to add one shape under Roy Olafsen and three shapes under Michele Jenkins. Once again the shapes are resized to fit, but the text that has been entered is now too small to read. This will be corrected later.

NOTE

Both Add Shape After and Add Shape Before insert new shapes at the same level. Add Shape Above inserts a new shape in the level above, which would be a superior position. Add Shape Below inserts a new shape in the level below, which would be a subordinate position. Add Assistant inserts a new shape between levels.

Exercise 7-11   ADD ASSISTANT AND COWORKER SHAPES

Assistant shapes are used for positions that provide administrative assistance or other support. They are inserted below a selected shape but above the next-lower level.

Coworker shapes are inserted at the same level as the selected shape and report to the same superior as does the selected shape.

1. On slide 8, select the level 1 shape.

2. From the SmartArt Tools Design tab, in the Create Graphic group, click the Add Shape button 🔲, and choose **Add Assistant**. A new shape is inserted between levels 1 and 2.

3. Select the shape below Michael Peters to add another shape at the same level. From the SmartArt Tools Design tab, in the Create Graphic group, click the Add Shape button 🔲, and choose **Add Shape Before**. A new shape is inserted at the same level—it represents a coworker.

4. Repeat step 3 to add one more shape under Roy Olafsen.

5. Now increase the slide size so that you can more easily see the text. From the View tab, in the Zoom group, click the Zoom button 🔍, and check **90%**; then click **OK**.

6. Scroll on the enlarged slide to locate the assistant shape below the level 1 shape; key **Troy Scott**, press Enter, and then key **Assistant** so that this text fits on two text lines.

7. In the three shapes under Michael Peters, key the following employee information on two text lines in each shape. After the text is entered, press F2 or Esc to deactivate the shape and then press Tab to move to the next shape.

MIS	**Billing**	**HR**
Chuck Warden	**Sarah Conners**	**Chris Davis**

8. After keying the text in Chris Davis's shape, press Esc to deactivate the text shape. Press Tab one time to move to Roy Olafsen's shape, and press Tab to move to the first shape under Roy Olafsen.

9. In the two shapes under Roy Olafsen, key the following employee information:

Events	**Marketing**
Ian Mahoney	**Evan Johnson**

10. In the first two shapes under Michele Jenkins, key the following (leave the last shape blank):

Kitchen	**Purchasing**
Eric Dennis	**Jessie Smith**

11. From the View tab, in the Zoom group, click the Fit to Window button 🔳. Notice that the organization chart again adjusted the text to a smaller size, as shown in Figure 7-16. The text is too small to be readable when projected in a presentation. You will fix this with the changes you make in the next two exercises.

Figure 7-16
Organization chart with small text

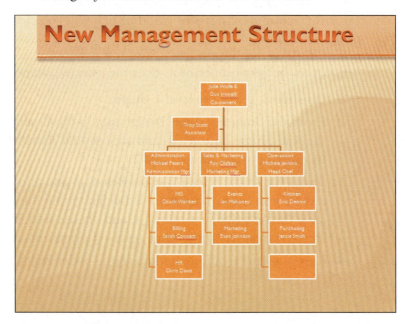

Exercise 7-12   CHANGE LAYOUT, DELETE SHAPES, AND REORDER SHAPES

The layout of the organization chart can be changed to show subordinates in a *standard* format or a *hanging indent* format. A shape can be repositioned to a higher level by promoting (moving up) or repositioned to a lower level by demoting (moving down). An entire group of connected shapes can be moved right or left. If you have more shapes than necessary, you can delete them at any time.

1. On slide 8, select the shape for Michael Peters. From the SmartArt Tools Design tab, in the Create Graphic group, click the Layout button, and choose **Standard**. The subordinate shapes below Michael Peters (coworkers) are now arranged side by side instead of in a vertical, hanging arrangement.

2. Select the blank subordinate shape below Michele Jenkins, and press Delete.

3. Select the shape for Eric Dennis, and click the Promote button. The shape moves up a level, and the connected shape moves with it. Click the Undo button.

4. Select Roy Olafsen's shape, click the Layout button, and choose **Standard**. Repeat this process to change the layout for Michele Jenkins's shape to **Standard**.

5. This arrangement communicates nicely the three levels of the organization, as shown in Figure 7-17; however, the text is very small. The next steps will rearrange the layout so that each shape can be a little larger.

Figure 7-17
Organization chart with standard layout

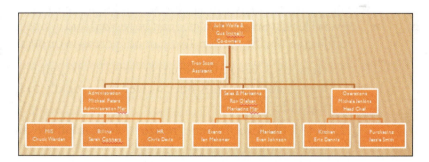

6. Select the shape for Michael Peters. From the SmartArt Tools Design tab, in the Create Graphic group, click the Layout button, and choose **Right Hanging**. Repeat this process to apply the **Right Hanging** indent to the other two level 2 shapes.

7. Select the shape of Sarah Conners, and click the Demote button. Now this shape is indented under Chuck Warden.

8. Select the shape of Evan Johnson, and click the Move Selection Up button ⬆ to move this shape above Ian Mahoney.

9. Select the shape of Eric Dennis, and click the Move Selection Down button ⬇ to move this shape below Jessie Smith.

10. Select the shape for Michael Peters, and click the Right to Left button ⇄. This entire branch of the chart is reordered to appear on the right, as shown in Figure 7-18.

Figure 7-18
Organization chart with hanging indent layout

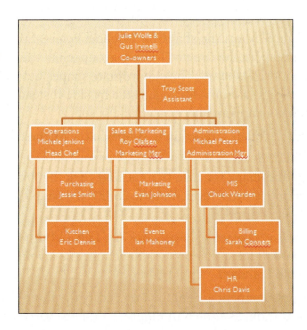

Exercise 7-13   CHANGE SHAPE SIZING AND STYLES

The entire SmartArt area can be made larger to accommodate charts with several levels. Selected shapes can be resized and connected shapes repositioned so that the text fits better. Text can be increased or decreased in size.

1. On slide 8, resize the SmartArt area by dragging its border to expand it horizontally on both sides as well as vertically to fill the open space on the slide.

2. Select the level 1 shape, resize it horizontally to make it wider, and then make both names fit on one line.

3. Select all three level 2 shapes, and resize horizontally and vertically to allow a little more room in each shape.

4. Select all of the chart's shapes, and increase the font size to 16 points and bold. Adjust the horizontal size of shapes if the text word-wraps.

5. Now spread apart the related shapes in the chart for easier reading. Select the Michael Peters shape and the related shapes below it. Hold Ctrl and press the right arrow → press about five times to move this branch to the right. The connecting lines automatically adjust.

6. Select the Michele Jenkins shape and the related shapes below it. Hold Ctrl and press the left arrow ← about five times to move this branch to the left.

7. With the SmartArt area selected, from the SmartArt Tools Design tab, in the SmartArt Styles group, click the Change Colors button, and select **Colorful – Accent Colors**.

8. You can also change the color of individual shapes. Select the Assistant shape; then from the SmartArt Tools Format tab, in the Shape Styles group, click the Shape Fill button, and choose a little lighter fill color but keep the text readable.

9. Select the entire SmartArt, and from the SmartArt Tools Design tab, in the SmartArt Styles group, examine the effect of different SmartArt Styles on the chart. Click the SmartArt Styles More button, and then choose the **Inset Effect** from the 3-D category, as shown in Figure 7-19.

10. Update the handout footer text to *[your initials]***7-13**.

11. Save the presentation as *[your initials]***7-13** in your Lesson 7 folder.

Figure 7-19
Completed
organization chart

Creating Other SmartArt Graphics

The eight types of PowerPoint SmartArt graphics offer many options to illustrate your thoughts in a visual way. This exercise will focus on three diagrams in the relationship category.

Exercise 7-14   CREATE A RADIAL DIAGRAM

A *radial diagram* starts with a central circle (level 1) and four circles (level 2) connected to and surrounding the center circle. You can insert as many additional circles as you need to illustrate your message.

1. Insert a new slide after slide 8 that uses the **Title and Content** layout. Key the title **New Customer Philosophy**.

2. From the content placeholder click the SmartArt button 📷.

3. Click the **Relationship** type; then double-click **Basic Radial**. A chart appears with four circle shapes that radiate from the center circle with text placeholders.

4. Click the center circle; then from the SmartArt Tools Design tab, in the Create Graphic group, click the Add Shape button 📷, and a new circle is added to the diagram. It becomes the selected circle.

5. With the new circle selected, press ⌦Delete to remove this new shape.

6. Click the center circle, and key **Customer**.

7. Think about your diagram's positioning as though you were referring to the face of a round clock. Click the top outer circle (12 o'clock position), and key the information shown under "12 o'clock" in Figure 7-20. Press Enter after the individual words so that the information appears on three text lines. (Because AutoCorrect capitalizes the words, you must make a correction to change the second and third words in each shape to lowercase.)

8. Click the circle at the 3 o'clock position, and key the corresponding text.

9. Working in a clockwise direction, key the remaining text shown in Figure 7-20 in the remaining outer circles.

Figure 7-20
Radial diagram text

12 o'clock	3 o'clock	6 o'clock	9 o'clock
Satisfy	Provide	Provide	Resolve
customer	courteous	excellent	problems
needs	service	quality	promptly

NOTE

If PowerPoint automatically capitalizes the second and third word in each circle, change the letters to lowercase. Automatic capitalization is caused by AutoCorrect. You can turn off this feature, if you wish, by following these steps: Click the **File** tab, choose **Options**, then choose **Proofing**. Click **AutoCorrect Options**, deselect **Capitalize first letter of sentences**, click **OK**, and then click **OK** again.

10. From the SmartArt Tools Design tab, in the SmartArt Styles group, click the Change Colors button 📷, and choose **Colored Fill – Accent 6**. Then click the SmartArt Styles More button 📷, and look at the effect of different options as you point to them. Choose the **Cartoon** style.

11. Drag the borders of the SmartArt area to increase the size of the diagram so that it fills the open space.

12. Choose the center shape; then from the SmartArt Tools Format tab, in the Shape Styles group, click the Shape Fill button and choose a darker shade of the shape fill color to emphasize the center, as shown in Figure 7-21.

Figure 7-21
Radial diagram

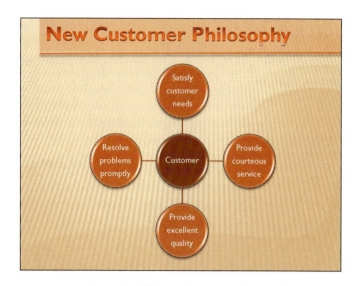

Exercise 7-15   CREATE A GEAR DIAGRAM

Gears have spokes that stick out from a round shape and lock with other gears to make them turn. The turning of each gear is dependent on the other gears. Therefore, the *gear diagram* communicates interlocking ideas that are each shown as shapes.

1. Insert a new slide after slide 9 that uses the **Title and Content** layout. Key the title **Interlocking Ideas**.

2. From the content placeholder, click the SmartArt button 📊.

3. Click the **Relationship** type, and then double-click **Gear**. A chart with three shapes and directional arrows appears. Key the text as shown in Figure 7-22.

4. From the SmartArt Tools Design tab, in the SmartArt Styles group, click the SmartArt Styles More button ⤓, and choose the **Sunset Scene** from the 3-D category.

5. Resize and reposition the SmartArt graphic so that it is balanced on the slide, with even spacing around the diagram.

Figure 7-22
Completed gear diagram

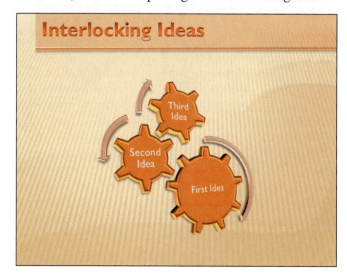

Exercise 7-16   INSERT A CONTINUOUS PICTURE LIST

The *continuous picture list* contains round placeholders for pictures and a horizontal arrow to communicate that the items shown represent interconnected information.

1. Insert a new slide after slide 10 using the **Title and Content** layout. Key the title **New Desserts**.

2. From the content placeholder click the SmartArt button .

3. Click the **Relationship** type, and then double-click **Continuous Picture List**. A chart appears with three shapes that each contain a small circle with a picture placeholder.

4. Click the first picture placeholder to access the **Insert Picture** dialog box. Navigate to your student files, select the **cake** picture, and click **Insert**. Or, if you prefer, you could double-click to insert the picture.

5. Repeat this process on the next two placeholders, inserting the **cookies** picture in the middle shape and the **strawberry** picture in the right shape.

6. Now key the following text below the pictures as shown in Figure 7-23, and the text will automatically resize:

   Fruit Cake Holiday Delight
   Oatmeal and Raisin Cookies
   Cream Cake and Strawberries

7. From the SmartArt Tools Design tab, in the SmartArt Styles group, click the More button ⊽, and select the **3-D, Polished** style.

8. Resize and reposition the SmartArt graphic on the slide.

9. Update the handout footer text to *[your initials]***7-16**.

10. Save the presentation as *[your initials]***7-16** in your Lesson 7 folder.

Figure 7-23
Continuous Picture
List

Changing SmartArt Graphics

Once a SmartArt graphic is created, the layout can easily be changed by selecting a different type of layout. However, the levels of your information may not translate well into some layouts. Shapes within the SmartArt area can also be repositioned by dragging them. SmartArt graphics can be converted to text or to shapes that can then be edited as drawing objects.

Exercise 7-17   CHANGE DIAGRAM LAYOUTS

At any time during the development of your SmartArt graphic, you can apply a different diagram layout. Level 1 information and level 2 information will be reformatted to fit the new layout, so the layout you choose must have matching levels to display all the text you entered.

1. Move to slide 3, and select it in the Slides and Outline pane. Press Ctrl+C to copy the slide; then move to slide 11, and press Ctrl+V to paste.

2. Now working on slide 12, select the SmartArt graphic; then from the SmartArt Tools Design tab, in the Layouts group, click on several different layouts to consider the different options that are available. Notice how the level 1 and level 2 information is arranged, and consider the emphasis that each level receives. The next three steps point out specific diagrams to try and what you should notice in each one.

>
> **NOTE**
>
> Because this is a list diagram, you see list layouts first. You could access all diagrams by clicking the All category.

3. Click **Table Hierarchy**. This layout does not distinguish between the levels; level 1 information is placed above level 2, but no color or lines are used to show any connecting effect or relationship between the levels.

4. Click **Grouped List**. Now it is easy to see that certain items relate to other items because the shapes used for level 1 create a "container" for the shapes used for level 2 information. This layout emphasizes level 2 text.

5. Click **Vertical Arrow List**. This layout clearly distinguishes between the two levels, and it works well for bulleted lists of information. The arrows that display level 2 information communicate that the level 2 information is an outgrowth of level 1. Click to apply this layout.

6. The fill color on the arrows blends too much with the slide background to be easily visible, so change the colors and the style to make the arrows stand out more. On the SmartArt Tools Design tab, in the SmartArt Styles group, click the Change Colors button ; then choose **Colorful Range – Accent Colors 5 to 6**. Click the SmartArt Style More button , and choose **Flat Scene** in the 3-D category.

7. Select the three arrows; then from the SmartArt Tools Format tab, in the Shape Styles group, click the Shape Fill button 🖌, and choose **White, Background 1, Darker 15%**. Now the arrows still blend with the theme design, but they are easier to see, as shown in Figure 7-24.

8. Resize the diagram to fill the slide.

Figure 7-24
Diagram with changed layout

Exercise 7-18   CHANGE THE ORIENTATION OF DIAGRAMS

Because of the particular information a diagram must contain, the information may need to be displayed in a different orientation than the original SmartArt shape provides. For example, instead of a top-to-bottom orientation, it might need to be left to right.

1. From the Slides and Outline pane, select slide 8 and copy it. Move to the last slide in your presentation, and paste the slide.

2. Now on slide 13, select the SmartArt graphic. From the SmartArt Tools Design tab, in the Layouts group, click the More button ▾, and choose the **Horizontal Hierarchy** layout. The shapes are now positioned horizontally as in a decision-tree diagram.

3. While the shapes are still connected, the sizes should be adjusted on some of them.

4. Select the three shapes for Michael Peters, Roy Olafsen, and Michele Jenkins. Resize them horizontally and vertically to increase the shape size so that all text prints on three lines and there is sufficient space above and below the text in each shape.

5. Select the MIS shape, all the ones below it, and the Billing shape. Resize these shapes horizontally so that each name fits on one text line, as shown in Figure 7-25.

6. Increase the vertical size of the Julie Wolfe & Gus Irvinelli shape.

Figure 7-25
Diagram with different orientation

Exercise 7-19 CONVERT SMARTART GRAPHICS TO TEXT AND SHAPES

If you need to use only the text of a diagram, you can convert a SmartArt graphic to text and then a bulleted list will be created to replace the diagram. Some diagrams convert well to bulleted lists; others will require more editing to create usable lists.

If you convert to shapes, the diagram becomes a drawing object that can be ungrouped and edited just as any other shape can. Once the shape conversion is done, however, the diagram cannot be edited as a SmartArt graphic.

1. From the Slides and Outline pane, select slide 12 and copy it. Move to slide 13, and paste the slide.

2. Now on slide 14 select the SmartArt diagram. From the SmartArt Tools Design tab, in the Reset group, click the Convert button ; then choose **Convert to Text**. The text is changed to a bulleted list showing two levels.

3. Click Undo to return this text to the previous diagram.

4. With the diagram selected, from the SmartArt Tools Design tab, in the Reset group, click the Convert button again, and then choose **Convert to Shapes**. Now the diagram is a grouped set of shapes.

5. From the Drawing Tools Format tab, in the Arrange group, click the Group button ⊞▾, and choose **Ungroup**. Now all the diagram parts are separate shapes.

6. Select the three shapes on the left. From the Drawing Tools Format tab, in the Shape Styles group, click the More button ▾, and click **Intense Effect – Orange, Accent 6**.

7. Change the alignment on these shapes to left.

8. Reposition the three arrows by moving them under the rectangles so that the bullet does not show before each item.

Figure 7-26
Diagram with changed layout

9. With the three arrows selected, from the Home tab, in the Paragraph group, click the Align Text button ▤; then click **Middle**.

10. Check the positioning of all six parts for even spacing on the slide.

11. Update the handout footer text to *[your initials]*7-19.

12. Save the presentation as *[your initials]*7-19 in your Lesson 7 folder. Close the presentation and submit your work.

Lesson 7 Summary

- SmartArt graphics are used to present information in a visual manner.
- SmartArt graphics are organized by eight different types that include a wide variety of layouts such as organization charts, radial diagrams, list diagrams, and relationship diagrams.
- The SmartArt Design tab has command buttons for inserting shapes and modifying the predefined layouts. Shapes can be added and removed.
- List layouts provide an alternative to listing information in a bulleted list because concise text can be placed on shapes that help to graphically communicate topics and subtopics.
- Process diagrams show a sequence of events or the progression of workflow.
- Cycle diagrams communicate a continuous or ongoing process.
- Hierarchy diagrams are used to depict a hierarchical structure, showing who reports to whom and who is responsible for what function or task.
- Pyramid diagrams show interconnected or proportional relationships.
- Relationship diagrams contain interconnected shapes that reflect relationships in some way.
- Matrix diagrams display two axes in related quadrants that emphasize the whole or the individual parts.
- An organization chart is a type of hierarchy chart in a tree structure, branching out to multiple divisions in each lower level.
- When an organization chart shape is promoted, it moves up a level. When a chart shape is demoted, it moves down a level.
- The SmartArt Text pane provides a quick way to enter text that labels SmartArt shapes.
- List diagrams can show both level 1 and level 2 information, but text must be concise for easy reading.
- Text entered in SmartArt shapes automatically resizes to fit the shape; if shapes are increased in size, the text they contain is also increased in size.
- An existing bulleted list can be converted to a SmartArt graphic.
- Quick Styles provide choices for color and effect changes such as outlines, beveling, and shadows that can be applied to any selected shape.
- SmartArt Styles consist of predefined effects that work well together for diagrams.
- An illusion of depth is created with 3-D style options.
- Shapes can be resized and repositioned within the SmartArt area.
- The Change Colors option provides many possible variations of theme colors.

- If color changes made to a SmartArt graphic are unacceptable, the colors can be reset to their original colors.
- Several layouts in the List type have placeholders for pictures.

LESSON 7		Command Summary
Feature	Button	Ribbon
Change back to original formatting		SmartArt Tools Design, Reset group, Reset Graphic
Change organization chart layout		SmartArt Tools Design, Create Graphic group, Layout
Change SmartArt Style		SmartArt Tools Design, SmartArt Styles group, More
Change text from a bulleted list to a graphical layout		Home, Paragraph group, Convert to SmartArt
Change the color of a selected shape		SmartArt Tools Format, Shape Styles group, Shape Fill
Create a graphical list or diagram on a slide		Insert, Illustrations group, SmartArt Graphic
Create additional shapes within a diagram		SmartArt Tools Design, Create Graphic group, Add Shape
Decrease the level of a selected bulleted item or shape		SmartArt Tools Design, Create Graphic group, Demote
Increase the level of a selected bulleted item or shape		SmartArt Tools Design, Create Graphic group, Promote
Pick from choices for shape color and effects		Home, Drawing group, Quick Styles
Rearrange layout direction or sequencing of shapes		SmartArt Tools Design, Create Graphic group, Right to Left
Select from variations of theme colors		SmartArt Tools Design, SmartArt Styles group, Change Colors

Please visit our Online Learning Center, *www.lessonapproach2010.com*, where you will find the following review materials:

- **Concepts Review**

    True/False Questions

    Short Answer Questions

    Critical Thinking Questions

- **Skills Review**

    Review Exercises that target single skills

    Lesson Applications

    Review Exercises that challenge students by testing multiple skills in each exercise

- **On Your Own**

    Open-ended exercises that require students to synthesize multiple skills and apply creativity and problem-solving as they would in a real world business situation

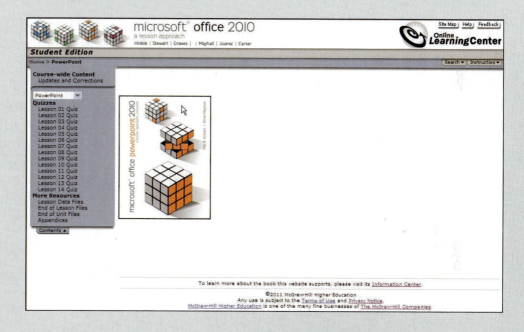

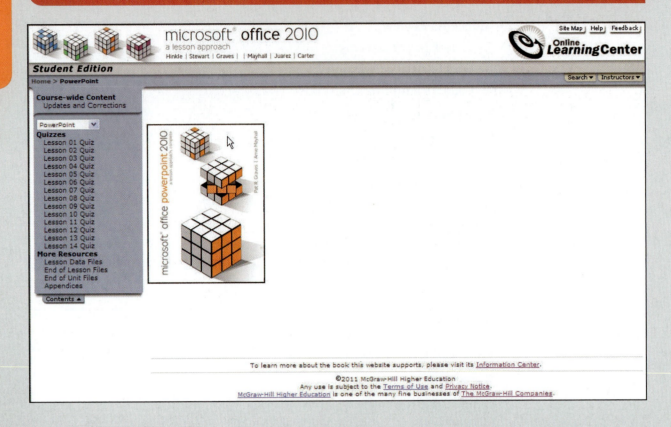

Please visit our Online Learning Center, *www.lessonapproach2010.com*, where you will find Unit Applications review materials.

Site Map | Help | Feedback

Online LearningCenter

microsoft® **office** 2010
a lesson approach
Hinkle | Stewart | Graves | | Mayhall | Juarez | Carter

Student Edition

Home > **PowerPoint**

Search ▾ | Instructors ▾

Course-wide Content
Updates and Corrections

PowerPoint ⌄

Quizzes
Lesson 01 Quiz
Lesson 02 Quiz
Lesson 03 Quiz
Lesson 04 Quiz
Lesson 05 Quiz
Lesson 06 Quiz
Lesson 07 Quiz
Lesson 08 Quiz
Lesson 09 Quiz
Lesson 10 Quiz
Lesson 11 Quiz
Lesson 12 Quiz
Lesson 13 Quiz
Lesson 14 Quiz

More Resources
Lesson Data Files
End of Lesson Files
End of Unit Files
Appendices

Contents ▴

microsoft® office powerpoint 2010
a lesson approach, complete
Pat R. Graves | Amie Mayhall

To learn more about the book this website supports, please visit its Information Center.

©2011 McGraw-Hill Higher Education
Any use is subject to the Terms of Use and Privacy Notice.
McGraw-Hill Higher Education is one of the many fine businesses of The McGraw-Hill Companies.

Microsoft® Office Access 2010

A Lesson Approach, Complete

There is more to learning a database management program like Microsoft Access than simply pressing keys. Students need to know how to use Access in a real-world situation. That is why all the lessons in this book relate to everyday business tasks that a database manager would perform.

As students work through the lessons, they are guided through routine business tasks as if they are employed as student interns for EcoMed Services, Inc., a fictional light located in Kansas City, Missouri.

EcoMed Services, Inc.

EcoMed Services, Inc. is a premier leader in the environmentally friendly distribution of lighting needs to medical facilities throughout the United States. The company's primary mission is to maximize effective ecology solutions for our medical clients without compromise. The Company was founded in 1972, the year before the United States experienced its first energy crisis, and has steadily grown to partnering with over 150 medical facilities ranging from small critical access clinics to large medical facilities with over 2000 patient beds.

The company stocks over three hundred standard and specialized light bulbs including diagnostic, surgical, utility-indoor and utility-outdoor. The well-established business relationships with our 29 vendors ensure that the company will have the type and shape of bulb that its customers need. Currently EcoMed Services stocks over 15 different common and specialized bulb shapes including: circuline, spiral, bayonet, canister, dish, mini-spiral, twin-tube, triple-tube, quadruple-tube, single-ended tube, and double-ended tube.

Ivon Gonzalez, the company's president and founder, promises that that the company's knowledgeable and professional employees will always meet or exceed its customers' expectations. Ms. Gonzalez has made it a company priority to Invest in Information management solutions including improving the database functions that support the company's needs. The company recently starting hiring student interns to help manage and update the Access database that has been supporting critical inventory, sales, and payroll functions of the company.

Unit 1

UNDERSTANDING ACCESS DATABASES

Lesson 1

Getting Started with a Database

OBJECTIVES *After completing this lesson, you will be able to:*

1. Identify basic database structure.
2. Work with a Microsoft Access database.
3. Identify components of Access.
4. Navigate Access recordsets.
5. Modify a datasheet's appearance.
6. Save and print a recordset.
7. Manage Access files.

Estimated Time: 1½ hours

Databases are part of everyday business. In this book, the database with which you will work involves a Case Study about EcoMed Services, Inc., a fictional company that sells illumination supplies to hospitals and medical centers. This book explains database usage and development as if you were a new student intern recently employed by the company.

EcoMed Services, Inc., uses several databases to take care of its business needs, such as payroll, shipping, and billing. Just like you, most student interns who work at EcoMed Services are somewhat familiar with databases through their school. You probably already know that your school uses databases to keep track of what courses you've taken, where you live, when you graduate, how to best contact you, and other important academic information. Just as you've learned to use your school's databases through your daily interactions, you will learn about EcoMed's business procedures and databases.

A *database* is a logically organized collection of data. The most common type of database in use today is relational. Other types of databases include flat, hierarchical, network, and dimensional. If you are familiar with spreadsheets such as Microsoft Excel, you have an understanding of a flat database. Excel has incorporated many simple database commands to be used in simple database structures. Microsoft Access creates relational databases that are much more complex than Excel spreadsheets.

Identifying Basic Database Structure

Microsoft Access follows the relational model for its design. Access databases are organized by major objects. In a relational database, all data are stored in tables. A *table* is the major database object that stores all data in a subject-based list of rows and columns. A database table can look similar to a table displayed in a spreadsheet program, or it can appear different.

Tables are made up of records and fields. A record is a complete set of related data about one entity or activity. A *record* is displayed as a row in a table. Examples of records include a phone directory listing, a sales transaction, or a bank deposit.

Figure 1-1
Data organization

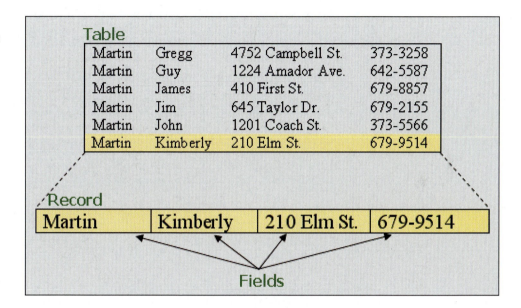

Records are composed of related fields. A *field* is the smallest storage element that contains an individual data element within a record. A field is displayed as a column in a table. A group of related fields make up a record. A group of related records make up a table, and a group of related tables make up a relational model database.

Figure 1-2
Data hierarchy

Although all data are stored in tables, often you use other objects to locate, organize, and modify recordsets. A recordset is a Microsoft object–oriented data structure consisting of grouped records. A *recordset* can be as small as a single field or as large as two or more combined tables.

Major objects in an Access database include the following:

- Tables store data about people, activities, items, and events. A table consists of records made up of fields. The information in a table appears in rows (records) and columns (fields), similar to an Excel worksheet.

- Queries display and organize data depending on the question being queried. You can specify criteria or conditions to show records and fields from one or more tables. You can also create queries to perform actions.

- Forms display data on a screen in user-friendly formats. Forms make data entry and editing simpler. With a form, you can view, add, and edit fields and records in a table.

- Reports organize and format data to be used as printable documents. Reports are professional looking, formal documents that display information, usually derived from database queries.

Figure 1-3
Major object
orientation

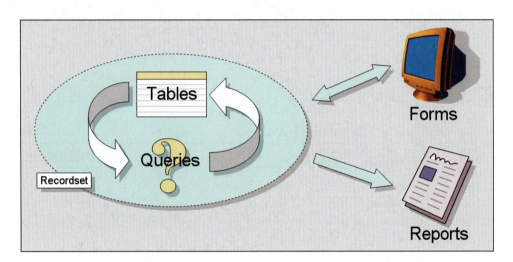

A recordset is most often displayed as either a form or a report. A form is a major database object used to display information in an attractive, easy-to-read screen format. Forms can be used to display, add, edit, or delete record-sets. A report is a major database object used to display information in a printable page format. Reports can only display recordsets.

Working with a Microsoft Access Database

Because of the complexity of a database, Access limits certain file operations that are available for other applications, such as Word or Excel. Access does not have the "Save As" file command. When a database is open, you cannot move or rename the file. Therefore, before you begin working with a database, you must place the file in a suitable storage location. The storage medium in which the database file is located (such as a USB flash drive) must provide enough space to allow the database to grow, and you must have rights to modify the file in that location. Some storage locations at your school or at EcoMed do not allow an average user to modify files. These locations can only be fully used by a person with administrative rights.

Exercise 1-1   MANAGE A DATABASE

At the beginning of each lesson, you will be required to copy the student lesson files onto a USB flash drive or a location where you have rights to copy, rename, and modify the database. The student lesson files are located online or are available from your instructor. The files you need for a lesson can be found in the folder that matches the lesson number. For example, in the first lesson, you will need the folder **Lesson 01**, which contains the database **EcoMed-01**. If you need help copying files to your computer, ask your instructor or lab manager for assistance.

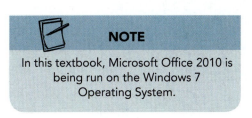

NOTE

In this textbook, Microsoft Office 2010 is being run on the Windows 7 Operating System.

1. Locate the **Lesson 01** folder.

2. Double-click the folder **Lesson 01** to see its content.

3. Right-click the file **EcoMed-01** and from the shortcut menu, and choose **Copy**.

4. Right-click an unused part of the folder and from the shortcut menu, choose **Paste**.

5. Right-click the new file and from the shortcut menu, choose **Rename**. Rename the file *[your initials]*-EcoMed-01.

6. Right-click *[your initials]*-**EcoMed-01** and from the shortcut menu, choose **Properties**. Make certain that the **Read-only** attribute check box is not checked.

Figure 1-4
Properties dialog box

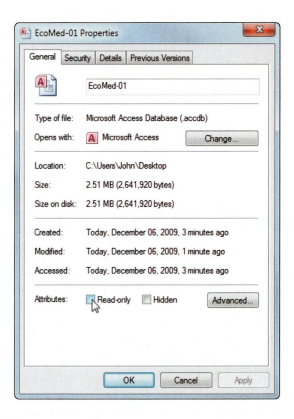

7. Click **OK** to close the dialog box. Close the Windows Explorer.

Exercise 1-2 START A DATABASE

The first screen that appears after starting Access is Getting Started with Microsoft Office Access. From this screen, you can create a new database, open an existing database, or view featured content from Microsoft Office Online.

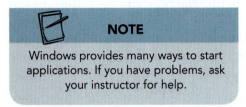

NOTE

Windows provides many ways to start applications. If you have problems, ask your instructor for help.

1. Click the **Start** button and choose **All Programs**.
2. Click on the **Microsoft Office** folder and choose **Microsoft Office Access 2010** to start Access in the Backstage.

Figure 1-5
Access Backstage

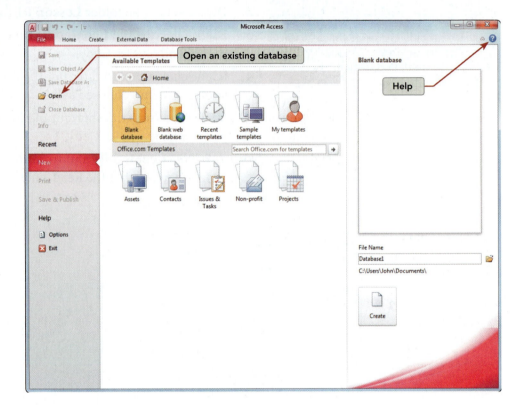

Exercise 1-3 OPEN A DATABASE

By double-clicking on the file icon of a database, you open it in the default mode. For most databases, the default mode is Shared. Shared mode is a method of opening a database in which multiple users may modify the file's data at the same time. In addition to Shared mode, Access databases can be opened in Read-only, Exclusive use, and Exclusive Read-only.

At most locations such as your school or EcoMed, each time you open a database, a security alert displays on the Message Bar. The Message Bar alerts you that the database may contain malicious code. Because all Access databases contain program code, this message normally displays. If you know that the database you are opening does not contain malicious code, enable the contents. After you enable the contents, you will be able to view and modify the contents of the database.

1. Click **Open** 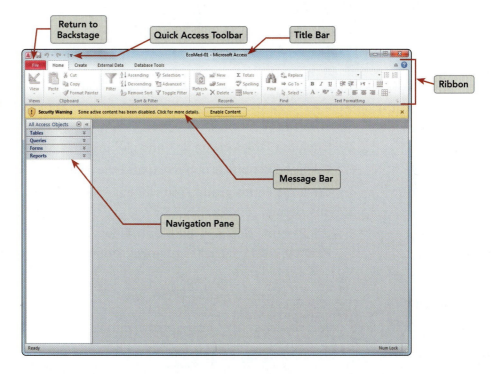 on the left of the screen.

2. Locate the folder **Lesson 01**. Select the file *[your initials]*-**EcoMed-01** and click **Open**.

3. In the Message Bar, a **Security Warning** message states that certain content is disabled. Click **Enable Content** to continue.

Identifying Components of Access

As with most Microsoft Office applications, in Access you will use Backstage View to print and manage most file operations. You will use command tabs and ribbons to complete specific tasks. The commands in each ribbon are organized by command groups. These groups are organized by command category.

In Access, you will use the Navigation Pane to control major database objects. The Navigation Pane is the rectangular area on the left side of the database window. The Navigation Pane organizes major database objects. When you become more familiar with general database functions, you will be able to use the Navigation Pane to organize database objects by business function such as payroll, inventory, or accounts receivable. All major database objects are accessed through the Navigation Pane.

Figure 1-6
Getting Started
window
EcoMed-01.accdb

Exercise 1-4 MANIPULATE THE NAVIGATION PANE

The Navigation Pane displays the major database objects. Microsoft Access allows you to organize major objects by categories and groups. You can open an object by double-clicking on the object or by right-clicking on the object and selecting Open from the shortcut menu.

The EcoMed Services, Inc., database organizes objects by the category Object Type and grouped by All Tables. Access allows you to change the layout of the Navigation Pane.

1. In the **Navigation Pane**, click the **Tables** group to expand the group and show all the tables in this database.

Figure 1-7
Navigation Pane
EcoMed-01.accdb

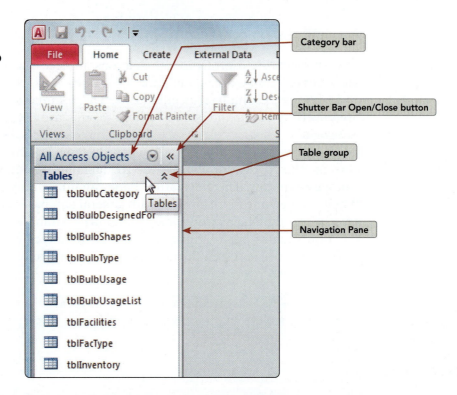

2. Click the **Tables** group again to collapse the group.
3. Click the **Reports** group to expand the group.
4. Click the **Forms** group. You can have multiple groups expanded at any time.
5. Click on the Category bar's drop-down arrow and select **Tables and Related Views**. Objects are now grouped by related major objects.

Figure 1-8
Navigation Pane
options
EcoMed-01.accdb

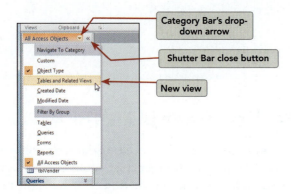

6. Click on the Category bar's drop-down arrow and select **Object Type** to return the **Navigation Pane** to its original layout.

7. Click the **Shutter Bar** button « to collapse the **Navigation Pane**. This action allows you to see more data on the screen.

8. Click the **Shutter Bar** button » to expand the **Navigation Pane**.

Exercise 1-5   EXPLORE TABS, RIBBONS AND GROUPS

Access uses tabs, ribbons, and groups, similar to other Microsoft Office applications. Some Access commands are the same as in Word and Excel. Other commands are unique to Access. Hovering over a command displays its ScreenTip. A *ScreenTip* is the name of or information regarding a specific object. This information can include images, shortcut keys, and descriptions.

When you click on a command tab, a unique set of command groups will appear in the ribbon. A *command group* is a collection of logically organized commands.

1. In the command tab **Home**, in the command group **Clipboard**, you will find the **Cut** button ✂. Hover your mouse pointer over this command to display its ScreenTip.

Figure 1-9
Viewing ScreenTips
EcoMed-01.accdb

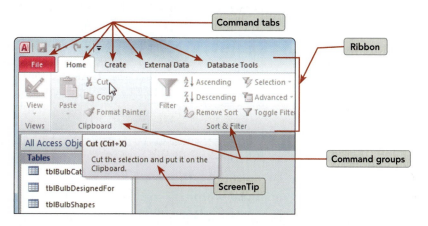

2. In the command tab **Create**, in the command group **Forms**, hover your mouse pointer over the **Form** button. Read the ScreenTip.

3. Click the **Home** command tab.

Exercise 1-6   OPEN AND CLOSE MAJOR OBJECTS

EcoMed Services, Inc., uses the internationally accepted Leszynski Naming Convention. The Leszynski Naming Convention is a method of naming objects that emphasizes the use of three-letter prefixes to identify the type of object. This naming convention does not allow the use of spaces or underscores. Although Access does not require the Leszynski Naming Convention to be applied, this convention is commonly used by software developers and programmers worldwide.

TABLE 1-1 Leszynski Naming Convention for Major Objects*

Prefix	Object Type	Example
tbl	Table	**tblBulbType**
qry	Query	**qryInvShort**
frm	Form	**frmInventory**
rpt	Report	**rptInvByVender**

*For a comprehensive list of control prefixes, see Appendix B-1 (Please see the Online Learning Center, www.mhhe.com/lessonapproach2010).

1. In the **Navigation Pane**, verify the **Tables** group is expanded.

2. Double-click the table **tblInventory** to open it. The table that contains the inventory's information is now open.

Figure 1-10
Open a table
EcoMed-01.accdb
tblInventory

3. Click the **Close** button ⊠ to close the table **tblInventory**.

4. In the **Navigation Pane**, collapse the **Tables** group.

5. Expand the **Queries** group, right-click the query **qryManageType**, and select **Open** from the shortcut menu.

6. Right-click the document tab for **qryManageType**, then select **Close** ⌧ from the shortcut menu.

Exercise 1-7 EXPLORE DATASHEET AND DESIGN VIEWS

In Access, each major database object has multiple views. The view that allows you to see a recordset organized similarly to an Excel spreadsheet is called Datasheet View. A *Datasheet View* ⊞ is a screen view used to display data in rows and columns. Records are displayed as rows, and fields are displayed as columns. Tables, queries, forms, and reports can be displayed in Datasheet View.

In addition to the Datasheet View, most major objects can be displayed in Design View. A *Design View* ⊠ is a screen view used to modify the structure of a major object. Switching between different views can be completed by:

- Selecting, from the **Home** command tab, in the **Views** control group, the option arrow for the **View** button.
- Using the **View Shortcut** button (lower right corner of the screen).
- Right-clicking the object and selecting the view.

1. In the **Queries** group of the **Navigation Pane**, double-click **qryManageContacts** to open the query in **Datasheet View**.

2. On the command tab **Home**, in the command group **Views**, click the bottom half of the **View** spilt button and select **Design View**. In this view, you can see the table that is used to create this query.

Figure 1-11
Switching views
EcoMed-01.accdb
qryManageContacts

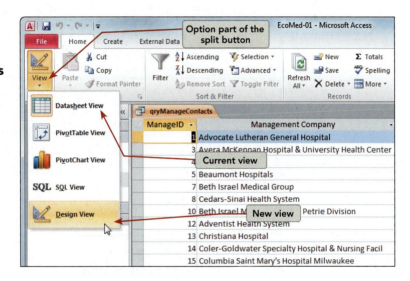

3. Right-click the document tab for the query, then select **Datasheet View**.

4. In the **Navigation Pane**, expand the **Tables** group.

5. Double-click **tblVender** to open the table in **Datasheet View**.

6. Right-click the document tab for the table, then select **Design View**. This view is where you define the structure of the table.

7. Right-click the document tab for the table, then select **Close All**. This action will close all open documents.

8. In the **Navigation Pane**, collapse both the **Tables** and **Queries** groups.

Navigating Access Recordsets

Now that you know how to navigate through the major objects in the **EcoMed-01** database, you now can learn how to navigate through records. Because most employees are familiar with Excel, you will first learn to edit data through Datasheet View.

Datasheet View has two modes: edit mode and navigation mode. *Edit Mode* is the mode in which changes to the content of a field can be made and the insertion point is visible. The insertion point looks like an I-beam. *Navigation Mode* is the mode in which an entire field is selected and the insertion point is not visible.

You will first learn to navigate around large datasheets by using the scroll bars, navigation buttons, and keyboard shortcuts. These procedures will be very similar to the procedures used in Excel.

Exercise 1-8   USE NAVIGATION BUTTONS IN A TABLE

In navigation mode, you can move between fields by using the keyboard shortcuts or record navigation buttons. A *Record navigation button* is an icon that moves the pointer within a recordset to the next, previous, first, or last record. The record navigation buttons are located on the navigation bar near the bottom of the window.

1. Expand the **Tables** group. Double-click the table **tblBulbUsageList** to open it. By default, the first record, first field, is selected.

Figure 1-12
Navigation buttons
**EcoMed-01.accdb
tblBulbUsageList**

2. In the Navigation Bar, click the Next Record button ▶ once. The **List ID** for the second record is highlighted.

3. Click the Previous Record button ◀ to return to the previous record.

4. Click the Last Record button ▶| to move to the last record in the table.

5. Click in the Current Record box. Delete the number in the box, key **75**, and press Enter. The pointer moves to the seventy-fifth record.

6. Right-click the document tab for the table, then select **Close**. Collapse the **Tables** group.

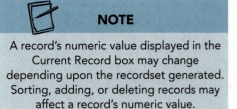

NOTE

A record's numeric value displayed in the Current Record box may change depending upon the recordset generated. Sorting, adding, or deleting records may affect a record's numeric value.

Exercise 1-9   USE NAVIGATION SHORTCUT KEYS IN A QUERY

Just as in a table's Datasheet View, you can use both the navigation buttons and keyboard shortcuts to navigate through a recordset. Often using the mouse seems the easiest for beginners. As you become more comfortable editing database information, using the keyboard shortcuts can be a faster method for entering and correcting data. You should use the method that works best for you.

1. Expand the **Queries** group. Double-click **qryManageContacts** to open it in **Datasheet View**.
2. Press Ctrl + End to move to the last field in the last record.
3. Press Home to move to the first field in the current record.
4. Press Ctrl + Home to move to the first field in the first record.
5. Press End to move to the last field in the current record.
6. Press ↓ to move to the last field of the second record.
7. Right-click the document tab for the table, then select **Close** and collapse the **Queries** group.

TABLE 1-2 Keyboard Shortcuts

Action	Shortcut
Move down one screen	PageDown
Move to the current field in the first record	Ctrl + ↑
Move to the current field in the last record	Ctrl + ↓
Move to the current field in the next record	↓
Move to the current field in the previous record	↑
Move to the first field in the current record	Home
Move to the first field in the first record	Ctrl + Home
Move to the last field in the current record	End
Move to the last field in the last record	Ctrl + End
Move to the next field	Tab or →
Move to the previous field	Shift + Tab or ←
Move up one screen	PageUp
Place the pointer in the Specific Record Box	F5
Save record changes	Shift + Enter

Modifying Datasheet Appearance

Not everyone likes seeing data in default view. Depending on the department at EcoMed, you may need to modify how the database looks. Although the data will remain the same, their appearance can be customized for each user. You can change the appearance of an Access datasheet very similarly to how you would change the appearance of an Excel worksheet. You can hide, display, and resize columns as well as rows.

You also can use formatting tools to change the appearance of text for the data displayed. Although the Datasheet View is similar in both Excel and

Access, in Access, format settings globally affect all text in every column and row. In Excel you can format individual cells, rows, and columns. Some commands, such as bold, underline, and italics, apply to the entire datasheet. Other commands, such as align left, center, and align right, can be applied to selected fields in the datasheet. Later you will learn to use Reports and Forms to better control the appearance of data.

Exercise 1-10   HIDE AND UNHIDE COLUMNS

EcoMed is a large company with large amounts of data. Some of the tables in its database contain many fields. When a table contains more fields than can be viewed on a single screen, you must scroll horizontally through the window to see all the information contained in a single record. To reduce the number of fields shown per record, you can hide columns within the datasheet.

1. Expand the **Tables** group. Double-click the table **tblFacilities** to open it. There are 17 fields in this table.

2. Click on the column header for the field **Facility Type** and drag through **Management Type**. The two selected columns are highlighted.

3. Right-click on the column header for the field **Management Type** and select **Hide Fields**.

Figure 1-13
Selecting multiple columns
EcoMed-01.accdb tblFacilities

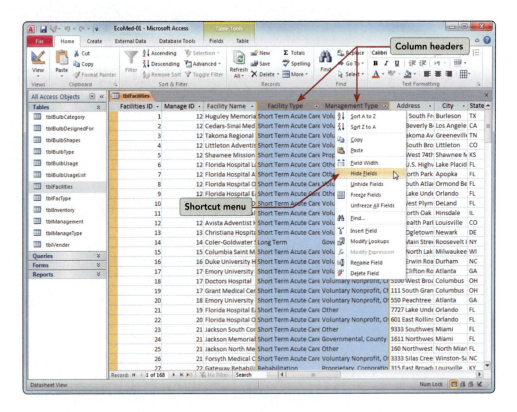

4. Right-click on the column header for the field **Facility Name** and select **Unhide Fields**.

5. Click the check boxes for the fields **Regions** and **Web Site** to remove their checkmarks. This dialog box can be used to hide and unhide fields.

NOTE

When you change the appearance or design of a major database object, Access prompts you to save the changes.

6. Click **Close**.

7. Right-click the document tab for the table, then select **Close**. A dialog box appears, prompting you to save the changes to the table. Click **Yes** to accept the changes.

Exercise 1-11 CHANGE COLUMN WIDTHS AND ROW HEIGHTS

By default, all columns in a datasheet are the same width. You can change the width of each column to optimize your view of the data in each field or to see the entire column title for each field. You also can make columns narrower if too much blank space is included.

Similarly to adjusting column widths, you can adjust row heights in Datasheet View. Although column widths can be set individually, row heights cannot. In Datasheet View, the row height is a global setting that applies to all rows in the entire datasheet.

1. Double-click the table **tblFacilities** to reopen it.

2. Place the pointer on the vertical border between column headers for **Facility Name** and **Address**. Notice that the pointer changes to a vertical bar between a two-headed arrow. This bar is the resize pointer.

Figure 1-14
Resize a column
EcoMed-01.accdb
tblFacilities

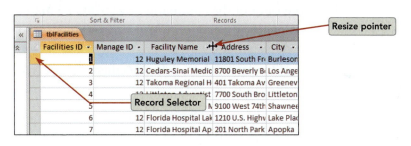

3. Drag the pointer to the right approximately three inches to allow enough space so the complete facility name is displayed for each record.

NOTE

The Best Fit command will widen a column based on the widest content visible but not the widest content in the column, like the same command in Excel.

TIP

You can save the changes to objects by using the keyboard shortcut, Quick Access toolbar, shortcut menu, or the Save dialog box.

4. Right-click the column header **Address**, and select **Field Width** from the menu.

5. In the **Column Width** dialog box, click **Best Fit**.

6. Right-click on the record selector for the first row.

7. From the shortcut menu, select **Row Height**.

8. In the **Row Height** dialog box, key **30** and click **OK**. Notice that all rows are now taller.

9. Right-click on the record selector for any record and select **Row Height**.

10. Click the **Standard Height** check box and click **OK**.

11. Press Ctrl + S to save the changes to the table.

Exercise 1-12   USE THE FONT COMMAND GROUP

You can increase the readability of data by applying specific format commands from the Font command group. Font commands, such as bold, underline, and italics, apply to the entire datasheet. Other commands, such as align left, center, and align right, can be applied to selected fields in the datasheet.

EcoMed allows some latitude of individual choices when displaying data. However, certain standards are maintained to reduce clerical errors when entering or editing data. Decimal numbers are aligned right. Short whole numbers can be aligned either right or centered. Long text is aligned left. Short text such as a title can be aligned either right or centered.

1. In the command group **Text Formatting**, hover your mouse pointer over the word **Calibri**. The ScreenTip states that this is the Font command.

2. Click the Font drop-down arrow and select **Microsoft Sans Serif**. The font has been applied to the entire datasheet.

3. The command to the right of Font is Font Size. Change the Font Size to **10**.

4. Place the resize pointer on the vertical border between column header for **Facility Name** and **Address**.

5. Double-click to automatically adjust the column width of **Facility Name**.

6. Select the field **Manage ID** by clicking its column header. Click the Center button 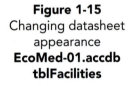. Only one field has been affected.

7. To the right of the command group **Text Formatting** is a button called Alternate Row Color ▦. Click its drop-down arrow to show the available colors.

8. In the **Standard Colors**, select **Medium Gray 2** (row 3, column 3) as the alternate color.

Figure 1-15
Changing datasheet appearance
EcoMed-01.accdb
tblFacilities

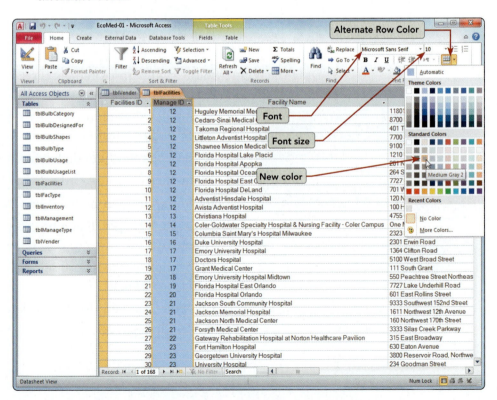

9. Right-click the document tab for the table **tblFacilities** and select **Save** 🖫.

10. Right-click the document tab for the table **tblFacilities** and select **Close** 🗙.

11. In the **Navigation Pane**, collapse the **Tables** group.

Saving and Printing a Recordset

To reduce paper waste, EcoMed has established best practices when printing. As an employee, you should follow these best practices. These practices include the following: (1) create electronic copies rather than paper copies, (2) preview all pages documents before printing, and (3) send documents as e-mail attachments. When possible, employees are asked to save electronic PDF or XPS files rather than printing to paper.

Any element in Access that can be printed can also be saved as a PDF or XPS file. *XPS* is the file extension used by a XML Paper Specification (XPS) file format that preserves document formatting and enables file sharing of printable documents. *PDF* is the file extension used by a Portable Document Format (PDF) for document exchange originally created by Adobe Systems in 1993 and released as an open standard in 2008.

The PDF or XPS format ensures that when the file is viewed online or is printed, it retains the original format without the viewer needing Access.

Exercise 1-13　PRINT A QUERY

If you are certain that you need to print an object, you have four methods of printing. These methods are:

- Click the **File** tab, from the **Print** option, choose **Quick Print** 🖶.

- Click the **File** tab, from the **Print** option, choose **Print** 🖶.

- Click the **File** tab, from the **Print** option, choose **Print Preview** 🔍. Click **Print** 🖶.

- Press Ctrl+P.

When you use the **Print** button 🖶 or the keyboard method, the **Print** dialog box displays to allow you to change print options. When you click the **Quick Print** button 🖶, Access sends the document directly to the default printer without allowing you to change print options.

1. Expand the **Queries** group. Double-click the table **qryManageContacts** to open it.

2. Press Ctrl+P to open the **Print** dialog box.

Figure 1-16
Print dialog box
**EcoMed-01.accdb
qryManageContacts**

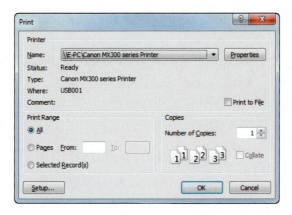

3. Depending on your class procedure, you can either print the table or cancel the print process. To cancel, click **Cancel**. To print the datasheet, click **OK**. If you are uncertain, ask your instructor.

4. To the far right of document tab for the query **qryManageContacts**, click **Close** ⊠.

5. Collapse the **Queries** group.

Exercise 1-14 PRINT A TABLE

Before printing a datasheet, you can use Print Preview to determine whether to change the page orientation from portrait (vertical layout) to landscape (horizontal layout). Landscape is often the better option when a datasheet contains numerous fields or wide columns. Printing in landscape mode can reduce the number of pages required to print the information.

1. Expand the **Tables** group. Double-click the table **tblVender** to open it.

2. Click the **File** tab. From the **Print** tab, choose **Print Preview** 🔍.

3. Click the **Last Page** navigation button ▶| to display the last page.

4. From the **Print Preview** command tab, in the command group **Zoom**, click **Two Pages** to view both pages.

Figure 1-17
Print Preview
**EcoMed-01.accdb
tblVender**

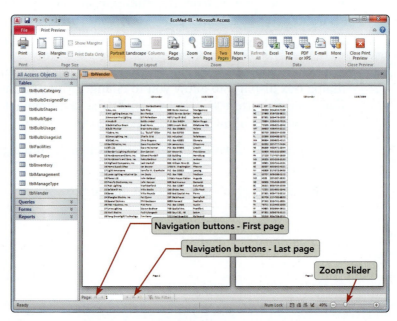

5. From the **Print Preview** command tab, in the command group **Page Layout**, click **Landscape** 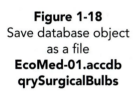 to reduce the total number of pages to print.

6. Based on your classroom procedure, you can either print the table or cancel the print process. If you are uncertain, ask your instructor.

7. From the **Print Preview** command tab, in the command group **Close Preview**, click **Close Print Preview** ☒. This action will return you to the table's **Datasheet View**.

8. Close the table and collapse the **Tables** group.

Exercise 1-15 SAVE A TABLE TO AN EXTERNAL FILE

Rather than directly printing to paper, you should first create an electronic XPS or PDF file. The electronic file can be saved, printed, and e-mailed. Often, the electronic file can be used just as effectively as a paper copy. The XPS and PDF file formats preserve the formatting of the document. The file can be viewed on a screen or printed by anyone who has a copy of the file.

When creating a PDF file, you can save the document in reduced quality or high quality. Reduced quality is similar to draft quality printing. High quality produces a better printout but also increases the size of the file saved.

After creating an electronic file, you should check the size of the file to make certain that it is not too large for the company's e-mail. The EcoMed e-mail server does not allow file to be larger than two megabytes.

1. Expand the **Queries** group. Double-click **qrySurgicalBulbs** to open it.

2. Click the **File** tab and click on the **Save & Publish** tab. From here, you can save the database or a major database object.

3. In the **File Types** section, click **Save Object As** option, and choose **PDF or XPS** from the next level in the cascading menu.

Figure 1-18
Save database object as a file
EcoMed-01.accdb
qrySurgicalBulbs

4. Change the location to the location where you will be storing your homework.

5. In the **File name** control, key *[your initials]*-01-15.

6. Click the **Save as type** option, and select **PDF**.

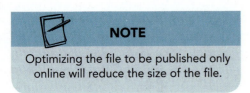

NOTE

Optimizing the file to be published only online will reduce the size of the file.

7. Make certain that the **Open file after publishing** check box is checked.

8. Click **Publish** to create the PDF file. Your file will open in a PDF Reader.

9. Depending upon your class procedure, you can print the PDF from the PDF Reader.

10. Close PDF Reader.

11. Right-click the **qrySurgicalBulbs** document tab and select **Close** 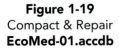.

12. Collapse the **Queries** group.

Managing Access Files

Access, similar to many database applications, is designed to display data quickly. To manipulate large amounts of data, space efficiency must be compromised. Normal database activities, such as adding, deleting, and moving data, can make the file unnecessarily large. After performing extensive work on a database, you should compact the data to save disk space. Depending on the type of work they do, employees at EcoMed are required to compact their databases periodically. Normally, databases are compacted at least once a week.

Regardless of how often employees compact their databases, all employees are required to back up their databases daily. A file can be backed up to the same location as the original file or to a new location.

Exercise 1-16   USE COMPACT AND REPAIR

The Compact and Repair Database command reclaims unused space and improves database efficiency. After compacting an inefficient database, many activities will perform quicker. Because you have only been looking at data rather than modifying data, compacting your current database may not change its size. Later, when you modify data and major objects, compacting your database will be very important.

1. Click the **File** tab to navigate to the Backstage View.

2. On the **Info** tab, click **Compact & Repair Database**.

Figure 1-19
Compact & Repair
EcoMed-01.accdb

Exercise 1-17   BACK UP A DATABASE

You should get in the habit of backing up your database regularly. By default, the backup file is saved to the same location as the original file. The default name of your backup file is the current date and time appended to the end of the original file name. You can change both default values by typing in a new name.

1.   Click the **File** tab to return to the Backstage.

2.   From the list of commands on the left, click the **Save Database As** option to open the **Save As** dialog box.

3.   In the dialog box's **Navigation Pane** (the left pane), select the location where you want to store your class work.

4.   Press ⌷Home⌷ to move the cursor to the beginning of the filename in the **File name** control. Do not delete the current file name from the control.

NOTE

Remember that you cannot use forward slash (/), semi-colon (;), or colon (:) symbols in filenames.

5.   Key **BK-*[mm]*-*[yy]*-** (mm = current two-digit month, yy = current two-digit year.)

6.   Click **Save** to close the old database and leave the backup copy of the database active.

7.   In the Message Bar, click **Enable Content**.

Exercise 1-18   CLOSE A DATABASE

Now that you have compacted and backed up your database, you can close your database and exit Access.

   You can use any of these methods:

*   From the **File** command tab, choose **Exit** ☒.

*   In the upper right of the Access window, click the Close button 🟥.

*   From the **File** command tab, choose **Close Database** 🖻.

*   Press ⌷Alt⌷+⌷F4⌷.

1.   Click the **File** command tab.

2.   From the list of command on the left, click the **Exit** button ☒.

Lesson 1   Summary

*   An Access database is relational, the most common type of database in use today.

*   Major Access database objects include tables, queries, forms, and reports.

*   A record is composed of related fields, a table is composed of related records, and a database is composed of related tables.

- A recordset is a Microsoft object–oriented data structure consisting of grouped records.
- A recordset is most often displayed as either a form or a report.
- An opened database cannot be moved or renamed.
- Shared mode is the default mode for most databases. This mode allows multiple users to use the database simultaneously.
- When opening a database for the first time in a location, a security warning displays on the Message Bar alerting you that the database may contain malicious code.
- In the Navigation Pane, major objects are organized by categories and groups.
- The Leszynski Naming Convention is a method of naming objects that emphasizes the use of three-letter prefixes to identify the type of object.
- Datasheet View and Design View are two methods of displaying each major object.
- Edit mode allows contents of fields to be changed.
- Navigation mode allows for movement among fields.
- The columns and rows of a datasheet can be hidden, displayed, or resized.
- Format changes to a datasheet affect all text in every column and row.
- In a datasheet, column widths can be changed individually; row heights must all be the same.
- In a datasheet, some format commands can be applied to individual fields; other commands apply to the entire datasheet.
- The Quick Print command sends a document directly to the default printer without allowing changes to print options.
- Documents can be printed or published in portrait or landscape orientation.
- A printable object can be saved as either an XPS or PDF file. The file preserves the document formatting in either reduced or high quality.
- Normal database activities such as adding, deleting, and moving data can unnecessarily increase the size of a database file.
- The Compact & Repair Database command reclaims unused space and improves database efficiency.

LESSON 1		Command Summary	
Feature	Button	Task Path	Keyboard
Close active object			Ctrl+W or Ctrl+F4
Close database		File, Exit	Alt+F4
Column width		Shortcut menu, Column width	
Collapse Navigation Pane	«		
Compact database		File, Compact & Repair Database	
Database Properties		Shortcut menu, Properties	
Datasheet View		Views, View, Datasheet View	
Design View		Views, View, Design View	
Expand Navigation Pane	»		
Export Data		File, Share, Save Object As, PDF/XPS	
Font Face		Font, Font	
Font Size		Font, Font Size	
Hide Fields		Shortcut menu, Hide Fields	
Jump to next screen or record			PageDown
Jump to previous screen or record			PageUp
Move to beginning of field text			Home
Move to end of field text			End

continues

LESSON 1		Command Summary *continued*	
Feature	**Button**	**Task Path**	**Keyboard**
Move to first record	⏮		Ctrl + Home
Move to last record	⏭		Ctrl + End
Move to next field			Tab
Move to next record	▶		
Move to previous field			Shift + Tab
Move to previous record	◀		
Open database	📂	File, Open	Ctrl + O
Page Layout		Design View, Page Setup, Page Layout	
Print Preview	🔍	File, Print, Print Preview	
Print	🖨	File, Print	Ctrl + P
Row Height		Shortcut menu, Row Height	
Save	💾	File, Save	Ctrl + S
Save record changes			Shift + Enter
Unhide Fields		Shortcut menu, Unhide Fields	

Please visit our Online Learning Center, *www.lessonapproach2010.com,* **where you will find the following review materials:**

Concepts Review

True/False Questions

Short Answer Questions

Critical Thinking Questions

Skills Review

Review Exercises that target single skills

Lesson Applications

Review Exercises that challenge students by testing multiple skills in each exercise

On Your Own

Open-ended exercises that require students to synthesize multiple skills and apply creativity and problem-solving as they would in a real world business situation

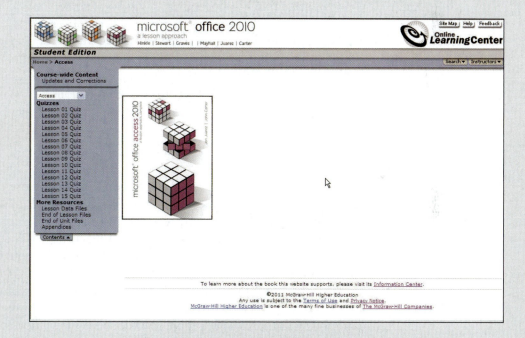

Viewing and Modifying Records

OBJECTIVES *After completing this lesson, you will be able to:*

1. Modify recordsets in a table.
2. Modify recordsets through a query.
3. Use Office edit tools.
4. View and modifying recordsets through a form.
5. Manage attachments.
6. Preview, print and save data through a report.

Estimated Time: 1½ hours

In Lesson 1, you learned general information about the database environment, including how to identify major objects in the EcoMed database such as tables, queries, forms, and reports. In this lesson, you will learn to add, edit, delete, and print data. You also will learn how to use time-saving edit commands like duplicate, copy, and paste. Finally, you will learn how to attach images to a record in tables.

As a student intern for EcoMed Services, Inc., you will work directly with data in tables or as a recordset through a query, form, or report. Although you can modify data through a table in Datasheet View, more often it is easier to use a query and form to limit the amount of data viewed at one time.

Modifying Recordsets in a Table

Records are routinely added to databases. For example, whenever a new student enrolls at your school, several records regarding the new student are added to your school's database. Whenever EcoMed Services, Inc., gets a new customer, you will need to add the customer's information to the database.

On other occasions, a record might be deleted if the information will no longer be used. However, not all databases allow records to be deleted. For example, when a bank customer closes an account, all records are not deleted. The account is moved to an inactivate status and is no longer accessible for use, but all information is retained indefinitely.

Exercise 2-1   OPEN A DATABASE

In a real company, you would be working with only one primary database. However, for the purposes of this textbook, you will use a new database for each lesson. For Lesson 2, the database and related files are located in the **Lesson 02** folder provided with the book. At the beginning of each lesson, you will use the appropriate database needed for the lesson. Before working with the file, you must copy and rename the file.

1.   Open the folder **Lesson 02**.

2.   Right-click the file **EcoMed-02** and from the shortcut menu, choose **Copy**.

3.   Right-click the file **EcoMed-02** and from the shortcut menu, choose **Rename**. On your keyboard, press ⎡Home⎤ to move to the beginning of the file name. Key your initials and then a hyphen. Press ⎡Enter⎤ to accept the new name.

4.   Right-click *[your initials]*-**EcoMed-02** and from the shortcut menu, choose **Properties**. Make certain that the **Read-only** attribute check box is not checked. Click **OK**.

TIP

If a Read-Only message appears in the Message Bar, you will need to close the database, deselect the Read-only property, and reopen the file.

5.   Double-click *[your initials]*-**EcoMed-02** to open the database.

6.   If the Message Bar's **Security Warning** appears, click the **Enable Content** button.

Exercise 2-2   EDIT FIELDS IN A TABLE

You do not need to "save" when you make changes to data in a record. Access automatically saves your changes as soon as you move the insertion point from the modified record to any other record.

You can determine if a record was saved by the shape of pointer in the *Record Selector*. If a shape does not appear in the record selector, then the record has already been saved. Two shapes can appear in the record selector:

• A pencil icon appears while you are adding or editing text. This shape indicates the record changes have not been saved.

• An asterisk marks a new record that does not have data in any field.

1.   In the **Navigation Pane**, expand the **Tables** group and double-click **tblManagement** to open it in **Datasheet View**.

2.   Locate the **ManageID** 3 and click in the second field **Management Company**. This action places the insertion point in the field.

NOTE

Notice the pencil icon in the record selector indicates that the record has been modified but not saved.

3. Press End to move the insertion point to end of the data in the field.

4. Press Ctrl + Backspace to delete the word to the right of the insertion point, "Center."

Figure 2-1
Modifying a record
EcoMed-02.accdb
tblManagement

5. Key **Complex**.

6. Press ↓. Notice that the pencil icon has disappeared from the record selector, which indicates that the changes to the record have been saved.

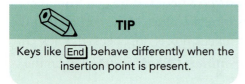

TIP

Keys like End behave differently when the insertion point is present.

7. Press ↑. The whole field is selected without an insertion point. Press End to move to the last field in the record.

8. Press Shift + Tab to move to the previous field.

9. Key **Butler** to change the last name.

10. Press Tab to move to the next field.

11. Press the space bar to delete the selected data.

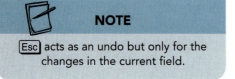

NOTE

Esc acts as an undo but only for the changes in the current field.

12. Press Esc to undo the deletion of the **ContractEnds** data.

13. Press ↓ to save the changes to the record.

Exercise 2-3   ADD A RECORD IN A TABLE

For a person familiar with spreadsheets, the simplest way to add records to a table is in Datasheet View. Datasheet View looks very similar to a worksheet. You add new records to the last row of the table. The last row of the table is marked by an asterisk in the record selector. You move to the new record row using any of the following steps:

- Right-click a record selector and on the shortcut menu, select **New Record** ⊞.

- From the Navigation buttons, click the New Record button ▸⊞.

- From the **Home** tab, in the command group **Records**, select **New** ⊞.

- Ctrl + +.

TIP

When a new record is being added to a table, a star icon will appear in the record selector of the new record.

NOTE

The first column lists field names. The second column contains data to be entered along with special characters and instructions. **Red** text is entered exactly as shown. **Black** symbols (such as in the phone number) automatically appear and do not need to be keyed. *Orange italic* indicates specific instructions for the field.

1. From the command tab **Home**, in the command group **Records**, click **New**. This action moves the insertion point to the empty record at the bottom of the table.

2. Key the information below to create a new record. Press ⎡Tab⎤ to move from one field to the next.

ManagementID:	*Press* ⎡Tab⎤
Management Company:	Rhode Island Hospital
Address:	593 Eddy Street
City:	Providence
State:	RI
ZIP:	02903
Phone Number:	(401) 444-4000
Contact First Name:	Kenneth
Contact Last Name:	Hammond
ContractEnds:	*Press* ⎡Ctrl⎤+⎡;⎤

3. Press ⎡Shift⎤+⎡Enter⎤ to save the changes without leaving the new record.

4. Press ⎡Ctrl⎤+⎡PageUp⎤ to return to the first field in the record.

Exercise 2-4 DELETE A RECORD IN A TABLE

There are times when you find that records are no longer needed and should be removed from a table. An example might be that you find a record that was entered into the wrong table.

  To delete one or more records, you must first select the record(s) that you intend to delete. After selecting the record(s) you can use one of four methods:

- Select a record and press ⎡Delete⎤.
- Right-click a selected record and on the shortcut menu, select **Delete Record**.
- From the command tab **Home**, in the command group **Records**, select **Delete** ⎡X⎤.
- ⎡Ctrl⎤+⎡-⎤.

REVIEW

The record selector is the narrow gray column to the left of the first field in the **Datasheet View** of a table or query.

1. In the **Datasheet View** of the table **tblManagement**, click in the record selector to select the record for "High Country Hospital" (**ManageID** 111).

UNIT 1 LESSON 2

Figure 2-2
Selecting a record
for deletion
EcoMed-02.accdb
tblManagement

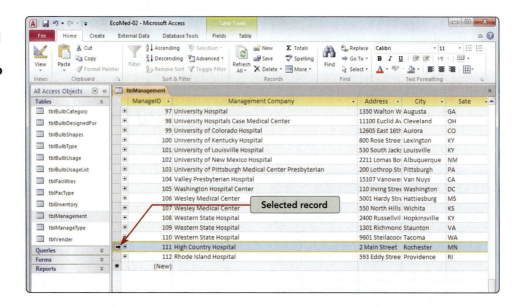

2. Press [Delete]. The record disappears, and a dialog box opens asking you to confirm the deletion.

Figure 2-3
Dialog box
confirming deletion
EcoMed-02.accdb
tblManagement

3. Click **Yes**. Access deletes the record.
4. Click in the record selector to select the record for "Western State Hospital" (**ManageID** 110).
5. Press [Ctrl]+[-] and then click **No** to decline the deletion.
6. In the **Navigation Pane**, collapse the **Tables** group. Do not close the table.

Modifying Recordsets through a Query

Modifying data through a table is not always practical. If the table is large, you will spend excessive time moving around the table. To be more efficient, you should use a query instead of a table. When you use a query to make changes to data, you are making changes to the recordset. Although the records display in the query, the data are actually stored in a table.

An advantage to editing through a query over a table is that the recordset of a query does not have to display all the records or fields in the table. Using a query allows you to view only the relevant fields and records. When you edit a record in a query, the data in the underlying table are changed automatically.

Exercise 2-5   EDIT FIELDS THROUGH A QUERY

When editing a record, you can insert text or use the Overtype mode to key over existing text. Use [Insert] to switch between Insert and Overtype modes.

1. In the **Queries** group of the **Navigation Pane**, double-click the **qryManageUniv**. Notice that there are only 22 records. This query is showing only management companies that are universities.

2. In the record for "Temple University Hospital," in the field **Contact Last Name**, click to the right of "-" in "Salamanca-Riba."

3. Press [Insert] to switch to **Overtype** mode. When you are in **Overtype** mode, "Overtype" appears on the status bar, and the insertion point becomes a block.

Figure 2-4
Overtype mode
EcoMed-02.accdb
qryManageUniv

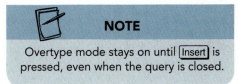

Methodist University Hospital	Wei	(901) 516-7000
North Shore University Hospital	Monagle	(516) 562-0100
Ohio State University Hospital	Jiang	(614) 293-8000
Robert Wood Johnson University Hospital	Kissiah	(732) 828-3000
Robert Wood Johnson University Hospital at Rahway	Ashigh	(732) 381-4200
Robert Wood Johnson University Hospital Hamilton	Fetterolf	(609) 586-7900
Shands at the University of Florida	Herd	(352) 265-8000
Temple University Hospital	Salamanca-Riba	(215) 707-2000 **Insertion point becomes a block**
Thomas Jefferson University Hospital	Shukla	(215) 955-6000
University Hospital	Conlee	(513) 584-1000

> **NOTE**
>
> Overtype mode stays on until [Insert] is pressed, even when the query is closed.

4. Key **Simm**.

5. Press [Insert] to return to **Insert** mode. The block returns to an insertion point.

6. Press [Ctrl]+[S] to save the record while leaving the insertion point in the field.

7. Click the document tab for **tblManagement** and click in the **ManageID** 87.

8. Press [Tab], then [End] to move to the last field in this record. The changes that you made to the last name in the query are saved in the table.

Exercise 2-6   ADD A RECORD THROUGH A QUERY

The additions made in a query's recordset are simultaneously made to the underlying table. In the EcoMed database, additions made through qryManageUniv are actually stored in tblManagement. The corresponding fields in the table are updated through a query, even though the query's recordset does not display all the fields in the source table.

1. Click on the document tab for **qryManageUniv** and press [Ctrl]+[+] to move to a new record.

2. Key the customer information below to create a new record. Press [Tab] to move from one field to the next.

Management Company:	University Hospital
Contact Last Name:	*Key [your full name]*
Phone Number:	(555) 555-1800

NOTE

In this text, to help identify your work, you often are asked to key an identifier such as your name or initials.

NOTE

The ManageID field has been set to assign a unique sequential number automatically. This unique number helps identify individual records.

3. From the command tab **Home**, in the command group **Records**, click **Save** to save the record.

4. Click the **tblManagement** tab and, using the record navigation button Last record ⏭, move to the last record.

5. From the command tab **Home**, in the command group **Records**, click **Refresh All**. This action forces the table to update changes to the record.

6. You should now see the record that you just created. Because the query did not display all the fields in the table, the newly created record is incomplete.

Exercise 2-7 DELETE A RECORD THROUGH A QUERY

Similar to adding a record through a query, you can delete a record through a query. The record will be removed from both the query (qryManageUniv) and the underlying table (tblManagement).

1. Click the document tab for **qryManageUniv** and click the record selector for the last record. This record should be the record for "University Hospital" that you entered earlier.

NOTE

When you deleted the record while in the query qryManageUniv, Access automatically refreshed the query. By selecting Refresh All, you force Access to refresh the data being displayed in all open objects.

2. Right-click the selected record. From the shortcut menu, select **Delete Record**. Click **Yes** to confirm the deletion.

3. Click the document tab for **tblManagement**. Notice that the record you deleted has "#Deleted" in each cell.

4. From the command tab **Home**, in the command group **Records**, click **Refresh All**.

5. Press Ctrl + End and then Home. Notice that the record with your name has now been deleted.

6. Right-click the **tblManagement** tab. From the shortcut menu, select **Close All**.

7. In the **Navigation Pane**, collapse the **Queries** group.

Using Office Editing Tools

Similar to Word and Excel, Access uses AutoCorrect. *AutoCorrect* is an application feature that automatically corrects commonly misspelled words. The AutoCorrect Options button appears next to text being automatically corrected. Choices within the button allow you to customize the correction process. You can undo the correction, cancel future automatic corrections for this error, or turn off the AutoCorrect option completely.

The Office Clipboard is a feature available in Microsoft Word, Excel, PowerPoint, Access, and Outlook. You can use this clipboard to collect and paste multiple items. You can copy items from any program that provides copy and cut functionality, but you can only paste items into a Microsoft Office application. If you have multiple Office programs running, the contents of the Office Clipboard are deleted after you close the last Office program.

Exercise 2-8 USE AUTOCORRECT

Text edit commands are used to make changes to the data within a record. AutoCorrect corrects commonly misspelled words as you key the text. For example, if you type "hte," AutoCorrect will change it to "the." AutoCorrect fixes many capitalization errors.

1. Click the **File** tab, and then click **Options** 🗎.

2. In the left pane, click **Proofing**.

3. In the right pane, click the **AutoCorrect Options** button to open the **AutoCorrect** dialog box.

Figure 2-5
AutoCorrect dialog
box
EcoMed-02.accdb

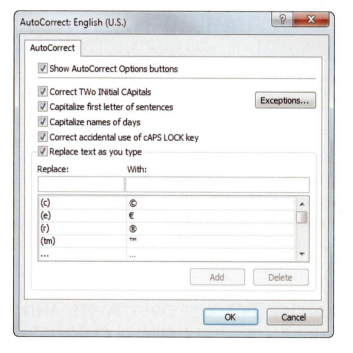

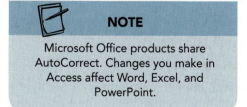

NOTE

Microsoft Office products share AutoCorrect. Changes you make in Access affect Word, Excel, and PowerPoint.

4. Make sure all checkboxes are checked. These are the automatic actions that AutoCorrect will perform during data entry.

5. Scroll down the list of entries to see which words are in the AutoCorrect dictionary.

TABLE 2-1 AutoCorrect Options

Options	Description
Show AutoCorrect option buttons	Option button appears after a word was automatically corrected.
Correct TWo INitial CApitals	Corrects words keyed with two initial capital letters, such as "THis."
Capitalize first letter of sentences	Capitalizes the first letter in a sentence.
Capitalize names of days	Capitalizes days of the week and months.
Correct accidental use of cAPS LOCK key	Corrects words keyed with Caps Lock on but Shift key pressed, such as cAPS.
Replace text as you type	Makes corrections as you work.

6. Click **OK** to close the **AutoCorrect** dialog box.

7. Click **OK** to close the **Access Options** dialog box.

8. In the **Tables** group of the **Navigation Pane**, double-click the table **tblVender**.

NOTE

The field **VenderID** has been set to assign a unique sequential number automatically.

9. Press Ctrl+ + to add a new record.

10. Press Tab to move to the **VenderName** field.

11. Key **ACN**.

12. Press the space bar. Notice that "ACN" changed to "CAN".

13. Place your pointer over the corrected word. Click the **AutoCorrect Options** icon 🗲. When it appears, select **Change back to "ACN"**.

14. Key **Inc.** to complete the field.

15. Press Tab to move to the **ContactName** field.

16. Key **TOm Heart**. Notice that AutoCorrect corrected the name to "Tom Heart."

17. Press Tab to move to the next field.

Exercise 2-9   USE COPY, PASTE, AND THE OFFICE CLIPBOARD

You can copy a block of text from one part of a table to another. There are three ways to copy and paste text:

- From the ribbon, click **Copy** 🗐, then click **Paste** 📋.
- Press Ctrl+C (copy), then Ctrl+V (paste).
- Right-click and from the shortcut menu, choose **Copy**, then **Paste**.

    When you copy the second text block, the Office Clipboard pane opens. You can use the Office Clipboard to paste multiple blocks of text. From that pane, you can select the item you want to paste.

You can use the duplicate command to copy one field at a time. You can duplicate the data from a field in the previous record to the same field in the current record by pressing Ctrl+' (apostrophe).

You can also paste an entire record from one location to another by using the Paste Append command. To use this command you must match all fields in both records.

TIP

Unlike the Office Clipboard, the Windows Clipboard only stores the last item copied. On both Clipboards, text can be pasted repeatedly. However, when you copy new information using the Windows Clipboard, the old information on the Windows Clipboard is replaced by the new information.

1. From the command tab **Home**, in the right lower corner of the command group **Clipboard**, click the dialog box launcher ⤵ to open the **Clipboard** pane.

2. Find the record for **VenderID** 27 and click to the left of the "C" in "Capitol." Press Shift+End to select all text to the right of the insertion point.

3. Press Ctrl+C to copy. Notice that the selected text has been added to the **Clipboard**.

TIP

In the Clipboard, the icon next to each copied item indicates the application from which the item was copied.

4. Hover your mouse over the copied text in the **Clipboard** pane. An option arrow appears to the right of the copied text.

Figure 2-6
Clipboard pane
EcoMed-02.accdb
tblVender

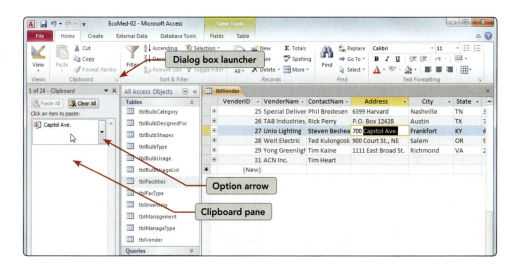

5. Press Tab to move to the **City** field.

6. Right-click the selected text and choose **Copy** from the shortcut menu. This text has been added to the **Clipboard** pane.

7. Press Tab to move to the **State** field.

8. From the command tab **Home**, in the command group **Clipboard**, click **Copy** 📋. You now have three items in the **Clipboard** pane.

NOTE

The Office Clipboard holds up to 24 copied items.

9. Click in the **Address** field for **VenderName** "ACN Inc." and key **2800**.

10. Press the space bar.

11. In the **Clipboard** pane, click the option arrow for "Capitol Ave." and select **Paste** from the menu. The copied text has been added to the field you were editing.

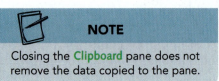

NOTE

Closing the **Clipboard** pane does not remove the data copied to the pane.

12. Press Tab. From the **Clipboard** pane, click "Frankfort."

13. Press Tab. From the **Clipboard** pane, click "KY."

14. Press Shift+Enter to save the changes to the record.

15. In the upper right of the **Clipboard** pane, click **Close** ×.

Exercise 2-10   USE UNDO

In a previous exercise you used Esc to cancel changes in a field. You will now use the Undo button ↺, which can affect fields, records, or even major objects.

Access remembers changes to the record and lets you undo most edits. If you accidentally delete text in a field, you can use the Undo command to reverse the action. One exception is if you delete a record, which cannot be undone. There are two ways to undo an action:

• On the Quick Access Toolbar click Undo ↺.

• Press Ctrl+Z.

1. Press Tab. Press Ctrl+' to copy the data from the field above into the current record. This number is not the correct ZIP for this record, but the point here is to show the keystroke shortcut.

2. In the Quick Access Toolbar, click Undo ↺. All unsaved changes to the record are removed.

Figure 2-7
Undo changes to a record
EcoMed-02.accdb tblVender

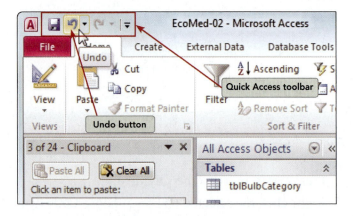

3. Click the Record Selector for vender "ACN Inc." and press Delete.

4. Read the dialog box and then click **Yes** to confirm the deletion.

5. Press Ctrl+Z to attempt to undo the deletion. Nothing happens because once a record is deleted, it cannot be undone.

6. Right-click the document tab for **tblVender**. From the shortcut menu, select **Close** ▱.

7. In the **Navigation Pane**, right-click the table **tblVender**, and from the shortcut menu, choose **Delete**.

8. In the dialog box, click **Yes**. The table is deleted.

9. Press Ctrl+Z to undo the deletion of the table.

10. In the **Navigation Pane**, collapse the **Tables** group.

Viewing and Modifying Recordsets through a Form

A form is a major Access object. A form is designed to be used on a computer screen. Through a form, you can enter, view, sort, edit, and print data. Most often when making changes to records, it is easier to use a form rather than a table. A form uses the same navigation buttons, scroll bars, and text editing features as a table.

Exercise 2-11　NAVIGATE THROUGH FORMS

A form is linked to a recordset. The fields displayed through a form are the same as in the table or query from which they originate.

1. In the **Forms** group of the **Navigation Pane**, double-click the form **frmVender**. This form is using the Single Form view.

2. In the **Forms** group of the **Navigation Pane**, double-click the form **frmVenderList**. This form is using the Multiple Items Form view to display data.

3. In the **Forms** group of the **Navigation Pane**, double-click the form **frmVenderSplit**. This form is using the Split Form view.

Figure 2-8
Multiple open documents
EcoMed-02.accdb frmVenderSplit

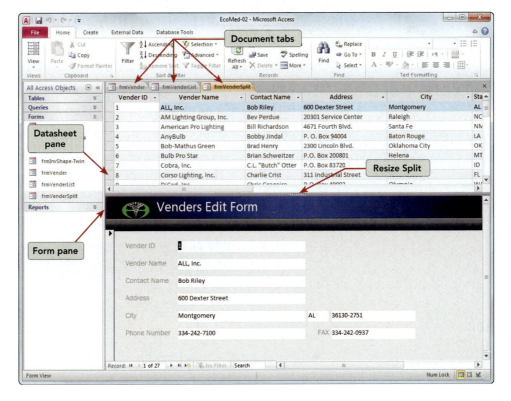

4. Click the document tab for **frmVenderList**.

5. Press Tab to move the cursor to the second field (**Vender Name**) in the first record.

6. Press Ctrl + PageDown to move to the second record in the same field.

7. Press Ctrl + End to move to the last field in the last record.

8. Click the document tab for the form **frmVender**.

9. Press Tab seven times. Notice the selected field order is not always left to right or top down.

10. Press PageDown to move to the next record. Notice that the field **State** is still selected.

11. In the record navigation tool, click the **Last Record** button ⏭. The record for vender 27 is now visible.

12. Click the document tab for **frmVenderSplit**.

13. Press Tab to move through the first record. Notice that the fields in the form are not in the same order as in the datasheet.

14. Press PageDown to move to the next record. Notice that the information in the selected record and the form are the same.

Exercise 2-12   EDIT FIELDS THROUGH A FORM

You can edit data in a form with the same shortcuts you use in a table or a query. For example, Backspace deletes a single character, and the keyboard combination Ctrl + Delete deletes everything to the right of the insertion point.

The data displayed in each field of a form is stored in a table. By using Datasheet View, you can also delete text from a form in the same way you can delete text from a table.

1. Click the document tab for the form **frmVenderList**.

2. Press Ctrl + Home to move to the first record.

3. Press Tab three times to move to the **Address** field.

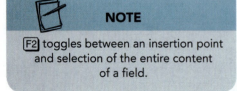

NOTE

F2 toggles between an insertion point and selection of the entire content of a field.

4. Press F2 to place the insertion point into the field.

5. Press Ctrl + Backspace to delete one word to the left of the insertion point.

6. Key **Blvd.** Notice the pencil icon in the record selector.

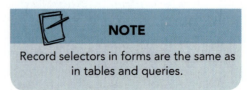

NOTE

Record selectors in forms are the same as in tables and queries.

Figure 2-9
Edit data in a form
EcoMed-02.accdb
frmVenderList

7. From the command tab **Home**, in the command group **Records**, click **Save** ▣.

8. Click the document tab for **frmVenderSplit**.

9. In the datasheet at the top of the form, click in the **Address** field for vender 8.

10. In the field, double-click the word Street and key **Blvd.**.

11. Press Shift + Enter to save the changes. Notice that the data in the **Address** field has not changed in the lower part of the form.

12. Press ↓ and then ↑. The changes now appear in the form.

13. Click in any field in the form (lower half.)

Exercise 2-13 ADD RECORDS THROUGH A FORM

A form can make it easier for you to add records. A well-designed form utilizes field placement to improve the efficiency of data entry. Forms in the EcoMed database are designed for effective and efficient data entry.

1. From the command tab **Home**, in the command group **Records**, click **New** ▣. The record selector will display an asterisk until you key new data.

2. Key the following new record, pressing Tab between entries:

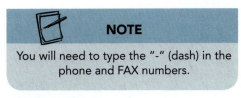

NOTE

You will need to type the "-" (dash) in the phone and FAX numbers.

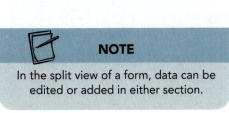

NOTE

In the split view of a form, data can be edited or added in either section.

Vender ID:	*Press* Tab
Vender Name:	*Key [your school's name]*
Contact Name:	*Key [your full name]*
Address:	825 Canal Street
City:	Cary
State:	NC
ZIP:	27513
Phone:	919-555-1601
FAX:	919-555-1602

Figure 2-10
Adding a new record
**EcoMed-02.accdb
frmVenderSplit**

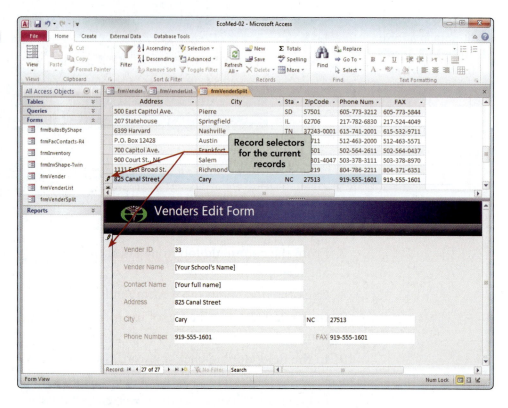

3.   Press [Ctrl]+[S] to save the new record.

Exercise 2-14   DELETE RECORDS THROUGH A FORM

You can delete the current record by using all the same methods you used when deleting a record in a table. The records will disappear from the form and the underlying table.

1.   Click the document tab for **frmVenderList**.

2.   Click in any field for the vender "EarthElectric, Inc." (**Vender ID** 10).

3.   From the command tab **Home**, in the command group **Records**, click the **Delete** option arrow ⊠ and choose **Delete Record** 🗙.

Figure 2-11
Delete options
**EcoMed-02.accdb
frmVenderList**

4.   Click **Yes** to confirm the deletion.

5.   Click the document tab for the form **frmVenderSplit**. Navigate to where vender 10 should be. Notice that there is a row with "#Deleted" in each field.

6. From the command tab **Home**, in the command group **Records**, click **Refresh All** 🔄.

7. Right-click the **frmVenderSplit** tab. From the shortcut menu, select **Close All**.

8. In the **Navigation Pane**, collapse the **Forms** group.

Managing Attachments

Some tables include an image with each record. The Inventory table and the Bulb Shapes table include a field with an image of the product. The attached images can be any type of image file including jpg, gif, or tiff.

In addition to images, you can attach certain types of data files such as documents, worksheets, or text files. The Attachments window allows you to add, remove, open, or save an attachment. Attached files cannot be larger than 256 megabytes or be non-data files such as programs, system files, or batch files.

Exercise 2-15   ATTACH AN IMAGE

When attaching an image, you must know the location of the file and in which record the file will be stored.

1. In the **Tables** group of the **Navigation Pane**, double-click the table **tblInventory**.

2. Click anywhere in the record for **InvID** 5.

3. Press F2 and then End to move to the last field in this record.

4. Press Shift+Tab. Double-click in the attachment field for the selected record. The **Attachments** dialog box appears.

Figure 2-12
Adding an attachment
EcoMed-02.accdb tblInventory

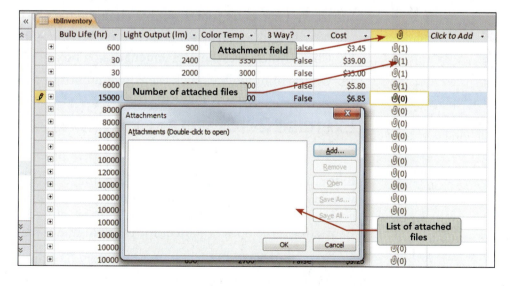

5. Any names of attached field will appear in this dialog box. Click **Add**.

6. In the **Lesson 02** folder, double-click the file **CL-10WL.jpg**.

7. Click **OK** to close the **Attachment** dialog box.

8. Press ⌈Ctrl⌉+⌈S⌉ to save the changes for the record.

9. Right-click the table's document tab, and choose **Close** from the shortcut menu.

10. In the **Navigation Pane**, collapse the **Tables** group.

11. In the **Forms** group of the **Navigation Pane**, double-click the form **frmInventory**.

12. Press ⌈PageDown⌉ until you get to **InvID** 5's record.

13. Click the picture. A mini toolbar appears above the image.

Figure 2-13
Attachments in
a form
**EcoMed-02.accdb
frmInventory**

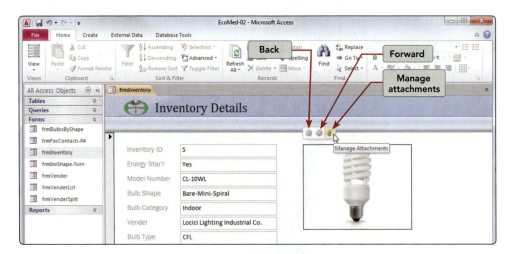

14. On the mini toolbar, click the Manage Attachments button 🔗 .

15. In the **Attachments** dialog box, click **Add**.

16. In the **Lesson 02** folder, double-click the file **CL-10WLc.jpg**. You now have two files attached to this record.

17. Click **OK** to close the **Attachment** dialog box.

18. On the mini toolbar, click the **Forward** button ⊕ to see the second file.

Exercise 2-16   EXTRACT AN IMAGE FROM THE DATABASE

Extracting is different than removing an image. When you remove an image, you delete that image from the record. When you extract an image, you save a copy of the image as a file that can be stored outside the database. Extracting a file does not affect the original image stored in the database.

1. Press ⌈PageUp⌉ until the data for **Inventory ID** 4 are displayed in the form.

2. Double-click the image of the product to open the **Attachment** dialog box.

3. Click **Save As**.

4. In the **Save Attachment** dialog box, change the **File name** to **Circuline.jpg**.

5. Check the file path in the location bar. Change if needed.

6. Click **Save** to save a copy of the image outside of the database.

REVIEW

If you close a major object after modifying or adding a record, Access will save the changes without prompting the user.

7. Click **OK** to close the **Attachment** dialog box.

8. Close the form by right-clicking the form's document tab and choosing **Close**.

9. In the **Navigation Pane**, collapse the **Forms** group.

Previewing, Printing, and Exporting Data through a Report

Just as forms are designed to view data on a screen, reports are designed to view data on paper. Forms are designed to fit on a standard computer screen, while reports are designed to fit on sheets of paper. From the Print dialog box, you can set a print range or change the page orientation.

Exercise 2-17　PREVIEW A REPORT

Print Preview shows you how the selected report prints on paper. *Print Preview* is a method for displaying on the screen how an object will appear if printed on paper.

TIP

To use the **Print Preview** ribbon for tables, queries, and forms, you must click the **File** tab and select the **Print** option.

1. In the **Reports** group of the **Navigation Pane**, double-click the report **rptInvShort**.

2. Right-click the report's document tab and choose **Print Preview** .

3. From the command tab **Print Preview**, in the command group **Page Layout**, click **Portrait** .

Figure 2-14
Print Preview
**EcoMed-02.accdb
rptInvShort**

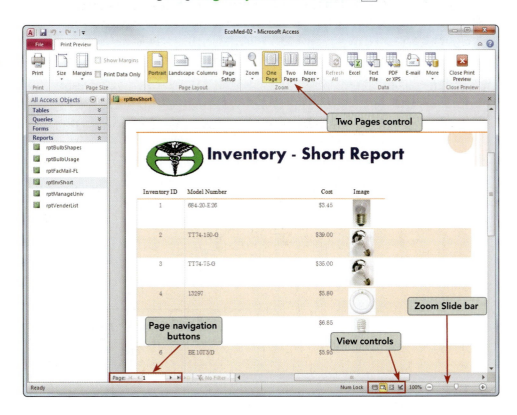

4. From the command tab **Print Preview**, in the command group **Zoom**, click **One Page** 🔲. Even though this command was already selected, clicking it again will resize the report so that the first page will fit fully on the screen.

5. In the Page navigation control located in the lower left corner of the **Print Preview** window, click Last Page 🔳. This report is 22 pages long.

6. Right-click the report's document tab and choose **Close** ◲.

Exercise 2-18   PRINT A REPORT

Depending on the size of the report, you may need to change the page orientation, margins, or both. You can set the print orientation to either portrait or landscape depending on the data being printed.

1. In the **Reports** group of the **Navigation Pane**, double-click the report **rptVenderList**.

2. In the right end of the status bar are the change view buttons. Click **Print Preview** 🔲.

NOTE

Most printers cannot print all the way to the edge of a page. Each printer may have a slightly different margin setting. Reports can act differently depending on your printer. If you do not get exactly the same results as depicted in this exercise, you may need to modify the report.

3. A warning dialog box appears. This report has a problem with its width. Click **OK**.

4. From the command tab **Print Preview**, in the command group **Zoom**, click **Two Pages** 🔲. Notice that this report has overflowed onto a blank page.

5. From the command tab **Print Preview**, in the command group **Page Size**, click the **Margins** option arrow 🔲 and select **Narrow**.

Figure 2-15
Changing margin settings
EcoMed-02.accdb
rptVenderList

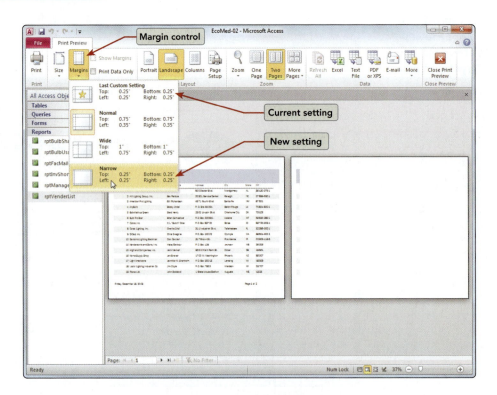

6. From the command tab **Print Preview**, in the command group **Print**, click **Print** 🖶. The **Print** dialog box opens.

7. Based on your classroom procedure, you can either print the report or cancel the print process. To cancel, click **Cancel**. To print the report, click **OK**. If you are uncertain, ask your instructor.

Exercise 2-19   SAVE A REPORT

You can save a report as an electronic XPS file. A saved report can be viewed or printed through XPS viewer, which is a standard Microsoft report format. Beginning with Office 2007, PDF is also a standard report format used by Microsoft.

1. From the command tab **Print Preview**, in the command group **Data**, click **PDF or XPS** 📄.

2. Change the location to the location where you will be storing your homework.

TIP

Use the Browse Folder button to help you store files in non-default locations.

3. In the **File name** control, type *[your initials]*-02-19.

4. Click the **Save as type** control, and select **XPS Document**.

5. Verify that the **Open file after publishing** check box is checked.

Figure 2-16
Save a report to a file
EcoMed-02.accdb rptVenderList

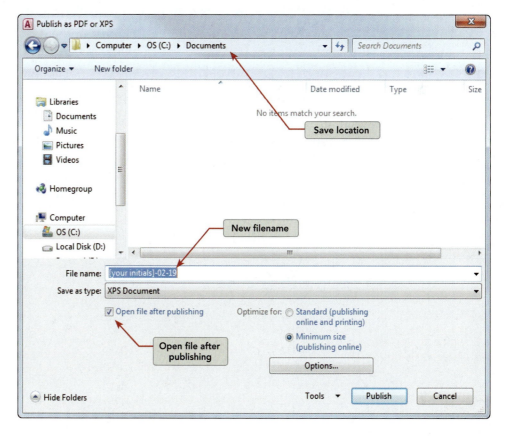

REVIEW

Optimizing the file for online exporting and printing increases the size of the file.

6. Click **Publish** to create the XPS file. Your file opens in Internet Explorer.

7. Close Internet Explorer. Click the **Close** button for the **Export-XPS** dialog box.

8. Right-click the **rptVenderList** tab. From the shortcut menu, select **Close**.

9. In the **Navigation Pane**, collapse the **Reports** group.

10. Click Close [x] to close the database.

Lesson 2   Summary

- Access automatically saves changes to a record when you move the insertion point to another record.
- Records are stored in tables.
- Records can be added, edited, and deleted in a table, through a query, or through a form.
- You can delete records from a table by clicking on the Record Selector and pressing the delete key [Delete].
- When editing a record, you can insert text or use the Overtype mode to key over existing text.
- AutoCorrect corrects commonly misspelled words.
- Press [Ctrl]+['] to duplicate the contents in the field from the previous record.
- Press [Ctrl]+[;] to enter the current system date into a field.
- Press [Ctrl]+[C] to copy and [Ctrl]+[V] to paste text.
- Click Undo [↩] to restore previously deleted text.
- You can attach an image or document file to a record.
- Print Preview displays on screen how an object will appear when printed.
- An exported object can be viewed or printed at a later time.

LESSON 2		Command Summary		
Feature	Button	Task Path		Keyboard
Add record		Home, Records, New		Ctrl + +
Attachment				
Copy		Home, Clipboard, Copy		Ctrl + C
Date, Current				Ctrl + ;
Delete record		Home, Records, Delete		Ctrl + −
Duplicate field				Ctrl + '
Export		MS Office, Print Preview, Data, XPS		
Margins		Print Preview, Page Size, Margins		
Paste		Home, Clipboard, Paste		Ctrl + V
Refresh All		Home, Records, Refresh All		
Save record		Home, Records, Save		Ctrl + Enter
Undo		Edit, Undo		Ctrl + Z

Please visit our Online Learning Center, *www.lessonapproach2010.com,* **where you will find the following review materials:**

Concepts Review

True/False Questions

Short Answer Questions

Critical Thinking Questions

Skills Review

Review Exercises that target single skills

Lesson Applications

Review Exercises that challenge students by testing multiple skills in each exercise

On Your Own

Open-ended exercises that require students to synthesize multiple skills and apply creativity and problem-solving as they would in a real world business situation

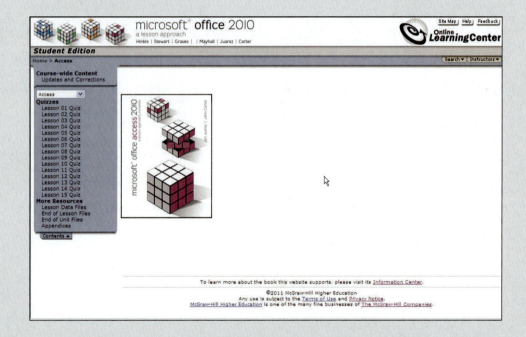

Finding, Filtering, Sorting, and Summarizing Data

OBJECTIVES *After completing this lesson, you will be able to:*

1. Find and replace data.
2. Use wildcards.
3. Sort records.
4. Add and modify the totals row in datasheets.
5. Use filters.
6. Use the database documenter.

Estimated Time: 1½ hours

The main purpose of the EcoMed database is to turn raw data into useful information. The data stored are too complex to find specific information easily, such as the total number of halogen bulbs currently in stock. To locate specific information, you can use standard Access tools to search, find, sort, and filter records. By applying the proper combinations of tools, the cumbersome data become useful information.

EcoMed Services, Inc., sells 316 different types of lighting devices that are divided into three different categories and five different bulb types. If you want to know which items are the most expensive for each category, you would sort the inventory by cost in descending order and filter by each category. You will often use a combination of tools to display specific information.

Finding and Replacing Data

Finding information can be time consuming if you have to scroll through several thousand records. Searches can be conducted quicker when fields contain unique data. For example, if you know the phone number of a particular facility, you can find that company quickly because no two companies share the same phone number. However, if you only know the company's area code, then the search can take quite a bit longer, because your database may contain numerous facilities that share the same area code.

Although most often you change single records, on occasion, you will find it necessary to update the same data listed in multiple records. Customers at EcoMed Services are classified by management type. If the management type for a group of customers changes, then these changes need to be reflected throughout the entire database. To make these changes, you will need to find the original management classifications and replace them with the new classifications.

Exercise 3-1 USE THE SEARCH TOOL

Using the Search tool is a quick way to find data in a recordset. The Search tool begins its search at the first field of the first record and stops at the first match. If the recordset contains more than one match, only the first match is found. Because of this limitation, the Search tool is best used when searching for unique data, such as a phone numbers or specific names. The Search tool can be used in tables, queries, and forms.

NOTE

The Search tool is not case sensitive. Access treats uppercase and lowercase text the same.

1. Locate and open the **Lesson 03** folder.

2. Make a copy of **EcoMed-03** and rename it *[your initials]*-**EcoMed-03**.

3. Open and enable content for *[your initials]*-**EcoMed-03**.

4. From the **Navigation Pane**, open the table **tblFacilities** in **Datasheet View**.

Figure 3-1
Search tool
EcoMed-03.accdb tblFacilities

5. In the Navigation bar, click in the **Search** tool.

6. Key **h**. Starting from the upper left, the first "h" is selected.

7. Key **o**. Starting from the upper left, the first "ho" is selected.

8. Key **u**. The selection has moved to the 37th record (Facilities ID 38).

9. Press [Backspace] three times to remove the content of the **Search** tool.

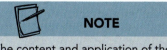

NOTE

The content and application of the Search tool will not be retained when you close an object.

10. Key **chic**. The selection has moved to the **City** field of the 32nd record.

11. Clear the content of the **Search** tool.

12. Key **303**. The selection has moved to the **Phone Number** field of the 4th record.

13. Clear the content of the **Search** tool.

Exercise 3-2   USE THE FIND COMMAND

Similar to the Search tool, the Find and Replace dialog box finds matches in a recordset. However, there are two major differences. First, the Find and Replace command begins a search at the insertion point, and second, this command includes options for fine-tuning how the text is matched.

TABLE 3-1 Find and Replace Dialog Box Options

Option	Description
Look In	Sets the search for the current field or the entire table.
Match: Any Part of Field	Finds records with matching characters anywhere in the field.
Match: Whole Field	Finds records in which an entire field matches the value in the Find What text box.
Match: Start of Field	Finds records in which the beginning of a field matches the Find What entry.
Search: All	Searches forward to the end of the table and wraps back to the beginning.
Search: Up	Searches in the Up (backward) direction only.
Search: Down	Searches in the Down (forward) direction only.
Match Case	Finds exact uppercase and lowercase matches.
Search Fields As Formatted	Enables you to key data in its display format. To find a date that is stored as 1/25/01, you can key 25-Jan-01. This is the slowest search.

There are two ways of opening the Find and Replace dialog box using the Find tab:

• From the **Home** tab, in the **Find** group, click **Find** 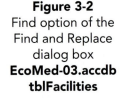.

• Press Ctrl + F.

1. Click anywhere in the table. Press F2 and then Ctrl + Home to move to the top of the table **tblFacilities**.

2. From the **Home** tab, in the **Find** group, click **Find** .

3. In the **Find What** control, key **jack**.

4. Click the drop-down arrow for the **Look In** control and choose **Current Document**.

5. Click the drop-down arrow for the **Match** control and choose **Any Part of Field**.

Figure 3-2
Find option of the Find and Replace dialog box
EcoMed-03.accdb
tblFacilities

NOTE

To see the results of a search, you can drag the **Find and Replace** dialog box by its title bar to a location on the screen that does not conceal the results of the search.

6. Click **Find Next**. The first occurrence of "jack" is located in the field **Facility Name**. To search in only one field, you must click in that field before starting the search.

7. Click in the **Contact First Name** field of the first record. You do not need to close the **Find and Replace** dialog box to interact with the underlying table.

8. Click the drop-down arrow for the **Look In** control and choose **Current field** and set the **Match** control to **Whole Field**.

9. Click **Find Next** to find "jack" in record 44.

10. Click **Find Next** to find the next occurrence, and continue until you reach the end of the table.

11. Read the message box and click **OK**.

12. Click **Cancel** to close the **Find and Replace** dialog box.

Exercise 3-3   USE THE REPLACE COMMAND

The Replace tab finds matches in the same way as the Find tab. With Replace, you not only find the match, but you can also replace each matched value with a new value. You can replace either a single occurrence or every occurrence of the value.

When using the Replace All option, you must be careful that all occurrences in the recordset are values that you plan to replace. Sometimes, unanticipated errors can occur. For example, if you try to replace the word "form" with "report," then a field containing the word "information" will become "inreportation."

There are two ways of opening the Find and Replace dialog box using the Replace tab:

- From the **Home** tab, in the **Find** group, click **Replace** .
- Press Ctrl + H.

1. In **tblFacilities**, widen the field **Facility Name** so that you can see all of the data.

2. Click in the field **Facility Name** for the first record.

3. Press Ctrl + H to open the **Find and Replace** dialog box.

4. In the **Find What** control, key **university**.

TIP

Make sure that you have keyed the period after "Univ.".

5. In the **Replace With** control, key **Univ.**.

6. Verify that the **Look In** control is set to **Current field**.

7. Click **Find Next**. A dialog box appears to tell you that this text string was not found. Click **OK**.

8. Click the drop-down arrow for the **Match** control and choose **Any Part of Field**.

9. Click **Find Next**. The first occurrence after the insertion point is selected.

10. Click **Replace** to replace the first occurrence of "university" with "Univ." and to find the next occurrence of "university."

11. Click **Find Next** to skip this occurrence of "university" and move to the next.

12. Click **Replace All**.

13. Read the message box about not being able to undo this operation and click **Yes**.

14. Click **Cancel** to close the dialog box.

Using Wildcards

Up to this point, you have used exact text when finding text. On occasion, you may not know the exact value you want to match. For example, you might need to find a particular facility but not know its exact name. You may know part of the name such as "Regional." Since you only know part of the name, you would need to search the name field using a wildcard. A *wildcard* is a character or group of characters used to represent one or more alphabetical or numerical characters.

Exercise 3-4 FIND DATA USING AN ASTERISK "*"

The asterisk (*) is a wildcard that represents one or more characters. If you search for "Mar*" as a name, you will match names such as "Mar," "Mart," "Martin," "Marigold," or "Marblestone." All fields matched will begin with "Mar" regardless of the remaining characters in the field.

1. In the table **tblFacilities**, click Ctrl+↑ to move to first record in the **Facility Name** field.

2. Press Ctrl+F to open the **Find and Replace** dialog box.

3. Click the drop-down arrow for the **Match** control and choose **Whole Field**.

4. In the **Find What** control, key **univ***.

5. Click **Find Next**. The "Univ. Hospital" is selected in record 30.

6. Click in the table and scroll down to "Indiana Univ. Hospital," **Manage ID** 47. This record was skipped by the **Find** utility because the **Facility Name** did not start with "Univ.".

7. Click **Cancel** to close the dialog box.

Exercise 3-5 FIND DATA USING A QUESTION MARK "?"

The question mark (?) is a wildcard that represents a single character. If you search for "Mar?" as a first name, you will find names such as "Mari," "Mark," "Marv," or "Mary." All fields containing only four characters and starting with "Mar" will be matched. Fields containing more than four characters or not beginning with "Mar" will not be matched.

1. In the table **tblFacilities**, click Ctrl+↑ to move to the first record in the **Facility Name** field.

2. From the **Home** tab, in the **Find** group, click **Find**.

3. In the **Find What** control, key **o??o**.

4. In the **Look In** control, select **Current field**.

5. In the **Match** control, select **Any Part of Field**.

6. Click **Find Next** to find the first occurrence of any field's content that has two charters between two "o." The first match is in the word "D<u>oct</u>ors."

7. Click **Find Next** a few more times to see the different words that can be found.

8. Click **Cancel**.

Sorting Records

In a table, records are displayed in the order in which they were entered. For example, whenever a new facility is added, its name is added to the end of a table. Most often though, this order is not useful when trying to find a specific record.

You can change the sort order of the recordset depending on the information you need. When creating a facilities phone list, you would sort the recordset by the facility name.

Exercise 3-6 SORT RECORDS IN DATASHEET VIEW

You can sort data in three ways:

> **TIP**
>
> A small up or down arrow appears on the column header of a sorted column. This sort order arrow appears to the right of the column header's drop-down arrow.

- From the **Home** tab, in the **Sort & Filter** group, choose **Ascending** 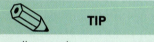 or **Descending** .

- On a column selector, click the option arrow and select the **Sort A to Z** or **Sort Z to A**.

- In a field, right-click and select the **Sort A to Z** or **Sort Z to A**.

1. In the table **tblFacilities**, in the **Facility Name** field, click the option arrow on the column header, and choose **Sort A to Z** .

Figure 3-3
Apply Sort to a column
EcoMed-03.accdb
tblFacilities

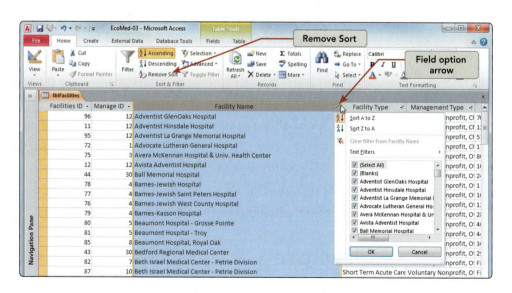

2. From the **Home** tab, in the **Sort & Filter** group, click **Remove Sort** 🐦. Notice that the sort order arrow no longer displays in the column header.

3. Select both the **Contact First Name** and **Contact Last Name** fields.

4. Right-click the selected column headers and choose **Sort Z to A** 🔽. The table is now sorted in descending order by first name and then by last name.

5. In the **Navigation Pane**, open the query **qryFacContacts** in **Datasheet View**. This query gets its data from **tblFacilities**.

6. Notice that the query is not sorted by contact names. Click on the document tab for **tblFacilities**.

7. Click in the **Revenue** field, click the option arrow on the column header, and choose **Sort Largest to Smallest** 🔽.

8. Right-click the table's document tab and choose **Save** 💾.

9. Right-click any document tab and choose **Close All** 📑.

Exercise 3-7   SORT RECORDS IN A FORM

A form can be set to view a single record at one time or multiple records at once. All forms can be sorted. When multiple records are displayed in a form, the sort order is observable. To see the results of a sort to a single record form, you will need to navigate through the recordset one screen at a time.

1. From the **Navigation Pane**, open the form **frmFacContacts** in **Form View**.

2. Click in the **Facility Name** field for the first record.

3. From the **Home** tab, in the **Sort & Filter** group, click **Ascending** 🔼. A different record is now displayed.

4. Press `PageDown` to move through all the records to see that the form is indeed sorted by **Facility Name**.

5. Click in the **Last Name** field.

6. From the **Home** tab, in the **Sort & Filter** group, click **Ascending** 🔼.

7. Use the Record Navigation buttons to move through the records and see the change.

8. Right-click the form's tab and choose **Close All** 📑.

9. From the **Navigation Pane**, open the form **frmFacContacts** in **Form View**. Notice that the form retained the last sort order.

10. From the **Home** tab, in the **Sort & Filter** group, click **Remove Sorts** 🐦.

11. Right-click the form's tab and choose **Close** 📄.

Exercise 3-8   SORT RECORDS IN A REPORT

The recordset displayed in Layout View of a report can be sorted similarly to a recordset in Form View of a form. Layout View of a report allows you to fine-tune the display of data, including sorting fields and adjusting column widths.

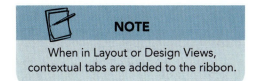

NOTE

When in Layout or Design Views, contextual tabs are added to the ribbon.

1. From the **Navigation Pane**, open the report **rptVenderList** in **Report View**. This report is sorted by Vender ID.

2. From the **Home** tab, in the **Views** group, click **View** and choose **Layout View** 📄.

3. Click the column heading **Contact Name** to select the entire column of data.

4. From the **Home** tab, in the **Sort & Filter** group, choose **Descending** 🔽.

Figure 3-4
Sort in a report
EcoMed-03.accdb
rptVenderList

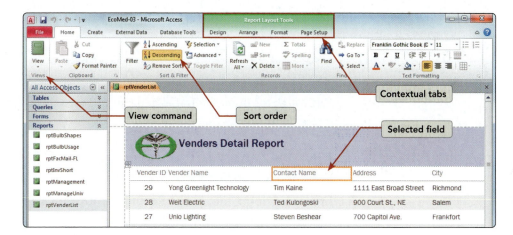

5. From the **Home** tab, in the **Views** group, click **View** and choose **Report View** 📄.

6. Right-click the report's tab and choose **Close** 🗙.

7. Click **Yes** to save the changes.

Adding and Modifying the Totals Row in Datasheets

The Totals row is a feature that you can use to summarize data quickly. For example, if you need to know the total annual revenue of your customers, you would need to create a sum total for the revenue field in the facilities table. In addition to being able to total a field, you can determine the average, count, maximum value, minimum value, standard deviation, and variance of the values.

Exercise 3-9   ADD A TOTALS ROW TO A QUERY

The Totals row uses an aggregate function to summarize a field. An *aggregate function* is a dynamic mathematical calculation that displays a single value for a specific field. Any change to a recordset automatically triggers recalculations of the aggregate functions located in the Totals row.

TABLE 3-2 Totals Row Aggregate Functions

Function	Description
Average	Calculates the average value for a column containing numeric, currency, or date/time data.
Count	Counts the number of items in a column.
Maximum	Returns the item with the highest value. For text data, the highest value is the last alphabetic value.
Minimum	Returns the item with the lowest value. For text data, the lowest value is the first alphabetic value.
Standard Deviation	Measures how widely values are dispersed from an average value.
Sum	Adds the items in a column containing numeric or currency data.
Variance	Measures the statistical variance of all values in the column containing numeric or currency data.

1. From the **Navigation Pane**, open the query **qryFacStats** in **Datasheet View**.
2. From the **Home** tab, in the **Records** group, click **Totals** Σ to add a **Totals** row at the bottom of the **Datasheet View**.
3. In the **Totals** row, click in the **Regions** field. A drop-down arrow appears on the left of the field.
4. Click the drop-down arrow to show the list of available functions.
5. Choose **Count** from the list. There are 167 records with **Regions** data.

NOTE

Aggregate functions will ignore fields that are blank for their calculations. In this case, every record has a **Regions** value so the result of the **Count** function equals the number of records in the recordset.

Figure 3-5
Adding Totals row to a datasheet
EcoMed-03.accdb
qryFacStats

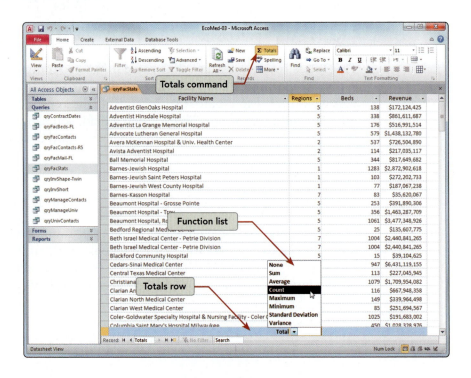

Exercise 3-10   MODIFY A TOTALS ROW IN A QUERY

A Totals row is always present. Once you've created a Totals row in a datasheet, you can never truly delete it. You either modify it with a new function or hide it. Each time you display the Totals row, the functions that you last saved will appear.

TIP

When you see "#####" in a field, it indicates that a number is in the field but is too large to be seen in its entirety with the current column width. To view the number, resize the column to make it wider.

1. In the query **qryFacStats**, click in the **Totals** row for the **Beds** field.

2. Click the drop-down arrow and choose the function **Average**. The average number of beds is shown.

3. In the **Totals** row, click in **Revenue**.

4. Click the drop-down arrow and choose **Maximum**. The largest yearly gross revenue of our client facilities appears.

5. From the **Home** tab, in the **Records** group, click **Totals Σ** to remove the **Totals** row.

6. Click **Close ×** to close the query.

7. Click **Yes** to save the changes.

8. Reopen the query **qryFacStats**.

9. From the **Home** tab, in the **Records** group, click **Totals Σ** to add the **Totals** row. Notice that the functions you added have been saved.

10. Click **Close ×** and then click **Yes** to save the changes.

Using Filters

A *filter* is a database feature that limits the number of records displayed. A filter uses a criterion to determine which records will be displayed. A *criterion* is a rule or test placed upon a field. When the tested field in a record matches the filter criterion, then the record is displayed. If the tested field does not match the filter criterion, then the record is not displayed.

Once you define a filter, you can toggle to either apply or remove it. When applied, a filter displays only matching records. When removed, the entire recordset displays. Whether applied or removed, the actual number of records in the underlying recordset remains constant.

Exercise 3-11   CREATE AND APPLY A FILTER BY SELECTION

Filter By Selection is a filter applied to a single field. The filter can be created to match the entire field or a portion of a field. The selection will be compared to field values in the recordset based upon a comparison option selected from a contextual menu. A contextual menu is a varying list of options based upon an item selected.

The filter options displayed depend upon the type of field and data selected. Options displayed for a date field differ from options displayed for a text field. Some options, such as "Begins With" or "Ends With," display only when the beginning portion or the ending portion of a text field is selected.

When filtering with more than one field, only records that match all filters will display. For example, if you need to list all nonprofit client facilities, you will need to create criteria for the management field. Only records that match "Voluntary Nonprofit, Other" will appear.

TABLE 3-3 Common Contextual Filter Options

Field Type	Filter Option
Date	Equals Does Not Equal On or Before On or After
Numeric	Equals Does Not Equal Less Than or Equal To Greater Than or Equal To Between
Text	Equals Does Not Equal Contains Does Not Contain Begins With Does Not Begin With Ends With Does Not End With

1. From the **Navigation Pane**, open the table **tblFacilities** in **Datasheet View**.
2. In the table **tblFacilities**, in the **Facility Name** field, click the option arrow on the column header, and choose **Sort A to Z** ⬇.
3. Click the **Search** tool and key **hos**. The Search tool finds the first case of hospital in the first record.
4. Double-click the word "hospital" to select the whole word.
5. From the **Home** tab, in the **Sort & Filter** group, click **Selection** 🍸.
6. From the menu, choose **Contains "Hospital"**. There are 142 records that contain "hospital" in their name. Notice that the word hospital can appear in any part of the facility name.

Figure 3-6
Creating a Filter By
Selection
EcoMed-03.accdb
tblFacilities

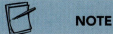

NOTE

The field **Facility Name** now has a small icon of a funnel in the column header to indicate the table has a filter by this field enabled.

7. From the **Home** tab, in the **Sort & Filter** group, click **Toggle Filter** to turn off the filter.

8. Press [Tab] to move to the **Facility Type** field.

9. From the **Home** tab, in the **Sort & Filter** group, click **Selection** and choose **Does Not Equal "Short Term Acute Care"**. You find 17 client facilities that are not a Short-Term Acute Care facility.

10. From the Navigation bar, click **Toggle Filter** to disable the filter.

11. Press [Tab] to move to the **Management Type** field.

12. Click the **Search** tool and delete the previous text.

TIP

When the insertion point is in a field with no characters selected, Filter By Selection assumes the whole field is selected.

13. In the **Search** tool, key **, s**. The search tool finds the **Management Type** "Governmental, State" in the 55th record.

14. Click in the selected field so that no text is selected and the insertion point is located between any two characters in the field.

NOTE

Clearing a filter deletes it from the object, unlike the **Toggle Filter** control, which just turns the filter on and off.

15. From the **Home** tab, in the **Sort & Filter** group, click **Selection** and choose **Equals "Governmental, State"**. Ten facilities have this type of management.

16. Click the drop-down arrow next to the funnel icon in the column heading for the **Management Type** field and choose **Clear filter from Management Type**.

Figure 3-7
Clear a filter
EcoMed-03.accdb tblFacilities

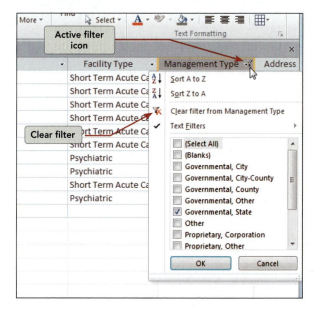

Exercise 3-12   FILTER FOR A SPECIFIC VALUE

When filtering for a specific value, you select one or more values from a predefined criteria list. Each item on a list can be "selected for" or "omitted from" the filter condition. When two or more criteria are selected, either criterion must match for the record to display. For example, assume you select "NY" and "CA" for the state; then, all records from New York as well as all records from California would display.

The criteria list is dynamically created based upon the unique values found in the field. The first two items in every criteria list will be "Select All" and "Blanks." "Select All" toggles between selecting and omitting all values. Selecting "Blanks" includes records for which the criterion field is left empty.

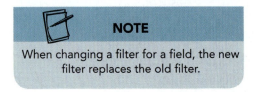

NOTE

When changing a filter for a field, the new filter replaces the old filter.

1. With the table **tblFacilities** open, verify that the focus (column header is yellow) is on the **Management Type** field.

2. From the **Home** tab, in the **Sort & Filter** group, click **Filter** .

3. In the menu, click the check box **(Select All)** to remove all checkmarks.

4. Click the check boxes for **Governmental, City** and **Governmental, State**. All records for both customers display.

5. Click **OK**. All records for both types of customers are displayed.

Figure 3-8
Filter logic: Specific value
EcoMed-03.accdb

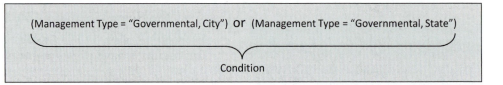

(Management Type = "Governmental, City") **or** (Management Type = "Governmental, State")

Condition

6. From the **Home** tab, in the **Sort & Filter** group, click **Filter** . From the menu, choose **Clear filter from Management Type**.

7. Press Tab until you are at the **Beds** field.

8. From the **Home** tab, in the **Sort & Filter** group, click **Filter** .

9. In the menu, click the check box **(Select All)** and then click the check box for **(Blanks)**.

10. Click **OK** to apply the filter. Only records that do not have data in the **Beds** field are shown.

11. Click the drop-down arrow for **Beds**. From the menu, choose **Clear filter from Beds**.

12. Click the **Close** button and then click **Yes** to save the changes.

Exercise 3-13   FILTER FOR A RANGE OF VALUES

Other contextual filter options, such as calendar filters, have even more options. If you filter on a date field, you can select to filter dates by days, weeks, months, quarters, or years. The options available will vary depending on the date selected and the current date. For example, if the date selected is within the current year, then "This Year" becomes an available filter option.

1. From the **Navigation Pane**, open the report **rptManagement**.

2. From the **Home** tab, in the **Views** group, click **View** and click **Layout View** .

3. Press Shift+Tab to move to the last field header, **Contract Ends**. Right-click this header and from the menu click **Date Filters**. From the menu choose **Between…**.

4. In the **Between Dates** dialog box, click in the **Oldest** control.

5. Key **1/1/2015** and press Tab.

6. Press the **Calendar** button 📅 for the **Newest** control.

7. Use the arrows to move through the calendar until you get to December 2015. Click the 31st to add the date to the **Newest** control.

Figure 3-9
Calendar control
**EcoMed-03.accdb
rptManagement**

8. Click **OK**. The report now only shows details of the management companies whose contracts expire in 2015.

Figure 3-10
Filter logic: Range of values
EcoMed-03.accdb

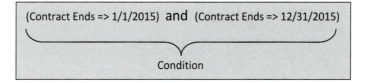

9. From the **Home** tab, in the **Sort & Filter** group, click **Toggle Filter** ▼.

10. Right-click the report's tab and choose **Close** ✕.

Exercise 3-14   CREATE AND APPLY A FILTER BY FORM

Filter By Form allows you to define a collection of criteria for one or more fields using a template. When using Filter By Form in a form, the template appears as a blank form. Alternatively, when using Filter By Form in a datasheet, the template appears as a blank datasheet.

Collections in Filter By Form are organized by tabs. The first tab is called "Look for" and is located in the lower left-hand corner of the template. In a tab, all conditions must be met for a record to be displayed. For example, in the "Look for" tab, if you defined the criterion "NY" for the state and the criterion "Albany" for the city, then only records from "Albany, NY" would be included in the active recordset.

1. From the **Navigation Pane**, open the form **frmFacContacts** in **Form View**.

2. From the **Home** tab, in the **Sort & Filter** group, click **Advanced** 📄 and choose **Filter By Form** 📄.

3. Click the drop-down arrow for the **Region** and choose **2**.

Figure 3-11
Filter By Form
EcoMed-03.accdb
frmFacContacts

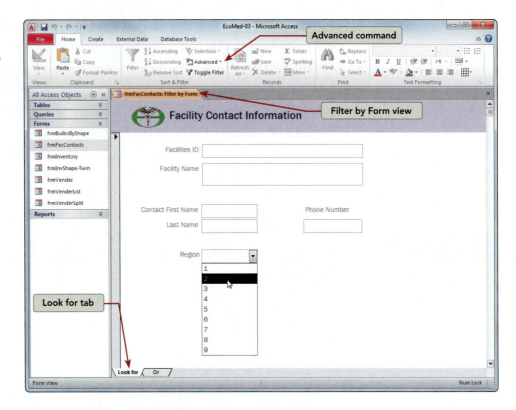

4.   From the **Home** tab, in the **Sort & Filter** group, click **Toggle Filter** ⟨▽⟩. This action returns you to the form and enables the filter, which 10 records match.

5.   Press ⌈PageDown⌋ to move through the records.

6.   From the **Home** tab, in the **Sort & Filter** group, click **Advanced** ⟨▤⟩ and choose **Filter By Form** ⟨▤⟩. The last setting for **Region** is still present.

TIP

The asterisk (*) can be used in a filter just like in the Find & Replace tool.

7.   Click in the **Facility Name** field, and key ***center***.

8.   From the **Home** tab, in the **Sort & Filter** group, click **Toggle Filter** ⟨▽⟩. Only four records display.

Figure 3-12
Filter logic: Filter By
Form
EcoMed-03.accdb

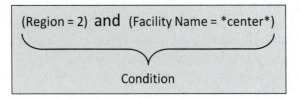

9.   Press ⌈PageDown⌋ to move through the records.

Exercise 3-15   USE FILTER BY FORM OR OPTION

In the previous exercise, you used Filter By Form to create a set of filters in a single tab. There are times that you may need to create a more complex filter using multiple tabs. The Filter By Form has the ability to add alternate sets of filters. Alternative collections of filters are located on the "Or" tab. When using multiple tabs, displayed records must match all conditions on the first tab or all conditions on the additional "Or" tabs.

Suppose that you need to display a list of client facilities in Kansas and Missouri. Although you might say "Kansas and Missouri," this request is actually an OR condition. You really want to display all the records that are in the state "KS" or the state "MO." Because both values are applied to the same field, you must place the first filter on the "Look for" tab and the second on the "Or" tab.

1. From the **Home** tab, in the **Sort & Filter** group, click **Advanced** and choose **Filter By Form**. The filter is set to find facilities that are in Region 2 and are "Centers."

2. Click the **Or** tab next to the **Look for** tab to open an alternative collection of fields.

3. Click the drop-down arrow for the **Region** and choose **3**.

4. Click in the **Facility Name** field, and key ***center***.

> **NOTE**
>
> Other symbols can be used in a Filter By Form. For numerical data, logical operators (>, <, >=, <=, =, and <>) can be used.

Figure 3-13
Filter logic: Filter By Form with Or
EcoMed-03.accdb

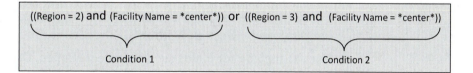

5. From the **Home** tab, in the **Sort & Filter** group, click **Toggle Filter**. There are eight records that match both conditions.

6. From the **Home** tab, in the **Sort & Filter** group, choose **Toggle Filter** to disable the filter.

7. Click the **Close** button ⊠ to close the form.

Using the Database Documenter

External documentation helps EcoMed's IT department document changes to its database. An easy way to document the structure of the database is to create a report using the Database Documenter. The *Database Documenter* is an Access tool that lists the indexes, properties, relationships, parameters, and permissions of major database objects.

Exercise 3-16   SAVE A REPORT FOR A TABLE

When documenting a single object, you often need to include details for fields and indexes. By default, the Database Documenter does not include fields or indexes in its report. It is always a good idea to check which options are selected before printing a report.

1. From the **Database Tools** tab, in the **Analyze** group, click **Database Documenter** 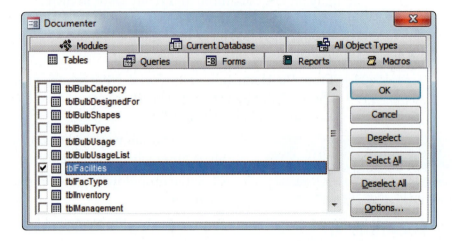.

2. In the **Documenter** dialog box, on the **Tables** tab, click the check box for **tblFacilities**.

Figure 3-14
Database
Documenter
EcoMed-03.accdb

3. Click **Options** to open the **Print Table Definition** dialog box.

4. For the **Include for Table** section, check **Properties**, **Relationships**, and **Permissions by User and Group**.

5. For the **Include for Fields** section, select **Names, Data Types, Sizes, and Properties** (third option).

6. For the **Include for Indexes** section, select **Names, Fields, and Properties** (third option).

7. Click **OK** to accept the changes and close the dialog box.

8. Click **OK** to view the report.

9. From the **Print Preview** tab, in the **Zoom** group, click **More Pages** and choose **Twelve Pages** from the menu. This nine-page report contains all the available information on the design of this table.

10. Click the **Close Print Preview** button.

11. From **Database Tools** tab, in the **Analyze** group, click **Database Documenter**.

12. In the **Documenter** dialog box, on the **Tables** tab, click the check box for **tblFacilities**.

13. Click **Options** to open the **Print Table Definition** dialog box.

14. For the **Include for Table** section, only check **Properties** and **Relationships**.

15. For the **Include for Fields** section, select **Names, Data Types, and Sizes** (second option).

TIP

In this book, you will be asked to generate a Documenter report when the structure of an object has been modified. To reduce the number of pages in the report, you will be asked to apply specific option settings.

16. For the **Include for Indexes** section, select **Nothing** (first option).

Figure 3-15
Print Table Definition
options
EcoMed-03.accdb

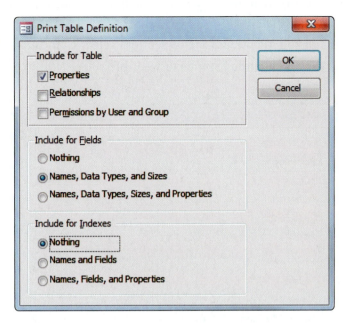

17. Click **OK** to accept the changes and close the dialog box.

18. Click **OK** to view the report. This version of the report is only one page.

19. From the command tab **Print Preview**, in the command group **Data**, click **PDF or XPS** 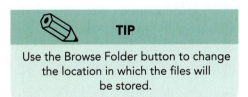.

> **TIP**
>
> Use the Browse Folder button to change the location in which the files will be stored.

20. Change the location to the location where you will be storing your work.

21. In the **File name** control, type *[your initials]*-**03-16**.

22. Click the **Save as type** control, and select **PDF**.

23. Verify the **Open file after publishing** check box is checked.

24. Click **Publish** to create the PDF file.

25. Close the PDF viewer. Click the **Close** button for the **Export-XPS** dialog box.

26. Click **Close Print Preview** ⊠.

Exercise 3-17   SAVE REPORT FOR OTHER OBJECTS

The documentable properties of a query are different than the properties of a table. Because a query has criteria, it also has an SQL statement. The SQL statement is a text representation of the query's criteria.

1. From **Database Tools** tab, in the **Analyze** group, click **Database Documenter** 📄.

2. In the **Documenter** dialog box, on the **Queries** tab, click the check box for **qryFacMail-FL**.

3. Click **Options** to open the **Print Query Definition** dialog box.

4. For the **Include for Query** section, only check the check boxes for **Properties** and **SQL**.

5. For the **Include for Fields** section, select **Names, Data Types, and Sizes**.

6. For the **Include for Indexes** section, select **Nothing**.

Figure 3-16
Print Query
Definition options
EcoMed-03.accdb

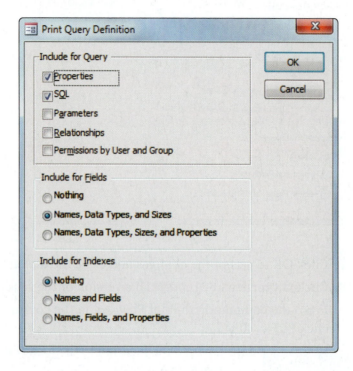

7. Click **OK** to accept the changes and close the dialog box.

8. Click **OK** to view the report. Notice that the information for the query fits on one page.

9. From the **Print Preview** tab, in the group **Data**, click **PDF or XPS**.

10. Change the location to the location where you will be storing your homework.

11. In the **File name** control, type *[your initials]*-03-17.

12. Click the **Save As type** control, and select **PDF**.

13. Verify that the **Open file after Exporting** check box is checked.

14. Click **Publish** to create the PDF file. This report is only one page.

15. Review the PDF file in the PDF reader, then close the file and the **Export-XPS** dialog box.

16. In Access, click the **Close** button [X] to close the database.

Lesson 3   Summary

- To locate specific information, you can use Access tools to search, find, sort, and filter.
- You can improve search speeds by specifying unique data.
- The Search tool begins its search at the first field of the first record and stops at the first match.
- The Find and Replace command begins a search at the insertion point and includes options for fine-tuning how text is matched.
- A wildcard is a character or group of characters used to represent one or more alphabetical or numerical characters.
- The Totals row is a feature that you can use to calculate aggregate functions quickly.
- Each time you display the Totals row, the functions that you last saved will appear.
- A filter is a database feature that limits the number of records displayed.
- When applying a filter to a recordset, only records matching the criterion will display.
- The Filter By Selection options displayed depend upon the type of field and data selected.
- When filtering for a specific value, you select one or more values from a dynamically created list.
- The date filter options available vary depending on the date selected and the current date.
- Filter By Form allows you to define a collection of criteria for one or more fields using a template.
- Filter By Form has the ability to add alternate sets of filters located on the "Or" tab.
- The Database Documenter is an Access tool that lists the indexes, properties, relationships, parameters, and permissions of major database objects.

LESSON 3		Command Summary	
Feature	**Button**	**Task Path**	**Keyboard**
Database Documenter		Database Tools, Analyze, Database Documenter	
Filter by Form		Home, Sort & Filter, Advanced, Filter By Form	
Filter Range of Values		Home, Sort & Filter, (data type) Filters	
Filter Selection		Home, Sort & Filter, Selection	
Filter Specific Value		Home, Sort & Filter, Filter	
Find		Home, Find, Find	Ctrl + F
Replace		Home, Find, Replace	Ctrl + H
Sort Ascending		Home, Sort & Filter, Ascending	
Sort Descending		Home, Sort & Filter, Descending	
Sort Remove		Home, Sort & Filter, Clear All Sorts	
Totals Rows		Home, Records, Totals	
Layout View		Home, Views, Layout View	
Report View		Home, Views, Report View	

Please visit our Online Learning Center, *www.lessonapproach2010.com*, where you will find the following review materials:

Concepts Review

True/False Questions

Short Answer Questions

Critical Thinking Questions

Skills Review

Review Exercises that target single skills

Lesson Applications

Review Exercises that challenge students by testing multiple skills in each exercise

On Your Own

Open-ended exercises that require students to synthesize multiple skills and apply creativity and problem-solving as they would in a real world business situation

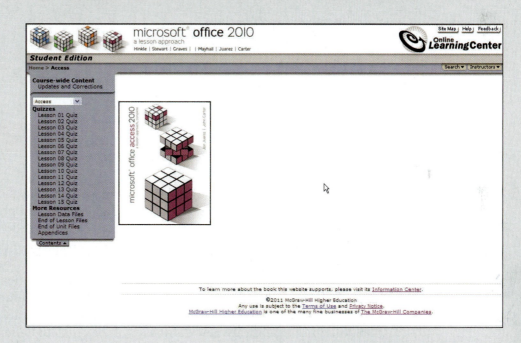

OBJECTIVES *After completing this lesson, you will be able to:*

1. Create a database.
2. Create a table.
3. Manage external data.
4. Control field appearance.
5. Control data integrity.
6. Add and delete fields in a table.

Estimated Time: 2 hours

EcoMed Services, Inc., maintains a database that tracks customer information, including contact names, facilities, addresses, and phone numbers. The database also tracks product information, including model numbers, product types, pricing, and technical specifications. All of these data are vital information necessary to operate a company on a day-to-day basis.

As the company grows, EcoMed's day-to-day activities may change. New procedures or new departments may need to be implemented. To meet the changing requirements, new data may need to be tracked and managed. Sometimes an entirely new database will be created. Other times, only a new table will be added.

The structure of a database is critical for a company's ability to convert data into useful information. A database must be both efficient and effective. It must be designed to improve data management and protect the integrity of the data.

Creating Databases

The president of EcoMed Services, Inc., has decided that the company should begin keeping up with technological advances in energy management. The sales department has been given the new tasks of attending energy conferences and tracking new contacts they make at the conferences. You have been directed to create two new databases to track the conferences and the contacts.

There are two methods for creating a new database. One method uses templates to create a structured database containing major objects (tables, queries, forms, or reports). The second method creates a blank database without any objects.

Exercise 4-1   CREATE A DATABASE USING A TEMPLATE

When creating a new database, you sometimes can find a database template on which to base your preliminary design. A *database template* is a ready-to-use database containing all the tables, queries, forms, and reports needed to perform a specific task.

For example, Access includes an events template designed for tracking events, which includes the event name, start time, end time, description, and location. The events template also includes two forms and five reports that can display the events by start time or event type. Creating this template will be useful for developing a functional conference database.

1. Click the **Start** button 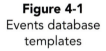 on the Windows taskbar and point to **All Programs**.

2. Click **Microsoft Office Access 2007** to start Access. (You might have to first point to a program group, such as Microsoft Office).

3. Access opens to the **Backstage** with the **New** tab selected.

4. In the **Available Templates** section, click **Sample templates**.

5. Click the **Contacts Web Database** template.

Figure 4-1
Events database templates

6. Click the **File New Database** button .

7. In the **File New Database** dialog box, navigate to the location where you want to store your class work. Change the **File name** to *[your initials]-Contacts*. Click **OK**.

8. Click **Create** to launch the template. The new database opens with a form already open.

NOTE

Microsoft templates do not follow the Leszynski Naming Conventions when naming major objects.

9. In the **Security Warning** message, click **Enable Content** to continue.

10. Click the **Shutter Bar Open/Close** button » to expand the **Navigation Pane**.

11. This database has two tables, one query, 13 forms, and six reports. Open a few forms and reports to see the layouts of the objects.

12. Open the table **Contacts**. Review the types of data that can be stored. Many of these fields are not needed for our company.

13. Right-click the document tab for the table **Contacts** and choose **Close**.

Exercise 4-2   SET DATABASE PROPERTIES

Database properties do not change the functionality of the database. They only provide useful information to help identify the file. Adding properties to a database can help you and other database managers identify the purpose of the database. Some database properties, such as the title, author, and company, are defined automatically when the database is created. The information automatically entered comes from the identification settings of the workstation on which the database is created.

When creating a new database, you should change the properties to reflect the purpose for which the database was created. Some properties, such as Compact on close, help keep the size of the database manageable.

1. Click the **File** tab. In the Backstage View, the **Info** option is selected. At the far right of the screen, click **View and edit database properties**.

2. Click in the textbox for the **Title** property and key the name of your class.

3. Change the value for **Author** to *[your full name]*.

4. In the property **Comments**, key **This database was created using Microsoft Contacts template on** *[today's date]*.

5. Click **OK** to close the dialog box.

6. While in the Backstage View, click the **Options** button .

7. In the left pane, click the **Current Database** category. Locate the **Compact on Close** property and click the check box to add a checkmark.

Figure 4-2
Changing properties

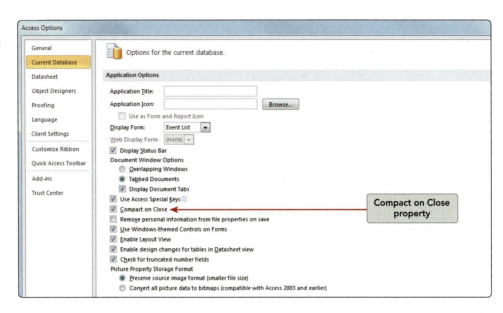

8. Click **OK** to close the **Access Option** dialog box.

9. A warning dialog box appears to inform you that the database must be restarted before your changes will be implemented. Click **OK**.

10. Click the **File** tab. Click **Close Database** 📇 to close the active database without closing Access.

Exercise 4-3   CREATE A BLANK DATABASE

If you cannot find a database template to meet your needs, you must create a blank database from scratch. The process requires you to name the database and specify the location in which it will be saved. Once the database is created, you will be able to add other major objects, such as tables, queries, reports, and forms.

1. In the **New** option tab, click **Blank database** 📄.

2. Click the **File New Database** button 📂.

3. In the **File New Database** dialog box, navigate to the location where you want to store your class work. Change the **File name** to *[your initials]*-EcoMed-Contacts. Click **OK**.

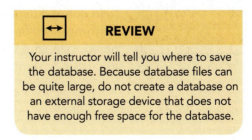

↔   REVIEW

Your instructor will tell you where to save the database. Because database files can be quite large, do not create a database on an external storage device that does not have enough free space for the database.

Figure 4-3
Create a blank
database

4. Click **Create** 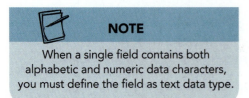. A new table opens in **Datasheet View**.

5. Click the **Close** button ⊠ for the table. Notice that because the table does not contain fields, it is not listed in the Navigation Pane.

Creating a Table

The company president wants EcoMed Services, Inc., to begin developing sales leads. You have been directed to create a table to store contact information for potential customers. In a well-designed database, each table should store data for a unique purpose. The new table that you create will store only new sales lead contacts.

Exercise 4-4 CREATE A TABLE IN DESIGN VIEW

NOTE

When a single field contains both alphabetic and numeric data characters, you must define the field as text data type.

Design View offers you the greatest flexibility when defining field names, types, and properties. The order and type of field defined depends on the data that will be stored. When defining new fields, you will need to determine the field name, size, and type. For example, prices should be stored as currency, names as text, and images as attachments.

TABLE 4-1 Access Data Types

Setting	Type of Data
Text	Alphanumeric characters. A text field can be a maximum of 255 characters long. Use Text as the Data Type for numbers that are not used in calculations, such as addresses or phone numbers.
Memo	Descriptive text such as sentences and paragraphs used for text greater than 255 characters in length or for text that uses rich text formatting.
Number	Numbers (integer or real). Data in a number field can be used in arithmetic calculations. Use Number as the Data Type when values will used in calculations.
Date/Time	Formatted dates or times used in date and time calculations. Each value stored includes both a date component and a time component.
Currency	Money values used for storing monetary values (currency). Values can be used in arithmetic calculations and can display a currency symbol.
AutoNumber	A unique numeric value automatically created by Access when a record is added. Use AutoNumber Data Type for generating unique values that can be used as a primary key.
Yes/No	Boolean value displayed as check boxes. Use Yes/No Data Type for True/False fields that can hold one of two possible values.
Attachment	Pictures, images, binary files, or Office files. Preferred data type for storing digital images and any type of binary file.
Hyperlink	Navigation element for an Internet site, e-mail address, or file pathname. Use Hyperlink Data Type for storing hyperlinks to provide single-click access to Web pages through a URL (Uniform Resource Locator) or files through a name in UNC (universal naming convention) format.

1. From the **Create** tab, in the **Tables** group, click **Table** ▦. A new table is created, and the ribbon now shows the contextual tabs **Fields** and **Table**.

2. From the **Fields** contextual tab, in the **Views** group, click the top part of the split button ⬗ to switch to **Design View**.

3. In the **Save As** dialog box, key **tblContacts** and click **OK**. The table is now in **Design View**.

UNIT 1 LESSON 4

Figure 4-4
Design View of
a table
**EcoMed-Contacts.
accdb
tblContacts**

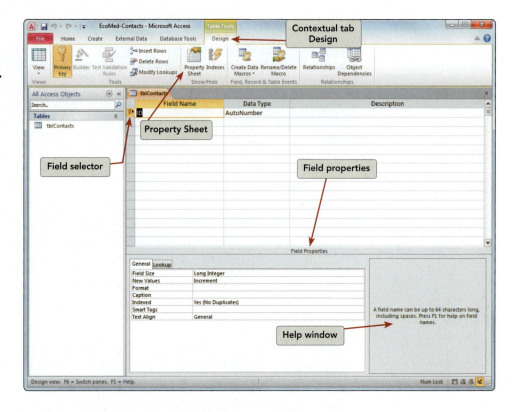

4. In the first row, in the **Field Name** column, key **ContactID**.

5. Press Tab to move to the **Data Type** column. The default **Data Type** for the first field in a new table is **AutoNumber**.

6. Press Tab to move to the **Description** column. Key **Contact identification number**.

7. Press Tab to move to the second field in the **Field Name** column. Key **LastName**.

8. Press Tab to move to the **Data Type** column. The default data type is **Text**.

9. Press Tab and key **Last name of contact**.

10. Enter the following fields:

Field Name	Data Type	Description
FirstName	Text	First name of contact
Company	Text	Contact's company
EmailAddr	Hyperlink	Contact's company Email
PhoneNum	Text	Office phone number
Fax_Num	Text	Office FAX number
FirstContact	Date/Time	Date that first contact was made
Notes	Memo	Comments about the contact

11. Click the **Close** button ✕ for the table.

Figure 4-5
Structure changes to
a table
**EcoMed-Contacts.
accdb
tblContacts**

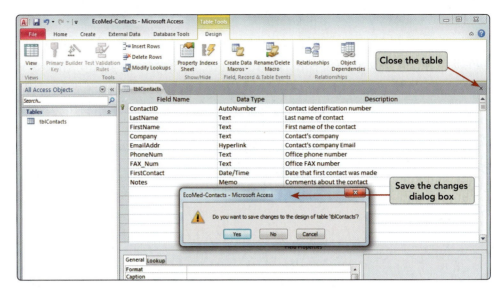

12. Click **Yes** to save the changes to the design of the table.

Exercise 4-5   MODIFY TABLE PROPERTIES

Table properties do not change the functionality of the table. They only provide useful information to help identify the object. Some properties, such as owner or date/time modified, are automatically updated according to the workstation settings.

1. In the **Navigation Pane**, right-click the table **tblContacts**, and choose **Table Properties**.

2. In the Description textbox, key **This table stores the information for EcoMed's contacts**.

Figure 4-6
Table Properties
**EcoMed-Contacts.
accdb
tblContacts**

tblContacts Properties

General

tblContacts

Type: Table
Description: This table stores the information for EcoMed's contacts|

Created: 12/20/2009 7:03:59 PM
Modified: 12/20/2009 7:27:02 PM
Owner: Admin

Attributes: ☐ Hidden

OK   Cancel   Apply

3. Click **OK**.

4. In the **Navigation Pane**, double-click the table **tblContacts**.

5. From the **Home** tab, in the **Views** group, choose **View** ✎.

6. From the **Design** tab, in the **Show/Hide** group, click **Property Sheet** 🗂. The **Property Sheet** appears. Notice that the **Description** property contains the text from Step 2.

7. From the **Design** tab, in the **Show/Hide** group, click **Property Sheet** 🗂 to close the **Property Sheet**.

8. Right-click the **tblContacts** document tab and choose **Close** ⬛.

Managing External Data

EcoMed Services, Inc., uses electronic data interchange whenever possible. *Electronic data interchange* (EDI) is the transfer of electronic data from one computer system to another. EDI transfers data from one system to another without re-entering or re-keying data. Importing data electronically prevents errors that may occur when data is re-keyed incorrectly.

Each time you import data, you duplicate the original data. The original data remain in the source application while you work with a copy of the data in your database.

Exercise 4-6   COPY TABLE STRUCTURE FROM AN EXTERNAL TABLE

When copying a table, you have three options: You can select to include only the structure, the structure and data, or only the data. When you copy only the structure, you create an empty table without any records. You can add records at a later time.

1. From the **External Data** tab, in the **Import & Link** group, click **Access** 🅰.

2. In the **Get External Data** dialog box, click **Browse**.

3. In the **File Open** dialog box, locate the **Lesson 04** folder and select the file **EcoMed-04**. Click **Open**.

4. Back in the **Get External Data** dialog box, make sure that the **Import table, queries, forms, reports, ...** option is selected. Click **OK**.

5. In the **Import Objects** dialog box, click the **Options** button.

6. Remove the checkmark from **Relationships**.

7. In the **Import Tables** section, select **Definition Only**.

8. Select the table **tblManagement** from the list of tables.

Figure 4-7
Import table options
**EcoMed- Contacts.
accdb
tblManagement**

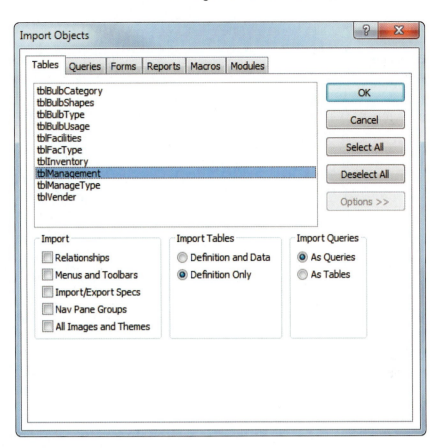

9. Click **OK**. Close the **Get External Data** dialog box.

10. In the **Navigation Pane**, double-click **tblManagement**. This table has no records. Only the table structure was copied.

11. Right-click the **tblManagement** document tab and choose **Close** ⬜.

12. Click the **File** tab. Click **Exit** ❎.

Exercise 4-7 EXPORT A TABLE TO ACCESS

You can export an Access table directly to another Microsoft application, such as Word or Excel. Access tables can also be exported directly to non-Microsoft applications such as dBASE and Paradox. For applications not supported by Access, you can export a table using a file format such as text, XML, or HTML. When exporting a table, you can save the steps used in the export operation. Saving the steps can greatly decrease the time it takes to export the same table next time.

1. Locate and open the **Lesson 04** folder.

2. Make a copy of **EcoMed-04** and rename it *[your initials]*-**EcoMed-04**.

3. Open and enable content for *[your initials]*-**EcoMed-04**.

4. Right-click the table **tblVender** in the **Navigation Pane** and choose **Export**, then **Access** 🅰.

Figure 4-8
Export a table
EcoMed-04.accdb
tblVender

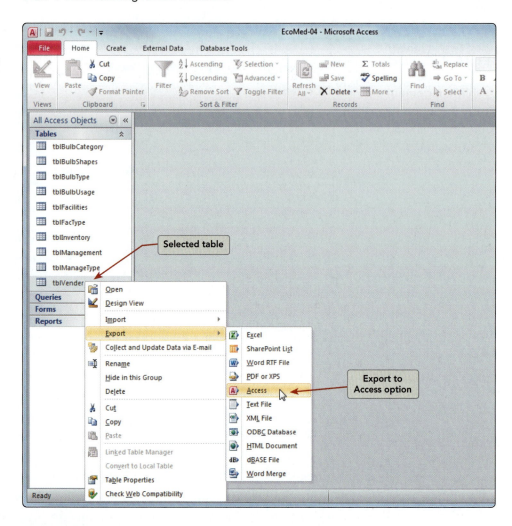

5. In the **Export – Access Database** dialog box, click **Browse**.

6. In the **File Save** dialog box, locate and click *[your initials]*-**EcoMed-Contacts**, which you created earlier in this lesson. Click **Save**.

7. Click **OK** to close the **Export – Access Database** dialog box.

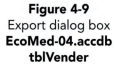

NOTE

Check with your instructor to verify the location of your student data files and the location in which you will be working. The folder "Documents" is often the default folder when you create or store files.

Figure 4-9
Export dialog box
EcoMed-04.accdb
tblVender

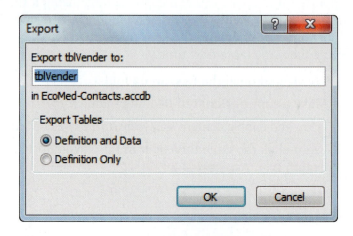

NOTE

You may want to open the database *[your initials]*-EcoMed-Contacts to verify that the table was exported.

8. Click **OK** to export the table **tblVender** with its data and structure.

9. In the **Export – Access Database** dialog box, click **Close**.

Exercise 4-8 EXPORT DATA TO WORD

You can export a table, query, form, or report to Microsoft Word using the Access Export Wizard. A copy of the object's data will be stored as a Rich Text Format (rtf) file. For tables, queries, and forms, the visible fields and records appear as a table in the Word document. Hidden or filtered columns and records are not exported.

1. In the **Navigation Pane**, select the query **qryUnivContacts**.

2. From the **External Data** tab, in the **Export** group, click **More** and then select **Word**.

3. In the **Export – RTF File** dialog box, delete "qry" from the file name.

4. Click the check box **Open the destination file after the export operation is complete**. Click **OK**.

5. View the table in Word, then close the application Word.

6. In the **Export – RTF File** dialog box, click **Close**.

Exercise 4-9 IMPORT DATA FROM EXCEL

For most non-Access applications, a wizard steps you through the import process. When importing from an Excel workbook, you may select all columns and rows from a worksheet or just a range of cells. The ease of importing data greatly depends upon how the information is stored in the source spreadsheet.

1. In the **Navigation Pane**, double-click the table **tblManagement**. Notice that there are 107 companies in this table.

2. Close the table.

3. From the **External Data** tab, in the **Import & Link** group, click **Excel**.

4. In the **Get External Data – Excel Spreadsheet** dialog box, click **Browse**.

5. In the **File Open** dialog box, locate the folder **Lesson 04**, and select the Excel file **New Management**.

6. Click **Open**.

7. Select the option **Append a copy of the records to the table:**, click the drop-down arrow, and select **tblManagement**.

Figure 4-10
Import data from
Excel
EcoMed-04.accdb
tblManagement

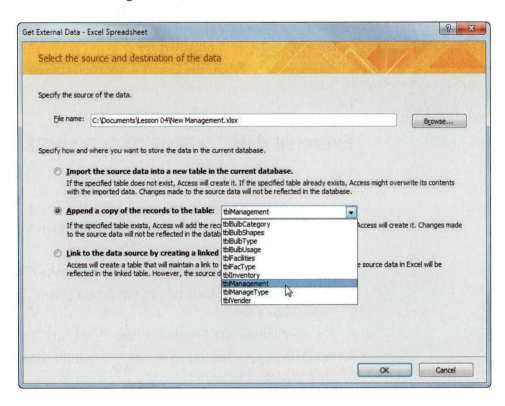

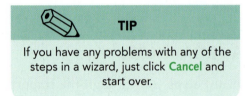

TIP

If you have any problems with any of the
steps in a wizard, just click **Cancel** and
start over.

8. Click **OK** to start the **Import Spreadsheet Wizard**.
9. In the first step of the **Import Spreadsheet Wizard**, you
   see the data from the Excel file. Click **Next**.
10. Access has identified the information in the first row
    as header information. These headers will be treated
    as field names. Click **Next**.
11. Click **Finish**. In the **Get External Data – Excel Spreadsheet** dialog box,
    click **Close**.
12. Open **tblManagement** in **Datasheet View**. There are now 110 records.
    Three records were imported. Close the table.

Adding and Deleting Fields in a Table

Although infrequent, sometimes the changes needed by EcoMed Services,
Inc., require that a table be modified. Adding and deleting require a different
level of care.

Before adding a field to a table, you first should make certain that it does
not duplicate an existing field's data. Adding a new field in one table to store
data that is already in another table creates an inefficient data design and can
lead to data entry errors.

Deleting a field can be much more dangerous than adding one. Before
deleting a field from a table, make certain that the data in the field will never
be needed in the future. Many database administrators would rather move
data to an archive table than delete historical information.

Exercise 4-10 ADD AND DELETE FIELDS IN DATASHEET VIEW

You also can insert and delete fields in Datasheet View. When inserting a text field in a datasheet, the default width of the field is 255 spaces. Each field will be named Field*n*, where n is a sequential number starting with one (1). Although the task of deleting a field from datasheet may appear similar to hiding the field, deleting a field is a permanent action that cannot be undone.

1. In the **Navigation Pane**, double-click the table **tblManagement**.

2. From the **Home** tab, in the **Records** group, click **More** and click **Unhide Fields** from the menu.

3. In the **Unhide Fields** dialog box, click the check box for **Click to Add**. Click **Close**.

4. Press End to move to the last field in the table.

5. Right-click the field header **Click to Add** and choose **Yes/No** from the shortcut menu. The field is now called **Field1**, and a new **Click to Add** column has been added.

6. Key **NonProfit** and press ↓. Check boxes appear in the new field. A checkmark equals "Yes," "True," or "On."

7. Press End and Shift+Tab to return to the last field.

TIP

In field names, using symbols other than dashes (-) or underscores (_) can cause problems. There are no such problems with captions.

8. From the **Fields** tab, in the **Properties** group, click **Name & Caption**.

9. Press Tab to move to the **Caption** textbox. Key **NonProfit?**.

10. Press Tab to move to the **Description** textbox. Key **A checkmark indicates that a company is a NonProfit organization**. Click **OK**.

11. Notice that the **Caption** setting is what you see as the field header. Also the **Description** now appears in the status bar.

12. Click on the column header for the **CEO**.

13. From the **Fields** tab, in the **Add & Delete** group, click **Delete**. Click **Yes** to confirm the deletion.

Exercise 4-11 ADD AND DELETE FIELDS IN DESIGN VIEW

Adding fields through Design View is more flexible than through Datasheet View. In addition to text, numeric, and date fields, you can define and size all field types.

NOTE

When you insert a field, the new row is placed in the row selected, and all fields below are moved down.

1. From the **Fields** tab, in the **Views** group, click **View** to switch to **Design View**.

2. Click on the field selector for **PhoneNum**.

3. From the **Design** tab, in the **Tools** group, click **Insert Rows**.

Figure 4-11
Inserting a row
EcoMed-04.accdb
tblManagement

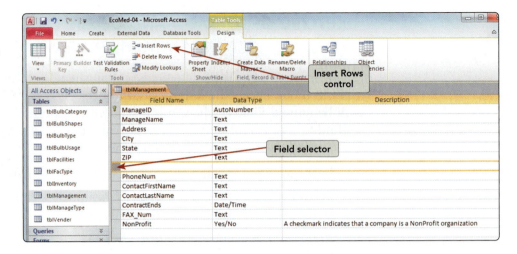

4. Click in the **Field Name** for the blank row and key **CellNum**.

5. Press [Tab]. The default **Data Type** is **Text**. Press [Tab].

6. In the **Description** for **CellNum** key **Contact's work cell number**.

7. From the **Design** tab, in the **Views** group, click **View** to switch to **Datasheet View**.

8. Click **Yes** to save the changes to the table's structure.

9. From the **Home** tab, in the **Views** group, click **View** to switch to **Design View**.

10. Select the field selector for **FAX_Num**.

11. From the **Design** tab, in the **Tools** group, click **Delete Rows**. Click **Yes** to confirm the deletion.

12. From the Quick Access Toolbar, click **Save**.

REVIEW

Changes to field data are saved automatically; however, you must save design changes to the table.

Controlling Field Appearance

Certain field properties control how a field appears to database users. A change to one of these properties only affects the field's appearance without changing the underlying structure or size of the field.

Changing a field's appearance may be necessary for functional reasons, not merely cosmetic ones. For example, when most records use the same area code, you may change the default value for the phone number. This simple change may improve the speed, accuracy, and consistency of your data entry.

NOTE

Spaces should not be used in field names. Spaces create complications when using fields in advanced objects such as Macros and Modules.

TABLE 4-2 Text Field Properties

Property	Purpose
Field Size	Controls the size of a text field and can be up to 255 characters.
Format	Defines the appearance of data. Custom formatting changes the appearance of the data without changing the underlying record.
Input Mask	Displays a pattern for entering the data. Examples are the use of parentheses around an area code or hyphens in a social security number.
Caption	Sets a label or title for the field. The Caption replaces the field name as the column title in a datasheet and as the control label in forms and reports.
Default Value	Specifies the value that automatically appears in a field when creating a new record. The value can be accepted or changed.
Validation Rule	Condition specifying criteria for entering data into an individual field. A Validation Rule of ">100" requires values to be larger than 100.
Validation Text	Error message that appears when a value prohibited by the validation rule is entered. For the Validation Rule ">100," the Validation Text might be "You must enter a value greater than 100."
Required	Requires entry of a value in the field when set to "Yes."

Exercise 4-12 CHANGE FIELD PROPERTY CAPTION

When no caption is defined, the name of the field displays as its column heading on a datasheet or as its control label in a form or report. When a field caption is defined, the caption will be used instead.

1. In the **Design View** of **tblManagement**, double-click the field **ManageID** to select the **Field Name**. Press Ctrl+C.

2. In the **Field Properties** sect ion, click in the **Caption** property.

3. Press Ctrl+V. Add a space between "Manage" and "ID".

4. Press ← and key **ment**.

Figure 4-12
Change the caption
property
**EcoMed-04.accdb
tblManagement**

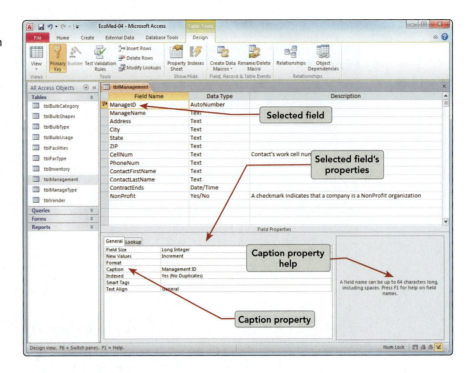

5. Double-click the **Field Name PhoneNum** and press Ctrl+C.

6. Press F6 to move to the **Field Properties** section.

TIP

When a **Field Name** is one word, you do not need a **Caption**.

7. Press Tab three times to move to the **Caption** property.

8. Press Ctrl+V. Add a space between "Phone" and "Num."

9. Press End and key **ber**.

10. Press Ctrl+S to save the changes to the table structure.

Exercise 4-13 CHANGE FIELD PROPERTY DEFAULT VALUE

Setting a default value is useful when a significant number of records contain the same field value. For example, if the majority of your employees live in the same state, you might choose to set a default value for the state field. All new records will display the default value, and previously entered records will not be changed. Whenever a record contains a different value for the field, the user can key a new value to replace the default value.

1. In the **Design View** of **tblManagement**, click the field selector for **NonProfit** and press F6.

2. Press Tab until you reach the **Default Value** property.

3. This property is set to "0," which represents the cleared check box.

4. Change the zero to a **-1**. The -1 value represents the checked check box.

5. From the **Home** tab, in the **Views** group, click **View** to switch to **Datasheet View**. Click **Yes** to save the changes.

6. Press Ctrl+End to move to the last record. Notice that the record selector with the asterisk (*) has a checked check box. This row is the new record row.

7. From the **Home** tab, in the **Views** group, click **View** to switch to **Design View**.

8. Key **0** to change the **Default Value** property for **NonProfit** back to "0".

9. Press Ctrl+S to save the changes to the table structure.

Exercise 4-14 CHANGE FIELD PROPERTY FORMAT

You can improve data entry by specifying formats. For example, you can set the format for a date to display the name of the month, set the format for currency to show dollar signs, or set the format for text to display as uppercase letters. For some data types, you can select from predefined formats. For others, you can enter a custom format.

1. In the **Design View** of **tblManagement**, click the field selector for **ContractEnds**, and press F6.

2. In the **Format** property, click the drop-down arrow and select **Medium Date**.

Figure 4-13
Setting Format property
EcoMed-04.accdb
tblManagement

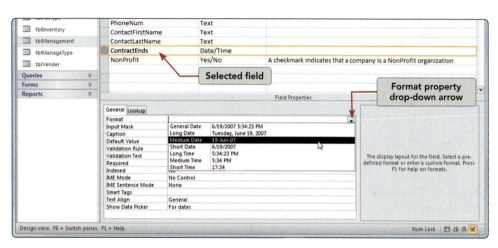

3. From the **Design** tab, in the **Views** group, click **View** to switch to **Datasheet View**. Save your changes.

4. Press Tab until you see the **ContractEnds** field. The appearance of the dates has changed.

5. From the **Home** tab, in the **Views** group, click **View** to switch to **Design View**.

6. Click the field selector for **State** and press F6.

7. In the **Format** property, key **>**. This will visually make the content of this field appear in upper case.

8. From the **Design** tab, in the **Views** group, click **View** to switch to **Datasheet View**. Save your changes.

9. In the **State** field for **Management ID** 1, key **il**. Press Tab. The data display as upper-case characters.

10. From the **Home** tab, in the **Views** group, click **View** to switch to **Design View**.

Exercise 4-15   CHANGE FIELD PROPERTY INPUT MASK

An input mask is used to format the display of data and control the format in which values can be entered. Input masks can be used for text or numeric data types. You can use the Input Mask Wizard for common formats, such as telephone numbers and social security numbers.

TABLE 4-3 Input Masks

Character	Description
0	Digit (0 through 9, entry required; plus <+> and minus <–> signs not allowed).
9	Digit or space (entry not required; plus and minus signs not allowed).
#	Digit or space (entry not required; blank positions converted to spaces, plus and minus signs allowed).
L	Letter (A through Z, entry required).
?	Letter (A through Z, entry optional).

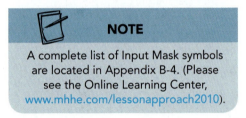

NOTE

A complete list of Input Mask symbols are located in Appendix B-4. (Please see the Online Learning Center, www.mhhe.com/lessonapproach2010).

1. In the **Design View** of **tblManagement**, click the field selector for **PhoneNum** and press F6.
2. Click the **Input Mask** property row.
3. From the **Design** tab, in the **Tools** group, click **Builder** 🖾.

Figure 4-14
Input Mask Wizard dialog box
EcoMed-04.accdb tblManagement

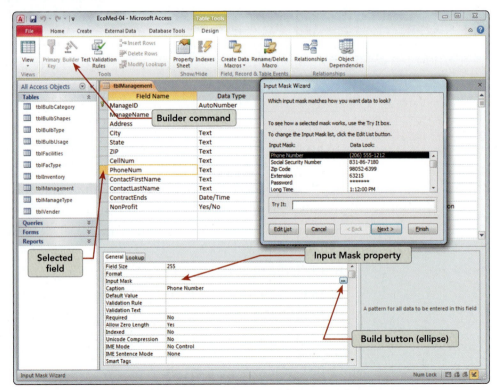

4. The **Input Mask Wizard** lists several common masks and shows how the data are displayed. Select the **Phone Number** mask.

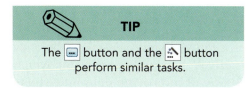

TIP

The ⊡ button and the ⬀ button perform similar tasks.

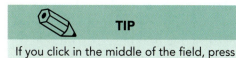

TIP

If you click in the middle of the field, press Home to move the insertion point to the beginning of the field.

5. Click **Next**. The wizard asks if you want to change the input mask. Click in the **Try It** entry box.

6. Press Home. Key your phone number.

7. Click **Next**. The wizard asks how you want to store the data. Select **With the symbols in the mask, like this:**.

8. Click **Next**. Read the final message and click **Finish**.

9. From the **Design** tab, in the **Views** group, click **View** ⊞ to switch to **Datasheet View**. Save your changes.

10. For the first record, press Tab until you reach the **Phone Number** field and try entering your phone number.

11. From the **Home** tab, in the **Views** group, click **View** ⬃ to switch to **Design View**.

Exercise 4-16 CHANGE FIELD PROPERTY DATE PICKER

Depending on the workstation's language settings, the date picker displays either to the right or left sides of a Date/Time field. Clicking the date picker launches a calendar control from which you can select a date. If the field is empty, the Date Picker will default to the current date.

1. In the **Design View** of **tblManagement**, click the field selector for **ContractEnds** and press F6.

2. Move to the **Show Date Picker** property, click the drop-down arrow, and select **For dates**.

3. From the **Design** tab, in the **Views** group, click **View** ⊞ to switch to **Datasheet View**. Save your changes.

4. Click in the first record's **ContractEnds** and click the **Date Picker** ▦.

Figure 4-15
Date Picker
EcoMed-04.accdb
tblManagement

ber ⌄	ContactFirstName ⌄	ContactLastN ⌄	ContractEnds ⌄	NonProfit? ⌄
10	Paola	Bandini	30-Apr-16	☐
90	Antonio	Lara		☐
00	Deanna	Zitterk		☐
00	John	Lovela		☐
	Sharon	MacKe		☐
10	Janie	Ward		☐
00	Joydeep	Mitra		☐
	Sandra	Hambr		☐
	Robert	Czerni		☐
00	John	Leyba	31-Aug-16	☐
11	Mildred	Latini	31-Dec-15	☐
	Roberta	Himebrook	30-Apr-16	☐
00	Roberto	Apodaca	31-Jul-16	☐
00	Anil	Runachingha	30-Nov-15	☐

Date Picker

April, 2016
Su	Mo	Tu	We	Th	Fr	Sa
27	28	29	30	31	1	2
3	4	5	6	7	8	9
10	11	12	13	14	15	16
17	18	19	20	21	22	23
24	25	26	27	28	29	30
1	2	3	4	5	6	7

Today

5. Press Esc to exit the field without saving any changes.

6. Click the **Close** button ✕ for the table.

Controlling Data Integrity

EcoMed Services, Inc., requires certain procedures to increase data efficiency but also to ensure data integrity. *Data integrity* is the condition through which data can be assumed to be accurate. One way of improving data integrity is by defining the field properties for tables.

Certain field properties restrict values stored in a field. A change to one of these properties can affect both the structure and the size of the field. Because these changes might alter your data, it is best to make them before adding records to a table. If a table already contains data and you are uncertain if your data will be affected, back up your database before making changes to field properties.

Exercise 4-17   SET THE PRIMARY KEY

Most tables contain a primary key. A *primary key* is a field or set of fields in a table that provide a unique identifier for every record. Each record must store a unique value in a primary key field. Most often primary keys are numeric data types; however, other data types can be used.

1. In the **Navigation Pane**, double-click the table **tblBulbType**.

2. From the **Home** tab, in the **Views** group, click **View** 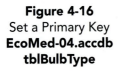 to switch to **Design View**.

3. From the **Design** tab, in the **Tools** group, click **Insert Rows** ▸.

4. Key **BulbTypeID** and press Tab.

5. In the **Data Type** column, key **a**. **AutoNumber** is the only data type on the list that starts with an "A."

6. From the **Design** tab, in the **Tools** group, click **Primary Key** 🔑.

Figure 4-16
Set a Primary Key
EcoMed-04.accdb
tblBulbType

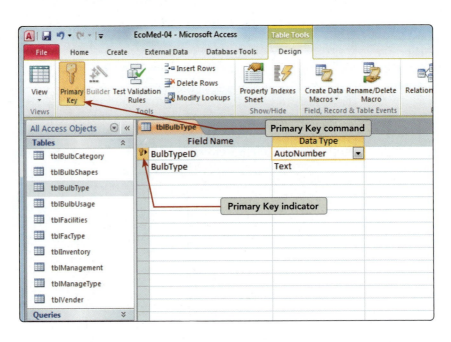

7. From the **Design** tab, in the **Views** group, click **View** to switch to **Datasheet View**. Save your changes.

8. The field **BulbTypeID** has now been populated with a unique number.

Exercise 4-18 SET THE FIELD PROPERTY FIELD SIZE

Changing the field size alters the space available to store data. The numeric value defined in the Field Size property is the maximum number of characters allowed for storage of data. Changing the field size in Design View is different than changing the column width in Datasheet View.

1. From the **Home** tab, in the **Views** group, click **View** to switch to **Design View**.

2. In the **Design View** of **tblBulbType**, click the field selector for **BulbType** and press F6.

3. In the **Field Size** property, change 255 to **15**.

> **TIP**
>
> Text fields should be wide enough to hold most data but not so unnecessarily wide that they waste storage space.

4. From the **Design** tab, in the **Views** group, click **View** to switch to **Datasheet View**.

5. Read the message dialog box. Click **Yes**. If any record stores more than 15 characters in the **BulbType** field, all characters beyond the first 15 characters will be deleted.

6. Right-click any document tab and choose **Close**.

Exercise 4-19 SET THE FIELD PROPERTY VALIDATION TEXT AND RULES

A *Validation Rule* is a condition specifying criteria for entering data into an individual field. You define a validation rule to control what values can be entered into a field. You also can enter an optional validation text to match your rule. *Validation text* is an error message that appears when a value prohibited by the validation rule is entered.

For example, you could define the validation expression ">=100" for a quantity field to prevent a user from entering values less than 100. For the corresponding validation expression, you could enter "You must enter a number equal to or greater than 100."

When you set a validation rule for a field that contains data, Access will ask if you want to apply the new rule to the existing data. If you answer yes, Access evaluates the rule against the existing data in the table. If any record violates the validation rule, you will be notified that the data must be corrected before the rule can be applied.

The Test Validation Rules button checks the current data in the field to see if it matches the Validation Rule. If it does not, Access displays an error message alerting you to the conflict.

1. In the **Navigation Pane**, double-click the table **tblManagement**.

2. From the **Home** tab, in the **Views** group, click **View** to switch to **Design View**.

3. Click the field selector for **ContractEnds** and press F6.

4. Tab to the **Validation Rule** property and key **>=1/1/2015**. This rule restricts users to enter a date before January 1, 2015.

5. Press Enter to move to the **Validation Text** property.

6. Key **All new contracts must terminate after or on 1/1/2015.**.

7. Press Ctrl+S to save the changes to the table. A data integrity dialog box appears asking if you want to test the current data with the new rules. Click **Yes**.

8. From the **Design** tab, in the **Tools** group, click **Test Validation Rules**. Click **Yes** in the dialog box.

9. The next dialog box tells you that all the data in this table pass the validation rule you just created. Click **OK**.

10. From the **Design** tab, in the **Views** group, click **View** to switch to **Datasheet View**.

11. Press Tab until you reach the **ContractEnds** field.

12. Key **1/1/2011** and press Enter.

Figure 4-17
Validation Text
dialog box
**EcoMed-04.accdb
tblBulbType**

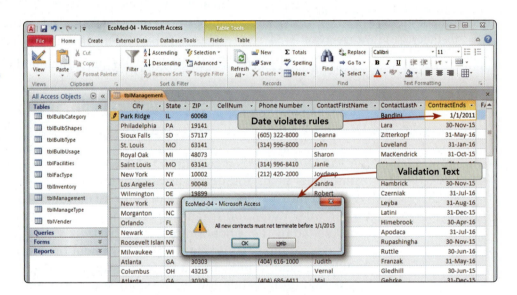

13. Click **OK** to close the dialog box. Press Esc until the original data reappear in the field.

14. Close the table. Compact and close the database.

Lesson 4 Summary

- The two methods for creating a new database are using a template or creating a blank database.
- A database template is a ready-to-use database containing all the tables, queries, forms, and reports needed to perform a specific task.
- A new database created as a blank database does not contain objects or data.
- Some database properties come from the operating system of the workstation on which the database is created.
- The two methods for creating a new table are using a template and creating a blank table.
- Table templates provide a quick and easy method to produce a table containing commonly used fields based on a specific need.
- When a single field contains both alphabetic and numeric data characters, you must define the field as text data type.
- When copying a table, you can select to include only the structure, the structure and data, or only the data.
- Before adding any field to a table, you first should make certain that it does not duplicate an existing field's data.
- When tables are created using Datasheet View, Access evaluates the data entered to determine the data type for the field to create.
- A Caption is a field property that displays as a column heading in Datasheet View or as a control label in a form or report.
- Spaces should not be used in field names. Spaces create additional requirements when using fields in advanced objects, such as macros and modules.
- An input mask is used to format the display of data and control the format in which values can be entered.
- Depending on the workstation's language settings, the date picker displays either to the right or left side of a Date/Time field.
- A primary key is a field or set of fields in a table that provide a unique identifier for every record.
- Changing the field size in Design View is different than changing the column width in Datasheet View.
- The data contained in a field defined as the primary key of a table must be unique.
- A Validation Rule is a condition specifying criteria for entering data into an individual field.
- Validation text is an error message that appears when a value prohibited by the validation rule is entered.
- Importing data prevents errors that may occur when re-keying data.

- Data can be exported to another Microsoft application such as Word or Excel or non-Microsoft applications such as dBASE and Paradox.
- Data imported from another Access database, a non-Access database, or a non-database application can be added to an existing table or used to create a new table.

LESSON 4		Command Summary	
Feature	Button	Task Path	Keyboard
Application Parts		Create, Templates	
Change field name		Fields, Properties, Name & Caption	
Database, blank		New, Blank database	
Database, new		File, New	
Delete column		Fields, Add & Delete, Delete	
Delete rows		Design, Tools, Delete Rows	
Export, Word		External Data, Export, More, Word	
Field, properties		Home, Views, Design View	
Field, properties, toggle			F6
Import, Excel		External Data, Import & Link, Excel	
Insert rows		Design, Tools, Insert Rows	
Paste		Home, Clipboard, Paste	Ctrl + V
Primary key		Design, Tools, Primary Key	
Table, create		Create, Tables, Table	
Table, properties		Right click object, properties	

UNIT 1 LESSON 4

Please visit our Online Learning Center, *www.lessonapproach2010.com,* **where you will find the following review materials:**

Concepts Review

True/False Questions

Short Answer Questions

Critical Thinking Questions

Skills Review

Review Exercises that target single skills

Lesson Applications

Review Exercises that challenge students by testing multiple skills in each exercise

On Your Own

Open-ended exercises that require students to synthesize multiple skills and apply creativity and problem-solving as they would in a real world business situation

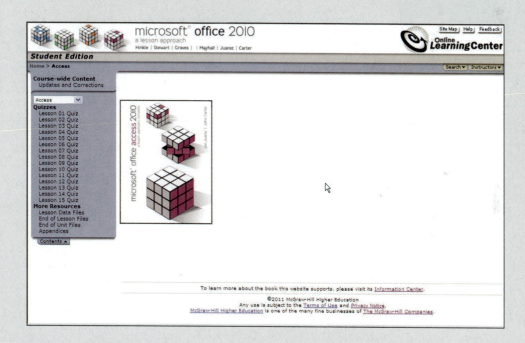

Please visit our Online Learning Center, *www.lessonapproach2010.com,* **where you will find Unit Applications review materials.**

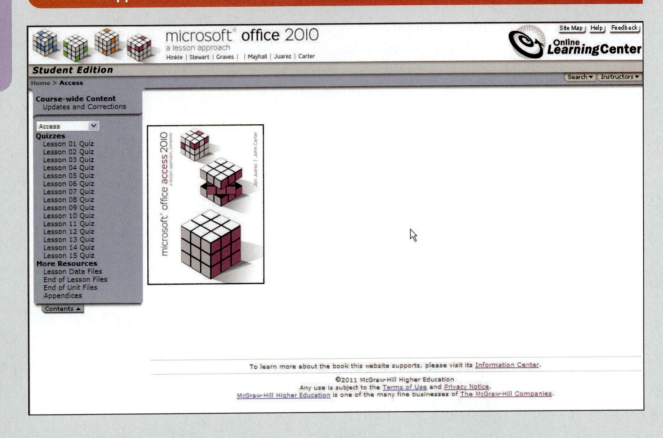

Unit 2

DESIGNING AND MANAGING DATABASE OBJECTS

Lesson 5
Managing Data Integrity

OBJECTIVES *After completing this lesson, you will be able to:*

1. Create relationships between tables.

2. Work with referential integrity.

3. Work with subdatasheets.

4. Use the Lookup Wizard.

5. Use Analyze tools.

6. Track object dependency.

Estimated Time: 1½ hours

A major advantage of a database over a spreadsheet is the ability to create relationships. A *relationship* is a link or connection of a common field between two tables, two queries, or a table and a query. Relationships change a flat data structure that contains isolated data into a linked data structure. For tables to be related, they must share common data and have a common field.

Relationships must be planned; they do not just happen. Understanding them—and how to set them—takes time and practice. As you work more extensively with databases, you will learn more about creating and maintaining relationships.

The EcoMed Services, Inc., database stores customer information in two tables. The facilities table stores the names and addresses of the medical facilities to which products are shipped. The management table stores the name and address of the parent organization to which invoices are shipped.

If each parent company managed only one facility, then a flat relational structure could work. However, each management company can have more than one facility associated to it. Therefore, a relational structure is required to link the two tables. After you create a relationship between the facilities table and the management table, you will be able to create forms and reports that can identify which management organization is responsible for which medical facility.

Creating Relationships between Tables

Relational database management systems, such as Microsoft Access, are the predominant structure used for business applications. In a relational database, related tables are connected by a join line. A *join line* is a graphical representation of the relationship created between two recordsets that are connected by common fields. In Access, the common fields must be the same data type and size; however, they do not need to use the same name.

When you select a primary key in both related tables, you create a One-To-One relationship. A *One-To-One relationship* is a relationship that occurs when the common field is a primary key in the first table and a primary key field in the second. This status means one record in the first table can relate to only one record in the second table.

When you select a primary key in only one field, you create a One-To-Many relationship. A *One-To-Many relationship* is a relationship that occurs when the common field is a primary key in the first table and not a primary key field in the second. This status means one record in the first table can relate to one or more records in the second table.

When you do not select a primary key in either table, you create an Indeterminate relationship. An *Indeterminate relationship* is a relationship that occurs when Access does not have enough information to determine the relationship between the two tables. An Indeterminate relationship occurs when the common fields in the first and the second table are not primary key fields.

Exercise 5-1 LOOK AT AN EXISTING RELATIONSHIP

The EcoMed database links or relates the Vender table to the Inventory table. You can see this link in the Relationships window. The *Relationships window* is a visual interface that displays, creates, destroys, or documents relationships between tables, queries, or both.

One or more relationships can be displayed at any time. When more than two tables are displayed, you should arrange and resize the table list boxes to allow optimum viewing of field names and join lines. You now will use the Relationships window to examine the relationship between the tables Vender and Inventory.

1. Locate and open the **Lesson 05** folder.
2. Make a copy of **EcoMed-05** and rename it *[your initials]*-EcoMed-05.
3. Open and enable content for *[your initials]*-**EcoMed-05**.
4. From the **Database Tools** tab, in the **Relationships** group, click **Relationships** to opens the Relationships window.

5. From the **Design** tab, in the **Relationships** group, click **All Relationships** . All tables that have a relationship with other tables will open. The line connecting two tables represents the relationship between the tables.

6. Click and drag the bottom and right edges of the **tblVender** Field List until all field names are visible.

Figure 5-1
Relationships window with Field Lists rearranged **EcoMed-05.accdb Relationships window**

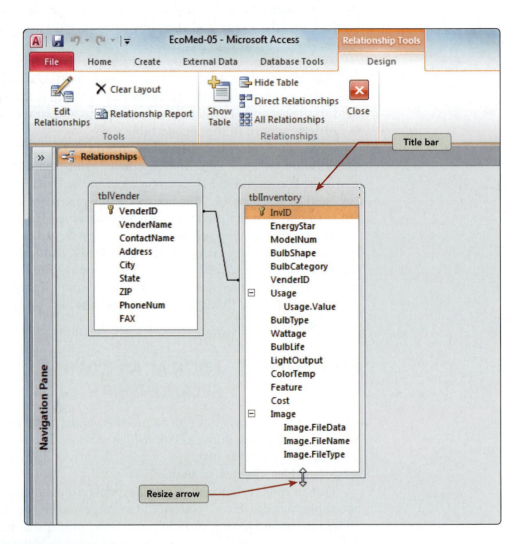

7. Resize the field list for **tblInventory** until all its fields are visible.

8. Right-click the sloping part of the join line between **tblVender** and **tblInventory** to open the shortcut menu for a join line.

Figure 5-2
Shortcut menu
**EcoMed-05.accdb
Relationships
window**

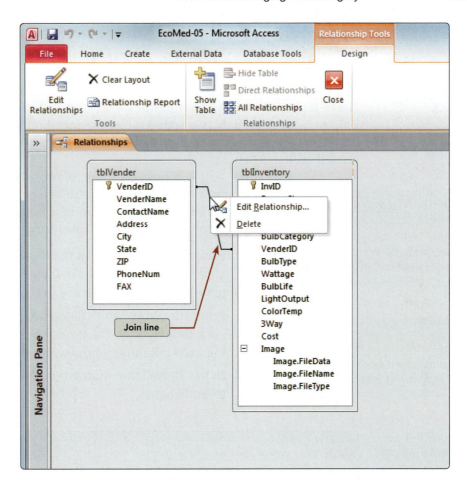

9. Choose **Edit Relationship** 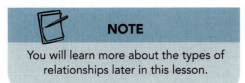. Notice that these two tables have a One-To-Many relationship using the common field **VenderID**.

Figure 5-3
Edit Relationships
dialog box
**EcoMed-05.accdb
Relationships
window**

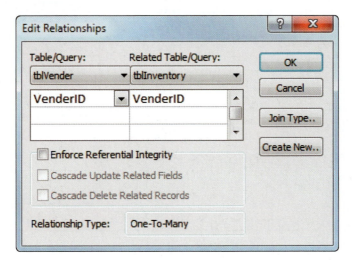

10. You will not be making changes to this dialog box, so click **Cancel**.

Exercise 5-2   CREATE A RELATIONSHIP IN THE RELATIONSHIPS WINDOW

You can create different types of relationships depending on whether you chose a primary key as a common field. When a primary key in one table links to a common field in another table, the common field becomes a foreign key. A *foreign key* is a common field that links to a primary key field in a related table.

NOTE

The Show Table dialog box sometimes opens automatically when no relationships are present in the database.

TIP

If you cannot see the field lists, move the Show Table dialog box by its title bar.

You will now create a relationship between the tables Inventory and Bulb Shapes. You will use the bulb shape field. The field bulb shape is a key field in tblBulbShape and a common field in tblInventory.

1. From the **Design** tab, in the **Relationships** group, click **Show Table** . The **Show Table** dialog box lists the tables and queries that are in the database.

2. From the **Show Table** dialog box, in the **Tables** tab, click **tblInventory**. Click **Add** to add the table's Field List to the Relationships window.

3. In the **Show Table** dialog box, double-click **tblBulbShapes**.

Figure 5-4
Show Table dialog box
EcoMed-05.accdb Relationships window

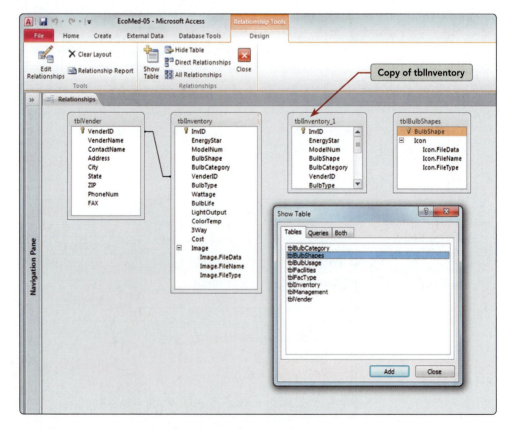

NOTE

Copies of field lists have "_#" added to the end of the table or query. "#" stands for the number of copies.

REVIEW

The Primary Key indicates that this field contains a unique identifier for each record.

4. In the **Show Table** dialog box, click **Close**.

5. The table **tblInventory** has been entered twice. Click on the field list **tblInventory_1** and press Delete to remove this copy.

6. In the **tblBulbShapes** Field List, click the **BulbShape** field. The field name has a key symbol because it is the primary key in this table.

7. Click and drag the **BulbShape** field from the **tblBulbShapes** Field List to the **BulbShape** field in the **tblInventory** Field List.

8. The **Edit Relationships** dialog box opens. The **Relationship Type** is One-To-Many because the common field **BulbShape** (primary key) appears only once in the table **tblBulbShapes**, but the **BulbShape** (foreign key) can appear many times in the table **tblInventory**.

9. Click **Create**. A join line links the common field names.

10. Resize and move each Field List to appear as shown in Figure 5-5.

Figure 5-5
Show Table dialog box
EcoMed-05.accdb
Relationships
window

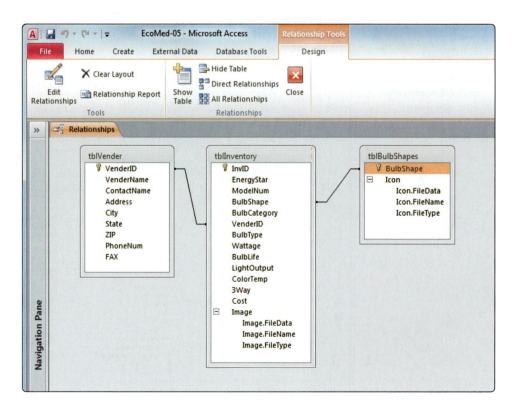

NOTE

The **Clear Layout** command X clears the way tables are arranged in the Relationships window but does not affect relationships.

11. From the **Design** tab, in the **Tools** group, click **Clear Layout** X.

12. Click **Yes** to clear the layout.

13. From the **Design** tab, in the **Relationships** group, click **All Relationships** ⊞.

14. Resize each of the field lists so that all their fields are visible.

15. From the **Design** tab, in the **Relationships** group, click **Close** ⊠. Click **Yes** to verify the changes to the layout of the Relationships window.

Exercise 5-3   SAVE RELATIONSHIPS

Generating a Relationship Report helps a database administrator document and manages data integrity. A *Relationship Report* is a graphical report displaying one or more relationships. Each Relationship Report you create must have a unique name.

1. From the **Database Tools** tab, in the **Relationships** group, click **Relationships** 🔳.

2. From the **Design** tab, in the **Tools** group, click **Relationship Report** 🖼.

3. From the Quick Access toolbar, click **Save** 💾.

4. In the **Save As** dialog box, key **rptRelInventory-Shape** and press **OK**. This saved report can opened or printed at any time.

Figure 5-6
Save a Relationship Report
EcoMed-05.accdb
rptRelInventory-Shape

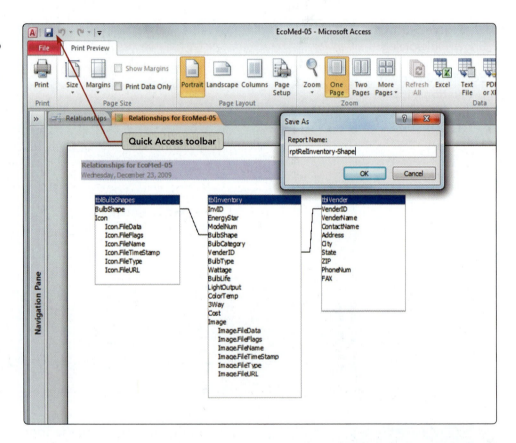

5. Right-click the **Relationships** document tab, and choose **Close All** 🖻.

Working with Referential Integrity

The use of referential integrity helps reduce human error through accidental deletions or other common errors. *Referential integrity* is a set of database rules for checking, validating, and tracking data entry changes in related tables. Enforcing referential integrity in two or more tables ensures that values stored in each table are consistent throughout the entire database.

For example, if you enforce referential integrity between the management table and the facilities table, then you can prevent someone from entering a new record for a medical facility without creating corresponding management information. This restriction would prevent shipping product to a company for which we do not have a billing address. The enforced integrity also would prevent someone from deleting a record for a management company without first deleting the associated facilities.

Exercise 5-4   ENFORCE REFERENTIAL INTEGRITY

You can enforce referential integrity between tables in a One-To-Many relationship. When referential integrity is enforced, the join line between the tables displays a 1 for the "one" side of the relationship and an infinity symbol (∞) for the "many" side. Referential integrity cannot be set for indeterminate relationships.

You can set referential integrity when the following conditions are met:

- The linking field from the main table is a primary key.

- The linked fields have the same data type.

- Both tables belong to the same Microsoft Access database.

1. Open **tblInventory**. In the first record (InvID #1), change the **Bulb Shape** to **Flood**. Press Ctrl+S to save the record.

2. Open **tblBulbShapes**. Notice that "Flood" is not listed as a **Bulb Shape**. Remember that the purpose of the "One" side of the relationship is to store a unique list of items to be used in the "Many" side of the relationship.

3. Close both tables.

> **NOTE**
>
> Before Access applies referential integrity rules to a relationship, the data in the two tables must pass the rules created. In this case, data exist in the "Many" side of the relationship that does not exist in the "One" side. The Bulb Shape "Flood" in tblInventory does not pass the rules.

4. From the **Database Tools** tab, in the **Relationships** group, click **Relationships** .

5. Double-click the sloping part of the join line between **tblInventory** and **tblBulbShapes**. The **Relationship Type** is One-To-Many.

6. Click the check box to select **Enforce Referential Integrity** and click **OK**.

7. Read the error message and click **OK**.

Figure 5-7
Enforcing referential
integrity
EcoMed-05.accdb
Relationships
window

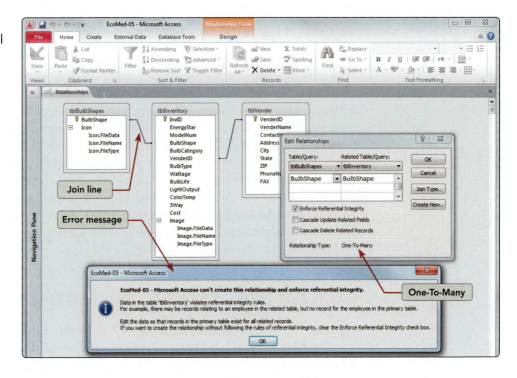

8. Click **Cancel** to close the **Edit Relationships** dialog box without saving the changes.

9. Open **tblInventory**. In the first record (InvID #1), change the **Bulb Shape** to **A-line**.

10. Close **tblInventory**.

11. In the document tab **Relationships**, double-click the sloping part of the join line between **tblInventory** and **tblBulbShapes**.

12. Click the check box to select **Enforce Referential Integrity** and click **OK**. This time, the changes were accepted, and the symbols "1" and "∞" have been added to the join line.

Figure 5-8
One-To-Many
relationship
EcoMed-05.accdb
Relationships
window

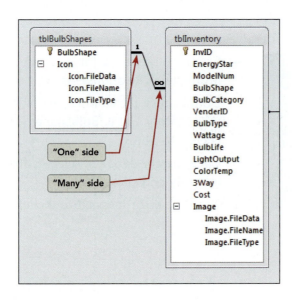

13. From the **Design** tab, in the **Relationships** group, click **Close** ⊠.

14. Open **tblInventory**. In the first record (InvID #1), change the **Bulb Shape** to **Flood** and press ⬇.

15. A message box alerts you to a problem.

Figure 5-9
Referential Integrity finds an error
EcoMed-05.accdb Relationships window

16. Click **OK**. Press Esc to reject the changes to the record.

17. Close the table.

Exercise 5-5   REMOVE REFERENTIAL INTEGRITY

Referential integrity is a property of a relationship. When you remove referential integrity from a relationship, you merely remove the validation rules while preserving the original relationship between the tables. Removing Referential Integrity does not destroy the relationship.

1. From the **Database Tools** tab, in the **Relationships** group, click the **Relationships** button ᴱᴳ.

2. Right-click the sloping part of the join line between **tblInventory** and **tblBulbShapes**.

3. Choose **Edit Relationship** from the shortcut menu.

4. In the **Edit Relationship** dialog box, remove the checkmark from **Enforce Referential Integrity**. Click **OK**.

5. From the **Design** tab, in the **Relationships** group, click **Close** ⊠.

Working with Subdatasheets

A table on the "One" side of a One-To-Many relationship, by default, has a subdatasheet. A *subdatasheet* is a datasheet linked within another datasheet. A subdatasheet contains data related to the first datasheet. The common field linking the two datasheets is the primary key field in the main datasheet and the foreign key field in the linked datasheet.

You can insert a subdatasheet into a main datasheet even when a relationship does not exist between the two objects. When a relationship does not exist, Access will automatically create one. You can insert a subdatasheet into any major object that has a Datasheet View such as a table, query, or form.

Exercise 5-6   INSERT A SUBDATASHEET

You can insert a subdatasheet into a main datasheet even when a relationship does not exist between the two objects. When you insert a subdatasheet, you must identify the table that will be used as the subdatasheet, the Link Child Fields, and the Link Master Fields. The child field is the linked field in the subdatasheet and the master field is the linked field in the master or source recordset.

When a relationship does not exist between the child and master, Access will automatically create one. You can insert a subdatasheet into any major object that has a Datasheet View such as a table, query, or form. You will now insert the inventory table as a subdatasheet for the table Bulb Shapes.

NOTE

In tables that have a relationship with the table to be used as a subdatasheet, the common field will be selected from the fields used in the relationship. If there is no relationship between the two tables, you can fill the properties Link Child Field and Link Master Fields by hand.

NOTE

You can expand or collapse all subdatasheets by using the Expand All or Collapse All commands found on the Home tab; in the Records group, click More, and choose Subdatasheet menu.

1. Open **tblBulbShapes** in **Design View**.

2. From the **Design** tab, in the **Show/Hide** group, click **Property Sheet** .

3. In the **Property Sheet**, the property **Subdatasheet Name** is set to **[None]**. Click on this property. Click the drop-down arrow and choose **Table.tblInventory**. Notice that Access has selected the field **BulbShape** as the common field and placed this field into the **Link Child Fields** and **Link Master Fields**.

4. From the **Design** tab, in the **Show/Hide** group, click **Property Sheet** to close the **Property Sheet**.

5. Switch to **Datasheet View** and save the changes to the table.

6. Notice that the beginning of each record now has an **Expand** icon symbol. Click the **Expand** icon for the **BulbShape** "Bare-Triple Tube." There are five bulbs in our inventory that have the shape Bare-Triple Tube.

Figure 5-10
Expanding a subdatasheet
EcoMed-05.accdb
tblBulbShapes

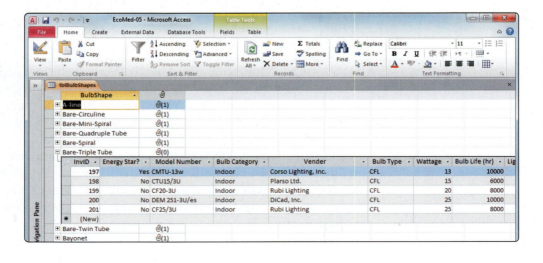

7. Click in the subdatasheet's first record. The Record Navigation buttons are now set to the subdatasheet.

8. Close and save the changes to **tblBulbShapes**.

Exercise 5-7   REMOVE A SUBDATASHEET

Not all subdatasheets need to be displayed in the master recordset. If most database users do not need to use the subdatasheet, you can remove it from the main datasheet.

1. From the **Navigation Pane**, open **tblVender** in **Datasheet View**.

2. Click the **Expand** icon ⊞ for the **VenderID** "AnyBulb." There are 15 bulbs that we buy from this vender.

3. From the **Home** tab, in the **Records** group, click **More** ▦, and choose **Subdatasheet**, then **Subdatasheet** ▦, from the menu. The common field is **VenderID**.

Figure 5-11
Viewing a subdatasheet's settings
EcoMed-05.accdb
tblVender

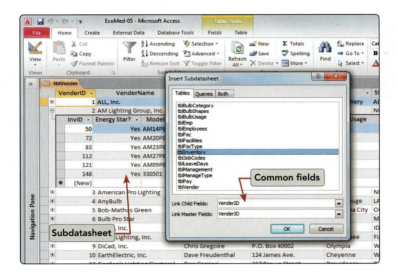

4. Click **Cancel** to close the **Insert Subdatasheet** dialog box.

5. From the **Home** tab, in the **Records** group, click **More** ▦, and choose **Subdatasheet**, then **Remove**, from the menu. The symbols are gone, but the relationship between this table and **tblInventory** is still present.

6. Close the table. You are asked if you want to save the changes. Adding and removing a subdatasheet counts as a structure change for the table. Click **Yes**.

Using the Lookup Wizard

A *Lookup field* is a field property that displays input choices from another table and allows these choices to be selected from a list. Lookup fields are used often when a company uses specialized codes within their databases. An example of a specialized code is the two-letter abbreviation for a state. Prior to the adoption of the two letter codes by the United States Postal Service in 1949, states were only identified by their complete name.

Codes use less space than lengthy text describing the record. Some codes are readily understandable, such as standardized abbreviations for common names such as NASA. Other codes are less obvious and need a Lookup field for a data entry operator to use.

In addition to reducing the amount of data stored in a table, a Lookup field can improve the efficiency and consistency of data entry. The best fields to convert to a Lookup value are those that contain a finite number of values. Lookup fields use list boxes to display a list of possible values.

Exercise 5-8   CREATE A LOOKUP FIELD

In Microsoft Access, you can add a field to a table to look up information in another table. You typically use this technique when you use a numeric code as a common field to relate the two tables. In the EcoMed database, we'll use a numeric value to identify the bulb category. By using this technique, we can reduce the storage size of the records in the inventory table.

NOTE

Lookup fields can use text or numerical data to link two tables. The numerical option takes up less space in the database.

1. Open **tblBulbCategory** in **Datasheet View**. There are four categories: Diagnostic, Surgical, Indoor, and Outdoor, each with a **BulbCategoryID** 1 through 4.

2. Open **tblInventory** in **Datasheet View**.

3. Click the field option arrow for the field **Bulb Category**. This field lists the four common categories contained in **tblBulbCategory**. Click **Cancel**.

4. While the **Bulb Category** field is selected, press Ctrl+H. Key **Diagnostic** in the **Find What** control and **1** in the **Replace With** control. Click **Replace All** and click **Yes** to confirm the replacements.

5. Repeat step 4 for the following data:

Find What	Replace With
Surgical	2
Indoor	3
Outdoor	4

6. Close the **Find and Replace** dialog box. Click the field option arrow for the field **Bulb Category**. This field should now only contain the numbers 1–4. Click **Cancel**.

7. From the **Home** tab, in the **Views** group, click **View** to switch to **Design View**.

NOTE

Lookups create relationships, and just like other relationships, the fields used in a relationship must be the same **Data Type**.

TIP

Always save the changes to your table before starting the **Lookup Wizard**.

8. The field **BulbCategory** has the **Data Type** of **Text**. Change the **Data Type** to **Number**. Notice that the field's **Field Size** property is now **Long Integer**.

9. Press Ctrl+S to save the changes. The warning message warns that some data may be lost. Click **Yes**.

10. Click the option arrow for the **BulbCategory** Data Type and choose **Lookup Wizard**.

11. The **Lookup Wizard** dialog box appears. Verify that **I want the lookup field to get the values from another table or query.** is selected. Click **Next**.

12. From the list of tables, choose **Table: tblBulbCategory** and click **Next**.

13. Click the Add All button [>>] to move both fields from the **Available Fields** to the **Selected Fields** area.

14. Click **Next**. Click the first drop-down arrow and choose **BulbCategory** as the sort order field.

15. Click **Next**. Double-click the right edge of the column header to resize the column to fit the widest data.

16. Click to remove the checkmark from the **Hide key column** control. The **BulbCategoryID** field is displayed.

Figure 5-12
Choose the value from the Lookup column.
EcoMed-05.accdb tblInventory

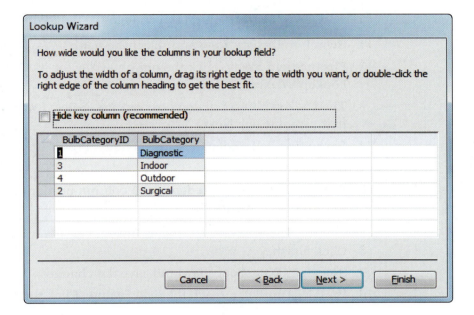

17. Click to add the checkmark to the **Hide key column** control. The ID will be stored in the field and the text will be seen in **Datasheet View**.

18. Click **Next**. Accept the default field name and click **Finish**.

19. Click **Yes** to save the table and return to **Datasheet View**.

Exercise 5-9   ADD DATA WITH A LOOKUP FIELD

In addition to reducing the size of records in the inventory table, adding data through a Lookup field reduces the number of keystrokes necessary to enter a value. Because values in a Lookup field are listed alphabetically in ascending order, you only need to type the first letter of the bulb category to display the corresponding category. You will now test the Lookup field you just created.

1. Click in the first record's **InvID** field and press ⎯Tab⎯ until you reach the **Bulb Category** field and key **s**. The combo box will display **Surgical** because only one option from the list starts with the letter "s."

Figure 5-13
Choose the value
from the Lookup
column.
**EcoMed-05.accdb
tblInventory**

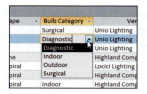

2. Press ⬇ to move to the next record.

3. Click the drop-down arrow to the right of the field to display the list of categories and choose **Diagnostic**. You no longer have to worry about a typographical error in this field.

Exercise 5-10   CREATE A LIST LOOKUP FIELD

You will now use the Lookup Wizard to modify the field named 3-Way. Currently the field is a Text. We now want to use the field to identify the bulb as capable of being used in a 3-Way or Dimmer fixture. You rename the field from 3-Way to Features and then change the field type to Lookup.

1. Switch to **Design View** and select the field **3-Way**. This is a **Text** field.

2. For the field **3Way**, click the option arrow for its **Data Type** and choose **Lookup Wizard**.

3. The **Lookup Wizard** dialog box appears. Select **I will type in the values that I want**. Click **Next**.

4. In the first cell under **Col1** type **3-Way**. Press ⬇.

5. Key **Dimmer**.

6. Double-click the right edge of the column header to resize the column to fit the widest data. Click **Next**.

7. You are asked to change the label. Key **Feature**.

8. Click **Finish**.

9. Switch to **Datasheet View** and save the changes.

10. Press Tab until you reach the field **Feature**. Click the drop-down arrow to see the choices.

11. Press Esc and return to **Design View**.

Exercise 5-11   MODIFY A LOOKUP FIELD

The list of values displayed in a Lookup field can be limited or editable. When you set the Limit To List value to yes, only the database designer can add new values to the list. When you set the Limit To List value to no, you allow the user to enter new values.

1. Click the field **Feature**.

2. In the properties section, click the **Lookup** tab.

3. Click the **Limit To List** property. Read the description in the Help window.

4. Change this properties value to **Yes**.

5. Double-click the property **Allow Value List Edits** to change the value from "No" to "Yes."

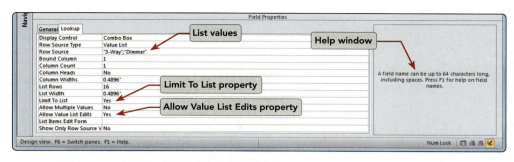

Figure 5-14
Change Lookup
properties
**EcoMed-05.accdb
tblInventory**

6. Read the Help window on this property. Save the table and switch to **Datasheet View**.

7. In the first record, click in the field **Feature** and click the drop-down arrow. A small icon appears below the expanded list.

8. Click the Edit List icon 🖉. The **Edit List Items** dialog box opens.

9. Key **None**.

10. In the **Default Value** control, select **None** from the list.

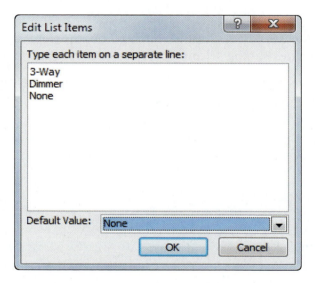

Figure 5-15
Edit a Lookup
field list
**EcoMed-05.accdb
tblInventory**

11. Click **OK** to close the dialog box.

12. Click the drop-down arrow for the field **Feature**. You now have three options.

Exercise 5-12 CREATE A MULTI-VALUED LOOKUP FIELD

A Lookup field can be set to be a multi-valued Lookup field. A multi-valued Lookup field is a Lookup field that can store more than one value per record. This type of field is very useful when it is possible for a single field to have multiple values. You will now create a multi-valued Lookup field for the bulb usage field.

1. Switch to **Design View**.

2. Click on the **Field Name BulbType**.

3. From the **Design** tab, in the **Tools** group, click **Modify Lookups** 🗔.
A new field has been added, and the **Lookup Wizard** dialog box opens.

4. Verify that **I want the lookup field to get the values from another table or query.** is selected. Click **Next**.

5. From the list of tables, choose **Table: tblBulbUsage** and click **Next**.

6. Click the **Add All** button ⏩ to move both fields from the **Available Fields** to the **Selected Fields** area.

7. Click **Next**. Click the first drop-down arrow and choose **Usage**.

8. Click **Next**. Double-click the right edge of the column header to resize the column to fit the widest data. Click **Next**.

9. Name the field **Usage**.

10. For the control **Allow Multiple Values**, click the check box.

11. Click **Finish**. Click **Yes** to save the changes.

12. Switch to **Datasheet View**.

Exercise 5-13   ADD DATA WITH A MULTI-VALUED LOOKUP FIELD

Each value stored in a multi-valued Lookup field is linked to the source record. Values can be selected or de-selected for any record.

1. For the fourth record, click the drop-down arrow for the field **Usage**.

2. Click the Check boxes for **Ceiling Mount**, **Fan**, and **Table Lamp**.

Figure 5-16
Multiple Values
Lookup field
EcoMed-05.accdb
tblInventory

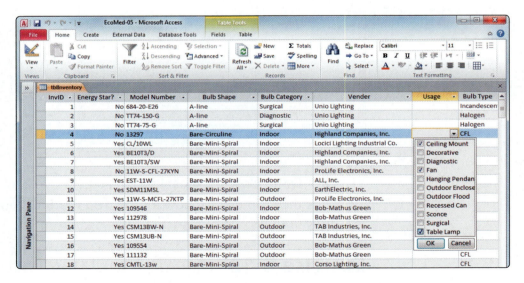

3. Close **OK**. Resize the column so you can see all the data. Each value is stored separated by a comma.

4. Switch to **Design View**.

5. Click in the **Usage** field. Notice the **Data Type** is **Number**. Only the **UsageID** is being stored in this field.

6. In the properties section, click the **Lookup** tab. The **Allow Multiple Values** property is set to **Yes**.

7. Save and close all tables.

Exercise 5-14   VIEW RELATIONSHIPS CREATED BY LOOKUP FIELDS

A Lookup field creates a relationship between the main table and the linked table. The relationship uses the Lookup field as the common field. This relationship can be displayed and documented in the Relationships window.

1. From the **Database Tools** tab, in the **Relationships** group, click **Relationships** .

2. From the **Design** tab, in the **Tools** group, click **Clear Layout** ⓧ. Click **Yes** to clear the layout.

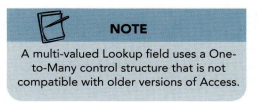

NOTE

A multi-valued Lookup field uses a One-to-Many control structure that is not compatible with older versions of Access.

3. From the **Navigation Pane**, drag **tblInventory** and **tblBulbUsage** to the Relationships window. A join line appears between the two tables. Creating the Lookup from one table to the other has created this relationship.

4. Arrange the field lists so you can clearly see all fields and relationships.

5. Double-click the join line between **tblInventory** and **tblBulbUsage** to open the **Edit Relationships** dialog box. This is a One-To-Many relationship. The main table is **tblBulbUsage**; it has the primary key. Click **OK**.

Figure 5-17
Relationships created by Lookups
EcoMed-05.accdb Relationships window

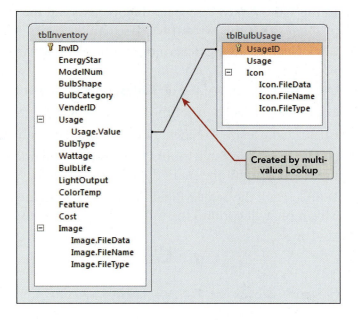

6. Close the Relationships window. A message box asks if you want to save the changes to the layout. Click **Yes**.

Using Analyzing Tools

The Table Analyzer Wizard is a tool that analyzes a database and recommends changes for normalization. *Normalization* is the process of restructuring a relational database for the purposes of organizing data efficiently, eliminating field redundancy, and improving data consistency.

The wizard analyzes table structures and field values. When the wizard identifies duplicated data or improper table structures, you are given the option to allow the wizard to make changes to your database automatically or for you to make changes manually. This type of analysis tool is used most often when designing a database or creating new structures.

Exercise 5-15   ANALYZE A TABLE

When the Table Analyzer identifies a significant number of records that contain repeating field values, the Analyzer will recommend that you split the table into two new tables. If you split the table, the structure and contents of the original table will be preserved.

1. Open **tblInventory** in **Datasheet View**. You can see there is redundancy in the **Bulb Type** information.
2. Close the table.
3. From the **Database Tools** tab, in the **Analyze** group, click **Analyze Table** 📇.
4. In the **Table Analyzer Wizard** dialog box, read the description of the problems that this wizard will try to address.
5. Click **Next**. Read the description of how the wizard will try to fix the problem.
6. Click **Next**. From the list of **Tables**, select **tblInventory**.
7. Click **Next**. Select **Yes, let the wizard decide**.
8. Click **Next**. Resize the Fields Lists so that you can see all the fields.
9. Double-click the **Table1** Field List header. Rename this table **tblInv**. This table will contain the main data for the inventory.
10. Double-click the **Table2** Field List header. Rename this table **tblBulbType**. This table will contain the unique data for the bulb types.

11. Notice that the wizard has selected both the **BulbShape** and **BulbType**. In the Field List **tblBulbType**, drag **BulbShape** back to the **tblInv** Field List under **VenderID**.

Figure 5-18
Table Analyzer
Wizard
EcoMed-05.accdb
Table Analyzer
Wizard

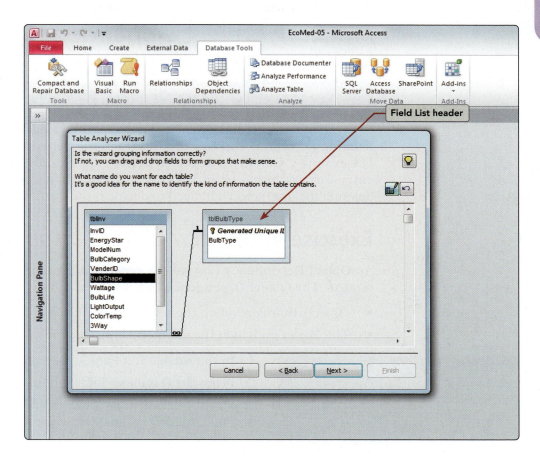

12. Click **Next**. In the field list **tblInv**, click **InvID** and click the Set Unique Identifier button 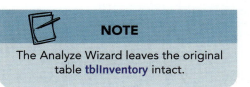 to make this field the Primary Key for the table.

13. Click **Next**. The wizard thinks that there might be some typographical errors in your data and gives you an opportunity to correct these errors.

14. The data shown are correct. Click **Next** and **Yes** to move to the next step. In the last step, select **No, don't create the query** option.

15. Click **Finish**. If the **Access Help** window appears, close it. You now have two new tables, **tblInv** and **tblBulbType**.

16. Click the **tblInv** tab. Press [End]. The wizard has placed the new Lookup field at the end of the table.

17. Click in the **Lookup to tblBulbType** field.

18. From the **Fields** tab, in the **Properties** group, click **Name & Caption**.

NOTE

The Analyze Wizard leaves the original table **tblInventory** intact.

19. Change the **Name** property to **BulbType** and the **Caption** to **Bulb Type**. Click **OK**.

20. Close and save both tables.

Tracking Object Dependency

Access provides a database tool to display information regarding dependencies among major objects. *Object dependency* is a condition in which an object requires the existence of another object. For example, the inventory form depends upon the inventory table.

Understanding dependencies helps maintain database integrity. Before deleting an object, you first should track the dependencies for that object. For example, you might decide to delete a query, only to discover that a data entry form is based upon that query rather than the source table. Before deleting the query, you will need to decide if the form will need to be changed.

Exercise 5-16 VIEW OBJECT DEPENDENCY

An Object Dependency List can be generated for tables, queries, forms, and reports. The Object Dependency List displays:

- Objects that depend on the selected object.
- The object on which the selected object depends.

NOTE

The first time this tool is used or when major objects are added and removed from the database, you will need to update the dependency information.

1. In the **Navigation Pane**, select **qryManageUniv**.

2. From the **Database Tools** tab, in the **Relationships** group, click **Object Dependencies** 🖳.

3. The **Object Dependencies** pane appears on the right side of your window. In the dialog box, click **OK** so the Access can update the dependencies.

Figure 5-19
Object Dependencies task pane **EcoMed-05.accdb Object Dependencies Task Pane**

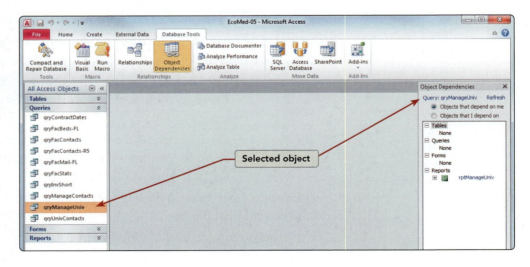

4. The first view is **Objects that depend on me**, and it shows that the report **rptManageUniv** depends on the query **qryManageUniv**.

5. Click **rptManageUniv** in the pane. The report opens in **Design View**.

6. From the **Design** tab, in the **Tools** group, click **Property Sheet**. In the **Property Sheet**, click the **Data** tab. Notice that the **Record Source** property is set to **qryManageUniv**.

7. Close the **Property Sheet** and the report.

8. In the **Object Dependencies** pane, click **Objects that I depend on**. This result shows that the query **qryManageUniv** depends on the table **tblManagement**.

9. Click **tblManagement** to open the table in **Design View**.

10. Close the table.

Exercise 5-17   VIEW A MISSING DEPENDENCY

If a database object is not functioning properly, you should look at its dependency list. For example, if a form does not display data, the record source upon which it depends might be missing. Viewing "Objects that I depend on" identifies the source recordset for that object.

1. In the **Navigation Pane**, select **qryFacMail-FL**.

2. In the **Object Dependencies** pane, click **Refresh**. Notice that this object needs the table **tblFacilities**.

3. Click **Objects that depend on me**. Notice that this query is needed by the report **rptFacMail-FL**.

4. In the **Navigation Pane**, right-click **qryFacMail-FL** and choose **Delete** from the menu. Click **Yes** to confirm the deletion.

5. In the **Navigation Pane**, select **rptFacMail-FL**.

REVIEW

Remember to backup your database!

6. In the **Object Dependencies** pane, click **Objects that I depend on**. Click **Refresh**. If a dialog box appears, click **OK**.

7. You can see that **qryFacMail-FL** is now missing. For the report to work, a new query would need to be created.

8. Close the **Object Dependencies** pane.

9. Compact and repair the database, and then close it.

Lesson 5   Summary

- Relationships between tables change a flat database, containing isolated data, into a relational database, containing linked data.
- Graphical relationships between tables can be viewed in the Relationships window.
- Related fields must be of the same data type and size but do not need to be named the same.
- A One-To-One relationship occurs when the common field is a primary key in the first table and a primary key field in the second.
- A One-to-Many relationship occurs when the common field is a primary key in the first table and not a primary key field in the second.
- An Indeterminate relationship occurs when Access does not have enough information to determine the relationship between the two tables.
- One or more relationships can be displayed in the Relationships window.
- When a common field is a primary key in the first table, it becomes a foreign key in the second table.
- A Relationship Report is a graphical report showing related tables.
- Referential integrity is a set of database rules for checking, validating, and keeping track of data entry changes in related tables.
- A subdatasheet is a datasheet linked within another datasheet containing related data.
- A Lookup field is a field property that displays input choices from another table and allows these choices to be selected from a list.
- A multi-valued Lookup field is a Lookup field that can store more than one value per record.
- The Table Analyzer Wizard displays options for improving table structures of your database based upon field types and the values stored.
- Object dependency is a condition in which an object requiring the existence of another object.

LESSON 5		Command Summary	
Feature	**Button**	**Task Path**	**Keyboard**
Collapse Subdatasheet	⊟		
Expand Subdatasheet	⊞		
Layout, Clear	✕	Database Tools, Relationships, Relationships, Tools, Clear Layout	
Lookup field, Create		Design, Tools, Modify Lookups	
Lookup field, Limit To List		Design View, Lookup, Limit To List	
Lookup field, Multi-valued, Create		Design View, Lookup, Allow Multiple Values	
Object Dependency		Database Tools, Relationships, Object Dependencies	
Primary Key, Set			
Referential Integrity, Enforce		Database Tools, Relationships, Edit Relationship, Enforce Referential Integrity	
Relationship Report, Create		Database Tools, Relationships, Relationships, Design Tools, Relationship Report	
Relationships, Show All		Database Tools, Relationships, Relationships, Design, Relationships All Relationships	
Relationships, Table, Show		Database Tools, Relationships, Relationships, Design, Relationships Show Table	
Relationships, View		Database Tools, Relationships, Relationships	
Subdatasheet, Insert		Design, Show/Hide, Property Sheet	
Subdatasheet, Remove		Home, Records, More, Subdatasheet, Remove	
Table, Analyze		Database Tools, Analyze, Analyze Table	

Please visit our Online Learning Center, *www.lessonapproach2010.com,* where you will find the following review materials:

Concepts Review

True/False Questions

Short Answer Questions

Critical Thinking Questions

Skills Review

Review Exercises that target single skills

Lesson Applications

Review Exercises that challenge students by testing multiple skills in each exercise

On Your Own

Open-ended exercises that require students to synthesize multiple skills and apply creativity and problem-solving as they would in a real world business situation

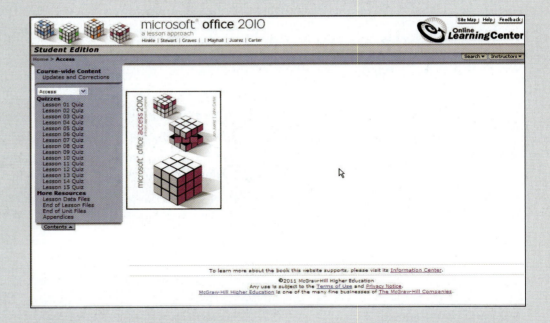

Lesson 6
Designing Queries

OBJECTIVES   *After completing this lesson, you will be able to:*

1. Create and modify select queries.

2. Add criteria and operators to queries.

3. Apply logical operators.

4. Modify query properties.

5. Add calculations to queries.

6. Create queries with wizards.

7. Apply PivotChart/PivotTable Views.

Estimated Time: 1½ hours

In most relational databases, queries locate, add, modify, and delete records. The effectiveness and efficiency of a query depends on its ability to access information quickly. A query is designed by selecting the appropriate fields, specifying appropriate criteria, and sorting recordsets.

Queries make data more manageable and often are the record source for reports and forms. For example, a report based on an employee table with 1,000 employees would show all 1,000 records. A report based on a query might show only a manageable subset of the entire table. The query might specify information, such as who is eligible for retirement, who is on vacation this week, or who has worked for the company for less than five years.

As with any computer application, executing a complex query takes processing resources. For a large database executing a very complicated query, the processing time might be extensive. To create effective queries, a skilled database administrator must be knowledgeable about the numerous types of queries available. In this lesson, you will learn to use common Access queries.

 REVIEW

A query is similar to a filter in some respects. However, a table can have only one filter but multiple queries.

Creating and Modifying Select Queries

In business situations, the most common type of query is a select query. A select query functions like a question that returns a different answer each time it is executed. For example, if you create a query to display names of employees who are over the age of 40 years, the results would be different depending on the day you executed the query and the employees who currently work for the company.

A select query locates data from one or more tables and displays the results as a datasheet. These results can be grouped, filtered, and sorted. In addition, a select query can calculate sums, averages, standard deviations, and other types of statistical functions.

In addition to Datasheet View and Design View, a query can be displayed in SQL View. SQL (*Structured Query Language*) is a computer language designed to manipulate data in relational databases. SQL was developed in the early 1970s, specifically designed to manipulate data in IBM's original relational database. In 1986 SQL was adopted as a standard by the American National Standards Institute.

Exercise 6-1   VIEW A SELECT QUERY AND ITS REPORT

You most often use the Query Design window to create and modify a query. The Query Design window has an upper and lower pane. The upper pane is the field list pane in which you choose the data source from one or more field lists. The lower pane is the design grid in which you specify criteria. The lower pane is also known as the QBE (Query by Example) grid.

The Design View of a query is the visual interface for the SQL statement. The Datasheet View displays the results of the SQL question asked of Access. The SQL statement is the actual code stored in an Access database.

1. Locate and open the **Lesson 06** folder.
2. Make a copy of **EcoMed-06** and rename it *[your initials]* **-EcoMed-06**.
3. Open and enable content for *[your initials]*-**EcoMed-06**.
4. Open **qryEmpPhone** in **Design View**. This query uses four fields from the table **tblEmployees**.

Figure 6-1
Query design
window
EcoMed-06.accdb
qryEmpPhone

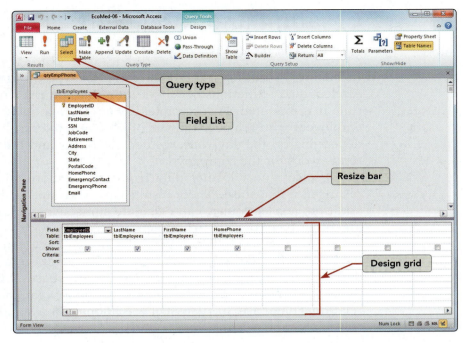

5.   Right-click the document tab for **qryEmpPhone** and choose **SQL View** .

Figure 6-2
SQL statement
EcoMed-06.accdb
qryEmpPhone

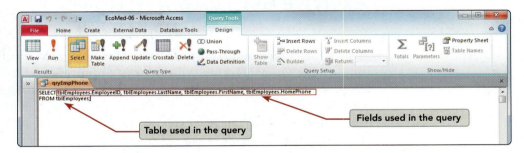

6.   Open **rptEmpPhone** in **Design View**.

7.   From the **Design** tab, in the **Tools** group, click **Property Sheet** .

8.   In the **Property Sheet**, click the **Data** tab. The **Record Source** property shows that this report is based on **qryEmpPhone**.

Figure 6-3
Report's property
sheet
EcoMed-06.accdb
rptEmpPhone

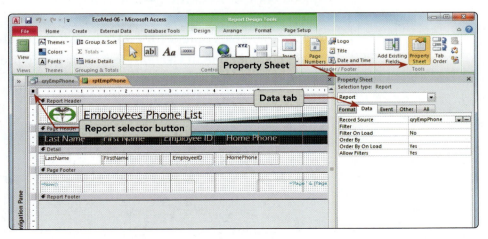

9.   Right-click the document tab for **rptEmpPhone** and choose **Close All** .

Exercise 6-2   CREATE A SELECT QUERY BASED ON A SINGLE TABLE

You will now create a query to display bulb prices. Rather than display all fields and records from the Inventory table, you will define appropriate criteria. You will define criteria and field lists in the Design View of a query. You then will display the resulting recordset through the datasheet of the query.

When you view the results, only the fields and records that you specified will display. The fields and records that you specify in the design grid create a dynaset. A *dynaset* is dynamic recordset that automatically reflects changes to its underlying data source.

1. From the **Create** tab, in the **Queries** group, click **Query Design** 📇.
2. In the **Show Table** dialog box, double-click **tblInventory**. The **tblInventory** Field List appears in the upper pane of the Query Design window.

Figure 6-4
Show Table dialog box
EcoMed-06.accdb
QryBuldPrices

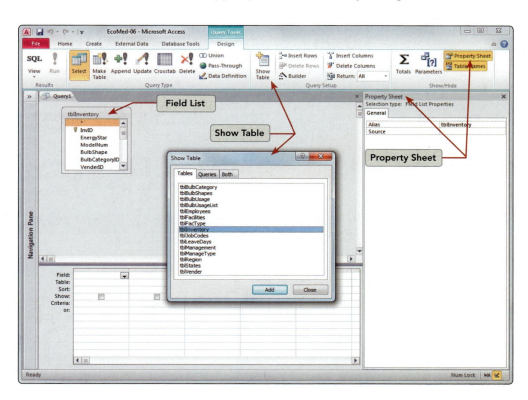

3. Click **Close** in the **Show Table** dialog box.
4. Resize the Field List so all fields can be seen.
5. If the **Property Sheet** is not open, click **Property Sheet** 📇.
6. Click the **tblInventory** Field List. The **Property Sheet** is now showing the properties of the table.
7. Click the blank area to the right of the Field List. The **Property Sheet** is now showing the properties of the query.
8. From the Quick Access toolbar, click **Save** 💾.
9. In the **Save As** dialog box, key **qryBulbPrices** and click **OK**.

↔ **REVIEW**

If you accidentally open two copies of the same Field List, right-click the second list and select Remove Table. You can also click the title bar of the Field List window and press ⌈Delete⌋ to remove the second copy.

Exercise 6-3 ADD FIELDS TO A QUERY

You can add fields to the design grid of a query by any of the three following ways:

- Double-click the field name in the Field List.
- Drag the field from the Field List to a Field row in the design grid.
- Click the Field row in the design grid and select a field name from the drop-down list.

1. From the Field List, double-click **ModelNum**. The field appears as the first field in the **Field** row in the design grid at the bottom of the screen.

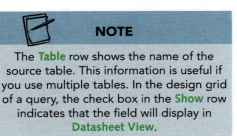

> **NOTE**
>
> The **Table** row shows the name of the source table. This information is useful if you use multiple tables. In the design grid of a query, the check box in the **Show** row indicates that the field will display in **Datasheet View**.

2. The **Property Sheet** now shows the properties of the field. Click **Property Sheet** 🗐 to hide the **Property Sheet**.

3. Drag the **BulbShape** field from the Field List to the **Field** row, second column.

4. In the third column, click the **Field** row, then click its drop-down arrow. Choose **Cost** from the list of field names.

Figure 6-5
Adding fields to the design grid
EcoMed-06.accdb qryBulbPrices

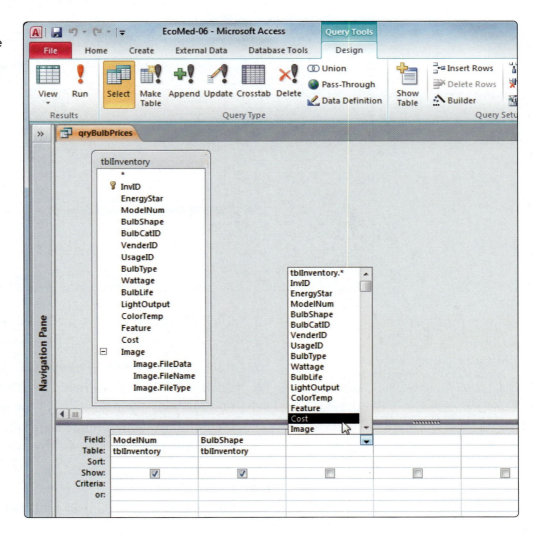

NOTE

Notice that the column headers in Datasheet View are not the same as the field names. These headers' values come from the Caption property of the fields, just like the Datasheet View of a table.

5. From the **Design** tab, in the **Results** group, click **Datasheet View** ⊞. Only the three fields that you selected are shown.

6. Save and close the query.

Exercise 6-4 CREATE A SELECT QUERY BASED ON TWO TABLES

A query is based on one or more field list. Each Field List is a recordset created by a table or query. When you use two or more Field Lists, you must link the Field Lists through a common field. This link will combine the matching records between the two tables. The link must be established through a field common to both tables.

1. From the **Create** tab, in the **Queries** group, click **Query Design** 🗐.

2. From the **Show Table** dialog box, double-click **tblInventory** and **tblBulbCategory**.

NOTE

When you use more than one table in a query, they must always show a join line.

3. Double-click **tblBulbCategory** again to add a second copy. Click **Close**.

4. The second copy of **tblBulbCategory** ends with "_1".

5. Resize and move the Field Lists so all fields can be seen.

6. From the **tblInventory** Field List, double-click **InvID** and **ModelNum**.

7. From the **tblBulbCategory** Field List, double-click **BulbCategory**.

NOTE

In a select query, the Run command 🔴 and Datasheet View command ⊞ produce the same results.

8. From the **Design** tab, in the **Results** group, click **Run** 🔴.

9. This query resulted in a dynaset of 1,240 records. Notice the many copies of the **Model Number**. Switch to **Design View**.

10. Right-click the **tblBulbCategory_1** Field List and choose **Remove Table**.

11. From the **Design** tab, in the **Results** group, click **Run** 🔴.

12. The dynaset now contains only 310 records. The extra records came from having a copy of a table in the query.

13. Save the query as **qryBulbList**.

14. From the **Home** tab, in the **Views** group, click the bottom half of the **Design View** 📐 and choose **SQL View** ᴤ. This SQL statement shows the tables used in the query and their relationship.

Figure 6-6
SQL statement for two-table query
EcoMed-06.accdb qryBulbList

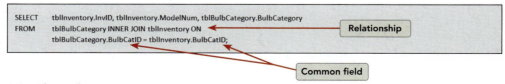

```
SELECT   tblInventory.InvID, tblInventory.ModelNum, tblBulbCategory.BulbCategory
FROM     tblBulbCategory INNER JOIN tblInventory ON
         tblBulbCategory.BulbCatID = tblInventory.BulbCatID;
```
Relationship

Common field

15. Close the query.

Adding Criteria and Operators to a Query

Adding criteria to a query is similar to adding criteria to a filter. One major difference is that more than one condition can be placed on multiple fields. When the query is executed, each condition placed as a criterion must be evaluated against field values for each record in the dynaset. The combination of conditions and operators is evaluated as a single criterion statement.

An *operator* is a word or symbol that indicates a specific arithmetic or logical relationship between the elements of an expression. Operators are used to create conditions. Operators can include arithmetic operators, such as the plus sign (+); comparison operators, such as the equals sign (=); logical operators, such as the word "And"; concatenation operators, such as & and +; and special operators, such as "Like," "Between," or "In."

In addition to operators, a condition can include one or more functions. A *function* is a procedure used in an expression. Most functions include multiple arguments. An *argument* is a reference in a function assigned as a single variable. Some functions such as "Date" do not require arguments. Other functions such as "DateDiff" contain both required arguments and optional arguments.

TABLE 6-1 Types of Operators

Type	Definition	Examples
Arithmetic operator	A word or symbol that calculates a value from two or more numbers.	+, −, *, /, \, ^
Comparison operator	A symbol or combination of symbols that specifies a comparison between two values. A comparison operator is also referred to as a relational operator.	=, <>, <, <=, >, >=
Logical operator	A symbol, word, group of symbols, or group of words used to construct an expression with multiple conditions.	And, Or, Eqv, Not, Xor
Concatenation operator	A symbol, word, group of symbols, or group of words used to combine two text values into a single text value.	&, +
Special operators		Like, Between, In, True, False

Exercise 6-5   USE A SINGLE CRITERION

Text, numbers, or expressions can be used as criteria. When you create criteria using text values, you must include leading and closing quotation marks around the text. Criteria using date values include leading and closing pound signs (#). Numbers and expressions do not require leading or closing symbols. You will now create a select query using a single criterion.

1. Open **qryBulbPrices** in **Design View**.
2. Click the **Criteria** row for **BulbShape**. Key **canister**.

Figure 6-7
Entering criteria
EcoMed-06.accdb
qryBulbPrices

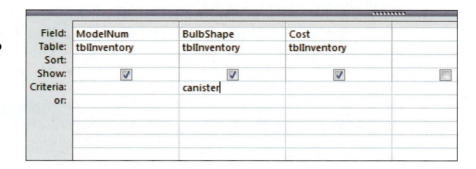

Field:	ModelNum	BulbShape	Cost	
Table:	tblInventory	tblInventory	tblInventory	
Sort:				
Show:	☑	☑	☑	☐
Criteria:		canister		
or:				

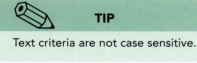

TIP

Text criteria are not case sensitive.

TIP

After you run a query, Access places leading and closing quotation marks around the text used as the criterion.

NOTE

This query has reduced the dynaset from 310 records to 6 records.

3. From the **Design** tab, in the **Results** group, click **Datasheet View** ▦. Only those products of **Bulb Shape** "canister" are shown.
4. Switch to **Design View**.
5. Click in the **Criteria** row for **BulbShape** and press F2 to select the criterion. Press Delete.
6. In the **Criteria** row for **BulbShape**, key **dish**.
7. From the **Design** tab, in the **Results** group, click **View** ▦. Only those products of **Bulb Shape** "dish" are shown.
8. From the **Home** tab, in the **Views** group, click the bottom half of the **Design View** ◤ and choose **SQL View** ▦. This SQL statement now shows the criteria.

Figure 6-8
SQL statement:
criteria
EcoMed-06.accdb
qryBulbPrices

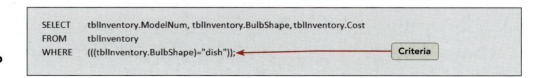

```
SELECT    tblInventory.ModelNum, tblInventory.BulbShape, tblInventory.Cost
FROM      tblInventory
WHERE     (((tblInventory.BulbShape)="dish"));            ◀——— Criteria
```

9. Switch to **Design View**.

10. Click in the **Criteria** row for **BulbShape** and press F2. Press Delete to remove the criteria.

11. Save and close the query.

Exercise 6-6 USE COMPARISON OPERATORS

Queries often use comparison operators to evaluate data. Comparison operators allow you to evaluate numbers, text, and dates. For example, the expression ">10/17/11" would display all records with a date after October 17, 2011. The expression ">=10/17/11" would display all records with a date on or after October 17, 2011.

When comparing text, fields are evaluated alphabetically. The expression <"smith" would display all records that appear in a dictionary before the word "smith".

TABLE 6-2 Comparison Operators

Operator	Meaning
=	Equal
<>	Not equal
<	Less than
<=	Less than or equal to
>	Greater than
>=	Greater than or equal to

1. Open **qryEmpLeave** in **Datasheet View** and notice that the dynaset is sorted by **Leave Date**.

2. Switch to **Design View**. Click in the **Criteria** row for **LeaveDate**.

3. Key **<=3/31/10** and press ↓. Access adds "#" around the date criteria.

4. Switch to **Datasheet View**. Records for which the **Leave Date** is on or before March 31, 2010, display (50 records).

5. From the **Home** tab, in the **Views** group, click the bottom half of the **Design View** and choose **SQL View** . This SQL statement now shows the criteria and sort order.

Figure 6-9
SQL statement: criteria and sort
EcoMed-06.accdb qryEmpLeave

```
SELECT    tblEmployees.EmployeeID, tblEmployees.LastName, tblEmployees.FirstName,
          tblLeaveDays.LeaveCategory,  tblLeaveDays.LeaveDate
FROM      tblEmployees INNER JOIN tblLeaveDays ON
          tblEmployees.EmployeeID = tblLeaveDays.EmployeeID
WHERE     (((tblLeaveDays.LeaveDate)<=#3/31/2010#))          ⟵ Criteria
ORDER BY tblLeaveDays.LeaveDate;                             ⟵ Sort by
```

6. Switch to **Design View** and delete the criteria for **LeaveDate**.

7. Save and close the query.

Exercise 6-7   USE WILDCARDS IN CRITERIA

In much the same way you would use wildcards in the Find command, you can use wildcards in a query. When using a wildcard in the Criteria row of a query, the Like operator compares the criterion condition to each record.

For example, in the first name field, the criterion Like "Joa" would display records that contain fields such as "Joan", "Joann", and "Joaquin."
When using a wild card, Access automatically adds the keyword "Like."

> **REVIEW**
>
> The wildcard * represents any number of characters. Thus, the criteria "f*" specifies the letter "f" followed by any number of characters.

You will now modify an existing query to display all facilities with the word "Hospital" in its name.

1. Open **qryFacDetails** in **Design View**.

2. In the **Criteria** row for **FacName**, key **f***.

Figure 6-10
Using the * wildcard
EcoMed-06.accdb
qryFacDetails

Field:	FacilitiesID	FacName	ManageTypeID	MedicareID	Revenue	
Table:	tblFacilities	tblFacilities	tblFacilities	tblFacilities	tblFacilities	
Sort:		Ascending				
Show:	☑	☑	☑	☑	☑	
Criteria:		*f				
or:						

3. From the **Design** tab, in the **Results** group, click **Run** ⚡. Records in which the **Facility Name** starts with "f" are displayed.

4. Switch to **Design View**. Access inserts the keyword **Like** and formats the text with quotes.

5. Press F2 and Delete to delete the criteria.

6. In the **Criteria** row for **FacName**, key ***hospital***.

7. Switch to view the dynaset. Records where the **Facility Name** contains "hospital" are displayed.

> **NOTE**
>
> When using the "?" wildcard, you must place the quotation marks around your criteria. Otherwise Access will tell you that you have a syntax error.

8. Switch to **Design View**. Delete the criteria.

9. In the **MedicareNum Criteria** row, key **"??2*"**. This criterion will look at the third number in the **Medicare Number**, which indicates the type of facility. In this case, "2" refers to Long-Term facilities.

10. Press ↓.

Figure 6-11
Using the * and ?
wildcards
EcoMed-06.accdb
qryFacDetails

Field:	FacilitiesID	FacName	ManageTypeID	MedicareNum	Revenue	
Table:	tblFacilities	tblFacilities	tblFacilities	tblFacilities	tblFacilities	
Sort:		Ascending				
Show:	☑	☑	☑	☑	☑	
Criteria:				Like "??2*"		
or:						

UNIT 2 LESSON 6

REVIEW

The wildcard ? represents a single character.

11. View the dynaset. Three records are displayed.

12. Return to **Design View** and delete the criteria.

Exercise 6-8 USE KEYWORDS IN CRITERIA

Only the keyword "Like" is automatically added to a criterion. All other keywords must be specified. Criteria expressions can be viewed in the Zoom box. You can open the Zoom box by pressing Shift+F2.

TABLE 6-3 Criteria Keywords

Keyword	Returns records where the field ...
Is Null	has no data, is "blank," or is "empty."
Between	value is between two numbers.
Like	value equals a defined text.
Not	value does not match the defined value.

1. In the **Design View** of **qryFacDetails**, in the **Criteria** row for **MedicareNum**, key **null** and press ⬇. Access has inserts the keyword "Is" to the criteria and capitalized "Null."

2. View the dynaset. There are 18 facilities that don't have **Medicare Numbers**.

3. Return to **Design View**.

4. Edit the **MedicareNum** criteria to show **is not null**.

5. View the dynaset. There are 146 facilities that do have **Medicare Numbers**.

6. Return to **Design View** and delete the criteria.

7. From the Fields List, add the field **Beds**.

8. Right-click in the **Criteria** row for **Beds** and choose **Zoom** 🔍.

9. In the **Zoom** dialog box, key is **between 100 and 300** and click **OK**.

10. View the dynaset. There are 38 facilities with between 100 and 300 beds.

11. Switch to **Design View**.

12. In the **Show** row, click to remove the checkmark for **Beds**.

13. View the dynaset. The numbers of beds are no longer showing, but the field is still being used for the criteria.

14. Switch to **SQL View**.

Figure 6-12
SQL statement:
Between keyword
**EcoMed-06.accdb
qryFacDetails**

```
SELECT    tblFacilities.FacilitiesID, tblFacilities.FacName, tblFacilities.ManageTypeID,
          tblFacilities.MedicareNum, tblFacilities.Revenue
FROM      tblFacilities
WHERE     (((tblFacilities.Beds) Between 100 And 300))
ORDER BY  tblFacilities.FacName;
```

Criteria using key word

15. Return to **Design View** and delete the criteria.

16. Close the query and save the changes.

Applying Logical Operators

An AND criterion or an OR criterion compares two conditions in a single statement. You use AND criteria when two conditions must occur simultaneously for the statement to be true. You use OR criteria when either condition must occur for the statement to be true.

The design grid of a query allows for AND and OR statements without using AND or OR as keywords. When you create an AND criteria, you enter all conditions on the same Criteria row of the design grid. When you create an OR criteria, you enter the conditions on different Criteria rows of the design grid.

Exercise 6-9   USE AND CRITERIA

An AND condition can be created for a single field or multiple fields. When an AND condition is placed on a single field, the keyword AND must be placed between the two conditions. When an AND condition is placed on multiple fields, the keyword is not entered. When more than one field contains a condition on the same Criteria row, then an AND condition is created automatically by Access.

You will now create a query that uses the AND condition. You will search for all facilities that are in the state of Florida and in the city of Miami.

1. From the **Create** tab, in the **Queries** group, click **Query Design** .

2. From the **Show Table** dialog box, double-click **tblFacilities** and click **Close**.

3. Resize the Field List so all field names can be seen.

4. Add the following fields to the query design grid: **FacName**, **Address**, **City**, **State**, **ZIP**.

5. In the **FacName** column, click the drop-down arrow in the **Sort** row and choose **Ascending**.

6. Switch to **Datasheet View** to see the results. Resize the columns so all data are visible.

7. Right-click the document tab for the query and choose **Save** . Key **qryFacAddress** and click **OK**.

8. Switch to **Design View**.

9. In the **State** column, key **fl** in the **Criteria** row.

10. Switch to **Datasheet View** to see how many facilities are in Florida. Return to **Design View**.

11. In the **City** column, key **miami** in the same **Criteria** row.

Figure 6-13
AND criteria on the same row in the design grid
EcoMed-06.accdb
qryFacAddress

Field:	FacName	Address	City	State	ZIP
Table:	tblFacilities	tblFacilities	tblFacilities	tblFacilities	tblFacilities
Sort:	Ascending				
Show:	☑	☑	☑	☑	☑
Criteria:			miami	"fl"	
or:					

12. Switch to **Datasheet View**. Only records that matched both the state and city criteria are shown. Return to **Design View**.

13. Click in the **Criteria** row for the **City** field. From the **Design** tab, in the **Query Setup** group, click **Delete Rows** ⇥×.

14. Click in the **Criteria** row for the **State** field. Key **tn and nc**.

15. Switch to **Datasheet View**. No records match the criteria because no facility's state can be both TN and NC.

Exercise 6-10   USE OR CRITERIA

An OR condition can be created for a single field or multiple fields. When an OR condition is placed on a single field, the keyword OR must be placed between the two conditions. When an OR condition is placed on two or more fields, the keyword is not entered. When multiple conditions are placed on multiple Criteria rows, then an OR condition is automatically created by Access.

You will now create a query that creates an OR condition. You will search for all facilities that are in the state of Tennessee or the state of North Carolina.

1. Switch to **Design View**. Point to the right of the word "Criteria" in the **Criteria** row to display a black arrow pointing right. Click to select the **Criteria** row and press ⌷Delete⌷.

Figure 6-14
Selecting a Criteria row
EcoMed-06.accdb qryFacAddress

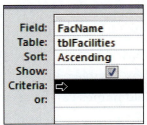

2. Click in the **Criteria** row for the **State** field, and key **tn**. View the dynaset to see nine matching records. Return to **Design View**.

3. Key **nc** in the row below "tn" to enter a second condition. The first **or** row is directly below the **Criteria** row.

Figure 6-15
OR criteria on separate rows in the design grid
EcoMed-06.accdb qryFacAddress

Field:	FacName	Address	City	State	ZIP
Table:	tblFacilities	tblFacilities	tblFacilities	tblFacilities	tblFacilities
Sort:	Ascending				
Show:	✓	✓	✓	✓	✓
Criteria:				"tn"	
or:				nc	

4. View the dynaset. Each record meets one of the "OR" conditions. Return to **Design View**.

5. Save and close the query.

6. Open **qryFacAddress** in **Design View**. Notice that Access has combined the two criteria to one row using the "OR" keyword.

7. Switch to **SQL View**.

Figure 6-16
SQL statement: Or criteria
EcoMed-06.accdb qryFacAddress

```
SELECT     tblFacilities.FacName, tblFacilities.Address, tblFacilities.City, tblFacilities.State,
           tblFacilities.ZIP                              ┌─────────────────┐
                                                          │ Criteria using OR │
FROM       tblFacilities                                  └─────────────────┘
WHERE      (((tblFacilities.State)="tn")) OR (((tblFacilities.State)="nc"))
ORDER BY   tblFacilities.FacName;
```

8. Switch to **Design View** and delete the criteria.

9. Save and close the query.

Modifying Query Properties

Queries display specific data and sorted data. By setting specific properties on a query, you can display top values and subdatasheets. For example, if you need to list the five facilities with the highest revenue, you would sort the facilities table by revenue in descending order and apply the Top Value property. The original query, including its criteria, would remain the same. You would only modify its properties to display the top values.

The Top Values property displays either a static number of records (such as the top 5) or a percentage of all records in the dynaset (such as the top 5 percent). Depending on the sort order, Top Values can display either the highest (top) or lowest (bottom) values. For example, when you sort a numeric field in ascending order, the "top" of the list will be the lowest numbers. When you sort a numeric field in descending order, the "top" values are the largest numbers.

Exercise 6-11　FIND THE TOP AND BOTTOM VALUES

When using the Top Values property, Access displays records based on the defined sort order. If a query is sorted by a numeric value, then the top values will be based on the sorted numeric field. If a query is sorted by a text field, then the top values will be based on the sorted text field.

To find the top 5 percent of the facilities that have the greatest annual revenue, you will apply the appropriate property to the FacDetails query. You must first sort the dynaset and then apply the top 5 percent property.

1. Open **qryFacDetails**.

2. Switch to **Design View**. Click in the **Sort** row for the **FacName** field. Click the drop-down arrow and choose **(not sorted)**.

3. Click in the **Sort** row for the **Revenue** field. Click the drop-down arrow and choose **Descending**.

4. Switch to **Datasheet View**. The facilities are sorted in descending order, starting with the facilities with the greatest annual revenue.

5. Switch to **Design View**.

6. From the **Design** tab, in the **Show/Hide** group, click **Property Sheet** 📇.

7. Click anywhere to the right of the **tblFacilities** Field List to make the **Property Sheet** display the **Query Properties**.

8. Click the property **Top Values** and the drop-down arrow. Choose **5**.

Figure 6-17
Top Values property
EcoMed-06.accdb
qryFacDetails

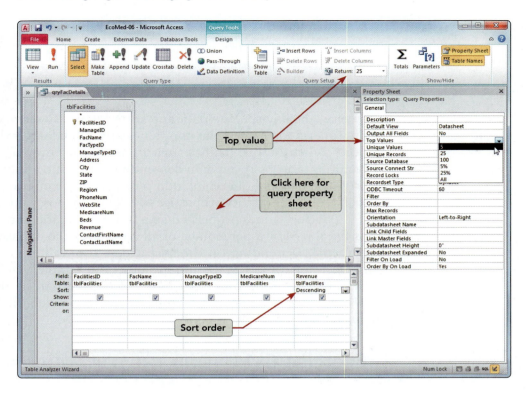

TIP

The **Top Values** property also can be changed in the Return list box found on the **Design** tab, **Query Setup** group.

9. Switch to **Datasheet View**. Because the field **Revenue** is sorted in descending order, the five greatest revenues are shown.

10. Switch to **Design View**. From the **Design** tab, in the **Query Setup** group, click the **Return** list box and select **5%**.

11. Switch to **Datasheet View**. The top 5 percent of facilities according to their revenues equals 9 records that are displayed.

12. Switch to **SQL View**.

Figure 6-18
SQL statement:
Top 5 Percent
EcoMed-06.accdb
qryFacDetails

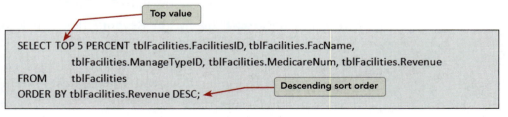

NOTE

Remember to reset the Top Values property to All. If you forget to reset the property and later prepare a report based on the query, you will print an incomplete dynaset.

13. Switch to **Design View** and reset the **Return** list box to **All**.

14. Close and save the query.

Exercise 6-12 CREATE A QUERY WITH A SUBDATASHEET

Just as a table can display a related table as a subdatasheet, a query can also contain a subdatasheet. A subdatasheet is created by defining a Subdatasheet Name as a query property. The sheets must be linked by a common field. You will now modify qryMgtContacts by linking the ManageID field between the tables management and facilities.

1. Open **qryMgtContacts**.
2. Switch to **Design View**. Open the **Property Sheet** if it is not already visible.
3. Click in the open space next to the Field List to select the query properties and not the field properties.
4. In the **Property Sheet** for the query, click the property **Subdatasheet Name** and click the drop-down arrow. Choose **Table.tblFacilities** from the list.

> **NOTE**
>
> If the **Property Sheet** shows "Field Properties," click again in the top pane. You may also need to resize the **Property Sheet** to see all values.

5. Click the **Link Child Fields** property and key **MgtID**.
6. Click the **Link Master Fields** property and key **MgtID**.
7. Close the **Property Sheet** and switch to **Datasheet View**.
8. Click the **Expand** button  for any record to see which facilities are managed by each company.
9. Collapse the subdatasheet.
10. Close the query and save the changes.

Adding Calculations to a Query

The queries you have created so far have been select queries. Select queries display the resulting dynaset as individual records, similar to a datasheet of a table. In addition to selecting fields and records to display, a select query can display results of calculations.

To display a calculation in a query, you use an aggregate function. An *aggregate function* is a sum, average, maximum, minimum, or count for a group of records. For example, you can create a query to display the total bed count for all facilities associated with a single management organization.

A select query also can have a calculated field. A *calculated field* is a field that uses an expression or formula as its data source. After creating a calculated field in a query, you can add those fields to forms and reports. In later lessons, you will learn to add calculated fields directly to the forms and reports.

A calculated field does not store data in the source dynaset. The value of a calculated field is generated each time you run the query. Only the definition and properties of the calculated field are stored in the query object, not the field values.

Because a calculated field is not part of the source dynaset, each calculated field must have a unique name. When a field does not have a name, Access assigns an alias name. The alias name for a calculated field displays as text followed by a colon, in front of the calculation.

Exercise 6-13   USE A FORMULA IN A CALCULATED FIELD

You will learn to create a calculated field by constructing an equation to calculate the sales price of inventory items. EcoMed marks up its inventory by 48 percent. The sales price is calculated by using the formula of cost times 1.48. That means an item that costs $1.00 will sell for $1.48, and an item that costs $2.00 will sell for $2.96.

Calculated fields can be entered directly into the design grid or can be entered using the Expression Builder. The *Expression Builder* is an interface used to create a function, calculation, or expressions.

TABLE 6-4 Expression Builder Components

Component	Description
Expression box	White area at the top of the window that shows the formula as you build it. (Also called the preview area.)
Expression Elements	List of elements available to build an expression.
Expression Categories	Subset of the elements found in the Expression Elements panel.
Expression Values	Subset of the categories found in the Expression Categories panel.

1. Open **qryInvShort** in **Design View**.
2. Click the empty **Field** row in the fifth column.
3. From the **Design** tab, in the **Query Setup** group, click **Builder** ⚟.

Figure 6-19
Building an expression for the query
EcoMed-06.accdb qryInvShort

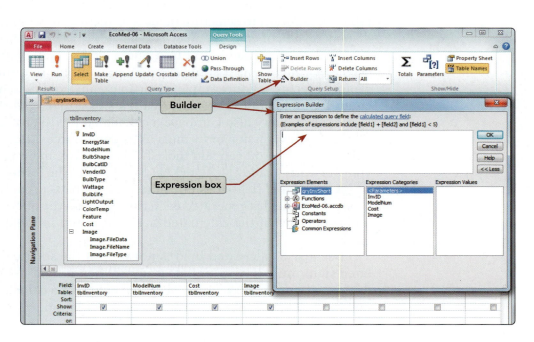

NOTE

The middle pane will display the field in the query as long as the query has been saved.

NOTE

Square brackets are used to surround field names.

Figure 6-20
Building a formula
EcoMed-06.accdb
qryInvShort

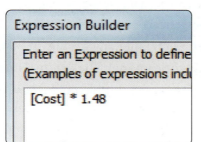

Expression Builder

Enter an Expression to define
(Examples of expressions incl

[Cost] * 1.48

REVIEW

To see the calculation more easily, you can open the Zoom window by using
Shift + F2 .

5

4. The current query is at the top of the **Expression Elements** panel. In the **Expression Categories** panel, click the field **Cost**.

5. In the **Expression Values** panel, double-click **<Value>** to paste the value of the **Cost** field to the Expression box.

6. In the **Expression Elements** panel, click **Operators**.

7. In the **Expression Values** panel, double-click ***** (the asterisk) which acts as a multiplication operator.

8. In the Expression box, key **1.48** as the numerical equivalent of a 48 percent markup.

9. Click **OK** to close the **Expression Builder**.

10. Switch to **Datasheet View**. Notice that the last column shows the markup cost of each item in the inventory.

11. Access has given the calculated field a label (or alias) of "Expr1." Switch to **Design View**.

12. Replace "Expr1" with **Retail**. Be certain to leave the colon between the label and the expression.

13. From the **Design** tab, in the **Show/Hide** group, click **Property Sheet** .

14. In the property **Format**, click the drop-down arrow and choose **Currency**.

15. Close the **Property Sheet**.

16. Switch to **Datasheet View**. The calculated field is now formatted.

17. Save and close the query.

Exercise 6-14 USE A FUNCTION IN A CALCULATED FIELD

In addition to constructing a calculated field directly, you can use the Expression Builder to look up and insert arguments and operators for a predefined function. For this exercise, you will use the DateDiff and Now functions to calculate the difference between two dates. The two dates that you will use are the employee's date of birth and today's date. The resulting difference will be the age of the employee.

1. Open **qryEmpDates** in **Design View**.

2. Click the empty **Field** row in the fifth column.

3. From the **Design** tab, in the **Query Setup** group, click **Builder** .

4. In the **Expression Elements** panel, double-click **Functions** and click **Built-In Functions**.

5. In the **Expression Categories** panel, click **Date/Time**.

6. In the **Expression Values** panel, double-click **DateDiff**. This function has five parameters or values. We need to fill three of them.

> **NOTE**
>
> Functions use leading and ending placeholders, << and >>. These placeholders identify the argument(s) used in the function.

7. In the Expression box, click on **interval** and key **"yyyy"**.

8. In the Expression box, click on **<<date1>>** to select the placeholder.

9. In the **Expression Elements** panel, click **qryEmpDates**. In the **Expression Categories** panel, double-click **DOB** to add the date of birth field to the expression.

10. In the Expression box, click on **<<date2>>**.

11. In the **Expression Elements** panel, click **Built-In Functions**.

12. In the **Expression Categories** panel, click **Date/Time**.

13. In the **Expression Values** panel, double-click **Now**. This function has no parameters but still needs to have its parentheses.

14. Press ⌈Delete⌋ until you have deleted the remaining commas and placeholders. Do not delete the right parenthesis.

Figure 6-21
Building a function
EcoMed-06.accdb
qryEmpDates

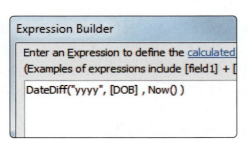

15. Click **OK**. Press ⌈↓⌋. Access has added the alias "Expr1".

16. Replace the alias with **Age**.

17. From the **Design** tab, in the **Show/Hide** group, click the **Property Sheet** . In the **Age Property Sheet**, click in the **Format** property and key **#" years"**. There is a space before the "y" in years.

18. Switch to **Datasheet View**. The newly calculated field shows the employee's age plus a text string.

19. Return to **Design View** and close the **Property Sheet**.

20. Save the query.

Exercise 6-15   USE A CONCATENATION EXPRESSION IN A CALCULATED FIELD

In addition to mathematical, date, and statistical functions, Access also includes text functions. Text functions allow you to extract or combine text. In this lesson, you will concatenate text. *Concatenate* is the operation of joining two or more character strings end to end. For example, the two text strings "twenty" and "three" can be concatenated with the symbol "-" to produce the single string "twenty-three".

1. Click the empty **Field** row in the sixth column.
2. From the **Design** tab, in the **Query Setup** group, click **Builder** 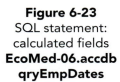.
3. In the **Expression Categories** panel, double-click **LastName**.
4. In the **Expression Elements** panel, click **Operators**.
5. In the **Expression Categories** panel, click **String**. There is only one string operator.
6. In the **Expression Values** panel, double-click the **&** (ampersand).
7. Click in the Expression box and key **", "** (double quotation, comma, space, double quotation).
8. Press [Spacebar] and key **&**.
9. In the **Expression Elements** panel, click **qryEmpDates**.
10. In the **Expression Categories** panel, double-click **FirstName**. Click **OK**.

Figure 6-22
Concatenation
expression
EcoMed-06.accdb
qryEmpDates

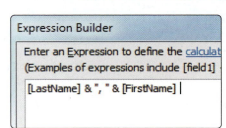

11. Edit the alias "Expr1" to **FullName**.
12. Switch to **Datasheet View**. The newly calculated field shows the last and first names of employees in one field.
13. For the first record, change the **Last Name** from "Abdone" to **Smith**.
14. Press [↓]. Notice the **FullName** value has changed to show the new last name of the employee.
15. Switch to **SQL View**.

Figure 6-23
SQL statement:
calculated fields
EcoMed-06.accdb
qryEmpDates

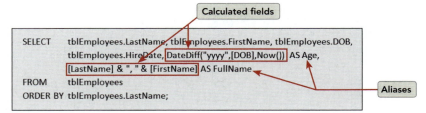

16. Save and close the query.

Creating Queries with Wizards

Relationships and referential integrity prevent data duplication or unmatched relationships. However, when using data from other sources, such as an on-line Web site, the table you create might not follow your relationship rules. Access provides two queries that assist you in verifying the accuracy of your data.

You use the Query Wizard to create the Find Unmatched Records Query and the Find Duplicate Records Query. The Query Wizard can also be used to create a Crosstab query.

Exercise 6-16 USE THE SIMPLE QUERY WIZARD

You have been asked to create a query that will display the name of the vender, the inventory model number, the shape of the bulb, and the image of the bulb. Because these four fields do not exist in a single table, you will need to create a query and link the appropriate fields. You can use the Query Wizard to create this query.

When creating a query using a wizard, you must select the record source and the associated fields. The record source can be one or more related tables or queries. The dynaset will generate on the basis of the relationship between the three tables.

1. From the **Create** tab, in the **Queries** group, click **Query Wizard** 🔍.

Figure 6-24
New Query Wizard
EcoMed-06.accdb

2. In the **New Query** dialog box, double-click **Simple Query Wizard**.
3. From the **Tables/Queries** list box, choose **Table: tblVender**.
4. In the **Available Fields** list, double-click **VenderName**.
5. From the **Tables/Queries** list box, choose **Table: tblInventory**.
6. In the **Available Fields** list, double-click **ModelNum** and **BulbShape**.
7. From the **Tables/Queries** list box, choose **Table: tblBulbShapes**.
8. In the **Available Fields** list, double-click **Icon**.
9. Click **Next**. The default type of select query is **Detail**. Click **Next**.
10. Delete the suggested title and key **qryVenInv&Shape**.

11. Click **Finish**. This dynaset lists the venders, inventory, and shape of each bulb.

12. Switch to **Design View**. Resize and move each Field List to match Figure 6-25.

Figure 6-25
Query created by the
Simple Query Wizard
**EcoMed-06.accdb
qryVenInv&Shape**

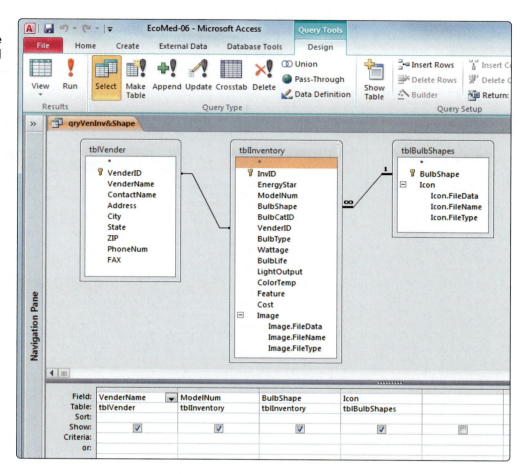

13. Notice that the tables are linked to one another with join lines. Close and save the query.

Exercise 6-17   USE THE CROSSTAB QUERY WIZARD

A crosstab query displays information similar to that in a spreadsheet. The Total row calculates sum, average, count, or other totals. The Crosstab row defines the fields used for the data, column headings, and row headings. Data are grouped by two fields, one listed on the left and the other listed across the top.

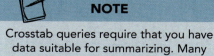

NOTE

Crosstab queries require that you have data suitable for summarizing. Many tables do not have fields appropriate to display as a crosstab.

1. Open **qryEmpLeave** in **Datasheet View** and sort by **Last Name** in ascending order.

2. Notice that each employee has taken multiple sick and vacation days. Close the query without saving.

3. From the **Create** tab, in the **Queries** group, click **Query Wizard** .

4. In the **New Query** dialog box, double-click **Crosstab Query Wizard**.

5. In the **View** control, click **Queries**. From the list, select **Query: qryEmpLeave**. Click **Next**.

6. From the **Available Fields**, double-click **LastName** and **FirstName** as the row headings. Click **Next**.

7. Select **LeaveCategory** as the column heading and click **Next**.

8. Select **LeaveDate** as the data to be shown and **Count** as the function. Click the check box **Yes, include row sums** to deselect the control. Click **Next**.

Figure 6-26
Crosstab Query
Wizard
**EcoMed-06.accdb
qryEmpLeave_
Crosstab**

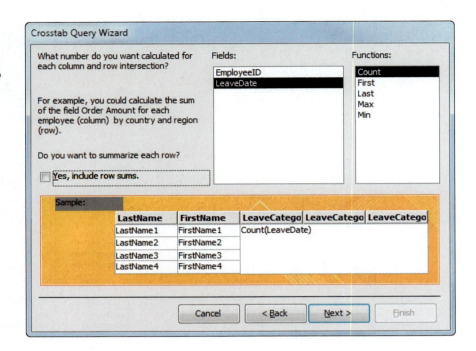

9. Accept the suggested title and click **Finish**. This query counts each sick and vacation day for each employee.

10. Switch to **Design View**. Two new rows were added to the design grid by the wizard: **Total** and **Crosstab**.

11. Close and save the query.

Exercise 6-18   USE THE FIND DUPLICATE QUERY WIZARD

The Find Duplicates Query Wizard analyzes a table for duplicate data. If duplicates are identified, you decide what action to take, including deleting or editing the records.

1. From the **Create** tab, in the **Queries** group, click **Query Wizard** .

2. In the **New Query** dialog box, double-click **Find Duplicates Query Wizard**.

3. From the list of table, select **Table: tblVender**. Click **Next**.

4. From the **Available fields** list, double-click **VenderName**.

Figure 6-27
Choose the field that might have duplicates.
**EcoMed-06.accdb
qryVenDuplicates**

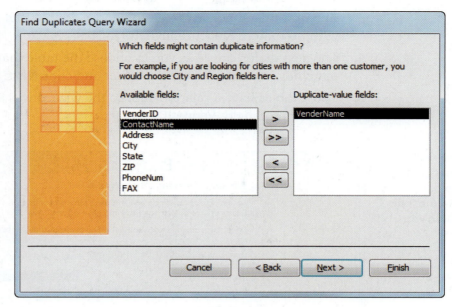

5. Click **Next**. Click the **Add All** button >> to show all fields in the resulting dynaset. Click **Next**.

6. Delete the suggested title and key **qryVenDuplicates** and click **Finish**. The query shows the two duplicate records.

7. From the **Home** tab, in the **Records** group, click **More** and choose **Subdatasheet**, then **Subdatasheet** from the menu.

8. In the **Insert Subdatasheet** dialog box, on the **Tables** tab, select **tblInventory**.

9. Using the drop-down arrows, set the **Linked Child Fields** and **Linked Master Fields** fields to the common field, **VenderID**. Click **OK**.

10. Expand both subdatasheets. Notice that **VenderID** 31 does not have any inventory related to it, so it is safe to delete this record.

11. Select the record for **VenderID** 31.

12. From the **Home** tab, in the **Records** group, click the **Delete** option arrow and choose **Delete Record**. Click **Yes** to verify the deletion.

13. From the **Home** tab, in the **Records** group, click **Refresh All**. The query is run again, but this time there are no duplicates.

14. Close and save any changes to the query.

Exercise 6-19 　USE THE FIND UNMATCHED QUERY WIZARD

The Find Unmatched Query Wizard finds unmatched, or orphaned, records. Orphaned records occur when referential integrity has not been enforced. When working on a database designed by someone else, it is can be beneficial to check if there are unmatched records.

1. From the **Create** tab, in the **Queries** group, click **Query Wizard**.

2. In the **New Query** dialog box, double-click **Find Unmatched Query Wizard**.

3. The first dialog box asks you to choose a table that might have records with no match. Select **tblInventory**. Click **Next**.

4. The next dialog box asks you to choose the table that should have the matching records. Choose **tblVender** and click **Next**.

5. These tables have a relationship, so the wizard was able to determine the common field, **VenderID**.

Figure 6-28
Match the common field.
EcoMed-06.accdb
qryInvNoVen

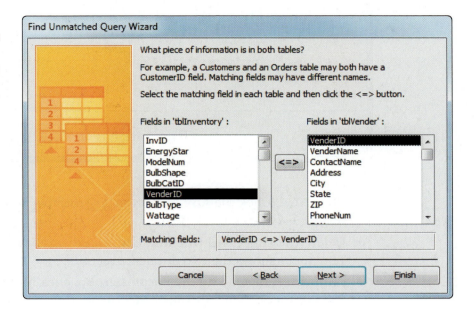

6. Click **Next**. In the **Available fields**, double-click **InvID**, **ModelNum**, and **VenderID**. Click **Next**.

7. Delete the suggested title, key **qryInvNoVen**, and click **Finish**. The query shows there are 15 bulbs in the inventory table without a vender. We will not be fixing this error at this time.

8. Close the query.

Applying PivotChart/PivotTable Views

PivotTables and PivotCharts are methods of viewing complex information in summarized formats. PivotTables and PivotCharts can automatically sort, count, and total data in a summarized format. You can change the summary's structure by dragging and dropping fields using a graphical interface.

You use PivotTables and PivotCharts to analyze related totals or to compare related information from a large data set. In a PivotTable or PivotChart, each column or field in your source data becomes a PivotTable field that summarizes multiple rows of information. When you rearrange the fields in a PivotTable, the changes appear as changes to columns in the related PivotChart. You can save changes to and print PivotTables and PivotCharts.

Exercise 6-20   USE PIVOTTABLE VIEW

A *pivot table* is an interactive table that combines and compares data in a summarized view. You create a pivot table by using a graphical interface to drag and drop fields into appropriate column, row, and data locations.

1. Open **qryInvCostByVen**.

2. From the **Home** tab, in the **Views** group, click the bottom half of the **View** button and choose **PivotTable View** 📊.

3. To open the **PivotTable Field List**, click the **Design** tab, and in the **Show/Hide** group, click **Field List**.

4. From the **PivotTable Field List**, select **VenderName**. Click the drop-down arrow in the lower right corner. It contains a list of all drop zones in the table. Choose **Row Area**. Click **Add to**.

Figure 6-29
Adding a field to a PivotTable.
EcoMed-06.accdb
qryInvCostByVen

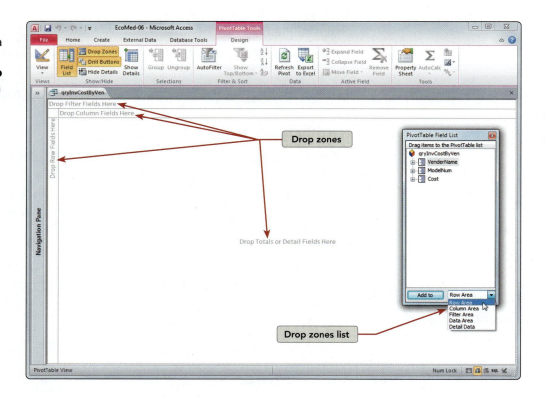

5. Drag the **ModelNum** field from the **PivotTable Field List** into the **Drop Totals or Detail Fields Here** zone of the PivotTable.

6. In the **PivotTable Field List**, select **Cost**. In the drop-down list at the bottom of the list, choose **Detail Data** drop zone. Click **Add to**.

7. From the **Design** tab, in the **Show/Hide** group, click the **Field List** 📋 to close the **Field List**.

8. In the PivotTable, click the **VenderName** button's drop-down arrow. Remove the checkmark for **All**. Add a checkmark to "Cobra, Inc." and click **OK**. This action adds a filter to the PivotTable.

NOTE

When the drop-down arrow of a Field Button turns blue, it means that not all choices are selected.

9. Click the **VenderName** button's drop-down arrow. Add the checkmark for **All** and click **OK**.

10. Close and save the query.

Exercise 6-21 USE PIVOTCHART VIEW

A PivotChart View displays the same information as a crosstab query, including counts and sums of numeric fields. A *PivotChart View* is an interactive graphical representation of data displayed in a PivotTable.

A PivotChart displays field values that can be switched or pivoted to display different views of the same data. You set different levels of detail by dragging fields and items or by showing and hiding items in the field drop-down lists.

1. From the **Create** tab, in the **Queries** group, click **Query Design**.

2. Double-click **tblInventory** and **tblBulbCategory** to add the tables to the grid, then close the **Show Table** dialog box.

3. Size the Field Lists.

4. From **tblInventory**, double-click **InvID** and **Cost** to add them to the design grid.

5. From **tblBulbCategory**, double-click **BulbCategory** to add it to the design grid.

6. Save the query as **qryCostByCategory**.

7. From the **Design** tab, in the **Results** group, click the bottom half of the **View** button and choose **PivotChart View**.

8. Select **BulbCategory** from the **Chart Field List**. Click the drop-down arrow in the lower right corner. It contains a list of all drop zones in the chart. Choose **Category Area**.

9. Click **Add to**.

Figure 6-30
PivotChart
EcoMed-06.accdb
qryCostByCategory

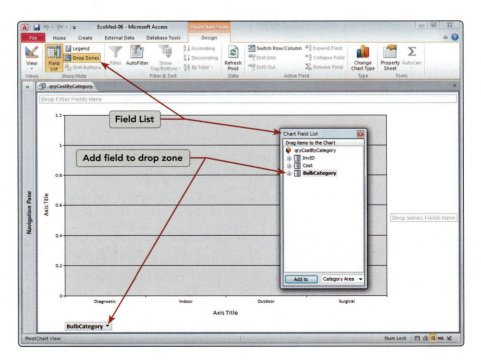

NOTE

The Chart Field List displays a field name in a bold font whenever the field is used in the chart.

TIP

When dragging a field to a drop zone, make sure that the drop zone "lights up" before you release the field. In the case of the Data Area, a blue box will appear above the chart.

10. Drag the **Cost** from the **Chart Field List** into the center of the PivotChart. The data is added to the chart, and the **Sum of Cost** field button is added to the top of the chart.

11. Right-click the **Category Axis Title** at the bottom of the chart. Choose **Properties**. Click the **Format** tab. In the **Caption** control, key **Bulb Categories**.

12. Click the **Value Axis Title** to the left of the chart. Clicking on a new object automatically switches the property sheet to that new object. Key **Base Cost** as the new **Caption**. Close the **Properties** sheet.

13. From the **Design** tab, in the **Show/Hide** group, click **Field List** to remove the **Chart Field List**.

14. From the **Design** tab, in the **Show/Hide** group, click **Drop Zones** to remove the unused drop zones.

Figure 6-31
Finished PivotChart
EcoMed-06.accdb
qryCostByCategory

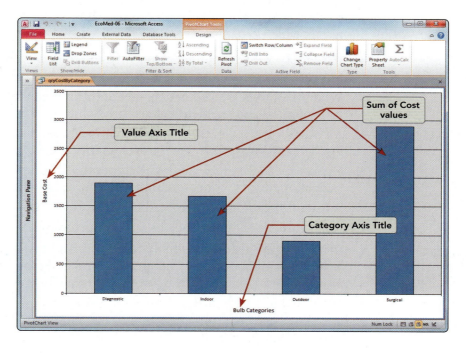

15. Switch to **Datasheet View**. Notice that making changes to the query's PivotChart has no effect on the dynaset. The **PivotChart View** is just another way of viewing the data.

16. Save and close the query.

17. Compact and close the database.

Lesson 6   Summary

- Queries make data more manageable and often are the record source for reports and forms.

- In addition to Datasheet View and Design View, a query can be displayed in SQL View.

- A select query, the most common type of query, locates data from one or more tables and displays the results as a datasheet.

- The Query Design window has an upper and lower pane. The upper pane is the Field List pane in which you choose the data source from one or more Field Lists. The lower pane is the design grid in which you specify criteria.

- A dynaset is dynamic recordset that automatically reflects changes to its underlying data source.

- In the design grid of a query, the check box in the Show row indicates that the field will display in the Datasheet View.

- When you use two or more tables in a query, the tables must be linked through a common field.

- In a query, more than one criterion can be placed on a single or multiple fields.

- When the query is executed, each condition placed as a criterion must be evaluated against field values for each record in the dynaset.

- An operator is a word or symbol that indicates a specific arithmetic or logical relationship between the elements of an expression.

- Operators can include arithmetic operators, comparison operators, logical operators, concatenation operators, and special operators.

- A function is a procedure used in an expression.

- An argument is a reference in a function assigned as a single variable.

- Criteria using text values include leading and closing quotation marks. Criteria using date values include leading and closing pound signs (#). Numbers and expressions do not require leading or closing symbols.

- When using a wildcard in the Criteria row of a query, the Like operator compares the criterion condition to each record.

- Only the keyword "Like" is automatically added to a criterion. All other keywords must be specified.

- Criterion expressions can be viewed in the Zoom box. You can open the Zoom box by pressing Shift + F2.

- An AND criteria exists when two conditions must occur simultaneously for the statement to be true.

- An OR criteria exists when one of two conditions must occur for the statement to be true.

- When using the Top Values property, Access displays records based on the defined sort order.

- The Top Values property displays either a static number of records (such as the top 5) or a percentage of all records in the dynaset (such as the top 5 percent).
- A calculated field is a field that uses an expression or formula as its data source.
- When a field does not have a name, Access assigns an alias name. The alias name for a calculated field displays as text followed by a colon.
- Calculated fields can be entered directly into the design grid or can be entered using the Expression Builder. The Expression Builder is an interface used to create a function, calculation, or expressions.
- Concatenate is the operation of joining two or more character strings end to end.
- A crosstab query displays information similar to that in a spreadsheet. Crosstab queries require that you have data suitable for summarizing. Many tables do not have fields appropriate to display as a crosstab.
- The Find Duplicates Query Wizard analyzes a table for duplicate data.
- The Find Unmatched Query Wizard finds unmatched, or orphaned, records.
- A PivotTable is an interactive table that combines and compares data in a summarized view.
- A PivotChart is an interactive graphical representation of data displayed in a PivotTable.

LESSON 6		Command Summary	
Feature	**Button**	**Path**	**Keyboard**
SQL View	SQL	Home, Views, SQL View	
Open Zoom dialog box	🔍		
Query, Add Top feature	▼10	Design, Query Setup, Return	
Create, Query wizard	📇	Create, Macros & Code, Query Wizard	
PivotTable View	📊	Home, Views, PivotTable View	
Open PivotTable Field pane	🎛	Design, Show/Hide, Field List	
PivotChart View	📊	Home, Views, PivotChart View	
View, Toggles Drop Zones	▤	Design, Show/Hide, Drop Zone	

Concepts Review

True/False Questions

Short Answer Questions

Critical Thinking Questions

Skills Review

Review Exercises that target single skills

Lesson Applications

Review Exercises that challenge students by testing multiple skills in each exercise

On Your Own

Open-ended exercises that require students to synthesize multiple skills and apply creativity and problem-solving as they would in a real world business situation

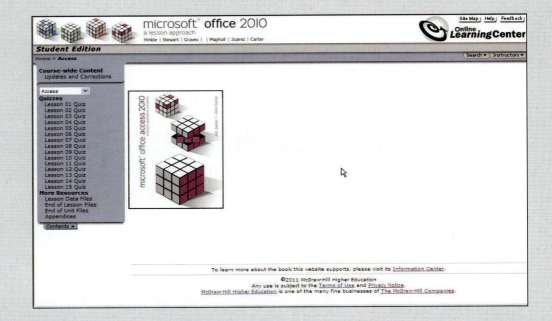

Lesson 7
Adding and Modifying Forms

OBJECTIVES   *After completing this lesson, you will be able to:*

1. Generate forms quickly.

2. Modify controls in Layout View

3. Work with form sections.

4. Modify controls in Design View.

5. Add calculated controls to a form.

6. Print/save forms.

Estimated Time: 2 hours

Although you can enter, edit, and delete data directly in the datasheet of a query or table, most often database operators will use forms to perform these activities. When you use the Datasheet View of a table or a query, the dynaset can display only in columns and rows. In Datasheet View, when each record of the dynaset contains numerous fields, the entire record cannot be seen on one screen.

The limitations of a datasheet emphasize the need for forms. A form can be designed to view an entire record on a single screen. Other advantages of forms include:

- You can arrange data in an attractive format that may include special fonts, colors, shading, and images.

- You can design a form to match a paper source document.

- You can include calculations, functions, and totals in the form.

- You can display data from more than one table.

Generating Forms Quickly

The quickest way to create a form is to use the Form Wizard or use a tool in the Forms Group. When using the Form Wizard, select the source dynaset(s), fields, layout, and style. The fields may be from multiple tables or queries, as long as a relationship exists between the recordsets.

When using a tool, all fields from the source dynaset are automatically placed on the form. You can use the new form immediately, or you can modify the form in Layout View or Design View. Database designers often use either the Wizard or a tool in the Forms group to create a beginning form that they can later modify and enhance.

Exercise 7-1   CREATE A FORM WITH A WIZARD

The Form Wizard lets you select fields, a layout, and a style. The layout determines whether the records are arranged in columns, rows, or a hybrid of columns and rows. The style automatically sets the colors, background, and fonts used for the form.

You will now create a form based on the facility beds query. The form will include all fields in the query except for the Web site hyperlink.

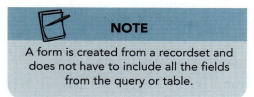

NOTE

A form is created from a recordset and does not have to include all the fields from the query or table.

1. Locate and open the **Lesson 07** folder.
2. Make a copy of **EcoMed-07** and rename it *[your initials]*-**EcoMed-07**.
3. Open and enable content for *[your initials]*-**EcoMed-07**.
4. From the **Create** tab, in the **Forms** group, click **Form Wizard** .

Figure 7-1
Form Wizard dialog box
EcoMed-07.accdb

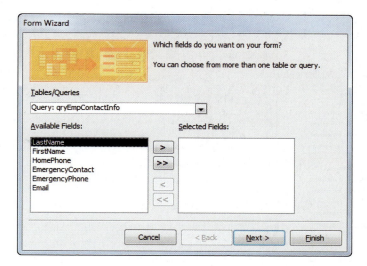

5. In the **Tables/Queries** drop-down box choose **Query: qryFacBeds**.
6. The dialog box asks which fields to use on the form. Click the Add All button to choose all fields.

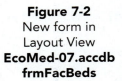
7. In the **Selected Fields** list, click **WebSite**. Click the Remove One button `<` to move it back to the list on the left.

8. Click **Next**. The dialog box asks you to choose a layout. Click each layout to see a preview. Select **Tabular**.

9. Click **Next**. The dialog box asks for a title for the form. This title is used both as a title and as the name of the form. Key **frmFacBeds**.

10. Select **Open the form to view or enter information** and then click **Finish**.

11. The form shows all 164 records, each on one row. Close the form.

Exercise 7-2   GENERATE A FORM WITH ONE CLICK

When using the Forms tool, you can create a Simple Form, Split Form, or Multiple Items Form by selecting the appropriate command button located in the Forms group. Each command uses all the fields in the source recordset to create a predetermined form.

The Simple Form tool creates a form for entering one record at a time. The Split Form tool creates a form that shows the datasheet of the source recordset in the upper section and a form in the lower section. The Multiple Items tool creates a form that shows multiple items in a datasheet, with one record per row.

1. In the **Navigation Pane**, select **qryFacBeds**.

2. From the **Create** tab, in the **Forms** group, click **Form**. The new form is now in **Layout View**, showing only one record.

Figure 7-2
New form in
Layout View
**EcoMed-07.accdb
frmFacBeds**

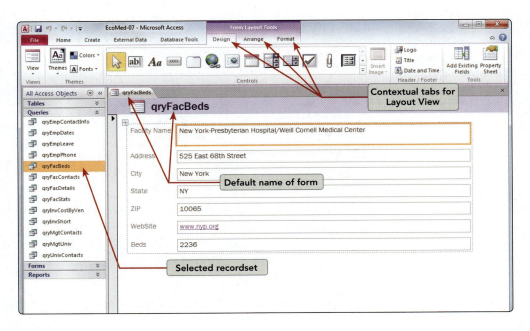

REVIEW

When creating a new form, you should use the Leszynski Naming Conventions. This method means forms are preceded by the prefix "frm," and the first letter of main words are capitalized with no spaces between words.

3. Right-click the new form's document tab and choose **Save**. The default name is the name of the recordset used to create the form.

4. In the **Save As** dialog box, key **frmFacBedsOne** and click **OK**.

5. In the **Navigation Pane**, select **qryFacBeds** again.

6. From the **Create** tab, in the **Forms** group, click **More Forms** and choose **Split Form**. The new form is now in **Layout View**, showing one record at the top and the recordset at the bottom.

7. From the Quick Access toolbar, click **Save** to save the new form.

8. In the **Save As** dialog box, key **frmFacBedsSplit** and click **OK**.

9. In the **Navigation Pane**, select **qryFacBeds** again.

10. From the **Create** tab, in the **Forms** group, click **More Forms** and choose **Multiple Items Form**. The new form is now in **Layout View**, showing all records.

11. Press Ctrl+S to save the new form.

12. In the **Save As** dialog box, key **frmFacBedsList** and click **OK**.

13. In the **Navigation Pane**, select **qryFacBeds** again.

14. From the **Create** tab, in the **Forms** group, click **More Forms** and choose **Datasheet**. The new form is now in **Datasheet View** showing all records. Even though this form looks like the **Datasheet View** of a table, it does not store data.

15. Press Ctrl+S to save the new form.

16. In the **Save As** dialog box, key **frmFacBedsData** and click **OK**.

17. Right-click any document tab and choose **Close All**.

Modifying Controls in Layout View

A *control* is a database object that displays data, performs actions, and allows you view and work with information. A control enhances the visual appearance of the interface, such as labels and images. Controls can be bound, unbound, or calculated.

A *bound control* is a control whose data source is a field in a table or query. You use bound controls to display values from the source recordset. The values can be text, dates, numbers, Yes/No values, pictures, and even graphs. An *unbound control* is a control without a source recordset. You use unbound controls to insert lines, symbols, or static pictures onto the form. A *calculated control* is a control whose data source is an expression rather than a field.

Exercise 7-3 MODIFY A CONTROL LAYOUT

Access uses a control layout function to group controls together. A control layout assists you to horizontally and vertically align grouped controls within a form. A control layout is similar to a table in which each cell is a control. A control layout has two controllable features: padding and a margin. *Control padding* is the space between the gridline of the form and the control. A *control margin* is the specified location of information inside a control.

1. From the **Navigation Pane**, right-click **frmFacilities** and choose **Layout View** ▤. The layout of the controls is known as **Stacked**.

Figure 7-3
Form Layout View
**EcoMed-07.accdb
frmFacilities**

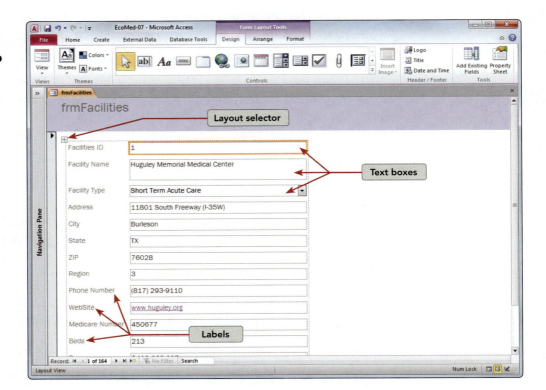

2. Click the **Layout Selector** ⊞ to select the entire control layout.
3. From the **Arrange** tab, in the **Position** group, click **Control Padding** ▤ and choose **Narrow** ▤. The space between all controls has been reduced.
4. From the **Arrange** tab, in the **Position** group, click **Control Padding** ▤ and choose **Medium** ▤. The space between controls has increased.

Exercise 7-4 RESIZE AND MOVE CONTROL LAYOUTS

Whenever you are in the Layout View of an object, you can easily see how resizing or moving controls within a form will affect the visibility of the data.

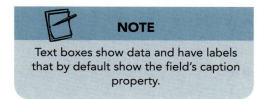

NOTE

Text boxes show data and have labels that by default show the field's caption property.

While viewing the source data on the form, you can rearrange the controls and adjust their sizes to improve the form's appearance and functionality.

1. Click the **Facility Name** text box. An orange box indicates the control is selected.

2. Place your mouse pointer on the right edge of the select text box. When you see the resize pointer, drag the control to make it smaller, but make sure all data can still be seen.

Figure 7-4
Resize a text box in Layout View
EcoMed-07.accdb frmFacilities

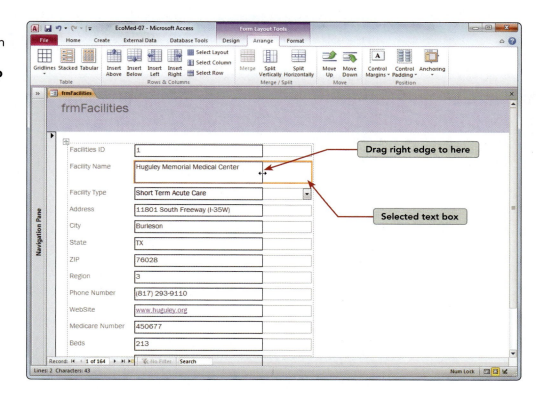

3. Click the **WebSite** label.

4. From the **Arrange** tab, in the **Rows & Columns** group, click **Select Row** ▦ to select both controls in the row.

5. While pressing Ctrl, click the labels for **Medicare Number**, **Beds**, **Revenue**, **Contact First Name**, and **Contact Last Name**.

6. From the **Arrange** tab, in the **Rows & Columns** group, click **Select Row** ▦ to select the six text boxes and their labels.

7. From the **Arrange** tab, in the **Table** group, click **Stacked** ▤. The six controls have created their own control layout.

8. Click the **Layout Selector** ⊞ for the new control layout and drag it to the right of the other control layout so that the top **Facilities ID** and **Website** controls are aligned.

Figure 7-5
Moving a control
layout
EcoMed-07.accdb
frmFacilities

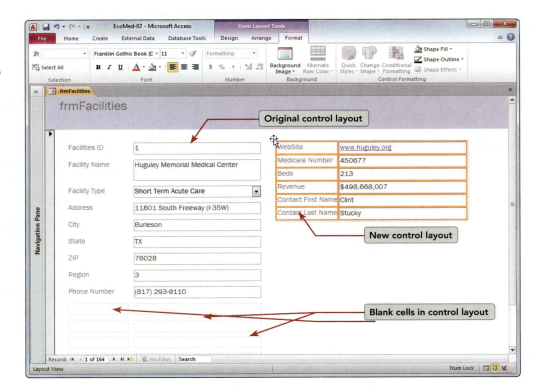

9. From the **Arrange** tab, in the **Position** group, click **Control Padding** ▦ and choose **Medium** ▦.

10. Save the form.

Exercise 7-5 ADD CELLS TO A CONTROL LAYOUT

Control layouts are like tables in Word and PowerPoint. In addition to inserting columns, you can also split and merge cells.

1. Click the **City** text box.
2. From the **Arrange** tab, in the **Merge/Split** group, click **Split Horizontally** ⊞. The **City** text box is now not as wide.
3. Click the blank cell to the right of the **City** text box.
4. From the **Arrange** tab, in the **Merge/Split** group, click **Split Horizontally** ⊞.

Figure 7-6
Adding cells to a control layout
EcoMed-07.accdb frmFacilities

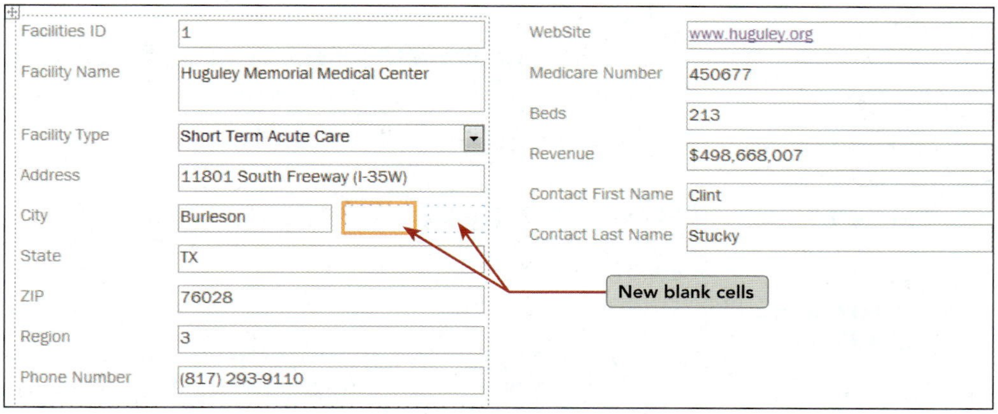

5. Click the **State** text box.
6. Left-click and drag the **State** text box to the blank cell to the right of the **City** text box. When the blank cell turns orange, release the mouse button.
7. Click the **ZIP** text box.
8. Left-click and drag the **ZIP** text box to the blank cell to the right of the **State** text box.
9. Click the **State** label and press ⌈Delete⌉.
10. Click the **ZIP** label and press ⌈Delete⌉.
11. Click the **City** label and press ⌈Delete⌉.
12. Save the form.

Exercise 7-6 ADD, DELETE, AND MOVE CONTROLS IN A CONTROL LAYOUT

A single form can have multiple control layouts. For example, you might have a tabular layout to create a row of data for each record, and then one or more stacked layouts underneath, containing more data from the same record.

In tabular control layouts, controls are arranged in rows and columns like a spreadsheet, with labels across the top. Tabular control layouts always span two sections of a form; whichever section the controls are in, the labels are in the section above.

In stacked layouts, controls are arranged vertically like you might see on a paper form, with a label to the left of each control. Stacked layouts are always contained within a single form section.

1. Click the **Region** label.

2. From the **Arrange** tab, in the **Rows & Columns** group, click **Select Row**.

3. Press [Delete] to delete both controls from the layout.

4. Click the **WebSite** label. From the **Arrange** tab, in the **Rows & Columns** group, click **Select Row**.

5. Drag the selected control to the blank cells above the **Phone Number** label.

6. Click the **Medicare Number** label. From the **Arrange** tab, in the **Rows & Columns** group, click **Select Row**.

7. From the **Arrange** tab, in the **Move** group, click **Move Up**.

Figure 7-7
Move a control in a control layout
EcoMed-07.accdb frmFacilities

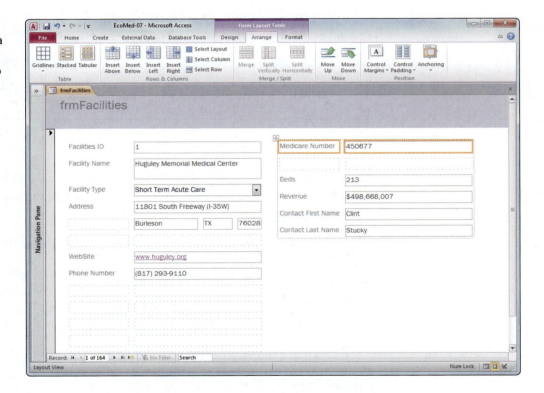

8. From the **Design** tab, in the **Tools** group, click **Add Existing Fields**. The top panel contains the recordset (**tblFacilities**) on which this form is based and its fields.

9. From the top panel of the **Field List**, click and drag **MgtTypeID** between the **Revenue** and **Contact First Name** text boxes until you see an insertion point between the two controls.

Figure 7-8
Use the Field List to
add a field
**EcoMed-07.accdb
frmFacilities**

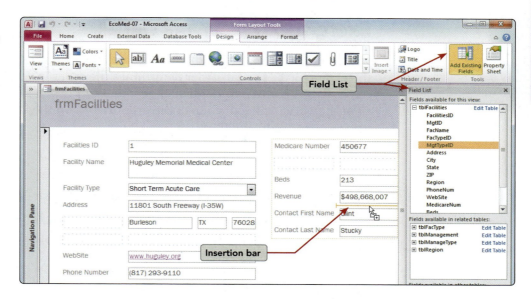

10. From the **Design** tab, in the **Tools** group, click **Add Existing Fields** to close the **Field List**.

11. From the **Arrange** tab, in the **Rows & Columns** group, click **Insert Below** to add a blank row in the control layout.

12. From the **Arrange** tab, in the **Rows & Columns** group, click **Insert Below** to insert a second blank row.

13. From the **Design** tab, in the **Header/Footer** group, click **Date and Time**.

Figure 7-9
Adding a Date and
Time control
**EcoMed-07.accdb
frmFacilities**

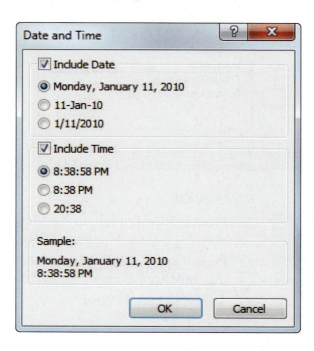

14. Click **OK**. The data and time control is added to the header of the form.

15. Save the form.

Exercise 7-7   SET TAB ORDER

Tab order is a form setting that determines the movement of the insertion point through a form. The tab order determines the order in which the insertion point moves from control to control. The usual tab order is top-to-bottom, left-to-right; however, you can change the order based on the layout of the form.

1. From the **Design** tab, in the **Views** group, choose **Form View** 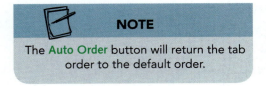.
2. Press [Home] to move the pointer to the first field. Press [Tab] to move through all the controls on the form. This order is the default tab order.
3. From the **Home** tab, in the **Views** group, choose **Design View** .
4. From the **Design** tab, in the **Tools** group, click **Tab Order** .
5. Click and drag the field selectors for **WebSite** through **PhoneNum**. Drag the two fields below **MgtTypeID**.

Figure 7-10
Tab Order dialog box
EcoMed-07.accdb frmFacilities

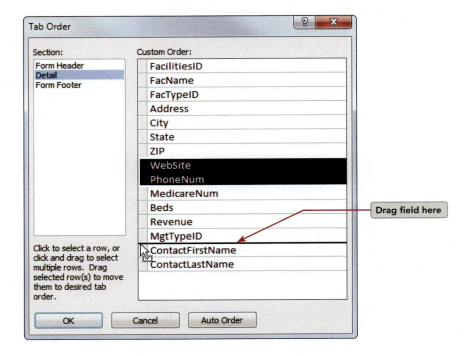

6. Click **OK**.
7. From the **Design** tab, in the **Views** group, click **Form View** to switch to **Form View**.
8. Press [Tab] to move from text box to text box. Notice that **Medicare Number** is now after **ZIP** in the tab order.
9. Switch to **Layout View**.

NOTE

The **Auto Order** button will return the tab order to the default order.

Exercise 7-8   FORMAT A FORM IN LAYOUT VIEW

You can easily refine the placement and size of controls through the Layout View. Layout View allows you to modify the properties of controls by viewing the source data in each control. In Layout View, you can navigate through the dynaset to determine the best layout for the controls.

1. Click below the label that contains the name of the form, "frmFacilities" and press Delete. The header of the form (purple background) reduces in height.

2. From the **Design** tab, in the **Header/Footer** group, click **Title** 🔳.

3. Key **Facility Information**. Press Enter.

4. Double-click the right edge of the title label to auto-size the label.

Figure 7-11
Selecting a standard color
EcoMed-07.accdb frmFacilities

5. From the **Format** tab, in the **Font** group, click Font Color 🅰 and choose **Automatic**.

6. Click in the blank area below the **Contact Last Name** the controls.

7. From the **Format** tab, in the **Font** group, click Background Color 🎨.

8. From the **Standard Colors**, choose **Purple 1** (eighth column, second row).

9. Switch to **Form View**.

10. Save and close the form.

Working with Form Sections

A basic form contains controls only in a single detail section. Advanced forms use multiple sections. Some sections display on every screen or on every page if the form is printed. Other sections display only at specific times. The five form sections are:

- The Detail Section is part of a form or report that displays data once for every row in the record source. This section makes up the main body of the form or report.

- The Form Header Section is a section of a form that displays once at the beginning of a form. This section often is used to display objects that would appear on a cover page, such as a logo, title, or date.

- The Form Footer Section is a section of a form that appears once at the end of a form. This section often is used to display summary information such as totals.

- The Page Header Section is a section of a form that displays at the top of each printed page. This section often is used to display title information or page numbers to be repeated on each page.

- The Page Footer Section is a section of a form that displays at the bottom of each printed page. This section often is used to display title information or page numbers to be repeated on each page.

The Page Header Section and Page Footer Section can only be seen in Print Preview or when the form is printed. The sections that initially appear in a form depend on the type of form originally created.

Exercise 7-9 OPEN AND SIZE FORM SECTIONS

When you scroll through a form, the Form Header always displays at the top of the screen. The Form Footer always appears at the bottom of the screen. The values in the detail section will change based on the values in the recordset.

1. From the **Navigation Pane**, right-click **frmFacContacts** and choose **Design View** 📉. This form is using two sections: **Form Header** and **Detail**.

2. Place the mouse pointer on the top of the **Form Footer** section bars. When the pointer changes to a two-headed arrow, click and drag up to the 3-inch mark on the vertical ruler. You have resized the **Detail** section of the form.

3. Place the mouse pointer on the bottom of the **Form Footer** section bars. When the pointer changes to a two-headed arrow, click and drag down ½ inch.

Figure 7-12
Open a form section
**EcoMed-07.accdb
frmFacContacts**

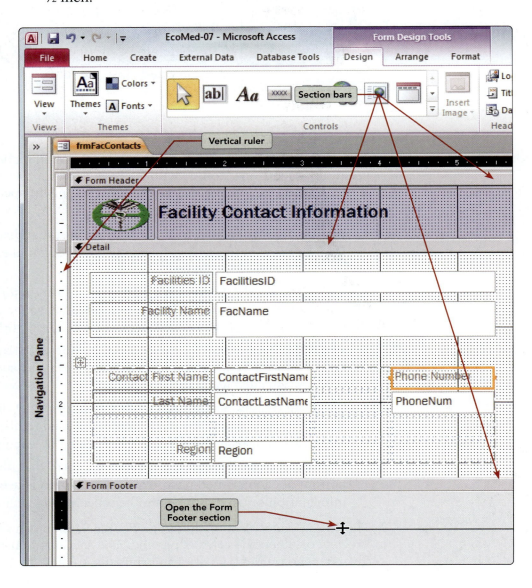

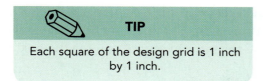

TIP

Each square of the design grid is 1 inch by 1 inch.

4. Right-click the **Detail** section bar and choose **Page Header/Footer** 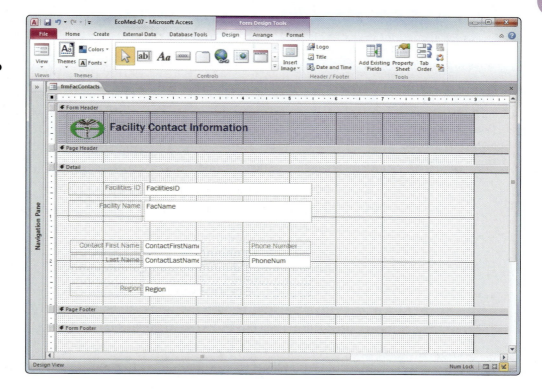. This command adds two more sections.

Figure 7-13
All form sections expanded
EcoMed-07.accdb frmFacContacts

5. The width of the form is 9-inches. Click and drag the right edge of the form to the 7.5 inch mark.

6. Save the form.

Exercise 7-10 ADD LABELS AND VIEW FORM SECTIONS

The Label tool in the Toolbox is used to enter text or titles in a form. The text displayed in a label is independent of the recordset and does not change when a new record is displayed.

When you select a label or any other object, selection handles appear around the object. Selection handles are eight small rectangles around an active object. The top left selection handle is known as the Moving handle and is used to move the object without resizing it. The other seven handles are known as sizing handles. Sizing handles are any selection handles on a control except the top left one, used to adjust the height and width of the object.

1. From the **Design** tab, in the **Controls** group, click Label ***Aa***. The pointer changes to a crosshair mouse pointer with the letter A.

2. Place the pointer in the **Form Header** section at the 6-inch mark. Click and drag down and to the right to draw a box about 1.5 inches wide and around 5 dots tall. When you release the mouse button, you see the box with a text insertion point.

3. Key **Form Header** and press ⏎Enter⏎. The label box is selected and displays the eight selection handles around its edges.

4. In the **Page Header** section, add a Label that is the same size as the one in the **Form Header** section. Key **Page Header** in the label.

5. In the **Page Footer** section, add a Label that is the same size as the one in the **Form Header** section. Key **Page Footer** in the label.

> **NOTE**
>
> Pressing ⏎Enter⏎ does not move the cursor to the next line in a label. It finishes the label and selects it.

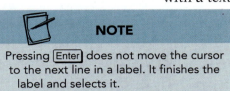

Figure 7-14
Adding a label to the Form Header
EcoMed-07.accdb frmFacContacts

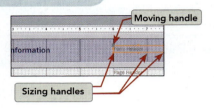

6. In the **Form Footer** section, add a Label that is the same size as the one in the **Form Header** section. Key **Form Footer** in the label.

7. Switch to **Form View**. The "Form Header" and "Form Footer" labels are visible.

8. Press ⏎PageDown⏎ to move to the next record. There is no change in the **Form Header** and **Form Footer** sections of the form.

9. Press ⏎Ctrl⏎+⏎End⏎ to move to the last record. There is no sign of the "Page Header" and "Page Footer."

10. Click the **File** tab, and from the **Print** option, click **Print Preview** . Click near the top of the preview to zoom in. You can see the "Form Header" and "Page Header" labels at the top of the first page.

11. Scroll down to see the "Page Footer" label at the bottom of the page.

12. In the **Page** navigation controls, click the **Last Record** button ⏭. After the last record, you can see the "Form Footer" label appear.

13. From the **Print Preview** tab, in the **Close Preview** group, click **Close Print Preview** ⊠.

14. Close the form and save the changes.

Modifying Controls in Design View

> **NOTE**
>
> A form inherits the field properties of the table. Changes to the form's properties do not affect the table's properties.

Certain actions cannot be completed in Layout View. To perform these tasks, you will need to switch to Design View. Design View provides a different and more detailed view of the form's structure. In Design View, you can view the Header, Detail, and Footer sections. Unlike Layout View, when the form is in Design View, the form does not display the recordset data in each control.

Exercise 7-11   FORMAT A FORM IN DESIGN VIEW

When using Design View to modify the format of a form, you can often begin by selecting a predefined format.

1. From the **Navigation Pane**, right-click **frmInventory** and choose **Design View** 📐.

2. Double-click the **Form Header** bar to open the **Property Sheet** for this section.

3. In the **Property Sheet**, on the **Format** tab, click the **Back Color** property. An drop-down arrow appears to the right of the property.

4. Click the drop-down arrow and choose **Access Theme 5**.

Figure 7-15
Assigning a theme
**EcoMed-07.accdb
frmInventory**

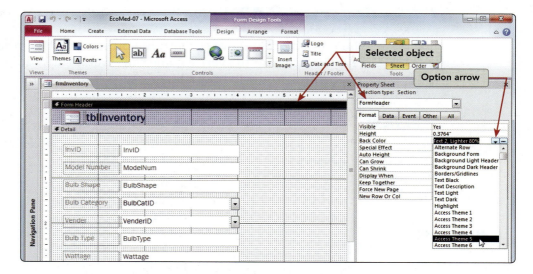

5. Click the **Detail** section bar. The **Property Sheet** now shows this object's properties.

6. In the **Property Sheet**, on the **Format** tab, click the **Back Color** property. Click the drop-down arrow and choose **Access Theme 2**.

7. Place your mouse pointer over the top edge of **InvID** text box. When a small black down arrow appears, click. All controls below the arrow are now selected.

Figure 7-16
Selecting multiple objects
**EcoMed-07.accdb
frmInventory**

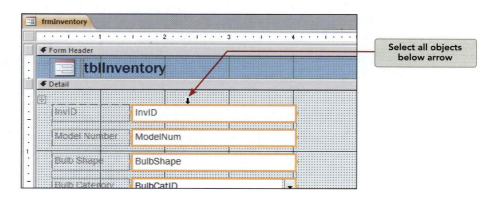

8. While pressing Ctrl, click the **Image** control to remove it from the selection.

9. Right-click the selected objects. From the pop-up menu, select **Special Effect**  and choose Special Effects: Shadowed.

10. Click the **Detail** section to deselect the text box controls.

11. From the **Design** tab, in the **Header/Footer** group, click **Title** and key **Inventory Details**. Press Enter.

12. Right-click the **Title** label and select **Size** and choose **To Fit**.

13. From the **Design** tab, in the **Tools** group, click **Property Sheet** to close the **Property Sheet**.

14. Save the form.

Exercise 7-12   RESIZE AND MOVE CONTROLS

When resizing and moving controls, you can use the gridline marks in Design View. You can use the vertical and horizontal rulers to position the edges of each control. You will now add an image control to the form.

1. Click the **InvID** text box.

2. From the **Arrange** tab, in the **Rows & Columns** group, click **Insert Right** twice. This action creates two new columns of blank cells.

3. Click the **Image** control. Drag the **Image** control to the upper-right-most blank cell.

Figure 7-17
Moving a control
EcoMed-07.accdb
frmInventory

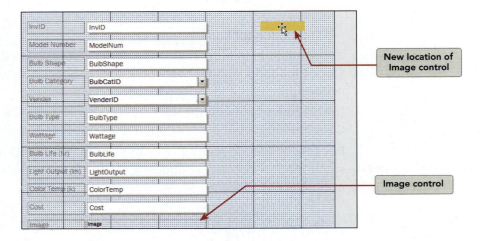

4. While pressing the Ctrl key, click the five blank cells just below the **Image** control.

5. From the **Arrange** tab, in the **Merge/Split** group, click **Merge**. The six selected cells are now merged into one cell.

6. Click any blank cell to the left of the **Image** control. Drag the right edge of the control left to the 4.5-inch mark on the horizontal ruler. This action reduces the width of the blank column.

Figure 7-18
Resizing a column
EcoMed-07.accdb
frmInventory

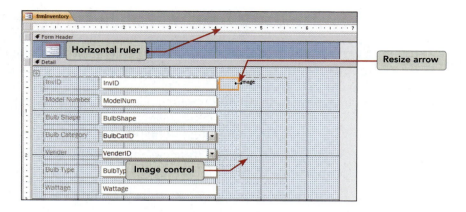

7. Click the **Image** control. Drag the right edge of the control right to the 6.75-inch mark on the horizontal ruler to widen the **Image** control and the column.

8. Click the **Image** control's label and press ⌜Delete⌝. This action deletes the label but not the cell.

9. Click the blank cell where the **Image** label was located and press ⌜Delete⌝. Because none of the cells in that row were being used, the whole row of blank cells was deleted.

10. Click the blank cell below the **Image** control. From the **Arrange** tab, in the **Merge/Split** group, click **Split Horizontally** ▦.

11. Click the label and text box for the **Cost** control. Drag both controls to the right-most blank cell from the step above.

12. Click the **Wattage** text box. From the **Arrange** tab, in the **Rows & Columns** group, click **Insert Above** ▦.

13. Switch to **Form View**.

Figure 7-19
New layout
EcoMed-07.accdb
frmInventory

Inventory Details	
InvID	1
Model Number	684-20-E26
Bulb Shape	A-line
Bulb Category	Surgical
Vender	Unio Lighting
Bulb Type	Incandescent
Wattage	20
Bulb Life (hr)	600
Light Output (lm)	900
Color Temp (k)	1250

Cost $3.45

14. Save the form.

Exercise 7-13 MODIFY PROPERTY SETTINGS

Every control has property settings. The property settings allow you to modify a control more precisely. For example, through the property settings, you can modify how an image will appear. The Picture Size Mode settings for an image include the following:

- Clip Mode sizes an image to its original size.
- Stretch Mode sizes an image to fit the control without regard to the proportions of the original image.
- Zoom mode sizes an image to fit the control while maintaining the proportions of the original image.

1. Switch to **Layout View** and click the **Image** control.
2. From the **Design** tab, in the **Tools** group, click **Property Sheet** 🖼️.
3. On the **Format** tab, click the **Picture Size Mode**. Click the drop-down arrow and choose **Clip**. This mode shows the image at normal size.
4. Change the **Picture Size Mode** to **Stretch**. This mode changes the shape of the image to make it fit the width and height of the control.
5. Change the **Picture Size Mode** to **Zoom**. This mode changes the size of the image until the image's width or height is the same as the controls.
6. In the **Property Sheet** for the **Image** control, click the **Picture Alignment** property.
7. Click the drop-down arrow and choose **Center**.
8. In the **Width** property, key **2.2**. This entry changes the width for all the cells in this column.
9. In the **Special Effect** property, choose **Shadowed**.
10. Switch to **Form View**. The image control now has the same effect as the other controls.
11. Switch to **Design View** and save the form.

Exercise 7-14 ADD A LABEL

Adding a label to a form helps identify the entire form or aspects of the form. For example, you might add a label to identify the department for which the form was created or a date on which the form was last modified.

1. Drag the bottom of the **Form Footer** section down ½ inch.
2. From the **Design** tab, in the **Controls** group, click Label 𝐀𝐚.
3. Place the pointer in the **Form Footer** section around the ¼-inch mark on the horizontal ruler. Click and key **Prepared by:** *[your full name]*.
4. Click the **Form Footer** bar. In the **Property Sheet**, change the property **Back Color** to **Access Theme 2**.
5. Close the **Property Sheet**.
6. Switch to **Form View** to see your new label.
7. Save the form.

Adding Calculated Controls to a Form

Access allows you to use a standardized format using a theme. A *theme* is a set of unified design elements and color schemes for bullets, fonts, horizontal lines, background images, and other elements of a database object. Using themes helps you create professional and consistent forms and reports.

Exercise 7-15   ADD UNBOUND TEXT BOXES

Although any control that has a Control Source property can be used as a calculated control, an unbound text box is the easiest control to change into a calculated control. You will now create a calculated control to calculate the retail price of items. First you must add an unbound text box to the form.

1. Switch to **Layout View** for **frmInventory**.

2. Click in the blank cell under the **Cost** control.

3. From the **Arrange** tab, in the **Merge/Split** group, click **Split Horizontally** 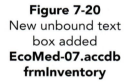. The size of the new cells match the **Cost** controls.

4. From the **Design** tab, in the **Controls** group, click **Text Box** [abl]. The pointer changes to a crosshair mouse pointer with the letters "ab."

5. Hover your mouse over blank cells in the layout. An orange box appears in the potential location of the new control. Click the blank cell below the **Cost** text box control.

6. Adding an unbound text box also means that you receive a label to the left of the text box. Double-click the new label and replace the text with **Retail**.

Figure 7-20
New unbound text box added
EcoMed-07.accdb
frmInventory

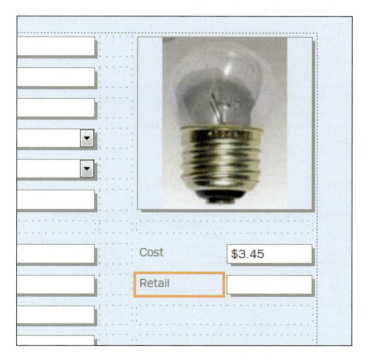

7. Save the form.

Exercise 7-16   ADD A CALCULATED CONTROL

You can use a calculated control to display the solution to a calculation. The calculation can be an expression or a function. For example, if you have a form displaying the number of items sold and the unit price for each item, you can add a calculated control to multiply the two fields and display a total price. In this example, you calculate the retail price of items. The retail price is 48 percent above the unit cost or 1.48 times the unit cost.

1. Switch to **Design View**.
2. Double-click the unbound text box to display its **Property Sheet**. Click the **Data** tab.
3. Click the **Control Source** property; read the description of this property in the status bar.
4. To the right of the control source property, you can see the Build button. The Build button appears as an ellipsis. Click the Build button  to open the **Expression Builder** dialog box.
5. In the **Expression Elements** panel, your **frmInventory** form is shown as the current object at the top of the list.
6. The object **frmInventory** is selected in the **Expression Elements** panel. In the **Expression Categories** panel, click the field **<Field List>**.

7. In the **Expression Values** panel is a list of fields from this form's recordset. Double-click **Cost** to paste the value of the **Cost** field to the Expression box.
8. In the **Expression Elements** panel, click **Operators**.
9. In the **Expression Values** panel, double-click "*" (asterisk).
10. In the Expression box, key **1.48** as the numerical equivalent for a markup of 48 percent.

Figure 7-21
Expression Builder with an expression
EcoMed-07.accdb
frmInventory

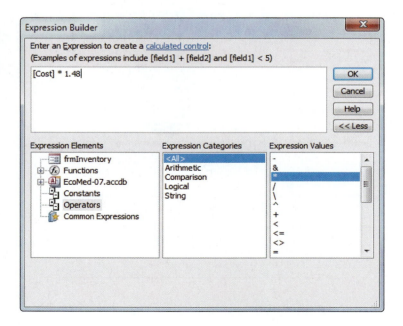

TIP

You must click the OK button to accept the changes in the Expression Builder.

11. Click **OK** to close the **Expression Builder**. The equation appears in the unbound text box.

12. Click the **Format** tab in the **Property Sheet**. Click the **Format** property and its drop-down arrow. Choose **Currency**.

13. Click the **Text Align** property. Click the option arrow and choose **Right**.

14. Click the **Cost** text box. Change its **Text Align** property to **Right**.

15. Close the **Property Sheet** and switch to **Form View**.

16. Press PageDown to view a few records.

Figure 7-22
Completed form
EcoMed-07.accdb frmInventory

frmInventory		
Inventory Details		

InvID: 2
Model Number: TT74-150-G
Bulb Shape: A-line
Bulb Category: Diagnostic
Vender: Unio Lighting
Bulb Type: Halogen

Wattage: 150   Cost: $39.00
Bulb Life (hr): 30   Retail: $57.72
Light Output (lm): 2400
Color Temp (k): 3350

Prepared by: [Student's full name]

17. Save and close the form.

Printing/Saving Forms

Although forms are designed to view data on a screen, on occasion you may need to print a form. If you choose to print the entire form, all records will display. Each record may display on a single page, on multiple pages, or on a portion of a page, depending on the size of the form and the size of the paper on which you print.

When printing a form, the Page Header section and Page Footer section will print on each vertical page. If a form is wider than the paper width, a single page of the form may print on two or more pages of paper. You can change the width of the form and the margins of the page to optimize the print quality of a form.

Prior to printing, you can select a single record. When you select a single record, you cannot use Print Preview. With forms, Print Preview can only be used when printing or saving all records or a range of printable pages.

Exercise 7-17   PRINT SPECIFIC PAGES

As with other Office applications, such as Word, you can print a specific page or range of pages. When printing a specific range of pages, you must enter a single page number, a list of page numbers separated by commas, or a page range including the first page through the last page.

1. From the **Navigation Pane**, double-click **frmVenderList**.
2. Click the **File** tab and from the **Print** option, click **Print Preview** .
3. From the **Print Preview** tab, in the **Zoom** group, click **Two Pages** . This form shows all records on two pages.
4. From the **Print Preview** tab, in the **Print** group, click **Print** .
5. In the **Print** dialog box, in the **Print Range** section, choose **Pages**.
6. In the **From** control, key **1**. The **To** control is now active.

Figure 7-23
Print dialog box
EcoMed-07.accdb
frmVenderList

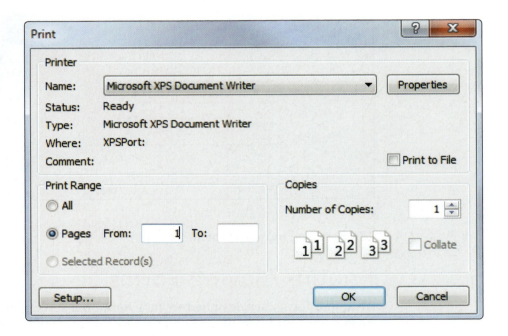

7. Click the **To** control and key **1**.
8. Based on your classroom procedure, you can either print the form or cancel the print process. To cancel, click **Cancel**. To print the form, click **OK**. If you are uncertain, ask your instructor.
9. From the **Print Preview** tab, in the **Close Preview** group, click **Close Print Preview** .
10. Save the form.

Exercise 7-18   PRINT ONE RECORD

When printing a single record, you must first select the record through the form. You cannot select to print a single record through the Options in the Print or Print Preview commands.

1. In the **Form View** of **frmVender**, press ⌨PageDown until you reach the record for the vender "AnyBulb."

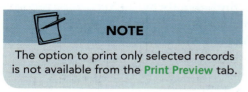

NOTE

The option to print only selected records is not available from the **Print Preview** tab.

2. Click the record selector on the left side of the form. The record selector is very tall in this form because the form is set to only show one record at one time.

3. Click the **File** tab and from the **Print** option, click **Print** 🖶.

4. In the **Print** dialog box, in the **Print Range** section, choose **Selected Record(s)**.

5. Based on your classroom procedure, you can either print the form or cancel the print process. To cancel, click **Cancel**. To print the form, click **OK**. If you are uncertain, ask your instructor.

Exercise 7-19   PRINT MULTIPLE RECORDS

Similar to printing a single record, you can print a contiguous range of records. The order in which the multiple records will print depends on how the dynaset is sorted.

1. Switch to **frmVenderList** in **Form View**.

2. Click the record selectors for **Vender ID** 1.

3. Drag down to **Vender ID** 4. These are all the venders whose names start with "A."

Figure 7-24
Multiple records selected
EcoMed-07.accdb
frmVenderList

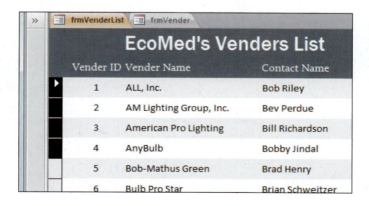

4. Click the **File** tab and from the **Print** option, click **Print** 🖶.

5. In the **Print** dialog box, in the **Print Range** section, choose **Selected Record(s)**.

6. Based on your classroom procedure, you can either print the form or cancel the print process. To cancel, click **Cancel**. To print the form, click **OK**. If you are uncertain, ask your instructor.

Exercise 7-20   SAVE A RECORD

Just as with other major objects, a form can be saved as a PDF or XPS file. To save a single record or range of records through a form, the record or records first must be selected. The process for saving a single record is the same process that you would use for saving a range of records.

1. Switch to the form **frmVender**.
2. Press ⌈PageDown⌋ until you reach the vender "Cobra."
3. Click the record selector on the left side of the form.
4. Click the **File** tab and from the **Save & Publish** option, click **Save Object As** 🖻.
5. In the **Database File Types** section, double-click **PDF or XPS**.
6. In the **Publish as PDF or XPS** dialog box, click the **Options** button
7. In the **Options** dialog box, in the **Range** section, click **Selected records** and click **OK**.

Figure 7-25
Saving selected records as a PDF
EcoMed-07.accdb frmVender

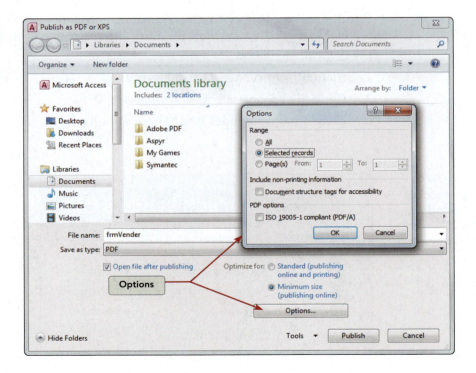

8. Change the location to match where you will be storing your work.
9. Name the file **07-20-10**.
10. Verify that the file type is **PDF** and click **Publish**.
11. Close both forms.
12. Compact and close the database.

Lesson 7 Summary

- A form can be designed to view an entire record on a single screen.
- A form can include calculations, functions, and totals.
- The quickest way to create a form is to use the Form Wizard or a tool in the Forms group.
- The Form Wizard lets you select fields, a layout, and a style.
- When using the Forms tool, you can create a Simple Form, Split Form or Multiple Items Form by selecting the appropriate command button located in the Forms group.
- A control is a database object that displays data, performs actions, or controls user interface information, such as labels and images. Controls can be bound, unbound, or calculated.
- A control layout assists you to horizontally and vertically align the controls within a form. A single form can have multiple control layouts.
- In Layout View of a form, you can rearrange and adjust the size of controls to improve the form's appearance and functionality.
- In Layout View, you can navigate through the dynaset to determine the best layout for the controls.
- Aligning a control is different than aligning the text within a control. Aligning the text within a control does not move the placement of the control on the form, only the contents of the control.
- The five sections of a form include Detail, Form Header, Form Footer, Page Header, and Page Footer sections.
- The Page Header section and Page Footer section can be seen in Print Preview or when the form is printed.
- When you select a label or any other object, selection handles appear around the object.
- When resizing and moving controls, you can use the gridline marks, vertical ruler, and horizontal ruler to position the edges of each control.
- The property settings of a control allow you to more precisely modify a control.
- A Picture Size Mode can be set to Clip, Stretch or Zoom modes.
- A label control is only associated with the major object to which it is attached.
- An unbound text box is the easiest control to change to a calculated control.
- A calculated control can contain an expression or a function.
- When printing a form, the Page Header section and Page Footer section will print on each vertical page.
- When printing a specific range of pages, you must enter a single page number, a list of page numbers separated by commas, or a page range including the first page through the last page.

- To print a single record, first you must select the record through the form. You cannot select to print a single record or range of records through the Options in the Print or Print Preview commands.
- The order in which multiple records will print depends on how the dynaset is sorted.

LESSON 7		Command Summary	
Feature	**Button**	**Path**	**Keyboard**
Controls, Date and Time		Design, Header/Footer, Date and Time	
Controls, Padding		Arrange, Position Control Padding	
Controls, Special Effects		Right-click control, Special Effects	
Controls, Tab Order		Design, Tools, Tab Order	
Controls, Text Box, Add		Design, Controls, Text Box	
Controls, Title		Design, Header/Footer, Title	
Fields, Background Color		Format, Font, Background Color	
Fields, Font Color		Format, Font, Font Color	
Fields, Remove One		Remove One	
Fields, Size to Fit		Right-click control, Size, To Fit	
Form View		Home, Views, Form View	
Form, Add New Column		Arrange, Rows & Columns, Insert Left or Insert Right	
Form, Add New Row		Arrange, Rows & Columns, Insert Above or Insert Below	
Form, Control Layout Selector		Arrange, Rows & Columns, Selector Layout	
Form, Create, Datasheet Form		Create, Forms, More Forms, Datasheet Form	
Form, Create, Multiple Form		Create, Forms, More Forms, Multiple Form	
Form, Create, Split Form		Create, Forms, More Forms, Split Form	

continues

LESSON 7		Command Summary	
Feature	**Button**	**Path**	**Keyboard**
Form, More Forms		Create, Forms, More Forms	
Form, Move control		Arrange, Move, Move Up or Move Down	
Form, Save As		File, Save As	
Form, View Page Header/Footer		Right-click section bar, Page Header/Footer	
Form, Wizard		Create, Forms, More Forms, Form Wizard	
Label, Add		Design, Controls, Label	
Layout, Merge Cells		Arrange, Merge/Split, Merge	
Layout, Select Row		Arrange, Rows & Columns, Select Row	
Layout, Split Horizontally		Arrange, Merge/Split, Split Horizontally	
Layout, Stacked		Arrange, Table, Stacked	
Print Preview, Two Pages		File, Print, Print Preview, Zoom, Two Pages	

Please visit our Online Learning Center, *www.lessonapproach2010.com,* **where you will find the following review materials:**

Concepts Review

True/False Questions

Short Answer Questions

Critical Thinking Questions

Skills Review

Review Exercises that target single skills

Lesson Applications

Review Exercises that challenge students by testing multiple skills in each exercise

On Your Own

Open-ended exercises that require students to synthesize multiple skills and apply creativity and problem-solving as they would in a real world business situation

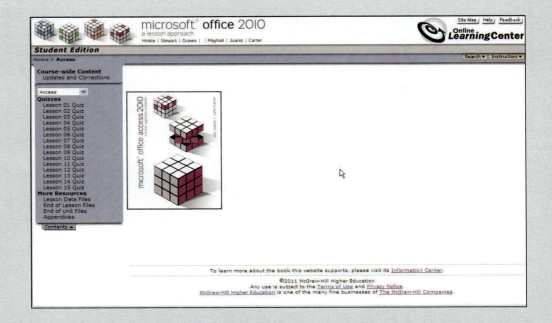

Lesson 8

Adding and Modifying Reports

OBJECTIVES   *After completing this lesson, you will be able to:*

1. Generate reports quickly.

2. Modify controls in layout view.

3. Work with report sections.

4. Work with controls in a report.

5. Use Format Painter and Conditional Formatting.

6. Create a multicolumn report and labels.

Estimated Time: 2½ hours

In a previous lesson, you learned how to create and design effective and efficient forms. Forms are the best way to view data on your screen. On occasions when you only are printing a limited amount of information, you can use the form to create a printout. However, if you need to print large amounts of information, you should create an appropriate report. In a report you can:

- Show data in an attractive format that may include variations in fonts, colors, shading, and borders.
- Show certain fields or records rather than the entire table.
- Group and sort records with summaries and totals.
- Add images.
- Display fields from more than one table.

In this lesson, you learn how to create reports quickly using the Report Wizard. You also will work in Layout View and Design View to insert, delete, and modify the controls within a report. Finally, you will learn to control section and page breaks when designing reports that group information by sections.

Generating Reports Quickly

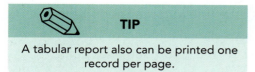

TIP

A tabular report also can be printed one record per page.

When you need to create a simple report that displays a limited number of fields per record, you can use the Report Wizard. The Report Wizard will allow you to select the source recordset and select simple format choices. A report usually has Report, Detail, and Page sections and can be either columnar or tabular.

Exercise 8-1   CREATE A REPORT WITH A WIZARD

You have been asked to create an inventory report that displays five fields, including an image field. Your manager recommends that you use the Report Wizard to design the report quickly.

1. Locate and open the **Lesson 08** folder.
2. Make a copy of **EcoMed-08** and rename it to *[your initials]*-EcoMed-08.
3. Open and enable content for *[your initials]*-**EcoMed-08**.
4. From the **Create** tab, in the **Reports** group, click **Report Wizard** 🔍.
5. In the **Tables/Queries** drop-down box, choose **Query: qryInvShort**.
6. The dialog box asks which fields to use on the form. Double-click the following fields to add them to the **Selected Fields** section.

    InvID
    ModelNum
    BulbShape
    Cost
    Image

Figure 8-1
Report Wizard dialog box
EcoMed-08.accdb

7. Click **Next**. This part of the wizard asks to add groups. This skill will be covered later in this lesson. Click **Next**.
8. Click the first combo box drop-down arrow and select **ModelNum**. The report will be sorted by this field. Click **Next**.

UNIT 2 LESSON 8

REVIEW

When creating a new report, you should use the Leszynski Naming Conventions. This rule means forms are preceded by the prefix "rpt," and the first letter of main words are capitalized with no spaces between words.

TIP

The pointer toggles between the last zoom size and Fit.

9. In the **Layout** section, select **Outline**, and in the **Orientation** section, select **Portrait**. Click **Next**.

10. Click **Next**. Modify the title to **rptInvShortOutline**.

11. You can choose to preview the report or modify the design. Select **Preview the report** and click **Finish**.

12. The report opens in **Print Preview**.

13. From the **Print Preview** tab, in the **Zoom** group, click **More Pages** 🔳 and choose **Twelve Pages**. This report shows the three products of inventory per page.

14. From the **Print Preview** tab, in the **Close Preview** group, click **Close Print Preview** ☒.

15. Close the report.

Exercise 8-2   GENERATE A REPORT WITH ONE CLICK

After reviewing the report you generated using the Report Wizard, your manager decides that perhaps you should create a simple report that displays more records per page. You will need to generate the report and then modify its controls and properties.

1. In the **Navigation Pane**, select **qryInvShort**.

2. From the **Create** tab, in the **Reports** group, click **Report** 🔳. The new report is now in **Layout View** showing multiple records.

Figure 8-2
Report in Layout View
EcoMed-08.accdb
rptInvShortList

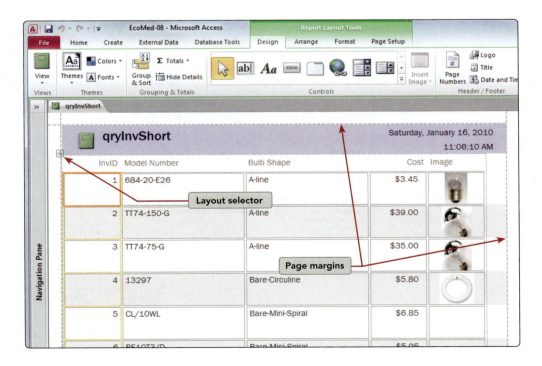

3. From the Quick Access toolbar, click **Save** 🔳 to save the new report.

4. In the **Save As** dialog box, key **rptInvShortList** and click **OK**.

5. From the **Design** tab, in the **Views** group, click **Report View** 🖻.

6. Scroll down the report. Notice that there appears to be only one very long page. Only **Print Preview** will show horizontal page breaks.

7. Right-click the report's document tab and choose **Print Preview**.

8. From the **Print Preview** tab, in the **Zoom** group, click **Two Page** 🖽.

9. In the **Page** navigation tool, click **Last Page** ⏭. This report has 21 pages.

10. From the **Print Preview** tab, in the **Close Preview** group, click **Close Print Preview** ❎.

Modifying Controls in Layout View

As with a form, you can modify an object's controls in Layout View. Layout View allows you to see not only the controls but also the actual data displayed for each record. Layout View allows you to modify the controls to effectively display all information for each record.

Exercise 8-3   FORMAT A REPORT IN LAYOUT VIEW

At EcoMed Services, each report must have a report title that identifies the report. The title should provide enough information to identify the source recordset and the purpose of the report. You should never use the same title for different reports. Your first tasks will be to add a title to the report and then add gridlines between records.

1. Switch to the **Layout View** for **rptInvShortList**.

2. From the **Design** tab, in the **Header/Footer** group, click **Title** 🗒.

3. Key **EcoMed's Inventory Quick Detail Report** and press ⌷Enter⌷. The title has wrapped to a second row.

4. Drag the right edge of the title control to the right until the title fits on one line with about a ¼-inch space at the end. This action will also move the date and time control to the right.

5. Click the **Date** control.

6. Drag the right edge to the left until the control is inside of the margin dotted line.

7. Click the title control.

8. From the **Arrange** tab, in the **Position** group, click **Control Margins** 🔲 and choose **Wide** to add inside space between the text and the controls edge.

9. Click the **InvID** label. From the **Arrange** tab, in the **Rows & Columns** group, click **Select Row** 🞖.

10. From the **Format** tab, in the **Font** group, click **Center** 🖹.

11. Click the **InvID** text box. From the **Arrange** tab, in the **Rows & Columns** group, click **Select Row** 🞖.

12. From the **Format** tab, in the **Control Formatting** group, click **Shape Outline** ✎ and choose **Transparent**.

13. Right-click the selected cells. From the menu, select **Gridlines** and choose **Horizontal** ▦.

14. Switch to **Report View**.

Figure 8-3
Formatting a report
in Layout View
EcoMed-08.accdb
rptInvShortList

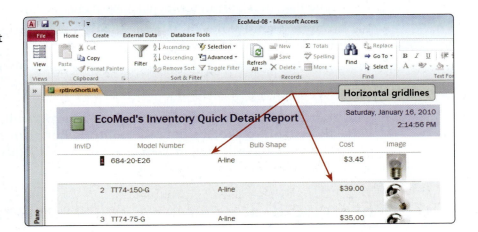

15. Save the report.

Exercise 8-4   ADD AND REARRANGE CONTROLS IN A REPORT

Your manager asks you to add vendor identification as the first column to the report you just created. You will need to use the Field List pane to select and insert the field. The Field List pane comprises of three sections. The top section displays the fields in the recordset. The middle section displays fields from tables that have a relationship to the recordset. Finally, the bottom section displays the fields from all tables in the database.

1. Switch to **Layout View** and click the column heading **Bulb Shape**.

2. From the **Arrange** tab, in the **Rows & Columns** group, click **Select Column** ▦.

3. Press ⌈Delete⌋. The other fields in the control layout have moved over to the left.

4. From the **Design** tab, in the **Tools** group, click **Add Existing Fields** ▦. The **Field List** pane appears.

5. If the **Field List** only shows one section, click **Show all tables**.

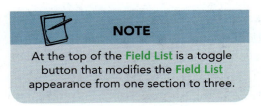

NOTE

At the top of the **Field List** is a toggle button that modifies the **Field List** appearance from one section to three.

6. From the **Field List**, in the **Fields available for this view:** section, drag the field **VenderID** to the left of **InvID** in the report until you see a vertical insertion bar.

Figure 8-4
Adding a field to a
report in Layout View
EcoMed-08.accdb
rptInvShortList

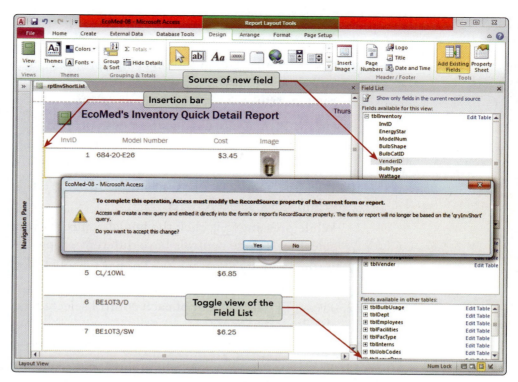

7. The warning dialog box states that the recordset for this form must be modified to include the table and field just added. Click **Yes**.

8. From the **Design** tab, in the **Tools** group, click **Add Existing Fields**  to remove the **Field List**.

9. Click the **Vender** text box. From the **Home** tab, in the **Sort & Filter** group, click **Ascending**

10. Save the report.

Exercise 8-5   FORMAT A REPORT USING THE PROPERTY SHEET

The vendor name that displays as the first field will need to be modified to display only once. You will need to hide the duplicate values per section. This process is an effective way of displaying information, but only if the records are sorted by the vender name. You also need to change the padding and margins. Just like with forms, the padding is the space between the gridlines, and the margin is distance between the edge of the control and the displayed information.

1. Click the column header **InvID** label.

2. From the **Design** tab, in the **Tools** group, click **Property Sheet** .

3. In the **Format** tab, click in the **Caption** property and edit the text to read "Inv ID."

4. On the **Format** tab, change the **Width** property to **.6**.

5. Click the **Inv ID** text box.

6. On the **Format** tab, in the **Text Align** property, click the drop-down arrow and choose **Center**.

7. Click the **Vender** text box.

8. On the **Format** tab, change the **Width** property to **2.3**.

9. In the **Hide Duplicates** property, click the drop-down arrow, and choose **Yes**.

10. Click the **Vender** text box. From the **Arrange** tab, in the **Rows & Columns** group, click **Select Row** ⊞.

11. While pressing Ctrl, click the **Image** control to remove it from the selection. Image controls have different properties than text boxes.

12. In the **Property Sheet**, on the **Format** tab, click in the **Top Margin** property and key **.15**.

13. Press ↓. The content of each control selected has moved down. Close the **Property Sheet**.

14. From the **Design** tab, in the **Views** group, click **Print Preview** 🔍.

15. From the **Print Preview** tab, in the **Zoom** group, click **Two Pages** 🔳.

Figure 8-5
Final report
**EcoMed-08.accdb
rptInvShortList**

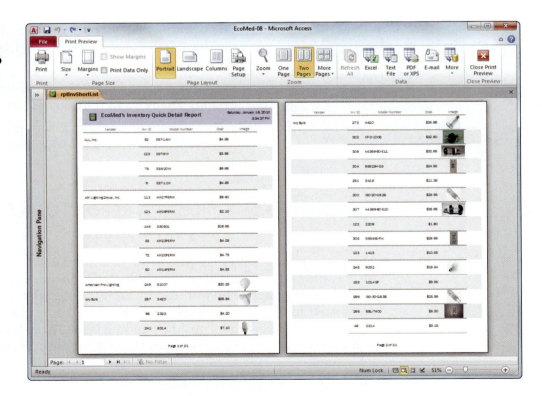

16. Save and close the report.

Working with Report Sections

Reports can have numerous sections. A report has a Detail section which shows records. The Report Header/Footer is a section of a report that prints once at the beginning or the end of the report (first or last page). Headers and footers can contain main titles, summary calculations, design lines, and even images. The Page Header/Footer sections that print at the top/bottom of every page are often used for page numbers and the date. Reports may also have one or more Group Header/Footer sections. Group Header/Footer are sections of a report that print before or after each defined group.

TABLE 8-1 Sections of a Report

Name of Section	Purpose
Detail Section	Prints each record from the table or query.
Group Footer	Prints once at the end of each group. It may include a total or other calculation for the group.
Group Header	Prints once at the start of each group. It may display a group title.
Page Footer	Prints once at the bottom of every page. It may include page numbers or a date.
Page Header	Prints once at the top of every page. It may include column headings, page numbers, or a date.
Report Footer	Prints once at the bottom (last page). It may include summaries or totals.
Report Header	Prints once at the top (first page). It may include a title, a logo, or an image.

Exercise 8-6   CREATE A GROUPED REPORT USING A WIZARD

The facilities table includes a field that contains the reported annual revenue for each facility. The sales department has asked that you create a report to display the revenues broken down by region. You will use the facilities revenue query as the recordset, group the records by region, and sort the records by state. A report group organizes or categorizes a recordset by a particular field.

1. From the **Create** tab, in the **Reports** group, click **Report Wizard** 🔍.
2. In the **Tables/Queries** drop-down box, choose **Query: qryFacRev**.
3. Click the **Add All** button `>>`.
4. Click **Next**. The wizard has determined that this report could be grouped by the field **Region**. We will keep this setting. Click **Next**.
5. Click the first combo box drop-down arrow and select **State**. The report will be sorted by this field.

UNIT 2 LESSON 8

6. Click **Summary Options**. You can pick what type of aggregate functions to have added to the report.

7. Click the check box for **Sum**.

Figure 8-6
Summary Options in
the Report Wizard
EcoMed-08.accdb

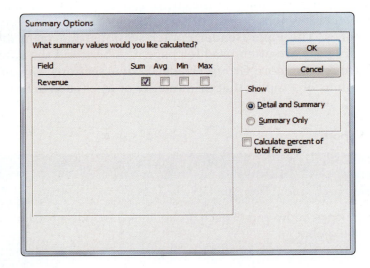

8. Click **OK** to close the **Summary Option** dialog box. Click **Next**.

9. In the **Layout** section, select **Stepped**, and in the **Orientation** section, select **Portrait**. Click **Next**.

10. Modify the title to **rptFacRevByRegion**.

11. Select **Preview the report** and click **Finish**.

12. Close **Print Preview** and switch to **Layout View**.

13. Adjust the width of the controls with "###" so that you can see all of the data without crossing the right margin (dotted line).

14. Scroll through the report. Notice the functions at the bottom of each **Region** grouping.

15. Switch to **Design View**. Notice that there are two new sections in the report: **Region Header** and **Region Footer**.

16. Save the report.

Exercise 8-7 ADD A GROUP SECTION IN DESIGN VIEW

You will need to sort the facility names. You first will need to add a state group and then select the state field as the sort value. To add a group, you add a Group Header/Footer to the report.

1. From the **Design** tab, in the **Grouping & Totals** group, click **Group & Sort** to open the **Group, Sort, and Total** pane. The wizard added one grouping and one sort.

Figure 8-7
Show Group, Sort,
and Total pane
**EcoMed-08.accdb
rptFacRevByRegion**

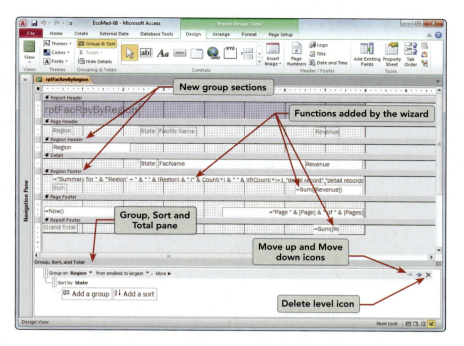

2. In **Group, Sort, and Total** pane, click the **Add a group** button and choose **State**. A new **State Header** section has been added.

3. At the right end of the **Group on State** row, click the **Move up** icon to move the **Group on State** above the **Sort by State**.

4. From the **Group, Sort, and Total** pane, in the **Sort by State** level, click the down arrow next to **State** and choose **FacName**.

NOTE

You do not have to add a Sort level for fields that have a Group level because a sorting option is included in the Group level.

Figure 8-8
Modifying a sort
order in a report
**EcoMed-08.accdb
rptFacRevByRegion**

5. In the **Region Footer** section, select all controls and press ⌈Delete⌋.

6. In the **Report Footer** section, select all controls and press ⌈Delete⌋.

7. In the **Page Header** section, place your mouse in the vertical ruler until you see the right black arrow. Click and drag down through the **Detail** section to select all of the controls in the **Page Header**, **Region Header**, **State Header**, and **Detail** sections.

8. From the **Arrange** tab, in the **Table** group, click **Tabular** ⊞ to add all the controls to a layout control.

9. Click in the **Report Header** to deselect the controls.

10. In the **Detail** section, click the **Revenue** label and drag it up into the **Page Header** section, above the **Revenue** text box.

11. Click in the blank cell to the left of the **Revenue** label and press [Delete]. This action removes the blank column from the layout.

12. Save the report.

Exercise 8-8 MODIFY GROUP OPTIONS

To make the report more versatile, you have been asked to print the average revenue values for each state and region and for all facilities. You will need to add calculated values to the footer sections of state, region, and report.

1. From the **Group, Sort, and Total** pane, click the **Group on Region** level. Click **More**.

2. Click **with no totals** drop-down arrow. Click the **Total On** drop-down arrow and choose **FacName**. For the **Type**, choose **Count Records**.

3. Click the check box **Show Grand Total** and **Show subtotal in group footer**. You now have added a control that will calculate the number of facilities in each region and a control to calculate the total number of facilities in the report.

Figure 8-9
Add an aggregate function to a group
EcoMed-08.accdb
rptFacRevByRegion

4. Without closing the **Totals** window, in **Total On**, choose **Revenue** and **Average** for the **Type**.

5. Click the check boxes for **Show Grand Total** and **Show subtotal in group footer**. This action adds the **Avg** function to both the **Region Footer** and **Report Footer** sections. Notice that the name of the option in the **Region** group is no longer "with no totals" but reflects the fields that now have functions added to the report.

6. From the **Group, Sort, and Total** pane, in the **Group on State** level, click **More**.

7. Click **with FacName, Revenue totaled** drop-down arrow. For **Total On**, choose **State** and **Count Records** for the **Type**.

8. Click the check boxes for only **Show subtotal in group footer**.

9. Without closing the **Totals** window, in **Total On**, choose **Revenue** and **Average** for the **Type**.

10. The option for **Show Grand Total** is already checked, because this function was added by a previous step. Click the check box for **Show subtotal in group footer**.

11. Press [Esc] to close the **Total** window. There should be a **Count** and **Avg** function in the **State Footer**, **Region Footer**, and **Report Footer** sections. Notice that two functions are the same; the only difference is the section in which it appears.

12. You can see there are no controls in the **State Header** section. In the **Group, Sort, and Total** pane, for the **Group on State**, click the **with a header section** drop-down arrow and choose **without a header section** to remove this section from the report.

Figure 8-10
Functions in report sections
EcoMed-08.accdb
rptFacRevByRegion

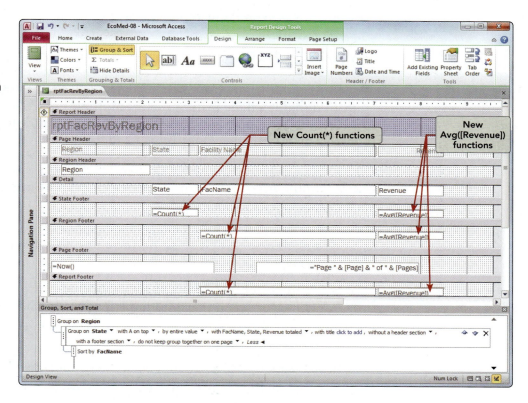

13. From the **Group, Sort, and Total** pane, in the **Group on Region** level, click **More**.

14. Click the **do not keep group together on one page** drop-down arrow and choose **keep header and first record together on one page**. This selection controls where page breaks are placed in the report.

Figure 8-11
Page break options
EcoMed-08.accdb
rptFacRevByRegion

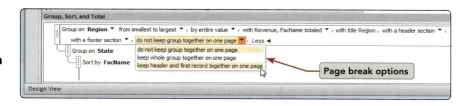

15. From the **Design** tab, in the **Grouping & Totals** group, click **Group & Sort** to close **Group, Sort, and Total** pane.

16. Switch to **Report View** to see the new functions. We will be sizing these new controls in the next exercise.

17. Switch to **Design View** and save the report.

Working with Controls in a Report

Just like a form, reports have bound controls (text boxes), unbound controls (labels), and calculated controls. You can move, size, align, and format controls using the same techniques that you learned when creating and modifying forms. When moving and sizing controls in a report, you should periodically preview your report to ensure that all values are visible.

Exercise 8-9   MOVE AND RESIZE CONTROLS

Depending on the amount of changes you will need to make to a report, you may find that it will be faster to select multiple controls and then resize them together, rather than resizing them individually. You will now resize the three controls displaying the count value in each section.

1. In the **Page Header**, click the **Region** label.

2. From the **Arrange** tab, in the **Rows & Columns** group, click **Select Layout** .

3. From the **Arrange** tab, in the **Sizing & Ordering** group, click **Size/Space** and choose **To Tallest** . All the controls in the layout now have the same height values.

4. Click in the **Report Header** to deselect the layout.

5. In the **Page Header**, select both the **Region** and **State** labels.

6. From the **Arrange** tab, in the **Sizing & Ordering** group, click **Size/Space** and choose **To Fit** .

7. In the **Region Footer** section, click the "Count" text box.

8. From the **Arrange** tab, in the **Merge/Split** group, click **Split Horizontally** .

9. Drag the selected "Count" text box to the blank cell to the right.

10. From the **Arrange** tab, in the **Merge/Split** group, click **Split Horizontally** .

11. In the **State Footer**, click the blank cell to the right of the "Count" text box.

12. From the **Arrange** tab, in the **Merge/Split** group, click **Split Horizontally** twice.

13. In the **State Footer**, click the "Count" text box and drag it to the right until it is above the "Count" text box in the **Region Footer**.

14. In the **Report Footer**, click the "Count" text box.

15. From the **Arrange** tab, in the **Merge/Split** group, click **Split Horizontally** twice.

16. In the **Report Footer**, click the "Count" text box and drag it to the right until it is under the "Count" text box in the **Region Footer**.

17. From the **Design** tab, in the **Tools** group, click **Property Sheet** .

18. In the **Property Sheet**, change the **Width** property to **.35**, which resizes the entire column.

19. In the **Detail** section, click the **FacName** text box.

20. In the **Property Sheet**, change the **Width** property to **5**.

21. Close the **Property Sheet**.

TIP

Reports in portrait layout should keep their page widths less than 7.9 inches.

NOTE

The **Remove Extra Report Space** command only reduces the width of the report to the right-most control in the report.

22. Right-click the report's tab and choose **Print Preview**. A dialog box opens to tell you that the width of the report is too wide. Click **OK**.

23. From the **Print Preview** tab, in the **Zoom** group, click **Two Pages** ⬛. The report's width needs to be reduced.

24. Close **Print Preview**. Notice that the Report Selector has a green triangle that indicates a possible error.

25. Click the Report Selector. Notice that a yellow diamond information icon appears.

26. Click the information icon and choose **Remove Extra Report Space**.

Figure 8-12
Adjusting report width
EcoMed-08.accdb
rptFacRevByRegion

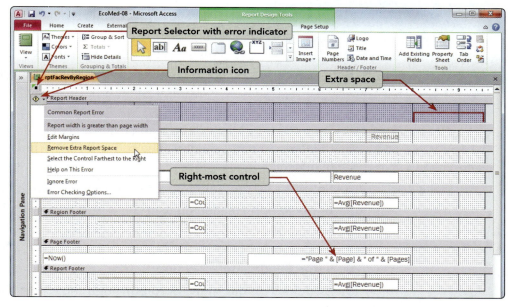

27. Switch to **Print Preview**. The report now fits within the page margins.

28. Close **Print Preview** and save the report.

Exercise 8-10   ADD AND MODIFY LABELS

When you add a value in a footer section, you should also add a label to identify the new control.

1. Switch to **Layout View**.

2. From the **Design** tab, in the **Controls** group, click Label . Move your mouse over the controls in the report. When you point over a blank cell, the cell turns orange.

3. Locate the blank cell to the left of the first "Count" function (in this view, the result of the first function is 3) and click to add the label.

4. Key **Count of Facilities by State** and press Enter.

5. From the **Design** tab, in the **Controls** group, click Label .

6. Click in the blank cell to the right of the count "3."

7. Key **State Average Revenue** and press Enter.

8. From the **Design** tab, in the **Controls** group, click Label . Click in the blank cell below the second appearance of the "Count of Facilities by State" label.

9. Key **Count of Facilities by Region** and press Enter.

10. From the **Design** tab, in the **Controls** group, click Label . Click in the blank cell below the second appearance of "State Average Revenue" label.

11. Key **Region Average Revenue** and press Enter.

12. Switch to **Design View**.

> **NOTE**
>
> In **Design View**, labels cannot be added directly to a control layout. Create the label in an open area of the report and then drag the label to a blank cell in the control layout.

13. From the **Design** tab, in the **Controls** group, click Label . Hover your mouse over the blank cell in the report. Notice that in this view, cells don't turn orange when your pointer is over them.

14. In the **Report Header**, click at the 4-inch mark on the horizontal ruler. Key **Total Number of Facilities** and press Enter.

15. Drag the new label to the blank cell to the left of the "Count" text box in the **Report Footer** section. The cell will turn orange when you are over a blank cell.

16. From the **Design** tab, in the **Controls** group, click Label .

17. In the **Report Header**, click at the 4-inch mark on the horizontal ruler. Key **Average of all Facilities** and press Enter.

18. Drag the new label to the blank cell to the right of the "Count" function in the **Report Footer** section.

19. Switch to **Layout View**. Scroll through the report to see all the new labels.

20. Press Ctrl+Home to return to the top of the report.

Exercise 8-11   FORMAT THE REPORT HEADER

Whenever you create a report through the Report Wizard, the report title is automatically created using the recordset name as the title. You now will need to delete the default title and add a new title.

1. Select the label at the top of the report and press Delete. With no controls in the **Report Header**, this section closes.

2. From the **Design** tab, in the **Header/Footer** group, click **Title** ▣.

3. Key **EcoMed–Facility Annual Revenue**.

4. Press [Ctrl]+[Enter] to add a second line to the label. Key **Detailed Report** and press [Enter].

5. From the **Design** tab, in the **Header/Footer** group, click **Date and Time** 🕔.

6. In the **Date and Time** dialog box, remove the checkmark for **Include Time** and click **OK**. The width of the **Title** control has been reduced.

7. From the **Design** tab, in the **Controls** group, click Label 𝐀𝐚. Click in the blank cell below the **Date** control.

8. Key **Prepared by:** *[your full name]* and press [Enter]. The new label shares the same font and size with the **Title** control.

9. From the **Format** tab, in the **Font** group, change the Font Size to **11**.

10. From the **Format** tab, in the **Font** group, click the **Align Text Right** ▤.

11. Click the **Title** control. Drag the control's bottom border up until the extra space below the title is removed.

Figure 8-13
Formatted Report
Header
EcoMed-08.accdb
rptFacRevByRegion

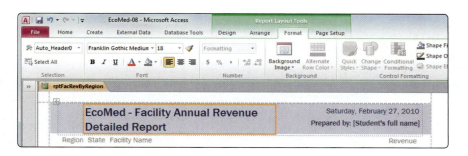

12. Save the report.

Exercise 8-12   ALIGN CONTROLS

There are two distinct activities when aligning controls. First, you can align the contents of a control. You can align a control to display its values left justified, centered, or right justified. Second, you can select multiple controls to align the outside edges of all the controls either to the left, right, top, or bottom. When you align the margins of multiple controls, the most extreme value will be used to set their positions. In other words, when aligning three controls to left alignment, the three controls will align even with the control farthest to the left. The same will occur for the three other alignments.

1. Click the **Region** text box that shows "1."

2. From the **Format** tab, in the **Font** group, click Center ▤.

3. Click the **State** text box that shows "KS."

4. From the **Design** tab, in the **Tools** group, click **Property Sheet** 🗔.

5. Change the **Text Align** property to **Center**.

6. Click the **Region** label. From the **Arrange** tab, in the **Rows & Columns** group, click **Select Row** ▦.

7. While pressing Ctrl, click the **Facility Name** label to deselect it from the others.

8. In the **Property Sheet**, change the **Text Align** property to **Center**.

9. Switch to **Design View** and close the **Property Sheet**.

10. In the **State Footer**, click the **Count of Facilities by State** label. While pressing Ctrl, click the other label in the section and the two labels in the **Region Footer** section.

11. From the **Format** tab, in the **Font** group, click Align Text Right ▤.

12. In the **Page Footer**, click the "Now" function and press Delete. It is not needed because we added a **Date** function to the **Report Header**.

13. In the **Detail** section click the **FacName** text box. While pressing Ctrl, click the page numbering control in the **Page Footer** section.

14. From the **Arrange** tab, in the **Sizing & Ordering** group, click **Align** 🔲 and choose **Left** ▮.

Figure 8-14
Aligning controls
EcoMed-08.accdb
rptFacRevByRegion

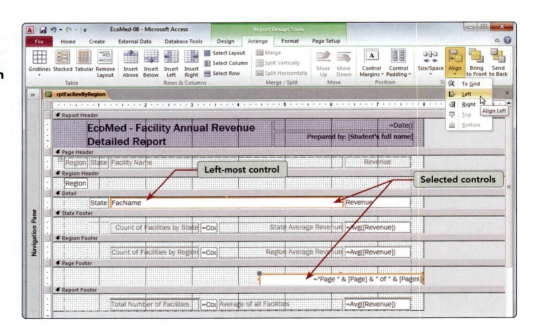

15. From the **Arrange** tab, in the **Sizing & Ordering** group, click **Size/Space** and choose **To Widest** 🔲.

16. Click the **Page Footer** bar to deselect the two controls. Click just the page numbering control.

17. From the **Format** tab, in the **Font** group, click Center ▤.

18. Switch to **Layout View** to see your changes. Save the report.

Exercise 8-13   ADD LINES AND GRIDLINES TO A REPORT

Many reports display a large amount of information. To improve the report's readability, you can add lines and gridlines. Lines and gridlines help the reader easily identify information.

1. Click the **Region** label. From the **Arrange** tab, in the **Rows & Columns** group, click **Select Row** 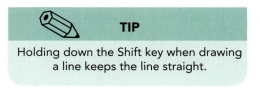.

2. Right-click the selected controls, select **Gridlines** and choose **Bottom**.

3. Click in the blank cell below "KS." There is a line at the top of the cell.

4. Right-click the selected control, select **Gridlines**, and choose **None**.

5. Switch to **Design View**. Deselect the controls. In the **State Footer**, click the "Avg" text box.

6. Right-click the selected text box, select **Special Effect**, and choose **Shadow**.

7. From the **Design** tab, in the **Controls** group, click the down arrow button to see the second row of controls. Click the Line control ⟍. Your mouse pointer is now a line and crosshair.

Figure 8-15
Controls in ribbon
EcoMed-08.accdb
rptFacRevByRegion

8. In the **Page Footer**, click in the far left of the section above the page numbering control and drag right, just shy of the 8-inch mark on the horizontal ruler. If your line is not straight, we will fix it.

9. Open the **Property Sheet**.

10. To create a straight horizontal line, its **Height** property must be **0**. Change the **Height** property to **0** if needed.

TIP

Holding down the Shift key when drawing a line keeps the line straight.

11. In the **Border Width** property, click the drop-down arrow and choose **2 pt**.

12. In the **Region Footer**, click the "Count of Facilities by Region" label.

13. In the **Property Sheet**, the property **Gridline Style Top** might be set to **Solid**. If so, change this value to **Transparent**.

14. Switch to **Print Preview**.

Figure 8-16
Report with lines
added
**EcoMed-08.accdb
rptFacRevByRegion**

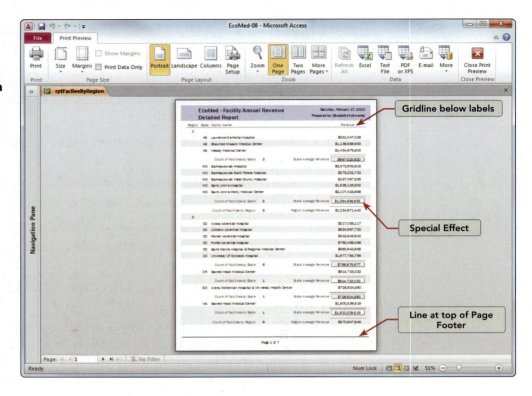

15. Save the report.

16. Close **Print Preview**.

Exercise 8-14   EDIT COMMON EXPRESSION CONTROLS

By default, the Page Header contains text boxes that use the common expression to display the current date. A common expression is a control with built-in commands to display dates, times, or page numbers. The Page Footer contains a text box that displays the current page number.

1. In the **Report Header** section, click the **=Date()**control. The **Property Sheet** shows that this is a text box.

2. In the **Property Sheet**, click the **Data** tab. The **Control Source** for this control is an Access common expression that displays the current date.

Figure 8-17
The =Date()
Property Sheet
**EcoMed-08.accdb
rptFacRevByRegion**

Property Sheet				✕
Selection type: Text Box				
Auto_Date			▼	
Format	Data	Event	Other	All
Control Source		=Date()	▼	...
Text Format		Plain Text		
Running Sum		No		
Input Mask				
Enabled		No		
Smart Tags				

3. Click the **Format** tab. Click the **Format** property drop-down arrow and choose **Medium Date**.

4. In the **Page Footer** section, click the page number control.

5. In the **Property Sheet**, on the **Data** tab, click the **Control Source** property. Click the **Build** button 🔲. The **Expression Builder** shows the Access code for this control.

6. Close the **Expression Builder** and click the **Format** tab. Change the **Font Italic** property to **Yes**.

7. Close the **Property Sheet**.

8. Switch to **Print Preview** and review the report.

9. Switch to **Design View** and save the report.

Exercise 8-15   CREATE A SUMMARY REPORT

You have been asked to create a summary report. After asking your coworkers in the IT department, you have discovered that the easiest way to create the report is to first create a detailed report that displays all records and then remove the detail section. Follow these steps to create the report.

1. From the **Design** tab, in the **Grouping & Totals** group, click **Hide Details** 📇. Notice that the **Detail** section of the report is still visible.

2. Switch to **Report View**. The details of each facility and their revenue are now hidden, but so is the **State** text box.

3. From the **File** tab, click **Save Object As** 📄.

4. In the **Save As** dialog box, key **rptFacRevSummary** and click **OK**.

5. Click the **Home** tab. Switch to **Design View**, which is the **Design View** for the new report.

6. Open the **Group, Sort, and Total** pane, click **Group on State**, and then click **More**.

7. Click the **without a header section** drop-down arrow and choose **with a header section**. Close the **Group, Sort, and Total** pane.

8. In the **Detail** section, click the **State** text box.

9. From the **Arrange** tab, in the **Move** group, click **Move Up** 📑 to move the **State** text box into the **State Header** section.

10. While pressing Ctrl, click the **Region** text box in the **Region Header** section to select both controls.

11. From the **Arrange** tab, in the **Sizing & Ordering** group, click **Size/ Space** 🔡 and choose **To Tallest** 📐.

12. In the **Report Header**, click the title label. Double-click the word "Detailed" and key **Summary**.

13. In the **Page Header**, click the **Facility Name** label and press Delete.

14. Save and switch to **Report View**.

Figure 8-18
Finished summary report
EcoMed-08.accdb rptFacRevSummary

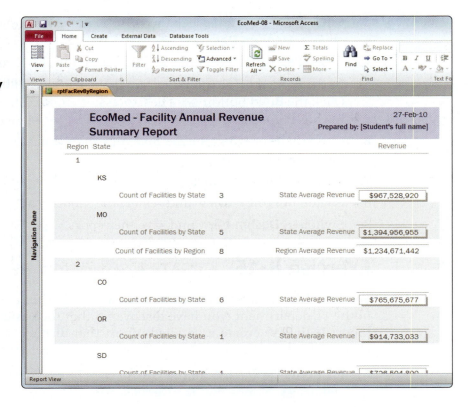

15. Close the report.

Working with Format Painter and Conditional Formatting

Access has a Format Painter like Word and Excel. The Format Painter is a tool that copies the font, size, color, and alignment from one control to another control. It saves you from having to set the individual properties for each control. To use the Format Painter, you first select the control that has the desired formatting, click the Format Painter button, and then click the control to be changed.

You can also apply conditional formatting. Conditional formatting is formatting that displays in certain conditions, such as a style, color, or other setting. For example, you can set conditional formatting to show values over $15,000 in a different color, bolded, and underlined.

Exercise 8-16   USE THE FORMAT PAINTER

The calculated control should have the same format as the other controls in the **Detail** section. Use the **Format Painter** to match the control characteristics.

1. Open **rptFacRevByRegion** in **Layout View**.
2. Select the **Count of Facilities by State** label.
3. From the **Format** tab, in the **Font** group, click Bold ⬛B⬛.

TIP

Clicking the Format Painter command 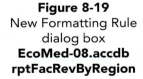 will allow you to format only one other control. Double-clicking the Format Painter command will allow you to format many other controls.

4. From the **Format** tab, in the **Font** group, change the Font to **Calibri** and Font Size to **12**.

5. From the **Format** tab, in the **Font** group, double-click **Format Painter**. The pointer changes to an arrow with a paintbrush.

6. Click the **State Average Revenue** label. The formats are copied.

7. Click the **Count of Facilities by Region** label.

8. Click the **Region Average Revenue** label. Press Esc to cancel the **Format Painter**.

9. Save the report.

Exercise 8-17 USE CONDITIONAL FORMATTING

Many database designers use conditional formatting to call attention to records that are outside a specified parameter. Often managers use reports to track sales, production, and inventory levels. Conditional formatting helps quickly identify exceptional or abnormal information. You have been asked to modify the current report to highlight any facility with revenue greater than or equal to $2 billion.

1. Click the first number under the **Revenue** label.

2. From the **Format** tab, in the **Control Formatting** group, click **Conditional Formatting**.

3. In the **Conditional Formatting Rules Manager**, click **New Rule**.

4. In the **New Formatting Rule** dialog box, you have the option of two different rule types. Select **Check values in the current record or use an expression**.

5. Press Tab twice to move to the second combo box. Click the drop-down arrow and choose **greater than or equal to**.

6. Press Tab and key **2000000000** (9 zeros).

7. Click Bold **B**, click Font Color **A**, and choose Dark Red (seventh row, first column).

Figure 8-19
New Formatting Rule dialog box
EcoMed-08.accdb rptFacRevByRegion

New Formatting Rule

Select a rule type:

Check values in the current record or use an expression
Compare to other records

Edit the rule description:

Format only cells where the:

Field Value Is ▾ | greater than or equal to ▾ | 2000000000 | ...

Preview: AaBbCcYyZz   **B** *I* U ⬢▾ **A**▾

OK   Cancel

8. Click **OK**.

9. Click **New Rule**.

10. Select the **Compare to other records** rule type.

11. In the **Bar color** control, click the drop-down arrow and choose Yellow (seventh row, fourth column). Click **OK**.

Figure 8-20
Conditional
Formatting Rules
Manager
**EcoMed-08.accdb
rptFacRevByRegion**

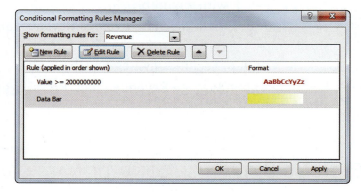

12. Click **OK**. Preview your report.

13. Save and close the report.

Creating a Multicolumn Report and Labels

In addition to columnar and tabular reports, you can format a report to show the data in more than one column. You can use Design View or the Report Wizard to organize fields in a single column, and then you can use the Page Setup command to set the number and width of the printed columns.

You can also create labels using the Label Wizard, which is an option in the New Report dialog box. The Label Wizard lists common label brands and sizes, including mailing labels, package labels, and even CD labels.

Exercise 8-18   CREATE A MULTICOLUMN REPORT FOR A QUERY

You will now create a multicolumn report to display inventory information using two columns per page.

1. In the **Navigation Pane**, select **qryInvShort**.

2. From the **Create** tab, in the **Reports** group, click **Report** 🗎.

3. From the Quick Access toolbar, click **Save** 💾. Key **rptInvMultiCol** and click **OK**.

4. Click the **Bulb Shape** label. From the **Arrange** tab, in the **Rows & Columns** group, click **Select Column** 🎛. Press ⌈Delete⌋.

5. Resize the **Model Number** control to just fit the data.

6. Resize the **Cost** control to just fit the data.

7. Resize the width of the **Image** control to make it square.

8. Switch to **Design View**. In the **Detail** section, resizing the InvID text box until the right edge of the **Picture** control at 4 inches on the horizontal ruler.

9. From the **Page Setup** tab, in the **Page Layout** group, click **Columns** ▦.

10. Set the **Number of Columns** to **2** and the **Column Spacing** to **.1**.

11. Set the **Column Size Width** to **3.9**.

Figure 8-21
Setting up a
multicolumn report
**EcoMed-08.accdb.
accdb
rptInvMuliCol**

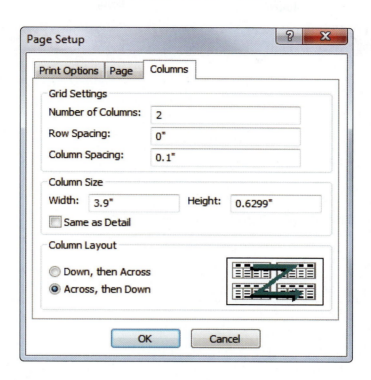

12. Click **OK**. Switch to **Print Preview** and view all 11 pages.

13. Close and save the report.

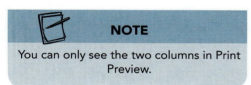

NOTE

You can only see the two columns in Print Preview.

Exercise 8-19 CREATE MAILING LABELS

The Label Wizard assists creating package labels. After you select a label type and size, the Label Wizard asks which fields to place on the label, which font to use, and how to sort the labels. You will now create a report to print mailing labels needed to mail information to our current vendors.

1. In the **Navigation Pane**, select **tblVender**.

2. From the **Create** tab, in the **Reports** group, click **Labels** 📋.

3. In the **Label Wizard** dialog box, in the **Filter by manufacturer** section, choose **Avery**.

4. In the **Unit of Measure** section, choose **English** and in the **Label Type** section, choose **Sheet Feed**.

5. In the top list box, choose the **Product number** "5160." Click **Next**.

6. Set the **Font name** to **Times New Roman**, the **Font size** to **8**, the **Font weight** to **Normal**, and the **Text color** to **black**. Click **Next**.

7. In the **Available fields**, double-click **ContactName** and press ⏎.

8. In the **Available fields**, double-click **VenderName** and press ⏎.

9. In the **Available fields**, double-click **Address** and press Enter.

10. In the **Available fields**, double-click **City**.

11. Key a comma and a space.

12. In the **Available fields**, double-click **State**.

13. Key two spaces.

14. In the **Available fields**, double-click **ZIP**.

Figure 8-22
Label Wizard
dialog box
EcoMed-08.accdb
rptVenderLabels

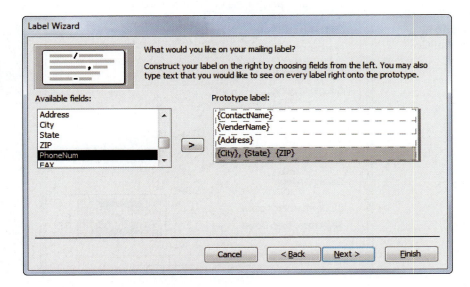

15. Click **Next**. In the next dialog box, double-click **VenderName** to add it to the **Sort by** section and click **Next**.

16. Edit the report name to **rptVenderLabels**. Select the option **Modify the label design**. Click **Finish**.

Figure 8-23
Design View for
mailing labels
EcoMed-08.accdb
rptVenderLabels

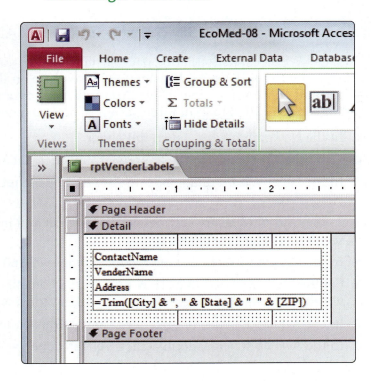

17. From the **Page Setup** tab, in the **Page Layout** group, click **Columns** ▤. The **Number of Columns** is set to 3. Click **OK**.

18. Right-click the **rptVenderLabel** document's tab and choose **Print Preview**.

19. If an information dialog box appears, just click **OK**. All the labels fit on one page.

20. Close **Print Preview**. Close and save the report.

21. Compact and repair the database, and then close it.

Lesson 8   Summary

- Before printing a report, it is good practice to view the report in Print Preview.

- In Print Preview, you can change the zoom size.

- Columnar style reports are most commonly used when the length of the data is too wide to display properly in tabular format.

- The properties of controls can be modified.

- Simple reports can be created using the Report Wizard.

- Horizontal lines in a report can be created, moved, or resized, just as any other object.

- In a tabular report, each record displays on a separate line.

- Section properties can be viewed and modified in the Property Sheet.

- Group sections can organize and summarize information based on categories.

- Page breaks can be forced to occur before and after group sections.

- Fields can be added to a report through the Field List window.

- When adding or moving fields in a report, care should be given to align other controls in the header or footer to match the detail section.

- Controls should be sized and aligned to make the report easier to read.

- The date and the page number are common controls created by the Report Wizard.

- The Property Sheet for each object in a report lists all the characteristics or attributes for that object.

- Calculated controls display the results of a numeric expression based on one or more fields in a record.

- A summary report can be created by hiding the detail section of a standard report.

- The properties of multiple objects can be set simultaneously through the Format Painter.

- Conditional Formatting applies the property only when certain conditions are met.

- Records in a multicolumn report or label display in two or more columns.

- The Label Wizard can create non-standard package labels.

LESSON 8		Command Summary	
Feature	Button	Menu	Keyboard
Add Line control		Design, Controls	
Align controls		Arrange, Sizing & Ordering, Align	
Align text		Format, Font	
Apply Conditional Formatting		Format, Control Formatting	
Apply Format Painter		Format, Font	
Apply Sorting and Grouping		Design, Grouping & Totals, Group & Sort	
Create Labels		Create, Reports	
Create Multicolumn Report		Page Setup, Page Layout, Columns	
Create Report		Create, Reports	
Create Report, wizard		Create, Reports	
Format, Bold	**B**	Format, Font	
Format, Grid bottom			
Format, Grid Horizontal			
Format, Shape Outline		Format, Control Formatting	
Format, Size, Tallest		Arrange, Sizing & Ordering, Size/Space	
Format, Size, Widest		Arrange, Sizing & Ordering, Size/Space	
Hide Detail section		Design, Grouping & Totals	
Promote a grouping level			
Remove gridlines			
Select Column		Arrange, Rows & Columns	

Please visit our Online Learning Center, *www.lessonapproach2010.com,* **where you will find the following review materials:**

Concepts Review

True/False Questions

Short Answer Questions

Critical Thinking Questions

Skills Review

Review Exercises that target single skills

Lesson Applications

Review Exercises that challenge students by testing multiple skills in each exercise

On Your Own

Open-ended exercises that require students to synthesize multiple skills and apply creativity and problem-solving as they would in a real world business situation

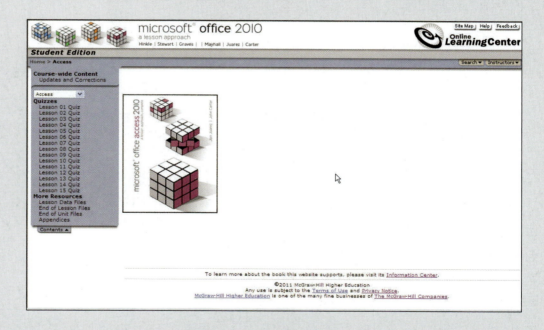

Please visit our Online Learning Center, *www.lessonapproach2010.com*, **where you will find Unit Applications review materials.**

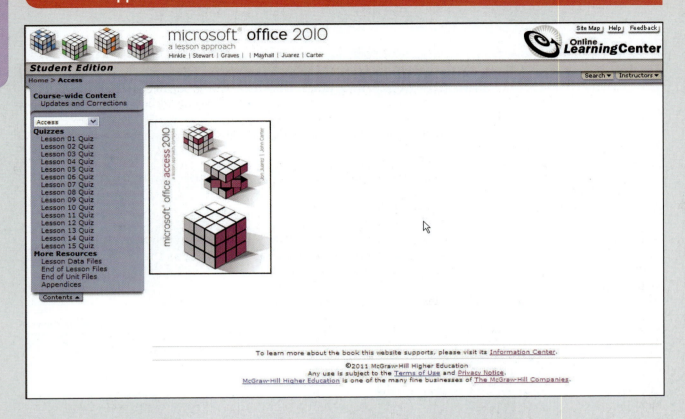

WORD GLOSSARY

() denotes Lesson number where term can be found.

Active window   Window in which you are currently working that shows the title bar and taskbar button highlighted. (6)

Antonym   Word that is opposite in meaning to another word. (3)

Ascending sort order   Arrangement that places items in first-to-last or lowest-to-highest order, such as from A to Z or 0 to 9. (5)

Attribute   Setting, such as boldface or italics, that affects the appearance of text. (2) (11)

AutoComplete   Automatic Word feature that suggests the completed word when you key the first four or more letters of a day, month, or date. (3)

AutoCorrect   Automatic Word feature that corrects commonly misspelled words as you key text. (3)

AutoFormat   Word feature that automatically changes formatting as you key text or numbers. (2)

AutoRecover   Word feature that automatically saves open documents in the background. The backup version of the document can be recovered in case the original is lost or damaged in a power failure or because of a system problem. (1)

AutoText   Word feature you can use to insert text automatically. (3)

Background pagination   Automatic process of updating page breaks and page numbers that occurs while you are creating or editing a document. (10)

Bar tabs   Used to make tabbed columns look more like a table with gridlines. A bar tab inserts a vertical line at a fixed position, creating a border between columns. (5)

Border   Line, box, or pattern placed around text, a graphic, or a page. (4)

Building Blocks   AutoText entries, cover pages, headers, footers, page numbers, tables, text boxes, and watermarks that are stored in galleries to be inserted in documents. (3) (10)

Bulleted list   List of items, each preceded by a bullet (•). Each item is a paragraph with a hanging indent. (4)

Character style   Formatting applied to selected text within a paragraph; includes font, font size, and font style. (11)

Click and type   Insert text or graphics in any blank area of a document. Position the insertion point anywhere in a document, click, and then key text. Word automatically inserts paragraph marks before that point and also inserts tabs, depending on the location of the insertion point. (4)

Clipboard   Temporary storage area in the computer's memory used to hold text or other information that is cut or copied. (6)

Color set   Feature for applying color. It includes four colors for text and background, six accent colors, and two colors reserved for hyperlinks. (11)

Contiguous text   Any group of characters, words, sentences, or paragraphs that follow one another. (1)

Copy   Method for copying text or other information, storing it on the Clipboard, and then placing it in a new location. (6)

Cut and paste   Method for moving text or other information by removing it from a document, storing it on the Clipboard, and then placing it in a new location. (6)

Descending sort order   Arrangement that places items in last-to-first or highest-to-lowest order, such as from Z to A or 9 to 0. (5)

Document theme   Feature that includes colors, fonts, and effects which affect the overall appearance of a document. (11)

Drag and drop   Method for moving or copying text or other objects short distances by dragging them. (6)

Drop cap   Large letter that appears below the text baseline, usually applied to the first letter in the word of a paragraph. (2)

Em dash   Dash twice as wide as an en dash and used in sentences where you would normally insert two hyphens. (4)

En dash   Dash slightly wider than a hyphen. (4)

Facing pages   Document with a two-page spread. Right-hand pages are odd-numbered pages, and left-handed pages are even-numbered pages. (8)

Field   Hidden code that tells Word to insert specific information, such as a date or page number. In a data source table, each item of information contained in a record. (3) (8)

File name   Unique name given to a document saved in Word. (1)

File tab   Tab that displays the Backstage View which lists the commands to create, open, save, and print a document. (1)

Find   Command used to locate text and formatting in a document. (7)

First-line indent   Indent for the first line of a paragraph. (4)

First-line indent marker   Top triangle on the left side of the ruler. Drag the indent marker to indent or extend the first line of a paragraph. (4)

Font   The design applied to an entire set of characters, including all letters of the alphabet, numerals, punctuation marks, and symbols. (2)

Footer   Text that appears in the bottom margin of a page throughout a section or document. (10)

Formatting mark   Symbol for a tab, paragraph, space, or another special character that appears on the screen, but not in the printed document. (1)

Gallery   List of design options for modifying elements of a page. (10)

Gutter margins   Extra space added to the inside or top margins to allow for binding. (8)

Hanging indent   Indentation of the second and subsequent lines of a paragraph. (4)

Hanging indent marker   Bottom triangle on the left side of the ruler. Drag the marker to indent the second and subsequent lines in a paragraph. (4)

Hard page break   Page break inserted manually. Does not move, regardless of changes in the document. (9)

Header   Text that appears in the top margin of a page throughout a section or document. (10)

I-beam   Shape of the mouse pointer when it is positioned in the text area. (1)

Indent   Increase the distance between the sides of a paragraph and the two side margins (left and right). (4)

Indent marker   On Word's horizontal ruler, small box or triangle that you drag to control a paragraph's indents. (4)

Insert mode   Mode of text entry that inserts text without overwriting existing text. (1)

Insertion point   Vertical blinking bar on the Word screen that indicates where an action will begin. (1)

Key Tips   Letters that appear over commands after you press the Alt key. Press the letter of the command you want to activate. The Key Tips may also be called *badges*. To turn off the Key Tips, press Alt again. (1)

Landscape   Page orientation setting in which the page is wider than it is tall. (8)

Leader characters   Patterns of dots or dashes that lead the reader's eye from one tabbed column to the next. (5)

Left and right indent   Indent left and right sides of paragraph (often used for quotes beyond three lines). (4)

Left indent   Indent paragraph from left margin. (4)

Left indent marker   Small rectangle on the left side of the ruler. Drag the marker to indent all lines in a paragraph simultaneously. (4)

Line break character   Character that starts a new line within the same paragraph. Insert by pressing Shift + Enter. (1)

Line space   Amount of vertical space between lines of text in a paragraph. (4)

Linked style   Paragraph formatting applied to selected text. (11)

List style   Formatting instructions applied to a list, such as numbering or bullet characters, alignment, and fonts. (11)

Margins   Spaces at the top, bottom, left, and right of the document between the edges of text and the edges of the paper. (8)

Mirror margins   Inside and outside margins on facing pages that mirror one another. (8)

Multilevel list   Numbering sequence used primarily for legal and technical documents. (4)

Negative indent   Extends a paragraph into the left or right margin areas. (4)

Nonbreaking space   Space between words, defined by a special character, that prevents Word from separating two words. Insert by pressing Ctrl + Shift + Spacebar. (1)

Noncontiguous text   Text items (characters, words, sentences, or paragraphs) that do not follow one another, but each appears in a different part of a document. (1)

Nonprinting character   Symbol for a tab, paragraph, space, or another special character that appears on the screen, but not in the printed document. (1)

Normal style   Default paragraph style with the formatting specifications 11-point Calibri, English language, left-aligned, 1.15 line spacing, 10 points spacing after, and widow/orphan control. (11)

Numbered list   List of items preceded by sequential numbers or letters. Each item is a paragraph with a hanging indent. (4)

Organizer   Feature that lets you copy styles from one document or template to another or copy macros from one template to another. (12)

Orientation   Setting to format a document with a tall, vertical format or a wide, horizontal format. (8)

Orphan   First line of a paragraph that remains at the bottom of a page. (9)

Overtype mode   Mode of text entry that lets you key over existing text. (1)

Pagination   Process of determining how and when text flows from the bottom of one page to the top of the next page in a document. (9)

Pane   Section of a window that is formed when the window is split. A split window contains two panes. (6)

Paragraph   Unique block of text or data that is always followed by a paragraph mark. (4)

Paragraph alignment   Determines how the edges of a paragraph appear. (4)

Paragraph mark   On-screen symbol (¶) that marks the end of a paragraph and stores all formatting for the paragraph. (1) (4)

Paragraph space   Amount of space (measured in points) before and after a paragraph; replaces pressing Enter to add space between paragraphs. (4)

Paragraph style   Formatting instructions applied to a paragraph; includes alignment, line and paragraph spacing, indents, tab settings, borders and shading, and character formatting. (11)

Placeholder text   In a template (or a new document based on a template), text containing the correct formatting, which you replace with your own information. (12)

Point   Measure of type size; 72 points equals 1 inch. (2)

Portrait   Page orientation setting in which the page is taller than it is wide. (8)

Positive indent   Indentation between the left and right margins. (4)

Proofreaders' marks   Handwritten corrections to text, often using specialized symbols. (1)

Property   Any information, such as the filename, date created, or file size, that describes a document. (1)

Quick Access Toolbar   Toolbar containing frequently used commands and which is easily customized. (1)

Quick styles   Various formatting options for text and objects that display as thumbnails in a gallery. (11)

Replace   Command used to replace text and formatting automatically with specified alternatives. (7)

Ribbon   Seven default tabs, each tab containing a group of related commands. (1)

Right indent   Indent paragraph from right margin. (4)

Right indent marker   Triangle on the right side of the ruler; drag the marker to indent the right side of a paragraph. (4)

Ruler   Part of the Word window that shows placement of indents, margins, and tabs. (1)

Sans serif   Font characteristic in which the font has no decorative lines, or serifs, projecting from its characters, such as Arial. (2)

ScreenTip   Brief explanation or identification of an on-screen item such as a Ribbon command. (1)

Scroll bar   Bar used with the mouse to move right or left and up or down within a document to view text not currently visible on screen. (1)

Section   Portion of a document that has its own formatting. (8)

Section breaks   Double-dotted lines that appear on screen to indicate the beginning and end of a section. (8)

Selection   Area of a document that appears as a highlighted block of text. Selections can be formatted, moved, copied, deleted, or printed. (1)

Serif   Font characteristic in which the font has decorative lines projecting from its characters, such as Times New Roman. (2)

Shading   Applying shades of gray, a pattern, or color to the background of a paragraph. (4)

Shortcut menu   Menu that opens and shows a list of commands relevant to a particular item that you right-click. (2)

Smart quotes   Quotation marks that curl in one direction (") to open a quote and curl in the opposite direction (") to close a quote. (4)

Soft page break   Page break automatically inserted by Word and continually adjusted to reflect changes in the document. (9)

Sort   To arrange items in a particular order, such as alphabetical or numerical order. Sorting is often done on tables and lists but can also be performed on text paragraphs within a document. (5)

Special characters   Characters such as the trademark symbol™ or those used in foreign languages. (4)

Split bar   Horizontal line that divides a document into panes. (6)

Split box   Small gray rectangle located just above the vertical scroll bar. You can drag it down to split a document into two panes. (6)

Status bar   Bar located at the bottom of the Word window that displays information about the task you are performing, shows the position of the insertion point, and shows the current mode of operation. (1)

Style   Set of formatting instructions that you apply to text. (11)

Style set   List of style names and their formatting specifications. (11)

Symbol   Special character, such as the copyright symbol ©. (4)

Synonym   Word that is similar in meaning to another word. (3)

Tab   Paragraph-formatting feature used to align text. (5)

Tab characters   Nonprinting characters used to indent text. (1)

Tab marker   Symbol on the horizontal ruler that indicates a custom tab setting. (5)

Tab stop   Position of a tab setting. (5)

Table style   Formatting instructions applied to a table, such as borders, shading, alignment, and fonts. (11)

Task pane   Pane to the right or left of the text area that provides access to a variety of functions. (3) (6) (11)

Template   File that contains formatting information, styles, and text for a particular type of document. (12)

Theme   Set of formatting instructions for the entire document. (2) (11)

Thesaurus   Tool you can use to look up synonyms for a selected word. (3)

Title bar   Bar that displays the name of the current document at the top of the Word window. (1)

Widow   Last line of a paragraph that remains at the top of a page. (9)

Wildcard   Symbol that stands for missing or unknown text. (7)

Wingdings   Font that includes special characters, such as arrows. (4)

EXCEL GLOSSARY

Parentheses ( ) denotes lesson number where term can be found.

3-D reference   A cell address that refers to a cell on a different worksheet. It includes the sheet name followed by an exclamation point (Sheet1!B7). A 3-D reference can also be a formula. (4)

Absolute reference   A cell address that does not change when copied in a formula. (4)

Accent   Mark or symbol above or below a character to show pronunciation or meaning. (9)

Active cell   The cell that is ready for data and outlined with a thick border. (1)

Add-in   Excel function, feature, or command that supplies enhanced capability. It is installed separately from the main program. (1)

Argument   Values or cell ranges between parentheses in a function; they are what a function needs to complete its calculation. (1)

Argument ScreenTip   Screen prompt while keying a formula or function that displays the syntax. (5)

Arithmetic mean   An average of values calculated by adding the values and then dividing the total by the number of values. (5)

Arithmetic operators   Math symbols for calculations (+, −, /, and *). (2)

Ascending sort   Order in which data are arranged from lowest to highest value or A to Z. (8)

AutoCalculate   Status bar area that displays sum, average, count, maximum, or minimum for a selected range of cells. (2) (4)

AutoComplete   Feature that displays a suggested label after one or more characters are keyed in a cell in the column. (3)

AutoCorrect   Feature that corrects certain types of keying errors automatically. (2)

AutoFit   Size a column to its longest entry, or size a row to the font. (1)

Axis   Horizontal or vertical boundary that encloses chart data. (7)

Axis title   Optional label for the categories or values in a chart. (7)

Background   An image that displays on-screen for the worksheet. (4)

Backsolve   What-if analysis in reverse. It involves setting results and then determining formula arguments. (9)

Border   Line around a cell or range of cells. (1)

Calculated column   A column in a table that has a formula. (8)

Calculated column exception   Cell in a table column that has a different formula or data. (8)

Cell   Intersection of a column and row in a worksheet with an address or reference, such as cell B5. (1)

Cell address   Column letter and row number that identifies a location in the worksheet. (1)

Cell alignment   Feature that describes and sets how the contents of a cell are positioned within the cell. (3)

Cell reference   The cell address or location in the worksheet. (1)

Cell style   Set of format attributes, including font, font style, font color, borders, alignment, and fill. (2)

Character space   Average width of a numeric character in the font. (1)

Character string   Sequence of letters, numbers, or other symbols. (3)

Chart   Object that uses cells in a worksheet to illustrate data in a graph; a visual representation or display of data (1) (7)

Chart area   Background of a chart. (7)

Chart floor   Base or bottom of a 3-D chart. (7)

Chart layout   Elements and location of those elements on a chart. (7)

Chart object   Chart that appears on the same sheet as the data. (7)

Chart sheet   Chart that appears on its own worksheet in the workbook. (7)

Chart style   Preset selection of colors and effects for overall appearance of a chart. (1) (7)

Chart title   Optional title or name for a chart. (7)

Chart wall   Vertical background or wall for a 3-D chart. (7)

Color scale   Data visualization that displays two or three color fill variations across a range of cells based on values within a range. (3) (9)

Column   Vertical group of cells in a worksheet identified by alphabetic letter. (1)

Combination chart   Chart that uses more than one chart type or more than one number scale. (7)

Conditional formatting   Cell formatting that is displayed based on the cell's contents. (3)

Constant   A value which does not change and which can be named. (5)

Constraint   A restriction or requirement for a cell value when using Solver. (9)

Context-sensitive tabs   Command tabs that appear only when needed or when a particular object is active. (1)

Custom format   Display format created in the Format Cells dialog box using Excel's format codes. (3)

Custom view   Display and print settings that can be saved with a workbook. (8)

Data bar   Bar-shaped fill in a cell based on values within a range. (3)

Data label   Chart element that displays the value, an optional title for each value. (1)

Data marker   Chart object, such as a bar or column, that portrays individual values. (7)

Data point   One value from a chart data series. (7)

Data series   Collection of related values in the worksheet. (7)

Data source   Worksheet row and column data used to build a chart or a PivotTable; data that are copied or imported into Excel from an external program (7)

Data table   Matrix below a chart that lists the values and categories displayed in the chart; a cell range that calculates and displays results of substituting different values in a formula. (7)

Data visualization   Format elements that display bars, colors, or icons for values. (3)

Defined name   User-created name for a range of cells. (5)

Descending sort   Order in which data are arranged from highest to lowest value or Z to A. (8)

Disclaimer   Statement that limits an obligation or legal right, often used in a header or footer. (2)

Display trigger   Keyboard character that displays a list of defined names in Formula AutoComplete. (5)

Document theme   Built-in set of fonts, colors, and effects used in a workbook. (2)

Drag-and-drop pointer   Four-headed arrow that appears when the pointer rests on the edge of a cell, used to copy or cut data by dragging. (3)

Duplicate row   A row in a table or list that has exactly the same data in one or more columns as another row. (8)

Electronic spreadsheet software   Computer software that produces reports with calculations, list management, or charts. (1)

Embedded chart   Chart object; a chart that appears on the same sheet as its data. (7)

Exponentiation   Math operation that raises a number to a power. (2)

Extension   Three or four characters, preceded by a period, added to file name. (2)

Field   A single category or column of data in a table or list. (8)

Field name   The column label in the header (first) row of a table or list. (8)

Field value   An individual piece of data in a cell in a table or list. (8)

File tab   Tab or button at the left of the Ribbon that opens Backstage view with document information and basic commands, such as Save and Print. (1)

File name   Name assigned when a workbook is saved and visible in Open dialog box, Computer, or Explorer. (1)

Fill   Background color or pattern for a cell. (1)

Fill handle   Square shape at lower right corner of a cell used to copy or fill data. (1)

Filter   Criteria that sets rules showing or hiding data; a subset of records from a list. (8)

Floating symbol   Currency symbol that is placed immediately to the left of the first digit. (2)

Folder   Storage location for work files on a disk or other media. (1)

Footer   Data at the bottom of each printed page of a worksheet. (2)

Formula   Equation that calculates an arithmetic result by performing a calculation on values in a worksheet. (1)

Formula AutoComplete   A list of built-in functions and range names that begin with the letter keyed while building a formula. (2) (5)

Function   Built-in formula for common mathematical, statistical, financial, or other calculations. (1) (5)

Function Arguments   Dialog box that displays help and entry areas for completing a function. (5)

Goal Seek   Command that backsolves or adjusts the value in a cell to reach a desired outcome. (9)

Gradient   A blend of colors used as fill for a cell or a chart element. (3) (7)

Gridline   Horizontal or vertical lines in a chart's plot area that aid in reading values. (7)

Header   Data at the top of each printed page of a worksheet. (2)

Header row   First row in a table or list with descriptive, unique labels or titles for each column. (8)

Highlight cells rules   Formatting based on conditions using relational or comparison operators. (4) (9)

Home   Cell A1. (1)

Horizontal (category) axis   Data that are shown in a chart, created from row or column headings. (7)

HTML   Hypertext markup language, which is used to format a Web page. (4)

Icon set   Set of three, four, or five icons displayed in a cell and based on values within a range. (3) (5)

Insignificant zero   A zero in a value that does not affect the actual value. (3)

KeyTip   Keyboard shortcut that appears on screen after [Alt] or [F10] is pressed. (1)

Label   An entry in a cell that begins with a letter. (2)

Landscape   Page orientation that prints a horizontal page that is wider than it is tall. (4)

Leading zero   A zero shown as the first digit in a value. (3)

Legend   Chart object that explains the colors, textures, or symbols used to differentiate series in the chart. (2) (7)

Link   A simple reference in a formula to another cell in the workbook; a live (active) connection to another file. (8)

Live Preview   Feature that displays design changes before they are applied. (2)

Macro   Visual Basic routine saved in a workbook; a sequence of commands and keystrokes that perform a routine task. (9)

Macro-enabled workbook   An Excel workbook with macros and an.xlsm extension. (9)

Marked as Final   Workbook property that prevents editing. (9)

Math hierarchy   Mathematical rules that determine which part of a formula is calculated first. (4)

Metadata   Information such as the computer name, user name, storage location, and creation date that is saved with a workbook. (9)

Mini toolbar   A toolbar with font-editing buttons that appears when text within a cell or chart object is selected. (1)

Mixed reference   A cell address that adjusts either the row or the column when the formula is copied. (4)

Name Box   Drop-down combo box in the formula bar that shows current cell address. (1)

Named range   A defined name for a range of cells. (5)

Negative value   Value that is less than zero. (4)

Numeric keypad   Set of number and symbol keys at the right of the keyboard. (3)

Object   Separate, clickable element in a worksheet that can be positioned, sized, and formatted. (1) (2) (7)

Objective cell   Formula cell parameter for a Solver solution. (9)

Office Clipboard   Temporary memory area that can hold up to 24 copied elements across Office products. (3)

Order of operation   Mathematical rules that determine which part of a formula is calculated first. (4)

Order of precedence   Mathematical rules that determine which part of a formula is calculated first. (4)

Page orientation   Print setting that determines landscape or portrait layout. (4)

Parameter   The data or information needed by Solver to determine a solution (objective and variable cells, constraints). (9)

PDF   Adobe portable document file. (1)

Pick From Drop-down List   Feature that displays a list of labels already in a column when a cell is right-clicked. (3)

Pixel   Measurement unit that represents a screen dot. (2)

Plot area   Rectangular chart area bounded by the category and value axes. (7)

Point   1/72 of an inch; used as a font measure. (2)

Portrait   Page orientation that prints a page that is taller than it is wide. (2) (4)

Print area   The range of cells to be printed. (8)

Property   Descriptive information about a workbook or metadata saved with a workbook. (1) (9)

Protection   Worksheet or workbook property that prohibits edits to locked cells, shapes, and objects. (9)

Quick Access Toolbar   Customizable toolbar with buttons for frequently used commands. (1)

Range   A group of cells that forms a rectangle. (2)

Range address   Upper-left and lower-right cell addresses separated by a colon. (2)

Range name   A defined name for a range of cells. (5)

Record   One row of data in a table or a list. (8)

Relative reference   A cell address that adjusts to the row or column where a copied formula is located. (1) (4)

Replacement string   Sequence of characters that is exchanged for existing data in the Replace command. (3).

Ribbon   A set of command tabs with buttons, galleries, and commands. (1)

Row   Horizontal group of cells identified by a number in a worksheet. (1)

Scale   The range of values used to plot a chart. (7)

Scaling   Ratio or percentage used to print or output a worksheet; a sizing method in which an object is resized by a percentage. (4)

Scenario   A saved set of values for a worksheet. (9)

Scenario summary report   A formatted description in outline style that lists changing and results cells for each scenario in a worksheet. (9)

Scope   Property of a range name that sets its location in the workbook to a particular worksheet. (5)

Secondary axis   Separate set of values for a chart data series. (7)

Selection handle   Small circles, squares, or other symbols at the corners and/or edges of an object used for sizing the object. (1) (7)

Selection pointer   White cross-shaped pointer used to select cells. Solid black arrow to select rows or columns. (2)

Series   List of label, values, dates, or times that follows a pattern. (1)

Sizing handle   Marker at bottom right corner of a table used to expand or contract a table. (8)

Solver   An Excel add-in that backsolves the value for a cell with a formula. (9)

Sparkline   Miniature line or column chart within a cell. (7)

Stop   One color used in a gradient fill. (7)

Structured reference   Defined name for an identifiable range in a table. (8)

Super ScreenTip   A box on screen that displays the name and purpose of a button, a keyboard shortcut, and possibly a preview of the dialog box. (1)

Synonym A word having the same meaning as another word. (9)

Syntax Required parts of a function or formula; rules for how a function is built. It includes an equal sign (=), the function name, and the arguments in parentheses. (5)

Table List of information with a row headers followed by rows of data. (8)

Texture Fill that appears as a grainy or nonsmooth background. (7)

Thesaurus Reference that lists words with the same and/or opposite meanings as the active label. (9)

Tick mark Small line on a chart axis that aids in identifying values. (7)

Trendline A line added to a chart the points out and forecasts future directions and trends in values. (9)

Trigger Keystroke that starts an action or command, such as displaying Formula AutoComplete and structured reference lists; a display trigger. (8)

Value An entry in a cell that begins with a number or an arithmetic symbol. (2)

Variable cells Cells that can be changed in a Solver problem. (9)

Vertical (value) axis Horizontal or vertical range of values on a chart. (7)

What-if analysis Procedure of varying values in a worksheet to forecast and predict future results. (9)

Whole number Value without a fraction or decimal. (4)

Wildcard Character that represents one or more letters or numbers. (3)

Windows Clipboard Temporary memory area that holds cut or copied data. (3)

Workbook Excel file that holds worksheets with data. A workbook has an.xlsx file name extension. (1)

Worksheet Individual page or sheet in a workbook shown by a tab at the bottom of the screen. (1)

Zoom size Magnification setting that controls how large data appear and how much of a worksheet appears at once on the screen. (1)

POWERPOINT GLOSSARY

Parenthesis ( ) denotes lesson number where term can be found.

Activate To select a placeholder by clicking it. An activated text placeholder can accept text that you key, or it can be moved or resized. (1)

Adjustment handle Yellow diamond-shaped handle used to change a prominent feature of a shape. For example, you can change the size of an arrowhead relative to the body of the arrow. (4)

Album layout Used to change how pictures are positioned in a photo album. (4)

Alignment Left, center, right, and justify attributes available for text positioning in various objects. Also refers to how objects are positioned on a slide. (5)

Animation effects Visual effects that control how text, pictures, movies, and other objects move on a slide during a slide show. May include audio. (1)

Animations See **Animation effects.**

Artistic Effect Effect that applies photo filters to pictures. Effects include Painting, Blur, Cement, Light Screen, Plastic Wrap, Pastels, and other effects. (4)

Assistant shape Shape in an organization chart that is usually placed below a superior shape and above subordinate shapes. Usually, an assistant shape has no subordinates. (7)

AutoCorrect Feature that automatically corrects commonly misspelled words as you key text. (2)

Autofit options Options for fitting text into placeholders. (2)

Axis Line that borders one side of the chart plot area. The Vertical (Value) Axis displays a range of numbers, and the Horizontal (Category) Axis displays category names. (6)

Background Removal Allows for the removal of the background of a picture to help the audience focus on the important part of that picture. (4)

Backstage view Contains quick commands that include file management and printing options such as print settings and a preview area so that you can review slides before printing. (1)

Banded Columns Table style option that provides columns in alternating colors. (5)

Banded Rows Table style option that provides rows in alternating colors. (5)

Bar chart Chart that compares one data element with another data element using horizontal bars. (6)

Bevel Effect that makes a picture or some other shape look dimensional; has several different options available. (4)

Bitmap pictures Made up of tiny colored pixels (picture elements). The more you enlarge a bitmap, the more blurred it becomes. Examples of bitmaps are pictures created in a paint program, photographs and other images that come from a scanner, and images that come from a digital camera. (4)

Black and White View that converts all colors to either black or white, eliminating shades of gray. Generally used for printing. (1)

Blank presentation Empty presentation. May be used to start a new presentation with no design elements such as colors, text, or other content. (2)

Body text Text on a slide, excluding titles. On a PowerPoint slide, body text placeholders usually display bulleted text. (1)

Brightness Adjusts the overall lightness of the colors in a picture. (4)

Bullet Small dot, square, or other symbol placed at the left of each item in a list. (1)

Cell Intersection of a row and a column in a table or a worksheet. (5) (6)

Cell Bevel Dimensional effect to make cells look raised and rounded or pressed in. (5)

Cell margin Space between the text in a cell and its borders. (5)

Cell pointer Pointer in the shape of a white cross used to select cells in a Microsoft Excel worksheet or Microsoft Graph datasheet. (6)

Chart Displays numbers in pictorial format, such as slices of a pie or columns in varying heights. Charts are sometimes called *graphs*. (6)

Chart Layouts Controls the position in which different chart elements appear on a chart. (6)

Chart Styles Preset styles that can be applied to a chart to enhance its appearance through colors matching the document theme colors. (6)

Clip art Ready-to-use media files including illustration, photograph, video, and audio files that you can insert in a presentation. Also called *clips*. (4)

Clipboard Temporary storage area in the computer's memory, used to hold text or objects that are cut or copied. (3)

Clipboard options Allow the control of settings of the Clipboard task pane. (3)

Clips See **Clip art.**

Collate To print all the pages of a document before starting to print the first page of the next copy. (1)

Color View that displays the presentation in full color for slide shows and printing. (4)

Color saturation Controls the intensity of colors, making an image less or more vivid as the percentage changes from 100 percent. (4)

Color tone Creates cool or warm tones by changing the temperature of image colors on a scale of 4,700 to 11,200. The low end of this scale has cool tones, and the high end has warm tones. (4)

Column chart Chart that compares one data element with another data element using vertical bars. (6)

Columns Individual cells aligned vertically in a table or worksheet. (5)

Command buttons Buttons designed to perform a function or display a gallery of options. (1)

Connection sites Red handles on an object that indicate where connector lines can be attached. (4)

Connector line Straight, curved, or angled line with special endpoints that can lock onto connection sites on a shape or other PowerPoint object. (4)

Constrain Used to draw objects in precise increments or proportions. For example, a line will be straight or angled in precise amounts, a rectangle will be square, and an oval will be round. When resizing an object, the correct size ratio is maintained. (2) (4)

Contiguous slides Slides that follow one after another, such as slides numbered 2, 3, and 4. (3) See also **Noncontiguous slides.**

Continuous Picture List SmartArt graphic that contains round placeholders for pictures and a horizontal arrow to communicate that the items shown represent interconnected information. (7)

Contrast Adjusts the intensity of the colors in a picture by adjusting the difference between the lightest and darkest areas. (4)

Copy Reproduces a selected object or text and stores it on the Clipboard without removing the selection from its original place. (3)

Corrections Modifies the brightness and/or contrast of a picture. (4)

Coworker shape Shape in an organization chart that is connected to the same superior shape as another shape. (7)

Crop To trim the vertical or horizontal edges of a picture. (4)

Cropping handles Short black markers on the sides and corners of a picture selected for cropping. When you drag one of these handles with the cropping tool, an edge of the picture is cut away (trimmed). (4)

Crosshair pointer Shape of your pointer when drawing objects. (4)

Cut Removes a selected object or text from a presentation and stores it on the Clipboard. (3)

Cycle SmartArt graphic Diagram that illustrates a continuous process. (7)

Data series Group of data that relates to a common object or category such as a product, geographic area, or year. A single chart may display more than one data series. (6)

Datasheet Table that is part of Microsoft Graph and in which you enter numbers and labels that are used to create a chart if you do not have Microsoft Excel installed on your computer. When you start a new chart, the datasheet appears automatically, containing sample data that you can delete or overwrite. (6)

Date and time Option that displays the current date and time to be updated automatically or keyed as a fixed date. (3)

Decrease list level To move text to a lower outline or heading level. (2)

Demote To decrease the level of a shape in a SmartArt graphic. (2)

Design theme Predesigned background graphics, theme colors, theme fonts, theme effects, and other formatting options that can be applied to presentations for a consistent appearance. These can be customized for a particular topic or unique design. (2) (3)

Destination When working with Clipboard objects, the presentation or other document in which the objects are pasted. (3)

Diagram Visual representation of information that can help an audience understand a presenter's message. (7)

Drag To move a selected object from one location to another by holding down the left mouse button while moving the pointer. (1)

Draw Table Method of inserting a table by using the pencil pointer to control the height and width as well as the vertical and horizontal lines within the table. (5)

Duplicate To make a copy of a selected object on the same slide or to reproduce slides. The duplicate is stored on the Clipboard without removing the selection from its original place. (3) (4)

Eraser Used to erase table cell borders. (5)

Explode To move a pie slice away from other slices in a pie chart to add emphasis. (6)

File name Unique name given to a PowerPoint presentation file, a Word document file, or files created by other applications. (1)

File tab Tab that provides access to opening, saving, printing, and sharing your PowerPoint file with others. (1)

Find Locates text in a presentation. (3)

First Column Table style option that emphasizes the first column of the table. (5)

First-line indent Indent in which the first line of the paragraph is indented farther to the right than the other lines in the paragraph. (2)

Fit to Window Changes from the current zoom settings so that the slide will fit in the window that is open. (1)

Font face Set of characters with a specific design such as Times New Roman or Arial. (2)

Font size Point measurement of characters in a font. (2)

Footer Text that usually appears at the bottom of a slide, notes page, or handout page. (3)

Format Painter Used to copy formatting from one object to another. (3)

Four-pointed arrow Used to move placeholders and other objects without resizing them; can also be used to select text in a bulleted list by clicking the bullet. (2)

Gallery Collection of thumbnails displaying different effect options. (1)

Gear SmartArt graphic Diagram that illustrates interlocking ideas. (7)

Glow Effect that adds a soft color around the object's edges, making the object stand out from the background. (4)

Graph See **Chart.**

Grayscale View that displays slides in shades of gray for printing on a black-and-white printer. (1)

Gridlines On a slide, evenly spaced vertical and horizontal lines that can be shown to help with alignment. On a chart, the background lines that aid interpretation of data quantities. (4) (6)

Group To combine selected objects so that they behave as one object. On the Ribbon, a set of related command buttons. (1) (4)

Guides Horizontal and vertical lines used to align objects. Guides do not display in a slide show or when printed. (4)

Handout Printout that contains one, two, three, four, six, or nine PowerPoint slides on a page. (1)

Hanging indent Indentation of the second and subsequent lines of a paragraph. Also, an organization chart format in which subordinate shapes are displayed under a superior shape. (2) (7)

Header Text that usually appears at the top of a slide, notes page, or handout page. (3)

Header Row Table style option that emphasizes the first row of the table. (5)

Help Reference tool for getting assistance with PowerPoint. (1)

I-beam Shape of the pointer when positioned in a text area; used to select text or mark the location at which you can insert text. (1)

Increase list level To move text to a higher outline or heading level. (2)

Indent marker On the horizontal ruler, a small triangle or rectangle that controls indent positions. (2)

Insertion point Blinking line that indicates where text will be inserted. (1)

Keyword(s) Word (or words) that describe the subject matter of your clip art search. (4)

Landscape Horizontal orientation for slides or printed pages in which the width is greater than the height; the opposite of portrait. (1)

Last Column Table style option that emphasizes the last column of the table. (5)

Layout See **Slide layouts.**

Legend Used to identify by color or pattern the data series or categories in a chart. (6)

Level In organization charts, the position in the hierarchy of the organization being diagrammed. (7)

Line spacing Amount of vertical space between lines of text and between paragraphs. (2)

Line weight Thickness of a line measured in points. (4)

List SmartArt graphic Diagram that illustrates information in groups and subgroups. (7)

Live Preview Feature that shows the result of applying an effect as you point to the effect thumbnail in a gallery before selecting the effect. (1)

Lock Drawing Mode Enables drawing the same shape multiple times without having to reactivate the shape tool. (4)

Merge cells To combine two or more table cells into one larger cell. (5)

Noncontiguous slides Slides that do not follow one after another, such as slides numbered 1, 3, 5, and 7. (3) See also **Contiguous slides.**

Normal indent Indent in which all lines are indented the same amount from the left margin. (2)

Normal view Displays the three parts of the PowerPoint window: the Slides and Outline pane, the Slide pane, and the Notes pane. (1)

Notes page Feature that prints a slide image on the top half of a page, with speaker notes on the lower half of the page. (1)

Notes Page view Displays speaker notes as they will appear when printed. (1)

Notes pane Area below the Slide pane where you can add speaker notes for a slide. (1)

Nudge To move an object in very small increments by using the arrow keys. (4)

OpenType fonts Provide more detailed letter shapes and more variations of character sets than do TrueType fonts. (2)

Organization chart SmartArt graphic that shows hierarchical relationships of an organization. (7)

Outline Presentation content in a text format showing slide titles and listed information. (1)

Page number Placed in the lower right corner of notes and handout pages by default. (3)

Paste Inserts an item stored on the Clipboard at the current location. (3)

Paste Options Button showing options that appears near a pasted item when the source formatting is different from the formatting of the destination presentation. (3)

Pencil pointer Used to draw and recolor table borders. (5)

Photo Album Creates a presentation consisting mostly of pictures that can be formatted to create electronic scrapbooks or photo albums. (4)

Picture Border Line that surrounds pictures. (4)

Picture effects Customizable special effects for pictures such as shadows, glow, bevel effects, and soft edges. (4)

Picture style Selection of preset effects to enhance the appearance of pictures. (4)

Pie chart Chart that shows the proportions of individual components compared to the whole. (6)

Placeholder Box that can contain title text, body text, pictures, or other objects. Most slide layouts contain placeholders. A placeholder's formatting, size, and position is set on a master slide and can be customized. (1)

Plot area Area of a chart that displays the shapes, such as columns or pie slices, that represent data. (6)

Points Measure of font size; 1 inch has 72 points. (2)

Portrait Vertical orientation for slides or printed pages in which the height is greater than the width; the opposite of landscape. (1)

Preset Effects or settings that are automatically available. (4)

Process SmartArt graphic Diagram that illustrates sequential concepts or events. (7)

Promote To increase the level of a shape in a SmartArt graphic. (2)

Proofreaders' marks Handwritten notations used to mark corrections on printed text. (1)

Proportions Relationships between the height and the width of an object. When resizing an object, its proportions will be preserved if both the height and the width of the object change at the same rate or percentage. An object that is out of proportion is either too tall and skinny or too short and wide. (4)

Pyramid SmartArt graphic Diagram that illustrates relationships based on foundational concepts. (7)

Quick Access Toolbar Toolbar located at the top of the PowerPoint window that provides access to frequently used commands. (1)

Quick Styles Preset effects that are displayed in a gallery and used to enhance the appearance of shapes. (7)

Radial SmartArt graphic Diagram that illustrates relationships focused on or directed at a central element. (7)

Reading view Displays the presentation in a view with the title bar showing that is easy to browse. (1)

Redo Reverses a previous action such as an editing change. Up to 20 actions can be reversed if the Save feature has not been used. (3)

Reflection Illusion of an object being reflected off another surface by displaying a semitransparent copy of the object as a mirror image. (4) (5)

Regroup Recombines objects that were at one time part of the same group. (4)

Replace Locates text in a presentation and replaces it with different text that you specify. (3)

Research Searches reference materials such as dictionaries, encyclopedias, and translation services to find information you need. (3)

Reset Picture Used to return a picture to its original state after its colors have been changed. (4)

Ribbon Consists of task-oriented tabs arranged at the top of the PowerPoint window that each contain commands organized in logical groups. (1)

Rotate Change the angle of an object. (2)

Rotation handle Green handle appearing above a selected object that you can drag to change the angle of the object. (4)

Rows Individual cells arranged horizontally across the table or worksheet. (5)

Ruler Measurement shown at the top and left side of the slide pane to help with object positioning, sizing, and tabs. (5)

Scale Specifies the range of values on a chart's value axis and the interval between values. (6)

ScreenTip Identifying information displayed in a small box that appears when you point to an on-screen item such as a command. (1)

Scroll bars Used to move what you see on the screen right or left and up or down. For example, you can use the vertical scroll bar to move from slide to slide. (1)

Shadow Effect that gives the illusion of light shining on an object, producing a dark area behind it. (4) (5)

Shape One of a group of predefined shapes that are easy to draw. Available shapes include rectangles, circles, arrows, flowchart symbols, stars, banners, callouts, lines, and connectors. (6)

Sizing handles Small circles and squares on the border of a selected object that are used to resize the object. (2)

Slide layouts Contain placeholders for slide content such as titles, bulleted lists, charts, tables, and SmartArt. (1) (2)

Slide number Placed on slides, usually in the lower right corner, depending on the theme. (3)

Slide pane Area where you create and edit presentation slides. (1)

Slide Show view View that displays slides sequentially in full-screen size. Slides can advance manually or automatically with slide timings, using a variety of transition effects. Slide shows can display movies and animated elements. (1)

Slide Sorter view Displays several thumbnails of slides, making it easy to reorder, add, delete, or duplicate slides and set transition effects. (1) (3)

Slide transitions Visual effects that enhance the way slides change during a slide show as you move from one slide to another. May include audio. (3)

Slides and Outline pane Area that can display either an outline of the presentation's text or thumbnails of the presentation's slides. You choose either Outline or Slides by clicking the appropriate tab. (1)

SmartArt graphics Shapes arranged in a diagram format to visually communicate information. (7)

Soft Edges Effect that changes a picture's normal hard edges to a soft, feathered appearance that gradually fades into the background color. (4)

Source When working with Clipboard objects, the presentation or other document from which the objects were cut or copied. (3)

Spelling Feature that corrects spelling by comparing words to an internal dictionary file. (3)

Split cells To divide a table cell into two smaller cells. (5)

Standard Layout for displaying an organization chart; also, can refer to standard colors such as red, blue, green, or yellow. (7)

Status bar Horizontal bar at the bottom of the PowerPoint window that displays information about the current presentation on the left and viewing commands on the right. (1)

Subordinate shape Shape in an organization chart that is connected to a superior shape reflecting a higher level. (7)

Table Arrangement of information in rows and columns. (5)

Table borders Lines forming the edges of cells, columns, and rows and the outline of the table. (5)

Table style Combination of formatting options based on theme colors. (5)

Tabs On the Ribbon, task-oriented groups of commands. Used with Tab, tabs can be used to indent text. Tab stops appear on the horizontal ruler. (1)

Template Preformatted presentation with a background design, font settings, and suggested content that is ready for input. (2)

Text box Free-form text object used to add text to slides. (2)

Text fill WordArt fill effect that can be a solid color, gradient fill, pattern, texture, or picture fill. (4)

Text outline WordArt outline effect that can be modified by color, width, and line style. (4)

Theme See **Design Theme.**

Theme colors Preset groups of colors for text, background, accent, and hyperlinks that can be applied to a presentation. (2) (3)

Theme effects Selection of built-in effects that can be applied to a presentation. (3)

Theme fonts Selection of fonts that can be applied to a presentation. (3)

Thesaurus Finds words with similar meanings. (3)

3-D Orientation that adds a perspective dimension to create the illusion of depth. (7)

3-D Rotation Effect that enables an object to be displayed in a variety of dimensional treatments. (4)

Thumbnail Miniature version of a graphic image. In PowerPoint, a miniature version of a slide is often referred to as a "thumbnail." (1)

Tick marks Small measurement marks on a chart's value or category axis. (6)

Title text Text that usually appears at the top of a PowerPoint slide. Title text is usually placed in a title text placeholder. (1)

Toggle button Switches between on and off when clicked. (2)

Total Row Table style option that emphasizes the last row of the table. (5)

Transform Effect that changes text into different shapes. (4)

Transition effects Visual or sound effects used when changing between slides during a slide show. (1)

Transitions See **Slide transitions.**

TrueType font Most common font format. (2)

2-D Orientation in which you see the shapes in dimensions of height (up/down measurement) and width (left/right measurement). (7)

Undo Reverses the last action, such as an editing change. PowerPoint can undo up to 20 actions if the Save feature has not been used. (3)

Ungroup To separate a group of objects. When an object is ungrouped, each of its parts behaves as an individual object. (4)

Vector drawing Illustration made up of lines and shapes that can be scaled to any size or aspect ratio without blurring. Vector drawings can be modified in PowerPoint by recoloring and by adding, removing, and rearranging individual elements. (4)

View buttons Four buttons located on the lower right corner of the PowerPoint window. You use these buttons to switch between Normal view (the default), Slide Sorter view, Reading view, and Slide Show view. (1)

Word wrap Text automatically continues to the next line in a placeholder or text box when a line is full. (2)

WordArt Text objects with fill and line colors plus special effects such as Shadow, Reflection, Glow, Bevel, 3-D Rotation, and Transform. (4)

Worksheet Area in Microsoft Excel in which you enter numbers and labels that are used to create a chart. When you create a new chart in PowerPoint, an Excel worksheet automatically appears containing sample data that you can delete or overwrite. (6)

Zoom Used to change the size at which you view an area of the screen. (1)

ACCESS GLOSSARY

() denotes Lesson number where term can be found.

aggregate function   A dynamic mathematical calculation that displays a single value for a specific field. (3)

aggregate function   A sum, average, maximum, minimum, or count for a group of records. (6)

argument   A reference in a function assigned as a single variable. (6)

arithmetic operator   A word or symbol that calculates a value from two or more numbers. (6)

AutoCorrect   An application feature that automatically corrects commonly misspelled words. (2)

bound control   A control whose source of data is a field in a table or query. (7)

calculated control   A control whose source of data is an expression, rather than a field. (7)

calculated field   A field that uses an expression or formula as its data source. (6)

command group   A collection of logically organized commands. (1)

comparison operator   A symbol or combination of symbols that specifies a comparison between two values. (6)

concatenate   The operation of joining two or more character strings end to end. (6)

concatenation operator   A symbol, word, group of symbols, or group of words used to combine two text values into a single text value. (6)

control   A database object that displays data, performs actions, and lets you view and work with information that enhances the user interface, such as labels and images. (7)

control margin   The specified location of information inside a control. (7)

control padding   The space between the gridline of the form and the control. (7)

criterion   A rule or test placed upon a field. (3)

data integrity   The condition through which data can be assumed to be accurate. (4)

database   A logically organized collection of data. (1)

Database Documenter   An Access tool used to display the indexes, properties, relationships, parameters, and permissions of major database objects. (3)

database template   A ready-to-use database containing all the tables, queries, forms, and reports needed to perform a specific task. (4)

Datasheet View   A screen view used to display data in rows and columns, similar to a spreadsheet. (1)

Design View   A screen view used to modify the structure of a major object. (1)

dynaset   A dynamic recordset that automatically reflects changes to its underlying data source. (6)

Edit Mode   The mode in which changes to the content of a field can be made and the insertion point is visible. (1)

electronic data interchange   The transfer of electronic data from one computer system to another. (4)

Expression Builder   An interface used to create a function, calculation, or expressions. (6)

field   The smallest storage element that contains an individual data element within a record. (1)

filter   A database feature that limits the number of records displayed. (3)

Filter by Selection   A filter applied to a single field (3)

foreign key   A field that links to a primary key field in the related table. (5)

function   A procedure used in an expression. (6)

Indeterminate relationship   A relationship that occurs when Access does not have enough information to determine the relationship between the two tables. (5)

logical operator   A symbol, word, group of symbols, or group of words used to construct an expression with multiple conditions. (6)

lookup field   A field property that displays input choices from another table and allows these choices to be selected from a list. (5)

Navigation Mode   The mode in which an entire field is selected and the insertion point is not visible. (1)

normalization   The process of restructuring a relational database for the purposes of organizing data efficiently, eliminating field redundancy, and improving data consistency. (5)

object dependency   A condition in which an object requires the existence of another object. (5)

One-to-Many relationship   A relationship that occurs when the common field is a primary key in the first table and not a primary key field in the second. (5)

One-To-One relationship   A relationship that occurs when the common field is a primary key in the first table and a primary key field in the second. (5)

operator   A word or symbol that indicates a specific arithmetic or logical relationship between the elements of an expression. (6)

PDF   The file extension used by a Portable Document Format (PDF) for document exchange originally created by Adobe systems in 1993 and released as an open standard in 2008 (1)

PivotChart   An interactive graphical representation of data displayed in a PivotTable. (6)

PivotTable   An interactive table that combines and compares data in a summarized view. (6)

primary key   A field or set of fields in a table that provides a unique identifier for every record. (4)

Print Preview A method for displaying on the screen how an object will appear if printed on paper. (2)

record A complete set of related data about one entity or activity. (1)

record navigation button An icon that moves the pointer within a recordset to the next, previous, first, or last record. (1)

referential integrity A set of database rules for checking, validating, and keeping track of data entry changes in related tables. (5)

relationship A link or connection of a common field between two tables, two queries, or a table and a query. (5)

Relationship Report A graphical report showing related tables. Each Relationship Report you create can be saved. (5)

Relationships window A visual interface that displays, creates, destroys, or documents relationships between tables, queries, or both. (5)

ScreenTip The name of or information regarding a specific object. (1)

special operator A symbol, word, group of symbols, or group of words used to express a relationship between two values. (6)

SQL (Structured Query Language) A computer language designed to manipulate data in relational databases. (6)

subdatasheet A datasheet linked within another datasheet. (5)

table A major database object that stores all data in a subject-based list of rows and columns. (1)

theme A set of unified design elements and color schemes for bullets, fonts, horizontal lines, background images, and other elements of a database object. (7)

unbound control A control without a source of data. (7)

Validation Rule A condition specifying criteria for entering data into an individual field. (4)

Validation Text An error message that appears when a value prohibited by the validation rule is entered. (4)

wildcard A character or group of characters used to represent one or more alphabetical or numerical characters. (3)

XPS The file extension used by an XML Paper Specification (XPS) file format that preserves document formatting and enable s file sharing of printable documents. (1)

WORD INDEX

POWERPOINT INDEX